# AN ECONOMIC HISTORY

# OF EUROPE SINCE 1750

# AN ECONOMIC HISTORY

# OF EUROPE SINCE 1750

BY

WITT BOWDEN

MICHAEL KARPOVICH

ABBOTT PAYSON USHER

HOWARD FERTIG

New York · 1970

First published in 1937 by American Book Company


HOWARD FERTIG, INC. EDITION 1969
Published by arrangement with Witt Bowden

Library of Congress Catalog Card Number: 68-9642

PRINTED IN THE UNITED STATES OF AMERICA
BY NOBLE OFFSET PRINTERS, INC.

## PREFACE

In this Economic History of Europe since 1750 we have endeavored to present the broad results embodied in the extensive special literature. We have included in this survey the literature on economic geography, the technology of industry and agriculture, the location of economic activity, the history of population, and recent studies of monopolistic competition. It has not been our intention to burden the reader with any restatement of the critical problems involved. For our purposes it is generally sufficient to use only the conclusions. In many instances, the results of these attempts at a broad synthesis appear only in revisions of older judgments of events and policies, or in new arrangements of material.

Problems of interpretation have been emphasized, because we feel that the shorter general treatises must play an active part in the progressive development of the subject. The field is so extensive that no single scholar could prepare a "full length" economic history of Europe. Even if such a book could be written, it is by no means clear that it would in any adequate way supplant the special literature. This special literature must be regarded as the basic element in the development of our historical knowledge. If this large mass of material is to be effectively utilized, there is great need of an up-to-date general treatise for purposes of instruction and synthesis — such as is embodied in this volume.

Economic history is treated as an integral part of general history. This is done not so much by the inclusion of the data of general history as by the plan of organization and by emphasis on the interaction of economic, political, and cultural factors. We have tried to avoid oversimplification but at the same time to emphasize boldly and clearly the significant economic institutions and forces as they have taken shape and direction since the eighteenth century.

It is our purpose to sketch in narrative form the development of Europe as a whole, by description of the nature of the economic contacts among the various countries, and by discussion of the consequences of the intensive development of particular regions. Comprehensive description of the internal development of particular countries is not possible on this scale. The more important episodes in the history of the leading countries have been treated with care, and the continuity of development is emphasized by graphs and by sketches of the history of primary industries.

iii

Great pains have been taken to emphasize both comprehensive geographical description and statistical totals. The detailed analysis of particular regions or industries is shown in relation to a larger whole. Description of representative types makes it possible to convey an accurate impression of conditions over the entire area. Analysis of strategic industries affords an accurate account of the primary features of industrial development.

These methods have made it possible to present a highly objective statement of the course of historical development, but complete objectivity is, of course, unattainable. Any interpretation of history will be influenced by one's concepts of historical process and by a number of important ethical and social judgments. We have endeavored to maintain a consistent position on all these aspects of historical science. We are not conscious of any significant differences of opinion on basic issues, so that collaboration has involved no suppression of individual convictions. The chapters on Russia were prepared by Professor Karpovich. The other chapters were divided equally between the other authors in conformity with their primary interests.

We are conscious of the difficulty of dealing objectively with recent events. No pains have been spared to apply rigorous principles of criticism and interpretation to the available material. The task is made somewhat less difficult because economic history suffers less than political history from incomplete disclosure of primary source material, but it is very difficult to see recent events in true perspective. It is recognized that in dealing with present-day societies differing in vital respects from our own there is a special difficulty in subordinating the preconceptions of one's own environment. But every effort has been made to understand the historical forces that have given rise to the economic systems of other countries and to interpret these systems fairly as phases of the European and the world economy.

Many primary sources have been used, as well as our own special studies in portions of the field covered, but a general treatise of this nature must rest primarily upon the special literature. Our obligations extend, however, not only to the writers of the large number of special studies that have been consulted, but also to numerous associates, past and present. To the stimulus of association with inquiring student minds we are also profoundly indebted.

THE AUTHORS.

# CONTENTS

## MAPS, GRAPHS, AND DIAGRAMS

# PART I. ECONOMIC CONDITIONS AND ORGANIZATION IN THE EARLY EIGHTEENTH CENTURY

## CHAPTER 1

## POPULATION AND RESOURCES

————◆————

### The Scope of Economic History

The movement of economic history is due to reactions among three distinct classes of factors : physical resources, the technologies developed for the use of resources, and social institutions. Failure to appreciate the significance of any of these classes of factors must necessarily render our understanding of events less adequate and less complete than the best scholarship requires. Each of these classes of factors may be studied separately and important contributions to economic history can be made from such studies, even though no actual synthesis of the various factors is attempted. Such partial studies, however, fail to reveal the full meaning of events.

No true synthesis is possible unless all classes of factors are shown in some organic relationship to one another. The study of economic history thus requires some knowledge of economic geography, and some understanding of the technical changes, as well as the analysis of institutional development. The broader features of the rise of capitalistic modes of production are now well established, and there is little difficulty in creating an interest in this phase of economic history. The geographical and technological aspects of economic history have long presented serious difficulties. These materials have been very imperfectly treated in much of the general literature of the subject. Within the last few years, however, important progress has been made in the analysis of these problems. It is therefore possible, now, to attempt a comprehensive interpretation of the movement of economic history.

Full discussion of the newer results would undoubtedly present very great difficulties to elementary students, but detailed treatment of these materials is not necessary. The primary results of the work can be made available to those who have no sustained interest in economic geography and technology. It is merely necessary to

1

recognize that economic history must include some account of the quantitative aspects of social change. We must achieve some positive judgment of the nature and the significance of changes in the mass and location of the population. We must realize that rates of growth are delicate indices of the rapidity of change. The results of intensive study of these problems can be presented in maps and graphs which should quickly reveal their meaning without discussion of the critical problems involved.

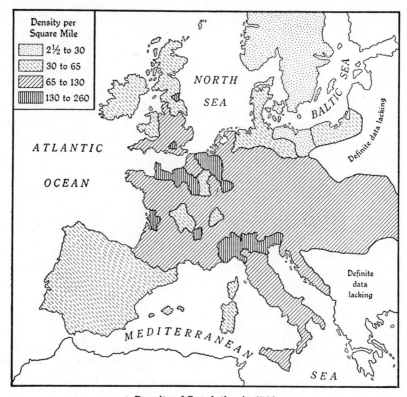

*Density of Population in 1700*

## The Distribution of Population in Europe in 1700

The study of population furnishes us with the most delicate measure of the intensity and direction of economic movement at any given time. The analysis of the economic condition of Europe in 1700 must thus begin with some consideration of the mass and distribution of population. We must consider the variations in density among different regions, and we must determine as best we may the relative importance of the urban population.

The broader features of the distribution of population in Europe may be seen most readily by study of the map on page 2. This map shows somewhat more detail than can be conveniently presented in a table, for we have full details for the counties of England and the generalities of France.[1] The following table shows the general figures for selected dates between 1700 and 1846. It will be observed that the highest densities did not exceed 130 persons per

APPROXIMATE DENSITIES OF POPULATION [2]

*Persons per Square Mile*

|  | 1700 | 1750 | 1800 | 1825 | 1846 |
|---|---|---|---|---|---|
| England and Wales | 90 | 106 | 162 | 210 | 278 |
| Scotland | 38 | 42.5 | 49 | 67 | 85 |
| Ireland | 45 | 68.6 | 124 | 216 | 252 |
| France | 109.5 | 114 | 129 | 147 | 164 |
| Sweden | 9.1 | 9.9 | 13 | 15 | 18.6 |
| Norway | 4.5 | 5.5 | 6.7 | 8.1 | 10.3 |
| Belgium | 137 | 183 | 250 | 300 | 370 |
| Holland | 98.5 | 130 | 160 | 176 | 224 |
| Denmark | 41 | 46 | 52 | 62.5 | 86.5 |
| Schleswig | 55 | 64 | 75 | 84 | 97.5 |
| Holstein | 57 | 68.5 | 95 | 113 | 138 |
| Hanover | 62 | 71.5 | 90 | 104 | 120 |
| Electoral Saxony | 99 | 107 | 126 | 150 | 200 |
| Württemberg | 103 | 145 | 180 | 193 | 221 |
| Bohemia | 72.5 | 100 | 145 | 176 | 213 |
| Neuchâtel | 91.5 | 107 | 152 | 170 | 221 |
| Prussia | 42 | 53 | 72.5 | 91.5 | 125 |
| Spain | 36.6 | 43.5 | 51 | 57.5 | 63.5 |
| Portugal | 45.5 | 70 | 89.5 | 92 | 103.5 |
| Lombardy | 137 | 146 | 222 | 270 | 310 |
| Piedmont | 137 | 146 | 165 | 174 | 200 |
| Sardinia | 32.4 | 38 | 51.7 | 52 | 58.5 |
| Tuscany | 96 | 108 | 129 | 148 | 186 |
| Naples | 74 | 107 | 142 | 162 | 186 |
| Sicily | 105 | 113 | 157 | 160 | 164 |

[1] Statistique Générale de la France, *Territoire et population*, Paris, 1837, vol. I, p. 154. Great Britain, Census of Population, 1841, *Commons Papers*, 1843, vol. XXII, p. 37.
[2] Dieterici, K. F. W., "Die Vermehrung der Bevölkerung Europas seit 1650," *Abhandlungen der k. Akademie der Wissenschaften*, Berlin, 1850, p. 115. Figures for some countries have been revised in the light of later studies.

square mile over any substantial area, though there were considerable masses of population in and around the largest cities — London, Paris, Genoa, and Venice. In several regions the density just exceeded the figure of 130 per square mile, taken as the line of demarcation between these groupings. It is especially significant to note on the map the wide range of territory covered by the shading for 65 to 130 persons per square mile. With very small exceptions, this classification of densities includes a large part of western and central Europe. On the borders are the less fertile areas — Spain, the Baltic countries, and parts of France and the British Isles.

These differences in density of population were closely related to the differences in the qualities of the soils. Only a few maritime regions imported any significant proportion of their basic food, and even these regions were largely dependent upon their immediate neighborhood for the major part of their requirements.

## The Interdependence of Industry and Agriculture

Although the distribution of population was dominated by the production of food, one must not assume that the population was primarily engaged in agriculture. Industry and agriculture were closely associated. In regions with abundance of food, large numbers of specialized industrial workers were maintained in close association with the agricultural workers. Some of these artisans were concentrated in small towns, some were distributed among the villages of the countryside. The farm households supplied large amounts of part-time labor, as many semiskilled processes were carried on in the farmhouses in intervals between housework and the casual farm chores that fell to the lot of the women and children. In the poorer agricultural regions the meager income from the land was supplemented by industrial work during the winter months.

This intimate relationship between industry and agriculture was due to the predominance of pure manual labor in all the more important branches of industry. So little power was used that the productivity of labor was low. Under these circumstances the weight of the food consumed was very much greater than the weight of the raw materials necessary to give employment to the artisans. The differences between the weights of food consumed and of the raw materials used were especially great in the case of the textile industries. Under such circumstances an industry based upon hand work can most advantageously be located with reference to the food supplies needed to maintain the workers.[1]

Wool loses only about one third of its weight in the process of manufacture. Silk, cotton, and linen lose much less. At the beginning of the eighteenth century a bale of wool weighing 240 pounds would give employment to 300 persons for a week, when engaged in the production of a medium grade of cloth. With full employment, 15,600 pounds of wool and other raw materials would furnish employment to the 300 persons for one year. At the standards of consumption recognized in famine time, eight bushels of wheat were allowed per person per year. Three hundred wool workers would thus require 144,000 pounds of wheat. Even if no allowance is made for fuel and for other direct requirements of consumption, it will be evident that raw materials could be moved to the supplies of food with a large balance of advantage.

It is, therefore, superficial to speak of eighteenth-century Europe as being largely self-sufficient because there was little movement of primary foods. The effective utilization of local food supplies required important movements of primary raw materials and finished products. The interdependence of regions upon each other in 1700 must be considered primarily with reference to raw materials, supplementary foods, and highly manufactured products. In 1600, two thirds of the wool produced in Spain was exported to England and northern Europe. In 1700, the Spanish wool trade had declined somewhat, but it was still important. Spain and the northern manufacturing districts were absolutely dependent upon trade with each other. We cannot now discover the precise proportion between the volume of trade and the total consumption of the population. Very likely the percentage of trade to consumption would seem small to us, but whatever the physical volume of trade it was vital to the prosperity of every part of Europe. We cannot understand the economic development of Europe unless we study Europe as a whole. The different regions and nations were associated by necessity in a common life which they understood very imperfectly.

## The Mass and Distribution of the Urban Population

It has long been known that there were very few large cities in Europe in the early modern period. Paris and London each

---

[1] Mr. W. H. Dean, Jr., is preparing a thesis on this subject under the direction of Mr. Usher. The treatment of locational theory, here and in later passages, owes much to Mr. Dean's work.

exceeded a half million as early as 1650, but thereafter growth was slow. The population of these metropolitan areas in the eighteenth century is not accurately known, but it is doubtful if either capital had a population much in excess of 750,000 in 1750. The inadequacy of our statistical material has made it difficult to form any detailed picture of the general conditions of town life at this period, but a neglected source of information makes it possible to present some interesting figures for France. The census of population attempted in 1697–1698 furnishes full details of the urban population for nearly half the total area, and as the regions covered in the complete enumerations are broadly representative, they afford a highly significant picture of the general structure of social life at that time. For towns in excess of 10,000 inhabitants figures are also available for parts of Italy. The results of a tabulation of these returns are shown in the tables below, which give the percentages of the total population living in towns of the various sizes. It will be observed that in a large part of France 10 per cent of the population

PERCENTAGES OF TOTAL POPULATION OF FRANCE IN TOWNS [1]

| Towns of | In 1697–1698, in: | | In 1911 |
|---|---|---|---|
| | 17 Generalities | 18 Generalities | |
| Over 100,000 | 8.7 | 7.15 | 14.56 |
| 20,000–99,999 | 4.2 | 6.1 | 11.64 |
| 10,000–19,999 | 3.5 | 3.24 | 5.83 |
| 5,000– 9,999 | 2.4 | 3.1 | 6.47 |
| 2,000– 4,999 | 4.7 | | 5.70 |
| Under 2,000 | 5.3 | | |
| Total towns | 28.8 | | 44.20 |
| Towns over  2,000 | 23.5 | | 44.20 |
| Towns over  5,000 | 18.8 | 19.59 | 38.5 |
| Towns over 10,000 | 16.4 | 16.49 | 32.03 |

PERCENTAGES OF TOTAL POPULATION IN TOWNS, IN PARTS OF ITALY [2]

| Towns of | Sicily, 1713–1714 | Naples, 1669 | States of the Church, 1700 | Tuscany, 1744 |
|---|---|---|---|---|
| Over 100,000 | 9.2 | 8.6 | 7.6 | |
| 20,000–99,999 | 5.5 | 4.2 | 4.9 | 12.3 |
| 10,000–19,999 | 13.3 | 10.2 | 4.5 | 2.8 |
| Towns over 10,000 | 28.0 | 23.0 | 17.0 | 15.1 |

[1] Boulainvilliers, Le Duc de, *État de France*, London, 1752.
[2] Beloch, J., "La popolazione d'Italia nei secoli XVI, XVII, XVIII," *Bulletin de l'Institut International de Statistique*, III, p. 41.

enumerated in 1697–1698 was living in towns of less than 5,000 inhabitants. Only about 8 per cent of the total population was to be found in cities of more than 100,000, and only about 13 per cent in cities of 20,000 and over. Fully one third of the total "urban" population was thus to be found in the really small units, and little more than half in the positively large towns and cities. The less detailed material on Italy is closely comparable for the units enumerated, and there is abundant ground for believing that the small towns there were no less important than in France.

Conditions in 1700 thus emphasize the importance of the primary distinctions to be drawn between urban and rural types of settlement. The bare antithesis tends to oversimplify the problem of describing the actual distribution of the population. Really complete description should distinguish the larger and smaller villages, as well as several gradations of urban concentration. As some highly characteristic rural types exhibit strong tendencies to agglomeration, the urban cannot be distinguished from the rural unit merely in terms of agglomeration. Furthermore, the large villages of the highly fertile rural areas are commonly as large as the smaller towns of the less fertile districts. Any definition that is to be applicable over wide geographical areas and considerable periods of time must therefore emphasize differences in function rather than mere differences in size. Urban settlements are distinguished by the services they render to the population of a larger area. Towns are, in most instances, centers for defense, trade, or administration; less frequently they are specialized centers for cultural, medical, or recreational activities. Urban settlement is thus to be associated with the development of centralized social organization and with the intensive utilization of special sites. In the Middle Ages and the early modern period the exercise of these special functions did not ordinarily require a great concentration of population. The relatively high cost of inland transportation and the relatively slow speeds of travel imposed sharp limitations upon concentration. All types of towns were affected by these factors. The modest volume of inland trade kept the commercial factors of town life within narrow limits, and the slowness of communication prevented any extensive administrative centralization. The organization of the church likewise tended to produce relatively small units as dioceses for bishops, for the slowness of travel hampered the ecclesiastics as much as the civil administrators. Defensive functions, too, might well be associated with quite small units, for some walled towns were

URBAN AND RURAL POPULATION, ENGLAND AND WALES, 1801-1931 [1]

| Price Williams | Large Towns over 20,000 | Small Towns [2] 2,000-19,999 | Rural Districts and Towns under 2,000 | Total |
|---|---|---|---|---|
| 1801 | 2,404,000 | 1,211,000 | 5,277,000 | 8,892,000 |
| 1811 | 2,878,000 | 1,369,000 | 5,916,000 | 10,164,000 |
| 1821 | 3,582,000 | 1,630,000 | 6,788,000 | 12,000,000 |
| 1831 | 4,520,000 | 1,874,000 | 7,502,000 | 13,896,000 |
| 1841 | 5,572,000 | 2,107,000 | 8,229,000 | 15,909,000 |
| 1851 | 6,885,000 | 2,328,000 | 8,713,000 | 17,927,000 |
| 1861 | 8,218,000 | 2,499,000 | 9,348,000 | 20,066,000 |
| 1871 | 9,800,000 | 2,775,000 | 10,135,000 | 22,712,000 |
| *Official Figures* | | | | |
| 1871 | 9,543,000 | 4,498,000 | 8,671,000 | 22,712,000 |
| 1881 | 12,452,000 | 5,182,000 | 8,340,000 | 25,974,000 |
| 1891 | 16,413,000 | 5,327,000 | 7,362,000 | 29,002,000 |
| 1901 | 18,938,000 | 6,114,000 | 7,469,000 | 32,527,000 |
| 1911 | 22,559,000 | 5,839,000 | 7,907,000 | 36,070,000 |
| 1921 | 23,655,000 | 6,235,000 | 7,851,000 | 37,886,000 |
| 1931 | 25,893,000 | 5,932,000 | 7,999,000 | 39,947,000 |

considered vital to the welfare of a region even at the beginning of the eighteenth century. Many towns were distinguished from the neighboring villages only by their rather more substantial walls; but this feature was merely a matter of quality and degree, for the structure of the village and even of the farm gave some heed to the requirements of defense.

The scale of urban concentration must thus be studied as a problem that is distinct in many ways from the functional services that really distinguish these specialized units of settlement. Even a thinly settled frontier region will hardly be without some urbanized centers, and the substantial rural populations of the Middle Ages and the early modern period required a large number of relatively small towns. Even in 1700 the towns enumerated in France were frequently of less than 1,000 inhabitants. We should hesitate to class them as towns, but they were walled market towns with corporate organization, and frequently they were judicial seats. It is this difference in the scale of urban life that is most characteristic of the changes within our period. This development is most adequately perceived if emphasis is placed upon the classification of

[1] Williams, P., "On the Increase of Population in England and Wales," *Journal of the Statistical Society*, vol. 43 (1880), pp. 466-467. Continued from census materials.

[2] The Census authorities (in the figures for 1871-1931) include settlements of over 2,000 as towns even if they possessed no distinctive legal organization.

PROPORTIONS OF URBAN AND RURAL POPULATION, ENGLAND AND WALES,
1801–1931 [1]

*Given in Percentages of the Total Population*

| Price<br>Williams | Large Towns<br>20,000 and over | Small Towns [2]<br>2,000–19,999 | Rural Districts<br>and Towns<br>under 2,000 |
|---|---|---|---|
| 1801 | 27.1 | 13.4 | 59.5 |
| 1811 | 28.3 | 13.4 | 58.3 |
| 1821 | 29.9 | 13.6 | 56.5 |
| 1831 | 32.5 | 13.4 | 54.1 |
| 1841 | 35.0 | 13.3 | 51.7 |
| 1851 | 38.3 | 13.0 | 48.3 |
| 1861 | 41.1 | 12.4 | 46.5 |
| 1871 | 43.2 | 12.2 | 44.6 |
| *Official Figures* | | | |
| 1871 | 42.0 | 19.7 | 38.3 |
| 1881 | 47.9 | 20.0 | 32.1 |
| 1891 | 56.6 | 18.2 | 25.3 |
| 1901 | 58.3 | 18.5 | 23.2 |
| 1911 | 62.0 | 16.1 | 21.9 |
| 1921 | 62.7 | 16.5 | 20.8 |
| 1931 | 65.1 | 14.8 | 20.1 |

towns by size rather than upon the mere division between the urban
and rural populations. Unfortunately, modern statistical enumerations seldom afford the detail necessary for adequate study of
the relative importance of the small towns. The general character
of the change, however, is indicated by a special tabulation of census
materials for England and Wales for the period 1801–1931 in the
tables on pages 8 and 9.

The larger towns absorbed the primary increase of population, so
that even in 1871, 43 per cent of the total population of England
and Wales was living in towns of over 20,000 inhabitants, as compared with the 12.9 per cent found in similar urban units in
France in 1700. In 1931, 65 per cent of the total population of
England and Wales was living in towns with more than 20,000
inhabitants.

## The Distribution of Population in Europe in 1935

The significance of the picture of conditions in Europe in 1700 will
be appreciated more vividly if it is compared with the picture of
Europe in 1935. The general features of the distribution of densi-

[1] See note 1 on page 8.                    [2] See note 2 on page 8.

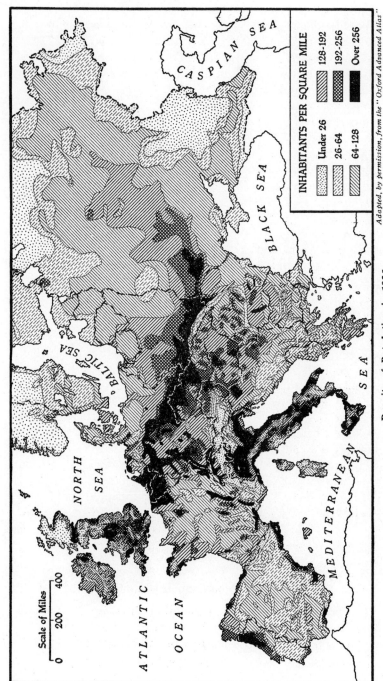

INHABITANTS PER SQUARE MILE

| | | |
|---|---|---|
| Under 26 | 128-192 |
| 26-64 | 192-256 |
| 64-128 | Over 256 |

CASPIAN SEA

BLACK SEA

BALTIC SEA

NORTH SEA

ATLANTIC OCEAN

MEDITERRANEAN SEA

Scale of Miles
0  200  400

Density of Population in 1935

Adapted, by permission, from the "Oxford Advanced Atlas"

10

ties of population are shown in the maps on pages 10 and 12.   Considerable areas, as shown on page 10, have developed a density of population in excess of 256 persons per square mile.   The area of maximum density extends in a somewhat broken belt from the industrial districts of England and Scotland to the industrial region of Poland.   There are extensive areas of dense population in northern and central Italy, southern Germany, and small maritime areas in France, Spain, Portugal, and Sicily.   A very much larger area is shown at densities between 128 and 265 persons per square mile. In 1935 the population had not only increased in mass, it had also become much more intensely localized.

Study of the distribution of population in 1935 in connection with the distribution of mineral resources will reveal the close relationship between the present localization of economic activity and the primary resources in minerals.   Excepting only Italy, small sections of France, and the Iberian Peninsula, the regions of maximum density in 1935 were regions with extensive deposits of coal and iron.   Coal is, on the whole, more important than other minerals as a factor in the localization of economic activity.   The relations of coal to modern industrialism have so long been recognized that there can be no need of insisting upon the fact.   The change from locational patterns dominated by food to locational patterns dominated by coal was brought about by the generalized application of power to industry.   The influence of the introduction of power upon a large scale appears in two aspects of the problem of the transport of materials.

The introduction of power increased the rate of production per capita.   The relation between the weight of raw materials and the weight of food required was changed.   A point might well be reached at which the significance of food would be offset by other considerations.   The use of coal as a source of power, however, created a new situation ; for coal would be consumed in the process of production no less completely than the food consumed by labor. In both cases the total weight used becomes a special factor in the industrial location because none of this weight enters into the finished product.   It is most economical to use such weight-losing materials at their original source.   Transportation costs incurred for moving such materials are a net addition to the cost of the finished product.

The importance of the fuel problem will be most vividly appreciated if we make a rough computation of the actual weights to be

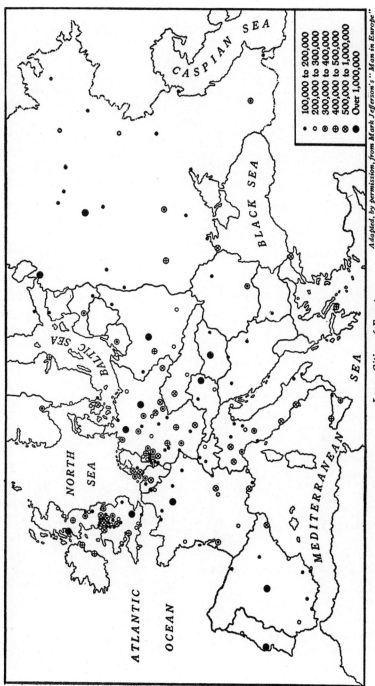

CASPIAN SEA

BLACK SEA

BALTIC SEA

NORTH SEA

ATLANTIC OCEAN

MEDITERRANEAN SEA

100,000 to 200,000
200,000 to 300,000
300,000 to 400,000
400,000 to 500,000
500,000 to 1,000,000
Over 1,000,000

*Adapted, by permission, from Mark Jefferson's "Man in Europe"*

*Large Cities of Europe*

moved.   On the basis of a 40-hour week there would be 2,080 hours in a working year.   At its best, the early Watt engine consumed 6.26 pounds of coal per horsepower hour.   To furnish a workman with one horsepower per hour for a year, over 13,000 pounds of coal would be required.   If we assume a 60- or 72-hour week, the fuel requirement would be correspondingly increased.   Even if we allow for improvements in the standard of living since 1700, the workman would hardly consume much more than 500 pounds of primary foods.   In the early textile industries the power supplied ranged between one-half horsepower and one horsepower per capita. The weight of fuel to be moved was, therefore, considerable even in the textile trades, which used much less power than the iron trade.

The new power technology thus created conditions in which food became progressively less important as a locational factor and coal rapidly became a paramount consideration in the location of industries using much fuel, either as a source of power or as a source of heat.   Food resources did not cease to be of importance, but sharp distinctions arose between hand processes and power proc- esses.   In most instances regions dependent upon hand processes were obliged to accept lower standards of living, because of low productivity.

### The Growth of Population, 1700–1935

We have established the general character of population patterns in 1700 and in 1935.   We must now consider briefly the magnitude of the change and above all the rate of change.

The inadequacy of our statistical information tends to obscure the extraordinary magnitude of the increase in population since the late eighteenth century.   Complete enumerations of population did not become an established practice until this period of economic development was well begun, and in consequence exact records give us no information about any other period in the history of population.   We have thus come to regard these phenomena of growth as an ordinary feature of social life, and many writers assume that the continuance of prosperity must necessarily be accompanied by the maintenance of these really remarkable rates of increase.   Both historical study and abstract analysis lead inevi- tably to the conclusion that such periods of increase in population are unusual.   In a discussion of the probable population of the world, G. H. Knibbs, the director of the Census Bureau of Australia, in a statement made in 1914, shows that the rate of increase in census-taking countries from 1906 to 1911 was 1.159 per cent per year and that the average rate of increase in the world as a whole for the period 1804 to 1914 was 0.864 per cent per year.  These rates may not seem very high, but even the lower rate for the world leads to doubling the population every 81 years.  Their significance becomes apparent only when we apply such rates of increase to relatively long periods of time.  Mr. Knibbs continues:

"Either this rate of increase [1.159 per cent per year] must be enormously greater than has existed in the past history of the world, or enormous numbers of human beings must have been blotted out by catastrophes of various kinds from time to time.  For, putting the present [1914] population at 1,649,000,000, at the average rate of increase of the years [1906-1911] this number would be produced from a single pair of human beings in about 1,782 years, that is to say since A.D. 132, or since Salvius Julianus revised under Hadrian the Edicts of the Praetors.  Even the rate given by the world populations between 1804 and 1914 [0.864 per cent] gives only 2,397 years, carrying us back only to B.C. 483, or since the days of Darius I of Persia." [1]

He concludes that the average rate of the increase of population over long periods of time must be less than the rate of 0.16 per cent per year exhibited by France in the later nineteenth century.  The rates of increase recorded in our statistics must thus be regarded as remarkable and unusual social phenomena, and we must be on our guard lest familiarity should make them seem commonplace.

The materials available for the study of the growth of population in Europe can be most readily analyzed by graphic methods.  Computation of annual rates of increase with the compound-interest formula is a laborious process.  Graphic methods are less exact, but the errors lie well within the limits of error in the statistical material.  On semilogarithmic charts, straight lines indicate constant rates of growth, and the rate per cent is a direct function of the slope of the line.  With a little care, percentages of increase can be read from the graphs by measurement of the slopes. [2]

The changes in the rates of increase of population during the eighteenth and nineteenth centuries are shown in the graphs on page 15.  Much of the material for the period 1700-1800 is merely an

---

[1] Knibbs, G. H., "The Mathematical Theory of Population," *Census of the Commonwealth of Australia*, 1911, vol. I, Appendix A, p. 32.

[2] For fuller explanation of these methods of analysis and of the semilogarithmic graphs shown in this book, see Appendix I at the end of the text.

approximation, either because of deficiencies of enumeration or by reason of difficulties in making adjustments to stated areas. The material from 1800 to 1910 is based upon comprehensive enumeration except for European Russia. Adjustments to the present areas of Prussia and of Germany have been made by government officials.

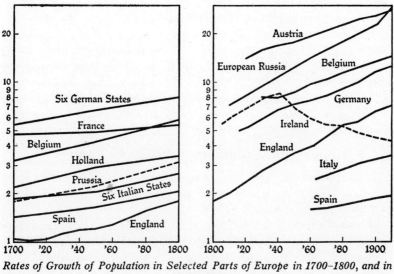

*Rates of Growth of Population in Selected Parts of Europe in 1700–1800, and in 1800–1910*

In order to simplify the arrangement of these graphs, the figures for Austria, Belgium, and several other lands have been plotted on scales different from the one shown. Only the slopes of the lines are significant.[1]

Study of the graphs discloses a marked acceleration in the rates of growth until 1850, with some notable shifts in the regions of most rapid growth in the latter part of the nineteenth century. The highest rate in the first half of the eighteenth century is the rate of 0.58 per cent per year in Holland, excepting only the decade 1730–1740, when England's population increased at a rate of 0.75 per cent. In the second half of the eighteenth century there is acceleration in England and in Prussia at rates of 1.0 and 0.66 per cent respectively.

[1] As data for 1700–1800 are available for most areas only at fifty-year intervals, the lines in the first graph are in effect linear trends. If more abundant data were available, all the lines would disclose variations in the rate of growth. The line for England and Wales, plotted from decennial figures, gives a more exact picture of the course of population growth, but it will be noted that the "curve" must be broken up into a series of linear trends for purposes of general analysis. On the scale shown here, the smaller differences in slopes are not accurately appreciated by the naked eye.

Italy and Spain show rates of about 0.5 per cent each.   In the first
half of the nineteenth century the rate of increase in England and
Wales reached the figure of 1.5 per cent.   Ireland disclosed a similar
rate for nearly a generation and in one decade a rate of 4.0 per cent
was reached.   Germany, European Russia, and for a single decade
Austria, exhibit rates of about 1.25 per cent, possibly 1.30 in
European Russia, though the figure for population in 1811 is uncertain.   A large portion of Europe was thus developing at rates which
would double the population in less than fifty-six years.   These
rates were not fully maintained in the second half of the century
except in Russia.   For the Continent as a whole there was certainly
a diminished rate of increase, though some portions of Europe have
no adequate records, and no general statement can be made with
confidence.

### Regional Differences in Rates of Growth

Comparisons of the development in different countries are
perhaps even more significant than these general features of the
graphs.   England and Wales, the most highly industrialized area
in the early nineteenth century, increased only a little faster than
European Russia, the most important frontier area in Europe.
The margin of difference would amount to five years in the time
required to double the population : fifty-six years against fifty-one.
This gives us the clue to much of this widely diffused growth of
population.   There were three general phases of growth represented
in the European area : intensive growth around the coal fields and
in the great commercial centers ; extensive growth on all the frontiers
of Slavic Europe ; increases in the maturely settled agricultural
districts, due jointly to improvements in agricultural productivity
and to the indirect influence of industrialization in neighboring
states.   Industrialization played an important part in the development of Europe as a whole, and its indirect influences upon the
less favored regions are perhaps the most striking indication of
economic interdependence.   The great coal and iron resources of
Europe must be reckoned as an asset not only by the countries which
actually possess them, but by their neighbors.   Unfortunately,
these matters become involved with matters of political prestige
and national pride, so that the economic gains are frequently ignored.
   Some features of development in particular countries should be
emphasized.   The record of Ireland in the nineteenth century
furnishes an almost unique case of remarkable increase in population

followed by an even more remarkable decline, for such decreases in population are rare. This episode is commonly explained as the result of a great change in the potato crop of Ireland, for the introduction of the potato there provided a great increase in the food supply, while the appearance of the black rot in 1845 restricted the crop and led to heavy emigration to Great Britain and the United States. Some details of the timing of growth in England and in Germany are also significant. The low rates of growth in England in the years 1700–1720 and 1740–1760 imply that the new technologies were not exerting any marked influence on the growth of population. The rapid growth in England in 1720–1740 can doubtless be best explained in terms of agriculture and food supplies; the densities of population were not carried above limits well within the margins of the older technologies of industry and agriculture. In 1760 growth begins which must be identified with the innovations in agriculture and industry. Three broad periods can be distinguished: 1760–1800, 1800–1880, and 1880–1910. The first and third periods disclose rates of growth of 1.0 per cent per year; the second period as a whole shows an average rate of 1.375 per cent, with some decades above and some below the general average.

The actual rate of increase is not itself so remarkable as the length of the period over which it was maintained. For more than one hundred fifty years this region, which had already achieved a density in excess of one hundred persons per square mile, maintained a rate of increase in excess of 1.0 per cent per year. Only in the Continental coal fields do we find any development that is comparable, but even in the Rhineland the increase has not been maintained as long, though the rates are higher: in 1816–1880, about 1.25 per cent per year; in 1880–1890, 1.75 per cent; in 1890–1910, 2.00 per cent.

This long period of rapid growth in England is significant in connection with the concept of an "industrial revolution" primarily confined to the latter part of the eighteenth century. The remarkable continuity of recorded growth and the acceleration in the early nineteenth century are hardly consistent with the heavy emphasis placed upon the eighteenth century in the commonly accepted concept. The changes of the eighteenth century were important, but they were only a beginning. The developments which followed were not merely the result of the accomplishments of that initial period, but the cumulative result of a continuing technological achievement. As the period of change was long and the

growth essentially continuous, it seems better to treat the movement as an evolutionary process.  In a certain sense these epoch-
making changes were "revolutionary," but they were not brought
about by a sudden and violent change.

Conditions in Prussia and the rest of Germany are also interesting.  The rate of growth in Prussia exceeded the rate in Germany as
a whole throughout the two centuries.

RATES OF INCREASE OF POPULATION IN GERMANY: RATE PER CENT PER YEAR

|                    | 1700–50 | 1750–1800 | 1800–50 | 1850–90 | 1890–1910 |
|--------------------|---------|-----------|---------|---------|-----------|
| Prussia            | 0.5     | 0.66      | 1.25    | 0.875   | 1.5       |
| Six German states  | 0.416   | 0.36      | 0.75    | —       | —         |

|                     |  |  | 1816–40 | 1840–70 | 1870–1910 |
|---------------------|--|--|---------|---------|-----------|
| German Empire       | — | — | 1.125   | 0.70    | 1.10      |
| Non-Prussian states | — | — | 0.875   | 0.585   | 1.0       |

This development of Prussia was due to a combination of factors:
progressive settlement of the frontier provinces; more complete
utilization of the agrarian resources of the more fertile provinces;
the introduction of the new technology in textiles and metals.
These factors cannot readily be separated, because their influence
was not felt in equal measure in all the provinces.  It is sufficient
to note the substantial importance of the first half of the nineteenth
century.  These data indicate clearly the danger of emphasizing
the establishment of the Empire as the beginning of a new period
in the economic history of Germany.  The differences between
Prussia and the non-Prussian states are due to the relatively greater
density of population in the South German states in 1700, and to
the lack of great resources of iron and coal comparable to the
resources of the provinces of Prussia.

The development of Belgium and Holland is so closely associated
with the coal fields of Flanders and the industrialized area of the
Rhine that it is not necessary to comment at length.  In France,
after modest increases in the first quarter of the nineteenth century
at rates of 0.52 and 0.66 per cent per year (in 1800–1819 and in
1820–1829), the net growth of population fell to very low rates.
No decade from 1840 to 1909 exceeded a rate of 0.40 per cent per
year, and two decades fell to 0.07 and 0.08 per cent (1860–1869 and
1890–1899).  These low rates were mainly attributable to losses in
extensive areas which were not more than offset by the gains in the
industrial and commercial regions.  Internal readjustments have

thus been more conspicuous in France than in the other countries of Europe. Even Italy and Spain were, at this period, less affected by such internal redistributions of population; but both Italy and Spain had experienced considerable internal stress at earlier periods. Their modest gains are none the less remarkable.

## Population and the Balance of Power

These changes in the distribution of population have exerted important influences upon the political power and the prestige of the various European states. In general, central Europe has gained in importance, and France has become relatively less important. Within the Germanic area of central Europe, Prussia has become more and more important, and Austria had lost much power and prestige even before her dismemberment at Versailles. Finally, the spectacular growth of Russia in the nineteenth century carried her far beyond the frontier phase of her development and made her quantitatively a compellingly important factor in the economic life of Europe.

Economic changes of this type make themselves felt very slowly, because there are many complicating factors. The mass of population has a certain significance in its relation to military strength, but in the eighteenth century this phase of economic influence was less directly felt than it has been since the introduction of a general obligation to perform military service. This change was an important contributory factor in the political significance of the capacities of Napoleon I. In a similar fashion increases in wealth were not an immediate factor in political changes. In most of the countries of Europe the privileges of the nobility limited the effective taxable resources of the state until the second half of the nineteenth century. The rapidity of the development of the power to tax varied widely among the different states, so that the political consequences of economic growth seldom appear simultaneously with the economic change. The economic changes commonly precede the political consequences by a wide interval.

Political changes, too, have been profoundly influenced by revisions of boundaries and by alterations in the structure and organization of the state. Such transformations have intensified the changes that would have inevitably accompanied the economic development of the various geographic regions.

In 1700 political power was only in part dependent upon the position of any political unit, as several important families had

APPROXIMATE POPULATION OF SELECTED EUROPEAN COUNTRIES,
IN THOUSANDS, 1700–1846 [1]

|  | 1700 | 1750 | 1800 | 1846 |
|---|---|---|---|---|
| United Kingdom | 8,635 | 10,012 | 14,997 | 27,220 |
| France (bounds of 1819–1846) | 23,600 | 24,600 | 27,800 | 35,400 |
| Spain | 7,250 | 8,600 | 10,480 | 12,650 |
| Portugal | 1,739 | 2,662 | 3,420 | 3,940 |
| Italy, Six states [2] | 9,205 | 10,380 | 13,405 | 17,035 |
| Italy — Area of 1910 [3] | 11,500 | 13,150 | 16,900 | 21,200 |
| Belgium | 1,610 | 2,150 | 2,960 | 4,350 |
| Holland | 1,100 | 1,460 | 1,795 | 2,505 |
| Norway | 587 | 705 | 1,050 | 1,325 |
| Sweden | 1,640 | 1,790 | 2,340 | 3,340 |
| Denmark | 665 | 745 | 845 | 1,400 |
| Prussia — Provinces of 1688 | 1,790 | 2,260 | 3,180 | 5,380 |
| Prussia — Boundaries of 1846 | 5,100 | 6,420 | 8,800 | 15,300 |
| Six non-Prussian states [4] | 5,208 | 6,350 | 8,400 | 11,948 |
| Approximate population of non-Prussian states of 1st Empire | 5,800 | 7,050 | 9,320 | 13,300 |
| Russia (without Finland) | — | — | 31,000 | — |

acquired control of widely scattered domains. The House of Hapsburg is the most conspicuous, but by no means the only, illustration
of this phase of political organization. Different branches of the
family held Spain, parts of the Low Countries (now Belgium and
Luxemburg), Austria proper, and parts of Italy. Some member of
the family commonly secured additional prestige as Emperor of the
Holy Roman Empire. The extinction of the Spanish line in 1700
led to the establishment of a Bourbon dynasty in Spain, but after
a period of war the outlying possessions were retained by the
Hapsburgs. In such a period conditions in particular regions are
less important in high politics than the dynastic combinations
created by war, diplomacy, and marriage. The rise of Prussia and
the Napoleonic wars clarified the political situation in some measure.
The unification of Italy and the later unification of Germany were
even more important steps towards the effective political organization of extensive geographic regions into compact territorial states.
Such political developments inevitably increase the interdependence
of economic development and political prestige, so that the politics
and diplomacy of the later nineteenth century must needs be

[1] Computed partly from the densities given in the table on page 3.
[2] Sicily, Naples, Piedmont, Sardinia, Tuscany, Lombardy — an area of 87,492
square miles.
[3] Area of 1910 — 110,550 square miles.
[4] Electoral Saxony, Hanover, Württemberg, Bohemia, Schleswig, Holstein.

POPULATION OF EUROPE, IN THOUSANDS, 1850-1910 [1]

|  | 1850 | 1865 | 1880 | 1910 |
|---|---|---|---|---|
| United Kingdom | 27,201 | 29,925 | 34,623 | 44,915 |
| France | 35,630 | 38,020 | 37,450 | 39,528 |
| Spain | — | 15,920 | 16,859 | 19,540 |
| Portugal | — | — | 4,551 | 5,958 |
| Italy | — | 24,950 | 28,211 | 34,377 |
| Belgium | 4,426 | 4,984 | 5,520 | 7,422 |
| Holland, or the Netherlands | 3,001 | 3,510 | 4,049 | 5,904 |
| Norway | 1,392 | 1,690 | 1,909 | 2,353 |
| Sweden | 3,462 | 4,092 | 4,572 | 5,499 |
| Denmark | 1,422 | 1,694 | 1,969 | 2,702 |
| Germany (bounds of 1871) | 35,310 | 39,545 | 45,093 | 64,568 |
| Austria | 17,629 | 19,650 | 22,075 | 28,427 |
| Hungary | — | — | 15,697 | 20,793 |
| Switzerland | — | [2,630] | 2,839 | 3,735 |
| Russia in Europe (without Finland) | 60,000 | 74,800 | 85,200 | 142,500 |
| Finland | 1,629 | 1,835 | 2,047 | 3,093 |
| Bulgaria | — | — | 2,008 | 4,317 |
| Rumania | — | 4,133 | 4,546 | 6,966 |
| Serbia | — | 1,186 | 1,724 | 2,916 |
| Greece | — | 1,395 | 1,702 | 2,600 |

analyzed with more explicit reference to economic conditions than would be necessary in any study of the eighteenth century.

It would be, perhaps, an error to attribute direct influence to economic factors in every case, but their outstanding importance is rarely more apparent than in the rise of Prussia to a position of decisive leadership in Germany. The history of the Customs Union shows clearly the importance of economic factors in bringing the South German states to associate themselves with Prussia in preference to Austria.

The record of economic development given in tables on pages 20 and 21 is thus merely the background of the complex political developments of the period. The figures certainly possess considerable significance, but they must be used with caution. It must be remembered, also, that the figures for the eighteenth century are approximations only, based upon marriages, births, and deaths computed in somewhat different ways for the various areas. But even when every possible allowance has been made, the change in the position of France is strikingly exhibited. The absence of reliable figures for Austria in the eighteenth century makes it impossible

[1] Statistique Générale de la France, *Statistique internationale du mouvement de la population*, (1907) I, pp. 2-42; (1913) II, Tableaux, pp. 3-18.

to follow all the phases of the comparative development of Prussia. The earliest trustworthy figure for Austria is for 1819–1820, when the population within the boundaries of 1914 is given as 13,851,000; the population of Prussia within the boundaries of 1846 was, in 1820, 14,414,000.   Speculation on the earlier history of population in Austria is purposeless.   Dieterici gives figures for Bohemia from 1772, but Bohemia was scarcely representative of the entire area. The returns for European Russia are also subject to considerable elements of error, though there can be no doubt of the general character of the development.   The acquisitions of territory in the south, the settlement of the great black-earth areas there, and the rise of the grain trade of the Black Sea made the economic history of Russia largely a record of frontier settlement that presents a close parallel to the economic history of the United States.

A classified Bibliography of books suitable for reference and for collateral reading is included near the end of this book. See first the plan of classification shown by the table of contents thereof.

# CHAPTER 2

# THE ORGANIZATION OF COMMERCE AND INDUSTRY IN 1700

———◆———

## A New Order Foreshadowed

The social structure of Europe at the beginning of the eighteenth century differs from the social system of our time in so many ways that at first glance it would seem different only in incidental details from the social system of the period of the Reformation. The rural life of the larger portions of the population was narrow; the number of large towns was very small, and the numerous market towns of less than 5,000 inhabitants fostered a type of provincialism that we associate with the Middle Ages. It is easy to draw the conclusion that no significant changes took place in economic and social life in the interval between the discovery of the New World and the invention of Newcomen's steam engine (1702). Nothing could be further from the truth. It is hardly too much to say that all the fundamental elements of modern business enterprise were developed during the sixteenth and seventeenth centuries. The basic features of the new social structure were worked out, but they were applied on a relatively small scale, and the economic changes found no adequate expression in the political life of the time.

There were thus present in the economic and social life of Europe many new elements whose significance could be appreciated only by those who were not misled by superficial appearances. The landed gentry were still the most prominent group in social and political life, but the businessmen and financiers were already able to exert significant pressure at particular points in the political system. Distinctions between the classes were softened in nearly all countries, and in some countries the wealthy traders and businessmen were rapidly assimilated by the ruling class. The village still preserved much of its former appearance even in England; but it was by no means the same village. In some sections the position of the agricultural workers was changed. In the industrialized regions the influence of the capitalists had become the dominant factor in both town and country. The cottage craftsman and the unskilled workers had lost much or all of their independence. In the towns, despite the protective shelter of some formal organization in a guild, the small master had become in fact the paid employee of a capitalist who dominated much of the process of production from some strategic stage of manufacture or from control of the sale of the final product.  Capital had already become a power, though its power was exercised through channels that are not readily perceived by the modern reader who is accustomed to slightly different forms of industrial organization.  The essential features of modern business organization appear before the factory system becomes the predominant form of industrial organization and long before the corporation supplanted the personal businesses and the partnerships that were still a conspicuous feature of the early nineteenth century.

Although we commonly think of the factory as the most characteristic feature of modern economic organization, it is merely one of many types of business enterprise.  Transport and merchandising are important elements in the economic system, and any adequate description must do full justice to all phases of economic activity. The primary characteristics of modern business enterprise are common to all forms.  The modern enterprise differs from the medieval enterprise in every essential feature: the accounting unit is more explicitly defined and its affairs are more adequately analyzed; the legal forms of association have been developed and the advantages of association have been more extensively exploited; finally, specialization of function has been carried much further than in the Middle Ages, so that relations of different classes of enterprise to one another are more explicitly defined.

### The Organization of Craft Industry

Industry in 1700 was organized in many different forms according to the widely varying circumstances of particular industries. The highly industrialized centers presented many features of capitalistic organization which we shall discuss presently.  There remained, however, a large field for the small craft shop.  The large number of small towns and villages offered only very restricted market areas for the crafts concerned solely with local consumption. The crafts concerned with the preparation of food and drink were necessarily organized with reference to small local markets.  The butchers, fishmongers, bakers, retail grocers, apothecaries, millers, chandlers, and like crafts were in all cases developed on a scale proportionate to their immediate market.  Even in the larger towns, the enterprises were characteristically small, as the individual establishment was essentially a neighborhood unit.  The building crafts, the small metal crafts working for domestic consumption, the clothing crafts, and shoemakers were likewise organized in small units. The aspect of industry was thus profoundly different in the two primary divisions: the major export industries were already dominated by capital; nearly all the industries serving local consumption, and some export industries, were carried on in small-scale establishments that had not outgrown the limits of the craft shop.

Taking the industrial field in its entirety, we find all the possible types of craft shop. In some industries the craft shop in the smaller towns and villages was merely a business carried on by an isolated craft worker. There was not enough work to justify even the employment of an apprentice. Furthermore, there were discriminations against apprentices taught in the small villages, so that the craftsman would not find it easy to secure an apprentice. The master might teach his own sons, but even if he did so there would be periods in which he had no apprentice. Normally, however, the craft shop was something more than an establishment with an isolated worker. In most industries the craftsman was assisted by apprentices and journeymen. Apprentices were boys learning the craft. The period of apprenticeship was commonly between five and seven years. Few of the crafts were really so difficult that this length of time was required for instruction, but a relatively long period was customary in order to enable the master to secure some compensation for time actually given to instruction and for materials spoiled or wasted. As boys were apprenticed at the age of twelve or thirteen, their physical strength was a limiting factor in some crafts. All things considered, the period of apprenticeship was not unreasonable, but there can be little doubt that the requirement of a period of apprenticeship was consciously designed to restrict the numbers of craftsmen. In some regions the number of apprentices was rigidly limited. It was even more common to require that the apprenticeship be served in the town or region.

Even when there were few formal restrictions, the craftsman was rarely able to set up a shop of his own as soon as he had completed his apprenticeship. Some of the older guild statutes say explicitly that no one shall set up a shop until he is married and has sufficient funds. Both conditions are suggestive. In most instances the craft work was done on the premises used for living purposes. The shop was merely a room or shed devoted to craft work. As the master was presumed to be in a position to accept apprentices, no one could really be a full-fledged master until he was married and had set up housekeeping; because apprentices had to be boarded and lodged, and in the earlier period even journeymen lived with the master. Genuine economic factors thus required some period of transition between apprenticeship and mastership. As long as the craft system retained all its implications, this period of transition was short. It was merely an interval of one, two, or three years within which the trained craftsman worked for wages, in the shop of a master. By saving something from his wages, he would soon be able to marry and set up a shop of his own.

Conditions in the sixteenth and seventeenth centuries, however, had become progressively unfavorable to the lower grades of industrial workers, and even in the crafts serving local consumption distinctions appeared between employer and employee. This development resulted in the emergence of groups that remained journeymen indefinitely. They married and lived in rooms of their own, but they never secured the right to set up shops of their own, and seldom accumulated the means that would have been necessary. It is difficult to appraise the factors involved in this development. In some crafts the shop became more pretentious and required an outlay beyond the means of the less capable and adaptable workmen. In the tailoring trades, for instance, there could be considerable gradation among the various establishments. Differences in skill in cutting, and differences in the capacity to deal with customers, might both become important factors in the development of the shop. The entire group of crafts ministering to luxurious consumption discloses a significant development towards a larger establishment, with considerable differentiation between the master and his workmen.

There were thus three primary types of craft shop: the shop with the isolated master; the shop with a fixed group of apprentices and journeymen; the shop with a basic permanent staff, and a floating group of journeymen hired from day to day or from week to week. In numbers, shops of the second type would not be likely to have fewer than two apprentices and two journeymen. Such an establishment would thus have a total of five persons including the master, who certainly worked full time. Such a shop might have a larger staff, but descriptions of craft shops seldom record more than ten persons in shops with an essentially permanent staff. The third type was definitely larger; the permanent staff would in most instances amount to four or five, and the floating journeymen would bring the numbers up well over ten in periods of active trade.

The development of the third type of craft shop created a new problem for the artisan. The short period of employment with any one master made it essential to organize some simple means of bringing the workmen into touch with the masters. In some of the large towns the journeymen seeking employment formed the habit of assembling each morning in a particular street or square. Gradually a formal house of call developed, with a formal roll of workers. In its fully developed form this arrangement involved a labor organization with a recognized monopoly of placement. The masters recognized that journeymen could be hired only at the house of call and only in the order in which their names stood on the roll. The journeymen recognized that they might secure employment only at the house of call, subject to the conditions imposed by the organization. They had to pay their dues to the organization. This general system was further amplified by the development of the journeyman's tour. In France the journeyman was expected to make an extensive tour upon the completion of his apprenticeship. The same practice appeared in many sections of Germany. In Spain movement was discouraged. It may be that this period of travel contributed something positive to the proficiency of the journeymen, but the primary purpose was to promote sufficient mobility of labor to prevent serious overstocking of the labor supply in the larger towns. The journeymen, once on the road, were practically forced to keep on the march until they reached a town which had some need of their particular skill. On reaching town the wandering journeyman proceeded to the house of call for his craft. If current labor conditions were bad, he was given some help and urged to go on to the next town. If accepted, his name was placed upon the roll and his chances of employment were equal to those of the rest of the craft. If, on the other hand, a journeyman was so ill-advised as to seek work on his own initiative, he would be treated as "scabs" have always been treated.

Organized journeymen's associations were more extensively developed in France than in either England or Germany. There was no significant development of this type in Spain; about Italy, we are not very well informed. The organizations in France were said to date from the period of cathedral building in the thirteenth and fourteenth centuries, but these claims are without documentary support. The organizations of which we have continuous record are not older than the sixteenth century, and many of the crafts have no formal records of a journeymen's association until the eighteenth century. These organizations were at times prohibited, and their activities were always subjected to severe regulation. The records are therefore incomplete, but we have some lists which are significant as indices of the range of crafts in which the floating journeymen created special problems. In 1789 there were journeymen's associations in Paris in the following crafts: basketmakers, carpenters, chamois dressers, curriers, dyers, founders, glaziers, harness makers, hatters, horseshoers, joiners, kettlemakers, linen drapers, locksmiths, nailers, planers, plasterers, ropemakers, saddlers, shearmen, slater-tilers, smiths, stonecutters, stovemakers, tanners, tinsmiths, turners, and wheelwrights. Dijon lists add: capmakers, printers, shoemakers, tailors. With the exception of the cloth workers these journeymen were almost certainly attached to craft shops of the general type described.

## The Craft Guilds

The guilds of the Middle Ages survived as regulative organizations and as benefit societies, but there were many changes in structure and function. The large towns presented some special problems. There were many craft organizations in all the greater towns, and their relations with one another and with administrative authorities were profoundly influenced by local circumstances. In London the wealthier craft guilds had become important at an early date and exerted significant influence upon the government of the city. Their power was definitely established early in the sixteenth century, and thereafter the twelve great livery companies were the dominant factor in the city government. The companies accumulated rich endowments, and retained their social importance until the latter part of the nineteenth century. In Paris the crafts still elected the Provost of Merchants, but his authority diminished steadily in importance after the middle of the sixteenth century. In Italy most of the larger towns lost their autonomy and the greater guilds lost their political importance and even their independence in the execution of their regulatory functions.

The structure of the crafts became much more complex in all the larger towns. Some crafts developed two classes of masters; one group, composed of the well-to-do, maintained large industrial or mercantile establishments in which the poorer masters and journeymen were employed. In many instances masters and journeymen of several different crafts were dependent upon a master of a different craft for their livelihood. Many cases appear in all large towns.

In London the authority of some of the great companies was extended to include subordinate crafts, but in many parts of Europe no adequate provision was made for the new problems created by these hierarchies of crafts.

The more characteristic changes in guild organization occurred outside the large towns.  In the Middle Ages there were few formally organized craft guilds in the small towns and villages.  The small numbers of craftsmen were able to maintain customary standards of workmanship and competition without much administrative machinery.  With the growth of monarchical power attempts were made to extend the general features of guild organization over the entire territory of the various states.  The French ordinances of 1581 and 1597 are especially important.  The policy was not without constructive elements, for it tended to facilitate freedom of movement among craft workers, who had previously found it difficult to move from the country to the towns or from one town to another.  Some restrictions remained.  Provisions were made to protect the great capitals such as Paris from provincial craftsmen who were presumed to be less skilled.  Despite these advantages, the broad comprehensive schemes of the great French ordinances tended to build up more organization than was necessary or desirable.  The poorer craftsmen were burdened with fees that they could ill afford; the close supervision of processes of production made industry less adaptable to changes in trade and technique.  The generalization of guild regulation, however, did not check the development of capitalist control, though this generalization made it more difficult for the small masters and journeymen to organize effectively to protect their interests.  The evils of the generalization of guild organization became progressively more serious.  Even by 1700, the modest gains were heavily offset by the disadvantages in nearly all the Continental countries.

English policy in this period was highly distinctive.  Instead of extending the guild system throughout the country, the system of apprenticeship was made obligatory.  The Statute of Artificers, sometimes called the Statute of Apprentices (1563), restricted the exercise of the skilled crafts to persons who had served a seven-year apprenticeship with an accredited master.  The guilds already in existence were fully recognized, and their position was carefully protected.  Entrance to a specified list of crafts was restricted to sons of members and to sons of persons possessing property.  In the provincial towns and rural districts in which no craft guilds existed, the administration of the new regulations was entrusted to the justices of the peace at Quarter Sessions.

This mode of meeting the problems of the time possessed all the advantages and entailed none of the disadvantages of the policy adopted on the Continent. Provision was made for the maintenance of a supply of skilled labor. Some guarantees were provided against overcrowding in particular crafts. But the industrial system was not burdened with needless organizations, rules, and restrictions. As conditions changed, some adjustments were made by allowing some of the provisions of the Statute of Apprentices to fall into abeyance. The local authorities proved to be more flexible in mind than the agents of the central governments that were responsible for industrial regulation on the Continent. The newer developments of the eighteenth century were not seriously obstructed in England, though later the woolen industries faced many uncertainties, which were relieved only by the suspension and ultimate repeal of the Statute (1813 and 1814).

### Beginnings of Capitalistic Control; the Merchant-Employer

The fondness of many writers for sharply defined classifications has long obscured the length of the period in which we find side by side both capitalistic and noncapitalistic forms of industrial organization. In a group of industries which was constantly diminishing we find until a late date craft shops that were definitely noncapitalistic. The master was a fellow worker, not an employer. Some use was made of capital instruments, but there was no specialized employer control. In a different group of industries we begin to find capitalist employers at a very early date. Sombart, the eminent Marxist historian, attempts to work out a chronology for the development of capitalism, based upon the relative importance of capitalist influences. Such schemes are clearly of significance as an expression of a mature judgment of the relative importance of capitalistic forms at various periods, but the periods can never mean more than that. It is perhaps less misleading to students to approach these industrial problems from the point of view of careful description of all the forms of organization that are found period by period. Such comprehensive descriptions include the judgments of relative importance emphasized by the periods, but they do not run the risk of distracting the attention of the student from the small-scale trades concerned with personal consumption.

Capitalistic forms can be found in medieval Europe as early as the twelfth and thirteenth centuries; and after the fourteenth century capitalistic industry is of great importance in a variety of export industries in the highly industrialized centers. The craft shop in its simpler forms survived over large areas until the second half of the nineteenth century, and in areas of limited importance it still survives in Europe. In India and the Far East the simple craft shop is still of great importance, though it is losing ground rapidly at the present time.

The simplest form of capitalist enterprise is the merchant-employer or putting-out system. The essential feature of this mode of organization is the rise of the wholesale merchant to a position in which he controls and finances the process of production, in whole or in part. In many instances this is precisely what happens in the course of development. The drapers or clothiers became employers of the craft workers. The wholesale merchants of silks at Lyon (or Lyons), in France, became employers. Less frequently, master workers became merchants; they abandoned actual craft work and became merchants who employed others in one or more related crafts. This system of industrial organization is extraordinarily adaptable. The merchant secures control of production by furnishing the raw materials to the craft workers and directing their efforts into the types and styles of goods most in demand. The craft worker continues to work in his shop without any direct supervision. The external aspects of industrial organization are thus scarcely disturbed. The dependent worker in the export trades turns his goods over to a merchant who has made an advance contract for them, whereas in the earlier stage the craft worker in these export trades sold the goods to some wholesale merchant in an open market. Capitalistic control thus developed without displacing the craftsman either as to the locus of the actual work or as to general regional distribution. The external aspect of the industrialized regions, therefore, changed very little in the long period dominated by this transition. It is thus correct to say that in 1700 the appearance of life in the industrial towns of Europe would not have seemed strange to an observer who had known these districts in the fourteenth century. But it should be noted that such a statement must be understood with absolute literalism. The appearance was unchanged; the real condition of industrial society had undergone profound changes. The growth of capitalistic control involved no shock. The new position of the merchant-employer seemed merely to make life a little more simple for the craftsman.

## Flexibility of the Merchant-Employer System

The merchant-employer might control the whole process of production, or only some specific stage.  In the southwestern counties of England the clothiers dominated the entire process from the purchase of wool to the sale of finished or partly finished cloth in London.  The wool was given out to women and children on the farms to be carded and spun.  The yarn was collected and again given out to weavers; some of these weavers were town craftsmen, but after the sixteenth century in England there was a noticeable drift to the country.  Before 1563 the clothiers introduced into the industry many workers who had served no apprenticeship, and the interests of the towns were expressed in the prohibitions of this practice in the Weavers' Act of 1555 and the Statute of Apprentices of 1563.  The cloth was fulled at a fulling mill owned by the clothier. If the cloth was to be dyed and sheared, it was again given out to craft workers.  The product was sold by the clothier at Blackwell Hall in London.  It was stated in 1618 that many of the Suffolk clothiers employed as many as five hundred persons.  Whenever we find any statistical material, the evidence all tends to show that these enterprises involved large numbers of persons, ranging from thirty or forty to no less than a thousand.

In Norfolk the process of production was divided, largely because there was substantial export of worsted yarn to the Continent all through the sixteenth and seventeenth centuries.  Accordingly, the master combers bought wool and had it combed and spun.   The finished yarn was sold to exporters in London or in the towns of Norfolk to independent craft workers who did the weaving on their own account.

The merchant-employer system was in many instances superimposed upon formally organized groups of craft workers.  In such cases, new distinctions were set up.  In Lyon the silk industry developed two groups of masters: the merchants, who secured almost complete control of production; and the master weavers, who did all the weaving.  Some of the master weavers made silks for sale in the open market even at the beginning of the eighteenth century, but it was only a small minority: one or two hundred out of three or four thousand.  As there were about two hundred master merchants, the average enterprise involved the employment of twenty master weavers by each master merchant.  Some of the merchants employed as many as one hundred master weavers.  The organization here presents the full complexity of the system, for these master weavers were not isolated workers. Most of them had three or four looms in their shops, and they necessarily had apprentices. There were journeymen, but the journeymen might work for a master merchant.

At Lyon the weavers were allowed to work for more than one master at a time, provided strict account was kept of the materials supplied and each piece was guaranteed to be the work of a single weaver. We must therefore think of the business of the master merchant as a very loosely organized enterprise. There was no well-defined body of employees, no great central shop; hardly more than an array of contracts with individual weavers. In consequence, industrial unrest frequently expressed itself as a contest among groups of masters. The organization was too fluid to create a positive issue between a group of employees and a specific employer.

### Early Factories

In the eighteenth and seventeenth centuries the most common form of capitalistic control is the merchant-employer system. There can be little doubt of its predominant importance in the textile industries of the exporting regions. We find also many individual cases of industrial establishments in which the workers are brought together in a special building or group of buildings and subjected to regular discipline and supervision. Many cases can be collected in England and in France. There are strong grounds for presuming the existence of many such establishments in Italy, though the Italian material for this period has not been extensively studied. In most instances this departure from custom is due to some special feature : the availability of large buildings left vacant by the suppression or transfer of some abbey or priory; the grant of special privileges to encourage the setting up of a new industry; the costliness of the raw materials and the desirability of direct supervision to prevent waste and embezzlement. Many are disposed to reserve the term *factory* for establishments which combine these features with the use of power machinery, but such a distinction would merely require the addition of another category. It is clearly unsatisfactory to classify these aggregated establishments as craft shops, and they are obviously different from the establishments organized under the merchant-employer system. The simplest solution of these problems of classification is provided by the grouping of all these establishments under the general class of factories, with appropriate subdivisions. In all, we find four primary types of factory : the small factory without power machinery; the small factory with power machinery; the large factory without power machinery ; the large factory with power machinery.

In general, the small factories of the nineteenth century developed out of the larger craft shops of the earlier period. The large factories developed as alternatives to the merchant-employer system. The transition from the craft shop to the small factory is obscure and difficult to trace. The distinction must needs turn upon gradual changes in the position of the master. If he participates actively in the work of the shop on a plane of equality with the men, the establishment is clearly a craft shop. If he becomes more explicitly an employer and less and less a "fellow worker," the establishment changes in character and can be more accurately described as a small factory. The printing trade affords some excellent illustrations of the complexity of this transition. The petty job printing shops remained typical craft shops down to a late date. The great book printers and publishers, however, had plants of a very different order, and one would naturally hesitate to classify the great printers as mere craftsmen.

The use of factory organization in connection with the establishment of new industries was common in both England and France in the sixteenth and seventeenth centuries. In both countries many of the establishments had a long continuous history. They were by no means casual experiments that flourished for a year or two and then failed. Documentary material is more abundant in France than in England, because in France many of these establishments were subsidized. There is a considerable amount of material in the public records, whereas in England even the establishments with patents of monopoly were left entirely free from public interference. Detailed descriptions are rare and seldom adequate.

In France there were establishments designed to introduce Dutch processes of cloth manufacture at Abbeville, Elbeuf, Sedan, and Saptes. Encouragement was also given to the development of other textiles. Under direct control of the state, a manufacture of tapestry and furniture was set up at the Gobelins, and other controlled manufactures were established at the Savonnerie, at Beauvais, and at Sèvres. Most of these new establishments were organized as factories.

The most famous of the private establishments was that of Van

Robais at Abbeville.  Van Robais emigrated from Middelburg in
1665, aided by special grants to cover the expenses of bringing his
machinery, and special religious privileges for his family and for
the Dutch workmen brought to give instruction.  He was granted
a subsidy upon condition of keeping one hundred looms at work.
This enterprise continued until the end of the eighteenth century.
We have comprehensive lists of the employees by occupations for
three dates.  At the close of the seventeenth century there were
753 men and 939 women employed ; a total of 1692.  A list of 1711
classifies the employees under the names of the twelve superintendents or supervisors.  There were then 1,391 persons employed.  In
1767 there were 1,441 employees, classified in the list by occupations.
We have also from the late seventeenth century a full text of the
shop rules of the manufacture of cloth of silver and gold at St. Maur
des Fosses, near Paris.  The value of the raw material afforded the
primary incentive to centralization.

These establishments were perhaps unusually large, but it is not
necessary to concern ourselves here with the scale of the average
establishment, nor even with the actual number of such establishments.  The important fact is the presence of these highly centralized industrial units prior to the general application of power
to the machinery used in the work.  Under special circumstances,
such units were advantageous.  It would seem simplest to classify
them as factories without power machinery, but in any event their
presence is indicative of the growth of capitalistic control.

### Accounting and the Unit of Business Enterprise

In the earlier periods of history business was largely personal, and
in many instances a single individual carried on many different
affairs.  The famous Medici family affords a striking illustration
of this combination of several enterprises in one hand.  The early
interests of the Medici were largely confined to the importation of
wool.  This contact led to participation in the manufacture of cloth ;
and later to active conduct of trading operations in the Near East.
Some banking was an inevitable accompaniment of these extensive
operations, and it was a short step from financing the activities of
the personal business to the conduct of a general banking business
for a considerable list of clients.  In enterprises of this general type
we see a first step towards modern business organization, because it
was essential that separate books of account should be kept for each
of these enterprises.  In strict analysis we must think of an enter-

prise not in terms of ownership or legal organization but in terms of the accounting unit.   These various activities of the Medici should be treated as separate enterprises for purposes of analysis in just such measure as separate accounts were kept.   The business enterprise was usually at that time smaller than the unit of ownership.   At the present time the effective unit of business enterprise is much larger than the basic corporate units, for in many instances the final unit of accounting is a group of corporations that are subject to centralized control, though ownership may be widely diffused even in the corporate sense.   The development of double-entry bookkeeping served to give explicit form to the notion of a separate accounting unit.   This practice began in Italy in the fourteenth century and spread rapidly to all sections of Europe.   But for a long period of time there was little or no analysis of the accounts.   No attempt was made to present summarized statements of the business as a whole.   This was true even of the largest business firms of the Middle Ages and the period of the Reformation.   Neither the Medici nor the great firm of the Fugger prepared balance sheets for their enterprises at stated intervals.   At the death of the head of the house, legal requirements made necessary a comprehensive statement of affairs, but only on rare occasions was any summary statement drawn up, and even then it did not assume the form familiar to us.   The modern balance sheet owes its form to the Dutch engineer and mathematician Simon Stevin (1602).   The full significance of this device to the merchant and his creditors was not fully explained until a half century later, when Jacques Savary recommended that balance sheets be drawn up at stated intervals. In order to protect creditors, the Code of Commerce published in France in 1673 required every businessman to draw up a balance sheet at least every two years.[1]

This development in accounting practice was closely associated with changes in the size of the average business enterprise and more especially with changes in the law and practice of business partnerships and associations.   The simple partnership is a legal device of great antiquity, so there was little need of any essentially new rules of law.   Changes in business conditions, however, led to many changes in practice.   Partnerships in business may be of two general types; there are partnerships for a particular transaction, and partnerships for the conduct of an enterprise over a period of time.

---

[1] Usher, A. P., "Sources of Modern Business Principles and Practice," *Harvard Business Review*, vol. III, p. 283.

In the Middle Ages and in the early modern period, both types of association were common, but partnerships for particular transactions or ventures were much more important than at later periods. In the thirteenth and fourteenth centuries a number of famous Italian partnerships played a dominant part in the commerce of Europe. The great German business houses of the fifteenth and sixteenth centuries were organized as partnerships. In both cases these "companies" were closely, though not absolutely, identified with particular families. The articles of association gave explicit legal form to an enterprise that was an outgrowth of an essentially personal business.

### Regulated and Joint-Stock Companies

The association for particular transactions was, however, the more common feature of early business organization, and in England this mode of conducting trade was fostered by a long series of great trading "companies," beginning with the Staplers and the Company of Merchants Adventurers. The development of trade in the sixteenth century was promoted by the formation of a number of companies for special purposes, which play a notable part in the history of business enterprise because their problems ultimately required changes in old practices and led to the establishment of the joint-stock company as a basic form of commercial and industrial organization.

The "regulated" company typified by the Merchants Adventurers was an association designed to hold trading privileges and to maintain warehouses and living accommodations for members in various foreign towns. It was an association of businessmen, but the company as such was not a business enterprise. The actual conduct of trade rested with individual members or groups of members. Ordinarily, the undertakings for each season were treated as independent ventures. Contracts were drawn; the purchases were made for export, goods for importation were secured abroad, and when these were sold, the transaction was completely liquidated. The "company" did not have a capital account, though it incurred various expenses which were met by collecting dues or assessments from the members. Its facilities for trade could not be used by traders who were not members, and accordingly trade was not open to all in the sense which we are prone to assume. The trade of the Hanseatic League was conducted in this general manner. We do not find "companies" of precisely this type in France or Mediterranean

Europe, as the privileges covering the trade of the Near East were applied to the states as such, and the external organization of trade corresponds more closely to modern practice.

This transition from the regulated company to the joint-stock company discloses a notably gradual development. Long-distance voyages to Russia and the Levant required more capital than could easily be furnished by a single group. It was therefore found desirable to make a single venture which members of the company might join. As it was not obligatory upon members to subscribe to each voyage, the venture was still, in form, a special partnership for a particular enterprise. The decisive step was really taken when participation in the venture became obligatory. Each venture then represented the entire membership in the company. From this stage to a continuous joint stock was an easy transition, made desirable by the length of these voyages and the delays involved in complete liquidation of the venture. Continuous joint-stock enterprises are to be found in various companies before the East India Company adopted the practice, but the generalization of this mode of organization is commonly associated with the changes in the practices of the East India Company and their ultimate embodiment in Cromwell's charter of 1657. The development in Holland was closely comparable.

The evolution of the joint-stock company also involves the transition from the concept of a partnership divided into shares to the limited-liability company with freely transferable stock. The division of partnerships into shares proportionate to the contribution of the individual was very old. It was an established practice in the twelfth century, when we first begin to have substantial documentary material on ships and shipping. Each partner contributed a specific fraction of the total amount involved and was entitled to share in the profits of the venture in that proportion. Shares in ships were bought and sold freely at Genoa even in the twelfth century, but ship ownership presented special problems.[1] An extensive application of share ownership appears also in the mining districts of Germany in the sixteenth century. But the normal partnership was for a particular venture, and transfer of the shares was not common until the larger trading companies adopted the practice of trading on a continuous joint stock. From this period, shares assumed the general features of the par-value shares of the

---

[1] Byrne, E. H., *Genoese Shipping in the Twelfth and Thirteenth Centuries*, Cambridge, Mass., 1930, p. 14.

modern corporation. They represented subscriptions of stated amounts and entitled the bearer to share in profits in proportion to his holdings. These shares were considered to be transferable, and dealings in shares became a feature of commercial life in Amsterdam, Paris, and London during the last quarter of the seventeenth century.

The grants of monopolies by Queen Elizabeth and by James I in England exerted considerable influence in fostering the development of the use of corporations in industry and trade, though this was hardly the object of the crown. These grants were in part designed to foster the development of new industries, and some brave pretense of encouragement to inventors is to be found in a large number of the patents. The rapid development of this system under James I led to concerted protest, and after a sharp struggle the famous Statute of Monopolies was passed in 1624. The prohibitions of the common law were restated and affirmed even against the crown, but the most important feature of the statute was the exceptions. Special grants to new industries were authorized, and grants of monopoly to inventors were explicitly sanctioned if limited to a period of fourteen years. This was the first explicit recognition of the property rights of an inventor, and it speedily became the basis of an activity in invention which found no counterpart in Continental countries, where the inventor had no means of securing a profit from his efforts unless he was able to keep his process a secret. This clause of the Statute of 1624 at once became the basis of a series of grants. The issue of patents for inventions was finally organized systematically in 1721 with a special staff of officials and a body of general rules. Laws closely modeled upon British law were adopted by the United States and by France in 1791. The Netherlands formulated patent laws in 1817; Austria in 1820. The significance of the leadership of England in this respect can scarcely be overestimated.

### Functional Middlemen

The character of business in the early modern period was profoundly affected by the development of specialized agencies for transport and finance. The merchants of the Middle Ages had been obliged to travel with their goods, because there were no common carriers ready to undertake the task of moving goods for long distances. In many instances one or more partners traveled with the goods while the others remained in residence in appropriate

towns.  Even maritime trade required the presence of the owner of
the goods or some accredited agent.  By the beginning of the
sixteenth century the broader elements of a general system of
transport had come into being.  Messages and small packages of
all descriptions were handled by the "posts."  Heavier freight was
handled by wagoners and boatmen on the roads and rivers of Europe.
The wagoners were closely associated with innkeepers, who collected
and stored the smaller packages and made arrangements for the
collection and delivery of large and bulky freight.  Relations
between shipowners and shippers were also transformed, so that
the shipowner became more definitely a common carrier acting
under contract for a shipper not directly represented by any person
on board the vessel.

The extent of these developments is indicated in part by the
route maps of France and Europe used by these carriers, and by the
organized post routes.  More attention was given to passenger
travel, both by road and by water.  In some sections of Germany
and in the vicinity of Paris regular service for passengers and freight
was established on the rivers.  These boat lines were given exclusive
rights to operate on stated days ; rates for goods and persons were
specified, and infringements of the franchise were contested.  Regular service was established on the rivers both above and below
Frankfort on the Main as early as the fifteenth century.  The
development around Paris dates from the beginning of the seventeenth century.

Under the influence of these developments in transport, wholesale
and retail trade began to assume the characteristic forms that are
familiar to us.  We find significant discussions of business policies
and practices in the treatises of Savary (1675) and Defoe (1713).
The merchant was free to give his attention to problems of merchandising.

The emergence of a highly specialized class of bankers was of great
importance to this development.  Some elementary banking operations are of great antiquity, and even in the early medieval period
there were some specialized banking businesses.  Banking functions
of a sort were exercised also by ecclesiastical houses — the abbeys
and priories, and notably by the Knights of the Temple.  Before
1300 the history of banking is obscure and uncertain, but the fourteenth century is marked by the beginnings of an active development
of deposit banking.

Doubts may be entertained in respect to the quantitative importance of the credit activities of bankers in the period between 1300 and 1700, but there can be no significant doubt of the importance of this development for the history of banking in the eighteenth and nineteenth centuries. The Bank of England is the final step in a long process of development which reaches far back into the Middle Ages.

### The Development of Credit

The banks of the early period were deposit banks : they accepted deposits in cash, to be held subject to the pleasure of the depositor, who was entitled to withdraw the funds in cash or to have them transferred to the credit of another person on the books of the bank. The convenience of this transfer on the books of the bank restricted actual withdrawals in cash to a modest percentage of the total volume of funds held by the banker. He was thus able to assume that he would never be required at any one time to furnish cash against the total amount of deposits. In consequence, some portion of the funds might be loaned to the city or to the king; funds might be loaned to private individuals; or the banker might himself invest the funds in some business venture. All these modes of employing funds were actually used. If the banker merely served as an intermediary in the transfer of specie from one person to another, there was no actual increase in the funds that might be spent. Theoretically, the credits on the books always originated in actual deposits of specie. But this was not the case. The banker might credit a person with funds in the bank in order to enable this party to transfer funds to a third party. The city might find its collections of taxes slow; or a businessman might need funds for some purchase. Various circumstances might convince the banker that the loan would be ultimately repaid, and accordingly he would be willing to transfer credit on the books although the party had no funds standing in his name sufficient to cover the transaction. In form, the borrower appeared on the books as a "depositor" to whom the bank owed money, though in this case the ledger aiso carried a record of an equal obligation to the banker. Once these entries had been made, the borrower might have credit transferred to another person, or he might withdraw some of the funds in cash. If no cash was actually withdrawn, the implications of the transaction were simple. The banker lent credit to the borrower, and the borrower met some current obligation by a transfer of credit. The party receiving this payment stood in the same relation to the banker as he would if cash had been deposited by the borrower or by himself. Even the simplest form of bank was thus able to exercise its highly distinctive function as a vehicle for the creation of credit.

In the course of the sixteenth and seventeenth centuries extensive modifications in banking law and practice made banks a more convenient source of credit, and opened up the important potentialities of note issue. In its primitive form, the bank did nearly all its business directly with its customers. The only business transacted in writing was business in foreign exchange. Technically, the contractual agreements between the bankers and their customers rested. upon verbal statements. For this reason, checks came into use only after a considerable interval. They were used in a limited way in the fifteenth century, but they did not become at all common until late in the sixteenth century. The bank note appeared even later, for its use involves the legal doctrine of negotiability.

The new legal doctrine does not appear until the close of the sixteenth century, and it was not established until the middle of the seventeenth century. Bills of exchange and promissory notes then began to pass from hand to hand by endorsement, and the banks were able to circulate demand notes to bearer. On the Continent checks remained nonnegotiable. In England they were treated as negotiable instruments. The issues of notes by the goldsmith bankers of London in Cromwell's time mark the effective beginning of this practice in England, and the rapid development of the London money market in the last half of the century paved the way for the founding of the Bank of England. This bank embodied all the elements of the new practices of banking. Its privileges and its connections with the government made it the most important bank in England and gave it a position of leadership which ultimately forced it to accept the responsibilities of a central bank.

Other consequences of the development of the bank note were not so fortunate. The new idea was adopted by the governments of the colonies of the American seaboard, and the first issues of government paper money were made in 1690 under the leadership of Massachusetts Bay. France experimented with government paper money in 1701 and later with heavy issues of bank notes. It is not certain that Law's bank was actually unsound, though his theoretical writings do not disclose the shrewd appreciation of the problems of bank credit that characterized his fellow countryman

Patterson, the founder of the Bank of England.[1] Whatever the possible merits of Law's bank, it became hopelessly involved in the Mississippi scheme and was forced into liquidation. This bitter experience dominated French policy for the remainder of the century. Despite one or two attempts to establish a large public bank, sentiment was too hostile to permit such an institution to secure any foothold. Banking remained in the hands of private individuals, and note issues were of little importance. The early chartered banks of Continental Europe were little more than institutions for centralized clearance through book transfers. England thus became the leader in the generalization of the extensions of the credit system made possible by the development of the doctrine of negotiability.

[1] Harsin, P., *Les doctrines monétaires et financières en France du XVI<sup>e</sup> au XVIII<sup>e</sup> siècle*, Paris, 1928. Harsin, P., *Crédit public et Banque d'État en France du XVI<sup>e</sup> au XVIII<sup>e</sup> siècle*, Paris, 1933.

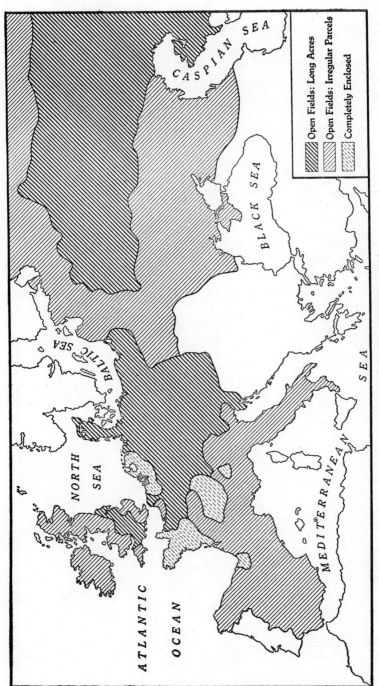

Types of Rural Settlement, about 1700

CHAPTER 3

# AGRICULTURE AND THE SURVIVALS OF FEUDALISM

———◆———

## External Aspects of Rural Life about 1700

The external aspects of rural life in Europe in 1700 had changed very little in the course of five centuries. The arable area had been extended; nearly all the better land had gradually been taken into cultivation; villages had become somewhat larger, and many hamlets had appeared in the regions of dispersed settlement. The general patterns of settlement, however, were not conspicuously different from the patterns of 1200, though the boundaries between the various types had undergone some alterations. The life of both village and manor house was dominated by survivals of the feudal regime. Rural Europe in 1700, therefore, appeared to be much closer to the Middle Ages than to modern times.

The reforms of the eighteenth and nineteenth centuries brought about extensive changes in all the basic elements of rural life, except in certain moribund regions of Mediterranean and south-central Europe. Despite isolated survivals of the older modes of rural organization in England and Germany, the conditions of 1700 now seem remote and unreal. In fact, rural life on the eve of the reforms is rather more difficult to understand than the rural organization of the twelfth and thirteenth centuries. A number of changes had taken place in the relations between lords and tenants which gave the tenant a degree of economic security that was inconsistent with feudal theory, though the general features of the feudal structure were not changed. An understanding of conditions in 1700 demands some appreciation of the relation of that period to its past as well as to its future. The reforms cannot be fully understood unless we realize precisely what progress had already been achieved when the attack on feudal survivals began actively in the eighteenth century.

Important clues to the significance of the feudal structure in 1700 are to be found in the basic patterns of settlement and village organization. The persisting modes of settlement had acquired new meanings, and differences in systems of settlement were related to important differences in the reform movements. The forms of settlement are a useful connecting link between past and present.

45

The rural landscapes of Europe about 1700 may be divided into the three broad types shown in the map on page 44. There were regions dominated by regular open arable fields, subdivided into small strips of about one acre each. Normally, these strips were ten times as long as they were wide; for this ratio of 1 to 10 persisted over an extensive area despite differences in the linear units prevailing in the various localities. In describing these fields as "open" we mean that there were no permanent fences or ditches between the strips in the arable fields. The entire area of arable land belonging to the village would commonly be protected by some kind of barrier to prevent livestock from wandering in from the woods or moors surrounding the plowed fields. The strips were separated from each other only by balks of unplowed turf. Small patches of meadow land might be carefully fenced, to serve as pasture for the draft animals. The conspicuous feature of such a landscape was the absence of all barriers in the large arable fields.

Open fields of a different type were dominant in Spain, southern France, Italy, portions of the British Isles, and over a large area in Russia. In these regions the parcels in the fields were irregular, in each village and holding. The parcels varied considerably in both size and shape, and although long acres might occasionally be found in these regions, they were exceptional. In many sections of Spain, southern France, and Italy the typical acre was square in shape. But the parcels in the hands of owners and tenants were seldom square, because they commonly contained several acres, and thus became rectangles or complex shapes adapted to the lay of the land. This seemingly small difference in the character of the land units is closely related to important differences in the economic functions of the villages of the two open-field regions, and these differences of function resulted in considerable differentiation of the reform movements.

A third type of landscape was also found, though in a more restricted area; here we find completely enclosed small fields. The large areas dominated in general by this type of settlement are shown on the map, but it is presumed that detailed study of the system of settlement would reveal enclosed areas in parts of Spain and Italy also. It is important to note that the enclosed regions were not confined to low-grade land in sparsely settled districts. The enclosed areas in Belgium and Holland and in sections of Normandy and Poitou were highly fertile. Enclosed agriculture was, therefore, something more than a survival of a primitive form in the poverty-stricken backwaters of rural Europe.

The origin of these different types of rural organization is still incompletely solved.  The research of the last twenty years has shown that the explanations of early writers were unsound.  These different modes of rural life cannot be explained in terms of racial culture.  Geographic factors have played an important, but by no means a decisive, part.  Some of these differences in type can be associated with differences in soils, and related differences in plows and systems of plowing.  The heavier soils were more adequately worked by the great plow with wheels.  The difficulty of turning this implement and its eight-ox team made it convenient to make a long furrow.  It is not quite so easy to understand why the unit of the holding was generally a single acre.  The long acres do, however, appear most systematically on the heavy soils of the great plow.  The irregular parcels and the square acres are associated with the lighter soils and the plow without wheels.  Shorter furrows were common, and in many sections the land was plowed along both axes of the plot.  But the lack of precise correlation between plow types and the boundaries between the two types of open fields suggests the presence of cultural factors.  These cultural factors were not as exclusively Teutonic as was once supposed, and the villages of the long acres probably acquired their definite organization long after the migrations.  We must presume, too, that there were notable fluctuations in the boundaries between the enclosed areas and the open-fields area with irregular parcels.  Subdivision of large holdings frequently resulted in the formation of open fields with many irregular parcels.  The persistence of the basic types of settlement over a long period must not lead us to assume that there were no substantial changes in the geographical boundaries of the three primary types.

### The Character of Villages with Regular Open Fields

The open fields necessarily entailed some measure of village organization, for in each type there were some restrictions upon the use of the land that comprised the individual holding.  The open-fields system bore witness to the fact that no individual had exclusive rights over the land he occupied.  The woods and the uncultivated moors and heaths were enjoyed in common, though their use was, in many regions, regulated by local rules.  The village arable, too, was opened to the herds for grazing as soon as the harvests were gathered.  The eighteenth-century jurist Eusèbe Laurière gave exact expression to this general custom in the statement: "No one may exclude others from his estate except when the land is under crop; when the crops have been harvested the land, by a kind of natural law, is common to all, rich and poor alike." In strict theory, none might enclose any portion of the arable fields of the village, even if a relatively large parcel of land was held in a solid block. In many regions, dominated in general by open fields, enclosed parcels were to be found, but these were commonly parcels of waste land that had been brought into cultivation after feudal structure had taken form. In England a number of owners were allowed to make enclosures of particular parcels if all the owners agreed. Under cover of these exceptions, small areas had been enclosed in England in the course of the sixteenth and seventeenth centuries, but the general rule limiting the right to enclose was still generally accepted in England and on the Continent throughout the region of the open fields. The area actually withdrawn from the older arable fields was small.

The system of agriculture practiced in these open-field villages involved a sharp separation between stock growing and arable culture. Prior to the reforms, which were of very restricted significance before 1700, little attempt was made to raise forage crops on the arable land. The stock grazed on the bare fields in the fall, and they were fed some of the straw after the grain was threshed, but their primary sources of food were the meadows and the uncultivated wood, moor, and heath. In the villages with long acres the village officers supervised all agricultural activity, both the cropping of the arable land and the management of the meadows and pastures. In villages with irregular parcels the cultivators managed their arable fields with no explicit interference from village officers, but the meadows and pastures were regulated and supervised by the village. In the long-acre villages the entire village was really the unit of management. The individual was completely subordinated to the group. This type has been described at times as a "village community," but the term is misleading. Some writers concluded that the village must have been originally "free," and as a consequence the feudal lords were deemed to be intruders who had encroached upon the rights of the villagers. It was assumed that the land originally "belonged" to the village as a whole, and that communism is thus the original form of land holding. Some Socialists at one time made much of the "village communities" of Great Russia; treating them as survivals of a primitive communism that might be revived and assimilated by the socialistic state of the future. But all these theories about the "village community" involve misleading suggestions. It is therefore desirable to avoid this otherwise useful term, so that it will be best to designate this type of open-field village as the communal village. The village with irregular parcels may be called "the individualistic village.'

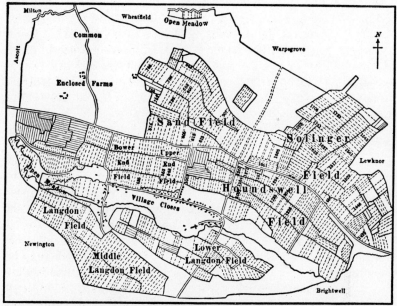

From H. L. Gray, "English Field Systems"

*Tithe Map of Chalgrove*

## The Village of Chalgrove

The problems and activities of the communal village will be most readily understood if we examine a typical village map. The tithe map of the village of Chalgrove in Oxfordshire, reproduced on this page, was drawn in 1841, but it represents a condition that had long existed. The map does not show specifically any holdings by a manorial lord, as the village belonged to Magdalen College, Oxford, and all the land was let out. The special significance of this particular map lies in its positive evidence of the systematic organization of the arable in three distinct fields. The original arable area was probably confined to the units Sand Field, Solinger Field, and Houndswell Field. The small divisions Bower End Field and Upper End Field were doubtless attached to Houndswell Field. Langdon

Field, Middle Langdon Field, and Lower Langdon Field are presumed to be later improvements, and their precise relation to the
field system is not made clear in this tithe survey. The enclosed
farms, in the northwestern corner of the village, were presumably
taken from the "waste," or common pasture.

At the time of the survey the area of the village lands was set at
2,358 acres, divided as follows: arable land, 1,620 acres; meadow
and pasture land, 431 acres; wood land, 8 acres; common pasture
or waste, 140 acres; homesteads, 48 acres; glebe, 69 acres; roads
and waste, 42 acres. The arable area was divided into nearly 2,000
narrow "lands" or selions, each containing an acre or less. Owing
to the reduced scale of the map reproduced, the full number of strips
cannot be shown. The full-size "lands" conform closely to the
standard acre.

The arrangement of the "lands" was such that many of them were
not directly accessible from the roads of the village. In these cases
the holders of certain groups of "lands" had a right of way over
particular strips up to stated dates. These strips therefore had to
be plowed later and harvested earlier. The pattern of the arrangement of the strips also involved the turning of the plow teams on
certain strips, commonly called "headlands." The strips numbered
755 and 1751 on the plan were headlands, though they did not over-
lap other strips throughout their length. Other headlands may be
found on the plan along the unnumbered strips. Headlands were
plowed later than the abutting strips. Such rights over property
of others, or "servitudes," occur when land is held in full proprietorship, but they detract in some measure from the value of the property burdened with them, and they are commonly an outgrowth of
special circumstances. In the open-field village, servitudes were
an inevitable consequence of the system of subdivision and were an
important factor in village life.

The holding of any particular villager consisted of parcels divided
more or less equally among the three primary divisions of the arable
fields. The copyhold for lives held by John Jones, consisting of
nearly 22 acres, was divided among the fields as follows: Solinger
Field, 7¼ acres in 15 parcels; Sand Field, 9 acres in 13 parcels;
Houndswell Field (including Bower End and Upper End), 5¾ acres
in 13 parcels. The locations of these parcels are shown by the
numbers given on the plan. The careful division of the holding
among the three fields was an essential consequence of the village
management of cropping. When the system was in actual use, each

general division of the arable would lie under a single crop or lie as fallow; thus, when Solinger Field lay under wheat, Sand Field would lie under barley or oats, and Houndswell Field would be plowed and cultivated but left as fallow without crop.  Unless each villager held a reasonable quantity of land in each field, his crops would be seriously affected by the succession of culture in the village fields.  If most of his land lay in one field, some years would leave him with no crop at all on that portion of the holding, and other years would leave his crops out of balance.  Village management thus entailed the division of each holding among the primary divisions of the village fields, whatever their number.

## Village Management

The village officers were thus charged with several general functions intimately connected with the agricultural management of the village land.  The general scheme of management, a system of bare fallowing [1] with a two- or three-year cycle, remained relatively stable over a long period of time.  The land was cultivated for one or two years under cereals, and for one year without a crop.  The system of bare fallowing can be traced back continuously into the history of Italy and Greece prior to the Christian Era.  In the earlier period the biennial fallow was most common.  After the eighth century there is evidence of a triennial fallow.  The choice between the different cycles was after all a subordinate detail.  These systems prevailed generally in all types of open-field villages and in many of the enclosed regions.  In no area was the choice of the cultural system a deliberate act renewed from year to year.  Until agricultural reform was far advanced this immemorial custom was accepted as a given condition of rural life.  When the village was managed as a unit, the village officers determined the details of culture : the time to plow, with special reference to laggards who might hold up the work of holders of headlands; the time to do harvesting; the time to let the livestock into the arable fields; the regulation of meadow grazing and hay cutting; the organization of the village herds grazing on the waste land.

If the village belonged to one or more nonresident lords, the external features of village life would not disclose any explicit evidence of their presence unless their lands were enclosed and separately administered.  As long as the demesne land of the lord or

[1] The general character of bare fallowing is explained in detail in the section of this chapter on that subject, pages 56–57.

lords lay in strips intermingled with the strips of the villagers, no special agricultural problem would be involved. Some of the village officers would be appointed by the lord, some were commonly elected by the villagers; with rare exceptions the various officials would necessarily deal with affairs affecting both lord and villagers.

If there was a manor, with a permanent official establishment, the presence of the lord would be symbolized by the great house. If the lord's land was not enclosed, the general organization of the village would not be affected, though the immediate presence of the lord might have practical consequences, to the interest or detriment of the villagers. The continuous presence of the lord or his steward was on the whole a source of danger. Under such circumstances there was added likelihood that portions of the uncultivated lands would be enclosed and improved by the lord, to the ultimate disadvantage of the villagers, who would sooner or later find that the remaining wild pasture or waste was really insufficient for the needs of the village herds. Then, too, if the lord developed land hunger, with or without adequate economic grounds, the villagers were inevitably subjected to pressure. If the tenancies were not definitely heritable and secure, the lord could certainly increase the area of his demesne farm in the course of time. A variety of circumstances would make it possible to displace tenants or their heirs. In the sixteenth and seventeenth centuries such processes altered considerably the proportions of the land in England under the direct control of the manorial lords.

In the course of time, in England, the lords were able to separate all or part of the demesne farm from the general village lands. The partial enclosures of the sixteenth and seventeenth centuries in England were predominantly separations of the demesne lands from peasant holdings. In some villages large landholders not possessed of manorial rights joined the lord in partial enclosure projects, but these modifications did not affect the general pattern of the movement. Such lands were merely withdrawn from village control and became separate units of land management. The enclosed farms of the Chalgrove map show how little such modifications really affected the general organization of the village. As long as there remained a substantial area of arable land subject to management by the village, the essential features of the communal village would remain. The enclosures of the seventeenth century, therefore, attracted little attention, despite the relatively large area of land withdrawn from the general arable area of the villages affected.

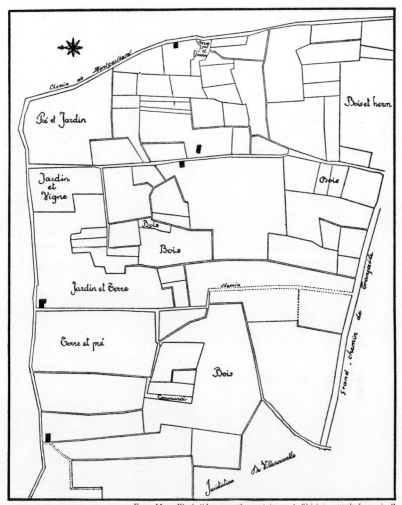

From Marc Bloch, "Les caractères originaux de l'histoire rurale française"

*Open and Irregular Fields near Montgaillard, Haute-Garonne, France*

### Irregular Open Fields

When the open fields lay in irregular parcels, the land map of the village cannot readily be distinguished from the map of an enclosed area.    The map above shows a portion of the village of Montgaillard in the Department of Haute-Garonne, twenty or twenty-five miles southeast of Toulouse.    The section of the map shown does not include the village itself, but a number of scattered farmhouses will be noted on the plan. The description of the village is not given, but the general character of these village plans is well understood. The land was divided into relatively large blocks, which were commonly close together, though not necessarily contiguous. These arrangements differ in no essential respect from those of enclosed areas. The villager managed his own lands. The arable, however, was commonly subject to some form of bare fallowing and to some common pasturing unless it was planted with vines. In the open-field village, even of this type, the right to graze livestock on the entire arable area after harvest time, was recognized.

From the point of view of land management, these villages were really more nearly similar to the enclosed areas, for they were in fact areas of individual farms, despite the general rights of grazing on the arable (for part of the year) and upon the wild pasture. In many cases no attempt was made to organize definite village flocks and herds, so that even the grazing was an individual responsibility. The economic functions of the village were then reduced to a bare minimum.

In Ireland, Scotland, and Wales irregular open fields were frequently created by the persistent subdivision of large farms. The following map shows the condition of 205 acres of a town land in Donegal, Ireland, as described in the report of the Devon Commis-

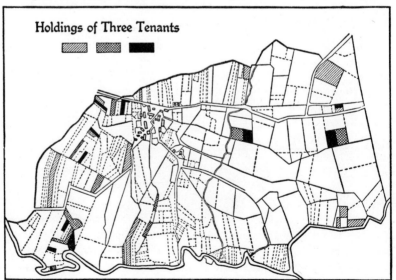

Holdings of Three Tenants

*From H. L. Gray, " English Field Systems "*

**Town Lands of Donegal**

sion of 1845. "The whole was occupied in one farm two generations ago; it then became subdivided into two farms, and those two have been since subdivided into twenty-nine holdings, scattered into 422 different lots. The average quantity of arable in each holding is four acres, held in fourteen different parts of the town land; the average quantity of pasture per farm is three acres, held in lots in common. . . . They had been in the habit of subdividing their lands, not into two when a division was contemplated, but into as many times two as there were qualities of land in the gross quantity to be divided. They would not hear of an equivalent of two bad acres being set against one good one, in order to maintain union and compactness. Every quality must be cut in two, whatever its size, or whatever its position. Each must have his half perches, although they be ever so distant from his half acres." Joint tenancy and subdivision among heirs had thus transformed a single farm into something like an open-field village.[1]

## Enclosed Farms

Within restricted limits were to be found completely enclosed farms, which exhibit all the features of the modern system of completely individualized management of the land. In some sections this type of settlement was very old, dating perhaps from the origins of settled agriculture in parts of Brittany and Belgium. In other regions the enclosures are associated with long acres in such a way that one would presume a positive breakup of open-field villages. The history of most of these regions has not yet been studied with sufficient care to warrant positive generalization. The areas shown as "completely enclosed" in the map on page 44 were certainly enclosed as early as 1700, but these boundaries cannot be assumed to represent the original system of settlement.

In Flanders and in Poitou we find characteristic illustrations of extreme dispersion. The major part of the population lived on scattered farms. The farm was the basic unit of settlement. The farms covered the whole countryside, with little regard even to the primary roads. The house with its adjoining farm buildings stood in the midst of an enclosure surrounded by great elms and thick hedges. At the crossroads a small cluster of houses and a church constituted the only symbol of organized rural life. In Flanders a considerable urban population had been associated with this widely dispersed rural population, so that the region has presented over a

[1] Gray, H. L., *English Field Systems*, Cambridge, Mass., 1915, p. 191.

long period an unusually sharp contrast between urban agglomeration and rural dispersion. In Poitou the region of scattered farms was more decisively rural. Towns and villages were small and infrequent. Little hamlets sufficed for a bare minimum of social contact and organization. The enclosures, as in Flanders, were formed of hedges interspersed with large trees, so that the region had the aspect of light woods with many clearings. Such regions thus came to be described as "*pays de bocage*," in antithesis to the open plains.

Enclosures were carried out in the manner best suited to local conditions. In parts of Brittany and in Quercy the fields were set off from each other by low walls of stone laid up without mortar. There were also regions in which the population was less widely dispersed. Compact villages and hamlets predominated over scattered farms in the enclosed regions of central France. The enclosed regions thus presented many diversities of external aspect. In some parts of Brittany enclosed villages possessed substantial areas of wild pasture which was used in common. At times, too, the meadows were used in common. Collective rights were not entirely absent even in enclosed regions, so that we really find a long series of types of settlement, ranging from the compact communal village — in which the individual was completely subordinated to the group — to the enclosed region with scattered farms in which all the land was subject to purely individual control. The problems of reform were profoundly affected by these wide variations in the range and character of collective rights. The communal villages could be reorganized only after a complete redistribution of all the arable land, and a complete revision of the place of the village in the economic life of the community. When the arable land was already under individual control, the obstacles to reform were less considerable.

### Bare Fallowing and Nitrate Accumulation

From antiquity to the nineteenth century, the culture of cereals in Europe was based upon the practice of bare fallowing. For one year in each two or three the land was plowed and cultivated without being planted to any crop. The value of this procedure was due to the destruction of weeds, to the improvement in the physical condition of the soil, and to the accumulation of nitrates in the soil during the summer. It maintained the supply of this important form of plant food. The relation of bare fallowing to nitrate accumulation was not known earlier than 1850, and not until the close of the century did we know the full detail of the process of nitrate formation. In the older literature bare fallowing was described as "resting the land." At one time it was supposed that residues from plant growth poisoned the land for an immediate repetition of that crop. Recent experiments at Rothamsted, England, have failed to discover any toxic substances in the soil, though some soils become acid after a period of years and require treatment with some form of lime. Acidity, however, should not be classed as a toxic condition. Modern research has demonstrated that the significance of bare fallowing is primarily due to the accumulation of available nitrates in the soil. The precise amount of nitrate accumulated depends upon the physical characteristics of the soil and upon its drainage, but on all soils significantly useful for general agriculture the amount of nitrate thus developed would be considerable.

Modern research shows that losses of available nitrates occur more largely through drainage than through utilization in plant growth. It may thus be readily understood that cultivation increases the drainage losses because the breaking up of the soil permits the surface water to pass more rapidly through the top soil to the subsoil and its drainage channels. The nitrates would soon be exhausted if these losses were not offset by the fixation of a portion of the nitrogen included in the soil atmosphere. Losses are also offset by the decay of organic matter in the soil: the roots of previous crops or annual herbage, the leaves of trees, or any stalks and herbage left to decay on the surface of the soil. The stock of nitrates in the soil at any one time is the resultant of the balance between positive and negative factors. There are two relatively stable points of equilibrium between the constructive and destructive forces, a point of equilibrium for land kept continuously under plow, and a point of equilibrium for land under natural or artificial herbage without removal of any vegetable matter. If nitrates are added to the soil, the stock of nitrate can be increased, but much of the nitrate is really lost in drainage. By means of bare fallowing the stock of nitrate can be maintained at a level only slightly lower than that characteristic of virgin soil under natural herbage. It is thus a rational system of land management. For high-grade soils not naturally deficient in phosphorus, bare fallowing maintains the vital supplies of nitrates so well that cultivation can continue over long periods at a significant level of productivity.

## Yields of Cereals after Fallowing

The practice of bare fallowing continued to be a dominant feature of cereal culture in Europe until the first half of the nineteenth century, but one must not conclude that there was no significant improvement in agricultural practice from the beginning of the thirteenth century to the beginning of the nineteenth century. The agricultural reformers of the eighteenth and nineteenth centuries make derogatory remarks about fallowing and the general practice of their less well-informed contemporaries, but these strictures involve much exaggeration. The significance of the improvements that had taken place is indicated decisively, even by the scanty material now available on agricultural productivity. The best material for the Middle Ages is furnished by the crop records of five manors of the Bishopric of Winchester for the period 1200–1449. The averages for the whole period are shown in the following table.

AVERAGE YIELD OF GRAIN ON FIVE WINCHESTER MANORS [1]

A. Bushels per acre

|  | 1200–49 | 1250–99 | 1300–49 | 1350–99 | 1400–49 |
|---|---|---|---|---|---|
| Wheat | 8.16 | 9.12 | 9.44 | 9.36 | 9.28 |
| Barley | 12.72 | 12.72 | 14.00 | 14.88 | 16.56 |
| Oats | 11.20 | 10.48 | 9.68 | 10.96 | 13.60 |

B. Ratio of product to seed

|  | | | | | |
|---|---|---|---|---|---|
| Wheat | 4.14 | 3.75 | 4.23 | 4.34 | 4.54 |
| Barley | 4.28 | 3.47 | 3.80 | 4.01 | 4.31 |
| Oats | 2.92 | 2.33 | 2.44 | 2.87 | 3.59 |

There is evidence of a little improvement in yield, but the increases are not great enough to be significant, except perhaps for oats. These records represent a high standard of management and are probably a little higher than the county or regional average which we might find in modern figures.

It is difficult to find representative figures for England in the eighteenth century for yields under a system of bare fallowing, but considerable material is available for Germany. The records of an estate in Saxony about 1750 afford full details on yields (table, page 59). The ratios of harvest to seed show only modest improvement over medieval standards, but heavy seeding gave good yields. The records of the manor of Crawley in England show some experimentation with heavy seeding, but without much success. During

[1] Beveridge, Sir W., " The Yield and the Price of Corn in the Middle Ages," *Economic History*, 1927, vol. I, p. 161; by permission of Macmillan & Co., Ltd., publishers.

the fourteenth century the two-bushel standard was adopted at Crawley, and English practice retained a standard of 2 to 2½ bushels of seed until the nineteenth century, with some increases on special soils.   Even with this lighter sowing, yields of about 18 bushels per acre were common in eighteenth-century England.

YIELDS OF CEREALS ON A SAXON ESTATE, ABOUT 1750 [1]

|  | Seed, Bu. per Acre | Ratio of Crop to Seed | Total Crop, Bu. per Acre |
|---|---|---|---|
| Wheat | 4.32 | 6.08 | 26.2 |
| Rye | 4.32 | 4.49 | 20.2 |
| Barley | 4.32 | 4.83 | 21.8 |
| Oats | 4.32 | 5.86 | 25.4 |

The experiments at Rothamsted in England supply important contributory evidence.   The check plots were cultivated, without the application of any manure, under each of the basic cropping systems: one plot was kept continuously under wheat, another plot was alternated between wheat and fallow.   This check plot thus presented the worst possible standard of a fallow system, distinctly below the level of most medieval and early modern practice, because in actual practice there was some addition of manure.   Even under the rigorous conditions of the unmanured check plots, the Rothamsted averages for fifteen years in the period 1855–1911 were 11.8 bushels per acre on the plot growing wheat each year, and 17.2 bushels per acre for the wheat alternated with fallow.   This result indicates clearly that the low returns in the Middle Ages and early modern period were due largely to poor tillage.   Even when some allowance is made for the standard of tillage attainable on a large area, the crudest system of bare fallowing would admit of extensive improvement over the medieval standard, which was only half the Rothamsted average.   Records show such improvements.   Tillage was improved; more use was made of manure and of composts of plant residues; acid soils were treated with lime; wet soils were drained by open ditches and in some cases by tile drains.   In many regions, with fuller utilization of wild pasture, there was a considerable increase in the number of livestock kept.   Thus, although the cultural system was nominally the same in 1700 as it had been in the time of Charlemagne, the standard of practice had been very greatly improved.

[1] Goltz, Freiherr Theodor von der, *Geschichte des deutschen Landwirtschaft*, Berlin, 1902–03, I, p. 261.

## Rotation Agriculture

The reforms of the early modern period were not general, but in cereal culture England and Germany led the way. In stock breeding, the earlier work was largely done in Holland and in France. The new practices were for a long period confined to the estates of the great landowners in sections where partial enclosure gave them an opportunity to experiment with new modes of culture. The greatest improvement in culture consisted in the substitution of two courses of forage crops for the bare fallow of the older system. The old system was described as one bread crop, wheat or rye; one drink crop, barley; and one year fallow. In regions ill adapted to barley less beer was consumed and this description did not fit the facts, but it was true that the arable land contributed very little to the support of the livestock. The cattle were fed the straw from the mature plant, but there was little positive food value in such forage. At times, a crop of peas provided a better grade of forage. The new rotation system substituted for the fallow year a course of turnips or Swedes, and a course of clover. The turnips were planted in rows and cultivated throughout the growing season. It was thus possible to clear the land of weeds without the complete sacrifice of a crop. The roots could be stored for winter use so that the cattle and sheep could be carried through the winter in better condition.

The other function of fallowing, the building up of nitrates, was accomplished by growing legumes. In the regions of mixed cereal and stock farming, clover or alfalfa (called "lucerne" in Europe) was the most common legume. This use of legumes is based on their capacity to promote the fixation of nitrogen. The plants act as hosts to bacteria which develop in colonies on the roots. These colonies appear as nodules, which are clearly visible to the naked eye. "Nitrogen fixation takes place in the nodule, which thus becomes richer in nitrogen than the rest of the root, and its final product is supposed to be a soluble protein which is passed on to the plant."[1] Experiments with yellow lupines at Rothamsted yielded the following results:

|  | Blossom Formed | Seed Beginning to Form | Seed Ripe |
|---|---|---|---|
| Nitrogen in nodule, per cent | 5.2 | 2.6 | 1.7 |
| Nitrogen in rest of root, per cent | 1.6 | 1.8 | 1.4 |

[1] Russell, E. G., *Soil Conditions and Plant Growth*, 4th ed., London, 1921, p. 206; by permission of Longmans, Green & Co., publishers.

The amount of nitrogen fixed can be determined by field experiments. One of the simplest experiments at Rothamsted consisted of a comparison between the effects of a crop of clover followed by barley and two crops of barley in successive years.

|  | *Plot Where Clover Was Grown* | *Plot Where No Clover Was Grown* |
|---|---|---|
| Nitrogen in crop (1873), lb. per acre | 151.3 (in clover) | 37.3 (in barley) |
| Nitrogen left in soil after crop of 1873 was removed, per cent | 0.1566 | 0.1416 |
| Nitrogen in crop (1874), lb. per acre | 69.4 (in barley) | 39.1 (in barley) |

The nitrogen fixation during the growth of the clover exceeded the requirements of the plants themselves, and left the soil in such condition that the yield of barley in the following year was 1.76 times the yield of barley on the adjoining plot upon which no clover was grown.  A course of legumes was fully as valuable as a bare fallow even when the entire crop was removed.  In practice, the effects were much greater.  If cattle were pastured on the clover, the forage value could be secured without much removal from the land of basic chemical constituents.  If a portion of the clover was plowed into the soil while still green, the addition of nitrates was greater and the organic matter was itself valuable. In practice, the legume crop was more of a stimulus to plant growth than the bare fallow.  By reason of its function, it was sometimes called "green" fallow.

Basic experiments at Rothamsted also yielded other highly significant results.  It appears that no benefit is secured from the growing of clover unless sufficient fertilizer is applied to produce a heavy crop.  It was also found that crops of beans do not produce gains in the subsequent crops under any circumstances.  The record of these field experiments is given in the table on page 62. It will thus be clear that the effective use of clover as a means of nitrate fixation is dependent upon a considerable change in the fertility program of the farm.  It is on this account that bare fallowing persisted until the nineteenth century.  Substantial amounts of barnyard manure would be necessary, and the best results could be obtained only by the importation of fertilizers.  The early development of the use of clover in rotation was consequently confined to the stock-raising districts, and generalization of practice was

EFFECT OF CLOVER AND BEANS ON FOLLOWING CROPS OF WHEAT. CROPS
GROWN IN ROTATION, AGDELL FIELD. TOTAL PRODUCE PER ACRE [1]

A

Clover crops: 1874, 1882, 1894, 1902, 1906, 1910
Wheat crops: 1875, 1883, 1895, 1903, 1907, 1911

|  | Clover Crops Cwt. | Wheat after Fallow Lb. | Wheat after Clover Lb. | Difference Due to Clover Per Cent |
|---|---|---|---|---|
| Unmanured | 14.0 | 4,028 | 3,696 | − 8.2 |
| Mineral manure | 47.0 | 5,147 | 6,052 | + 17.6 |
| Complete manure | 50.1 | 5,493 | 6,093 | + 10.9 |

B

Bean crops: 1854, 1862, 1866, 1870, 1878, 1890, 1898
Wheat crops: 1855, 1863, 1867, 1871, 1879, 1891, 1899

|  | Bean Crops Lb. | Wheat after Fallow Lb. | Wheat after Beans Lb. | Difference Due to Beans Per Cent |
|---|---|---|---|---|
| Unmanured | 1,888 | 4,907 | 4,373 | − 10.9 |
| Mineral manure | 2,615 | 5,528 | 5,447 | − 1.5 |
| Complete manure | 3,177 | 6,092 | 5,929 | − 2.7 |

possible only in the early nineteenth century, when cheap guano and bone meal enabled farmers to secure important supplementary stocks of fertilizers at low cost. Bare fallowing was essential in Europe generally until the introduction of commercial fertilizers enabled the farmer to develop his fertility program by systematic importation. Arthur Young and Albrecht Thaer were therefore unwilling to recommend the abandonment of bare fallowing in the cereal districts of Europe. The rotations led to pronounced differentiation in agricultural practice. The heavier and moister soils proved to be especially adapted to mixed stock and cereal farming. The essence of this system lay in the possibility of leaving the clover and artificial grass for three, four, or five years before the land was plowed again. Each plot of arable land was then used for field crops for not less than four years, and then "lay in grass" for three or more years. The grass could be cut for hay or grazed on the ground.

In regions adapted to such a system, the new modes of using land could not be introduced without comprehensive enclosure. It was essential that each holding should be under individual management, and the primary divisions of each holding had to be enclosed

[1] Hall, A. D., *The Book of the Rothamsted Experiments*, 2d ed., London, 1917, p. 200.

in order to permit the systematic alternation between field crops and forage crops. The geography of enclosure in the eighteenth and nineteenth centuries was dominated by the boundaries between the cereal farms and the mixed cereal and stock farms. The English midlands and sections of northern Germany were the regions most deeply affected by enclosure. In other regions the land came into individual management, but there was no necessity for investing large sums in hedges or other forms of fences or walls.

## Feudal Tenures

The rural organization of Europe in 1700 was profoundly influenced by feudalism, but even in the most backward sections feudalism had lost its original meaning. The increased power of the central government of the territorial states had qualified significantly the political importance of the nobility and the clergy, though these classes still retained important privileges, which enabled them to obstruct the development of centralization. At times this opposition was of real significance in checking abuses of monarchical power, but more frequently these activities merely delayed the social reforms that were clearly desirable. The relations of the nobles to the peasants had likewise undergone many changes. Rights of lordship had been converted into forms that closely resembled rights of ownership. The resemblance, however, was superficial, and land holding was governed by complex rules which preserved most of the objectionable elements of feudal law and failed to achieve any of the advantages of a positive system of private property. The result was thoroughly unsatisfactory from every point of view.

In the tenth and eleventh centuries the lord had been the only representative of public authority with whom the peasant came in contact. The lord protected the peasant from external violence and afforded legal redress from wrong suffered at the hands of his fellow villagers. The lord also protected the peasants from the depredations of the wild animals of the forest. The peasants were subject to various obligations, which were in part comparable to taxes and in part comparable to rent for the use of the land they occupied. The close interdependence between the lord and his peasants afforded some guarantee against unintelligent exploitation. Excessive exactions from the peasants would inevitably affect the lord's household. The peasants could run away, if conditions became very bad ; but, even apart from this ultimate check, the policy of the lord and his stewards was modified by their own selfish interests. A shortsighted policy would soon bring disaster. It was a social system dominated by intensely personal relationships. It was thus profoundly different from the society fashioned by eighteenth-century liberalism upon the basis of pure private property. Even under merely average conditions, feudalism in its original form had definite elements of strength and merit.

The processes of social change had transformed the relations between lord and tenant. Rights of lordship became rights of ownership. The noble of the eighteenth century thought of himself primarily as a landowner collecting a money revenue from a portion of his estate and possibly holding a large farm directly administered for money gains. Much of the produce was of course consumed on the estate, but an important proportion was sold. At the worst, this landlord had ceased to live on his estate. The land was let out to peasants by a resident agent or steward and the revenues were sent to the absentee, who lived at court. Absentee landlordship became general over large sections of France during the seventeenth century. In England and Germany it was not so common, but absenteeism was a factor everywhere, because the greater nobles necessarily owned land in many different localities and they made no attempt to visit all their domains personally even if they did not live at court.

In England the lords had lost all their significant legal privileges, though some manorial courts survived with greatly restricted jurisdiction until 1926. On the Continent of Europe judicial privileges were still significant in 1700. Many lords still had jurisdiction over capital crimes committed on their estates, and as a consequence the gallows was a symbol of the privileged character of the lord. All the subordinate features of the feudal relationship survived. Lordship was acknowledged by some money payment or by presentation of produce on accession to an inheritance, at marriage, and at stated seasons of the year. The symbols of lordship were thus still retained by personages who had ceased to exercise the significant functions of lordship. The change is strikingly apparent in the interpretation of hunting rights, one of the most irritating features of eighteenth-century lordship. The lords now claimed the right to maintain game preserves for sport, even if the birds and animals did serious damage to the peasants' crops. In many parts of France large flocks of pigeons were kept by the lords at the expense of the peasantry. Any attempt on the part of the peasants to keep the game in check was resented, and if the peasants entered the game preserves, their "poaching" was severely punished. This abusive perversion of feudal rights was extensively defended as an inherent right of property.

### The Perpetual Lease

The feudal tenures by which the peasantry had held their land were also transformed in this process of converting feudal lords into landowners; it is important to realize that most of these changes were beneficial to the peasants. The villein tenure of the early feudal period was gradually converted into a perpetual lease. In its original form the villein tenure left the peasant completely subject to the will of the lord. The labor services to be rendered were not limited or defined; the contribution in produce was not fixed in advance; the tenant might be evicted or his heir excluded from the inheritance. Mutual convenience resulted in the commutation into money of labor services and rents payable in kind. The major obligations of the tenant thus became certain. In England, in the sixteenth century, the courts held that the "will" of the lord was to be found in the custom of the manor; as systematic eviction of tenants had never been practicable, the appeal to custom necessarily guaranteed the right of succession. This was, however, a palpable reversal of the original meaning of the conditions of tenancy. The full detail of the process can be traced in England; in France a similar change cannot be followed as readily. In both countries the tenancies that were developed out of the villein tenure became perpetual leases, though they passed under different names. In England the new tenancy was called a "copyhold," because the tenant received a copy of the entry in the manorial records. In France the tenancy was called a "censive," because the tenant paid money dues, or "cens." Perpetual leases were common also in Germany (Erbzinspacht) and in southern Europe.

In southern Europe the perpetual lease was frequently called an "emphyteutic lease." The emphyteutic leases did not differ in any essential feature from the perpetual leases of northern Europe, but they originated in Greco-Roman law, and as a legal form survived the migrations and the development of feudalism. Closely related to the perpetual lease, notably in English law, was the "lease for lives." The commonest form of this lease was an engagement for the duration of the lives of three persons named in the lease. In many instances these lives had no connection with the transaction. The lessee was entitled to name a new "life" when one of the parties died, subject to the payment of a fine to the lessor. The payments made on the lease included an element of risk based on the probability of the survival of the parties named. Both parties to the lease became interested in mortality tables, in order to calculate the prices of such leases. When the lease expired, the landlord secured the benefit of any improvements made in the property.

In England many of the estates of the nobility were subject to rigid entail, or to family settlements. In such cases the head of the family himself had only a life interest in the estate. His activities were restricted in many ways and it was almost impossible to sell any portion of the estate. In other countries similar effects were achieved by similar legal devices. The great estates passed on from generation to generation, except for confiscations in time of civil war and the possible failure of all heirs. A society dominated by great landlords and perpetual leases thus became a very rigid form of social organization; insensitive to change and well-nigh incapable of reforming itself. Those of noble birth, no less than the peasant farmers, were dominated by a complex tangle of contractual and social obligations which they could not easily modify. The framework of rural life in 1700 was in many ways less plastic and flexible than the feudal structure which it had supplanted. At the best, the peasant had achieved security, but he had little freedom of action. The personal servitudes of feudalism had been commuted into money payments, but the land itself remained legally subject to a variety of servitudes both to the lord and to the fellow villagers.

These rigidities made the achievement of agricultural reform difficult. To the natural inertia of a custom-ridden peasantry there were added a number of positive legal obstacles. The peasant cultivator was not free to change his methods of cultivation. The great landlords were better able to experiment with new cultures, but they were not free to introduce new practices except in such measure as they had succeeded in enclosing their lands and separating the demesne farm from the village arable. Under such circumstances the reformers naturally concentrated all efforts on the achievement of pure individualism. The eighteenth-century reformer, whether merely an agricultural reformer or a political radical, was inevitably an individualist. Both assumed that freedom would solve the great economic and social problems of the day.

# PART II. NEW PHILOSOPHIES AND A NEW INDUSTRIALISM, 1750–1789

## CHAPTER 4

## MERCANTILISM AND LAISSEZ FAIRE

———◆———

### Background and General Nature of Mercantilism

During the decades immediately preceding the French Revolution, several earlier tendencies gained momentum — tendencies that vitally affected the course of European history and extended their influence to our own times. Long-prevalent ideas and policies affecting the relations of government to private enterprise were subjected to criticism and change. Dramatic if not decisive scenes were enacted in the international struggle for power and empire. These decades were marked by important stages in the transition to modern modes of business organization and modern technology of agricultural and industrial production. New ideas emerged, affecting the relations of classes to each other and to the state. These various changes were particularly prominent in western Europe. Other regions remained relatively unchanged internally and suffered a decline in comparative economic status. This chapter deals with the system of state regulation of economic life commonly described as " mercantilism," and with the emergence of opposing views and policies.

A distinctive feature of the sixteenth, seventeenth, and eighteenth centuries was the growth of commerce. Trade between the various regions of Europe expanded rapidly, but the discovery of America and the opening of commercial relations between Europe and the Far East by way of the Cape of Good Hope gave peculiar importance to overseas trade and colonization. The newly developing national states of Europe adopted a set of ideas and policies which, because of the growing importance of commerce, came to be described as mercantilism but which included many phases of economic activity. Many writers have given them the appearance of a logical and consistent system, although they were developed gradually and were variable and often conflicting in nature.

Mercantilism may be described broadly as the prevailing mode, during the early modern era, of regulating economic life for the attainment of wealth and political power.   During the first part of that period, banks and credit instruments were so slightly developed that the extension of trade and industry and the maintenance of nonfeudal armies and governmental activities depended largely on the command of gold and silver as mediums of exchange.   The mercantilistic emphasis on the importance of the precious metals led Adam Smith and other critics of mercantilism to hold the erroneous view that mercantilists confused gold and silver with wealth.

### Demand for Gold and Silver

There were various circumstances, political as well as economic, which explain the emphasis on the acquisition of monetary metals. One of these circumstances was the progressive increase in nonlocal trade.   The Mediterranean towns of Europe had long carried on extensive trade with Asia Minor and the Far East, and interregional European trade in the fourteenth and fifteenth centuries expanded rapidly.   The medieval village economy had been relatively self-sufficient, and local trade was often on a barter basis. But nonlocal trade required a medium of exchange.   Distant and hazardous commercial enterprises inspired by the age of discovery called for extensive resources.   There was a gradual development of banking, of credit instruments, and of bookkeeping and clearinghouse devices for canceling out mutual obligations with a minimum of money.   This process, however, was necessarily slow and uncertain, even in dealings between the various regions of Europe, as the Italian and German towns or the Flemish and English towns. The monetary systems were extremely varied and subject to the whims and avarice of rulers and to varying standards of fineness of the metallic content of the coinage.   Under such circumstances it was natural for merchants and other businessmen to view as of primary importance the possession of gold and silver.

Other reasons for the emphasis on command of precious metals were political in nature.   During the Middle Ages the feudal economy then prevailing was based largely on agriculture and the direct control of the products of peasant and handicraft labor in the villages and baronies.   Money, to be sure, was coveted, and as the tastes and ambitions of feudal lords and suzerains expanded, there was increasing need of a medium of exchange for buying luxuries and for engaging in the Crusades and other adventures and enterprises. But they were able to command the plainer essentials of living directly from their estates, which often included towns and crude mining and industrial enterprises. Under feudalism the overlords required little money for maintaining armies, courts, and legislative bodies, for the feudal rights and duties of vassals included such activities as fighting, holding court, and attending council meetings. But vassals were likely to view their obligations lightly and to emphasize their rights. Thus in England the vassals of King John forced him in 1215 to sign the Great Charter; and later kings turned more and more to the townsmen and the smaller landlords for support against their great vassals, whether churchmen or lay landlords. The transition from government by feudal lords to government in the modern sense involved the hiring of soldiers and sailors, the buying of military and naval equipment, the maintenance of courts and administrative agencies by taxation rather than by dependence on the services of vassals, and various other expenditures requiring a medium of exchange.

The townsmen depended on metallic money for financing their rapidly expanding enterprises. Landlords sought it for buying luxuries and paying the costs of their adventures and wars. Kings found it to be essential to their plans for making themselves independent of their vassals by means of paid armies and civil servants, for commanding the resources of their subjects, and for engaging in ambitious enterprises of war and expansion. Among the outstanding founders of powerful early modern states were Louis XI of France (1461-1483), Henry VII of England (1485-1509), and Charles I, who became king of Spain in 1516 and in 1519 assumed the crown of the Holy Roman Empire as Charles V. Monarchs, feudal lords, and merchant princes vied with one another for command of the limited quantities of the precious metals afforded by European mines. Desire for the luxury goods of Asia tended to maintain a trade balance calling for the export of metals eastward.

## Modes of Acquiring Treasure

Before the age of Columbus and da Gama, an outstanding problem was how to increase the store of gold and silver. The voyages of discovery enabled the Portuguese and the Spaniards to solve the problem by plundering the natives of India and of the New World and by developing the mines of Mexico, Peru, and Brazil. Other countries were less successful in gaining direct control of the sources of bullion but were able to share the Spanish and Portuguese treasures partly by capture and partly by trade. Spain and Portugal failed to develop a balanced and well-rounded economic life, and depended on the manufactures of other countries, especially of England, France, Flanders, and Holland. These latter countries, partly because of their failure to gain control of the principal sources of the precious metals, depended more largely on manufacturing and trade for securing gold and silver — a fact which gave them ultimately a great advantage over Portugal and Spain.

### Modes of Maintaining a Favorable Balance of Trade

If trade was to be utilized for securing gold and silver, there had to be a "favorable balance of trade" — more goods, in value, had to be exported than were imported. An outstanding problem of public policy, therefore, was the devising of methods for buying as little as possible, in terms of value, and selling as much as possible abroad. To be sure, this crude conception was gradually supplemented by inclusion of services and other items now sometimes described as part of the "invisible" balance of trade but more adequately expressed, in common with trade in the narrow sense, as the "balance of indebtedness." In promoting a "favorable" balance, various methods were used.

(1) Prominent among mercantilist policies was the encouragement of the consumption of goods produced at home by sumptuary laws regulating food, clothing, etc., and by subsidies or other aids to industry. Conversely, the use of foreign-made goods was discouraged by tariffs, prohibitions, or other means.

(2) Since manufactured goods sell for more than raw materials, the latter, when not produced in sufficient quantities at home to supply the demands of trade, should be imported, manufactured, and sold abroad. The difference between cheap raw materials and dear manufactured goods would thus be paid by foreign buyers and added to the favorable balance of trade. Similarly, raw materials produced at home should not be exported if by any means they could be sold abroad in the form of manufactured goods.

(3) But ability to sell manufactures abroad in competition with other countries depended on the cost of production, which consisted mainly of the wages of workers. The idea of a subsistence wage grew up with the system of wage labor following the decline of serfdom. Mercantilists adopted the conception and made it a fundamental part of their doctrines. Labor was viewed as the primary source of "national" wealth, and the poorer the laborer the larger was his contribution to the wealth of the country. Low

wages — substantially at the level of subsistence — were viewed as essential for two reasons. In the first place, employers held that wages above the subsistence level would induce the worker to spend part of his time in idleness, which would decrease the amount of labor available. Secondly, it was held that high wages would increase the costs of production, and that this would undermine the nation's competitive power, on which depended a favorable balance of trade. It was even contended that employers were justified in paying wages below the subsistence level if this should prove to be necessary to maintain their competitive power in foreign markets, the government assuming the burden of poor relief as a supplement to insufficient wages. Supplementing wages with poor relief was ultimately, indeed, more a part of public policy than of theory. The doctrine of "the utility of poverty" (applied, of course, by those who held the view, not to themselves but only to the working classes) was widely accepted both before and after the period of mercantilism, but its logical development and extensive embodiment in public policy were distinctive aspects of mercantilism.

(4) By securing colonies and controlling the trade and industry of the colonists, it was believed that there could be maintained a dependable source of goods not produced at home and a continuous market or "vent" for surplus products. Two types of colonies were viewed as particularly serviceable in maintaining a favorable balance of trade. One type consisted of colonies that were adapted to the production of silk, sugar, tobacco, rice, and other noncompetitive goods. The other type included territories that could either produce in their own mines or secure from rivals of the mother country enough gold and silver to pay the difference between the value of the goods they sold to the mother country and the value of their purchases.

(5) By developing the arts of navigation and maintaining shipping facilities for carrying the country's goods and, if possible, a part of the goods of other nations, the store of money could be still further increased. Gradually there was developed the conception known later as the "invisible" balance of trade, including income from investments, payments by ambassadors and by tourists, and services such as shipping facilities as distinguished from the sale of commodities. Most of the mercantilists of the eighteenth century recognized this broader base of international exchange and of the balance of payments, but they continued to emphasize the "favorable" balance in the narrower sense.

(6) Still another phase of mercantilism, implicit in the various aspects already described, was a detailed regulation by the state not only of exports and imports but also of production, of the monetary system, and even of the consuming habits of the people. Regulation was in part by means of the state's own administrative machinery and in part by means of guilds and corporations.   Thus as late as 1721 the English Calico Act imposed heavy fines and informers' fees on those who wore clothing made of calico or who used calico in household furnishings or in any other way; merchants were forbidden to sell calicoes or manufactures containing calico. The purpose was to protect English woolens and silks from the competition of cottons imported from India.

Contemporaneous writers who dealt with economic subjects were mainly pamphleteers either advocating or opposing mercantilism. There were few writers who analyzed the subject objectively or scientifically in the manner of modern economists, and even Adam Smith was propagandist as well as scientist.   Later economists, to be sure, were likely to express personal opinions and advocate policies under the guise of principles and even "laws" of nature; but much progress has been made in the scientific compiling and interpreting of economic data.   Mercantilism was primarily not a system of theory or a school of thought but a gradually developed series of statutes and administrative policies.

### Colbert as a Mercantilist

Jean Baptiste Colbert, who in 1661 became the principal minister of King Louis XIV of France, so firmly impressed his policies on his age that they gave rise to the term " Colbertism," used synonymously with "mercantilism."   His views transcended mercantilism in the narrow sense, to be sure, and some of his policies even removed restrictions on economic freedom.   As in England, the regulatory functions of the guilds were restricted, but the absolute authority of the state was substituted.   His promotion of industrial education may be said to have stimulated individual initiative, but he attempted to control for purposes of state policy the channels in which initiative found expression.   He opposed local restrictions on interprovincial trade, but his promotion of internal freedom of trade in agricultural products, as well as his control of the export of grain, seems to have been due largely to his desire to maintain an abundant and cheap supply of food for the industrial population — a distinctively mercantilist policy.   For the same purpose, and also for aiding in the export of surpluses, he improved the highways and constructed canals, notably the famous Languedoc Canal (Canal du Midi) connecting the Atlantic and the Mediterranean.

Colbert's attitude toward industry was perhaps narrower and more nationalistic than that of the English mercantilists. Its political and fiscal aspects are indicated by his view that "manufactures will produce returns in money, which is the single aim of commerce and the only means of increasing the greatness and power of the state." Even more explicit was his assertion that "I believe that agreement is fixed upon the principle that it is only the abundance of money in a state that determines its greatness and power." Economically, his policy was based on his desire to free France from dependence on foreign manufacturers. He was disturbed by the fact that Italians, Flemings, Dutch, Englishmen, and Germans sold to Frenchmen various costly manufactures requiring special skill. Among these were steel, jewelry, porcelain, lace, tapestry, and many woven goods. He encouraged the immigration of skilled craftsmen and the introduction of foreign methods and devices. He simplified the tariffs in 1664, and three years later increased the duties on most manufactured goods. Extensive bounties and subsidies were granted to manufacturers, and special efforts were made to encourage the crafts devoted to the more artistic and highly skilled productions — a policy which left a permanent impress on French industry. From his administration dates the purchase by the government (1662) of the famous Gobelin works, which served as a school for the training of artists and craftsmen in the making not only of tapestries but also of fine textiles for clothing and other artistic manufactures. In characteristic mercantilist manner Colbert believed that an abundant supply of cheap labor for industry was essential, and to this end he secured a reduction in the number of holidays connected with church festivals, and a curtailment of membership in monasteries.

For the encouragement of shipping facilities and of trade with foreign countries, he sought to facilitate the export of grain, during years of surplus, and of wine, brandy, and manufactures. To the same end he established free ports; provided for drawbacks or refunding of duties on imports intended for re-exportation; levied duties on the shipping of foreigners; and granted bounties to French shippers and shipbuilders. He also promoted commercial companies such as the East India Company, and greatly extended the French colonial empire, the trade and industry of which he sought to monopolize for Frenchmen.

In the enforcement of mercantilist policies, Colbert formulated codes for the detailed regulation of industry, and appointed royal inspectors responsible to the state. He desired flexibility in adaptation to varying localities and conditions, and he never lost sight of larger national aims, particularly independence from foreign manufacturers and the attainment of superiority in artistry and quality of products. But he was a thorough absolutist, and his successors extended his system and stifled industry by minute regulations which lost sight of larger aims and became a mere expression of the authority of the state. It was this system which was attacked by some of the physiocrats and uprooted by the French Revolution.

In spite of the absolutism of the monarchy, however, provincialism survived in France, and indeed contributed to the obscuring of the larger national aims of Colbert and to the preoccupation of his successors with routine details of regulation.

### The English Navigation System

In England the strong monarchs of the Tudor line, especially Henry VII, Henry VIII, and Elizabeth, imposed their will during the sixteenth century with slight difficulty, partly because the country was relatively small and homogeneous and partly because their policies were in accord with a popular reaction against the turbulence and tyranny of the feudal lords. After the triumph of Parliament in the seventeenth century, the mercantile and industrial classes exerted such influence on Parliament as to assure the continuance of mercantilist policies, but with greater flexibility and opportunity for initiative than in France. These policies were embodied in various laws, notably the Navigation Acts, and in the work of the Privy Council, the Board of Trade, and other administrative agencies.

The most noted phase of English mercantilism was the navigation system embodied in the Acts of Trade. The first comprehensive act was passed in 1651 during the rule of Oliver Cromwell. Upon the restoration of the Stuart dynasty in the person of Charles II in 1660, the law of 1651 was re-enacted with minor changes, and from time to time various amendments were added. In 1696, after the triumph of Parliament in the Revolution of 1688, an act was passed primarily intended to strengthen the administration of earlier laws.

Thereafter there were few important changes until the system began to decline a century later.

The Acts of Trade were sometimes obscure and inconsistent in detail and not easily interpreted. But the main provisions and purposes stood out in bold relief.

(1) *Exports from the English colonies.* — By the middle of the eighteenth century the overseas expansion of western European states had given to their colonies a place of outstanding importance. In the case of England, insular, small in territory, and restricted in resources and in opportunity for continental expansion, colonies played an increasingly dominant role. The Acts of Trade required that exports from the colonies should be in ships owned, built, and largely manned by Englishmen; but colonists were classed as Englishmen and might use their own ships, although under restrictions which benefited the ships of the mother country, especially the ruling that return cargoes must come from England. The Irish were generally excluded; but Scotchmen, by common law after the union of the crowns in 1603, and by the interpretation of the Act of Union of 1707, were permitted to share the export trade from the colonies. To encourage the building and use of English ships, various bounties and other aids were granted from time to time. Many colonial products (the so-called " enumerated " commodities), such as tobacco, rice, cotton, sugar, and naval stores or materials required for ship construction and repair, could be exported only to England. These were goods desired by Englishmen, either for domestic use or for manufacture and re-export. Other commodities might be sold to foreigners; and indeed some of them could not be shipped to England, on the ground that they would compete with English products.

(2) *Imports into the colonies.* — The legal provisions with regard to ships to be used for importing goods into the colonies were essentially the same as for exports from the colonies. England was regarded as the "staple" for colonial imports — with few exceptions, all goods which the colonists imported had to be shipped from England or by way of England, no matter where the goods might be produced. This enabled England, in so far as the laws were enforced, not only to impose English manufactures on the colonists but in many cases to use English as distinguished from colonial ships in supplying colonial needs.

(3) *Imports into England other than from her own colonies.* — Noncolonial imports into England were subject to complicated and

changing regulations. In general, imports from the colonies of other countries (the French, Dutch, Spanish, and Portuguese colonies) could come into England only in English vessels. Goods from a foreign country other than a colony could not be sent to England by the ships of a third country except when the usual port of shipment of the goods was in a third country. By way of illustration, French wines had to come direct from France in French or English ships; the Dutch, for example, against whose powerful merchant marine the laws were at first mainly directed, were unable to ship French wines through Holland to England or even direct from France to England. Some goods, as Dutch spices, were barred entirely.

(4) *Coastwise shipping.* — England's monopoly of coastwise trade is indicated by a passage from the law of 1660: No foreigner shall transport goods "from one port or creek of England, Ireland, Wales, Islands of Guernsey or Jersey, or town of Berwick upon Tweed to another port or creek of the same." After the Act of Union with Scotland in 1707, the Scottish coastwise trade was also subject to Parliamentary regulation.

(5) *Fisheries.* — Formerly the fisheries were comparatively important, not only because of the product but because they served as "nurseries of seamen" and a stimulus to shipbuilding and shipping. In addition to fish as food, whale oil and whalebone were important commodities. After the Protestant Reformation, when there was a tendency to abandon Catholic customs regarding abstinence from meat, laws and regulations attempted to force a continuance of the eating of fish, but on economic rather than religious grounds. Among the regulations designed to favor English fisheries was a provision imposing double duties on the ships of aliens bringing fish to English markets.

### Other Phases of English Mercantilist Policy

English mercantilism found expression not only in the navigation system, some of the outstanding features of which have been described, but also in various regulations concerning manufactures in the colonies. These restrictions were embodied in administrative policies even more largely than in statutes. The commission issued to the Board of Trade in 1697 emphasized the duty of the members of the board to prevent the development of colonial manufactures, and instructions to colonial governors usually included the same policy, especially the preventing of colonial action for encouraging manufactures. Among the laws governing colonies, passed by Parliament, were acts to prohibit the making of woolens for the market, although of course household industry was not prohibited. In 1732 the making of hats was restricted, and after 1750 the making of ironware and steel was forbidden, though the pig-iron and bar-iron industry was encouraged.

Some colonial industries were stimulated instead of restricted. Thus the smelting of iron was encouraged by the removal of duties on the importation into England of colonial pig iron and even of bar iron. In addition to preferential duties or free importation in the case of certain goods, bounties were paid at various times for encouraging the colonial production of such goods as naval stores, hemp, indigo, and silk. In various other ways efforts were made to stimulate certain colonial industries. But these policies were themselves significant illustrations of mercantilism, as they were for the purpose of making the colonies a source of supply for goods needed by Englishmen, in return for which Englishmen would supply the colonies with manufactures. In this way England would be able to exchange dear manufactures for cheap raw materials, strengthen the basis of her general export trade, and increase her favorable balance of trade with other countries as well as with the colonies.

There were various other phases of policy substantially mercantilist in nature. Restrictions were imposed on the export of wool. The import of grain was discouraged and usually prohibited, while bounties were paid to encourage the export of surplus grain. General tariff regulations, embodied in the "book of rates," favored the import of goods needed in England and imposed duties on foreign goods which would compete with English products, especially manufactures. Various laws prohibited the emigration of skilled workmen and the export of tools, implements, and machines, and models, drawings, or designs of the instruments used in manufacture. Detailed regulation of industrial processes, and sumptuary laws for controlling consumption, although not abandoned, were less prominent in the eighteenth century than earlier.

## Opposition to Mercantilism

The views of mercantilist writers and statesmen regarding the regulation of economic life placed the trading and manufacturing classes on a seemingly impregnable basis. The interests of these groups came to be regarded as practically identical with the interests of the nation.   The monopolistic position of the leading mercantile and manufacturing groups was widely viewed as a moderate price to pay for the maintenance of the all-important favorable balance of trade.   But other groups gradually became more critical. The landlords, who had lost their feudal power and had been opposed by the kings during the rise of dynastic states, were more assertive in the eighteenth century and less inclined to accept the claims of mercantilists as to the superior value and national importance of trade and manufacturing.   Producers of raw materials, whose markets were restricted in many cases to the demands of the manufacturers of their own country, were becoming restive and finding such powerful champions as Arthur Young and Adam Smith in England and the physiocrats in France.

There was opposition, also, even from some of the trading and manufacturing groups.   The English East India Company, for example, imported indigo, silks, cotton goods, and other costly materials which required the shipment of considerable amounts of money out of England.   The calicoes and other fabrics imported from India came into competition with English products, especially woolens and silks.   The company was thus forced to defend itself against attacks from mercantilists on the twofold basis of its draining precious metals out of the country and its competing with English manufacturers.   It is true that many mercantilists rallied to the defense of the company, but the conflicts between the company and other groups did much to discredit the idea of identity of the interests of the nation with the interests of the mercantile and manufacturing classes, and to create a wholesome if disconcerting recognition of the growing complexity of the economic system. Mercantilism was further weakened, among the more aggressive and competitively powerful manufacturers and merchants, by retaliatory policies abroad.   It became apparent that extreme protective measures, such as prohibiting the export of wool and the import of manufactures, incited other countries to raise their barriers, which hindered the expansion of trade.

### Abatement of the Struggle for Gold and Silver

The growth of opposition to mercantilist regulations was largely due to new conditions differing from those of the era of the rise and ascendancy of mercantilism.   The struggle for gold and silver was abated by their increasing abundance and by the repeal or evasion of export restrictions.   The long-continued import of the metals from the New World by Spain and Portugal at length greatly increased their volume throughout Europe. Much of the treasure imported by Spain and Portugal found its way into other countries through the buccaneering activities of such men as Hawkins and Drake, and through captures in wartime. Much of it was commanded by the superior industrial skills of other countries. Imports of precious metals from the New World were progressively larger, and at the same time the exports of precious metals to the Far East were smaller. The use of Oriental spices declined; and the fine fabrics of the Far East, as silks, calicoes, and porcelains, were successfully duplicated or imitated by westerners. The comparative abundance and freedom of export and import of the precious metals was an important factor in the relaxation of emphasis on economic regulation for the purpose of securing and retaining gold and silver.

While the precious metals were becoming more abundant, the importance of gold and silver coins as mediums of exchange was declining. This was due to such circumstances as the rise of banks, the use of substitutes for coins, and the increased velocity of circulation of mediums of exchange.

### Banks and Credit Instruments

The importance of "bank money" in the eighteenth century is described by Adam Smith. "There are several different sorts of paper money," he states, "but the circulating notes of banks and bankers are the species which is best known." He goes on to explain how these notes, in connection with a small amount of gold or silver, multiply the amount of money in circulation. "A particular banker lends among his customers his own promissory notes, to the extent, we shall suppose, of a hundred thousand pounds. As those notes serve all the purposes of money, his debtors pay him the same interest as if he had lent them so much money. The interest is the source of his gain. Though some of these notes are continually coming back upon him for payment, part of them continue to circulate for months and years together. Though he has generally in circulation, therefore, notes to the extent of a hundred thousand pounds, twenty thousand pounds in gold and silver may, frequently, be a sufficient provision for answering occasional demands. By this operation, therefore, twenty thousand pounds in gold and silver perform all the functions which a hundred thousand could otherwise have performed."

Although goldsmiths, merchants, and bankers seem first to have developed the idea of issuing large amounts of paper money on the basis of a comparatively small reserve of gold and silver, and to have profited immensely in the exercise of an essentially public function, governments were not slow to utilize the method for meeting their obligations or for expanding their financial resources. Both banks and governments failed frequently to resist the temptation to issue excessive amounts of paper money.    But the significant fact in the history of mercantilism is that the device of issuing credit instruments and paper money on a small metallic base vastly expanded the circulating medium and abated the mercantilistic and nationalistic struggle for gold and silver.

Similar in effect was the development of such credit instruments as bills of exchange and ordinary bank checks.    These were used not only between two original parties to a bargain, contract, or obligation, but by endorsement they became negotiable and were used in satisfying complicated obligations involving extensive transactions in widely separated areas.    These instruments were based not on gold and silver but mainly on the deposits and accounts of patrons of financial institutions.    Deposits themselves came to be based largely on a network of credits representing goods and services, stocks, bonds, mortgages, and other securities, and promissory notes based often merely on faith in the integrity and competence of the debtor.    A bill of exchange, check, draft, or note signed merely by a local individual or the agent of a local organization could not become extensively negotiable because the integrity and competence of the individual or the organization and the security back of the instrument were known only in local circles.    It was in this fact that banking institutions largely had their basis.    They became reservoirs of innumerable small local resources of depositors and patrons, as well as of the investments of the stockholders or owners.    The local resources, combined in a single institution, enabled that institution to stand in the place of the individual and to make his credit valid in remote and extensive transactions.    As a result of the development of banking institutions throughout Europe, and especially in Italy, Spain, Augsburg, Antwerp, Amsterdam, and London, there was a progressive decline in the proportion of gold and silver required for international and interregional as well as for local exchange.    Large-scale transactions, including wholesale trade, came to be handled largely by means of paper money, credit instruments, and clearinghouse operations;    and coins were by no means the only medium of exchange, even in everyday retail transactions.

One of the main arguments of the early mercantilists had been that gold and silver were necessary to enable governments to defend their peoples in wartime. By the eighteenth century, however, the expenses of governments during wars were met only in small part by means of coins and bullion, as Adam Smith pointed out with keen relish in his attacks on mercantilism. He estimated that the Seven Years' War (1756–1763) cost Great Britain more than £90,000,000, and that two thirds of this was spent in distant countries. But the total gold and silver money then in circulation he estimated as only about £18,000,000. He concluded that ability to finance foreign wars had little relation to the stock of gold and silver at the command of governments.

### Increasing Velocity of the Circulation of Money

The comparative importance of the precious metals was much reduced also by the increasing velocity of circulation of the various mediums of exchange. One shilling used for five transactions in a day was equal, in effect, to five shillings each of which was used only for one transaction. There were many factors tending, in the eighteenth century, to increase the velocity or frequency of circulation alike of coins and of other mediums of exchange. The general *tempo* of business had quickened; transportation facilities were being rapidly improved; and the modes of transferring credits had become increasingly efficient.

The older mercantilists thought of the balance of trade literally as the difference, in value, between exports and imports of commodities, but this conception was gradually modified by a realization of the complexity of economic relations. Some of Adam Smith's most vigorous attacks on mercantilism were aimed at the older, narrower view of the balance of trade, already virtually superseded.

### Emergence of *Laissez-Faire* Ideas

It is true that mercantilists of Adam Smith's time recognized, as do modern economists, that the actual balance is composed of numerous items in addition to the difference between the exports and the imports of commodities. But there were some fundamental differences in point of view between the mercantilists and such critics as Smith and his predecessors, the physiocrats of France. Mercantilism was essentially a system of nationalism, with rigorous control of economic activities for the attainment of national wealth and power.  The physiocrats and Adam Smith and later the classical economists were not opposed to the attainment of national wealth and power, but they were primarily individualists and advocates of the point of view summed up by the term *laissez faire*. This doctrine opposes governmental intervention and control except for maintaining competitive conditions.  *Laissez faire* assumes that under the automatic controls or adjustments of a competitive price system, the unfettered interests of the individual will be forced into conformity with the general interest.

### The Physiocrats

The connection of the group of Frenchmen known as physiocrats with the idea of *laissez faire* is indicated by the meaning of the term physiocracy — the "rule of nature." They called themselves "*les économistes*," although the term "physiocrats" was suggested in 1768 by one of the group (DuPont de Nemours, in his *Physiocratie, ou constitution naturelle du gouvernement le plus avantageux au genre humain*), and later writers have properly reverted to the term which indicates the distinctive idea of the group.  The conception of a "natural order," to be sure, was not originated by them. The idea of government as a social contract, the original terms of which were the "natural order," was familiar to John Locke in the seventeenth century and even to earlier writers.  Jean Jacques Rousseau, the author of the *Contrat social*, advocated a return to a "state of nature."  But the physiocratic conception of the "natural order" had little in common with the "natural rights" which political theorists regarded as the terms of the original social contract.  The physiocrats referred to an economic, not a political, "order of nature."  Their attacks were not on feudal, ecclesiastical, and social privilege but rather on the monopolistic position of merchants and craftsmen — a position these classes were able to maintain by means of governmentally sanctioned guilds and corporations and of the mercantilistic regulations which had survived from the time of Colbert.

The leader of the group was François Quesnay, who died in 1774, two years before Adam Smith published his *Wealth of Nations*. Quesnay's approach to economic problems was affected by the fact that he was a physician and a student of physiology.  He believed that the production, distribution, and utilization of wealth were comparable to the circulatory and other natural processes of the body. Among other advocates of these or similar ideas were the father of Mirabeau, noted figure of the Revolution; DuPont de Nemours, who originated the term "physiocracy"; Turgot, who, as minister of Louis XVI, made an effort to put into practice certain liberal policies, though he was not a member of the "sect," as he called the group; and Vincent de Gournay, a businessman and public official, whose views and influence found expression through his friend Turgot.

## The " Natural Order "

The physiocratic conceptions of the order of nature in economic life are far from definite or consistent, but to them is largely traceable, through Adam Smith, the view which many have continued to hold, namely, that the general welfare as well as the advantage of the individual is best served when government allows each individual to seek his own interests under the competitive conditions of a free market. But in the age of the physiocrats, the competitive conditions of a free market could be established only by repealing the monopolistic and restrictive policies associated with Colbertism and mercantilism. One of the group asserted, in typical manner, that if all the futile, unfair, and contradictory laws were repealed, little would remain for legislators to do. Their aim, however, was not to dispense with public authority, but rather to utilize it for maintaining the conditions they regarded as essential to the functioning of the "natural order."

## The Exaltation of Agriculture

The mercantilists had recognized the fundamental importance of agriculture in furnishing food and the elementary materials of industry and trade, but their emphasis was on the transformation of cheap crude materials into dear manufactured goods and on the interchange of goods for swelling the balance of trade. The physiocrats, on the other hand, reverted to a primitive emphasis on agriculture. They held that the production of new wealth, even in agriculture, requires the destruction of a certain amount of previously created wealth — as the seed sown for a new harvest. But in agriculture alone, so they held, is the new wealth produced in excess of the old wealth destroyed or used up. This is because the farmer is the agent of nature, the only true creator. Nature, with the aid of the farmer, actually creates wealth. But the craftsman, the trader, and all others merely take the grain or the wool or the timber already produced and do nothing more than change its form or transfer it from place to place.  Industry and trade, therefore, instead of being exalted above agriculture in national economy, were declared to be "sterile" or unproductive in the sense of creating no new wealth or yielding no "net product."

This "net product" the physiocrats assigned to the landlord, although by their own analysis it was the creation of nature aided not by the landlord but by his tenants and laborers.  Later economists, especially David Ricardo, asserted that the "net product" assigned by the physiocrats to the landlord is merely rent appropriated by him, not in accord with an inviolable natural order but merely because he owns the land.  It is apparent, too, that the "sterility" attributed to industry and trade was based on a purely physical conception of wealth.  To a hungry man a loaf of bread produced by artisans and placed before him by traders would have had greater utility than a barn full of grain fresh from the hands of the farmer as the agent of creative nature.  The physiocratic exaltation of landlords above merchants and manufacturers because of the "net product" of agriculture and the "sterility" of non-agricultural pursuits was even more illusory than the mercantilistic exaltation of merchants and manufacturers because of their connection with the national balance of trade.  But the illusion was historically important as a phase of the reaction against mercantilism and as a vital part of the movement toward *laissez faire*.

## Influence of the Physiocrats

The physiocrats were not without influence on the course of events in France.  Their ideas appear in various early edicts (1763, 1766, and 1774) repealing many of the restrictions on the export and import of grain and the movement of grain between provinces.  Their opposition to the monopoly of the privileges of carrying on various trades by members of guilds and corporations was reflected in Turgot's edict of 1776 for abolishing the guilds.  These were later restored, but their privileges were largely swept away during the Revolution.  The reciprocal Treaty of Commerce of 1786 with Great Britain was distinctly physiocratic in favoring French agrarians.  Their ideas regarding taxation (which, they held, should be based on the "net product") influenced the tax policy of the Constituent Assembly during the Revolution.  Not the least significant of their influences, moreover, was the reflection of their ideas in Adam Smith's *Wealth of Nations*.

## Adam Smith's " System of Natural Liberty "

The philosophers believed in the "natural rights of man" first formulated as the terms of the mythical social contract. Physiocracy in essence was the "rule of nature." Adam Smith's counterpart of these ideas was his "system of natural liberty." But Smith's conception was far more definite than the earlier doctrines, and it pervaded his whole system of economic thought.

In its negative aspect, his "system of natural liberty" found expression in a noted passage in the *Wealth of Nations* in which he defined what he regarded as the appropriate functions of government and carefully excluded therefrom the regulation of economic life. "According to the system of natural liberty," he asserted, "the sovereign has only three duties to attend to." One of them was defense against internal violence and against invasion; the second was maintenance of "an exact administration of justice" for protecting citizens from injustice or oppression; and the third was support of certain public works and institutions needed in the general interest but beyond the scope of private initiative or profit.

In its positive aspects, the "system of natural liberty" is described in great detail as the operation throughout economic life of the motive of self-interest, restrained and subordinated to the general interest, not by law or authority, but by the forces of competition. In the *Wealth of Nations* Smith attempted to show that in the use of capital or "stock" the "natural interests and inclinations" of investors coincide with "the public interests." In meeting the economic requirements of society in a "system of natural liberty" there is constant competition for the profitable use of capital. "Without any intervention of law, therefore, the private interests and passions of men naturally lead them to divide and distribute the stocks of every society among all the different employments carried on in it, as nearly as possible in the proportion which is most agreeable to the interest of the whole of society." He assumed that in the absence of governmental intervention, not only interest and profits but wages and rents would find natural competitive levels which would harmonize the interests of the individual and the group.

Adam Smith, however, was no mere theorist. As an observer of exceptional keenness and candor, he recognized the fact that in reality there was a conflict between individual profits and the interests of society. The "natural" and "most advantageous" conditions of free competition were "deranged," so he charged, by "the regulations of the mercantile system." Thus the "system of natural liberty" based on unrestricted competition was merely hypothetical. Indeed Smith was convinced that the monopolists of the mercantile system were so firmly entrenched as to make vain the hope of establishing his "natural liberty," at least in the realm of trade. He never tired of denouncing "the interested sophistry of merchants and manufacturers," whose "monopolizing spirit" made impossible the establishment of free trade. The interests of the landed class, on the other hand, he believed to be "strictly and inseparably connected with the interests of society."

## Support of *Laissez Faire* by Manufacturers

It is one of the ironies of history that the agrarians became the last-ditch opponents of free trade and that the influence of the merchants and manufacturers finally accomplished the overthrow of the old regulatory system and the introduction of *laissez faire*. The triumph of the new economic liberalism was deferred till the nineteenth century, and was even then limited by many regulations and by important legal and natural monopolies. But the newer types of industrialists associated with cotton, iron, and pottery were veering toward *laissez faire* even before the French Revolution.

The change of sentiment among the English industrialists is traceable not so much to the theoretical view of the advantages of "a system of natural liberty" as to the pressure of new forces and conditions. Among these was the obsolescence of old regulations, as those embodied in the excise laws and in the Statute of Apprentices, when applied to the newer, rapidly changing industries. But the outstanding cause of the shift of the point of view of the industrialists was their competitive power based on the new machines and methods, combined with their desire to overcome mercantilist obstacles in other countries in the way of an expansion of their exports. These circumstances were back of the support of the Treaty of Commerce with France in 1786 for the reciprocal reduction of duties, and of their demand for similar treaties with other countries. As early as 1788 the English cotton manufacturers petitioned the government to negotiate additional treaties on the principles of the French treaty for the purpose of opening "new channels of consumption for the increased quantity of . . . cotton goods which have been and will be made in Great Britain in consequence of the great extent of the power of machinery and human labor which have been applied to this manufactory."

CHAPTER 5

# THE STRUGGLE FOR EMPIRE

———◆———

## The Eighteenth-Century Crisis of Imperialism

In the long history of European overseas expansion the eighteenth century was pre-eminently an era of conflict between France and England. At the beginning of the century the duel for empire between these two states was in its early stages. Although final decision as to the ascendancy of Great Britain was delayed by the rise of Napoleon, the outcome was ensured by the conditions of the eighteenth-century struggle, and particularly by the economic transformation of England during the early stages of the industrial revolution. The triumph of Great Britain determined the future racial and political complexion of vast areas of the world and affected vitally the course of European economic and political history.

The expansion of trade and the exploitation of dependent territories had proceeded since the age of discovery in accordance with mercantilist principles. England's notable triumphs in the application of these principles, as in the Seven Years' War, were soon followed by the first momentous breach in the system — the American Revolution. Although there was not immediately apparent any vital effect of this Revolution on imperial policy, the revolutionists were reinforced by the economists, led by Adam Smith, and by the free-trade and *laissez-faire* views of the newer types of industrialists. Significant, also, was the influence of the ideals of individualism, liberty, equality, and nationalism of the French Revolution. The ultimate outcome was a new type of imperialism, involving a much larger degree of colonial self-government and a much smaller degree of compulsory conformity to modes of economic life prescribed by the central authority.

## The Commercial Revolution

The background of the eighteenth-century struggle for empire extends to the age of discovery. Before the era of Columbus and da Gama, western Europe was the frontier of the civilization which centered in the Mediterranean, and especially in the cities of Italy. The discovery of America by Columbus under the flag of Spain and the opening up of the route around Africa to the Far East under

Portuguese auspices inaugurated changes so profound as to warrant the term "commercial revolution."

Genoa and Venice had established empires essentially commercial but with a territorial basis in the control of various eastern Mediterranean areas. The wealth and power of the great Italian city-states were based largely on their favorable location for mediating commerce between the various regions of Europe and the countries to the east — the Far East and the populous and wealthy cities of western Asia and Egypt, such as Constantinople, Bagdad, and Alexandria. Venice sent fleets of merchant vessels to Constantinople, the Black Sea, Syria, Egypt, the Barbary Coast, and western Europe. For generations a notable annual event in the lives of Englishmen and other westerners was the visit of the Flanders fleet of the Venetians. On overland routes to the towns and fairs of Germany and other inland areas there was an extensive trade in goods brought by Italians from the East and in wares manufactured in Italy. Over the same routes and subject largely to Italian control was the trade in the cruder products of central, northern, and western Europe moving southward in exchange for the commodities imported or produced by Italians. Thus the Italian cities were the centers of commercial relations extending from the British Isles and the Baltic countries to China and the East Indies.

The changes associated with the commercial revolution included the decline of the Mediterranean cities and the rise of towns and commercial nations on the Atlantic seaboard. Western Europe, no longer the frontier, became the center of the stirring events connected with exploration, the quest for treasure, colonization, trade, and the Europeanization of the world. But before Frenchmen and Englishmen played the major parts, the Portuguese, the Spaniards, and the Dutch built up their empires.

### Earlier Empires — the Portuguese Monopoly of Oriental Trade

Portugal, one of the Christian kingdoms carved out of the Moorish dominions of the Iberian Peninsula, began its career of expansion in 1415 by capturing from the Moors one of the two "Pillars of Hercules," the fortress of Ceuta south of the Strait of Gibraltar. Then followed in succession a crusade against the Moslems in Bilad Ghana, "land of wealth," in the Senegal River valley beyond the Sahara; a futile effort to expand eastward in a direct attack on the centers of the Moslem faith; the rise of the slave trade as a means of financing further expansion; the colonization of islands along the western coast of Africa; evolution of the idea of sailing around Africa to the Far East; the rounding of the Cape of Good Hope in 1486; and finally, in 1497-1498, under the stimulus of the first voyage of Columbus, the expedition of da Gama to India.

Along the shores of the Indian Ocean and eastward to China and the East Indies the Portuguese came into contact with an extremely populous and wealthy region. The commercial and industrial traditions of the region extended to a remote antiquity. The native governments had fallen into a state of decay, and trade was dominated by the Arabs. The Portuguese were able to gain ascendancy by virtue of the superiority of their ships, their long-range guns, and the art of maneuvering and using their merchant vessels on occasion as military machines. Generations of experience in fighting the Moors and in exploring the western coast of Africa had made the Portuguese the finest and boldest seamen of the age. By 1511 they extended their control of strategic African and Indian Ocean centers to Malacca, commanding the route to China and Japan and the Spice Islands through the straits between Sumatra and the Malay Peninsula. Within another decade the northern portions of Sumatra and Java and several of the Spice Islands or Moluccas had fallen under their sway. They thus achieved mastery of the Far Eastern trade, wresting control alike from the Moslem Arabs of the East and from the Italians as European distributors. This gigantic undertaking was supplemented by the continued exploitation of various regions in Africa in the quest for slaves and for gold, and by the discovery and extensive colonization of Brazil.

The Portuguese Far Eastern Empire, however, was in ruins within a century after its establishment. Its decline was hastened by the union of Portugal with Spain in 1580. Portugal was thus involved in Spanish troubles, and the Dutch, at war with Spain, were barred from Lisbon, the great distributing center for Oriental goods imported by the Portuguese. As a result, the Dutch opened up direct connection with Far Eastern centers, and by the early seventeenth century the Portuguese empire in the Far East had been largely taken over by the Dutch.

### Spain in the New World

In the sixteenth century the power of Portugal was exceeded only by that of Spain. In 1516, hardly a quarter of a century after the first voyage of Columbus to America, King Ferdinand V died and his grandson became Charles I of Spain.  Three years later, in 1519, occurred the death of Charles's paternal grandfather, the Emperor Maximilian, and he became Charles V of the Holy Roman Empire.  His dominions included the two Sicilies, the Netherlands, Burgundy, the Holy Roman Empire, and the satellite territories of Bohemia, Moravia, Silesia, and Hungary, as well as Spain and a large part of the New World.  Among the native peoples of the Americas there was no effective resistance to the Spanish invaders, who had become skillful fighters in wars against the Moors;  and not until the seventeenth century was there serious competition from Europeans.

The natural inclinations of the warlike Spaniards in America prompted them to seek primarily for treasure.  These inclinations were confirmed by the abundance of silver and gold among the natives, though the appearance of abundance was somewhat misleading, due to the free use of the metals for ornaments.  The tendency of the invaders to neglect the basic economic development of the New World in favor of a quest for treasure was further strengthened by the current demand in Europe for gold and silver during the transition from feudalism and barter to a money economy alike in public affairs and in economic enterprise.  Other Europeans were perhaps no less eager in their efforts to seize the silver and gold of conquered peoples, but were less favored with opportunities.  Furthermore, the merely exploitative activities of the Spaniards and the Portuguese must not be allowed to obscure the fact that they extended their civilization over  large parts of South America and large areas in the southern part of North America.  The natives were not exterminated but instead were measurably civilized.

The Portuguese and Spanish rulers of the sixteenth century were enriched by a fabulous flow of treasure.  But the wealth acquired so readily was dissipated in activities which consumed and destroyed rather than created economic resources.  The European connections of the Spanish rulers, Charles V and Philip II, brought temporary prestige and splendor, but the ultimate effects were disastrous.  Costly wars were waged against Italians, Turks, the English, and the people of the Low Countries.  Holland, which formed a mere fragment of the gigantic Spanish Empire, rose in revolt and began the building up of the outstanding financial, commercial, and colonial empire of the seventeenth century.

## The Dutch Empire

The revolt of the Dutch against Spanish rule began in 1568. It was not until eighty years later, in the Treaty of Westphalia ending the Thirty Years' War, that Spain formally recognized the independence of Holland. But during the interval, sometimes described as the Eighty Years' War for Independence, the Dutch were extremely active in the arts of peace as well as of war. Much of the capital needed for their commercial and colonial enterprises they acquired by seizure of Spanish vessels bearing gold and silver from the New World.

Antwerp in the southern Netherlands rose rapidly in the sixteenth century to a place of prominence in finance, trade, and industry, but suffered severely during the revolt against Spain, and especially during the "Spanish Fury" of 1576. Beginning in the latter part of the sixteenth century, Amsterdam, which managed to maintain its defenses against the Spaniards, became the outstanding financial and commercial center of Europe. The Bank of Amsterdam was founded in 1609, and more than a century and a half later Adam Smith, in his *Wealth of Nations*, stated that the bank "has, for these many years past, been the great warehouse of Europe for bullion."

The Dutch made full use of their limited resources for agriculture, manufactures, and shipbuilding, and of their exceptional opportunities for developing fisheries; but their most remarkable success was in the carrying trade. It was the interruption of their enterprise in this field by their expulsion from the Lisbon trade that led them into the field of colonization. The Portuguese had made Lisbon the emporium for the European distribution of Far Eastern goods, and from Lisbon the Dutch had built up a lucrative carrying trade. When Portugal in 1580 was joined to Spain, the Dutch, who were in rebellion against the Spaniards, were barred from Lisbon. Soon thereafter they successfully challenged the Portuguese monopoly by going directly to the Orient, and this in turn led to seizure of Portuguese trading centers and the building up of the Dutch Empire in the Far East. So energetic were the new masters of the spice trade that the markets were soon glutted, and steps were taken not only to monopolize the European distribution but to supervise the production of spices by such methods as the pensioning of native rulers for discontinuing the growing of spices. After the separation of Portugal from Spain in 1640 the Dutch retained the richer and more strategic areas that they had seized from the Portuguese.

For a time even Brazil was under the rule of the Dutch, and in Surinam, or Dutch Guiana, they secured permanent footing. While the Puritans were establishing themselves in New England, the Dutch were developing the fur trade with the Indians and making settlements in the strategic and fertile valley of the Hudson, which they named New Netherland. Dutch companies, particularly the Dutch West India Company, attempted to make settlements in various regions and succeeded in building up an extremely profitable carrying trade. But the commercial and colonial expansion of the Dutch antagonized the English, and their power in Europe was challenged by the French under Louis XIV. The ensuing conflicts marked the decline of Dutch trade and empire.

### English Conflicts with Portugal, Spain, and Holland

While the Portuguese and the Spaniards were building their empires, the interests and activities of Englishmen remained largely insular. Their adventures in France during the Hundred Years' War had been largely dynastic and feudal, and had virtually come to an end in the middle of the fifteenth century, though Calais was retained until 1558. John Cabot, a Venetian, had sailed westward, to be sure, under the flag of England and with a charter granted by Henry VII, but little came of the voyage except the establishment of claims to areas long regarded as of secondary value. There is a curious entry in the account book of the parsimonious king, "To hym that founde the new isle, ten pounds." Much exploratory work was done in the sixteenth century, but Englishmen lagged behind the Dutch as well as the Portuguese and the Spaniards.

The sixteenth-century conflict between Spain and England was more largely political and religious than economic. Englishmen profited greatly, it is true, by preying upon the commerce of the Spaniards, but before the defeat, in 1588, of the Spanish Armada, which attempted the conquest of the country, the rulers of England made little serious effort either to establish colonies in the New World or to challenge the supremacy of Spain in western trade or of Portugal in the exploitation of the Far East. The disrupting of the Portuguese Empire was largely the work of the Dutch. The decline of Spanish power was largely a result of internal weakness, overextension in the New World, and dissipation of resources in European adventures, though it was hastened by the attacks of

English sea rovers such as Hawkins and Drake and by the aid given by England to the Dutch.

Englishmen shared with the Dutch the Far Eastern trade which had been controlled in the sixteenth century by Portugal. They were compelled, however, to content themselves largely with trading centers on the mainland, the Dutch having gained ascendancy in the Spice Islands, then chiefly coveted. By the time Dutch independence was finally acknowledged by Spain in 1648, Englishmen were embroiled in the Puritan Revolution, and many of the early colonists were people who left England because of discontent with political and religious conditions. Already English policy was veering away from hostility to Spain and attempting to check the maritime ascendancy of Holland. The efforts of James I and Charles I to form an alliance with Spain had been resented by Englishmen, and there had been intimate political and religious ties between England and Holland. But commercial interests prevailed over religious and political sympathies, and an outstanding policy of the Puritan government of Cromwell was its hostility to the Protestants of Holland. This found expression in alliances, in the Navigation Act of 1651 intended largely to curb the Dutch carrying trade and fisheries, and in the first of a series of naval wars with the Dutch. The conflict thus begun with Holland was continued under the Restoration from 1660 to the Revolution of 1688.

English writers described, in terms disparaging to their own countrymen, the Dutch economy and skill in shipbuilding and navigation, their advanced methods of banking and finance, especially in foreign exchange, their low tariff duties, and their exact workmanship and uniform standards of manufacture. They advocated, on the one hand, imitation of Dutch methods, and on the other hand the adoption of policies designed to thwart the Dutch in the use of these methods. Lord Shaftesbury, leader of the Parliamentary opposition to Charles II, pointed to Holland in 1673 as "England's eternal enemy, both by interest and inclination." The Cromwellian alliance of 1655 with France against Holland was renewed by Charles II. The Navigation Act of 1651 was re-enacted and strengthened. Cromwell's war against Holland in 1652 was renewed under Charles II in 1665 and again in 1672. It was as a prelude to the war of 1665 that the English in 1664 seized New Netherland.

However, with the rise of French trade and colonialism under Colbert, minister of Louis XIV, the "eternal" enmity of England

and Holland subsided and English hostility, toward the end of the seventeenth century, was directed against France. Then began a series of armed conflicts extending to 1815, sometimes described as the Second Hundred Years' War with France — intermittent wars accompanied for a century and a quarter by continuous imperial rivalry.

## The Rise of French Imperialism

Jacques Cartier explored the lower St. Lawrence valley as early as 1534, and the beginning of colonization at Port Royal and Quebec was as early as the first decade of the seventeenth century. The northern fisheries and the fur trade with the Indians had been exploited even earlier. Various trading companies were organized in the early seventeenth century, notably the Canada Company in 1627, and efforts were made to emulate the Dutch and the English in the establishment of trading centers in the Far East. But the wars of religion, the dynastic wars, and the Continental ambitions of the French rulers combined to deter extensive commercial and colonial expansion until the latter part of the seventeenth century. Even then, the aim of Louis XIV was primarily the maintenance of French ascendancy in Europe.

The attitude of Englishmen in viewing France as their outstanding rival was due to the disturbance of the balance of power in Europe by the aggressive policies of Louis XIV (1643–1715) and the naval, commercial, and colonial activities promoted by Louis XIV's great minister, Colbert. England had no ambition to gain direct control of Continental territories, but Englishmen were keenly conscious of the advantages of maintaining political influence through alliances and subsidies, thereby preventing any Continental rival from gaining either territorial or diplomatic ascendancy. They willingly accepted the aid of France in weakening Spain and Holland; but when Louis XIV undertook a series of wars for territorial conquests in the Spanish Netherlands and Holland, and later exulted at the virtual union of the crowns of France and Spain when his nephew inherited the Spanish crown, England undertook a series of alliances and wars to check the Grand Monarch.

The English were alarmed not only by the Continental aggressions of Louis XIV but also by the revival and expansion of French activities in naval, commercial, and colonial affairs. Colbert, who served as principal minister from 1661 to 1683, wrote in 1669 that "the seaborne commerce of Europe employs about 25,000 vessels; in the natural order of things, each nation would possess a share of this tonnage proportionate to its power, population, and the extent of its coasts. But the Dutch have 15,000 to 16,000 ships, and the French not more than 500 or 600." His policies, which have already been described in connection with mercantilism, radically altered the status of France not only in respect to the merchant marine but also in naval strength, in colonial enterprise, in finance, and in manufactures. His aim was principally to challenge the supremacy of the Dutch; but the outcome of his policy, combined with the Continental aggressions of his sovereign, was the inauguration of the epochal struggle for empire between France and England.

## The Struggle for North America

Portugal, Spain, and Holland continued long after the seventeenth century to play important roles in imperial affairs, but after the era of Colbert and Charles II the center of the stage was occupied by France and England. The principal issues were the colonization of North America and the control of the more lucrative branches of overseas trade — West Indian sugar, African slaves, and the spices and fine fabrics of the Far East.

In 1689, at the beginning of the long series of imperial wars in which France and England were the main contestants, the French possessions in North America were much more extensive than the English. The area of the English settlements extended only a short distance inland, and included a narrow strip of coastal country from the vicinity of Charleston, South Carolina, to the Kennebec River in Maine. English claims, largely uncolonized, extended far westward, overlapping part of the French claims, which included a large area south of the St. Lawrence River and the Great Lakes, and extended from the Appalachians to the Rocky Mountains. To the south the claims of Spain overlapped those of both France and England. The French and the English both claimed Newfoundland and the Hudson Bay country. The French colonies, trading posts, and frontier fortresses were widely scattered from Newfoundland and Acadia southwestward along the St. Lawrence, the Great Lakes, and the Mississippi to the Gulf of Mexico.

The Treaty of Ryswick in 1697, ending the War of the League of Augsburg (King William's War in colonial annals), brought no decisive change. The Treaty of Utrecht in 1713, ending the War of the Spanish Succession (Queen Anne's War), recognized the claims of Great Britain to the region of Hudson Bay and to New-foundland, although the French retained certain fishing rights in the vicinity of Newfoundland. The Treaty of Aix-la-Chapelle in 1748, ending the next great armed conflict, the War of the Austrian Succession (King George's War), was indecisive, as the territories seized during the war were restored. The final overthrow of French power in North America was achieved during the Seven Years' War (the French and Indian War), which was concluded by the Treaty of Paris in 1763. Canada and most of the land east of the Mississippi River were ceded to Great Britain. The Louisiana territory, mostly west of the Mississippi, was given to Spain, but later was returned to France, which sold it to the United States in 1803.

Although the final acquisition of French territories in America by the British was in the course of successful wars, the decisive factors were geographical and economic. At the time of the appeal to arms in the Seven Years' War there were more than a million British colonists in the strategic areas of the Atlantic sea-board, with ready access to the resources of the home country and with a diversified and comparatively advanced economic life of their own. In all of North America there were probably less than a hundred thousand Frenchmen, and they were widely dispersed from the Gulf of St. Lawrence to the Gulf of Mexico. Their economic activities were largely confined to farming, the fisheries, and the fur trade. Britain's command of the sea extended beyond mere naval superiority and included the mercantile marine, enabling both the home country and the colonists to maintain effective commercial as well as military and naval connections alike in war and in peace.

The various wars beginning with the War of the League of Augsburg in 1689 involved most of the countries of Europe, and the issues were by no means restricted to colonization and trade. Indeed, the ambitions of French rulers were more largely bound up with Continental military power, territorial expansion, and political prestige than with overseas empire. It was this fact, combined with the clever utilization of the resulting antagonism against France on the Continent, that accounts largely for the ultimate ascendancy of England over France in the struggle for empire. This is the meaning of the familiar saying that England won her overseas empire from France in Germany. But various other European as well as colonial circumstances contributed to the triumph of

England. Among these were the advantages of her insular position, the blow dealt to French industry and enterprise by the persecution of the Huguenots, the freer, more flexible nature of English commercial and political institutions, and the friendly union of Scotland with England (1707) in the United Kingdom of Great Britain.

## The West Indies

Throughout the colonial period of the history of the American continents, the most coveted of the mainland regions were controlled by Spain and Portugal, with the exception of the short-lived Dutch regime in Brazil; and these regions were pre-eminent as sources of gold and silver. The mainland of North America north of Mexico was less highly prized than were the West Indies. Some of the reasons for this attitude were stated by Sir Josiah Child in his *New Discourse of Trade* in the latter part of the seventeenth century. "New England," he complained, "is the most prejudicial plantation to this Kingdom." The people were frugal, industrious, and temperate, he admits, but they raised corn and cattle, built ships, carried on manufactures and fisheries, and competed with Englishmen for the trade of the other colonies. In a word, their economic activities were not complementary but competitive in relation to English enterprise. In lesser degree, Child's complaint applied to the other mainland colonies. The West Indies, on the other hand, were almost exclusively complementary in character.

The chief product of the islands was sugar (indeed, they were often called the sugar colonies), and their other products were such as Europeans desired but could not readily produce — notably cotton, tobacco, and indigo. The European colonists in the islands produced goods desired in Europe and bought European goods in return; and at the same time they made little effort to build ships or handle their own goods, and thus provided a lucrative opportunity for European shipping. They utilized African slave labor and furnished, before the rise of the mainland cotton industry, a principal basis for the slave trade carried on largely by Europeans, though in part by mainland colonists. The planters sent their children to Europe to be educated, and frequently returned to Europe to spend their declining years and their fortunes. Most of the capital invested in the islands was provided by Europeans who enjoyed large dividends without suffering the inconvenience of residence in the islands. While Spain held most of the islands, many of the nationals of other European countries prized their footholds as bases for piracy, privateering, and military operations against the Spaniards.

Sugar had long been produced from sugar cane in the Far East and in Arabia and Persia, and from the latter countries had been imported by Europeans, but only in small quantities as a luxury and for medical uses. As an important article of commerce used by the common people, its production dates from the development of sugar-cane plantations operated by slave labor in Brazil and the West Indies.

From the juice of the sugar cane there were made not only sugar but also molasses and rum. The sugar colonies were valuable indirectly in enabling the other colonies, notably New England, to secure money with which to pay for their imports from Europe. New Englanders sold fish, lumber, and other goods to the sugar planters, and also shared the African slave trade. In return for their products and for slaves they received either money or molasses. From the molasses they made rum, a widely used beverage. The money received from slaves and rum enabled them to buy European manufactures. The most important economic aspect of the sugar colonies, aside from the production of molasses, rum, and sugar, was the basis they furnished for the slave trade. To Europeans there was an incidental advantage in colonial slave labor. It was held that slaves would "confine the plantations to planting only" and prevent the development of industries such as would compete with European enterprise.

For more than a century Spain's position in the West Indies was virtually uncontested. In 1625 Englishmen occupied St. Christopher (St. Kitts) in the Leeward Islands to the east, and the French gained a footing about the same time. The Dutch had established themselves on the mainland in Dutch Guiana (Surinam) even earlier, but their main interest seems to have been the development of the carrying trade. Throughout the seventeenth century piracy and privateering flourished, and many of the early European outposts in the West Indies were merely havens of sea rovers who preyed upon legitimate trade and Spanish treasure ships.

In 1689 the Spaniards still controlled Cuba, most of Hispaniola (Haiti), Puerto Rico, and various minor islands. England had gained possession of Jamaica, the Bahamas, Barbados, and several small islands in the Leeward group. The Bermudas, far to the northeast, afforded Englishmen a strategic center for operations not only in the West Indies but on the mainland as well. France had won several lesser islands and a part of western Hispaniola. The Dutch had won Curaçao, near the mainland of South America, and some smaller islands.

As a result of the wars beginning in 1689, important changes occurred in the status of the various nations in the West Indies. The Treaty of Ryswick in 1697 restored conquered territories. The War of the Spanish Succession, ended by the Treaty of Utrecht in 1713, greatly weakened the sea power and the carrying trade of the Dutch and correspondingly strengthened the position of Great Britain. Louis XIV agreed to renounce his claims to special advantages for Frenchmen in the trade of the Spanish Empire — claims which had been based on the accession of his grandson, Philip, to the throne of Spain. France was weakened in the struggle for empire in the West Indies and elsewhere by the exhaustion of her resources on the European Continent and by the capture or destruction of a large part of her naval and mercantile vessels. It was during this war that Great Britain gained decisive control of the sea. The growth of British power was recognized by Spain in the "Asiento," a special compact which enabled the British to drive a wedge into the monopoly of Spaniards in Spanish-American trade. By this treaty the British were granted for thirty years a virtual monopoly in the sale of slaves to the Spanish colonies. One British vessel was also permitted to exchange cargoes once a year at Puerto Bello on the Isthmus of Panama — a source of much friction later, due to the transfer of its cargo to other ships and reloading contrary to the spirit of the agreement.

Friction with Spain, discontent with the monopolies granted to the trading companies, the supplying of slave labor to rival colonies under the Asiento, and the rapid revival of French activities in the West Indies combined to threaten the ascendancy won by Great Britain. The French sugar colonies were able to undersell the British, partly because of the efforts of the British to confine the sugar trade to Great Britain and the British colonies, and partly because of British regulations against the refining of sugar in their colonies. In the mid-century wars which came to an end in 1763 in the epochal Peace of Paris, the British again forged ahead of the French both commercially and territorially. The end of French rule in North America, already described, was accompanied by important British gains in the West Indies, including the cession by France of Grenada, St. Vincent, Dominica, and Tobago. But thereafter there was a gradual decline in the economic importance of the islands as compared with other areas of European imperial expansion.

### The Trading Companies and Territorial Aggrandizement in the Far East

In the race between France and England for ascendancy in North America, the stakes were territories valuable primarily for colonization by Europeans, although the fisheries and the fur trade were prizes dependent on a comparatively small number of settlers. The West Indies were coveted for the products of slave labor, especially sugar, molasses, and rum, for the profits of the slave trade, and for the strategic advantages of the islands as approaches to the mainland. The western and southern coasts of Africa furnished appreciable quantities of gold and ivory and a limited opportunity for trade with the natives, but were chiefly prized as sources of slaves and as way stations on the route to the Far East. The Far East may be broadly defined as the vast area extending from the western shores of the Indian Ocean to Japan, the East Indies, and Australia. The continent of Australia and some of the islands, as well as South Africa, were later to afford extensive opportunities for colonization, but large migrations of Europeans were delayed until the nineteenth century. Most of these regions were not well adapted to colonization by Europeans, or were already populous and well advanced in the arts of industry and trade. Before the nineteenth century the struggle for empire in the Far East was mainly for the control of trade with the natives. The lands bordering on the eastern Mediterranean had earlier played a large part in European economic life, not only as agents for the interchange of European and Far Eastern goods but because of their own trade and industry. In the nineteenth century they were again to have prominent roles in the drama of European empire, but in the seventeenth and eighteenth centuries they were relatively unimportant, European interest being diverted westward by the commercial revolution and by the ascendancy of the Turks.

In the Far Eastern trade, luxury goods were pre-eminent. Among these were the spices, largely controlled first by the Portuguese and later by the Dutch. Pepper, less expensive than most of the other condiments, was imported in vast quantities. The finer silk and cotton textiles, porcelains, precious stones and pearls, dyestuffs, and raw cotton and silk were more largely imported from the mainland. Many of these commodities, as silks, cottons, and porcelains, came to be widely produced or imitated in the West. The industries of the Far East thus vitally affected those of Europe. A notable instance is the cotton industry. The importation of Indian silks and cottons by the English East India Company led to the extension of the laws for protecting English woolen and silk manufacturers. The ultimate result of such protective measures as the Calico Act of 1721 was to stimulate the manufacture of cotton goods in England to such an extent that the woolen and silk interests found themselves confronted by domestic competition which profoundly altered the structure of the textile industries.

The early phases of the struggle for the Far East centered about the control of the spice trade. This trade the Dutch succeeded in taking over in large part from the Portuguese. For the maintenance of monopolistic prices, they destroyed many of the trees and ruthlessly exploited the natives. The English, in order to secure a footing in the Spice Islands, began early in the seventeenth century to exchange mainland textiles for spices. But the Dutch were able to maintain their superiority in the spice trade, and the English were mainly dependent on trade between Europe and their factories or trading centers on the mainland of India. The East India Company, which had a monopoly of trade with England, had established extensive centers of trade at Bombay on the west coast of India, at Madras on the east coast, and at Calcutta in Bengal, in the rich and populous delta region of the Ganges valley. The French had sent expeditions to the Far East early in the sixteenth century, and their activity had been revived by a monopolistic charter to the French East India Company in 1664 and by grants to the company from public funds. Their main centers of trade were at Pondichéry near Madras in southeastern India and at Chandernagor near Calcutta. Before the Seven Years' War beginning in 1756 the conflicts between the French and the English were primarily between the trading companies, although these were chartered by their governments and were granted political and military as well as commercial powers.

Early in the seventeenth century the once powerful Mogul Empire fell into decay, and the French and English companies began to take advantage of the weakness, jealousy, and cupidity of the native princes for the purpose of extending their political as well as commercial influence. Dupleix, who assumed his duties as governor of the French East India Company January 13, 1742, gained for the French an early lead in the process of territorial aggrandizement.   By fortifying the French posts, making treaties with the native princes, and enlisting native soldiers, he soon extended French influence over southern India and threatened the position of the British in Bengal.   But during the Seven Years' War the British, under the brilliant leadership of Robert Clive, a company clerk turned warrior, retrieved their losses, extended their rule in Bengal, conquered Pondichéry, and won ascendancy from the French over the native princes of southern India.   The Treaty of Paris in 1763 restored several of the French posts to the French East India Company but barred their fortification, and the company was not long able to survive its reverses. Thenceforth the struggle of the British was not with Europeans but with native princes — a conflict which resulted in the ultimate establishment of the authority of the British government over most of India, and, allegedly for the defense of India, over adjacent regions as well.   The process of transferring authority from the East India Company to the crown began soon after the Seven Years' War but was not completed until a century later.

As a result of the series of events culminating in the Seven Years' War the British won a position on the mainland of India which enabled them ultimately to gain ascendancy in the Far East. But the Dutch retained their extensive empire, especially in the highly prized area of the Spice Islands, and continued to enjoy a lucrative trade.   Intensive efforts were made to increase European exports to India, but with so little success that many mercantilists continued to denounce the trade as detrimental because of the "unfavorable" balance and the attendant export of bullion.   Some cloth, lead, tin, iron, and other commodities were exported, but the British Far Eastern possessions afforded no extensive market for European manufactures until after the development of the textile industries on a factory basis.   Most of the goods imported from the Far East were such as Europeans were unable to produce and yet were insistent on consuming, and it was therefore argued that the trade was advantageous, even though bullion had to be exported. Proponents of the trade also held that it should be encouraged as a basis for re-export to countries without direct trading relations. The principal attacks on the English East India Company centered around the importation of calicoes, on the ground that they competed with the woolen manufacture.   The ultimate result, as already indicated, was the development of cotton manufacturing in England and a far-reaching readjustment of the entire textile industry.

Other important Far Eastern industries had already been introduced, as the manufacture of silks and porcelains and the culture of the sugar cane in the West Indies.

The Far East was an important source of wealth in the form of taxation, tribute, the salaries of officials, and direct exploitation. During the Seven Years' War the East India Company forced the Great Mogul to grant it the right to administer the revenues of Bengal. Support of native princes against their rivals was often conditioned on the making of large grants to company officials. Clive himself acquired a fortune and on his return to England declared in self-defense that he marveled at his moderation. The vast revenue flowing to England from India in the eighteenth century was one of the important sources of wealth which stimulated consumption and the investment in capital goods accompanying the industrial revolution.

## Changes in Imperial Policy

Adam Smith, whose *Wealth of Nations* was published in the year of the American Declaration of Independence, denounced "the folly and injustice" of European policy in the original conquest of other peoples and in the prohibitions and monopolies attending the colonization and government of overseas possessions. His attack on mercantilism, already described, was substantially an attack on imperial policies. "The monopoly of the colony trade," he asserted, "like all the other mean and malignant expedients of the mercantile system, depresses the industry of all other countries, but chiefly that of the colonies, without in the least increasing, but on the contrary diminishing, that of the country in whose favor it is established." Smith proposed for the American colonies a system of representation in the British Parliament; and for the empire as a whole, the abolition of the monopolistic privileges of the commercial companies and "a moderate and gradual relaxation of the laws which give to Great Britain the exclusive trade to the colonies, till it is rendered in a great measure free."

During the century following the publication of the *Wealth of Nations*, the trend of British imperial policy in its economic aspects was in the direction advocated by Smith. His point of view was emphasized by the loss of the Thirteen Colonies. In adopting his view, Englishmen were influenced not so much by his theoretical conception of the advantages of "perfect liberty" as by the events of the industrial revolution. England's precedence in mechanical technology established the basis of a competitive power which made possible the virtual monopoly of colonial trade without legal compulsion; and the repeal of the monopolistic laws aided Englishmen in overcoming the barriers to the expansion of their trade beyond their own empire.

The American Revolution made a serious breach in the imperial system and gave warning to Europeans that at least the cruder and more obvious forms of imperial greed and compulsion would have to yield to a system of complementary economic relations based more largely on mutual advantages maintained by competitive efficiency. This warning, reinforced by the doctrines of the economists, by the ideals of the French Revolution, and in the case of the English by early competitive advantages, wrought far-reaching and significant changes in the spirit of empire. The cruder forms of mercantilistic monopoly, the slave trade, and ultimately slavery itself gave way before the forces which gained momentum in the late eighteenth century. Exploitation of subject peoples continued, and destructive imperial rivalry combined with monopolistic policies in new forms later became once more an outstanding feature of European economy. But for a century the early modern forms of imperialism were decisively altered.

CHAPTER 6

## TECHNOLOGICAL CHANGES

———◆———

### The Effect of Commercial Expansion on Industrial Methods

In recent generations the efficiency of industrial production has
caused producers to exert increasing pressure on world markets.
This new force was apparent in England as early as 1788, when the
English cotton manufacturers sought through reciprocal treaties to
open "new channels of consumption" for the increased quantities of
cotton goods even then being produced "in consequence of the
great extent of the power of machinery." But before the rise of
modern technology, the initiative was taken by the merchants, who
sought new methods of production and transportation for the purpose of taking full advantage of opportunities for trade.

During the middle decades of the eighteenth century there was
an exceptionally rapid expansion of exports from England and of
tonnage in the foreign trade. But the improvement of industrial
techniques was stimulated less by the actual increase of trade
than by the opening up of new commercial opportunities. These
opportunities resulted from the acquisition of overseas territories,
the growth of sea power, and the control of trade routes. Furthermore, the areas under British control were for the most part
complementary in nature: they afforded markets for English manufactures and at the same time supplied Englishmen with raw materials and other goods that England could not readily produce.
The full utilization of these opportunities required improvements
in modes of manufacturing and transportation. The expansion
of trade further stimulated industry by the introduction of new
commodities and the development of new manufactures. The
cotton industry grew out of the importation of calicoes and raw
cotton, and the stimulus of commerce marked the rise of various
other important industries, as silk, sugar, tobacco, and pottery.

The economic basis of industrial expansion was not only in the
increased opportunity for export, but also in surplus wealth for
enlarged consumption at home and for investment in the facilities
and materials of production. Throughout the eighteenth century,
and especially during the decade following the Seven Years' War,
writers continually noted the increase in wealth and in demand for

a great variety of goods and services. A writer in 1767 stated: "That our riches are, in fact, amazingly increased within a few years, no one who is in the least acquainted with this country can entertain a doubt." According to this writer, the increase in British wealth was largely a result of the Seven Years' War and "the immense riches flowing in since that period from our commerce, extended over every quarter of the globe."

Industrial production had been largely under the direction of guilds. The earlier guilds had assumed important responsibilities for maintaining standards and fair prices, allocating materials and markets, and preventing monopolistic abuses. But they ultimately emphasized their privileges more than their responsibilities, and failed to establish a basis for dealing with the intricate problems of securing raw materials and selling their products in distant markets. In an age of rapid expansion their policies continued to be based on the simple and restricted conditions of local trade. Control of production as well as of interchange tended therefore to pass from the guilds of producers to the mercantile classes, as in the development of the merchant-employer or putting-out system. Thus the system of production was directly influenced by the merchants and was made more flexible and more readily susceptible to expansion and the adoption of the new technology.

## Science and Technology

The incentives for the improvement of industrial techniques were primarily economic, but the intellectual background and the instrumentalities of change are to be found in the evolution of the scientific spirit. Francis Bacon in his *Novum Organum* called attention to the prescientific explanations of inventions and discoveries in ancient times as gifts of the gods to men, as in the Promethean myth of the origin of fire. He then described the three great modern "mechanical discoveries," printing, gunpowder, and the compass, as having "changed the face and state of things in all the world: the first in letters, the second in war, and the third in navigation." He asserted that "the empire of man over things is founded on the arts and sciences only; for nature is only governed by obedience. If the utility of any one particular discovery has so affected mankind as to make us think that he who could oblige the whole human race with any benefit must be greater than man, how much higher will it seem to discover some method by means of which all other things may be rapidly discovered!"

Bacon's conception of the method for rapidly discovering "all other things" was described in his philosophical writings and applied in his ideal commonwealth, the New Atlantis. It was in essence the doctrine of natural laws and their discovery and application by the techniques of observation, experiment, and mathematical analysis. Bacon's contemporaries and successors in various countries applied these techniques in the development of astronomy, mathematics, physics, mechanics, anatomy, and ultimately the entire range of modern sciences. Almost a century before Bacon's *Novum Organum*, Copernicus observed the stars through openings in the walls of his house and initiated the modern system of astronomy which Galileo, Kepler, and Newton extended by telescopic studies and the formulation of the laws of planetary motion and of gravitation. William Harvey in 1628 published his demonstration of the circulatory system in animals. Boyle, Lavoisier, and Priestley inaugurated the modern science of chemistry. Organized scientific research was promoted by the founding of societies, the building of observatories, the sending out of scientific expeditions, and the publishing of journals.

The inventions of the early scientists were mostly scientific instruments — the telescope, the compound microscope, the barometer, the thermometer, the air pump, and the manometer. But their indirect connection with the process of invention in the field of industrial technology is apparent in several ways. Their work first gave prominence to the conception of natural laws and of mastery of nature by obedience to the laws of nature. They developed the techniques of observation and experiment. They formulated the principles of mathematics and applied these principles in the study of mechanics. Even the untutored workingmen of the eighteenth century who devised many of the epochal industrial inventions were influenced by the scientific point of view. In a sense they were themselves scientists because they applied the techniques of observation and experiment and made use of mathematical and mechanical principles.

## Evolution of Technology

The three great inventions, printing, gunpowder, and the compass, described by Francis Bacon as having "changed the face and state of things in all the world," came into extensive use in Europe in the early modern period and are more significant as indications of the transition from the medieval to the modern age than are many of the events traditionally described as marking the transition. Even more momentous than those three inventions in shaping the course of civilization, were various innovations in earlier epochs of culture. The use of natural objects as tools and weapons, the chipping and polishing of stones, the use of handles, the control of fire, the domestication of plants and animals, the making of pottery, the smelting of copper and tin and the making of bronze, the introduction of the hard metal, iron — these various changes, spanning hundreds of thousands of years, marked the advance of man from his primitive stage to the culture of the early modern era. These changes were accompanied by the use of the simpler mechanical devices such as levers, pulleys, and cranes, usually operated by hand, the wheel, the water wheel, the sail, the pump, and the windmill. But even when the simpler machines came into extensive use, human labor remained the primary productive force, both as a cost and as a directive agency. The simpler machines, like tools, were instruments of production entirely dependent upon labor for their significant use.

The distinctive feature of the era of technological history which began in the eighteenth century is the increase in the scope of mechanization. Power was applied to machinery in more generalized forms, and a larger number of machines became essentially automatic. These achievements were not at first conspicuous, because power was applied on a very small scale. The lighter machines were turned by a crank operated by hand; heavy apparatus was driven by a windlass operated by one or more horses, or by water power. The use of windmills was narrowly restricted. But once it was possible to apply power in a generalized form, even on a small scale, it was a relatively simple matter to increase the scale of operation. Such changes rapidly transformed the relations between labor and machinery. A machine for spinning, whether the motive power is human, as in the case of the Hargreaves spinning jenny, or mechanical, as in the case of the later spinning devices, is not a mere aid or supplement to the hand but a substitute for it, in the actual process of controlling, drawing out, and twisting the fibers into thread.

The outstanding feature, then, which distinguishes the period since the industrial revolution from the ages preceding it, is the extent of the use of machines as substitutes for manual labor. There are various other distinctions, such as are illustrated by the use of coke instead of charcoal, and the discovery and varied utilization of petroleum and other natural resources. But these, on analysis, are found to derive their significance largely from their connection with machines. The smelting and refining of iron by means of coke made possible the extensive use of iron for making machines; and oil, gasoline, and electricity revolutionized motive power for the operation of machines.

## Use of the Term " Revolution"

The term "industrial revolution" has often been criticized, but popular usage persists and calls at least for an explanation. The ordinary meaning of the term "revolution" seems to involve three main elements. In connection with any series of events described as a revolution there is first what may be called the natural, normal process of change and adaptation; secondly, an obstacle or obstruction in the current of change; and thirdly, a more or less abrupt removal of the obstruction with correspondingly rapid and often violent readjustments. Important aspects of the economic history of England in the eighteenth century exhibit these general features and seem to warrant the qualified use of the term "revolution." The prevailing trend since the medieval period had involved the transformation of a localized and comparatively self-sufficient economy into a nationalistic-colonial-commercial empire. This process had culminated by the end of the Seven Years' War (1756–1763) in unprecedented opportunities for profitable trade throughout the world and in the accumulation of a vast amount of wealth by Englishmen for increased consumption and for new fields of investment. But the comparatively slight improvements in methods of production and transportation interposed a serious obstacle in the way of the full use of the opportunities afforded by territorial expansion, control of trade routes, and the increased income of Englishmen. The obstacle was removed by relatively sudden changes in the methods of production and transportation, with correspondingly abrupt and radical readjustments in the social structure.

In the extent and rapidity of change, the eighteenth-century transition in England to modern technology was unprecedented if not revolutionary; but the process of transition conformed to a well-known and universally applicable "pattern of behavior." Whatever we do, as individuals or groups, is part of a general circuit or pattern. First there is a sense of incompleteness or inadequacy. This in turn gives rise to a quest for means to meet the need or complete the circuit of experience.   Finally, if the search for instrumentalities to satisfy the need is successful, these are utilized to achieve the end in view.

In the eighteenth century, Englishmen experienced a keen sense of the inadequacy of certain accustomed ways of doing things, as the supplying of an expanding market for farm produce by medieval methods, freeing their mines from water by the crude pumps then in use, smelting and forging with charcoal, furnishing weavers with yarn by means of the spinning wheel, and the transporting of goods by pack horses and clumsy, heavy-wheeled wagons over almost impassable roads.   The feeling of inadequacy in turn gave rise to a nation-wide interest in the problems of improving the material facilities of production and transportation.   The outcome was the development of experimental farming and of the process of devising and applying a multitude of technological improvements in those fields of production and transportation where older methods had been least adequate for meeting the prevailing needs and opportunities.

## Growth of Technological Interests in England

The growth of technological interests in the latter part of the eighteenth century was by no means restricted to England.   Various regions on the Continent had long excelled England.   After the middle of the century a relaxation of corporate monopolies in France was accompanied by new inventions, new enterprises on a larger scale, and efforts to introduce improved methods.   Inventors were well received and, as in England, were sometimes granted special rewards.   A popular English view, almost proverbial, was that Continentals, especially Frenchmen, excelled as inventors, while Englishmen were superior in the development and industrial application of inventions.

Great as was the indebtedness of Englishmen to foreigners, by the end of the eighteenth century they had applied the more recent techniques far more successfully and extensively than had Continentals.   The decisive stages in the transition from medieval to modern industrial methods occurred first in England.   Historians therefore have ample reason for emphasizing the English phases of eighteenth-century technological change.

It has often been stated that the technological changes of the eighteenth century were brought about by a few individuals who were popularly opposed and ill-rewarded.   This view was encouraged and exaggerated by the attorneys of Richard Arkwright in their defense of Arkwright's patent claims, and also by various writers who either desired to secure changes in the patent laws or to discredit working-class opposition to laborsaving machines. It is true that a few names stand out among the inventors of the age, that the rewards of inventors were often meager, and that there was occasional opposition by workers who were being displaced or forced to change their occupations. But interest in more efficient methods and in the rewarding of inventors was virtually nation-wide and was shown alike in the work of thousands of individuals and in organized public and private activities.

Popular interest found expression in England in a large increase in the number of patents. During the hundred years before 1760 there were only 616 patents, and many of these were not for inventions in the modern sense, whereas from 1760 to 1790 there were 976 patents when letters patent were issued almost exclusively for original devices or processes. There were innumerable unpatented inventions, many of them of great importance. Among the many inventions and improvements by the great potter Josiah Wedgwood and his associates, only one was patented. The process of securing a patent was costly and complicated, and there was much opposition to the patent laws. The Society for the Encouragement of Arts, Manufactures, and Commerce granted its awards only for unpatented inventions.

Organized interest in science had found expression much earlier, as in the Royal Philosophical Society. During the latter half of the eighteenth century associations with more practical aims became popular. Among these were the Society for the Encouragement of Arts, Manufactures, and Commerce, the Manchester Literary and Philosophical Society (which carried on activities hardly consistent with its name), and various agricultural societies. These organizations offered rewards to inventors, maintained exhibits, published journals, and promoted experimentation in agricultural and industrial technology. Governmental participation included not only the issuing of letters patent for inventions, but also the granting of special awards and the enactment of laws designed to maintain for Englishmen a monopoly in the use of new inventions and methods.

The modern patent-law policy of England dates from the Statute of Monopolies of 1624. This law was passed by the Parliament of James I primarily for the purpose of curbing the crown in the sale of "commissions, grants, licenses, charters, and letters patent" to individuals and corporations "for the sole buying, selling, making, working, or using of anything within this realm." An exception was granted, however, in the case of patents for "the sole working or making of any manner of new manufactures within this realm to the true and first inventor and inventors of such manufactures," provided "they be not contrary to the law, nor mischievous to the state, by raising prices of commodities at home, or hurt of trade, or generally inconvenient." The term "invention" was applied at that time to a new industry or trade as well as a new device or process, and an "invention" as thus defined might be patented by an Englishman even though already used or carried on abroad by foreigners. By the late eighteenth century, court decisions and administrative practice had narrowed the meaning of the term to substantially the present usage.

The patent system was criticized by manufacturers, who desired the free use of inventions. Others held that the interests alike of inventors and of the public could best be served by a mode of rewarding inventors such as would more adequately maintain their rights and at the same time promote the freer and more general use of new inventions. But the system survived and became a model for the patent laws of many other countries, notably the United States.

### Innovations in Agriculture

It is a curious paradox that the ferment of eighteenth-century technological interests first produced significant results in agriculture. A contributing factor was the political situation. Tory landlords, usually described as inflexible in their opposition to political and social change, lost their influence at court and in national politics after the triumph of the Whigs in 1714, and set about the more intensive cultivation of their estates. Whig as well as Tory landlords were jealous of the rapid rise of the mercantile classes and were eager to maintain their status by increasing their income. Country gentlemen, both Whigs and Tories, were prominent members of the Royal Philosophical Society and were influenced by the scientific and rational spirit of the age. Many of them were acquainted at first hand with agricultural advances on the Continent. The expansion of trade, the growth of towns, and the subsidizing of Continental allies during the wars of the period were opening up new markets for agricultural products.

The varied activities of such prominent innovators as Jethro Tull,

Lord Townshend, Robert Bakewell, and Arthur Young are described in another connection (Chapter 8). Ordinary farmers, especially yeomen and small tenants, were usually opposed to innovations, but there were notable exceptions. Arthur Young in his *Six Months' Tour of the North of England*, published in 1770, credited one Cuthbert Clarke, a tenant farmer, with several inventions. Among these were a machine for draining swamps (for which he received a prize), a mechanical turnip slicer (important in preparing turnips for feeding to livestock), and a threshing machine ("the grand machine on which he builds his reputation"). To Farmer Clarke, Young even ascribed experimentation with electricity for stimulating the growth of plants.

Societies as well as individuals took up the work of experimentation and especially of publishing the results of experiments. Most of the organizers and patrons of the Society for the Encouragement of Arts, Manufactures, and Commerce were country gentlemen, and in its early work this organization emphasized the improvement of agriculture.

A serious obstacle in the way of agricultural innovations was the survival of small holdings and commons in many parts of the country. The obstacle was removed by a renewal of enclosures, described later. Enclosures made possible the use of the new methods and the extension of large-scale, capitalistic farming. Yeomen and small tenants lost their holdings and sought employment in the growing industrial centers. Subsistence farming was largely supplanted by market farming, and the growth of market farming focused attention on the need for better modes of transportation.

## Improvements in Transportation

Before the great expansion of commerce in the nineteenth century, facilities for transportation by sea were comparatively adequate. The motive power in remote antiquity was a combination of sails and oars. By the eighteenth century a series of improvements in the art of shipbuilding had evolved a magnificent and effective sailing ship, and its use had been facilitated by the improvement of harbors, lighthouses, maps and charts, by the perfecting of the compass, and by the devising of new instruments, notably the "marine watch" for finding the longitude at sea. Before this latter device was invented, the British Parliament as early as 1713 offered a reward of £20,000 for such an instrument, and the last installment of the reward was paid to John Harrison in 1773.

In contrast with marine transportation, the prevailing modes of inland transportation were extremely crude and inadequate. The condition of the roads was an almost universal subject of complaint on the part of eighteenth-century travelers, and even the main highways, before the age of turnpikes, were almost impassable in wet weather except on horseback. A frequent practice was to build a narrow causeway or "pack and prime way" about four feet wide for horses in single file, with a virtually unimproved roadbed on each side for carriages. After a flood the roadbed was likely to be either a bog or a ravine. Transportation was mainly by pack horses. The cost of transporting freight about 1750 between London and Birmingham, little more than a hundred miles, was £5 a ton. Whenever practicable, goods were transported by coastwise vessels. Coal was thus carried so commonly that it was known as "sea coal."

The maintenance of roads was traditionally the duty of the parish officials. Turnpikes to be constructed and maintained by trusts or companies on the basis of tolls were authorized in the seventeenth century, but little progress was made even in the building of toll roads until the middle of the eighteenth century. The uprising of the Young Pretender's forces in 1745 in an effort to restore the Stuart dynasty called attention to the inadequacy of the highways for military purposes and reinforced the demand for better roads by farmers and merchants. The result was the rapid extension of the turnpike system under national authority, to supplant the inertia of parish officials. The enclosure movement facilitated the building of roads, as many of the enclosure acts passed by Parliament made provision for roads as a condition of combining small holdings and commons under the acts. So rapid was the progress that a writer declared in 1767 that "there never was a more astonishing revolution accomplished in the internal system of any country." He stated that the number of horses required for the carriage of freight, and the time required for traveling, had been cut in half "within the compass of a few years," and that "everything wears the face of dispatch."

Travelers continued to complain of impassable roads. Scientific road and bridge building was delayed until toward the end of the century, when, under the guidance of an English genius, blind John Metcalfe, and of two Scotch engineers, Thomas Telford and John Loudon McAdam, the modern highway system began to take shape.

While the roads were being transformed by the turnpike trusts, a network of canals and rivers was rapidly extending transportation by inland waterways. England had been backward in road building, improvement of rivers, and construction of canals, partly because of the exceptional facilities for the interchange of goods by means of coastwise shipping. As early as 1681, Frenchmen had constructed the remarkable Languedoc Canal or Canal du Midi, connecting the Bay of Biscay in the Atlantic with the Gulf of Lyon in the Mediterranean. This canal, 148 miles long, piercing a mountain, attaining an elevation of 620 feet above sea level, and including 119 locks, caused Arthur Young, on visiting it in 1787, to exclaim, "Here, Louis XIV, thou art truly great!" Little further progress was made in France in canal construction until the Napoleonic era.

In England there was a long history of isolated improvements in river courses, but the first important canal was not built until the Duke of Bridgewater and his engineer, James Brindley, completed the seven-mile Manchester-Worsley canal in 1761. The channel was entirely artificial, to prevent flooding and silting, and locks were avoided by the use of tunnels and aqueducts. The canal was regarded as a most remarkable engineering achievement such as would convey the duke's name "with peculiar brilliancy to the latest posterity." Coal had been carried from Worsley to Manchester by pack horses at 9 to 10 shillings a ton. Manchester profited by the canal, as the price of coal was cut in half. Bridgewater also constructed the Manchester-Mersey canal, which greatly reduced freight charges between Manchester and Liverpool. The Grand Trunk Canal, opened in 1777, connected the Irish Sea and the North Sea by way of the Mersey and the Trent, and made use of five tunnels, five aqueducts, and seventy-five locks, with part of the canal at an elevation of 395 feet above sea level. By the end of the century continuous canal and river navigation facilities connected Liverpool, Manchester and the other principal cotton centers, Leeds, York, and the other woolen centers, the port of Hull, the Staffordshire potteries, Birmingham and the Black Country of coal and iron, and the great ports of Bristol and London.

Thus the principal industrial and commercial centers of the country were connected by a network of inland navigation. Improved roads, connecting with rivers and canals, promoted intercourse between the rural areas and the towns, mines, and factory centers. Regular coach services were established on the main highways. Wagons and canalboats began to take the place of pack horses. The commercial traveler appeared with his samples, taking orders, and supplanting the petty chapmen (peddlers) and the merchants of the fairs and markets who carried their goods with them. Market farming, the growth of towns, the rise of new industries, and the general expansion of business were greatly facilitated. In the internal economy of England, these changes were perhaps as significant as those wrought by the railroad and the steamboat in the nineteenth century and the automobile and the airplane in the twentieth century.

## Coal and Iron

The eighteenth-century expansion of the coal industry illustrates the interdependent nature of the economic changes of the period. The first canals were mainly for the transportation of coal. Canals tapping the coal fields vastly extended the coal industry, and cheap coal in turn laid the basis for the rise of new industrial centers, as those connected with iron and pottery. The coal and iron industries were phases of the exploitation of landed estates. At the same time they were the main foundation on which nineteenth-century industrialism was based.

Coal had long been used in small quantities for domestic heating and certain specialized industrial processes, as in forge work and in the operation of various types of kilns, vats, and crucibles. For smelting and refining, charcoal was chiefly used. The increasing demand for coal was due not only to the growth of towns and of industry but also to the using up of the forests and the exhaustion of the supply of wood fuel. The eighteenth-century revolution in the coal industry was rapidly accelerated by the discovery of methods for using coke in the smelting furnaces.

The primitive method of mining coal was the pit or quarry method with natural drainage. Horizontal shafts or tunnels (adits) were at first mere extensions of pits or quarries. Later, vertical shafts were sunk for connecting with underground coal beds, and from the vertical shafts the seams of coal were followed, the coal being raised in baskets by ropes and windlasses. In the eighteenth century the increasing depth of the shafts entailed dangers of noxious gases, explosions, displacement of supports, and flooding. There were various eighteenth-century improvements in mining. The pumping of water from the mines was one of the main incentives for the development of the steam engine, and in some mines steam power was used to raise the coal. Gunpowder was introduced for blasting.

Railroads with wooden rails were used before the eighteenth century. Iron rails were introduced as early as 1767. Wagons on rails carried the coal, when possible by gravity, to the road, river, canal, or port for transportation to market. Efforts were made to utilize such by-products as pitch, tar, oil, vitriol, sulphur, and copperas. Outstanding technological changes were indirectly connected with mining — namely, improvements in transportation and the utilization of coke for smelting iron.

Iron smelting had been in a sense a by-product of agriculture. It had been a part of the development of great landed estates. The location of furnaces had been determined by the availability of suitable iron ores, of wood for charcoal, of stone for building the furnaces, and of lime for flux. The furnace hands and their families were usually workers on the estates and were likely to divide their time between farming and furnace work. From the furnaces the molten metal was ladled out and poured into prepared molds for various cast-iron articles (such as firebacks, pots, engine cylinders, pump barrels, pipes, gun carriages, and manacles for slaves); or the metal was allowed to run out of the furnace into a bed of sand with a main trench (a "sow") and small lateral trenches ("pigs"), and the resulting "pig iron" was later refined and used in the various metal-working trades. A good average output of pig iron by charcoal furnaces was five tons per week.

The earliest forges made wrought iron from the better ores without smelting the ore into pig iron by the furnace process. The ore was heated and softened into a pasty "bloom" and repeatedly hammered to get rid of the dross and to toughen the texture. The usual eighteenth-century forge was mainly for making bar iron out of pig iron for fabrication by ironware craftsmen, although many simpler forms of wrought-iron wares were made directly in the forges from pig iron. The pig iron was put through successive heatings and hammerings, the larger hammers being operated by water power. The making of ironware out of wrought iron or bar iron from the forges was largely by handicraftsmen. Few machines were used, and great skill was often required. Steel and its products required further refinements and a high degree of skill, so that the use of steel was greatly restricted.

### Transformation of Iron Technology

A far-reaching change in the iron industry was the transition from charcoal to coke in the smelting of iron. Charcoal burning had been an important business.  For the hearth the sod was cut away, and several cords of wood were stacked on the cleared space in an irregular cone with an open center to serve as a chimney.  The opening was filled with kindling, the cone was covered and capped with sod, the kindling was lighted with a coal at the top, and the wood was allowed to burn without a flame for about a week, when it was dismantled with speed and caution to prevent its bursting into flame.  The charcoal was stored in stone buildings to prevent spontaneous combustion.  The problem of an adequate supply of wood for charcoal became increasingly serious due to enclosure of the commons and increase of tillage and to the growing demand for iron.  Before the use of coke, the output of pig iron in England declined and imports increased.

Coal was unsatisfactory because of lack of adequate draft and the presence of sulphur in the coal, which made the iron brittle. The first successful use of coke was in the early eighteenth century, but the perfecting and spread of the method was a slow process, partly due to the fact that much of the coal was not adapted to coking.  At first the use of coke-smelted iron was limited to castings direct from the foundry.  The use of coke in making pig iron suitable for refinement in the form of wrought iron was not perfected until after the middle of the century.  After 1763 the coking of coal was improved by the use of coking ovens in place of open piles as in the making of charcoal.  Somewhat later John Smeaton's iron-blowing cylinders were perfected at the Carron iron works in Scotland. They supplanted bellows of wood and leather; their pistons were operated by water power; and they not only made the use of coke practicable but resulted in a fourfold increase in the output of the furnaces.  In 1776 John Wilkinson introduced the steam blast, using one of Watt's engines, and thereafter coke for smelting rapidly supplanted charcoal.

These changes enabled the ironmasters to use coke for making pig iron suitable for further use in the refining processes of producing wrought or malleable iron.  There remained, however, the fuel problem in making malleable iron out of pig iron.  The making of a ton of bar iron (a form of malleable iron) required about 50 per cent more charcoal than the smelting of a ton of pig iron.  Coal was used to some extent in forges, but the main fuel was charcoal. The first important step toward the use of coal was the introduction of the reverberatory furnace, a refinery furnace based on the principle of throwing the flame back from a vaulted top upon the metal to be fused. It was first limited mainly to making malleable iron for nails. In 1784 Henry Cort patented a reverberatory furnace which had openings in the furnace door for puddling or stirring the molten metal to aid in the burning and escape of impurities.

With the efforts to solve the fuel problem by the use of coal there were associated fundamental changes in manipulation. The most significant of these changes were also introduced by Henry Cort. In addition to his improved reverberatory furnace with its puddling process, he developed a method of rolling instead of hammering the metal. The puddled iron was separated into lumps or "loops," and these, while still in the furnace, were reduced to a welding heat. They were then taken to a forge hammer and beaten into red-hot and still slightly soft "half-blooms" and then passed through rollers. Cort's method effected a great saving in fuel, but its revolutionary nature was chiefly apparent in a fifteenfold increase in output per hour and a revival and rapid expansion of the iron industry. The British output of pig iron in 1720 was about 25,000 tons. During the mid-century period there was a decline. By 1788 the output was about 68,000 tons; by 1796, more than 125,000 tons; and by 1804, 250,000 tons. Furthermore, the use of rollers made possible the much more efficient shaping of the metal for subsequent use than by hammering, and led to the introduction of sheet iron and various other forms of structural iron.

The three main forms of iron were cast iron (pigs, sows, and foundry goods), malleable iron (bar iron, sheet iron, and other products of the refinery furnaces), and steel (refinery iron with a small percentage of carbon, to give hardness and temper). There were important eighteenth-century changes in the making of steel as well as of cast iron and malleable iron. The most notable improvement was made by Benjamin Huntsman from 1740 to 1742. His crucible steel-casting process, although crude and expensive, remained generally in use until it was supplanted by the Bessemer process after the middle of the nineteenth century.

A most vital phase of the transformation of industrial techniques was the development of machine tools. Without machine tools the modern age of iron and steel would have been impossible. Watt constructed his model steam engine in 1765, but twelve years were required to perfect a true cylinder. The general principle of the machine tool is the mechanical and automatic control of the contact point between the material to be shaped and the tool for shaping it. Although much progress was made in the eighteenth century, the application of the principle of the machine tool in the metal-working trades was mainly in the nineteenth century.

### Pottery and the Beginnings of Industrial Chemistry

The making of unglazed, unfused earthenware was one of the earliest of the arts. Later came the glazing of the surface and later still the making of stoneware with clay and silica fused throughout. The finer pottery or porcelain ware was made in antiquity, and the art was acquired by Italians in the fifteenth century. Although the making of crude "peasant pottery" was a native English art, the finer forms of pottery were introduced from Holland, Italy, and the Orient in the seventeenth and eighteenth centuries. In the late seventeenth century Englishmen used ordinary "friable" or "throwing" clays for working on the wheel; lighter, colored clays of looser texture, called "slips," for decoration; and powdered lead for the glaze burned on the surface in the kiln.

Beginning in the late seventeenth century, a series of innovations transformed the industry. About 1680 salt was used instead of the more expensive powdered lead for the glaze. About the same time various improvements were made in the clay body. About 1720 powdered flint came to be used for mixing with the clay for white and cream-colored wares. Soon thereafter liquid lead glaze was introduced for certain types of pottery, and lead poisoning, which had been abated by the substitution of salt for powdered lead, again afflicted the craftsmen. Other changes included the use of new pigments and acids. About 1755 deposits of kaolin, resembling the fine Chinese clays, were discovered in Cornwall and Devon, but because of such advantages as coal and skilled workers in the north, the making of porcelain from kaolin gradually shifted to Staffordshire.

Accompanying the use of new materials were new methods and devices. For the liquid lead glaze, a dipping process greatly reduced the amount of work required. For the popularly used types of pottery, the clay was forced into a series of molds, and the throwers, or men at the potter's wheels, worked thereafter only on the finer grades. In place of the "sun pans" for preparing the decorative "slip" clays, "slip kilns" came to be used. The grinding of flint was described in 1732 as a process of "breaking and pounding the stones while dry and afterwards sifting the powder through fine lawns." This method, it was declared, "hath proved very destructive to mankind, occasioned by the dust suckled into the body, which . . . fixes so closely upon the lungs that nothing can remove it." By a new method the stones were sprinkled to avoid dust, and ground by a mill operated by water, wind, or horses, and later by steam engines, and the powder was afterwards reduced mechanically to an oily paste. Among the many innovations of Josiah Wedgwood was a lathe, first used in France, for cutting and shaping various types of pottery. The printing or stenciling of designs began to supplant hand painting on the less expensive types of pottery as early as 1756, when John Sadler and Guy Green stated under oath that they, alone, unaided, had printed, in six hours, "upwards of 1,200 earthenware tiles of different patterns, . . . more in number and better and neater than 100 skillful painters could have painted in the like space of time, in the common and usual way of printing with a pencil." After 1780 the pattern was commonly applied before glazing. This method was particularly successful with the willow patterns of Josiah Spode. Thereafter only the finest pottery was painted entirely by hand.

In its dependence on chemistry, the pottery industry was a significant forerunner of modern industry. Josiah Wedgwood's only patent covered a chemical procedure for encaustic painting in imitation of Etruscan and Roman antiques.

Closely associated with the development of the industry was the improvement of transportation methods, already described. For the hauling of raw materials and fuel and the handling of the bulky and fragile wares, the older methods were peculiarly inadequate. In 1762 a turnpike was built through the potteries. The rapid expansion of the industry dates from the opening of the Grand Trunk Canal in 1777, with various branches, notably to the works of Josiah Wedgwood at Etruria near Hanley. These branch canals performed the functions of the later railroad spurs and sidings. Wedgwood estimated that one tow horse could draw as much tonnage as forty horses on land, and with much less breakage.

## Textiles: Early Improvements

In 1792 Josiah Wedgwood wrote that the effort to describe the rapidity of change in pottery making and especially in the iron industry "makes my head giddy. I feel it just as impossible . . . as to number the sands of the sea. The difficulties are nearly equal with respect to the cotton trade; with this difference, indeed, that one must here shoot flying, for this darts forward with such an amazing rate as to leave all others far behind.   This business is supposed to have increased with ten times the celerity of any other, owing chiefly to the machinery invented by that truly great man, Sir Richard Arkwright."

While the credit accorded Arkwright as inventor may be questioned, the remarkable transformation of the textile industries was the most spectacular phase of the eighteenth-century technological revolution.   Although the woolen industry was less rapidly affected than the cotton industry, the use of the new inventions in the making of woolens and worsteds wrought economic and social changes even more vital; for cotton manufacturing was comparatively recent, while the age-old woolen industries had run deep and nation-wide roots in the lives of the people.

In the making of cloth as distinguished from wearing apparel and other finished goods, there were four basic processes: preparation of the fiber for spinning; the spinning of the fiber into yarn or thread; the weaving or knitting of the yarn; and the finishing process.   These main stages, and especially the preparatory and finishing processes, varied widely with the kind of fiber and of finished product and involved a large number of subordinate stages and occupations, as cleaning, sorting, carding or combing, roving, fulling, bleaching, dyeing, and printing.

Prominent among the technological innovations previous to the invention of machines for spinning was the stocking frame of William Lee in 1598.   This was a complicated mechanism for knitting.   It was opposed in Nottinghamshire, the great center of the knitting trade, and Lee was patronized by Henry IV of France. His invention was later reintroduced into Nottinghamshire, where it became the basis of a transitional stage of industry, the machines being owned by employers but operated in the homes of the workers. Another early innovation was the Dutch loom for weaving ribbons, tapes, and other small wares.   By 1725 it was widely used at Manchester and with it the weaver, instead of weaving one piece at a time, could make more than a dozen.   Still another early eighteenth-century innovation was the silk-throwing machine, introduced by John and Thomas Lombe from Italy, for twisting the cocoon filaments into thread.   Lombe's establishment near Derby on the Derwent River was described as "amazingly grand," and it seems indeed to have been a factory in the modern sense.

The first of the series of epochal inventions which transformed the cotton and woolen industries was the fly shuttle (or flying shuttle) of John Kay, in 1733.   A grooved runway was made on each side of the loom, and along these grooves the shuttle, carrying the weft, was propelled by hammers with springs and cords operated by a handle or treadle.   Thus one weaver instead of two could operate even a broad loom, and weaving was speeded up by the more rapid movement of the shuttle.   The drop box, devised by Robert Kay in 1760, applied the principle of the fly shuttle in the use of two or three shuttles with weft of different colors for making figured patterns. These inventions so increased the demand for yarn as to call for improvements in spinning.

In 1738 Lewis Paul patented a roller spinning machine which he and John Wyatt had invented.   Although it was used for a time for spinning cotton, its mechanical imperfections led to its abandonment.   By 1760 the increased demand for yarn led the Society for the Encouragement of Arts, Manufactures, and Commerce to offer rewards for a spinning machine.   There were several contestants, but the first successful device for spinning more than one thread at a time was the spinning jenny invented by James Hargreaves about 1764 and patented in 1770.   The jenny retained the wheel for rotating the spindles, but the drawing out and twisting of the roving were mechanized, whereas on the spinning wheel these processes were performed by hand.   There was a movable carriage with several spindles and bobbins, and the rovings were held by clasps. The hand that drew out the roving for spinning on the spinning wheel was used, on the jenny, to open and close the clasps and move the carriage.   The early jennies contained only eight spindles, but the number was rapidly increased.   The spinning jenny could not be used to twist thread hard enough for warps.   It was operated by hand power and was ordinarily used, like the spinning wheel, in homes, not in factories.

### The Era of Arkwright and Crompton

The transition to power spinning in factories was a result of the invention of the throstle or water frame, patented in 1769 by Richard Arkwright, and the mule, invented by Samuel Crompton in 1779. Important improvements in accessory processes, as carding and roving, were patented by Arkwright in 1775.   The water frame utilized the principle of rollers, as did Wyatt and Paul's machine. The rovings were drawn out or attenuated by rollers revolving at different speeds, and the threads were twisted and wound by flyers and bobbins operating continuously.   Although not originated by

Arkwright, roller spinning was perfected by him and made commercially profitable. The same principle was soon applied to the making of rovings. The machine was run at first by water power, but the steam engine was soon successfully used. The thread was twisted so abruptly as to be suitable chiefly for calico warps.

Machine-made yarns for finer goods, as muslins, awaited the invention of mule spinning by Crompton. The mule contained, like the jenny, a movable carriage with the spindles, but rollers were used for automatically feeding the rovings to the spindles. When the yarn was partly spun, the feed rollers were stopped and the spinning was completed at high tension. This made possible the spinning of the finer threads for muslins. The winding or reeling of the thread was done by reversing the carriage. This involved the principle of intermittent spinning, whereas the throstle system of the water frame was continuous. These two basic processes have continued to be used side by side in the modern textile industry. As in the case of the water frame, the mule could be run either by the water wheel or by steam power. Economically, the peculiar significance of the mule was in the spinning of the finer counts of thread for the making of muslins, cambrics, and other delicate and fashionable fabrics. Thread could be spun far finer than by the human hand. It was estimated in 1812 that from one half to two thirds of the cotton industry depended on mule-spun thread.

The preparatory processes, especially carding, combing, and roving, were rapidly mechanized. Although Edmund Cartwright patented a power loom in 1785, it was so crude as to have little effect on weaving until various improvements were made in the early nineteenth century. More significant in the eighteenth century were changes in the various finishing processes. The traditional methods of bleaching had required several months, a large amount of labor, and risk of loss in process. The basis of chemical bleaching was laid by Scheele's discovery of chlorine in 1774, Berthollet's experiments in 1785, and the work of Thomas Henry and others at Manchester in the use of chlorine for bleaching vegetable fabrics. The picturesque bleaching fields were rapidly displaced by chemical methods. The cylindrical method of printing calicoes, later used in principle for the printing of books and periodicals, was patented in 1784 by Thomas Bell and was soon widely used in place of the laborious and expensive method of hand printing by means of blocks or copper plates. The new method made possible a hundredfold increase in output and yet required less skill.

## Steam Power

Although steam engines were used in a few factories before the end of the eighteenth century, the essential features of the transition to modern machines and factories in the textile industries were introduced by means of water power. Most of the epochal innovations already described were not a result of the use of steam power, for the new inventions and industries were at first largely dependent on water power. Water power had long been used for grinding grain, lifting water and minerals, and operating bellows, hammers, saws, rollers, stamps, stone crushers, and various other devices. Its use in textile factories was so extensive that in 1791 a traveler reported that "there is scarcely a stream that will turn a wheel through the north of England that has not a cotton mill upon it." But water power restricted industry to the streams, aggravated the problems of access to raw materials, markets, and labor, and prevented the full utilization of the new inventions and the free development of industry. The result was the gradual improvement of mechanisms for the utilization of steam power.

In 1690 Denis Papin devised an experimental engine with a piston which was forced through a cylinder by steam and forced back by the vacuum resulting from the condensation of the steam. About 1702 Thomas Newcomen developed an engine with a piston and cylinder, a separate boiler, hand-operated valves, and a lever beam for transmitting the power.[1] With various improvements, this crude device was used extensively for pumping water out of mines. James Watt, who was assigned the task of repairing a Newcomen engine in 1763 at the University of Glasgow, was disturbed by the waste of three fourths of the fuel by the condensing of the steam in the cylinder. Two years later he hit upon the idea of a separate condensing chamber. In 1769 he took out his first patent, and with the aid of various associates gradually worked out modes of utilizing the principles of his patent. In this type of engine the piston was forced through the cylinder in one direction only by steam, the reverse movement being produced by the weight of the plunger of the pump. In 1782, Watt patented the "double-acting" principle, utilizing steam alternately at both sides of the piston head. When one end of the cylinder was receiving steam from the boiler, the other end was discharging into the condenser, and *vice versa*. Later

[1] It is sometimes said that Newcomen patented this engine in 1705; but there is no record of such a patent. See Jenkins, Rhys, *Collected Papers*, London, 1936, pp. 77-78.

improvements by Watt included automatic control of the steam pressure by a governor. His first engines had no mode of transforming to-and-fro motion into rotary motion for running machinery. In 1781 he patented a system of gears (the sun-and-planet system) for transmitting the power from the piston, but the prevailing device came to be the crank and shaft for transforming the reciprocal or to-and-fro motion of the piston into rotary motion for operating machinery.

The cylinder of Watt's engine, especially the double-acting cylinder, required a precision beyond the capacity of the metal workers of the time. The cost of making experimental engines and the equipment required for the experimental work exhausted Watt's resources and credit until Matthew Boulton came to his aid with the mechanical and financial resources of the Soho plant near Birmingham. The first successful engine was not constructed until 1776 and was made possible by the use of John Wilkinson's boring machine, invented in 1774. Although many engines were used in the eighteenth century for such varied work as pumping water out of mines, lifting coal, operating furnace blasts and forge hammers, and running the machinery of factories, the perfecting of the engine awaited the nineteenth-century era of machine tools. But its revolutionary significance was foreseen, as when a writer in 1787 declared that it was destined to "change the appearance of the civilized world." Its immediate significance was the freeing of invention and industry from the geographical and mechanical limitations of water power.

CHAPTER 7

# THE REORGANIZATION OF INDUSTRIAL ENTERPRISE

———◆———

## Technology and Industrial Organization

The most revolutionary and spectacular phases of the industrial revolution in the eighteenth century were the changes in technology, although the abruptness of the transition has at times been over-emphasized. Accompanying the technological revolution, and connected with it partly as cause and partly as effect, was the integration of enterprise. Integration assumed two forms: an increase in the size of plants or units of production, finding typical expression in the factory; and an enlargement or concentration of units of capital, involving primarily an extension of large-scale ownership and control to the field of industrial production.

There had been a progressive accumulation of wealth by merchants, landlords, bankers, and investors in shares of joint-stock companies and in the securities issued by governments to finance the wars of the period. This accumulation of wealth was particularly extensive in England, and was a factor in the encouragement of invention and especially in the utilization of improved methods. Large-scale capitalization had long characterized certain branches of enterprise, and its extension to industrial undertakings had been promoted by the merchant-employer system of manufacturing. Machines, mechanical power, and the various other technological improvements furnished the final stimulus not only for the transition to the factory system but for the more rapid extension of large-scale capitalization to industrial enterprises.

There have been numerous definitions of the factory system, some of which would limit the factory to a plant which uses machinery and mechanical power. A more adequate view would include other establishments with a concentration of capital and labor and with centralized control. Even a workshop employing handicraftsmen and involving centralized control of labor, materials, and output is economically and socially hardly distinguishable from an establishment which utilizes machinery and mechanical power. Whether the narrower or the broader view is accepted, factories were not unknown before the eighteenth century. The problem is simplified when it is recalled that changes so fundamental as the transition to new modes of production can never be confined within the exact boundaries either of definitions or of periods of time. The factory system derives its main importance from its contrast with other modes of production, especially those connected with households, villages, small handicraft shops, and the merchant-employer system. All of these forms of industrial production survive to the present day even in the most advanced countries; and factories existed long before they contributed significantly to the total volume of production. The fact of essential significance is that the technological changes of the eighteenth century, combined with the expanding opportunities for profitable sale of goods and with the capitalistic organization of the markets, created conditions which made large establishments with centralized control characteristic rather than exceptional.

Technological changes, it must be remembered, were by no means restricted to the invention of machines. Hardly less important were canals, better roads, the new technique of farm production for interchange with the output of industry, the use of coke, and new materials and processes for making pottery. These changes were not primarily mechanical, although in many cases, as in the blast for the coke-burning furnace, mechanical power was indirectly involved. These various changes, as well as those which primarily involved the invention of machines and the substitution of mechanical power for hand power, made economical and virtually imperative a progressive increase in the size of plants and in the number of workers per plant, together with some form of organized and centralized control of raw materials, production, labor, and output. These characteristics are the essentials of the factory system.

The integration of units of capital was less vitally affected by technological changes, for the capital used for industrial production was already owned extensively by wealthy merchants, landlords, and master craftsmen. Most of the modern forms of capitalization had long been known. Wealthy individuals, partnerships often with "sleeping partners" who supplied nothing but their capital, and joint-stock corporations had invested large amounts of capital in virtually all forms of business, although less extensively in manufacturing than in many other forms of enterprise. Before the collapse, in the early eighteenth century, of the speculative bubbles centering around the South Sea Company in England and the schemes of John Law in France, the investment of surplus capital in joint-stock enterprises had assumed large proportions in connection with industrial as well as commercial and financial undertakings. The subsequent ill-repute and legal disabilities of joint-stock companies retarded this form of investment, and the integration of industrial capital in the eighteenth century was largely by individuals and partnerships on the basis of rapidly accumulated profits derived from utilization of the new techniques. There was nevertheless an increasing investment by sleeping partners whose income was derived from trade, agriculture, banking, and loans to governments. Some writers have held that the integration of capital was the cause alike of technical innovations and of factory organization. But cause and effect are always elusive except in simple cases of a clear sequence of events, and their study is perhaps less significant than description of changes and analysis of the interaction of economic forces. In reality each phenomenon — the accumulation of wealth available for capital investment, and the progress of technology — was both cause and effect. The former helped to stimulate and make possible the use of inventions, and the latter greatly accelerated the rate of capital accumulation and concentration.

## Large-Scale Enterprise before the Industrial Revolution

In most of the countries of Europe agriculture had long been dominated by large estates. These ranged in size from the single manor or agricultural village held by the lord of the manor, to the barony, which, in feudal times, might in theory be an entire kingdom owned by the king as feudal suzerain or overlord. These manors and baronies, to be sure, were more than agricultural estates, for manufacturing and local trade were carried on and they were comparatively self-sufficient. The villagers held their lands by stable tenures, but with the exception of a comparatively small number of freeholders they were dominated by the landlords even before the enclosure movements, which were particularly prominent in England in the sixteenth and eighteenth centuries. In the sixteenth century, enclosures were largely for converting the small cultivated holdings and the commons into "sheep walks" to meet the increasing demand for wool. In the eighteenth century the movement was resumed, but more largely for the purpose of large-scale market farming. Thus the medieval aspect of farming as a "way of life" with landlords and peasants living in comparative self-sufficiency under a stable regime of mutual obligations fixed by custom, had largely disappeared by the end of the eighteenth century, especially in England. Landlords had come to be businessmen, conducting capitalistic, large-scale, specialized farming for markets. A large proportion of the former tenants and holders of small plots by customary title had lost their holdings and had become hired workers or had been forced to seek industrial employment.

Even before the age of discovery, commercial enterprise, especially in the older Mediterranean centers, had assumed a large-scale, capitalistic form when it involved the carrying on of distant trade relations, but in most of the countries of Europe interchange of goods was ordinarily on a small scale in local markets and towns and by petty chapmen or peddlers. Even at the great regional fairs a large proportion of the business was done by small merchants, little more than peddlers, although numerous associations of merchants were formed. As interregional trade expanded and increasingly involved transportation by sea, extensive capital was required. At the larger fairs, middlemen played prominent roles. In the organization of merchant fleets, cities aided the merchants and in some cases owned and manned the vessels. Money-changing, loaning of money, insurance, and the gradual emergence of banking functions associated with the financing of wars and of trade, stimulated the development of large-scale finance. The explorations and the colonial and commercial ventures of the Spaniards and Portuguese were largely financed and managed by public authorities. When Holland, England, and France entered these fields of enterprise, the governments refrained for the most part from direct participation in financing trade. But they extended occasional subsidies, granted monopolistic charters, made treaties, adopted protective measures such as the English Navigation Acts, and waged commercial wars for the control of markets, territories, and trade routes. The chartered companies, which at first were mere associations of merchants, later assumed the form of joint-stock enterprises, thus inaugurating the modern regime of joint-stock corporate finance.

Thus before the industrial revolution agriculture, interregional trade, and finance were organized on the basis of large-scale capitalization. Individuals and dynastic groups were prominent, as, for example, the powerful mercantile and banking family of Fugger, originating at Augsburg. More important were the companies, either associations such as the Merchants Adventurers, or joint-stock corporations such as the later trading companies and the Bank of England.

Manufacturing, local trade, and even mining remained until the industrial revolution largely on the basis of small units and capitalization by master craftsmen and petty traders. Even in these fields guilds had traditionally acquired monopolistic privileges and extensive powers of regulation, although the actual operation and financing of business units remained in the hands of individual members of the guilds. In England and to some extent on the Continent many master craftsmen before the industrial revolution were able to evade or modify the restrictions on the number of apprentices and journeymen in their service, and thus there was a tendency to increase the capitalization and scale of operations. The master craftsmen and their guilds were losing control of many aspects of industry by virtue of the development of the merchant-employer system, which was largely financed and to some extent supervised by the merchants. There had long been many instances of large capitalization and of concentration of wage earners in mining, smelting, and mill and furnace industries requiring power, but these, before the late eighteenth century, were exceptional forms of industrial organization.

## Survivals of Small-Scale Industries

An age-old form of industrial production is handicraft industry associated with households, farmsteads, and villages. Even in the most highly industrialized countries today there are survivals, as dairying, canning, sewing, and the making and repairing of tools. During the period of prohibition in America the extensive revival of home brew was a reversion to a once-prevalent mode of production. In frontier communities domestic industry provides the households and farmsteads with a large proportion of fabricated goods. In Europe, village economy, with a simple division of labor, continued for a long time to furnish the manors or agricultural villages with both agricultural products and most of the crude fabricated goods that were available. The villages were largely self-sufficient, and production for sale was mostly for local interchange, often by barter, in the local markets.

In the market towns and to some extent in the larger agricultural villages there was a more extensive division of labor. Industrial processes were carried on increasingly in specialized handicraft shops. These shops were in a sense a modified form of household industry, for the home and the shop were ordinarily combined, as is often still the case with petty tradesmen, cobblers, and other craftsmen who attempt to maintain an independent status in the midst of factories and large mercantile establishments. In most of the European countries the handicraft shop, even after the industrial revolution, continued to be an important unit of industrial production for supplying the markets.

In various countries where interregional trade was highly developed, and especially in England, the merchant-employer system continued to be a prominent factor in production long after the rise of factories. It was important both in rural areas and in the vicinity of towns. The system was most widely adopted in the cotton and woolen industries, but was not limited to textiles. Thus it is estimated by T. S. Ashton in his *Iron and Steel in the Industrial Revolution* that about 1737, within ten miles of Birmingham, 9,000 tons of bar iron were annually made into ironware "under a domestic system of production." Present-day survivals include lacemaking, tailoring, and various other processes.

There were various industrial activities which were on the boundaries of household industry, the handicraft shops, and modern industrial establishments. These included smelting furnaces, foundries, forges, flour mills, breweries, distilleries, kilns, and various other mill and furnace industries, and also quarrying and lumbering. These various activities were often carried on as adjuncts of household and village economy, as manorial forge work and grinding of grain. Even when utilized for supplying the markets they were usually on so small a scale as to require slight capital. Most of the workers were craftsmen, and many of them belonged to guilds. But some of the mills and furnaces were on a large scale. This was especially true of the enterprises that produced raw materials or partly finished materials for use by household and handicraft shopworkers, as in the case of the smelting of iron, the crushing of flax, the sawing of lumber, and the fulling of cloth. These establishments were important connecting links with modern units for industrial production.

Before the sixteenth century various Continental countries were more advanced industrially than England, not only in mill and furnace industries but also in weaving and spinning and other handicrafts. Thereafter Englishmen, making extensive use of Continental skill and capital, advanced so rapidly as to lead recent writers to compare the period beginning with the dissolution of the monasteries and the enclosures with the later industrial revolution. By the eighteenth century, leadership alike in technological progress

THE REORGANIZATION OF INDUSTRIAL ENTERPRISE 133

and in the integration of industry was rapidly shifting to England. While it is true that before the epochal technological changes of the eighteenth century there had been large establishments and occasionally even a combination of processes under unified control, extending, for example, from mining to the marketing of the products of foundries and forges, these were exceptional. Eighteenth-century technology created conditions which greatly increased the degree of integration even in the mill and furnace industries, not only by making large firms and establishments typical instead of exceptional but by vastly expanding the size of units alike of capitalization and of production. This is true even of the brass and copper industries, in which there had been a long history of capitalistic organization.

## The Copper and Brass Industries

Early instances of large-scale enterprise in England are to be found in the copper, calamine (zinc), and brass industries. Two joint-stock companies were chartered in 1568 — the Mines Royal Company and the Mineral and Battery Works. Both were based largely on German skill and capital. The smelting of copper at the Keswick plant of the Mines Royal Company in 1573 required more than 4,000 loads of charcoal, more than 26,000 loads of peat, 215 loads of "stonecoal," 1,180 loads of lime, and 357 bushels of kelp. The smelting of copper and the making of brass, wire, household utensils, etc. utilized large amounts of capital and large factories. During the seventeenth century these industries declined and the companies lost their monopolies. On the basis of legislation passed in 1689 and 1693, there was a reorganization, and the eighteenth century witnessed a progressive improvement of technology, increase of capitalization, and expansion of the size of companies and establishments.

The total output of copper by the monopolistic Mines Royal Company in 1570 was only 1,261 cwt. 28 lb. The company's capitalization in 1569 was £20,400. Workers engaged by the company in smelting seem to have numbered not more than twenty-five. In 1697 the total output of copper was estimated at 160 tons, half of which was made by one company. One of the largest copper and brass companies had capital stock worth in 1692 about £40,000. By 1767 one of several companies claimed a capitalization of £200,000, with employees numbering 2,000. Twenty years later the output of copper was more than 8,000 tons, controlled largely by two groups of companies acting for a time in concert, and the manufacturers of Birmingham alone consumed from 1,500 to 2,000 tons annually. In 1794 the establishment of a single company had an output of nearly 1,000 tons.

These remarkable changes indicate that even in an industry which had long been marked by a comparatively high degree of integration the eighteenth century witnessed an expansion of output and of units of production and capitalization which may well be described as revolutionary. Accompanying the expansion and largely responsible for it was a series of technological changes extending from improvements in the smelting and refining of copper about 1690 to the high degree of mechanization, a century later, in the works of Boulton and Watt at Soho, near Birmingham, where brass and copper were extensively used in various processes of manufacture.

## Iron and Steel

The ironworks of Ambrose Crowley established in 1690 at Swalwell and Winlaton are described by T. S. Ashton in his *Iron and Steel in the Industrial Revolution* as a "remarkable" and "surprisingly modern" undertaking. At Crowley's death in 1713 his estate was valued at £200,000. His products included commercial bars, sheets, and rods, steel, heavy forge work, as anchors, and a large variety of iron and steel implements and utensils. He had no smelting furnaces, but maintained foundries for castings from pig iron, various types of forges, steel furnaces, rolling mills, slitting mills, and workshops for making ironware. In addition to the wage earners in his own plants, many household workers and shopworkers were employed in making ironware out of the materials supplied by his factories, often on credit. These workers ordinarily owned their tools but sold their output to Crowley and were required to conform to regulations prescribed by him.

Another comparatively early instance of integration in the iron industry is the Coalbrookdale establishment of Abraham Darby. After encountering difficulties in the use of clay molds for iron castings, he visited Holland in 1704 to study Dutch methods. He brought back skilled Dutch ironworkers and introduced the method of casting in wet sand. In 1708 he leased the Coalbrookdale furnaces and soon thereafter introduced the epochal coke-smelting process. By 1715 his Coalbrookdale plant was worth at least £5,000. After his death in 1717 his widow formed a partnership. The firm at first made merely the simpler forms of cast-iron goods, such as firebacks and boilers, but expanded its activities to include engine castings, forge work, coal mining, and coking.   The partners increased their business rapidly, especially after the middle of the century, built houses for their workmen, and developed their activities into a typical modern enterprise.

The iron industry, as already stated, was in a declining condition during the first half of the eighteenth century, and most of the large-scale enterprises either originated or attained importance during the second half of the century, after the general adoption of coke as a fuel and of the power blast, puddling and rolling, and other technological improvements.   Two examples must suffice: the Walker family and the company in charge of the Carron works.   In 1741 Samuel, Aaron, and Jonathan Walker began business as founders on so small a scale that their first year's output was only five tons.   Within a decade it had grown to 256 tons, and the making of crucible steel by the Huntsman process was added to their activities.   In 1796 their business was valued at more than £200,000. The Carron foundry, in Scotland, was established in 1759.   The capital was divided into twenty-four shares, held by seven persons. In 1773 the firm became a chartered joint-stock corporation with 600 shareholders and a capital of £150,000.   A writer in 1789 described the Carron establishment as "the greatest perhaps of its kind in the world: the weekly consumption of coals amounts to 11,000 tons, at 4s. per ton; and the consumption each day is equal to that of the city of Edinburgh for a whole week.   As many coals, therefore, are consumed in the Carron foundries as would suffice to supply a city of 700,000 inhabitants.   A thousand workmen are daily employed in this manufactory, whose wages amount to £700 per week and £36,400 per annum.   The demands from abroad, and particularly from Spain, continue to increase."   This was written, it is to be noted, on the eve of a quarter century of warfare, which greatly stimulated the iron industry.

In 1761 Smeaton constructed for the Carron works a blast of four gigantic cylinders, with air pumps operated by water power, and made possible more than a fourfold increase in output of pig iron. The later use of the steam blast and other improvements led to a progressive enlargement of size and output of blast furnaces.   By 1804 the total output of pig iron was about 250,000 tons as compared with estimates of 18,000 to 25,000 tons for 1720 and, because of the decline of the charcoal industry, even smaller quantities up to the middle of the century.

## The Industries of Birmingham

The iron industry as it expanded after the middle of the eighteenth century was located mainly in the Black Country west of Birmingham, in the south of Scotland, and in southern Wales.  Forges were more widely distributed, especially after the development of canals and steam power.  The potteries were centered largely in Staffordshire northwest of Birmingham.  The more progressive woolen centers were in the West Riding of Yorkshire.  The cotton industry was mainly in the vicinity of Manchester.  Birmingham had long been noted for the making of ironware, but the difficulty of transporting heavy goods, the constructing of forges and foundries in the new iron centers, the growth of demand for artistic wares and luxury goods, and the abundance of skilled metal workers and other craftsmen combined to direct the attention of the citizens to new trades. These included artistic novelties, toys, buttons, shoe buckles, locks, guns, plated wares, coins, and various other articles requiring extensive use of copper, brass, and silver.  Most of these trades required special skill and small capital for tools and equipment, and they were carried on mainly throughout the century in handicraft shops and even in households.  But many of the merchants and master manufacturers acquired considerable wealth.  A writer as early as 1783 stated that 209 residents of the city were each worth £5,000 or more, and of these eighteen had fortunes ranging from £30,000 to more than £100,000.  A large proportion of this wealth was from the profits of manufactures, although the profits went largely not to the craftsmen but to enterprising merchants who rapidly extended their sales abroad as well as in England and gained increasing control of manufactures.

## Boulton and Watt

Although the factory can hardly be said to have become a predominant or even typical form of organization in eighteenth-century Birmingham, there were notable instances of factories.  Of these, the most important were the establishments of Boulton and Watt at Soho, which later merged with the city.  Matthew Boulton was the son of a prosperous toymaker of Birmingham.  The building of his first plant at Soho, on a "barren heath," was begun as early as 1759.  By 1765 there were five buildings worth £9,000, large enough to employ 600 workmen.  By 1774 the plant employed a thousand workmen and made a large variety of goods, such as toys, shoe buckles, buttons, and gold, silver, brass, and plated ornaments.

By the end of the century it was the center of a modern industrial community with a series of plants adapted to specialized functions, including a mint and a large foundry.   There were "many ingenious mechanical contrivances" operated by steam power.

From the beginning Boulton had used the most advanced mechanical devices, but he soon found that the water supply was inadequate. For the purpose of conserving the supply, he installed an engine for pumping the water back to the millrace.   Not the least of his claims to distinction was his partnership with James Watt for the perfecting and marketing of the steam engine.   Boulton's early arrangement with Watt was mainly for the purpose of exploiting Watt's patent by means of royalties from the use of the steam engine.   The rapid increase in the demand for engines in England and abroad led to the sale as well as the leasing of engines under royalty contracts, and to the development of what has been described as the first factory in the modern engineering industries.

Boulton had various other business connections, and he extended his activities and interests far beyond the development of steam power and the carrying on of the manufacturing operations at Soho. He was prominent in the development of canals and roads, in the mining of copper and tin, in various local business ventures, in the promotion of associations of manufacturers, in national politics, and in the extension of markets abroad.   He became his own merchant, thus reaping a "double profit" and reversing the former status of the manufacturer as subordinate to the merchant.

## The Potteries

In the pottery industry there was comparatively little mechanization except in the grinding and mixing of materials, but these, with various other changes, already described, brought about an integration of capital and a rise of factories.   The new methods of production, combined with improved transportation, the substitution of earthenware for pewter, the growth of coffeehouses and clubs and more elaborate tastes, and the skillful organization of marketing facilities, led to a rapid expansion which gave the industry national importance.   Such changes as the mechanical grinding and mixing of materials, the substitution of molding for throwing on the wheel, the stenciling or printing of decorative patterns on the surface, and the use of "slip" kilns in place of "sun pans" required specialization of labor and processes, centralized supervision, and comparatively large capital.   The importation of raw materials and the sale of the product in distant markets also promoted integration.  Formerly a master potter had a single oven and employed about five or six workmen.  Throughout the eighteenth century, and especially during the latter half, many of the master potters increased the number of their ovens and expanded their operations.  With the introduction of various improvements in manufacture and transportation, the scattered shops and domestic establishments gave place to the thriving Five Towns dominated by a few wealthy manufacturers.  By the end of the century the Staffordshire potters gained ascendancy even in the making of porcelain from the kaolin deposits of the southwest.  Previously, the principal porcelain works had been in London, Derby, and Worcester, where factories had been built about the middle of the century.

## Josiah Wedgwood

Among the various master potters of the new type the most fa-mous was Josiah Wedgwood.  He was born in 1730, at Burslem, a member of a family of potters.  The family business went to his brothers, and one of these employed him as an apprentice.  At twenty-one he was given charge of a small establishment belonging to another potter.  In this shop he made such varied articles as snuffboxes, candlesticks, pickle dishes, and teapots, and had opportunity to make experiments in color, shape, and texture.  By this time many of the technological changes described in an earlier chapter had already begun to have their effect in expanding the size of the business unit, and Wedgwood was soon able to form partnerships with other potters who had capital and who wished to utilize his skill and experimental bent.  In 1759 he leased workrooms, sheds, two kilns, and a cottage and set up in business for himself.  The business expanded rapidly and in 1766 he established a sales agency of his own in London.  In the same year he formed a partnership with Thomas Wedgwood, a cousin, and bought an estate for £3,000 for the purpose of building a new factory.  In 1769 a partnership was formed with Thomas Bentley, a merchant of Liverpool, who contributed not only his capital but also the facilities of his mercantile firm and his connections abroad for exporting pottery, and his knowledge of classical art, which was to give peculiar distinction to Wedgwood pottery.

On the estate purchased in 1766 the partners gradually established the famous Etruria works near Hanley.  Complete removal of the business from Burslem to Etruria was not accomplished until

1774. The new establishment had two distinct units, one for ordinary pottery, the other for ornamental wares. The partnership with Thomas Wedgwood was continued and was utilized for making "useful" pottery, which came to be defined as tableware, while the partnership with Bentley was primarily interested in ornamental pottery other than "such vessels as are made use of at meals." Other partnerships and connections were formed from time to time by Josiah Wedgwood alone or by him and Bentley, as with the Cornish Clay Company, with the Potters' Clay Company, with a firm of flint grinders, and with various groups interested in canals and road construction. These personal, flexible connections illustrate the fact that industrial organization in the eighteenth century was largely in the form of individual enterprise or of the simple partnership rather than the joint-stock corporation. Funds for capital expansion came extensively if not predominantly from the large profits derived from the newer types of industrial enterprise. The rapid accumulation of profits is illustrated by the case of Wedgwood, who began his career as an apprentice entirely without capital and ended it in 1795 with extensive lands and a personal estate of about £240,000.

The earlier potters, like most of the other manufacturers, depended on merchants for raw materials other than those of local origin and for nonlocal sale of their products. Wedgwood's policy is an illustration of the trend among the newer types of manufacturers. He took an active part in organizing and controlling the raw-materials markets, as in his connections with the Cornish Clay Company, the Potters' Clay Company, and a flint-grinding firm. In the marketing of his products he adopted policies which affected merchandising in general and which aided in reversing the former subordination of the manufacturers to the merchants. Among these policies were the maintenance of his own showrooms and sales agencies in various towns; the building up of mercantile facilities and connections in various parts of the world; the substitution of retail stores for peddlers and handicraft shops; the payment of transportation charges; guarantee of safe delivery; and dependence for profits on low prices and large sales rather than on "a high price with a diminished sale."

The Etruria works included separate workshops, ovens, and yards for "useful" and for ornamental wares, and extensive housing facilities for the workmen. During prosperous times several hundred workmen were employed. Wedgwood himself in 1783 described the remarkable changes that had taken place within his own memory, not only at Etruria but throughout the Potteries. During his boyhood the houses were "miserable huts," the lands "yielded little of value," and the almost impassable roads virtually cut off the region from the rest of the world. In contrast he described the "happy change" wrought by industry, with "houses mostly new and comfortable, and the lands, roads, and every other circumstance bearing evident marks of the most pleasing and rapid improvements." The Potteries were described in 1805 as an area of "about nine miles in extent, the whole of which is now so covered with manufactures and dwelling houses that it has the appearance of a large, scattered town."

## Textiles

Large-scale capitalization and the rise of factories in the textile industries in the eighteenth century were peculiarly significant for several reasons. In the first place, these industries were exceptionally important because of their widespread geographical distribution in rural areas as well as in the towns, and because of the large number of people directly affected. In the second place, the changes involved not only an expansion and a net addition to wealth and economic activity (there was a rapid expansion, especially in the cotton industry) but also a transformation, change of location, and shifting of emphasis from one textile industry to another. The expansion of the cotton industry, for example, was partly at the expense of the woolen, silk, and linen industries. In the third place, the transition in the textile industries, especially in cotton, was comparatively radical and abrupt, involving a change from the primitive household system to factories. The transition involved a more extensive uprooting and transplanting, a greater stress and strain attending the necessary economic and social readjustments, than in many of the other industries. The ordinary textile firm was comparatively small and was based on a comparatively small investment, many firms using second-hand or even rented equipment. Profits were large and were ruthlessly plowed back into industry. The mortality rate was high in spite of rapid expansion of markets, and one of the gravest problems of the period was the excessive use of income for capital formation as opposed to domestic consumption.

The fly shuttle, although invented in 1733, was not extensively used until after the middle of the century. Hargreaves invented the spinning jenny about 1764. Neither of these devices utilized power, and the spinning jenny even tended to prolong the system of cottage industry. After the introduction of Arkwright's water frame in 1769 and of Crompton's mule ten years later, the spinning industry underwent rapid transformation. Soon thereafter preliminary stages of fabrication, such as carding and roving, and later processes, such as dyeing, bleaching, and printing, were extensively affected by technological innovations. Even weaving, which awaited the early nineteenth century for the perfecting of the power loom, came increasingly under the control of capitalists, who often assembled handlooms in their workshops and attempted a closer supervision of the weavers in their homes and shops. A writer as early as 1788 stated that there were 143 water-power spinning factories in England, Scotland, and Wales, distributed as follows: in Lancashire, 41; in Derbyshire, 22; in Scotland, 19; in Nottinghamshire, 17; in Yorkshire, 11; in Cheshire, 8; and in other places, 25. It was also stated that in 1788 there were 550 mules with as many as 90 spindles each, and more than 20,000 hand jennies. In 1794 Nottinghamshire was reported as having 31 cotton factories as compared with 17 in 1788. In 1795 Scotland is said to have had 39. In the same year Stockport, in Cheshire (the entire county having only 8 in 1788), had "23 large cotton factories, four worked by steam," and in addition, many smaller "spinning shops." A traveler reported in 1791 that in the north of England there were cotton mills on virtually every stream large enough to turn a water wheel. By that time the steam engine was rapidly being introduced.

### Richard Arkwright

Among the many "new great cotton lords," as Robert Owen described them, the outstanding eighteenth-century figure was Richard Arkwright. He was born at Preston in north Lancashire in 1732. He early became a barber and later a dealer in hair for the making of wigs, much worn in the eighteenth century. His early activity in the cotton industry is obscure, but it is known that with the aid of mechanics he made improvements in the roller-spinning process devised by Wyatt and Paul. In 1768 he moved to Nottingham in quest of capital, and in 1769 patented his water frame. In 1771 he formed an extremely valuable connection with Jedediah Strutt and Samuel Need, hosiery merchants who had organized an extensive putting-out system based on the use of the stocking frame.   In the same year he moved to Cromford and built a cotton mill on the River Derwent near Lombe's silk factory.   In his mill he at first spun thread for use by Strutt and Need in the making of hosiery, but as early as 1773 weaving shops were opened in Derby for making cloth exclusively of cotton.   This led to the repeal of the act of 1735, which had required the use of linen warps, and opened the way for the rapid expansion of the calico industry. In 1775 he took out a second patent covering various preparatory processes, especially carding.   By 1779 the Cromford mill employed about 300 workmen.   Thereafter Arkwright and his various partners rapidly extended their operations over the north of England and sold licenses to various other manufacturers for the use of their patents, the licensees having invested, according to Arkwright, £60,000 by 1782.   In addition, a large number of manufacturers had challenged his patent rights by refusing to pay premiums.   His patent of 1769 was declared invalid in 1781, two years before its expiration, but in 1785 his second patent was upheld.   Other manufacturers then organized and in the same year brought about a reversal of the court's action.   Thereafter the expansion of factory production was extremely rapid, due not only to the canceling of Arkwright's patent of 1775 but to the increasing use of Crompton's mule of 1779, which was soon so improved as to be adapted to the use of power, although the perfecting of automatic operation awaited the nineteenth-century " self-actor " mule.

The end of Arkwright's monopoly greatly expanded the factory system and checkmated his ambition for personal domination, but his enterprises continued to expand.   As early as 1785 he corresponded with Boulton and Watt, and soon thereafter began to introduce steam power.   His fortune at his death in 1792 was estimated at £500,000.

During the last decade of the eighteenth century, the more progressive woolen centers of Yorkshire rapidly adopted the factory system for spinning and accessory processes, and the older centers, which adhered to the wheel and the spinning jenny, were in a state of decline.   This was due in part to the competition of cottons. In 1794, on one estate not far from Manchester, there were three woolen establishments, one of which included a six-story building, dyehouses, other extensive buildings, and a steam engine.   Benjamin Gott's factory known as Bean Ing, near Leeds, was begun in 1792, and by 1800 it carried on twenty-nine processes of woolen manufacture, made use of a 40-horsepower steam engine, and employed about 1,000 workers.  Merchants of Leeds declared as early as 1791 that "the scribbling mill, the spinning frame, the fly shuttle, have reduced manual labor nearly one third."

### The Printing of Textiles: Robert Peel

The textile-printing industry had long been carried on in work-shops which in some instances resembled factories, but with the invention of cylindrical printing there was a rapid integration of capital and of processes.  In this field Robert Peel occupied a position resembling that of Arkwright in spinning, although Peel also engaged in spinning and bleaching.  He claimed as early as 1785 to employ 6,800 workmen.  His works near Bury were described ten years later as finding "constant employ for most of the inhabitants of Bury and its neighborhood, of both sexes and all ages."  Peel himself stated, in describing his reasons for introducing the Factory Bill of 1802, that at one time his firm employed nearly a thousand children of the class known as pauper apprentices.

### Associations of Businessmen

In medieval and early modern history, before the rise of the joint-stock corporation, associations were almost universal.  The derivation of the word *company*, from the Latin *cum* or *com-*, with, and *panis*, bread, emphasizes the idea of companionship or, literally, of dining together.  The guilds of merchants and of craftsmen were associations of individuals not for pooling their capital and their profits but rather for mutual protection and for regulation of work-manship, markets, and the details of enterprise.  Even the early trading companies were not joint-stock undertakings but associa-tions for maintaining the monopolistic rights of the group and regulating the conditions under which the members carried on their separate enterprises.  In the system of mercantilism many of the regulatory functions which had been exercised by medieval and early modern associations were taken over by the state.  Later, under the influence of *laissez faire* and unrestricted initiative and competition, concerted action became increasingly difficult.  The rise of joint-stock enterprise interposed a further obstacle and at the same time afforded in a sense a substitute for associations of individuals and partners.

Gradually the disruptive tendencies of the competitive regime gave rise to the modern forms of association, such as cartels, cham-bers of commerce, trade associations, and informal combinations.

These have been traced by some writers to the medieval and early modern associations, but there is no evidence of continuity. They are traceable, not organically to be sure, but in type and in function, to associations of businessmen of the early stages of the industrial revolution.

Various local and temporary committees of businessmen were formed from time to time for the purpose of dealing with specific problems of common interest, such as taxation, poor relief, and roads and canals. During the last quarter of the eighteenth century several groups were formed in Great Britain with permanent organization and continuity of function for dealing with a variety of common interests. Probably the earliest of these was a committee formed in Manchester in 1774, the forerunner of the Manchester Chamber of Commerce. The committee was reorganized in 1781 and was concerned with a large variety of activities, including opposition to Arkwright's patents, encouragement of invention, reciprocal trade treaties, an increase in the supply of raw materials, especially cotton, and relations with employees. As early as 1777 the principal ironmasters had a definite organization which held quarterly meetings and dealt with such problems as prices, markets, taxes, and commercial treaties. In 1777 the worsted clothiers and manufacturers of the West Riding of Yorkshire, Lancashire, and Cheshire formed an organization known as the Worsted Committee, authorized by law to handle certain phases of the administration of the laws against alleged frauds and embezzlements connected with the merchant-employer system. The committee soon expanded its activities to include the encouragement of invention and the use of machinery, lobbying, and other work characteristic of modern associations. In 1783 Birmingham organized a General Commercial Committee with interests and activities resembling those of the other groups. A similar tendency toward organization was exhibited by the potters and also by the manufacturers of Glasgow.

### The General Chamber of Manufacturers

One of the functions of the Manchester committee and also of the Birmingham group was to correspond with manufacturers in other centers. William Pitt's cotton excise bill of 1784, which was based on earlier excise measures applicable to a simpler system of production before the rise of factories and of wealthy and powerful manufacturers, aroused widespread opposition and led to the first

instance of concerted action by the various local groups.   The success of the manufacturers in their opposition to the cotton tax was
soon followed, in 1785, by the organization at London of the General
Chamber of Manufacturers of Great Britain.   The members were
for the most part delegates of local committees or chambers, the
further organization of these being a special object of the central
body.   Its first main enterprise was its opposition to Pitt's Irish
policy, but it formulated a comprehensive program and established
an office at London.   Its principal support came from the larger
manufacturers of the newer types at Manchester and Birmingham
and in the iron and pottery centers.   But its principal weakness
lay in the voting strength of delegates from the older, more conservative industries.   Josiah Wedgwood, the great potter, complained that "a man who should get a delegation from the tooth-
brush makers of London would have a vote equal with a delegate
sent from Birmingham or Manchester."   The result was that in
connection with the reciprocal treaty of commerce with France in
1786, the older, more conservative interests, in opposition to the
treaty, succeeded for a time in gaining control.   The men who
had been responsible for the organization of the Chamber gained
their ends in the adoption of the treaty, and the Chamber, cleverly
discredited by Pitt, was gradually abandoned by its sponsors.   It
was nevertheless a significant forerunner of modern types of associations among businessmen.

# CHAPTER 8

## AGRARIAN REORGANIZATION AND REFORM IN THE EIGHTEENTH CENTURY

————◆————

### The General Features of Enclosure in England

The reorganization of the agrarian system in England has always been described as a process of enclosure, because the extinction of the various kinds of common rights was commonly followed by the construction of permanent hedges and ditches, not only around the boundaries of the property of each individual but also around the primary field divisions of each individual estate. In some sections of England and over wide areas in Continental Europe, the extinction of common rights did not lead to such extensive hedging and fence building. In the literal sense, therefore, many sections of Europe did not experience any enclosure movement, but such sharp emphasis upon the external aspects of the agrarian reforms tends to obscure many of the essential legal, social, and agricultural features of the movement. The primary objective, in England as in Continental Europe, was the establishment of absolute individual control of the use of land. The details of the process present wide variations, because the effective resistance to reform was profoundly influenced by all the local differences in land tenure, custom, and agricultural practice. The immediate purposes of reform were likewise varied, because the desired changes in agricultural practice always involved greater diversification of culture in order to adapt methods more closely to the requirements of different soils and climatic conditions.

Some aspects of the reforms were very imperfectly recognized by the agricultural writers of the eighteenth century. Arthur Young in England, his admirers in France, and Albrecht Thaer in Germany assumed that reform involved the adoption of specific methods of farming. Young was willing to recognize the different requirements of the heavier and the lighter soils, but he had little sympathy for the actual problems of farming in many sections of England and France. Any departure from his rigid standards of practice was unsparingly condemned, though increased knowledge of agricultural science and of farm management enables us to explain many of these supposedly unsound practices. We must not be too

146

quick to accept the definitions of the problems to be found in the literature of the period, and for this reason it is desirable to divide the general problem into its essential aspects.

The simplest problem of reform was the extinction of the rights of pasturage on arable land that had always been subject to individual management. The general boundaries of the area that thus stood outside the system of communal agriculture have been mapped by Professor Gray, whose results have already been shown on the map on page 44. Nearly 40 per cent of the total area of England was subject only to the least important of the collective servitudes of common use: the right to pasture animals on the arable after harvest. The extinction of this right presented little difficulty. In so far as the holders of arable land had their proportionate share of livestock they might exclude the cattle of other villagers on the principle that they were reserving their fields for their own stock. If a principle of stinted pasture were to be adopted, nothing could be more reasonable than to adjust the rights of pasture to the size of the arable holding, and no one could object to a fully individualized grazing system.

The character of reform in this general area is easily inferred from the material supplied by the reports to the Board of Agriculture at the close of the eighteenth century. Slater summarizes the material for Wessex (Hampshire, Wiltshire, Berkshire, and Dorsetshire) as follows: "It may be described as at present a country of very large farms, with a very large proportion of open down, the cultivated land itself remaining remarkably open, being divided into large irregular fields by hedges which are full of gaps. Rights of common here more than elsewhere have decayed, irrespective of actual enclosure; and using the word enclosure in its broad sense, it may be said that in Wessex the process of enclosure has least of all taken visible shape, either in the growing of hedges, or building of walls, or in the conversion of arable to pasture, or pasture to arable, or in the scattering of the habitations of the inhabitants over the whole parish; but it has most profoundly affected the social life of the villages." [1]

The voluntary character of this process of reform leaves us with little knowledge of the timing of the process. Important inferences can be drawn from the reports of travelers. Gonner holds that the extinction of common rights was largely completed in this area

[1] Slater, Gilbert, *The English Peasantry and the Enclosure of the Common Fields*, Constable and Company, Ltd., London, 1907, p. 234.

before 1700. The reports of the late eighteenth century leave no reasonable doubt of the substantial completion of the reform in this area before the close of the century.

## Enclosure of Waste

By the statute of Merton (1235) lords of manors were authorized to improve and enclose portions of wasteland, provided that sufficient wild pasture and forest remained to meet the requirements of the villagers. Until 1893 there was no effective procedure to protect the interests of the villagers, though for many generations the amount of wild land was so largely in excess of requirements that there was little danger of serious injury to the interests of the peasants. Land thus enclosed became the exclusive property of the improving lord. It might be administered directly or leased to tenants on short-term leases. It is commonly supposed that little land from this source was leased on copyholds or other forms of long lease. Enclosure of this type could not be effectively opposed. The initiative rested with the manorial lords, and this privilege was an important factor in the formation of the great properties in the hands of the nobility. Large areas of arable and pasture lands were brought into use from the wild state in all sections of England, most particularly in the great grazing areas of the north and the Welsh border.

Interest in the improvement of waste lands during the Commonwealth led to the proposal to authorize the enclosure of waste by act of Parliament. Various bills were brought in subsequently, but none was passed. Their significant effect would have been to open up improvement to persons other than manorial lords. The projects and patents for the drainage of the fens should doubtless be associated with this movement for more liberal provision for improvement of wild land.

Although no general provision was made for such projects, precedents were definitely established in the eighteenth century for the use of a special act of Parliament in each case. This change is in part a feature of the increase in the scope of Parliamentary authority, but these acts of Parliament had new consequences. Persons other than lords of manors might participate or initiate an improvement; furthermore, agreement of representatives of the major portion of the property might lead to an authorization to distribute the entire area of the common pasture among the holders of pasturage rights.

In the course of the eighteenth century the agricultural improvers developed great zeal for the comprehensive enclosure of the common pastures. These common grazing grounds were alleged to be a source of all that was bad. The large herds of village stock led to progressive deterioration through uncontrolled breeding. Epidemics were quickly diffused over wide areas. Persistent overstocking of the pasture precluded the development of good stock that might yield a true profit. As one contemporary said, the commons were places where "a few lean sheep starved, and two rabbits struggled for each blade of grass." For these evils, the act of Parliament provided a complete and expeditious remedy. The record of enclosure of common pasture and waste by act of Parliament is as follows:[1] in 1727–1760 (34 years), 74,518 acres; in 1761–1792 (32 years), 478,259 acres; in 1793–1801 (9 years), 273,891 acres; in 1802–1815 (14 years), 739,743 acres; in 1816–1845 (30 years), 199,300 acres; in 1846–1907 (62 years), 334,906 acres; total, in 1727–1907 (181 years), 2,100,617 acres.

Unfortunately, this extensive breakup of the wild pastures entailed serious social and economic consequences. These commons had long been an important resource to the poorer craftsmen of the villages and to the agricultural laborers who had no actual claim upon the village arable. By general assent these squatters had been allowed to enclose small portions of the commons for a cottage site and garden. In some sections the squatters held that they acquired positive rights if they built a habitable cottage over night. The lawyers and the landlords were on the whole unwilling to accept this point of view. The prevailing legal opinion assumed that these squatters had no positive right to any use of the commons. Comprehensive partition of the common pastures inevitably excluded these squatters from all share in the land. Many persons, too, with very small tenancies found that the process of enclosure left them with so little land that it had no practical value, or so little that it had to be sold to pay the apportioned expense of enclosure. The reckless breakup of the common pastures deprived many of uses of land which they had long enjoyed, and this narrow legalistic policy detached the artisans and agricultural laborers from the land. This displacement of the squatters and poorer cottagers was certainly a factor in the increased need of poor relief, but the increases in the poor rates were not of course directly related to the progress of enclosure.

[1] Slater, G., *op. cit.* (page 147), p. 267.

## Enclosure of Arable

The difficulties of reorganization were most serious in the area characterized by communal regulation of tillage. Reform involved a complete reconstruction of village life, and such a change was not easily brought about. Parts of the arable area of such villages might be enclosed by agreements among the owners of adjacent parcels who agreed to exchange parcels in order to throw their holdings into larger units. The lord of the manor and a few large property holders might arrange for the consolidation and enclosure of their parcels, but it was rare that any substantial portion of a village could be enclosed by unanimous agreement. The smaller holders preferred the existing system. Portions of the arable fields were enclosed by agreement during the sixteenth and seventeenth centuries, but the general structure of rural life was not palpably altered. The actual changes were in fact somewhat more extensive than appeared on the surface, for we now know that the consolidation of farms began at an early date and was already far advanced at the beginning of the period of extensive enclosure by act of Parliament. The material is obscure and incomplete, but the studies of the Land Tax returns by Gray, Johnson, and Davies leave no grounds for reasonable doubt of the primary facts. Economic conditions became less and less favorable to the "yeoman" farmer, or small proprietor. The system of combined stock and cereal farming that was growing up in the enclosed areas of the Midlands required a larger unit than the single family holding of thirty acres of arable. The new farm unit utilized approximately the same cereal acreage, but the green crops of the new system occupied a larger area than the old fallow, and a considerable area lay for several years under artificial grasses. More capital was necessary, and some hired labor was indispensable. All through the sixteenth and seventeenth centuries there was a steady increase in the number of large farms. The change was at once a cause and a result of enclosure. The increased profits of the new system furnished the chief incentive to enclosure, but the new system could not be established until the land was freed from all the servitudes of common pasture, and united in large parcels adapted to the new needs.

The less careful small proprietors inevitably suffered losses, which forced them to sell their holdings. Some died without heirs, or without successors capable of managing the holding. If there had been no special advantage in readjustment, these properties would merely fall into the hands of new small proprietors.  In actual fact most of the land coming on the market was systematically acquired by large proprietors to be consolidated into new units for management.  Land that could not wisely be administered directly by the lord's steward would be laid out in appropriate units and leased for a term of years to some tenant.  These tenants might be recruited in part from the group of peasant farmers, but they could not be classed as occupying owners.

At the close of the sixteenth century, copyholds were not always secure hereditary tenancies.[1]  Copyholds for lives were especially precarious.  Unexpected deaths of some of the persons named in the deed might place the copyholder under the necessity of paying a heavy premium to assure his occupancy of the holding.  In hard times this payment might not be feasible, or might seem unwise. Some lords even refused to allow the holders to nominate new lives and left the copyholder with a holding that would be terminated by the caprice of the hazards to which the remaining lives were exposed.  Enclosure by agreement thus fostered a process of consolidation of landholding that radically altered the numerical proportions between the large and the small proprietors.  The economic and social subordination of the villagers to the lord of the manor was thus considerably increased.

The necessity of unanimous consent inevitably made it difficult to bring about the enclosure of areas involving many proprietors. The small proprietors, too, had less to gain from the reorganization. The process involved many expenses, which were at best an unwelcome burden to the small proprietor.  The small farms could not advantageously be enclosed, as the areas were not large enough to justify the expense of hedging, nor suitable for management under such a system.  The small proprietors, as a group, were likely to oppose enclosure, and the holders of the smallest parcels were certain to oppose reform.  In so far as these proprietors were really secure they could successfully prevent any comprehensive breakup of the open-field arable.  The use of a special act of Parliament made it possible to override the objections of the minority, and as voting was in terms of property values, a considerable number of small proprietors might well find themselves outvoted by a few large holders.

[1] Tawney, R. H., *The Agrarian Revolution in the Sixteenth Century*, London, 1912, pp. 289-301.

## Procedure under Act of Parliament

The first special act of Parliament authorizing or approving enclosure is the act of 1706 for the enclosure of parts of Marden and Bodenham. Two acts were passed in the reign of Anne, and sixteen under George I. These early acts were primarily confirmations of voluntary agreements, so that the new elements appear only if the individual acts are studied with some care. Procedure developed rapidly after 1760. In theory the rights of all were recognized, but even at best the equities of some of the parties were imperfectly protected. In 1801 the form of the special acts was prescribed by general statute, but actual enclosure still required a special act. Procedure was simplified further by acts of 1836 and 1845; the authority to approve projects for enclosure was vested first in a Parliamentary committee and later in two commissioners. The details of local procedure, however, were not greatly changed.

The records of enclosure by act of Parliament show conclusively that this mode of procedure merely supplemented the other methods. Tabulation of the awards is somewhat unsatisfactory, as the areas are not always given, and at times appear in terms of virgates or other units which cannot be reduced to precise acreage. The results available show that the enclosures by act of Parliament, of common arable, with some meadow and waste, were as follows: [1] in 1700–1760 (61 years), 237,845 acres; in 1761–1801 (41 years), 2,428,721 acres; in 1802–1844 (43 years), 1,610,302 acres; in 1845–1907 (63 years), 187,321 acres; total, in 1700–1907 (208 years), 4,464,189 acres.

The combined area of waste and open-field arable enclosed by act of Parliament during the eighteenth and nineteenth centuries amounted to about 20 per cent of the total area of England. Even in individual counties there were few instances in which Parliamentary enclosure exceeded 50 per cent. It is clear that the breakup of the open arable fields, the extinction of common rights, and the breakup of the waste were largely accomplished by the less formal procedures. The reports to the Board of Agriculture lead one to conclude that the major portion of unrecorded enclosure occurred before 1790. Many counties were entirely enclosed by that date, and even in counties where much Parliamentary enclosure was necessary, the unenclosed areas were small. The detailed

[1] Curtler, W. H. R., *The Enclosure and Redistribution of Our Land*, The Clarendon Press, Oxford, 1920, p. 148.

tables given by Gonner show extensive Parliamentary enclosure in the period 1790–1810. One may therefore conclude that after 1810 unenclosed areas can hardly have exceeded 35 per cent of the total in individual counties, and for England as a whole the unenclosed areas can scarcely have exceeded 20 per cent of the total area.

## General Features of the Reforms in France

Owing to differences in climate and soil types, the development of agriculture in France presents some sharp contrasts both to English and to North German practice. The agricultural writers of the eighteenth century took little interest in the special problems of France, and most of them condemned French agricultural practice without qualification. The persistence of most of the characteristic types and better understanding of the economics of agriculture enable us to appreciate more justly this differentiation in practice. The general predominance of small farms, notable specializations between stock raising and cereal culture, and the importance of viticulture distinguish the agriculture of France from that of the British Isles. In many sections of France the establishment of completely individualized control of the land did not lead to enclosure as in England. The French landowners were unwilling to incur heavy expenses for building additional roads and for making permanent hedges or ditches. It is well known that some enclosures in England did not justify the costs, and it is likewise evident that the French peasants have been subjected to many inconveniences and costs by reason of the necessity of working many small parcels of land at a considerable distance from the farm buildings. No generalization can safely be made about the relative merits of these policies. In many instances the English improvers proceeded with undue optimism, whereas the French peasants pursued a penurious and shortsighted policy. The broader differences in the purposes and procedure of reorganization, however, rest upon substantial differences in the economic geography of these regions.

The right to pasture livestock upon the stubble of the arable fields after the harvest was the chief limitation of individual control over large sections of France, as we have seen in the study of the different types of village settlement. This right of common pasture was the first of the communal servitudes to be challenged by the new doctrine of individualism. The limitations upon this right appeared first in Provence. There was much wild pasture in Provence, so that the arable fields were not really a necessary resource. The influence of Roman law emphasized the doctrines of individualism that underlay the entire reform movement. It is thus hardly surprising to find even in 1469 a declaration against common grazing of the arable fields. This declaration was premature, for though it applied to the province generally, it was not recognized by all the local authorities. Actual extinction of this right came about by local action in the course of the sixteenth and seventeenth centuries. The proprietors were not required to put up any permanent fences; but they were entitled to drive livestock off their land if their land was posted. In Normandy the right of the owner to enclose arable land was recognized early in the sixteenth century. It was explicitly stated when the customs of the province were authoritatively reduced to writing in 1585. It was also held that grazing might be prohibited by any proprietor on land from which the crops had not been gathered. When applied to the extensive apple orchards in Normandy, this doctrine became highly important, because the fruit was not gathered until November. As grass or oats was commonly planted among the trees, these orchards were a type of improved pasture. In 1743 it was held that a proprietor might prohibit grazing on a field if it were planted with clover, or even if oats were mixed with the clover. A proprietor was also authorized to prohibit grazing on his arable fields if he had enough sheep to graze his own fields. These areas thus established at an early date the doctrines on which the general reform movement was based.

At the time of the inquiry of 1766–1767 there was little common pasture of arable in the west or south. With or without enclosure, the right had been extinguished in Flanders, Brittany, Normandy, Poitou, Languedoc, Provence, and Dauphiné. There was much enclosure in Saintonge, Guyenne (or Guienne), Berry, and Bourbonnais. In the central and northeastern provinces the older practices persisted with little change. Declarations by the courts in 1766 afforded authorization for the completion of this process in Languedoc, Normandy, Roussillon, and in some sections subject to the Parlement of Paris.

The administrative authorities then proceeded to encourage reforms in the other provinces. A series of edicts were issued for specified provinces between 1767 and 1777, authorizing enclosure of arable and extinction of all rights of common pasture over land so enclosed. The regions affected were the important agricultural districts of the upper Seine and Marne, the eastern provinces, and three regions on the Spanish border. Throughout most of this area neither the large proprietors nor the peasants wished to undertake enclosure. The more energetic farmers wished to protect forage crops without actual enclosure, but there was no formal authorization of this important intermediate solution, and as a result the effective reform of grazing on the arable was deferred until after the Revolution.

### Improvement of Waste Land in France

The waste lands adjoining the villages were likewise the object of much reforming activity. The great improvements of waste lands in France took place in the twelfth and thirteenth centuries. It was then recognized that the lord might improve waste land, provided that the needs of the villagers were not injured. This doctrine was recognized in the provincial customs, but the gradual reduction of the amount of waste land gave new importance to the qualifications. Complaints of abuses of the privilege by the lords at the States-General at Blois led to prohibition of further encroachments by the lords by an ordinance of 1667. But this ordinance was very imperfectly enforced, and additional protective measures were taken later in the reign. Villages and towns which had sold their waste lands under pressure were allowed to recover their rights. An edict of 1683 forbade the alienation of these waste lands. The ordinance of 1667 refused to recognize the right of the lord to one third of the remaining waste, but this position could not be maintained and the claims of the lords were recognized with certain qualifications. Whatever the immediate practical effects of these ordinances, they established the doctrine that the waste land belonged of right to the village or town, subject in some regions to the lord's right to one third. The primitive feudal principle was modified in favor of the villagers.

In the eighteenth century the reformers directed attention to these waste lands, and the general criticism of old practices included these wild pastures in their condemnation. After 1754 local edicts authorized the division of wild pastures in the provinces of Bearn, Languedoc, and Burgundy. Bertin, as Controller General and Secretary of State, and D'Ormesson, as Intendant of Finance, encouraged the division of these wild pastures, though no general ordinances were issued. Between 1769 and 1781 provincial ordinances were issued for Lorraine, Metz, Alsace, Cambresis, Flanders, Artois, Burgundy, Pau, and Auch. In other provinces division of the waste was authorized in many villages, and some portions of the waste were enclosed by lords.

No single policy was followed in this movement.   The lords and the richer peasants wished to follow a narrowly legalistic policy, by restricting shares in the waste to persons having some specific holding in arable land.   This principle would have excluded the agricultural laborers and artisans who had no arable land under any kind of tenure.   The lords claimed one third of the existing waste.   The administration, both central and local, exerted all its influence to prevent the adoption of such a policy.   They urged distribution to each family in the village.   Although much land was allotted to individuals, the movement proceeded slowly because of the sharp conflicts of interest among the various classes.   The government withdrew its support, because it proved to be difficult to protect the interests of the poorer villagers.   The peasantry as a group were indisposed to recognize the lord's right to one third.   The grazing interests, notably in the mountain regions, were strongly averse to any distribution of the wild pasture.   There was further division of wild pasture during the Revolution, but the second period of reform was likewise brought to an end by a tardy but genuine recognition of the interests of the poor.   In the end, considerable amounts of wild pasture survived in the eastern and southern provinces.   A little survived in the west, but in northern and central France the waste passed into individual ownership.

## Predominance of Small Farms

These reforms were dominated by the solicitude of the central government for the welfare of the poor and by the large mass of small cultivators.   Even in the eighteenth century France was characteristically a country of small farms.   These holdings were in the hands of three general classes of tenants: freeholders, perpetual leaseholders, and lessees for short periods of years.   The perpetual leaseholders were not owners in the sense of the Civil Code of the Revolution, but their position was fully comparable to the eighteenth- and nineteenth-century copyholders of English law, who have always been grouped with the freeholders in discussing the "yeomen" farmers as a class.   Despite a few writers who have taken the extreme position of recognizing only the freeholders, the majority of the students of conditions in France have adopted this general position.   All recent studies are based on the recognition of heritable leaseholders as peasant proprietors along with the freeholders. These leaseholders fall into two main classes, the *censiers* and the emphyteutic lessees. When the problem is thus defined, the tax rolls and Revolutionary documents leave no possible doubt of the dominant position of these peasant proprietors in eighteenth-century France.

The analysis of the materials is still incomplete, so that we have only approximate figures for large sections of France, but the general results are clear. The area owned by the nobles ranged from 9 to 44 per cent. The nobility were most important in the south. The possessions of the clergy rarely exceeded 20 per cent. Their larger holdings were concentrated in the north, in the plains of Cambrai and Hainaut. The bourgeoisie, industrialists and traders of the towns, held between 12 and 45 per cent of the area in different regions. The peasant proprietors held areas ranging from 22 to 70 per cent.

The general impression that one would form from the history of this agricultural reorganization may seem to be inconsistent with the violence displayed by the peasantry during the Revolution and with the complaints of abuses in the Memorials of Abuses (*cahiers des doleances*) submitted to the States-General in 1789. The explanation of these features of the rural situation is to be found in the pronounced feudal reaction in the second half of the eighteenth century. Increasing need of revenue from land impelled the nobles to search their title deeds for new sources of income. Obligations that had long been forgotten were revived, if there was no positive legal obstacle to the lord's claim. Many obligations to render services were revived and rigidly enforced, though they were not a significant source of revenue. The rights of preserving game were pushed to great lengths: pigeons, rabbits, and pheasants were bred for sale in the markets despite complaints from the peasants that the crops were ruined by the game. Such an attempt to revive the most irritating aspects of feudal lordship could lead to nothing but bitterness and defiance. The standard of living of the peasantry was undoubtedly low; as a class, the peasants were ruthlessly exploited by the collectors of the land taxes, and they concealed their savings whenever it was possible.

### Areas of Large and Small Farms in Germany

Agrarian conditions in Germany invite comparisons both with England and with France. The southwest was predominantly a region of small farms early in the eighteenth century, so that the

general features of agricultural exploitation were closely comparable
with French practice.   The history of tenure and feudal rights also
offers many parallels to the history of the agrarian regime in France.
In the northeast, on the other hand, conditions were more nearly
comparable to conditions in England.   The land was more directly
under the control of the nobility and landed gentry; large areas
were consolidated in the demesne farm and administered by the
lord's steward as in England.   Part of the land was let out to tenants whose status left them at the mercy of the caprice of the lord
and his stewards.   In the northeast stock raising was more
important than in the southwest, and in the last decades of the
eighteenth century the methods of culture on these great estates were
profoundly influenced by Flemish and English practice.   The detailed history of the region, however, presents sharp contrasts to
the history of the English Midlands, because the status of the
peasants was markedly inferior to that of the English peasantry,
and because the enclosures took place so much later.

The studies of Knapp and his pupils have identified the general
boundary line between these sharply contrasted regions with the

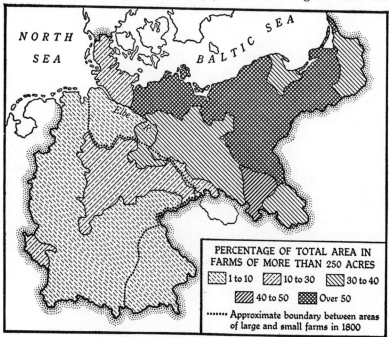

*Proportion of Large Farms in Germany, 1895*

course of the Elbe. This boundary is therefore almost identical with the boundary between the areas of large and of small farms in 1895. Bavaria has been included within the area of large farms in 1800 on the basis of Hausmann's study, but in the absence of statistical material the classification must remain uncertain. The middle German states, with only 10 to 30 per cent of the area in large farms in 1895, occupied about the same relative position in the eighteenth century. There were more large farms than in the Rhineland, but they were not such an important feature as they were east of the Elbe.

In the eighteenth century these holdings were for the most part unenclosed both in the southwest and in the northeast. The arable fields lay open, and the parcels of the lords were intermingled with the parcels cultivated by the peasants. The general scheme of culture, according to a three-course system with bare fallow, was obligatory for lord and peasant alike. In many portions of the territory east of the Elbe the establishment of the open-field system took place during the process of colonization. German or Slavic colonists were established on great estates; sooner or later the arable was divided into the characteristic parcels, and individual shares were allotted in the three primary divisions of the arable area. Although these great estates were thus formed in part by a process of improvement of waste land, they were not taken into unrestricted individual control as in England. The differences in the advantages between the larger and smaller units were thus more largely determined by legal and social conditions than by purely technical agricultural conditions. One must assume that labor was more effective when the peasants were predominantly concerned with an individual holding worked under conditions which assured them a definite right to a portion of the produce fixed in advance. In the maturely settled cereal districts there was thus a tendency towards the development of security of tenure, limitation of the obligations to the lord, and diminished importance of a demesne cultivated by compulsory labor service or hired labor.

### The Relations between Lords and Peasants in Germany

In German historical literature the differences between the west and the east are described in terms of the position of the lord. In the west the original rights of the manorial lord had suffered attrition as regards his relations both with the state and with his dependent tenants. The judicial rights, which were originally an important obligation, had been largely absorbed by the sovereign princes in southwest Germany in the sixteenth and seventeenth centuries.   In England the manorial courts continued to sit, but the scope of their activity was so largely restricted after the seventeenth century that they were of merely nominal importance.   In France and in eastern Germany these judicial functions remained important.   The military and fiscal functions of the feudal lord were likewise significantly curtailed in England, France, and southwest Germany.   The transformation of the erstwhile feudal lord into a landlord with a revenue from quitrents was, perhaps, more complete in southwest Germany than in either England or France.   But conditions of land tenure still contained so much feudal law that it would be extremely misleading to describe these personages as "landlords."   Though the authority they had possessed in the Middle Ages had been irretrievably lost, many of the symbols of power still survived, so that the condition in the eighteenth century is more adequately described as "lordship" (*Grundherrschaft*).

In the northeast the feudal lords were gaining new power and prestige throughout the sixteenth and seventeenth centuries.   They improved waste; they evicted many of the peasants and added the holdings to the demesne; the new tenancies created were invariably granted on precarious terms, and extensive labor services were required.   The eighteenth century thus found these lords solidly entrenched in a position which strongly resembled that of the great feudal magnates of the eleventh century.   They exercised many of the political and judicial functions characteristic of the feudal period, and by reason of their extensive domains they enjoyed resources which made them a power in the state.   Much of the land in their possession was not let out to tenants, but was administered by their stewards and cultivated by labor services.   These great estates closely resembled the administrative manors of early English law, in which the demesne farm likewise constituted a substantial portion of the total area of the village.   Despite important peculiarities in details, these estates can best be described as a type of the "administrative manor" (*Gutsherrschaft*).

The status of the peasantry in the southwest differed only in small details from conditions in France.   There were a few serfs, even towards the close of the eighteenth century.   They were perhaps more numerous in southwest Germany than in the eastern sections of France, but their legal disabilities were softened somewhat by custom.   In strict law the serf might not acquire any property on his own account.   Accordingly any personal property accumulated reverted to the lord at the death of the serf.   Thus, small movables and livestock accumulated by a serf would revert to the lord.   In practice this legal disability was reduced to the presentation to the lord of a single object in each class.   In some instances a money payment might be required in some stated ratio to the value of the holding.   The heirs, of course, had no right to inherit; but commonly the lord would accept the heir, or at least some one of the sons.   The serf was subjected to unlimited obligations to perform labor services.

The peasants, who had once been villeins with insecurity of tenure and obligations to render labor services, had secured their freedom. They became perpetual leaseholders with security of tenure and fixed money rents.   There were many small differences in the details of these tenures, but the broader features are common over large areas.   Peasants holding under short leases for specified terms of years were technically free, but their economic position was insecure and in many ways less favorable.   In southwest Germany the original holdings of the peasants had been subdivided, so that many no longer held enough land to support a family.   Such peasants had to serve as hired laborers or to supplement their agricultural income by craft work in industry or transportation.   Subdivision of peasant holdings tended to break down the distinctions between the peasants and the cottagers, though the legal description emphasized the original character of the holding.   A quarter peasant was one who held one fourth of the holding required for the full support of a family.   The holder might be no better off than a cottager, but he was classified separately.

In the east there were substantial numbers of serfs in several sections, but the majority of the peasants were technically somewhat better off.   Their tenure (*unerbliches Lassbesitz*) was in strict law a type of villein tenure.   They could acquire property, and in that sense they were better off than a mere serf, but their tenure was insecure and the heirs had no positive right to succession, though in most instances the lord would designate some son as successor. These peasants were required to perform labor services at the discretion of the lord, and their children were required to serve in the lord's household for a period of years.   In effect, there was little to distinguish them from serfs, and the Prussian emancipation edicts of the eighteenth century make no distinction between the two groups. In the absence of statistical material it is difficult to make comparisons, but one is left with the impression that the status of the peasantry east of the Elbe represents one of the lowest levels reached in any part of Europe over a period of many centuries. It did not represent a perpetuation of an earlier condition, but actual loss of privileges.

Unfortunately, one cannot assume that the difficulties were merely legal. Frederick William I and Frederick the Great were both deeply concerned with the "barbaric" treatment of the peasants. Frederick William I declared that he had himself seen peasants beaten with cudgels and whips, driven to their work like cattle. The ordinance of 1738 forbade such mistreatment of the peasants under pain of imprisonment for the first offense and for the second offense death. In 1750 the Countess Gessler was sentenced to six years imprisonment for "inhuman" treatment of her maids. Frederick the Great declared the sentence to be too mild, and ordered reconsideration. The Countess had escaped, however, and fled to Poland, where she remained in exile, despite the attempts of her husband to secure clemency.[1] At the end of the century, after some improvement, the condition of the peasantry was incredibly bad. For purposes of comparison, it is important to remember that the French peasantry, whose condition has been so widely publicized, were in law and fact "free" peasants in secure possession of more than one half the total area of France, subject only to fixed money rents and sundry obligations which were mere symbols of the past power of their lords. Conditions in eastern Germany were so many degrees worse that accurate comparison is really impossible.

Although the general condition of Germany was most unfavorable, agrarian reforms were attempted. The actual achievement was small. In the south, at Kempten, enclosures were made as early as the sixteenth century, but it was only a local movement. There were a few enclosures in Hanover (or Hannover) in the early eighteenth century, but there were no large results. In Prussia, under Frederick the Great, persistent attempts were made to reorganize the field arrangements and to introduce better methods of culture. It was impractical to attempt compulsory reforms in the state as a whole, but much was done on the extensive domains of the crown. Waste land was improved and enclosed. The demesne farms of many of the estates were "separated" from the lands of the peasants

[1] Goltz, Theodor, Freiherr von der, *Geschichte der deutschen Landwirtschaft*, Berlin, 1902, vol. I, p. 430.

and brought together in substantial parcels to be administered independently. In some cases, the parcels of the peasants were "consolidated," and the common rights of grazing on the stubble were extinguished. Some reforms were carried out on land of the royal domain between 1750 and 1753, but the primary reform work was subsequent to the Seven Years' War. There was much opposition from the administrative officials. In 1770 a Superior Commission was established to organize the work of separating demesne land from the parcels of the peasants. A general ordinance was issued for Silesia in 1771. The actual accomplishments were modest. In Brandenburg, prior to 1775, enclosures had been made in 385 villages, but in most of these cases nothing more was involved than the separation of demesne land from the peasants' parcels. The movement was important, however, in two respects: it furnished administrative experience which dominated the development of reform in the nineteenth century; and the experience with the modest numbers of enclosed estates developed new methods of agricultural practice in accordance with the requirements of the various regions.

### Improvements in Agricultural Practice in England

The early history of the rotation of crops is very inadequately known. The artificial grasses began to be used in England in the sixteenth century. Clover and the root crops did not appear until the middle of the seventeenth century. The date is marked, in a sense, by the treatise of Sir Richard Weston, *Discours of the Husbandrie used in Brabant and Flanders* (1645). But Flemish methods were very ill known in England, and modifications in the details of practice were essential. The extensive development of the new agricultural system did not take place until the eighteenth century. We have no details upon the history of mixed arable and stock farming in the Midlands. On the light soils the pioneer work was done by the second Viscount Townshend after his retirement to his Norfolk estates in 1730. It was not, however, until 1776 that Coke of Holkham introduced the standard four-course rotation, commonly known as the Norfolk system. The lean, dry pastures of the region were brought into cultivation, and with two forage crops interspersed with the cereals more stock could be carried than on the old pastures. The cereal production of the region was considerably increased. This general system ultimately had a wide vogue in all the cereal districts of England.

Pioneer work was also done by Jethro Tull, one of the glorious failures in the history of agriculture. He became convinced that the chief defect of agricultural methods lay in imperfect tillage and wasteful seeding. He was correct in his judgment of the importance of improved tillage, but he was seriously at fault in his contention that no fertilization was necessary. He opposed the use of stable manure, because the manure served as a carrier for weed seeds. His practical recommendations were therefore unsound in the form in which he made them, but he brought out important new types of agricultural machinery, and was the first modern experimentalist to make any systematic study of the physical preparation of the soil. His drill seeder was first brought out in 1701, but 'his systematic treatise " Horse-Hoeing Husbandry" was not published until 1731 (in the more widely read form, not until 1733). His experiments were repeated in France by Duhamel de Monceau, and later in England by Harte and by Arthur Young. The characteristic feature of Tull's system was the planting of the cereal crops in widely spaced drills or rows. Large returns were secured in proportion to the seed used, but Harte and Young showed that the yields per acre did not assure any clear profit above the costs.

All agricultural writing in the eighteenth century was necessarily empirical, because the unsatisfactory condition of chemical science made it impossible to deal adequately with the problems of organic chemistry involved. No aspect of soil fertility and plant growth could be thoroughly analyzed. The great improvements were thus based on direct experience. In the second half of the century formal field experiments began in all the more important countries, but the technique of these experiments was faulty though it was greatly improved by Arthur Young in England and by Albrecht Thaer in Germany. Judgment of the writers of the period must therefore be tempered by an appreciation of the conditions under which they worked.

Arthur Young is best known as a keen observer of local usage and as a vivid journalist. The journals of his tours appealed to the larger public, and under the circumstances possessed more permanent interest than the systematic works, but they do not give any adequate impression of Young's scientific interests and capacities. He was deeply concerned with systematic experimentation and with the general formulation of objective standards of agricultural practice. Both aspects of his work are significantly represented throughout his active career.   The first tours in England were made during the years 1767 to 1770, and all three journals were published before 1771.   The last of the county surveys made for the Board of Agriculture was not published until 1809, when Young's capacity for work was already seriously limited by approaching blindness. The first general studies were embodied in the *Farmer's Letters*, published in 1767, shortly followed by the *Rural Economy* (1770) and the *Course of Experimental Agriculture* (1770).   In 1775 Young began work on his *Elements of Agriculture*, a treatise intended to represent all established knowledge of agricultural problems.   In so far as existing literature and experience was inconclusive, new experiments were to be made.   He was still engaged in this vast enterprise in 1814, though his eyes made work slow and difficult. This project remained incomplete, but ten folio volumes of the manuscript are now in the British Museum.   Most of his personal contributions had doubtless appeared in print in the *Annals of Agriculture*, or in the essays, but it would be interesting to have a little more description of the unfinished manuscript than is available in print.   Young pushed his scientific research as far as the science of his time permitted.   In 1781 and 1783 he became interested in the actual constituents in the soil solution, but though he sent samples to Priestley for analysis, the attempts were without significant results.   It was not until 1837 that Boussingault demonstrated the relation of nitrates to plant growth.   The scientific work led to no generalizations of permanent significance, but it is important to remember that the observational work embodied in the tours and surveys was definitely based upon the field experiments at Bradfield in the years 1763–1767.   The *Journals* of the earliest tours thus expressed judgments that had been carefully tested by experimental method.

The tours were of great importance to the development of agriculture in England, because they diffused knowledge of careful management during the crucial period of great activity in enclosure.   The literary success of the published journals was, of course, only one phase of the matter.   All the material was collected by personal visits to large selected lists of farmers.   On many of the trips Young was extensively entertained.   In Ireland, for instance, he traveled four hundred miles without once stopping overnight at an inn.   He himself believed that few farmers ever changed their methods by reason of anything they had read in a book.   So we must think of the published journals as a symbol of Young's influence rather than as the primary factor in the introduction of new methods. For more than forty years Arthur Young was the greatest of the agricultural improvers in England. Government support was confined to the activities of the Board of Agriculture, established in 1793, but though Young obtained the secretaryship, his influence on the work of the board was subordinated to the inferior talents of Sir John Sinclair, its first president.

### Agricultural Science in Germany

In Germany the development of agriculture was dominated by the encouragement to systematic study afforded by the establishment of courses in agriculture in the universities early in the eighteenth century. The first chairs were established at Halle and Frankfort on the Main in 1727. Instruction was developed in the other universities in the course of the next generation, so that it was an accepted feature of the curriculum throughout Germany in the last quarter of the century. A body of systematic literature inevitably developed. The most important of the earlier works were the treatises of J. G. Leopoldt (1750) and J. G. Eckhardt (1754), and the collected essays of J. C. Schubart (1783-1785).[1] Most of this writing involved much premature generalization, but the work of Albrecht Thaer (1752-1828) was based upon so much concrete experience that it retained its practical significance long after the development of organic chemistry had destroyed the underlying assumptions of the analytical chapters.

Thaer had been trained as a doctor of medicine, but his interests were never entirely satisfied by his practice. About the time of his marriage (1785), he purchased a small farm near Celle (Hanover). He felt dissatisfied with current local practice, and proceeded to read widely in agricultural literature in order to apply scientific methods. The earlier German and English literature left him still dissatisfied, but about 1790 the English originals of much of Arthur Young's work came into his hands. He proceeded at once to put his own material into systematic form, though his first considerable work was published as an "Introduction to a Knowledge of English Agriculture" (1798-1800).[2] The general method of treatment

---

[1] Leopoldt, J. G., *Einleitung zu der Landwirtschaft* (Introduction to Agriculture), 1750; Eckhardt, J. G., *Experimental-Oekonomie* (Experimental Economics), 1754; Schubart, J. C., *Oekonomisch-kameralistische Schriften* (Essays in Economics and Administration), 1783-1785.

[2] The actual German title is: *Einleitung zur Kenntniss der Englischen Landwirtschaft*.

was not greatly changed in the maturer study published as the "Principles of Rational Agriculture" (1809–1810).[1] These notable treatises were the most carefully generalized studies of agriculture that had been published in any country.  The basic concept rested upon the thesis that plant growth removed certain elements from the soil, so that continuous pursuit of agriculture would be impossible unless these elements were returned to the soil.  Rational agriculture therefore required the maintenance of the fertility of the soil, and Thaer took this rather literally as requiring fertilizers that would add exactly the constituents removed.  This perception of the importance of a consciously conceived fertility program marks the beginning of a truly scientific concept of the problems of agriculture.

In the absence of adequate analysis of the processes of plant growth, Thaer was obliged to make a number of crude estimates as to the requirements of the plants and the effect of the different systems of field management.  He had no knowledge of the role of minerals in plant growth, though his theory was most significantly applied to the mineral problem.  His methods and even his generalizations were modified rather than invalidated by the development of scientific analysis, so that his works remained important and vital for fully two generations after his death.

Although the farm near Celle served as a basis for experimentation and reflection, it was administered upon sound economic principles and yielded good profits.  Thaer thus developed a reputation as a practical administrator, and as early as 1799 some students were in residence learning his methods.  A formal institute was opened in 1803, with lectures on agriculture by Thaer and in the natural sciences by Einhof.  Some instruction was given in mathematics and accounting.  Frederick William III of Prussia invited Thaer to come to Prussia, and in June, 1804, Thaer moved his institute to an estate at Möglin, a little above Rathenow on the Havel.  Despite the disturbed political conditions, registration in the institute rose to 106 in 1809.  After complete suspension of all work from 1813 to 1815 it recovered its position, and in 1819 was placed specifically under the patronage of the crown as the Royal Academic Institute of Agriculture.

In Thaer's work we find the best analysis of the system of mixed farming that developed in Holstein and Mecklenburg in the course of the eighteenth century.  Earlier descriptions were so imperfect

[1] The actual German title is: *Grundsätze der Rationellen Landwirtschaft.*

that the system was commonly supposed to be identical with the English system. Thaer shows that this North German system represents an intermediate stage in the development from fallow agriculture to rotation agriculture. In Holstein the system appeared conspicuously in the second half of the eighteenth century, as a system of alternating arable and pasture with enclosure. The main features of the system were developed in Mecklenburg almost simultaneously, but without enclosure. A fallow course was followed by one winter cereal crop and three or four summer cereal crops. There then followed a clover course, and after that several years of improved pasture. The system differs from the Anglo-Flemish system in the persistence of the fallow course and in the absence of any turnips. The cereal crops, too, stood in a different relation to the whole. The descriptions of field management in the English grazing districts are so incomplete for the sixteenth and seventeenth centuries that no certain identifications can be made, but it would seem likely that the process of transition from the triennial fallow was much more complex than is commonly supposed. The persistent use of artificial grasses throughout the early period would have required occasional plowing of the improved pastures, and once the land was plowed it is likely that some cereal crops would be grown. There is thus a strong presumption that this North German system of alternating cereals and grazing must have had some counterpart in the earlier history of English agriculture.

## Stock Breeding

In the early modern period livestock farming was largely a specialized type of enterprise. The grazing districts were located in the regions that were too wet or too dry for successful cereal culture. In large areas of France, Spain, Switzerland, and Italy the summer pastures were in the mountains and the winter pastures in the plains. The flocks or herds were driven substantial distances in Spain, in southern France, and in Italy. The longest drives were the great sheep drives of the Merino sheep in Spain, which moved the sheep from the winter pastures in Estremadura and Andalusia to the summer pastures in the foothills of the Pyrenees. There were long drives, also, in Italy and in Provence. This system of migration, called "transhumance," presented complex legal problems. The march of the sheep was protected by legal privileges held by associations of migratory sheep owners. Strips of land were reserved for the drives, and local arable farmers were forbidden to enclose for arable culture any portions of the reserved area. Restricted rights were claimed for grazing the sheep on the wild pastures of the villages on the route, though the villages contested these rights. All through Spain and Italy the contest between the shepherds and the arable farmers persisted throughout the early modern period. Agricultural reform in the regions of transhumance involved restrictions of grazing rights in favor of arable agriculture. The extinction of the servitudes of common use of grazing land thus assumed a special form, but here, as in the north, improvement in agriculture necessarily involved the development of the exclusive control characteristic of the system of private property in land.

More intensive forms of livestock-raising appeared at an early date in the marshy regions: portions of the Lombard plains, parts of Flanders and Holland, parts of Normandy, Brittany, and Poitou. In many of these regions cereal culture was not entirely supplanted by grazing, and it was from these regions that the modern systems of mixed farming developed.

We have little knowledge of the methods of stock breeding in vogue in the sixteenth and seventeenth centuries. We know that there were many distinct types of all classes of farm livestock, but little or no attention seems to have been given to problems of selection. New interests in crossbreeding developed in connection with horse racing, in England. A few fine horses were imported from Arabia and the Barbary states about the middle of the seventeenth century, and the great race horses of the eighteenth century were developed from their descendants. The most famous of the early eastern horses were the Leeds, the Darley, and the Godolphin Arabians, and D'Arcey's White Turk. By the close of the eighteenth century the English breeders had developed the English Thoroughbred, which won general favor as a fine saddle horse.

The introduction of Merino sheep in north Europe was probably of greater general economic importance. There are unsupported references to an importation of Merinos into England in the reign of Henry VIII, but the first authentic importation into north Europe was by Sweden in 1723. The experiment had no large consequences. A flock of Merinos was brought to Saxony in 1765, and another importation was made in 1778. From this second flock was developed the Saxon Merino which became so important a factor in fine woolgrowing in the nineteenth century. There were importations into Hungary (1775), Denmark (1786, 1797), and Prussia (1786). The flock brought to Rambouillet in 1786 became the basis of a distinct type which was of great importance to France. Flocks were brought to England in 1788 and 1791 ; from them are descended the crossbred sheep of the southern counties and later of Australia.

The most distinctive achievement, however, was Bakewell's improvement and standardization of types by judicious inbreeding. His contemporaries believed that breeding within the prohibited degrees of kinship was unwise and dangerous. Bakewell, however, showed that the standards of particular types could be substantially and quickly improved by close breeding from the best individuals. Beginning only about 1760, he had achieved notable improvements upon the Leicestershire sheep within a decade. He also worked with cattle, and produced much heavier animals than any before known. So great a secrecy was maintained about all of Bakewell's work at Dishley that we have only the most general notions of his methods and principles. In selecting his stock, he placed new emphasis on the ideal type to be produced, and in setting up these new types he gave more attention to meat than did his contemporaries. His work was thus new in method and in purpose. There was much discussion of the merits of his Dishley sheep, and some thought his cattle too fat. One wit said that his animals were too expensive to buy and too fat to eat. Neither his sheep nor his Longhorns entirely justified the expectations that Bakewell entertained, but his principles became the basis of most of the work subsequently done with livestock.

# CHAPTER 9

## ECONOMIC CLASSES

———◆———

### Historical Background: the Agrarian Classes

A broad view of European society before the commercial revolution reveals three main economic groups : landlords, lay and clerical; agricultural workers, who not only tilled the soil but also carried on various industrial activities in a comparatively self-sufficient rural economy; and the peddlers, merchants, and craftsmen of the markets, towns, and fairs. By the eighteenth century, economic classes had become far more numerous and interdependent, but their evolution and status and their radical transformations in the eighteenth and nineteenth centuries can be understood adequately only in the light of their medieval origins.

Many church officials were landlords, for much of the land was held by the church and administered by bishops and abbots. Even the parish clergy controlled estates known in England as "glebe" lands. During the era of turbulence and insecurity when Roman imperial authority was declining and being displaced by religious and feudal institutions, the church acquired extensive lands in the form of gifts and through its administration of wills and inheritances. Clergymen were forbidden to marry, and the wealth acquired by the church was rarely alienated. Its properties thus grew by a cumulative process till they included vast estates throughout Europe. Bishops and abbots claimed immunity from the suzerainty of secular rulers, but gradually conformed to the customs of the feudal and manorial system.

Invasions, conquests, and civil warfare devastated Europe, and owners of land, as well as the landless classes, were deprived of the political and military protection such as imperial Rome had provided and such as modern governments afford to their citizens. Defense was therefore organized by the more powerful or more fortunately situated landlords. Castles, monasteries, and even cathedrals became walled fortresses. To the barons, abbots, and bishops the smaller landowners surrendered their lands, either willingly or through force, and thus there grew up the system of feudal and manorial tenures based on an elaborate arrangement of customary duties and rights. The landlords organized armed forces and courts,

171

ruled their vassals and serfs, and collected rents, and in return owed the obligation of maintaining order and protecting their subjects. Later, when central governments arose and took over the public duties and obligations of the landlords, the latter retained their rights and privileges without counterbalancing responsibilities. This was the situation which existed in the eighteenth century in varying degrees virtually throughout Europe, and especially on the Continent.

The agricultural workers in most of Europe were reduced to a state of serfdom. They had certain rights established by custom or by court procedure, such as the hereditary right to till a small amount of land, ordinarily in the form of strips in the cultivated fields of the village or manor, and the right to use the fallow fields, the common pasture, and the woods and wastes. But they were deprived of the right to sell their holdings or to move, and were thus bound to the soil as a part of the property of the lord of the village. They were required to pay rents, usually in the form of a part of their crops; to cultivate the land reserved for the lord's own use; and in many cases to render various personal services to the lord. Customary obligations and rights varied widely from place to place, and underwent extensive modification by the eighteenth century; but where, as in England, serfdom no longer prevailed, rights largely disappeared with obligations, and the status of the peasants was in fact hardly less servile and often less secure than it had been under the medieval regime of custom.

## Historical Background : Classes in the Towns

Many of the early modern towns had grown up around the castles, cathedrals, and monasteries of the medieval landlords. The agrarian landlords viewed the towns with few exceptions as part of their fiefs, and imposed upon the townsmen various feudal and manorial obligations. The early stage of urban evolution was primarily commercial. The townsmen served mainly as middlemen for the interchange of goods. A natural development was the fabrication of materials coming into the hands of the townsmen, the merchants utilizing the labor of their families and other townsmen to increase the value of their commodities and thereby add to their profits. The former stage was marked by the rise of guilds of merchants, who were also in many cases handicraftsmen; the latter stage, by the growth of specialized guilds in which industrial craftsmen predominated. The guildsmen of the towns, unlike the peasants, were able to throw off their feudal and manorial obligations or to convert them from personal obligations into collective taxes paid by the town. They were also able to secure monopolistic privileges and regulatory powers which made the guilds quasi-public organs of municipal legislation and administration. Thus the burghers played an important historic role in conflict with feudal overlords. In some countries, particularly France and England, the kings utilized the hostility of the townsmen to the feudal barons for increasing their own power. In general, the townsmen gave expression to the dynamic evolutionary forces in conflict with the *status quo* of the immobile landed classes.

## The French Landed Aristocracy

The secular landlords early acquired hereditary titles of nobility and special privileges such as the holding of the principal offices, a superior social status, and, in many countries, virtual exemption from taxation. By the eighteenth century their economic influence was undermined in most of western Europe by the mercantile classes; but even in France and England they retained their titles, their social prestige, and many of their special privileges, such as exemption from most of the tax burden in France, and membership in the House of Lords in England. Many of the privileges of the secular landlords were shared by the upper clergy, including the bishops and the more powerful abbots. But the status of the clergy was adversely affected after the sixteenth century by the dissolution or decay of the monasteries, the confiscation and secularization of church properties, and the rise of simpler types of church organization and more individualistic forms of worship.

The position of the French landed aristocracy in the eighteenth century is particularly significant because of its relation to the revolutionary movements beginning in the latter part of the century. Titles of nobility in France as in other countries were hereditary, but new titles could be obtained with comparative ease. Patents of nobility were issued by the crown, and the royal revenues were increased by sales of patents to wealthy members of the middle classes. Some of the offices of state conferred hereditary nobility on the occupants, and there was thus established the nobility of the robe in contrast with the older nobility of the sword. The prestige of aristocracy might be acquired even by the purchase of a nobleman's estate. From time to time efforts were made to enforce more rigorous requirements, but by 1750 there were probably 80,000 noble families, many of them gravely impoverished. The more recent nobles from the bourgeois classes were often even more arrogant in the assertion of their privileges than were those of ancient origin. Although many of the aristocracy were not primarily landlords, land remained directly or through taxation in most cases the chief economic basis of their income as well as of their social status. They owned not far from a third of the land.

The bishops and the principal abbots were members of the nobility, although the monastic properties in the eighteenth century were predominantly urban. It has been estimated that the church owned directly perhaps no more than 6 per cent of the land of France at the time of the Revolution, but this was held almost entirely by the higher clergy, who also, like the secular landlords, received extensive manorial revenues from peasant properties. In addition, the higher clergy were the chief beneficiaries of the tithe, which, although usually less than the literal tenth, was often more burdensome than the dues connected with the manorial system.

In the eighteenth century, under the frivolous and prodigal Louis XV and under the serious-minded but weak and vacillating Louis XVI, the government of the country was largely dominated by the greater nobles, the higher clergy, and the court favorites. Their irresponsibility was cloaked by the absolute authority of the crown. Their dominant aim was to control public offices and public funds for private uses. Judges and administrative officials had often been drawn from the bourgeoisie, but high office conferred nobility, and members of the middle classes who acquired offices and titles usually sought estates to enhance their social prestige and to increase their income. Many of the nobles who lived at the court had small estates, many of them dissipated their wealth, and most of them neglected their lands. "The nobility in France," wrote Arthur Young in his *Travels in France during the Years 1787, 1788, and 1789* (1794), "have no more idea of practicing agriculture and making it an object of conversation, except on the mere theory as they would speak of a loom or a bowsprit, than of any other object the most remote from their habits and pursuits." They sought to maintain their incomes by delegating the collecting of manorial dues and rents to middlemen and by obtaining pensions and sinecures at the court, in the army and navy, and in the church. A large proportion of the taxes, which bore most heavily on the peasants, was diverted to the court favorites in the form of gifts and pensions as well as sinecures. There is the case of a duke who became a colonel at the age of seven. Abbeys, with their extensive revenues, were widely held *in commendam*, without the duty of exercising the functions of abbots. Some of the "commendatory abbots" were mere children. The extravagance of the royal household and the wholesale diversion of public funds and church revenues to private uses by pensioners and holders of sinecures led an eighteenth-century Frenchman to speak of the court as a "bottomless pit" and "the nation's grave."

### The English Landlords

In England the number of noble families was more successfully restricted than in most Continental countries, but there was a large body of landed gentry who belonged to the lesser aristocracy. It is often stated that the English landlords had fewer privileges and more responsibilities than the same groups in France. While this is true, it is a fact of great historical importance that as early as 1660 the English Parliament, controlled by the landlords, freed the large estates from feudal obligations and extended to the landlords the right of absolute ownership. In place of the dues which had been paid as a condition of tenure, Parliament substituted excises and customs paid by the nation at large. At the same time the land-lords continued to collect rents for themselves from the peasants, whose tenures thus remained subject to manorial obligations. Many of the English nobles extended their economic basis to include not only land but also investments in commercial, colonial, and industrial enterprises. Many of them, especially in the early eighteenth century, received extensive pensions from the state and held lucrative public offices with nominal duties. But in spite of the throwing off of feudal dues, they were not exempt from general taxation, and they often devoted themselves to larger public affairs. They encouraged their younger sons to use their own energies as well as turn their family prestige to account in working out careers in the House of Commons, in the army, the navy, or the church, in administrative posts at home or in the colonies, in diplomacy, and even in business enterprises.

As for the higher clergy, the bishops of the established church retained many of their medieval privileges, as membership in the House of Lords and a social status second only to that of the lords temporal. The more important monasteries had been dissolved in the sixteenth century, and most of their estates had been con-fiscated. The hereditary lords and the bishops alike, although they formed a powerful class and retained important privileges, identified themselves with the life and work of the nation to a greater extent than had the nobility in France. As a result, they were able to weather the storms of revolution and indeed to profit for a time by the reaction against the French Revolution.

Below the lords (the dukes, marquises, earls, viscounts, and barons) were the baronets, knights, esquires, and "gentlemen." Gregory King in 1688 estimated their total number as 16,400. Their land titles were no longer encumbered by feudal obligations, and they enjoyed various privileges connected with office holding and social status. Unlike the impoverished lesser nobles of France, they were usually well to do and active in the economic, social, and political enterprises of their townships and counties. They had responsibilities as well as privileges, such as the payment of taxes and the holding of local and Parliamentary offices without compensation. On the other hand, as justices of the peace, sheriffs, and members of the House of Commons they naturally were inclined to pursue policies in their own interest, as when they secured the passage of innumerable enclosure acts which virtually extinguished peasant land tenures.

The privileges of the landed aristocracy in England were somewhat tempered by responsibilities; and class distinctions, although rigorous, were ameliorated by a certain intimacy of relations and by a constant crossing of the boundary lines of classes. In Continental countries, as well as in England, the landed aristocracy had long been recruited from the ranks of traders, but in England the extent of interchange of agricultural, commercial, and industrial wealth in the eighteenth century indicated a peculiarly significant mobility and adaptability on the part of economic groups.

### Peasant Proprietors in England

A distinctive feature of medieval Europe was the restricted nature of land tenures. This is indicated, indeed, by the term "tenure," which is from a word meaning literally not "to own" but "to hold." Even the most powerful of landlords owed obligations, as a condition of their tenures, both to their suzerains and to their vassals and serfs. Many of the conditions of feudal tenure had disappeared throughout Europe, and especially in England, by the eighteenth century, but possession in fee simple was far from prevalent.

In England the larger landlords had acquired absolute title to their lands so far as feudal obligations to the state were concerned, but much of their land was still subject to the customary or copy-hold tenures of the farmers. These tenures yielded dues and rents to the landlords, and at the same time gave to the occupying farmers hereditary claims to their holdings. There were also many leaseholders for life or even for lives extending beyond a generation. Such long-term leaseholders should be regarded as having a proprie-tary interest. Farmers with freehold tenure owned their lands without obligations to the larger landlords, and some of them had holdings large enough to warrant the employment of hired labor or even the renting of land to tenants. In addition to the free-holders, the copyholders, and the long-term leaseholders, there were many cotters to whom custom accorded a proprietary interest in their cottages and garden plots and in the commons and waste lands. Even squatters, building crude hovels on the waste lands, were accorded in many regions the privilege of using the commons and wastes. But cotters and squatters depended mainly on wage labor and had only a slight and increasingly precarious proprietary interest in the land.

Gregory King's estimates in the latter part of the seventeenth century indicate that the number of peasant proprietors in England was approximately equal to the number of tenants, and that the amounts of land occupied by the two groups were also about equal. A large proportion of the land, whether owned or rented by the occupiers, was in the form of scattered strips or plots in open fields. Owners and tenants and even cotters had the right to use the fallow fields and the common woods and waste lands. Most of the common rights varied in extent with the amount of land held in the cultivated fields. The open-field system prevented the adoption of improved methods and placed the small farmer at a disadvantage economically as compared with the holders of large enclosed estates. The enclosures of the sixteenth and seventeenth centuries had consolidated many of the open fields and commons into large estates, and some of the small holders had maintained their rights in the form of farms somewhat resembling the compact holdings of American farmers. In the latter part of the eighteenth century the renewed enclosure of open fields, commons, and wastes, com-bined with the engrossing or enlarging of farms, virtually completed the work of abolishing peasant proprietorships. An eighteenth-century writer estimated that from 1740 to 1788 between 40,000 and 50,000 small properties were absorbed into compact enclosed farms, mostly into larger estates, though some of the enclosures

remained in the possession of the actual cultivators.   Readers of
Oliver Goldsmith's *Deserted Village*, published as early as 1770,
will recall the poet's view of the disastrous effects on the villagers.
After 1770 the progress of enclosures and engrossing became much
more rapid.   Many of the small holders of strips and of rights of
commons were virtually forced to sell their holdings to the landlords, who usually controlled the administration of the Enclosure
Acts.

### Peasant Proprietors on the Continent

French students of eighteenth-century conditions have estimated
that in parts of France as much as half of the land was held by
peasants with some form of proprietary interest.   But the long-
continued subdivision of peasant properties, described by a contemporary Englishman as "minute and vicious," gave to the
ordinary peasant in many regions not more than a hectare (2.471
acres).   Ordinarily five hectares were regarded as necessary for
the maintenance of a family.   One cause of the smallness of holdings
was the equal division of the land among the heirs.   Much of the
land was held by customary tenures requiring payment of dues.
Tenures completely free from seignorial rights were exceptional.
Most of the proprietors resembled the copyholders of England,
although there remained a considerable number whose tenures
were servile.   The number of French serfs in the eighteenth century
was probably about a million.   The freeing of the serfs had been
going on for several centuries.   Emancipation had included the
right to transfer properties by sale or by will, but the landlords had
retained various privileges.   Among these were the *corvée seigneuriale*, requiring peasants to work on their estates without wages;
the levying of fees for transfer and inheritance and for the use of
the manorial wine press, mill, and oven; the exacting of tolls for
the use of roads and streams; and the monopoly of game, which
often involved the destructive pursuit of game over the peasant's
holdings.   Many of the medieval personal obligations of the serfs
had been commuted to money payments.

Sée, in his *Economic and Social Conditions in France in the Eighteenth Century*, ascribed the modern predominance of peasant ownership of the land in France to the eighteenth-century survival of the
manorial system, combined with the idleness and irresponsibility
of the nobility.   The landlords were not interested, as in England,
in capitalistic farming by means of improved methods, nor were

they as powerful politically as in England, where peasant rights were destroyed by the sanction of acts passed by a Parliament controlled by the aristocracy and the middle classes. Many of the French landlords were interested merely in collecting revenues from their estates, and to this end preferred to maintain their seignorial rights. But these rights were swept away by the Revolution, while peasant rights survived without the encumbrance of manorial restrictions. Thus the gradual transformation of the manorial system in England, largely by the landlords themselves, resulted in freeing the English landlords from the limitations of peasant holdings, which were enclosed and engrossed for large-scale, capitalistic pasturage and farming. In France, on the other hand, the attempted preservation of the manorial system by the landlords for the sake of dues and rents from the peasants went so far as to revive many obsolete obligations. The result, finally, was the revolutionary overthrow of the system and the freeing of the peasant proprietors from the exactions of the landlords.

Land tenures and peasant conditions were far from uniform in France and England, and in other countries of Europe an even greater diversity existed. In southwestern Germany almost as much progress had been made toward peasant ownership of land as in France. In northeastern Germany, on the other hand, and especially in the Slavic areas, large estates prevailed, and although the peasants were usually allowed certain customary rights, such as the cultivation of a garden plot and the limited use of commons or of waste lands, there were many who had not even these rights. Most of the peasants in this region were even more servile and precarious in status than the typical medieval peasant. In some of the smaller countries, notably in Holland, Switzerland, Norway, Sweden, and Piedmont in northern Italy, much progress was made by the peasants toward the acquisition of landed rights comparatively free from manorial obligations. In a large part of the Continent the rights and duties prescribed by age-old customs afforded some measure of security but at the same time retarded the progress of improved methods of production and confined the peasants within the bounds of servile tenures.

### Peasants as Contractual Tenants

Peasant land titles generally in the eighteenth century had an element of tenancy. Most of the peasant holdings were subject to various payments. In those regions where serfdom survived, the peasants were also required to render personal services and in respect to residence, occupation, and even marital status were subjected to control by the landlords. But in England, France, western Germany, and some of the smaller countries, tenancy in the modern contractual sense had already developed extensively. Much of the land in these regions was rented to the cultivators or to capitalistic farmers. The conditions of tenancy varied widely. In southern Ireland, for example, the usual form was tenancy at the will of the landlord or rather of his agent, for absentee landlordism was prevalent. The tenant was usually required to make various improvements, which remained the property of the landlord on eviction or on the termination of the lease. At the other extreme were the long-term leases held under comparatively favorable conditions by large-scale, capitalistic farmers in parts of England and France.

As peasant tenures in England gave way, in connection with enclosures and engrossing, to large estates, many of the landlords personally managed their pastures and farms, or engaged superintendents, and carried on operations by means of hired labor. But tenant farming was rapidly extended, and as early as the seventeenth century tenancy at the will of the landlord began to give way to leases more favorable to the farmers, the landlords finding that in this way they encouraged improved methods and better care of their properties. During the eighteenth century, when enclosures and enlargement of farms brought about the virtual extinction of peasant ownership, leases were ordinarily extended on their expiration, and many leases were for long periods and even for life. Improved methods and the increasing demand for agricultural products added greatly both to the rents of the owners and to the profits of the farmers. Some of the yeoman farmers (a term somewhat loosely used to include all of the comparatively independent small occupying owners) willingly sold their holdings to the larger landlords and became prosperous tenant farmers. But most of the former peasant proprietors seem to have been less fortunate, and in any case tenancy involved a lower social and political status.

In France also there was a large class of tenant farmers without any claim to ownership. During the century preceding the Revolution, many of the landlords deserted their estates and lived in the towns, especially at the court. The lands which they owned outright, without secondary peasant tenure subject to manorial obligations, were rented to *métayers* (tenants who shared the produce with the landlord) or to farmers who paid a money rental. In some regions special forms of tenancy prevailed, as in Lower Brittany, where the tenant owned the improvements, and in the region of Nantes, where the vineyards belonged to the tenant. As in the case of peasant proprietors, the amount of land held by tenants varied greatly, being so small in a large proportion of cases as to reduce the tenants to the necessity of supplementing their income by wage labor. This was true especially of the métayers. They ordinarily depended on the landlord for seed, stock, and even tools. Half of the crop usually went to the landlord, and in some regions an additional payment in money was exacted. Tenants who paid a money rental held comparatively large tracts and had resources to finance their operations. Some of them, like the more prosperous tenant farmers in England, were able to secure long leases, to live in excellent houses, and to become village "cocks of the walk." Some of them even sublet their lands to métayers. But these wealthy farmers, who formed an "agricultural bourgeoisie," were exceptional, and many who paid a money rental were hardly better off than the share-cropping tenants. In addition to the burden of rents due to the landlords, the taxes bore mainly on the peasants, and discouraged enterprise by penalizing the appearance of well-being and initiative. Furthermore, the absentee landlords, desiring to avoid the inconvenience of collecting and marketing their rentals, fell into the habit of commissioning middlemen to perform these duties, and these middlemen or agricultural contractors were often extremely exacting and unscrupulous. And yet before the Revolution the condition of tenant farmers had improved, largely due to the rise in prices and the growing demand for agricultural products.

### Landless Peasants

In all of the countries of Europe where the feudal and manorial system prevailed, the peasants in theory had security of tenure, although the tenure was ordinarily that of a serf who was bound to the soil and viewed as a part of the manorial property. But even in the Middle Ages there were many landless peasants. Before the rise of handicraft shops in the towns, there was often a considerable degree of specialization in the villages, some of the villagers devoting their time primarily to crude industrial pursuits and having no rights in the land except a limited use of the commons and wastes. The larger manorial establishments required many domestic servants. In some regions the growth of population exceeded available resources of arable land. The landless classes were also increased by adventurers, vagabonds, and offenders against the laws and customs of the community. Serfs often obtained emancipation at the cost of their rights to the land. These were some of the circumstances which had long been increasing the number of landless peasants.

In France tenant farming on a comparatively large scale was encouraged in the eighteenth century as capitalistic farmers were able to make improvements and pay higher rents. The share-croppers, on the other hand, were progressively impoverished and many of them were forced into the ranks of day laborers, as were many of the smaller peasant proprietors. Enclosures, the clearing of forests, and the reclamation of waste lands, although less exten-sive than in England, nevertheless curtailed the customary privi-leges of the landless classes and the small proprietors and tenants in the supplementing of their income by use of the commons. The growth of domestic industry in the form of the merchant-employer or putting-out system gave at least meager opportunity for employ-ment. Because of the progressive decrease in the size of peasant properties due to equal division among the heirs there was a large class of peasants who owned fragments of land and were therefore formally classed as proprietors but who depended mainly on day labor. They sought employment either from landlords or more prosperous tenants or from merchants or manufacturers in connec-tion with the domestic system of industry. Similarly, many of the share-croppers retained their status as tenants but depended largely on labor for wages.

In other countries as well as in France and England many of the peasants and townsmen were dependent on casual employment, partly agricultural and partly industrial. An eighteenth-century curé observed that in large areas of the Low Countries the rural workers were slaves of two masters — the landlord or farmer and the industrial employer. P. Bonenfant, a recent historian of the Low Countries, states that "if there is one thing concerning which all the sources are in accord, it is the misery of the workers in rural household industry." From the ranks of the wretched land-less classes came most of the petty criminals, beggars, and vaga-bonds, though their condition seems to have been hardly more miserable than that of many of the small proprietors and tenants.

In England, as has already been indicated, there had been a progressive increase in the number of landless rural workers since the enclosure movement of the sixteenth century. Indeed the abolition of serfdom, which gained headway in the fourteenth century, was accompanied by the growth of wage labor on the large estates and by the gradual loss of those customary privileges which had given to the serfs an element of economic security. The transition from peasant ownership to tenancy, which had been going on since the sixteenth century and which gained momentum in the second half of the eighteenth century, was marked by comparatively large tenant farms, whereas in France most of the share tenants (the métayers or share-croppers) held extremely small farms. Furthermore, the abolition of rights in the commons proceeded much farther in England than in France. As a result, the proportion of landless peasants in England was much larger than in France, and their dependence on day labor was more nearly complete. At the same time, capitalistic farming for the market led to the fullest possible utilization of farm produce for profits by sale in the growing industrial centers, and deprived the day laborer of many former opportunities for gardening and for the consumption of surplus products. The decline of domestic industry due to the rise of factories further restricted the opportunities of farm workers to supplement their income. To some extent these disadvantages were counterbalanced by the opportunities for employment afforded by the development of large-scale farming and by the growth of the new industries connected with the industrial revolution. But the condition of the landless farm workers remained extremely wretched.

## The Bourgeoisie before the Industrial Revolution

The term *bourgeoisie* is usually applied to several groups, primarily urban, between the hereditary aristocracy and the working classes. The principal bourgeois groups were the wholesale merchants and shippers; the merchants and master manufacturers who organized industry under the merchant-employer system; operators of the larger manufacturing establishments, mines, and other industrial enterprises; the financiers; some of the professional classes, especially lawyers; and some of the more prosperous tradesmen. The term "petty bourgeoisie" includes, in its application to eighteenth-century classes, the ordinary master craftsmen, tradesmen, and professional groups who had establishments or businesses of their own and who attempted to maintain an independent economic status. Their ideals and ambitions were bourgeois, and some of them were able to attain wealth and independence.   Usually, however, they were not far removed in status and standards of living from the wage-earning classes, into which, under the pressure of the industrial revolution, increasing numbers were ultimately destined to fall.   Although the term *bourgeoisie* applies by derivation to urban classes, the wealthier tenant farmers and even the yeomen have been described as an agricultural bourgeoisie.

### Ascendancy of the Merchants before the Industrial Revolution

Before the industrial revolution, mercantile capital was dominant. Mercantile theory and policy exalted commerce to a position of pre-eminence in national economy.   In France, despite the reverses suffered during the wars of the eighteenth century, there was a fourfold increase in foreign trade during the seventy-five years preceding the Revolution.   The wealth of landlords was largely in the comparatively immobile form of land and its produce, and was widely scattered over large areas.   Mercantile wealth was more mobile, more largely concentrated in strategic centers, and more readily subject to instant command for such use as best suited the interests of its owners.   The knowledge and experience of the merchants gave them a flexibility of mind and a capacity to use their resources for controlling political as well as economic forces and policies.   Kings and parliaments early found that they could readily tap the reservoirs of mercantile wealth through fees, licenses, loans, and taxes in return for monopolies, patents of nobility, and other favors.   Merchant princes vied with the landlords in the splendor of their mode of life, and often indeed won for themselves or their children titles of nobility.   "Merchants are commonly ambitious of becoming country gentlemen," Adam Smith observed, "and when they do, they are generally the best of all improvers. A merchant is accustomed to employ his money chiefly in profitable projects; whereas a mere country gentleman is accustomed to employ it chiefly in expense.   The one often sees his money go from him, and return to him again with a profit; the other, when once he parts with it, very seldom expects to see any more of it."

The financiers — moneylenders, money-changers, deposit bankers, and dealers in bills of exchange and securities of governments and joint-stock companies — were originally for the most part merchants who extended their activities to include financial operations.   The Medici of Florence, the Fugger family of Augsburg, and various other early modern financial dynasties were intimately associated with commerce. The Bank of Amsterdam, the Bank of England, and similar institutions were largely controlled by merchants and were mainly designed to facilitate commercial operations. As was pointed out by Adam Smith, they enabled merchants to pay their bills, especially in other countries, "not in common currency, but by an order upon or a transfer in the books of a certain bank established upon the credit, and under the protection, of the state." In the eighteenth century, banks even as fiscal agents of governments utilized their resources largely for financing commercial wars and colonial expansion. Financiers, to be sure, often had no direct interest in trade, and profited by the embarrassments of merchants as well as of princes and governments, but in general the mercantile classes were closely allied with financiers even when commercial and financial activities were not carried on by the same individuals or groups.

The wealthier mercantile classes, especially in western Europe, gained ascendancy over industry and local trade as well as over finance. The craft guilds had flourished in an age of local industry and trade and of government by towns and feudal states. With the growth of national states, especially in western Europe, governments increasingly assumed the duties of regulating trade and industry, either directly or by subordinating the guilds to their purposes. These tendencies were especially evident in the sixteenth-century policies of the Tudors in England and the system developed by Colbert in seventeenth-century France. Grants of monopolistic privileges and of regulatory functions continued to be made, to be sure, but mainly to associations for capitalistic enterprises, such as the trading companies. Craft guilds retained extensive privileges but were subjected to public authority, and since they failed to adapt themselves to the new conditions of nonlocal industry and trade, they rapidly declined. This was true especially of the guilds of handicraftsmen. Some of the more important guilds, as the Livery Companies of London and Six Corporations of Paris, came under the control of wealthy merchants and financiers and were ultimately utilized mainly for ceremonial and social functions. Others came under the control of closed corporations in the towns. But regardless of the fate of the guilds, the craftsmen, whether connected primarily with industry or with trade, became increasingly dependent on nonlocal sources of materials and tools and on wealthy wholesalers even for the local sale of their products. The ascendancy of the mercantile classes over industry was hastened by the extension of domestic industry under the merchant-employer system beyond the limits of guild monopolies and regulations.

## Craftsmen before the Industrial Revolution

The craft guilds which arose during the era of specialization, following the decline of the guild merchant, included merchandising and service crafts or occupations, as well as industrial crafts or those connected primarily with the production or fabrication of goods. Many of the occupations of the era of guilds remained unorganized. Even in the eighteenth century there was no sharp distinction between industrial, merchandising, and service crafts, although there are clearly defined instances of each, as the masons, the fishmongers, and the barbers. Before the industrial revolution, most of the manufacturers were literally handicraftsmen, as the derivation of the word implies, or were in any case masters with a small number of journeymen and apprentices. Traditionally the sale as well as the fabrication of goods had been under the control of the master craftsmen, although many of the merchandising crafts depended on importers and wholesalers, especially when trade rapidly expanded and local self-sufficiency declined. The craftsmen made strenuous efforts to maintain their guilds, and in many towns, even in western Europe, they succeeded throughout the eighteenth century in retaining legal monopolistic rights and regulatory functions. But in most of the guilds none of the apprentices and journeymen and few even of the master craftsmen had any effective influence on craft policies. These policies were adopted and administered either by the state or by a small number of wealthy merchants and masters. Moreover, such apparent victories as the craft guilds achieved were largely nullified by the transfer of production and employment either to domestic workers beyond the jurisdiction of the guilds or to large establishments such as were ultimately to absorb both guildsmen and domestic workers. Many of the craftsmen, to be sure, such as barbers, shoe repairers, carpenters, and petty tradesmen, were slightly affected by the merchant-employer system and even by technological changes and capitalistic organization, and were able to maintain at least a precarious economic independence.

The extensive utilization of the rural labor supply by merchants and master manufacturers in the seventeenth and eighteenth centuries under the merchant-employer system led to the rise of a large class of semi-industrial craftsmen in various parts of Europe.

As early as 1665 the employment of agricultural workers in manufacturing alarmed the authorities of Burgundy, who expressed fears that farms and vineyards would suffer from lack of cheap labor. A century later the textile industries in the vicinity of Rouen alone gave employment to about 180,000 rural workers. In England, as early as the fifteenth century, craftsmen began to migrate from the towns, where the regulations of the guilds and corporate authorities restricted their freedom, and to establish themselves as spinners and weavers of wool, combining gardening with industry. The enclosures and loss of peasant holdings in England created a large class of landless peasants; while in France the holdings of peasant proprietors and share-cropping tenants were often far too small to afford support for a family. Landlords and tenant farmers were usually eager for their workers to supplement their farm wages with income from spinning, weaving, and other industrial employments. Merchants and master manufacturers who organized the industrial workers, on the other hand, were equally eager to employ people who could depend in part on their farm wages and their garden plots and who were less inclined to organize in journeymen's guilds and raise questions as to wages and conditions of work. Thus there grew up in various countries, and especially in England and France, a large class of workers partly agrarian and partly industrial.

The craftsmen of the eighteenth century had a direct and personal connection with their employers and with the creative processes of the workshops. The shaping of articles of use and ornamentation on the lathe, the last, the loom, the anvil, or the potter's wheel gave to many workers an opportunity for expressing their personalities in their work. Such advantages were largely counterbalanced by adverse conditions. Hours were long. The Abbé Bertholon observed an extreme instance in 1787 at Lyon, where many craftsmen worked regularly eighteen hours per day with only fifteen minutes for meals. In most of the industrial centers, as well as in the rural districts, the customary wages were so low and work was so irregular as to require frequent resort by the workers to poor relief. Governments imposed severe restrictions on the freedom of movement and especially on the organization of workers. In spite of opposing laws and authorities, the journeymen, especially in France, organized extensively in societies resembling in various particulars modern mutual benefit clubs, trade-unions, and secret societies.

## The Great Industrialists

As has already been indicated, there were instances of large industrial establishments before the industrial revolution, even if the phenomena included under the term "industrial revolution" are regarded as extending back to the early eighteenth century. These earlier establishments seem to have been larger on the Continent than in England.  Perhaps the most remarkable early modern concentration of capital and labor was the famous Arsenal at Venice for building and repairing ships and making naval stores and munitions of war.  There were such enterprises in France as a linen factory near Rouen with 350 looms as early as the late sixteenth century; a silk-stocking factory that cost 300,000 livres and a tin-plate factory that cost 50,000 livres, both about the middle of the seventeenth century; and sugar refineries in the eighteenth century at Cette on which nearly 500,000 livres were expended. In mining and smelting there were exceptionally large concentrations of capital.  The royal factories and those under royal patronage established by Colbert were distinctively modern except for their comparative dependence on hand labor.  The concentration of capital and labor in eighteenth-century France seems to have been due mainly not to technological changes but to the desire for greater control of the process of production than was possible under either the domestic system or the guild system, although toward the end of the century the effects of English mechanical innovations began to be felt.  In France, as in England, deforestation resulting from increased demands for fuel and lumber led to an expansion of coal mining on a capitalistic basis, with improved methods of mining.  As early as 1744 the French government promoted large-scale enterprises by an attempt to confine the coal industry to companies or individuals operating under royal concessions.  The slight development of large-scale establishments in Belgium in the eighteenth century is indicated by the results of a governmental inquiry in 1764.  The largest establishment reported was that of a firm of clothmakers under public patronage employing 434 persons, and of these all but 175 were employed by the company in their homes.

The rise of the great industrialists or the industrial "high bourgeoisie" and of factory labor in the eighteenth century was limited, except for a few notable instances, to the British Isles, and was a characteristic phenomenon of the industrial revolution.  The great industrialists of the rapidly expanding coal, metal, pottery, textile, and transportation industries have already been described in connection with the reorganization of enterprise. Their economic significance lies primarily in their competitive power, which was based on the superiority of the new technology, the concentration of capital, and the centralization of management. They frequently paid relatively high wages and drew workers from agriculture and the older industries. They produced cheaply new and attractive products such as porcelains and fine textiles; manufactured on a mass-production basis the articles of everyday consumption; transported their materials and products more cheaply than small-scale producers; and controlled marketing and credit facilities formerly under the domination of merchants. There were constant complaints, from the older manufacturing centers, of the "prodigious disuse" of goods made from wool and of the country becoming "cotton mad," but it is particularly significant that such complaints rarely came from the more progressive woolen centers of Yorkshire. The superior competitive power of the new industrialists in foreign markets as well as at home was early recognized. A writer in 1788 complained that the new great manufacturers, by means of machines, were destroying industry in the homes of the people, "engrossing" native markets, and mastering "the gainful tide of commerce" of other countries. The new type of industrial bourgeoisie in the eighteenth century exhibited little interest in political reform for increasing their direct participation in Parliamentary and administrative activities. But they were keenly interested in public policies and, because of their competitive superiority, were rapidly shifting from the old mercantilistic regulatory system to a demand for unrestricted individual enterprise at home, and removal of foreign trade barriers by reciprocal treaties of commerce, as in the treaty of 1786 with France.

### Factory Workers

Workers in the larger mines, smelteries, foundries, and manufacturing establishments before such enterprises became typical instead of exceptional, were often engaged for long periods and were granted comparative security of employment. This was partly because of the fact that labor was less mobile than under the later factory system. In addition, a larger proportion of skilled workers requiring experience and apprenticeship was necessary than in later more highly mechanized establishments. Many of the mining and metal-working enterprises were carried on under conditions resembling the agrarian manorial system, the workers being regarded as a part of the estate and dividing their time between industrial and agricultural work and domestic service for their employers. In Scotland the coal miners were regarded as serfs until 1775, though they worked for comparatively high wages, and their emancipation was described ironically by a writer in the *Edinburgh Review* as "in the same great cause they were enslaved in — the cause of low wages." In some of the great factories established under royal patronage in France, the workers were often employed under long-term contracts which could be ended only after notice had been given. But workers were subjected to a rigorous regimentation as to hours, control by overseers, specialization, place of residence, and even personal habits outside of working hours. Furthermore, their tenure of employment became increasingly insecure because of the competition of landless rural workers, small proprietors and tenants, and even of women. Even before the legalization of the employment of women in France as weavers, there were complaints that men were "on the streets without work while girls are employed at the loom." The cheap labor of rural workers and of women, combined with rising prices, undermined wages as well as security of employment in England and France alike.

The first large-scale transition to modern factory labor accompanied the growth of factories in England and southern Scotland in the latter part of the eighteenth century. At Manchester "cartloads and boatloads of people of both sexes and all ages" poured into the city, and the entire region experienced a "rapid and prodigious increase" which was described as "unparalleled in the annals of trading nations." Two thirds of Birmingham's 12,000 houses in 1790 had been built within thirty years. Within a generation the Five Towns of the pottery district expanded from crude country villages into an almost continuous industrial center. The manufactures of Manchester "enflamed the emulation of Glasgow," which rapidly became an industrial as well as a commercial center. Leeds, with 53,000 people in 1801, had more than trebled its numbers in thirty years. Innumerable towns expanded with unprecedented rapidity. And yet a large part of the factories were in rural areas. The location of the early factories was limited by the use of water power and by the extremely crude and costly modes of transportation. As a result, the old restrictions on the movement of workers from parish to parish were broken down and labor acquired an unprecedented degree of mobility. At the same time, the workers, when transferred to the new industrial centers, were almost completely dependent on their employers. This was especially true of the pauper apprentices — the children of persons dependent on poor relief — who were sent in large numbers from various parts of the country to the factories for the purpose of reducing the parish taxes for the support of the poor. With the building of roads and canals and the development of steam power, factories were more widely distributed, and at the same time the mobility of labor was increased. Workers were recruited from the farms, from the older industries, from the mountains of Scotland and Wales, and from the vast reservoir of indigent tenant labor in Ireland.

Mechanization, combined with the new mobility of labor, broke down the rules of apprenticeship, made obsolete many of the older skills, and subjected employment increasingly to a supervised routine. Enterprise came more completely under the sway of the profit motive, and the larger undertakings were controlled by salaried managers whose positions depended on the amount of profits they earned for their employers. These changes weakened or destroyed the customary relations which had traditionally prevailed between employers and workers. These relations had been based on the prevailing conception of master and servant with the master's influence and interest predominant. But the personal factor, reinforced by custom and by certain legislative measures, such as the apprenticeship laws, was not without advantages to the workers.

The transfer of workers to the new industrial enterprises, which were located in many cases in rural regions, accentuated the problems of housing, public health, education, recreation, morality, and prevention of crime. The traditional forms of community life and modes of social control were disrupted ; and modern conceptions of social responsibility appropriate to industrial communities were as yet almost entirely undeveloped. Individualistic employers, driven by keen competition and dominated by a desire for large profits and wealth quickly won, were rarely willing, even if able, to provide security of employment or more than minimum inducements to obtain an ample supply of labor for their immediate needs. The fact that they were able to command an abundant supply of labor under the conditions which prevailed in the early factories is perhaps not so much an indictment of the new types of employers as a revelation of the condition of the working classes outside of the new industrial communities and of the general eighteenth-century attitude toward "the laboring poor."

## Comparative Status of Old and New Types of Workers in Eighteenth-Century England

The "rapid and prodigious increase" of England's industrial population in the latter part of the eighteenth century was but the prelude to a cumulative expansion which was to continue for a century and to become a characteristic feature of nineteenth-century European society. But in England even in the eighteenth century many of the distinctive traits of the modern industrial working classes were apparent. The wretched conditions of the early factory workers and the individualistic and antisocial policies of many of their employers have often been described. The workers' status and the obstacles which prevented them from sharing more adequately the benefits of the unparalleled increase of wealth made possible by their labor can be understood and appraised only in the light of a comparison with their earlier conditions and with the conditions of those who remained in the older employments.

That the wages of workers in the newer industrial centers were higher than wages on the farms and in the older centers is attested by the widespread complaints of landlords, farmers, and other employers and by the rapid movement of workers to the factories. The men who compiled county reports during the last decade of the century for the Board of Agriculture were in remarkable accord to the effect that wages varied conversely with the distance from manufactures. These men, who were inclined to favor rural employers, made such typical complaints as were voiced by the Lancashire reporter when he wrote of "the advance of wages and the preference given to the manufacturing employment by the laborers in general." There were even complaints of "the influx of wealth amongst the laboring class," the formation of extravagant habits, and "the corruption of the workmen," who "see their advantage" in industrial employment, thus forcing the landlords and farmers to pay "high wages" for less efficient workers than formerly. Rural employers had traditionally paid low wages because their laborers could supplement their income either by gardening and the use of the commons or by domestic industry. Industrial employers of the older type, on the other hand, had paid low wages because their workers could depend in part on agricultural income. Furthermore, the system of poor relief had developed into a subsidy to employers in a large proportion of cases. The combined wages of rural families from both agricultural and industrial employments were increasingly inadequate, even for a subsistence, and were supplemented by poor relief. Enclosures and market farming, combined with the decay of domestic industry, left a vast number of workers with virtually no means of livelihood except the poor rates, which were usually much higher in the rural areas than in the industrial centers.

The early factories employed large numbers of women and children under conditions often extremely unwholesome. But the children of the working classes had traditionally been required to work either at farming or in domestic industry at as early an age as their strength permitted. The philanthropic Society for Bettering the Condition of the Poor approved the rearing of children in cottages, "half naked and indifferently fed," because thereby they became "hardier and better laborers than those in parish workhouses." Pay by the job in agriculture was favored by the society because the father would be more likely to take "his sons to the field with him as soon as they can handle a hook or raise a mattock" and at an early age inure them "to industry and weather." A clergyman who was regarded as an advocate of the laboring classes favored allowing no poor relief "on account of any child above six years of age who shall not be able to knit" or "of any child above nine who shall not be able to spin." Women were almost universally expected to work either in the fields or at domestic industry as regularly as their family duties made possible. Many dairymaids were required by contract to work from 3 or 4 o'clock in the morning until 10 at night, and much of their work, as in handling heavy cheeses, was such as to impair their health. Arthur Young's "model" family budget assumed that the wife would earn one fourth as much as her husband, a child of ten as much as the mother, and a child of fifteen half as much as the father. The joint family income, according to Young's ideal, should be no larger than would support the ordinary family in which the father, mother, and children were regularly employed. Others should expect to depend on charity. To the enterprising landlords, merchants, and master manufacturers who enclosed the commons, engrossed the peasants' lands, and paid wages which required a subsidy in the form of poor relief, the binding out of the children of the rural poor to the cotton "lords" by the parish authorities was but a natural incident in the policy of attempting to reduce the poor rates.

It has been held that one of the disadvantages of factory labor was the insecure and casual nature of employment. Traditionally, the farm worker and the apprentices and journeymen of the crafts had been protected in a measure by such laws as the Statute of Apprentices of 1563 and the Poor Law of 1601 and by customary rights such as the use of the commons. The laws provided for such regulations as the nature of the apprentice's contract, and affirmed the duty of the state to "set the poor on work" or to provide relief. But law and custom alike had largely broken down before factory workers became numerous. Casual labor alike on the farms and in the crafts was a prominent feature of the eighteenth century. Enclosures increased the number of landless peasants, and the rise of the merchant-employer system emphasized employments which depended on the vicissitudes of the export trade and the highly variable demands of capitalistic employers.

The comparatively unfavorable status of labor before the industrial revolution was not peculiar to England. Idyllic pictures sometimes painted of labor in workshops and on the farms before the coming of the factory system are no nearer to reality in Continental countries than in England. By way of illustration the case of Belgium must suffice. Among 340 rural communes of Brabant in 1755, the indigents in only 54 communes numbered less than 10 per cent. In 44 communes the proportions ranged from 10 to 20 per cent; in 63, from 20 to 30 per cent; in 66, from 30 to 40 per cent; in 47, from 40 to 50 per cent; in 31, from 50 to 60 per cent; in 22, from 60 to 70 per cent; in 12, from 70 to 80 per cent; and in one commune, 90 per cent were indigent. In five towns the number of indigents ranged from 15 to 43 per cent. The evidence, largely nonstatistical, indicates that later in the century the proportion of indigents greatly increased. In Brussels the number of infants reported abandoned by their parents increased from 1,220 in 1776 to 2,570 in 1785.

The factory system arose during a transitional period of social theory. Mercantilism involved a conception of detailed regulation in which the working classes occupied a prominent place, as their labor was regarded as the chief source of national wealth. They should therefore, it was held, be kept at work, if work was available at a profit to their employers, but at a subsistence wage. True national wealth was regarded as wealth above and beyond the subsistence wage of the workers — wealth owned by their employers and taxed, when needed, by the state. With the decline of mercantilism there arose the "system of natural liberty" or competitive individualism, based on the theory that the competitive quest of individual interests works out in the interest of all. The new individualism was applied in practice for the most part to employers only, and the problem alike of old and new types of workers was to overcome the one-sided nature of the prevailing *laissez-faire* policies which, for example, gave to employers the right of organization but regarded combinations by workers as conspiracies in restraint of trade.

But factory workers had certain advantages, under the new system of *laissez faire*, for their concentration in comparatively large groups made possible the beginnings of organized self-help. Furthermore, there was a sharper focusing of attention on the conditions and needs of the newer types of workers. This was due to several circumstances. The mere fact of their being gathered together in large groups made them more conspicuous and at the same time facilitated collective action to seek a hearing for their grievances. Unsanitary conditions and contagious diseases endangered not only the workers but the entire communities in which they lived. The conflicts of interest between the landlords and industrial employers over such questions as the corn laws, the incidence of the poor rates, and the higher level of wages in the towns, which tended to draw the better farm workers away from rural employments, caused the landlords to call attention to the conditions prevailing in the factories. Out of the new conditions of factory labor and the focusing of attention thereon a new sense of social responsibility gradually emerged. This found expression ultimately in a relaxation of the laws against collective self-help by the workers, as the Friendly Society Act of 1793, the Arbitration Act of 1800 for the cotton industry, and the repeal of the Combination Acts in 1824. It found expression also in the Factory Acts beginning in 1802 and in various measures, local and national, for promoting public health, education, and legal equality.

In many ways the condition of the workers was less grievous in the factories than elsewhere. The most serious factory conditions were attributable largely to influences originating outside of the industrial centers. The workers came largely from what may be termed the polluted reservoirs of nonfactory labor — pauper apprentices, landless peasants, and wretched casual laborers of the farms, the mountains of Scotland and Wales, and the hapless tenants-at-will of Ireland. The breakdown of custom, which had afforded traditional protection at least to the extent of a subsistence, may have been accelerated by the rise of factories, but was largely independent of the new industries. The guilds had long been declining; the Statute of Apprentices was obsolescent; the Poor Law had become an instrument for subsidizing employers, whose wage payments, especially in farming and domestic industry, were increasingly inadequate to support their workers; and the peasant's stake in the land was being destroyed by enclosures. The reaction accompanying the French Revolution checked the efforts of the factory workers to improve their lot by collective self-help, and at the same time postponed for a generation the effective expression of the newly emerging sense of social responsibility. The result was the triumph of an unrestrained and one-sided *laissez-faire* policy dominated by employers.

CHAPTER 10

# EUROPE ON THE EVE OF REVOLUTION

————◆————

## Disturbed Equilibrium

The twenty-five years of war and social upheaval begun by the French Revolution of 1789 gave rise to a body of historical writing probably more voluminous than the literature relating to any other period of the same length. Most of the records and writings have emphasized the military, political, and biographical aspects. From the point of view of the economic historian, the era is less dramatic and spectacular. Some students of economic history are inclined to minimize the importance of such periods. But an era of such profound disturbance, in which there has subsequently been an almost universal interest, requires at least an explanation in economic terms, and an evaluation of its significance in economic history. This chapter summarily analyzes the historical origins of the stresses and strains and of the social and regional disequilibrium that characterized the eve of the Revolution.

In the field of economic theory there has grown up an elaborate system of equilibrium economics, centering around such conceptions as supply and demand, prices and volume of money, marginal profits and employment. Our interest here is in the broader field of historical experience. In this larger sense, social equilibrium is a state of comparatively harmonious relations between individuals and groups and a comparatively satisfying adaptation of men to the natural environment. If these conditions are not maintained by gradual adjustments, they are likely to be sought by means of sudden and violent measures, such as those of the era of revolution in the latter part of the eighteenth century. Equilibrium is not to be confused with absence of change; for any society which aims at remaining static is destined to frustration by unforeseeable natural forces or by intrusion of rival groups, if not by uncontrollable internal friction. Many societies have destroyed or crippled themselves by resistance to change, which has prevented adaptability, thwarted gradual adjustment, and made impossible the continuity of the processes of life and progress. Such was the situation in Europe in the latter part of the eighteenth century.

In most of the countries of Europe the landed aristocracy had

failed to shift its economic basis to the rapidly developing commercial and industrial forms of wealth, and yet had refused to recognize the claims of the bourgeoisie to a share of political power and
social status.   The struggles of the revolutionary era resulted in the
ultimate victory of the middle classes.   Their ascendancy was virtually unchallenged for a century ; but the rise of the working classes
and the resistance of the propertied classes then created a new type
of social disequilibrium.

The revolutionary period was no less significantly marked by a
regional struggle for commercial and colonial advantages, especially
between France and Great Britain.   The outcome was not a reduction of regional inequality but an increase of British advantages.
These advantages Great Britain long retained, though other
countries, by the development of strong governments and modern
techniques, were ultimately able to reduce the disequilibrium.   The
importance of Britain's unique position and the basis of her ascendancy may be made clearer by a brief account of the earlier status
of rival regions and the historical background of British power.

### Decline of Southern Europe

In early modern history several circumstances aided the Italians
in playing a leading role.   They were the principal heirs of Roman
and Byzantine civilization.   Italy was the center of the Roman
Catholic Church, with its prestige and power and its vast wealth
drawn from all Christendom.   The extensive and highly profitable
trade between Europe and the East and between southern and northern Europe was largely controlled by Italians.   The country was
also highly developed in respect to agriculture, manufacturing,
finance, and the fine arts.

The later growth of civilization in other regions was necessarily
accompanied by a decline in the comparative importance of Italy.
This change, already under way, was accelerated by the Protestant
Reformation, the disruptive conquests by the Turks, the discovery
of the New World, and the shifting of Oriental trade from routes
controlled by Italians to the route around Africa.   But the decadence of Italy as contrasted with a decline in its comparative importance is traceable to other causes.   Italy retained good harbors,
an excellent location for carrying on extensive trade with important
Mediterranean centers and central Europe, a favorable climate,
rich agricultural resources, great wealth, highly developed industries,
and superior skill and economic organization.

Among the causes of Italian decadence was an antiquated political system. After the fall of the ancient Roman Empire, the peninsula fell under the sway of feudal principalities and city-states. When commercial enterprise expanded into world trade and colonization and when other regions of Europe developed powerful dynastic and national states, the city-states of Italy no longer sufficed either for fostering the new forms of economic activity or for protecting the country from internal disorder and from external aggression. Local despots and oligarchs prevailed or gave place to foreign invaders. Native and alien governments alike were interested primarily in a policy of extorting a maximum of immediate revenue by means of taxes on trade, industry, banking, and agriculture, and in gaining advantages over rival cities. Industry was further retarded, and in many regions disrupted, by the restrictive and monopolistic policies of guilds and corporations.

With the invasion of Italy by Charles VIII of France in 1494 began the long and dismal era of alien rule in Italy. The principal rivals were the kings of France and the Spanish and Austrian monarchs. On the eve of the French Revolution, Venice and Genoa were republics, though shorn of their earlier wealth and power. The Papal States, including Rome, remained at least nominally independent of alien control. Modena and Lucca, small duchies northwest of Tuscany and the Papal States, also retained a nominal independence. The Kingdom of Sardinia, including the island of Sardinia and Piedmont adjacent to France, was ruled by a native dynasty. Parma and the so-called Kingdom of the Two Sicilies were controlled by Spain, and Milan and Tuscany by Austria. Political divisions, guild restrictions that retarded initiative and large-scale industry, tariffs and taxes that weighed heavily on all forms of enterprise and that were utilized for the aggrandizement of petty local rulers and foreign courts — these circumstances accounted for a decadence even more serious than the decline inherent in the westward shift of the centers of trade and finance.

The decline of Portugal and Spain, after a spectacular but unsoundly based imperial expansion, has already been described. By 1789 they were no longer vital factors in imperial rivalry.

### Central Europe: Wars and Localism

Although lacking the advantages of a strong central government and of ready access to the sources of wealth opened up by the commercial revolution, the German peoples in the fifteenth and sixteenth centuries were prosperous and influential. Their prosperity was based on rich natural resources and a central location in relation to European trade routes. They carried on trade in all directions: with the Italian cities and especially Venice over the passes of the Alps; with the peoples of the Danube valley and eastern Europe; with their neighbors to the west; and with the regions of the North Sea and Baltic Sea. The economic functions of a central government were performed in a measure by the Hanseatic League, consisting mainly of North German cities. The trade of northern Europe was long dominated by this organization. Germans even shared the wealth flowing into Europe by way of the new route to India by means, for example, of firms from southern Germany established at Lisbon. The textile industry spread from the Low Countries into the Rhine towns. Industrial organization began to outgrow the limitations of the guilds, and large firms such as the Fuggers carried on enterprises throughout Europe in various branches of manufacturing, mining, commerce, and banking.

But prosperity and economic development were short-lived. The central government, the Holy Roman Empire, was essentially medieval and was never an effective unifying agency. After the Protestant Reformation its powers were merely nominal. The Thirty Years' War, which came to a close in 1648 with the Treaty of Westphalia, left Germany in a ravaged condition, with much of her territory absorbed by neighboring states and with the people subjected to the rule of about 300 petty local sovereigns. Most of these rulers were essentially feudal lords, interested mainly in dominating and exploiting their peasants and in exacting tribute from the townsmen for the maintenance of anachronous castles and of pretentious imitations of the French court. Gradually two outstanding states emerged — Austria and Prussia — and some of the rulers encouraged a revival of industry and trade. But wars continued to drain the country of its resources, especially the wars of Louis XIV, the War of the Austrian Succession, and the Seven Years' War. The petty sovereigns continued their sway. Thus the Germans, in spite of their great cultural achievements and their vast potential resources, remained comparatively weak and economically undeveloped throughout the eighteenth century.

### Wars and Absolutism in France

France in ancient times — the Diocese of Gaul — shared extensively the economic development as well as the general culture of

Roman civilization.   Later the ideals of feudal society found super-
lative embodiment in the feudal states of France.   But from the
middle of the fourteenth century to the end of the sixteenth century
the country was disrupted by the Hundred Years' War, the Black
Death, political weakness and discord, and the wars of religion.
The invasions by the English kings during the Hundred Years' War
came to an end in 1453.   Out of the disorder and weakness of the
feudal era emerged a strong monarchy, but the kings refused to
content themselves with the work of unifying and building up their
French possessions, and engaged in wasteful adventures in Italy
and the Holy Roman Empire, beginning with the invasion of Italy
by Charles VIII in 1494.   In the sixteenth century the wars of
religion ravaged the country, weakened the central government,
and made impossible the orderly development of economic life.

Henry IV, the first of the Bourbon kings, at length led the way
toward a solution of the religious problem by issuing the Edict of
Nantes of 1598 based on the principle of religious toleration.   It
was in the reign of Henry IV that the modern economic reconstruction of France began, with a reform of taxation, building of roads,
fostering of agriculture, encouragement of the silk industry and
other manufactures, and the establishment of New World colonial
enterprise on a permanent basis.   The reign of Henry IV also marks
the beginning of Bourbon absolutism, which rescued the country
from the grave disorders of the feudal era and of religious conflict
and therefore made possible the revival and continuity of economic
development.   But absolutism proved to be a heavy price to pay
for economic security.   The disruptive tendencies of the feudal
lords were curbed, but their extensive privileges, their comparative
freedom from taxation, and their powers to exploit the peasants
remained and contributed prominently to the causes of the Revolution.   Industry and trade were fostered by royal subsidies and
protective legislation.   At the same time, however, the tendency of
monopolies, mercantilistic regulations, and guild restrictions was to
throttle initiative and efficiency and to prevent adaptability to
changing techniques and expanding markets.   New industries were
introduced and foreign workers were encouraged to settle in France,
but the persecution of the Huguenots, culminating in the revocation of the Edict of Nantes in 1685, caused irreparable loss in the
emigration of highly skilled and enterprising workers and businessmen to competing countries.   Absolutism was costly in other ways.
The government was inefficient and corrupt in its handling of taxa-

tion through the farming or contract system of collecting revenues. It made an extravagant and enervating use of public funds for patronage and pensions, for the luxury and ostentation of court life, and for carrying on destructive wars of conquest. Thus in spite of her rich resources and natural advantages, the position of France on the eve of the Revolution was inferior in many ways to that of England.

### Russia: Absolutism and Isolation

Russian history and economic development have been profoundly affected by the outstanding geographical feature of the country — the Great Plain of northern Europe and northern Asia. There is much diversity of climatic conditions, natural resources, and races, but in comparison with the other countries of Europe there is a remarkable degree of uniformity. This in turn has promoted political unity and facilitated the building up of a state with more than twice the area of the United States with its territorial possessions. In the maintenance of absolutism the czars made effective use of the church. The powers of the early czars were traceable in large degree to their having assumed leadership, as princes of the region of Moscow, in freeing Russia from the Mongols, Asiatic tribesmen who had conquered a large part of the country in the thirteenth century. Later the Romanov czars associated themselves with expansion and the building up of the empire. Locally, the landlords held despotic sway over the peasants on their estates, but recognized the absolutism of the czars in national affairs.

The role of Russia in the economic life of Europe was limited by geographical isolation. Access to the main sea routes and to the great economic currents of the world was seriously restricted in every direction. To the north were the Arctic regions. Eastward of European Russia was the Great Plain of northern Asia, sparsely inhabited by warlike nomads. Access to the Persian Gulf and the Mediterranean Sea was obstructed by the Turks and other peoples. The trade of southwestern Russia was largely controlled by the Germans. To the westward, the Baltic and North seas offered only an inhospitable intercourse with the world because of inadequate harbor facilities and the maritime superiority of Germany, the Scandinavian countries, and England.

Russia was predominantly agricultural, although by the eighteenth century a considerable trade had developed by means of local markets and interregional fairs as at Nizhni-Novgorod. Transportation facilities were afforded by the great rivers. Russians had long been expanding eastward and had established themselves on the Pacific in the seventeenth century. In the following century they even laid claim to Alaska. But before the age of the railway, access to the Pacific had comparatively little economic significance for Russia as a European power. More important was expansion southward and westward, notably under Peter the Great, who died in 1725. By conquest Peter gained access to the Baltic Sea and built the city of St. Petersburg (much later renamed Petrograd, and then Leningrad). From the Turks Catherine II later won access to the Black Sea. Peter and Catherine pursued far-reaching policies not merely of breaking down the country's geographical isolation but of developing ports, encouraging trade, building state factories, and westernizing the economic and cultural life of Russia. By the end of the century Russia was one of the great powers of Europe, but difficulties in the way of world intercourse remained outstanding characteristics of the country.

### Decline of Poland, Sweden, and Holland

When the king of Poland acquired Lithuania in 1386, his realm became the largest country in northern Europe. In the fifteenth and sixteenth centuries Poland was the strongest nation of the north. Although primarily agricultural, the kingdom controlled the eastern and southeastern shores of the Baltic Sea, with strategic trade centers, fertile soil, extensive forests and natural resources, and opportunities for the development of trade and industry. Its natural advantages were neglected. An extreme form of serfdom prevailed, and most of the landlords contented themselves with a crude, semibarbaric manner of life. The potential wealth of natural resources and of the forests remained undeveloped. No one was responsible for building roads and maintaining conditions favorable for trade and industry. Townsmen as well as peasants were severely restricted, especially by laws extorted from the king by the Diets of 1493 and 1496. Legal status was given to the domination of the peasants by the landlords. The middle classes were denied the right to buy land. Various commercial and industrial monopolies were reserved to the landlords. Industry was discouraged by the general preference of the aristocracy for imported goods.

While the kings of France, England, and Russia were becoming more powerful and were fostering trade, navigation, industry, and colonial expansion, the kings of Poland were becoming increasingly subject to the landlords. After 1572 each new king was elected by the nobles, who were mainly interested in maintaining their powers and privileges. In the next century the members of the Diet, the parliamentary body, acquired the *liberum veto*, or right of an individual member to defeat any measure proposed by the Diet. A single member might even thwart the action of an entire session of the Diet and force its disruption. This opened the way to foreign intervention through influencing or bribing a member of the Diet. Under such circumstances it is not surprising that Poland lost its opportunity for developing into a modern state and that its Baltic provinces were seized by Sweden and Russia. Finally, in three successive partitions, in 1772, 1793, and 1795, the whole of Poland was seized by Russia, Prussia, and Austria.

In the sixteenth century Sweden superseded Denmark as the chief Scandinavian power. A separate dynasty was established in 1523 and its position was greatly strengthened by the secularization of church lands and monastic properties. By conquests from Poland, Sweden acquired important provinces on the eastern shore of the Baltic; and by participation in the Thirty Years' War she secured the German territories of Western Pomerania, the bishoprics of Bremen and Verden, and the island of Gotland — extremely important commercial centers which enabled Sweden to challenge the power of the German mercantile classes in the Baltic.

The natural resources of Sweden — forests, minerals, fisheries — were developed, and the iron, lumber, and textile industries were promoted, partly by utilization of foreign skill and capital. The power of the nobles was restricted. Extensive lands were sold to the peasants, in the latter part of the seventeenth century, and an independent farming class was established. A successful struggle was waged against the monopolistic power of the Hanse merchants. Commercial treaties were negotiated with Holland, England, France, and Russia. In 1656 the Bank of Sweden was organized. Trading and commercial companies were chartered and colonization was undertaken.

Economic progress was checked by the military ventures of Charles XII. In a series of brilliant campaigns Charles defeated the armies of Denmark, Russia, and Poland. He then attempted to destroy King August of Poland, and even ventured an invasion of Russia for an attack on Moscow, but his army was swallowed up, as was that of Napoleon a century later. Charles fled into Turkey, and Sweden lost its Baltic provinces and its territories in northern Germany. After these disastrous military adventures, sound economic development was resumed, but on a restricted basis. The failure of Sweden's brief bid for an ambitious role as a great power left the field to other peoples, and immediately to the western nations.

The remarkable rise of Holland and the circumstances accounting for the decline of the Dutch commercial and colonial empire have already been briefly described. The country was reduced to a secondary role by the continental ambitions of Louis XIV of France and the commercial rivalry of the English.

## Continuity of England's Development

The outstanding position of Great Britain in nineteenth-century world history was the cumulative result of a long and gradual evolution. The English had the peculiar advantage of conserving small gains and transmitting them virtually without interruption or impairment from generation to generation.

Before the eleventh century the British Isles were conquered in whole or in part by several invading peoples — in historic times by Romans, Germans, and Scandinavians. The Normans, who conquered the country in the eleventh century, were originally from Scandinavia but had long been under the influence of French culture. These various invasions were in fact mass migrations which contributed vitally to the racial and cultural amalgam of modern Britain. After the Norman conquest in 1066, the expansion and consolidation of the power of the invaders involved much warfare and disorder in various parts of the islands, especially in Ireland. The Wars of the Roses of the fifteenth century marked the disruption and decline of feudalism. The Puritan Revolution of the seventeenth century was accompanied by civil warfare and a destructive conquest of Ireland. Invasions of Ireland and local feuds in both Ireland and Scotland retarded orderly, peaceful development. But for the most part the early invasions provided the basis for the evolution of British civilization. After the Norman conquest the British Isles outside of Ireland were comparatively free from the disruptive effects of invasion and civil war or domestic upheavals.

Thus the outstanding position of Great Britain in modern world economy is traceable primarily to the cumulative effects of a comparatively peaceful and uninterrupted evolution. While her Continental rivals were invading and despoiling each other and engaging in frequent domestic revolutions and upheavals, the

English were slowly but continuously developing and transmitting from one generation to another the social heritage which was the essential basis of their ascendancy.  Their political experience included the development of the common law based on custom and precedent, Parliamentary representation on the basis of a gradually expanding franchise, and a flexible administrative system indirectly responsible, through the House of Commons, to the electorate. Scientific knowledge underlying modern technology evolved on the one hand out of the work of theoretical scientists throughout Europe and on the other hand out of the predominantly pragmatic and experimental traits of the English.  Educational and cultural facilities profited peculiarly by the comparative freedom from disruptive wars and upheavals.  The country's productive resources of labor, skill, capital, and economic organization were developed with slight interruption and were frequently augmented by the movement of skilled workers and of financial resources from Continental revolutions, persecutions, and wars.  Because of these conditions and by the aid of the traditional balance of power policy in dealing with Continental countries, the British were able to acquire and retain many of their overseas territories and commercial advantages.

### Great Britain's Natural Advantages

The comparatively uninterrupted and cumulative development of British civilization was closely connected with the country's natural advantages.  Among these was the geographical location, affording the benefits of separation from the Continent and at the same time of close association with it.  When Rome was the center of civilization, Britain, to be sure, was a primitive frontier country. But with the expansion of European economy, to the advantages of separation and nearness in relation to the Continent was added a comparative accessibility to the great non-European land masses and centers of population and enterprise.  The location, combined with the numerous excellent harbors of a highly indented coast line, facilitated protection from invasion and contributed to the expansion of trade and the control of trade routes.

The climate of the British Isles is mild, with abundant moisture and moderate winds.  Among its direct economic effects were the promotion of sheepraising and the textile industries.  The climatic conditions are peculiarly favorable to spinning.  Efficient and economical spinning, especially of the finer types of yarn, requires a restricted range of temperature and a comparatively high and regular degree of humidity. These conditions in the British Isles, and especially in Lancashire, made possible the development there of the world's greatest textile centers. The indirect climatic effects were even more important. Mild but invigorating, with few extremes, the climate stimulated outdoor life and sports and provided a constant and steady flow of energy. Obviously, no single influence, environmental or hereditary, can be isolated. But the climatic factor, in combination with other favorable influences, resulted in a long-sustained national expenditure of energy and in a cumulative achievement exceptional in variety and quality.

The natural resources of the British Isles are restricted by the limited area — less than half the size of the state of Texas and smaller than Norway. But the exceptional variety and abundance of resources contributed vitally to British power, both directly and by affording a basis for the acquisition of supplementary resources from other regions. The land, though not exceptionally fertile, made possible a varied agricultural and pastoral development which, until the latter part of the eighteenth century, furnished most of the domestic food supply, supplemented by the extensive fisheries, and provided in addition a large volume of exports. During the early development of British economy, when most of the exports were raw materials, tin and lead were among the "staple goods" or standard commodities handled by the Merchants of the Staple. Potter's clay, long used for the cruder forms of earthenware, became the basis, in the seventeenth and eighteenth centuries, of an important branch of industry. Iron ores were abundant, and after the development of the coking process for supplanting charcoal, they became, with coal, the principal basis, in natural resources, of the country's remarkable industrial advance. The abundant streams furnished power for industrial plants and also extensive transportation facilities readily expanded by a network of canals.

## Evolution of British Economy

In respect to enterprise and skill and various other advantages as well as natural resources, some of the peoples of the Continent were long superior to the English. It was a peculiar combination of advantages, making possible an exceptional continuity of development, that resulted in the evolution of an economic society in the British Isles with superior competitive power and that gave to the British a long-sustained economic ascendancy.

Before the industrial revolution, hand labor predominated and competitive power depended even more than in an age of mechanization on low labor cost as an element in the cost of production. English employers had important advantages. The supply of industrial labor was augmented alike by domestic changes and by Continental conditions. The transition by means of enclosures from village agriculture to sheepraising in many parts of England in the sixteenth century, and the renewal of enclosures in the eighteenth century for large-scale market farming, forced large numbers of country people to seek employment in the towns. Highly skilled workers from France, the Low Countries, and Germany found refuge in England during the religious persecutions and the frequent wars and political turmoils of the Continent. Many skilled Flemish artisans migrated to England, under royal encouragement and protection, as early as the thirteenth century, and aided especially in the promotion of the textile trades. Highly trained, independent, and vigorous-minded artisans and tradesmen migrated to the British Isles from the Low Countries during the wars with Spain in the sixteenth century and the later wars with France and with local princes; from Germany during the wars of religion and later during Louis XIV's invasion of the Palatinate; and from France at various times, especially after the revocation of the Edict of Nantes and the renewed persecution of the Huguenots. The development of the brass, copper, iron, and steel industries depended vitally on German and Dutch immigrants. The thousands of Huguenot refugees provided the initial skill and to some extent the capital on which were based such varied industries as the manufacture of silk, linen, cambric, damask, velvet, and other fine fabrics, felt hats, paper, plate glass and crystal glass, pendulum clocks, mathematical instruments, and toys.

Industry on the Continent remained for the most part subject to the obsolescent restrictions of guilds and corporations, and dependent politically on comparatively weak local governments or on the vicissitudes of shifting dynastic and imperial authority. These political conditions were especially characteristic, in central and western Europe, of Germany and the Low Countries. In France and Spain irresponsible absolutism restricted business enterprise. England, on the other hand, enjoyed conditions far more favorable for the protection and expansion of industry. Among these were circumstances, already mentioned, which attracted large numbers of skilled workers from the Continent. Various industries, especially textile manufactures, grew up outside the towns or in the more recent municipalities of the north, where guild restrictions were readily evaded and where new techniques and new types of industrial organization could be introduced.  The national government undertook the supervision of industry, utilizing the guilds to some extent as administrative agencies but gradually acquiring a flexible centralized control.  For a time the indiscriminate sale of monopolies by the crown counteracted the advantages of centralized control; but in the year 1624 the Statute of Monopolies restricted domestic monopolies to the granting of temporary letters patent for new inventions (including new industries) and laid the basis for the modern patent law.  Monopolistic charters continued to be granted for purposes of colonization and distant trade, but under circumstances which required national protection.  Furthermore, the joint-stock method of financing the chartered companies facilitated widespread participation and large-scale, flexible organization necessary for overseas expansion.  The Statute of Apprentices of 1563 and the Poor Law of 1601 marked the early stages of a policy of compromise between the interests of conflicting groups.  Wages, hours, and labor contracts were controlled primarily in the interest of employers; but the system of apprenticeship was recognized and the government assumed responsibility for the maintenance of at least a subsistence wage and for public relief for persons unable to secure work.

The gradual and cumulative evolution of British economy is apparent in the modes of utilizing natural resources, in the growth of wealth, and in the development of industrial organization. The ownership of land in the British Isles, as in most of the other countries of Europe, was highly centralized, and the rewards of ownership were high but were conditioned by taxation and by public responsibilities.  There was a tradition of personal management of estates by landlords, who were receptive, especially in the eighteenth century, to ideas of soil conservation and agrarian progress.  The land was freed at a relatively early date from feudal servitudes, and an individualistic tradition favored innovation.  The limited forest resources were so rapidly exploited that they were nearing exhaustion when the transition to coal, coke, and water power fortunately permitted conservation of the timbered areas.  The comparatively abundant natural resources were constantly augmented by expanding supplies of raw materials from abroad and were utilized with cumulative skill and efficiency.

The wealth of the country was diverted in part to warfare, but even the wars were singularly effective in promoting colonial and commercial expansion. Wars were fought to a large extent by allies won in many cases by subsidies and by the balance of power policy, with a minimum of direct participation by Englishmen. From early times there was an almost constant flow of wealth into England. The Lombard bankers gave name to London's great financial center, Lombard Street. Capital for the development of manufacturing was furnished extensively by foreigners. In the sixteenth century Germans largely financed the brass and copper industry. The Huguenots in the seventeenth and eighteenth centuries devoted their financial resources as well as their skill to the development of textiles and other manufactures. The long conflict with Spain brought vast sums into the country through the seizure, in peace as well as war, of Spanish treasure ships. The slave trade was one of the most lucrative of the many sources of income. The exploitation of the vast wealth of India brought salaries, taxes, and tributes as well as the profits of trade. With the growth of colonies, overseas investments began to swell the modern balance of invisible exports and imports. The evolution of British economic skills and business organization has been described in earlier chapters. This evolution was a result of the peculiar advantages enjoyed by Great Britain. It was in turn a significant factor in the continued maintenance of British ascendancy until other peoples, in recent decades, were able to adopt similar techniques and modes of organization.

## Strategic Position of the New Classes in Europe

The increasing pre-eminence of Great Britain in the eighteenth century contributed significantly to the instability of regional relations which culminated in the epochal struggle of France and Great Britain. Other regions played important but secondary roles. Within the various regions, the ascendancy of the aristocratic classes, in conflict with the growing wealth and ambitions of the middle classes, created serious social tensions. The rigidity of the institutional structure prevented an adequate readjustment of class relations, and the tensions found release in revolution.

The aristocracy maintained its privileges and political power, but the middle classes gradually gained many strategic advantages. The environment of the landed aristocracy was relatively restricted and sheltered; the contacts and experiences of the middle classes were varied and sharply competitive.  As a result, members of the middle classes were likely to be keener and more alert.  Their wealth and income, connected with trade, industry, and finance, were constantly gaining in relative importance and were comparatively mobile and adaptable to changing conditions and new uses.  Kings, in their struggles for power, became increasingly dependent on monetary income, which could most readily be acquired by encouraging as well as taxing industry and trade or by borrowing funds from merchants and bankers.  Landlords also borrowed extensively from the middle classes and, in the case of the petty princes of many parts of Europe, exercised the power of taxation.  These circumstances, during the transition to an economy of money and credit, were largely responsible for the development of mercantilism, already described.

The political advantages of the middle classes, finding expression mainly in the policies of mercantilism, were achieved for the most part indirectly.  Governmental agencies remained under the immediate control either of absolute rulers or of the aristocracy.  Indirect political influence was not without temporary advantage to the middle classes, for it enabled them to profit by public policies without assuming political responsibilities.  But irresponsible power was one of the principal charges against the aristocracy; and mercantilism itself was subjected to critical scrutiny.  The issue of a fundamental change in class relations could not long be postponed.

### Stresses and Strains on the Eve of Revolution

The disequilibrium of regions and of social classes persisted and found expression in the wars and revolutionary movements of the end of the century.  The stresses and strains of the period may be described in terms of dynamic ideas and ambitions in conflict with static or inflexible institutions.

The natural sciences since the era of Copernicus and Galileo had been rapidly developing, with dynamic and even revolutionary effects.  Science was based on reason and experiment in opposition to the prevailing concept of authority.  It fostered a new attitude of mind that found expression in the idea of natural laws, such as the Newtonian law of gravitation.  It gave rise to a new conception of mastery of the natural environment through knowledge of natural laws.  The method and point of view of the scientist contributed vitally also to the adoption of a new attitude toward social life and institutions.  Scientific and philosophical thought became increasingly critical of prevailing conceptions of authority in state and church, such as the divine right of kings, and class distinctions and privileges based on birth.  In social and economic life the ambitions of the middle classes acted as ferments analogous to scientific and philosophical ideas in the intellectual world.  Beneath the middle classes were the peasants and the workers of the towns, who, though ordinarily passive and silent, were far from contented or immune from ideas of change and improvement of their status.

When one turns from the dynamic ideas and ambitions of the eighteenth century and considers the institutions of that time, there is apparent, in striking contrast, a rigidity, a resistance to change.  The unyielding nature of the institutional structure thwarted alike the Parliamentary reformers of Great Britain and the intellectuals such as Voltaire and Rousseau of France and even the enlightened despots such as Joseph II of Austria.

With few exceptions governments were hereditary and absolute.  Even in Great Britain, the House of Commons, because of the restricted franchise and the extremely unequal rotten-borough system of representation, was dominated by the hereditary aristocracy.  Everywhere the ruling classes, profiting by the *status quo*, and irresponsible in their exercise of power, opposed the changes which the middle classes and the intellectuals were demanding.

In the realm of religious institutions, after the struggles of the sixteenth and seventeenth centuries between Protestants and Catholics had subsided, the relative status of the two main groups of western Christendom was clearly defined.  Reforming zeal declined, although there were zealous nonconformist movements, as Methodism in England.  Both the Catholics and the Protestants emphasized forms and ceremonies and exerted themselves most vigorously for the maintenance of their privileged position in respect to titles and dignities, ecclesiastical properties, official recognition, and taxation.

Urban institutions had grown out of the struggles of townsmen to free themselves from the feudal lords.  Town governments were usually based on charters which, when granted, represented a significant advance toward self-government.  But in most of Europe, even in a large proportion of British municipalities, nominal self-government had degenerated into government by closed corporations interested mainly in preserving for themselves the privileges which had been won by the whole body of citizens.  Thus the charters, originally instruments of liberty, had become bulwarks of special privilege and of resistance to change. The guilds and industrial corporations, like the town governments, had early stood for municipal liberties and had exercised important functions, protective and regulatory. But by the eighteenth century they were restrictive, monopolistic, and opposed to change. Their influence had declined, and other institutions, as the great mercantile and banking houses and joint-stock companies, had brought about, in many regions and aspects of economic life, a reorganization of enterprise. But many of these "exclusive companies," as Adam Smith called them, as well as the earlier guilds and corporations, were described by the great Scotch writer as "nuisances in every respect." "The usual corporation spirit," he wrote with a fine scorn, "wherever the law does not restrain it, prevails in the regulated companies."

The aristocratic classes, with irresponsible power and with special privileges embodied in the hereditary institutions of government and of obsolescent feudalism, were the main bulwarks of the old regime. At the same time, even the towns, with their varied interests, many-sided activities, and progressive influences, afford evidences of the prevailing resistance to change. It is true that institutional life normally tends to assume fixed forms utilized for the maintenance of vested interests; but the eighteenth century was characterized not only by unusual institutional inflexibility but also by the rapid emergence of new ideas and group interests. The result was the creation of social stresses and strains which culminated in revolution. The revolutionary movement soon involved other countries as well as France, and regional as well as social disequilibrium became an outstanding factor in the quarter century of conflict.

# PART III. THE AGE OF REVOLUTIONS, 1789–1832

CHAPTER 11

## THE FRENCH REVOLUTION

————◆————

### Revolutionary Economic and Social Thought

Adam Smith and the physiocrats, whose criticisms of mercantilism were summarized in the discussion of that subject, extended their attacks to other phases of the old regime.  Adam Smith, for example, described many of the universities and learned societies as "sanctuaries" of "exploded ideas and obsolete prejudices."  These writers shared the critical, rational, and individualistic views of a large group of thinkers, among whom Voltaire achieved outstanding fame and influence.

There were thousands of books and pamphlets and many periodicals which exhibited as a common characteristic a skeptical and critical view of contemporary society and institutions.  Voltaire's pre-eminence was based not so much on his originality as on his versatility, cleverness, and ability as a popularizer of ideas.  A stream of essays, histories, plays, poems, and letters flowed from his pen.  He early accepted the skeptical ideas and imitated the ironical method of Pierre Bayle's *Critical and Philosophical Dictionary*, published in 1697.  While in exile in England Voltaire became an admirer of English "liberty," and in his *Letters Concerning the English Nation* (or *Lettres Philosophiques*) he wittily contrasted his more or less imaginary conceptions of English life with conditions in France.  The individualistic control of the land in England promoted a limited form of liberalism among the aristocracy, who at the same time had a far greater sense of social responsibility than the nobility of France.  The powers of the crown and the privileges of the church had also been greatly curtailed.  Voltaire's special aversion was the church, but hardly any phase of contemporary society in France and other Continental countries escaped his withering wit and sarcasm.

A multitude of other writers, not only in France but in other countries as well, advocated ideas which were essentially destructive.  They paid little attention to constructive plans for replacing what

215

they wished to overthrow. Most of them in reality were not opposed to political absolutism and were strongly attached to conceptions of private property, social inequality, and even aristocracy. They had somewhat vague ideas of a "natural" order of society; but their influence was primarily critical and destructive, and yet they had little conception of the forces which were being unleashed by their attacks on the old order.

In contrast with the critical and rational writers exemplified by Voltaire, there were various others who attacked the old regime in a different manner. They were more inclined to recognize the non-rational, emotional, and social aspects of life. Many of them advocated constructive programs based on such conceptions as the social contract, natural rights, the will of the people, and even the socialization of capital. This group of thinkers, or type of thinking, was exemplified pre-eminently by Jean Jacques Rousseau.

Rousseau, like Voltaire, borrowed freely from other writers, foreign as well as French. He owed much to John Locke's doctrine of government as a social contract based on the laws of nature, and also to Locke's *Thoughts Concerning Education* and *Letters on Toleration*. His skepticism concerning the adequacy of reason resembles the attitude of Montaigne, who, in the sixteenth century, argued that reason alone cannot suffice for attaining the truth. Rousseau's personal maladjustments and experiences gave to his writings a deep emotional tone. He began his famous treatise on education, *Émile*, by declaring that "All things are good as their Author made them, but everything degenerates in the hands of man." He denounced "the vicious social institutions" in which men are submerged, and counseled men to "observe nature and follow the path she traces." In his *Social Contract* and other works he declared that men are naturally virtuous but have been corrupted by the selfish interests of the few, who had acquired domination by the power of private property and of social institutions and customs based on property. He held that natural rights and natural virtue could be restored only by uprooting existing institutions and establishing a society based on natural laws and the unfettered will of the people.

The idea of private property as the source of social evils had been taught by various writers, as by Thomas More in his *Utopia* and by certain obscure writers of seventeenth-century England, such as Gerrard Winstanley, who proposed a system of laws for the government of a communistic commonwealth. Morelly and Mably, contemporaries of Rousseau, utilized the same general conceptions of natural rights, inherent equality, and native human virtue, but went farther even than Rousseau in developing an elaborate program for social reconstruction on the basis of the socialization of capital. These writers, like Rousseau, emphasized the role of education in rescuing men from their debased condition and in guiding and disciplining the will of the people in the new society to be established on the ruins of the old.

Few of the revolutionary thinkers of the age, whether belonging to the rationally critical type, as Voltaire, or to the emotional group exemplified by Rousseau, possessed any adequate historical knowledge or sense of the organic nature of social change. But their combined influence in precipitating revolutionary change was perhaps enhanced by this defect. Men of the skeptical and rational type destroyed faith in existing institutions and provided an armory of facts and ideas. Men of the emotional type, with their emphasis on natural rights, natural virtues, equality, and the doctrine of the sovereignty of the people, stirred the feelings, furnished a vague but popular program, and stimulated the impulses and the will to act. In a vital sense the French Revolution was a product of the union of the "enlightened" thought of such men as Voltaire and of the far deeper and more compelling impulses to action generated by the philosophy of men of the type of Rousseau.

## The Pressure of Events

The critics of the old regime were confronted by an institutional system which was irresponsible and theoretically absolute but which in fact proved to be powerless either to bring about the minimum of reform necessary for its own preservation or to suppress criticism. Ministers of the king, and especially the great churchmen, occasionally tried to silence the critics, but many of the brilliant wits in court circles were viewed as sources of amusement and diversion.

Louis XIV, who died in 1715, had warned his grandson and heir against pursuing his own follies of war and extravagance. The Duke of Orleans, regent during Louis XV's minority, and the king himself when he came of age, ignored the advice. They plunged the country into a succession of wars, already described in connection with the eighteenth-century struggle for empire. They maintained and increased the extravagances of court life, supporting a growing army of greedy sycophants, pensioners, and holders of sinecures. They financed their expenditures by an antiquated, inequitable, and oppressive system of taxation, supplemented by an increasing dependence on loans. Louis XVI, during whose reign the Revolution occurred, was an absolute monarch in name only and was in reality a victim of the irresponsible system and the army of beneficiaries which it had created.

The system of taxation included the *taille*, or land tax; personal taxes on certain forms of income; the *corvée*, a work tax for road construction and upkeep; and other direct taxes falling mainly on the peasants. There were also various indirect taxes, such as levies on the sale and transport of goods, excises on salt and tobacco, and tariffs on imports. Many of the wealthier landlords were exempt from the land tax, and the personal taxes were levied with extreme inequality. Types of taxation and modes of collecting them varied in different parts of the country. Some of the indirect taxes were collected by contractors or tax farmers, who paid the government a lump sum and exacted from the people as much as possible in addition. The opposition to taxation was caused not so much by its nature as its lack of uniformity, its inequalities, and the exemption of those who could most readily pay; by the inefficient and oppressive methods of collection; and by the extravagant, corrupt, and irresponsible expenditures.

In 1774 the administration of finances was placed in the hands of Turgot, a friend of the physiocrats and a 'vigorous but somewhat tactless reformer. He was soon forced to resign because of the opposition of pensioners, tax-exempt nobles and clergy, tax farmers, and monopolists in trade and industry. Turgot's successor, Necker, a banker, temporarily won the support of the privileged classes by a policy of liberal expenditures. He won the confidence of the public by his *Compte Rendu*. This first public statement of royal finances purported to reveal the condition of the treasury but in fact juggled the figures for the purpose of bolstering the public credit. Finally Necker began to face realities, including the problem of financing the intervention of France in the American Revolution. His proposals for returning to Turgot's policy of reform and retrenchment, combined with factional opposition of other members of the king's ministry, led to his downfall. His successors found it increasingly difficult to float loans. The government was faced with the necessity of curtailing expenditures or of reforming the system of taxation by abolishing exemptions and inequalities. The interest on the debt had indeed become so large that any possible curtailment of expenditures would have been insufficient. But neither economy nor reform was acceptable to the courtiers and advisers of the king, and his ignorance and weakness of will subjected him to their domination.

Public debts incurred in wars and ever augmented by the insatiable greed of pensioners, courtiers, and tax-exempt nobles and clergymen culminated finally in the acknowledged bankruptcy of the government. The Assembly of Notables, called together in January, 1787, refused to concede to the king's ministers the right to tax them, and even demanded the dismissal of Calonne, the new minister of finance. Calonne's successor, in his attempts to levy new taxes and float new loans, encountered the hostility of the Parlement of Paris, a judicial body, which declared that the States-General should be called to deal with the financial crisis. The abolition of the Parlement was then decreed, but this aroused an ominous popular clamor in support of the judges of the Parlement and in favor of the calling of the States-General. It was under these circumstances that Louis XVI decided to convene the States-General as the only remaining expedient for securing financial support. In accordance with precedents which had governed the medieval election of members of the States-General, local groups of electors were directed to present *cahiers* containing suggestions as to the work to be done.

Most of the constituencies drew up *cahiers*, and these documents reveal on the one hand the conditions immediately preceding the Revolution and on the other hand the nation-wide acceptance of the ideas of such men as Voltaire and Rousseau. The election conformed to the medieval tradition of representation of the three estates — clergymen, nobles, and commoners — and the *cahiers* afford evidence of the point of view of the three classes.

The *cahiers* of all three of the estates were in agreement as to the desirability of constitutional government in place of royal absolutism, although the commoners went farther in their criticism of absolutism and in their views concerning the powers of the States-General and the reforms it should bring about. So grave was the financial status of the government, and so thoroughgoing had been the criticism of the fiscal system, that even the clergy and the nobles bowed to the inevitable and in most of the *cahiers* agreed to give up their exemptions from taxation. Proposed reforms and innovations included virtually every phase of French social life. The most popular demands in the *cahiers* of the third estate concerned the elimination of the privileges and inequalities not only of the nobles and the clergy but also of the monopolistic guilds, royal pensioners, and officeholders. They urged that appointments to public positions, whether in civil offices or in the armed forces or in the church, should be based on talent and ability; that members of the nobility should be allowed to engage in business and the professions without loss of status; and that the monopolistic and restrictive powers of the members of guilds should be eliminated. The idea seems to have prevailed that the desired changes could be achieved readily and peacefully.

## The National Assembly's Policy of Liberation

When the States-General (or Estates General) assembled on May 5, 1789, the representatives of the third estate demanded that the three estates meet jointly and vote by head and not separately with vote by estates. In order to enforce their view they finally resorted to the first revolutionary act by declaring themselves, contrary to the order of the king, a National Assembly, and by inviting the nobles and clergy to join them. Faced with a situation which he dared not oppose by force of arms, the king yielded and ordered the nobles and clergy to join the commoners.

The demands for reform in the *cahiers* were soon reinforced by popular uprisings. In Paris the storming of the Bastille, a state prison, on July 14 became the symbol of national liberation. The ancient royal government of the city of Paris was transformed into a commune controlled by the electors. Throughout France more than three hundred outbreaks occurred between March and July. Many of these were occasioned by the distress resulting from the bad harvest of 1788 and the severe winter following it. But in a broader sense the uprisings were the result of a cyclical rise in prices with no corresponding rise in wages. The great landlords and bourgeois proprietors and in some degree the peasant proprietors benefited by the rise in prices. But the masses of the peasants and the wage earners experienced a decline in the purchasing power of their incomes. In the spring of 1789 the cyclical movement was reinforced by the seasonal rise in prices, by the effects of the poor harvests of the previous year, and by the widespread agitation for reform in connection with the elections to the States-General. The disturbances of 1789 were far more than mere bread riots. In many places the people refused to pay taxes, destroyed the defenses of the towns, and burned the records of land ownership in the seignorial courts. Local police and soldiery were often sympathetic.

It was under these circumstances that the "great fear" of 1789 spread over France and reached its culmination significantly while the National Assembly was considering the reforms demanded by the electorate. It is not surprising, therefore, that the Assembly voted with virtual unanimity, early in August, to abolish the most serious inequalities and privileges of the old regime. The abolition of the feudal system was decreed, and all dues and obligations surviving from serfdom were annulled without compensation to the landlords. Other feudal dues were to be indemnified, but the distinction between servile and nonservile obligations proved to be impracticable and in 1793 the last vestiges of seignorial rights other than ordinary rentals were abolished. The August decrees also annulled special privileges with respect to hunting, fishing, maintenance of dovecots, etc. Church tithes, fees of country curés, and the holding of more than one office (pluralities) were abolished, and also tax exemptions, lay and clerical. The sale of offices was forbidden, and action was taken to abate the evil of royal pensions and sinecures.

In August, 1789, the Declaration of the Rights of Man and of the Citizen was adopted. This famous document reflected the philosophy of Rousseau except for its vigorous defense of private property as "a sacred and inalienable right," and in this respect it foreshadowed the essentially bourgeois course of the Revolution. The "liberty" proclaimed by the Declaration closely resembled the *laissez-faire* conception of the physiocrats and of Adam Smith. Men were to be free in the political sense of being subject to no authority save the laws made and administered as an expression of "the general will"; but a reasonable interpretation of the Declaration implies that not even "the general will" could question certain "natural" rights, as, for example, "the sacred and inalienable right" of property. Men were declared equal in respect to rights, and equal in the eyes of the law. The application of the doctrine of equality as intended by the framers of the Declaration is clear from the further statements that all offices and employments should be open to all solely on the basis of their capacities, virtues, and talents; and that no one should be subjected to public action or penalty except by due process of law applied impartially to all.

The National Assembly's general policy of freeing the country from the restraints of the old regime found expression in various laws for the control of the church, which was regarded as the main bulwark of privilege and reaction. Decrees were adopted for the transfer and sale of church properties, for the dissolution of monastic orders, and for the election and compensation of church officials, who were to be regarded as public officials. Plans were adopted for the reorganization of local government and of the courts on a more uniform and democratic basis. In June, 1790, the hereditary nobility was abolished, and the use of titles, liveries, and armorial bearings was forbidden.

The Assembly, although dominated by bourgeois elements, at length applied its principles of liberty and equality, or more precisely, the principles of individualism and *laissez faire*, to trade and industry. Early in 1791 it decreed the abolition of monopolies in business enterprise and proclaimed freedom to everyone "to engage in such business or to practice such profession, art, or craft as he may find profitable." A later law went much farther and revealed the attitude of the members of the Assembly as that of employers desiring to free themselves on the one hand from the restrictions and monopolies of guilds and corporations, and on the other hand from interference with wages and conditions of employment by the concerted action of workers. The suppression of "corporations of the citizens of the same calling and profession" was declared to be "one of the fundamental bases of the French constitution." Organized action by employers, shopkeepers, workers or journeymen of a trade was forbidden. Agreements for refusing to work except at "a settled price" for "their skill or labor" were forbidden and the instigators of such agreements were to be fined and deprived of the rights of citizenship. Attempts to prevent others from working at a lower wage were to be punished by fine and imprisonment; threats of violence "against workers who use the liberty granted by the constitutional laws," that is, against strikebreakers, were to be regarded as criminal offenses; and assemblies or "mobs" of workers attempting to restrain other workers from "the free exercise of skill and labor" were declared to be guilty of sedition and were to be dispersed by force.

Similar tendencies were apparent in the constitution of 1791, which was the culminating work of the National Assembly. Under the constitution, the supreme powers of government were vested in a Legislative Assembly, elected indirectly by electors chosen by "active" citizens — by persons at least twenty-five years of age paying direct taxes and furnishing proof of various other qualifications, such as the taking of an oath of citizenship and loyalty. Persons in domestic service were excluded from active citizenship.

Thus in its initial stages the French Revolution is revealed as essentially a bourgeois movement. In an era of revolutionary ideals, enthusiasms, and conflicts, numerous eddies and crosscurrents were inevitable. But after the privileges, monopolies, and anomalies of the aristocratic old regime were swept away, the main current of the Revolution moved with minor deviations in the channel of bourgeois property rights to be maintained in accordance with the principles of individualism, legal equality, and *laissez faire*.

## The Legislative Assembly's Conflict with the Old Order

The constitution of 1791 retained the monarchy but restricted the power of the king to ceremonial and nominal functions. The new government, which was controlled by the Legislative Assembly, was confronted by the opposition of the various elements affected adversely by the revolutionary changes. At the same time it disappointed many who desired further changes or who found that the new regime was not achieving the results they had expected. The peasants acquired freedom from feudal obligations, tithes, and obnoxious taxes; but the urban working classes, supported by many idealistic or ambitious middle-class leaders, began to demand that liberty and equality be translated into terms of economic opportunity for employees and those without property. There was a current of socialistic thought, but the demand for the abolition of private capitalism was never a significant force. Businessmen and intellectuals demanded the liberation of private enterprise from state regulation and guild control; while the common people expected the new government to exercise its regulatory functions for the defense of the masses against high prices, inequitable taxes, unemployment, and domination by landlords and employers. Many even among the middle classes showed signs of disaffection, especially in respect to the decrees abolishing guilds and corporations. The leaders of the Revolution were far from agreement regarding revolutionary policy at home or abroad. It became increasingly apparent that royalists, aristocrats, and churchmen throughout Europe, under the influence of the *émigrés*, were rapidly forming a common front for the purpose of overthrowing the revolutionary government and restoring the old order.

Many signs of trouble and impending conflict had appeared even under the National Assembly. The measures against the nobles and the clergy caused many of these classes to leave the country, and these *émigrés* attempted by means of propagandist agents and literature to arouse hostility within France and to enlist the military support of foreign governments against the new regime. Louis XVI, who at first declared his acceptance of the limited monarchy, became increasingly restive under the unaccustomed restraints. As early as October, 1789, he was forced to remove his court from Versailles to Paris, and thereafter he was hardly more than a prisoner in his palace. The Pope declared the laws for the reorganization of the church to be schismatic. The king, who signed these and various other laws against his will, became increasingly intent on an appeal to foreign powers. In June, 1791, he attempted to escape but was arrested and brought back to Paris. In July and August, 1791, the rulers of Austria and Prussia plainly indicated their intention "to restore the liberty and honor" of their fellow sovereign and "to put limits to the dangerous extremes of the French Revolution."

Louis XVI accepted the constitution of 1791 but he refused to sign two measures passed by the Legislative Assembly in November, 1791, for suppressing the opposition of the *émigrés* and of the hostile churchmen (the nonjuring clergy). Instead, he secretly solicited the aid of foreign courts. The Legislative Assembly, confronted with internal and external enemies intent on its overthrow, declared war on Austria and Prussia, ordered the expulsion of the nonjuring priests, and prepared to send armed forces to defend the frontier. The king continued in communication with foreign enemies, and the queen found means to reveal to the Austrians and Prussians the French military plans.

The final overthrow of the monarchy, as well as the consolidation of the revolutionary forces, was made inevitable by a statement issued by the Duke of Brunswick, commander of the Austro-Prussian forces, on July 25, 1792. This manifesto declared that the purpose of the sovereigns he represented was to stop the attacks "on the throne and the altar" and to restore Louis to full sovereignty. Not content with this avowal of purpose, it outraged the profoundest of French sentiments by threats against the homes and the lives of Frenchmen who opposed the invading armies. If the king or queen were affronted and their preservation and liberty were not immediately provided for, the city of Paris would be "delivered over to military execution and to complete ruin." Two weeks later the king was dethroned; and within two months the Republic was formally proclaimed. The Legislative Assembly itself, which was moderate in policy and desirous of maintaining the limited monarchy, was swept aside. The National Convention, elected directly by popular vote, met in September charged with the herculean tasks of drawing up a constitution for the newly proclaimed republican government while at the same time defending France from internal chaos and from invading armies.

## The Defense and Extension of the Revolution by the National Convention

The National Convention, which met September 20, 1792, undertook simultaneously to repel invasion, to suppress internal rebellion, to solve the grave problems of financial and industrial disorganization, and to extend and consolidate the revolutionary program.

The armed forces were reorganized on the basis of conscription and of leadership chosen without regard to birth or social status but because of tested ability. Conscription applied not only to the armed forces but to the civilian population. To the various classes appropriate tasks were assigned. Artisans and workingmen were conscripted for the national program of manufacturing munitions and supplies. The decree of August 23, 1793, containing these provisions, also directed that property as well as persons be conscripted and that an "extraordinary manufacture of arms of every sort" be undertaken by the Minister of War.

In foreign relations the National Convention formulated a policy of far-reaching significance. In December, 1792, it issued instructions "to be followed by the armies of the Republic in the countries where they shall carry its arms." The sovereignty of the people was to be proclaimed; existing authorities were to be overthrown; tithes, seignorial rights, serfdom, monopolistic corporations, and all special privileges were to be suppressed; and democratic governments, based on "peace, assistance, fraternity, liberty, and equality," were to be established. On April 13, 1793, a more moderate decree was adopted, avowing a policy of nonintervention in the government of other countries, but asserting that the Convention would "sooner be buried under its own ruins than suffer that any power should interfere in the internal regime of the Republic." But the long succession of French conquests was actually accompanied by the overthrow, in many parts of Europe, of the old regime, economically and socially as well as politically.

In the internal affairs of France the response of the National Convention to the threats of foreign governments, the intrigues of the royal family, and the disaffection of nobles and clergy was the execution of several thousand opponents of the Republic including the king and queen.   The Reign of Terror began as a life-and-death struggle to save the Republic and the Revolution from a seemingly irresistible combination of enemies.   Although it degenerated into a struggle of factions guilty of utmost excesses, it saved the revolutionary movement from collapse and rescued the French people from a reactionary vengeance which could hardly have been less extreme.   It is not without interest that the guillotine, symbol of the Terror, was introduced as a less barbarous and cruel mode of execution than the prevailing method of decapitation by the ax. The old regime was inflexibly opposed to its own reformation.   As a seemingly insurmountable obstacle in the way of change, it was destroyed.   The methods used by the National Convention were extremely brutal, but the Convention's creative activities were carried on in the face of extreme difficulties and were made possible by the powerful pressure of revolutionary forces throughout the country.

When the National Convention assembled, it was confronted not only by enemies at home in league with invading armies, but also by industrial and financial disorganization.   Invasion and internal disorders were inevitably accompanied by economic disturbances. The revolutionary government inherited a bankrupt treasury and a system of taxation requiring thoroughgoing reform.   Crown lands, extensive church properties, and the estates of the émigrés were nationalized, and the sale of these properties was originally designed to liquidate the debt inherited from the old regime.   The idea of utilizing these properties as the basis for money occurred to the National Assembly, and the first issue of assignats was made in December, 1789.   These were regarded as mortgage bonds.   They were to be restricted to the value of the confiscated properties, were to be withdrawn from circulation after the sale of the properties, and were to be used primarily to extinguish the national debt.   But new tax policies, never popular, were formulated and enforced with difficulty;  and the extraordinary expenses incurred for repelling invasion led to a progressive increase in the volume of the assignats. By July, 1792, a short time before the National Convention met, the assignats had already depreciated until 60 livres in coin were worth 100 livres in assignats.   Thereafter depreciation continued until the assignats by 1797 became worthless and were repudiated.

The inflation of the currency, the increasing scarcity of supplies due to general economic disorganization, and the increasing demand for supplies due to wartime requirements combined to force prices rapidly upward. Various measures were adopted for fixing the value of the assignats and for regulating prices. In September, 1793, the Law of the Maximum fixed the maximum prices of the principal commodities in everyday use and also the rates of wages and salaries. But the Convention assumed no responsibility for carrying on economic activities, for controlling the volume of production, or for rationing the supply of goods and labor. It was inevitable, therefore, that the laws for fixing prices were ineffective. The principal results of the government's fiscal policy, unaccompanied as it was by any correlative policy of economic controls affecting supply and demand, were economic demoralization, inflation, and a transfer of wealth and income from creditors to debtors and from the more conservative classes to speculators. Thus in the field of finance the policies of the revolutionary governments before 1797 were far from successful or constructive. But the old inequitable system of taxation and the royal pensions were wiped out and the way was prepared for the modern fiscal system.

The National Convention extended the policy of emancipating the peasants by granting them complete freedom from seignorial dues without compensation to the landlords. There were many small proprietors in France before the Revolution, but the clear predominance of small estates in modern France dates from the Revolution. The nationalized properties were sold extensively in small tracts on easy terms, and payment was facilitated by monetary inflation. Another policy adopted by the Convention promoted small proprietorships by requiring that estates be divided equally among the heirs. A law providing for the division of common lands also tended to promote peasant proprietorship.

Much of the confiscated land was sold in comparatively large tracts to persons who rented it or hired workers to farm it. It has been urged that many farm tenants and rural wage workers after the Revolution were hardly better off economically than were their ancestors. The laws giving equality to all the heirs tended to cause a minute subdivision of the land, and holdings were already far too small in many cases to afford a livelihood. The laws permitting the division of common lands deprived many poor peasants of the use of these lands. But the net gains of the peasants were extremely important. The strength of modern France, rooted as it is so largely in its free peasantry, intensely devoted to the soil and to republican institutions, is perhaps the most significant result of the Revolution.

The National Convention inaugurated the first national system of public education.   The plan included special schools for instruction in such subjects as agriculture, engineering, mining, navigation, veterinary science, medicine, and architecture.   A museum of applied arts and sciences was established.   Weights and measures were standardized on a scientific basis by the adoption of the metric system.   A beginning was made in the formulation of the modern laws of literary and industrial property and in the reform of the civil and penal codes.   Slavery in the colonies was abolished in 1794, although it was temporarily restored in 1802 by Napoleon.

From the establishment of the Republic in September, 1792, to July, 1794, the National Convention, although divided into factions, was dominated by the commune of Paris.   In the Paris commune the classes without property were influential, although many idealistic or ambitious bourgeois leaders utilized and encouraged the radical tendencies of the working classes for their own purposes. The later and more brutal excesses of the Reign of Terror were largely a result of the factional struggles of the leaders of the Convention, and especially of Danton and Robespierre.   The fall of Robespierre in July, 1794, was followed by the suppression of the commune, the end of the Reign of Terror and of the worst of the factional conflicts, and the beginning of a bourgeois reaction.

### The Bourgeois Reaction

The fall of Robespierre and of the Paris commune marked the ascendancy of the propertied and professional groups.   But the National Convention remained favorable to the ideals of legal equality and individualism and to the Republic in opposition to the old regime.   A year before the fall of Robespierre a constitution had been drafted (in June, 1793 — the Constitution of the Year I of the Republican calendar).   This constitution, based on the doctrines of Rousseau, was ratified by the people but was never put into operation.   A new constitution was drawn up and put into effect in 1795 — the Constitution of the Year III.

In contrast with the document of 1793, the second constitution framed by the National Convention revealed clearly the bourgeois tendencies of the Convention.   Citizenship and the right to vote were restricted to persons who had lived a year in France and who paid a land tax or personal property tax.   Domestic servants were denied citizenship.   Special property qualifications were required of officeholders.   The bicameral legislative system was reintroduced, and elections were indirect. The executive branch, to be chosen by the upper and more conservative chamber of the legislature, consisted of five Directors. The "inviolability" of property was affirmed : "It is upon the maintenance of property that the cultivation of the land, all the productions, all means of labor, and the whole social order rest." The constitution, while containing these various explicit provisions for eliminating the political power of the propertyless classes, also included safeguards against aristocratic and clerical influence. The return of the *émigrés* was barred, and the confiscation of their estates was affirmed. The new owners of the nationalized properties of the crown, the church, and the *émigrés* were confirmed in their titles. The church was to remain separated from the state, without state support, and no one was to be required to contribute to the church. Inheritance of titles and of authority, though not of property, was declared to be inconsistent with equality before the law.

The government of the period of the Directory in carrying out the policies of the new constitution was opposed on the one hand by those who favored a return to the old regime and on the other hand by advocates of further economic and social change. The measures undertaken by the Directory in combating opposition are illustrated by the law of 1796 against public enemies. Persons guilty of discourse or of writings for the purpose of dissolving the legislature or the Directory or of instigating the murder of officials, or of re-establishing the monarchy, or of pillaging or partitioning public or private property, were to be put to death. Gatherings thus instigated were declared to be seditious mobs. Among the radicals there were secret associations devoted to promoting economic as well as legal equality. The abortive constitution of 1793 was viewed by these groups as a step toward equality, while the constitution of 1795 was denounced as an undemocratic charter which riveted the people's chains instead of breaking them. Babeuf, a prominent leader of the radicals, formulated a program for the nationalization of property, to be gradually consummated by the abolition of private inheritances. The program called for the administration of enterprise by a democratically controlled national community. A plan for the overthrow of the Directory was betrayed, and in May, 1797, Babeuf and several other leaders were executed. A royalist plot in the same year was also betrayed, but the leaders were merely transported to the penal settlement in Cayenne, French Guiana. Later, in July, 1799, when the Directory was threatened by widespread disorders instigated by royalists, the law of hostages was enacted for placing on the royalists the responsibility for maintaining order, on pain of execution of hostages taken from the families of former nobles and *émigrés*.

The Directory was harassed by factions, plots, and intrigues, by monetary inflation and virtual bankruptcy, by widespread corruption, and by the disintegration of local administration, business enterprise, and social customs. Peasants had profited by emancipation and by the acquisition of confiscated lands, but they were discontented because of new taxes, compulsory military service, and the disruption of traditional modes of life. Many of the townsmen welcomed the new freedom from restrictions on industry and trade and profited from contracts for war supplies and from speculative opportunities opened up by monetary inflation. But others suffered disruption of their enterprises. Thousands of workshops were closed, and foreign trade was gravely curtailed. Vast numbers of the working classes were unemployed, and public relief on a large scale became necessary. In spite of the gravest of obstacles the armies of the Directory had achieved a series of striking military victories beyond the frontiers of France, but in 1799 reverses threatened France once more with invasion. The cumulative discontent within France, instead of subsiding in the face of foreign danger, found expression in a move for the overthrow of the Directory — a movement which culminated in the military dictatorship of Napoleon Bonaparte.

## Organization of Revolutionary Forces by Napoleon

When Napoleon Bonaparte returned from his Egyptian campaign in October, 1799, France had passed through ten years of unparalleled revolutionary upheaval. The country at large detested the old regime. Small groups of survivors of the privileged classes intrigued, to be sure, for restoration; and many idealistic or ambitious leaders still dreamed of pressing forward toward economic and social as well as legal equality on the basis of somewhat vague programs of socialism. General Bonaparte keenly sensed the desires of the dominant bourgeois classes of the towns and of the masses of peasants for political stability and for security in the enjoyment of the gains which the Revolution had brought to them. All classes were discontented with terroristic methods, the corruption of the bourgeois Directory, and the inability of the revolutionary governments to embody revolutionary ideals in an orderly social system.

Bonaparte and his associates took advantage of these conditions to establish a disguised military dictatorship. At first the Consulate which he organized maintained republican forms. In 1802 Bonaparte was made First Consul for life, with the right to nominate his successor. In 1804 he became Emperor Napoleon I, with the right of succession in his family. The efforts of earlier revolutionary governments to bring about uniformity in local government and to subject local authorities to central control were more successfully continued by the Napoleonic regime. The principal local officials were chosen by the central government, and the new administrative divisions with centralized control remained a permanent part of the French political system. The immediate effect of these changes was to strengthen the military dictatorship. Their ultimate economic significance was to give to the modern democratic government of France, in a period of rapid economic change and integration of business enterprise, a capacity to carry into effect vital national policies of taxation, social legislation, and industrial control which strong local governments could have blocked.

The Consulate (so called from the fact that the executive consisted of three consuls) and later the Empire undertook as one of the main tasks the conciliation of the disaffected classes — the clergy and the *émigrés*, together with their relatives. The skill of Napoleon and his advisers was apparent in their winning the allegiance of most of the members of these groups without surrendering the more important gains of the Revolution. The Roman Catholic Church was restored and most of the priests were allowed to return to their posts with public salaries, but on condition of allegiance to the new government. Church lands were not returned and the monasteries were not re-established. The principal churchmen were to be nominated by the government, but the bishops were to be invested or given their official authority by the Pope. As for the nobility, their confiscated estates, in so far as they had been sold, were not to be returned. Persecution ceased and most of the *émigrés* returned. The hereditary aristocracy was not re-established, and offices were bestowed on the basis of merit or of allegiance to the government. The pomp and ceremonies of court life were revived, and honors were granted, as membership in the Legion of Honor, but for life only and on the basis of personal achievements.

Taxation was simplified, equalized, and made administratively feasible, although financial pressure led to increasing dependence on some of the detested indirect taxes of the old regime, as tobacco and salt taxes.   Corruption was punished.   A sinking fund was created in connection with the national debt.   The Bank of France was established.   Public administration was placed on a comparatively efficient and economical basis.   Economic recovery and expansion were promoted by orderly government and by a vast system of public works.   War contracts also continued to provide a temporary stimulus.   Public works were carried on in part by the labor of prisoners of war.   Among the enterprises were extensive roads and canals, harbor improvements, and the draining of swamps and marshes.

The new government attempted to reduce to a minimum the opposition of the clergy and of the aristocracy, but its main source of strength was the support of the middle classes.   Napoleon vigorously maintained the revolutionary policies for emancipating the peasants and for freeing the middle classes of the towns from corporate and guild restrictions, from national regulations associated with mercantilism, from the obstructive anomalies of local governments and tariffs, and from the galling political and social inequalities associated with the old regime.   As an expedient for the more effective control of the food industries, which vitally affected the military plans of Napoleon, there was a temporary reversion to a form of guild organization, but the old system of monopolies and minute regulation was not restored.

The continued ascendancy of the bourgeoisie is illustrated by the labor provisions of the civil and penal codes.   In the relations between workers and employers, the master-and-servant doctrine prevailed.   In spite of the theory of legal equality, the worker had virtually no legal recourse in case of a disagreement, because the law required the courts to accept the testimony of the employer as against that of the employee.   Furthermore, self-help by concerted action was illegal, because the law forbade workers to form organizations of more than twenty members, and defined strikes and picketing as crimes.   Workers were subjected to oversight by the police as well as to control by their employers by means of books containing records of successive employments.   On applying for a new job, each worker was required to present his book containing approval of his record by his last employer.   The number of wage earners was small, and the earlier efforts to exalt the proletariat as a significant revolutionary force were doomed to failure because of the predominance of peasants and of independent tradesmen and owners of small enterprises.   The Napoleonic system merely followed the natural course of the Revolution in assuring the ascendancy of well-to-do peasants and urban middle classes.

The principal features of revolutionary legislation for legal equality, administrative and judicial reorganization, emancipation of the peasants, individualism in business enterprise, and public education were embodied either in special legislation or in the Napoleonic Code. The revolutionary ideals of liberty, as of the press, and the doctrine of popular sovereignty were subordinated to the military dictatorship. The immediate results were national unity, comparative efficiency, and a series of remarkable achievements in the reorganization of the national economy and in the temporary defeat of a large part of Europe in league against the Revolution. The ideals of liberty and of the sovereignty of the citizens at the polls survived alike the dictatorship of Napoleon and the monarchical reaction of 1814 and later again found embodiment in French institutions.

### Reaction against Revolutionary Tendencies

The revolutionary wars from 1789 to 1815 involved most of Europe. Their origin was in the hostility of other governments to the Revolution. The French at first fought primarily to defend their soil and to prevent the overthrow of the revolutionary system by invaders. They soon became convinced that they could defend their revolutionary ideals only by spreading them and by aiding other peoples to throw off the restraints of the old regime. By an easy transition they acquired a love of power and military glory which prolonged the conflict and greatly extended its area. This aspect of the struggle affected most vitally the relations between France and Great Britain and led the British to assume the most persistent and vital role in opposition to France as an imperial power even more than as the champion of revolutionary ideals. The French, directed by the overmastering ambitions of Napoleon, overreached themselves. Their defeat was partly due to self-exhaustion. More significant was the hostility of outraged nationalism, which Napoleon had stimulated but which turned against him as the self-seeking master of Europe. Another vital factor in the defeat of France was the superiority of the British in economic development and in sea power, by means of which they subsidized their allies, maintained their own trade, virtually destroyed that of France, and protected themselves from the direct ravages of war.

The international settlement at the Congress of Vienna in 1814–

1815 marked the rise of Prince Metternich of Austria as Napoleon's successor in the attempt to direct the affairs of Europe. The agreements at the Congress of Vienna were primarily political but they affected the course of economic development throughout Europe. The French conquests had been accompanied not only by the overthrow of governments but by the abolition of serfdom, of class privileges, and of guild and corporate restrictions. The principles of the Napoleonic legal code were widely adopted. Under the direction of Metternich as the most influential agent of reaction, the Congress of Vienna undertook not merely a restoration of the former ruling families but a return to the old order in respect to class rule, relations between peasants and landlords, and other phases of social and economic life. There was also formulated a rigorous program of repression for preventing reforms as well as revolutions. Metternich held that the first and greatest concern of a nation is with stability — never with change. The duty of governments is to "maintain the foundations of their institutions, both ancient and modern; for if it is at all times dangerous to touch them, it would certainly not now, in the general confusion, be wise to do so."

In France the devotion to the revolutionary ideals was so strong that Louis XVIII, even when supported by the arms of the conquerors of Napoleon, dared not attempt a full restoration of the old regime. In his Charter of 1814 he claimed authority by divine right but granted representative government and recognized the revolutionary transfers of confiscated property and other outstanding economic and social changes. Gradually the reactionary royalists gained control and pursued policies which led to the Revolution of 1830. In most of the countries which had come under the sway of Napoleon or under the influence of revolutionary ideals, extreme reaction prevailed. Even in Great Britain, which had escaped the direct ravages of the wars and which had effectually checked revolutionary and even reform movements in the early years of the revolutionary period, the decade following the fall of Napoleon was marked by extreme repression and by a resurgence of aristocratic influence.

### Survival and Significance of Revolutionary Influences

Although strenuous efforts were made after 1815 to destroy the effects of the French Revolution, European economy remained profoundly altered. In Germany, the beginnings of nationalism and unification are traceable to the Napoleonic era, when the Holy

Roman Empire was overthrown, together with a vast number of petty principalities. In parts of Germany, especially in Westphalia and the Rhenish Palatinate, the French abolished the guild system, reformed the laws, built roads, and in general demonstrated the disadvantages of the old regime and the constructive possibilities of the revolutionary impulse. The weakness of disunited Germany with an antiquated economic and social system enabled Napoleon to impose his will and to exploit the country. At the same time Germans themselves were inspired to attempt the regeneration of their country. In Prussia serfdom was abolished, although under conditions which tended to transform the peasants not into free proprietors but into dependent wage workers or tenants. Laws defining the economic status and restricting the economic activities of landlords, peasants, and townsmen were repealed, and free enterprise, with freedom of occupational choice, was legalized. In Belgium the French occupation cleared away local restrictions and corporate monopolies, stimulated trade and industry, opened up new markets, and prepared the way for the leadership of Belgium in adopting British industrial methods. In other regions, also, the revolutionary impulses continued to have important effects even during the era of reaction. In most of the countries which had been permeated by French ideas the attempted restoration after 1815 was reversed by the middle of the century. Thereafter the new conceptions of a free peasantry, freedom of enterprise, equality before the law, and representative government rapidly gained ascendancy.

It may be urged that the gradual operation of evolutionary forces would have brought about the transformation of European society independently of the French Revolution. Hostility to the Revolution in fact united the opponents of change and stiffened their resistance. Twenty-five years of warfare destroyed resources, checked the development of new techniques, and retarded the adoption of British industrial methods. The fact remains, however, that the actual course of economic change was inseparably associated with the Revolution. Furthermore, the nature and significance of the Revolution as a Continental movement, especially in its economic and social aspects, can be appreciated by Americans only when evolutionary British institutions are contrasted with the comparatively inflexible nature of Continental society in the eighteenth century.

The American Revolution and the Declaration of Rights were expressions of the forces already dominant in American society.

These forces were in part derived from British traditions and institutions; and they were in part an outgrowth of the New World environment, which afforded abundance of land and comparative freedom of opportunity and gave rise to individualism and a tendency toward social equality.  By a long process of historical evolution, the British people had already achieved an evolutionary and adaptable system of law, legal equality, representative institutions, comparative freedom of enterprise and of occupational choice, the abolition of serfdom, and individualistic control of the land.  The privileges of the aristocracy, though important, were counterbalanced by obligations and a sharing of tax burdens and were tempered by comparative elasticity of class lines.  The colonial and commercial expansion of the British and the rapid changes of the industrial revolution contributed to the fluidity of British society and to the flexibility of British institutions.

In America, British traditions and institutions were reinforced by the frontier environment.  In consequence the American Revolution was a struggle for the maintenance of basic institutions and traditions already established and for the formal recognition of rights already in substance enjoyed but challenged by the personal government of George III.  Americans and Englishmen had institutions essentially evolutionary in nature, as the common law, representative government, and competitive business enterprises outside the limits of guilds and state monopolies; and their sparsely settled territories and colonies afforded opportunities for expansion of population, the easing of social tensions, and the mitigation of social inequalities.

In all of these respects most of the peoples of the Continent afforded sharp contrasts.  They were subjected to a social and institutional framework that was far more rigid and inflexible and to territorial limits that prevented expansion save by the conquest of neighbors.  They were dominated by the nonevolutionary principle of autocratic, divine-right absolutism.  This principle might occasionally find expression in a "benevolent" or "enlightened" despotism, as in Austria under Joseph II, but it was essentially, as Joseph II discovered, the bulwark of the established order and of the privileged classes in opposition to change.  In Continental countries, therefore, basic changes were brought about by a revolutionary break with the past.  The Revolution in France, the march of Napoleon across Europe, and especially the spread of revolutionary ideas, effected such a break with the past and released forces which ultimately transformed the Continent.    The main permanent change of an economic nature was the emancipation of the peasants. The Revolution also promoted individualism and freedom of enterprise, but these changes, especially outside of France, were associated significantly with the extension of the industrial revolution to the Continent; and in much of the Continental environment they were destined to give way, after the World War, to new types of economic society associated on the one hand with communism and on the other with Fascism.

From the British point of view the French Revolution wrought no basic change in the social structure, but it affected Englishmen significantly. It checked rather than accelerated the evolutionary process in England. By monopolizing the energies and resources of Continental countries it retarded the extension of British technology to the Continent, facilitated British commercial and colonial expansion, and prolonged the era of British ascendancy.

# CHAPTER 12

# ECONOMIC PROBLEMS OF THE REVOLUTION AND THE WARS

## The National Debt in France

The downfall of the old regime in France was precipitated by financial collapse, first revealed to the nation by Calonne's "Plan for the Improvement of the Finances" (August 20, 1786). This document laid bare the full gravity of the situation, and the shock was intensified by its unexpectedness. Necker (Calonne's predecessor in 1776–1781) had felt confident of the future. He was convinced that the existing taxes would continue to meet the reasonable needs of the government, and condemned Calonne unsparingly for his extravagances and incompetence. There is little reason to doubt the sincerity of Necker, though his good faith was questioned at the time, and his self-deception is really the most significant feature of the crisis. Despite his confidence, the state was literally at the end of its resources, without the slightest hope of balancing revenue and expenditure unless through a complete reorganization of the fiscal system. Looking back over the history of the century, it is now easy to understand both the reality and the gravity of the crisis. Five times during the eighteenth century the government had canceled a portion of the state debt and readjusted its obligations. Successive finance ministers had sought out new taxes, with apparent success. It was recognized that the government had the authority to increase the amount of the land tax (*taille réelle*) and to increase the income taxes (*taille personelle*, and *vingtième*). Half the revenue was derived from indirect taxes, some of which could be varied in amount according to need. Nominally, the government was able to reach all types of taxable capacity, and there was every appearance of reasonable distribution of burdens among the different classes of incomes. In reality, the entire system was perverted by the exemptions of the privileged groups.

Exemptions relieved the wealthy property holders from any significant burden of taxation on land or upon incomes from land. The nobility and the clergy were exempt by reason of feudal privileges. The ranks of the nobility were not closed; in the time of

Louis XIV, patents of nobility could be purchased for 6,000 livres. Nobility might be acquired also by the purchase of an estate to which the privileges of lordship were attached. Many offices of state conferred hereditary nobility, and nearly all these offices were to be had for a price. Towards the close of the century there were more than four thousand privileged offices open to persons not of noble birth. It was thus literally true that the only way to escape taxation was to become rich. The newer income taxes (*vingtièmes*) theoretically fell upon all classes alike. The privileged orders, however, had secured the right to have their assessments made personally by the chief administrative officer of their district, and the assessments were thus adjusted to the "circumstances" of the individual. If we include some of the wealthy bourgeois among the exempt, more than half the property of the kingdom was wholly or partially exempt. The burden of the direct taxes thus fell upon the peasantry and the lower middle class, and it was impossible to increase the revenue very much by increases in the rate of taxation. The chief burden of the indirect taxes likewise fell upon these poorer classes. The duties on internal trade raised the prices of food, and hindered the development of industry and commerce.

Calonne realized the futility of any attempt to build up the revenues of the government without a large extension of taxation of privileged persons. At his instance an Assembly of Notables was summoned to consider a comprehensive reorganization of the finances of the kingdom. All three estates were represented in the assembly, though the nobles and the clergy predominated. The disastrous collapse of the fiscal system was explained to the assembly in great detail. The members were at first incredulous. Calonne was severely criticized, and presently he was forced to resign. Strangely enough, the privileged orders were not unwilling to recognize the necessity of an abandonment of their exemptions, but it is evident that they assumed that they could secure control of the new government. Nobility and clergy thus joined in a determined attempt to force the king to summon the States-General. Failure to secure any substantial grants of new taxes from either the Assembly of Notables or an Assembly of the Clergy forced the government to yield. So little was coming in from taxes that in August, 1788, the government was obliged to divert funds from the hospitals to meet current expenses. On August 8, the date for the meeting of the States-General was set for May 1, 1789; on August 16 the government was obliged to issue treasury notes, bearing interest, to meet three eighths of the current obligations for salaries and pensions. A few days later Necker was recalled. His influence with the bankers made it possible to secure loans sufficient to meet immediate needs pending the assemblage of the States-General.

## Paper Money and the National Lands

When the States-General assembled in May, 1789, the government had already incurred increasing deficits for eight years. According to Calonne's statements, the deficits had increased from 70,000,000 livres [1] in 1781 to 160,000,000 livres in 1788. In 1788 the ordinary expenditures amounted to 286,000,000 livres. The government debt had been increased by loans amounting to 653,-000,000 livres during the four years 1783–1787. On May 5, 1789, Necker estimated that the year's receipts would be 475,000,000 livres, and placed the service of the debt and allied charges at 255,-000,000 livres, or 53 per cent of the revenue.

In this emergency Necker proposed that the powers of the Caisse d'Escompte (Discount Office) be increased. As a powerful national bank with extensive privileges of note issue, the Caisse might have been a great resource. But popular distrust of banks was so great that this project could not be pressed. The current needs of the government, however, were extensive. Antagonism toward the clergy led ultimately to a vote for the confiscation of the property of the church, and (December 19, 1789) a special form of paper money was devised in association with these new national assets. In form, the assignat was primarily a device to facilitate the sale of confiscated clerical property and to place purchasing power in the hands of the government before the sales were executed. For the first year or two the assignats did not have clear legal status as paper money. They were not legal tender; and until June, 1791, the government was presumed to destroy any assignats paid for church lands. Many members of the Assembly undoubtedly thought that they had skillfully evaded the issue of paper money, but the financial officers were not laboring under such an error, and circumstances soon made it impossible to misunderstand the true status of the assignat. Metallic currency was being hoarded even in 1788, so that dearth of the circulating medium became serious. The early issues of assignats were in large denominations, 1,000, 500,

---

[1] The *livre* originally, in Charlemagne's time, meant the value of a pound of silver; but it was gradually reduced. In 1788 its value was about 19 cents. In 1795 the livre was replaced by the franc.

and 200 livres. There was urgent need of smaller currency; accordingly in the fall of 1790 various municipalities authorized local agencies to issue "notes of trust" (*billets de confiance*). At first the term *bank* was avoided, though it was used frequently in 1791. These agencies issued currency to the amount of nearly 150,000,000 livres. In a few cases, this privilege of note issue was abused, but despite much severe criticism at the time later investigation showed that this currency was not seriously depreciated. It contributed to the development of the assignat. On December 26, 1791, the Assembly voted to issue 300,000,000 livres of assignats in denominations of 50, 25, 15, and 10 sous, and after this date there was no serious deficiency in small denominations. These issues, of course, were clearly intended to serve as a circulating medium.

The assignats, mandats, and the church lands with which they were redeemed were the most important financial resources of the revolutionary governments from May, 1789, until the abandonment of paper money in July, 1796. Taxes continued to be collected, but the depreciation of the paper money made them less and less important. The average monthly receipts have been compiled by Professor Harris, with reductions of nominal values to the value of the currency in May, 1789; and the total issue of assignats has been estimated by him — as shown by the tables on page 242.

The amounts of assignats authorized were somewhat greater, notably after August, 1794, and some writers have confused the amounts voted with the amounts actually issued. To the end of July, 1794, total issues amounted to 20,210,000,000 livres, about two thirds having been redeemed in land. Whatever valuations be placed upon the assignats as redeemed, it is clear that this means of disposing of the confiscated lands was a notable resource to the revolutionary governments. It is also evident that the issues of assignats were also a direct means of transferring purchasing power to the government.

### The Depreciation of the Assignats

The rates of depreciation shown by the table have been taken from the materials used in 1797 to adjust payments upon long-term debts. The treasury used a series of rates that were largely based upon the premiums on gold and silver. In the provinces, rates were calculated which gave weight to commodity prices. As gold and silver scarcely circulated at all, the premiums on the metals do not afford a good measure of depreciation, and until substantial studies have been made of commodity prices, the averages of the local tables of depreciation are the most trustworthy measure. The monetary problems created by such a currency, which are highly complex in any case, were especially complex in revolutionary France. Trade conditions were depressed in 1789 and 1790, and the exchanges were unfavorable to France. The credit of the government was seriously impaired by the financial crisis. It is therefore remarkable that there was no clear depreciation in the early period. Harris says that gold was at a premium because of special conditions, though there was no change in the price level that suggests depreciation of the currency. Subsequent depreciation was due only in part to overissue. The value of the currency was profoundly affected by political events, as in the case of the greenbacks issued by the United States during the Civil War.

AVERAGE MONTHLY RECEIPTS OF THE FRENCH GOVERNMENT [1]

| | Taxes | | Assignats and Other Sources | | Proportion of Taxes to |
|---|---|---|---|---|---|
| | *Nominal* | *Gold* | *Nominal* | *Gold* | *Total Revenue* |
| [1789] [2] | 33.0 | 33.0 | 36.0 | 36.0 | 48 per cent |
| 1790 | 16.0 | 16.0 | 38.0 | 38.0 | 30 ” ” |
| 1791 | 19.5 | 17.5 | 103.0 | 93.0 | 16 ” ” |
| 1792 | 30.5 | 23.0 | 90.5 | 67.5 | 25 ” ” |
| 1793 | 28.0 | 15.0 | 266.0 | 35.0 | $9\frac{1}{2}$ ” ” |
| 1794 | 41.0 | 16.5 | 214.0 | 90.5 | 15 ” ” |
| [1795] [3] | 118.0 | 6.5 | 1,334.0 | 75.5 | 8 ” ” |

*in Millions of Livres:*

ISSUES OF ASSIGNATS AND THEIR VALUE [1]

| | Amount, in Millions of Livres: | | Value at End of Period, in Per Cent of Face Value | |
|---|---|---|---|---|
| | *Issued during Period* | *Circulation at End of Period* | *Local Tables* | *Treasury Tables* |
| 1790–1791 | 1,860 | 1,490 | 86 | 77 |
| Jan.–May, 1792 | 2,200 | 1,660 | 72 | 58 |
| June–Dec. 1792 | 2,750 | 2,250 | 75 | 72 |
| Jan.–Aug. 1793 | 4,950 | 4,050 | 39 | 22 |
| Sept. 1793–July 1794 | 8,450 | 7,200 | 41 | 34 |
| Aug. 1794–Nov. 1795 | — | 19,700 | 0.8 | 0.8 |
| Jan. 28, 1796 | — | 39,000 | — | — |

[1] Harris, S. E., *The Assignats*, Harvard University Press, Cambridge, 1930, pp. 51, 57, 166–205.

[2] May 1–Dec. 31, 1789.          [3] Jan. 1–Nov. 30, 1795.

After the fall of Robespierre the value of the assignat declined precipitously.  The government was irresolute; the price controls were discontinued, and official decrees attempted partial devaluation of the currency.  These measures tended to discredit the assignat, and matters grew steadily worse because the government was unable to procure other resources.  Even with improved facilities for printing, the presses were scarcely able to turn out enough currency in a day to meet the requirements of the morrow.  Inflation can assist materially in the meeting of a serious financial crisis, but issues of new currency cannot entirely take the place of other resources.  Although some efforts had been made to reorganize the system of taxation, the work had not progressed far enough to yield significant results.  Uncertainties of the future discouraged the financial interests, and loans could not be placed.  Distrust of organized banking prevented any substantial development of the banking system.  The Directory, therefore, took over (October 27, 1795) a treasury which was perhaps in even more hopeless disorder than at the beginning of the Revolution.  All emergency expedients had been exploited and found wanting; no sound constructive work had been accomplished.

It was not possible to dispense with the assignats at once, but they were devalued and liquidated early in the following year. This law of March 18, 1796, however, authorized an issue of new paper (2,400,000,000 livres) under the name *mandats territoriaux*. These notes were secured by state property and receivable for its purchase at a price of twenty times the actual income from the property in 1790.  In theory, therefore, the *mandat territorial* should have had the value of the currency of that year.  Assignats could be converted into mandats at a rate of 30 francs in assignats for 1 franc in mandats — a rating wholly inconsistent with the valuation of the mandat for the purchase of land.  Despite or because of these complex ratings, the mandats depreciated rapidly, so that they ceased to be of practical significance in July, 1796. On June 26 the government ordered that the land tax be paid in grain or in accordance with the price of grain.  On July 31 the government refused to accept mandats for the purchase of land except at the market rating, and a few days later it was ordered that all taxes be paid in specie or in mandats at the market rating. A month later all the accounting departments of the government were placed on a specie basis.  The paper currency was not formally abolished until February 4, 1797.  Mandats were receivable until March 21, for arrears of taxes or land purchases, at one per cent of their face value: after March 21 they might be exchanged for certificates that were receivable in part for purchases of land.

## The Finances of the Consulate and the Empire

These currency reforms by no means made an end of the critical condition of the treasury, despite the increase of tax receipts. On September 30, 1797, two thirds of the state debt was canceled. New resources were found in the development of the house and chimney taxes, but the government lived by casual expedients. At the time of the *coup d'état* of 18–19 Brumaire (November 9–10, 1799), there were only 167,000 francs in the treasury, most of which had come in the day before. The office opened at two o'clock each day, and closed when the money on hand was exhausted.

It seems likely that these grave financial problems were not without influence upon the projected *coup d'état*, though the formal plans of Sieyès seem to have been more largely preoccupied with fears of a royalist movement leading to a restoration of the monarchy. The *coup d'état* was certainly supported by powerful financial interests concerned alike with the maintenance of the Republic and the reorganization of the finances. The increased authority of the executive branch of the government gave these reform elements a freer hand, and they found unexpected support in the administrative talents of Napoleon.

The first days of the Consulate were inevitably colored by the distressed treasury inherited from the Directory. The memoirs contain references to a number of casual receipts in specie, and the general impression is given that for the first month or two the treasury was dependent upon casual receipts. Within a month, the bankers of Paris were induced to underwrite a loan of 12,000,000 francs against the receipts from an increase in the land tax. The loan was not fully subscribed, but funds were raised by a lottery. By various expedients the Consulate survived these critical months; in 1800 a reform of the land tax assessments ensured added revenue, and the establishment of the Bank of France created a financial agency that freed the government from dependence upon the private bankers. The Bank of France was first established as a fiscal agent of the government without any important special privileges (February 13, 1800). In 1803 it was given a monopoly of note issue; the intimacy of its relations with the treasury led to the establishment of control in 1806, assuming the form which it retained until the reform of 1936. Napoleon proposed that his military operations should finance themselves. In the most literal sense the armies were expected to live off the subject territories. In the earlier Napoleonic wars, this policy was achieved in some measure. Tribute from subject states, contributions from allies, and forced levies in newly conquered territory provided important resources. The actual records of sums collected, however, show that the language of Napoleon's letters and speeches must not be taken too literally. The foreign wars were not a dead weight upon the French budget, but even Napoleon was unable to make the vanquished pay all the costs of war. The system of forced contributions failed utterly in Spain (1810), and again in Russia (1812).

### Taxation and Finance in Great Britain, 1688–1815

The history of taxation and finance in Great Britain presents many significant contrasts to the experience of France. In the first place, we have complete statistical information for the history of public finance after 1688. England could not avoid a great increase in expenditure, because she was inevitably involved in the wars of the eighteenth century, and her colonial expansion required a great increase of the military and naval establishments even in time of peace. The services, which had required £1,112,000 in 1700, demanded an expenditure of £3,859,000 in 1774. In the same interval, interest on the public debt increased fourfold. England was able to meet these increased charges by the levy of new taxes. There were no continuing deficits in years of peace; the current expenses of the government and the service of the growing debt were at all times covered without addition to the permanent debt. The amount of the debt was slightly reduced during the longer intervals of peace, but the reductions were small. War expenditure always entailed new borrowing, though there were increases in taxes that covered about two thirds the average annual expenditure of these periods of war. During the early years of the wars with Revolutionary France, the government was obliged to borrow large sums. But after 1798 new taxes yielded additional revenue and thereafter taxes were increased progressively to meet the mounting expenditure. Even during this period, tax receipts supplied about half of the total expenditure. The general features of British policy are shown by the two following tables, on page 246.[1]

[1] Accounts relative to Public Income and Expenditure (H. W. Chisholm), *Commons Papers*, 1868–1869, vol. 35, I, p. 428, and II, pp. 298 ff.

ANNUAL RECEIPTS AND EXPENDITURES OF GREAT BRITAIN,[1] IN THOUSANDS
OF POUNDS STERLING,[2] IN SELECTED YEARS OF PEACE

| | Interest on Debt | Army and Navy | *Expenditures* Civil Government | Total Current Expenditure | *Receipts* Total, Excluding Loans |
|---|---|---|---|---|---|
| 1686–88 (average) | 336 | 1,112 | 720 | 2,168 | 2,268 |
| 1700 | 1,250 | 1,250 | 699 | 3,201 | 4,343 |
| 1715 | 3,275 | 2,218 | 733 | 6,228 | 5,547 |
| 1725 | 2,795 | 1,468 | 1,251 | 5,515 | 5,960 |
| 1738 | 2,059 | 1,779 | 885 | 4,724 | 5,716 |
| 1754 | 2,822 | 2,164 | 1,043 | 6,030 | 6,827 |
| 1765 | 4,828 | 6,138 | 1,049 | 12,016 | 10,927 |
| 1774 | 4,612 | 3,859 | 1,094 | 9,566 | 10,613 |
| 1786 | 9,480 | 5,482 | 2,014 [3] | 16,977 | 15,245 |
| 1792 | 9,310 | 5,577 | 2,065 [3] | 16,953 | 18,607 |

THE BRITISH NATIONAL DEBT,[1] 1688–1817 [4]

| Character of Preceding Period | Year | Debt,[5] Millions of Pounds | Approximate Population, Millions | Approximate Debt, per Capita |
|---|---|---|---|---|
| | 1688 | 1.0 | 6.2 | 3s. |
| War | 1697 | 14.5 | 6.2 | £2  6s. |
| Peace | 1701 | 12.5 | 6.2 | 2  0 |
| War | 1714 | 36.1 | 6.4 | 5  12 |
| War | 1721 | 54.3 | 6.4 | 8  10 |
| Peace | 1739 | 46.3 | 7.0 | 6  12 |
| War | 1749 | 77.1 | 7.2 | 11  0 |
| Peace | 1755 | 72.4 | 7.5 | 9  12 |
| War | 1766 | 131.0 | 8.2 | 16  0 |
| Peace | 1775 | 126.0 | 8.8 | 14  6 |
| War | 1785 | 243.3 | 9.6 | 26  10 |
| Peace | 1792 | 237.4 | 10.1 | 24  0 |
| War — 1st phase | 1801 | 517.5 | 14.9 | 34  18 |
| War — 2d phase | 1817 | 839.3 | 20.0 | 40  4 |

## Distribution of the Burdens of British Taxation

The increases in revenue from taxation were made possible by the placing of additional burdens upon the propertied classes. The

[1] See footnote on page 245.

[2] The pound sterling in the eighteenth century had about the same value as in later normal times — equal to about $4.86.

[3] Civil expenditures include, in 1786, £361,000, and in 1792, £501,000, for expense of administering a lottery.

[4] Great Britain, 1688–1792; United Kingdom, 1801–1817.

[5] Unredeemed capital, exclusive of capital value of annuities.

record of the eighteenth century thus shows that even the unreformed Parliament was sensitive to the new needs of government. Even in the eighteenth century the new resources fell into the primary groups that became the basis of the fiscal system under Peel and Gladstone. There were taxes on property, from which the less well-to-do were largely if not entirely exempt. There were taxes on luxuries, and customs and excise taxes on tea, alcoholic beverages, and tobacco. It was only necessary to eliminate the relatively unproductive protective duties to bring this system of taxes into conformity with the theory of the classical economists who exerted a direct influence upon the system from the time of the publication of Smith's *Wealth of Nations.*

The change in the distribution of burdens is best shown by comparing the taxes in force in 1815 with the taxes levied prior to the Revolution of 1688,[1] because some new taxes were introduced immediately after the accession of William and Mary.

RECEIPTS FROM THE PRINCIPAL TAXES IN ENGLAND AND WALES, 1687–1688

|  | Thousands of Pounds | Per Cent of Total |
|---|---|---|
| I. Direct taxes: | | |
|     Hearth money | 200 | 11.2 |
| II. Taxes on articles of consumption: | | |
|     The old subsidy, tunnage on | | |
|         wine, duty on woolen cloth | 577 | 31.6 |
|     Special duties of 1685: | | |
|     Wine, vinegar, tobacco, sugar, | | |
|         linen, brandy, silks | 415 | 23.0 |
|     Excise duties: | | |
|     Alcoholic beverages, vinegar, | | |
|       tea, coffee, chocolate, wine | | |
|       licenses | 620 | 34.2 |
| | 1,812 | 100.0 |

The small proportion of direct taxation in 1687 inevitably placed a heavy burden of taxation upon the lower classes, for the customs and excise duties on luxuries would not place a proportionate burden upon the well-to-do.

The distribution of the burden of taxation was notably different in 1815, as shown by the table on page 248.

[1] Dowell, S., *A History of Taxation and Taxes in England*, London, 1884, I, pp. 42, 239-249. See *Commons Papers*, 1868-1869, vol. 35, for somewhat more detail, less conveniently classified.

The revenue of Great Britain in 1815 was largely secured by direct taxes on property and taxes on a small number of articles in the general class of food, drink, and tobacco. The sugar duties afforded some protection to planters in the British West Indies, but with this exception the duties enumerated in this category afforded no protection. The duties on corn (grain) were prohibitive and yielded no revenue. The protective duties on raw materials and manufactures were not important sources of revenue, amounting to only 8.87 per cent of the total.

RECEIPTS FROM TAXES, GREAT BRITAIN, 1815

|  | Millions of Pounds | Per Cent of Total |
|---|---|---|
| I. Direct taxes: | | |
| Houses and establishments | 6.50 | |
| Income tax | 14.60 | |
| Inheritances | 1.29 | |
| Other taxes on property | 2.38 | |
| Total of above | 24.77 | 36.20 |
| Coaches, cabs, shipping | 0.64 | |
| Total direct taxes | 25.41 | 37.35 |
| II. Taxes on articles of consumption: | | |
| 1. Salt, sugar, currants, pepper, vinegar | 5.11 | |
| Malt liquors and licenses | 9.79 | |
| Wine and spirits | 8.60 | |
| Tea | 3.59 | |
| Coffee | 0.27 | |
| Tobacco | 2.02 | |
| Total — food, drink, tobacco | 29.38 | 43.00 |
| 2. Raw materials for manufacture | 6.06 | 8.87 |
| 3. Manufactures | 4.08 | 5.94 |
| 4. Stamp duties | 2.74 | 4.00 |
| 5. Miscellaneous | 0.58 | 0.84 |
| | 68.25 | 100.00 |

It is impossible to discover the precise relation of these taxes to the relative wealth of different classes in the kingdom, but it must not be forgotten that local rates and tithes were largely a burden on property. It is evident, however, that property as such bore an important part of the burden of government. The income tax exempted incomes under £60, and the rate was increased on incomes in excess of £200. The taxes on houses were also mildly progressive, and the tax on coaches was frankly designed to place burdens upon the conspicuous consumption of the wealthy. We cannot form any opinion of the net effect of these elements of progression, but they clearly forced the wealthy to acknowledge their civic responsibilities. The fiscal system presents a sharp contrast to the system in pre-revolutionary France.

The reforms of the eighteenth century were consciously directed toward the objectives that were so unmistakably achieved in the war budgets. The attempt to tax property directly began in the reign of William and Mary. Early experimentation took the form of a general property tax, not unlike the general property taxes that were introduced in the American colonies in the eighteenth century. Personal property largely escaped taxation, however, and the general property tax became a fixed tax on land. The house tax was introduced in 1696; a tax of 2 shillings on each house, with additional taxes on each window in excess of seven. The rates were raised in 1747, and the elements of progression were further emphasized. In 1748 Pelham also introduced a tax on private carriages. In an attempt to increase the yield of the customs duties, Pelham in 1745 reduced the duties on tea to such a low figure that smuggling was made unprofitable. Later ministers raised the customs duties to unproductive levels, but low duties on tea were again restored by Pitt in 1784, and the Commercial Treaty with France (1786) was based on the general principle of setting the duties below the cost of smuggling. Reforms of the customs and excise continued into the nineteenth century.

The inhabited house tax was established in 1778; a levy upon an assessment directly related to the rental value of the house. The old window taxes were continued, however, for many years. In 1799 Pitt established an income tax. Ten per cent was levied on incomes in excess of £200 a year, incomes between £60 and £199 were charged lower rates, and all incomes below £60 were exempt.

The reforms were thus imposed directly upon the older fiscal system. The new taxes were added, but the old taxes were not repealed. Until Pitt's time this process involved a continuous increase in the administrative complexity of the system. The doctrine of Parliamentary control was applied literally. Each tax was granted for a specified purpose, so that each new imposition was separately recorded, even when several impositions were charged against the same commodity. Fifteen separate assessments were made against wine in 1784. In 1785 a special committee reported upon the condition of the public accounts and made recommendations for their simplification, which were embodied in the Act of 1787. The receipts from all taxes were paid into a single fund, thereafter called the Consolidated Fund. All disbursements were to be made from this fund. All compound rates of duty were reduced to single rates. The reform was merely a matter of simplification of administrative practice, but it was a necessary prelude to the reforms of policy.

## The Development of the Bank of England

No description of British public finance would be complete without some reference to the development of the banking system. The early history of private banking in England was not especially noteworthy. A primitive type of deposit banking appears in England, as on the Continent, at an early date. Various forms of private banking activities were far advanced in the sixteenth century. The development of the doctrine of negotiability in the seventeenth century made it possible to deal more conveniently in bills of exchange and promissory notes. Notes payable to bearer on demand afforded the holder sufficient legal protection to make them generally acceptable, and the private banks of England, Holland, and Italy were able to circulate demand notes to bearer, though the volume of such issues seems to have been small. Many schemes for a large joint-stock bank were proposed after the Restoration, but no charter was actually issued until 1694. The urgent needs of the new government led to the acceptance of a scheme worked out by William Patterson and financed by a notable group of men in the City of London. The company agreed to lend the government £1,200,000 in perpetuity in consideration of being granted the privilege of issuing notes to this amount. This loan made by the Bank of England marks the substantial beginning of the funded debt, and the establishment of the bank gave new importance to the practice of issuing notes. The volume was increased rapidly until bank notes became an important part of the circulating medium. England, the American colonies, and France all indulged in experimentation with paper money at about this time. Both the colonies and France had unhappy experiences with government paper. France, under John Law, likewise experienced a bitter disillusionment with a chartered bank of issue. The Bank of England was the only one of all these ventures to achieve permanent success. Its experience, therefore, has exerted an especially important influence upon the development of modern banking practice. For more than a century it occupied an absolutely unique place in public and private finance. It acquired a leadership in the banking system of the country that gave it great responsibilities, and it rendered services to the treasury that were inestimable.

The organization and privileges of the Bank of England were developed in three statutes (1694, 1697, 1708). The first Bank Act provided only for the issue of notes to the amount of the loan to the government. The second Bank Act (1697) authorized issues in excess of this amount, if such issues were appropriately distinguished. It was also specifically required that all notes should be redeemed in specie on demand, though it is likely that the courts would have held the bank fully liable even without additional legislation. The second Bank Act also gave the Bank of England a guarantee that no other joint-stock company would be authorized to carry on banking activities within the kingdom, and in 1708 it was provided that no bank notes should be issued by any partnership consisting of more than six persons. The advantages of limited liability were thus restricted to the Bank of England, and even large partnerships were not allowed to extend their credit in the form of notes. These provisions resulted in the perpetuation of the private banks of London as essentially personal enterprises. Most of the banks of the seventeenth century continued in the hands of single families until the late nineteenth century, and a few famous names have survived even the extensive consolidations of the last thirty years.

There was not a little division of interest between these private banks and the Bank of England. The great bank interfered with their note issues and took over all the business of the government, but in the course of time specializations of activity developed which left the private bankers a large amount of highly profitable business. When banking houses began to develop in the provincial towns, it became essential for them to have correspondents in London, and the Bank of England made no attempt to enter this field. During the second half of the eighteenth century London became the focus of a substantial circulation of funds between the agricultural and industrial counties. The banks in the agricultural counties had surplus funds which could not be invested at home. The banks in industrial counties found that their clients brought them more bills of exchange and notes than they could wisely carry themselves. It became the established practice to rediscount or sell these bills in London where local bankers took them up on their own account or on behalf of the banks of the agrarian counties for which they acted as agents.

The private banks in London and in the provinces found that there was no necessity of holding large reserves of specie. The country banks were in constant contact with their London agents, and the balances in the hands of their agents were an important part of their assets. The London bankers usually had accounts in the Bank of England, and soon came to rely upon that bank for any sums of specie beyond the casual requirements of daily till money. If they needed specie unexpectedly they assumed that they could always secure specie against their deposits or by the rediscount of bills of exchange with the Bank of England. The Bank of England thus held the primary reserves of the whole banking system and as possessor of the central reserve it inevitably became the lender of last resort. As the banking system thus assumed its modern form, the cyclical fluctuations in industry and trade developed new features which appeared in acute form in 1788, 1793, and 1799. Systematic discussion of banking policy began in 1793, and the currency problems of the period of the wars resulted in a notable development of monetary theory.

### The Bank of England and the Currency, 1797–1815

When Great Britain entered the European war, she not only possessed an unusually strong treasury, but also a singularly mature banking system. The people were thoroughly familiar with the use of bank notes, and it soon appeared that the government could turn these habits to good account. The government relied upon the Bank of England for short-time loans and made use of its facilities for the remittance of funds to the Continent. In addition to the expenses of British forces, large sums were sent to the allies as loans or subsidies. The years 1795 and 1796 also involved heavy demands for credit on commercial account. The Bank of England could not satisfy both the government and the traders without endangering its solvency. After considerable discussion between the bank and the government, the government issued an Order in Council (February 27, 1797) forbidding the bank to pay out specie to its private clients. This Order in Council was confirmed by act of Parliament and continued in force until 1821. The order affected only the Bank of England, so that technically both the government and the private banks were under obligation to pay specie on demand. The government made little use of specie in England, as all domestic payments were made through the Bank of England. The private banks made no change in their old habits, continuing to use Bank of England notes as equivalent to specie. Bank notes were not made legal tender, but a mass meeting of bankers and merchants passed a resolution agreeing to accept Bank of England notes, and thus by agreement rather than by force of law the bank note became the effective currency of the United Kingdom. To meet the new requirements of circulation one-pound notes were authorized. The country banks followed the lead of the Bank of England, and their issues expanded considerably. Despite the ambiguity of their legal status the issues of the whole group of country banks were nearly equal to the issues of the Bank of England.

Exempt from the obligation to meet domestic demands in specie, the Bank of England was able to place its resources unreservedly at the command of the government. Large sums were remitted to the Continent in specie. Despite a great increase in its total liabilities, the reserve diminished steadily : in the third quarter of 1814, against total liabilities of £65,000,000 the Bank held a reserve of only £2,200,000, or 3.4 per cent ; not more than one tenth of the reserve that would have been necessary under ordinary circumstances.

This is the first instance of credit and currency inflation through a central bank. There can be little doubt that these credit facilities were indispensable to the conduct of the war, and despite the criticism of contemporary and later theorists, it must be confessed that the government and the Bank of England showed remarkable moderation and restraint in the use of the great powers at their disposal. In 1814 the general price level was about double the level of 1790. The rise in prices was less extreme and much more gradual than in the World War. The return to the former price level was also more gradual. Not until 1826 did the general price level again reach the level of 1790. If we attempt to measure depreciation in terms of the premium on Spanish silver, the gravity of the crisis is perhaps more vividly presented. The highest premium on Spanish silver was 38.2 per cent (in 1813). This would suggest an exchange rate of $3.41 per pound sterling between New York and London. It must be remembered, however, that there was no formal mechanism for control of exchange and no attempt to "peg" the exchanges as was done during the World War.

The attempts of contemporaries to explain these phenomena contributed much to monetary theory, but their analysis of the problem was imperfect in many respects and their information was defective. At that time no index numbers of prices had ever been constructed, and no substantial analysis is possible without several series of price indexes. David Ricardo and the group associated with the Bullion Report also misunderstood and misinterpreted many credit phenomena. They were in error about the relations between the Bank of England and the country banks, and they assumed that deposit credits were less important than note issues. There has been considerable discussion of this episode in recent years, but despite a great enlargement of our knowledge it is difficult to feel that the final word has been said.

### Neutrals and Enemy Trade, 1793–1803

Upon the outbreak of war with France in 1793, Parliament passed (May, 1793) a Statute on Traitorous Correspondence, which prohibited the export to France of any military stores, foodstuffs, clothing, commercial paper, or specie. The statute itself contemplated some exemptions and provided for the issue of licenses to permit trade with the enemy. The prohibition, therefore, became a basis for controlled trade, and subsequent redefinitions of the prohibition merely resulted in modifications and extensions of the license system. Whatever the significance of the various Orders in Council or statutes for the history of international law, their actual importance for the history of trade was completely dominated by the system of trade controls worked out in the license system. This novel system, developed at first by executive decrees (Orders in Council), was authorized in a mature and highly generalized form by the statutes of 1799 and 1800.

These statutes recognized explicitly the complete abandonment of the restrictions of the Navigation Acts. Since Cromwell's time British trade had been restricted to British ships, or, in respect to European goods, to the ships of the country in which the goods originated, or of the country controlling the usual port of first shipment. The war emergency forced Great Britain to give extensive recognition to all the neutral carriers, regardless of the origin of the goods. The European wars never entirely engulfed the small states of the North Sea and Baltic Sea. The United Provinces, the Scandinavian countries, the Hanse towns Lübeck, Bremen, and Hamburg, the port of Danzig, all served for longer or shorter periods as ports of entry and as sources of neutral shipping. American vessels also played a large part in the carrying trade of Europe. Trade contacts existing at the outbreak of the wars brought many American vessels to France and to Great Britain with exports from the United States, but only a portion of the return cargoes was taken from the British Isles.   Neutral shipping and neutral ports therefore afforded the simplest vehicle for maintaining trade with the enemy. At this early stage, neutrals were not even required to secure licenses for the import of grain from enemy or nonenemy territory.   The wars thus modified the conditions of trade.   Even the blockades were not strictly enforced.   In December, 1800, neutrals were guaranteed immunity from seizure by British war vessels or privateers if they were bringing supplies to Great Britain from enemy ports, whether blockaded or not blockaded.

The status of neutrals was adversely affected by the Navigation Act of the Revolutionary government in France.   The French act of September 21, 1793, and a supplementary law of October 9, applied to France all the characteristic features of the early English Navigation Acts.   The trade of France was reserved to French vessels, navigated by French crews, excepting only vessels of other countries bringing their own products.   Neutrals engaged in carrying British goods from British ports would be excluded by these navigation laws.   Neutrals shipping a cargo in France after landing cargo from their own country could not be prevented from landing the cargo in Great Britain.   In the earlier phase of the wars, however, France exerted no serious pressure on neutrals.

Crop failures in 1799 created a serious shortage of food in Great Britain, which was intensified by the modifications of usual trade contacts and special conditions of European demand.   Production in England was about half of the normal yield, and foreign crops were likewise below normal, so that emergency supplies were difficult to secure.   From a quotation of 49 shillings 6 pence per quarter in January, 1799, the price of wheat rose to 93 shillings 10 pence. There was much distress in the larger towns; soup kitchens were opened, and wheat was sold to the needy at cost.   Wheatless meals and days were ordered.   The assize of bread, which regulated the processes of baking and retail trade, was amended in small details, but no attempt was made to make the use of coarse bread compulsory.   Export of cereals was prohibited; starch making and distilling were restricted.   Bounties were offered on importations of food at certain ports, and all duties on importation were remitted. The emergency was partly met, but the scarcity of cereals in Europe gave England her first clear intimation of her food problem.   The surplus available in northern Europe would no longer suffice to meet demand in periods of deficient harvests.   Opinion at the time was sharply divided on the analysis of the crisis. Some members of the government and a number of well-informed experts realized perfectly the full meaning of the crisis. This view was later confirmed by the careful surveys of the wheat resources of Europe made in 1818-1820 by William Jacob. Many contemporaries, however, assumed that the crisis was due to the wars, or to the restrictive Corn Laws, or to the failure to extend proper encouragement to agriculture.

Prices continued high throughout 1800 and 1801. The first general enclosure act was passed; much new land was improved and brought into arable culture, and much emphasis was placed upon better methods of culture. Sir John Sinclair and his followers maintained stoutly that with proper protection and proper methods Great Britain could provide for her own needs. The stimulus afforded by this crisis contributed much to the relief of pressure on food supplies in the later years of the wars when some positive pressure was exerted to close the Continent to British trade.

### The Continental System and the Blockade

The Peace of Amiens, March 25, 1802, afforded a short period of relief from war controls, but military operations began again in 1803, and on May 16 the English laid an embargo upon all French shipping, which soon resulted in the re-establishment of the system of licensed trade. The extension of Napoleon's authority on the Continent, however, soon gave a new turn to events. Prussia was forced to close her ports to British trade on March 5, 1806, and the British government replied (April 16, 1806) by declaring a blockade of the coast from the mouth of the Elbe to Brest. The Berlin Decree of Napoleon (November 21, 1806) gave more explicit form to the French position. The British Isles were declared to be in a state of blockade; all commercial intercourse with Great Britain was forbidden even to neutrals; no vessels coming directly from Great Britain or her colonial possessions were to be allowed entrance in any French port; all vessels making false declarations were declared lawful prize.

Despite the shattering effect of these declarations upon established principles of international law, the actual movement of trade was not greatly altered. Few seizures of neutral vessels were made under the Berlin Decree until after the Treaty of Tilsit (July 7, 1807), and the British license system was progressively transformed to meet the changed circumstances of the trade. The order of February 4, 1807, declared that neither British naval vessels nor British privateers would stop neutrals going to the United Kingdom with importable goods, even though the goods seemed to be "enemy property," provided only that the ship had not cleared from a port actually blockaded by the British fleet. This meant, in effect, that the British would not seize a neutral vessel that had cleared from one French port nominally bound for another French port, if the vessel in fact were proceeding to a British port. With this order the system of controlled trade entered its final stage of sophistication : the clearance papers of the trading vessels ceased to have any certain meaning. Vessels with French papers were safe only if they proceeded to the British Isles. Vessels with neutral papers and a neutral flag might in fact be French vessels that had been officially "neutralized." Neutrals might have documents from both sides : a license from Great Britain to pass them by the British cruisers, and French papers to secure their clearance from a French port. These final developments were a direct result of the famous measures of 1807. A British Order in Council (November, 1807) required neutrals to enter a British port and pay customs duties before proceeding to European ports. Napoleon's Milan Decree of December 17, 1807, declared that neutral vessels would be seized if they recognized the British order, whether by actually paying customs in a British port or by submitting to visit by a British naval vessel. Trade between the British Isles and the Continent continued in spite of these measures, and in spite of the more extensive blockade declared April 26, 1809, covering all ports under French control from the Ems to northern Italy. The nominal effects of the primary declarations were profoundly modified by the licensed trade of neutrals, fictitious or real. Most of the trade between the enemy countries passed through some neutral port, but in 1810 the French harvests were so large that there was no hope of disposing of them except in the British Isles, and direct export was permitted under license. More than three million bushels of wheat were exported to Great Britain from France and Flanders, about one quarter of all the wheat imported by the British in that year. In November, 1811, negotiations were begun through intermediaries for an exchange of French wine for British sugar. An arrangement was actually concluded in January, 1812, and though the quantities involved were not large, it is noteworthy that even at this particular date there was no disposition to attempt a complete cessation of all trade with the enemy. In fact, both France and Great Britain were on the point of withdrawing their basic decrees and orders, under pressure from the United States.

In the light of the full descriptions of licenses and trade controls, it is evident that neither Great Britain nor France was able to attempt a drastic application of economic pressure. All economic measures invariably produced domestic reactions which no government could ignore. The use of economic pressure was therefore qualified by the necessity of avoiding ill effects at home. It was possible to subject the adversary to much inconvenience, and the practical objective was to create as much distress as possible with the least possible damage to the home market. In this economic contest the command of the sea gave the British a decisive advantage. France suffered considerable inconvenience from dearth of tropical and semitropical commodities. Nominally, France was in a position to curtail the food supply of her antagonist, but the explicit influence of war measures was largely confined to the years 1811 and 1812. Even in those years there is no evidence of any determined attempt to starve England into submission. The failure of the Russian campaign and the revolt of Prussia against Napoleon made an end of any pretense of closure of the Continent against England.

# CHAPTER 13

# AGRARIAN REFORMS IN EUROPE, 1789–1870

## The Night of the Fourth of August

Events in Paris in the summer of 1789 led to much disorder in the provinces. Peasants refused to pay rents to their lords, and many chateaux were attacked. It was generally assumed that the fall of the Bastille marked the downfall of the old regime. The National Assembly was obliged to take some step to prevent the spread of disorder. At a meeting on August 3 letters from the provinces were read, disclosing this grave crisis. A Committee of the Assembly proposed a resolution urging the peasants to recognize existing obligations until the constitution was completed, as the Assembly would then deal suitably with the problem. After brief debate, the Committee was instructed to bring in an amended draft of the resolution. On the afternoon of August 4 the Committee presented a resolution couched in sharper terms than the first draft; it declared that the riots threatened "the sacred rights of property and of personal safety." The discussion of this commonplace declaration was suddenly given an unexpected significance by speeches from two members of the nobility. Feeling that the growing antagonisms of the peasantry might best be checked by timely concessions, some nobles had already renounced certain of the more odious feudal privileges. The Duc d'Aiguillon planned to give wider scope to such a policy by proposing the general commutation of various feudal obligations. The Duc de Noailles happened, however, to speak first, and offered a still more generous concession: abolition without compensation of the labor services, and of all personal servitudes. The Duc d'Aiguillon gave his support to this proposal and debate followed, though without much evidence of general support for this momentous proposal. One member thought that the Assembly was actually on the point of adopting the resolution of the Committee, when the entire character of the debate was changed by the speech of Le Guen de Kerangall, a member of the third estate. Dressed in peasant costume, he delivered a ringing speech on the rights of man and the injustices of feudalism. The rest of the session was one of the most extraordinary in the Revolution, and when the Assembly finally adjourned at one o'clock the next morning, it had voted a series of resolutions which led ultimately to the abolition of all feudal rights without compensation.

The resolutions of August 4 contained only a general declaration of policy, so that more formal expression of their aims was made in a series of decrees voted in the course of the following week.   The new legislation was put in final form by the decree of August 11 : "The National Assembly destroys entirely the feudal regime, and decrees the abolition without compensation of all feudal dues and rents pertaining to serfs or involving personal servitude.   All other obligations may be redeemed at rates and under conditions to be determined by the National Assembly."   Other articles abolished all jurisdictional rights, and the exclusive rights of hunting and of keeping pigeons or rabbits.   Tithes were ordered abolished, but were to be collected until more suitable provision could be made for the support of the clergy.   Rents payable under perpetual leases of all kinds were recognized as nonfeudal payments for the use of land, but all such obligations could be extinguished by payment of the equivalent capital sum.

Even this later resolution was a statement of policy rather than a mature legislative act, and there were serious elements of ambiguity. The declaration that the feudal regime was abolished was a gross overstatement of the actual scope of the measure.   The only concession of substantial pecuniary importance was the renunciation of the fines and fees incidental to the administration of civil and criminal law in the seignorial courts.   The primary sources of feudal revenue were not touched. All classes of ground rents and all dues on transfers and successions were retained.   These notable reservations were emphasized in the decree of March 15, 1790, which defined administrative procedure to be followed in execution of the decree of August 11.   Furthermore, the rates prescribed May 3, 1790, for the redemption of ground rents were held to be excessive. Rents payable in money were to be extinguished by the payment of a capital sum amounting to twenty times the annual rent; in effect, capitalization at 5 per cent.   Rents payable in kind could be extinguished only by payment of twenty-five times the annual rent; equivalent to capitalization at 4 per cent.

### Emancipation without Compensation, 1790-1793

The refinements of legal reasoning embodied in all these qualifications made no impression on the minds of the peasants.   They were told that feudalism was abolished, and to them the meaning was clear — that all the rights of the feudal lords were abolished. Attempts to collect rents were met by persistent refusal and obstruction. The peasants became convinced that the lords were evading the clear meaning of the new laws. Violence increased, and the National Assembly found itself obliged to take concerted measures for the repression of this spirit of revolt. But other decrees inevitably served to emphasize the radical interpretation of the peasants. On June 19, 1790, further use of titles of nobility was prohibited, and in April, 1791, all special honors were abolished. The nobility were required to discontinue the use of special pews in the choirs of churches and chapels. They were required to take down the gallowses and pillories which had long been the symbols of jurisdictional rights. Weather vanes, which had also been a symbol of privilege, were henceforth to be freely used by all. Social equality was achieved at an early stage of the reforms.

Continued disorders and the changed complexion of the new Legislative Assembly ultimately led to further concessions to the peasantry. The law of August 18, 1792, abolished all dues on transfers and successions. The important law of August 25, 1792, required documentary proof of title of all feudal lords, both in respect of further collection of the rents admissible and in respect of continued possession of woods and pastures. It appeared that a considerable number of lords actually possessed documentary titles to their estates, while others did not, so that discriminations arose. Some peasants escaped all payment of dues and acquired full ownership of their lands, whereas others attached to a different estate still remained subject to the payment of rents. In the meantime, the movement of revolutionary thought had broken down what little conservatism had remained, so that the Convention finally completed the destruction of feudalism by the law of July 17, 1793. All feudal rights were abolished, even if they rested on documentary title. All perpetual leases were assumed to be equivalent to full ownership, and the lessees were thenceforth recognized as owners without payment of any compensation to the lessors. The only rents still recognized were the rents due on share tenancies and rents due on leases for a stated number of years. All feudal documents and titles were ordered to be deposited with the municipal authorities within three months; on August 10, 1793, all the documents collected were to be burned, and the remainder within three months. The promises of August 4 and August 11, 1789, were thus fulfilled.

### The Formation of the National Domain

The laws of 1792–1793 stripped the clergy of their tithes and the nobility of all revenues not derived from the direct exploitation of their land or from their share tenancies and leaseholds. Measures of a different category affected the property of the church and all persons who emigrated from France. The law of November 2, 1789, placed all ecclesiastical property at the disposition of the kingdom. On December 21 the National Assembly authorized the sale of ecclesiastical property to the amount of 400,000,000 francs, and in July, 1790, the sale of all the property of the church was authorized. The state assumed all the debts with which this property was charged, and provision was to be made for the support of the clergy, but even with these deductions the diversion of funds was considerable. These properties, together with the immediate possessions ef the crown, were known as the national domain of primary origin.

The property of the *émigrés* and the condemned constituted a distinct portion of the national domain. A law of November 9, 1791, declared the *émigrés* collected near the frontier subject to capital punishment and forfeiture of their estates unless they dispersed before January 1, 1792. On December 13, 1791, it was provided that no *émigré* should receive any pension from the state. Property of *émigrés* was sequestrated February 9, 1792, and by July 27 it was recognized in principle that the property of *émigrés* should be sold. The administrative procedure to be followed in these sales was defined by laws of August 14 and September 2, 1792.

The landed estates of importance in this second category of the national domain were largely but not exclusively the property of nobles. The victims of the Terror included many members of the third estate, and many proscribed persons of humble circumstances fled across the frontiers. The official list of *émigrés* included more than 130,000 names, though applications for the restoration of estates did not exceed 30,000. The laws abolishing feudalism confiscated without compensation nearly all the revenues not derived directly from exploitation; the former noble was thus left his chateau, his woods, and the lands worked by hired laborers or share tenants. Those who remained in France and escaped the Revolutionary tribunals were left in the enjoyment of their immediate estates. A few of the nobles thus maintained their position; but by far the larger number lost all their property.

The Revolutionary legislation was intended to provide for the sale of the confiscated lands in small parcels, so that the number of peasant proprietors might be largely increased. The objective was achieved in part. About half the land formerly held by the church was purchased by bourgeois. The individual parcels were small, but it is generally presumed that the bourgeois did not intend to work the land themselves, and the combination of parcels gave many of them gross holdings of appreciable size. The restitutions to the *émigrés* ultimately led to the restoration of a distinct class of large landowners. The number of peasant proprietors, however, must have increased somewhat, even if we count as peasant proprietors under the old regime the numerous holders under perpetual lease.

The gross amounts of these redistributions of wealth are very imperfectly known. Lecarpentier estimates the value of church property sold at 2,500,000,000 francs of 1790. The real estate of the *émigrés* apparently amounted to about 1,500,000,000 francs of 1790; the capital value of the property unsold in 1814 amounted to about 187,000,000 francs, and the losses were officially computed as 1,297,000,000 francs of 1790. The church lands were sold rapidly during the earlier Revolutionary period, and the greater part of this portion of the national domain was sold before the end of the Terror. Sales of the property of *émigrés* proceeded much more slowly, and only about half of the property sold was conveyed even by May 31, 1795. The status of these sales aroused many doubts, and definitive validation of all titles to new holders became a serious political issue. Despite misgivings, none of the governments subsequent to the Terror was in a position to question the permanent guarantee of all titles of bona fide possessors of property purchased from the state. The restoration of Louis XVIII could be assured only upon the condition of the recognition of all new possessors.

### The " Milliard of the Émigrés "

The dispossessed also presented a problem which increased steadily in gravity. The general amnesty granted the *émigrés* April 26, 1802, provided for the restitution of certain confiscated property which had not actually been sold. Some forest land was to be retained by the state. Buildings converted to public use were retained, and no restitution was authorized if the value of the property of the applicant exceeded 100,000 francs. In individual cases exceptions were made, but restoration of property under the

Empire was not of large significance. After the fall of Napoleon the problem became acute. The *émigrés* were eager to secure full restitution of all property lost, but it was evident to all in authority that such a policy was politically impossible. The Charter of 1814 guaranteed titles to purchasers and holders of national property. A law of December 5, 1814, however, authorized the restitution of all confiscated property remaining unsold; provided for the payment of an indemnity for property in public use, and for the payment to the original owners of any balances still due the state.

The property available for distribution under this law had a rental value of 9,380,000 francs, or a capital value of about 187,600,000 francs. It consisted largely of forests (9,000,000 francs revenue), and 46 per cent of these forests had been previously owned by the Duc de Conde and the Duc d'Orleans. As a resource to the general body of *émigrés*, this act of restitution was therefore of modest significance, amounting to less than 7 per cent of the official computation of the direct losses. It is thus easy to appreciate the intensity of the feelings of the *émigrés*, and despite the extravagance of many of their demands, the payment of some indemnity was a simple act of justice. Political circumstances made its achievement a matter of considerable difficulty, and it was not until 1824 that a formal project was laid before the Chambers.

The law of April 27, 1825, provided for the payment of an indemnity amounting to a little less than 1,000,000,000 francs. An attempt was made to compute the value of the estates lost as of 1790; from this amount certain deductions were made on account of debts discharged by the state, and of restitutions under the law of 1814; the balance was paid in bonds yielding interest at 3 per cent. In many instances the *émigrés* were able to buy back portions of their estates, but the number of parcels was so great that actual reconstruction of the old domain was difficult if not impossible. As a class, the *émigrés* received substantial restitution; there were, however, many inequalities in the administration of the laws: some received amounts in excess of the values lost; others, less.

This "milliard of the *émigrés*," however, was not intended to afford any compensation for the rents and dues abolished by the law of July 17, 1793, and the earlier laws directed towards the abolition of the feudal regime. The restoration did not alter in any detail the general effect of the primary legislation of the Revolution. All feudal rights, and many that were not really feudal, were suppressed without compensation. There is no means of forming any correct idea of the extent of these losses. In the early days of the Directory one of the officials declared that the rents formerly received from perpetual leases of all classes amounted to 120,000,000 francs, representing a capital value of about 2,500,000,000. The true feudal rents must have reached a substantial sum, and there was some net revenue from the fees and fines derived from the seignorial courts. The rents suppressed without compensation may well have accounted for two thirds of the income of the feudal lords.

## Reforms in " Liberated " Territory

The eighteenth century witnessed the beginnings of reform in the condition of the peasantry of most of the leading European countries, but the effective accomplishment was so narrowly limited in scope that we commonly associate the reform of agriculture with the nineteenth century. The political ideals of Revolutionary France contributed much to the progress of reform, and the conquests of the armies of France contributed as much or even more. But the appearances are in some respects misleading. The Revolution and its conquests were an important factor in the timing of the reforms, but the actual progress of reorganization was the product of local needs combined with the liberal-radical philosophy that was so widely diffused during the eighteenth century. It must be remembered that attacks upon the privileges of the nobles and the clergy were fostered by the growth of monarchical power as well as by new democratic ideals. New concepts of agricultural policy were suggested by the development of economic thought in England and in France. Both the physiocrats and the English liberals criticized absentee landlordism and urged measures to give more security and independence to the peasant cultivators. In Savoy, Piedmont, Tuscany, and Naples, and in Spain, the beginnings of reform were definitely associated with the development of the authority of the crown. Many feudal privileges were curtailed or abolished, and the position of the peasantry correspondingly improved. It is true that many of the privileges affected by these reforms had already ceased to be of much practical importance, but it was nevertheless a step forward to clear away these obsolete features of the old regime. In Naples and in Spain some attention was given the important problems created by the rights of pasturage possessed by the associations of owners of migratory flocks and herds. The extension and improvement of arable agriculture made it desirable to curtail the privileges of the grazing rights of the sheep and cattle on the march between winter and summer pastures; but this problem was less difficult than the problems presented by enclosure in England and northern Europe. The antagonisms between farmers and shepherds were of long standing both in Spain and in Italy. The crown found that it had important fiscal motives for the adoption of policies more favorable to settled agriculture and to the support of larger numbers of taxpayers. The genesis of the reform movement was thus a matter of considerable complexity. Practical needs were combined with legal and political ideals of great diversity. The influence of the French Revolution was largely due to this extensive preparation for a substantial reorganization of the status and position of the peasantry.

French influence was directly extended beyond the old frontiers by the conquests of the armies. The territory of Belgium and the whole of the left bank of the Rhine were incorporated in the territory of France, and French legislation was applied. The decrees abolishing feudal rights were put into effect there by decrees of 1795 and 1798, and executed with such thoroughness that none of these rights and privileges were subsequently restored. Holland, though organized independently as the Batavian Republic and later as a kingdom, was likewise legally assimilated to France. Decrees of 1801 and 1804 abolished feudal privileges and feudal tenures. Some privileges were subsequently restored, but the main achievements of reform were not disturbed.

In Italy, French law and institutions were promulgated in the various states established by Napoleon. The laws relating to the abolition of feudal rights and privileges were applied to Piedmont and Sardinia in 1797; to Naples, Lombardy, and Venetia in 1806; to Tuscany in 1808; to the States of the Church in 1809; and to Sicily in 1810. Problems of administration varied considerably among the different sections. In the north and in Tuscany little remained of the onerous obligations of feudalism. Naples and Sicily, however, presented a more serious problem. The administrative commission charged with the execution of the reform discovered 1,395 distinct feudal rights and privileges. As a concession to the nobility, rights were recognized if positive title could be proved. This qualification protected many estates, and as the projected abolition of entails was unsuccessful, the broader features of the agrarian regime were not destroyed.

## The Reaction in Italy

The reaction after the fall of Napoleon was severe. Practically every section of Italy nominally restored all the old laws, but in actuality the restoration was less complete than appeared on the surface. Civil and criminal jurisdictional privileges were largely qualified even when nominally restored. The entailed estates were restored in nearly every section of Italy, so that the large landholders as a class were not destroyed, nor significantly dispossessed. Their rights, however, were more nearly proprietary. All the older tenures were restored in slightly modified forms: the perpetual leaseholds (emphyteusis), share tenancy (métayage), and the leases for periods of years at money rents. Church lands were restored in part, though in many instances the rights were merely rights to receive rents from perpetual leases.

The significance of this reversal of policy is still a matter of considerable difference of opinion. Some believe that it was socially undesirable to re-establish the great estates; others feel that the merits of peasant proprietorship may be seriously exaggerated. Both share tenants and perpetual leaseholders were significantly dependent upon their landlords; at the most the share tenants might be reduced to a condition bordering on peonage. Their obligation frequently exceeded their means of payment, so that they were continuously in debt to the proprietor. It is alleged that the division of produce was unfair to the tenant, and that these tenants actually received less for their work than the day laborer. But it is certainly significant that an idealist of the attainments of Sismondi could feel so firmly convinced that share tenancy assured the greatest possible degree of independence and well-being to a class without sufficient means to lease and equip a holding. "The Tuscan peasant receives from the hand of nature all provision for his subsistence; he needs scarcely any money, as he has no payments to make; he has no knowledge of taxes, because they are paid by the proprietors; and as he can have no dispute with the government, he is generally deeply attached to it. He lives on his holding as if it were an inheritance, improving it with confidence in the future, knowing that his fields will be worked after his death by his children and his grandchildren. . . . He has all the advantages of ownership without the inconvenience of being obliged to defend it." [1]

[1] Sismondi, J. C. L. Simonde de, *Études sur l'économie politique*, Paris, 1837, vol. I, pp. 291–294.

Sismondi was writing from direct personal knowledge of his own estates and the life of that section of Tuscany. He was, of course, identified with the landowning class, but his views were dominated by his ideals rather than by his social position. Bowring says that Sismondi "looked at the question as a philanthropist, seeking the result of his theories in the content and happiness of the laboring poor." Bowring himself makes a most illuminating comment upon the "independence" of the métayer. "There is a point of view," he says, "which has not excited sufficient attention; this is the universal isolation of the peasantry, which is a necessary condition of the mezzeria system. Where there is no association there must be much ignorance. Every peasants' family in Tuscany stands as it were alone; this is indeed a great security for the public tranquillity; but it is tranquillity purchased at a fearful price, at the price of a stationary and backward civilization. I do not perceive how education can break down the barriers which surround every *contadino* [peasant] family. I had occasion more than once to see four generations inhabiting the same cottage; but the last had not added a particle of knowledge to the ignorance of the first : the same gross superstitions, the same prejudices against books, the same unwillingness to introduce any species of improvement in husbandry, the same reference to ancestral usages. In innumerable cases families have occupied the same farms for hundreds of years, without adding a farthing to their wealth, or a fragment to their knowledge ! Can the system be changed ? Certainly not by direct or violent legislation, nor by individual efforts, which have failed again and again, because they have struggled against the vis inertia of generations." [1]

In Tuscany and in the States of the Church it was commonly held in Bowring's time that the proprietors of lands let on share tenancy received as net gain no more than one quarter and sometimes as little as one sixth of the gross produce. A number of costs were borne by the proprietor, and in any event the maintenance of the tenant was in effect a first charge on the produce. It was in the interest of the proprietor to insure reasonable provision for basic needs, but even a grasping proprietor might find it hard to circumvent the wiles of peasants, cunning with the experience of generations in dealing with proprietors and their agents.

Although the results of the Parliamentary inquiry of 1883 seem to

---

[1] Bowring, Sir John, "Report on the Statistics of Tuscany, Lucca, the Pontifical, and the Lombardo-Venetian States," *Commons Papers*, 1839, vol. XVI (Cd. 165), p. 40.

furnish a less favorable view of the position of the métayers, Grizi, writing in 1909, presents later evidence which makes it necessary to qualify the official conclusions of the report. He holds that the métayer is definitely better off than the agricultural laborer, and that this form of tenancy is so well adapted to the requirements of extensive regions that there is no ground for substituting other forms of tenure for it. In so far as the reactionary policies of the various restored monarchs merely preserved the great estates and the broad elements of the older tenures, the policies were by no means without constructive merit. The ideals of the Revolutionary period contained much that was unsound and extravagant, and even in France many features of the original program were abandoned.

### The Work of the Spanish Liberals

In Spain the advance of the French armies led to the formation of a Regency directed by a committee charged with national defense. Reform elements were dominant in the leadership of the government, as in the membership of the Cortes of 1811 which formulated the new constitution. The reform legislation was therefore the work of the Spanish liberals, and not merely an application of French legislation to a conquered or "liberated" area. The agrarian reforms were embodied in four statutes enacted by the Cortes, but not incorporated in the constitution of 1812. The statute of August 6, 1811, abolished feudal rights and gave full ownership to possessors of seignorial estates and to peasant proprietors. The law of June 11, 1813, was directed against the privileges of the owners of migratory sheep and the general concept of common grazing. All general rights of pasturage were extinguished on pastures, arable land, and other land. The law of July 19, 1813, abolished feudal rights exercised by the crown in various localities in Aragon. The law of January 4, 1813, provided for the division of all land held in common, excepting only enclosed common pasture. Only the first of these laws is of much permanent significance, as all the others were annulled by decree of Ferdinand VII, May 4, 1814. The law of August 6, 1811, became the basis of all subsequent reforms of property in Spain. This law provided for the abolition of all surviving feudal rights without compensation, so that the general principle is similar to the Revolutionary legislation in France, but there were important differences in detail. The actual reform of the agrarian tenures was much less drastic than in France. All seignorial rights of jurisdiction were vested in the national government. The law abolished all personal services and all obligations based upon rights of lordship and not derived from a free contractual engagement provable by extant titles. It also abolished all feudal rights of an exclusive or restrictive character, such as the rights of hunting and fishing reserved hitherto to territorial lords, the obligation to use the lord's oven and the lord's mill, and exclusive control of water rights and of forests. Compensation was allowed only when positive documentary title could be exhibited. Rights formerly enjoyed by territorial lords and by peasant proprietors were converted into rights of full ownership. Estates reverted to the nation if their possessors had failed to perform the services in consideration of which the estate had been granted.

The chief differences between this law and the French laws lay in the interpretation of the expression "free contractual engagement." Spanish administrators recognized as contractual the rents paid by lessees holding under perpetual leases. These payments were held to be rents, with no contaminating element of feudal subservience. This interpretation was legally sound, and although it protected the position of the great proprietors, it may well have been sound policy. In France the essential features of the perpetual lease were preserved in a lease that was nominally limited to twenty-nine years. As no formal act of renewal was required, common consent made the tenancy in effect a continuing relationship.

After the Restoration, acts of the Regency and the Cortes were annulled, but jurisdictional rights were not restored. The execution of the law of August, 1811, was suspended until the re-establishment of constitutional government in 1820. In 1821 a law was passed to deal with a number of problems of administration. New emphasis was laid upon the production of documentary titles. Lordships might be recognized as estates in full ownership only after proof of title, and collection of rents was suspended until title was established. It was further provided that payments of rent under perpetual leases should not exceed 2 per cent of the value of the property. At this time, too, complete abolition of entails was voted (October 11, 1820). But the application of these reforms was again delayed by the overthrow of the constitutional government, and it was not until 1836 and 1837 that the effective execution of these laws was attempted. The laws of 1811 and 1821 were re-enacted August 26, 1837; the abolition of entails was again voted August 30, 1836, but the reform was not fully recognized until 1841.

## The Genesis of Reform in Prussia

In the portions of central Europe not profoundly influenced by French ideas and legislation, Prussia is the most important and most distinctive area. It will therefore be most helpful to study conditions in Prussia in some detail. The reforms in Prussia assumed a highly characteristic form, differing in many respects from both French and English types. In some of the smaller states, notably Denmark, the policies followed were also distinctive and significant, but for the most part the agrarian reforms in the other states of central Europe present only secondary variations from the French or Prussian types. A clear understanding of the differences in policy is more important than geographical comprehensiveness.

Lehmann and some other writers have held that the reforms in Prussia were significantly influenced by French thought and legislation. He even went so far as to attribute large importance to French thought in the formation of the liberal policies of Stein. But this view is unsound. In so far as foreign influences are to be found among the German liberals of the period, English influences predominate. Hanover was an important source of contacts with English thought and institutions, and there were many important literary contacts. Adam Smith and Arthur Young were well known to small but important groups of experts and administrators. Despite the importance of French literary influences in the time of Frederick the Great and the continued influence of the language and manners, the radical tendencies of French thought made no deep impression. With the outbreak of the Revolution the reactions of the nobles and the bureaucracy were predominantly hostile. French influence, therefore, was important only in those areas placed under the direct administrative control of France, and some immediately adjacent territory. The Rhine provinces of Prussia came under these influences, so that in the description of the distinctive agrarian reforms it must be understood that the areas primarily involved are the portions of Prussia largely east of the Elbe: Brandenburg, Silesia, Pomerania, and the province of Prussia. The reforms of the nineteenth century were at one time dated from the edict issued October 9, 1807 (often called Stein's Edict), but modern researches have emphasized their continuity with the reforms of the eighteenth century.

The policies of the nineteenth century were not new, but they assumed new significance because the critical condition of the state

made it possible to require some sacrifices of the nobility.   Furthermore, the disasters of 1806 finally forced the king to abandon his
favorites and to give effective authority to the heads of the great
administrative departments.   The recall of Stein in September,
1807, gave real power to the great administrative system that had
been gradually building since the accession of Frederick the Great.
The leading administrators had long realized the imperative need of
far-reaching social and political reforms, and many elements of the
program were clearly formulated in their minds.   Stein's Edict
was actually prepared in the midst of the crisis leading to Stein's
recall, so that the final text was actually published (October 9, 1807)
only eight days after Stein's first audience with the king.   The
memoirs and papers of the leading ministers disclose completely the
advanced stage which had already been reached in the formulation
of the reforms that followed, though the care taken in the preparation of the ordinances frequently required a substantial interval
of time.   We know, for instance, that the preliminary studies for
the ordinance on the Division of Commons were begun within a
few weeks of Stein's recall, though the ordinance was not issued
until June 7, 1821.   It is rare that any legislation is prepared with
as much regard for the knowledge of experts and the practical
requirements of a concrete social system.   Foreign influences cannot be excluded, but the achievement was highly characteristic
both in concepts of policy and in the details of administration.

Conditions in Prussia presented a wider range of problems than
were to be found in France and the Mediterranean countries.   The
peasants were more abjectly dependent upon their lords than in
France or even in Spain and Italy.   The task of emancipation was
therefore more difficult and complex.   The characteristics of soil
and climate made desirable a substantial change in methods of
agriculture.   In Prussia, east of the Elbe, a great increase in stock
raising was required if the land were to be used to the best advantage.
It was therefore necessary to abolish the old practice of common
pasturage on the arable fields, and many meadows and arable fields
needed to be enclosed.   The reforms fall into these two divisions:
(a) emancipation from personal subjection and from servile dues of
feudal origin, and (b) the abolition of all rights of common.   The
lords received more consideration than in France or in areas significantly influenced by France.   Compensation was awarded for all
dues and burdens charged upon the land.   The award of land as
compensation for dues surrendered was a novel feature of Prussian

policy which was probably wise, despite certain dangers. The abolition of common rights and the subsequent enclosure presents similarities to the English enclosure movement, but the differences were of the utmost importance. The English procedure of the eighteenth and early nineteenth centuries was characterized by the comprehensive enclosure of the entire area of the village. Prussian procedure was much more flexible; the demesne lands of the lords were separated from the peasant holdings, but no pressure was placed upon the peasants to enclose their land. Many peasants were thus allowed to reorganize their holdings as small farms without incurring many of the costs that would have been imposed upon them by comprehensive enclosure. Furthermore, peasants whose rights did not entitle them to a parcel of land that could be economically worked received an award of a capital sum or an annual rent. A conscientious attempt was certainly made to treat meadows, pastures, and woods from a broad, social point of view. Each case was examined on its merits. It is now generally recognized that the English enclosure acts provided inadequate safeguards in these respects. The Prussian reformers treated an extremely difficult problem with keen judgment and with genuine regard for social welfare. All the details of the earlier laws were profoundly influenced by Albrecht Thaer, the great agriculturalist, and they bear eloquent witness to his knowledge.

### Emancipation and Commutation in Prussia, 1807-1858

The edict of October 9, 1807, established free trade in land, assured to all a free choice of occupation, and abolished the humiliating obligations of serfs. Restrictions upon the purchase and sale of land by particular classes were abolished; nobles could buy town land or peasant holdings, and members of the lower classes might buy "noble" land. Procedures were established for breaking entails and trusts. With the consent of the authorities lords might combine peasant holdings or attach them to the demesne. These provisions were designed to enable impoverished nobles to secure funds needed for repair of war damage without burdening the land with mortgages. It was deemed wisest to keep the land unencumbered. Freedom of choice of occupation was granted all classes in order to promote readjustments between the urban and rural populations. Personal subjection was abolished: immediately, in respect of all who held land under heritable tenures or by perpetual lease; on Martinmas, 1810, in respect of all other peasants. The orders of 1808 and 1809 gave a narrow interpretation to these sections. The more important obligations of the peasants were not modified: rents in money or in kind; labor services rendered by the peasants, with or without their teams; dues on transfers; dues of craft workers; court fees; all these obligations remained. The edict abolished the dues payable for personal emancipation; the obligation of the peasant's children to render labor services for three years at the manor house at nominal wages; the fees due from persons seeking subsistence outside the manor. It exempted peasants of twenty-four years or over from the obligation to accept cottages in the village charged with the burdens of obligatory service. Although this edict marks the beginning of the general reforms, it was not intended to abolish feudalism or even to define the general procedure for the reorganization of agriculture.

The general policy of the reformers was embodied in the edicts of 1811, 1816, and 1821.[1] In the adjustment of relations between the peasants and their lords the general principle was followed of allowing compensation varying in amount according to the security of the tenure. Perpetual lessees were granted full ownership of their holding upon payment of twenty-five times the amount of the annual rent. Peasants holding land by heritable customary tenure were required in 1811 to cede one third of their land. Peasants holding life tenancies or leases for a fixed number of years were required to cede one half their land. It was assumed in 1811 that these adjustments would be quickly made; but such was not the case. The declaration of May 29, 1816, modified procedure significantly and delayed the completion of the reforms for a generation. The poorer peasants were excluded from the operation of the law. Adjustment was made more complex by provision for computation of equivalents in each case. Finally, it was provided that if both lord and peasant found the existing condition satisfactory, nothing need be done. The edict of March 2, 1850, made provision for the completion of the abolition or conversion of feudal dues and services. Twenty-four enumerated rights, obligations, and dues were abolished without any compensation. Surviving perpetual leaseholds were converted to full proprietorships and the general principles of adjustment were made applicable to the small holders excluded from the earlier laws. A later order brought the process of commutation to a close by refusing to recognize petitions after December 31, 1858.

[1] On September 14, 1811, and again on June 7, 1821, edicts were issued on both phases of the reforms, described respectively as *Regulierung* and *Gemeinheits-Theilung*.

PROGRESS OF COMMUTATION, PRUSSIA [1]

| | Number of New Owners | Number of Morgen of Area Gained [2] | Number of Days' Service Abolished | |
|---|---|---|---|---|
| | | | Team Service | Hand Labor |
| 1811–1820 | 18,256 | 1,550,000 | 920,000 | 950,000 |
| 1821–1848 | 52,326 | 3,600,000 | 5,050,000 | 15,910,000 |
| 1849–1865 | 12,706 | 350,000 | 360,000 | 6,680,000 |
| 1866–1895 | 572 | 710,000 | 30,000 | 60,000 |
| Total | 83,860 | 6,210,000 | 6,360,000 | 23,600,000 |

Official returns of adjustments of feudal rights are incomplete, but they afford an approximate index of the progress of adjustment. The area reported yields the results given in the above table. But the area covered by the returns is less than 10 per cent of the area reported in the returns on abolition of rights of common. The area is also less than 10 per cent of the area in the hands of small and medium proprietors in 1859.

There are two obvious omissions: first, some of the poorer peasants never succeeded in adjusting their dues; secondly, the perpetual leaseholders were probably not reported in these returns. But even with such allowances, a large deficiency remains unexplained.

### The Extinction of Rights of Common in Prussia

The suppression of rights of common was of the greatest importance to the improvement of agricultural practice. Withdrawal of land from rights of common use by others was first authorized in Prussia by the ordinance of 1771, which applied to Silesia only. The general principle was recognized in the General Land Law promulgated in 1794. The abolition of common use was held to be desirable from the point of view of the best use of the land. It was therefore allowable when proof could be offered of general advantage. In respect of separation of demesne lands from village lands it was sufficient if a certificate of public convenience was granted by an expert. If a villager petitioned for withdrawal of land from common use, it was necessary to offer proof of convenience to the village as a whole. In England the position taken in the enclosure acts was more individualistic; it was necessary to secure votes from the owners of the major part of the area involved. The

[1] Meitzen, A., *Boden und Landwirtschaftliche Verhältnisse des Preussischen Staates,* Berlin, 1865-1901, I, pp. 431-434; VI, pp. 272-273.

[2] One *Morgen* = .63 acre.

German theory favored the enclosure of the demesne land by the lords, and thus fostered a process carried out in England with less supervision by the courts in the sixteenth and seventeenth centuries.

The extinction of common use was furthered by the edict of September 14, 1811, on the division of commons. All landholders were given full cultural control over one third of the area of their holdings. No provision was made for consolidation of separate parcels, and no holder was under any obligation to sell or exchange his parcels. Sale or exchange by voluntary agreement was, of course, allowable. A village might abolish common pasturage of the arable fields, by unanimous vote, but right of common might be restored upon petition of one quarter of the interested parties. Provision was made for limited enclosure of meadows, and for strict regulation of the use of wild pasture and forests.

The edict of June 7, 1821, gave full effect to the general policy for division laid down in 1794. Land might be withdrawn from common use on petition of one or more participants holding as lord, freeholder, or perpetual lessee. Others might petition for withdrawal of land only with the consent of the lord. Separation might be made unless proof was offered that it would result in damage to the soil. The essential features of the law lay in the careful description of procedure to be followed in determining the value of the rights of the various parties, and in the flexibility of the adjustments. Participants might receive the equivalent of their former holding in land, in money, in annual payments in money or in kind. No one need accept a parcel of land which would require him to change the method of farming previously followed. Wild pasture and forest land might be converted into arable fields if the soil was suitable, but forests might not be divided if division was likely to interfere with the practice of sound forestry. Rights of use of forests were covered by rents equivalent to the average value of the rights enjoyed. If common rights were not abolished, procedure was defined for the regulation of common use over all classes of land.

The edict of 1821 was the primary basis of the reform of the field systems in Prussia; but the ordinance was supplemented by many administrative orders, some general in scope, others applicable to specified areas. When the poorer peasants were given the opportunity of commuting their labor services (March 2, 1850), the process of extinction of rights of common was extended to meet their needs by an ordinance of the same date. The edict of April 2, 1872, provided for further extensions of the principles of separation and consolidation, and established principles by which the process of reform might be made more comprehensive. The provisions of the edict of 1821 were extended to the lands not subject to rights of common, which had been excluded at that time. New provisions dispensed with the need of unanimous consent of all the parties affected by the proposed reform. The holders of one half the area lying in scattered strips might petition for the consolidation of the entire area. If the area included land still subject to rights of common, such rights had to be extinguished prior to consolidation. This law provided the means of completing the work of reform.

Separation and consolidation were not, however, carried out systematically throughout Prussia. The reforms were fairly comprehensive in the eastern provinces, but in the west rather more than half the area still lay in scattered strips in 1895. In this region of small farms, consolidation was less necessary. Some statistical material is available, but it is confused by the additions to the territory of Prussia in 1866. The records of the extinction of rights of common are more nearly adequate; about 84 per cent of the area of land in private use is included in the returns, so that the figures given in the following table should afford a rough measure of the progress of these reforms.

AREA, IN HECTARES, AFFECTED BY SEPARATION AND EXTINCTION OF COMMON RIGHTS [1]

|  | Average per Year | Total Area | Per Cent |
|---|---|---|---|
| Before 1820 | — | 685,000 | 3.40 |
| 1821–1848 | 380,000 | 10,247,000 | 52.00 |
| 1849–1855 | 377,000 | 2,267,000 | 11.50 |
| 1856–1860 | 254,000 | 1,270,000 | 6.45 |
| 1861–1865 | 160,400 | 802,000 | 4.04 |
| 1866–1870 | 194,200 | 971,000 | 4.90 |
| 1871–1875 | 106,000 | 530,000 | 2.65 |
| 1876–1880 | 74,200 | 371,000 | 1.88 |
| 1881 | 61,000 | 61,000 | 0.31 |
| 1882 | 70,000 | 70,000 | 0.35 |
| 1883 | 64,000 | 64,000 | 0.32 |
| In Hanover, before 1867 | — | 2,410,000 | 12.20 |
| Total |  | 19,746,000 | 100.00 |

The net effect of these reforms upon the peasantry was less considerable than one might suppose. Substantial amounts of land changed hands; many owners parted with some of their

[1] Schlitte, B., *Zusammenlegung der Grundstücke*, Leipzig, 1886, I, p. 226.

property, others gained.   Former owners disappeared, new owners came upon the records.   But the net change was small.   There was a small decline in the number of cultivators having teams and cultivating areas ranging between 15 and 150 acres : the number fell from 351,607 in 1816 to 344,737 in 1859, a loss of 1.95 per cent. The area in their hands decreased from 34,425,000 morgen to 33,498,000 morgen, a loss of 2.69 per cent.   In some provinces the changes were more considerable, notably in Pomerania and Silesia, where the area diminished by 13 and 12 per cent respectively. But even these changes are not startling.   A far-reaching agrarian reform was carried out with little displacement.   The balance between the primary rural types was not significantly disturbed.

### The Concentration of Ownership and Its Social Significance

The conversion of feudal lords into landlords was likely to produce some measure of concentration in the ownership of land. The natural tendencies were intensified in some countries and in some regions by the special adaptability of the soil to large-scale farming.   Regions favorable to livestock raising became regions of large farms, and in all regions of large farms the holdings of the great landowners increased, before or after the agrarian reorganization of the eighteenth and nineteenth centuries.   The cereal, wine, and olive districts exhibit somewhat different tendencies. The land was worked in small units in the period before the reforms, and the reforms converted the perpetual leaseholders into owners. Most of these regions show some increase in the number of small proprietors.   Differences in the distribution of ownership were thus related in part to differences in use.   In all regions of large farms, the great landowners participated actively in the revision of agricultural practice and made the large investments necessary to adapt the land to new uses.   In the long discussions of the merits of small farms from the social point of view, these technical contributions of the great landowners are commonly forgotten.   It is now generally recognized that agricultural methods had to be adapted to conditions of soil and climate, so that differentiation of practice was necessary and inevitable.   Small farms are most successful in some regions; large farms are necessary to success in others.

Concentration of ownership, however, created a number of social and economic problems, which were in many countries intensified by the laws of entail.   The practice of establishing entails arose in the later Middle Ages and was widely used in nearly all European countries. The entail prevented dissipation of estates through subdivision among the heirs; a designated heir, usually the eldest son, succeeded to the entire estate. Other members of the family had claims upon the estate for assistance, but they had no direct control. The head of the house enjoyed the estate, but he could not dispose of it by will nor was he allowed to make destructive or wasteful use of the estate. He had only a life interest. In so far as entails or equivalent devices existed and survived the feudal system, they made the social system extraordinarily rigid. No portion of an entailed estate could be sold without the formal consent of every living member of the family. In the course of the nineteenth century, entails were abolished by positive laws, or procedures were defined by which they might be broken. With the exception of Prussia, countries characterized by concentrated ownership were profoundly influenced by the system of entail until the latter part of the nineteenth century. In Prussia the entails were significantly qualified by the edict of 1807. Except in Prussia and regions dominated by the French legislation it was very difficult to buy land. Large areas were in effect entirely withdrawn from the market. The ownership of land, therefore, conferred distinction and power : distinction, because it could not be freely bought ; power, because the great estates were inevitably leased to tenants over whom the proprietor could exercise many types of control, direct and indirect.

The economic advantages which fostered the development of large holdings, and the historical circumstances which explain their development out of feudalism, do not justify the social system built around the rigidities of the law of entail. This system created a kind of stability, and if stability is really desirable, much might be said for such a system of organization. It has generally been assumed, however, that progress and even survival are promoted when our social institutions become more flexible and not more rigid. Legal reforms and depressed prices of agricultural commodities have resulted in the breakup of many of the old estates. The third quarter of the nineteenth century marked the highest degree of concentration of property in land, and for this period we have statistical material for France, England, and Prussia.

### Regional Differences in Prussia

In Prussia in 1861 the small proprietors were an important group, but the large proprietors were more important. The returns for

## Ownership of Land in Prussia [1]

(Omitting Hohenzollern and Hunting Lands)

(a) Area of Land Held; Thousands of Morgen

| Size of Holding | Prussia | Posen | Brandenburg | Pomerania | Silesia | Saxony | Westphalia | Rhineland |
|---|---|---|---|---|---|---|---|---|
| 0–3.1 acres | 120 | 59 | 145 | 80 | 273 | 266 | 245 | 1,006 |
| 3.2–18.9 acres | 679 | 527 | 647 | 400 | 1,478 | 956 | 1,022 | 2,611 |
| 19.0–189 acres | 9,212 | 3,326 | 5,337 | 2,863 | 3,865 | 4,088 | 3,793 | 3,302 |
| 190–378 acres | 1,740 | 447 | 899 | 572 | 514 | 645 | 547 | 663 |
| Over 378 acres | 9,015 | 5,863 | 6,979 | 6,569 | 6,438 | 2,581 | 1,120 | 2,218 |
| Total | 20,766 | 10,222 | 14,007 | 10,484 | 12,568 | 8,536 | 6,727 | 9,800 |

(b) Per Cent of Area Held

| Size of Holding | Prussia | Posen | Brandenburg | Pomerania | Silesia | Saxony | Westphalia | Rhineland |
|---|---|---|---|---|---|---|---|---|
| 0–3.1 acres | .58 | .57 | 1.03 | .76 | 2.17 | 3.1 | 3.6 | 10.2 |
| 3.2–18.9 acres | 3.28 | 5.06 | 4.72 | 3.82 | 11.75 | 11.3 | 15.2 | 26.6 |
| 19.0–189 acres | 44.52 | 32.70 | 38.05 | 27.31 | 30.80 | 47.8 | 56.3 | 33.9 |
| 190–378 acres | 8.10 | 4.27 | 6.40 | 5.45 | 4.08 | 7.5 | 8.1 | 6.7 |
| Over 378 acres | 43.52 | 57.40 | 49.80 | 62.66 | 51.20 | 30.3 | 16.8 | 22.6 |
| Total acres | 100.00 | 100.00 | 100.00 | 100.00 | 100.00 | 100.0 | 100.0 | 100.0 |

[1] *Preussische Statistik*, 1864, V, p. 21.

the kingdom of Prussia as a whole are given in the following table. It is important, however, to compare these returns with the figures for the individual provinces, as there were profound differences.

DISTRIBUTION OF THE OWNERSHIP OF LAND IN PRUSSIA IN 1861 [1]

Area Owned, in Morgen (1 morgen = .63 acre)

| Size of Holding | Morgen | Per Cent |
|---|---|---|
| By cottagers, 0–3.1 acres | 2,227,000 | 2.4 |
| By small proprietors: | | |
| 3.2–18.9 acres | 8,427,000 | 9.0 |
| 19.0–189 acres | 35,914,000 | 38.4 |
| | | 47.4 |
| By large proprietors: | | |
| 190–378 acres | 6,072,000 | 6.4 |
| Over 378 acres | 40,914,000 | 43.8 |
| | | 50.2 |
| Total | 93,554,000 | 100.0 |

The table on page 280 discloses the sharp contrast between Westphalia and the Rhineland on the one hand and the region of the great estates, Pomerania, Posen, and Silesia. It is important to note that even in these regions there were many independent owners of one-family farms. All types of units of ownership and exploitation are represented in all regions. Broad description in terms of general categories tends to close our eyes to the fact that serious social problems are created by differences of proportions amounting at times to no more than 10 or 20 per cent. Effective social organization is to be achieved by proper adaptation to varying conditions. It is a matter of flexibility and balance, rather than of the general establishment of the "best" type of farm or the "best" form of industrial enterprise.

### Small Proprietorship in France

In France the great proprietors had been less important than in England or Prussia even before the Revolution. The Revolution weakened the position of the great landowners, and it is commonly presumed that they held less land in 1884 than after the Restoration. The best returns are for the year 1884, as shown below. Cottagers would be partly dependent upon some means of support other than their land, with the possible exception of some market gardeners. Some of the "small proprietors" might be dependent

1 *Preussische Statistik*, 1864, V, p. 21.

upon other means of support, but normally these owners would be able to work their holding without hired labor, and would be able to support themselves and their families. They were the predominant class in France.

DISTRIBUTION OF THE OWNERSHIP OF LAND IN FRANCE, IN 1884[1]

Area Owned, in Hectares (1 hectare = 2.471 acres)

| Size of Holding | Hectares | Per Cent |
|---|---|---|
| By cottagers, 0–4.94 acres | 5,211,000 | 10.53 |
| By small proprietors: | | |
| 4.95–14.8 acres | 7,543,000 | 15.26 |
| 14.9–123.5 acres | 19,217,000 | 38.94 |
| | | 54.20 |
| By large proprietors: | | |
| 123.6–594 acres | 9,398,000 | 19.04 |
| Over 594 acres | 8,017,000 | 16.23 |
| | | 35.27 |
| Total | 49,386,000 | 100.00 |

### Concentration of Ownership in England

The return of landowners in England (1872–1873), commonly called the New Domesday, shows that the great landowners actually controlled a somewhat larger portion of the total area than even the Prussian Junkers of Pomerania. The return is not satisfactory in respect of the numbers of owners, because there was a great deal of double counting. Parcels held in different counties were recorded as belonging to different owners. The results were not even tabulated in the official return, because it was feared that the records would encourage radical attacks on the propertied class. The tabulation given on page 283 is the work of John Bateman. The classifications of owners having less than 300 acres cannot be compared directly with the classes given for France and for Prussia, but those who owned more than 300 acres controlled 67.6 per cent of the total area. This intense concentration of control was probably equaled in southern Spain, and possibly in parts of Italy, but we have no adequate statistical material for either of those countries. The power and prestige of the English landowners were used with an unusual sense of social responsibility. The position of the landowner was notably qualified by the importance of the great industrial fortunes and, after the great electoral reforms, by the influence of the great industrial constituencies. Whatever judgment one may

[1] Foville, A. de, *La France économique, 1887*, p. 64.

| | Average Area Held by Each Owner | Area Held, in Acres | Per Cent |
|---|---|---|---|
| Public bodies and waste | — | 2,950,000 | 8.6 |
| Cottagers, less than one acre | 0.21 acre | 150,000 | 0.4 |
| Small proprietors, 1–100 acres | 18 acres | 3,930,000 | 11.4 |
| Lesser yeomen, 101–300 acres | 169 acres | 4,140,000 | 12.0 |
| Greater yeomen, 301–1,000 acres | 498 acres | 4,780,000 | 13.9 |
| Squires, 1,001–3,000 acres | 1,708 acres | 4,310,000 | 12.5 |
| Great landowners, commoners having over 3,000 acres | 6,597 acres | 8,490,000 | 24.6 |
| Peers | 14,320 acres | 5,720,000 | 16.6 |
| | | 34,470,000 | 100.0 |

form about the merits of the British social system, there can be no doubt that the distinctive achievements of nineteenth-century Britain were in many ways the product of a society based upon an unusually intense concentration of a quasi-feudal control of land.

## The Beginnings of Agricultural Science

Agriculture continued to be an essentially empirical pursuit until nearly the middle of the nineteenth century.   Scientific analysis of problems of soil condition and plant growth was impossible until the general procedure of organic chemistry was established about 1830, largely under the inspiration of Justus von Liebig, and the great field experimenters Boussingault and John Bennett Lawes. Results were incomplete and inaccurate for an appreciable interval after the basic work of the decade of the 1830's.   Although the initial achievements consisted largely of rationalizations of established methods, progress in research speedily led to essentially new modes in preparing fertilizers from animal residues and crude minerals, and to great refinements and economies in the use of the new materials. The ultimate development of commercial processes for the fixation of atmospheric nitrogen was a logical and natural outcome of the scientific inquiries of the early nineteenth century.   The influence of science upon agriculture has been no less important than the

[1] Return of the name and address of every owner of one acre and upwards, with estimated acreage and annual gross estimated rentals.   England and Wales, Scotland, *Commons Papers*, 1874, vol. 72, Parts I, II, III.   Summary of the returns of owners of land in England and Wales, *Commons Papers*, 1876, vol. 80.   Bateman, J., *The Landowners of Great Britain and Ireland*, London, 1883, pp. 515 ff.   Broderick, G. C., *English Land and Landlords*, London, 1881, pp. 157-197.

applications of science to industry and commerce, though the applications are less obvious to the average citizen and their significance scarcely appreciated.

The accumulation of scientific data upon agricultural chemistry began to assume substantial proportions early in Priestley's career (1770), but the work done in England and France was fragmentary, and the significance of many observed facts was imperfectly perceived. Even those whose knowledge was correct were unable to demonstrate convincingly the errors of the older views, so that many competing theories are to be found in every aspect of the problems of plant growth. In nearly every case the views most widely held were most seriously in error. Thaer, Sir Humphry Davy, and the Swedish chemist Berzelius still believed that humus (decayed organic matter in the soil) was the chief source of the carbon found in plants. Basic experiments had been made on the respiration of plants by Senebier (1782) and by Theodore de Saussure (1804). It was shown conclusively that the actual source of carbon was carbon dioxide such as is exhaled by animals. It was known that the process of assimilation required the energy derived from light. But even professional chemists such as Davy and Berzelius were unimpressed.

It was known that a number of minerals were to be found in the ashes of plants, and even in the sixteenth century it was known that such ashes exerted a significant influence on plant growth. The presence of nitrogen was known, but its significance was not understood, and nothing was really known of the process by which nitrates are formed and assimilated. Thaer's *Principles of Agriculture,* published in 1809, and Sir Humphry Davy's *Lectures* (1802–1812), published in 1813, afford a comprehensive picture of the state of expert opinion immediately before the extensive development of organic chemistry and its applications to agriculture.

The new developments were not the work of any single man, nor were the procedures entirely new. Laboratory and field experiments had been made systematically during the whole of the last generation of the eighteenth century. Arthur Young had even secured the co-operation of Priestley in certain analyses in conjunction with some of his field experiments. The techniques of experimentation, however, had been insufficient. Systematic research over wide fields was impossible in the laboratory before the decade of the 1820's, and field experiments were not associated in any adequate fashion with the technique of chemical analysis.

The new achievements were an outgrowth of improved technique of experimentation, and the early work was accomplished by persons whose greatest gifts lay in this field.

## The Work of Liebig and Wöhler

In so far as any priority can be given to the great leaders, the place of honor must be given to Justus von Liebig. He was interested in chemistry, and the ineffectiveness of instruction in Germany forced him to study abroad. Paris was chosen in preference to Sweden, because more work was being done in what we now call organic chemistry, though boundary lines were then uncertain. Liebig studied in the private laboratory of Gay-Lussac, and after an interval returned to Germany to take a chair in chemistry at Giessen (1824). In 1828 he offered laboratory instruction to all students who desired to register. Never before had there been any public provision of laboratory facilities or instruction. One of his first tasks was an improvement in laboratory procedure. He invented the combustion furnace, and perfected a technique for the analysis of organic compounds. As early as 1831 Liebig had perfected the technique of analysis that is still in use. In 1836 F. Wöhler became Professor of Chemistry at Göttingen; though trained in Sweden under Berzelius, he soon found himself working on problems closely associated with those engaging Liebig's attention, and much important work was prosecuted and published jointly. Together they laid the foundations for the development of chemistry in Germany, and their pupils carried their methods to foreign countries.

Singly and jointly, Liebig and Wöhler made important contributions to research and to the pure theory of organic compounds. Their achievements in this field are less generously appraised today by English writers than by Germans, and judgment is difficult, because the great generalizations in organic chemistry were made by their successors. In the related field of agricultural chemistry, however, Liebig made a notable synthesis, which was important both for its influence upon contemporary opinion and for its fruitfulness as a foundation for further work. These notable generalizations were embodied in the treatise, issued simultaneously in German and in English in 1840, under the title *Organic Chemistry in Its Relations to Agriculture and Physiology*. The English translation was the work of one of Liebig's students, Lord Playfair. Although it dealt with much new research, the treatise was addressed to a wide circle of readers and exerted a great influence upon public opinion.  The humus theory and all "pre-chemical" agricultural notions were destroyed beyond all hope of revival.  The interrelations between animal and vegetable life were accurately described in general, though many details clearly required further research, and insufficient data led Liebig into error on a number of important points.

The views of Liebig can be summarized very compactly.  Plants derive their supply of carbon from the air, by the process of respiration first accurately described by de Saussure.  Liebig built the older observations into a chain of reasoning whose logic could not be resisted.  The supply of nitrogen was presumed by Liebig to be derived from the ammonia present in the atmosphere.  Insufficient data led Liebig to assume a precipitation, in rain water, of 70–85 pounds of ammonia per acre.  Modern observations show no more than 15 pounds per acre under the most extreme conditions recorded, and Sir A. D. Hall presumes that the average precipitation would not exceed 4 or 5 pounds per acre.  This error of observation led Liebig to presume that the supply of nitrogen does not constitute a serious problem.

Liebig presumed that minerals are essential to plant growth in the precise proportions in which the minerals are present in the ash.  As both carbon and nitrogen were presumed to be abundantly supplied by the atmosphere, Liebig concluded that the actual limiting factors in plant growth are deficient supplies of particular minerals, especially phosphorus and potash.  This view became the basis of all the practical recommendations subsequently made, and the basis of sharp criticisms of agricultural practice.  Liebig also held that plants did not absorb their food from the soil solution, but from particles of soil in direct contact with the roots of the plant.

## The Correction of Liebig's Errors

Liebig's incorrect views were at variance with empirical experience in a number of respects, but no adjustment was possible unless the doubts created by experience could be expressed in accurate and systematic experiments.  Two great series of field experiments had the immediate object of resolving the conflicts between theory and practice.  The first field experiments fully implemented with chemical analyses were those conducted by Jean Baptiste J. D. Boussingault at the farm Bechelbronne.  These experiments, begun in 1834, demonstrated the practical importance of additional supplies of nitrogen, but the results were not sufficiently conclusive to compel the rejection or modification of Liebig's position. Similar experiments were begun at Rothamsted in England in 1843 on the farm of John Bennett Lawes under the joint direction of Lawes and J. H. Gilbert. Gilbert was a young chemist who had just completed his training in Liebig's laboratory. These experiments, like those of Boussingault, were planned on a generous scale, designed to throw light upon all the fundamental problems of science and practice. The original experiments were designed to exhibit the problems of the more important rotation systems then in vogue, with careful control plots to provide contrasts. Results soon led to sharp controversy with Liebig, but in the end the Rothamsted work made a number of corrections in Liebig's original position. Inasmuch as some corrections are embodied in late editions of Liebig's work, some care must be exercised in citing his views.

By 1855 the following points had been established by the work at Rothamsted. The proportion of minerals required to promote plant growth is not correctly indicated by the constituents of the ash. This is especially notable in the case of turnips: they contain little phosphorus, but they respond notably to applications of phosphate. It was shown that nitrates are not sufficiently supplied by natural conditions except for the legumes. No explanation of this nonconformity of legumes was then possible. The beneficial effect of fallowing was shown to be due to an increase in the supply of nitrates.

The problem presented by the legumes remained unsolved for thirty years. The nodules on the roots of legumes offered a focus for study, but the methods used to control the experiments prevented the bacterial action that lay beneath the whole problem. After early failures, bacterial studies were resumed in 1877 by Schloesing and Müntz, and finally in 1886 Hellriegel and Wilfarth were able to announce the solution of the problem. Bacteria living in the nodules were able to fix some of the nitrogen contained in the atmosphere in the soil. This solution opened up a new series of nutritional problems. It was clear that the processes taking place in the soil were not mere chemical reactions; a wide range of bacterial phenomena are involved. The development of colloidal chemistry added other complexities to the processes of plant nutrition and plant growth, though the basic quantitative and qualitative concepts of the earlier period were not overthrown.

CHAPTER 14

# RUSSIA BEFORE THE EMANCIPATION

——————

## Population and Territory

One of the outstanding facts of the history of Russia during the eighteenth century and the first half of the nineteenth is the considerable extension of her boundaries.  Prior to 1700, as far as we can judge, the population of Russia for at least a century remained more or less stationary.  After the time of Peter the Great, however, we find a steady and rapid increase of population (besides a large increase of territory), as shown by the following table:

THE POPULATION OF RUSSIA [1]

|  | Within the Boundaries of 1725 | Within the Boundaries of the Year Cited |
|---|---|---|
| 1725 | 13,000,000 | 13,000,000 |
| 1762 | 19,000,000 | 19,000,000 |
| 1796 | 29,000,000 | 36,000,000 |
| 1815 | 30,000,000 | 45,000,000 |
| 1851 | 39,000,000 | 67,000,000 |

From 1725 to 1851 the population of the Russian Empire increased more than fivefold.  This increase was due in part to rapid growth within the limits of the empire in 1725.  The rates were 1 per cent per year from 1725 to 1762, 1.25 per cent per year from 1762 to 1796; and 0.58 per cent per year from 1796 to 1851.  These rates were higher than in any country of western Europe during the eighteenth century.  Part of the increase, as is shown by the table, was due to the acquisition of new territories.  The territorial growth of Russia was proceeding more rapidly and on a much larger scale than that of any other country in Europe.  While in most of the European countries the national boundaries had been established at an earlier period and remained constant, subject to only minor changes, the Russia of the eighteenth century and the first half of the nineteenth was still an empire in the making.

Most of the new territorial acquisitions had not only political but also economic importance.  The conquest of the Baltic prov-

[1] Miliwkov, P., *Ocherki Po Istorii Russkoi Kultury*, St. Petersburg, 1909, vol. I, p. 24.

inces and of Finland placed Russia firmly on the shores of the
Baltic Sea and opened to her a direct and convenient way for commercial relations with northwestern Europe. The acquisition of
the north coast of the Black Sea, including the mouth of the Danube,
opened a way to the Near East and to the Mediterranean. The
conquest of the Caucasus and the advance southward along the
western and the eastern shores of the Caspian Sea brought Russia
nearer the markets of Persia and central Asia, while the acquisition
of Polish territories along the western land frontier brought Russia
into direct contact with the countries of central Europe.

Some of the newly acquired territories, such as the Baltic provinces and part of Poland, with their more developed economic life,
a larger number of towns, and a more numerous middle class, directly
increased the economic resources of the Russian Empire and in
course of time became important centers of industrial production.
Others, such as the Caucasus, added to the country's wealth in
natural resources. Finally, some of these acquisitions had a
primary importance for the extension of agricultural settlement,
having opened vast new regions for mass colonization. The Russian
development of the period exhibited a more dynamic character than
that of any other European country. Nowhere else could one see a
similarly wide and intense movement of population from one part of
the country to another. Prior to the eighteenth century a comparatively dense and settled population in the Russian Empire was to
be found only in the center of the plains of European Russia: the
region of Moscow with the immediately adjoining provinces, and
the upper valley of the Volga. Somewhat less densely settled were
the northern part of the Ukraine, and the ancient Smolensk and
Novgorod regions, to the west and northwest of Moscow respectively. Finally, starting from central Russia, a narrow strip of
fairly dense settlement stretched out toward Archangel, along the
river Dvina; and another strip was to be found along the middle
course of the Volga and farther east, in the direction of Siberia. To
this limited area of comparatively dense settlement now was added
a vast territory in the south and the southeast of European Russia.

### Frontier Expansion

The acquisition of the Black Sea coast opened for mass colonization the fertile prairies of New Russia. After the conquest of the
Caucasus and the shores of the Caspian Sea, colonization also
became possible in the regions of the lower Volga, north Caucasus,

and the territory near the southern end of the Ural range.  It is significant that during the period in question the population of all these newly settled regions increased much more rapidly than that of central Russia and the north.  The colonization of the border regions at the expense of central Russia was proceeding in several different ways.  Large groups of population were moving there of their own free will in quest of better living conditions.  Landlords acquiring estates there were transporting their serfs to the new regions, while the government, in its turn, was settling large numbers of crown peasants there.  If in the days of Peter the Great approximately two thirds of the population still were concentrated on the ancient territory of the czardom of Moscow, probably no more than one third of the total population was living there in the middle of the nineteenth century.

With the growth of population in the southern and southeastern regions of European Russia, the importance of these regions in the economic life of the country increased.  By the beginning of the nineteenth century there was already established a fairly clear economic differentiation among the various parts of European Russia, in accordance with the differences in soil and climate.  The fertile prairies of the south became the "Granary of the Empire," producing practically all of Russian wheat, and it was there also that Russian cattle breeding was concentrated.  The so-called black-earth region of central Russia remained the region of oats and rye, while the nonagricultural part of central Russia, as well as the northwest, became the principal industrial regions of the empire.  Until the middle of the nineteenth century, mining and the metallurgical industries were concentrated almost entirely in the Ural Mountains. Siberia remained a region of secondary importance in the economic life of the country.  Inadequate means of communication made the whole of northern Asia, acquired by the czardom of Moscow in the course of the seventeenth century, a remote colony, loosely connected with the European parts of the empire.  Even by the middle of the nineteenth century the entire territory from the Urals to the Pacific Ocean contained scarcely more than 2,500,000 Russians. Obviously, both the mass settlement of Siberia and the exploitation of its natural resources were still in the future.

Not only in the eighteenth century, but throughout the first half of the nineteenth century as well, the population of Russia remained overwhelmingly rural.  In 1724 the urban population of the country was 328,000, or 3 per cent of the whole population; by

1796 it rose to 1,301,000, or 4 per cent, and by 1851 to 3,482,000, or 7.8 per cent. The majority of towns were relatively small. According to the data available for the end of the period, of about one thousand Russian towns, excluding Poland and Finland, eight hundred seventy-eight had less than 10,000 inhabitants each, only thirty-two had over 20,000, and only two (Moscow and St. Petersburg) had more than 150,000. For the eighteenth century one naturally has to assume even smaller numbers. It should be said also that many of these towns were primarily administrative centers, and that only a small part of their inhabitants were typically urban so far as their occupations were concerned.

## The Nobles and the Clergy

The Russian Empire of the eighteenth century inherited from the czardom of Moscow a social organization based on the division of the population into several "estates," in accordance with the nature of obligations which these groups had toward the government. Already in the eighteenth century, however, and even more so in the nineteenth, the legal terms used to designate the various "estates" covered in each case a fairly heterogeneous group. The farther one advances in this period, the more often one sees differences in economic status cutting across the legal structure of society based on the division into the "estates."

At the top of the social ladder stood the nobility (a little over 1 per cent of the population). In the eighteenth century this class included elements of various historical origins: the remnants of the old feudal aristocracy, the descendants of the "military servicemen" of the sixteenth and seventeenth centuries, and finally some nobles recently created by the monarchy since the days of Peter the Great. In this way the nobility of birth and the nobility of service became merged into one class, which towards the end of the century acquired all the characteristics of a privileged order, with a corporate organization of its own. All the nobility enjoyed certain personal privileges, such as exemption from the poll tax and from the obligation to send recruits into the army, and in addition they possessed also some important economic privileges. With some exceptions, which will be noted below, throughout all this period the nobles alone had the right to own serfs. For a short period at the end of the eighteenth century they even enjoyed the monopoly of land ownership. This was abolished in 1801; but even without such a monopoly fixed by law, the nobility remained in possession of most of the privately owned land in the country.[1]  In the first quarter of the eighteenth century the old distinction between the hereditary "patrimonies" and estates granted in return for military service had been abolished forever.  All the traces of conditional land tenure finally disappeared, and all the land in the hands of the gentry became their full property.  But within this group of legally equal noblemen there were great differences so far as distribution of wealth was concerned.  The number of land magnates owning enormous estates and tens of thousands of serfs was very small.  Most of such great estates were formed in the eighteenth century, chiefly through the grant of crown lands widely practiced by the monarchy, and most of the wealthiest landlords of the time belonged to the nobility of service of a very recent origin.  The bulk of the nobility were far behind this favored group in the extent of their land ownership.  Even the general mass of the relatively large landowners (counting all who had over 500 serfs) formed on the eve of the Emancipation (1861) less than 4 per cent of the nobility, while about 20 per cent owned between 100 and 500 serfs, and the rest less than 100 serfs.

In contrast with prerevolutionary France, the Russian clergy of the time (about 1 per cent of the population) scarcely can be considered a privileged order.  Even the fundamental civil and personal rights of clergymen were not definitely fixed by law until the 1830's.  Actually, with the exception of a small group of the upper hierarchy, the social status of the clergy remained an inferior one, while the economic situation of the parish clergy, more particularly in rural districts, did not differ very much from that of the peasants.  The church as a whole lost its economic power and independence with the secularization of monastic estates in 1764, when the lands and the serfs previously owned by the church were taken over by the crown.

## The Urban Classes

Among the urban classes of the population the law of the period distinguished three different groups: the merchants, the artisans, and the manual workers.  Of these the first group possessed in the second half of the eighteenth century some of the personal rights enjoyed by the nobility and the clergy.  But even this merchant class held a position in the social hierarchy of the country far below that of the nobility.  Because of the peculiar conditions of its

[1] On the eve of the Emancipation the crown held 67.6 per cent of the land; the nobility, 30.6 per cent; and all the other groups, only 1.8 per cent.

historical development, the Russian bourgeoisie of the eighteenth century was still very far from having reached that stage of independence, social weight, and organization which on the whole characterized the contemporary bourgeoisie of western Europe. It is significant that the first attempts to give the Russian bourgeoisie a corporate organization and to hand over to it the management of municipal affairs came from above, and that the efforts of the government in this direction proved to be largely fruitless, partly because of the lack of solidarity and the indifference of the group itself. Among the merchants only a very small number possessed substantial capital, while the great majority consisted of small traders whose material condition was not far above that of the artisans.

The artisans were even less organized than the merchants. In this case again, in contrast with western Europe, Russian history had not developed sufficiently strong forms of social organization. Prior to the eighteenth century Russia did not know any guild system, and attempts to introduce it from above, by governmental legislation, were not very successful.

## The Peasants

The overwhelming majority of the population of Russia consisted of peasants, or "rural inhabitants" as they began to be called in legal documents. In the second half of the eighteenth century about 55 per cent of this class were in a state of personal bondage. Serfdom in Russia reached the highest peak of its development in the later part of the eighteenth century. By that time the Russian peasant, who originally had been fixed to the soil and not to the person of the landowner, found himself in complete dependence on the latter. The landlord had the right to dispose of the person of his serf as well as to exploit his serf's labor without compensation. In addition, he exercised police authority over his serfs and he was their sole judge in all but grave criminal cases. He was responsible to the government for the fulfillment by the serfs of their obligations towards the state, such as payment of the poll tax and sending recruits into the army. On the other hand, it was his duty to provide food for his serfs in periods of bad harvests and famine, and he was prohibited by law from maltreating them.

By the terms of law the serfs had no right to own property, but there is enough evidence to show that both in the eighteenth century, and more particularly in the nineteenth, this provision was not strictly adhered to. Contemporary accounts point out that every serf considered his house and his household effects, as well as his horses and cows, to be his personal property, and that although legally the landlord could deprive him of this property, cases of such seizure were extremely rare. Moreover, recent studies have brought to light a fairly large number of instances in which serfs were buying land and sometimes a very considerable amount of it. In some cases land was bought with peasants, so that there was the paradoxical situation of serfs owning serfs. As a rule such land bought by the peasants was used by them independently, without any interference on the part of their master, and it remained free from any dues in favor of that master. In spite of the fact that the deed had to be made in the name of the master, who in this way held the legal title to the land, cases of abuse on the part of the masters seem to have been very rare. Thus the law of 1848 which allowed the serfs to acquire real estate with the permission of the landlord merely sanctioned a practice that had been in existence for some time before that.

Besides the serfs belonging to private landowners, the main body of the rest of the peasants consisted of various categories of crown peasants living on land belonging to the state. Although attached to the soil and subject to certain limitations so far as their property rights were concerned, the crown peasants, unlike the serfs, were considered to be personally free. In flagrant violation of this principle, however, in the course of the eighteenth century a large number of crown peasants (about 1,000,000 of male "souls") were transformed into serfs by means of granting state lands to private landowners.

Territorially, serfdom was predominant in the central parts of European Russia (under Catherine II it was extended also to the Ukraine), while in the border regions, particularly in the north and in the southeast, the great majority of the rural population were either crown peasants or free agriculturists.

### The Corvée System

The organization of the landlord's economy, based on serf labor, took different forms, depending on local conditions prevailing in various parts of Russia. Most typical of serfdom was a system under which the landlord reserved for himself a considerable part of land on the estate, and the chief obligation of the serfs consisted of the corvée (bárshchina), that is, the work on the master's land.

In the eighteenth century the landlords as a rule retained for their own exploitation about one third of the land, while on the eve of the Emancipation the landlord's part usually formed more than half of it.   An imperial decree published at the end of the eighteenth century proclaimed three days a week as the normal amount of time to be spent by the serfs in working on the master's land, but there are good reasons to assume that in many cases the actual duration of the *corvée* went beyond that norm.   In some extreme cases all the land was reserved by the master for his own exploitation, and the peasants were reduced to the position of slave laborers receiving their subsistence from the landlord, but such cases apparently were rare.

The *corvée* system prevailed in all those regions in which nature favored agriculture.   It was almost a general rule in the fertile south, in those estates which used serf labor, and it was predominant in the agricultural part of central Russia and along the Volga, where about three fourths of the serfs were employed in this way.   On the contrary, in those parts of central Russia which lay outside the black-earth region, as well as in the north, where both soil and climate were less favorable to agriculture, the landlords in most cases found it more advantageous to reduce their own agricultural exploitation of the land to a minimum, and to employ the work of their serfs otherwise.   Here the master's part hardly ever formed more than one fourth of the whole land in the estate, and a relatively small number of serfs were assigned to its cultivation.

## The Quitrent System

Many serfs were not subject to the *corvée;* they had to pay the landlords a quitrent (*obrók*), partly in kind and partly (and in course of time, mostly) in money.   The amount of the quitrent was determined by an agreement between the landlord and his serfs, and it was not subject to any governmental regulation.   To pay this quitrent the serfs had to rely not so much on the products of their own agriculture, which were barely sufficient for their own subsistence, as on their other earnings of a nonagricultural nature.   It was precisely in those parts of Russia that one could find a particularly strong development of various peasant handicrafts, for the products of which there was a fairly wide demand.   With the masters' permission, the serfs of these regions commonly found employment outside the estates as seasonal laborers, factory workingmen, or as traders engaged in petty retail trade in the towns.   Under the quitrent system agriculture was reduced to secondary importance. Among the owners of the estates there were many absentee landlords, while many of their peasants remained peasants in name only. This system, in its extreme development, could lead to a complete liquidation of the landlord's own agricultural exploitation, and to the transfer of all the land to the use of the peasants. Such cases, however, were very exceptional. Even in those provinces where the quitrent system predominated, about 40 per cent of the peasants still continued to perform the *corvée*. After 1800 the cases of substituting the quitrent for *corvées* became more numerous, parallel with the development of money economy in the country, but on the whole the quitrent system grew but slowly. According to some calculations, on the eve of the Emancipation about three fourths of the serfs in European Russia still were employed under the *corvée* system, and only one fourth were paying the quitrent instead.

Besides these two major groups of serfs, there was also one comparatively small group (in the middle of the nineteenth century numbering about 1,500,000 out of 20,000,000) which consisted of the so-called "household serfs." These were serfs who did not receive any land from the landlord, and were kept by him in the immediate vicinity of his house. They supplied the numerous personnel of house servants, or ministered to the various needs of the master's household as craftsmen and manual workers.

### The Communal Village

The outstanding trait of peasant agriculture, among both the crown peasants and the serfs, was the communal landholding. The origin of the communal village in Russia is one of the most debatable points in Russian economic history. Many volumes have been written to prove or disprove the connection between the later-day communal organization of the Russian peasantry and the primitive commune of earlier times. However, the prevailing opinion among the authorities tends to view the most characteristic features of the rural commune in modern times as a product of comparatively late historical development. By the beginning of the eighteenth century many peasants, more particularly in the central part of European Russia, began to suffer rather acutely from the insufficiency of land at their disposal, and as free land was no longer available, there arose a strong demand for a redivision of land on a more equitable basis. As a result there was gradually established in the village communes a system of periodical redistribution of land, in accordance with

changing needs and working capacity of the different peasant households. The same purpose of establishing an equality of conditions
was served by the introduction in all the peasant communes of the
"strip" system under which all the arable land was divided into
several portions, according to the quality of the soil, with every
household of the commune entitled to its share in each of these
portions. Finally, in Russia as elsewhere the natural concomitant
of communal landholding was the compulsory course of husbandry
from which the individual members of the commune were not permitted to deviate.

In technique, the peasant agriculture in Russia remained on a
rather low level. In the eighteenth century, in those regions where
land was still abundant, fallowing, without any alternation of crops,
continued to be used. In central Russia, however, the three-field
system prevailed, sometimes still in its less developed form when
more than one third of land was left fallow. There was no noticeable
progress in the methods of cultivation, and rather rudimentary implements continued to be used. The situation was not much better
in the majority of landlords' estates, where as a rule not only was
the land cultivated with serfs' labor, but the peasants contributed
their livestock and their implements as well. On the whole, such a
system of cultivation, more particularly in the agricultural part of
central Russia, prevailed to the time of the Emancipation. Only
gradually and rather slowly were more advanced forms of agriculture
introduced here and there. After 1800 the growth of the grain market moved the more enterprising and more progressive among the
landlords to attempt intensive methods of cultivation. Institutions
such as the Free Economic Society in St. Petersburg and the
Moscow Society of Agriculture ardently preached various technical
improvements, while Russian economic literature of the early
nineteenth century was full of discussion of the new English agriculture with its manifold advantages. The cases of practical application of these theories, however, remained rather isolated
phenomena, and they did not affect the general agricultural situation in the country to any considerable extent.

### Industry

For a long time there was a tendency among the Russian economic
historians to regard the large-scale industry of the eighteenth
century as an "artificial" and "premature" creation of Peter the
Great. Today such a point of view is no longer tenable. We know

that in the seventeenth century there already existed in Russia fairly large industrial undertakings, both in the field of metallurgical industry and in textile manufacture.  Some of these were government-owned factories and foundries, created with the help of foreign specialists, but there were also private enterprises in the form of "manorial factories" established on the estates of some large landowners.  It is true, of course, that after Peter's time the development of large-scale industry in Russia proceeded at a much more rapid pace, assuming at the same time a more continuous character.  But it is clear, on the other hand, that the industry of Peter's time could not have achieved its relative success if it had not been for the fact that the economic life of the country offered a favorable field for such an achievement.  In most cases the initiative of establishing new factories still belonged to the government, anxious as it was to satisfy the needs of national defense and to increase the revenues of the state.  But from the outset it was joined by private initiative, and with the progress of the century private initiative was acquiring an ever-increasing importance.

Already in Peter's time the majority of Russian industrialists were native capitalists, most of whom belonged to the merchant class, while the others came from the landowning nobility.  Thus both commercial and agrarian capital contributed to the building up of the new industry.

Relatively speaking, the amount of private capital invested in these undertakings was very substantial.  From available data referring to some individual enterprises, we know that government support, in the form of subsidies and loans, played only a secondary, and in some cases not even a very important, part.  Moreover, many of the government factories were soon transferred to private hands.  It is true, of course, that private establishments continued to receive vigorous support from the government.  In addition to subsidies and loans, they were granted monopolies and various other privileges, and many of them had a guaranteed market for their output in the form of government orders.  At the same time they were protected from foreign competition by high tariffs, and in some cases by a total prohibition of the importation of certain products into Russia.  These, however, were conditions common to all the countries of Continental Europe in the seventeenth and eighteenth centuries.  Moreover, it should be remembered that in the 1760's the economic policy of the Russian government abandoned many features of earlier protectionism, including the granting of monopolies, and that after that time government tutelage over industry assumed a somewhat milder form.

It was in the field of labor recruitment that Russian conditions differed most from those in western Europe. Practically everywhere forced labor was used in industry to some extent, but nowhere else had it reached the same proportions as in Russia. The reasons for its much wider use in Russia are obvious. The absence of a sufficiently numerous class of city artisans, and the spread of serfdom, which kept a considerable part of the population attached to the estates of the private landowners, confronted Russian industry with a particularly difficult task so far as the supply of labor was concerned. The problem was solved by the extension of serfdom to industry. Large numbers of state peasants were assigned to work in government-controlled factories, and a law promulgated in 1721 granted the merchant-manufacturers the right to buy serfs to be employed as factory workers. Such serfs came to be known as "possessional workers," and the factories where their work was wholly or predominantly employed were called "possessional factories." However, the legal position of possessional workers was somewhat different from that of an agricultural serf, for they were attached not to the person of the factory owner but to the factory, and their labor could not be employed otherwise than in the factory.

There was still another type of factories based entirely on forced labor. These were the so-called "manorial factories" established on the estates of the landlords, where all the workers were serfs belonging to the owner. The number of these manorial factories increased rapidly in the second half of the eighteenth century, and this type was particularly important in the field of cloth industry.

The insufficiency and unreliability of labor statistics for the whole of the period make it extremely difficult to establish, with any degree of accuracy, the ratio between the forced and free hired labor.[1] According to some calculations, free labor constituted about 40 per cent in the 1760's, about 50 per cent in the early nineteenth century, and about 60 per cent around 1825. These figures are disputed by some writers as being too high, and, curiously enough, the data for the period after 1825 are even less sufficient than for the preceding time. One cannot doubt, however, that the general tendency was

---

[1] Of course it should be remembered that among the free hired laborers a very considerable number were serfs working on the outside under the quitrent system. In view of the particularly strong development of various peasant crafts precisely in the quitrent regions, we may be sure that it was in this group that the Russian industry found its first supply of skilled labor.

in the direction of the increasing use of free labor.  This is particularly true of light industry, while in the mines and the metallurgical works of the Ural region forced labor predominated until the Emancipation.  However, it is significant that both the possessional and the manorial factories were in decline towards the end of the period. When in 1840 a law was promulgated permitting the owners of the possessional factories to liberate their serf workers, a considerable number of owners quickly availed themselves of the opportunity to replace forced labor with that of free workers.  Simultaneously, the manorial factory was rapidly losing its importance in the economic life of the country.  In 1830 the ratio of serf laborers employed in these factories to the whole number of factory workers in Russia fell to about 15 per cent, and in the 1840's to about 5 per cent.

We are not on much firmer ground when it comes to determining the general extent of Russia's industrial development during the period.  Official statistics used the term "factory" indiscriminately to cover a variety of industrial establishments, widely differing from one another in size and degree of centralization.  In addition to the big factories, very small establishments were listed, which did not deserve the name, even if judged by the standards of the time.  Moreover, no distinction was made between a "factory" where production was concentrated in one building and others which consisted of a series of small workshops under the same management. In some cases only the final part of production took place in the "factory" building, while all the preliminary operations were performed by the workers in their own workshops.  Finally, there are reasons to suspect that sometimes official reports listed as "factories" enterprises which still were operated under the merchant-employer system.  No wonder, therefore, that the estimates of the number of factories in Russia in the eighteenth and nineteenth centuries, made by modern scholars, vary considerably.  For the later part of the period, an approximate estimate is given in the following table:

FACTORIES AND FACTORY WORKERS [1]

|  | Factories | Workers |
|---|---|---|
| 1800 | about  2,000 | about 100,000 |
| 1825 | over    5,000 | over   200,000 |
| 1854 | about 10,000 | over   450,000 |
| 1861 | over  14,000 | over   500,000 |

[1] Tugan-Baranovsky, M., *Russkaia Fabrika v Proshlom i Nastoiashchem*, 1926, p. 66; with some later figures.

Estimates of the number of workers employed at the beginning of the nineteenth century vary from about 100,000 to about 200,000. There is less discrepancy in the estimates for the later dates. Recently, a careful study has been made of some of the principal branches of Russian industry in the eighteenth century,[1] which has shown that few of the establishments had less than fifty workers, while there were large numbers of factories employing more than one hundred workers, and many factories employing more than one thousand. For the nineteenth century one can assume even a larger concentration of labor.

If one accepts the above data as substantially correct, one is forced to abandon the familiar picture of a pre-Emancipation Russia lagging far behind the rest of Europe in her industrial development. It is significant that none of the contemporary western European authors who have written on Russian economics in the late eighteenth century and the early nineteenth speaks of Russia as an economically backward country. In fact, during some part of the eighteenth century, Russian industry, at least in some branches, was ahead not only of all the other Continental countries but of England as well. This was particularly true of the metal industries. In the middle of the eighteenth century Russia was the world's largest producer of both iron and copper, and it was not until the 1770's in the case of copper, and the very end of the century in the case of iron, that English production became equal to that of Russia.

It was only in the nineteenth century that England began to outrun Russia at a rapidly increasing pace in volume of production as well as in technique. In comparison with the prodigious English development, the progress of Russian metallurgy then appeared very unimpressive. In the 1860's the production of iron was hardly twice as large as in the beginning of the century, and the reasons for this are fairly obvious. Enjoying a virtual monopoly within the country and using cheap forced labor, the iron works of the Ural region lacked the motive for radical technical improvement. On the eve of the Emancipation they were mechanized in only a very small degree; iron was still commonly smelted with charcoal, and coke was used only in rare cases. In general, in Russia as in many other countries of the Continent, the introduction of machinery was a very slow process, and by the middle of the nineteenth century it had not proceeded very far. Technical progress was compara-

[1] Liubomirov, P., *Ocherki Po Istorii Russkoi Promyshlennosti, v XVIII i Nachale XIX Veka*, Leningrad, 1930.

tively rapid in the new cotton industry, which attained a considerable degree of development during the early decades of the century. It benefited from the constantly rising and widespread demand for inexpensive cotton goods and from the prevailing low prices on imported English yarn. This was the one branch of Russian industry which by 1840 was entirely based on free labor, and it depended less on government support than any other industry in the country. After 1842, when exportation of spinning machinery from England was permitted by the British government, Russia began to increase the production of its own yarn, and in the course of the next decades it underwent a thorough reorganization under the influence of the English technique.

The period that saw the formation of large-scale industry in Russia was also a period of considerable growth for the peasant craft industry within the country. There are no data that would enable us to establish, with any degree of accuracy, the relative importance of the two in the economic life of the country. There can be no doubt, however, that in many fields peasant craft industry, far from being crowded out by the new factories, was able not only to hold its own but even to increase its production. Generally speaking, the craft industry satisfied the demands of the domestic market for the less expensive and more widely used goods, while the factories, in most cases, worked for the government and for foreign export, or produced goods in demand among the upper classes of society. By the second half of the eighteenth century the peasant craft industry became thoroughly commercialized, and the overwhelming majority of craftsmen worked for the market, selling their produce to the middlemen. Some branches of this industry acquired a national importance, as, for instance, the linen industry of Ivanovo-Voznesensk, which later on became one of the largest centers of textile manufacture in Russia. In this case large-scale industry grew on foundations that were laid by peasant craftsmen. In fact, the first factory owners in Ivanovo were former serfs who had been able to accumulate wealth and to buy their freedom. We have here the interesting phenomenon of the appearance among the Russian industrialists of a new social group — that of the "peasant bourgeoisie."

## Foreign Trade

One of the most important factors in the development of Russia's foreign trade was the firm establishment of Russia on the shores of the Baltic Sea. Prior to the eighteenth century practically the only point of commercial contact between Russians and western Europeans was faraway Archangel, separated by a long distance from central Russia and situated on the shores of the White Sea, frozen for eight months of the year. After the first quarter of the eighteenth century, Archangel rapidly lost its importance, and the Baltic period in the history of Russia's foreign trade began. In the days of Peter the Great it was still necessary for the government to use compulsory methods for shifting trade from Archangel to St. Petersburg; but in 1727 all restrictions upon the trade of Archangel were abolished. By that time the natural advantages of St. Petersburg had become so obvious that compulsion was no longer necessary. Riga and Libau (Liepaja) were also developed as important Baltic ports in the later part of the eighteenth century, affording still more convenient access to some important regions.

In the south, Russian Black Sea trade did not begin to develop until the opening of the nineteenth century. After 1774 Russia enjoyed the right of navigation in the Black Sea, and her commercial ships were allowed by Turkey to go through the Straits to the Mediterranean Sea. But in view of the insufficiency of Russia's merchant marine no foreign trade of considerable volume could develop until the Straits were opened to the commercial ships of western European nations as well. Time was needed also for the economic development of southern Russia and the construction of Russian ports on the shores of the Black Sea; in this connection the rise of Odessa, acquired in 1792, was of great importance. With these preliminary conditions fulfilled, Russia's Black Sea trade began to grow, showing a steady increase during the first half of the nineteenth century. However, the Baltic trade remained supreme until the middle of the century, more particularly with regard to imports. In the beginning of the century its share in the sea trade of Russia constituted about 91 per cent of the exports and 85 per cent of the imports. In the middle of the century the figures were 61 per cent and 84 per cent, respectively. With regard to imports the situation remained almost unchanged, but about one third of the export trade by sea had passed from the Baltic to the Black Sea.

As to the land trade, it played an altogether minor part in the eighteenth century (less than 6 per cent of Russia's foreign trade), but its importance was gradually increasing during the first half of the next century. By the middle of the nineteenth century it already constituted about 27 per cent of the exports and about 37 per cent of the imports. During the same period the total volume of Russia's foreign trade increased almost three and a half times.

Both in the eighteenth century and in the early nineteenth Russia's chief customer was England. In the eighteenth century the English controlled about one half of Russia's European trade. In 1846–1848 their share still amounted to one third. The second place was then occupied by Germany (11 per cent), and the third by France (10 per cent). Throughout all the period in question Russia had an excess of exports, and in the eighteenth century the excess was very large. During the first half of the nineteenth century the import trade developed steadily, and by the end of the period it was nearly as large as the export trade.

Some of the advantages that Russia could derive from this situation were lost by her because of the passive character of her participation in foreign trade. Both the initiative and the actual carrying of trade remained in the hands of foreigners. Russian merchants still lacked the required energy, the knowledge of foreign languages, and the familiarity with western commercial practices needed to carry operations into foreign territory. In most cases business was conducted in Russian seaports with representatives of foreign firms and foreign brokers. At the same time, in spite of strenuous efforts on the part of the government, the Russian merchant marine remained negligible for most of the period. In the eighteenth century practically all shipping was in the hands of the English and the Dutch. They played the part of intermediaries between Russia on the one hand and France and southern Europe on the other. At the end of the century attempts were made to free Russian trade from foreign domination. In 1787 commercial treaties were concluded with France, Naples, and Portugal. Simultaneously there was noticeable a certain increase in the number of Russian commercial ships carrying foreign trade. But the development was a painfully slow one, and in the middle of the nineteenth century most Russian goods were still carried on foreign ships, while foreign firms predominated in St. Petersburg, and Greek and Italian merchants in the Black Sea ports.

The chief items of export in the eighteenth century were raw materials, such as hemp, flax, and timber, products of the Russian metallurgical industry (particularly iron), and textiles (chiefly linen and canvas). In return Russia imported mostly wine, fruits, coffee, sugar, silk tissues, and fine cloth, all of which (including coffee and sugar) were articles of luxury.

The nineteenth century brought with it some significant changes. Russia still continued to export a considerable volume of raw materials, supplying the world market with 70 per cent of its total amount of hemp and flax. To these was now added wool, the appearance of which among the items of Russian export was connected with the successful development of sheep breeding in southern Russia. On the other hand, the exportation of both iron and textiles underwent a sharp decline as a result of the remarkable development in the corresponding branches of English industry. The most significant change, however, was in the rapid growth of grain exports from Russia. In the eighteenth century they were almost negligible, but by 1850 they constituted about one third of the total Russian export trade. Generally speaking, Russia's trade with western Europe consisted more largely of agricultural products than in the eighteenth century.

There were significant changes in the nature of goods imported into Russia from the West. There was a considerable increase in the imports of manufactured articles, both in volume and in variety. In connection with the development of the Russian cotton industry, an increasing amount of cotton yarn and raw cotton began to be imported from England. Finally, towards the end of the period, there was a noticeable increase in the importation of machinery, particularly for the needs of the cotton industry.

# CHAPTER 15

# THE PERFECTING OF THE NEW TECHNOLOGY

――――◆――――

## The Continuity of Technological Development

The period 1760–1790 was marked by a number of inventions of unusual importance to the development of the technique which we associate with modern industry, but these inventions mark only the beginnings of the new technology. Its full accomplishment required not merely an extensive application of the machines invented at that time but a continuous development of invention over a wide field. Not even the primary features of the new technology were effectively established until the close of the careers of the inventors and engineers who gave such distinction to the first third of the nineteenth century. That generation has rarely received its full share of attention because achievements at their stage in the process of development are not readily appreciated by the general public. There is a tendency also to feel that the more meritorious inventions occur only at early stages in the process of technical development. But these ideas are seriously in error. They are due to the failure of the general public to distinguish between the individual invention and the general process of achievement by which mechanical developments of a particular class are made of practical value to the community. All great accomplishments rest upon a long series of inventions spread over a considerable period of time. Unfortunately there is a strong tendency to concentrate attention on one or two incidents in this process.

The inventions which compose these longer processes of development vary in their importance and in respect of the technical difficulties to be overcome. It is quite clear that the originality and merit of inventions have little to do with their place in the long series which constitutes the process of achievement. Some inventions of commanding importance are made very early in the sequence of development, and other inventions are made very late. The notable contribution of James Watt to the development of the steam engine really stands at a relatively late stage in the process. All engineers today recognize the quality and significance of the work of Newcomen. The general public and many historians seldom make any attempt to deal with the whole process of achievement and persistently allow some single conspicuous invention to represent the entire process. Even the selection of the invention so publicized has frequently been dominated by caprice and misunderstanding of the actual history of the technical advance.

The attitude ordinarily taken towards the inventions of the generation dominated by Arkwright, Crompton, and Watt is merely a conspicuous illustration of this general habit of mind. People have been quick to assume that all the technological changes of the nineteenth century were explicitly foreshadowed by the great inventions of the eighteenth century. Even historians have been slow to recognize the amount and the quality of effort that was necessary to carry through to its true conclusions the development begun at that time. The actual extent of the accomplishment in 1790 was very narrowly limited. In the textile industry, which was so deeply involved in the changes, the new machines did not constitute a complete series. Spinning and the preparatory processes were fairly adequately covered, though there was no possibility of meeting all the needs of the woolen and worsted industries. The combing machines then available were very imperfect and ill-adapted to an application of power. There was no effective power loom, although Cartwright had gone far towards working out the primary problems of principle. Machines for cloth finishing had not been significantly improved. Much of the machinery was not adapted to the intensive use of power. Crompton's mule constitutes the most important illustration of this limitation of the early machines. The operator supplied the motive power as well as a great deal of guidance in the operations of the mechanism. The ribbon frames and the knitting frames presented similar characteristics, though both of them were much more automatic than the mule. Finally, none of these machines could be built of the harder metals with any precision. They were commonly constructed of wood, and many of their shortcomings were due to the limitations of materials and to the absence of refinements of design which could be achieved only by a professional group of machine makers.

### The Lighter Instruments of Precision

The perfection of the technique of production so effectively launched in the late eighteenth century was made possible by the application, to heavy-duty machinery, of standards of precision first achieved in the field of light engineering. The public is perhaps a little slow to think of clocks and watches as important types of machinery. The small amount of power used and the small scale of the mechanism itself frequently close our eyes to the great refinement of mechanical design embodied in these instruments. They stand out as the most conspicuous examples of instruments of precision. The lessons learned by the craftsmen of these trades formed the basis for the development of the engineering sciences in the late eighteenth century and the early nineteenth century. These timekeepers presented a substantial array of notable devices for the control of motion. These devices involved all the primary problems of geared mechanisms. The marine chronometer required delicate adjustments to the expansion and contraction of metals during small changes of temperature. The pendulum clocks presented important problems in the theory of dynamics. The development of the pendulum clock rested upon a complete mathematical treatment of the forces operating in a pendulum. The escapements of both clocks and watches called for considerable refinements in the design of the gear teeth, and the problems received full mathematical treatment in the course of the eighteenth century.

The importance of work done on clocks and watches will be readily appreciated by all attentive students of the biographies of inventors and technicians in the late eighteenth century and the early nineteenth. Much of the work done for Arkwright on the spinning machine was entrusted to a clockmaker. George Stephenson learned much of his mechanics by repairing and studying clocks. The rapid development of the engineering sciences after Watt's inventions was largely due to the extensive mathematical treatment of the problems of dynamics involved in the construction of these small instruments of precision.

The field of light engineering also includes the development of the lathe. Until the sixteenth century the lathe did not advance notably beyond the forms that it had assumed early in the Middle Ages. In its primitive form it was little more than a device to rotate a rather small and light object. Early in the sixteenth century attempts were made to increase the compass of the machine. It was made capable of holding larger and heavier pieces of work, and considerable progress was made in the application of various devices to assist the workman in guiding the tool for the performance of accurate and complex cuts. Elements of a crude slide rest appear specifically in the work of Jacques Besson, who died about 1568. He was able to cut screws of any pitch in wood; this could be done on work of varying diameter, and right- and left-hand screws could be produced at will. Other attachments enabled him to produce elliptical, conical, and various composite forms. Practical applications of all of this fancy turning appear in the making of furniture. Another type of lathe which accomplished somewhat similar ends was the mandrel lathe. In this machine special motions were imparted to the spindle by which the work was turned, so that specific motion was given to the work itself while the tool performing the work was held in fixed position. Lathes of this sort were extensively used for screw cutting and for a variety of special types of work. By the close of the eighteenth century there were several types of lathes available for light work in which the workman was largely, if not entirely, emancipated from the task of guiding the tool. Some special applications designed particularly to meet the problems of the clock and watch trades achieved a very high degree of precision in their work. As early as 1763 the Fusee engine had achieved the distinction of being a positive instrument of precision. Within a limited field of light engineering the problem of precision had been thoroughly mastered, although at this time engineers such as Watt could scarcely secure materials capable of functioning at all. For many years the efficiency of steam engines was seriously impaired by the inaccuracy of the cylinders and the errors in the cutting of gears. The perfection of the new technology demanded the extension of the methods of precision from the field of light engineering to the new field of heavy-duty machinery.

## Heavy-Duty Instruments of Precision

The earliest development of heavy-duty tools is to be found in the boring engines developed by John Wilkinson. Boring machines operated by power were by no means new. Pump barrels and pipes had been bored from wood prior to the fifteenth century, and in the sixteenth century power devices were developed capable of boring cannon of bronze or cast iron. The earliest machines were merely intended to finish a casting which was already roughly formed. The characteristic boring engine of the early modern period was the vertical engine fully developed at the close of the seventeenth century. These instruments were all designed for the manufacture of cannon. The cannon was suspended in a frame over the drill and was held against the drill by its own weight. The drill was attached to a windlass and turned by one or two horses. This drill was developed to such a point that it was possible to bore cannons from solid castings. When the Newcomen engine was developed, these boring engines were soon adapted to making cylinders for the engines, though the large diameter of the cylinders made it difficult to achieve any high degree of accuracy. The first important improvements were made by John Wilkinson in a device that was patented January 27, 1774; designed originally for boring cannon, this machine was set to work two years later on cylinders and condensers for Boulton and Watt. It achieved a measure of accuracy until then unknown. The design of the boring engine was subsequently changed in some particulars. The earliest dated drawings are from the year 1795. At this time the drill head was carried on a heavy rod which ran completely through the cylinder and was supported at both ends. The drill was carried through the work by a rack-and-pinion device contained within the supporting rod. For many years the power required to operate these boring machines was supplied by horses turning a windlass, the heavier engines having as many as four horses on the windlass.

The development of the lathe as an instrument of precision in heavy-duty work involved two decisive changes. It was essential that the lathe be built entirely of iron. Any lathe constructed wholly or partly of wood would be subject to changes of alignment and position sufficient to make accuracy unattainable. It was also essential to have the iron lead screws cut with extreme accuracy. At the close of the eighteenth century all lathes were built of wood and there were no screws of any kind that achieved any significant measure of accuracy. Without minutely accurate screws precision could not be attained. The large screws then used in heavy-duty machines were all produced from castings which were corrected in part by filing. This process of production was both costly and unsatisfactory. The first objective of the great lathe makers was the production of good lead screws. The pioneer work was done by Henry Maudslay in England and by David Wilkinson in the United States. Their early work was very nearly simultaneous and the similarity of the basic features of their machines is quite striking. There can be no doubt of the substantial independence of their work, but as Wilkinson's work was not carried effectively beyond its initial stage, the primary achievement is undoubtedly the work of Maudslay. Maudslay's lathe fulfilled all of the requirements of a completely satisfactory heavy-duty machine.

The first all-metal lathe was set up in Joseph Bramah's shop for the manufacture of his newly patented lock. The lathe was constructed entirely of iron and embodied the principles of the slide rest which were already fully developed in a variety of forms in various light wooden lathes and in the Fusee engine. The head and tail stops and the slide rest were carried by a triangular bar mounted on castings. The triangular form was chosen in order to simplify the task of surfacing, because these surfaces had to be prepared entirely by chisel and file. The slide rest was governed by a lead screw running the whole length of the machine. The machine at this time was not large enough to be applied to the heavier kinds of work, but after 1800 a great deal of time was given by Maudslay to the problems of screw cutting.

The engineering trades at that time had great need of minutely accurate lead screws of great length and diameter. The solution of the problem involved not only the development of considerable mechanical facility in handling large pieces of work but the elaboration of special procedures for the study of errors in the pitch of the thread. Several screws were carefully prepared by hand, and the best of these were selected for further work in specially constructed lathes. In this way a very fine brass screw was constructed nearly seven feet long in which the error amounted to less than one sixteenth of an inch. A device was then constructed to remedy this error and the screw so produced was examined with micrometric apparatus. It then appeared that there were many errors of detail; there were irregularities in the width of the cut and in the pitch of the screw. Further corrections reduced these errors to such small proportions that they ceased to be of any practical significance. This protracted effort was the basis of the development of the engineering trade in the years that followed. The historian of the lathe, Holtzapffel, says: "Mr. Maudslay effected nearly the entire change from the old imperfect and accidental practice of screw making . . . to the modern exact and scientific mode now generally followed by engineers; and he pursued the subject of the screw with more or less ardour and at an enormous expense until his death in 1835."

From this point the development of the whole set of machine tools proceeded rapidly. Pattern-turning lathes for copying irregular shapes were developed by Bentham, Brunel, and Blanchard. These lathes were based more or less directly on various types of the lighter lathes formerly constructed of wood. The planing and milling machines presented more elements of novelty in design, but their development presented little difficulty, once the basic work on the heavy-duty lathes had been accomplished.

## Interchangeable-Part Manufacture

The development of accurate methods for the manufacture of individual objects, particularly of metal, made it possible to apply new methods to the manufacture of many articles consisting of separate parts. As soon as it should become possible to manufacture the individual parts with a high degree of accuracy, it would be possible to produce the parts separately in large quantities to be assembled into the finished object. The economy of such a method of production was perceived at an early date. A Swedish engineer, Christopher Polhem, endeavored to apply such methods to the manufacture of various metal objects in a plant set up at Stiernsund about 1700. Water power was applied to all possible stages of manufacture, and individual parts were made which were later finished and assembled. Machinery was not then sufficiently developed to give adequate effect to the brilliant idea, and it was fully a century before substantial achievement of such results became possible. In 1785 a Frenchman named LeBlanc began the manufacture of muskets on the principles of interchangeable-part manufacture. Little is known of the details of the methods he employed, but from Whitney's experience we may infer that the essence of his procedure lay in the filing of the different parts of the lock of the musket with jigs as guides for the workmen. These French developments seem to have had no conspicuous consequences. The general system of manufacture, however, was established at a slightly later date, both in Great Britain and in the United States.

The most important work along these lines was done by Eli Whitney and Simeon North in connection with the manufacture of firearms under contracts with the United States government. As we cannot properly follow the details of this development, it will be sufficient to note that the work of Eli Whitney was a vital factor in the whole technique of a considerable group of Connecticut industries. Although the work in its earliest stages involved only a modest amount of mechanical equipment, the development of special machine tools proceeded with great rapidity.

In England the most notable achievement was the work of Brunel and Bentham in the manufacture of pulley blocks for the navy. Brunel had had experience in the United States and it is possible that some of his ideas were influenced by the projects and methods of American engineers. The essential details of the scheme, how-

ever, were not taken directly from American sources.   The project
for the systematic manufacture of blocks was independently conceived by both Brunel and Bentham.   They were brought together
at an early date so that the scheme as ultimately developed was the
work of the two men.   With the security afforded by a contract
to supply all the requirements of the British navy, they designed
a set of machinery embracing forty-four separate machines capable
of performing a large part of the work required for the production
of the finished block.   The machines fell into four general groups.
(1) There were sawing machines for roughing out the blocks.
(2) There was a group of machines designed to do the work of boring,
mortising, and shaping the blocks.   (3) The third group of machines
were designed to turn and bore the sheaves, to rivet the brass liner,
and to finish the facing of the sides.   (4) The iron pins serving as
an axle for the sheaves were hand forged in dies and subsequently
finished on lathes and polished.   These machines were built by
Maudslay and represented a high standard of workmanship.   With
them ten unskilled men performed work that otherwise would have
required one hundred ten highly skilled workmen.   This installation
was thus highly successful (though other woodworking machines,
designed by Brunel, were less effective).   Despite this notable
demonstration, the general features of such a system of manufacture
were not clearly perceived, and such methods were not extensively
introduced into England until their success in the United States
attracted attention to them.

## The Development of the Power Loom

The hand loom is a somewhat unusual type of machine because
it is merely a device for holding the work which engages the attention of the operator.   It presents, therefore, a striking example of
certain features of the problem of definition : the number of parts
and their relations to one another make it clearly impossible to
describe the apparatus as a tool, but it must be confessed that it is
far removed from the concept of a machine popularized by Ure and
Karl Marx.   The general features of a developed hand loom are
shown in the diagram on page 314, which is highly simplified.
The number of threads in the warp has been very greatly reduced,
and all the supports of the various parts have been omitted so that
one sees the bare essentials of the operative mechanisms.   The
warp unrolls from the beam at the right-hand side of the diagram.
The threads of the warp are separated by the laze rods $L\,L$ into

series of odd and even threads. Each of these groups of threads is controlled by one of the heddles supported by the pulleys *P P*. Each thread of the warp passes through a small opening in the threads of the heddle frames. By means of these heddles the various series of warp threads may be lifted. In the diagram, which displays the apparatus for absolutely plain weaving, only two heddles *H H* are shown. If it were desired to produce simple geometrical patterns, a larger number of heddles would be necessary.

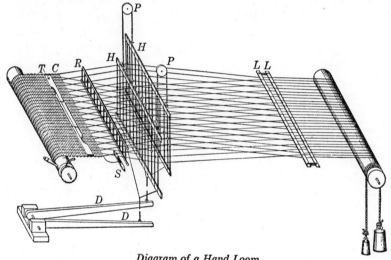

*Diagram of a Hand Loom*

In that event the threads passing through each heddle would have to be selected with reference to the kind of pattern to be produced. From an early date the heddles of the developed hand loom were controlled by pedals *DD*. Next in order of arrangement we see the reed *R*. In the old hand loom the reed was suspended from the overhead frame of the loom. The reed consists of a large number of fine wires between which pass the threads of the warp. After each throw of the shuttle *S* the reed is drawn up against the finished cloth, to beat into the fabric the strand of yarn just deposited by the shuttle. In the actual loom as set up, the warp threads pass over a broad strip across which the shuttle passes when it is thrown by the weaver. The diagram also shows the temple *T* which was used to maintain the full width of the woven fabric.

The hand loom as described above reached an essentially mature form early in the Middle Ages, and from that date until the invention of the fly shuttle (or flying shuttle) in 1733, no significant change occurred in the general structure of the broad loom. A project for the application of power to the loom was developed by Leonardo da Vinci. His attempts, however, were unsuccessful. Other projects involving slightly different mechanical features appeared in France in the seventeenth century, but nothing was accomplished. These early attempts failed because they afforded no possible solution for the free movement of the shuttle through the warp. The problem of the shuttle was solved on the ribbon loom because it was not necessary that the shuttle should be free, but this arrangement contributed nothing to the development of the broad loom. The first intimation of a solution of this difficult problem is afforded by the fly shuttle developed by John Kay in 1733. The reed frame was enlarged in order to carry the runway necessary for the shuttle, and the reed frame was built out so as to provide space for the shuttle beyond each end of the reed. The shuttle boxes at each end of the reed frame were equipped with small devices mounted on runners by which the shuttle could be put in motion. These devices could be controlled by strings mounted over the center of the reed so that the operator could control the shuttles for any width of loom from the center of the apparatus. For the broadcloth looms engaged in making goods a yard and three quarters, or even two yards, wide, it was obviously a matter of great convenience to be able to operate the shuttles from the center of the loom. Without the fly shuttle, the broadcloth loom required the attendance of two weavers. It may seem strange that nearly a century elapsed before the full consequence of this invention was developed, for the fly shuttle really carried the promise of the achievement of an automatic power loom. The reason for this long interval and for the thirty years of struggle at the end of the eighteenth century lay in the very great difficulty of controlling the motion of a free shuttle.

The true nature of the problem is vividly revealed by Cartwright's description of his early experience with the power loom. Discussion of the spinning inventions had attracted his attention to the need of increasing the productivity of the loom. After considering this problem for a short time, Cartwright produced his first loom; and he describes his experiences in the following passage : "It struck me that as plain weaving can only be three movements which were to follow one another in succession, there would be little difficulty in producing them and repeating them. Full of these ideas I immediately employed a carpenter and a smith to carry them into effect. As soon as the machine was finished, I got a weaver to put in a warp which was of such material as sail cloths are usually made of. To my great delight, a piece of cloth, such as it was, was the product. The reed fell with the weight of at least half a hundredweight and the springs which threw the shuttle were strong enough to have thrown a Congreave rocket. In short, it required the strength of two powerful men to work the machine at a slow rate and only then a short time. I then secured what I thought was a most valuable property by a patent on April 4, 1785. This being done, I condescended to see how other people wove, and you will guess my astonishment when I compared their easy modes of operation with mine. It was not until 1787 that I completed my invention and took out my first weaving patent." [1]

There is a great tendency to assume that the problem of the power loom was effectively solved by Cartwright's inventions. Many have failed to realize that nearly thirty years elapsed before a practical power loom was available in England. A successful loom, to be sure, was introduced somewhat earlier in the United States, but important improvements were essential even to the Lowell loom. This long period of struggle involved much more than a mere critical refinement of the principles sketched in by Cartwright. The essential problem of the loom was the effective control of the relatively violent motions necessary to successful operation of the shuttle. Although the loom is in no sense of the word an instrument of precision, the production of a practical loom presented the kind of problem that characterizes the instrument of precision. It was not enough merely to produce certain motions; it was absolutely essential to control them with delicacy. The accomplishment of this truly difficult task required supplementary parts and regulative mechanisms which must be ranked as inventions of a very high order. Even in the developed loom of the present time the shuttle presents a number of very difficult problems. The statement of an experienced textile expert is significant and interesting. Speaking of the problem of the shuttle, he says: "Experience has proved it to be uncertain in action, costly to keep in order, and by far the most dangerous part of the machine. . . . When a shuttle is negatively driven, an enormous waste of power results, partly on account of the impossibility of accurately gauging the force required, and partly because the best of motors is liable to variations in speed. A shuttle

[1] Ellison, Thomas, *The Cotton Trade of Great Britain*, London, 1886, p. 25.

must never be permitted to rebound after reaching a shuttle box, consequently swells are employed in such a manner that it has been affirmed that the force required to drive a shuttle into or out of a shuttle box is equal to that required for driving it through a shed. On this assumption three times the actual power required for useful work is taken from the engine, and twice the necessary power must be created by springs or other appliances. . . . The movement of a negatively driven shuttle is essentially a jerky one and frequently produces the most disastrous results." [1]

The inventors of the late eighteenth century therefore faced a number of peculiarly difficult mechanical problems even after the primary parts of the power loom had been given their characteristic functions. The Cartwright looms were never effectively used, although looms on his principles were installed in one or two factories. Older accounts neglect the work of John Austin of Glasgow. He began work on a power loom in 1789 and applied for a patent, though no patent was actually taken out at that time. A loom embodying many improvements was exhibited before the Chamber of Commerce at Glasgow in 1796. Two years later thirty looms were set up at the spinning mill of J. Monteith at Pollockshaws, four miles outside of Glasgow. Additional looms were installed by the same company at a later date. A model of this loom was sent to the Society of Arts at London in 1806 and is still in their Museum. The machine was provided with stop motions for both weft and warp, and it was capable of sixty traverses of the shuttle per minute. It would produce two yards of web per hour. One weaver with a boy could tend five looms on coarse work, or three or four on fine work. The precise influence of Austin's loom in England is not accurately known, but it is presumed that his work was familiar to the Englishmen working on the loom at the beginning of the nineteenth century. The work of William Radcliffe in 1802 and that of Thomas Johnson between 1803 and 1805 was probably independent. We cannot be as certain of the important patents taken out by Horrocks in 1813 and 1821. These patents were fully developed by the firm of Sharp & Roberts in 1822. Looms were put on the general market, and they were rapidly adopted by the industry in the course of the decade.

The development of fancy weaving was dominated by the development of the Jacquard action. This notable achievement of French

[1] Fox, T. W., *The Mechanism of Weaving*, London, 1894, pp. 266-276; by permission of Macmillan & Co., Ltd., publishers.

textile men will be briefly described in Chapter 22. Any full description of this accomplishment would require more space than is here available, and undoubtedly would try the patience of the general reader. It is important to note, however, that this great step forward in textile machinery took place only in the early nineteenth century, and that the application of power to looms with the Jacquard action was quite late.

## Developments in Spinning and Finishing

The water frame or throstle for continuous spinning reached an essentially mature form in the hands of Arkwright. Crompton's mule, however, long resisted any general application of power. It presented the peculiar problem of a succession of essentially different movements. The motion of the carriage to and from the rolls was not, perhaps, a peculiarly difficult problem. The spindles had two motions, the direct rotation for spinning and the reverse motion for winding, and these motions had to be co-ordinated with the stopping and starting of the rolls. The machine as a whole presented, therefore, a much more complex mechanical problem than the throstle, all the motions of which were continuous. The application of power to the mule required a number of notable inventions, and the machine in its final form is commonly regarded as one of the most notable accomplishments of the early nineteenth century. It would be a great mistake to assume that the application of power was a simple affair requiring no more than ordinary technical competence. As early as 1790, attempts were made by Strutt to apply power to the mule, with modest success. The basic inventions were the work of Richard Roberts of the Sharp & Roberts firm, who produced a definitive "self actor" in 1825. A somewhat different model was patented in 1834 by William Smith, and nearly all modern mules are based on these two models. These improvements of the mule reduced the labor costs of spinning 30 or 40 per cent within a few years of their introduction.

The period was also marked by significant work upon the machines required for finishing, and upon the difficult problem of wool combing. Early work on the shearing engines, both in France and in England, was dominated by the notion of applying power to a large pair of shears. Several machines were brought out on these principles in the period 1792 to 1815. They were only moderately successful. The modern development has been dominated by the American patents of 1792 and 1793 which worked out the details for the use of curved knives set on a cylinder working against a bed plate. The principle is now familiar to all in the lawn mower. The lawn mower was, in fact, suggested by the cloth shearing engine. Needless to say, the adjustments of the shearing engine are much more delicate. It is not necessary to describe in any detail the long struggle of inventors with the problem of the combing machine. It is significant to note, however, that the most important work on this problem was done in France, and that the basic work of Heilman was not completed until 1845.

The record of invention in the textile industry thus shows that the full accomplishment of mechanization was not achieved until the second quarter of the nineteenth century.

## The Invention of the Turbine Water Wheel

The term "turbine" was first used by Burdin in 1824. The term is designed to emphasize the fact that in such wheels the water is moving over the vanes of the wheel. In all of the other types of water wheel there is no motion of the water relatively to the buckets or floats of the wheel. In the turbine wheel the power is derived from the impulses or reactions set up between the flow of water and the curved passages within which it is contained. The force generated by reaction appears in many forms. The common lawn sprinkler with jets turned in opposite directions at each end of the hollow crossbar embodies the basic elements of a reaction turbine. This form, however, cannot be used conveniently as a source of power without profound modification. Nearly all forms of turbines demand the strict enclosure of the rotating member in a stationary casing. The slow development of this type of wheel is probably due to the mechanical problems involved in the fitting of the casing around the wheel.

One of the very early suggestions of the turbine principle appears in the notebooks of Leonardo da Vinci at the close of the fifteenth century. The sketch shows explicitly a competently conceived set of vanes, but the wheel is provided with no casing at all, so that a large part of the force must have been lost. There is an interesting sketch involving elements of the turbine principle in the work of Besson in 1568. There was a notable installation at Toulouse at the beginning of the eighteenth century, and wheels of the type used there were extensively applied in southern France and in Italy. They fall short by a very small degree of achieving all the distinctive features of the mature turbine. A great deal of work was done on the problems of the water wheel in the second half of the eighteenth century. Scientists and engineers in several European countries were seriously engaged in analytical and experimental work. The difficulty of achieving an adequate solution of the problem is strikingly indicated by the failure of all of this work to produce a decisive accomplishment. The list of students included the notable mathematician Euler and the English engineer Smeaton; both the theorist and the practical engineer failed. Work continued into the nineteenth century, especially in France, where Burdin at the technical school of St. Étienne made important studies of the reaction turbine. His concepts of the problem embodied many important features of the final solution, but there were vital defects of design which stood in the way of a successful accomplishment.

Burdin's work, however, was of great importance because it brought the problem to the attention of one of the students at St. Étienne, Benoit Fourneyron. Fourneyron began active study of the problems of the turbine in 1823. By 1827 he had produced a small turbine capable of developing about 6 horsepower. A few years later he moved to Besançon to work on the problem of the turbine with the financial assistance of Caron, the master of an iron forge at Fraisans. Fourneyron designed a small wheel rated at 10 horsepower for the blowing engine and a larger wheel rated at 50 horsepower for the forge hammers. The 50 horsepower wheel, completed in 1832, presented the first adequate solution of the turbine. A patent was taken out and a memoir was submitted to the Society for the Encouragement of National Industry. Three other inventors had submitted designs in competition for the prize offered by the society, but the prize of 6,000 francs was awarded to Fourneyron. This achievement must be regarded as one of the very great technical accomplishments of the nineteenth century. It was not only the basis for an extensive utilization of water power in Continental Europe throughout the century, but it was also the basis of important developments of water powers in the United States throughout the industrialized sections. This type of wheel, moreover, is capable of a very great variety of applications, so that it becomes possible to utilize the energy of falling water whatever its volume or whatever the height of the fall. The invention of the turbine, therefore, opened up the full possibilities of the utilization of water power, and became of the greatest importance when the development of electricity made it possible to distribute energy over considerable distances.

# CHAPTER 16

## COMMERCIAL POLICY, 1789–1834

---

### Smuggling and the Treaty of 1786

Both England and France became deeply committed to protective policies in the second half of the seventeenth century, and tariff barriers were raised steadily throughout the eighteenth century. The importation of many commodities was prohibited, and there were also long lists of commodities whose movement was in effect prohibited by high duties. The facility with which the Channel could be crossed in small boats encouraged smuggling, and the illegal entry of wines, spirits, tea, and tobacco became a source of great concern to England. France suffered in like fashion, especially along the Dutch border. Tobacco and Indian textiles were regularly smuggled. In 1745 the British authorities were so completely baffled by the smugglers that an amnesty was offered to all smugglers who appeared before a certain date and described their methods of procedure. But this merely checked operations for a short interlude, and illegal trade was soon in full swing once more. There were well-known offices in Paris and London at which parcels could be delivered for illegal entry. The charges had been reduced to about 10 per cent of the value of the goods. Tea was an even more lucrative commodity than tobacco or spirits for the English smugglers. In 1745 it was estimated that consumption mounted to 4,000,000 pounds, of which only 20 per cent paid duty. In 1787 it was presumed that only 40 per cent of the tea consumed in Great Britain paid duty. Consumption had increased to 13,000,000 pounds. East India officials engaged in private trade shipped tea in foreign vessels to Continental ports where it was sold to tea companies that supplied the smugglers. The British authorities assumed that there were, in 1787, 5,000,000 pounds of tea at Hamburg and 3,000,000 pounds at Ostend, awaiting smugglers. With the addition of spirits and tobacco, the enterprise became very extensive. "Forty thousand persons were supposed to be engaged, by sea and land, in the various branches of the contraband trade, with large and connected capitals, from which an immense profit was derived. . . . The farmers near the coast have already changed their occupation: and instead of employing their horses

321

in tilling the soil, . . . they use them for the more advantageous purpose of carrying smuggled goods inland." [1]

The development of liberal thought in England and in France was therefore contemporaneous with practical problems of customs administration that were favorable to reform of the customs system. The doctrines of Adam Smith's *Wealth of Nations* and the liberal program of the physiocrats in France provided ready defense for reformist policies which appealed to statesmen largely on practical grounds.

The earliest manifestation of liberal tendencies was the commercial treaty negotiated between France and Great Britain in 1786. It was supposed at one time that this treaty was forced upon France as a condition of peace in 1783. The French sources show that the treaty was the outcome of a deliberate attempt on the part of the physiocrats to force their liberal ideals upon an unwilling and unconvinced public. Dupont de Nemours urged Vergennes to insert a clause in the treaty of 1783 providing for the negotiation of a commercial treaty. He presumed that Britain would be glad to enter into such an arrangement, and it was his opinion that it would be highly beneficial to France. The clause was inserted, but the British government would never have negotiated a treaty if the French had not forced the issue, in May, 1785, by increasing the duties levied on British goods. Even after negotiations were begun, the treaty was so unpopular in England that there was no possibility of success unless France made great concessions to the demands of British manufacturers. The treaty finally signed (1786) was unfairly advantageous to England, both in its major provisions and still more in the finer details of the schedules. France reduced duties on hardware, textiles, leather, and porcelains, in some cases, to 10 per cent ad valorem; and in no case did the duties exceed 15 per cent. Great Britain removed the discrimination against French wines and spirits that had been established by the Methuen Treaty in favor of Portugal. The duties were reduced also to about one half of the preceding rates.

The actual effect of the treaty is hard to determine, because the low duties discouraged smuggling, and some of the effect on trade was nominal rather than real. The effect upon public opinion in France, however, was most explicit. Traders and manufacturers felt that the British had secured all the advantages, and that many

---

[1] Tomline, George, *Memoirs of the Life of the Right Honorable William Pitt*, Philadelphia, 1821, vol. I, pp. 282-283.

French industries had been sacrificed by the idealism of the French negotiators. The severity of competition with British goods soon intensified the conviction that protection was essential to the industries of France. The treaty was denounced in 1789, and thereafter France became deeply committed to a policy of protection. The agricultural regions were no less insistent than the industrialists, so that the liberal groups were left in a hopeless minority. Even under the Second Empire, the Chambers were so hostile to relaxation of duties that Chevalier and Louis Napoleon were obliged to embody their liberal measures in commercial treaties that lay entirely outside the jurisdiction of the legislature.

## Pitt's Reform of the Customs

British policy was dominated almost entirely by practical considerations, but the accomplishments were important and mark the actual béginning of the revision of the customs system. The principle of Parliamentary control of expenditure had gradually produced an intolerable confusion in the public accounts. Each specific need of revenue was met by the levy of a specified tax upon some commodity. Many commodities were charged with levies for different purposes, so that it was not only necessary to account separately for the revenue from each commodity but even to record separately the product of each separate levy. In 1785 a Committee on Public Accounts made a notable report on the intricacies of the customs, and an act was passed in 1787 to carry out the recommendations of the committee. The reform merely effected an administrative simplification. This act was no more than a beginning, but the outbreak of the French Revolution and the following wars prevented further reform at that time. The tendencies of Pitt's thought are, however, clearly indicated by the proposed change in the Corn Laws.

Until 1770 Great Britain regularly exported a considerable quantity of grain. The trade was complex, because there were exports from ports of the west that were partly offset by some imports on the east coast. But there was none the less an excess of exports over imports. It was intended to prohibit export entirely in years of dearth, and to discourage importation unless prices were at a high level. After 1770 there was a net balance of imports, not large, to be sure, but practically continuous. From 1770 to 1788 cereals were imported to the average annual value of £291,000, about half of the average annual value of the net exports in the period 1746 to 1765.  The change in the direction of trade led to some relaxation of duties in 1773, in order to encourage importation. Increasing concern was felt about the food supply, and some attention was given to the sources of foreign supplies.

### The Corn Bill of 1790, and the " Landed Interest "

In 1790 the Committee on Trade and Foreign Plantations undertook a systematic study of the export surplus of the regions of northern Europe, then the chief sources of supply.  They reached the conclusion that the effective surplus for export was very small, so that any measurable crop failure would make it necessary to rely upon the supplies of North America.  Further reduction of the obstacles to importation was recommended.  The government introduced a bill which reduced the duties on the various cereals at certain price levels.  The law of 1773 had permitted importation at three price ranges, with a nominal duty at the highest price range, and relatively high duties for both the intermediate range and the low price range.  For wheat, the duties were as follows:

THE CORN LAW OF 1773: WHEAT SCHEDULE

| Price of Wheat, per Quarter [1] | Duty |
|---|---|
| 48 shillings or over | 6d. |
| Over 44s. but under 48s. | 17s. 0d. |
| 44s. or under | 22s. 0d. |

There were similar schedules of duty for all the other grains and the primary legumes, peas and beans.  The term " corn " covered these legumes and all the northern cereals.  The bill of 1790 proposed to leave the price levels unchanged throughout, but the duties at the intermediate price range were drastically reduced.  For wheat, the duty was reduced from 17 shillings to 2 shillings 6 pence.  The significance of these price levels may be seen by referring to the graph on page 325 showing the price of wheat.  The presumptions of the debates, of course, are best reflected by the price levels prevalent up to 1790, for prices were subsequently affected by the currency troubles and the war emergency.

The proposals of the government seem modest enough, but a group in Parliament were deeply roused by the clear implication that the government expected England to be dependent upon some supplementary importation of food.  This group was led by Lord

---

[1] A "quarter" is a measure equal to about 8 bushels.  The abbreviation s., of course, is for shilling; and d. for pence.

Sheffield, who remained the leading champion of agriculture until his death. The debates in Parliament are very imperfectly reported, but the substance of the case of the opponents of the government is embodied in Lord Sheffield's *Observations on the Corn Bill.* He recognized that England was becoming dependent upon importations of food "to an alarming degree"; but he was convinced that the country was "capable of raising sufficient food for its own consumption." He proposed, therefore, that every possible encouragement be held out to growers of grain. He recognized the necessity

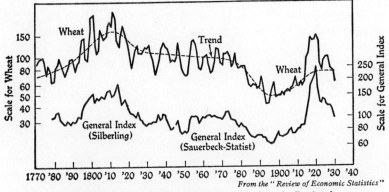

*Prices of Wheat, and General Index of Prices, in England*

of a higher price level, and with this in view proposed various amendments to the bill. The government proposed to permit warehousing in bond, in order to encourage importation in anticipation of price increases. Lord Sheffield attacked this clause, and (March 11, 1791) the House divided 62 to 62, the Speaker casting a vote with the Noes, so that the government was defeated. When the schedules of prices were debated in April, Lord Sheffield again defeated the government; he carried, by a vote of 59 to 53, an amendment which raised the price level for the low duty on wheat from 48 shillings per quarter to 52 shillings.

These amendments may not seem to present very important issues, but it must be remembered that they represent the victory of an agricultural bloc opposed to the government. By these small margins Parliament refused to accept a broad-visioned policy that would have afforded a sound basis for the development of British agriculture and finance. The government did not propose to apply a free-trade policy, but in this phase of finance as in others, it proposed to move towards liberalism. The government felt that a warehousing clause was essential to any workable scheme and accordingly offered to make a compromise. The price levels governing the duty on importation were raised somewhat higher (from 52 shillings to 54 shillings for wheat), and warehousing in bond was permitted.

## The Blockade and the Corn Law of 1815

The problem of the food supply became very serious during the wars with Napoleon. Conditions became acute in 1799 and 1800. Prices rose to unprecedented levels, and statutory restrictions were imposed on the use of wheat. Pastry making was restricted; the dilution of flour with bran was recommended and legalized. High prices stimulated production. The enclosure of waste land brought new areas into cultivation, much of it land that had never before been plowed, and some of it so heavy that it could hardly be plowed at all. Enclosure of the existing arable area also proceeded rapidly, as the rearrangement of fields offered prospects of increased supplies of grain and increased profit. The "landed interest," as the agricultural bloc was called, was jubilant. They "pointed with pride" to the "great achievement" of the British farming class. The possibility of substantial self-sufficiency was, in their eyes, conclusively demonstrated. The rising price levels gave them little concern, despite the fact that wheat stood at 123 shillings per quarter during the crisis in 1801, averaged 76 shillings between the years 1802 and 1809, and finally reached 130 shillings 10 pence per quarter in 1812.

The price schedules of the Corn Laws were revised in 1804, but the prices rose so much above the schedules that the laws were of little practical importance. The problem was brought to the attention of the House of Commons by an apparently innocent attempt of Sir Henry Parnell to do something for Ireland. Though Ireland had been a part of the United Kingdom since 1801, Irish trade was nevertheless handicapped by discriminatory duties. Exports within the British Empire, as well as exports to foreign countries, were heavily taxed, if not prohibited. Parnell proposed to have a committee make an inquiry into the conditions of the grain trade of Ireland. The motion was amended to cover the grain trade of the United Kingdom, and the entire problem was thus brought before Parliament (1813). The committee was dominated by the landed interest, and all the doctrines of Lord Sheffield's *Observations* were written into the report. In order to protect agriculture, the committee proposed to stabilize existing conditions.   The wheat schedule suggested was as follows :

| Price of Wheat per Quarter | Duty |
|---|---|
| Over 135s. 2d. | 6d. |
| Under 135s. 2d. but over 105s. 2d. | 2s. 6d. |
| Under 105s. 2d. | 24s. 3d. |

To protect the milling interest, all importation of flour was prohibited.

A bill was introduced in April, 1813, following the general lines of the committee report, but with higher rates of duty than suggested by the committee.   Before the bill was far advanced, grain prices broke sharply, and the decline in price continued in 1814.   It was agreed to postpone consideration of the bill.   When discussion was resumed in May, 1814, the price of wheat had fallen to 73 shillings 6 pence per quarter.   Napoleon had been defeated and peace was in sight.   The menace of war had ceased to be a factor, but the farming class was faced by disaster precipitated by a combined effect of bad harvests, falling prices, and high costs.   The agricultural elements were not unopposed.   The industrial towns, then seriously underrepresented, made themselves heard.   Large numbers of petitions were submitted, with thousands of signatures.   The opposition was so impressive that the government urged the postponement of final action on the bill for six months.

In February, 1815, the plight of the farmers had become even more serious.   The best grain was selling at a price that would yield no profit even if the land were rent free.   Many were utterly without means of paying taxes ; others raised money for taxes only by selling produce far below its prime cost.   A new Corn Bill was introduced by the government and given priority even over the budget.   Substantial changes of schedules were necessary, because of further change in price levels, and a new principle was adopted.   It was now proposed to prohibit importation of grain when the price was below a stated figure, and to admit grain free of duty above that figure.   For wheat, the critical price was set at 80 shillings per quarter.   It was presumed that this scheme would maintain prices at 80 shillings, but the framers of the law failed to consider the effect of domestic production.   With good harvests domestic production alone resulted in price levels well below 80 shillings.   Only an export bounty, when the domestic price was under 80 shillings, would have maintained the 80-shilling level for wheat.   Despite the protests of the manufacturing districts, the bill was passed because it was felt that "something must be done for agriculture." The law proved to be a disappointment. Prices fell to a new low in 1815, and though they rose above 80 shillings in 1816, 1817, and 1818, they fell again to low levels. These price changes were due in part to currency readjustments associated with the resumption of specie payments, but the law was hardly likely to have had the intended effect. The revisions of the import prices and duties in 1822 and 1828 introduced new features, but the actual change in the effect of the laws was small.

### Huskisson and Tory Liberalism

The great liberal reforms of economic policy in nineteenth-century Britain were accomplished by three men whose careers were closely identified with the Tory party. William Huskisson and Sir Robert Peel were lifelong Tories; Gladstone began his career under Peel in the Tory ranks and remained in the party until the shock of the repeal of the Corn Laws split the Tories and forced the entire progressive wing into an alliance with the Whigs. The fusion of these groups created the Liberal party, which gave Gladstone the power to complete the reform of economic policy.

The history of the development of economic policy in England presents a number of extraordinary paradoxes. The careers of all of these leaders disclose important changes of policy; they were not systematic thinkers, but they were accessible to external influences and sensitive to the requirements of social needs. When Huskisson and Peel entered political life, the great parties were not very sharply distinguished in opinion. Lines of demarcation were dominated by social and regional considerations rather than by matters of principle. Furthermore, Pitt undoubtedly proposed to carry through important measures of administrative reorganization, and not even the sharp reaction from the radicalism of the French Revolution destroyed the conviction that new social conditions required some modification of British policy. None of these leaders, at the beginning of their careers, held sharply formulated views. They were determined to face new problems with courage and an open mind. At the outset, Tory Liberalism was hardly more than an enlightened conservatism, but the open-mindedness of the outstanding personalities in the group made them singularly accessible to the influence of the economists. In matters of economic policy, Huskisson, Peel, and Gladstone were gradually won over to a frank acceptance of the doctrines of the economists, and in the later stages of their careers these doctrines were formulated sharply as general principles of policy.

The years 1820–1821 mark the crisis in the development of Huskisson's thought. Participation in committee work on commercial policy and the Corn Laws brought him into close contact once more with Ricardo, and these problems raised issues of greater political importance than the currency problems before the Bullion Committee. Huskisson was profoundly impressed with the Ricardian criticism of both the Navigation Laws and the Corn Laws. When the suicide of Castlereagh left the leadership of the party in the hands of Canning (1823), Huskisson was ready to sponsor a systematic economic policy. He had progressed so rapidly that on many points he was in advance of his colleagues in the "Liberal" wing of the party. He was, however, sufficiently astute to appreciate the necessity of making haste slowly. His measures were thus designed to accomplish such reforms as would be accepted by the party and by the country at large.

The reforms of the Corn Laws in 1822 and in 1828 represented very incompletely the changed attitude of Huskisson; but no more could be accomplished at that time. The reform of the Navigation Laws offered a more hopeful field. A large mass of legislation was still nominally in force, though many acts had long since fallen into abeyance. A beginning had been made before Canning became Prime Minister. In 1822 the Wallace-Robinson code revised the whole body of law on shipping and navigation. Three hundred obsolete statutes were repealed. The Navigation Act of 1660 was amended. Restrictions on trade with the Spanish West Indies, and on Dutch trade, were removed. British colonies were allowed to trade directly with the United States and with many parts of Europe.

Huskisson proceeded further to liberalize the navigation system. The Warehousing Act of 1823 laid the foundations for the transit trade with Continental Europe which soon became very important. Before that time England had served as an *entrepôt* for the imports and exports of her colonies, but Dutch carriers had served the Continental countries. Similar in purpose, too, was the Reciprocity Duties Act of 1823, which permitted the negotiation of reciprocity treaties and became the basis of an important series of treaties modeled on the treaty with Denmark (June 16, 1824). Concessions of this general character were ultimately granted the United States in 1830, and trade relations were placed upon a more amicable footing than at any other time since the Revolution.

There was nothing new in principle in the removal of restrictions then operative in the Scotch linen industry and in the silk industry. With the repeal of the Statute of Apprentices in 1813–1814, the repeal of restrictive legislation was clearly foreshadowed. The repeal of the Spitalfields Acts, however, was an indication of the increasing accessibility of Huskisson to reasoning from liberal principles. The repeal was strongly urged by Ricardo and McCulloch. The significance of the arrangements for collective bargaining embodied in the act was not well understood at the time, so that it is now difficult to share the enthusiasm of the economists over the repeal and over the principle of unregulated individual wage contracts. Happily, the procedure of formal wage negotiation between masters and groups of employees continued both in London and in Coventry, despite the withdrawal of statutory sanctions.

The attack on prohibitive duties was more constructive, and it happened that the silk trade was selected as the first conspicuous demonstration of the merits of a more liberal fiscal system. The new duties, replacing absolute prohibitions or prohibitive high duties, were roughly equivalent to 30 per cent ad valorem. It was presumed that this amount of protection would be sufficient to safeguard the industry without sterilizing all initiative by giving the security of a complete monopoly of domestic trade. These new rates of duty, too, made smuggling less attractive.

Before these new silk schedules went into effect, the general principle was extensively applied in the budget of 1825. The general features were sketched by Robinson, as Chancellor of the Exchequer, but much of the detail was left to Huskisson. All duties designed to be protective were reduced to 30 per cent ad valorem, on the ground that "a greater protection is only a premium to the smuggler" and an unwise bounty to an incompetent manufacturer. Rates of duty on articles not specifically enumerated were also reduced: on manufactured articles, from 50 per cent to 20 per cent; on unmanufactured articles, from 20 per cent to 10 per cent. There were many sharp reductions on manufactures in which British producers were presumed to possess competitive advantages over foreign producers. Duties on cotton goods were thus reduced to 10 per cent — an amount presumed to be sufficient to cover the duties on the raw materials used. These reforms, urged on broad principles, were probably as extensive as could wisely be attempted. The budget was in no sense a true "free trade" budget; there was no attempt to impose taxes "for revenue only"; but notable evils were removed. The yield of the lowered duties was encouraging, and industry did not suffer from the reductions. This was especially notable in the case of the silk industry; the quality of British goods improved, and exports to France increased. Positive experience under a relatively liberal regime convinced manufacturers of the unreality of their fears. The transition from the protective system to "free trade" covered the relatively long period between the budgets of 1825 and 1860. The dramatic struggle over the Corn Laws tends in many ways to obscure the significance of the general progress in budgetary policy.

## The Prussian Tariff of 1818

The history of the customs system in Prussia and other German states is of unusual complexity, because the customs system was intimately involved in the struggle to achieve political unity in Germany. Aspirations for unity gained new force during the "War of Liberation," and the problem was one of the most difficult issues presented to the Vienna Congress. It soon appeared that no significant solution was feasible. The mutual jealousies of Austria and Prussia, together with the stubborn spirit of independence in the small states, made it impossible to achieve any significant measure of unity. The Germanic Confederation actually established was a feeble makeshift; neither Prussia nor Austria was willing to bring all their territory into the Confederation. Both desired to retain their status as entirely independent powers. It is noteworthy, however, that the future objectives of Prussian policy were clearly formulated by Humboldt before he left Vienna. In an important Memorandum dated September 30, 1816, Humboldt reviewed the entire situation. He pointed out the inadequacy of the constitution of the Confederation, and danger of assuming that it could become the basis of German unity. "The real achievement of common institutions," he said, would come through negotiations with the individual states. "The policy of Prussia will consist in bringing her neighboring states to accept her political and administrative system."

This broad statement would have meant little, even to contemporary diplomats, for in 1816 there was nothing especially attractive or praiseworthy in the administrative institutions of Prussia. The kingdom was itself a mere assemblage of scattered territories which were only loosely bound to Berlin. There were many divergences in administrative procedure and in substantive law. But the leading administrative officials were not thinking of the Prussia that was then known to the chancelleries of Europe. Ever since the establishment of Baron von Stein as Minister in 1807, a small group of talented administrators had been planning far-reaching reforms that would create a new Prussia and give her a new importance in Germany. The great reform edict of 1807 would inevitably lead to a complete reorganization of the fiscal system of Prussia, and the new fiscal system was designed to give Prussia the means of "bringing her neighbors to accept her administrative institutions." There can be no doubt of the deliberation with which each step was taken in the accomplishment of this truly extraordinary plan.

Until 1807 Prussian administration distinguished sharply between town and country. It had proved to be impossible to levy indirect taxes in the country districts, but in the towns increasing use had been made of indirect taxes since the end of the fifteenth century. As a result, the territorial unit for all indirect taxation was the individual town. Administrative centralization led to some uniformity in the amounts of taxes collected from the towns of particular provinces, but there were variations from province to province. In the late eighteenth century the schedules of the tax ordinances included all the taxes levied in the towns: direct taxes as well as indirect, local customs as well as local excises. The term *Akzise* (excise) was nevertheless applied to the system as a whole, though it was in many ways misleading and inappropriate. The direct taxes of the developed system comprised taxes on land, on draft animals, on milch cows, and on sheep, together with poll taxes on artisans and laborers. The tax system included agricultural land situated outside the town walls, so that the municipal units dealt with some agricultural production. The indirect taxes fell into two general classes: taxes on consumption, which were excise taxes in the strict sense, and taxes on trade and circulation. Taxes were levied on all the primary articles of consumption: animals slaughtered for food, grain and breadstuffs, beer and wine. Nothing escaped. Cattle killed by the owner for personal consumption were taxed. Grain brought into the towns from land belonging to citizens was taxed. There were, of course, discriminations; local produce was favored over the produce of other towns in the same province. The produce of other provinces and of foreign states was still more heavily taxed.

The duties on trade and circulation fell into three general classes. All food products were charged with duties amounting to as much as 3 per cent; these duties were collected from the purchaser at the weekly market. Commodities other than food were also taxed at the weekly market: hay, firewood, clay, coal, lumber, cooperage, and the like. Finally, there were taxes on articles in general trade: manufactures generally, jewelry, notions; some taxed ad valorem, some at specific rates. Administration had long since passed out of the hands of the municipalities themselves. The consequences of such a system were unfortunate in many ways. Obstacles to local trade were intensified, whereas long-distance trade was not affected as long as the packtrains and wagons skirted town walls without entering the towns. There were, of course, tolls on roads and rivers, that had survived from the Middle Ages, but these obstacles to trade were being steadily removed, and many disappeared during the Napoleonic wars.

This fiscal system in Prussia led to an extraordinary separation of interest between town and country. Migration between town and country was practically prohibited. Sale of land was restricted to townspeople or to country people respectively. The Edict of 1807 removed all these restrictions and laid the foundations for a new administrative system. The next step was obviously the reform of the taxes, in order to establish uniformity between town and country. The tariff of 1818 was thus an integral part of the great reform program begun in 1807. This new tariff act established a uniform system of customs and excise duties throughout all the Prussian dominions. The customs duties were levied at the frontiers, and applied to all trade, to transit trade as well as to goods entered for consumption. The duties on goods in transit were not high, but for that matter none of the duties were high.

In order to simplify problems of administration the duties were in almost all cases specific rates in terms of number, weight, or measure. Raw materials of foreign origin were admitted free of duty. Foreign manufactured goods were charged at rates which were not intended to exceed 10 per cent. Rates of duty on tropical and semitropical products were intended to amount to about 20 per cent. In addition to these customs duties, specified foreign manufactures retained for consumption were subject to excise duties amounting to 10 per cent. For the most part, export was free to all, but a few export duties were levied. The fiscal monopolies in the production of salt and playing cards were protected by positive prohibition of all importation. Foreign goods in transit were subject to the import duties, and to the export duties, if any. They were not liable for the excise duties, and might even be warehoused for an interval if proper declarations were made. The domestic trade of Prussia was absolutely free. The law contained some general statements of the policy to be pursued in negotiations with other states. Favors enjoyed by Prussian subjects in the other states would be recognized by the grant of equivalent favors, and appropriate treaties would be negotiated. On the other hand, if the trade of Prussian subjects were obstructed, retaliatory measures would be taken.

This tariff act is cited at times as the first "free trade" tariff in nineteenth-century Europe. The act was indeed an outcome of the liberal influences which then played such an important part in Prussian administration, but it is misleading to describe it as "free trade." The duties were indeed low, but they were not revenue duties in the strict sense. Furthermore, the net effect of the law was not a lowering of the fiscal barriers to trade. For much of the trade of central Europe the law of 1818 created new barriers, and there can be little doubt but that it was the deliberate intention of the framers of the law that these new barriers should be created.

## The Strategic Position of Prussia

The effect of the new law upon German trade may be most readily perceived by a study of the map of central Europe. The more important industrial regions of Germany were the southern states, Saxony, Bavaria, Württemberg, and Baden. Although they still preserved some trading contacts with Austria and Italy, their chief outlet was to the north. By way of the valleys of the Rhine and the Elbe they reached the ports of the North Sea. Much trade was actually water-borne, but even the land routes followed the river valleys. Prussia commanded both of these primary trade routes; the valley of the Rhine was completely dominated by the Rhenish provinces, the valley of the Elbe by the older provinces of the Electorate. The strategic significance of this position had been fully appreciated by the Prussian statesmen, and this geographic position was the basis of the political steps taken by them to secure a Customs Union. Through the Customs Union they expected to achieve a unification of Germany under Prussian leadership.

The purposes of the Prussian policy are revealed by the public statements of Hardenberg and Bernstorff in the months immediately following the publication of the law. Various groups of merchants were deeply concerned with this change and made inquiries about the future of Prussian policy. The earliest statement of importance appears in Hardenberg's letter of June 3, 1818, to the merchants of Ried (Rhineland): "The difficulties arising out of the scattered position of the Prussian states, and out of the length of their borders, the advantages that would accrue from a union of several German states in a common industrial and commercial system, have not escaped the attention of the government. These matters turn on obvious relations. The plan which has just been endowed with the force of law has been matured with specific reference to these matters. It is no less within the spirit of this plan to retaliate against foreign discriminations than to reward a spirit of reciprocity and a neighborly disposition to unite for the common good." [1]

In 1819 there was correspondence with Gotha and some of the other Thuringian states which throws considerable light upon general policy and also indicates some uncertainty on the part of Prussia as to the precise nature of the next step to be taken. At this time there was no suggestion of complete amalgamation with the Prussian system. Both Bernstorff and Hardenberg urged the smaller states to unite with each other so that they might join Prussia on a basis of equality. Saxony made overtures to Prussia but refused to negotiate a customs treaty. Prussia was unwilling to proceed upon any other basis. The general attitude of Prussia is expressed in the address of Hardenberg to the Association of German Merchants, December 25, 1819: "The Prussian government would be rejoiced if all the German states could unite on the principles of a common commercial system. The Prussian government would willingly extend its hands to contribute its share. It must not be forgotten, however, that the diversities of constitution of the various states constitute an obstacle, and that at present particular states that find their position difficult might unite with each other." [2]

There is, thus, decisive evidence of the purposes of Prussia and of the prompt recognition of the importance of the new situation created by the promulgation of the tariff of 1818. The difficulties presented by the variety and complexity of conflicting interests made it impossible to proceed at once. Negotiations were therefore

---

[1] Eisenhardt Rothe, W. von, and Ritthaler, A., *Vorgeschichte und Begrundung des deutschen Zollvereins, 1815-1834*, Berlin, 1934, I, p. 79.

[2] Treitschke, H. von, *Die Gründung des deutschen Zollvereins*, Leipzig, 1913, p. 39.

begun independently of Prussia in Bavaria and Württemberg and among some of the Thuringian states. These aspects of the history of the tariff of 1818 were imperfectly known for many years, so that some writers were unduly impressed by the famous Memorandum of Nebenius. This memorandum on the economic condition of Germany was prepared late in 1818 or early in 1819. In April, 1819, it was submitted confidentially to the Landtag of Baden, and in the fall of 1819 it was communicated to the various German ministers at Vienna. Nebenius urged the formation of a customs union, the reciprocal abandonment of protective duties on the goods of other German states, and the adoption of a common tariff policy against foreign countries. This was not an essentially new concept, as there had been considerable discussion of the idea of a customs union ever since the Vienna Congress. The essence of the problem lay in the procedure to be followed, and in this respect Nebenius advocated the least hopeful procedure. He proposed that action be taken by the Confederation. This involved the participation of Austria, and a well-nigh hopeless three-cornered negotiation between Austria, Prussia, and the larger South German states. It is difficult to believe that the memorandum of Nebenius made any significant contribution to the negotiations of the decade that followed the promulgation of the Prussian tariff.

## The Negotiation of the German Customs Union, 1819–1834

No states were more painfully affected by the law of 1818 than the enclaves — certain states and fragments of states — completely surrounded by Prussian territory. Anhalt consisted of two primary pieces of territory and five smaller fragments. The largest part of Schwarzburg-Sondershausen, two fragments of Weimar, and one section of Gotha were also completely surrounded by Prussia. The general relations between Prussia, these enclaves, and other Thuringian states may be best studied on the map on page 337. The solution of their problems was developed in the course of negotiations with Schwarzburg-Sondershausen in 1819. This state was closely associated with the Hohenzollerns, so that there were no serious obstacles to negotiation on either side. The treaty signed October 25, 1819, became the model for all subsequent treaties with the very small states. The Prince of Schwarzburg-Sondershausen agreed to accept unconditionally all changes in customs legislation made by Prussia, and all customs treaties negotiated by Prussia with other states. The collection of customs

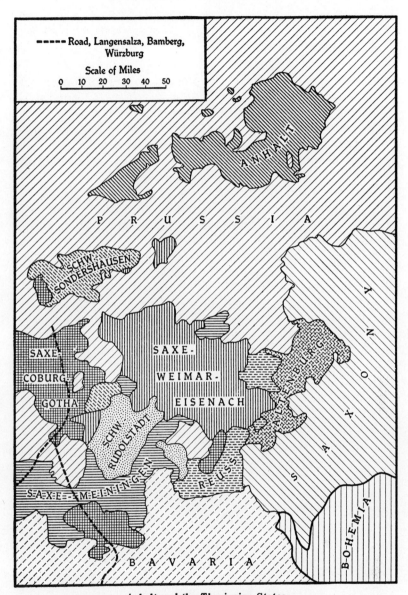

*Anhalt and the Thuringian States*

Each of these eight states is shown with a distinct style of heavy shading. Notice the exclaves (outlying fragments) of seven of them. Notice also three exclaves of Prussia completely surrounded by the territories of Anhalt, Saxe-Coburg-Gotha, and four other states.

duties was assumed by Prussia, and all duties were thereafter to be collected at the external boundaries of Prussia, so that the territory of the principality, so far as foreign trade was concerned, was completely assimilated with Prussian territory. The proceeds of the customs duties were shared in proportion to population. This arrangement was in reality highly favorable to all the small states, as their per capita consumption was considerably less than the average in Prussia. The small states regularly secured increases of revenue by reason of this arrangement. Prussia thus made generous financial sacrifices in the interest of unity. Inspections with reference to excise taxes were to be made in the principality by officials of the principality. Several treaties of this general type were concluded with other small states in the interval prior to the critical year of 1829, but these arrangements had little bearing upon the development of the Customs Union.

In the meantime, negotiations proceeded among the other German states. In 1824 treaties were signed between Baden and Hesse-Darmstadt, and between Württemberg and a group of enclaves. Prussian influences were brought to bear upon Bavaria and Württemberg and negotiations between them soon came to be regarded as a preliminary step to union with Prussia. In April, 1827, a provisional agreement was drawn up, and in January, 1828, Bavaria and Württemberg signed a treaty which set up a joint customs administration.

Shortly afterward (February 14, 1828) Hesse-Darmstadt concluded a treaty with Prussia, which was the general model followed in all subsequent negotiations with the larger states. Hesse-Darmstadt accepted the customs schedules of the Prussian system and agreed to introduce the more important excise taxes of the Prussian system. Commissioners from both states were to cooperate in establishing the new customs administration in Hesse-Darmstadt. The supervision of the new customs frontiers was divided between officials of both states. Both states appointed controllers to supervise the customs administration. A conference of plenipotentiaries was to be held each year to divide the joint revenue in proportion to population. All changes in customs and excise were to be made by common consent, but Prussia reserved the right to denounce the treaty. This clause proved to be of great significance in the history of the Customs Union, for Prussia exercised her right to denounce the treaties when the small states endeavored to join hands in order to force new concessions from

Prussia; whereupon, the negotiations for new treaties would proceed between Prussia and the individual states.

These treaties of 1828 rapidly brought matters to a head.   Saxony became the focus of the opposition to Prussia, and in March, 1828, an agreement was reached between Saxony, Electoral Hesse, and several of the Thuringian states.   This agreement became the basis of a series of treaties which set up a Middle German Customs Union

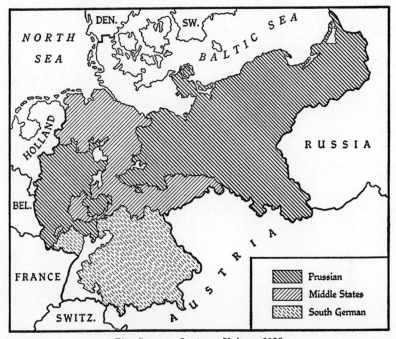

*The German Customs Unions, 1830*

(September 24, 1828).   This group in its final form included Saxony, Electoral Hesse, the Thuringian states (with the exception of Schwarzburg-Rudolstadt), Oldenburg, Hanover, Bremen, and Frankfort on the Main.   These states pledged themselves to grant reciprocal favors for the transit trade and to complete the roads needed to assure communication between the southern states and the North Sea.   They also agreed not to enter any other customs union as individuals for a period of six years.

These arrangements came as a surprise to Prussia, as it had been presumed that the neighboring states would quickly associate themselves with Prussia.   But even this unexpected opposition was not a serious check to the Prussian scheme.   The first response to the threat of the Middle German Customs Union was the negotiation of a treaty with Bavaria and Württemberg.   Preliminary arrangements were concluded as early as March, 1829, though the final treaty was not signed until March, 1833.   This achievement made a deep impression upon the anti-Prussian group, but it did not entirely destroy the Middle German scheme.   The decisive counterstroke was the conclusion of an agreement for a toll-free road connecting Prussia with Bavaria and Württemberg by way of Gotha, Saxe-Meiningen, and Coburg.   The opportunity was created by the strategic location of a large Prussian exclave between Gotha and Saxe-Meiningen.   These small states had projected a road largely for local communication, and it proved practically essential to go through Prussian territory.   Prussia now offered to contribute to the undertaking provided that the road should be extended into Prussian territory in the north, to a terminus at Langensalza, and to Bavaria in the south, to Würzburg and Bamberg (map, page 337). It was agreed further that the road should be free to transit trade. This arrangement was concluded in July, 1829.   At about the same time, another route agreement was concluded with Mecklenburg, providing free use of the road on a section of the right bank of the Elbe, assuring uninterrupted use of the land route to Hamburg. By these means the intended effect of the Middle German Customs Union was nullified.   Free access to Bavaria and Württemberg was achieved, and the great Elbe route to Hamburg was open throughout its whole length.   The selfish interests of the smallest states thus made possible the final destruction of German separatism.

For a brief period a bitter trade war was carried on between Saxony and Prussia, but the route arrangements were a fatal blow to the projects of the Middle German group.   Saxony was in fact encircled, and the pressure of commercial interests soon forced the administration to yield to the inescapable pressure of location. By 1830 Saxony admitted defeat and opened negotiations with Prussia.   In August, 1831, Electoral Hesse signed a treaty with Prussia.   The final treaty between Prussia and the southern union of Bavaria and Württemberg was signed in March, 1833.   In May, negotiations with the Thuringian states were concluded, and in March, 1834, the treaty with Saxony brought to an end all serious opposition to the Customs Union.   The adhesion of other states followed at intervals, but the ultimate success of the Prussian policy was no longer subject to any doubt.

# PART IV. THE ASCENDANCY OF BRITISH ENTERPRISE, 1832–1870

# CHAPTER 17

# THE TRIUMPH OF FREE TRADE IN GREAT BRITAIN

## The Enfranchisement of the Middle Class

The development of economic policy in the 1830's and 1840's was closely associated with the political reforms which greatly increased the political influence of the middle class in Parliament, in the municipalities, and in local government. The system of representation in 1830 was archaic, and the general forms of local administration were likewise survivals from a remote past. For this reason the entire political structure was steadily becoming less and less representative of the economic interests of the industrial and commercial classes. The extensive internal migrations of population and the rise of a number of new industrial and commercial centers had produced important changes in the social and economic structure of Great Britain. The political structure had changed little since the Revolution of 1688. Parliament was composed of representatives from the counties and from the boroughs, but the borough was merely a unit of settlement which possessed a corporate form of government and the right to Parliamentary representation. A number of the boroughs were important centers of middle-class interests, and in some the franchise was liberal, including even many workingmen. The majority of the boroughs, however, were small, rights of citizenship were narrowly restricted, and, in many, political control was not even exercised by the body of "citizens." In fact, 186 boroughs of the 237 investigated were closed corporations. The municipal council, which exercised all authority, filled all vacancies in its membership without reference to any external authority. These self-perpetuating councils thus exercised autocratic control over all the affairs of the town. The management of municipal property, the raising of taxes, the control of accounts were all subject to this irresponsible body, and in most instances its activities were completely withdrawn from all public supervision. With the exception of 59 of the larger boroughs, the Parliamentary franchise was in the hands of small groups of freemen, property owners, or councilors who were not even representative of the total population of the borough. The boroughs had thus become a peculiarly unfortunate vehicle for the influence of propertied interests. Many boroughs were in the hands of the gentry, directly or indirectly, so that members of the House of Commons were in effect "appointed" by the great landowners. Happily, the range of interest of those possessed of political rights was very wide, and the unreformed House of Commons was accessible to the broad currents of popular opinion, but some reforms were clearly desirable.

The issue of Parliamentary reform was raised by the revolutions of 1830 in France and Belgium. Fear of disorder in England led Earl Grey, leader of the opposition, to propose reform. The Tory ministry under Wellington was unwilling to consider any reform, but the ministry was defeated on other issues (November 15, 1830) and resigned. Earl Grey was able to form a notable ministry combining Whigs with some of the Tories who had followed Canning, thus foreshadowing the more permanent alliance between the Whigs and the Tory Liberals after the repeal of the Corn Laws. The first Reform Bill passed its second reading by a small majority, but the government was defeated at a later stage in the debates and called for a dissolution. The government secured a substantial majority in the extraordinary general election that followed. The Second Reform Bill, however, was rejected by the House of Lords. Demonstrations occurred in many places and tension was acute. A Third Reform Bill passed the House of Commons and was sent to the Lords (March 26, 1832). Fear of a creation of new peers (to change the vote in the House of Lords) reduced the opposition, and the second reading was carried; but a hostile amendment was subsequently carried, and the government resigned. Wellington's attempt to form a ministry failed because Peel refused to assist in the passage of any reform bill whatsoever, on the ground that they had pledged their opposition to the bill in the general election. The Whig government returned to power, and the king promised to create new peers if it should prove to be necessary, but the House of Lords surrendered, and the Reform Bill was passed (1832).

The reform accomplished established important new principles: 57 boroughs were completely disfranchised; the representation of 30 was reduced to one member each; 62 new seats were given to the counties; 63 new seats were given to towns and boroughs hitherto unrepresented. The franchise was defined by the act: in the boroughs, all holders of houses of a rental value of £10 were given the vote; in the counties, copyholders, and leaseholders for lives paying rentals of 40 shillings or more, were given a vote. Tenants at will paying £50 in rent were also enfranchised. Some working-men were disfranchised, but the act made Parliament roughly representative and added greatly to the direct influence of the middle class.

## Administrative Reforms

The Poor Law of 1834 and the Municipal Corporations Act of 1835 completed the great political reforms that became the basis of a comprehensive reorganization of public administration. The Poor Law of 1834 is important not only for the suppression of abuses but also as an administrative measure. Local administration had been left in the hands of unpaid officers subjected to little supervision and very imperfectly guided by the general statutes which defined their powers. The principle of Elizabethan administration had been to grant complete local autonomy in the administration of the broadly defined national policies. In the absence of central control, wide variations in administration developed, and in many regions auto-cratic control of the organs of local government made it possible to make the system of poor relief a means of furthering the private advantage of special interests. Property owners used the Poor Rates as a means of guaranteeing the rents of their tenants; farmers used the rates as a means of reducing the costs of agricultural labor, and at the worst as a means of reducing the laborers to a condition of virtual peonage. The financial burdens of all this maladministra-tion fell largely upon the commercial and industrial classes, who paid local taxes though largely excluded from effective participation in local government.

The act of 1834 established a Poor Law Board of three members, possessed of extensive authority over all local bodies and officers. For local administration, parishes were grouped into Poor Law Unions, each subject to the authority of a Board of Guardians elected by the taxpayers. Each taxpayer had at least one vote, but an additional vote was given for each £50 of annual income assessed, not exceeding six votes as owner and six as occupier. An occupying owner might thus have twelve votes. The guardians were salaried officers. The broader principles of relief administra-tion were sketched in the act, but the bill as passed had been seri-ously weakened by amendment. The rigors of the original project were preserved without any of the more forward-looking elements. Outdoor relief was to be prohibited; relief was to be made less eligible than self-support, both in respect of the standard of food and comfort and in respect of the establishment of workhouse discipline.

These principles were not without their merit, as regards the able-bodied — an irresponsible group, demoralized by injudicious relief. No adequate provision was made, however, for the aged, the infirm, and the children. It was the original intent to segregate these groups for treatment appropriate to their needs, but opposition to any substantial centralization made segregation impossible, and perpetuated the "mixed workhouse" in its most offensive form. The necessities of subjecting the able-bodied to some measure of physical discomfort were incompatible with the needs of the children, the infirm, and the aged. It was not possible to abolish outrelief entirely, so that the actual standards of poor relief were an unhappy compromise between sound concepts of reform and hostility to the centralization of administration. Even in 1909 the country was unwilling to adopt a thoroughgoing principle of segregation by classes proposed by the Royal Commission on the Poor Law.

The Municipal Corporations Act of 1835 was also an important administrative reform. The municipal corporation was in effect a survival from the Middle Ages — in its financial resources and methods, in its structure, and in its administration. The abuses were extensively explored by the notable commission of inquiry, and the diversity of conditions revealed defies any brief summary. The act of 1835 made residence a condition of citizenship. The administration of justice was separated from local government, and placed in the hands of appointees of the crown. Primary authority was given to the municipal Council, elected by the citizens. The Council elected the Mayor and the Aldermen. The Mayor and Aldermen, acting with the Council, made all appointments and supervised all the administrative work of the borough.

## Parnell's " Financial Reform "

Progress towards fiscal reform is first marked in the 1830's by the publication, in 1830, of Sir Henry Parnell's treatise *Financial Reform*. In fact, three editions were exhausted in as many years. Parnell proposed to levy "the revenue which is wanted for the public service in such a manner as to occasion the smallest possible loss of money and enjoyment to contributors, and the least possible impediment to the progress of national industry and national wealth." He recognized, however, that remissions of duty would reduce revenue and cause unfavorable reactions in industry. It would therefore be necessary to proceed slowly. The immediate program called for the repeal of duties on raw materials; substantial reductions of duties on foreign manufactures; reductions on taxes correct in principle but excessive in amount, such as those on sugar, tea, dried fruits, tobacco, wine, and spirits. The immediate loss in revenue from these reductions was to be met by an income tax of $3\frac{1}{2}$ pence to 5 pence per pound ($1\frac{1}{2}$ to 2 per cent), and by a general policy of retrenchment, especially in military and naval expenditure.

An interesting feature of the treatise is the solicitude shown throughout for the immediate financial problem. It is a presentation of the fiscal aspect of the case for a liberal policy. It advised raising the amount of revenue by reducing duties, in the conviction that increased consumption would more than offset the reduction in the rate of duty. The whole treatise was based upon the kind of considerations which had dominated Huskisson's thought, but the analysis of the case was pushed much further.

Parnell was a member of the Whig cabinet in 1831, and it is commonly presumed that the budget of 1831 was profoundly influenced by these principles. This budget, however, was a failure. The reductions in duties were extensive, and the losses were serious; more serious in many instances than was anticipated. The new taxes designed to offset the losses were unpopular; taxes on raw cotton, on exports of coal, and a tax of one half of one per cent on transfers of land or securities. This failure made the Whigs timid, and no extensive reforms were subsequently attempted. Despite attempts to reduce expenses, there were increases in expenditure, and, as a result, a series of deficits. Peel believed that the Radicals in the Whig ranks deliberately refused to vote sufficient funds to permit any increase in military and naval expenditure.

The fiscal reformers continued active, and in 1840 Joseph Hume secured the appointment of a Committee to Investigate the Customs System. Parnell was a member of this committee, and the report was in effect a new version of Parnell's treatise, equipped with a vast array of statistical material. The report of the committee showed that the receipts of revenue were largely derived from the taxes upon a very small number of articles, as grouped in the table on page 346.

CUSTOMS RECEIPTS, 1838-1839 [1]

| Group | Number of Articles | Amount of Revenue from Each Article | Total Revenue Received | Per Cent of Gross Revenue |
|---|---|---|---|---|
| 1 | 349 | Less than £100 | £8,050 | 0.036 |
| 2 | 132 | £100-£500 | 31,629 | 0.141 |
| 3 | 45 | £500-£1,000 | 32,056 | 0.143 |
| 4 | 107 | £1,000-£5,000 | 244,733 | 1,100 |
| 5 | 63 | £5,000-£100,000 | 1,397,324 | 6.290 |
| 6 | 10 | £100,000-£500,000 | 1,838,630 | 8.290 |
| 7 | 9 | Over £500,000 | 18,575,071 | 84.000 |
| 8 | 147 | Net loss through drawbacks | − 5,398 | — |
| | 862 | | £22,132,891 | 100.000 |

It thus appears that the 19 articles in groups 6 and 7 produced
92.29 per cent of the net revenue.   The losses on the 147 articles of
group 8 are also noteworthy.   Most of the customs duties imposed
heavy burdens on the community without any benefit to the government.   Many thoughtful persons had become convinced by Huskisson's experience that British industries no longer needed protection
against foreign competition.   The industrialists themselves were
slow to admit their independence of protective duties, but the increasing requirements of the government made it essential to modify
the fiscal system, and important groups in both parties were pressing
for a customs system designed to foster consumption.   Lower duties
on increased imports of basic commodities promised the needed
revenue.   This report, however, had no clear influence upon Whig
policy.   In fact, the raising of a sharp party issue on the subject of
the Corn Laws and the sugar duties represented a significant change
in policy.

### Richard Cobden and the Anti-Corn-Law League

The final bid for power made by the Whigs in 1841 was undoubtedly an attempt to make political capital out of the work of Richard
Cobden and his associates in the Anti-Corn-Law League.   The
entire career of Cobden was an index of the magnitude of the changes
produced by the Reform of 1832.   In the unreformed Parliament
political leadership had been largely confined to the leisure class.
It was not in any strict sense a prerogative of birth, but it was closely
associated with wealth and social connections.   The careers of both
Peel and Gladstone were characteristic of the mechanisms by which
the wealthy industrialists attained social position and political

[1] *Commons Papers*, 1840, vol. V, "Import Duties," p. iv.

importance.   The great public schools, especially Eton and Harrow, matriculation at the "right" college at Oxford or Cambridge, and a good degree placed a man socially, and practically assured political preferment.   The universities were regularly searched for bright young men with political ambitions.   Benjamin Disraeli was an exception.   Though of Jewish birth, he was brought up a Christian, because of the political disabilities of the Jews.   Privately educated, he lacked the usual social connections, and his career in Parliament was correspondingly difficult.   As a free lance, he lost no opportunity to distinguish himself.   Even such shocking things as bottle-green waistcoats and the admitted authorship of novels were after all means of distinguishing himself from the disciplined mass of "brute voters" whose numbers gave power to the leaders.   Extraordinary qualities brought him a commanding position in the Tory party when it was disorganized by the "great betrayal" of Sir Robert Peel. But even then, before Disraeli actually assumed leadership, his friends set him up with a country estate and did their best to make him a "country gentleman" in the conventional sense.   Land ownership conveyed prestige, however recent the acquisition ; complete assimilation into the ranks of the gentry might be achieved through marriage and the educational system established for the leisure class.   The "City" was by no means without political influence, but as such it furnished few leaders.

At an early date Cobden became convinced that the businessman should enter politics of his own right.   He was fascinated by the careers of the great merchant princes of Italy, and he saw no reason why British merchants should not cherish the ambition of becoming great political figures like the Medici.   He complained that British industrialists and merchants lacked imagination and accepted too complacently the social structure which left all high political activity to the landed gentry and the gentlemen of leisure associated with them.   The agitation for the repeal of the Corn Laws was thus a concrete issue by means of which he hoped to educate the industrial class to a more adequate appreciation of their interests and of their newly acquired power.

Agitation on the Corn Law issue was first organized systematically by a notable group of radicals in Parliament, including Grote, Molesworth, Joseph Hume, and Roebuck.   An Anti-Corn-Law Association was formed in 1836, and many speeches were made in Parliament.   Results were negligible.   The essentially rational appeals of the radicals left their audiences unmoved.   A group of

Manchester radicals formed an Anti-Corn-Law Association October 1, 1838, under the leadership of the journalist Prentice.   This group laid the subject before the Manchester Chamber of Commerce, which was then preparing a petition to Parliament.   Cobden entered the lists at this stage; he urged the adoption of a policy of total repeal, and (December 20, 1838) laid before the chamber a full draft of a petition embodying all the basic arguments later made famous by the Manchester school.   He pointed out that industry had become more important to England than agriculture; that the pressure of foreign competition was increasing notably, especially since the removal of restrictions on the export of machinery; that the future of England's export industries depended upon the reduction of the price of food to the levels prevalent in Continental Europe.

Cobden's draft was adopted and at once became the basis of a more active agitation.   In January the Manchester Association raised £6,000 to carry on the work, and local associations were formed in other towns.   Conferences of delegates from the local associations, at London in February, 1839, and at Manchester in March, formulated plans for a permanent union of the local associations under the name of the Anti-Corn-Law League.   A central office was established at Manchester.   Lecturers were engaged. Systematic publicity was furnished by many newspapers, and a registered periodical was established to maintain contacts among the various local associations and their members.   In the rural districts the speakers encountered many difficulties; they were refused the use of the halls ordinarily available for political meetings; outdoor meetings were harassed and disturbed by organized groups of roughs.   A meeting at the University of Cambridge was broken up by the students.   But all this agitation produced little reaction in Parliament.   No attempt was made even to consider the modification of existing Corn Laws.

Cobden was bitterly disappointed by the failure of the effort made in 1839, but plans were laid for an increase in activity both in Parliament and in the country at large.   The new effort was not without effect.   The Whigs, who had been growing steadily weaker in Parliament, finally decided to take advantage of this new fervor. In 1841 they proposed drastic reductions in the Corn Laws and in the duties on sugar.   The espousal of this new policy led to a general election.   The prominence given these proposed changes in tariff policy, and the sharp division of opinion fostered by the activities of the Anti-Corn-Law League, inevitably dominated the campaign. The situation was complex and confusing, however, because tariff policy had never before been made a party issue. Both parties contained large progressive groups. The Tory party still included a large section of "Canningites," who were ready to proceed with gradual reforms of the tariff, even though they might be hostile to the reduction of particular duties at a given moment. In 1841, however, this phase of Tory opinion was ineffectively led. The death of Huskisson had left the Tory Liberals without a spokesman, and the issues of the decade had forced into prominence the more reactionary elements of Tory thought. On these issues both Peel and Gladstone had followed Wellington without reservation. Peel was therefore able to accept the Whig challenge with complete sincerity. The Tories went before the country pledged to a moderate revision of the Corn Laws and the sugar duties. Events showed that the Whigs had completely misjudged the movement of public opinion, for the Tories were returned with a majority of ninety. Peel became Prime Minister.

## Peel's Budgetary Program

The confused position of the parties on tariff issues is shown by the introduction of a general budget whose principles were scarcely distinguishable from the proposals of Parnell's treatise which had inspired the early Whig budgets and the inquiry of 1840 into the customs. The development of this policy can be followed in great detail in the correspondence of Peel from as early a date as November, 1839. Peel's policy was essentially based on the determination to put an end to the deficits which had weakened the Whig administration. He realized that expenditure was likely to increase unless the military and naval establishments were seriously weakened. It was therefore necessary to find new sources of revenue which could be developed to meet the requirements of the government. More than a month before the resignation of the Whig ministry, Peel had decided to use an income tax as a source of a substantial revenue. He hoped that it would not be permanent, but he was convinced that it was necessary. The burden of this tax would be offset in part by extensive reductions in taxes upon consumption. It was not without difficulty that he secured the support of his colleagues, but they were finally persuaded of the necessity, so that they were agreed upon the major features of fiscal policy by the time that they were actually installed in office.

Financial needs had thus led Peel to undertake a revision of fiscal policy which carried him rapidly towards free trade. When the actual decision was made, neither Peel nor Gladstone was fully conscious of the implications of the new policy. A minister nominally elected on an issue of maintaining protection thus laid down a program of tariff reduction which could lead only to complete freedom of trade. Up to this time Gladstone had given little attention to economic problems, and it was only with reluctance and misgiving that he finally accepted the important post of Vice-President of the Board of Trade. The immediate consequences of all these decisions are described in striking language by Gladstone in an autobiographical fragment written years afterward: "When Sir Robert Peel assumed the government he had become deeply committed to protection, which in the last two or three years had become a subject of commanding controversy. I suppose that at Newark I followed suit, but I have no records. . . . [Once established at the Board of Trade] the stones of which my protectionism was built up began to get uncomfortably loose. When we came to the question of the tariff, we were all nearly on a par in ignorance, and we had a very bad advisor in MacGregor, Secretary to the Board. . . . My assumption of office at the Board was followed by hard, steady, and honest work; and every day so spent beat like a battering ram on the unsure fabric of my official protectionism. By the end of the year, I was far gone in the opposite sense. I had to speak much on these questions in the session of 1842, but it was always done with great moderation." [1]

We are less well informed of the state of Peel's mind, but apparently his convictions likewise passed through an extensive transformation. Morley says: "The situation was essentially artificial. There was little secret of the surrender of protection as a principle. In introducing the proposals for the reform of the customs tariff, Peel made the gentlemen around him shiver by openly declaring that on the general principle of free trade there was no difference of opinion." [2] It must be remembered, however, that neither Peel nor Gladstone proposed at this time to attempt an immediate reduction of all tariff duties. The essential feature of their whole fiscal policy was an adaptation of policy to circumstances, so that there should be no serious loss in revenue at any moment, nor any

---

[1] Morley, J., *Life of W. E. Gladstone*, 1903, I, p. 250; by permission of Macmillan & Co., Ltd.

[2] Morley, J., *op. cit.*, I, p. 262.

shock to established industries. It was in essence the policy of Huskisson and Parnell, so deeply conscious of fiscal need that it was far removed from any form of doctrinaire free trade. Although the implications were clear to Gladstone in 1842, the principles then recognized were not fully embodied in the budget until 1860. The history of the intervening years, however, cannot be properly appreciated unless we have clearly present to our minds both the conscious acceptance of the broad principle and the restraint shown in its application to concrete problems of policy.

The budget of 1842, as introduced March 11, provided for an income tax of 7d. in the pound (2.92 per cent) on all incomes over £150. For purposes of administration five classes of incomes were distinguished: income from land received by owners; income from land received by occupants of leased premises; income from public funds; profit of trades and professions; incomes of public officers. The tariff duties were reduced all along the line. Such prohibitions of import as still remained were repealed, and duties of a prohibitory character were reduced. Duties on raw materials were reduced to nominal amounts; they were retained only as a basis of records; in scarcely any instance did duties in this category exceed 5 per cent. Duties on partly manufactured commodities were reduced to levels which in no case exceeded 12 per cent. On manufactured articles the duties never exceeded 20 per cent. Export duties on manufactures were abolished. Of 1,200 items in the tariff, reductions were made in 750. There were no reductions on wines, brandies, or dried fruits, nor on sugar, tea, and coffee. The loss of revenue anticipated from remissions was computed as £1,140,000. In 1844 the sugar duties were reduced, but colonial sugar was still given preference, and there were heavy discriminations against the slave-grown sugar of Brazil and Cuba. The budget of 1845 made important reductions in 520 rates of duty, extending further the broad principles of 1842.

## The Corn Laws, 1842–1845

The Tories had pledged themselves to revise the Corn Laws, though it was assumed that the changes would still recognize the principle of protection. Properly speaking, this policy was consistent with the reforms proposed in the general tariff, and there was thus nothing in the actual proposals of the government that could occasion surprise. The correspondence between Peel and his colleagues shows that his opinions were more advanced than those of his party, but he insisted merely upon moderation, not upon the abandonment of the principle of protection.  Writing to Lord Ripon in October, 1841, Peel said : "I think the degree of protection you propose is too great. . . .  The principle on which we ought to proceed in reviewing the Corn Laws is to disregard the consideration of future clamour, or extravagant expectations on either side, and to bear in mind as far as we can the permanent and comprehensive interests of the country, among which encouragement to domestic production occupies a prominent place; but surely a duty of £1 when the price here is 56 shillings a quarter is more than is requisite."  [1]

Some members of the ministry were unable to accept Peel's proposals, and there were resignations before the introduction of the bill.  There can thus be no doubt of the presence of some divergence between the views of Peel and Gladstone and the views of the rank and file of the party.  Peel's achievement of leadership had revived the division between the Tory Liberals of Canning's time and the "die-hards" who had found a more congenial leader in Wellington, despite the capacities for "strategic retreats" which he had exhibited on the issue of Catholic Emancipation and Reform.  Under such circumstances moderation was not only a matter of principle but also a political necessity.

The Corn Law of 1842 adopted the sliding-scale feature of the law of 1828, but with new price scales and an absolutely uniform reduction in the amount of duty.  When wheat was 50 shillings per quarter or less, the duty was 20 shillings; as the price rose above 50 shillings, the rate of duty diminished one shilling for each shilling of increase in price.  At a price of 73 shillings per quarter the duty would thus be one shilling; thereafter no further reduction was made.  Consequently, when domestic prices were between 50 shillings and 73 shillings, the net preference on domestic wheat would be unchanged, but importation would be permitted under all conditions of price.  Cobden denounced the bill "as a bitter insult to a suffering nation."  In a few localities hostile demonstrations occurred.  Peel's effigy was carried on a gibbet through the streets and thrown into the flames amid jeers and cries.

The passage of the Corn Law was a setback for the Anti-Corn-Law League, and for a few months nothing was attempted.  By the fall of 1842, however, Cobden rallied his forces, and plans were laid for a

[1] Parker, Charles Stuart, *Sir Robert Peel, from His Private Papers*, London, 1899, vol. II, pp. 296–297; by permission of John Murray, publisher.

new campaign on an even larger scale ; it was now proposed to reach the working class, both urban and rural.   Every registered voter was to receive a packet of literature covering the whole argument. Lecture tours were extended, both single speeches and joint debates. Although the approach of the League was primarily logical, Cobden lifted the agitation to an emotional plane which led him into many extravagances.   In a speech in the House of Commons February 17, 1843, his language was so unguarded that Peel took it as a personal insult that might even be interpreted as a threat of violence.   Like all great agitators, Cobden possessed that power of concentration which made everything else seem unimportant in comparison with the cause.   Even when the outlook was as discouraging as it must have seemed in 1843, he was sanguine of ultimate victory.   "The Thing is on its last legs," he wrote.   "The wholesale admissions of the government must prove destructive to the system in no very long time."

With our present knowledge of the personal opinions of Peel and Gladstone, we can well understand the encouragement derived by Cobden from the debates forced upon the House by the motions for repeal which were introduced at regular intervals as a test of opinion. There is much material in Peel's papers on the changes in his opinions on the Corn Law issue itself.   He had followed the debates with an open mind, and the case presented made a deep impression upon him.   He could not ignore the importance of "the conflict of arguments on the principle of protection"; he was forced to accept "the concurring proofs that the wages of laborers do not vary with the price of food"; he found it increasingly difficult to resist "the application to articles of food of those principles which had been gradually applied to so many articles."   The change in his opinions had proceeded to such length by June, 1845, that one of the Whigs, Lord Howick, pointed out that his speech on Villiers's motion for repeal of the Corn Laws advanced no ground for the rejection of the principle, so that issue was joined solely on the question of immediate and total repeal.

### The Failure of the Potato Crop in Ireland

Within two months of this truly important debate, the occurrence of the potato blight in Ireland created a grave crisis which brought into sharp focus all these conflicting aims and opinions on the general and the specific issues of tariff policy.   The fungus disease known as the "black rot" appeared in Ireland for the first time.   Its onset was spectacular, and to the ignorant peasantry terrifying in the extreme. Fields of apparently vigorous potato vines would be stricken and laid flat within twenty-four hours. Even if the potatoes were gotten out of the soil apparently unharmed, they rotted quickly in storage. The blight appeared in August, 1845; and though attempts were made to prevent alarmist spread of the news, the ministry was kept fully informed of the spread of the disease. By the end of September conditions were extremely serious.

Peel's personal decision was made as early as October 15, when he wrote Lord Heytesbury : "The remedy is the removal of all impediments to the import of all kinds of human food; that is, the total and absolute repeal forever of all duties on articles of subsistence. You might remit nominally for one year. But who will re-establish the Corn Laws, once abrogated?"[1] Peel assumed that it would ultimately be necessary to open the Irish ports at low or nominal rates of duty, and that even a temporary reduction of the duties in Ireland would make it necessary to grant similar favors in England. The immediate necessity was hardly great enough to make this reasoning impressive, as was revealed when the Cabinet met at the end of the month. The emergency was discussed at length, but Peel found it inadvisable to force a decision. After an adjournment of a week, Peel proposed (November 6) to issue an Order in Council opening the ports to foodstuffs at reduced rates ; to summon Parliament to confirm this Order in Council; to give notice of the introduction, after Christmas, of a bill to modify the Corn Laws. Only three ministers were willing to approve of this policy, and it was agreed to postpone a decision until the following month.

Towards the close of November the serious nature of the emergency could no longer be concealed from the public. Lord John Russell, one of the Whig leaders, issued a public letter to his constituents, criticizing the dilatory policy of the government. Writing from Edinburgh, November 22, he pointed out the need of a vigorous policy. He expressed amazement at the inaction of the government. He went on to say: "Observation and experience have convinced me that we ought to abstain from all interference with the supply of food. Neither a government nor a legislature can ever regulate the corn market with the beneficial effects which the entire freedom of sale and purchase are sure themselves to produce. . . . Let us, then, unite to put an end to a system which has been proved to be the blight of commerce, the bane of agriculture, the source of bitter

[1] Parker, C. S., *op. cit.* (page 352), vol. III, p. 224.

divisions among classes, the cause of penury, fever, mortality, and crime among the people." [1]

The Cabinet met December 2, but even the increasing severity of the crisis left some important members of the Cabinet hostile to any proposals involving the explicit abandonment of the principle of protection. Peel, therefore, resigned (December 6, 1845). Lord John Russell was asked to form a ministry, but he found many sources of difficulty. There was no assured Whig majority in the Commons, and among his prospective colleagues there were differences of opinion which he found it difficult to reconcile. After protracted negotiations the attempt to form a ministry was finally abandoned, and Peel was asked to withdraw his resignation (December 20, 1845).

Peel had become convinced that the immediate emergency in Ireland could be met without resort to Orders in Council or special reductions in duties. The purchase of Indian corn (maize) in the United States had been suggested as early as November 5. On the 27th of the month the treasury appointed a commissioner to take charge of relief measures, and on December 9, actually after Peel's resignation, a credit for £100,000 was opened with Baring Brothers for the purchase of Indian corn in the United States. By this time it was presumed that about one half the potato crop was lost, so that with deductions for seed only three eighths would be available for consumption. Actual need would not arise until late in the spring, and the deficiency in food would be met by the government's import. This policy was developed rapidly after Peel withdrew his resignation, though the measures were kept secret. Supplies began to arrive in Ireland late in January. Grinding and milling problems were effectively solved with the advice of an officer who had had extensive experience in the United States. Instructions were prepared to teach the people how to use this new foodstuff. The first rations of corn meal were issued at the Waterford Poor House, March 19, and general distribution began at the end of the month. Reactions were unfavorable in some sections, but these adverse sentiments were quickly overcome, as the prices were low. With small supplementary supplies of oatmeal from military and naval stores, the Indian corn provided for all essential needs. Relief works were set up to enable the poor to buy food. The government advanced £185,000, and ultimately recovered about £135,000.

[1] Walpole, Spencer Horace, *The Life of Lord John Russell*, London, 1889, vol. I, pp. 406-409.

The actual importance to Ireland of the repeal of the Corn Laws was revealed in the years that followed.  The black rot was seriously destructive in the next two seasons, so that the free admission of Indian corn and rice proved to be of great importance.  In fact, Ireland was never again able to produce the supplies of food that had been the basis of the great increase in population.  Population declined steadily for more than a generation.  Without recourse to cheap foods, distress during this long period of adjustment would have been greatly increased.

## The Repeal of the Corn Laws

The assurance of adequate provision for the emergency in Ireland made it possible for Peel to address himself to the task of Corn Law reform without haste or panic.  It was his intention to make the new Corn Law an integral part of the series of progressive fiscal reforms which were already far advanced.  As early as January 6, 1846, he wrote to Edgerton: "I meditate not a mere dealing with the Corn Laws, but the continued and more extensive application of those principles which governed the introduction of the tariff of 1842." [1]  The law as passed permitted free entry of cereals from all portions of the empire, and made great reductions in the duties on foreign grain.  Maize (Indian corn) and rice were admitted free. On wheat the duty was 10 shillings when wheat was under 48 shillings per quarter; as the price rose, the duty declined one shilling for each shilling of increase in price.  At 53 shillings and over, 4 shillings remained as a fixed duty.  After February 1, 1849, the duty on wheat was reduced to one shilling a quarter regardless of price. The industrialists were also asked to make sacrifices.  Reductions were made in the duties on tallow and timber.  The duties on the coarser textiles were entirely removed, and the duties on the finer grades were reduced from 20 to 10 per cent.  Duties on silks were fixed at 15 per cent.  On other manufactures duties were reduced to a level of about 10 per cent.

The Corn Bill was introduced in January, and was finally carried through the House by the votes of three groups: a section of Tories numbering a little more than one hundred, the greater part of the Whig following, and a small number of Radicals.  The opposition was furnished by about two thirds of the original Tory group.  It was on this occasion that Disraeli rose to commanding prominence. The debates in the House were protracted and bitter; and the

[1] Parker, C. S., *op. cit.*, vol. III, p. 323.

antagonisms of the moment made it difficult to restore unity in the Tory party.   It was soon recognized that the Corn Bill would surely pass, and it then became the concern of the opposition to ensure the defeat of Peel at the earliest possible moment thereafter.   Many feared that the public regard for Peel would make it possible for him to establish a government independent of party.   His worst enemies declared that it was his avowed intention to do so, but there is not the slightest basis for any of these allegations.   Whatever Peel's intentions, the opposition displayed a rather low type of cunning to ensure his defeat.   The unpopular subject of coercion in Ireland was before the House, and by astute parliamentary tactics vote on this measure was delayed until the Corn Law was far advanced in the House of Lords.   The Whigs and the Protectionists then combined to defeat the government.   Wellington urged a dissolution and appeal to the country.   Peel refused to dissolve. Three days after the Corn Bill passed the Lords, he resigned and retired from public life.   Even today there is the widest diversity of judgment expressed in regard to Peel's capacity and conduct, but few statesmen ever made vital decisions of policy that stood the test of time so well.   Every major statute passed during Peel's ministry remained an unchallenged feature of the economic structure of Great Britain for the remainder of the nineteenth century.   It was a notable achievement, and to an unusual degree a personal achievement.

### Gladstone's Fiscal Policies, 1853–1860

Although Peel had taken the initial steps towards a mature free-trade policy, the permanence of the trend in the direction of liberalism was by no means admitted on all sides.   The income tax was unpopular, and though the Corn Law repeal was secure, the Protectionist group in the Tory or Conservative party really dominated its policy.   The Whigs were irresolute, and despite accession to office under essentially favorable conditions, they held no sure command of Parliament or of the country.   A new period of tension and difficulty began in 1851, when the Whigs were defeated by a combination hostile to the retention of the income tax and were disposed to raise the question of some form of protection to agriculture. The complexities of the financial problems and of party affiliations made any solution difficult.   The former followers of Sir Robert Peel were still nominally associated with the Conservative party, and though they numbered scarcely more than forty, the distinction of their leaders made them a force to be reckoned with.   There had been talk of a coalition with the Whigs, but personalities made such a union difficult.

In a general election notable for the confusing presentation of issues, the Conservatives secured a majority that was absolutely dependent upon the support of the Peelites.   A sharp crisis was therefore precipitated when the sympathy of this group was completely alienated by a peculiarly offensive and unskillful budget. Gladstone led the opposition against Disraeli in a memorable debate. The government was defeated and resigned.   Under the circumstances, nothing was possible except a coalition between the Whigs and the Peelites, and after negotiations of great delicacy the arrangements were concluded.   The new Cabinet contained six Whigs, six Peelites, and one Radical; though the Whigs numbered 270 and the Peelites only 40.   Lord John Russell was obliged to relinquish the position of leader and Prime Minister to Lord Aberdeen; Gladstone became Chancellor of the Exchequer and soon revealed powers which made him the chief support of the government.   This coalition brought to an end the confusion of opinion in the great parties which had been a source of disruption and complexity ever since the conversion of Huskisson to the Liberal program in 1821. During these thirty years every positive advance toward a liberal fiscal policy had originated with the group of Liberals in the Tory party.   The completion of the task now fell to Gladstone, with the support of what may be appropriately called the Liberal party.

The budget was the primary problem for the new government. The income tax had actually expired, so that the entire question was reopened.   Gladstone proposed to restore the income tax for a period of seven years at the old rate.   The limit of exemptions was to be reduced to £100, and a tax at a lower rate was proposed for Ireland.   A number of small amendments were made in the details of several schedules, and some revisions were made in the other direct taxes.   The only concession made to public opinion was a provision for the possible extinction of the income tax in 1860.   To make abandonment of this resource less difficult, the rates of duty were to be reduced in the last three years.   The explicit provisions of the proposed measure afford no adequate notion of its importance. The actual schedules were less significant than the convictions which Gladstone was able to create in the minds of his colleagues and his party.   All the waverers were won over by Gladstone's persuasive powers.   When the measure was laid before the House April 18, the success of the coalition was assured, and Gladstone became the man of the hour.   The triumph of that great budget speech was the foundation upon which was built the Liberal party and Gladstone's leadership of the party in the House of Commons.   Although in reality nothing substantively new was achieved at that time, the maintenance of the liberal policy was an event of first-class importance.

The final achievement of the reforms implicit in the famous budget of 1842 was postponed until 1860. . The budget of that year swept away all but 48 of the 419 duties then levied.   Only 15 articles, or classes of articles, contributed significantly to the revenue : spirits, sugar, tea, tobacco, wine, coffee, corn, currants, timber, chicory, figs, hops, pepper, raisins, and rice.   Despite the progressive reductions in customs duties, the revenue had increased a little since Peel's budget of 1842.   Excise taxes produced considerably more, and the income tax had become a much more important contributor.   Expenditures had increased from £51,100,000 in 1842 to £72,800,000 in 1860, and it is clear that the increased needs of the government could not have been met by increases in the rates of customs and excise duties.

BRITISH REVENUES IN 1842, AND IN 1860 [1]

|  | 1842 | 1860 |
| --- | --- | --- |
| Customs | £20,700,000 | £23,300,000 |
| Excise | 12,500,000 | 19,400,000 |
| Stamps | 6,900,000 | 8,300,000 |
| Income tax | 2,400,000 | 10,900,000 |
| Other revenues | 6,200,000 | 8,300,000 |
| Total revenue | £48,700,000 | £70,200,000 |

## The Cobden-Chevalier Treaty

The commercial treaty with France negotiated towards the close of 1859 stands somewhat outside the general scheme of fiscal policy developed in this period.   This treaty was presumed by many to be the basis for a general reduction of European tariffs, and a beginning of the generalization of the British fiscal policy.   As the ultimate significance of the treaty was much less considerable, it seems less important to us than it did to contemporaries.   British Liberals had reached the conclusion that reductions of duty might best be made by each country on its own initiative.   Attempts to negotiate treaties in Peel's time had not been satisfactory or successful, and

[1] Northcote, Sir S. H., *Twenty Years of Financial Policy*, London, 1862, pp. 376, 394.

the growing conviction of the merits of free trade made procedure by reciprocity treaties seem unnecessarily clumsy and indirect. Although the treaty was long known as the Cobden treaty, the idea did not originate with Cobden or with the British government. Both were somewhat reluctant and were persuaded by the French liberal Michel Chevalier, because the treaty was a necessary means of initiating a reform in France.

General opinion in France had been strongly protectionist ever since the Revolution. French industry felt especially in need of protection against England's superiority both in textiles and in metals. The agricultural interest, also, was predominantly protectionist. A few intellectuals formed a nucleus for the development of liberal thought, but their influence was small. When Louis Napoleon rose to power, he was accessible to some of the liberal economists.

This group realized the hopelessness of any reduction of the tariffs by ordinary processes of legislation, but the treaty-making power lay solely in the hands of the emperor. Chevalier thus conceived the idea of proceeding by way of a commercial treaty with Great Britain. To be effective, the proposal must seem to originate in Britain. Chevalier therefore urged Cobden to consider the feasibility of such a treaty. When the project was first suggested in 1856, Cobden was indifferent and unimpressed. The entire scheme seemed uncongenial. The tension in the period after the close of the Crimean War created new grounds for a gesture of friendship between England and France. The desirability of counteracting political apprehensions on both sides, and the increased importance of the Manchester group, gave Chevalier his true opportunity in 1859.

He renewed the correspondence with Cobden. Gladstone was approached and found well disposed. Cobden soon became thoroughly convinced of the merits of the scheme, and during Chevalier's visit to England in October, 1859, there were several meetings at which the basic features were agreed upon. The plan called for the presentation of Cobden to the emperor in an apparently casual manner. Cobden would then be able unofficially to suggest the advantage of a commercial treaty. This feature of the scheme was completely successful. The emperor was genuinely impressed. Arrangements were made for formal negotiations, and the treaty was signed January 23, 1860. Ratification by Parliament followed quickly, and though there was some opposition, it was overcome.

The treaty contributed much to an improvement of public sentiment in both countries, and the commercial significance of the treaty was by no means inconsiderable. With renewals, the treaty remained in force until 1880.

France agreed to abolish all prohibitions directed against British goods, and to establish duties not exceeding 30 per cent at various specified dates between July 1, 1860, and October 1, 1861. British coal and coke, iron, machines, and tools were all benefited by this opening of the French market. The French iron industry was unable to supply the requirements of the railroads, and though some small charcoal iron works were forced to close, the large works survived and the country secured the benefit of lowered prices. Conditions in the textile industry were more complex, both as respects the detail of actual competition and the conditions of production in France. No generalizations can be made.

Great Britain agreed to admit French goods free, excepting only French wines and spirits. The duty on wine was reduced from 15 shillings per gallon to 1 or 2 shillings per gallon, according to the alcoholic content. The duties on brandies and spirits were reduced from 15 shillings to 8 shillings 4 pence per gallon. These important reductions were later qualified by Great Britain's establishing new duties on Portuguese wines which continued the preference for Portuguese wines so obnoxious to France.

CHAPTER 18

# THE PROTECTIONIST MINORITY IN CENTRAL EUROPE, 1834–1865

## The Reaction from Liberalism

At the beginning of the nineteenth century the German states had made little progress towards any formal expression of a commercial policy. Austria and Hungary followed a sharply prohibitive customs system; the other German states could have no organized policy towards foreign trade until the adoption of the border customs system. Accordingly, the modern history of commercial policy in the greater part of Germany begins only with the early border tariffs, adopted by Bavaria in 1807, by Württemberg in 1808, by Baden in 1812, and by Prussia in 1818. In Prussia liberal influences prevailed in administrative circles, and the natural interest of the greater portion of Prussia required an essentially liberal policy. Fiscal expediency, too, made it desirable to adopt low schedules. The South German states were more strongly disposed towards protection, but in effect fiscal motives were more important than any formal principle of free trade or protection.

The bureaucratic character of the administration in all these states, also, served to subordinate any conscious consideration for specific interests to the immediate needs of revenue. Old traditions led to the shortsighted view that high rates of taxation would produce large revenues; but such notions scarcely deserve to be ranked as protective policies. There was nothing in German thought that could be explicitly compared with the deliberate purpose of protection of vested interests which dominated so much of British legislation in the eighteenth century and the early nineteenth. In France, too, there was more formal thought on matters of commercial policy, and industrial interests were not without influence at Versailles.

As early as 1819 Friedrich List was able to interest an association of German merchants in a project for a customs union designed to serve as a basis for retaliation against foreign states. The Prussian tariff of 1818, despite its low schedules, created new barriers to foreign importation, though they were not of material importance on account of the great superiority of the British industries equipped with power.    However, all details of commercial policy were inevitably subordinated to the problems of particularism until the formation of the Customs Union of 1834.    The domestic problems were more important than the foreign problems, and divergent views respecting the general scales of duty were necessarily sacrificed to the need of greater unity in fiscal administration.

Furthermore, the interests of industrialists were by no means identical.    In many fields of industry skilled hand workers with low standards of living were long able to compete successfully with foreign industry.    In some instances lower labor costs were of decisive advantage to Germany; in other instances foreign machinery was not applicable to the types of goods made in Germany. This was especially true of the small wares of iron and steel made from high-grade charcoal iron.    The products did not compete directly with the puddled coke iron of England, and though Germany was in many ways far behind England in technical development, her workmen did not suffer seriously from competition.    Cutlery and the special steel dies produced by Krupp at this time are characteristic examples.

Even in the textile industries, the limitations of the machine technique in Great Britain left important branches of the industry in secure possession of the skilled artisans of Germany.    Weaving by power was so much less successful than spinning that large quantities of cotton yarn were exported by Great Britain to the weaving districts of Prussia, Saxony, the Thuringian states, Brunswick, and parts of Bavaria.    The spinning districts of Bavaria, Württemberg, and Baden suffered severely.    The linen industry was seriously affected by the rapid strides made in Ireland and in England.    But the textile interests were far from being united.

The establishment of the Customs Union in 1834 gave new stimulus to foreign and to internal trade because of the great simplification of the fiscal system and the reduction in the number of customs barriers.    The immediate reactions of manufacturers in southern Germany were hostile to Prussia and to the essentially liberal system of 1833.    But these complaints were nullified by the brilliant financial results of the new system and by the stimulus given to industry by the great enlargement of the domestic market.    The revenue of the Customs Union increased from 14,500,000 thaler in 1834 to 16,500,000 thaler in 1835, an increase of 13.7 per cent.    The results over the first decade were even more striking.    New accessions had added $9\frac{1}{2}$ per cent to the population, but the revenue had increased by 82 per cent; a notable fiscal achievement even when allowance is made for the increase in the population of the original states of the Customs Union. These financial returns made an end of any hostility that might be felt towards Prussia. The gains in revenue soothed the pain of losing complete independence.

### Early Increases in Rates of Duty

The earliest moves towards the conscious adoption of a protective policy were designed to foster the beet-sugar industry. The issue was first raised by Bavaria in 1835, but the proposals were not extensively considered. There was further discussion in 1838, but again nothing was done. Then Prussia discovered that it was possible to establish the industry within Prussian territory, and certain modest favors were granted. Refineries of cane sugar were allowed to make beet sugar, thus securing the benefit of the duties charged against cane sugar. Beet sugar refineries were also authorized to make cane sugar in the off season, when no sugar beets were available. These modest encouragements cut deeply into the business of the Dutch sugar refiners, and negotiations ultimately led to the first reciprocity treaty signed by the states of the Customs Union (January 21, 1839).

The Customs Union was given the benefit of reductions of duty on specified goods exported to Holland and her colonies. The shipping of the Customs Union was guaranteed the reductions and exemptions from duty enjoyed by the Dutch in the Lower Rhine. The concessions to Holland were considerable: partly refined sugar, hitherto charged the full rate, was to be admitted at one half the rate on refined sugar; the duties on refined sugar were reduced from 11 thaler to 10 thaler per hundredweight; the duties on butter, cheese, and cattle exported by Holland were reduced to one half the former figure; the duty on rice from the Dutch colonies was reduced. The grant of bounties to the Dutch refineries nullified the adjustments on sugar, and in 1841 the Customs Union was obliged to take further action on beet sugar.

In the meantime industrial conditions were changing. Pressure on the spinning districts of southern Germany was becoming serious. The hand industry suffered from the increased efficiency of British manufacturing processes; and the beginnings of power spinning in Germany were hampered by sharp competition. The German manufacturers alleged that the British were selling below the cost of production in order to stifle the new industrial development in Germany. Furthermore, the transformation of the iron industry had begun under the stimulus of the building of the first railroads, which created an extensive demand for heavy iron products. Coke smelting, puddling, and rolling mills were introduced, but heavy importations were necessary, and the rapid increase in railway building led to a corresponding increase in the import of British iron. By 1844 imports provided for one half of the domestic consumption, whereas they had formerly amounted to no more than 20 per cent.

In addition to the chambers of commerce already in existence, merchants' associations were established in Baden and in Württemberg. A committee of ironmasters was formed at Saarbrücken, and cotton manufacturers organized at Leipzig. In 1841 Friedrich List's *National System of Political Economy* was published, and in 1843 a protectionist periodical was established under the name *Zollvereinsblatt*. List's writing contributed much to give body to the protectionist movement. Though his thought was deeply colored by prejudices and antagonisms, the historical material gave it a measure of dignity and a professional tone that lifted the whole controversy to a higher plane.

The immediate effect of this new pressure was small. The adoption of a slightly smaller unit of weight had the effect of increasing by 3 per cent all duties levied in terms of weight. Falling prices altered somewhat the economic effect of the rigidly defined specific duties. But the positive concessions to protection were limited to changes in the duties on iron in 1844 and to very modest increases on textiles in 1846. The duties on iron checked importation appreciably, and though the approximate ad valorem rates may not seem high today, they did afford some protection. At the average prices for the years 1853–1855, the approximate ad valorem rates were as shown in the following table:

APPROXIMATE RATES OF DUTY IN THE CUSTOMS UNION, 1855[1]

| | | | |
|---|---|---|---|
| Raw sugar, 62.5% | Pig iron, 18.5% | Cotton yarn, | 10.7% |
| Coal, 12.5% | Rails, 48% | Machine-spun linen yarn, | 3.5% |
| Flax, 1.3% | Bar iron, 35 to 58% | Woolen yarn, | 0.7% |

Beet sugar and iron thus enjoyed significant protection from foreign competition. The textiles were not assisted to any appreciable extent.

[1] Benaerts, P., *Les Origines de la Grande Industrie Allemande*, Paris (Thèse, 1933), p. 241.

## The Fiscal Union

The general policy of the Customs Union became deeply involved in the political problems raised by negotiations with the northern states and with Austria for the extension of the union. The inclusion of Nassau in the Customs Union was delayed for a time by a projected treaty with France which would have made it difficult for her to join. This treaty, however, was rejected by the French Chamber, and Nassau straightway entered into negotiations with Prussia. The treaty was signed December 10, 1835. The Free City of Frankfort on the Main found that her trade was seriously curtailed by her independence, so that her acceptance of the Customs Union was inevitable. This treaty was signed January 2, 1836. The Baltic states and the Hanse towns remained outside the union for a considerable interval. They had little to gain. With direct access to the sea, they showed little concern over the establishment of the border customs system of the Customs Union.

Hanover (German name Hannover) was closely associated with England, as the four kings George I, George II, George III, and George IV all retained their rights in Hanover despite their accession to the throne of Great Britain. Brunswick and Oldenburg were ready to accept Hanoverian leadership, and in 1834 a "Fiscal Union" (*Steuer Verein*) was formed which included these three states and some small enclaves. Mecklenburg negotiated a reciprocity treaty with France (1836) which guaranteed the maintenance of existing conditions for ten years. The north was thus organized independently and afforded little hope of any extension of the Customs Union. Hanover was aggressively independent, and the most that Prussia could accomplish was a modest rectification of the customs frontier by the exchange of small enclaves for purposes of taxation (1837). The death of George IV, involving the separation of the crowns, made the prospects for negotiation even less promising. The Duke of Cumberland, who inherited the throne of Hanover as Ernst-Augustus I, was especially insistent upon maintaining the independence of his kingdom.

The adhesion of these northern states, however, was especially important to Prussia, and persistent efforts were made to bring these states into the Customs Union. Difficulties arising between Brunswick and Hanover opened the way to the detachment of Brunswick, and high hopes were entertained in Prussia, because parts of Hanover were cut off by a portion of Brunswick. This pressure proved to be insufficient, and the adjustment was made by Brunswick. The treaty of October 19, 1841, provided for separate treatment of part of her territory. The main mass was brought within the frontier of the Customs Union; the rest of the territory remained in association with Hanover and Oldenburg. No further progress was made in this region until the Austrian question forced Prussia to make extensive concessions to Hanover.

## The Policy of Austria

The development of the Customs Union had not left Austria unmoved. In 1833 Austria tried to forestall the Prussian Union by proposing the formation of an all-German customs union under the auspices of the German Confederation. There was provision for such procedure in Article 19, but in this instance, as in so many others, the mechanisms of the Confederation were incapable of producing positive results. It was also perceived that any form of customs union would require a comprehensive administrative reform in Austria; the existing fiscal system emphasized the provinces rather than the frontier of the Hapsburg Monarchy, and the tariff schedules were sharply restrictive. There were many complete prohibitions, and many duties were so high that they were in fact prohibitive. Even the bitter antagonism to Prussia did not furnish a sufficiently powerful motive to overcome the inertia and conservatism of the Austrian administration.

Many industrialists were opposed to this essentially unintelligent fiscal system, and the group urging reform adopted a program looking towards the inclusion of Austria in the existing Customs Union. The tariff of 1838, however, was dominated by the reactionary group, so that all action seemed to be indefinitely postponed. In 1840 Baron Kübeck began a systematic attack on the prohibitory system, but his efforts did not lead to much positive result, despite the large amount of information collected by a commission of inquiry. A few slight changes were the only concessions to reform.

The Revolution of 1848 produced important changes in the entire Austrian administration. Schwarzenberg and Brück became the dominant forces in the higher administration. They were determined to make some effective challenge to the growing importance of Prussia, and both were quick to perceive the importance of fiscal reform and entrance into the Customs Union. The new policy was publicly announced in a series of inspired articles in the Vienna *Gazette*, beginning October 26, 1849. The objectives of the new administration were declared to be : a reciprocity treaty with the Customs Union; a complete reorganization of the Austro-Hungarian customs system; and the formation of an Austro-German Customs Union.

The new policy was described in further detail in an official memorandum of December 30, 1849. This document defined the duties and the objectives of a newly appointed Federal Commission on Commercial Relations. The commission was instructed to proceed forthwith towards the building up of a policy of national protection in Austria and in the commercial districts of Germany. That is to say, the protectionist minority in the Customs Union was to be offered the assistance of Austria in their efforts to change the general policy of the Customs Union. The Customs Union tariff would be made more acceptable to Austria, and by leading the protectionists Austria might regain much of the influence she had lost in Germany. The problem of commercial policy thus became deeply involved in all the major issues of high politics. The new administration was definitely protectionist, but its protective policy was after all an enlightened one. The ministers proposed to encourage domestic industry by establishing complete freedom of trade within the protected area. They therefore proposed to destroy all existing obstacles to the freedom of internal commerce. They also proposed to encourage the importation of raw materials and partly manufactured products.

The full implications of the new policy were explicitly stated in a memorandum of May 30, 1850, which laid down a scheme differing on every vital point from that of the Prussian Customs Union. The Federal Commission was to have authority to summon a congress for the discussion of commercial policy. The results of the deliberations were to be embodied in a series of treaties to be ratified by the various states. The control of future policy was to be vested in four departments to be organized by the Confederation, and in general the policy was to give due weight to both types of regional interest. The "free trade" policy of Prussia was to be qualified sufficiently to make adequate provision for the needs of the industrial districts. It was pointed out, also, that the proposed new customs union would lay the foundations for political union.

Prussia refused to enter into any discussions of commercial policy through any agencies of the Confederation. True to the general principle of direct negotiation with individual states, Prussia declared her willingness to negotiate directly with Austria. Under these circumstances Austria changed her plan in some details and bent her energies to the task of gaining admission to the existing Customs Union.   To this end, her overtures to the South German states were of value.

The general issue was sharply formulated by the activities of Prussia; the Hanoverian problem was partly independent, but it could not at this date be treated as a wholly separate issue.   Any change in the balance between liberal and protectionist forces would surely be of importance in Customs Union circles, and any further liberalization of the tariff schedules would seriously interfere with the adjustments necessary to make the Customs Union schedules fit the needs of Austria and the immediate requirements of the political situation in the Austrian states.

### The Treaty with Hanover and the Crisis of 1851–1852

There can be no doubt that all the Prussian ministers were fully conscious of the intimate bearings of the Hanoverian negotiation upon the Austrian question.   Hanover was forced to reconsider her position.   Her isolation from her neighbors was making itself felt.   Revenues were declining, and the ministers had proposed important increases.   Oldenburg refused to accept these proposals, and the Fiscal Union of the two states was thus imperiled.   Without any notification to the other states in the Customs Union, Prussia opened negotiations with Hanover.   The entire proceeding was kept secret until the treaty was formally ratified by both states September 11, 1851.   The terms were extraordinarily favorable to Hanover.   Prussia needed her support, and recognized the necessity of paying the price.   Hanover was to receive 75 per cent more than the share of the customs revenue directly proportionate to population.   She was allowed to import rails and other materials for the construction of her railroads free of duty, and special reductions of duty were granted on colonial products.   Prussia's gains were less tangible, though the customs frontier was shortened, and portions of Prussia secured an unimpeded access to the North Sea.

The communication of the treaty to the other German states and to Austria produced a profound reaction.   Members of the Customs Union were outraged by the high-handed procedure of Prussia. They felt that they should have been consulted when such substantial issues of policy were involved.   Bavaria and Württemberg were nearly ready to withdraw from the Customs Union unless the Hanoverian treaty was denounced.   They were therefore the more favorable to the overtures from Austria, which offered support against Prussia in return for assistance in gaining admission to the Customs Union. If this attempt should fail, Austria urged the southern states to withdraw from the Customs Union and form a new association looking towards the Danube.

Under these auspices the conference for the renewal of the Customs Union treaties began (September, 1851). The conferees were sharply divided at once on the question of procedure. The protectionists proposed to consider first the question of the admission of Austria, because the character of the tariff would be affected by the decision. Prussia proposed to negotiate the new treaties first, in order to be able to deal with Austria as a group already organized for the coming decade. The conference remained deadlocked on this issue of procedure, because it was obvious to all that the decision of the Austrian question would be actually determined by the order in which these matters were discussed. Prussia finally assumed control of the crisis by announcing (September, 1852) that all general negotiations were to be suspended, and that she would negotiate only with individual states.

The combination between the South German states and Austria was completely broken up by the negotiation of a new treaty between Austria and Prussia. This treaty, signed in February, 1853, provided for the postponement of the entrance of Austria into the Customs Union. A joint commission was to be set up in 1860 to work out plans for the admission of Austria in 1865. In the meantime many new and partly manufactured products were to pass between the states free of duty. Duties on a list of enumerated articles were to be reduced between 20 and 50 per cent. The terms of this treaty were to extend to any states in the Customs Union with Prussia.

The signature of this treaty was decisive. All tension was relieved by this compromise, and even the most hostile South German states found themselves under pressure from the industrial and commercial classes, which had at all times insisted upon the necessity of maintaining the Customs Union. By April the Customs Union treaties were ratified for another decade, and it was generally assumed that the permanence of the association was definitely assured.

## The Exclusion of Austria

The Austro-Southern group were slow to recognize the full significance of the Prussian attitude, and not without reason. Statements had been made that political problems were not involved in any way, and Austria was now so definitely embarked upon a policy of fiscal reform that there were grounds for the belief that all the difficulties might be adjusted. The Austrian ministers kept the matter before the public. A detailed scheme was submitted to the Customs Union states at the close of 1856, and conferences were held with Prussia at Berlin in 1857. The Prussians were not accommodating, and neither these discussions nor further conferences in January, 1858, led to any result. In the meantime Austrian diplomats were doing their utmost to secure sympathy and support among the states of the Customs Union. The protectionist sympathies of the southern states were encouraged, and their spirit of independence praised. In the north the Free Cities of the coast were approached with intimations of support and protection for the maintenance of their privileges. Enough was accomplished to create real apprehension in various quarters in Prussia, but the leaders were slow to move.

The defeats suffered by Austria in Italy furnished a propitious opportunity, and Prussia decided to undertake a revision of the tariffs of the Customs Union in the direction of free trade. It was intended that the reform of policy should be sufficiently drastic to make the adhesion of Austria impossible. Overtures from Austria in August, 1860, gave the Prussian ministry an opportunity to declare that no negotiations based on the treaty of 1853 could involve the question of the admission of Austria to the Customs Union. Prussia would not consent. Not long after this Prussia opened negotiations with France looking towards a reciprocity treaty. When this became known, Austria declared that it would be an insurmountable obstacle to her acceptance of the Customs Union treaties. Prussia persisted, and the treaty was initialed in March, 1862. Apart from relatively low schedules of duties, the treaty guaranteed most-favored-nation treatment to both parties. This would involve the nullification of the preferences then existing in favor of Austria. The announcement of the negotiation to Austria and to the states of the Customs Union (April 7, 1862) precipitated a major diplomatic crisis.

Saxony, Baden, and the North German states were ready to accept the French treaty, but five southern states were bitterly opposed. The hostility was predominantly political. Bavaria, Württemberg, Hesse-Darmstadt, Hesse-Cassel, and Nassau resented the assumption of authority by Prussia, and felt that their effective independence would be hopelessly lost if Prussia could at any time

commit them to decisive acts of policy without preliminary discussion.   Austria was thoroughly roused; and, lest all opportunity
be lost ever to enter the Customs Union, she offered to make substantial sacrifices.   Her ministers agreed to accept the existing
schedules of the Customs Union tariff; to accept a complete co-
ordination of customs administration; to guarantee payment of
revenues from customs in specie, or in Austrian paper on a specie
basis; and finally Austria agreed to accept a reduced share of the
revenue, three eighths of the percentage of the population of Austria
to the total population of the Union.

Prussia proceeded, however, with the French treaty, and ratification was completed August 2, 1862.   Bavaria and Württemberg
refused to accept the treaty.   Bernstorff notified them that this
refusal could only be interpreted as unwillingness to renew the
Customs Union treaty.   Bavaria announced that she would propose
that Austria be included in the Customs Union.   Bismarck declared
that any such proposal would result in the withdrawal of Prussia
from the conference.   Thus, even before the opening of the formal
conferences for the renewal of the treaties, Prussia and the South
German states were deadlocked.   Within a month of the opening
of the conferences (December, 1863), Prussia denounced the general
treaty and declared that all negotiations must proceed with individual states.

For some months the resistance of the southern states continued
with no signs of capitulation, despite pressure from the commercial
interests and assurances from their neighbors that no support could
be expected.   But the resolution of the governments was weakening.
The accession of Louis II to the throne of Bavaria at this juncture
made it less difficult for Bavaria to modify her position, and private
assurances were given to the French ambassador that matters would
ultimately be adjusted.   The united front in the south was finally
broken by the defection of Hesse-Cassel, June 20; and the completion of negotiations with all but four southern states left the
opposition in a hopeless position.   On October 12 the four southern
states accepted the new treaties.

In the spring a new reciprocity treaty was negotiated between
Prussia and Austria, but it merely accentuated the differences between Austria and the Customs Union.   All preferences were withdrawn, and many duties were raised.   From this date there was no
serious likelihood of the inclusion of Austria in the Customs Union,
and the future of Germany seemed clearly to involve a progressive

weakening of Austrian influence. The union of all the Germanic peoples was indefinitely postponed.

## Friedrich List

Although the protectionist groups were unable to exert any large influence upon the policy of the Customs Union, it is wrong to assume that these developments were without importance. Nominally, Prussia was deeply committed to a liberal policy, but all this liberalism had been dominated by the major problems of high politics. These decisions of policy did not possess the significance for the future that was clearly present in the great decisions of British policy in this period. The adoption of a protective policy by Bismarck is not especially surprising, because all the foundations for such a reversal of policy were really laid in this period. Furthermore, the professional statement of the case for protection by Friedrich List [1] was of great importance for the future of German scholarship and German policy. These aspects of the early development of the protective movement should not be neglected.

List was a strange character: too farsighted to be a practical businessman or administrator; too much the man of action to be a sound or consistent thinker. His career and all his material interests were sacrificed to his devotion to liberal reform and to the rights of individual freedom, but his published work was a great factor in the development of extensive government interference in industry and trade. Born in an artisan family in Reutlingen, Württemberg, List secured sufficient education to enter government service as a clerk. An appointment requiring residence at Tübingen afforded an opportunity for university training which revealed conspicuous talent. Liberal tendencies brought List to the attention of the minister Wagenheim, and in 1817 List was appointed Professor of Administration and Politics at Tübingen. The fall of Wagenheim before the close of the year weakened List's position, but there is no reason to suppose that any serious difficulty would have been encountered if it had not been for List's participation in a movement looking towards a Customs Union.

During a visit to Frankfort in April, 1819, List came in contact with a group of German merchants interested in the development of a customs union as a means of retaliating against foreign tariff discriminations. List threw himself into this movement with enthusiasm, became secretary to the organization, and drew up a

[1] The name is often seen also in the English form " Frederick List."

memorial which was submitted to the Federal Diet.   The authorities in Württemberg took offense, holding that List had no right to engage in activities with a "foreign" state without permission. List defended himself, asserting that the German Federation was in no sense a "foreign" state, but he was nevertheless dismissed from his professorship (May, 1819).   He started the "German Industrial and Commercial Magazine" to serve as an organ of the Union of German Merchants.   The Union also undertook negotiations in favor of a customs union at various courts, but none of these efforts led to positive results.   A misunderstanding with the treasurer of the Union of German Merchants created difficulties for List, and he withdrew from the organization.

In the meantime List had become involved in local politics at Reutlingen as defender of the people against various forms of arbitrary government interference.   He was elected to the assembly, but was refused a seat because he was under the required age. Elected once more a year later, he at once introduced three projects for laws involving drastic reforms.   He proposed that measures be taken to revive the depressed industries of Württemberg; that the taxes be adjusted to the capacity of the country to bear the burdens; that the upper house should meet each year and submit an annual budget.   He also prepared a memorial on behalf of Reutlingen which contained sharp criticisms of the existing administration. This came to the notice of the authorities, and just before the printed copies were issued, the offending material was seized and List was arrested.

The charge of sedition disqualified List as member of the assembly. List contested the case, which dragged on for more than a year, but the decision was against him.   He was sentenced to ten months' imprisonment and nearly all the costs of the case.   He appealed, but fled to Strasbourg.   After travels in France and in England, he returned to Württemberg and was at once arrested.   He was released before the sentence was fully served, and given a passport to leave the country.   Contacts with Lafayette, made in Paris, and some friendships in Germany led him to set out for the United States (April, 1825).

The five years spent in the United States exerted a controlling influence upon his thought.   The rapid growth of the country impressed him deeply, and suggested his famous generalizations upon the stages of economic growth.   The striking appreciation of the value of agricultural land was interpreted as a direct and simple result of the development of manufactures, so that these gains might be treated as the gains secured from protection of native industry. Contacts with various figures in industry and politics soon made him an important personage in the protectionist controversy, so that his partially formed ideas were rapidly developed under the stimulus of an active agitation. Several short papers were written, and a large treatise was planned.

The American experience also impressed List deeply with the importance of railroad transport. His correspondence with the Bavarian Minister of Mines discloses remarkable grasp of these problems as early as 1827, before any really practical locomotive had been developed anywhere. The development of anthracite coal properties in the Schuylkill valley gave him much concrete experience. It was necessary to construct a canal and a railroad in order to reach a navigable waterway, but the completion of these works made the mine a profitable undertaking. Part interest in this property gave List more economic security than he had had at any other time in his career.

In November, 1830, List returned to Europe. At the moment, he hoped to secure status as United States Consul at Hamburg, but political difficulties arose and List himself abandoned the scheme. Somewhat later he was able to secure an appointment as United States Consul at Leipzig, accredited to the Customs Union. As the salary was nominal, the value of the post lay in its official character. Throughout this period his time was divided between literary work and agitation for the development of railroads. Much time was spent both with government officials and with the capitalists interested in the promotion of railways. List hoped to persuade the state governments to embark on a large scheme of railroad building upon the basis of a planned network. It was not possible to accomplish more than the completion of particular lines by groups of private capitalists. List contributed much, however, to the intelligent planning of these routes, both in the detail of location and in their relationships to the general network that ultimately emerged.

His literary work was notably stimulated by the competition for a prize announced by the French Academy in 1838 for an essay dealing with problems of tariff policy. List submitted an essay, and though no prize was awarded, this essay inspired *Das nationale System der politischen Ökonomie*, ultimately published in May, 1841 (English translation, *The National System of Political Economy*, 1856). The enthusiastic reception of this work led the publishers to establish the *Zollvereinsblatt* (the "Customs Union Journal"), a weekly periodical devoted to protectionist activities. List edited this paper and wrote extensively for it.

Throughout this period List was harassed by financial strain. His health was affected, and at times he became despondent. Business contacts with railway committees were not free from tension. The journalistic work led to much sharp controversy. Constant travel wore down his reserves of physical energy. For several years his health was uncertain, and by 1846 it was seriously impaired. On November 30, 1846, he committed suicide, while in the Tyrol seeking rest.

### The National System of Political Economy

List's chief work is more important for its ultimate influence upon German policy and scholarship than for its specific content. It furnished vital elements in the doctrines of the younger Historical school, and it was the most important single factor in the rebirth of Protectionist literature. These developments were closely related, but they should not be confused. The *National System* is therefore a book of notable historical significance, though it can hardly be called a great book. One must consider its implications rather than its explicit doctrines.

List's defense of protection was based largely upon what he called the doctrine of productive powers. The wealth and prosperity of a country were in his view largely dependent upon its technical skill and its framework for the organization of social and economic activity. Although the production of exchangeable values was the immediate end of economic activity, the wisdom of a given policy could not be measured without considering its effect both upon exchangeable values and upon the productive powers of the country. To explain his position, List used an illustration from the life of individuals. Suppose there are two families having farms of equal extent, each family composed of the parents and five sons. In one family all effort is put into the land and no attention is given to any improvements in the technique of production. Land, labor, and capital are devoted solely to the production of exchangeable values. The father of the other family deliberately sacrifices a certain amount of immediate enjoyment in order to develop the capacities of his sons. Two are trained in agriculture, three in the professions. List assumes that with improved methods, two are able to produce as much from the land as the five sons of the other family, and that the professional income of the other three is clear gain. The wise policy, therefore, entailed a temporary sacrifice of consumable commodities.

The illustration is perhaps unsound in various particulars, but it does suggest the general course of List's argument. The agricultural community could improve its position by well-chosen protection. A sacrifice of the immediate standard of consumption, through the acceptance of expensive and inferior manufactures, would lead to ultimate gains. The costs of manufacture would fall. The increase in the total population, through the development of manufactures, would give added value to agricultural land. The capital gains from social development would outweigh any possible costs of protection. List was too ready to believe that all these changes would be due to protection; too little inclined to consider methods of developing productive powers other than the protective tariff. This was, however, the essence of his case: against the immediate costs of protection, which he frankly admitted, there should be balanced the large and intangible gains from the entire process of social growth.

List's reading of history led him to believe that the more important changes in economic and social organization were always the result of wise acts of policy. He felt that the classical writers were indifferent to the evident facts of history, and that they used only such historical material as happened to suit their purpose. Adam Smith, he thought, though well read in history, was dominated by a narrow interest in the division of labor and its effects, so that he failed to appreciate many important phases of economic and political history.

List never thought of himself as a mercantilist, because he assumed that the mercantilists failed to realize that protection was a sound policy only under certain conditions and for a limited period of time. Furthermore, List never used any of the arguments for protection characteristic of the mercantilists. He approached the mercantilists most closely in his discussions of the relations between the temperate zones and the tropics. There are passages, indeed, which might lead one to think of List as a militant imperialist, looking towards colonies as a necessary basis for the development of the great manufacturing states of the temperate zones. But though he clearly recognized the tendency towards tropical colonization, he did not associate imperialism with economic self-sufficiency. Neither for the nation nor for the imperial power did List assume self-sufficiency to be an object of policy.   Later developments of nationalism in the nineteenth century therefore lead one away from List's thought.

With List, the nation was a functional unit in a world system.   Its policies, to be realistic, should recognize all the features of its position : its climate and resources, the relative degree of technical and cultural development, and its position in the world system. The nation was not at any time treated as a closed system, in the fashion so characteristic of Schmoller and the later Nationalists. List's thought was on a higher plane.

"The highest object of rational politics is, as we have explained in our second Book, the association of nations under the reign of law. This object can only be attained by the elevation of the most important nations to a degree as equal as possible in culture, prosperity, industry, and power : by the change of antipathies and quarrels which divide them, into sympathy and good understanding.

"In our days, nations are estranged from each other by various causes.   In the first rank are questions of territory and boundary. The political division of Europe does not yet correspond with the nature of things. . . .   But, in our time, it is vain even to think of a rational division." [1]

The final chapters on the history of English policy laid heavy emphasis upon the reversal of British policy after the full achievement of industrialization.   List surveyed the policies of the early modern period with genuine insight, though his documentation was slender.   The significance of many of the restrictive policies is not to be denied, though the effects were not always intended.   No attention is called to the very great importance of the eighteenth-century laws for the protection of property rights in new inventions, though it would be wholly consistent with List's thought to foster the development of productive powers by such means.   List concludes that England's industrial supremacy was largely due to the skill with which new industries had been developed by protection. The reversal of the general policy, and the statement of the free-trade policy in general form, he took to be evidence of the consummate hypocrisy of the English.   Having achieved a distinguished position, they wished to prevent the development of their rivals by recommending a policy that was clearly known to be unsuited to the state of development of all these less advanced nations.   These bitter

---

[1] List, F., *The National System of Political Economy*, Philadelphia, 1856, Book IV, Chapter II, pp. 476–477.

strictures on the English liberals undoubtedly lower the tone of the book and exhibit all the weaknesses of List at their worst.

The book was of substantial influence in the field of practical politics, especially in Continental Europe, but its larger significance appears in its influence upon the development of economic history. Despite the limitations of its scope, and the real limitations of its author, it was undoubtedly one of the most notable factors in the development of an evolutionary concept of the processes of economic history.   It was the most suggestive and thought-provoking book of many that dealt with economic history.   By implication rather than by direct statement it did much to focus attention on three problems essential to any systematic analysis of historical process.

List interpreted history as a dynamic process in which individuals and social groups are truly creative factors. Without actually putting it in words, he worked with a concept of dynamic adaptation. He conceived economic activity as dominated at any given moment by resources, but the limitations imposed by these resources might be overcome in part by the transformation of technique and social organization.   The classical economists recognized the significance of improvements in the arts, but List recognized that technical and social change was a continuous process to which the state might make some positive contribution.   The attention of the Classical School of economists was directed towards a static analysis of the equilibrium of economic forces.   List was concerned with the dynamic processes of historical change.   His book thus represents a fundamentally different method of treating the problems of economics, and his contribution was in many respects unique.

List also denied the general validity of much of the classical reasoning.   In respect of matters of policy, he explicitly declared that all decisions of policy must be carefully related to all the conditions of the moment.   No single line of policy could be followed under all circumstances.   This important but limited application of the doctrine of relativity was of great significance to the development of economic thought.   Controversy raged throughout the century.   The theorists took refuge in the position that there were two kinds of truth; a higher kind of scientific truth whose findings were universal and absolute; a lower order of knowledge in which all findings were conditioned by circumstance, and hence merely relative.   Latterly, however, a broadly generalized theory of relativity has been developed in philosophy, mathematics, and the physical sciences, so that today we no longer feel that there is such a wide separation between the "genetic sciences" and the "exact sciences." But even at the present time, the meaning of relativity in the historical sciences is very incompletely explored.

List also contributed much to our recognition of the importance of institutions. He protested against the indifference of individualists, who recognized no function for the state beyond a mere keeping of peace and order. He believed that acts of state policy might and perhaps even would necessarily play a constructive part in the development of organized social life. He was thus in some sense of the word an institutionalist. But these phases of his thought were not explicitly developed. His writings give us no clear formulation of any principles about institutional development, nor any extended discussion of the influence of institutions upon the activities of individuals.

The insight of List is shown notably by his concepts of the appropriate applications of steam power to transport. A recent biographer has embodied his various schemes in a single world map, which represents List's thought between 1820 and 1844. This world transport system involves three great transcontinental railway lines: New York – Washington – St. Louis – San Francisco; Hamburg – Vienna – Constantinople – Bagdad – Bombay; Paris – Moscow – to an undetermined point in China. The plan also provides for canals at Panama and Suez; with a network of steamer lines, which use Marseille as the terminus for the Suez route to India. List possessed the vision that underlies the great careers in business and finance, but the world in which he lived had little use for such powers of imagination. The best that Germany in his time could offer such a talent was a career in literature and scholarship.

# CHAPTER 19

## THE AGE OF IRON AND STEEL

———◆———

### The Consumption of Iron

The conspicuous economic transformation of Europe and the United States in the mid-nineteenth century was so closely associated with the development of the heavy metal trades that the period is frequently characterized as the age of iron and steel. The term is by no means inappropriate, but careful study of the economic problems requires more precision of statement. The extent of the development of the heavy metal trades will be most readily perceived if we direct our attention to the per capita consumption of iron. Despite the shortcomings of our statistics the approximate annual consumption in Great Britain can be computed for some critical dates in the eighteenth century, and for the whole of the nineteenth century. Statistics of production are accurate only within 5 or 10 per cent of the total, even in the latter part of the nineteenth century. Scrap iron was used in some measure throughout the period, so that we can deal only with newly made iron, the net addition to existing stocks. Exports of some highly manufactured objects of iron and steel are not comprehensively enumerated, so that we lose a small percentage of the actual total. These qualifications, however, apply throughout the period, so that the figures in this table probably exhibit the general features of the changes.

APPROXIMATE PER CAPITA CONSUMPTION OF PIG IRON IN GREAT BRITAIN [1]

| | Pounds per Year | | Pounds per Year | | Pounds per Year |
|------|------|------|------|------|------|
| 1735 | 15 | 1866 | 110 | 1895 | 262 |
| 1800 | 26 | 1884 | 266 | 1900 | 292 |
| 1830 | 77 | 1890 | 303 | 1930 | 293 |

In 1735 the technique of coke smelting had just been established, and the Darbys had developed the process of casting in green sand so that the smaller castings had been generally introduced. But the use of iron and steel was still narrowly limited, confined to minor

[1] Computed from materials in Beck, L., *Geschichte des Eisens*, vol. III, p. 1072; IV, pp. 164, 326; and general statistical manuals.

domestic uses and to small tools and hardware. The figure 15 pounds per year per capita probably represents only a slight increase over the consumption of the late Middle Ages. The notable feature of the table is the small increase in per capita consumption by 1800. The introduction of puddling and the rolling mill in 1783 had opened up new potentialities, and production had increased notably, but the changes had affected the balance between domestic production and foreign trade more profoundly than the domestic consumption of iron. Imports had become much less important, and a substantial export trade had developed. The great increase in the use of iron began in the first third of the nineteenth century, preceding the development of the modern railway.

This period was marked by an important increase in the use of iron for structural purposes; for bridges, buildings, and vessels for inland and coastwise waterways. The first iron bridge in England and probably in the world was built at Coalbrookdale between 1773 and 1777. Cast iron was used, but the characteristics of the new material were imperfectly understood and the venture long remained an isolated case. Experiments with canalboats were begun as early as 1790, but the generalized application did not follow immediately. In 1801 a cotton mill was built at Manchester by Boulton and Watt. Iron girders and columns were used to reinforce the masonry. The beams were of cast iron. Although the design of the beam was not economical of material, this technique of construction was more and more frequently used, because it afforded hope of fireproof construction for mills and warehouses. In 1824 systematic study of the breaking strength of beams began, and the design of cast-iron beams and girders was rapidly improved. Individual girders of forty feet span were extensively used. Arched bridges, with specially designed units, were constructed in many places after the success of the 236-foot span at Sunderland designed in 1790 and completed in 1796. Other famous cast-iron bridges of this general type were: the bridge over the Thames at Southwark, consisting of three spans of 210, 240, and 210 feet; the bridge over the Neva at St. Petersburg (Leningrad), consisting of seven spans varying between 107 and 156 feet.

Shipbuilding and railway construction, however, required wrought iron, and improvements in production and in the design of rails and beams reduced costs sufficiently to make the general use of wrought iron possible. The famous bridge over the Menai Strait proved to be an important factor in this change. The depth of water and the character of the strait made it almost impossible to set up the scaffolding and false work that would have been necessary if cast iron had been used. Furthermore, a clear span of 460 feet was necessary for one section. George Stephenson and William Fairbairn designed an entirely novel type of wrought-iron bridge and devised new methods of erection. Extensive study was made of the strength and properties of wrought iron and of the design of composite wrought-iron girders. After the completion of the bridge in 1850, the use of wrought iron was greatly extended. When wrought iron was used, only half as much iron was necessary as had been required in the cast-iron beams and girders. This economy of material must be considered when we study the changes in per capita consumption, because the progressive economy in the use of material obscures in part the increase in the use of the material. Many of the 110 pounds used in 1866 were doing twice as much effective work as was done by any of the 77 pounds used in 1830. In recognizing the comparative importance of the development of consumption before and after 1830, also, we must not allow the significance of the railroad era to be overlooked.

The consumption of iron in Great Britain is, of course, a rough index of the rate of change in Europe as a whole. Figures for the first half of the nineteenth century are not readily available, but even in 1864 most of the European countries were less advanced than England in these new modes of consumption. The results embodied in the table below are subject to the same general qualifications as the figures for Great Britain. The uncertainty of the computation is clearly indicated by the divergence of the figures for 1864 and for 1866. Coming from different sources, they reflect the inaccuracies of our primary statistics. The low consumption of iron in Italy,

ANNUAL CONSUMPTION OF PIG IRON, IN POUNDS PER CAPITA [1]

|  | 1864 | 1866 | 1884 | 1890 | 1895 | 1900 |
|---|---|---|---|---|---|---|
| England | 169.4 | — | — | — | — | — |
| Great Britain | — | 110.0 | 266.0 | 303.0 | 262.0 | 292.0 |
| Germany | 41.8 | 41.8 | 176.0 | 176.0 | 155.2 | 289.7 |
| France | 74.8 | 58.3 | 127.6 | 127.6 | 107.8 | 152.4 |
| Austria-Hungary | 22.8 | 20.9 | 44.0 | 53.4 | 64.0 | 68.2 |
| Belgium | 110.0 | 71.5 | 206.8 | 151.1 | 140.8 | 205.9 |
| Sweden | 57.2 | — | — | — | — | 127.6 |
| Italy | 14.3 | 17.6 | — | — | 30.8 | 39.8 |
| Russia | 6.6 | 8.8 | — | 17.6 | 34.7 | 56.9 |
| United States | 101.2 | 110.0 | 193.6 | 351.5 | 296.7 | 351.3 |

[1] Beck, L., *op. cit.*, VI, pp. 233, 1385.

Austria, and Russia is especially noteworthy. Equally notable is the character of consumption and the timing of changes in the United States, Germany, and France. It would probably be possible to find positive evidence of a direct correlation between these figures and the rate of railway construction, especially in the late nineties.

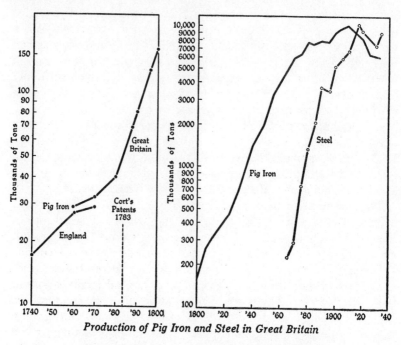

*Production of Pig Iron and Steel in Great Britain*

## The Production of Iron in Great Britain

The expansion of the iron industry in Great Britain was even more rapid than the rise of domestic consumption per capita; partly because the growth of population was considerable, and partly because of the important export trade in iron and iron products. The general course of the development of the industry is shown by the tables on pages 385, 386, and in the graphs above. The extraordinary rise of the Scotch industry after 1833 is notable, due in large measure to the introduction of the hot blast about 1828. This new process opened up the Scotch coal deposits on an impressive scale. This incident affords a notable illustration of the dramatic effect of technical changes on particular sources. The transfer to steel after 1865 is indicated notably by the table on page 386 and by the second graph on page 384. These figures emphasize the early railway era more clearly than the figures for consumption, though even here the introduction of cast iron is responsible for the dating of the primary period of expansion from 1823 instead of from the mature railway of 1830. The average rates of change, per cent per year, in the production of pig iron in Great Britain were as follows:

| | | | |
|---|---|---|---|
| 1740–1780 | 2.12% increase | 1860–1880 | 3.20% increase |
| 1780–1800 | 7.25% increase | 1895–1910 | 1.90% increase |
| 1806–1823 | 3.50% increase | 1910–1925 | − 2.87% decrease |
| 1823–1860 | 5.90% increase | | |

The above rates are for the linear trends as shown on the graphs on page 384.

THE ANNUAL PRODUCTION OF IRON, IN TONS, IN GREAT BRITAIN, 1740–1860 [1]

| | In England | In Scotland | Total in Great Britain [3] |
|---|---|---|---|
| 1740 | 17,300 | — | — |
| 1760 | 27,000 | 2,000 [2] | 29,000 |
| 1770 | 29,500 | 3,000 | 32,000 |
| 1780 | — | — | 40,000 |
| 1788 | 61,300 | 7,000 | 68,300 |
| 1790 | — | — | 80,000 |
| 1791 | 67,500 | 12,400 | 79,900 |
| 1796 | 108,900 | 16,000 | 125,000 |
| 1800 | — | — | 156,000 |
| 1806 | 235,200 | 22,800 | 258,000 |
| 1810 | — | — | 300,000 |
| 1823 | 417,500 | 24,500 | 442,000 |
| 1830 | 615,900 | 37,500 | 653,400 |
| 1833 | — | 44,000 | — |
| 1840 | 1,155,400 | 241,000 | 1,396,400 |
| 1843 | — | 248,300 | — |
| 1848 | 1,458,600 | 539,900 | 1,998,500 |
| 1855 | 2,390,600 | 827,500 | 3,218,100 |
| 1860 | 2,889,700 | 937,000 | 3,826,700 |

[1] The records of iron production to 1854 are all taken from unofficial sources. They vary somewhat in comprehensiveness and various versions of production appear in the different private compilations. To 1806, the figures given here are taken from Beck, L., *Geschichte des Eisens*, vol. III, pp. 1069, 1073, 1075, 1079; vol. IV, 160, 318, 657, 665. Scrivenor, H., *History of the Iron Trade*, pp. 88, 97, 99. Records for the period 1806–1854 are given by Marshall, J., *Digest of All the Accounts*, 1833, pp. 33–33 *; Banfield, T. C., *The Statistical Companion for 1854*, L. 1854, p. 56.

[2] See Beck, *op. cit.*, III, p. 1073 — 4 charcoal furnaces, estimated production at 500 tons each.

[3] Production in Ireland was negligible. The official figures after 1854 are designated United Kingdom, though it would be more correct to continue to use the term Great Britain.

## The Transition from Malleable Iron to Steel

English writers frequently make a distinction between the malleable-iron (wrought iron) period and the age of steel. The change was momentous for England, because her iron and coal resources were especially suited to the production of cast iron and puddled malleable or wrought iron. The processes of steel production required types of ore and of ore deposits that were less extensive in England than in Germany or the United States. The introduction of the modern technique of steel production was thus unfavorable to England from a broad competitive point of view. Many of the iron mines of west-central England were abandoned, pig-iron production slowed down, and large quantities of ore were imported from northern Spain and from Sweden. Even in 1905

ANNUAL PRODUCTION OF PIG IRON AND STEEL, IN TONS, IN GREAT BRITAIN
(UNITED KINGDOM), 1854-1935 [1]

|  | Pig Iron from British Ores Only | Total Pig Iron | Steel |
|---|---|---|---|
| 1855 | 3,218,000 | — | — |
| 1860 | 3,826,000 | — | — |
| 1865 | 4,819,000 | — | 225,000 |
| 1870 | 5,963,000 | — | 286,000 |
| 1875 | — | 6,356,000 | 723,000 |
| 1880 | — | 7,749,000 | 1,320,000 |
| 1885 | — | 7,415,000 | 2,020,000 |
| 1888 | 5,130,000 | 7,998,000 | — |
| 1890 | 4,848,000 | 7,904,000 | 3,676,000 |
| 1895 | 4,394,000 | 7,702,000 | 3,444,000 |
| 1900 | 4,666,000 | 8,959,000 | 5,130,000 |
| 1905 | 4,760,000 | 9,607,000 | 5,983,000 |
| 1910 | 4,976,000 | 10,012,000 | 6,374,000 |
| 1918 | 4,582,000 | 9,108,000 | 10,434,000 |
| 1920 | 3,953,000 | 8,035,000 | 9,202,000 |
| 1925 | 3,043,000 | 6,262,000 | 7,385,000 |
| 1930 | 3,604,000 | 6,192,000 | 7,326,000 |
| 1934 | 3,176,000 | 5,969,000 | 8,850,000 |

[1] After 1854 the confusion of statistical returns continues, and the growing importance of production from foreign ores adds a new difficulty. Official returns do not include production from foreign ores until 1876, and they are first separately given for 1888 (*Statistical Abstract*, 1888-1902). Returns in the British and American trade yearbooks publish figures which do not agree with the official figures, but no explanation is given. The pig iron figures in the table are taken from the *Statistical Abstracts* of the United Kingdom. The figures for steel production are taken from *The Mineral Industry* (N. Y.), 1892 and later volumes, by permission of McGraw-Hill Book Company, publishers.

foreign ores were the basis of about half of the total production of pig iron. Large increases in production in Germany and in the United States brought about a profound change in the relative position of the three major producers of iron.

These changes in the production of primary heavy products were of course closely related to important changes in the trade and commerce of the leading nations. Some writers went so far as to attribute the industrial supremacy of England in 1880 to the system of secondary education and the form of the family. Several writers have attributed the rise of Germany to special qualities of the Teutonic "race." Many attribute the change to a kind of social senility supposedly revealed in the business and social life of England in the later nineteenth century. It is much easier to explain the precise nature and timing of all these changes if we pay close attention to the relation of changed methods of production to the basic resources of the various areas.

The early development of the British iron industry was fostered by the close proximity of coal and iron over large sections of central and northern England, and in the great valley of Scotland. The mines, both of coal and iron, were well adapted to production on a modest scale, and the presence or absence of phosphorus and sulphur in the ores was not a matter of serious moment. Little was known of the chemistry of iron, and ores that were unsuitable for making wrought iron were used for castings of one sort or another. By 1830 it was realized that there were great differences in the strength of the various irons produced. But all these difficulties were offset by the accessibility of coal, iron, and the limestone used as a flux. In Germany and in the United States the great ore bodies were unknown or unusable for lack of cheap transport. English conditions were more favorable than those of any other country to the development of the heavy metal industries of the malleable-iron period.

The invention of the Bessemer converter brought this period to an abrupt close. For more than twenty years the successful use of the process was limited to pig iron produced from ores entirely free from phosphorus or from the charcoal pig iron still imported in small quantities from Sweden. There were large bodies of ores free from phosphorus, notably the red hematites, but England was not well supplied with them. The ores of Staffordshire and the Midlands were for the most part unsuitable. As soon as the importance of the phosphorus content was realized, these ores declined in value and many workings were abandoned.  The development of the open-hearth process (1867) and the basic process of Thomas and Gilchrist (1878) ultimately relieved the pressure in part.  But the new processes were most favorably conducted on a larger scale, and the massive ore bodies of the United States and Lorraine assumed primary importance.  Even with extensive utilization of Spanish ore, Great Britain was not able to maintain her position in the export trade. ˏ The notable development of the iron industry outside Great Britain was in part due to the diffusion of the new technique, but the readjustments in Great Britain show conclusively that the net effect of the new technique was unfavorable, especially as regards the production of pig iron.  The decline was not due to exhaustion of resources, but to selective factors unfavorable to many of the British deposits.  The general features of the changes in regional distribution of the iron industry are shown in the tables on page 389, and in the second graph on page 384.  In 1865 the four countries named in the tables produced 84 per cent of the pig iron produced in the world, and 90 per cent of the steel.  In 1930 they produced 72.8 per cent of the pig iron, and 74 per cent of the steel.

The new technique made it possible to produce more varied and superior products at lower costs.  The demand for labor was reduced and the delicacy of control of the product was in the end notably increased.  The original purpose was no more than the production of malleable iron at a reduced cost.  The development of chemical analysis and process control was unintended, but it soon appeared that commercial utilization of the product required a great improvement in the control of chemical reactions until then entirely unsuspected.

## The Bessemer Inventions

The Bessemer process was, in its conception, merely a new means of eliminating the carbon present in pig iron.  As in puddling, this was to be accomplished by combustion.  In the reverberatory, or "air," furnace, combustion took place on the surface of a shallow bath of molten casting iron.  The temperature of the bath was maintained by a fire in a separate compartment of the furnace; the heated gases from the fire were led over the molten iron and by constant stirring the carbon was gradually removed.  The process was laborious and required much skill.  Bessemer proposed to achieve the same end by passing a powerful blast of compressed air through a modest charge of molten iron.  The heat required by the

THE ANNUAL PRODUCTION OF PIG IRON, IN THOUSANDS OF METRIC TONS,
1865-1935 [1]

|      | United Kingdom | United States | Germany | France | The World |
|------|------|------|------|------|------|
| 1865 | 4,897 | 843 | 882 | 989 | 9,099 |
| 1870 | 6,060 | 1,692 | 1,391 | 1,178 | 12,259 |
| 1875 | 6,469 | 2,056 | 2,029 | 1,416 | 14,102 |
| 1880 | 7,875 | 3,897 | 2,729 | 1,725 | 18,547 |
| 1885 | 7,363 | 4,110 | 3,751 | 1,629 | 19,791 |
| 1890 | 8,033 | 9,353 | 4,637 | 1,970 | 27,630 |
| 1895 | 8,022 | 9,597 | 5,788 | 2,005 | 29,858 |
| 1900 | 9,003 | 14,009 | 7,549 | 2,714 | 39,599 |
| 1905 | 9,746 | 23,340 | 10,987 | 3,077 | 54,054 |
| 1910 | 10,380 | 27,636 | 14,793 | 4,032 | 66,210 |
| 1915 | 8,794 | 30,415 | 11,529 | 5,586 | 65,100 |
| 1918 | 9,184 | 39,680 | 11,754 | 1,306 | 66,399 |
| 1920 | 8,136 | 37,520 | 5,550 | 3,468 | 59,870 |
| 1925 | 6,236 | 36,702 | 10,047 | 8,323 | 72,100 |
| 1930 | 6,197 | 31,752 | 9,649 | 10,100 | 79,360 |
| 1933 | 4,123 | 13,345 | 5,266 | 6,327 | 48,781 |
| 1935 | 6,529 | 21,715 | 12,800 | 5,799 | 73,000 |

THE ANNUAL PRODUCTION OF STEEL, IN THOUSANDS OF METRIC TONS,
1865-1935 [1]

|      | United Kingdom | United States | Germany | France | The World |
|------|------|------|------|------|------|
| 1865 | 225 | 13 | 97 | 41 | 419 |
| 1870 | 286 | 68 | 169 | 83 | 703 |
| 1875 | 723 | 396 | 370 | 258 | 1,900 |
| 1880 | 1,320 | 1,267 | 660 | 388 | 4,273 |
| 1885 | 2,020 | 1,739 | 1,202 | 533 | 6,276 |
| 1890 | 3,637 | 4,346 | 2,161 | 566 | 12,096 |
| 1895 | 3,444 | 6,212 | 3,941 | 899 | 16,659 |
| 1900 | 5,130 | 10,382 | 6,645 | 1,565 | 28,727 |
| 1905 | 5,983 | 20,354 | 10,066 | 2,110 | 43,900 |
| 1910 | 6,374 | 26,512 | 13,698 | 3,506 | 58,656 |
| 1915 | 8,688 | 32,687 | 13,288 | 1,088 | 66,613 |
| 1918 | 10,434 | 45,178 | 13,756 | 1,807 | 77,381 |
| 1920 | 9,202 | 42,811 | 7,710 | 2,961 | 62,600 |
| 1925 | 6,137 | 45,394 | 12,176 | 7,290 | 83,400 |
| 1930 | 7,298 | 40,699 | 11,539 | 9,402 | 93,430 |
| 1933 | 7,002 | 23,232 | 7,585 | 6,526 | 67,121 |
| 1935 | 9,942 | 34,000 | 16,325 | 6,101 | 95,988 |

[1] *The Mineral Industry*, N. Y., 1892, p. 282; 1896, p. 334; 1905, p. 339; 1914, p. 413; 1921, p. 368; 1932, p. 287 — by permission of McGraw-Hill Book Company, publishers. See, also, Meisner, M., *Weltmontanstatistik*.

process was supplied by the intense combustion produced, and both silicon and carbon were completely eliminated if the process was maintained a proper length of time. This general method of refining iron was also developed in the United States by William Kelly at Eddyville, Kentucky (1851). The process was not as fully developed by him as it was by Bessemer, and the mechanical appliances used were ill suited to production on a large scale. Bessemer's work was entirely independent, though the public announcement was in fact later than Kelly's early demonstrations. Kelly's work was subsequently recognized by the United States patent office, but Bessemer was granted a separate patent on the converter itself.

When Bessemer announced his invention in August, 1856, at the meeting of the British Association for the Advancement of Science, he had no intention of identifying himself with the iron industry. The acclaim with which the paper was received made it easy to lease rights to use the process. But within a few months the lessees complained bitterly that the process was a failure. In some cases the iron produced could not be forged; in other cases it was brittle and weak. Bessemer thereupon repeated his experiments with the original results; but all his experiments had been based on Swedish charcoal iron, the purest pig iron obtainable. Experiments with British iron yielded a fantastic variety of results; and like many other inventors, Bessemer found that his invention was merely the beginning of trouble. It was necessary to push the chemical analysis of the process much further. He also made more detailed analyses of the various ores and varieties of pig iron.

Protracted study finally revealed several sources of difficulty. The converter iron that would not forge was found to be oxidized by the excessive action of the air blast. It was not an entirely new difficulty, but it was seldom a serious problem in a well-managed puddling furnace. This defect was remedied by the addition of a manganese flux. The credit for devising this mode of treatment is sometimes attributed to Mushet, and some critics have intimated that Bessemer made an unfair use of Mushet's work. Much detail of the history of this development is now known, but the equities of the case still remain obscure. Bessemer was working on the problem before Mushet's patent was taken out, in September, 1856. There were earlier studies of the problem by Heath (1845), whose patents had expired. The details of the treatment proposed by Mushet were alleged to be impractical. There are thus strong grounds for presuming that both Bessemer and Mushet were working more or less independently along similar lines, but without the complete independence of each other's work that is characteristic of parallel invention. There must have been some technical difficulty involved in Mushet's process, for despite the obvious importance of the treatment, he did not pay the annual fees required in England to retain exclusive rights over an invention. The recognition of Mushet's rights in the United States has contributed to the confusion of the incident.

## The Basic Process and the Open Hearth

Analysis of the various types of British ores and of the iron made from them revealed the phosphorus problem already mentioned. The new process was an utter failure with ores containing more than a trace of phosphorus. Bessemer and his associates acquired interests in several British deposits of hematite ores, free from phosphorus, and also interested themselves in the development of the iron deposits of northern Spain which were also suitable for use with this process. The great difference between the value of "Bessemer" and "non-Bessemer" ores stimulated research by independent investigators, and much work was done in search of modes of chemical treatment that would make the process workable with phosphorus-bearing ores. This research was finally brought to a successful conclusion by two chemists, Thomas and Gilchrist, in 1878. They succeeded in preparing a heat-resistant lining for the converter, in which manganese played the new role of promoting a chemical reaction with the phosphoric acid in these refractory ores. The phosphorus combined with the bases of the lining and left the iron free from all impurity. The converter had to be relined at stated intervals, but the lining could be broken up and sold for fertilizer, as it was rich in one of the most important mineral constituents of plant life. The other substances in the lining were also valuable for the treatment of the soil. The iron industry thus aided in the solution of the farmers' phosphorus problem.

The introduction of this "basic" process was of very great importance for the economic geography of the iron industry. This process made it possible to utilize fully the large deposits of the Cleveland district in England, which has long been one of the very important centers of iron production in that country. It also brought into use the great deposits on the international boundaries of Luxemburg, France, and Germany. These ores had long been known, but little importance was attached to them. They were not very rich in iron, and they contained so much phosphorus that they could not be used. After 1878 the association between these great ore bodies and the coal fields of the Ruhr and Saar became the basis of the extraordinary development of the heavy iron industry in Germany. The basic process, therefore, was relatively more favorable to Germany than to England.

The Bessemer process was originally intended to serve as a means of producing malleable iron, but it also made possible the production of new types of steel at a low cost. The puddling furnace yielded malleable iron in a solid state, in the form of balls collected on the ends of the stirring rods. The conversion of this material into steel required an entirely separate process of treatment. In the converter, the metal was liquid, and there were two possible means of producing steel. Theoretically, it would be possible to produce steel by stopping the blast before all the carbon was burned. This was difficult and uncertain. Very small differences in the carbon content produce profoundly different qualities of steel. It was therefore more practical to produce steel by adding a known quantity of carbon to the charge in the converter after the charge had been entirely cleared of its original carbon. This could be done by adding in liquid form some alloy of iron with a carbon content sufficiently high to produce the desired result in the final product.

The Bessemer plants in England, during their first decade, produced considerable quantities of malleable iron, but the iron so produced was not as suitable for many purposes as was the puddled iron, and the older methods have still continued to be used. The types of steel that could be produced, however, were distinctly superior for general structural purposes to the malleable-iron products. The converters were therefore gradually diverted to the making of mild steel for rails, ship plates, and the various rolled forms for bridge and structural work. At the outset the new steels were somewhat more expensive per ton than malleable iron, so that there was not a little resistance to the introduction of the new product. Furthermore, the new steel industry was not able to solve immediately all the difficulties involved in producing uniform qualities of steel of the various grades required. The untrustworthiness of the malleable-iron products in the United States created more favorable markets for Bessemer steels there. In the late 1860's a large proportion of the steel rails produced were exported to the United States. But the substitution of mild steel for malleable iron in England proceeded rapidly in the following decades.

In 1867 an additional process of steel production was developed by C. W. Siemens in collaboration with Émile and Pierre Martin. This "open-hearth" process was a development of a refining furnace heated by jets of gas. The original purpose of Siemens was to produce mild steel by the fusion of malleable-iron scrap with a certain amount of new cast iron. The carbon content of the new iron would be reduced by the addition of the relatively large mass of malleable iron. The general features of the process were readily demonstrated, but the details of furnace construction and management were a serious problem. Siemens granted licenses to several ironmasters, but they were not successful. In 1867 he erected furnaces at Birmingham at which the process was developed and perfected. Commercial success turned on refinements of procedure : the cooling of the bottom of the furnace by a current of cold air, the careful preparation of the bottom of the furnace by fusing thin layers of special grades of sand, and the use of accessory furnaces to heat the charge.

The economic importance of the process is due to two features of its application : the use of scrap metal is, of course, important, and in addition it appears that the open-hearth furnace is adapted to the treatment of classes of ores ill suited to the Bessemer converter. Ores containing some phosphorus can be treated successfully without special fluxes, and the use of the basic lining of Thomas and Gilchrist makes it possible to treat a wide range of ores which cannot be handled as well in the basic Bessemer process. The processes are complementary.

### The Railway and the Locomotive, before 1829

We are prone to think of the railway and its rolling stock as an integrated technique of transport, but the actual development of this transport system was complex. Railways were long in use around the coal mines; and, though we are tempted to dismiss this phase of the story lightly, it is a matter of considerable importance, for the railway as we know it was very definitely the handiwork of the mine superintendents and their engineers. The locomotive was developed to handle a transport problem that was placing great pressure upon the possibilities of a line operated by horse-drawn wagons. Few achievements represent so complex a synthesis of separate elements.

Mere plank ways were used in some collieries in the seventeenth century. In the second half of the eighteenth century cast-iron rails and cast-iron wagon wheels came into use.   The new material offered many appealing potentialities.   In 1789 William Jessup introduced the edge rail to be used in conjunction with cast-iron wagon wheels having an inner flange.   In 1797 rails were braced with cross ties.   But these developments represented only the best practice.   In many coal mines the railway consisted merely of flat plates, or at best of angle-shaped sections laid with the flange on the outside.   These cast-iron rails were brittle, especially in cold weather, and as early as 1805 tests were made of malleable-iron rails. The technique of rolling was developed, and by 1820 rolled rails of good design were produced by Birkenshaw.   To simplify the problem of rolling, the rail was designed to be laid in cast-iron chairs. The early cast-iron rails were short sections of three or four feet, bridging the gap between the supports.   The wrought-iron rails were being produced in twelve- and fifteen-foot lengths when the Stockton and Darlington line was chartered in 1821.   The technique of construction of the roadbed was largely complete before there was any locomotive that could compete in economy of operation with horses.

The history of the noncondensing engine and of the locomotive is too complex to admit any adequate statement.   Several steam carriages were designed to operate on the highway, forming an interesting series of precursors of the steam automobile.   Even as late as 1830 it was presumed that the steam carriage on the highway would be the significant mode of passenger transport.   There was then no adequate appreciation of the importance of surface condition and grades.   The highways of the early nineteenth century were unsuited to the operation of any motor vehicle, and they could not have been made suitable for motor traffic at any reasonable cost.

The more significant line of experiment, therefore, was opened up by Richard Trevithick.   He built a locomotive in 1803 to operate the railway at the Pen-y-darran iron works at Merthyr Tydvil in South Wales.   The engine was cumbersome, but it was demonstrated successfully at the mines.   It moved a train carrying ten tons of bar iron over nine miles of line at the rate of nine miles per hour.   This engine was used only a short time, as its weight was too great for the cast-iron rails of the line.   There was so much breakage of rails that Trevithick's locomotive was taken off the line and used as a stationary engine.   This engine marks the beginning of the series of heavy-duty locomotives.   Trevithick built another engine, originally designed for operation on the highway.   There is no trustworthy information about its design, nor about its demonstration near London. The picture, so frequently reproduced, was in actuality drawn years afterward and is without any technical or historical significance.

Experimentation continued around some of the coal mines in the north. The initial attempt at the Wylam colliery was inspired by Trevithick's work in South Wales. An engine was built for the coal company in 1804 by John Steel, who had worked with Trevithick on the Pen-y-darran engine. On account of similarities in design this engine has sometimes been attributed to Trevithick. The engine proved to be so heavy that it could not be operated on the wooden line then in use at Wylam, and nothing further was done until 1811. By that time the line had been relaid with cast-iron rails and a new effort was made to develop a locomotive. After 1811 experimentation was continuous, and proceeded concurrently at several mining centers. The work covered a wide range, but the results were unsatisfactory. The engines were operable, in some measure, but they were more costly than horse traction. Some began to lose faith in the possibilities of the locomotive, and experiments were made with cable haulage.

While matters were still in this unsatisfactory state, the Stockton and Darlington Railway was projected. The plan necessarily involved a more ambitious scheme than the construction of a mere coal road, as it would incidentally connect Darlington with the port of Stockton, and thus presented possibilities of developing passenger traffic. The scheme assumed the general form of a canal project, both in procedure and in the details of the charter granted April 19, 1821. Here, as in a few other instances of less importance, the legal concept of the railroad as a common carrier preceded the effective development of a locomotive. But the special character of the railroad was not appreciated, as there was no realization of the desirability of treating the whole system as an operating unit. The charter provided for the operation of wagons on the line by private individuals, but this was rarely done. For several years, however, the right to operate passenger coaches was leased to various individuals, in addition to some service furnished by the company. The primary concern of the company, however, was the coal traffic, which was handled in part by horses and in part by locomotives.

Stephenson confidently expected to be able to move all the coal traffic by steam, and an engine works was established to furnish the locomotives.  Results of operation were at first unsatisfactory. The performance of the locomotive at the opening ceremony on September 27, 1825, was not reassuring, though the performance was a distinct improvement over that of earlier locomotives.  The experience of operation in 1826 and 1827 raised grave doubts of the existence of any real economy in steam traction.  The increase of traffic required the use of additional horses.  The difficulties were not frankly recognized in the public reports, but the full records show that the committee on management was on the point of voting to abandon locomotive traction.  The managing engineer, Timothy Hackworth, offered to make a new locomotive embodying various improvements, and urged postponement of any decision until this new type could be tested.  He was authorized to proceed, and the *Royal George* was built.  This engine was specially designed to move heavy freight, and as a freight locomotive it deserves as much credit as is generally awarded the famous *Rocket*, which was designed primarily for speed.  The *Royal George* was tested in September, 1827, and set to work on the line in November.  The records of its achievement show clearly that it was the first locomotive to realize decisive economy in operation.

Its success was due to increased heating surface in the boiler, and to the singularly successful use of exhaust steam to create a forced draft.  Added heating surface was secured by running a U-shaped flue through the boiler.  This involved the inconvenience of firing the boiler from the front, as the smokestack and fire door were necessarily placed side by side.  The primary controls were at the rear, managed from a platform.  The tender, with water and the coke used as fuel, was in front.  The multitubular boiler first used in the *Rocket* was, of course, a much more adequate and elegant provision of added heating surface, but the U-shaped return flue was sufficient to make the critical addition of heating surface.  The truly notable feature of the *Royal George* was the cone-shaped jet which led the exhaust steam into the center of the smokestack in the most efficient manner possible.  This feature was based on careful trial and experiment by Hackworth, and was later applied to the famous *Rocket* when it was remodeled after the Rainhill trial (October, 1829).  The actual achievement of practical steam traction on a railway was the work of the staff of the Stockton and Darlington Railway, and the decisive achievement dates from the *Royal George* in September, 1827.  Horses continued to be used also, because there were not enough locomotives to handle even the coal traffic.

### The Liverpool and Manchester Railway

The Liverpool and Manchester Railway was the public demonstration of the achievements of George Stephenson and Timothy Hackworth at Stockton.  But much faith was required on Stephenson's part to urge the Liverpool and Manchester Company to rely exclusively on locomotives.  The analysis of that project and the carefully conceived principles of survey constitute George Stephenson's great contribution to the technique of the modern railway. His tests of grade resistance settled the great dispute between the relative advantages of the railway and motorized highway transport, and laid the rational foundation for a comprehensive railway system.

The doubts of some of the promoters as to the proper system of traction were met only in part by direct study of the records of the colliery lines and the Stockton and Darlington.  Accordingly, a test for locomotives was arranged, scheduled to be held at Rainhill, near Liverpool, October 1, 1829.  The Stephensons built the *Rocket* for this contest, in association with Henry Booth, who suggested the use of a multitubular boiler.  It is strange that this important feature appeared so late in the history of the British locomotive.  John Stevens, an American, had conceived the idea as early as 1787 and had taken out a United States patent in 1791.  In England, too, some use had already been made of such boilers for stationary engines, but the true significance of this type of boiler was not appreciated until 1829.  The incident thus bears striking testimony to the magnitude of the task of primary synthesis.  The precise significance of the various separate elements is not readily perceived.

Timothy Hackworth built for this contest a locomotive based on the primary features of the *Royal George*, though reduced in weight to meet the conditions set by the Liverpool and Manchester committee.  There was also a locomotive by John Ericsson, a steam coach of the pattern then projected for highways, and two contrivances worked by horses in treadmills.  The opening of the contest was postponed until October 6, and the trials occupied several days.  Ericsson's *Novelty* attained a speed of 28 miles per hour, but its construction was seriously defective and it broke down before the test was completed.  Hackworth's *Sanspareil* was officially rated at 500 pounds overweight, but was allowed to compete.  It was running well at a maximum speed of 15 miles per hour, when a cylinder gave way on account of a defect in boring.  The *Rocket* met all the tests, achieving speeds ranging between 13 and 16 miles per hour.  The *Rocket* was declared the winner.

It is frequently cited as the first truly successful locomotive, but this judgment is unfair to Hackworth.  Neither locomotive embodied all the essential features of the mature design.  The *Rocket's* exhaust jet was crude and ineffective.  The boiler of the *Sanspareil* was clearly inferior to the multitubular boiler of the *Rocket*.  The *Rocket* was remodeled after the tests, and fitted with an improved exhaust jet.  The *Sanspareil* was bought by the Liverpool and Manchester and operated for many years, but Hackworth adopted the multitubular boiler for all his later locomotives.  The Rainhill contest marked the close of the stage of tentative experiment in locomotive building, but the achievement was definitely not the work of any one man or even of any one firm of engine builders.

After the opening of the Liverpool and Manchester Railway in 1830, railway projects became numerous, but until the Great Western was chartered, none of the projects contemplated an interconnected system serving a large territory.  Lines were chartered and built in relatively short links which were subsequently combined for purposes of operation.  The development of the railway network in Great Britain was controlled only by the action of the special Parliamentary committees whose primary concern was the protection of investors by a careful study of the likelihood of securing a volume of traffic sufficient to cover the costs of the outlay.  These purposes were, of course, realized throughout the earlier period when the primary stems of the railway network were under construction.  The first important general declaration of public policy was embodied in the Railway Act of 1844, but these problems of policy can be best treated in other connections.

### The Steamboat and the Iron Ship

The invention of the steamboat preceded the development of steam traction on the railway, but the early steamboat was of very modest significance in Great Britain and in Europe.  Both inland and coastwise waterways were workable by wind or towpath under conditions which showed a large margin of superiority over the performance of early steamers.  American waterways, and most notably the Hudson River, were less easily utilized by other means.  American inventors, therefore, worked more tenaciously on the steamboat, and were able to achieve important practical results at an earlier stage in the technical development of the apparatus.

The full record of this achievement is therefore of secondary significance for the history of transport engineering in England and Continental Europe. The earliest American and the earliest British efforts were independent; though very nearly simultaneous, the important work of Fitch seems to have priority over the early experiments in Scotland and England. But after 1793 the travels of the American engineers made their work known in Europe, and gave them the benefit of many important engineering contacts, so that the ultimate achievement was not in any accurate sense a regional or national accomplishment. After 1800 the differences in the history of this application of steam must be attributed to the selective influence of the varying physical features of the inland and coastwise waterways.

The steamer, however, was not an entirely negligible factor in England, even during the first half of the nineteenth century. The British registers of merchant shipping reveal a substantial growth in the tonnage of small steamers after 1827.[1] They show, for the year 1827, 232 steamers, with a total tonnage of 23,000; for 1837, 531 steamers with a total tonnage of 51,000; and for 1847, 924 steamers with a total tonnage of 116,000. The records for France are not available, though there were some small steamers in use on the rivers and along the coasts. Experiments were made with long-distance voyages, at first with combined use of sail and steam (1819), later with steam as the primary source of power. The effective demonstration of the seagoing steamship did not take place until 1838. In that year four steam vessels crossed the Atlantic. The *Sirius* was not primarily designed for oceanic service, and her crossing was incidental to operation in Canadian waters. The *Great Western* was definitely designed for service, and her performance fulfilled the expectations of her owners, though she used 650 tons of coal outbound and 393 homebound, amounting, respectively, to 48 and 29 per cent of her carrying capacity. On the basis of these results, the Cunard Steamship Company inaugurated their steamship service in 1840 with a fleet of four steamships, which were obliged to use about 40 per cent of their carrying capacity for fuel. For another generation the use of steam on the oceans was largely confined to special mail and packet service on the North Atlantic. The use of the steamer was greatly extended by refinements in construction which made it possible to build compound engines using high pressures in the first of two or three

[1] Clepham, J. H., *History of Modern Britain*, vol. I, p. 438.

cylinders. In 1830 average practice showed a consumption of 9 pounds of coal per horsepower hour; in 1840 the rate of fuel consumption was reduced to about 5.3 pounds; and successively each decade to 4 pounds, 3 pounds, and in 1870 to 2.3 pounds. Further economies were subsequently secured, and after 1860 the significant use of steam developed rapidly. The Suez Canal, opened November 17, 1869, afforded a greatly shortened route to the East through the important traffic territory of the Mediterranean, and with this development oceanic commerce assumed the highly characteristic form of the late nineteenth century.

The development of the seagoing steamer added greatly to the carrying trade of Great Britain, because the capricious distribution of coal made it necessary to establish coaling stations over wide areas, notably in the Mediterranean, and this coal trade came largely into the hands of Great Britain and her ships. A great fleet of tramp steamers grew up to carry coal out from Great Britain, and to move the heavier foods and raw materials in towards British and other northern ports. This general structure of the shipping industry persisted until the World War, despite the emergence of new conditions created by the introduction of oil as a marine fuel.

The shipping business of the second half of the nineteenth century was profoundly influenced also by the introduction of iron as a material for the construction of ships. The increasing costs of ship timber in Europe had become a serious problem towards the close of the eighteenth century. Canada and the United States became important shipbuilding centers, and the teak and mahogany of India were an important resource. Ships were built in India on British account, and heavy timber was imported to supplement the wasting stocks of British and Baltic timber. Cheap timber gave American shipyards a commanding advantage over British and European yards, but the demand for tonnage made it necessary to continue to utilize European supplies. Rising costs of construction did not explicitly check the increase of the tonnage of the British merchant fleet until after 1840, but by that time the technique of iron-ship construction had been mastered and the British began to build iron ships at lower costs than American wood. This achievement of the British shipbuilders was not merely the basis of the maintenance of British control of the carrying trade, but an indispensable provision for greatly increased need of shipping space. The remarkable increase in the physical volume of trade would have been impossible without this enlargement of the supply of the raw materials of construction. The iron ships, whether under sail or under steam, were a vital part of the economic system based on the new technology, and this phase of the system of the nineteenth century gave sharp emphasis to the geographic position and resources of Great Britain.

The perfection of the technique of iron-ship building was an achievement of the malleable-iron period, for though some use could be made of castings, ship construction really demanded malleable iron or steel. The effective achievement was thus definitely limited by the somewhat late introduction of wrought-iron girders and beams, though the possibility of the use of iron was demonstrated soon after the development of the heavy-duty rolling mill. With the rolls it was possible to produce iron plates at low cost. Plates were used for boiler construction as early as 1786, and in the year following John Wilkinson built a canal barge seventy feet long, with iron plates applied to a wood frame. A barge was built on the Severn in 1789. We have no record of further use of iron in shipbuilding until the close of the Napoleonic wars. Iron canalboats were in use in Staffordshire in 1812 and 1813, but the work seems not to have had any continuing significance. In 1822 a small iron steamer was built for use on the Seine between Paris and Le Havre, but again without significant consequences.

Determined efforts to master the new material were made in 1830, when the proprietors of canals began a series of experiments to meet the competition which was threatened by the establishment of the locomotive on the railway. Early projects called for the construction of light iron barges driven by steam. Work was undertaken in several localities, and a number of iron barges were built. A small iron vessel was constructed for the exploration of the Niger, and its satisfactory performance on the voyage to Africa did much to establish confidence in the new construction. The Lairds at Birkenhead (1832), Fairbairn at Millwall Docks in London (1835), and Robert Napier on the Clyde (1839) were the pioneer firms. By 1850 Fairbairn had built about a hundred iron ships.

Prejudice against the new construction was by no means overcome, but the new technique was sufficiently established to win its way despite the conservatism and forebodings of the Admiralty and the insurance underwriters. The Admiralty experimented halfheartedly with the new material until the demonstration of the French ironclads in the Crimean War marked out decisively the course of the future development of naval construction.

## The Influence of the New Technique of Transport on Social Life

The achievements of the heavy-metal industries were closely associated with the development of an essentially new technique of transport on land and water.  It is not necessary to insist upon the essential novelty of the steam-operated railway, for it was convincingly new in every important feature.  Cost of transport was greatly reduced, speed of transport was notably increased, and the relative importance of the various routes was modified in many ways.  A two-track railroad was definitely superior to the best canal, and competed closely with the best rivers.  Although inland waterways could be developed so that they gave the appearance of forming a comprehensive network, the actual movement of traffic on the inland waterways was in fact restricted by many factors that do not appear conspicuously on the map.  The movement of goods over ranges of hills and watersheds was strictly limited.  Traffic did not move freely over the network of waterways.  The railway networks that had been created even as early as 1860 and 1870 constituted an integrated transport system in an entirely new sense of the word.  The social and economic consequences were profound, and though we are keenly conscious of the magnitude of the change, the precise significance of the new forces in social life is not always clearly appreciated.  The fascinations of the factory system have obscured the causes of many changes which are primarily due to the modifications of the transport system.

The novelty of changes in the system of oceanic transport is not so obvious, because the changes are largely changes in degree rather than in kind, but the magnitudes involved produced many highly novel effects.  The effective limits to the size of the wooden vessel had been reached just as the iron ship became a completely practical achievement.  Four or five thousand tons' burden is recognized as the limit for wooden vessels, largely because stem and stern posts must each be a single piece.  The steady increase in the size of iron and steel ships has created important changes in the distribution of shipping among the ports of the world.  The economy of large units tends to concentrate shipping more and more exclusively in the best ports available in each region.

The introduction of steam and the construction of the great oceanic canals have profoundly modified the basic seaways.  Reductions of cost have created an intensity of interregional competition entirely unforeseen by theorists of the early nineteenth century. The relatively sudden impact of these changes undoubtedly contributed much to the widespread demands for tariff protection that characterized the late nineteenth century. We deliberately nullify in part the economies we achieve by new inventions. A concept of protection as a kind of social shock absorber might be defended, if carefully hedged about with controls; but if it is rational to strive for technological improvement and lowered costs, it is hardly consistent to nullify the effects so extensively as the advocates of national self-sufficiency recommend.

The positive significance of all these changes in the structure of the transport system has been persistently minimized by the emphasis placed upon industrial organization by many early writers and most notably by Marx and his followers. The famous Communist Manifesto was not merely an economic interpretation of history, but in strict analysis an " industrial" interpretation of history. All the stress was laid upon class differentiation and the relation of the development of the capitalist modes of production. Much of this analysis was true, but it was one-sided. Intensive concentration on problems of class structure obscured an important class of phenomena that affected society as a whole — capitalists and proletarians alike. New patterns of social life were created, which are largely independent of the precise detail of the internal organization of particular societies.

Attention has already been called to the influence of the application of power to industrial processes. The increase in the rate of productivity per capita changes the locational significance of foods and weight-losing raw materials. Fuels involve relatively larger weight losses than foods, and in consequence population moves toward power and fuel sites rather than to food supplies. Specialization between industrial regions and food-producing regions becomes possible on a scale hitherto unknown. These broad regional changes are largely though not exclusively the outcome of modifications in industrial technique. The precise effects are, of course, also dependent in part upon the nature of the transport system. If costs of transport are falling at the same time, changes in the location and distribution of population assume large proportions.

Changes in the technique of transport, however, are in many ways independent, and the specific influence of changes in transport exerts its most characteristic effects upon the pattern of population within particular regions.  In general, the distribution of population reflects the geographic distribution of the resources useful to a society under the current conditions of technical development. If agriculture is predominant, population is likely to be more uniformly dispersed throughout the region than in the case of a society dominated by the deposits of coal, iron, and the nonferrous metals. The distribution of population is also affected by all the details of the topography of the region; notably by the details of the occurrence of supplies of drinking water and by the pattern of routes suitable for transport.  The specific influence of changes in the technique of transport appears most explicitly in the changing significance of topography under the influence of new techniques of transport.

When the problem is stated in this form, it should be clear that new techniques of transport are likely to lead to an increase of urban population.  This result is due to two slightly different aspects of improvement in the technique of transport.  The reduction of costs inevitably leads to larger movements of traffic, so that the system as a whole becomes more important, and the settlements at intersections of routes, or nodes, become proportionately larger.  The most significant features of the change, however, are due to the varying adaptabilities of new modes of transport to topography.

In a system of inland transport based upon pack horses or wagons, distance is the primary consideration.  Grade resistances are very much less important than actual mileage.  For canals and railroads, grade resistances are definitely more important than mileage. Differences between alternative routes become much more considerable than they were under the more primitive technique, and discriminations between primary and secondary routes become commandingly significant.  Differences between terminal points and intermediate points also become greater, because with greater speed and wider spacing of incidental services much traffic passes through intermediate points without stopping.  Thus, a road map of the sixteenth century will show post stations at distances determined by the needs of food and rest both for men and for animals. These needs in themselves create business for the post villages, quite apart from any actual local traffic.  Service problems for a canal or railroad are entirely different.

Selective factors also operate on the great terminals which serve as transfer points between land and water transport, most notably the great ports which serve as terminals for primary oceanic routes and as export and import centers for inland trade. Improvements in the technique of transport thus lead to progressive selection of the better routes and the better sites. The growing traffic is concentrated on particular routes and in a smaller number of towns. The old balance between urban and rural population is changed, and there is a notable increase in the large towns. These general theses can be developed in great detail by careful analysis of the economic geography of transport in the nineteenth century. The growth of cities finds its most complete explanation in the changed significance of topography under the influence of progressive changes in the technique of industry and transport. Industrial power, in part, but more especially new means of transport, destroyed the old social system based on the rural village and the market town. Society has become predominantly urban, and the large urban unit has become so characteristic of the new social order that the "small town" is as hopelessly "provincial" as the most remote rural village. The motorcar and rural electrification introduce new elements whose significance is still imperfectly explored.

# CHAPTER 20

# BRITISH TRADE AND EMPIRE

———◆———

## Territorial Expansion and Colonization

During the second and third quarters of the nineteenth century the ascendancy of Great Britain as a colonial, commercial, industrial, and financial power was virtually unchallenged. The basis of this ascendancy is apparent from circumstances already described in some detail. These include the geographical advantages of the British Isles; the stable and yet evolutionary and adaptable nature of British political institutions in contrast with those of the Continent; the accumulation of surplus capital and the long and varied experience of economic organizations in its utilization; the superior competitive power accruing from the industrial revolution; and the comparative freedom of the British Isles from the disruptive effects of the wars and revolutions characteristic of Continental states.

Before the last quarter of the nineteenth century the potential European rivals of Great Britain had little opportunity or inclination to enter the race for overseas territories or to acquire control of areas which impinged seriously on the British Empire. Englishmen themselves were divided in opinion as to the value of overseas territories directly under control of the government. But a comparison of maps of the British Empire of 1815 (following the Congress of Vienna) and of 1870 reveals a remarkable growth.

Cape Colony in South Africa was awarded to Great Britain in 1814. By 1836 the colony had expanded to the Orange River. In 1843 Natal was claimed by the British. By the middle of the century, British influence extended to the Vaal River and soon thereafter to the Transvaal, which had been occupied by the Boers, the Dutch settlers, in an effort to maintain their independence. Basutoland on the Orange River between Cape Colony and Natal came under British control in 1868. On the west coast of Africa the old slave-trade centers of Sierra Leone and the Gold Coast were reorganized, and by 1872 the Danish and Dutch settlements in this region were acquired. Nigeria was explored and claimed for Britain. The island of St. Helena was made a crown colony in 1834. The island of Mauritius in the Indian Ocean was colonized by settlers from India. Aden, to the east of the southern end of the Red Sea, was acquired in 1839; and the island of Perim, to the west, in 1852. In the Far East the monopoly of the East India Company was abolished in 1833, and in 1858 the government of India was transferred completely to the crown.  British rule was vastly extended to include virtually the whole of the peninsula and the adjacent regions of the Indus valley to the northwest, Kashmir and the Punjab to the north, and Assam to the northeast.  The way was thus prepared for Disraeli's action in 1876 in declaring Victoria Empress of India. In the Straits Settlements, southeast of India, Singapore, destined to become one of the greatest of a mighty chain of fortified ports, was occupied as early as 1819, and Malacca was regained from the Dutch in 1824.  Sarawak in northern Borneo was acquired in 1842; and in the same year, after the Opium War, China was forced to cede the strategic island of Hong Kong, on her main trade route.

In Canada the extension of the frontier and the growth of population led by 1852 to the beginning of the Grand Trunk Railway. The Red River colony grew by 1870 into the province of Manitoba. In Australia, a primitive outpost of the Empire in 1815, colonization proceeded rapidly throughout the period, and was promoted by emigration schemes, large-scale financing of sheepraising and agriculture, and the discovery of gold.  In New South Wales, where a penal colony at Botany Bay had been established in 1788, little progress was made until the second quarter of the nineteenth century, when the Australian Agricultural Company bought land and promoted colonization.  The same quarter century witnessed the beginnings of colonization in other portions of Australia and also in New Zealand.

British emigration was largely to the United States, Canada, Australia, and New Zealand.  Colonization of South Africa was mainly after 1870.  Before 1828 the annual emigration to Australia and New Zealand was less than a thousand.  Thereafter the number increased until 1841, when 32,625 went to these colonies.  After a temporary decline, the number in 1849 was again more than 32,000. Between 1850 and 1870 the smallest number was 12,332 in 1868, and the largest number was 87,881 in 1852.  To British North America the annual emigration increased from less than a thousand in 1815 to 23,534 in 1819.  This number was not again attained until 1830, when it rose to 30,574.  In 1832 the number was 66,339. After another decline the number suddenly jumped in 1847, under the influence of the Irish famine and of industrial discontent, to 109,680.  From 1848 to 1870 the smallest number was 6,689 in

1859 and the largest number was 43,761 in 1854. The very large emigration to the United States tended to promote trade relations and to increase remittances to the British Isles.

The colonization of Canada, Australia, and New Zealand, and the economic development of these and other regions of the Empire, especially South Africa and India, provided a rapidly expanding basis for the export of British manufactures, for the re-export of British imports, and for the investment of surplus income. These were the most important aspects of British imperial economy.

### Growth of Trade

The official values of exports and imports before 1871 are not on a comparable basis, and the validity of the figures before the introduction of free trade is impaired by a large and variable amount of smuggling. The growth of shipping is indicated by the clearances at United Kingdom ports. British vessels cleared from 1821 to 1830 averaged 1,782,000 tons a year; and from 1861 to 1870, 10,122,000 tons. Foreign vessels cleared during the earlier decade averaged 662,000 tons a year, and during the later decade 5,276,000 tons. Foreign clearances at United Kingdom ports increased at a more rapid rate than the British, but from a very low level, and in 1870 were only about half as large, in spite of the liberalizing of British navigation policies.

During the third decade of the century, registered British vessels had a tonnage of somewhat more than 2,000,000. Continuous figures of registered tonnage are available from about the middle of the century. In 1853, 25,224 sailing vessels with a tonnage of 3,780,000 were registered in the United Kingdom. Steam vessels numbered 1,385, with a tonnage of 250,000. The total figures are: vessels, 26,609; and tonnage, 4,030,000. For 1870 the figures are: sailing vessels, 23,189, with a tonnage of 4,578,000; steam vessels, 3,178, with a tonnage of 1,113,000; and totals, 26,367 vessels, with a tonnage of 5,691,000. The actual expansion of transportation facilities, moreover, was much greater than the figures indicate, due to progressive improvements in navigation and in port facilities, safeguards against hazards, and increase of speed. Much coastwise shipping had been supplanted by railway traffic. The British had tonnage of more than five and a half millions in 1870, the Germans less than a million, and the French slightly more than a million.

The nature of British trade is significantly illustrated by the growth in imports and exports of a few of the principal commodities.

The importation of wheat was over sixteen times greater from 1861 to 1870 than from 1821 to 1830. The annual average during the earlier decade was 517,000 quarters (a quarter being about eight bushels) and during the later decade, 8,391,000 quarters. The amount of cotton imported increased nearly five and a half times, from an annual average of 200,871,000 pounds to an average of 1,087,154,000 pounds. These and the following averages are for the decades 1821-1830 and 1861-1870. There was an almost ninefold increase in wool imports, from an average of 25,059,000 to an average of 216,269,000 pounds. The amount imported in 1861 was 147,173,000 pounds; and in 1870, 263,250,000. The largest increase in exports of major commodities during the same period (from 1821-1830 to 1861-1870) was the increase in coal exports, from an annual average of 335,000 tons to an average of 9,645,000, nearly twenty-nine times as great. The exports in 1861 were 7,855,000 tons; and in 1870, 11,703,000. In terms of values, the export of cotton goods and yarn increased about three and one half times, from an average of £17,248,000 to an average of £59,506,000. The figure for 1861 is £46,872,000; for 1870, £71,416,000. The export of woolen goods and yarn increased more than fourfold, from an average of £5,575,000 to an average of £23,482,000, the value in 1870 being £26,658,000. There was almost a sevenfold increase in silk exports, from an average of £330,000 to an average of £2,230,000. The nine-year annual average of iron and steel exports from 1822 to 1830 was £1,046,000, and during the years from 1862 to 1870 the average was fifteen and a half times as great, or £16,213,000. The value in 1870 was £23,538,000. From 1827 to 1830 the average declared value of exports of machinery and millwork was £232,000; and from 1867 to 1870 the average was almost twenty-two times as great — £5,028,000. The actual shipments of machinery during the earlier period were somewhat larger than is indicated by the declared values, due to evasions of the export license system.

These figures illustrate some of the main aspects of British economy. There was a remarkably rapid expansion of trade and shipping, and the growth was more significant than the expansion on the part of Continental countries, because these countries at the beginning of the period had very small volumes of foreign trade and of tonnage, whereas Great Britain began the period with a very large volume of trade and with unprecedented facilities for transportation. The British definitely abandoned the conception of a favorable trade balance in the narrow sense of an excess of exports over imports and entered an era of dependence on other sources for the balance of payments, as freight charges, brokerage and insurance commissions, and returns from overseas investments. The declared value of imports in 1871 was £331,015,000, and of exports, £283,575,000. The high degree of industrialization and specialization is indicated by the vast increase in the imports of food and raw materials and in the exports of manufactured goods. The increase in coal exports indicates the high degree of development of the coal industry in England as compared with the Continent and also the imperfect development and integration of transportation facilities from Continental coal centers to the coal markets. The increased exportation of iron and steel and machinery and to a less extent the expansion of coal exports indicates the abandonment of the futile policy of attempting to monopolize the new techniques.

### Export of British Capital

Estimates of foreign investments even for recent decades vary widely. For the period before 1870, information is fragmentary and estimates are rough approximations. With the exception of occasional periods of extreme speculation, government securities remained the principal form of investment. By the middle of the century, the total of British investments abroad in government securities and private enterprises probably amounted to £300,-000,000. In 1870 the total was probably about £800,000,000.

After about the middle of the eighteenth century, surplus incomes (that is to say, incomes which the owners could not normally spend either for consumption goods or for investment in profitable enterprises at home) had accumulated with great rapidity. Enclosures, market farming, and commercial ventures brought large fortunes. The national debt was vastly increased as a result of the wars, and interest payments on debts previously incurred were met in considerable measure toward the end of the Napoleonic wars by further borrowing. After 1815 the cessation of wartime expenditures brought about a decline of income from all forms of enterprise, but the decline in prices, in profits, and in domestic consumption gave added stimulus to the quest for stable investments with fixed returns. Domestic industrial enterprises were largely financed out of profits, and the income from agriculture, trade, and government securities flowed readily into colonial and foreign channels.

Domestic enterprises were equipped with the new techniques, and agriculture had been transformed by various innovations; and the country's productive facilities had been geared to large-scale production to meet the seemingly inexhaustible demands of wartime. After the war the distress of the people at home and the cessation of demands from abroad created a powerful pressure for markets. The export of capital facilitated the purchase of British goods. This fact was not always clearly perceived, and it was perhaps not prominent as a conscious motive among individual investors, but it nevertheless increased the pressure which tended to force surplus income into foreign and colonial investment channels. There was of course the possibility of expanding the home market, by means of a different apportionment of income among the large consuming groups living at a subsistence level. Such a reapportionment of income could have been effected measurably by the indirect method of taxation. But no serious consideration was given even to a reform of taxation for this purpose, save by a few individuals who were likely to be viewed as subverters of law and order.

The forms of overseas investment varied widely and changed in nature from decade to decade. Loans were extended to the French for the payment of the war indemnity. Revolutionary governments of the third decade of the century were financed (contrary to the prevailing attitude in English political circles) in Spain, Spanish America, and Greece. The Spanish-American financial ventures were not unrelated to the desire to break down Spanish colonial monopolies and to gain access to new markets. In 1824 and 1825 a mania developed, but soon subsided, for financing innumerable speculative ventures — a boom resembling the South Sea Bubble of the early eighteenth century. The movement for internal improvements in the United States absorbed extensive British capital until the panic of 1837, and according to a contemporary American estimate for 1839, European (mainly British) investments in American stocks that year amounted to $200,000,000. The railway age called forth a vast volume of British capital. In 1857 British holdings of American railroad stocks alone probably amounted to £80,000,000. Investments throughout the world included mines, public utilities, and factories. After the middle of the century, administrative facilities were organized in London for the supervision of enterprises as well as for handling investments. The flow of capital abroad was facilitated by various changes in company law, soon after the middle of the century, notably by the introduction of limited liability. Loans to governments continued, and involved grave problems of diplomacy and international relations, as, for example, the efforts to strengthen the decrepit Turkish Empire as a buffer state against Russian expansion southward. Investments alike in public securities and in private enterprises promoted the development of the policy of "diplomatic support" and even of armed intervention in behalf of British interests throughout the world. This policy found expression as early as 1842 in the Opium War against China and in 1847 to 1850 in threats of war against Greece in behalf of Don Pacifico, a British subject at Athens.

### British Ports and Seaways

Early in the nineteenth century there was a rapid development of ports and harbor facilities. A network of canals connected inland Britain conveniently with the coast in virtually all sections of the country. Ships were small, and port facilities were not excessively expensive. The rapid growth of market farming and of new industries in the Midlands and the north gave an unprecedented stimulus to widely dispersed shipping activities. But by 1870 the smaller ports were declining. Railways had largely taken the place of canals and had absorbed much of the coastwise traffic. The size of sailing vessels had increased, and steamships accounted for almost a fifth of the registered tonnage. The average size of sailing vessels registered in the United Kingdom increased from about 150 net tons in 1853 to about 200 tons in 1870. Steamships and many of the larger sailing vessels required facilities found only in the greater ports.

In 1830 the total tonnage of the United Kingdom was 2,202,000. London in 1829 had about one fourth of the total. On the eastern coast the tonnage of Newcastle was more than 200,000; the nearby port of Sunderland had 108,000 tons; and Hull, 72,000. On the west coast, Liverpool, rating below Newcastle, had only 162,000 tons; Whitehaven, 73,000; and Bristol, hardly 50,000. Glasgow had less than 50,000. During the four decades from 1830 to 1870 there was a progressive concentration of shipping at London, Liverpool, Hull, and Glasgow. Although many of the lesser ports were decadent, others were growing. Cardiff was rapidly becoming a rival of Newcastle as a coal-exporting center. Railway connections gave Southampton renewed vigor. Aberdeen and Grangemouth were making valiant efforts to maintain the commercial importance of eastern Scotland by handling an extensive coastwise trade and imports from the Baltic countries.  In all of the main ports vast harbor improvements had been made or were under way to meet the new conditions of rapidly expanding traffic, connections with railway terminals, and larger vessels, many of them made of iron and moved by steam.  The shipping of London remained extremely varied.  Liverpool specialized in cotton imports and the export of cotton manufactures.  At Hull the grain trade and the fishing fleets were particularly important.  Glasgow shared with Liverpool the cotton trade, imported materials for its gigantic shipbuilding yards, and exported iron, steel, and machinery.  Newcastle's coal export remained important but its general trade with the Baltic countries was also extensive.  Cardiff was primarily a coal-exporting center.

The relative importance of British seaways in 1868, the year before the opening of the Suez Canal, is indicated by the following tabulation, by values, of imports from and exports to the principal areas of the world.

### The Distribution of British Trade in 1868

| Region from Which British Imports Were Received, and to Which British Exports Were Sent | Value of Imports into the United Kingdom | Value of Exports from the United Kingdom |
|---|---|---|
| Neighboring countries | | |
| Portugal | £ 2,711,000 | £ 1,722,000 |
| Spain | 13,614,000 | 5,899,000 |
| France | 34,006,000 | 10,677,000 |
| Belgium | 8,255,000 | 3,150,000 |
| Netherlands | 11,466,000 | 11,246,000 |
| Denmark | 2,545,000 | 1,745,000 |
| Sweden and Norway | 6,215,000 | 1,393,000 |
| Germany | 18,173,000 | 22,774,000 |
| Russia | 20,052,000 | 4,250,000 |
| Total | £117,037,000 | £62,856,000 |
| Italy and the Eastern Mediterranean | | |
| Italy | £4,024,000 | £5,017,000 |
| Greece | 1,148,000 | 977,000 |
| Turkey | 6,237,000 | 7,556,000 |
| Rumania | 1,422,000 | 635,000 |
| Austria-Hungary | 2,030,000 | 1,077,000 |
| Egypt | 17,585,000 | 6,056,000 |
| Total | £32,446,000 | £21,318,000 |

(*Continued on the following page*)

THE DISTRIBUTION OF BRITISH TRADE IN 1868 (*Continued*)

| Region from Which British Imports Were Received and to Which British Exports Were Sent | Value of Imports into the United Kingdom | Value of Exports from the United Kingdom |
|---|---|---|
| Africa (except Egypt) and the Far East | | |
| (1) Foreign countries | | |
| West coast of Africa | £ 1,884,000 | £ 917,000 |
| China | 11,482,000 | 6,312,000 |
| Japan | 181,000 | 1,113,000 |
| Total | £13,547,000 | £8,342,000 |
| (2) British territories | | |
| British West Africa | £ 539,000 | £ 633,000 |
| British South Africa | 2,715,000 | 1,591,000 |
| Mauritius | 1,055,000 | 384,000 |
| India | 30,072,000 | 21,252,000 |
| Ceylon | 3,671,000 | 828,000 |
| Straits Settlements | 2,050,000 | 1,539,000 |
| Hong Kong | 236,000 | 2,186,000 |
| Australia and New Zealand | 12,571,000 | 12,075,000 |
| Total | £52,909,000 | £40,488,000 |
| Total, foreign and British | £66,456,000 | £48,830,000 |
| North America | | |
| (1) Foreign countries | | |
| United States | £43,062,000 | £21,432,000 |
| Mexico | 351,000 | 849,000 |
| Total | £43,413,000 | £22,281,000 |
| (2) British territories | | |
| Canada and Newfoundland | £6,772,000 | £4,848,000 |
| Total, foreign and British | £50,185,000 | £27,129,000 |
| West Indies, Central America, and South America | | |
| (1) Foreign countries | | |
| Central America | £ 940,000 | £ 160,000 |
| Venezuela | 31,000 | 265,000 |
| Colombia | 1,096,000 | 2,515,000 |
| Brazil | 7,456,000 | 5,352,000 |
| Uruguay | 1,138,000 | 930,000 |
| Argentina | 1,496,000 | 1,927,000 |
| Chile | 4,367,000 | 1,963,000 |
| Peru | 3,400,000 | 1,132,000 |
| Total | £19,924,000 | £14,244,000 |
| (2) British territories | | |
| West Indies and British Guiana | £6,566,000 | £2,459,000 |
| Honduras | 141,000 | 134,000 |
| Total | £6,707,000 | £2,593,000 |
| Total, foreign and British | £26,631,000 | £16,837,000 |

The imports and exports shown in the table were carried in both foreign and British vessels.  The seaways of the British Empire are indicated more definitely by the tonnage of British vessels, exclusive of the coasting trade, entered and cleared in 1868 at the principal ports of the outlying parts of the Empire.

### BRITISH VESSELS IN EMPIRE TRADE, IN 1868

| *Entered and Cleared at Ports of* | *Tonnage in 1868* |
| --- | --- |
| Canada and Newfoundland . . . . . . . . . | 4,280,000 tons |
| British West Indies  . . . . . . . . . . | 993,000 tons |
| New Zealand  . . . . . . . . . . . . | 528,000 tons |
| Australia . . . . . . . . . . . . . | 3,419,000 tons |
| British West Africa  . . . . . . . . . | 116,000 tons |
| British South Africa . . . . . . . . . . | 469,000 tons |
| India . . . . . . . . . . . . . . . | 3,197,000 tons |
| Ceylon . . . . . . . . . . . . . . | 1,071,000 tons |
| Straits Settlements  . . . . . . . . . | 839,000 tons |
| Hong Kong . . . . . . . . . . . . . | 1,232,000 tons |

For contact with western North America, especially after the discovery of gold in California, and for the transportation of the Australian wool clip, the Cape Horn route was extensively used.  But most of the Far Eastern traffic rounded the Cape of Good Hope.  The predominance of this traffic, as shown by the table above, reveals the vast importance of the opening of the Suez Canal in 1869, its later expansion, and its control, after 1875, by Great Britain.  The distance to Bombay was shortened by two fifths; to Calcutta, by a third; and to Hong Kong, by a fourth.

## Critics of Empire

The empires of Portugal, Spain, Holland, and France had risen and declined, and the British had lost the Thirteen Colonies.  The system of colonial monopoly was in disrepute, and British trade was predominantly with foreign countries.  During the middle decades of the nineteenth century many economists and statesmen accepted Adam Smith's views that Britain derived "nothing but loss" from her colonies and that the best policy would be to part with them as "good friends" and "faithful, affectionate, and generous allies" on a free-trade basis.  Jeremy Bentham as early as 1793 advocated the freeing of colonies.  The dominant school of free-trade and *laissez-faire* economists denounced the old colonial system and were more concerned with international arrangements for free trade than with the maintenance of a territorial empire.

Richard Cobden, spokesman of the textile manufacturers in the anti-protection crusade, denounced the colonial system and asserted in 1842 that free trade would "gradually and imperceptibly loose the bonds which unite our colonies to us by a mistaken attitude of self-interest." John Bright, manufacturer and statesman and associate of Cobden, was charged with proposing "to make a great empire into a little one." More than one prominent official of the British Colonial Office was a "Little Englander," such as Lord Blachford, who asserted that "the destiny of our colonies is independence." Gladstone, four times prime minister, looked forward to ultimate separation of the colonies from Great Britain. Even Disraeli, who, as prime minister, was to become the archchampion of imperialism, declared in 1866 that Great Britain should not undertake the defense of Canada and should abandon the territories in West Africa.

Too much importance, however, may readily be ascribed to these views. No significant move was made to restrict the bounds of empire; and, as has already been seen, throughout the period of criticism existing territories in Canada, Australia, India, and South Africa were rapidly extended and many new areas were acquired. No serious rivals appeared to claim unoccupied areas, and Great Britain had ample territories for assimilation. The grave defects of imperial administration and policy, surviving from the age of mercantilism, called for corrective measures, and much of the criticism was aimed not at imperialism itself but at the obsolete methods of administering the system. Englishmen were more largely interested in the breaking down of trade barriers in order to extend their markets in the populous areas outside the empire. But when the more serious defects of imperial policy were corrected, and when other countries, instead of accepting free trade and British imports without question, began to adopt the new industrialism, to revert to trade barriers, and to look about for colonies, there was a quick revival of imperial sentiment.

## Imperial Reforms

By the middle of the nineteenth century the free-trade movement had struck from the imperial system most of the anomalies of mercantilism denounced by the American colonists, by Adam Smith and later economists, and by the free-trade industrialists. Various other reform measures also were adopted.

Administrative reforms, although not primarily a part of economic history, had indirectly a great influence on colonial economy and on the survival of imperial connections. The Colonial Office dealt with remote problems and conditions with which neither Parliament nor the Colonial Secretary was likely to be thoroughly acquainted. The permanent officials of the Colonial Office were therefore exceptionally influential. Lord Durham, Edward Gibbon Wakefield, Charles Buller, and other critics of colonial administration complained of the irresponsibility and arbitrary character of rule by the undersecretaries. India was long ruled by a private corporation, the East India Company.

A rebellion in Canada in 1837 called attention acutely to the defects of colonial administration. Lord Durham was sent as High Commissioner to investigate the situation and to make recommendations. He proposed, and the government ultimately adopted, not only for Canada but for most of the other English-speaking areas, a system of colonial self-government. It was based on the English system. The nominal authority of the king was exercised by a royal governor; there was an elective parliament; and the executive was responsible not to the governor but to the colonial parliament.

In 1853 the East India Company was denied the right to make appointments to the Indian civil service, and a system of competitive examinations was established. In 1858 the government of India was transferred entirely to the crown. The competitive civil service was gradually extended, and colonial as well as home administration was placed on a much more adequate and efficient basis. The civil service was gradually opened to natives of the principal non-English-speaking areas.

Colonial policy underwent a significant change not only in the abandonment of the system of monopolizing colonial trade and controlling colonial industry but also in respect to emigration and land policy. Wakefield, an emigrant to Australia, formulated ideas which became the basis of the National Colonization Society, formed in 1830. Wakefield's plan was highly praised by John Stuart Mill, who described it as "self-supporting emigration," voluntary (in contrast with penal transportation), and financed by the sale of lands at moderate prices. The price fixed for land was to be so regulated as to encourage emigration but to provide funds in lieu of excessive taxation; to establish a proper balance between rural and urban population; and to discourage poorer emigrants from becoming landowners and thereby curtailing the supply of laborers.   These ideas were widely adopted in other colonies as well as in Australia.   In the absence of restrictions on the accumulation of landed property, many of the disadvantages of landlordism, characteristic of European society, appeared in the colonies.   The system of transportation of penal offenders to the colonies declined and was abandoned in 1857.

### Mid-century Imperialism

The Reform Bill of 1832 marked an epoch in British constitutional history and signalized the ascendancy of the middle classes.   The Chartist Movement, which attempted the democratization of the House of Commons on the basis of the enfranchisement of the working classes, virtually came to an end in 1848.   The intervening period was characterized by a predominant interest in domestic reform and free trade.   Other circumstances in addition to the defeat of the Chartists contributed, after the middle of the century, to the ebb of reforming zeal and to the diversion of British interests and activities into foreign and imperial channels.   Among these was the revolutionary movement which, beginning in France in 1848, rapidly spread over the Continent, overthrew Prince Metternich of Austria and his European system of reaction, and raised again the bogy of revolution in England.   The famine years in Ireland led to insurrectionary movements there.   The short-lived Second Republic of 1848 in France soon gave way to the Empire of Napoleon III.   Agitation was renewed for the unification of Italy.   Russia had long been restrained by the astute diplomacy of the British, particularly of Lord Palmerston, from gaining ascendancy in the Black Sea and the Straits connecting it with the Aegean and the Mediterranean, but was giving renewed evidence of ambitions to wrest control of this strategic area from Turkey.

The outstanding instance of the mid-century predominance of imperial interests was British participation in the Crimean War (1853-1856).   The war was a phase of the historic urge of Russia toward the sea.   Great Britain's part in the war against Russia and on the side of the Turks was a phase of the historic British policy of the balance of power, involving the utilization of lesser countries as buffer states against the expansion of actual or potential rivals. The Suez Canal had not then been constructed, although various proposals had been made; and the British had long been interested in the development of Asiatic lines of communication to the Far East to supplement the route around Africa.   It was believed that these routes, even more than British interests in the eastern Mediterranean, were menaced by the southward advance of the Russians. It was feared that Russia would expand through Persia to the Persian Gulf and even threaten British ascendancy in India. The refusal of Persia to accept an agreement for the safeguarding of British interests led in 1856 to a war against Persia, which revealed the far-reaching Asiatic nature of British ambitions in the Crimean War. Great Britain in alliance with France defeated Russia, and imposed a treaty which neutralized the Black Sea, driving both Russian and Turkish warships from its waters and arsenals from its shores. Persia, in alliance with Russia, was decisively defeated and was forced to give up her claims to Afghanistan on the borders of India. "We are beginning," said Lord Palmerston, "to repel the first opening of trenches against India by Russia."

It was during the mid-century period that China and Japan were forcibly brought into direct contact with Western imperialism. As early as 1839 the British government intervened to "protect" British merchants at Canton, where they had been importing opium from India contrary to prohibitions by the Chinese authorities in an effort to curb its use in China. Several cities were bombarded and seized, the island of Hong Kong was retained permanently, and the Chinese were forced to pay £5,750,000 to the British and to open up to British trade five ports from Canton to Shanghai. These arrangements were concluded in 1842. Fifteen years later the British government again intervened to "punish" the Chinese for the seizure of a vessel which they claimed was piratical but which, under false pretenses, had registered under the British flag. Even this registry had expired, but the local British representatives claimed that the Chinese were unaware of these circumstances and should be penalized for an attack on what they regarded as a British vessel. In reprisal the city of Canton was bombarded.

In the opening up of Japan the United States took the lead, in the visit of Commodore Perry in 1853. The visit was followed by treaties not only with the United States but also with Great Britain and other European countries. But antiforeign sentiment developed, and the slaying of a British agent resulted in the bombardment of Kagoshima in 1863. In 1864 the city of Shimonoseki was attacked by British, French, Dutch, and American warships, on the ground that a local official had attacked foreign vessels. Soon thereafter the Japanese reversed their attitude and welcomed foreigners, largely for the purpose of learning the secrets of their power.

## British Imperialism and the United States

Aside from the threat of Russian expansion into the areas of British interests in Asia, a threat which was averted by the Crimean War, there was no serious European rivalry in the way of British imperialism between the defeat of Napoleon and the last quarter of the nineteenth century. But before the Civil War, the United States not only restricted the extension of British rule in the New World but for a time rivaled the British in shipping and commerce.

The limits of British territorial expansion in the New World were restricted and defined by a series of controversies and agreements extending from the Monroe Doctrine of 1823 to the Clayton-Bulwer Treaty of 1850. The Monroe Doctrine was tacitly accepted by Great Britain because her ambitions at the time were not primarily for territorial expansion but rather for the encouragement of the Latin-American peoples in their move to throw off Spanish and Portuguese control. The British hoped in this way to break down the Spanish and Portuguese colonial monopolies and expand their trade, or, as William Cobbett, a democratic reformer, viewed the policy, to secure a market for their calicoes and to subject the Latin-Americans to the "slavery" of British financial and commercial control. In any case, the development and application of the Monroe Doctrine set bounds to British territorial expansion to an extent hardly foreseen by the British at the time of its promulgation.

Canadian boundary disputes were adjusted in 1842. British attempts to intervene in the revolt of Texas against Mexico for the purpose of obtaining a sphere of influence in Texas hastened the annexation of Texas to the United States in 1845. The Oregon country, by an agreement between Great Britain and the United States, was to be occupied jointly by the two nations pending adjustment of disputed boundaries. After much controversy and a threat of war, it was agreed in 1846 that the parallel of 49° north latitude, west as well as east of the Rocky Mountains, should become the southern boundary of the British domain.

Before the acquisition of Texas and California and the discovery of gold in California, American interest in the Caribbean area was secondary to that of Great Britain. The acquisition of the Texas coastline, and particularly the rapid settlement of the Pacific coast, revived interest in the Caribbean area, Central America, and the Isthmus of Panama, and in the control of transportation facilities, particularly of a projected Isthmian canal. Both countries sought concessions, and in the Clayton-Bulwer Treaty of 1850 they agreed to the neutralization of the proposed canal and to equality of rights. This treaty was later abrogated in favor of the United States. Its significance was primarily in checking British advances and preventing British ascendancy in this extremely strategic area, vital alike for political influence and for naval and commercial power.

The United States offered a challenge to British imperial expansion also in shipbuilding, shipping, and trade. The gross tonnage of vessels built in the United States and documented for American shipowners from 1821 to 1830 averaged only 89,372 a year; from 1831 to 1840, 118,960; from 1841 to 1850, 185,309; and from 1851 to 1860, 366,603. The documented gross tonnage of the merchant marine in 1830 was 1,192,000, and in 1860, 5,354,000. The tonnage employed in foreign trade in 1830 was 538,000, and in 1860, 2,379,000. Vessels of the United States entering United Kingdom ports in 1830 totaled 214,000 tons, and in 1861, 1,749,000 tons.

After the Civil War, American rivalry in shipbuilding and shipping no longer menaced British ascendancy. American gross tonnage engaged in foreign trade in 1870 was 1,449,000 as compared with 2,379,000 in 1860, and before 1890 it had fallen below 1,000,000. American vessels entered at United Kingdom ports in 1870 had a tonnage of only 629,000 in contrast with 1,749,000 in 1861. Among the causes were the Civil War, the diversion of energy and capital into railroad construction and internal development, and the transition to iron ships equipped with steam power, in the construction of which the British had decisive advantages.

## The Revival of Imperialism in Other Countries

The second and third quarters of the century were characterized by an unparalleled ascendancy of British imperialism and trade. This ascendancy was menaced by the appearance of a new set of circumstances that were destined to alter profoundly the status of Great Britain in world economy and world politics. Among these circumstances was the growth of nationalism.

The American Civil War restricted for a time the role of the United States as a world power but gave unquestioned authority to the Federal government and ascendancy to the industrial interests of the East. The temporary preoccupation of Americans after the Civil War with the settlement and development of the frontier soon gave place to a revival of interest in commercial and territorial expansion beyond their borders. The Franco-Prussian War of 1870 overthrew the Empire of Napoleon III but led to the establishment of the Third Republic in France on an intensely nationalistic basis. The government of the Third Republic, although unstable in the personnel of its cabinet, proved to be highly flexible and responsive to the interests of the commercial and industrial groups already committed, under earlier governments, to colonial expansion. The political unification of Germany and of Italy prepared the way for the emergence of new imperialistic ambitions. Russia, although checked by the Crimean War, soon resumed her expansion southward toward the Mediterranean, the Persian Gulf, and India, and continued her development of Far Eastern connections. The reorganization and westernization of the Japanese government was accompanied by imperialistic ambitions.

Paralleling the rise of strong nationalistic governments was the spread of industrialism. The adoption of new techniques and forms of business organization was accompanied by the growth of industry and trade and of urban centers; by new requirements for imported food and raw materials; by an intensified pressure on export markets; by a flow of surplus large incomes not needed for investment at home into foreign and colonial channels; by the establishment of world-wide commercial and financial connections; and by the pressure of the interested groups on their governments to utilize public agencies for the world-wide advancement and protection of their interests. The opening up of China and of Africa was in part a result of these developments, and in turn it provided a powerful stimulus to imperial rivalry. The economic depression of the years 1874 to 1879 revealed the dependence of private industrial enterprise on an expanding economy for the profitable utilization of accumulations of surplus income beyond the control of the masses of domestic consumers. The depression contributed materially to the succeeding era of intensified imperial rivalry.

# CHAPTER 21

# ECONOMISTS, REFORMERS, AND CHARTISTS

———◆———

## The System of Natural Liberty

The growth of opposition to monopolies and to the regulatory policies of mercantilism was accompanied by the development of theories of natural liberty, the natural rights of man, individualism, pursuit of self-interest, and *laissez faire*. These doctrines found expression in the writings of the physiocrats, Adam Smith, and the "philosophers" such as Voltaire and Rousseau. They were dominant in the American Revolution, the French Revolution, and the new industries which were transforming England in the latter part of the eighteenth century.

The advocates of these ideas were naturally confronted with the problem of reconciling individualism and the free pursuit of self-interest with larger social and group interests. It was urged that in an ethical or ideal sense the *ego* and the *alter* are not antagonistic but complementary. Actually, conflicts of interest exist, and these were recognized and even emphasized by many of the advocates of individualism and *laissez faire*. These conflicts were alleged to be aggravated, however, by monopoly and by public regulations and restrictions on competition. It was urged that in a state of free competition, conflicting interests are balanced and counteracted in an equilibrium which assures the greatest possible general welfare. Competition, wrote John Stuart Mill in his *Principles of Political Economy*, published in 1848, is not a "baneful and antisocial principle"; on the contrary, "every restriction of it is an evil, and every extension of it, even if for the time injuriously affecting some class of laborers, is always an ultimate good."

The beneficence of competition was attributed largely to the relationship between demand, supply, and prices. Demand is the basic fact of economic society, the force which animates economic activity. It was maintained that if the supplying of demand is actuated by competitive production, efficiency becomes necessary, profits will be merely sufficient to induce producers to supply the demand, prices will be as low as competitive costs of production permit, and consumers will have the benefits of competitive prices.

## The " Laws " of the Classical Economists

T. R. Malthus, David Ricardo, Nassau Senior, John Stuart Mill, and other writers of the classical or individualistic school developed a comprehensive system of " laws" applying to competitive society. Most of the writers asserted that these "laws" were in accord with social well-being, but the economist, they held, is on the same plane as the physicist, whose function is primarily to understand physical laws and secondarily to facilitate man's adaptation thereto. The physicist deals with the dual universe of matter and energy. The economist is concerned with the dual system of producing and consuming wealth. But the physicist makes no assumptions as to an "ideal" physical universe or as to what would happen in a hypothetical world; he concerns himself with what happens in the actual world. The classical economists, however, assumed as "ideal" or "natural" a state of individualism and free competition; they described what they believed would happen in such a state; and they then made the unwarranted assumption that these hypothetical occurrences are in accord with natural "laws." They observed the actual course of producing and distributing wealth, and, while recognizing limitations on free competition, held that scientific analysis must deal with the hypothetical state of perfect competition. "Our reasonings," wrote Mill, "must, in general, proceed as if the known and natural effects of competition were actually produced by it."

Three principal forms of income were recognized — the profits of owners of capital (as distinguished from land) and of entrepreneurs or "undertakers" (interest being regarded as a form of profit); the wages of labor; and the rent of land or "natural agents" (including returns on capital spent for permanent improvements). Profits in the form of interest were viewed as a reward for abstinence or saving; the profits of entrepreneurs were the difference between interest and gross profits and were described as "the wages of super-intendence" or rewards for "the exertions and risks of the under-taker." Separate provision for risk took the form of payments for insurance. Thus the three forms of profit were interest, insurance fees, and wages of superintendence, corresponding to the functions of abstinence, risk, and exertion.

Although variations were recognized in rates of profit, it was held that perfect competition would bring about a minimum rate compatible with inducement to exercise the functions of abstinence, risk, and superintendence, and would tend to create an equality in the rates for the various users of capital; for the unimpeded law of supply and demand would bring about a constant transfer and redistribution of capital in accord with varying opportunities for profit. This is a typical instance of the hypothetical nature of the classical "laws." The system of investment and enterprise was assumed to be an unimpeded flow, actuated by supply and demand under competition, whereas, if figurative language is permissible in scientific analysis, it may more significantly be described as a structure. Transfers of capital and labor take place but are inevitably impeded by rigidities and obstructions incident to institutions, customs, localized attachments, property rights, natural if not legal monopolies, and the varying and uncertain effect of abstinence. Abstinence from consumption was regarded as a positive function correlative with competitive investment and desire for profits. The actual condition of centralized ownership of income and potential capital, even in the days of the early classical economists, gave to abstinence a quality of hypothesis and unreality as a motive for investment and a basis for reward. Owners of large incomes were often free to invest or to refrain from investing their income, and to transfer or refrain from transferring their investments. Rewards going to owners of capital were mainly determined not by the "natural law" of abstinence but by the juridical or political laws of ownership. John Stuart Mill, himself, held that while "the laws and conditions of the production of wealth partake of the character of physical truths," with "nothing optional or arbitrary in them," the distribution of wealth "depends on the laws and customs of society." This much-quoted passage is in his chapter on property, and he referred primarily to the ownership of property rather than to the distribution of income. He recognized the effects of ownership, particularly of land, on the proportionate shares of income, but he failed to recognize the limitations of abstinence as a motive for investment or a basis for reward. The large rewards go not to abstainers from consumption in any vital sense but to owners of property sufficient to afford a surplus income beyond their own needs; and the fact of ownership enables the owners to impose an involuntary abstinence or to prevent a voluntary abstinence from consumption on the part of nonowners.

The rewards of productive labor — wages — were described as depending, in the case of aggregate wage payments, on a fixed "wages fund" consisting substantially of the income used, as "circulating capital," for financing the productive process. The amount of the "fund" is "fixed" by the strength of the inducement to abstain from consumption (to save) for investment in the productive process, and is thus controlled by economic "laws."

The demand for productive labor was thus viewed as restricted to the use of this fixed fund; and the average rate of wages was regarded as dependent on the supply of laborers who offer themselves for hire. Since the aggregate wage was held to be beyond control, it was believed that if some laborers receive higher rates, others must work for less or be thrown out of work, unless the number of available laborers is reduced. But the Malthusian "law" of population — the tendency of population to increase and to press upon the means of subsistence — means that wages, through competition for jobs, tend to remain near the subsistence level, that is, near the cost of rearing workers or the cost of production applied to labor as a factor in the general process of production. Some of the classical economists, however, occasionally indulged in moods of compassion for the worker and allowed themselves to entertain the hope that the general progress of society might lead to amelioration through the workers' voluntary control of the size of their families.

John Stuart Mill was long a rigorous exponent of the so-called "iron law of wages." In 1869, in an article in the *Fortnightly Review*, he modified his views. The "wages fund," he then stated, was not already produced and merely allocated to wages in the current stage of production, but was derived from current production; and a rise in wage rates might be possible by reducing the proportion of the product which would otherwise go to employers. This amended view was not included in the subsequent edition of his *Principles of Political Economy*, and he continued to regard a reduction in the size of workers' families as the crux of the problem of working-class amelioration.

The classical economists failed in general to sense the fact that employment and wage schedules are based largely on anticipated gross income; that gross income depends on the market for the product (volume of demand and price); and that the market for the product depends vitally on the allocation of income, including the amount going to employees. It is true that the employees of a given employer count so slightly in his particular market that this fact, in a competitive struggle for restricting the costs of production, is likely to be an insignificant force. As a result, the consumer market among workers is restricted, and the larger nonworker incomes devoted to investment tend to become sterile because of the restricted demand for the output of business enterprise.  These facts constitute a dilemma not merely for wage earners but for the entire economy.  The total wage was correctly viewed as being limited by the amount of capital available for the employment of labor, and the average wage as a function of demand and supply.  But significant analysis begins with these facts and must include particularly an understanding of the forces which affect the use of capital for the employment of labor.

Profits, which, in Mill's phrase, included interest, insurance, and the rewards of superintendence, were explained by abstinence, risk, and exertion.  Wages were viewed as an element in the cost of production, the aggregate amount being fixed by the "wages fund" saved from consumption, and the average wage being fixed in general by the supply or number of laborers.  Both profits and wages, it was held, involve either abstinence or risk or effort, although in the case of labor the effort is not the basis of the reward, and both fall within the system of competitive production costs.

The third form of reward — rent — was frankly recognized, however, as being beyond the competitive system.  Rent is the reward to the owners of "natural agents," mainly land.  The use of land requires labor and capital, and the competition of workers and capitalists will tend to reduce their rewards from the use of land to the general levels of wages and profits, whether the labor and capital are applied to the most productive land or to land that will yield an output barely equal to the costs of production.  Since the more productive land has an output above the costs of production necessary to bring it into use, the output above this level goes to the owner as rent.  The additional output is rent in the economic sense, whether the land is used by the owner or by others.  It is a reward not of abstinence or of risk or of exertion, but of ownership.  The "law" of rent is associated particularly with the work of David Ricardo.  Nassau Senior even went so far as to designate as rent all income above the competitive cost of production.  Even inheritance was viewed as rent.  By a logical subterfuge he was thus able to escape the dilemma of differential rates of profit and of wages and salaries above the level fixed by competitive costs, and yet to preserve in appearance the validity of the "laws" of competition.

Rent in the sense of a differential between the net output above cost of production from different units of land of varying productivity is implicit in the varying productivity of different units of land. The differential, as Mill pointed out, goes, "by the arrangements of society," to those who possess "exclusive power" over the land, that is, to the owners. But outside of a purely hypothetical regime of perfect fluidity of labor and capital — of absolutely unrestricted competition — such a differential exists in respect to capital as well as land, and indeed in respect to labor also, the differential in the case of employees going mainly to the purchaser of the labor (the employer) or, through the payment of interest by the employer, to the owner of capital. In the case of capital and of purchased labor as well as of land, the rewards are based essentially on ownership. In the case of large incomes from capital, abstinence from consumption is one of the will-o'-the-wisps pursued by the classical economists in their efforts to escape from the quagmire of actual economy into the competitive upland of their imagination.

## The System of Natural Liberty: *Laissez Faire*

British policy in the nineteenth century tended in the direction of the ideas of free competition and *laissez faire* embodied in the teachings of the economists. On the eve of the century, in 1795, a member of Parliament asserted that "trade, industry, and barter would always find their natural level, and be impeded by regulations which violated their natural operation, and deranged their proper effect." Even earlier the economic trend had been in the direction of individualism and new forms of competitive enterprise. A significant phase of the industrial revolution was the superior competitive power of the industrialists who adopted the new techniques and the more flexible modes of organizing production and markets. Because of the industrial revolution and of Great Britain's peculiar advantages in respect to colonies, trade, sea power, and government, British economy as a whole had achieved a superior competitive power, and exporters were interested in the removal of obstacles in the way of the expansion of the world market. It was therefore no accident, no merely casual exercise of the intellectual faculties of Englishmen, that created the classical system of economic thought. In a sense that system was an attempt to rationalize and give intellectual sanction to the practices and the ambitions of businessmen, although the economists, in a manner characteristic of men of thought, imputed to the emerging system of enterprise a logic and consistency hardly recognizable by businessmen themselves.

While classical economic thought was in a sense a by-product of the new system of enterprise, the economists nevertheless exerted much influence on public policies in the direction of *laissez faire*, and the new policies in turn facilitated the progress of individualism and competitive enterprise. The new economic doctrines were extremely important because they retained their ascendancy throughout the nineteenth century and in modified form are still widely accepted.

The most notable development in the field of *laissez faire* was the introduction of free trade, which extended even to the repeal of restrictions on the export of machinery and on the emigration of skilled workers. This remarkable transformation of public policy has already been described. The first notable victory of *laissez faire* over industrial regulation of the mercantilistic type was the repeal in 1784 of William Pitt's excise law, which had imposed on the cotton industry a detailed system of regulation characteristic of the earlier legislation. The law was opposed significantly on the ground that it deprived the manufacturers of "personal liberty and the free exercise of their property." In Great Britain there had been a comparatively early and extensive decline of monopolies and of guild and corporate restrictions. The decadence of public control of employers in respect to their employees was evidenced by the repeal in 1813 and 1814 of the wages and apprenticeship clauses of the Statute of Artificers of 1563. Thereafter employers had full legal freedom in respect to "hiring and firing." The Statute of Artificers of 1563, commonly called the Statute of Apprentices, and various other laws had regulated hours and required justices of the peace to adjust wages in accord with fluctuations in prices on the basis of "scarcity or plenty." Although these laws had long been obsolescent, their repeal was opposed by the workers. Because of the repeal or obsolescence of these laws, public policy for the protection of workers was limited substantially to the grant of poor relief to support the unemployed and to supplement the income of those whose wages were below the subsistence level. Even this policy was altered by the new Poor Law of 1834, under which, in the contemporary phrase, the Poor Law guardians who administered the law were viewed as guardians not of the poor but of the poor rates. Detailed regulatory measures applying to various industries were repealed, as the laws relating to the woolen industry of the West Riding of Yorkshire in 1822; the linen industry of Scotland in 1823; the Spitalfields silk industry in 1824; the leather industry in 1824 and 1827 ; and baking and the sale of bread in London in 1822 and elsewhere in 1836.   The Combination Acts of 1799 and 1800 and various earlier laws restricting working-class action were repealed in 1824, although a more moderate measure was enacted in 1825, and common-law limitations on labor organizations remained.   In 1833 land tenures and transfers were simplified, the East India Company's commercial monopoly was abolished, and the powers of the Bank of England were extended.   The new Poor Law of 1834 included among its provisions a modification of restrictions on change of residence by the poor and facilitated the flow of labor from place to place.   The usury laws were repealed in 1854.

Such measures as these, together with the abandonment of the elaborate and detailed protective system, wrought a remarkable transformation in public policy, although many of the laws had long been disregarded.   Thus a woolen manufacturer testified, in connection with the repeal of the law for regulating the industry in the West Riding of Yorkshire, that he had technically incurred a fine of £100 daily for twenty-five years.

A significant aspect alike of economic theory and of public policy in the system of *laissez faire* under competitive private enterprise was the status of labor.   A logical consequence of the system was the conception of labor as an element in the cost of production. Labor, like machinery or materials, was purchased by entrepreneurs for use in the process of production, and was therefore viewed as falling under the laws of competition and supply and demand. Labor organizations, when utilized for interfering with the free, competitive purchase of labor, were therefore regarded as contravening both the "laws" of economics and the common-law provisions against monopoly and restraint of trade.   Individualism and *laissez faire* thus applied to laborers as possessors of capacity to work, in quest of purchasers of labor.   But ownership of land and capital is distinguishable from the individuals who own them ; while capacity to work, on the other hand, is a part, and in the case of the worker dependent on his labor, a most essential part, of the personality.   This was recognized by some of the exponents of individualism and *laissez faire*, as John Stuart Mill, who advocated small peasant proprietorships and co-operative industrial production. For the only escape of the laborer from his dilemma was in ceasing to sell his labor and in becoming an owner of property or an entrepreneur.   This in turn was possible only under a system of one-man enterprise or under its antithesis, a system of socialized enterprise.

## Dissenters

Many economists were not in accord with the doctrines commonly described as the classical system or with the *laissez-faire* policies of government, but they were overwhelmed by their more noted contemporaries.   John Stuart Mill himself, although he came to be recognized as the outstanding exponent of the system, was in a sense convinced against his will.  He accepted in general the Malthusian view of population, the "iron law of wages," the Ricardian doctrine of rent, and the other "laws" of the "dismal science." But in conflict with his ideas were his warm social sympathies and his desire for reforms.   He referred to the "provisional" nature of economic doctrines as applying only during the survival of the system of private property.

Mill asserted that an economic system "which divides society absolutely into two portions, the payers of wages and the receivers of them, the first counted by thousands and the last by millions, is neither fit for, nor capable of, indefinite duration."  In a much-quoted passage he stated that "if the institution of private property necessarily carried with it as a consequence, that the produce of labor should be apportioned as we now see it, almost in an inverse ratio to the labor — the largest portions to those who have never worked at all, the next largest to those whose work is almost nominal, and so in a descending scale, the remuneration dwindling as the work grows harder and more disagreeable, until the most fatiguing and exhausting bodily labor cannot count with certainty on being able to earn even the necessaries of life; if this or communism were the alternative, all the difficulties, great or small, of communism would be but as dust in the balance."  But he believed that the existing wage system might be supplanted by co-operative industrial production; that small proprietorships in agriculture might be developed, as in France; that rent, large inheritances, and other large incomes based on property should be progressively socialized by means of taxation; and that the laws of property should be subjected to radical revision.

Objection and dissent found expression in various forms.   Jeremy Bentham's philosophy of utilitarianism — summed up by him in the dictum, "The sole object of government ought to be the greatest happiness of the greatest possible number of the community" — gave rise to a voluminous literature and was made the basis of many conflicting conceptions.   Bentham, born in 1748, was influenced by individualistic eighteenth-century philosophy. But he discarded its pseudo-historical basis, as the doctrine of the social contract. A believer in individualism, he nevertheless refused to accept the new economic doctrines as natural "laws," and insisted that all institutions, traditions, legislation, and customs should be subjected to critical scrutiny and rejected, accepted, or reshaped in the light of his general principle of utility. He was disappointed in his early ambition for a political career, but he profoundly influenced the course of legislative reform. He was described by Mill as "the most influential and on the whole the most eminent philosophical writer of recent times."

Among literary men there was a tradition of dissent and even of revolt. An outstanding critic was Thomas Carlyle. In a strident, dyspeptic style — which incited a contemporary to say that its author ought to starve — he denounced the economic doctrines of the time as a "pig philosophy," Mammonism, "naked egoism, vulturous greediness." The workhouse "bastilles" he compared with Dante's hell. In sarcasm he denounced the philosophy of overproduction, which he ascribed to the "governing class." "We accuse you of overproducing: you are criminally guilty of producing shirts, breeches, hats, shoes, and commodities in a frightful over-abundance. And now there is a glut and your operatives cannot be fed!" If men cannot control their destinies but must starve under *laissez faire*, with its "inane jargons and temporary market-cries" and "ever-new forms of quackhood," England "will cease to exist among nations," in spite of her "cotton-spinning and thrice-miraculous mechanism." Carlyle poured scorn upon the contemporary governing class but had no faith in democracy. He believed that hope lay in a vaguely defined leadership of true aristocrats, who would make themselves worthy of the adulation and devotion of the masses by presiding over "the distribution and apportionment of the wages of work done" and seeing that "there went no laborer without his hire."

William Cobbett, a somewhat earlier and extremely popular writer, denounced the ruling classes no less vigorously than Carlyle but held that the extension of democracy was essential. In his numerous books and especially in his journal, the *Political Register*, he advocated Parliamentary reform, supported working-class organizations, and in general represented and powerfully stimulated the protests of the lower classes against the prevailing conditions of labor and the policies of the government. He held that low wages and unemployment were caused by lack of demand for the products of labor, and that this lack of demand was due to "want of means in the nation at large to purchase the goods." He was particularly scornful of "tax-eaters" who drained the country's wealth through interest on the public debt, and of philanthropists who sought to free the West Indian slaves but "wallowed in luxuries" proceeding from the labor of British workers forced to subsist on cold potatoes while the "black slaves" dined on "Indian meal, pork, and rice."

Cobbett was scornful of Wilberforce and other aristocratic reformers and philanthropists, but they were the ones who first made effective protests against *laissez faire*. The struggle of the industrialists for Parliamentary representation and for the repeal of the Corn Laws led many of the aristocratic landed classes to inquire into conditions in the factories and to advocate the regulation of factory labor. With few exceptions the employers of industrial labor bitterly opposed such legislation, and they were supported by most of the economists. Among the manufacturers a notable exception was Robert Owen, who favored rigorous factory laws. This, however, was a minor aspect of his dissent from the prevailing political and economic system. He worked out an elaborate philosophy and a detailed social plan, which, in its economic aspects, involved working-class organization and co-operative production.

### Revival of Regulatory Functions: the Factory Acts

The abandonment of regulatory functions by the British government, as evidenced by the repeal of the law relating to apprenticeship and various other laws, was partly a result of the obsolescence of these laws and their lack of applicability to changed industrial conditions. New laws adapted to the new conditions were long delayed because of the prevailing individualism and hostility to any form of restriction of business. The most significant revival of the regulatory function in the nineteenth century was the control of the conditions of factory labor. The nature of the mass of evidence concerning the status of factory workers under *laissez faire* and unrestricted competition may be illustrated by the testimony before a Parliamentary committee in 1816. A cotton manufacturer stated that children as young as five years of age were employed; that the usual hours of work were fourteen, some mills requiring fifteen; and that some mills allowed no intermission for meals. A magistrate testified that the warm, humid, unventilated mills, with cotton lint, or "flew," polluting the air, induced a condition which required the frequent administration of emetics. A physician whose father-in-law owned a large mill testified "with the greatest reluctance" that the children, when they first came to the mills, with the close, humid atmosphere and high temperature, were seized with a mild fever and were subject to a subsequent debility. There was no protection from the machinery, and he had "too often" seen workers crushed to death, and the mangling of the hands of the children was "a very common thing." He stated further that children, so far as he knew, were never allowed to sit down during working hours; that they frequently walked two miles from their homes to the mills; and that the factories in his community usually operated from 6 o'clock in the morning until 7 o'clock at night in summer, and from 7 until 8 in the winter. Among the workers "scrofula is common indeed, and consumption extremely common."

The first Factory Act, passed in 1802, applied to the children of paupers — the "pauper apprentices" who were bound out by parish officials to cotton manufacturers. The law provided that the factories and dormitories should be washed twice a year with quicklime and fitted with windows or openings for ventilation; that the hours of actual work of the "apprentices" should be not more than twelve, between 6 A.M. and 9 P.M.; that they should be furnished with more than one set of garments; that not more than two children should be forced to use the same bed in the dormitories; and that they should be required to attend church and be "instructed in the principles of the Christian religion." The law was not regarded as a violation of the rights of employers and of the principle of "freedom of contract," because the children were the wards of the parishes. Perhaps the most significant fact regarding the law was that it remained from the beginning virtually a dead letter. Richard Arkwright, Jr., fourteen years later said that he believed his mills had been visited by inspectors only twice during the fourteen years.

In 1819 an act was passed applying to free children in cotton factories, barring children under nine from the mills, and limiting the hours of those from nine to sixteen years old to twelve per day except for the making up of lost time. This law also was not enforced. The law of 1833 applied to children in textile mills. It excluded children under nine, provided for the gradual introduction of a nine-hour day for children from nine to eighteen, and imposed a number of moderate restrictions. The law was chiefly notable, however, for providing for paid inspectors and machinery of enforcement. In 1842 the Coal Mines Regulation Act extended the regulatory principle to women. Women not already employed and girls were excluded, as well as boys under ten years of age. In 1844 provision was made for the half-time employment of children; and in 1847 the Ten Hours Act applied to women and young people, but in practice affected men as well. Men were excluded out of deference to the principles of *laissez faire* and freedom of contract. There were numerous provisions relating to such matters as sanitation, the fencing of dangerous machinery, and the education of children who worked in the factories. The regulations gradually became so detailed and elaborate as to form a code. An important codification of the laws was made in 1878.

### Development of Governmental Functions in the New Industrial Society

Prominent among the functions of modern governments is their statistical work. The first British census was in 1801, and the information then collected was fragmentary except for an approximately full count of the population. Various writers of the eighteenth century had begun to emphasize the importance of "political arithmetic" and had made efforts to estimate the extent of changes, especially in population. Official statistics mainly concerned public finances, including revenues from trade, and incidentally some information regarding volume of trade. Patent records, later collected and classified, are comparatively adequate. Parliamentary inquiries and special investigations from time to time in connection with controversial questions and the formulation of public policies afford the principal sources of statistical information, but they include a vast amount of unreliable statistics presented for the purpose of influencing opinion or policy.

After the first census of 1801 there was a rapid expansion of the field covered by the censuses and an improvement in the technique of collecting data. In the field of business the progress was rapid in the collecting of data relating to trade, shipping, shipbuilding, minerals, joint-stock companies, banking, and the finances of friendly societies. The latter were not business enterprises, but in the economic as well as the social life of the working classes and the lower middle classes they played a considerable role. Statistics of joint-stock companies and of friendly societies were collected by public registrars concerned with these institutions, and there were also registrars of births, deaths, and marriages.

Inspectors of various kinds also collected statistical and other data in connection with their other functions. There were poor-law inspectors, railway inspectors, and inspectors of factories, of mines, and of weights and measures. The collecting of statistics was in part a mere matter of fact-finding for the information of the public, and in part merely incidental to public administration, as in the case of trade statistics connected with the customs and excise laws. But the growth of statistical services was facilitated by the development of positive and regulatory functions of government and in turn it promoted the extension of these functions, as in connection with the factory laws and public health administration.

Among the mid-century extensions of the functions of government were services relating to education and public health. In 1848 the General Board of Health was created. In 1833, following the reform of Parliament in 1832, the first national grant of £20,000 was made for elementary education. In 1870, three years after the extension of the franchise to the working classes, school boards were established and provision was made for an elementary school, to be subject to public inspection, in every district. These measures were not primarily economic, although they were clearly attempts to adapt the work of government to the needs of the new industrial society. Since they were essentially noneconomic, they were not really opposed to the prevailing *laissez-faire* conception. Certain other measures, however, were distinctly in the field of enterprise.

The government had long maintained a postal service, but on a very small scale and at rates which restricted communication except by private means. In 1840 penny postage was adopted, the prepayment of letters by stamps was introduced, and the service was reorganized and vastly expanded. The number of pieces handled increased from 82,000,000 in 1839 to 877,000,000 in 1870. In 1848 books as well as letters and newspapers were accepted for mailing; and in 1863, trade patterns and samples. The general parcel-post system was not adopted until 1882. The handling of money orders was begun in 1838, and after 1861 the principal post offices served as savings banks. In 1868 the telegraphic system was acquired by the government and placed under the administration of the Post Office; and later the telephone was nationalized.

## The Early Labor Movement and Its Failure

The working-class heritage from the medieval guild system was the journeyman's guild. In some of the skilled trades, combinations of journeymen served as nuclei for trade-unions of the modern type, but the transformation of industry by the industrial revolution further reduced the importance of an already obsolescent system of labor organization. Another form of organization among workers was the friendly society. This was extremely popular among workers but was primarily devoted to social and mutual-benefit activities. This fact led to the legalization of friendly societies and to their public encouragement "to alleviate that immense charge with which the public is loaded in the support of the poor and provide by savings of industry [the wages of members] for the comfort of distress." The friendly societies, especially in the new industries of the north, had shown tendencies toward illegal trade-union activities. As a result, the various acts applying to them provided for public supervision and limitation of their activities to their avowed functions of maintaining and administering mutual-benefit funds. Before the legalization of trade-unions, many of the friendly societies were nevertheless in purpose disguised trade-unions. They were even more significant in affording experience and self-discipline as a preparation for the later trade-union movement.

In addition to the common-law restrictions on labor organization, such as the master-and-servant doctrine and the prohibition of conspiracies in restraint of trade, there were many statutory limitations, notably a section of the Statute of Artificers of 1563 which forbade workers to leave their work unfinished. The repeal in 1824 of the Combination Acts of 1799 and 1800 and of various earlier statutory limitations was followed by an outburst of trade-union organization. The movement was encouraged and in a measure directed by Robert Owen, a prominent cotton manufacturer. Owen formulated an elaborate plan for social reorganization on a co-operative basis. The plan grew out of his realization of the vast increase in the productive powers of industry, combined with the failure of society to make "proper arrangements" for the "advantageous application" of the new productive powers. In his *Report to the County of Lanark* (1821), he formulated plans for "practicable arrangements" by which "the whole population might participate in the benefits derivable from the increase of scientific productive power." These arrangements were to consist primarily of co-operative communities as "the first nucleus or division of society." Opposition from various sources led Owen to direct his attention more and more to the possibilities of utilizing working-class organizations. His optimistic and somewhat vague ideas of social reorganization were reflected in the early trade-union movement.

The first organizations formed after the limited legalization of unions in 1824 were soon disrupted by the enforcement of surviving legal restrictions and by the depression following the collapse of the boom of 1824-1825. Soon thereafter Owen became active in the movement. In 1829 efforts were made to form a Grand General Union of the United Kingdom among spinners and piecers. In 1830 a more comprehensive organization was launched — the National Association for the Protection of Labor, including workers in a large number of industries. In 1832 a Builders' Union was formed on a national scale. The movement reached its culmination and its debacle in the Grand National Consolidated Trades Union of 1834, inspired directly by Owen. This organization included heterogeneous units throughout the kingdom. Its avowed aims included co-operation, education, and other features of Owen's larger plan. But its main immediate object was the eight-hour day, to be achieved if necessary by means of a general strike. Owen, in advocating the eight-hour day, stated that the demand was moderate and in reality a concession to "the old prejudices of society," and that a four-hour day, "under proper arrangements," would "saturate the world with wealth." Before the strike could be organized, employers resorted to widespread lockouts and to "the presentation of the document" — an offer to restore workers to their jobs only on condition that they renounce all connection with combinations.

In addition to the internal weakness of heterogeneous local units hurriedly formed and loosely joined together in a national organization, various other factors contributed to the failure of the early trade-union movement. Common-law weapons were still effective when enforced against combinations, and such tactics as the threat of a general strike kindled enforcement zeal. The hostility of employers was reinforced by the prevailing social conceptions of the subordinate and submissive role of employees, and also by the accepted economic doctrines, especially the Malthusian "law" of population and the "wages-fund" theory. A typical opponent of unionism argued in 1834, on the basis of economic "laws," that "wages are not dependent on the will of those who pay them," and "can only be altered by changing the proportion between the number of laborers and the funds set apart for their maintenance." Workers "might as well attempt to turn the sun from its course as

to extract from their employers the same wages as at present, and
to give a third less of their labor in return." In addition, working-
class interests were increasingly diverted into other channels, such
as the agitation for the reform and democratization of Parliament,
the work of the Anti-Corn-Law League, and the co-operative
movement.

## The Chartist Movement

The working classes supported their employers in the struggle
for the Reform Bill of 1832, but were gravely disappointed when
they discovered, according to the London Working Men's Association, that only 14 per cent of the adult male population could vote
for members of Parliament and that from various causes the members of the reformed Parliament had "interests for the most part
foreign or directly opposed to the true interests of the great body of
the people." With the complete failure in 1834 of the movement
for organizing the workers, there was disillusion with trade-unionism
as well as with political action by the reformed Parliament. Working-class leaders then reverted to agitation for the further reform of
Parliament. In this way they hoped to achieve desired changes in
public policy and to remove political obstacles from the path of
trade-union organization.

To this end, various political associations were formed, notably
the London Working Men's Association of 1836. Early in 1837 this
association presented to Parliament a petition calling for electoral
districts approximately equal in population; universal suffrage for
adult males; removal of property qualifications for membership in
the House of Commons; payment of members; secret ballot; and
annual election of members of the House of Commons. The petition containing these proposals was formulated as a bill, which came
to be known as the People's Charter, and the ensuing nation-wide
organization for its advocacy came to be known as the Chartist
Movement. But while the movement was political in its immediate
objects, its ultimate aim was essentially economic. The People's
Charter stated that government as then organized deprived persons
of rights and powers and vested them in property, and that this
meant in effect that a few thousand property owners were given
"tremendous power" over "the lives, liberty, and labor of the unrepresented millions." The military and civil forces, the revenues,
the relief of the poor, the press, and the monetary arrangements
were thus controlled in a manner "by which the laboring classes

may be silently plundered or suddenly dismissed from employment." Such arrangements, the Charter stated, make impossible the exercise of the true function of government, which is the securing of "the greatest amount of happiness to all classes of society."

The leaders of the movement included philosophical radicals inspired by Bentham's utilitarianism; Tory reformers, notably Richard Oastler and Rev. J. R. Stephens, advocates of factory legislation and opponents of the Poor Law of 1834; and Owenites, devoted to a co-operative reorganization of society as a means of escape from the dilemma of the wage system. Some of these were not from the ranks of labor. Many of the working-class leaders, more strictly speaking, had no clear-cut ideas or program save the breaking up of what they denounced as the alliance of government with employers to exploit the workers. These leaders, especially in the north, appealed to "unshaven chins, blistered hands, and fustian jackets." In the south the skilled workers and their Benthamite and Owenite followers believed in "moral force." In the north the hard-pressed factory workers, led by such men as the fiery Feargus O'Connor, rapidly became adherents of "physical force" as a necessary mode of achieving their aims. There was a division, also, over the question of giving aid to the middle classes in their fight for the repeal of the Corn Laws, but the remembrance of the futile alliance with employers for the reform of Parliament in 1832, combined with the fear that the free importation of wheat would merely mean, for the workers, a reduction of wages, checked the movement toward a new alliance with the middle classes.

Several factors contributed to the decline of the movement. Long-continued failure to achieve its aims led on the one hand to discouragement and on the other hand to an accentuation of internal differences regarding aims and tactics. The advocacy of physical force led to the arrest of many of the leaders, to the breakup of gatherings, and to the dispersion of strikers. A rise of wages, a fall in retail prices, better enforcement of the Factory Acts, and a modification in 1847 of the Poor Law of 1834 contributed to a slight alleviation of distress. The final collapse of the organizations supporting the movement was occasioned by the ridicule attending the discovery of a large number of fictitious names on the petition of 1848. With the exception of annual Parliamentary elections, all of the six points of the Charter were finally adopted, but after the Chartist organization had collapsed.

## Co-operation

Robert Owen in 1834 stated that more than half a century earlier he had "discovered that there was some grievous error deep in the foundations of society." He repeatedly emphasized the paradox of the vast increase of productive powers accompanied by an increase of unemployment and a decrease of opportunity to consume the fruits of labor due to lack of "means of exchange coextensive with the means of production." His remedy was a reorganization of society on the basis of co-operative communities associated together for the mutually advantageous exchange of their surplus products. To this end he hoped to be able to utilize such organizations as the Grand National Consolidated Trades Union. This union included in its "Program and Manifesto" a somewhat vague plan for co-operative production and distribution, but was almost immediately disrupted. Numerous co-operative ventures were undertaken under the general impulse of Owen's ideas, and some are traceable to an earlier period, but most of them were short-lived.

John Stuart Mill, like Owen, perceived the paradox of the wages system in its failure to provide an income to wage earners as producers on the basis either of their production or of their needs. He asserted that if mankind is to "continue to improve," the predominant form of association must be "not that which can exist between a capitalist as chief, and workpeople without a voice in the management, but the association of the laborers themselves on terms of equality, collectively owning the capital with which they carry on their operations, and working under managers elected and removable by themselves."

The first co-operative organization which achieved outstanding success, the Rochdale Equitable Pioneers, founded in 1844, embodied in its aims the general conceptions of Owen and Mill but confined its immediate activity to the narrow field of retail trade. This fact, combined with the adoption of a set of simple principles of procedure, gave it a vitality and a permanent basis which previous groups had lacked. In consequence its members became literally the pioneers in one of the most important of modern economic movements, alike in capitalistic and in socialistic societies. The founders were 28 weavers of Rochdale, near Manchester. Their total capital consisted of £28. Their first store was the home of one of the members, and their stock in trade consisted of a few staple groceries. Goods were sold at prevailing market prices, and thus the antagonism of ordinary dealers was avoided. Each member was credited with a share of the surplus in proportion to his purchases. Sales were for cash only and thus the society avoided risks and financed its operations largely out of the current income of its members. Interest on the capital invested was limited to 5 per cent. A portion of the surplus of gross income over costs of operation was devoted to educational purposes. Larger questions of policy were subject to action by majority vote of the members without regard to the number of shares' held.

Within three decades the membership grew to about 8,000 and the volume of business to about £300,000. Many branches were established; and a wide variety of merchandise was handled, some of which was made in the society's own establishments. The Rochdale plan was widely adopted elsewhere, not only in England but also in other countries. In 1852 the societies were legally allowed to return to members their shares of the surplus in proportion to their purchases. They were also given, by various laws, the right to sell to nonmembers, to invest their funds in other societies, to incorporate under the limited liability laws, and to engage in wholesale trade. In 1863 the Co-operative Wholesale Society was formed. Production of some of the staple commodities was undertaken, and transportation facilities were acquired. A Co-operative Congress assembled in 1869 and authorized the establishment of a Co-operative Union with important educational and advisory functions.

Consumers' co-operation was in a sense self-propagating because it could be financed largely out of current purchases. Production, on the other hand, entailed problems of ownership, monopoly, investment, and risk which co-operative methods failed to solve except in limited fields for the most part subordinate to the consumers' societies. During the third quarter of the century, when consumers' co-operation was rapidly growing, there was a progressive expansion of British markets and improvement of working-class conditions, and attention was diverted, for the time, from efforts to utilize co-operation for the solution of the larger problems posed by Owen and Mill.

### Mid-century Revival of Trade-Unionism

The early trade-union movement declined rapidly after the disruption of the Grand National Consolidated Trades Union of 1834. The organizations associated with the Chartist Movement collapsed with the failure of the petition of 1848. But individual unions survived and became the organizing centers of a new type of unionism. One of the unions formed soon after the limited legalization of combinations in 1824 was the Journeymen Steam Engine and Machine Makers' and Millwrights' Friendly Society, dating from 1826. Based on craft-union principles and devoted to limited ends, it surmounted the various obstacles in the way of unionism during the second quarter of the century. Before the middle of the century the membership of its numerous branches totaled about 7,000, and the treasury of the society contained reserves amounting to £27,000. Each local branch had definite administrative duties, but there was a strong central organization. In 1851 smaller groups of national societies in the same general field were persuaded to join this group to form the Amalgamated Society of Engineers. The combined membership totaled 11,000, and the weekly contribution of one shilling by each member provided a solid financial basis not only for benefits to the members but also for concerted trade-union action on a large scale.

The Amalgamated Society of Engineers assumed an informal leadership in the organization of similar societies in other fields. Within a few years there were strong national federations not only of engineers but also of iron founders, carpenters, masons, and bricklayers. Each of these five societies was independent, but the leaders were regarded as an informal labor "cabinet," sometimes called the "Junta." In the northern textile centers trade-unionism of the new type soon developed, and in 1863 the Miners' National Union was formed. These various unions favored factory legislation and other public policies in the interest of labor, especially a further reform of Parliament and the extension of the ballot to workers. But their main interest was the improvement of the conditions of work for their own members — shorter hours, higher wages, and the exclusion of nonmembers through what came to be known as the union shop. The first annual Trades Union Congress was held in 1869.

In addition to national societies formed of local groups in the same craft or closely related crafts, there were local councils composed of various types of local unions. The Glasgow Trades Council was formed in 1857, and workers in several other cities soon followed the example of Glasgow. The London Trades Council, formed in 1861, was viewed as representing informally the interests of the unions throughout the country in legislation affecting labor.

### The Legal, Political, and Economic Advance of the Workers

The ill-defined legal status of trade-unions before 1867 is illustrated by the fact that the protection of their funds and the judicial settlement of disputes among members depended on resort to a provision of the law relating to friendly societies. Any other society that was not illegal was permitted by the law to record its rules with the Registrar of the Friendly Societies and to appeal to the courts for protection against maladministration of its funds. But early in 1867 a final decision was rendered against the Boilermakers' Union in a suit between the union and one of its local treasurers. The decision was based on the ground that trade-unions were illegal.

As a result of this judgment, the unions proposed an investigation by a royal commission. Employers also urged an investigation of alleged cases of violence by unions in their dealings with nonunion workers, particularly at Sheffield. A commission was appointed, and its report prepared the way for the removal, in 1871, of some of the legal obstacles in the way of the unions. Thereafter they were able to protect their funds, but picketing, "obstruction," "intimidation," and various other activities were punishable as criminal offenses, and the unions remained at the mercy of the courts, often unfriendly. The master-and-servant doctrine, although modified in 1867, continued to regard a breach of contract by an employee as an offense punishable by imprisonment, while such a breach by an employer was merely a civil offense. Trade-union law was further liberalized in 1876.

The year 1867 was a turning point in the political as well as the legal history of British labor. In that year the right to vote was extended to urban workers and a further move was made toward equal electoral districts. The secret ballot was adopted in 1872. In 1874 two labor members were elected to the House of Commons.

Various reform measures applying largely, although not exclusively, to the working classes included the abandonment of transportation for penal offenses, repeal of the laws allowing imprisonment for debt, amelioration of the penal code, improvement of prison conditions, and the development of elementary education. The lot of the working classes was improved by provisions in the Factory Acts for safeguards against dangerous machinery and unsanitary conditions. The hours of labor of children, young people, and women were reduced by successive Factory Acts, particularly the Ten Hours Act of 1847, and men were benefited indirectly because of the fact that their work could not be isolated from that of others in the same establishment.

The Ten Hours Bill was opposed vigorously by employers, as when John Bright asserted that it would force wages down and would have to be repealed as "a delusion practiced on the working classes." But the actual course of wages after its enactment was upward. Wages declined somewhat during the second quarter of the century, but since retail prices fell more rapidly, the purchasing power of workers' earnings was greater in 1850 than in 1825. During the third quarter of the century real wages rose approximately one third. But in 1825 wages had been so low that they were supplemented by poor relief in the case of a large part of the working population. The Poor Law of 1834 tended to force upon wage payments a larger part of the cost of supporting the workers. This was a period of rapid expansion — the "golden age" of British enterprise. Forms of income other than wages increased seemingly without limit. Wages, as an element in the cost of production, were basically restricted to competitive levels. But three important factors enabled the wage-earning classes to check for a time the devastating effects of competition and to improve their condition in an absolute sense if not in comparison with the status of other economic groups. These three factors were association, the changing structure of industry, and the dominant role of Great Britain in world economy. After the middle of the century the growth of trade-unions, friendly societies, and co-operative societies strengthened the influence of the workers alike on employers and on the government and enabled them to make more effective use of their earnings in improving their standard of living. The changing structure of industry increased the proportion of workers in the heavy industries as compared with agriculture, textiles, etc., and thereby increased the proportion of skilled male workers able to command higher wages. The increased export of British capital gave employment to low-paid labor in other regions and made British investments increasingly profitable. This circumstance, combined with the commanding position of Great Britain in world commerce and shipping, gave to British labor a favored position not unlike that of the "aristocracy" of organized skilled labor in contrast with the mass of unskilled labor within each country.

CHAPTER 22

# THE DEVELOPMENT OF INDUSTRY IN FRANCE, BELGIUM, AND GERMANY, 1830–1870

◆

## The Growth of Industry in France

An observer considering France as an isolated area could hardly fail to be impressed with the industrial development of the country during the first half of the nineteenth century. The Revolution freed industry from the restrictions of the rigid prescriptions of the codes and from the limitations upon the movement of skilled workmen imposed by the statutes of the craft guilds. The Patent Law of 1791 gave new encouragement to inventors and industrialists. The wars were a stimulus to industry in many ways, directly and indirectly. The restrictions imposed upon trading with the enemy afforded considerable protection against British manufactures, not only in France, but throughout a large portion of Continental Europe. Population increased substantially, after a long period of almost complete stabilization. Production increased even more rapidly than population.

APPROXIMATE PRODUCTIVITY OF INDUSTRY IN FRANCE, 1788–1850 [1]

| | Authority | Value of Final Products, in Millions of Francs | Value of Product per Capita, in Francs |
|---|---|---|---|
| 1788 | Tolosan | 931.4 | 37 |
| 1812 | Montalivet | 1324.4 | 45 |
| | Chaptal | 1820.0 | 63 |
| | Partial enumeration | 3037.4 | 87 |
| 1850 | Estimated total | 4037.4 | 115 |
| | Total including flour milling | 5215.7 | — |

It is now held that Chaptal's estimates were extravagant, and if that is true, the primary growth of French industry occurred in the period following the wars. The average rate of growth from 1788 to 1850 was 2.3 per cent per year if flour milling is excluded, and 2.9 per cent per year if flour milling is included. The material is too uncertain to make it wise to place much emphasis upon these

[1] Moreau de Jonnés, *Statistique de l'industrie de la France*, Paris, 1856, pp. 330–331.

446

specific rates of growth, but it is clear that the period was one of active growth. Trade statistics point to the same conclusion. The combined totals of exports and imports show a substantial increase during the period. In terms of sterling, the totals were: in 1801, £28,700,000; in 1848, £65,700,000. The rate of increase was about 1.5 per cent per year.

Despite this apparently satisfactory growth, French industrialists and statesmen were querulous, apprehensive, and dissatisfied. Demands for protection were persistent. French industries were said to be backward, unprogressive, and inefficient. The basis of all this pessimism and complaint was, of course, to be found in the rapid development of British industry and trade. Contemporary opinion was dominated by the comparative position of French industry. British trade had grown twice as fast as French trade, increasing from a total of £66,900,000 in 1801 to £295,800,000 in 1848. The total was thus a little more than twice the French total in 1801, but more than four and one-half times the total in 1848. But contrasts in the volume of production were even more distressing. Great Britain was rapidly becoming industrialized so that despite a smaller total population the industrial population was about equal to the industrial population of France and certainly more productive.

## The Changed Position of France

Until the latter part of the eighteenth century, France was really the leading industrial region of Europe. England was too small to challenge the industrial prestige of France. With scarcely more than one third of the population of the major Continental power, and no commanding difference in productivity, England occupied a clearly secondary position until the closing decades of the eighteenth century. For a considerable period the influence of the new technology was too restricted to affect the general industrial situation, but the differences became more and more important as the wars drew to a close. The France of Louis XVIII therefore felt keenly conscious of a loss of prestige in the economic world as well as in the world of high politics.

The economic condition of France in the early nineteenth century thus presents a striking instance of the need of careful consideration of both the international and the internal phases of economic growth. From the point of view of the general international situation, the position of France was getting steadily worse, and might well cause apprehension. From the standpoint of a pure isolationist, France was making an entirely satisfactory growth. The extreme pessimism and apprehension of those who thought exclusively in terms of prestige was certainly not justified. It must also be clear today that no economic policy could have made it possible for France to "hold her own" with Great Britain. The primary features affecting the international position of France were not within the limits of social control. The maintenance of industrial "leadership" was not within the power of France, nor was it necessary to her welfare.

On the other hand, it is idle to pretend that the changed international position was not a serious factor in the contemporary economic problem. The tone of economic development is profoundly affected by pressure or stimulation at certain critical points. Particular industries or occupations may well exercise an influence upon economic activity that may seem disproportionate to the precise quantitative importance of the industry or occupation.

At this time, both the cotton industry and the iron industry were especially important. The cotton industry was better suited to spinning and weaving by power machinery than any other branch of the textile industry. It developed rapidly; costs and prices fell more rapidly than the costs and prices of other textiles. Consequently, cotton goods were extensively used as substitutes for other textiles, sometimes merely because they were cheaper, sometimes because they offered novelties in style and design that could not be as readily produced in the other textiles. The growth of the cotton industry, in fact, created serious pressure of competition throughout the entire textile group. Growth occurred in the other branches of the textile group despite this pressure; but the presence of the menace of the cotton industry was inevitably a source of apprehension to manufacturers of woolens, silks, and linens in all countries. Thus the extraordinary growth of the British cotton industry was viewed with dismay by French textile manufacturers generally. The modest development of the cotton industry in France was no compensation, despite a substantial rate of growth. Lower standards of living made it possible to compete effectively in certain lines; but at every turn the French manufacturer was obliged to consider British costs and British prices. Such conditions of competition produced a sense of inferiority.

The iron trade was perhaps even more important. The British industry was forced to resort to coal and coke at an early date in the eighteenth century. After a long period of experimentation, the new technique was mastered and high-grade malleable iron was produced at greatly reduced costs. New modes of refining and working malleable iron reduced costs still further and opened up the new uses of iron already considered. The French iron industry was better supplied with wood than with coal, and consequently found little incentive to apply the new technique. Special properties of charcoal iron promised a modest market for this product despite competition with puddled iron, but this market became more and more restricted. The industry was subjected to persistent pressure from competition with the newer puddled iron, and in this field protection was sought. Behind the shelter of substantial tariff duties, the charcoal industry made appreciable growth.

With the coming of the railway, the French industry was unable to meet the demand for the heavy iron products that could be effectively produced only by the puddling process and the rolling mills. Dependence upon imports of iron and upon foreign engineering work again emphasized the important advances of technique in England. Under such circumstances, the modest growth of French industrial production could not possibly seem satisfactory, nor could the record distract attention from the fact that the position of France in the economic world had been profoundly changed.

## The Coal Resources of France

The new technology gave predominant importance to power resources capable of furnishing power in relatively large units. Windmills and the older types of water wheel were not large enough to afford a permanent basis for industrialization of the new type. The development of the turbine water wheel, however, after 1832, gave new importance to water power and in several sections of France and the United States water power became the predominant source of energy. Normandy and Alsace were able to build their industries around their water powers. Some use was made of water power in other parts of France, but conditions were not favorable to extensive industrialization. The possibilities of general industrial development in the new fields depended very largely upon the extent and character of the coal resources of France.

The general distribution of coal in France is best shown on the map (page 450). Small coal fields occur in many parts of France, but most of these deposits are very small, so that the actual re-

*Adapted from " The Mineral Industry," Vol. V, by permission of McGraw-Hill Book Company*
### Coal Resources of France

sources are neither extensive nor well distributed. The relative importance of the various coal fields is best indicated by the output near the beginning of the present century:

PRODUCTION OF COAL IN FRANCE, IN 1911 [1]

| Coal Field | Tons | Per Cent |
|---|---|---|
| Valenciennes | 26,100,000 | 66.6 |
| St. Étienne | 3,600,000 | 9.2 |
| Le Creusot | 1,800,000 | 4.6 |
| Alais | 2,000,000 | 5.1 |
| All other | 5,700,000 | 14.5 |
| | 39,200,000 | 100.0 |

[1] International Geological Congress, Toronto, 1913, *Coal Resources of the World,* I, pp. xix, xxviii.

The great field on the Belgian frontier is thus seen to be the chief coal resource of France.  In effect, this northern coal field is an integral part of the Belgian coal field, and careful analysis of economic phenomena should not ignore this feature of regional geography.  Some Belgian coal is exported to France, and the requirements of Belgium are covered in part by imports from England.  The Belgian section of this coal field was developed extensively long before workings were opened on the French side of the frontier, as there were special obstacles to exploitation.

The coal fields of St. Étienne and Le Creusot afforded the basis for an important development of the heavy metals as well as supplying the general requirements of a large section of central France. But the volume of production is not sufficient to develop massive industrialization.  The coal field at Alais in Languedoc is likewise of local importance.  Without these resources, central and southern France would doubtless have declined in economic and industrial importance.

The annual production of coal in France in typical years from 1787 to 1870 is shown in the following table:

PRODUCTION OF COAL IN FRANCE [1]

| | Metric Tons | | Metric Tons |
|---|---|---|---|
| 1787 | 215,000 | 1840 | 3,003,000 |
| 1802 | 844,000 | 1850 | 4,433,000 |
| 1811 | 773,000 | 1860 | 8,309,000 |
| 1820 | 1,093,000 | 1865 | 11,652,000 |
| 1830 | 1,862,000 | 1870 | 13,179,000 |

France developed her coal production rapidly after the Revolution. The output was still small relatively to that of Great Britain, though closely comparable with production in other countries.

APPROXIMATE PRODUCTION OF COAL IN VARIOUS COUNTRIES, IN 1840

| | Tons | | Tons |
|---|---|---|---|
| Great Britain | 31,024,000 | France | 3,003,000 |
| Belgium | 3,929,000 | United States | 2,070,000 |
| Prussia | 3,091,000 | Austria | 479,000 |

If these figures are compared with the figures of 1912 for production and estimated reserves, as shown in the table on the following page, it will be evident that France was not really backward in the de-

---

[1] Saward, F. E., *The Coal Trade*, Philadelphia, 1879, p. 47.

velopment of her available resources. France produces more tonnage in proportion to her actual reserves than either Great Britain or Germany. The annual production in France in 1910 was .009 of her actual reserves, whereas the annual production of Great Britain and Germany was respectively .0018 and .0021 of the actual reserves. The difference was even greater in 1840. The disparity in effective resources is so great that this comparison is perhaps of little genuine significance, but it is the most objective index we have of the truly energetic use of these very modest resources in France.

COAL RESOURCES OF LEADING COUNTRIES IN MILLIONS OF TONS [1]

|  | Production 1910 | Actual Reserves | Total Reserves, Actual and Probable |
|---|---|---|---|
| United States | 445.8 | — | 3,838,657 |
| Great Britain | 264.5 | 141,499 | 189,533 |
| Germany | 221.9 | 104,178 | 423,356 |
| France | 38.5 | 4,203 | 17,583 |
| Belgium | 23.1 | — | 11,000 |

The graph on page 471 shows that coal production was actually expanding at the substantial rate of 5 per cent per year.

It will be observed, however, that in respect of the production of coal the general position of France changed for the worse during the second half of the century. Neither Prussia nor the United States had made any effective use of their great resources in 1840. Great Britain and Belgium were therefore the only outstanding industrial rivals of France in 1840.

### The Iron Production and Resources of France

Analysis of the iron resources of France is more complex. There are many small deposits well suited to the older technique of production in which charcoal was used as fuel. When charcoal was used, the heavy consumption of fuel prevented much concentration of smelting or refining. Small, easily worked deposits were therefore especially useful. The total quantities required were not large, and the presence of impurities was not a very serious factor, as they were largely eliminated in the processes of reduction and refining. The extensive dispersion of the industry is indicated by the map of ore production and iron working (page 453). About 70 per cent of the ore raised was produced in the dotted area,

[1] International Geological Congress, Toronto, 1912, *Coal Resources of the World*, I, pp. xix, xxvii; by permission of The Macmillan Company of Canada, Ltd.

which is considerably more restricted than the area producing pig iron and malleable iron. The production of iron in the various districts in 1837 is given in the table on page 454.

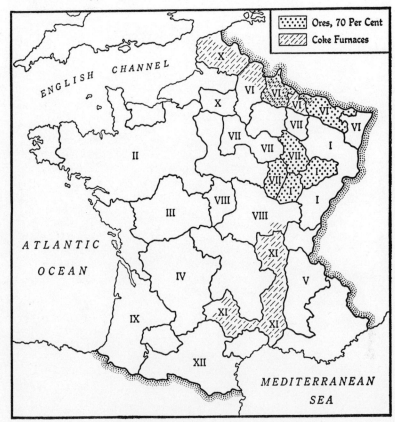

*Iron-Producing Districts of France in 1837*

The regions associated with the coal fields were already making use of coal or coke. Coal was the predominant fuel in the south, in the north, and in the immediate vicinity of Le Creusot. Elsewhere charcoal was used, with some supplementary reliance on coal in refining the crude iron. In 1837, 16 per cent of the pig iron was smelted with coal or coke. The true significance of this widespread use of minor deposits of iron appears when the figures for production are compared with the actual reserves. The revision of the boundary in 1918 makes the modern figures strictly applicable to France in 1837.

IRON PRODUCTION IN FRANCE, IN 1837 [1]

| District | Pig Iron | | Malleable Iron, |
| | Tons | Per Cent | Tons |
| --- | --- | --- | --- |
| I. Haute Saône, Doubs, Jura, Haut-Rhin, Meurthe, Côte-d'Or, Vosges | 55,570 | 18.1 | 29,339 |
| II. Eure, Orne, Mayenne, Morbihan, Sarthe, Loire-Inf., Côtes-du-Nord, Eure-et-Loir, Ille-et-Vilaine, Manche, Loir-et-Cher, Maine-et-Loire | 24,117 | 7.8 | 11,351 |
| III. Indre, Vienne, Indre-et-Loire, Deux-Sèvres, Northern Haute-Vienne | 5,911 | 1.9 | 2,914 |
| IV. Dordogne, Charente, Tarn-et-Garonne, Corrèze, Lot, Southern part of Haute-Vienne, NE. Lot-et-Garonne | 15,119 | 4.9 | 9,202 |
| V. Isère, Drôme, Vaucluse | 2,056 | 0.6 | 286 |
| VI. Ardennes, Moselle, Bas-Rhin, Aisne, Northern Meuse, Southern part of Nord | 46,937 | 15.3 | 30,914 |
| VII. Haute-Marne, SW. Côte-d'Or, Aube, Southern Meuse, Seine-et-Marne | 82,740 | 26.9 | 42,953 |
| VIII. Nièvre, Saône-et-Loire, Cher, Allier | 37,555 | 12.2 | 27,440 |
| IX. Landes, Gironde, Lot-et-Garonne, Basses-Pyrénées | 7,226 | 2.3 | 3,729 |
| X. Nord, Pas-de-Calais, Oise | 2,260 | 0.7 | 9,327 |
| XI. Loire, Rhone, Ardèche, Gard, Aveyron | 28,872 | 9.3 | 27,690 |
| XII. Ariège, Pyrénées-Orientales, Aude, Haute-Garonne, Tarn, [Basse] et Haute-Pyrénées | — | — | 9,491 |
| XIII. Corsica | — | — | 119 |
| | 308,363 | 100.0 | 204,755 |

It will be observed that the most important ironmaking region in 1837 possesses in fact the least important deposit of iron now counted as a major reserve (map, page 455). Lorraine contributed considerable amounts of iron in 1837, but all of this iron was derived from alluvial deposits of minor importance. None of the minette ores were used before 1844, and only modest quantities of minette were in use in 1860. They were not adapted to charcoal processes, and were of limited use when coke was used, though the phosphorus content was not as serious a factor when the cast iron was puddled. These ores were of course entirely unsuitable to the Bessemer

[1] Beck, L., *Geschichte des Eisens*, IV, p. 671.

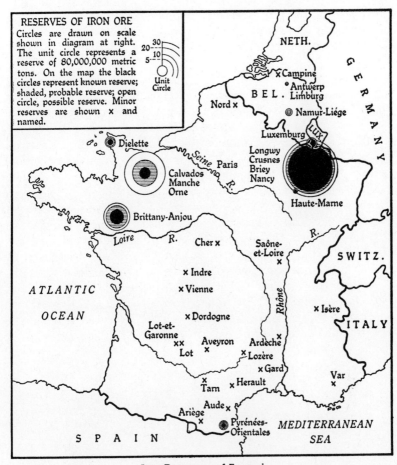

**RESERVES OF IRON ORE**
Circles are drawn on scale shown in diagram at right. The unit circle represents a reserve of 80,000,000 metric tons. On the map the black circles represent known reserve; shaded, probable reserve; open circle, possible reserve. Minor reserves are shown x and named.

*Iron Resources of France*[1]

IRON ORE RESERVES, 1921, IN MILLIONS OF TONS OF METALLIC IRON [1]

|  | Known | Probable | Possible |
|---|---|---|---|
| Lorraine (Longwy, etc.) | 1,548.0 | 375.0 | 450.0 |
| Calvados | 77.0 | 400.0 | 800.0 |
| Dielette | 28.0 | 25.0 | 25.0 |
| Brittany-Anjou | 115.0 | 230.0 | 230.0 |
| Pyrénées-Orientales | 16.5 | 16.5 | 16.5 |
| Haute-Marne | 5.5 | — | 4.5 |
| Other deposits | — | 7.1 | — |
|  | 1,790.0 | 1,053.6 | 1,526.0 |

[1] U. S. Geological Survey, Bulletin 706.   Roesler, M., *The Iron Ore Resources of Europe*, Washington, 1921, pp. 65, 69.

process or to the acid open-hearth process. The large resources
of Normandy, Brittany, and Anjou were very imperfectly utilized.
There was no fuel effectively available for the large ore bodies of
Calvados.

Looking backward, with full appreciation of all the technical
difficulties, one must recognize the magnitude of the obstacles to
the adoption of the British technique of production. In France,
Germany, and the United States the change in basic fuel required
a difficult and costly relocation of the industry. All three countries
possessed extensive forests, so that all were able to produce charcoal
at low costs. In France and in the United States the complete
relocation of the industry was scarcely possible before the development of the railroad supplied new facilities for transport over an
extensive network. The timing of the development of the massive
iron industry was thus affected in part by a number of important
geographic considerations. It was not primarily a matter of
technical incompetence, nor of indifference to change. The rates
of growth shown in the graph on page 471 are significant. Apart
from the remarkable spurt from 1850 to 1855, at a rate of 15 per
cent per year, the increases of $3\frac{1}{2}$ per cent per year were really above
the general average for industry in France. The figures are given
in the following table.

PRODUCTION OF IRON IN FRANCE [1]

| | Tons | | Tons |
|---|---|---|---|
| 1825 | 200,000 | 1850 | 405,000 |
| 1830 | 266,000 | 1855 | 850,000 |
| 1835 | 295,000 | 1860 | 967,000 |
| 1840 | 348,000 | 1865 | 1,226,000 |
| 1845 | 439,000 | 1870 | 1,178,000 |

In England, coal and iron were very closely associated, and the
Scotch iron industry was based in part on the famous blackband
ironstone, an ore body consisting of alternate layers of coal and
iron. When a hot blast was used, the iron could be smelted with
the fuel mined with the ore. Both as respects the quantities of
coal and iron and as respects their location in relation to each other,
every detail of production during the malleable-iron period was
especially suited to the characteristics of the coal and iron resources of Great Britain. Special difficulties, geographic or economic, were present in all the other iron-producing countries. The

[1] Meisner, M., *Weltmontanstatistik*, Stuttgart, 1926, I, p. 84.

extraordinary development of the iron industry in Great Britain between 1780 and 1860 was in large measure due to this remarkable adaptation of her resources to the special features of the technique of producing coke pig iron for refining by the puddling process.

## Invention and Innovation in France

The broader features of the history of industry in France can certainly be explained by careful analysis of the relation of her resources to the new technology. It is not safe, however, to ignore the presence of some purely social factors. French industrialists were somewhat less alert to the potentialities of innovation than their contemporaries in the United States. The contribution of France in the field of industrial invention is not proportionate to the contribution of France in the field of pure science. These relatively intangible aspects of social life cannot be measured. Even the number of patents for inventions is hardly an adequate index, because small differences in administration might include or exclude large numbers of innovations on the border line between positive novelty and mere ingenious use of existing knowledge. Nevertheless, the presence of some differences of a social character should be considered.

In these respects, the heritage of the eighteenth century was unfortunate. Industry had long suffered from the rigid restrictions of the series of codes first introduced in Colbert's time. For more than a century innovation was systematically discouraged except in narrowly restricted fields. In these cases, too, all the emphasis had been placed upon copying the established methods of foreign competitors. Economic conditions had then been favorable to stabilization, so that the policy was by no means disastrous, though it must have tended to reduce positive innovation to a minimum.

This tendency of the codes was intensified by the absence of any protection of property rights in inventions. From time to time prizes were offered for particular inventions or discoveries. The prize offered for a chronometer is perhaps one of the best-known instances of such a practice. Although it was not an isolated case, such means of encouraging invention were utterly inadequate. The amounts offered were too small; in many cases, scarcely enough to cover the expense of experiment. Without security in the enjoyment of properly defined rights of proprietorship, industrial invention could not justify the efforts and expense involved in the preliminary work. The absence of any patent law in France until 1791 must therefore be counted as a serious factor in the reduction of innovation to the bare minimum that emerges despite every discouragement. Even after the recognition of property rights in invention, the development of technology was not fully comparable to the developments in Great Britain and the United States, where the social background was more favorable. Pure science continued to attract the more original minds.

### Large-Scale Industry in Belgium

In the seventeenth and eighteenth centuries the importance of capitalist control in a portion of the industrial field produced a sharp division between the crafts and large-scale industry. In the earlier period the capitalist financed and controlled the process of production, without attempting to bring the operatives together in one place. That system of administration is called the "merchant-employer system." Under special conditions it was at times convenient to collect the workers in one place, so that factories are to be found occasionally throughout the early modern period. The history of large-scale industry is thus much longer than the history of the factory system. With the use of power, the factory system supplanted the merchant-employer system; but even in the textile industries the application of power was a relatively long process because some fibers and some stages of the process of manufacture presented serious difficulties to the application of power machinery. Power was not effectively applied to the loom until 1822, and even then only to the simplest form. For another generation all complex patterns were done largely, if not entirely, on hand looms. Power was not applied to mule spinning until 1825, nor in any decisive fashion to wool combing before 1845.

The precise details of the history of power must be kept in mind if one is to understand the development of the textile industries of Continental Europe in this period. For reasons that were in part purely historical, but in some measure geographic, Great Britain came at an early date to specialize in the phases of these industries most completely dominated by power. Belgium and France introduced power somewhat more slowly, and emphasized in increasing measure the processes and fabrics to which power could not successfully be applied. Selective specialization along lines of natural economic advantage thus tended to slow down the generalization of the use of power on the Continent. It is erroneous to presume that the course of industrial development ought to be the same in all three countries.

At this time, even in Great Britain, the generalization of the use of power was really *predominant* only in the cotton industry.   In 1840, 83 per cent of the persons employed in the cotton industry were in factories using power.   In the woolen and worsted industries, only 44 per cent of the workers were in factories.   Of the silk, flax, and hemp workers, 50 per cent were in factories.   There was hence a large place for hand labor in the textile industries, and the special- izations which had long existed made hand labor a somewhat more important factor in Europe than in England.   Sound judgment of the history of the industries of Continental Europe requires that special attention be given to this somewhat neglected portion of the industrial field: the surviving groups in large establishments under the merchant-employer system, and the craft industries.

INDUSTRIAL ESTABLISHMENTS AND WORKERS IN BELGIUM, 1846 [1]

| | Large Establishments | | Small Establishments and Crafts | | Total Workers |
| | 1 | 2 | 3 | 4 | (cols. 2, 3, 4) |
| | Number | Workers | Number | Workers | |
|---|---|---|---|---|---|
| Linen and hemp | 2,401 | 17,229 | 18,732 | 42,794 | 78,755 |
| Wool | 768 | 18,153 | — | — | 18,153 |
| Cotton | 350 | 14,318 | 43 | 362 | 14,723 |
| Silk | 27 | 675 | — | — | 675 |
| Hats, ribbons, lace | — | — | 1,074 | 3,010 | 4,084 |
| Dress | — | — | 10,036 | 11,057 | 21,093 |
| Total textiles | 3,546 | 50,375 | 29,885 | 57,223 | 137,483 |
| Metallurgy | 243 | 21,312 | 14,204 | 20,977 | 56,493 |
| Glass | 35 | 3,694 | 595 | 265 | 4,554 |
| Paper | 142 | 2,671 | 611 | 2,705 | 5,987 |
| Total | 3,966 | 78,052 | — | — | — |
| Coal and coke | 202 | 46,186 | — | — | 46,168 |
| Quarries, slate, tile | 1,613 | 19,976 | 6,786 | 11,789 | 38,551 |
| Heat | — | — | 12 | 71 | 83 |
| Light | — | — | 1,690 | 3,133 | 4,823 |
| Food | 8,434 | 22,404 | 7,928 | 7,457 | 37,789 |
| Wood | 1,032 | 1,722 | 20,636 | 19,235 | 41,593 |
| Leather | 968 | 2,692 | 11,841 | 10,459 | 24,992 |
| Chemicals | 417 | 1,453 | 1,240 | 1,627 | 4,320 |
| Miscellaneous industry | — | — | 2,691 | 7,416 | 10,107 |
| Total | 16,632 | 172,485 | 98,119 | 142,357 | 412,961 |

[1] *Statistique de la Belgique, 1846; Industrie,* Brussels, 1851, pp. x-xi.

The excellent census of occupations taken in Belgium in 1846 enables us to secure an unusually comprehensive picture of the industrial field in this complex period of transition. The table on page 459 shows the results of this enumeration, reclassified in some details for purposes of comparison. The large establishments as enumerated include over 40 per cent of the workers, but we should not today recognize as "large" establishments many of the units classified as large in the food, wood, leather, and chemical plants. The linen and hemp plants, averaging only about seven workers each, would also seem to be overrated in this classification. If we exclude all these, and also the coal mines and quarries, the total of large industrial establishments would be reduced to 1,565, employing 60,823 workers, or about 15 per cent of the total workers. The average number of workers per establishment in this reduced group of large establishments was nearly 40. This section of Belgian industry is very closely comparable to the portion of British industry reported by the Factory Inspectors. Power was used to a considerable extent throughout this section of the industrial field, though the amount of power per wage earner was somewhat less than in Great Britain. All these workers may be classed as factory workers.

### Large-Scale Industry in Great Britain and in France

Approximate comparison with Great Britain is possible if we combine the returns of the occupational enumeration in 1851 with the returns of the Factory Inspectors for 1850. The results given in the table on page 461 reveal the modest number of workers employed in the strategically important factories and metallurgical work. Less than 14 per cent of the total of industrial workers were the basis upon which was built the commanding position of British industry at this moment of extraordinary predominance. In the primary strategy of international competition, a large proportion of the craft workers simply do not count. The dominant tone of local industry is determined by the competitive strength of a modest fraction of the whole. The service industries, building, construction, and furnishings fluctuate with the changes in the prosperity of a group of primary consumers whose welfare dominates the welfare of all. These tables show clearly that the strategically placed industrial groups include no more than 15 or 20 per cent of the total number of workers. The precise percentage is subject to some doubt because the limits of the occupational classification are vague.  The inclusion of large numbers of part-time workers and general laborers may increase the total.  For this reason, no precise comparisons among different countries are really possible.

PERSONS EMPLOYED IN INDUSTRY IN GREAT BRITAIN, 1850–1851 [1]

| | Male | Female | Total | Per Cent |
|---|---|---|---|---|
| Reported by the Factory Inspectors, 1850 | 246,867 | 349,215 | 596,082 | 10.9 |
| Iron works, machinery, iron mining, 1851 | 154,590 | 1,632 | 156,222 | 2.8 |
| Coal mining | 216,366 | 2,649 | 219,015 | 4.0 |
| All other industrial workers [2] in groups XII, XIII, XIV, 1851 | 2,011,982 | 427,740 | 2,439,722 | 44.2 |
| Dress and apparel VI, 3, 1851 | 471,351 | 855,168 | 1,326,519 | 24.2 |
| Arts and crafts XI, 1851 | 746,431 | 16,905 | 763,336 | 13.9 |
| Total industrial workers | 3,847,587 | 1,653,309 | 5,500,896 | 100.0 |

Many features of the distribution of industrial workers in France are disclosed by the incomplete returns of the Census of Production attempted in France about 1847.  The returns did not include Paris, and a large portion of the south was never effectively covered. Apparently, the returns were not rigidly restricted to any specified date.  The results are consequently very unsatisfactory, but they are nevertheless indicative and constitute the only substantial statistical survey of French industry available for this date.  The census of 1851 classifies as industrial a considerably larger fraction of the total population.  The general results of the enumeration are given in the following table (page 462), with additions made at the time by Moreau de Jonnés.[3]

The commanding importance of the textile industries is clearly shown.  The totals employed in iron production compare favorably with the British total, but the modest number of coal miners discloses the vital weakness of French industries at this time.  The balance between large-scale industry and the crafts is also indicative. If appropriate adjustments of classification are made, the large-scale industries account for approximately one fifth of the total of industrial workers.  Conditions in the three countries (Belgium, France, and Great Britain) are closely similar.  But large-scale industry

---

[1] *Commons Papers, 1852–1853*, vol. 88, Part I.   Census of Population, 1851, Ages, Civil Condition, Part I, pp. xci, ccxviii.   *Commons Papers, 1851*, xxiii, Report of Factory Inspectors, Oct., 1850, p. 15.
[2] The number of factory workers has been deducted from the occupational return.
[3] Moreau de Jonnés, *Statistique de l'industrie de la France*, Paris, 1856, pp. 317, 340.

in France was less uniformly organized on the factory system. We know positively that power was less generally used, but the returns of 1850 are too incomplete to justify any specific numerical statement of the average power used per wage earner. Generalized description warrants the presumption that the merchant-employer system was much more important than it was either in Great Britain or in Belgium. In itself, this persistence of the older form of organization is not of great significance, but this form of organization was associated with the industries that were growing slowly and responding sluggishly to the improvements in the technique of using power. The survival of the older forms of organization was, therefore, an index of the extent to which France failed to share in the gains from the new technique of production.

PERSONS EMPLOYED IN INDUSTRY IN FRANCE, ABOUT 1850

| | Persons | Per Cent |
|---|---|---|
| Large-scale·industries: | | |
| Textiles | 710,996 | 13.15 |
| Iron and iron mining | 135,933 | 2.52 |
| Coal mining | 23,392 | 0.42 |
| Quarries | 121,000 | 2.25 |
| All other large industries enumerated | 66,561 | 1.23 |
| Total enumerated | 1,057,972 | 19.57 |
| Paris (Chamber of Commerce figures) | 131,638 | 2.46 |
| Estimated omissions in the south | 413,460 | 7.67 |
| Total | 1,603,070 | 29.70 |
| Arts and crafts | 3,800,000 | 70.30 |
| Total industrial workers | 5,403,070 | 100.00 |
| Total population | 35,783,170 | |
| Specialized industrial workers: | 15.4 Per Cent of Population | |

## The Tariff and the New Technology in France

To determine the precise significance of tariff policies is a matter of the greatest difficulty. Many facts are misrepresented by interested parties; on many matters positive information is not available; some facts, actually known, present difficulties of interpretation. It is rare that any specific problem in the history of tariff policy can be judged in the light of adequate knowledge of the relevant facts. The history of industry in France in the first half of the nineteenth century presents all these characteristic difficulties, but some inferences can be drawn if we make careful use of the experience of the decade of the 1860's when the treaty with Great Britain reduced the amount of protection on a long list of articles.

Competition with British industries was deeply involved in matters of technology, but French industrialists could not honestly demand protection on the ground that Britain was using new processes which were not understood in France.   After the Restoration, the differences in the application of power and machinery were not seriously affected by proficiency in engineering and machine making.   It is, of course, an error to represent the new technology as a peculiarly British achievement, despite the fact that a large number of critically important machines and processes were developed in England.   Technical progress was far enough advanced in France to make transfers easy, and much new work was being done in France.   But apart from such refinements, whatever obstacles might have existed were certainly overcome during the period of the Revolution and the Empire.

The distinctive textile machines were introduced in France and the recovered provinces of Belgium by the three famous British emigrants, John Holker, William Douglas, and William Cockerill. Holker, a Catholic Jacobite, emigrated from Manchester in 1757. He became interested in cotton spinning around Rouen, and between 1780 and 1792 he brought into use the more important English machines.   The cotton industry was relatively new and presented many problems, but the new technique was effectively established in Normandy even before the outbreak of the Terror. The woolen industry was successfully mechanized by Douglas and Cockerill.   As the export of British machinery was prohibited, this achievement was based upon the development of machine shops.   It is commonly held that Douglas turned out machines that were rather unsatisfactory and inferior in design.   The Cockerill shop at Liége developed a much better product, fully capable of competition with British machines.

The crucial problem of the woolen industry was combing. Despite the invention of a power comb by Cartwright in 1790, the British industry was not successfully established on a power basis until 1825, and even then the machine could not compete with hand combing for fine work.   Ternaux spent much time on mechanical combing, beginning with a machine developed by Douglas.   Mechanical combs were brought into use between 1810 and 1812, and a much improved comb was brought out in 1816 by the French inventors Godard and Collier.   This comb was used successfully until supplanted by the notable invention of Josué Heilman of Mulhouse, brought out in 1845. The development of mechanical combing was thus dominated by the French. French work on the shearing engine and the power loom was not significant.

The greatest single contribution to the textile industry by any French inventor was the Jacquard loom. This remarkable development of the draw loom brought to a close a series of efforts extending over nearly a full century. The complex figured fabrics characteristic of the silk industry were produced upon a large loom operated by not less than three persons. The weaver, or weavers, required the assistance of two persons to draw in appropriate groups the individual lead strings by which the threads of the warp were controlled. In its original form the loom had been brought from China to the Near East, at the beginning of the Christian era. Few changes were made until, in the seventeenth century, the French began to simplify the labor of the helpers. All the early efforts were directed towards the systematic control of the warp threads, so that the loom tender need only perform some simple series of movements. The solution of the problem achieved by Jacquard made it possible to apply power to the loom, but no serious attempt was made to adapt this loom to the use of power for forty years.

The famous Jacquard loom was a synthesis of earlier inventions by B. Bouchon (1725), Falcon (1728), and J. de Vaucanson (1745-1750). The present form of the loom was not achieved by Jacquard until 1804, when a brilliant solution of a number of critical difficulties opened a new era in the weaving of fancy goods. The mechanical features of the machine could not be explained even in the most elementary fashion without a long series of diagrams, and knowledge of the mechanical detail is not essential to an understanding of the primary economic significance of the achievement. Without the Jacquard loom, laborious hand work would have been necessary for the production of any fabric involving any pattern that was not a pure geometrical figure. Although designed to meet certain demands in the silk industry, the Jacquard loom has been extensively applied also to cottons and linens. On it, too, there have been made a large array of textile novelties which could not have been produced cheaply enough by hand looms to reach the market.

### The Competitive Position of the Textile Industries in France

The period of the wars, 1793-1815, saw the substantial introduction of machinery into the textile industries of France and Belgium.

Some of the machines were copied exactly from English models; some were modified; and at least two new and important contributions were made. All the machines were being currently built in France and Belgium. These facts are especially important from the standpoint of tariff policy. In careful studies of the tariff policy of the United States, Professor Taussig takes the position that much weight must be given to the degree to which a country is dependent upon others for the design and production of machinery. If a country is not dependent upon the importation of foreign machinery, there is little basis for a presumption of significant technical inferiority. Selective specialization may occur within the general limits of the industry, but such differentiation must not be confused with "technical inferiority" in any strict sense of the word.

The prohibition of the export of machinery from England makes it impossible to draw any direct inference from the fact that French and Belgian makers were supplying the textile factories of the Continent. The leadership of France in the development of mechanical wool combing does, however, afford the basis for inferences. The development and application of the Jacquard loom is also significant. These advances were partly offset, in the decade of the 1820's, by the development in Great Britain of the self-acting mule and the production of a thoroughly practical power loom. It is commonly held that these machines made their way in France rather slowly. Precise judgment of the timing of the adoption of the machines in France is made complex by practical limitations of the machines in their early state. They were not, at the outset, capable of performing all varieties of textile work. They were certainly ill-suited in this period to many of the fabrics in which the French specialized. In the face of all these considerations, it is difficult to believe that the French textile manufacturers could justify their demands for protection on the ground of technological inferiority.

The woolen and the silk industries were subject to some special strains. In France, as in Great Britain, the wool supply was a source of great concern. The wool clip of Europe was not expanding rapidly enough to meet the increased demand for textiles stimulated by decreasing costs of manufacture. The attempt to stimulate the domestic production of wool by protective duties is hardly surprising. Duties of 30 per cent were imposed by a series of acts (1816–1826), but the result was not particularly helpful to the woolen industries. Wool production at home did not increase, and the industry found no adequate supply of raw material until the development of wool growing in Australia and Argentina. Duties on wool were reduced sharply in 1856 and entirely abolished May 5, 1860. The silk industry was profoundly affected by an epidemic disease of silkworms which persisted in varying intensity from 1843 to 1865. The ravages of the disease were finally checked after research by Pasteur had established the nature of the malady, but Chinese and Japanese raw silks were by that time firmly established in the European market, and the local production of raw silk did not regain the ground lost.

Whatever the incidental benefits of protection to particular firms, there is no ground for presuming that it had promoted healthy readjustment in any large degree. The small group of reformers who urged a liberal policy upon the Emperor in the 1850's may have exaggerated the evils of protection, but there was much to justify their contention that protection was no longer necessary. The negotiation of the commercial treaty with Great Britain, despite the clearly expressed dismay and hostility of the industrialists, was an unusually courageous act of statesmanship. The government, however, did not feel it expedient to expose industry to British competition without some cushioning of the shock. The iron industry was promised continued protection; other manufacturers were assured free importation of raw materials; and the government set aside the sum of 40,000,000 francs to be loaned to industrialists in need of funds for new equipment (October 24, 1860).

At the time of the first report of the Commission in charge of the loans (April, 1861), 15,060,000 francs had been loaned to 88 textile manufacturers. The grants were largely to the cotton manufacturers; a few grants were made to woolen and worsted establishments, but only one application was received from the silk industry. The severity of the crisis caused by the cotton famine made it necessary to grant subsequent loans to some of the cotton manufacturers. No complete record of the activities of the Commission now exists, but it is fairly certain that the full amount authorized was never loaned. No grants were made after 1865, and at that time little had been repaid. The loan was a factor in assisting manufacturers to adjust themselves to a freer market, but the actual amount granted seems small. If this sum is in any adequate sense representative of the need, the competitive strength of French industry must have been much greater than had been assumed even by the liberal advocates of the treaty of 1860 with Great Britain.

That treaty was bitterly denounced by the ironmasters, but in reality the effects were not very serious.  There was a considerable increase in imports from Britain in the years 1861–1863, but the production of iron in France maintained its rate of increase until 1867.  In specific years the domestic market was somewhat over-supplied, but the margins were not large.  The transition from charcoal to coke as fuel for the furnaces was well under way in 1860, so that the influence of the treaty was merely supplementary. Professor Dunham feels that the treaty did little harm, and exerted some beneficial stimulus to improvement of methods of production.

The cotton industry suffered serious strains in all countries in the decade following the promulgation of the treaty of 1860.  At the outbreak of the Civil War in the United States, the industry was suffering from overproduction both in Great Britain and in France. The earlier phases of the interruption of the cotton trade brought some relief to the manufacturers.   The crisis was, however, a severe shock to the industry, as it came at a most unfortunate moment. New supplies of wool and silk, and the widespread applications of the mechanical technique, had created sharp competition among the various textiles, and this time cotton suffered the most serious strains.   These strains were really common to the industry as a whole, and were not peculiar to France.

Competition between the woolen industries of Great Britain and France was sharp, but without decisive advantage to either region. There was much selective specialization, and each maintained itself within restricted fields.  The evidence is confused, but there is no ground for presuming that the French industry suffered any significant losses by reason of freer trade.   In respect of linens and silks, there can be no serious question of the competitive strength of the French industries.  In these industries there was much selective specialization, but the preponderant advantages were more clearly with the major centers of production in France.

### The Introduction of the Steam Engine in Germany

The development of Germany in the nineteenth century presents a sharp contrast to the history of industry in France.   Germany contributed little that was original to the new industrial technique ; English machinery and methods were introduced much later than in France ; and German industrialists received a minimum of tariff protection.  Despite all these obstacles, and a depressing sense of industrial inferiority, German industry developed with great rapidity after the formation of the Customs Union and the introduction of the railroad. The new development centered about the coal fields and the metallurgical industries. The production of coal began to increase notably after the introduction of the steam engine in 1820, and the development became more rapid after the introduction of deep mining in 1838, with further acceleration upon the reform of mining law in 1851. Pig-iron production grew slowly until 1850, but from 1850 to 1869 developed at an extraordinary rate of 9 per cent per year. The character and location of primary resources was clearly the predominant factor in this growth, which, even in 1870, had merely established the primary foundation for the mature achievement.

The steam engine was first brought to Germany to be installed in barges on the Rhine; pumping engines were set up in two coal mines in the following year; and in 1822 a spinning mill at Chemnitz was equipped with steam power. Progress was slow, however, as there were no skilled workmen or shops competent to build engines. The toolmaking equipment was limited to the old-style lathes suitable only for the lighter tasks such as lockmaking. Dinnendahl declared that it was impossible to find a smith in all Westphalia capable of making a machine screw. Cylinders, tubing, and valves all presented serious problems. It is therefore hardly surprising to find that there were only 419 steam engines in Prussia in 1837. The generalization of the use of steam took place largely after 1840. Comprehensive statistical material is available from 1846. Returns for 1846 and 1861 are given in the following table:

STEAM ENGINES INSTALLED, GERMAN CUSTOMS UNION [1]

| | [ | 1846 | ] | [ | 1861 | ] |
|---|---|---|---|---|---|---|
| | Number | Horse-power | Per Cent of Total H. P. | Number | Horse-power | Per Cent of Total H. P. |
| Mines | 340 | 10,664 | 40.4 | 2,059 | 72,350 | 38.0 |
| Metallurgy | 143 | 4,164 | 15.8 | 763 | 18,634 | 10.0 |
| Machine building | 139 | 1,687 | 6.4 | 618 | 6,584 | 3.5 |
| Textiles | 261 | 4,744 | 18.2 | 1,394 | 30,638 | 16.0 |
| Agriculture | 164 | 2,050 | 7.7 | 1,693 | 21,183 | 11.5 |
| Miscellaneous | 369 | 3,045 | 11.5 | 3,586 | 35,260 | 21.0 |
| | 1,416 | 26,354 | 100.0 | 10,113 | 184,649 | 100.0 |

The modest equipment of textile factories with power indicates, better than any other available statistical item, the slow advance

[1] Benaerts, P., *Les origines de la grande industrie allemande*, pp. 377–378.

of power machinery in the German textile trades. Some water power was used, but the fact remains that the textile industry responded slowly to changed conditions. This was due in part to the importance in Germany of linen and woolen weaving. These branches were least suited to the machine technique of the time, and in them, with some increased emphasis on specialties, hand processes would naturally maintain themselves longest. Cotton spinning by power made considerable growth, but it did not acquire the predominance that it had achieved in Great Britain. In the absence of comprehensive statistics for the Customs Union area as a whole, it is impossible to sketch the changes in the textile industries with any satisfactory degree of precision. Boundary changes in 1866 and 1871 add to the difficulties of any statistical generalization. Technically, the German textile industries were distinctly inferior to the industries of Great Britain. Even when allowance is made for selective specialization in the least progressive branches, the German industry was clearly subject to severe competitive pressure. The German industry maintained itself only because the workers accepted very low standards of living.

The condition of the German textile trades is doubtless largely responsible for the common impression that the industrial development of the period before 1870 was relatively unimportant. This judgment of the industrial history of Germany takes inadequate account of the notable reorganization of mining and of the metallurgical industries. The primary accomplishments of the period before 1870 occurred in these fields. The technical procedures were fully developed and the quantitative achievement was substantial.

### The Development of Coal Mining in Germany

Although coal had been used in northern Germany for centuries, the technique of mining was very simple. In many parts of the Ruhr formation the coal measures came to the surface, and in places they were exposed on the hillsides. The modest quantities needed for local domestic use could be secured with little elaboration of technique, and inadequate transportation made it impossible to reach a large market. Open workings were all that was necessary in many places. In favorable locations galleries could be driven into the hillsides and could be drained of water by the natural slope of the gallery. Mining law was a survival from the period of maximum territorial decentralization, so that the great Ruhr basin was subject to no less than four codes of law. Mining was closely regulated by the state, and in several fields many mines were operated by the state.

The beginning of the modernized industry dates from the sinking of the first deep pit in the Ruhr field, where, a short distance from Essen, a thick vein of coal was located 1,782 feet below the surface. This pit was developed and went into operation in 1841, as the Graf Beust mine. Other borings led to further discoveries, and little by little the extent of the deeper deposits became known. The surface outcrops to the south were abandoned, and production developed rapidly. Markets were opened up by river, and ultimately by rail, and the iron furnaces adopted coke as their basic fuel. The technique of deep mining was soon extended to the Saar basin despite technical difficulties, and the Saar became one of the primary centers of mining technology. With the development of the railroads, the Saxon deposits and the deeper coal measures of Silesia were brought into productive use.

Prussian mining law was reformed. The first important act was the law of May 12, 1851, which gave individuals and companies full control of the regulation of production and sale, and reduced taxes to 10 per cent of the net product. Supplementary laws of 1854, 1856, 1860, and 1861 developed the general policy of private control subject to public regulation. Special attention was given to the legal problems of appropriate concentration of control, as earlier regulations had made it very difficult to secure clear title to concessions of sufficient size to form convenient units of administration. The series of legal reforms was consolidated in a systematic code for Prussia, June 24, 1865.

The production of coal in Germany increased rapidly after 1830, as shown by the following table and graph. The figures for Prussia

THE PRODUCTION OF COAL AND LIGNITE IN GERMANY [1]

| | Prussia, Tons | | Germany, Tons |
| --- | --- | --- | --- |
| 1825 | 1,418,000 | | |
| 1831 | 1,747,000 | | |
| 1839 | 3,090,000 | 1848 | 5,800,000 |
| 1845 | 4,643,000 | 1857 | 14,884,000 |
| 1861 | 12,821,000 | 1867 | 30,802,000 |
| 1865 | 20,667,000 | 1870 | 34,002,000 |

[1] Dieterici, K. F. W., *Statistische Uebersicht der wichtigsten Gegenstände des Verkehrs und Verbrauchs des Preussischen Staats*, Berlin, 1838-1848, vol. I, p. 384; II, p. 315; III, p. 472; IV, p. 487. Saward, F. E., *The Coal Trade*, 1879, p. 47; 1882, p. 61.

reveal increase at an average rate of 6.5 per cent per year from
1831 to 1861.   For Germany, as a whole, the greatest expansion
occurred in the years 1849 to 1857, when the rate was about 11 per
cent per year.   In Prussia the rate of production increased most
rapidly after 1861.   This achievement laid the foundations for the
development of Imperial Germany.

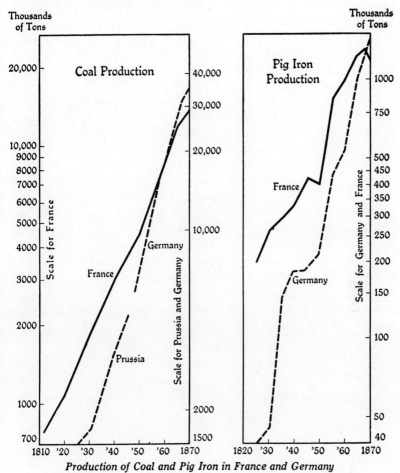

*Production of Coal and Pig Iron in France and Germany*

## The Reorganization of the Iron Industry in Germany

The transformation of the iron industry in Germany faced some
of the obstacles encountered by the French industry.   The abundance of wood and of dispersed deposits of easily worked iron

discouraged the relatively large investment required by coke-burning furnaces. The greater productivity of the coke furnace required larger supplies of ore. These could be secured either by developing new deposits with more elaborate procedures of mining, or by concentrating for smelting the production of the smaller mines. The development of the coke furnace thus involved in Germany as in France a substantial displacement of the industry. The use of coke for refining developed somewhat earlier than the use of coke in smelting because it involved a less serious displacement of the industry. The timing of this transformation was affected more largely by economic considerations than by any lack of technical knowledge.

The first coke furnace in Germany was built at Gleiwitz in Upper Silesia in 1794, twelve years after the building of the coke furnace at Le Creusot. But this project had little immediate consequence. In 1802 another furnace was built at Königshütte (later Królewska Huta in Poland), and in 1812 two more at Alvensleben. In 1836 five more furnaces were built. No coke furnaces were built in other parts of Germany until 1839, and very few were constructed, outside of Silesia, before 1850. In 1834, in the territory of the Customs Union only 4.5 per cent of the iron was produced with coke; and by 1850 the proportion smelted with coke was only 10.8 per cent. The introduction of the new process in the Ruhr in 1850 marked the beginning of an important development. The importance of the change at this date will be apparent from the record of production presented in the following table and in the graph on page 471.

THE PRODUCTION OF PIG IRON IN GERMANY [1]

| | Tons | | Tons |
|------|---------|------|-----------|
| 1825 | 40,000 | 1850 | 215,000 |
| 1830 | 46,000 | 1855 | 420,000 |
| 1835 | 144,000 | 1860 | 529,000 |
| 1840 | 183,000 | 1865 | 988,000 |
| 1845 | 185,000 | 1870 | 1,390,000 |

The volume of production was very small in 1825, and, despite the remarkable increase in the years 1830–1835, production was much less than in England or France. From 1835 to 1850 production increased at the rate of 2.5 per cent per year. For the five years 1850 to 1855 production increased at a rate of 14 per cent per year, and after 1855 the increase continued to 1870 at a rate of

[1] Meisner, M., *op. cit.* I, 84.

8.5 per cent per year.  The new technique and the development of railroads were favorable to concentration around the massive mineral resources.

The important technical achievements of Krupp began in the decade of the 1840's.  The business had originally been concerned with the preparation of high-grade crucible steels for making the dies and rolls used in mints.  This business was subsequently expanded by a notable application of rolls to the production of flat silver with embossed designs.  About 1842, experiments with crucible steels led to the development of a seamless steel tire for locomotive wheels and to the use of crucible steel for firearms and armor.  The techniques of these new processes were perfected, so that by 1850 Krupp was supplying railroads with a growing list of high-grade specialties.  The work on firearms did not become commercially significant until late in the decade of the 1850's.  After 1859 the Prussian state became an important purchaser.  The breech-loading mechanism was developed between 1859 and 1861.  Contacts with Russia were established, and after 1863 large supplies of ordnance were sold to Russia.

# CHAPTER 23

# THE MIDDLE CLASS AND WORKERS ON THE CONTINENT

## The Aristocratic Reaction after the Congress of Vienna

The defeat of Napoleon was followed by an effort throughout Europe to restore the class relations and hereditary privileges of the old regime. The liberal tendencies of the revolutionary era were curbed by laws and administrative policies for controlling the press, the schools, and the theaters, and for dissolving the various secret societies. The long period of warfare had checked the growth of trade and industry and had in this way tended to prolong the pre-eminence of agriculture and the domination of the landed aristocracy. In France the peasant proprietors, businessmen, and professional classes were strong enough to salvage the essential gains of the Revolution. But in most of the countries of the Continent opposition to the old regime had no adequate basis in the economic strength of the urban middle classes or of the peasants. Nevertheless, there were many adherents of the individualistic and democratic doctrines of the Revolution, and opposition to the old regime gradually grew stronger. It was reinforced by nationalistic aspirations in Italy and Germany, by the spread of the ideas of the English classical economists, and by the emergence of socialistic views.

Nationalistic tendencies had been strengthened by the high-handed policies of Napoleon in utilizing for his own ambitious aims the various peoples who came under his rule. These tendencies were prominent especially in Germany, Belgium, and Italy, and were soon to spread to the Balkans and South America. Metternich opposed the movement because it threatened the authority of Austria over subject peoples and her ascendancy among the Germans. His opposition, as well as that of rulers elsewhere, was intensified by the fact that nationalism was associated with liberal and democratic ideals and was supported by the middle classes.

In France the reactionary movement was less extreme than in other countries. The Bourbon dynasty was restored by the power of the victors, but Louis XVIII was careful to recognize and accept the principal changes brought about by the Revolution. The

474

Napoleonic Code, predominantly bourgeois in character, was retained. It was the effort of Charles X to restore autocratic rule and to favor the *émigrés* — "the grasping and traitorous aristocrats" — that led to the Revolution of 1830. In other countries effective resistance to autocratic rulers and hereditary aristocracy awaited the growth of the industrial classes, who were later to afford an economic basis for the achievement, in varying degrees, of political and economic liberalism. In France not only the middle classes of the towns but the emancipated and landowning peasants furnished a basis for the strength and persistence of liberalism. Throughout the Continent the industrial workers were unable to exert effective pressure either against the aristocratic reaction or against the growing influence of their employers.

## The Revolutions of 1830

The revolutionary movement of 1830 began in France and spread rapidly over a large part of the Continent. Charles X, who succeeded Louis XVIII in 1824, antagonized the middle classes in several ways. He forced through a refunding of the national debt at reduced interest in order to secure funds to indemnify the *émigrés* for their losses during the Revolution. In 1829 he appointed an *émigré* as prime minister. The elections of 1830 returned a hostile Chamber of Deputies, but Charles arbitrarily dissolved it before it met, muzzled the press, and called a new election under a decree disfranchising about three fourths of the voters. The result was a union of the middle and lower classes and the overthrow of Charles. But the bourgeois elements, favoring a limited monarchy, prevented the establishment of a republic and placed Louis Philippe on the throne, subject to the will of the bourgeois Chamber of Deputies. The French workers were in substantially the same position as the British workers when, in 1832, they aided the middle classes in securing the passage of the Reform Bill but found themselves as powerless as before. But the landowning peasants of France were much more influential than were the tenants and farm laborers of England. Moreover, small-scale enterprise was predominant in the towns, and bourgeois influence was much more widely diffused than in England, where factory owners and the great merchants and bankers were taking the place of the landlords as the dominant classes.

In Belgium the Revolution of 1830 was mainly for the purpose of bringing about the separation of Belgium from Holland and the establishment of a constitutional monarchy. Belgian industries had profited by the alliance with revolutionary France. The political connection with Holland also brought many advantages. But the obstinate and shortsighted policy of the Dutch king in respect to political and cultural matters aroused the nationalistic ambitions of the Belgians. The new government, like that of Great Britain after 1832 and of Louis Philippe in France, was dominated by middle-class ideals and interests. In Germany, Austria, Italy, and Poland the uprisings of 1830 were unsuccessful. Business enterprise was almost everywhere on a small scale, the guild system and the merchant-employer system were widely prevalent, and with the exception of a few comparatively unimportant areas, as some of the smaller states of western Germany, most of the peasants were not landowners but serfs, tenants, or wage earners. Divine-right monarchy, hereditary aristocracy, and landlordism therefore retained their ascendancy.

### Bourgeois Economic Doctrines and Policies before the Revolution of 1848

During the second quarter of the century, industrial changes such as had been transforming England gradually permeated the Continent. New problems arose and new demands were made upon governments. On the one hand, efforts were made to free enterprise from the regulations and monopolies incident to the older systems of production and trade; and on the other hand the rise of factories, the building of railroads, the growth of towns, and the emergence of industrial classes led to demands for positive action for factory laws and other adaptations to new conditions. Before 1848 few changes in policy occurred. Notable exceptions were the formation of the Zollverein or Customs Union in Germany and the enactment of the Prussian child-labor law of 1839, the French child-labor law of 1841, and the Prussian Industrial Law of 1845. The law of 1845 restricted the powers of master craftsmen and extended occupational freedom in certain industries throughout Prussia.

The transformation of economic ideas and doctrines outran the changes in policy. J. B. Say published his *Treatise on Political Economy* in 1803, and before his death in 1832 four revisions appeared. It was translated into several languages and was extremely effective in spreading his own ideas and those of his master, Adam Smith. He enlarged Smith's views of production by analyzing land, labor, and capital as the factors in production, and by developing the conception of the entrepreneur. He held that production automatically finances consumption and that supply begets demand. He attempted the role of an abstract, objective scientist, and compared economics with physics. Frederic Bastiat, born in 1801, wrote various pamphlets and minor works of a popular nature and in 1849 published his *Economic Harmonies*. He advocated free trade and individualism and believed that the social "laws" tend inevitably toward a harmony of interests and the perfecting of humanity. He emphasized the importance of demand and consumption, and recognized the inequalities of income, but held that interest rates tend downward, and with them the rewards going to capital, while wages tend upward. He combated the pessimistic conclusions derived from the writings of such men as Malthus and Ricardo and became an outstanding exponent of the view that the prevailing economic system was predominantly beneficent.

French economic thought of the bourgeois type, although not without a measure of originality, was largely derived from the British classical school. In Germany Friedrich List's *National System of Political Economy* was published in 1841. List's general conception was mercantilistic, but the development of his views was original, and his work was extremely influential. He built up a theoretical and historical argument against free trade as a universal doctrine and in favor of protection for the safeguarding of national interests and the development of new industries — the nurture of "infant" industries. He also advocated the exercise by the state of protective functions on behalf of labor. In method he was a forerunner of the historical school founded by William Roscher. Roscher's first important work appeared in 1843. He proclaimed the need for turning away from the hypothetical abstractions of the theorists to a study of economic history and environmental conditions for an understanding of economics.

## The Rise of Critical and Socialistic Thought

Sismondi (1773–1842) was a writer whose vigorous and many-sided contributions to economic thought defy classification. He was born in Geneva but his family connections were Italian and French as well as Swiss. He traveled in England and early became an admirer of Adam Smith, whom he continued to call " the master." But he lamented Smith's lapses into abstractions, and he severely criticized the later English economists and their imitators in France for attempting to formulate principles or laws apart from the facts of the social environment. He felt keenly the " vicious " nature of prevailing modes of distributing " the fruits of labor " but confessed that he saw no means of supplanting private property, to which he attributed contractual inequality and the conflict between individual interests and social welfare. His suggestions were limited to govermental action, contrary to *laissez faire*, for promoting a wider diffusion of ownership and for protecting the nonpropertied classes from the more serious evils of inequality of contractual strength. In his ideals he resembled the English utilitarians; in his method he was a forerunner of the historical school; and in his vigorous criticisms of landlordism and bourgeois industrialism he furnished an armory of weapons to the socialists.

Socialistic thought found expression more extensively among Frenchmen and later among Germans than among Englishmen, but there were notable British forerunners. Robert Owen, of Welsh origin, formulated an elaborate theory of co-operative communities which he believed would transform society. William Thompson, an Irishman, antedated Marx in turning the classical labor theory of value into an attack on the system of private enterprise as being the basis of the spoliation of the workers. On the Continent during the first half of the century many writers contributed to the development of socialistic thought.

Claude H. Saint-Simon, a nobleman, has been called the founder of French socialism. His writings can hardly be called socialistic, but his followers extended his ideas. He believed that the destruction of traditions and institutions by the French Revolution and by the growth of industrialism opened the way for a new social system, and he viewed himself as its herald. Somewhat vaguely but fervently he and his followers advocated the organization of the nation as a workshop or an integrated industrial enterprise. The prevailing ideals were to be somewhat like those of Bacon's New Atlantis. The plan called for scientific and benevolent supervision, efficient production, and the ultimate elimination of idlers or drones. The new society was to be a collectivism not of ownership — private property was recognized — but of ideals, discipline, and productive activity. But after the death of Saint-Simon in 1825 his followers became convinced that private ownership of capital was inconsistent with the achievement and maintenance of their ideals, and they therefore may be classed as socialists in the modern sense.

Charles Fourier formulated a plan for organizing society in communities (*phalanstères*) in which the normal interests and passions would find expression but would be reconciled and harmonized by the principles of co-operative association. His plan, somewhat fantastic and certainly impractical when viewed literally, embodied many fruitful conceptions. Modern hotels and apartment houses, the transition from domestic to collective production in many of the service industries, and the diffusion of ownership by the joint-stock principle have been cited as a few of the many instances of his prophetic insight. In his communities generous rewards were to go to capital. But wage earners were to be transformed into capitalists by means of joint-stock ownership. In each member of the community there was to be a harmonious and democratic fusion of the functions of ownership and labor, and also of production and consumption. The separation and lack of correlation of these complementary functions he regarded as the principal sources of conflict and maladjustment.

Louis Blanc, another associative or co-operative socialist, published his *Organization of Labor* in 1839, two years after the death of Fourier. Although it made no original or distinctive contribution to socialistic thought, its conciseness and clarity and the simplicity of its plan for co-operative workshops gave it great popularity. Pierre Joseph Proudhon's famous attack on private property — "property is theft" — allied him with the socialists in their central doctrine of the socialization of wealth. But his extreme individualism — his "liberalism gone to seed" — places him more accurately among the philosophical anarchists.

The beginnings of socialistic thought in Germany are found in the early writings of Karl Rodbertus, Ferdinand Lassalle, Friedrich Engels, and Karl Marx. Rodbertus owed much to the French socialists. He and most of the other German socialists were inclined, however, to favor state socialism as opposed to co-operative associations and to the Utopian schemes of Saint-Simon, Fourier, and Owen. They also showed a greater interest in the doctrines of the classical economists and gave intimations of the later trend of Marxian thought in turning classical "laws" against the system of private enterprise.

## Mid-century Uprisings

The growth of industrial classes on the Continent was accompanied by the divergent interpretations of industrialism briefly outlined above. These interpretations were influenced also by observations of the more advanced industrialism of England and by a desire to direct the course of anticipated industrial changes on the Continent. Engels's *Condition of the Working Classes in England* was published in 1844. The *Communist Manifesto*, which was first read before a group of radicals in London in 1847 and published in enlarged form in 1848, declared that Germany was "on the eve of a bourgeois revolution" involving the fall of the "reactionary classes," and that immediately thereafter the Communist party should lead the movement for a "proletarian revolution." Fourier's collectivism was based largely on anticipations of the growth of industrialism. List recognized the slight development of capitalistic business enterprise in Germany and proposed his program for the fostering and directing of private enterprise by the state. The "orthodox" economists of the Continent desired the removal of restrictions for the purpose of permitting enterprise to develop along lines of free competition and *laissez faire.*

These various trends of thought were prominent in the uprisings of 1848, but other influences were also apparent. In central and eastern Europe the demand for the emancipation of the peasants was an important issue. In Italy, Hungary, Bohemia, and Germany nationalism played a prominent part. Everywhere the intellectual liberals, supported in varying degrees by workers, businessmen, and peasants, demanded such distinctively liberal policies as an extension of the franchise, freedom of speech and of the press, and removal of restrictions on occupational choice.

In France, where the revolutionary movement began, credit inflation and rapid building of factories beyond immediate market demands for output were followed by a business crisis and widespread unemployment, aggravated by extremely high prices, especially of wheat and wine. The government of Louis Philippe, which was dominated by bankers and wealthy industrialists, met the widespread demand for reform with repressive measures. The incident which precipitated the revolt was the prohibition by the government of a banquet announced by reform leaders for February 22, 1848. On that date students and workingmen gathered in protest and were fired upon by the soldiery. Paris was almost immediately transformed into a city of barricades and of belligerent workers demanding not merely reform but the overthrow of the monarchy. Louis Philippe at once abdicated and sought refuge in England.

The bourgeois leaders and the intellectuals, fearful of the socialistic tendencies of the workers, acceded to the proclamation of a republic and proposed various reforms. They even made a show of accepting Louis Blanc's plan for national workshops. But Blanc had proposed a system of co-operative associations under governmental auspices for supplanting private enterprise, whereas the plan as adopted and carried out by officials hostile to Blanc's ideas was merely an arrangement for relief of the unemployed under bourgeois control — a revival of what had been called charity workshops. In June even the subsidies necessary for this perversion of Blanc's plan were withdrawn. Working-class revolt flared up again, but was repressed with much bloodshed. In the midst of the discord and confusion, Louis Napoleon Bonaparte, nephew of the great Napoleon, skillfully played the parties against each other, first becoming president and in 1852 emperor. But throughout the rapidly shifting political scene the middle classes, with the passive support of the peasants, retained their ascendancy.

Outside of France the principal immediate economic effects of the revolutions of 1848 were agrarian. In Hungary the landlord's power of life and death over his dependents was revoked and many copyholds were changed into freeholds. In Austria, Bavaria, Prussia, and some of the other states of Germany, the movement toward emancipation was accelerated, although in many parts of Germany and in Hungary the larger landlords were strengthened and many peasant proprietors were forced into the ranks of wage earners. In England, France, and some of the smaller countries, notably Belgium, the characteristic features of middle-class rule had already become prevalent. In most of the countries where revolutionary uprisings occurred in 1848, bourgeois rule awaited the extension of industrialism, the growth of cities, and the triumph of nationalism in Italy and Germany. Nevertheless the repressive system of Metternich was overthrown and the way was prepared politically for the gradual extension of economic liberalism.

## Extension of Bourgeois Doctrines and Policies after 1848

During the decades immediately following the uprisings of 1848, there was little change in the system of economic theory stemming from Adam Smith's *Wealth of Nations*, but there was a continued extension of its influence. The era of rapid expansion gave rise to an assertive optimism. Thus Bastiat's *Economic Harmonies* (1849) and the writings of H. C. Carey, an American economist, denied the gloomy implications of the doctrines of population, wages, and rent, and tried to prove that an increasing share of income goes to wage earners. Carey later became a protectionist. The principal departure other than in socialistic thought was made by the historical school. This phase of economic thought had already been foreshadowed in the writings of Sismondi, List, and especially Roscher. The evolutionary conception in the study and interpretation of economic life was strengthened by the development of the biological sciences. Charles Darwin's *Origin of Species* appeared in 1859. The "orthodox" economists retained their ascendancy in Great Britain, France, Holland, and Belgium, and exerted much influence elsewhere, especially in Italy. But economic nationalism exemplified by List, the criticisms of such men as Sismondi, and the opposition of the historical school to abstract and doctrinaire conceptions of economic "laws" became increasingly effective, especially in Germany, in checking the extension of "orthodox" economics.

The *Communist Manifesto* of 1848 contained the germs of Marxian doctrines, and socialistic thought was not without influence on legislation. But public policy was dominated by middle-class enterprise and by agrarian interests. Agitation for parliamentary reform, for social legislation, and for socialistic reorganization continued after the uprisings of 1848, and in Italy and Germany nationalistic aspirations assumed new forms. But the dominant economic interests of the peoples of western and central Europe were the building of roads and railroads and factories, the development of trade, and the organization and financing of new forms of enterprise.

In France under Louis Napoleon as president and emperor, business enterprise was carefully fostered. Two credit institutions, the *Crédit Foncier* and the *Société Générale de Crédit Mobilier*, were founded in 1852 to supplement the Bank of France in extending aid to landowners and in promoting the financing of business. They were in part responsible for the inflation which culminated in the crises of 1857, but were able to survive the crises. The *Crédit Lyonnais*, founded at Lyon in 1863, rapidly grew into a national institution by means of a system of branch banks. In Holland and Belgium there was also a rapid expansion of credit, but largely through existing institutions. French joint-stock companies with limited liability were not encouraged by law, but Belgian companies were granted admission to France in 1857 and British companies in 1862. In 1863 French law was modified and in 1867 still further liberalized. The result was a rapid extension of enterprise by limited-liability joint-stock companies. The government of Napoleon III also encouraged railway construction and after the depression of 1857 guaranteed interest to the railway companies. Napoleon tried to please all classes, but his policies were pre-eminently such as met the favor of businessmen by affording liberal contracts for public works and by promoting the industrial, commercial, and colonial expansion of France.

In France, Belgium, and Holland, as well as England, the remnants of guild control of trade and handicrafts had already disappeared. In many of the states of Germany guild regulations survived. The master craftsmen attempted to utilize the revolutionary agitation of 1848 for strengthening their control of industry and trade against the new industrialists. They held that the use of steam power should be restricted and that an extension of the guild system to all industry would safeguard Germany from the evils of the new industrialism and from the spread of socialism. In Prussia, the movement for curtailing the power of the guilds was checked by a law of 1848. It was not until the decade beginning in 1860 that compulsory membership in guilds and subjection both to guild regulations and public supervision were legally abandoned. During that decade there was a rapid extension of individualism and *laissez faire* in the choice of occupations and of place of business and employment, and in modes of carrying on the handicrafts and trades formerly subject to the guilds.

In the meantime, the economic basis of the traditional forms of industry and trade was being undermined. The German banking system was being reorganized and expanded to meet the demands for credit and investment in the new types of business enterprise. The Bank of Prussia had been established in 1846, and it became the basis of the modern Reichsbank. Twenty-five note-issuing banks appeared in Germany within two decades after 1850. A Prussian law of 1843 provided for joint-stock companies. This law, later liberalized, together with similar legislation in other German states, promoted the unwise utilization of the new credit facilities and aggravated the crisis of 1857. Company laws varied widely in the different states of Germany, but changes in the laws tended in general to facilitate the development of new forms of enterprise.

In Italy, the kingdom of Sardinia after 1848 underwent a significant economic transformation. This kingdom included the island of Sardinia and the areas of Italy adjacent to France and south-western Switzerland. A constitutional system in accord with British principles was accepted by the king in 1848, and on this political basis Count Cavour took the lead in reconstructing the economy of the country. Petty local tariffs were abolished, liberal trade arrangements were made with other countries, taxation was reformed, the building of railroads was promoted, and the modernization of agriculture and industry was undertaken. Cavour advocated the development of irrigation projects and aroused the country to the possibilities of water power as a substitute for coal. Sardinia alone would have been insignificant but it became extremely important as a nucleus for the political unification of Italy in 1861 and as a model for economic reconstruction throughout the kingdom of Italy in accord with the principles of British economic and political liberalism.

### Labor and Social Legislation

The rise of trade-unions on the Continent was hindered even more than in England by legal and administrative obstacles. In addition the workers of the Continent, especially in Germany, continued to exhibit a greater interest in politics than in trade-union organization and activity. In Germany, the journeymen in many industries maintained organizations. In connection with the mid-century conflicts over the status of guilds, the journeymen, in opposition to the masters, demanded freedom of migration, freedom to seek employment outside of the guild system, especially in factories, legislation for minimum wages and maximum hours, and the creation of a ministry of labor. But the future of labor was with workers outside of the handicrafts and guilds. In 1848 a Workmen's Congress was held in Berlin, a Central Committee was formed and later transferred to Leipzig, a bulletin was published by the Committee, and many local branches were formed. The movement was checked, however, by the reactionary influences that gained ascendancy after the Revolution of 1848.

In Germany after 1848, as in England after the decline of Chartism, co-operation became popular. Societies were formed by Franz Hermann Schulze-Delitzsch in the early 1850's, a central organization was founded in 1859, and favorable legislation was obtained in Prussia in 1867 and later for all of Germany. Credit societies and banks were established, as well as co-operative stores. Numerous workingmen's educational associations were also formed.

Thus in spite of discouragements after 1848, workers formed numerous local groups, mostly co-operative, educational, and political in nature, and held occasional congresses. With this movement Ferdinand Lassalle became prominently associated. But he vigorously opposed the existing co-operative societies as merely palliative and advocated organization for political action. He held that universal suffrage was the first objective, but that it should be merely the means for transforming privately owned enterprise and the system of wage labor into a system of co-operative production for delivering the workers from bondage to the "brazen law of wages." The Workingmen's Association of Leipzig, which had adopted the Schulze-Delitzsch plan of co-operation, invited him in 1863 to explain his views. This meeting was followed by various others, and the outcome was the transformation of a large proportion of the co-operative societies into a political movement. The German General Workingmen's Association of 1863, founded by Lassalle, made rapid progress previous to the death of Lassalle in a duel in 1864, but thereafter suffered from incompetent leadership.

In the meantime, the followers of Karl Marx, who favored direct state action rather than production by co-operative societies, were consolidating their influence over various educational and co-operative groups. In the Marxian groups, Wilhelm Liebknecht and August Bebel assumed leadership. The outcome was the formation, in 1869, of the Social Democratic Workingmen's Party. This organization and the group formed by Lassalle were formally united in 1875. The united group approved the idea of state assistance to producers' associations, but in general the program of the party was in accord with Marxian principles. The origins of the most important trade-unions (the so-called free unions as distinguished from the Christian unions) are traceable to the movement inaugurated by Lassalle in 1863.

Labor legislation in Germany before the founding of the empire was concerned more largely with the obsolescent guilds than with modern industrial conditions. As early as 1839, however, a Factory Act was passed in Prussia. Children under nine years of age were not to be employed, and children from nine to sixteen were to be employed not more than ten hours a day. Provisions for school attendance were also included. Further restrictions were embodied in a Prussian law of 1853. Many of the other German states passed similar laws. But neither the Prussian nor the other laws made provision for effective enforcement. The formation of the North German Confederation in 1867 was followed two years later by a detailed code applying to industrial employments throughout the Confederation, but enforcement remained lax even during the early imperial era.

The most important factory legislation in France before the Third Republic was the child-labor law of 1841. This act applied to factories using machinery and employing as many as twenty workers. Children below eight years of age were not to be employed. Children from eight to twelve were restricted to eight hours a day, and those from twelve to sixteen to a twelve-hour day. Educational provisions were included. In the more important industrial regions, serious efforts seem to have been made to enforce the law. In 1848 a general twelve-hour day in factories and workshops was provided for by law, but the act was not extensively enforced.

Labor organizations in France were rigorously restricted by legislation extending back as far as 1791. The act of 1791, by the revolutionary National Assembly, was declared by the Assembly to be inapplicable to chambers of commerce and was interpreted as applying only to workingmen. Various later laws re-enforced the act of 1791.

In spite of legal obstacles, three types of organizations maintained their activities, either secretly or with the connivance of the authorities. These were the early modern journeymen's organizations (*compagnonnages*), friendly societies (*mutualités*), and trade-unions of an early type (*sociétés de résistance*). Many of the journeymen's associations and friendly societies were in reality disguised trade-unions. After 1848 many co-operative societies were formed, some of them with public aid, but they soon disappeared. Napoleon III's government was at first hostile to all forms of labor organization, but friendly societies were later encouraged. After 1860 the persistence of the workers in the face of legal obstacles was rendered less difficult by the desire of Napoleon III to cultivate their good will. In 1864 the law against association was modified, and a restricted right to strike was conceded. There was a further modification of legal restrictions in 1868, workingmen's organizations being legally and theoretically "tolerated" on the same terms as associations of employers.

In the meantime the conception of militant defense embodied in the *sociétés de résistance* was giving place to a doctrine of co-operation to be carried into effect by unions which came to be called "syndical chambers." Strikes were deprecated except as a last resort, and the unions claimed legal recognition for the immediate purpose of obtaining peaceful agreements with employers. But many of the unions placed their faith in co-operative activities — credit societies, co-operative stores, and ultimately a system of co-operative production. This movement met grave reverses in 1868, and the workers then began to favor socialism of the Marxian type. The International Workingmen's Association (the First International) became popular in France.

## Marxian Socialism

Socialistic thought after 1848 was increasingly influenced by the powerful mind of Karl Marx, a middle-class German Jew born in 1818. He early came under the influence of Hegel's philosophy of change through the opposition of contradictory ideas and the emergence of a new synthesis from the conflict. As early as 1844 Marx applied this conception not to ideas but to economic forces. He pointed out the conflict between the system of private property and the rapidly emerging wage-earning class — a conflict which would bring about the dissolution alike of private capitalism and the wage system and lead to the formation of a new social economy. The *Communist Manifesto* of 1848, the varied editorial and journalistic work of Marx, and his great masterpiece, *Capital*, the first volume of which appeared in 1867, were essentially elaborations of this general conception. But he modified the philosophical dialectic of Hegel and attempted to found his doctrines on historical causation and economic analysis. He was influenced even more by English and French economic theories and conditions than by those of Germany.

Underlying the Marxian conception was the economic interpretation of history. This he defined in general terms as meaning that the legal, political, and cultural aspects of life and the forms of social consciousness are decisively affected by the stage of development of economic life, by prevailing modes of production, and by the material conditions of life. The conception of a historic conflict of interest between the owners of capital and the wage-earning classes found vigorous expression in the *Communist Manifesto*. This document asserted that "the history of all hitherto existing society is the history of class struggle," but that modern industrialism creates a new condition in which the class struggle is

simplified by the concentration of ownership of capital and the forcing of an ever-increasing proportion of the people into the ranks of
the nonpropertied wage workers. "All society is more and more
splitting up into two opposing camps, into two great hostile classes,
the bourgeoisie and the proletariat."

Marx held that in the new alignment of classes conflict of interests was inescapable. The economic basis of this view was
found in "orthodox" economic doctrines, particularly the labor
theory of value. David Ricardo, a banker-economist, in writing
of goods freely reproducible by labor and entering freely into the
competitive market, declared that "the value of a commodity, or
the quantity of any other commodity for which it will exchange,
depends on the relative quantity of labor which is necessary for its
production, and not on the greater or less compensation which is
paid for that labor." The compensation of wage labor is determined by competition, for it is itself bought and sold and is subject
to increase or diminution according to the general laws of supply
and demand. Therefore, wrote Ricardo, the "natural" rate of
wages is the price necessary to enable the laborer to maintain himself
and his family in accord with the standards of living which, through
habit, have become necessary to his existence.

Marx held that the labor required for the production of goods
is the measure of the value not of particular commodities in terms
of their market prices but of the aggregate value of all wealth
produced. Labor he viewed as the sum of human energy devoted
to production, not merely wage labor. But he pointed to the growth
of large-scale industry and the concentration of ownership in the
hands of a small group of capitalists, while the masses of the people
were becoming wage laborers. Thus an increasing proportion
of value (exchangeable wealth) was being produced by wage labor,
while the wage workers were receiving merely a subsistence. Nor
was this due to the wickedness or avarice of employers, but to
the operation of the economic laws of privately owned enterprise.
Wage workers were recipients of a mere subsistence due to the fact
that their labor power was owned by others who bought it in the
competitive labor market and controlled the "surplus value."
The dilemma of wage workers (condemned to competitive subsistence wages while producing "surplus value" going to others)
was described as an unavoidable aspect of competitive private
capitalism. Workers, however, were being brought together in
cities and large establishments under conditions which formed a

natural basis for association and "solidarity" of interests; and it was held that the growth and concentration of capitalistic enterprise would inevitably find culmination in proletarian action for the purpose of transforming private enterprise into socialized or collectivist capital as the only possible escape from the dilemma.

But Marx held that not only wage workers but their employers as well, and indeed the whole system of private capitalism, were confronted with an economic dilemma resulting from the peculiar position and increasing economic importance of wage labor. Wages are fixed by the competitive position of labor as an element in the cost of production, and workers can find work only when their labor has "surplus value" — when their labor is profitable. But profits depend on markets, and the workers, even when employed, have no purchasing power corresponding either to their need for consumption or to their capacity for production. On the other hand, those to whom goes "surplus labor value" (profits, rent, interest) have no capacity for consumption equal to their income. Nor do they have opportunity for profitable investment corresponding to their surplus income, because workers as consumers are unable to buy the products of labor under full employment of labor and capital. The results include a destructive struggle for markets, crises, unemployment, deflation of unused income, social disorder, and the disintegration of private capitalism. The only alternative was described as " collectivism " or concerted action for socializing capital and for distributing the product of industry to the whole body of producers, thus maintaining equilibrium between consumption and productive capacity. This outcome might be postponed but could not be averted by imperialistic expansion and the widening of the area of "expropriation" of "surplus labor value."

These various doctrines had been formulated by earlier writers. The basic importance of economic factors, the prevalence of conditions provocative of conflict between employers and employees, the Marxian views of wages and surplus value produced by labor, and the disequilibrium of productive capacity and consumption — all of these ideas had been embodied repeatedly in the writings of both socialists and nonsocialists. The labor theory of value as stated by Marx has no greater claim to scientific precision than many of the other "laws" of the classical economists. Nor is such a theory a necessary basis for socialism, or for the view that surplus value goes to nonproducers and creates economic disequilibrium, or even for the doctrine of the class struggle.

What, then, is the explanation of the dominant role of Marx in the history of socialism? An important source of strength was his simplification of the socialistic thesis. He brushed aside the various earlier forms of socialistic thought as inconsistent with historical evolution and as vague or Utopian or merely reformist. The whole force of his attack was directed against private capitalism, and the whole force of his positive argument was directed toward collective capitalism not merely as theoretically desirable but as the natural culmination of historical and contemporary forces. Although few of his ideas were original, his work as a whole was a distinctive synthesis of familiar conceptions. He adopted the most widely accepted doctrines of the economists and, on the basis of their own premises, turned the logic of classical economy into a powerful weapon against private capital and competitive production. He appealed not merely to logic but to history and to contemporary social change — the decline of handicrafts and small business; the building of factories, railroads, and other large-scale enterprises; the concentration of ownership; the transformation of other classes into wage earners; the international characteristics of capitalistic enterprise; and the recurrence of crises due at least in part to the disequilibrium of productive capacity and the purchasing power of laborers as consumers. Finally, he identified himself with the movement for working-class organization and political action.

### Beginnings of the International Labor Movement

The idea of internationalism in respect to the interests and aims of labor long antedated international organization. During the middle decades of the century, and especially during the crises beginning in 1837, 1847, and 1857, attention was directed to the growing interdependence of nations and to the acute sufferings of the unemployed. The new type of industrialism was rapidly being extended. Markets and banking were becoming more largely international. Employers were becoming increasingly dependent on the competitive expansion of markets in other countries for profitable sale of their "surplus" products, and this was believed to be largely due to the fact that workers as consumers had no income corresponding to their output, with a resulting disequilibrium of productive capacity and opportunity to consume the output of industry. The struggle for markets was provocative of international conflicts. National and international problems alike were believed to be traceable mainly to the exploitation of labor, which was viewed as inherent in the system of privately owned enter-prise. Workers, it was held, should therefore organize on an international basis for putting an end to the exploitation of labor.

An interchange of views was facilitated by the fact that the various revolutionary uprisings and the repressive policies of governments, especially in central Europe, caused an extensive movement of political refugees. Many of these exiles who were interested in labor organization were intellectuals. The outstanding instance was Karl Marx. An early effort at international organization resulted in the Communist League, formed in London in 1847. Its aims were international but it was largely restricted to German refugees. Its main importance was the adoption of the *Communist Manifesto* as its program. The term "communist" was adopted to distinguish it from other socialistic groups and programs, which were regarded by Marx as either Utopian or merely reformist. The *Manifesto* was based throughout on the conception of the international character of industry and trade and of the interests of labor. The aim of the League was described as "the union and agreement of the democratic parties of all countries." The conclusion of the *Communist Manifesto* was the slogan, "Workers of all lands, unite!"

The Communist League was never in reality international, nor was there at that time a sufficient basis in national groups for the support of an international organization. The repressive policies of most of the governments of Europe after the revolutionary movements of 1848 for a time checked the labor movement. But with the rapid advance of industrialization, the organization of labor was resumed, and in 1864 there was a new attempt to bring about a union of national groups.

Opportunity for extensive international contacts was afforded by the International Exhibition at London in 1862. A large group of French workmen and smaller numbers from other countries visited the Exhibition, and these visitors, together with refugees, held conferences with British labor leaders. The contacts then made were continued from time to time, and in 1863 formal proposals were made for a union of French and English groups. In 1864, at a meeting in St. Martin's Hall, London, a formal organization was launched. It was named the International Working Men's Association and was later known as the First International. Germans, Italians, Poles, and Swiss, as well as Frenchmen and Englishmen, took part in the organization.

The elements represented in the organization were far from harmonious.  Leadership in formulating a program and a plan of organization was undertaken by Marx.  For the sake of concerted action he abandoned his own extreme views and prepared a series of declarations not altogether consistent but on the whole acceptable to the various groups.  Private enterprise was declared to be incapable of remedying the plight of the workers, but no positive affirmation of collectivism was introduced.  Reformist measures, such as the British Ten-Hours Bill, were approved.  Co-operative societies were praised as demonstrating the possibilities of independent action by the workers as producers, but the ultimate aim of the International was declared to be the achievement of political power and the utilization of government in the interest of the masses. The International was based on autonomous national organizations or "sections," and plans were made for an annual congress and a permanent General Council.

The history of the International was marked by several conflicting tendencies.  (1) There was an element, largely Italian, which hoped to utilize the organization for promoting revolution for nationalistic ends, but the purely nationalistic group, followers of the Italian patriot Mazzini, soon withdrew.  (2) Many leaders, especially of the English type, held that labor organizations should concern themselves primarily with improving the lot of employees by bringing their influence to bear on employers in respect to wages, hours, and working conditions, and should limit their political activities to the securing of factory acts or other reforms directly affecting labor.  (3) Others, especially the French leaders before 1868, favored a thoroughgoing economic reorganization but by means of free co-operative societies aided when necessary by the state.  (4) A group led by Michael Bakunin, a Russian exile, believed in the overthrow of the political state as well as the destruction of private title to capital, and the establishment, in a vaguely defined manner, of equality and freedom by means of co-operative production.  At the end of his life Bakunin renounced his extreme individualism and accepted the view that man is "really a member of a collective whole."  (5) Marx and his followers held that title to private capital must be abolished but that the only practicable method for achieving this end and for providing a substitute was the utilization of the state for transforming private capital into public capital.  This "collectivist" economy was to be attained by "solidarity" of action of the masses of nonpropertied workers.

The Marxists maintained their ascendancy but acted with moderation in respect to forcing their doctrines upon the national groups.  Financial aid was given to various groups of strikers, and efforts were made to prevent the transfer of strikebreakers.  The formation of national groups was promoted, and the International became an influential organization.  But its internal disunity made effective action in a crisis impossible.  On the other hand, real unity on a Marxian basis could be achieved only at the cost of losing the support of important sections and of arousing still further the already intense fear and hostility of employers and governments.

The first critical test of the International was the Commune of Paris of 1871, following the overthrow of Napoleon III.  The instigation of the Commune was popularly, though erroneously, attributed to the International.  The officers of the International issued a declaration upholding the part played by the workers in the Commune and condemning the violent and bloody overthrow of the movement.  This was followed by a severe reaction against working-class organizations and by loss of the support of many of the more moderate trade-unions.  Soon thereafter the struggle between Marx and Bakunin culminated in the expulsion of Bakunin and his adherents.  This was followed by the nominal transfer of the General Council to New York in 1872, but in reality by the end of the International.

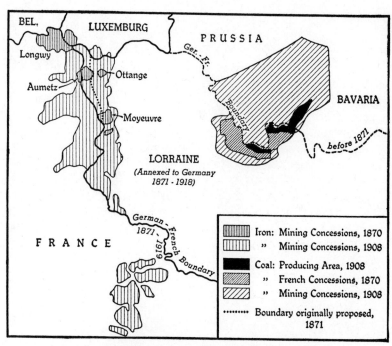

*Iron and Coal Resources of (and near) Lorraine*

Legend:

Iron: Mining Concessions, 1870
      "   Mining Concessions, 1908
Coal: Producing Area, 1908
      "   French Concessions, 1870
      "   Mining Concessions, 1908
·········· Boundary originally proposed, 1871

Map labels: BEL, LUXEMBURG, PRUSSIA, BAVARIA, Longwy, Ottange, Aumetz, Moyeuvre, LORRAINE (Annexed to Germany 1871 - 1918), FRANCE, Ger.-Fr. Boundary, before 1871, German - French Boundary 1871 - 1919

# PART V. THE STRUGGLE FOR THE WORLD MARKET, 1871–1914

# CHAPTER 24

## GERMAN INDUSTRY AND THE WORLD MARKET

———◆———

### The Boundary of 1871 and the Lorraine Ores

Germany's annexation of Alsace and Lorraine in 1871 affected the distribution of primary economic resources between France and Germany. In Alsace, France lost her largest and most prosperous cotton-manufacturing district; in Lorraine she lost important reserves of iron ore and some coal. The purposes of Bismarck in requiring this cession of territory were predominantly military. The rectification of the boundary was designed to make the threat of a French invasion at this point more determinate in direction. The earlier boundary, before 1871, gave a French army in Lorraine the choice of two widely divergent routes into Germany. Defense of the frontier, therefore, had required the massing of nearly twice as great a force on the German side.

In the early stages of the negotiations for peace, the Lorraine ores were not a factor in the German proposals for the location of the new boundary. The relation of the boundaries to the ore deposits, and to concessions granted before 1870, is shown by the map on page 494. The primary ore field then in use, the Longwy basin, was not included in the proposed annexation in the preliminary negotiations; nor was the smaller mining area at Aumetz inside the famous "green line" on the earliest maps, though this basin included important bodies of alluvial ores better adapted to smelting than the oölitic ores of the larger formation known as the "minette" or weak ores. The alluvial ores were known as "strong iron" (*fer fort*). The "minettes" could be safely used only in conjunction with the alluvial ores. The early stage of the negotiation thus gave to Germany only the smaller fields at Ottange and Moyeuvre, though the area of oölitic ores included was considerable. Some ores would have been transferred, but the transfer would have been merely incidental to a boundary line dominated by defensive considerations. Military strategy required certain control of the

495

highland on the left bank of the Moselle. Bismarck was determined to have complete possession of the area which he described as the "key of his house."

The arrangements of the preliminary treaty were modified in the course of discussions of the precise extent of the area "dominated" by Belfort (*rayon de Belfort*). The French experts held that this must mean at least the area within the range of existing heavy artillery. This interpretation would have included all territory within ten kilometers of Belfort. The French experts also pointed out that Germany would secure no advantage from the small region between this line and the water parting between the Rhine and the Rhone. The experts contended that this was the only intelligible interpretation of the preliminary agreement, and that no exchange of territory elsewhere could be claimed as a consideration for such a settlement of this portion of the boundary. The Germans, however, refused to accept this position and proposed lines which would have rendered Belfort utterly indefensible. Thiers was so deeply concerned over Belfort that he acceded to the general principle of an exchange of territory. It was therefore agreed that the boundary southerly from Luxemburg should be revised. Bismarck became ore conscious between the signature of the preliminaries and the appointment of the commissions to discuss the revisions of the Lorraine boundary. Minerals did not become a primary issue of policy, but he became sufficiently interested to appoint to the German staff a mining engineer, Hauchecorne, who was enthusiastic over the prospect of annexing ore fields.

The extreme demands of the Germans would have taken a small portion of the Longwy basin and deprived France of any direct contact with Luxemburg. Bismarck conceded three villages giving access to Luxemburg and restoring some currently operated iron works. The main elements of the French claims around Belfort were conceded, but additional ores were secured in Lorraine as shown on the map. The new boundary in the ore district of Lorraine was largely the work of Hauchecorne; it was based on the notions then current about the value of the minette deposits. Though the total area was known to be large, it was then presumed that the ores could be used only within two or three kilometers of the actual outcrops of ore at the surface. With this principle in mind, it was not difficult to draw a boundary that would include the greater part of the supposedly "workable" ores outside the Longwy district.

The immediate transfer of iron production was considerable.

In 1869 there were forty-five blast furnaces in the two departments Meurthe and Moselle.   Five of these were still burning charcoal; but the increase in coke furnaces had been more considerable than in any other section of France, and the increase in coke pig iron in this region more than offset the decline in the production of charcoal iron throughout France.   In 1869 these departments were producing 420,000 tons of pig iron, amounting to one third of the total production.   In 1871 there remained in this region only eighteen blast furnaces on the French side of the new boundary: their production was only 95,000 tons of pig iron.   By 1873 the number of blast furnaces had increased to thirty-five, producing 270,000 tons of pig iron.   At that time the production of iron in Germany (1,400,000 tons) was only slightly in excess of the production in France (1,300,000 tons); hence the net transfer of about 300,000 tons' capacity in pig-iron production was about 22 per cent of the total French production.

## The Basic Process and the Briey Basin

The serious extent of the transfers is revealed only in part by the productive capacity then in operation.   The future was intended to be involved even more than current production, for the major portion of the reserves then known lay within the new German boundary.   The discovery of deep beds of ore on the French side

IRON ORES IN LORRAINE, 1911, IN MILLIONS OF METRIC TONS [1]

|  | Known in 1870 | Developed since 1870 | Total Amount | Per Cent |
|---|---|---|---|---|
| France |  |  |  |  |
| Longwy Basin | 300 |  |  |  |
| Crusnes Basin | 600 |  | 900 | 30.0 |
| Germany |  |  |  |  |
| North of the Fentsch | 1,126 |  |  |  |
| Between the Fentsch and Orne | 385 |  |  |  |
| South of the Orne | 330 |  | 1,841 | 61.7 |
| Luxemburg | 250 |  | 250 | 8.3 |
| Total 1870 | 2,991 |  | 2,991 | 100.0 |
| France |  |  |  |  |
| Briey Basin | — | 2,000 | 2,000 |  |
| Nancy Basin | — | 200 | 200 |  |
| Total France, 1911 |  |  | 3,100 | 60.0 |
| Total Germany, 1911 |  |  | 1,841 | 35.4 |
| Total Luxemburg, 1911 |  |  | 250 | 4.6 |
| Total Lorraine, 1911 |  |  | 5,191 | 100.0 |

[1] Roesler, M., op. cit. (page 455), p. 63.

of the boundary has changed the situation, but the basins are so easily identified that every phase of the development can be followed. The table on page 497 gives a very conservative estimate of the ores definitely located in 1911.

This substantial diversion of primary resources proved to be much more important than anyone could have imagined in 1870; for the basic process developed within the decade following the war made these ore reserves the most important single factor in the iron production of Europe. In 1869 Lorraine produced 420,000 tons of pig iron; Europe as a whole produced 9,888,000 tons of pig iron, so that Lorraine contributed 4.2 per cent of the total for Europe. In 1913, however, Lorraine produced 47 per cent of all the ore produced in Europe. Because of the extensive exports of ore to other areas the precise contribution in pig iron is not clearly shown in the statistics of production.

The ore reserves in other parts of Germany are largely massed in the two general areas classed as the East Rhine and Weser districts. The ores vary in character and do not constitute a single field in either area, but the masses of ore are considerable and they are conveniently situated with reference to the great coal field of the Ruhr. The reserves of the East Rhine field are estimated as 118,900,000 tons; the Weser field is estimated to contain reserves of 98,900,000 tons. Together these fields represent about 85 per cent of the reserves in Germany outside Lorraine. If the Lorraine ores had not been acquired by Germany in 1871, the German ores, amounting in all to reserves of 255,600,000 tons, would have been the sole domestic supply of ore. The extensive coal fields would have attracted importations, but the detail of development would certainly have been different. The annexation of Lorraine was an event of first-class economic importance, affecting not only the national distribution of primary resources, but many details of regional development in Belgium, France, Germany, and Sweden. One must assume that large amounts of ore would have been imported by Germany, but it is not clear that Lorraine would have supplied so large a portion of them.

### The Textiles of Alsace

The iron ores have attracted so much attention over many years that the position of the Alsatian cotton industry is frequently overlooked. In 1868 there were in Alsace 2,131,000 cotton spindles, 48,536 looms, and 100 calico-printing machines. In Germany,

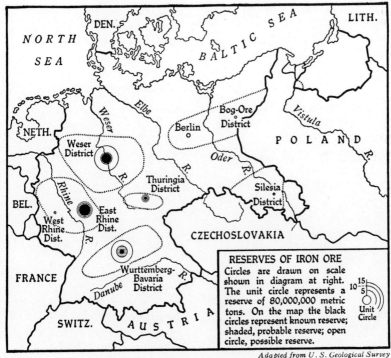

*Adapted from U. S. Geological Survey*

*Iron Resources of Germany, after 1920*

at that time, there were about 3,000,000 cotton spindles and 37,000 looms. As the Alsatian industry was technically more advanced, there can be little doubt but that its output in cotton yarn and cloth was somewhat greater than the output of all the German states. Alsace also produced a certain amount of woolens and silks, and both of these industries had reached a high level of technical efficiency, for machinization with power was as far advanced there as in any section of Europe.

The territory annexed in 1871 thus contributed largely to the textile industries of the newly formed German Empire, and subtracted this important amount from French production. The treaty entailed serious economic losses to France, and added materially to the sense of inferiority that was already too keenly felt for the best development of France.

The vigorous reaction in certain quarters belied the depressed state of mind so common in France. The discovery and development of the iron ores of the basins of Briey and Nancy were notable evidence of the technical competence and resourcefulness of the French, but despite genuine achievements in many fields the generation following the Franco-Prussian War looked into the future with misgiving and apprehension.

## The Predominance of Craft Industry in 1875

The industrial development of Germany in the eighteenth century and the early nineteenth had been profoundly influenced by the obstacles to trade created by the subdivision of the territory and the earlier systems of taxation in the various states. These factors had retarded industrial expansion until the formation of the Customs Union, and the narrow localization of much trade had been especially favorable to small industrial units. In many areas peasant industries were extensively developed even for export, and throughout the first half of the nineteenth century the independent master craftsman was the dominant element in all the occupations requiring skill. Capitalistic control in Germany was less conspicuous than in England, France, or Belgium. There were very few factories, and even the merchant-employer system was of clearly secondary importance.

The forms of industrial organization were not conspicuously changed even in the generation subsequent to the formation of the Customs Union. There were notable developments in coal mining and in the iron industry, but the general characteristics of the old industrial order persisted. In the textile industries the peasants and small masters clung to their old spinning wheels and to their hand looms. In woodworking and the leather industries there was little direct competition between power machinery and the simpler mechanisms of the craft shop. The supremacy of power spinning was clearly established as early as 1860, but heavy imports of British yarns limited the development of power spinning in Germany. The hand-loom weavers, however, were still able to compete in the highly specialized types of woolens, silks, and linens. The conservatism of the peasants and craftsmen emphasized very sharply the lines of demarcation between the older and the newer forms of industrialization. In the Ruhr basin and around some of the other coal fields the new order was fully established at the time of the formation of the Empire. In the kingdom of Saxony, the Thuringian states, and even in Bavaria the old forms persisted with little or no change.

The earliest comprehensive industrial statistics are for the year 1875. The broader features of the results are striking. If we make reasonable estimates of the average size of establishments with 5 to 10 wage earners, and with 11 to 50 wage earners, it is possible to distribute the total personnel among the various classes of establishments, as follows:

INDUSTRIAL POPULATION OF GERMANY, 1875 [1]

| Number of Wage Earners per Establishment | Total Number of Wage Earners | Per Cent of Total |
|---|---|---|
| Less than 5 | 4,159,000 | 64.3 |
| 5 to 10 | 189,000 | 2.9 |
| 11 to 50 | 891,000 | 13.8 |
| Over 50 | 1,231,000 | 19.0 |
| | 6,470,000 | 100.0 |

The position of large-scale industry is roughly comparable with conditions in France about 1850, but in Belgium concentration was further advanced even in 1846.   In England in 1850 only about 10 per cent of the industrial population was reported by the Factory Inspectors, but there was much large-scale industry not at that time subject to regulation.   There can be no doubt of the relatively slow development of large-scale industry in Germany.   The proportion of specialized industrial workers to the total population was smaller than in Belgium and Great Britain.   In these respects, the relationships between industry and agriculture were of the older type, characteristic of the eighteenth century, but it is hardly justifiable to say, as many do, that Germany in 1870 was an "agricultural" country.

The actual number of industrial workers in Germany was about equal to the number in France or England.   Even with slightly lower productivity per capita, the industries of Germany contributed much to the general trade of Europe.   Furthermore, Germany was producing as much iron as France, and nearly twice as much coal. British production of these basic commodities was very much greater, but the British industries were older, and the mineral deposits were closer to the sea.   Germany in 1870–1875 was nearly, if not fully, abreast of France in respect of the volume and value of her industrial output.   It is rather artificial to characterize as "agricultural" the country which ranked second or third in the world in industrial production.   It is better to refer specifically to the changes in the scale of industrial concentration and the use of power.

[1] *Statistik des Deutsches Reich*, vol. 34, p. 544; vol. 35, p. 852.

## The Use of Power and Large-Scale Enterprise

By 1895 the transition towards large-scale industry was far advanced. In the strictly industrial groups only 31.7 per cent of the persons gainfully employed were in the small units: as isolated workers, or in establishments with less than six wage earners. The other classifications were new, so that direct comparison with 1875 is not possible. Establishments having 6 to 20 wage earners were classed as medium size, and all establishments having more than 20 wage earners were classed as large. The large establishments in 1895 reported 51.7 per cent of the total number of wage earners; the medium scale establishments, 16.6 per cent; and the small establishments, 31.7 per cent. The preponderance of large-scale industry was thus beyond dispute.

Large-scale production is clearly advantageous only over certain portions of the industrial field, but there seems to be ground for presuming that there will always be a place for the smaller units. In Great Britain the careful Census of Production of 1907 reported 19.4 per cent of the workers in small establishments. Belgium in 1910 reported 26.78 per cent in small establishments (of under 5 wage earners). Germany in 1907 reported 29 per cent in small establishments. The Census of Manufactures in the United States omits so many of the small establishments counted in Europe that the general returns are very misleading. The materials in the census of occupations provide means of supplementing the other returns, and though the corrections involve elements of uncertainty it is clear that about 20 per cent of those gainfully employed in industry were working in small establishments. Small units were relatively more important in 1906 in France than in any of the other countries mentioned — employing 48 per cent of the total workers.

This increase in the importance of large-scale industry in Germany was closely associated with the introduction of power. The general features of this development are shown in the following table.

Although power was in use over a wide field in 1875, the amounts used were small. Power machinery was to be found only in the larger establishments, and only in those processes in which its use was most decisively established. In the textile field, spinning was largely done by power, but weaving was predominantly a hand process. In 1875, 527,000 looms were reported in the textile industries, whose total personnel amounted to 926,000. Fifty-nine per cent of these workers were employed in small establishments.

POWER EQUIPMENT OF INDUSTRY IN GERMANY: HORSEPOWER INSTALLED
PER PERSON [1]

| | 1875 | 1895 | | 1907 | |
| --- | --- | --- | --- | --- | --- |
| | *Establishments with More Than 5 Workers* | *Establishments with Less Than 5 Workers* | *Establishments with 5 or More Workers* | *All Establishments* | *Establishments with over 51 Workers* |
| Total Industry, (Groups III–XVIII) | — | 0.21 | 0.60 | 0.82 | 1.17 |
| Mining, etc. III | .94 | 1.30 | 1.88 | 3.02 | 3.06 |
| Preparation of metals V | .18 | 0.05 | 0.37 | 0.59 | 1.02 |
| Machinery VI | .16 | 0.13 | 0.38 | 1.18 | 1.11 |
| Textiles IX | .38 | 0.07 | 0.69 | 0.86 | 1.09 |
| Food and drink XIII | .33 | 0.58 | 0.77 | 1.03 | 1.48 |

In the clothing industry only one person in ten had a sewing machine that was worked by a treadle. German industry was heavily specialized towards those crafts and processes demanding skilled hand labor, and it must be remembered that in 1875 this field was still large and important. The relatively low wage scales in Germany also affected the boundary between hand work and machine work in the trades using power. As a consequence we find that the amount of power used even in mining was low in comparison with countries such as England or Belgium. Despite a great increase in the use of power between 1875 and 1895, hand labor was used more extensively in Germany in 1895 than in England, Belgium, or the United States.

The timing of the change to the use of power is difficult to explain. It is important to note that coal production increased less rapidly in the period 1875 to 1895 than either earlier or later. It is barely possible that technical problems in the use of lignite were responsible for this reduced rate of increase, but it is most likely that the primary explanation is to be found in the cheapness of skilled hand labor. Power came into use very rapidly in the United States because labor was very scarce and dear. In many industries power was introduced in the United States sooner than in England. In Germany the reverse was true. Highly skilled labor was abundant and cheap. A

[1] *Statistik des Deutsches Reichs*, vol. 35, Part II, pp. A 244–249; Neue Folge, vol. 113, pp. 130 ff., 396 ff.; vol. 214, pp. 2–3; *Statistisches Jahrbuch für das Deutsche Reich*, 1912, pp. 52–53.

machine then had to be extraordinarily productive and efficient if it was to compete effectively, and many of the early machines were effective only for plain standardized work. As late as 1860 many presumed that machinery would never cut very deeply into the fields dominated by highly skilled craftsmanship. This view underestimated the importance of the possibilities of improving the machines and reducing operating costs. But it is none the less true that many were too quick to assume that the skilled craftsman was entirely displaced by machinery. The German craftsman held his position longer, not because the German engineers were less competent than elsewhere, but because the higher grades of craft skill were cheaper in Germany than in other countries.

### Germany as an "Industrial" State

Contemporary opinion was deeply impressed by the rapid advance of large-scale production in Germany during the last decade of the nineteenth century. Production of primary heavy products of iron and steel exceeded production in other Continental countries and created significant competition for British industries, though the actual volume of production was still below the levels of British production. The increased use of power improved the competitive position of many branches of industries producing consumer goods, such as textiles, leather, and the small metal wares. These changes exerted a great influence on public opinion in all countries. Germany was recognized as an equal competitor with England. The commercial and industrial "supremacy" of England was clearly threatened, and some were quick to assume that the "decline" of England had already begun. An important group of German writers declared that the essential characteristics of German economic life had changed, and that German policy must be revised to meet the requirements of this "industrial" state which had emerged.

These characterizations of the underlying economic changes were not without elements of truth, but they were infelicitous and superficial. It is not possible to formulate any sharp distinction between an "industrial" and an "agricultural" state, and it is certainly unsound to take the position that Germany was an "agricultural" state in 1870 and had become an "industrial" state in 1895. Small regions may become intensively industrialized, so that the casual observer thinks of such a region as exclusively industrial. Even in such regions, an accurate census of occupations reveals unsuspected numbers of persons dependent upon agriculture. Belgium, despite intense industrialization around the great coal fields, still maintains an agricultural population of importance: 1,259,000 persons are gainfully employed in industry; 516,000 persons are gainfully employed in agriculture. Over large areas, the differences in the resources in different regions inevitably produce a close balance between the relative importance of industry and agriculture. With reference to a large area, we can only speak of such differences in the importance of industry and agriculture.

Underlying all the loose discussions of industrialization is the realization that some industries are more important than others. The "industrial" state of late nineteenth-century discussion was in reality a state able to take a commanding position in the production of primary heavy minerals. There can be no doubt of the strategic importance of the primary minerals, but it is best to make it perfectly clear that this is the real issue. The most important industrial regions, the focal centers of economic development and change, are the regions which contribute largely to the production of the primary heavy metals. The essence of the matter lies in the strategic significance of a particular group of industries, not in the mere totals of persons employed in the various occupational groups.

The general occupational statistics are important, however, as an index of the approximate importance of the different classes of resources. There are some variations in the detail of classifications in the various countries, but for broad comparisons the returns are adequate. The changes in the relative importance of the various occupations in Germany are shown in the following table. It will be observed that the relative position of agriculture and industry has been reversed, and that the importance of trade and commerce has increased notably. The enumeration in 1895 marks the change

PROPORTIONATE IMPORTANCE OF THE PRIMARY OCCUPATIONS IN GERMANY [1]

Shown by Percentages of the Total Gainfully Employed

|  | 1871 | 1882 | 1895 | 1907 | 1925 | 1933 |
|---|---|---|---|---|---|---|
| Agriculture and forestry | 47.3 | 42.2 | 36.4 | 34.0 | 30.5 | 28.9 |
| Industry | 32.8 | 34.3 | 37.9 | 39.1 | 42.1 | 40.4 |
| Trade and commerce | 9.0 | 8.6 | 10.9 | 13.9 | 16.4 | 18.4 |
| Public and private service | (10.9)[2] | 5.7 | 6.7 | 6.6 | 6.7 | 8.4 |
| Domestic service |  | 9.2 | 8.1 | 6.4 | 4.3 | 3.9 |
|  | 100.0 | 100.0 | 100.0 | 100.0 | 100.0 | 100.0 |

[1] *Statistisches Jahrbuch für das Deutsche Reich*, 1880, p. 15; 1934, p. 16.
[2] Includes persons living on incomes from property.

from a modest preponderance of agriculture to a modest preponderance of industry.

In France, industry is still somewhat less important than agriculture. Even the changes that have occurred since the World War have not carried the industrial group above the agricultural group, and in the percentage distribution industry has lost a little because of gains in trade and commerce. These features of the distribution of occupations, as well as the records of production of coal and iron, afford a basis for ranking Germany above France as a center of industrial activity. The materials warrant changing the rating of the countries at least as early as 1890. France has thus lost rank successively to England and to Germany: to England, at least as early as 1790; to Germany about one hundred years later.

The occupational structure of Great Britain seems to be profoundly different from that of the Continental countries, for the agricultural group in 1921 accounted for only 13.7 per cent of the total number of persons gainfully employed. The classification reported by the Census reports 35 per cent in industry, 19.7 per cent in trade and commerce; 11.7 per cent in personal service; and 19.9 per cent in the professions, public employment, and clerical work. It would be easier to make comparisons if the clerical workers were distributed between industry and trade, but the outstanding feature of the social structure is the small portion engaged in agriculture. The position of agriculture has been discussed from many points of view. Some have declared that agriculture has been sacrificed to the interests of the industrial class. Others have declared that agricultural interests have been subordinated to the amenities of country life, because the parks surrounding residential property are not as heavily taxed as agricultural land. It is doubtless true that both tariffs and local taxes have made the position of the farmer more difficult in England, but the gradual decline in the proportionate importance of agriculture has been more largely due to the development of industry than to the decline of the absolute numbers of the agricultural group. Until the great depression of 1878–1885, there were increases in acreage under crop and in numbers employed. Since that time there has been some decline, an inevitable readjustment to competition with imports. Conditions in England are unusual only in the degree to which soil types emphasize dairying and stock breeding, which employ fewer hands than crop raising.

Comparisons on a national basis are affected by the size of the areas compared. Even since the Versailles treaties, Germany is more than three times as large as England and Wales. The large area of Germany presents a much greater degree of regional differentiation than the relatively small area of England and Wales. No totals for an area the size of Germany could present such sharp contrasts as the totals for a small area. The figures for the smaller divisions of Germany are more nearly comparable to the English figures. The agricultural group, in 1933, accounted for less than 13 per cent of the gainfully occupied persons in Westphalia, the Rhineland, and Saxony. For an area about half the size of England the degree of industrial concentration was roughly comparable, even without including any administrative and commercial center comparable to London. Significant analysis of the detail of industrialization must needs have reference to well-defined geographic regions, sufficiently restricted in extent to possess some unity. Germany, France, the United States, and Russia are so large that averages for the area as a whole will have little significance.

### The Relation of Coal to Industrialization

Coal is the most important of the primary minerals. The diversity and importance of its uses give it priority over all the metals. Even with the development of water powers, coal is the more convenient source of power when readily available, for industrial plants as for railways. Many industrial processes require heat energy in forms that can be most readily supplied by coal. From the point of view of location of economic activity, coal is especially important because the heavy weight losses make the coal fields a powerful factor in the location of all industries using substantial quantities of fuel. Coal is thus the most important single factor in the location of the primary heavy industries. It is not necessary that the industry be located at the mine head, but the effective range of movement of coal for primary industries is narrowly restricted. Throughout the nineteenth century, progress in intensive industrialization was closely associated with the utilization of coal. The leadership of England was based upon leadership in the utilization of coal. This problem of industrialization involved, in its entirety, not only the technique of mining coal, but even more largely the technique of adapting industrial processes and transportation to this kind of fuel.

The adoption of the new technique by the Continental countries was delayed by difficulties affecting every phase of the process, but the more serious limitations were encountered in the economic and social factors. The transformation is so extensive that a substantial interval of time is required even if the rate of change is rapid. In Germany, the period of intense development begins about 1830 and the notable rates of increase do not slacken until 1910. In Great Britain the process extended over a longer interval because a greater number of primary inventions were involved. The process of change in England extended from 1730 to 1890. The close of the period of change is most objectively indicated by the general trends of production of primary minerals, such as coal and iron. But the explanation of these trends must be sought in the relation between production and total resources. Active change will proceed until all of the primary resources are brought into utilization on a scale proportionate to their importance. Judgment of the historical movement thus involves some examination of the relative resources of the different countries. In the case of France, we have already seen that the production of coal and iron was roughly proportionate to her resources at as early a date as 1845–1850. Her position, therefore, was determined by the character of her resources, and not by any failure to make use of the possibilities of the new technology.

Germany was in a profoundly different position. She possessed 56 per cent of the total coal reserves of Europe, as estimated in 1910; more than twice the reserves of Great Britain, whose reserves were rated in 1910 as 24 per cent of the total reserve of Europe. The estimates of total reserves involve many uncertainties, and it must be noted that the relative position of Great Britain was more favorable if only immediately available resources were counted. The immediately available reserves were stated in 1910 as 104,178,000,000 tons in Germany with the boundaries of 1914, whereas such reserves in Great Britain were 141,499,000,000 tons. Despite these great reserves, Germany in 1870 produced only about one third as much coal as Great Britain. Germany was a country of undeveloped potentialities.

Coal had been worked in Germany in a small way since the fourteenth century, but the abundance of wood and the difficulties of mining and using coal had left the coal mines largely undeveloped. Furthermore, the German coals are somewhat inferior in quality to the British coals and much less conveniently distributed.

## The Production of Coal in Germany, 1865–1935

The bituminous coals of Germany contain rather more foreign matter than the British coals, so that careful preparation is essential.

The seams are thinner and mining costs average somewhat higher. The chief difference, however, is due to the extensive use of lignite. In 1871 lignite constituted 22 per cent of the total production in Germany; in 1910, lignite accounted for 31 per cent of the total, and in 1921 for 51 per cent of the total. Some lignite contains so much water and dirt that it affords only one third of the thermal units of good coal. Anthracite coal averages between 8,000 and 8,600 calories (1 calorie = 1.8 British thermal units) per pound. The highest grades of bituminous rate a little higher, yielding between 8,400 and 8,900 calories. The poorest bituminous coal yields at least 6,600 calories. The highest grades of lignite fall just below the poorest bituminous, averaging between 5,500 and 7,200 calories. Selected lignite from Bohemia would fall within this class, but the average Bohemian lignite yields only 4,000 to 5,600 calories. The large lignite deposits of the Halle district and Saxony are of a lower rating. In their crude states, these lignites yield only 2,000 to 3,200 calories, or barely one third the heat units of the better grades of bituminous and anthracite.

The low heating values of lignite are of economic importance in two respects: the cost of fuel in terms of actual heat units is increased, and the range of distribution is reduced. Such low-grade fuels are not sufficiently valuable to bear much transport. The use of lignite has, however, been appreciably extended by additional processing. Briquettes were prepared by the wet process even before 1870, but this process required special binding agents and a long period of outdoor drying. After 1880, the dry process was developed. The lignite is pulverized and partly dried. It is then formed into briquettes at a pressure of 1,200 to 1,500 atmospheres. Under these conditions, the bitumens in the lignite are liquefied sufficiently to serve as a binding agent. The product is superior in many ways, and is independent of the weather. The heating power of the product is greater, averaging 4,500 to 5,300 calories per pound. Though still inferior to coal, the product would bear transport costs. Some of the poorer coals are also processed and made into briquettes.

The location of the coal and lignite deposits is shown by the map on page 510. The greater part of the true coal was produced in the Ruhr, the Saar, and in Upper Silesia. The Versailles treaties transferred a large part of the Upper Silesian field to Poland, so that German production has suffered severely by reason of the revision of the boundaries. The transfer of the Saar to France, for

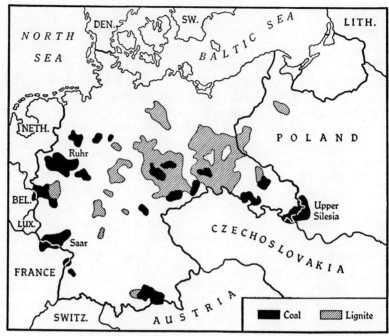

*Areas in Germany Producing Coal and Lignite*

a limited period of time, was also a serious diversion of resources. The primary coal deposits were thus inconveniently located with reference to the important industrial district in Saxony, the Thuringian states, and parts of Brandenburg. The development of this region would have been seriously affected if it had not been possible to utilize the lignite of the region. To what extent application of power was positively retarded by the cost and quality of local fuel, it is impossible to determine. A high grade of lignite was secured from Bohemia in the earlier period of industrialization, and small amounts of bituminous coal were available. It is by no means impossible that fuel costs should have retarded the generalization of steam power in central Germany in the critical period 1875 to 1895. Coal production in the principal European countries is given in the table on page 511.

The graph showing the production of coal and iron in Germany from 1865 to 1935 (page 512) brings out this retardation in both industries. Coal production was increasing at a rate of 5.5 per cent per year in the years 1865 to 1875; the rate declined to 3.9 per cent per year in the period 1875 to 1895, rising thereafter to a rate of

COAL PRODUCTION OF THE WORLD, IN MILLIONS OF METRIC TONS [1]

|      | United States | Great Britain | Germany (includes lignite) | France | Belgium | Total |
|------|------|------|------|------|------|------|
| 1864 | 22.8  | 94.3  | 26.1  | 11.2 | 11.1 | 173.7 |
| 1865 | 24.7  | 99.7  | 28.3  | 11.8 | 11.8 | 182.0 |
| 1870 | 29.9  | 112.2 | 34.8  | 13.3 | 13.6 | 217.8 |
| 1875 | 48.2  | 135.4 | 48.5  | 16.9 | 15.0 | 285.3 |
| 1880 | 66.8  | 149.3 | 59.1  | 19.3 | 16.8 | 339.3 |
| 1885 | 102.1 | 161.9 | 73.6  | 19.5 | 17.4 | 412.8 |
| 1890 | 141.6 | 184.5 | 89.2  | 26.0 | 20.3 | 513.1 |
| 1895 | 171.7 | 194.3 | 103.8 | 28.2 | 20.4 | 562.3 |
| 1900 | 243.4 | 228.7 | 149.5 | 33.4 | 23.4 | 765.1 |
| 1905 | 351.1 | 239.8 | 173.6 | 36.0 | 21.8 | 928.0 |
| 1910 | 445.8 | 264.5 | 221.9 | 38.5 | 23.1 | 1,143.7 |
| 1915 | 531.6 | 283.5 | 259.1 | 19.9 | 15.6 | 1,270.0 |
| 1920 | 598.0 | 233.2 | 252.3 | 25.3 | 22.3 | 1,317.0 |
| 1925 | 527.7 | 247.0 | 272.3 | 48.0 | 23.0 | 1,372.0 |
| 1930 | 487.0 | 247.7 | 301.7 | 54.9 | 27.4 | 1,413.0 |
| 1933 | 342.3 | 210.3 | 247.1 | 47.9 | 25.2 | 1,154.0 |
| 1935 | 381.2 | 226.5 | 292.0 | 47.1 | 26.4 | 1,327.0 |

4.5 per cent per year.  It will be remembered that the rates of increase from 1830 to 1865 were very high, though the quantities involved were small.  Coal production in Great Britain increased at an approximate average rate of 1.9 per cent per year, from 1870 to 1910.  The rate of increase in France was greater — 2.7 per cent per year.  The iron trade in Germany shows a similar retardation; increase at a rate of 10 per cent per year, from 1865 to 1875; at a rate of 4.6 per cent per year, from 1875 to 1900; at a rate of 7 per cent per year in the period 1900 to 1910.  These variations in the rates of change in the early years of the German Empire have not received much attention.  Many writers have ignored the important growth under the Customs Union.  The economic development of Germany has been associated primarily with the period since 1870, but these graphs and the graphs for the earlier period show conclusively that the actual beginnings of the industrial reorganization of Germany must be associated with the establishment of the Customs Union.

The general trend of iron production does not show any sharply defined increase after the introduction of the basic processes of steel making in the Bessemer converters and open-hearth furnaces.  This process, developed in England in 1878, made it possible to utilize

[1] *The Mineral Industry*, selected volumes.

freely the great oölitic iron deposits of Lorraine. The influence of this technical development does not appear in the statistics of iron production, because the change was in fact more gradual than many have presumed. The transfer from the alluvial ores to the oölitic ores was already far advanced when the basic process was

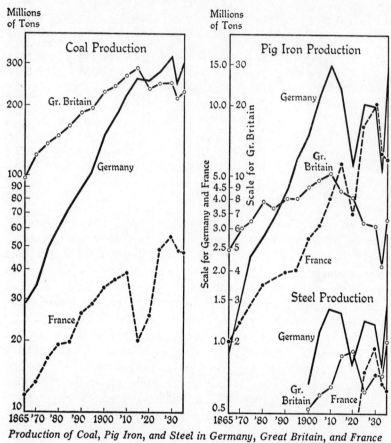

*Production of Coal, Pig Iron, and Steel in Germany, Great Britain, and France*

perfected. The new ores were not suddenly brought into the market, with an abruptness that would show clearly even in the statistics of production in Lorraine. The development of the iron industries of the Continent could not have continued as it did without full utilization of these resources, but even this unusually important discovery did not produce a demonstrable shock to the industry.

## The Position of the Heavy Industries since 1918

The trends shown on the graphs indicate that the great period of growth of the nineteenth century was reaching its term in the years immediately preceding the World War. New demands for coal did not exceed the economies achieved in the use of coal. Reduced rates of railroad building affected the demand for iron, and increased quantities of scrap iron further reduced the demand for new pig iron. Steel production continued to increase for a time after the iron market showed clear signs of stabilization, but even steel production increased less rapidly than before.

The position of Germany in the prewar world was more nearly in accord with the mass and quality of her resources. She produced slightly less coal [1] than Great Britain; 221 million tons as compared with 264 million tons for Great Britain. Germany, however, produced much more pig iron, and somewhat more than twice as much steel. Germany might well claim the distinction of being the leading producer of heavy industrial products in Europe, but this distinction was subject to some important qualifications. Germany had not secured the place in the world market that had been held by England during the greater part of the nineteenth century. The development of the United States overshadowed Germany: the American production of primary heavy products exceeded that of any European country by large margins, and the extent of the resources of the United States makes it perfectly clear that the position of the United States will become even more commanding. Furthermore, though the absolute volume of production in Great Britain was less than in the Germany of 1910, the differences were not large. Germany would never have come to dominate the industrial development of twentieth-century Europe. Great Britain would have remained a close rival.

The territorial adjustments of 1919 have altered the relative economic positions of France, Germany, and Great Britain. The most important section of the Upper Silesian coal field is now incorporated in Poland, and though some coal is exported to Germany, much iron ore is sent from Germany to Poland. In terms of current production the loss involved to Germany amounts to about 15 per cent. The loss of actual reserves amounts to only 8 per cent, but the loss of potential reserves amounts to nearly 40 per cent. The fuel resources of Germany, as now constituted, are not significantly

[1] Definitely less than Great Britain, if allowance is made for the low heating value of lignites.

superior to those of Great Britain. The redistribution of iron reserves, involved in the restoration of Lorraine, leaves Germany in a distinctly inferior position. The data for the leading countries are given in the following table.

IRON RESERVES OF EUROPE, IN MILLIONS OF METRIC TONS [1]

| Country (Boundaries of 1918) | Known | Probable | Possible | Total | Per Cent |
|---|---|---|---|---|---|
| France | 1,790.0 | 1,053.6 | 1,526.0 | 4,369.6 | 35.2 |
| United Kingdom | 317.5 | 464.3 | 1,472.3 | 2,254.1 | 18.2 |
| Sweden | 442.9 | 376.1 | 729.6 | 1,548.6 | 12.5 |
| Germany | 255.6 | 207.4 | 911.7 | 1,374.7 | 11.1 |
| Russia (European) | 269.5 | 277.0 | 412.5 | 959.0 | 8.5 |
| Total Europe | 3,735.6 | 2,898.2 | 5,771.2 | 12,405.0 | 100.0 |

These five countries account for 85 per cent of the total iron reserves of Europe. Spain would add 5 per cent. Six countries thus contain 90 per cent of the iron in Europe. The deficiencies of fuel in Sweden seriously affect her position, and doubtless much Swedish ore will continue to be exported to Germany. The future of Germany thus depends largely upon her fuels, and the supply of fuel does not hold out hope of much increase in industrial production. If no further boundary adjustments occur, Germany will be one of the leading industrial countries of Europe, but she can scarcely achieve even the measure of predominance that she might well have assumed in 1913.

## The Development of German Trade

The great changes in the industrial importance of Germany were of course reflected in the development of her trade. The changed relationships with other countries are revealed most clearly in the new commercial contacts. One of the most conspicuous changes appears in the development of independent contacts between Germany and the remote parts of the Far East and the southern hemisphere.

In the eighteenth and the early nineteenth century Great Britain became an important center of concentration for the products of the Far East, India, and the southern hemisphere. London was the great entrepôt for the Old World; Liverpool was the primary center for the trade with the New World and with Africa. Amsterdam retained some measure of importance, but her position had long since

[1] Roesler, M., op. cit., p. 18.

ceased to be comparable with that of London.   The structure of the primary trade routes made Great Britain the predominant center of north European trade long before the iron ship gave her a clear predominance in the maritime carrying trade.   The development of Australia, with its highly important wool trade, added another general line to the great long-distance trades under British control. The Suez Canal modified the system of trade in some particulars, but did not affect the general position of Great Britain.   The develop-ment of German industry, however, created a volume of trade that could not be handled conveniently through London.

Changes are perceptible in the early 1890's.   New business re-quired harbor improvements at Hamburg, Rotterdam, and Antwerp. New facilities attracted still more trade.   The North Sea ports of the Continent became steadily more important, so that the volume of trade at the leading Continental ports was nearly equal to that of the leading British ports.   If the coastwise trade is included, the total of the British ports is greater; but the foreign trade of the European ports was greater than the foreign trade of the British ports.   This decline of the transit trade marks the passing of the "commercial supremacy" of Great Britain.

The significance of this change was misinterpreted by contem-poraries just as the changes of the earlier nineteenth century were misinterpreted in France.   British trade had not declined; the changed relationships were produced by the rapid development of Germany.   The changes were also in a very real sense due to general changes in the volume and character of trade throughout the world.   Railroad building in the United States, in India, in South America, and in Australia furnished new masses of freight for export.   Lower ocean freights diminished the resistances to long-distance trade.   Business at the great ports developed upon such a scale that nearly all ports were obliged to make extensive improve-ments to accommodate trade.   The timing of these improvements varied.   The Continental ports were slightly in advance of British ports, but the differences were not great and in 1914 the reconstruc-tion of the port of London was far advanced.   All the ports were crowded, and in no case is there any clear evidence that trade was really lost on account of the condition of the harbor.

The necessity of achieving every possible economy in cost led to the development of new modes of dealing with long-distance trade. The privilege of diversion in transit afforded important economies. Cargoes of grain and cotton could be sold while afloat; the bill of lading would then be endorsed to the buyer. When the vessel stopped at a designated port of call, she would be directed to proceed to any destination desired. London and Liverpool retained some financial control over the transit trade even after the ports ceased to serve as entrepôts for the actual goods. However, in due time, new primary wholesale markets for cereals, cotton, and wool developed in Continental centers.

These broader underlying causes of change were not unknown to the better informed contemporaries, but popular opinion was impressed only by the facts themselves. Germans were unduly exuberant over the rise of German trade and industry. They were prone to ascribe the change to intrinsic superiority in business methods. Much was said about German thoroughness and their innate sense of order and discipline.

British empiricism was sharply criticized under the opprobrious characterization of muddling. Short hours and long week ends were cited as evidence that Britons had been softened by prosperity. Consular agents reported incidents of all kinds as evidence of German superiority in intelligence or in guile. Writers were not lacking who hinted at a German conspiracy to secure control of all the trade of the world. The German government was represented as standing behind the trader, and sinister motives of all kinds were attributed to these new industrialists and traders. Whatever truth may lie beneath all these incidents, innuendoes, and suspicions, it must be evident to any objective observer that the primary cause of all this development of industry and trade was the massive importance of the mineral resources of Germany. In 1830 they were scarcely touched; in 1910 they were being fully utilized with a degree of skill and efficiency that compared favorably with the technical development of other industrialized countries. In this record of development there is nothing essentially mysterious; in its economic aspects, nothing truly sinister.

## The Geographical Distribution of German Trade

The trade rivalries of the late nineteenth century led to a notable revival of many features of mercantilism, and the extravagances of protectionists were as great in Germany as in any country. All this literature exhibits a persistent distrust of competing industrial countries, and there is ever an implication that the greatest economic gain lies in trade with the tropics and semitropics which supply raw materials but do not compete in the production of manufactured products. This notion is by no means new. It was sharply formulated by Friedrich List in his system of national economy, and it was a dominant feature of eighteenth-century mercantilism. It is, therefore, especially interesting to note that the major part of German trade has involved her immediate European neighbors and the United States. Her best customers have been her closest industrial rivals.

GEOGRAPHICAL DISTRIBUTION OF GERMAN TRADE,
IN PER CENT OF TOTAL VALUE [1]

| Country of Origin or Destination | German Imports | | | | German Exports | | | |
|---|---|---|---|---|---|---|---|---|
| | 1893 | 1903 | 1909 | 1933 | 1893 | 1903 | 1909 | 1933 |
| Great Britain | 15.9 | 13.2 | 8.5 | 5.7 | 20.7 | 19.3 | 15.4 | 8.3 |
| Austria | 14.0 | 11.9 | 8.8 | 5.9 [2] | 13.0 | 10.3 | 11.6 | 7.3 |
| Russia | 8.5 | 13.2 | 16.0 | 6.7 [2] | 5.7 | 7.4 | 6.7 | 7.7 [2] |
| France | 5.8 | 5.4 | 5.7 | 4.4 | 6.3 | 5.3 | 6.9 | 8.1 |
| Netherlands | 5.2 | 3.1 | 3.0 | 5.5 | 7.4 | 8.2 | 6.9 | 12.6 [2] |
| Belgium | 4.2 | 3.3 | 3.4 | 3.3 | 4.5 | 5.2 | 5.3 | 5.7 |
| Switzerland | 3.4 | 2.7 | 1.9 | 2.0 | 5.8 | 5.9 | 6.3 | 7.2 |
| Scandinavia | 3.2 | 2.9 | 3.7 | 6.6 | 5.9 | 6.7 | 7.0 | 8.6 |
| Total for countries listed | 60.2 | 55.7 | 51.0 | 40.1 | 69.3 | 68.3 | 66.1 | 65.5 |
| United States | 11.1 | 14.9 | 14.8 | 11.5 | 10.9 | 9.1 | 9.2 | 11.6 |
| Asia | 6.0 | 7.3 | 8.0 | 12.7 | 4.8 | 4.6 | 4.5 | 7.6 |

The broader features of the geography of German trade are shown in the above table. In 1893 trade with the neighboring countries accounted for 60.2 per cent of the imports and 69.3 per cent of the exports. Trade with the United States added a little more than 10 per cent to both totals. The decline in the importance of imports from her European neighbors is largely due to the establishment of somewhat more direct contacts with the outside world. It is noteworthy, however, that the exports continue to find their best market in the neighboring countries of Europe and in the United States. The importance of the exports to most of these countries has even increased a little since the World War.

The same features of geographic distribution appear in the shipping records, which lend themselves conveniently to analysis over a somewhat longer period.

[1] Prepared from materials in the *Statistisches Jahrbuch für das Deutsche Reich.*
[2] Approximate trade with same areas as in 1909.

GEOGRAPHICAL DISTRIBUTION OF GERMAN SHIPPING, IN PER CENT OF TONNAGE WITH CARGOES [1]

| | Entered | | | Cleared | | |
|---|---|---|---|---|---|---|
| | 1873 | 1893 | 1908 | 1873 | 1893 | 1908 |
| Coastwise | 11.7 | 19.4 | 17.4 | 15.7 | 26.5 | 25.4 |
| Non-German Europe | 67.3 | 54.3 | 52.4 | 63.7 | 46.3 | 43.2 |
| Non-European | 21.0 | 26.3 | 30.2 | 20.6 | 27.2 | 31.4 |
| | 100.0 | 100.0 | 100.0 | 100.0 | 100.0 | 100.0 |

These materials are fairly representative of the large mass of material available for the analysis of foreign trade. The predominant importance of trade with neighboring countries or countries of the same general climatic zone is an outstanding feature of the history of trade in Europe and in the United States. These materials afford the clearest possible evidence of the importance of the differentiation of resources within the same general climatic zone. Differences of interest may exist, and businessmen may feel more conscious of trade rivalry than of common interests, but the fact remains that the great industrial regions find their best customers in the other intensely industrialized regions of the world.

The natural geographic regions are necessarily dependent upon each other, and the economic interests of the various states of Europe are even more closely interwoven. Many important boundaries have been determined by political considerations, which ignore many of the primary features of economic geography. The survival of the state system, as we know it, will depend in no small measure upon the frankness with which common economic interests are recognized.

The shipping records, also, throw some light upon the economic importance of the German colonies. In 1908 the tonnage coming from the colonies amounted to 0.53 per cent of the total: the outbound tonnage going to them amounted to 0.92 per cent. Fisheries on the high seas employed three times as much shipping as the colonial trade. It is, of course, possible to suggest that the true value of colonies will emerge only after their resources are fully developed; but it must be remembered that the proportionate importance of the trade will even then depend upon the relative importance of the various regions. The notion of a self-sufficient empire is as unreal as the notion of the self-sufficient industrial state. Each great industrial region must needs trade with all the major regions of the world.

[1] Prepared from materials in the *Statistisches Jahrbuch für das Deutsche Reich.*

# CHAPTER 25

# COMBINATION AND MONOPOLY IN INDUSTRY AND TRANSPORT

## The Nature and Importance of Competition

Monopolies were an important feature of economic organization in all the countries of Europe throughout the early modern period. Some of these monopolies were different in form and purpose from the combinations and monopolies of the nineteenth century. Others were closely comparable to the combinations of the recent period. The great companies of colonization have had some successors in the nineteenth century, though they have been less conspicuous. The Royal Niger Company and the companies organized to develop Rhodesia and British East Africa were similar in form to the British East India Company and the chartered companies of the seventeenth and eighteenth centuries. Companies of colonization were used also by other countries besides Great Britain. There are few modern representatives of the Royal Manufactures of France, though some of the companies have survived. The guilds and corporations of craft workers have been abolished or reduced to the role of clubs or charitable and educational foundations. The forms prominent in the past have lost the significance they formerly enjoyed, but other types, then of little importance, have come to be a dominant factor in our economic life. Neither monopoly nor big business is a new phenomenon, but they have assumed new forms. Furthermore, public opinion has been rudely shocked by the realization that the tendencies of economic development were completely misjudged by the economists and political theorists of the early nineteenth century.

Economists of the liberal school had led the attack on the monopolies of the eighteenth century. They presumed that their victory was complete and that they had laid the foundations for a free industrial society in which pure competition would be a dominant force. It was their belief that full monopoly power would rarely be achieved unless a positive franchise was granted, and in these cases appropriate measures of control could be taken. This presumption rested upon a train of reasoning that was not without merit, though recent analysis has shown that the reasoning was unsound. It was recognized that many industries and trades presented cases which were intermediate between pure monopoly and pure competition. The cases fall into two general classes.  In some trades, the number of competing firms is small, so that the withdrawal or addition of any firm would make a substantial difference to the market.  In other trades, products are so highly diversified that each firm has a real monopoly of its own special product, but full monopoly control cannot be achieved because the different products compete to an important degree.  The classical economists held that neither case presented any serious qualification of pure competition.  They held that even in these cases the price structure would be dominated by costs and that production would not be consciously controlled.

Recent developments of economic theory have shown that these presumptions are unsound.  If competitors are not very numerous, they are likely to take a keen interest in each other's activities.  If each adjusts prices and the volume of production to the policies of the others, the result approximates closely to the result that would be achieved by a pure monopoly.  As soon as any effective exchange of information is achieved, the difference between a loose association of producers and a pure monopoly lies merely in the degree of stability.  A loose association might be broken up if one member thought he could gain at the expense of the others.  But the best permanent interest of each competitor requires him to recognize the effect of his action upon the others, and this leads him to accept a policy of regulated prices and controlled production.  Theoretically, formal agreement among the competitors is not essential : conditions would approximate monopoly conditions as soon as each of the firms recognizes the *continuous* presence of each of the others.  This conclusion is essentially in accord with the history of all price wars.  Their true purpose is the destruction of one or more competitors so that the profits derived from exploiting the market need not be divided among so many firms.  Monopolistic conditions thus really emerge earlier than was formerly supposed; before formal combination of the firms.  Actual combination is significant because it guarantees more adequately the permanent survival of each firm.

Product differentiation under patents and trademarks affords less opportunity for the development of full monopoly, but profits within this field of industrial production are profoundly influenced by monopoly conditions.  Prices do not fall as rapidly as costs.  Improvements in the processes of production and distribution are not shared with the public until a considerable interval of time has elapsed. The elements of monopoly are not obvious, because the prices of such goods or services may fall appreciably. The gains of particular producers, however, may be very large. Even though the gains of progress are ultimately shared with the public, the industrial structure can hardly be treated as purely competitive if the primary source of gain lies in the use of monopoly power to slow down the distribution of gains from technological advance.

Although this new analysis of monopolistic competition has not yet been applied to the history of combinations or to the criticism of public policy, it is already clear that extensive revision of judgment will be necessary over a large field. The faith of the nineteenth-century liberal in the sufficiency of competition was not justified. More government control was necessary than the liberals presumed. In Europe actual errors of policy were less serious than in the United States. British policy was dominated by a cautious empiricism which avoided the dangers of either extreme and gave time for the development of analysis. In France, Germany, and most of the other Continental countries liberalism was not strong enough to offset the established influence of strong administrative systems based on more generous concepts of the role of the state. In Great Britain and the United States, however, there was a strong tendency to favor an essentially liberal concept, so that the early theory of competition was accepted as an adequate analysis of the economic order. Doubts were felt as to the need of vigorous action by the state, and in many instances the only action recommended was prohibition of monopoly and the enforcement of a code of fair competition. Combinations and monopolies were recognized only with many misgivings, even when steps were taken to prevent the abuse of monopoly power.

### The Early Development of British Railway Policy

In Great Britain railway policy was largely dominated by the liberal policy of maintaining competition among regulated private enterprises. The policy was never pushed to extremes, and at the beginning of the present century it became increasingly clear that little significant competition remained. In 1921 the principle of regional monopoly was frankly accepted. The transition from a policy of competition to the recognition of regional monopolies was singularly gradual, because the authorities were at all times ready to recognize loose forms of association and rate agreements which made it possible to achieve some unity of action whenever it was really necessary. Furthermore, in regions which promised only modest volumes of traffic railway construction was restricted to lines with an assured prospect of profitable operation. Under such circumstances no competing lines were ever authorized, so that the eastern counties and the southern coast were in fact served by regional monopolies. The general effect of railway policy in England presents many contrasts to the history of railway policy in the United States, where the general principles were nominally the same. The authority of the state was vigorously asserted in Great Britain, from the very beginning, and determined efforts were made to protect the interests of the public.

In the early years of railway building control expressed itself chiefly in careful scrutiny of each railway project. Railway charters were granted by Parliament, passing through a procedure established for private bills. The essential features of the process lay in the study of the project by a standing committee and in the hearing of complaints by any parties who felt that their interests were adversely affected. In the language of modern public administration, each project had to secure a certificate of public convenience. Every project was considered on its merits; the committee was required to examine the scheme on all the more obvious points, and the opposition might bring up any other considerations.

Important qualifications of the policy of competition were soon developed as a result of this rigid inquiry into the schemes submitted. The attempt to restrict construction to schemes with reasonable assurance of profit led Parliament to refuse charters to competing lines, unless competition was restricted to unimportant points. After 1843, when traffic had developed on a large scale, alternative routes were recognized if there was a real need of service at intermediate points. Even then, duplication of existing construction was not permitted if it seemed likely that the needs of traffic could be accommodated with the existing facilities. The existing line was, in such a case, required to grant running powers to the new line. This refusal to build lines in excess of the requirements of traffic led to the adoption of a principle of regional monopoly in several sections of England.

The map of primary railway systems in 1843 (page 523) shows the earlier results of this principle of policy. The map for 1853 (page 525) shows the next stage in the development of construction, when the establishment of alternative routes had created significant

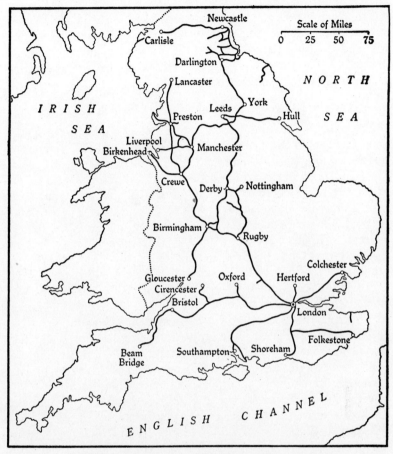

*Railways Operating in England December 31, 1843*

competition in Scotland, Lancashire, and the West Riding of York. The London and North Western competed directly with the Great Northern for the traffic of Edinburgh and Glasgow. The associated lines in Scotland were still nominally independent, but they were operated as a single continuous system. At that time, however, the development of operating relations among some of the railways resulted in projected combinations which would have greatly extended the principle of regional monopoly. The London and North Western was to be combined with the Midland; the Caledonian, with the Edinburgh and Glasgow; the London and South Western, with the London, Brighton and South Coast. The London and

North Western was already closely associated with the Caledonian so that effective operating unity would have been assured over the Midland counties, Lancashire and the Northwest, and the Scottish lowlands. The direct and indirect effects of this proposed combination presented a serious issue of national policy.

## The Maintenance of Competition in British Railways

The schemes for combination were carefully studied by a special committee under the chairmanship of Edward Cardwell. The committee approved of the combination of three railways in the region between York and the Scotch border, but it was unwilling to recommend the other combinations proposed. It was held that loose associations of companies might well be without danger to the public interest, but a permanent consolidation of one quarter of the railway mileage in England seemed to be too dangerous. Many witnesses declared that consolidation should necessarily proceed to great lengths, so that competition between systems would cease to be of any significance. But neither the committee nor Parliament was, at that time, prepared to accept the principle of regional monopoly as the exclusive basis of railway construction and operation.

This decision resulted in an appreciable increase in the emphasis upon competition, though not immediately. The Midland entered into a secret agreement with the London and North Western for a complete community of interests. This arrangement was discovered by the Great Northern in 1857, and the relations between the roads were seriously affected by the exposure of the secret. The Midland became more friendly to the Great Northern, but the directors realized that sound development required independent connection with London. Connections had been available at Rugby, and, after 1857, at Hitchin, but the increased volume of traffic made it difficult to furnish adequate service even with running powers over the Great Northern line from Hitchin to London. Work on a London terminal was begun in 1860, but the independent entrance to London was not brought into operation until 1869. These developments involved important additions to the terminal facilities of London, but they were fully justified by the volume of the traffic. There was, however, little need of the long extension northward to Scotland. Neither the line to Carlisle nor the lines in Scotland opened up any significant traffic at intermediate points, and the Scotch lowlands were already served by the important routes by the east and west coasts.

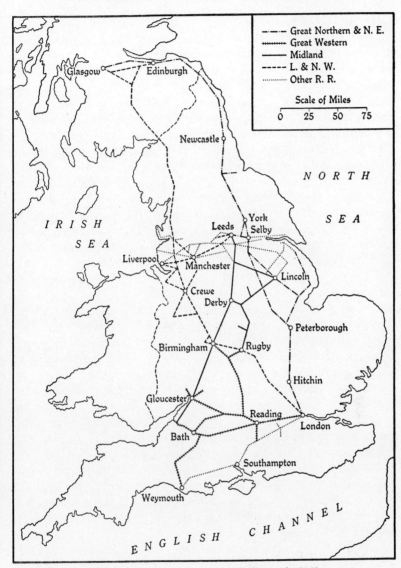

| | |
|---|---|
| —·—·— | Great Northern & N. E. |
| ········· | Great Western |
| ———— | Midland |
| - - - - | L. & N. W. |
| ·········· | Other R. R. |

Scale of Miles

0    25    50    75

*Main Lines of Primary British Railways in 1853*

The Midland system controlled an important freight traffic from the coal fields of Derby and Nottingham, but the system attracted less passenger traffic than either of its rivals. The attempt to attract passengers induced its directors to offer improved facilities for third-class travel. In 1872 third-class coaches were put on all trains, and in 1874 the first and second classes were combined at rates that were considerably lower than the old first class. The other roads were obliged to show more consideration to third-class travel, and after a short interval the quality of accommodation was notably improved on all British roads. These changes were the most tangible result of the decision of Cardwell's committee to reject the project for amalgamation in 1853. Against these positive benefits must be set some needless construction in the north.

In the combinations formed early in the present century, the Midland and the London and North Western led the way. In 1908 an agreement was made for joint use of all facilities and unification of control. The following year the Lancashire and Yorkshire was formally brought into the system, though this act was little more than a mere form, as the Lancashire and Yorkshire had been closely associated with the London and North Western since 1862. The lines on the east coast were also drawn closely together by private agreements. The government made no attempt to prevent these combinations.

Despite some agitation for public ownership, the railroads were returned to the companies after the World War, and in 1921 provision was made for the formation of four great companies, to control all the railroads within designated regions. The companies were allowed to prepare plans to give effect to these combinations, arranging among themselves all the details involved in the exchange of the securities of the existing companies for securities in the new companies. If plans were not completed before a specified date, arrangements were to be made or completed by the government. The new companies were based on existing associations, and in the first instance no attempt was made to simplify the structure by the exchange of lines which ran into territory primarily served by another company. Provision was made for subsequent adjustments. The Great Western Railway retained its name and the general features of the system already in existence. Some lines attached to the system by agreement or lease were now definitely incorporated in the new company. The London, Midland, and Scottish consisted of the companies associated by the agreements of 1908 and 1909, together with incidental additions designed to give the system complete control of the west coast route to Scotland via Liverpool and Manchester. The London and North Eastern brought together in one company the group of lines serving the east coast route. The main elements of the company had long been functioning as a unit.

The Southern Railway combined all the lines south of the Thames, from Kent to Cornwall.

The act of 1921 repealed the system of statutory maximum rates established under the act of 1894, but never effectively enforced. The companies were authorized to make rates subject to the approval and control of a special tribunal created for the purpose. This tribunal had full authority to fix and vary the rates of each company in such a way as to produce a standard revenue. The act also provided for a series of councils subject to the general authority of a National Wages Board. The councils are composed of freely elected representatives of the companies and the employees. The general features of the scheme had already been agreed upon by the companies and the unions of railway men. The act extended the scope of existing organization and conferred positive authority upon the National Wages Board. The Railways Act of 1921 was thus in all its essential features a formal recognition of policies and arrangements which had already been established. It marks the final abandonment of the theory of competition and of individual wage contracts in this important field.

### The Planning of the Railway Network in France

Experimentation with the locomotive began in France before the locomotive was an assured success, and use was made of steam traction on the coal lines around St. Étienne even before 1830. An important demonstration was given in 1832, but no railroads were projected until 1835. The government then proposed to charter a line from Paris to Le Havre to be controlled by a private company assisted by the state. In 1837 and 1838 lines were proposed between Paris and the Belgian frontier and between Paris and Marseille by way of Lyon. The debates raised the issue of state ownership. None of the projects were authorized, but no alternative policy was adopted. The government authorized some railroad construction in 1837, and loans were made to three companies, but the only authorized line of any great importance was a line from Paris to Rouen. In 1840 interest was guaranteed on a loan to a company chartered to build a railway between Paris and Orléans. The general policy of the government was not defined until 1842, when the construction of the primary stems of a railroad network was authorized. By this law, the state was brought into close association with private enterprise. It was hoped that the railways would be taken over by the government and operated directly by the state, but the pressure of circumstances led toward a larger measure of private initiative with government regulation.

The law of 1842 provided for the construction of a systematic network of railways radiating from Paris, supplemented by a line from Bordeaux to Marseille by way of Toulouse. The lines radiating from Paris were directed toward the various frontiers and coasts: to the Belgian frontier, by way of Lille; to the Channel ports; to Germany, by way of Nancy; to Marseille by way of Lyon; to Spain, by way of Tours, Bordeaux, and Bayonne; to the Atlantic coast by way of Tours and Nantes. The distinctive feature of the scheme was its comprehensiveness. Some general projects were suggested in England, but no general scheme was seriously discussed. This French project laid down all the primary elements of the railroad network of France. Largely because of the nature of the geography of transport in France, the plan was really based on the principle of regional monopoly. There would be no significant competition between any of the six great systems called for in the plan. There was water competition in some instances, though it was not, in France, a dominant factor in rates.

Public ownership and operation was not contemplated in the immediate future, but both the national government and the departments were to co-operate with private enterprise in the execution of the scheme. The state acquired title to the land required for the right of way and for buildings and railroad yards. The necessary funds were to be advanced by the national government, but two thirds of the cost was to be met ultimately by the departments. The state undertook also to prepare the roadbed, complete with tunnels and bridges. At this stage, portions of the lines were leased to private companies, with the obligation to finish all work of construction, to provide all rolling stock necessary, and to meet all operating expenses. Provision was made for acquisition by the government at the expiration of the 36- or 40-year lease. Strangely enough, the leases covered rather small portions of the network. None of the major systems was leased in its entirety to a single company. The principle of regional monopoly implicit in the structure of the network was thus obscured. The general framework of railway legislation was completed by two laws passed July 15, 1845. One act laid down the basic rules for operation and for the prevention and investigation of accidents. The other law, in the form of the concession for the line between Paris and the Belgian frontier, established the general features of the railway charters.  The capital structure was carefully defined, and an attempt was made to prevent speculation in railway shares.

### Regional Monopoly in France

When the lines were brought into operation, the absence of positive unity of control caused much inconvenience, so that consolidations were arranged among the concessionary companies. The relations with the state were also modified.  Leases were extended to 99 years, and the companies undertook to meet all the expenses of new construction.  Reorganization proceeded rapidly, so that within five years (1852–1857) the various companies were formed into the six great regional monopolies so clearly defined in the original conception of the network.  The main stems are shown on the map on page 531, with indication also of the approximate volume of traffic.  The Northern Railway (1852) was formed by a consolidation of three companies operating between Paris and the Belgian frontier.  The Paris-Orléans Railway (1852) was a combination of four companies operating in central France in the general region between Paris and Bordeaux.  The important traffic territory between Paris and Marseille was taken over by the Paris-Lyon-Mediterranean Railway (1852, 1857), which was composed of five companies and parts of what was originally the Grand Central. The Southern Railway (1852) was also given control of the canal of the Garonne valley.  The Eastern Railway (1853) was formed by the combination of eight small companies in the region between Paris and the German frontier.  The Western Railway (1853) was also a combination of eight small companies, which controlled the primary routes between Paris and the ports of Normandy and Brittany.

The railway network in France presents a sharply defined case of regional monopoly, because the movement of traffic follows such a definite radial pattern that the regional systems do not compete with each other for any significant traffic.  The British network is notably different in this respect, because all Scotch traffic has a fairly free choice between the east-coast and the west-coast routes to London, and Lancashire and the West Riding of York have important choices between the two great systems.  Furthermore, the Great Western competes with the London, Midland, and Scottish for much of the heavy freight of the port of Liverpool.  These features of the railway networks exert an important influence on the rate structures, because the normal influence of distance is modified in many ways by the presence of route competition. Analysis of these problems is impossible here, but it can be shown that the influence of route competition is not in any way dependent upon ownership. The problem presents an especially interesting demonstration of the importance of the recent developments in the theory of monopolistic competition and oligopoly.

Although the full recognition of the principle of regional monopoly in France was undoubtedly wise, this grant of monopoly power aroused much public apprehension. The turn of events was destined to make both the government and the railroads thoroughly unpopular. The railroads had undertaken extensive obligations for new construction, but long before the work was complete the crisis of 1857 cut deeply into the revenues and credit of the companies. The companies asked to be relieved of their obligations. The government was anxious to complete the network, and rather than abandon the program for construction, a state guarantee of interest was given on all construction work begun subsequent to a given date (the Franqueville agreements, February and June, 1859). This led to a most complex system of accounting, and created opportunities for friction between the government and the companies. The detail of the arrangement led some to presume that the railroads were securing important government subsidies that were entirely unnecessary. The truth cannot be readily ascertained. Some assistance was certainly necessary, if construction was to be pushed forward as rapidly as the government desired. Some construction, too, was not likely at any time to earn a full return on the investment. But it is quite likely that some of the companies actually secured more assistance than was strictly necessary or just.

After 1870 there was a considerable increase in pressure for an extension of state control. The great companies were unpopular; it was believed that construction was proceeding less rapidly than was desirable; in some quarters, public ownership was advocated as a solution. The larger problem was discussed, but no action was taken. But the hostility to the great companies resulted in the purchase by the state of ten small companies in the region between the Loire and the Garonne. It would have been easier to combine these small fragments with the Western or with the Paris-Orléans, but public opinion was too hostile, so the government undertook the operation of 2,615 kilometers of railway in one of the most hopeless sections of the entire national area. Some new lines were constructed in order to make an operable system; and these costs and

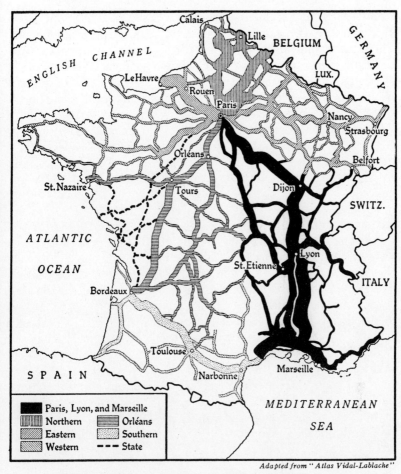

*Relative Volumes of Traffic on the Main Railways in France*

some improvements in service doubtless amounted to more than any interest payments that need have been given to the companies, either in their original form or as combined with the Western or the Paris-Orléans.  In 1908 the Western was purchased by the state and combined with the "State system" of these unhappy days.

### The Guaranty of Dividends in France

Political considerations led Gambetta and J. B. Léon Say to advocate extensive plans for new construction in all sections of France.  Hopes were entertained of reductions in rates and new economies in management.   It was proposed to add about 8,000 kilometers to the existing network of about 24,000 kilometers. Three thousand kilometers had already been projected.   Five thousand kilometers were to be built in the poorer sections of France on the grounds of social and military convenience.   Two thousand kilometers were to be classed as first-class roads and rebuilt on a broad gauge.   The detail of this vast scheme was worked out by Freycinet, the Minister of Public Works, and announced in January, 1878.   The state undertook to meet all expenses of construction, but no arrangements were made for operation.   Leases were made with new companies, when the work of construction was far advanced.

Towards the close of 1882 the construction program was far advanced, but no adequate arrangement had been made for operation of the greater part of the new lines.   The six great companies were anxious to secure concessions for much of this new line; but they were so unpopular that some concessions on rates were essential. The government needed financial assistance to complete the new construction.   Negotiations with the companies resulted (1883) in the signature of a series of conventions, which were so bitterly resented by the public that they were for years stigmatized as the "crooked conventions."   The state induced the companies to undertake the obligation of operating all the lines constructed; and it must be remembered that much of the mileage entailed serious liabilities.   The companies agreed to finish construction work still in progress.   They recognized frankly the authority of the state over rates and conditions of operation.   Some reductions in existing rates were granted.   In return the state gave a simple guarantee of dividends at stated rates.

The railroad network was thus developed far beyond the point of remunerative operation.   The state was required to pay out considerable sums on railway securities for more than a decade. Charges on the budget were heavy after the crisis of 1893, but towards the end of the century traffic increased in volume and in 1911 only the Paris-Orléans required any substantial guarantee. The more prosperous systems were able to repay the capital of some of the loans.

After the war, despite direct experience with government operation, there was no serious demand for government ownership. Relations with the great companies were finally redefined by the act of October 28, 1921.   This law provided for a certain measure of centralized control without destroying the separate identity of the six great companies. The railroads are subject to the authority of the Minister of Public Works, but the details of central policy and administrative co-ordination are largely determined by two Councils. The Superior Council of Railways consists of representatives of the state, the railways, and the shippers. The council must be consulted on all issues affecting the railroads as a whole, and upon such problems affecting particular systems as may be referred to it by the Minister of Public Works. The Administrative Council is composed of persons chosen from the administrative personnel of the six great companies. Its duties are more technical, though largely similar in scope to the duties of the Superior Council. Final authority over rates is vested in the Minister of Public Works, and, with the consent of the Ministry, he may disregard the advice of the Superior Council.

Each company remains financially independent, but there is a special railway budget. A common fund is set up to equalize returns among all the railway systems. If the excess returns of the prosperous roads are insufficient to meet the total deficits of the poorer roads, the rate level must be raised; if a net surplus is realized, the rate level is lowered. The ultimate answer to the strong and weak road problem is thus found in complete financial unity. The railroad network as a whole should produce a standard income. In order to assure efficiency of operation premiums are given to the entire personnel of each system; from chief administrator to crossing tenders, each shares in proportion to his wages. Systems realizing profits distribute 3 per cent of the excess of receipts over the receipts of 1920; or if there are deficits, 1 per cent of any amount by which the deficit has been decreased since 1920.

### State Ownership of Railways in Germany and Elsewhere

In many parts of Europe, railway construction was actively assisted by the state, and parts of the network were owned and operated by the state. None of the larger states, however, carried through a policy of comprehensive nationalization until the construction of the network was already far advanced. In the development of state ownership and operation, Germany took the lead. The movement was most successful in the smaller German states, in the early years of railway building. Hanover in 1842, Baden in 1843, Bavaria in 1844, and Württemberg in 1845 adopted the principle of state ownership.

The policy was strongly urged in Prussia, but there were difficulties in law as well as the special difficulty created by the separation of the Rhenish provinces from the primary body of Prussian
territory. The state undertook some railroad building in 1849;
and in 1853 the law of 1838 looking towards state purchase was re-
enacted. The development of state ownership was hindered by
the liberal opposition in the lower house of the Prussian parliament. In 1860 the state administered a little more than one third
of the total railway mileage, and the proportion had not increased
much when the German Empire was established. Bismarck was
anxious to establish generalized state control over the railroads
of the Empire as a whole. An Imperial Railway Office was established in 1873, ostensibly to secure co-ordination in respect of technical details of administration and operation. Even these aims
were very imperfectly accomplished, and the hopes of establishing
imperial ownership were soon shown to be entirely unfounded.

The Prussian Ministry resolved, in 1876, to proceed with a policy
of state ownership, but the policy was not announced until February 7, 1879. At the time the decision was made, the government
owned only 32 per cent of the mileage of railroads in Prussia. Purchases were made in the interval before the policy was announced,
but the primary acquisitions were made in the years immediately
following the public declaration of policy. Towards the end of
1882, the state owned 15,305 kilometers, and operated 2,142 kilometers that remained in private ownership. Private companies still
operated 3,850 kilometers. Additional purchases in 1884 gave the
government substantial control of the entire railway network.

In the meantime, nationalization had made headway in Belgium.
An extensive program of state purchase was begun in 1870. The
state then owned barely one fourth of the total mileage, but the
new program soon gave the state substantial control of the entire
network. In 1898 Switzerland nationalized her railways. Italy
and Japan adopted comprehensive state ownership in 1906 and in
1907 respectively.

The advantages and disadvantages of state ownership and
operation have been widely discussed, but the results of the discussion are singularly inconclusive. Each railroad system is so
deeply affected by all the features of the region served that no
valid comparisons are possible. We cannot reach any positive conclusion as to the relative merits of state ownership or of private
ownership. Careful analysis of rate structures and of policies leads,

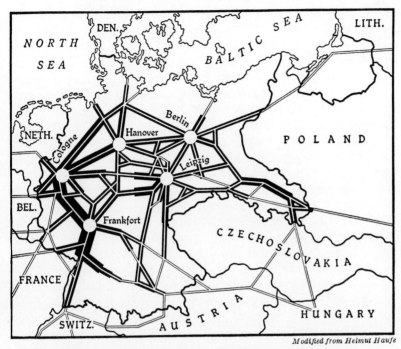

*Modified from Helmut Haufe*

*Relative Volumes of Traffic on the Principal German Railways*

on the whole, to the opinion that the form of ownership is less important than unity of administration and sound concepts of public interest.   The actual relations between the railways and the public are determined by the policies adopted in respect of rates, service, and continuing investment.   State-controlled systems reveal errors of policy and, at times, deliberate sacrifice or neglect of important public interests.   Privately owned systems exhibit faults of a different character.   Both types of management can achieve high degrees of efficiency; each type presents opportunities for the realization of the best interests of the social group.

### Industrial Combination: Resource and Process Considerations

The development of large enterprises and combinations in the industrial field presents many elements of essential similarity to the development of combinations among railroads.   But these similarities emerge only when the process of abstraction is carried to great lengths, so that general analysis can be developed most conveniently if we emphasize the special characteristics of industrial enterprise. The production of electric power presents special problems, also, which will be treated in Chapter 32. It is desirable to concentrate attention now upon the large group of strictly industrial enterprises, excluding transportation and power production. In this field, the tendencies toward large-scale production rest upon a number of factors, whose combined effects frequently lead to combination and monopoly. The factors leading towards concentration of industrial control fall into three general classes : (1) localized natural resources; (2) economies arising from the centralized control of the entire process of production from raw material to basic products or final consumption goods; and (3) economies achieved through large-scale organization for the marketing of diversified products over a large area.

Highly localized deposits of natural resources offer many tempting advantages to a combination of producers. The Newcastle Coal Vend is a characteristic illustration. The Newcastle coal field, effectively open to early utilization, was a relatively small area within fifteen or twenty miles of tidewater. The coal was sold in London and at other coastal points. No other coal was available for the supply of the market. An effective combination of producers — the Newcastle Coal Vend — appeared in the seventeenth century. Prices and production were restricted, so that the London market was largely dominated by the Vend throughout the early modern period. The organization continued, despite some attempts at regulation, until the coal trade was completely reorganized after the development of the railway. When the Midland collieries were able to reach the London market, the power of the Vend was broken. All cases of this general class rest upon the analysis of oligopoly — the control of an industry by a small number of companies. Circumstances force each company to recognize the effect of its policies upon the others, and under such conditions trade agreements can advantageously be made for the control of prices and production.

The most notable influence of natural resources upon the scale of enterprise appears in the oil industry. It is now recognized that the most effective technical procedures for the extraction of petroleum require unified control of production over the entire "pool." It is necessary to conserve the pressures exerted by natural gas. Wells should be driven in limited numbers at carefully selected sites. The wells should be run or pumped only in such measure as the crude oil can be effectively marketed. The crude oil is difficult to store without deterioriation, so that there is an obvious advantage in not producing oil that cannot be readily marketed. These considerations played a large part in the development of the producers' association in the Russian oil fields at Baku after 1888.

Tendencies toward combinations of producers appear in connection with many other highly localized deposits. The dominant factor seems to be the extent of the market controlled by the particular deposit. The Ruhr coal field, the German potash deposits, the Lorraine ores present instances of this type. The salt combinations show the operation of similar tendencies among a small number of deposits scattered over a restricted area.

Process considerations appear in many industries, but they are of particular importance in the iron and steel trade. The early iron industry was so largely dominated by charcoal fuel that the furnaces and foundries were necessarily small. With the introduction of coal as fuel more concentration was possible, but plants did not begin to expand to any great scale until wrought iron came into extensive use. The great iron works were obliged to carry the process of production further. Larger quantities of iron were refined and made into wrought iron, and the wrought iron was rolled into large forms as rails, structural shapes, and plates. Rolling mills became important adjuncts of the blast furnace.

The scale of the plant was increased still further after the introduction of the Bessemer converter and the open-hearth furnace. The demand for wrought iron and mild steel increased enormously, and the nature of the process made necessary a great increase in the size of the individual plant. The steel plant became a unit consisting of blast furnaces, converters or open-hearth furnaces, and rolling mills. The metal was carried through the whole process of production without being allowed to cool down beyond the point necessary for the next stage in the process. When new processes were introduced for making coke, the gases produced in coke making could be used to run the engines that operated the rolling mill. It was therefore advantageous to locate the coke furnaces at the steel plant as a primary unit in the works.

Continuous operation of so large a plant required precise timing of deliveries of all the primary raw materials — ore, limestone, and coal. Experience showed that it was dangerous to rely exclusively upon independent producers of ore and coal. The great steel works therefore extended their operations to the basic mining enterprises, by the acquisition of existing firms or by establishing new enterprises. The industrial unit in the iron and steel industry became an integrated unit capable of producing primary heavy products from the raw materials. Many firms carried integration further, so that more elaborately finished products were produced. Ships, ordnance, and railway supplies were produced in many instances by completely integrated enterprises. Under such circumstances, the industry came to be dominated by a small number of very large firms, such as Krupp, Creusot, Armstrong, Vickers-Maxim, and the great shipbuilding firms of the Clyde, the Tyne, and Hamburg. Further combination might be brought about by other circumstances.

## Industrial Combination: Market Considerations

Market considerations brought about combinations over a very wide field of diversified products protected by patents, copyrights, and trademarks. Unless the goods produced are distinctive in some fashion, control of the market is possible only in the case of highly localized resources which restrict the number of producers. The development of patents, copyrights, and trademarks afforded opportunities of great importance as soon as the railway made it possible to sell manufactured specialties over large market areas.

This great field was opened up by the industrial development of the nineteenth century. Patent laws were adopted early in the nineteenth century by all the European countries, and the economic importance of patents in Great Britain was greatly increased by the new industrial development. The new machine tools made it possible to produce all kinds of specialties under conditions of quantity production, which set a great premium upon extension of both plant and marketing organization. A million items could be produced at the merest fraction of the unit costs incurred in the production of two or three thousand items. Under such circumstances the scale of the enterprise would be closely related to the extent of the market.

Many demands formerly satisfied by the individualized work of local craftsmen came to be gratified by new specialties manufactured on a large scale and sold by high-pressure advertising throughout the national area and even in foreign countries. In some instances the new specialties are technically better products; in some they are cheaper in substance as in price. In every respect they are different, and their production has resulted in profound changes in the industrial and social structure. From the point of view of abstract analysis product differentiation merely assumed a new form, but the differences were important.   The production of some specialty on a small scale by a secret process or unusual skill may yield a high rate of profit which contains many elements of monopoly.   But the Versailles apothecary producing a special cold cream for a strictly local clientele does not present such an industrial and social problem as exists today in the great perfume makers, like Coty.

The organizations arising out of marketing considerations present a very wide range.   Some of the great organizations have control of groups of patents which give them an important measure of control of particular national markets.   A notable example of such a combination is furnished by the German dyestuffs combination formed in 1925 (*I. G. Farbenindustrie Aktien Gesellschaft*).   The mere enumeration of the component firms requires nearly two pages, and the activities of the combination include a wide range of chemical manufactures outside the field of dyestuffs.   But this is merely one illustration from the long list of combinations built around product differentiation.   In some instances the differences are substantial; in other fields, such as soaps and tobacco, one may wonder if the individuality of the products is sufficient to justify the outlay in advertising.   In many markets, keen competition among rival products closes people's eyes to the essentially monopolistic character of the profits.   The price level for the entire class of products is considerably above the cost level, and the impulse to combination is furnished by this possibility of establishing a price level sufficient to assure a substantial margin above all the special outlays for publicity.   Such industries are likely to be free from gross abuse of economic power, but it is not clear that they are entirely free from objectionable features.

The influence of tariff policy upon combinations has been extensively discussed in both Germany and the United States.   The problem is complex, but it seems clear that the tariff is not a primary cause of combination.   A high protective tariff, however, affords many opportunities for the abuse of economic power.   Some of the differences in the history of the movement in Germany and in Great Britain are doubtless due to differences in tariff policy.   The earlier British combinations were not permanent, because they were exposed to more foreign competition.   In Germany the domestic market was so completely secure that surplus production could be "dumped" in Great Britain without any fear of reaction upon the home market.   The experience of the United States confirms these inferences. Protective tariffs seem to bring about the formation of permanent combinations at an earlier date than would be likely in a free-trade area, and the price policies of such sheltered combinations are less likely to be modified by competition from abroad.

This external factor is, however, only one of many causes of differences in the timing of the combination movement. In the analysis of particular combinations it is tempting to stress some one of the three primary elements — resource considerations, process considerations, òr marketing considerations. But this is an oversimplification. All factors are present in some measure, and the distinction between these different factors is not always clear-cut. Variations in the precise nature of these details, or variations in respect of the combination of the different factors, produce striking differences in the result. A bewildering array of patterns of combination is thus created by different arrangements of a small number of primary elements.

### Characteristic Types of Combination

Descriptions of the combination movement have suffered severely from the lack of any terminology suited to the problem. Terms are used loosely in each country, and the meaning of primary terms varies from country to country. In the United States the term " cartel " is seldom if ever used; combinations are described as "pools," "trusts," or "mergers." In Germany nearly all combinations were described as " cartels " until quite recently, when new terms have appeared with special meanings. The terms "pool" and "cartel," as commonly used in the United States and in Germany, really cover much the same ground, though the kinds of "pools" most frequently found in the United States were less formally organized than the kind of "cartel" most frequently found in Germany. As these distinctions of degree of centralization of control are of great importance in tracing the progress of combination, it will be useful to confine the use of each term to the type of organization with which it is most commonly associated.

If we give precise meanings to the terms "pool" and "cartel," a series of forms of association can be distinguished which covers the whole range of combination. Trade associations provide means for exchange of information, and afford means of some loose informal agreements as to prices and policies of production. As there is no compulsion, the organization is merely a means of modifying the policies of the various firms. Such forms of association are not likely to persist, unless there are legal obstacles to more formal modes of organization. Such associations were not important in either Germany or Great Britain. The "pool," in the strict sense, is an organization which seeks to establish a positive price policy or a positive policy for production or marketing. The organization would have a small official staff, and many pools attempted to exercise positive control over members by imposing fines. The weakness of the pool lay in the fact that such engagements were, in all countries, classified as unenforceable contracts. In Great Britain, as in the United States, they were held invalid under the common law as contracts in restraint of trade. In France and Germany, they were denied protection under interpretations of the codes. Pools were, however, common in Germany and in Great Britain in the earlier stages of the movement. In Europe, public opinion was never sufficiently hostile to drive the movement underground.

The "cartel" represents a more advanced stage of organization than the pool, because a formal and permanent organization is formed for the control of sales. Common price policies and unified control of production can be effectively secured only if the members of the combination join in a unified system for marketing their product. In its most characteristic form, the cartel becomes an incorporated sales organization which takes over all the goods produced, and remits a return in accordance with the policy of the organization. The cartel did not destroy or even qualify the independence of the member firms. As producing units they retained complete autonomy; they were under no obligation to share technical information about processes or administrative methods. The cartel was not in any way concerned with raising the whole industry to the standard of efficiency achieved by the strongest firms.

"Mergers" would necessarily take this step towards complete administrative control. In a complete merger the individual firm loses its identity. The merger would make it possible to abandon inefficient plants, or to reorganize plants that were physically worth-while, though ineffectively administered. Complete merger might be accomplished by various devices. The "trust" in its primitive sense was the simplest means, because it required no public approval. The trust agreement would concentrate all power in the hands of a group of trustees appointed to hold and vote the stock of the constituent companies. The "holding company" accomplished the same end by more formal methods that are more flexible and more convenient. Complete consolidation in a single corporation is rare.

## The Combination Movement in Germany

Combinations of a modern type appeared in Germany even in the first half of the nineteenth century. An agreement between four Prussian alum works was concluded in 1836. In the late 1840's, some iron works in Nassau formed an association which developed a formal sales organization in 1869 and possibly earlier. Other associations, which were hardly more than pools, appeared in tin (1862), rails (1864), salt (1868), and potash (1870). Two or three new combinations were formed after the crisis of 1873, but the large development of combinations began after the adoption of the protective tariff in 1879, though the tariff was not the primary cause.

The combinations were still predominantly pools, with production quotas and agreements not to reduce prices below a stated minimum. In some instances agreements were made for division of sales territory. The combinations were not entirely successful or permanent. The coal pool for the Ruhr basin formed at Dortmund in 1879 was not renewed in 1884, and the attempt to revive the pool in 1885 failed. The coal trade engaged for a period in unregulated competition. In 1888 a sales agency was formed to cover sales of coke in foreign markets. In 1890 sales in the domestic coal trade were controlled, and in 1893 this association was reorganized as the Rhenish-Westphalian Coal Syndicate.

Most of the great cartels were formed on this model. The Coal Syndicate was incorporated as a joint-stock company with a capital of 900,000 marks. The stock was held by the various mining companies, but voting in the general assembly was proportionate to allotted output rather than to stock ownership. These companies are thus co-operative societies of a highly specialized type. The primary authority in the Coal Syndicate was vested in the general assembly, and all basic questions of policy were decided by the assembly. Administration was vested in three smaller groups elected by the assembly: the committee, the commission, and the executive. The commission fixed the total output each year and allotted percentage quotas to members. The executive fixed the selling price to customers and the price of account at which it took over the production of the mine owners. The Syndicate handled all coal, coke, and briquettes produced by the members. As the Syndicate was a recognized legal organization, it had the means of enforcing its policies upon the members.

The twenty years preceding the World War were marked by a

rapid development of combinations in the form of cartels. It is not easy to determine the precise number formed, as the lists of combinations include many pools not organized with incorporated sales agencies. Since the war there has been a tendency towards further consolidation. The less formal types consist of firms which recognize a "community of interest" without giving up their legal independence. Agreements are signed providing for a pooling of profits, a division of competitive territory, or for unified policy on particular matters. The more formal types involve combination under a holding company with more or less complete subordination of the various units. Recent developments, therefore, mark the beginnings of mergers on a large scale with a considerable increase in monopolistic control. The cartel seems to be less satisfactory than German writers were wont to believe in prewar days.

After a long period of sympathetic toleration of all the intermediate forms of combination, the German government finally promulgated an ordinance for the regulation and control of combinations. Authorized October 13, 1923, the ordinance was officially published on November 2, and went into effect as of November 20, 1923. This ordinance is of great interest because it makes a direct attack upon the essentials of the problem. The purpose is suggested by the title, which is equivalent to "ordinance against the abuse of economic powers." There is here no prohibition, nor any fine distinction between monopoly and competition, merely a direct statement that any agreements contrary to the public interest may be declared invalid. All agreements designed to influence production, sales, or prices must be in writing. All verbal stipulations or promises in amplification of written agreements are declared void. If the welfare and interest of the public is endangered, the Minister of Economic Affairs may follow any one of three procedures. He may declare void any agreement or any clause of an agreement which endangers public welfare. He may authorize parties to the agreement to break the contract without notice to other signatories. He may provide that he shall be shown copies of any order in pursuance of the offensive clause. The ordinance characterizes as "endangering the public welfare" any action which "unjustifiably" limits production, restricts sales, maintains or raises prices; or any action by which economic freedom is affected through buyers' or sellers' boycotts, or by the establishment of discriminatory prices or conditions. A Cartel Court is established to review all action involving the ordinance.

# CHAPTER 26

# THE LABOR MOVEMENT

———◆———

## Economic and Political Forces Affecting Labor, 1870–1914

Industrial workers became increasingly important during the closing decades of the nineteenth century because of the rapid extension of industrialism and the concentration of enterprise in large establishments. These tendencies were particularly striking in Germany. In 1871 the population in towns and cities of 2,000 people or more was only 36 per cent of the total; in 1900 it was 54 per cent; and in 1910, 60 per cent. The growth of population was almost exclusively in the larger towns and cities. Italian industry, under the stimulus of national unity and of the economic policies inaugurated by Cavour, expanded rapidly. French industry was retarded for a time by the defeat of France in the Franco-Prussian War of 1870–1871. Recovery was rapid, but French industry remained secondary to agriculture, and the typical industrial establishment remained small. Furthermore, the extreme bitterness of the reaction against the Commune of 1871 long hindered the progress of working-class organization. But ultimately in France as in other countries of western and central Europe the growth of industry gave increasing importance to industrial workers and their organizations.

In the field of economic theory, the wages-fund doctrine and the "iron law of wages" in their crude early forms were abandoned. Many economists attempted to find a theoretical basis for collective bargaining by labor organizations and for a larger role by the state in modifying the conditions of labor. Even the socialists, especially the German group known as state socialists and the English Fabians, accepted a policy of reform and compromise in place of rigorous interpretations of the labor theory of value and the class struggle. But there was wide acceptance by economists of a new theory of wages not radically different in its implications from the earlier classical doctrine. This was the theory of marginal productivity. A simple, unqualified form of this theory was to the effect that an employer will increase his labor force as long as an additional unit of labor is barely profitable enough to warrant the use of labor. Successive additions give him a diminishing amount of profit, and the wage he can afford to pay is correspondingly smaller. But workers doing the same kind of work, or capable of doing it, are interchangeable with the final or marginal workers, and the wage paid to each worker in a given group is therefore no greater than the wage the employer can afford to pay to the marginal or least profitable worker. This theory, or various refinements of it, came to be widely accepted by economists as an explanation of what actually happens to wages viewed comprehensively, and it offered little more to the wage worker than did the earlier "iron law of wages."

Changes in the economic status of wage earners in the nineteenth century as affected by wages and cost of living have been traced in England in greater detail than in any other major country. Estimates of changes in "gross money wages" (substantially equivalent to changes in wage rates) made by J. Kuczynski, who based his work on earlier studies by G. H. Wood, A. L. Bowley, and others, indicate an increase of about 33 per cent from 1870 to 1900 and a further increase of 7 per cent from 1900 to 1913. Kuczynski attempted to adjust money wages to losses and gains due to changes in cost of living, part time, unemployment, and social insurance payments. The resulting index of real wages per worker, including the unemployed, shows an increase of 47 per cent from 1870 to 1900, and a decline of 5 per cent from 1900 to 1913. His estimates for Germany show a much greater variability but indicate an increase of 30 per cent in real wages between the cyclical periods 1860–1867 and 1894–1902, and a small decline from 1894–1902 to 1909–1914. Wages in France also were highly variable. Kuczynski estimates an increase of 30 per cent in real wages between the cyclical averages of 1859–1868 and 1895–1903, and a further slight increase between 1895–1903 and 1909–1914. Recent studies of wages and cost of living in Sweden by the Institute for Social Science of the University of Stockholm indicate that the real annual earnings of employed workers in manufacturing and mining in Sweden rose 75 per cent from 1870 to 1900, and, in contrast with real wages in England, France, and Germany, made a further substantial advance from 1900 to 1913.

As Kuczynski and others have pointed out, there is probably an upward bias in most of the available figures of money wages because the data pertain mainly to larger industrial centers, well-organized industries, and the more stable and skilled occupations. The cost-of-living indexes are even more unsatisfactory than the indexes of money wages, and it is known that for certain periods they exaggerate the purchasing value of wages. Staple commodities, forming the chief basis of these indexes, probably tended to decline more or to increase less in price than the cost of essential services; and with the decline of opportunity for maintaining household services, workers became increasingly dependent on money wages for services as well as commodities. There was also a decline in the quality and durability of many goods produced in factories.

There was nevertheless an unmistakable increase in real wages in the latter part of the nineteenth century. During this period the industrialized countries exported vast sums for capital investment in other parts of the world. The rapid expansion of industry and trade and the unprecedented development of natural resources gave to these countries an economic basis for wage increases without impairing profits, even though the capitalization on which profits were paid did not always represent the investment of actual savings. Indeed the profitable operation of the productive system often called for higher wages. The shift of emphasis to the heavy industries employing a large proportion of skilled male workers, the more rapid tempo of mechanized production, and the greater demands on the energies of workers made desirable an increase in wages for promoting the productivity of labor. The bargaining power of labor organizations and the protective measures embodied in social legislation were factors in aiding workers to obtain higher wages, but the primary factor was the rapid expansion of European economy, which made possible an unprecedented increase in profits, partly at the expense of low-paid labor employed by the capital of the industrialized countries in other regions. When the era of expansion and easy profits came to an end, the upward trend of real wages was checked or reversed even before the World War. Thereafter the deterioration of labor from unemployment, part time, taxation, and financial instability, if not from reductions of money wage rates, was an outstanding feature of European economy.

Kuczynski and others have attempted to estimate changes in "relative" wages — that is, the average worker's comparative share of national production and income. Kuczynski defines the relative wage as the ratio of the average real wage to national per capita production adjusted to price movements. He holds that during the closing decades of the nineteenth century, when real wages advanced rapidly, the relative status of wages declined. His estimate for England shows a decline of 24 per cent from 1859–

1868 to 1895–1903; and for Germany, where national production expanded with amazing rapidity, a decline of 55 per cent from 1860–1867 to 1894–1902. Estimates of national production for this period are even less satisfactory than estimates of wages and cost of living; and the figures of relative wages are at best merely a pioneer effort to utilize the meager available data. There appears, however, to be a basis for the author's view that real wages tend to increase and relative wages tend to decrease during periods of business expansion; while real wages tend to decrease and relative wages tend to increase during periods of depression. The income of workers is used mainly for immediate consumption and does not ordinarily include any large surplus beyond what is necessary for consumption; while most of the non-wage forms of income consist more largely of surpluses representing investment and capital goods, and during a depression there is a rapid deflation of capital values and of incomes from investment. But an increase in the relative wage under such circumstances is usually accompanied by a decline in the absolute status of labor due to the curtailment of national production. At the same time, some forms of non-wage income, especially interest and salaries, decline less in depression than wages; and even dividends are likely to be maintained for a time out of reserves.

During the earlier decades of the period from 1870 to 1914, the organization of labor was retarded everywhere by legal restrictions. These were gradually abandoned. In addition, by 1914 the working classes had generally acquired the right to vote and to elect members of their own groups to serve in legislative bodies. Some of the complaints of the workers regarding their status in competitive enterprise had been met by means of social legislation, as the Factory Acts. Free public education had been widely adopted, and low-priced books and periodicals, including numerous labor journals, were available to workers. These legal, political, and cultural changes were in part a result of agitation and pressure by workers' organizations. At the same time, the adoption of policies more favorable to labor was partly for the purpose of counteracting the arguments of socialistic leaders that a fundamental change in the economic system was the only recourse of workers for an improvement of their lot. During this period the economic basis of such improvement as the working classes achieved was the rapid expansion of industry and trade, which increased the demand for labor and created vast surpluses for profits. There was therefore no

severe test of the status of industrial labor under the newly developing and rapidly expanding system of large-scale, capitalistic, and
imperialistic enterprise. Such a test was to come later, under
conditions of contracting and unstable markets and intense nationalism after the World War.

### Organized Labor in Great Britain

The Amalgamated Society of Engineers, organized in 1851, came
to be known as the "New Model" union. This union, with similar
groups, waged successful campaigns against truck or non-cash payment of wages; and also against "long pays" or long intervals
between pay days, involving debt and reduction of the purchasing
power of wages. These groups also had much to do with the enfranchisement of workers by the Reform Bill of 1867 and with the
legalization of unions by laws passed in 1871 and 1875. Extensive
funds were available for strikes but were used conservatively.
Friendly societies, social clubs, and co-operative societies continued
to attract large numbers of workers and in many cases they reinforced the trade-union movement.

Some of the gains won by the "New Model" unionism were lost
during the depression of the late 1870's. During the ensuing period
of industrial revival and trade expansion, workers were in a much
more favorable position than ever before. Co-operation, the laws
against truck, and the shortening of intervals between pay days
enabled workers to make more effective use of their earnings. After
1880 the trend of money wages was upward, while retail prices before
1895 moved downward. Experience in organization enabled the
workers to avoid many earlier mistakes. The extension of popular
education led to a much wider diffusion of knowledge, although the
tone of education was determined largely by aristocratic traditions.
The Factory Acts and reductions of hours afforded more leisure and
more favorable working conditions. Henry George's *Progress and
Poverty*, widely read in England, and also the teachings of the
Christian socialists, the Fabians, and other groups, broke down the
earlier pessimistic views associated with Malthus and Ricardo.
There was gradually formulated, in economic theory, a basis for the
belief that organized effort and public action for improving the
lot of the wage earners were not proscribed by economic "laws."
The enfranchisement of industrial workers in 1867 and of agricultural workers in 1884 made possible the direct participation of labor
in politics.

These circumstances profoundly affected organized labor in Great Britain. In the first place, organization became far more widespread by the inclusion of unskilled workers and by the growth of industrial unions in contrast with craft unions. In the second place, narrow trade-union aims and tactics were supplemented by political action and ultimately by the comprehensive political program of the Labor party.

An outstanding early instance of the extension of unionism among unskilled workers was the Dockers' Union. The London dock strike of 1889 was supported not only by other unionists but also by many outside the ranks of the workers. The success of the dock workers was followed by the extensive organization of unskilled workers. Local trades councils, formerly composed of representatives of local groups of skilled workers, came to be known in many cases as "trades and labor" councils. Industrial unionism, already prevalent in mining, won adherents in other groups. The Amalgamated Society of Railway Servants, for example, which was originally composed of skilled workers, absorbed other groups, both skilled and unskilled. Thus the railway workers, together with the miners, led the way in the extremely important shift from the craft to the industry as the basis of affiliation and concerted action.

It was the railway union which, in 1901, bore the brunt of a judicial attack on the legal position of unions. The Taff Vale Railway Company in that year obtained a verdict in the House of Lords, acting as a court, to the effect that a branch of the Amalgamated Society of Railway Servants had violated its contract with the company by a strike and that the Society as a whole was responsible for damages, amounting to £23,000. In 1906 Parliament passed the Trades Disputes Act, exempting unions from damage suits in connection with strikes or other activities authorized by law. In the meantime trade-union activity had been seriously checked by the Taff Vale decision at a time when prices were rising more rapidly than money wages. But the net result was to make the unions more aggressive. From 1892 to 1902 the number of members grew from about 1,500,000 to about 2,000,000; from 1902 to 1905, the number was less than 2,000,000; and in 1912 there were almost 3,500,000 members. Beginning in 1911 there were several important strikes, especially among railway workers and miners, and in 1914 the Triple Industrial Alliance was formed, consisting of railway, mining, and transport workers' unions. The chief economic function of the several groups of unions was "collective bargaining" between representatives of the unions and of employers for the purpose of concluding agreements regarding wages and working conditions. Many of the leaders, particularly in the Triple Alliance, were beginning to look beyond the trade agreement and to think in terms of the organization of the major industries into national guilds or corporations essentially socialistic in character.

The direct participation of unions in politics may be said to date from the formation of the Labor Representation Committee at the Trades Union Congress of 1869. Five years later two representatives of miners' unions were elected to the House of Commons. In 1893 the Independent Labor party, a socialistic group, was formed. In 1899 the Labor Representation Committee of the Trades Union Congress was directed to formulate a plan for promoting more effective political action, and the outcome was the Labor party, although the name was not adopted until somewhat later. As early as 1891 the Trades Union Congress had voted in favor of nationalization of key industries, but the Labor party before the World War was not avowedly socialistic. It sought to bring together certain socialistic groups and the co-operative societies as well as the trade-unions, on the basis of a moderate program of reform.

The Taff Vale decision of 1901 greatly stimulated the movement which culminated in 1906 in formal organization of the Labor party, and the 29 members of the party elected to the House of Commons in 1906 exerted much influence in securing the passage of the Trades Disputes Act. Members of Parliament at that time served without public pay, and the Labor members depended on the allocation of union funds. Another adverse judicial action, the Osborne decision of 1909, declared that the use of union funds for this purpose was illegal. This action, like the Taff Vale decision, strengthened the determination of the unions to extend their political influence and led to a law, in 1910, for public payment of members of Parliament. In December, 1910, the party secured 42 seats. Before 1914 it pursued in general a policy of co-operating with the Liberal party in the program of national insurance and other social legislation.

Participation by labor in local politics was made possible by a series of laws extending the local franchise to virtually all citizens. Municipalities had already, in the later decades of the nineteenth century, widely adopted "municipal trading" or ownership and operation of various public utilities. Such a program was inaugurated at Birmingham, for example, by Joseph Chamberlain as mayor in 1873. The growth of trade-unions and the extension of their activities to politics gave a new impulse to municipal socialism, by means of which essential services were provided at prices which materially increased working-class well-being and the purchasing power of workers' incomes.

## The French Syndicates

The French labor movement after 1871 was profoundly affected by the terrorism and hatreds associated with the overthrow of the Commune of 1871. Workers were shot in masses, survivors were exiled, amnesty was deferred for eight years, and legal disabilities of unions were not removed until 1884. But unions or syndicates of a mild type, under the leadership of Barberet, a Parisian journalist, survived the Commune. They disavowed resort to strikes and adopted among their aims a program of education and co-operation. Separate unions were not proscribed by the government, but an attempted federation was broken up. In 1876, however, a labor congress was allowed to assemble at Paris, where unions, friendly societies, and co-operative groups were represented.

By 1879 a bolder tone was apparent. At a labor congress held at Marseille the socialists under the leadership of Jules Guesde gained control, but the more conservative elements refused their co-operation. Among the socialists themselves there were two main groups, one adhering to evolutionary and reformist policies, the other favoring the formation of a revolutionary Marxist labor party. After the removal of legal restraints in 1884, labor exchanges (*bourses du travail*) were formed, the first in Paris in 1887. They somewhat resembled the American and English trades councils or central labor unions of the cities. They were designed to provide meeting places and centers of local activity for the various local unions and also to serve in a sense as employment offices. In many places they obtained financial support from the municipalities but claimed to be independent of political control. In 1892 these organizations formed a national federation, in opposition to the earlier more radical federations.

Thus the labor movement was divided into factions with conflicting aims and ideas as to tactics. It was retarded also by the fact that most of the unions were small, scattered, and unable to obtain adequate financial support. French enterprises were typically on a small scale, and the spirit of individualism characterized both businessmen and the extremely influential landowning peasants.

The co-operative movement had made little progress. The social-istic unions or syndicates were obstructed both by divided counsels and by the prevailing individualism. Internal conflicts and frus-trated aims encouraged the growth of a somewhat naïve faith in a vague but sudden and comprehensive transformation of the eco-nomic system by means of a general strike.

These various circumstances gave rise in 1895 to a new federation of revolutionary syndicates opposed alike to the labor exchanges and to the socialistic unions, which were devoted to political action by means of the franchise and labor representation in governmental agencies. The new organization was the General Confederation of Labor (*Confédération Générale du Travail*). It has been estimated that in 1894, on the eve of the formation of the C. G. T., there were 2,178 syndicates in France with a membership of more than 400,000. The C. G. T. attracted 700 syndicates, but most of these failed to pay dues and to participate in the earlier work of the federation. From 1895 to 1902 there was continued conflict, especially between the C. G. T. and the Federation of Bourses (labor exchanges), although hostility gradually abated and the two groups were united in 1902. In the meantime the socialistic parties had made strenuous efforts to win the support of the syndicates, and the C. G. T. was the main source of opposition to political action on the part of the workers. Reliance continued to be placed in direct action, with the hope of an ultimate general strike, reinforced by sabotage and the boycott.

Although the union of the two principal groups in 1902 was a victory for the theory of the general strike, there were many mod-erate elements in the new C. G. T., and many syndicates refused to join the Confederation. Furthermore, the policies actually pur-sued were rendered more moderate by the hostility of the govern-ment, as when Premier Briand, a socialist of the reformist type, arrested the leaders in a railway strike and called the striking workers to the colors. There were frequent strikes for such traditional trade-union objectives as higher wages, shorter hours, and weekly rest days, and these were predominantly successful. Nor was the Confederation averse to obtaining favorable legislation. In 1914 the Confederation had only about 600,000 members, and many of these were merely nominal adherents of the doctrine of revolutionary syndicalism. The membership of the reformist unions was almost as large as that of the Confederation. The number of unorganized workers was much larger than the total number of unionists. France remained predominantly a country of individualistic peasants, professional classes, and men of small enterprises.

### German Labor and the Social Democratic Party

In Great Britain the labor movement from 1870 to 1914 was at first essentially nonpolitical, and throughout the period there was emphasis on direct relations between employers and representatives of the unions. In France the socialistic leaders for a time won the support of many of the syndicates, but there was a gradual loss of faith in political action, and also a reluctance to enter into binding agreements with employers, the ultimate aim being a revolutionary transformation of national economy into a nonpolitical system of industrial syndicates on a somewhat vague socialistic or guild basis. The German trade-union movement affords contrasts to both the French and the British movement. Before 1890, unions were illegal. Even after that date collective action for exerting influence on employers was gravely restricted by the doubtful legal status of picketing, by the responsibility of representatives of unions in alleged breaches of contract, and by the extensive discretion of the police and administrative bodies in the application of the law. The working classes of Germany early came under the influence of Lassalle and Marx, and political action for the socialization of industry remained a prominent aspect of the labor movement, although collective bargaining, as in England, was the immediate goal of the unions.

The formation of the Social Democratic party in 1875 was soon followed by a bitter struggle with Bismarck, first Chancellor of the Empire. Before the law of 1878, proscribing socialistic groups, there were only about 50,000 trade-unionists, but the Social Democratic party polled about half a million votes. In spite of the law of 1878, which was invoked against trade-unionists as well as socialists, unionism survived in secret and disguised forms. Although the law was not repealed until 1890, its enforcement was relaxed during the 1880's. Bismarck attempted to undermine socialism and unionism alike by his comprehensive system of social legislation, but the socialist vote increased rapidly and in 1890 numbered about 1,500,000. Thereafter both the socialistic vote and the membership of the unions increased steadily. In 1913 there were about 3,600,000 trade-union members, and the Social Democratic party commanded 4,239,000 votes, about one third of the popular vote, and held 113 of the 397 seats in the Reichstag — the most numerous party in that body. It has been estimated that three fourths of the trade-unionists supported the party.

By far the largest trade-union membership was in the socialistic or "free" unions. Their origins are traceable to the efforts of Lassalle, Marx, Liebknecht, and Bebel to direct the early co-operative and educational societies into socialistic channels. These groups were the principal support of the Social Democratic party. In 1912 there were about 2,500,000 members of the socialistic unions. Another group, the Christian unions, was formed during the last decade of the century, in opposition to the socialistic and allegedly anti-clerical attitude of the free unions. They were not associated directly with the churches but were predominantly Roman Catholic. They were especially strong among mining, railroad, and textile workers. In 1912 their membership exceeded 300,000. Most of the trade unionists who were not connected with either the free or the Christian unions were members of a third group of societies going back to the 1860's. They were commonly known as the Hirsch-Duncker unions. Their models were the British unions and their members were mostly skilled craftsmen such as engineers, metal workers, cabinetmakers, and shoemakers. Their aims were even more moderate than were those of the Christian unions.

The German unions were thoroughly organized locally, and each of the three groups mentioned above had a strong central organization. The activities of the unions included the administration of sickness and unemployment benefits from membership dues; the carrying on of research, education, and propaganda, especially by means of numerous labor journals; and the obtaining of more satisfactory wages and working conditions by means of collective bargaining or, if necessary, by strikes. In 1914 the number of workers directly affected by trade agreements or collective bargains with employers was about 1,500,000. Most of the great industrialists were strongly opposed to unions and were able to resist the demands for collective agreements.

Virtually all types of unions attempted to influence the course of legislation, and working-class pressure was largely responsible, indirectly, for the comprehensive system of social legislation. The free unions were far more active, politically, than were the other groups, and in the organization and program of the Social Democratic party they offered an agency and a comprehensive policy for the government of the country. But many who voted for the party candidates were not socialists, and the party itself abandoned the uncompromising attitude of the early Marxians and adopted a policy of social reforms embodying a gradual approach to the problem of socializing private capital. The influence of trade-unionists and the Social Democratic party was probably more effective in local than in national politics. Extensive progress was made locally in the socialization of public utilities and in the carrying on of various municipal enterprises such as savings banks, theaters, fire insurance, and housing.

Continental unions and socialistic organizations outside of France and Germany followed the German pattern more commonly than the French. Trade-unions were predominantly socialistic but there was much conflict as to tactics. In Italy the unions grew rapidly during the two decades preceding the World War. There were struggles over tactics, but the principal groups of unions adopted the French conception of opposition to parliamentary methods and of adherence to revolutionary syndicalism for achieving the socialization of capital. In Austria and most of the other Continental countries the more important unions followed the lead, as in Germany, of the parliamentary socialists. They favored political reforms, "gradualism" in the socialization of capital, and the promotion of collective bargaining in dealing with employers.

## Obstacles in the Way of Concerted Action

After the disruption and virtual end of the First International in 1872, little progress was made for two decades toward concerted action on the part of the various national groups of socialists or trade-unionists. There was a widely accepted but unwarranted view that the Paris Commune of 1871 had been instigated by the First International, and prevalent ideas as to the aims and powers of the International were greatly exaggerated. As a result, various governments virtually outlawed the organization. The unification of Italy and Germany, the humiliation of France in the Franco-Prussian War, and the erection of tariff walls created a nationalistic atmosphere which was unfavorable to the international point of view. There were serious conflicts among the supporters of international organization.

Socialists were most actively interested in a union of the workers of the world, but they were confronted with various questions which prevented a union among themselves. Should they attempt to achieve socialism by revolutionary methods, or by "gradualism" — an evolutionary transformation of the economic system as proposed by Edward Bernstein and the German "revisionists" of Marxism and by the English Fabians? Should they refuse to compromise with private capitalism and its proponents, or collaborate with nonsocialistic parties in promoting social legislation and reform by parliamentary methods? Should the socialized ownership of capital be brought about by political action and the mere extension of the functions of government, or by some form of economic organization, as the French syndicates or the industrial guilds later proposed by the British guild socialists? What should be the attitude of socialists toward such questions as nationalism, imperialism, and war? Should socialists collaborate with nonsocialistic trade-unions, or oppose them in favor of unions committed to the abolition of private capitalism?

The trade-unions themselves were divided. Many of the unions, especially in Germany and the lesser countries, favored Marxian socialism. Others, as the groups affiliated with the General Confederation of Labor (the C. G. T.) in France, accepted the general doctrine of the socialization of capital but held that socialization should be achieved by the direct action of economic groups such as co-operative societies or the French syndicates, and not indirectly by governmental action. A third type, prominent in the United States and in Great Britain before the rise of the Labor party, accepted political action, but only for promoting legislation favorable to labor and for supplementing collective bargaining and the direct influence of the unions on employers. A fourth type held that labor organizations should abstain from politics, and especially from affiliation with political parties, and should limit themselves to employer-employee relations and the promotion of educational, social, and mutual-benefit activities among their members. Unions of this type usually consisted of skilled workers organized according to their skills or crafts. But unskilled workers had no craft basis for organization; and in many of the basic industries, such as mining, transportation, and iron and steel, conditions became increasingly unfavorable for craft unionism even among skilled workers. The impact of technological change on occupational skills tended to disrupt the traditional alignments. The highly integrated corporate ownership and management of enterprise, especially in the great basic industries, called for a similar integration of labor organizations. But the craft unions — the "aristocracy of labor" — clung to their form of organization in a manner resembling the conservatism of the earlier guilds.

## The International Labor Movement

Thus the working classes experienced numerous crosscurrents and conflicts in respect to forms of organization, aims, and modes of action both economic and political. As a result, unity of action was impossible, even on a national scale. But efforts were repeatedly made to overcome the obstacles in the way of international action, and during the quarter of a century preceding the World War measurable success was achieved. Strenuous efforts were made by the leaders to avert war, and their worst fears as to the effects of war in destroying the solidarity of labor were borne out by the disruption of the movement on the outbreak of the World War.

The formation of an international group comparable to the First International proved to be impossible before 1889. In that year an International Exhibition was held in Paris to celebrate the hundredth anniversary of the French Revolution. Among the many international congresses which met in connection with the Exhibition were two rival labor congresses. One of these was essentially a trade-union assembly, called together by the British Trades Union Congress. The other, attended by 391 representatives of socialistic and trade-union groups from twenty countries, was initiated by the socialists of Germany. It was this latter group which inherited the traditions of the First International and which came to be known as the Second International.

In 1896, after a series of congresses and bitter struggles with the anarchists, reminiscent of the conflict between Marx and Bakunin in the First International, the anarchists and antiparliamentary groups were expelled. The Second International won extensive support from the trade-unionists of most of the countries of the Continent, but the French General Confederation of Labor opposed the parliamentary method of attempting to introduce socialism, and the British Trades Union Congress was unwilling to commit the British unions unequivocally to socialism in any form. The attempts of the International to unify the diverse and conflicting elements led to many compromises regarding tactics and secondary aims, but there was a persistent adherence to the principle of socializing the major instruments of production and to political action supported by the working classes as the method of achieving socialism. There was agreement also in opposition to armaments and war, but not as to methods of preventing war under private capitalism. In 1900 the International Socialist Bureau was organized, with an office at Brussels, for maintaining constant international contacts.

The main support of the Second International was from the working classes, organized either in trade-unions or in socialist parties, but there was an influential middle-class element, especially among the leaders. The revolutionary syndicalists, especially in France, and many of the conservative unions in Great Britain, the United States, and elsewhere, were unwilling to support the Second International but were interested in the promotion of international understanding and voluntary concerted action. The International sought to direct the ideas and policies of the unions into socialistic channels, but it was inclined to recognize the conservatism of many of the unions and to promote internationalism among them, even on a nonsocialistic basis. It therefore placed its facilities at the disposal of trade-union leaders and encouraged them in the organization of international trade-union offices or secretariats. During the two decades preceding the World War the more important national unions formed such secretariats with permanent offices which served as clearinghouses of information and occasionally as agencies for aiding strikers and promoting the organization of labor.

In 1903 a central office or secretariat was instituted for promoting concerted action by the various types of national unions and by the international trade-union offices. This was first called the International Secretariat of National Trade Union Centers, but at the request of American delegates the name was changed in 1913 to the International Federation of Trade Unions. The organization adopted the general rule of autonomy for the constituent unions of the various countries. It was therefore neither socialistic nor anti-socialistic, but unions affiliated with the Second International held a prominent place. The initiative in its organization was taken by the socialistic German unions. The Federation avoided controversial questions of policy and dealt with such matters as the development of statistical services, the collecting and allocating of funds to aid strikers, the restraining of the international migration of strikebreakers, and the promotion of international agreements affecting labor. In 1912 the membership of the unions affiliated with the Federation was more than 7,000,000.

## The Growth of Co-operative Societies

The co-operative societies, like the socialist parties, were not composed exclusively of wage earners, but their members were mainly either industrial workers or peasants. Although the leaders of the co-operative movement usually avoided political connections, co-operation is in theory a form of socialism. Robert Owen and other early advocates of co-operation viewed it as an agency for transforming the economic system. The Rochdale Equitable Pioneers of 1844 professed adherence to this conception as their ultimate aim. John Stuart Mill proposed associations of workers "collectively owning the capital with which they carry on their operations" as avenues of escape from the dilemma of low wages based on competitive costs of production under private capitalism.

Karl Marx, although criticizing as Utopian the views of Owen, Fourier, and other associative socialists, nevertheless approved of workers' co-operative societies, especially for production, and asserted that "the value of these great social experiments cannot be overestimated." His main interest, however, was in the political organization of the working classes for the purpose of achieving a socialistic state. The Social Democratic party ultimately adopted the Marxian view in place of Lassalle's conception of socialism to be attained by co-operative societies aided by the state. In Belgium the co-operative movement, beginning in the 1880's, was from the first intimately associated with the socialistic trade-unions. The British Trades Union Congress tried to induce the co-operative societies to join the trade-unions and the socialistic groups in the formation of the Labor party. The co-operatives preferred to abstain from direct affiliation with the party, but their relations with other groups were intimate and their members were mainly members also of these other groups. The French syndicalists were vague and not always consistent in their aims, but the syndicates were viewed as the organizing centers of the future socialistic economy. This conception of economic activity and control centering around spontaneously organized groups of producers was an outgrowth of the associative or co-operative school of economic thought. The opposition of the syndicalists to co-operative societies under the auspices of the government grew out of their experiences with the government, especially the manner in which it had sabotaged the national workshops after the Revolution of 1848. Their attitude was strengthened by the violent overthrow of the Paris Commune of 1871. Later, their distrust of political action for the attainment either of co-operative production or of state socialism was accentuated by what they viewed as the betrayal of the workers by Millerand, Briand, and other socialistic politicians.

The skepticism of both syndicalists and Marxian socialists regarding consumers' co-operative societies was vindicated in some degree by the fact that these societies tended to lose sight of their earlier conception of co-operation as a method of achieving a new economic system. But the co-operative store with its auxiliary activities was the most successful form of co-operation among industrial workers. Co-operative societies for carrying on production encountered difficulties of capitalization and management which they were in most cases unable to overcome. It is true that there were many successful co-operative associations of producers, especially in agriculture, but in agriculture the members remained independent producers. Their co-operative agencies were used for obtaining credit, for facilitating the marketing and in some cases for the processing of their products, and for carrying on certain other auxiliary activities, such as insurance, home building, education, and recreation.

Among co-operative associations of producers, progress from 1870 to 1914 was particularly significant in agriculture. The number of societies in France before the World War was about 5,000, with a membership of about 750,000. Their activities included marketing, insurance, banking, group buying of fertilizers, seeds, etc., and the processing of certain products, as in dairies. There was an extensive development, also, of consumers' societies in France, largely among industrial workers. In 1913, 2,980 consumers' societies reported a membership of 865,000 and a business amounting to 375,573,000 francs.

In Germany, agricultural co-operation, initiated by village credit societies founded by F. W. Raiffeisen about the middle of the nineteenth century, expanded rapidly after 1870. These village societies performed many other functions, such as the group buying of farm supplies. Before the World War Germany experienced a rapid development of various types of societies. In 1914 there were five large central organizations. With these agencies were associated most of the co-operative societies: 16,969 credit societies with 2,313,187 members; 7,331 societies devoted primarily to such work as buying, manufacturing, and processing, with 697,767 members; 1,372 consumers' societies with 2,024,581 members; and 250 building societies with 71,936 members. The prominence of the urban working classes in consumers' societies is indicated by the fact that in 1918, 72 per cent of the members were industrial wage earners, 5 per cent were public employees and professional workers, and 13 per cent were persons without fixed occupations, including pensioners, largely from the working classes. Most of the producers' organizations and credit societies were agricultural, but the Schulze-Delitzsch share-capital banks were largely urban.

In Holland in 1914 there were 811 consumers' societies, 362 being agricultural; 1,052 producers' societies, including 798 creameries; 715 savings and loan societies; 47 insurance groups; and 269 building associations. In Switzerland, retail societies affiliated with the Swiss Co-operative Union served approximately one third of the families of Switzerland. Probably the most highly developed system of co-operative associations among agricultural producers was in Denmark. Co-operation assumed many forms, with emphasis on dairies, bacon-packing establishments, and the exporting of farm produce. Denmark's predominantly agricultural character, combined with the democratic system of land tenure, gave the peasant groups a comparatively free field for co-operative activity. In Ireland agricultural co-operation was an outstanding feature of the transition to peasant proprietorship. In most of the countries of Europe, agricultural co-operation had as one of its most important consequences the strengthening of the small proprietor; while consumers' co-operation not only increased the economic well-being of the industrial classes but also afforded experience in self-discipline and group action.

The early co-operative movement in Great Britain was described in an earlier chapter (pages 441–442). Great Britain, the home of consumers' co-operation, retained the lead in this field. The estimated number of societies in 1872 was 930, with 324,000 members. In 1914 there were 1,385 societies, with 3,054,000 members and a turnover of £88,000,000. The Co-operative Wholesale Society, which traces its origin to 1863, and the Scottish Co-operative Wholesale Society, founded in 1868, were designed primarily to serve merely as buying agencies for the co-operative stores. But their functions were extended in various directions. The C. W. S. acquired tea-growing estates in the Far East, operated factories of various kinds, notably flour mills, maintained shipping facilities, and owned banks with assets in 1914 approximating £7,000,000.

The extension of co-operation was promoted by national organizations such as the English Co-operative Union, with an Irish section, and by the International Co-operative Alliance. The latter organization, founded in 1895, held congresses, organized international co-operative exhibitions, and published a journal, the

*International Co-operative Bulletin.* The International Institute of Agriculture, established in 1905, devoted much attention to the promotion and improvement of agricultural co-operation.

## Factory Acts and Social Insurance

Co-operative societies and trade-unions were mainly devoted to self-help rather than the promotion of state action. There were also many friendly societies, mutual-benefit clubs, and similar groups which provided a simple form of group insurance against such contingencies as sickness, accident, and unemployment. Many trade-unions, especially before they obtained full legalization for concerted action in dealing with employers, used part of their funds for the assistance of needy or unfortunate members.

But changing economic conditions made increasingly inadequate the methods of mutual self-help against the hazards of industry. Large-scale enterprise reduced to an impersonal basis the relations between workers and employers and even between the members of labor groups, and at the same time forced an increasing proportion of the population into the dependent wage-earning classes. Labor became increasingly mobile, and workers shifted from region to region and from one occupation to another, with a disturbance of the stable group connections necessary for adequate self-help. The hazards of industrial diseases and accidents and especially of unemployment were accentuated by early factory and housing conditions and by recurring depressions. Industrial instability, the growth of cities, and the shifting of population weakened family ties and undermined the traditional basis of mutual dependence within the family circle. These were some of the circumstances that provided arguments in favor of public responsibility for regulating labor conditions and protecting the working classes from industrial hazards. At the same time the growing economic and political strength of labor organizations and the effects of popular education enabled the workers to bring pressure to bear upon governments for the enactment of social legislation.

The main features of factory legislation had already been worked out in Great Britain before 1870, but after that date there were several important changes. The Factory Acts were codified in 1878 and again in 1901. There was an increasingly rigorous control of dangerous trades and processes. The definition of factories and workshops was broadened, as by the extension of regulation in 1912 to such establishments as restaurants and retail stores or shops.

Among the many improvements in the administration and enforcement of the acts was the appointment of workingmen and, after 1893, of women, as factory inspectors.

Factory legislation was initiated in France, Germany, and some other countries before 1870, but the main developments were after that date.   These laws were detailed and highly technical in nature, and were gradually extended, as in Great Britain, to new fields of industry successively occupied by new techniques and large-scale organization.   The laws were designed primarily for the protection of women and children but were extended to include men.   The earlier laws emphasized limitations on the age of workers and restrictions on hours, especially of women and children.   The principal regulations affecting wages dealt not with wage rates but with such questions as fines or other deductions from wages, and payment in truck in place of money.   There was a progressively detailed and rigorous formulation of standards for ventilation, lighting, cloakrooms, lavatories, and other arrangements for the efficiency, health, and comfort of workers.   Special standards were developed for dangerous trades and processes.   Provisions for inspection and enforcement became increasingly rigorous, and administrative discretion was extended for adaptation of the laws to special circumstances.

Great Britain led the way in factory legislation, but in the group of laws known as social insurance, the initiative was taken by Germany.   The exigencies and hazards against which a greater or less degree of social protection was ultimately provided included industrial accidents, sickness, maternity, industrial or occupational diseases, invalidity, old age, dependency of women and children due to loss of the breadwinner, and unemployment.   Most of the measures popularly described as social insurance were not based on rigorous actuarial principles, but the purpose, namely, the distribution of losses and the elimination or reduction of individual risks, was virtually identical with the purpose of insurance as technically defined.   The losses were not distributed exclusively among the direct beneficiaries but were assumed in part by employers and by governments.   It is this fact which essentially distinguishes social insurance from ordinary commercial insurance and from the work of such groups as friendly societies.

Social insurance was an outgrowth of conditions and hazards beyond the range of the actuarial principles and procedure of commercial insurance, and beyond the control of individuals, families, and self-help groups such as friendly societies. Among these circumstances was the competitive fixing of wages mainly on the basis of labor as a factor in the cost of production. Another basic factor was the prevalence of involuntary unemployment due to recurring depressions, technological changes, occupational obsolescence, and other causes. In a mobile industrial population, family, group, and community ties were necessarily relaxed, and dependence due to loss of the breadwinner became increasingly a governmental problem. Probably the most immediate and obvious basis of demand for social insurance was the increasing use of dangerous machinery and the carrying on of industries and processes with abnormal rates of industrial diseases and accidents.

These circumstances influenced the government of Germany under Bismarck in 1878, when the problem of national sickness and accident insurance was first seriously considered. German economic thought had been comparatively free from the preconceptions of individualism and *laissez faire* which dominated the British and the French, and the leading economists advocated state intervention. Notable among these were Friedrich List, neo-mercantilist (d. 1846); Wilhelm Roscher, founder of the historical school; Adolph Wagner and Gustav Schmoller, state socialists; and Bishop von Ketteler, author of *The Labor Question and Christianity*. The followers of Lassalle and Marx also advocated public protection of the workers, but on the basis of the socialization of capital. The desire to curb the Marxian socialists was one of Bismarck's principal motives in advocating social insurance. He believed that such a policy would reinforce the antisocialistic legislation of 1878 and strengthen the allegiance of the workers to the new imperial government. He frankly announced that the policy was designed to draw the workers away from what he called the "siren song" of the socialists.

Insurance against sickness was adopted in 1883, and against accidents in 1884. In 1891 provision was made for protection against old age and invalidity; and in 1911 survivors' insurance, for widows and orphans, was added to the system. In the field of unemployment insurance, Germany made no attempt before the World War to establish a national system, but in some of the cities local plans were adopted. As early as 1894 Cologne, and later some other cities, made use of a plan originating in Switzerland. Unemployment benefits were made available to small groups of workers on a subsidized, semi-charitable basis. Other cities adopted a much more adequate system devised at Ghent in 1900.

This plan extended, by means of muncipal aid, the out-of-work benefits administered by trade-unions or mutual-benefit societies.

The various national insurance laws of Germany were codified in 1911, and a centralized administration, the Imperial Insurance Office, was set up, the costs of administration being borne by the government. Local workers' groups, many of which had long provided small benefit payments for their members, were extensively utilized for the local administration of the system. For sickness insurance, workers contributed two thirds and employers one third. For old-age and invalidity insurance, the contributions were equal, but public subsidies were added. Payments to widows and orphans were mainly from public funds, supplemented by contributions previously made to the old-age and invalidity funds. Accident insurance or workmen's compensation was based on the principle of employers' liability, the immediate cost being borne by employers.

The German system stimulated the movement for similar legislation in other countries, and the experience of Germany provided a basis for the formulation of laws elsewhere. Workmen's compensation for accidents, on the principle of employers' liability, was adopted before the World War by most of the countries of Europe. Provision was made for old age, in the form either of insurance based on contributions, or of subsidies and pensions, in Great Britain, France, Italy, Belgium, Spain, Denmark, and Serbia. Great Britain, Austria-Hungary, Russia, Norway, and Serbia followed Germany's example in the establishment of compulsory sickness insurance, and subsidies for noncompulsory sick benefits were granted in France and several smaller countries. Local organizations for the payment of unemployment benefits were widely subsidized, either by municipalities or by national governments. In 1911 Great Britain adopted the first national system of compulsory unemployment insurance. Unemployment insurance applied at first only to building and construction, engineering, machinery, shipbuilding, and sawmills — trades characterized by a high degree of seasonal and cyclical fluctuations in employment. Great Britain also developed an elaborate system of public employment offices (labor exchanges). Perhaps the most radical departure from *laissez-faire* principles was the British Trade Boards Act of 1909, providing for minimum wages in sweated industries. In 1912 the plan was extended to coal miners. But throughout Europe the outstanding contribution to national labor policy before the World War was the principle of social insurance.

CHAPTER 27

# MONETARY STANDARDS, PRICES, AND THE PRECIOUS METALS, 1770–1914

## The Development of the Gold Standard in England

Throughout the Middle Ages and the early modern period gold and silver were used for currency under conditions which present all the external features of bimetallism. Both metals were legal tender, and coins were struck from both metals in prescribed proportions. These monetary systems, however, were not true bimetallic systems. In many countries, over long periods of time, no attempt was made to enforce the valuation placed on the coins at the mint. Premiums were therefore easily established, and under such circumstances both metals circulated at the market ratio. More commonly, the monetary system became in fact a single standard. Few countries enjoyed equal facilities for procuring both gold and silver, and custom established a clear preference for one metal or the other. In such cases, the mint ratios soon came to favor one metal. We cannot now be certain that this was the result of deliberate policy, though in some instances there are strong grounds for presuming that it was. In any event, unfavorable ratios had the effect of restricting actual coinage to a single metal.

The working of early currency systems was also profoundly affected by the restrictions placed upon the export of coin and bullion. In many countries, export of specie was prohibited, but the ordinances made certain exceptions in favor of specified trades and in most instances special licenses could be secured. All these restrictions increased the cost of specie movements and hampered exchange business and currency adjustment. Until the eighteenth century the mints charged substantial fees for coinage, which added another factor of cost and possible mischief. The monetary systems of the early modern period are thus rather deceptive. They seem to be more nearly identical with nineteenth-century systems than they were in reality.

England was one of the first countries to establish a single standard with unrestricted rights to export and import specie. A free market for coin and bullion was established by a statute of Charles II (1663): "Forasmuch as several considerable and advantageous

566

trades cannot be conveniently driven and carried on without the
species of money or bullion, and as it is found by experience that
they are carried in the greatest abundance (as to a common market)
to such places as give free liberty for exporting the same . . . be it
enacted that from and after the 1st day of August, 1663, it shall
and may be lawful to and for any person or persons whatsoever to
export out of any port of England and Wales . . . all sorts of foreign
coin or bullion of gold or silver. . . ." The administration of this
statute was' difficult, and it was qualified by various orders and
restrictions for longer or shorter periods, but it remains the primary
basis of English policy and laid the foundations for the great importance of the free gold market in London.

The adoption of the gold standard was largely the result of the
operation of a mint ratio that was seriously biased against silver.
France offered a highly favorable rate for silver at her mints.
England discriminated against silver. Little silver was presented
for coinage in England, and it was not easy to maintain adequate
supplies of fractional currency. The silver coins remaining in
circulation were clipped and sweated so that they contained much
less than their legal weight. This condition of the silver coinage
was the occasion for the limitation of the legal-tender quality of
silver. A statute of 1774 limited the legal-tender quality of silver
to amounts not exceeding £25, unless the silver was tendered on a
basis of its bullion value. The act was limited to two years, but it
was subsequently continued. This statute really established a gold
standard, because gold coin became the sole legal monetary standard
at the rate defined in the mint ordinances then in force.

There could be no question of the authority of Parliament to
vary the monetary standard, but there had been a strong drift of
opinion towards an unvarying standard. In all these matters,
public opinion had been increasingly influenced by a pure commodity
theory of money. It was held that the state was under an obligation of honor to maintain an unvarying currency standard. Currency debasement was regarded with disdain as dishonest and
unwise. English writers and businessmen were deeply shocked by
the persistent debasements of currency in Spain, France, and
Germany. The currency of England had been maintained at a high
standard after the sixth year of the reign of Edward VI, though there
was a small reduction in the fine content of the shilling in 1601. No
country of Europe had maintained a longer record for sound currency. The act of 1774 was thus in effect an enactment designed

to adopt an unvarying gold standard. The specific terms of the act were supplemented by a firmly established policy.

During the wars with France the coinage and circulation of gold were practically suspended by the operations of the Restriction Act, though the statute is concerned solely with the Bank of England. The Bank was forbidden to pay its creditors in gold or to issue any gold except for army and navy supplies under a specific Order in Council. Notes of the Bank of England were to be receivable for taxes at par, and should be deemed equivalent to specie for use in all transactions, if accepted by the creditor. No one might be imprisoned for debt, however, if bank notes to the amount of the debt had been deposited for the account of the creditor. It will be observed that the notes were not made legal tender. They circulated by common consent. The notes of the Bank of England were supplemented by issues of private bankers in London and in the provinces. Specie rose to a small premium at once, but the premium did not exceed 5 per cent until 1800. In 1800 and 1801 Spanish silver stood at 11.2 and 15.9 per cent premium. Conditions improved somewhat, but during the climax (1813) of the struggle with Napoleon the premium rose to 38.2 per cent.

Government policy and the conduct of the Bank of England were praiseworthy. There was some credit inflation, but the amount was not large. Taxation was increased rapidly and after the war the currency was gradually readjusted with less shock than after the World War.

In anticipation of the resumption of specie payments, the gold standard was formally adopted and some technical changes were made in the mint ordinances. The guinea was discontinued, and the new sovereign issued at a rating of 20 shillings. The statute, June 22, 1816, declared gold to be the sole standard of value at the rate of 113 grains of fine gold to the pound sterling. The sovereign contained 123.27 grains of gold eleven-twelfths fine. Coinage was gratuitous, though a small charge was made if the owner of bullion demanded currency immediately upon delivery of bullion. The Troy ounce of gold was rated at £3 17s. 10½d; new coins were delivered without delay at the rate of £3 17s. 9d per ounce.

The act of 1816 limited the legal-tender quality of silver coins to 40 shillings. The silver content of all the silver coins was reduced far below the face value of the coins, so that they became typical token coins for subsidiary circulation.

## The Use of Silver in Continental Europe, 1789–1850

The history of the modern French coinage begins in 1785 with the rerating of the gold and silver coinage by Calonne. Changes in the market ratio between gold and silver led him to believe that gold was becoming more valuable. In order to be certain of maintaining the silver circulation, he therefore raised the ratio to 15.5 to 1. The mint ordinances of that time did not state this relationship in the form of a ratio, but the relations between the coins were specifically defined. Calonne was a bimetallist in the sense that all early modern statesmen were bimetallists: he defined a relationship between the gold and silver coins, but had no hope that both coins would remain in circulation. The ratio previously in force was 14⅝ to 1, and in the United States shortly afterwards a ratio of 15 to 1 was adopted. Calonne thus made a strong bid for a supply of silver. Subsequent discussion led finally to the acceptance of this ratio.

After the outbreak of the Revolution, Mirabeau proposed (December 12, 1790) a systematic reform of the coinage. The coinage system of the old regime had used the *livre tournois* as a denomination of account. All prices and value relationships were expressed as livres; but until 1720 the coins rarely corresponded precisely to the livre or its multiples and fractions. Alteration of the currency had been achieved by restating the values of the coins without changing their metallic content. Mirabeau proposed to establish a direct correspondence between the denomination of account and the primary coins. The livre was to be described as a given weight of silver of stated fineness. An unchanging monetary standard was implied, and Mirabeau proposed to simplify the old system by adopting silver as the standard. Gold was to be coined, but the value of the gold coins was to be determined by the market. Seigniorage was to be abolished, and the decimal system was to be introduced.

None of these reforms were adopted at this time, but the larger elements of the proposal dominated subsequent discussion. In 1793 the currency system was discussed, and resolutions were passed which called for a bimetallic system at a ratio of 15 to 1. A decimal coinage was to be issued, but the weights of the coins would have been materially changed. The predominance of paper money left these resolutions without effect. In 1795 further discussions of currency resulted in the definition of the new monetary unit as the *franc*, containing 5 grams of silver 0.9 fine. This monetary unit was closely related to the silver unit of the old regime, which had a fine silver content of 5 grams, though at the old standard of the mint (.958) the gross weight of the coin was 5.23 grams. The new unit was thus suggested in a sense by the old mint standard, but it is incorrect to identify the old livre with the franc as is sometimes done. The franc of 1793 was actually nine tenths of the old unit. The resolutions of 1795 made provision also for a gold coin of 10 grams, but without any declared value. In 1797 a bimetallic system was proposed, but no action was taken.

The bimetallic system was definitely re-established in 1803, by the law of April 7, sponsored by the Minister of Finance Gaudin. The silver franc of 5 grams was used as the basis of the system. Gold coins of 20 and 40 francs were authorized, at weights of 6.45 grams and 12.90 grams respectively. These weights were based on Calonne's ratio of 15.5 to 1. Standard gold and silver coins were to be struck from metal nine-tenths fine. The concept of bimetallism held at this time was probably less mature than the concept developed in 1865 at the time of the foundation of the Latin Monetary Union. The literature of the early nineteenth century shows no indication that the ministers of the period expected to bring the market ratio between gold and silver into close adjustment with the mint ratio. In 1803 Gaudin was merely setting a price on silver which would insure an adequate supply for a substantial silver coinage. There is no evidence that he expected gold to circulate without a premium.

In fact, little gold was offered for coinage. Between 1821 and 1850 the value of gold minted in France amounted to 453,000,000 francs. In the same period the silver coinage reached a total of 3,190,000,000 francs. During this period, gold commanded a premium ranging between 2 and 5 per cent. Its use was narrowly restricted. The experience of the United States was similar, as its mint ratios overvalued silver until 1834 and thereafter overvalued gold. Effective circulation of both metals was never maintained at the ratings of the mint ordinances. In Central Europe, as in Spain and Italy, silver was the primary basis of the currency, though there was provision for the coinage of gold at stated ratios to silver.

The use of silver in Continental Europe was not attended by any serious inconvenience during the first half of the nineteenth century. The mints of most of the European countries overvalued silver, and the flow of silver to the mints continued without serious interruption. These currencies were all severely upset by the sharp change in the ratio between gold and silver after the discoveries of gold in California and Australia in 1849. Gold production had increased substantially after 1840, so that the annual output in the years 1841 to 1848 was nearly three times the annual output of the earlier decades of the century. Production in 1849 rose to 3,100,000 ounces as compared with 1,800,000 ounces in 1848. By 1853 production reached 6,700,000 ounces, a level which was maintained for the critical years 1850 to 1873.

## The Appreciation of Silver, 1850–1865

As early as December, 1850, the ratio between silver and gold fell to 15.33, and the flow of silver to the Continent was abruptly checked. French imports of silver fell from 244,000,000 francs in 1849 to 73,000,000 in 1850; in 1852 there was a net export of silver to the amount of 3,000,000, and thereafter silver was exported in varying amounts until 1865.

The Central European countries met these new difficulties by monetary reforms common to the signatories of the German Customs Union and Austria. A convention concluded at Vienna January 24, 1857, provided for a uniform silver currency for all the countries adhering to the convention. The basic coin was a thaler of 18.66 grams of silver. Fractional coins were authorized at lower standards of fineness and of limited legal-tender quality. Gold coins were authorized, but they were not given any fixed value and were not given legal-tender quality. The convention thus established a silver standard. The reforms were not particularly successful, as the new coinage never really supplanted the older coinages of the various states. Agitation for further reform continued within the Customs Union. Austria withdrew from the union in 1867, and though discussions continued, no action was taken before the outbreak of the war with France. The German currency was reorganized by laws of 1871 and 1873. The strong drift towards gold favored the adoption of the gold standard. Gold coinage was authorized by a law of December 4, 1871, with a new monetary unit in the mark, a coin containing 2.79 grams of gold, nine-tenths fine. The gold standard was formally adopted July 9, 1873. Silver coinage was authorized, but the new silver coins were to be limited in legal-tender quality to sums of 20 marks, and issues were not to exceed 10 marks per capita. Old silver coins were to remain legal tender until withdrawn from circulation. The smaller coins were retired by 1879, but the thalers remained in circulation until October 1, 1907.

In Latin Europe events took a different course. Belgium, Switzerland, and Italy had accepted the larger features of the French monetary system, but without close conformity to the mint standards in respect of fineness. The condition of the currency was therefore peculiarly inconvenient, because the primary standard coins seemed to be more nearly alike than they were in fact. In the period following 1850, moreover, Belgium, Switzerland, and Italy all became strongly disposed to adopt a gold standard that would give formal effect to conditions that were being in fact established by the operation of the changed conditions in the markets for gold and silver bullion. These opinions were not shared in France.

A French committee appointed in 1858 to review the currency problem minimized the gravity of conditions. The change in the ratio between silver and gold was explained as being due to the joint influence of the drain of silver to the East and the increased production of gold. The committee held that the production of gold was not likely to continue long at the level then attained, and that the market ratio was likely soon to rise to its former relationship to the mint ratio. This impression must have been strongly held by the officials and directors of the Bank of France and the great private banks.

The committee advised against any change in the mint ratio, but they showed little faith in the permanence of a bimetallic system. The report is as significant for what is left unsaid, as for its positive commitments. It reveals the presence of powerful elements of conservatism and of opposition to a frank acceptance of the gold standard.

In order to prevent the exportation of the subsidiary silver coins, the fineness of the French pieces of 20 and 50 centimes was reduced (May 24, 1864) from .9 to .835. Belgium made overtures to France which resulted in a general conference late in 1865. The smaller countries wished to precipitate a general discussion of the monetary standard, in hopes of securing the adoption of a gold standard. The French took the position that none of the delegates had received any authority to discuss the question of the standard, and out of deference tb France the issue was not pressed. The problems were discussed briefly, and the preferences of the smaller countries for a gold standard were clearly indicated. But there was no general debate, nor any expression of approval for a bimetallic system.

The convention established a Latin Monetary Union by the act of December 23, 1865. The smaller states concurred in the nominal continuance of the bimetallic system at the ratio of 15.5 to 1. After discussion, the French standard for subsidiary coin was adopted. The coins were to be of uniform weight and fineness; coinage was to remain under the control of the various states, but the amount of subsidiary coin was limited to six francs per capita. The coins were legal tender up to 50 francs in payments between private individuals, up to 100 francs at all public offices. Each state was required to redeem all its own subsidiary silver in standard coin, and signatory states were required to redeem stated amounts of coin issued by other states. Provision was made for the coinage of 5-franc pieces of standard fineness. They remained legal tender in unlimited amounts; some states provided for redemption, others treated them as standard coin.

### The Demonetization of Silver

Increases in the production of silver in the late sixties were followed by a rise in the market ratio. In 1867 the market ratio was very slightly higher than the mint ratio and silver began to appear in the French mints. The trading and commercial interests feared a displacement of gold, and wished to prevent any large importation of silver by the explicit adoption of the gold standard. An inquiry was held in 1868, which revealed added strength in the advocacy of a gold standard. The Bank of France and the great private banks still exerted all their influence in favor of bimetallism, with a view apparently to the profits in the bullion market. The suspension of specie payments after the Franco-Prussian War eased the strain of the falling prices of silver for France, but other countries of the Latin Monetary Union were under severe pressure. Belgium authorized the limitation of coinage of 5-franc pieces, December 18, 1873.

Early the following year, a convention of the Latin Monetary Union finally resolved to limit the coinage of 5-franc pieces in each state. As a result, a certain amount of silver was coined, which created added burdens in later years. The states were not required to coin their quotas. The Swiss mints were closed to silver in 1875; France and Belgium forbade further coinage of 5-franc pieces in 1876. Free coinage of silver was completely abandoned by the Latin Monetary Union in 1878, and the action of the conference was ratified by the various states in the following year. The organization had served its purpose, but its life was continued in order to provide facilities for the redemption of the silver already outstanding.

Under the influence of spectacular increases in the production of silver in the United States, the ratio rose steadily. In 1874, at 16.16 to 1, it exceeded the ratio that had long been legal in the United States. In 1889 the ratio stood at 22.10. In 1893, after the repeal of silver purchase acts in the United States, the ratio rose to 32.57. In the present century the ratio fell sharply for the four years 1916–1920, but afterward rose rapidly to former highs.

The production of gold increased at modest rates throughout the critical period of transition to the gold standard, but new sources of supply began to contribute to production after 1892. The process of leaching gold from the hard quartz of the Transvaal was a technical innovation of considerable importance. Production increased from 7,600,000 ounces in 1893 to 14,800,000 ounces in 1899. New mining districts in Alaska and Siberia contributed additional quotas, so that production continued to increase until 1910. Production declined in the years immediately following the war, but latterly there has been some recovery.

### Money and Prices

The early classical economists held that a sound monetary system would and should exert little significant influence upon economic life. They presumed that it was merely a medium for the transmission of the forces inherent in the economic organization of society. Honestly conceived and administered, the monetary system would not itself generate any special forces or exert any specific influence upon social life. This view of the matter was not quite as simple or as naïve as it might seem to be, for these economists laid great stress on their notions of what was "sound" and "honest." Only specie, or something having the value of specie, could be "sound"; no tampering with the standards of the coinage, nor any issue of currency not redeemable in standard specie could be called "honest." These economists were ready to admit that evil could and would befall any society whose monetary system was not "sound" and "honest." The essence of their position lay in the conviction that virtue would be rewarded; that no distress or inconvenience could arise, if the monetary system were based on specie of unvarying weight and fineness. The great rise in prices in the sixteenth century was not entirely forgotten; but it seemed very remote, associated with unusual and extraordinary circumstances.

The expectations of the economists of the early nineteenth century were mistaken. Fluctuations in the production of the precious metals were greater than in any century except the sixteenth. The net changes were probably fully equal in magnitude to the changes in the sixteenth century, but silver had ceased to be a factor in primary price movements before the great increase in production that began after 1860. Had silver continued in use on the Continent, a sensational rise in prices might have occurred. Changes in the production of the precious metals were not, however, the only element in the monetary problem that was misjudged by early economists. They were prone to identify the monetary system with the standard coin ; all other forms of money were supposed to be tied to the standard in such a way that all primary monetary problems centered about standard specie. Their reasoning was correct in respect to subsidiary coin, and other forms of token money. They failed to appreciate the importance of bank credit in both its forms, notes and deposits. We now know that these forms of purchasing power exert influences on prices that do not differ in nature or magnitude from the effects of changes in the standard specie.

Once the importance of credit is recognized, monetary problems assume a different aspect. The price level depends not only upon conditions affecting the production and use of specie, but also upon the credit policies followed by the banks, consciously or unconsciously. The price level is not merely nor primarily controlled by cost of producing gold and silver ; the price level is dominated by acts of policy. Acts of policy are involved even in many of the matters associated with the use of specie. We must, therefore, approach all these problems of money and prices with a mind more frankly alert to the complexity of the phenomena. Currency and credit are deeply involved in our entire social system. The monetary system is not dominated by external circumstances beyond our control. It is an instrument of economic and social policy ; acted upon by our purposes and desires, it is also capable of exerting profound and unexpected influences upon our economic and social activities. We face, therefore, the difficult task of analyzing economic phenomena which are often very incompletely understood. It is especially important that we should not allow ourselves to be unduly influenced by their misconceptions of the problems they faced. It is only fair that we should judge their policies with due regard to the incompleteness of their knowledge and understanding.

## The Movement of Prices in England

An index number series for prices in England in the nineteenth century is shown in the graph on this page.  The graph also shows wheat prices and their trend.  The wheat prices have been a matter of comment in Chapter 16, and they need not be of immediate concern.  The index of general prices is largely based on the whole-sale prices of primary commodities.  In the terms of recent price

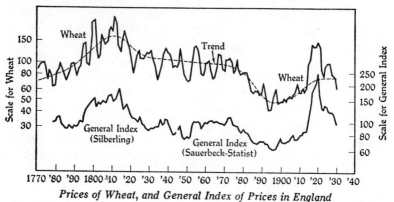

*Prices of Wheat, and General Index of Prices in England*

analysis, it is a wholesale price index.  Although it is not the best type of index for all purposes, it affords the best available basis for comparison with other periods.

The nineteenth century was a period of relatively great price disturbance.  No period in which currency standards were stable discloses changes of significantly greater magnitude.  The rise in prices in the sixteenth century was intensified by currency deprecia-tion in some countries, but the change in the price level in terms of specie was no greater than the changes in the nineteenth century. From 1370 to 1470 specie was relatively scarce and prices would have fallen sharply if a "sound" money policy had been pursued. Scarcely any country attempted such a policy, and the period was actually dominated by an extraordinary confusion of measures and expedients.  There are grounds, therefore, for believing that no earlier period exhibits such a long-continued decline in actual prices as occurred in the nineteenth century.

The nineteenth century is also striking in respect of the conspicu-ous departures from the predominantly downward tendency.  The disturbances due to the European wars, 1793-1815, are clearly marked.  One might think of this period as one marked by war inflation with a subsequent return to "normal." The movement of prices from 1852 to 1873 is also curiously inconsistent with the general downward tendency. The disturbances of the World War are likewise conspicuous.

The movement of prices in France after 1820 was closely conformable to the movement in England. The general tendency was downward, and the course as well as the amount of the decline was closely parallel to the price movement in England. The only difference of moment occurred in the period 1857 to 1867. The downward movement was pronounced in France, whereas in England prices exhibited a degree of stability that is curiously nonconformable to the general movement. The price index for the United States exhibits the same general features, but the fluctuations are more violent, and the crisis of 1836 was much more conspicuous than in the Old World. Although the price series for the other countries of Continental Europe have not been fully studied, we may fairly presume that the general features of the history of prices in the nineteenth century were common to all countries. No class of economic phenomena shows more clearly the essential interdependence of the economic activity of different countries and different regions.

## Cyclical Fluctuations

The price series of the nineteenth century also disclose cyclical fluctuations that were entirely unsuspected by economists of the early nineteenth century. The business cycle did not begin to attract attention as a regular phenomenon until 1825. Distressing crises occurred in England in 1793 and again in 1797, but they were not understood. The period of the wars was marked by some sharply defined emergencies, but these matters received little attention, as there was no technique available for the study of such price movements. After 1825 these fluctuations in business activity were studied with increasing care. Their cyclical character was recognized, and attempts were made to prevent the collapse of credit.

The precise nature of these fluctuations is not very adequately revealed by the graph. The character of such fluctuations is not fully revealed until the general movement of the series is represented by a carefully computed line such as is shown in the wheat series, which is then used as a base line for plotting deviations. Recent studies have shown that there are several cyclical movements extending over varying periods of time: a short cycle of about forty-one months, longer cycles of nine or ten years, and still longer cycles of about thirty years. The forty-one-month cycle has been identified in recently constructed indices of eighteenth-century prices, so that we have grounds for presuming that these phenomena are not entirely new, though they were not previously perceived.

### Factors in the Instability of Prices

The nineteenth century exhibits all three major types of price instability: disturbances due to wars; specific secular trends, tendencies extending over such long periods that they cannot be described as cyclical or recurrent; finally, the various types of cyclical fluctuation. The factors underlying these various kinds of disturbance are of course numerous, and we should presume them to present a truly wide range. Some of these phenomena have only recently been recognized, so that much research has necessarily been devoted to the statement of the problem. The study of causes is not very far advanced. We have learned that problems presumed to be simple are, in fact, highly complex. Decisions that seemed to our forebears to require nothing more than common honesty, now seem forbiddingly difficult. We must, therefore, approach the subject with the modesty that is always becoming to scholarship.

The disturbances due to wars present the least difficult of all problems. Protracted warfare involving large areas leads inevitably to inflation. Even if taxes are raised boldly and loans are placed in substantial amounts, the financing of war sooner or later leads to inflation. This need not be dishonest or unwise. There are degrees of inflation and important differences in type. Crude depreciation of the specie standard or the issue of inconvertible paper money are unskillful devices that are likely to fail. The issues of the assignats by the French Revolutionary government afford one of the classic illustrations of disastrous paper inflation. Pitt's concepts of war finance, on the other hand, reveal an extraordinary insight into the power of a system of credit that was then very imperfectly understood. The essential wisdom of his action is as notable as the folly of Revolutionary finance in France. Pitt suspended specie payment, and deliberately allowed the banks to expand their issues without the restraining influence of a reserve requirement. Recent experience has shown that serious inflation may occur without leading to a suspension of specie payments. This is hardly likely to happen unless circumstances are unusual, but it is essential to recognize that in speaking of war finance by means of credit inflation we do not imply that inflation begins only when specie payments have been suspended.

In so far as inflation is a positive evil, it must be treated as one of the evils of war. As with war itself, the evil does not end with the coming of peace. Interesting problems of policy arise when the war emergency ends. Is it more "honest" to return to the old specie standard, or to create a new standard consistent with the existing price level? In 1815 no one seriously discussed the problem.. It was assumed that resumption necessarily implied the restoration of the old standard. Modern economists would certainly raise the issue, and many hold that it is wiser and more honorable to adjust the currency to the price level than to cause widespread ruin by the sharply falling prices of a period of deflation. The distress of the years 1816 to 1820 was largely caused by the contraction of credit made necessary by the determination to restore the old standard for sterling. We sometimes forget that such a decision to "restore" the past is in fact a new decision which profoundly affects the future.

The decline of prices during the greater part of the century was at one time confidently ascribed to the demonetization of silver. The withdrawal of silver from circulation reduced the stock of standard specie and caused a decline in prices. Although Great Britain did not use silver in any quantity, the new demand for gold affected her price level, so that her prices followed those of Continental Europe and the United States. This explanation in its cruder forms leaves many questions unanswered. The decline during the first half of the century is not readily explained, if the pressure on the gold supply is supposed to begin only with the actual transition to the use of gold on the Continent. This general view appears in a refined form in the work of Warren and Pearson. Here all the stress is placed upon the inadequacy of the stock of gold to meet the growing demands of Europe. The drift toward gold was sufficiently strong, even in the first half of the century, to make this explanation plausible. Despite a large amount of statistical material, the case against gold and the gold standard is not entirely convincing. Some of the statistics are ineffectively analyzed, and with different treatment the material would lead to a different conclusion. But the primary difficulty rests upon a general issue of monetary theory. It is assumed that the general price level is directly controlled by the supply of standard specie. This assumption is not in accord with recent developments of monetary theory, and for some periods there is clear statistical evidence that the price level is not directly related to the total stock of standard specie.

Recent studies of Carl Snyder put forward an explanation of the general trends in terms of the changes in the volume of credit. The statistical analysis does not cover the whole of the nineteenth century. The immediate interest of Mr. Snyder was the period of postwar expansion in the United States. But the view presented would be broadly applicable to the nineteenth century as a whole, and it has the merit of being more nearly in accord with the developments of modern monetary theory. Mr. Snyder holds that the general price level falls when the total volume of bank credit is expanding less rapidly than the secular trend of the volume of trade. Conversely, prices rise if credit expands more rapidly than the trend of trade. Full statistical analysis has been worked out for the United States since 1860. There is a strong presumption in favor of this view as an explanation of the situation in Europe.

The business cycle presents one of the most difficult problems of modern theory, and opinion is still sharply divided between monetary theories and industrial theories. The monetary theorists attribute primary significance to the influence of an expansion of credit upon the price level. A period of moderate business activity leads to increased lending by the banks. Prices rise. Business becomes more optimistic. The banks supply added amounts of credit, so that prices continue to rise until at last more goods are produced than the consumers can buy. There can be no doubt of the importance of the influence of credit expansion upon prices. The vital issue in the monetary thesis is the assertion that the cycle is generated solely by monetary factors. The industrial theorists point out that new industries and new technical processes play a significant part in creating an expectation of profit. Gains from technical innovation contribute notably to the initiation and to the development of the upward phase of the cycle. These more general features of the cycle are complicated by incidents peculiar to particular periods, for the cycles are historical phenomena in the strict sense. They are not mere recurrences of identical elements. Despite remarkable progress in analysis, it has not yet been possible to achieve a satisfactory synthesis. Knowledge of particular phases of the cycle has advanced more rapidly than a mature understanding of the problem as a whole.

# CHAPTER 28

# EUROPEAN AGRICULTURE AND OVERSEAS COMPETITION, 1870–1914

———◆———

## The Development of Overseas Trade in Cereals

The new techniques of transport were important to Europe in supplying service at costs which enabled her industries to reach distant markets overseas. Food and raw materials could be procured in new abundance and at prices which were reduced through the combined influence of cheaper transport and extensions of the cultivated area on the agricultural frontiers of all the more distant continents. But the trade in agricultural products subjected European agriculture to severe competition and led to complex readjustments of agricultural enterprise over large sections of Europe. The primary pressure was most severe in the markets for wheat, wool, and fresh meat.

The geography of wheat culture and wheat export had been a matter of great concern in England throughout the first half of the nineteenth century. The need of importing supplementary supplies of primary foodstuffs was realized as early as 1790, but effectively accessible sources of supply were limited by costs of transport. In 1800 the larger export surpluses were commonly found in Poland, southern Russia, and North America. Competition for Polish grain was keen, and much of the grain was commonly taken by countries nearer than England. The potentialities of the great steppes of southern Russia became known at this time, but they were not an important resource until after the close of the Napoleonic wars. The development of Odessa as a port gave this region an outlet which became important despite the difficulties of transport from the interior. The Black Sea was a major source of British imports of wheat all through the first half of the nineteenth century. Some wheat was received from the United States, though the actual quantities seem small in comparison with the amounts shipped in the last quarter of the century.

Costs of transport restricted the area growing wheat for export to the immediate vicinity of cheap inland water transport. The areas involved were not large enough to force prices down, and maritime freights were high enough to insure the European producer a remunerative price. Until 1846 the British producer received some benefits from the protective duties, and French wheatgrowers were protected by a complex system of duties. Throughout this period, therefore, the agricultural interest shared extensively in all the gains of industrial progress. The increase in density of population kept demand well in advance of supply. After 1825 the general tendency of farm prices was upwards, and land values rose. In England the thirty years following the repeal of the Corn Laws were the "golden age" for agriculture. Profits were substantial, and under this stimulus the advances in the technique of intensive farming were impressive. The "high farming" of the great estates was looked upon as the model with which all cereal and stock farming could be compared. France and Germany were improving their methods rapidly, but the English still regarded Continental practice as inferior. The anticipations of persistent pressure of population upon the land led everyone to assume that the foundations of agriculture were secure, and that in this aspect of social life there would be no change.

The illusion was roughly shattered by the events of the 1870's. Attention was called to the influence of "improvements in the arts" upon rents, land values, and the use of land. Nothing occurred that was not in some form recognized in the theories of Malthus and Ricardo, but people had fallen into a way of ignoring the possibility of vital changes. The timing of the change is closely associated with the development of the railroad network in the United States and with important reductions in ocean freights arising out of competition between the shipping lines operating regular services and the "tramp" freighters free to adapt their sailings to the immediate demands for tonnage. Of the two factors, the development of railroads in the United States was the more important. The railroads crossed the Appalachians in 1852-1853. Through service to Chicago was begun within a year over the Lake Shore route, and in the course of a decade a network of railroads developed north of the Ohio.

The railroads brought new prosperity to the region. In earlier times, the primary mass of agricultural products had moved south by the Ohio and Mississippi rivers. The counties along the Great Lakes could reach New York, but this area was a small fraction of the total area. Settlement pushed out beyond the Mississippi. Horse-driven agricultural machinery made it possible to harvest acreages which would have been beyond the powers of the labor force available.   The chronology of this development is vividly indicated by the increases in wheat acreage and exports, as shown in the following tables:

ACREAGE UNDER WHEAT IN THE UNITED STATES [1]

| Year | Acres | Year | Acres |
|---|---|---|---|
| 1849 | 8,000,000 | 1875 | 26,300,000 |
| 1859 | 14,500,000 | 1880 | 37,200,000 |
| 1869 | 20,000,000 | 1889 | 38,100,000 |

ANNUAL EXPORTS OF WHEAT, IN BUSHELS, FROM NORTH AMERICA, RUSSIA, AND INDIA [2]

| Annual Average | North America | Russia | British India |
|---|---|---|---|
| 1831–40 | 240,000 | | — |
| 1851–60 | 5,500,000 | 41,100,000 | — |
| 1861–70 | 22,000,000 | 75,000,000 | — |
| Year | | | |
| 1875 | 55,000,000 | 53,500,000 | 4,000,000 |
| 1880 | 150,500,000 | 34,400,000 | 12,300,000 |
| 1881 | 75,200,000 | 46,200,000 | 33,000,000 |
| 1882 | 106,300,000 | 72,000,000 | 23,500,000 |
| 1883 | 70,300,000 | 79,000,000 | 34,600,000 |
| 1884 | 84,600,000 | 63,500,000 | 26,500,000 |
| 1885 | 57,700,000 | 86,700,000 | 35,000,000 |
| 1886 | 101,900,000 | 48,500,000 | 35,300,000 |
| 1887 | 65,700,000 | 73,200,000 | 22,500,000 |
| 1888 | 46,400,000 | 119,000,000 | 29,300,000 |
| 1889 | 54,300,000 | 107,100,000 | 23,000,000 |

The record of exports from the primary exporting countries shows both the great increase in the volume of the export trade of the United States and the change in the relative importance of the United States and Russia as sources of supply.   The increase in exports is notably greater than the increase in acreage under wheat. The importance of Russian exports after 1881 may be astonishing to those who are familiar with British trade, for North America was a predominant factor in British trade.   Russian exports found a nearer market in Mediterranean Europe.   After 1880 the deficits of several of the Continental countries increased rapidly, so that southern Russia was able to market large stocks without sending the wheat all the way to England.   These elements of wheat movements are

[1] Buchenberger, A., *Agrarwesen und Agrarpolitik*, Leipzig, II, p. 554.   For a complete series from 1867 see the *Statistical Abstract of the United States*.
[2] Buchenberger, A., *op. cit.*, II, p. 555.

shown by the changes in the sources of British imports, given in the
following table:

PERCENTAGE OF BRITISH WHEAT IMPORTS (INCLUDING FLOUR EXPRESSED
IN WHEAT) DERIVED FROM DIFFERENT COUNTRIES [1]

| | 1875–77 | 1881–83 | 1893–95 | 1904–13 | 1914–18 | 1924–27 | 1928–30 |
|---|---|---|---|---|---|---|---|
| Western Europe | 20.8 | 10.7 | 4.7 | 1.2 | — | 1.2 | 3.5 |
| Russia | 16.7 | 11.5 | 16.6 | 14.0 | 1.6 | 1.4 | 5.2 |
| United States | 47.0 | 59.0 | 55.5 | 38.7 | 76.6 | 29.3 | 21.4 |
| Canada | | | | | | 34.3 | 31.1 |
| India | 6.1 | 11.4 | 6.8 | 15.5 | 6.3 | 5.2 | 1.4 |
| Argentina | — | — | 11.0 | 17.6 | 8.3 | 14.7 | 24.3 |
| Australia | — | — | — | 9.6 | 6.1 | 12.5 | 11.4 |
| Other countries | 9.4 | 7.4 | 5.4 | 3.4 | 1.1 | 1.4 | 1.7 |
| | 100.0 | 100.0 | 100.0 | 100.0 | 100.0 | 100.0 | 100.0 |

The decline in the exports from European countries to England
indicates accurately the timing of the new pressure upon the local
supplies of Europe.  Increasing population absorbed the small
surpluses of France and Germany that had moved out over some
borders, even when wheat was coming in across other borders of the
same country.  But neither France nor Germany became dependent
upon foreign imports to the degree that was true of Great Britain.

Changes in the production and import of the other cereals were
not as striking, and the reactions upon European agriculture were
less severe.  In the period 1873 to 1893, for the world as a whole,
wheat acreage increased 19 per cent; barley acreage increased 5 per
cent; rye acreage declined 5 per cent.  Oats was the only cereal
whose acreage increase exceeded that of wheat, with an increase of
28 per cent.  There was some shift in consumption from rye to
wheat, but in general the rye-producing districts suffered less than
wheat-producing districts because the prices of rye did not fall as
rapidly as the prices of wheat.  The prices of oats remained extremely steady throughout the period of severe strain.  Despite
the increase in acreage, the pressure among the cereals was therefore
largely confined to wheat.

### Woolgrowing in the Southern Hemisphere

Towards the close of the eighteenth century, Great Britain began
to import wool on a considerable scale despite the large domestic

[1] Venn, J. A., *Foundations of Agricultural Economics*, Cambridge University Press,
London, 1933, p. 372.

production.  The expansion of the textile industry created new demands for raw material which eighteenth-century Europe was unable to satisfy completely.  Spain could not supply the needs of northern Europe for fine wool.  The improvement of the breeds of sheep in France and Germany, by importing stock from Spain, provided in some measure for the new requirements of the wool trade.  But supplies developed more slowly than demand, prices ruled high, and the industries based on wool suffered severely from competition with cotton.  The raw material was less well suited to the use of machinery, and wool was scarce.  The woolen and worsted industries grew slowly, and lost much ground to cotton, as cotton supplanted wool in uses adapted to the cheaper fiber.  After the Napoleonic wars, woolgrowing developed rapidly in Germany, as the Merino sheep developed in Saxony were especially well suited to the agricultural system and produced a high grade of fine wool.  Germany became one of the most important centers of production of fine wool.  By 1831 Germany was exporting to England six times as much wool as Spain.

In the meantime new sources of supply were being developed in Australia.  A convict colony was established at Botany Bay in what is now New South Wales.  For some years the colony was hardly more than a military post entirely dependent upon imports for all its supplies.  The development of an export commodity was entirely due to the efforts of Capt. John MacArthur, a member of the military force sent out with the second fleet in 1791.  He observed a notable change in the quality of wool of the Cape of Good Hope sheep brought to the colony to provide mutton.  Planned experiments were carried on with Cape sheep for four years (1793–1797), despite the ridicule of his colleagues in the garrison.  He was then able to secure a few merinos.  With these as a basis, he made further improvements in Cape sheep.  MacArthur was sent to England in 1803, as the result of friction in the garrison, and the opportunity was used to work for a complete reconsideration of the position of the settlement.

A committee of Parliament reported favorably upon the quality of MacArthur's samples of wool.  Various persons in the industry brought pressure to bear upon the Secretary for Colonies.  A memorial was submitted to the Treasury setting forth the situation of the wool trade: ". . . Fine cloths are made entirely of Spanish wool. . . . So great for some time past has been the increasing scarcity and advanced price of Spanish wool, that not only are large

BRITISH IMPORTS OF FOREIGN AND COLONIAL WOOL, IN THOUSANDS OF POUNDS [1]

| | Spain | Germany | Russia | Other European Countries | Australasia | Argentina | South America | India | Total Import | Total Re-export |
|---|---|---|---|---|---|---|---|---|---|---|
| 1796 | 3,339 | 14 | — | 81 | — | — | — | — | 3,484 | — |
| 1800 | 6,036 | 421 | — | 1,925 | — | — | — | — | 8,608 | — |
| 1810 | 5,952 | 834 | 32 | 3,879 | — | — | — | — | 10,873 | — |
| 1820 | 3,536 | 5,221 | 76 | 732 | 99 | 69 | — | 8 | 9,776 | 65 |
| 1830 | 1,644 | 26,787 | 203 | 1,635 | 1,967 | 19 | — | — | 32,313 | 659 |
| 1840 | 1,267 | 21,837 | 4,519 | 3,998 | 9,721 | 617 | — | 2,441 | 49,448 | 1,015 |
| 1850 | 441 | 9,196 | 3,556 | 7,569 | 39,018 | 1,862 | — | 3,473 | 74,327 | 14,389 |
| 1860 | 1,000 | 9,954 | 8,730 | 18,551 | 59,166 | 2,875 | — | 20,214 | 145,502 | 30,735 |
| 1870 | 25 | 4,405 | — | 19,280 | 175,081 | — | 12,693 | 11,143 | 263,250 | 92,542 |
| 1880 | — | 7,173 | 20,082 | — | 300,626 | — | 10,282 | 29,190 | 463,508 | 237,408 |
| 1890 | — | 6,733 | 24,785 | — | 418,771 | — | 11,173 | 34,238 | 633,028 | 340,712 |
| 1900 | 1,630 | 5,432 | 9,679 | — | 386,367 | — | 35,589 | 30,751 | 558,950 | 196,207 |
| 1910 | 2,965 | 3,434 | 3,798 | — | 505,197 | — | 69,629 | 53,334 | 803,295 | 335,222 |
| 1920 | 423 | 73 | 1,905 | — | 662,774 | — | 74,967 | 41,918 | 876,943 | 220,424 |
| 1930 | 537 | 1,385 | 1 | — | 431,706 | — | 126,529 | 34,263 | 786,452 | 290,064 |

[1] Journal of the Statistical Society of London (1870), vol. 33, A. Hamilton, "On Wool Supply," pp. 502-506. After 1866, The Statistical Abstract of the United Kingdom.

orders frequently rejected for want of raw material to furnish the supply, but the exorbitant price of what is to be had and contingent expenses of trade make it impossible to supply the Continental markets." It was stated that Spanish wool sold in the early part of the eighteenth century for between 1s. 3d. and 2s.; that it was currently selling for between 7s. and 10s.

MacArthur was heard by the Privy Council. The Council recommended that the project should be encouraged. MacArthur was granted 5,000 acres of land with the promise of as much more if the experiments succeeded. He was also allowed to purchase a number of pure-bred merinos from the flock at Kew. With this support, MacArthur collected a small group of sheep growers and artisans, and the entire company embarked upon a small ship which was christened the *Argo*. The vessel set sail from England with a golden fleece hung from the prow.

The adventure was by no means finished. The governor of the colony was furious with MacArthur, and vowed that he would never be allowed to keep his land or develop his project. The governor actually arrested MacArthur, and proposed to bring him before a court. The older officers intervened, led the troops against the governor, and placed him under arrest (January, 1808). The major in command of the garrison remained in control of the colony until a new governor was sent out from England. From this time on, the agricultural policy made steady progress, though politics in the colony remained divided between the military group and the agriculturists. Under Governor Macquarie, the Blue Mountains were explored, and wagon roads carried over the main passes. The further slopes proved to be remarkable grazing country, so that the flocks increased rapidly. In 1810 there were 25,000 sheep in the colony; in 1820 there were 99,400 sheep. The export of wool increased rapidly: from 14,000 pounds for Australasia, as a whole, in 1816, exports rose successively to 175,000 pounds in 1821; to 1,106,000 pounds in 1826. In 1834, the year of Governor Macquarie's death, the export was 4,347,000 pounds. This was only slightly less than the Spanish export to England in the early years of the century.

The development of the wool trade is exhibited by the table on page 586. These decennial figures afford a rather imperfect picture of the movement of trade, as the fluctuations of imports are of substantial magnitude, but the primary features of the record are clear. After 1850 Australia and New Zealand contributed 50 or

60 per cent of a greatly increased total production. Substantial supplies came also from South America, India, and South Africa, though the details of the development of South Africa are not shown in the table. There was a rapid increase of woolgrowing in Germany, and a notable development of woolgrowing in many European countries in the second half of the century. Though the amounts were not large in comparison with the huge totals from Australasia, the demand for wool was an important factor in the history of European agriculture.

### The Frozen-Meat Trade

Hides became an increasingly important import commodity for Europe during this period. The earlier stages of stockraising in South America were largely dominated by the value of hides, horns, and tallow. The further developments of stock-raising were profoundly affected by the perfection of the technique of refrigeration. Overseas shipment of live cattle from the United States was practical though not very satisfactory. Experiments were made as early as 1868, but continuous trade did not develop until after 1876. The eighties and early nineties were most conspicuously identified with this trade. The more distant stock-growing regions were not able to enter the British and Continental markets with live cattle.

In Australia, as in the United States, attention was given at an early date to packing meat in tins. But the various tinned products provided an inadequate and unsatisfactory outlet for the great volume of meat products available. Studies of chilling and freezing were begun in Australia in 1843, under the stimulus of the interest of T. S. Mort, a wool broker. Freezing proved to be superior in every way, and in 1861 the first freezing plant in the world was established at Sydney. The works remained for some time in an essentially experimental stage, and it was not until 1875 that the company was really prepared to supply even the local market with any regularity. The final developments were perfected in the later seventies by several firms in America, England, France, and Australia. All the successful techniques were based on ammonia compression processes. Trial shipments were made in 1877 and 1878. The Australian work culminated in the equipment of a 2,000-ton vessel, the *Strathleven*, with a complete refrigerating plant capable of freezing the meat on board. The vessel sailed from Sydney November 29, 1879, with forty tons of beef and mutton. The meat arrived in perfect condition. Continuous shipments of frozen meat from the United States began in 1874, and after 1876 the development was rapid. In 1874, exports from the United States amounted to 1,095 cwt.; in 1876, to 144,336 cwt.; in 1889, to 1,275,948 cwt.

## The Crisis in British Agriculture

No part of northwestern Europe was unaffected by the rapid development of southern Russia and the various overseas countries which became contributors to the world's supply of agricultural staples. But the impact of these new forces was not evenly distributed. Competition made itself felt most keenly in regions which had been devoted to cereals under the stimulus of the high price levels of the first decades of the century. Pressure was most severe in the poorest lands growing wheat in 1870. Some pressure was felt in sections producing grades of wool which were directly affected by the Australasian wools. The most conspicuous changes in land utilization were confined to England. In England, wheat acreages fell off sharply, declining from the record acreage in 1869 of 3,900,000, to 1,400,000 in 1895.

The decline of wheatgrowing in England led to a great change in the use of land. Many acres were wholly withdrawn from cereal culture and converted to pasture. The new cultures yielded smaller returns and afforded employment to smaller numbers of persons. The change in English agricultural life is not readily appreciated unless the statistical record is visualized with much concrete detail. The losses, which would have been serious enough at the best, were further magnified by a succession of poor harvests. British weather was singularly unfavorable, and curiously enough the abnormalities of cold and rain did not extend across the Channel. Cereal yields in France and Germany were of average volume throughout the period.

The material has been worked over with great care by Professor Venn. The average yield of wheat for the years 1853 to 1863 was 29.6 bushels per acre; for the years 1870 to 1880, the average yield was 24.4 bushels per acre; for the years 1882 to 1892, the average yield was 29.4 bushels per acre. The entire decade of the seventies was a period of distinctly low yields, and this period of poor harvests reached its culmination in the year 1878, when the yield of wheat fell to 15.5 bushels per acre, scarcely more than half the average crop of the sixties or the late eighties and nineties. The losses were confined to wheat, but wheat was of course the most important source of income.

These losses in yield were not offset by increased prices, because the heavy importations dominated the market and prices fell to levels usually reached only in years of bumper crops. The average price for the year 1878 was 47.9 shillings per quarter; and in 1879, when prices would usually have risen sharply, the price fell off to 45.2 shillings per quarter, the lowest price since 1865. As a result, tenants were unable to pay the rents on their farms. Through this caprice of nature, the full force of competition with the new sources of supply was felt by the wheatgrowers in a single season. Crops were below the normal expectation for the three following seasons, so the farmer found no relief. In Norfolk and in the fen country much land was entirely abandoned. Rents fell off sharply. Over large areas in the eastern counties less than half the former rental was actually collected. The better wheat lands of the Midlands did not suffer as severely, though the losses amounted to more than one third of the former income. In the grazing regions the losses were under one third; at times no more than 10 per cent.

The losses in wheat acreage were not offset by gains in any other arable crop. The minor cereals very nearly held their own, but there were small losses even among these grains. Considerable areas were added to the permanent pasturage. Market gardening and dairying afforded relief to small areas, but the general picture is one of decline.

Before the Royal Commission of 1895–1897, many witnesses pointed out that the decline in prices in this period was not confined to agricultural products. Attention was called to the progressive demonetization of silver, and it was asserted with great conviction that the true source of agrarian distress lay in the monetary system. It is not necessary to discuss this monetary theory of the depression, as the problem has been covered in the preceding chapter. The Royal Commission was not deeply impressed by the arguments of the silver group, though some members were ready to admit that monetary policy was a contributory factor. Recent discussions of monetary problems have reopened these questions, but despite much industry in the accumulation of material, little has been added to the subject. The greatest weakness of the monetary view lies in its failure to throw light upon the differences in the experience of different countries. England, the worst sufferer, had not used silver for a full century. France, which suffered least, had used silver more freely and clung more tenaciously to nominal bimetallism than any other European country. The differences in the impact of foreign influences afford a more delicate basis for the understanding of the essentially complex changes of the period.

## Losses in France and Germany

France did not suffer pressure which resulted in any marked change in the use of land or in the details of livestock raising. Lowered international prices were offset, in part, by tariff duties which kept domestic prices above the world price. France suffered serious losses in her vineyards and among the silkworms. The vines were attacked by a group of aphids known as the phylloxera. These devastating pests were brought to France from the United States on nursery stock used for developing new varieties of grapes. The phylloxera were observed in southern France as early as 1863, but the period of most serious damage extended from 1882 to 1892. The area in vines before the phylloxera devastation began was 2,400,000 hectares (5,928,000 acres); in 1882 this area had been reduced to 2,190,000 hectares, and in 1898 to 1,700,000 hectares (4,199,000 acres). The actual losses were somewhat greater, because large areas were replanted with new stock bred from American varieties of grape that were less seriously affected. The technique of protective spraying was highly developed, and towards the end of the century the vineyards had achieved a strong position. New modes of culture secured greater yields of wine from smaller areas.

The culture of raw silk presented a somewhat more complex combination of factors. The culture was abruptly checked in the early fifties by an epidemic disease of the silkworm. Production of raw silk fell from 25,000,000 kilograms to 12,000,000 in 1852, and to 9,700,000 in 1862. The best solution possible was afforded by breeding new stock that was more resistant to disease. But before the culture had fully recovered, trade with China and Japan introduced large quantities of raw silk at greatly reduced prices. This narrowly restricted culture was thus exposed to severe stress. Despite new protective duties the culture has not regained its former position.

Analysis of conditions in Germany cannot be carried into much detail, as the primary series of agricultural statistics do not begin until 1878. There are no comprehensive returns of acreage under various crops before that date and the materials available are not easily comparable because of boundary changes. We know that there was no reduction in the area under wheat or other cereals after

1878, but there was a period of low price levels in Germany in the years 1857–1867. Changes in the classes of livestock began in 1867, and it is not impossible that readjustments in arable agriculture had occurred before we have any full record. After 1878 there were increases in the acreage under potatoes and under sugar beets, so that there was a net increase in the area under field crops.

Livestock raising underwent notable changes, that seem to be closely associated with the development of the wool trade. Sheep had been an increasingly important factor in stock farming after 1828. In 1867 this movement was checked. The number of sheep in Prussia had increased from 12,500,000 in 1828 to 19,500,000 in 1867. In 1892 only 8,100,000 sheep were reported; and in 1902 the decline continued to 4,700,000. This extensive change in the number of sheep, though highly characteristic, should not have involved heavy losses, because there were corresponding gains in all other classes of livestock. Horses, cattle, swine, and goats all increased in number, at rates which correspond closely with the decline in the number of sheep.

There was pressure in Germany; complaints were widespread; official inquiries were made in Prussia, Württemberg, Hesse-Cassel, and Alsace. Unofficial studies of the depression were made by various organizations. Land values declined in some measure; the burden of mortgage indebtedness presented serious problems; towards the close of the period criticism of the speculative produce exchanges resulted in the complete prohibition of all speculative trading for a short period. But the actual distress was certainly much less severe than in England, and the losses of the French vinegrowers were probably more serious than any losses suffered by any single region in Germany.

## Agriculture in Denmark

The history of agriculture in Denmark is of special significance because the decline in cereal culture was met by a transfer to highly specialized dairying with complete freedom from tariff duties. Cereals and oil cake were imported in large quantities, but Danish agriculture prospered and conquered new markets for butter, cheese, and eggs. These changes were made with somewhat less shock than the changes in other countries, because the beginnings of the transition to dairying preceded the crisis by a considerable interval. Danish agriculture was profoundly affected, too, by the care taken to protect the interests of the peasants in the reorganization of the field arrangements begun on a large scale under the ordinances of 1781 and 1792. By 1802 half the land in Denmark was enclosed, and in 1840 only one per cent of the land remained subject to common pasture or feudal dues. The state was successful in preventing any marked increase in large farms and made a determined effort to improve the standards of agriculture among the peasants.

In the period following the repeal of the British Corn Laws the increased market for cereals led to some increase in cereal culture in Denmark. With the proceeds the peasants bought their holdings. Methods of culture were ill considered, however, for the peasants were not accustomed to the use of chemical fertilizers or provided with a sufficient number of livestock to enable them to maintain the relatively intensive system of cereal culture then established. As early as 1860 the decline of the yield per acre made it clear that some changes were necessary, and the obvious remedy for the immediate trouble was to increase the number of livestock. Numbers increased so rapidly during the sixties that imports of feeding stuffs began about 1870. Maize was brought in from the United States, barley from the Black Sea, and later oil cake from the cotton belt.

At this time the peasantry were so unskilled in the handling of dairy products that their butter and cheese were really unfit for any market requiring a high standard. It is perhaps true that there was no marketing system adapted to handling peasant products, but the essential factor was the poor grade of the product. The Royal Agricultural Society had already (1860) begun to provide training in the problems of dairy management, and a professorship in Dairy Science was shortly afterwards established at the Royal College of Agriculture in Copenhagen. Students were given systematic instruction and demonstrations.

The development of dairying was profoundly influenced by the invention of the mechanical cream separator. The first machine of any practical importance was that of L. C. Nielsen, brought out in 1878, but almost at once surpassed by the machine of de Laval (1879). This afforded new possibilities of concentrating the work of butter and cheese making so that the product of the small dairy farm could be treated by the best methods. The utilization of these new techniques was beyond the means of the peasants, but both commercial and co-operative dairies were tried as devices for concentrating the supply of milk. A small co-operative was established at Kaslunde, Fünen, in 1875. Lack of publicity made its historical importance very slight. In 1882, however, a dairy was built in southern Jutland at Hjedding, which became the model of most of the co-operatives. The members were bound to deliver all their milk to the co-operative; they shared the profits in proportion to the milk delivered. An experienced buttermaker was employed to manage the dairy and market the product. As opened, the dairy was based on co-operators controlling 400 cows.

The early years of the depressed cereal markets were thus marked by the spread of the co-operative movement among the peasant dairy farmers. Danish agriculture was thus far advanced towards reorganization before the cereal markets were significantly affected. The later years of the depression were marked by new technical advances which placed the dairying industry on an entirely new basis. Difficulties had been experienced on one of the great estates, from an offensive taste in the butter even after all the usual care had been exercised. The Laboratory for Agricultural Research, on appeal, sent an expert and established a bacteriological laboratory on the estate. It appeared that a certain type of bacteria was present in the dairy and in one of the wells on the farm. The offensive taste was entirely due to the presence of these bacteria. It was shown that the bacteria might be destroyed by pasteurization, and that the cream could be used for buttermaking if fermentation were induced by the addition of buttermilk or a pure culture of lactic acid. The final report on these investigations, made in 1891, marked a new era in the development of the dairy industry. The technique of large-scale buttermaking from separator cream was placed on a level far superior to any small-scale venture dependent upon natural fermentation. The co-operatives were able to introduce these methods more rapidly than the great estates, and in consequence the quality of the co-operative butter improved. In 1888 the great estates took fifteen out of sixteen silver medals, and all but four of eighteen bronze medals. In 1894 the co-operatives took all but one of seven silver medals, and all but two of sixteen bronze medals. Danish butter naturally won a strong place for itself in the English markets. The success was due to a singularly determined attempt to master all the technical problems of the industry and to vigorous efforts to diffuse quickly the results of scientific and practical research.

### Agriculture in Germany and Great Britain in 1914

On the eve of the World War there was much discussion of the position of British agriculture and much criticism of British policy toward agriculture. Pressure of competition brought with it a sense of inferiority, and there was a strong disposition in many quarters to believe that agriculture had been sacrificed to the demands of the industrialists for cheap food. Statistics show that Germany produced more food per acre than Great Britain, and supplied a larger proportion of the total food requirements of the population.

COMPARATIVE ANNUAL PRODUCTION PER 100 ACRES OF CULTIVATED LAND [1]

|  | Great Britain | Germany |
| --- | --- | --- |
| Number of persons supported | 45–50 | 70–75 |
| Tons of cereals | 15 | 33 |
| Tons of potatoes | 11 | 55 |
| Tons of meat | 4 | 4.5 |
| Tons of milk | 17.5 | 28 |
| Tons of sugar | trace | 2.75 |

Measured by the older standards, this record would indicate that British agriculture was seriously inferior. The modern economist, however, contends that productivity per acre is less significant than productivity per man. The number of persons employed per 100 acres of cultivated land was as follows:

|  | Male | Female | Total |
| --- | --- | --- | --- |
| Great Britain | 4.6 | 1.2 | 5.8 |
| Germany | 8.3 | 10.0 | 18.3 |

If we take the total food production as the best single index of productivity per acre, it appears that Great Britain produced about two thirds as much food per acre. This work was accomplished, however, by less than one third of the labor force required in Germany. The rate of productivity per person per 100 acres in Great Britain was twice the rate of productivity in Germany.[2] Such a computation is, of course, very crude; but it will serve to suggest the nature of the issue. If the agricultural worker in Germany produces only half as much as the agricultural worker in Great Britain, it is not likely that the German worker will have as

[1] *Commons Papers*, 1916, vol. IV. Middleton, T. H., *The Recent Development of German Agriculture*, p. 6.

[2] If the product in Germany is called a unit, Germany produces 1 unit per 100 acres; Great Britain .66 unit. Then Germany produces $\dfrac{1}{18.3}$ units per person per 100 acres = .055 unit; Great Britain produces $\dfrac{.66}{5.8}$ units per person per 100 acres = .113 unit.

high a standard of living. Even if he works his own holding, the German worker must be content with only half as much as his British comrade. Even hired labor in Great Britain must be presumed to fare better than hired labor in Germany.

These differences, however, are not entirely a result of deliberate choices of policy. It is fairly certain that differences in the standard of living between Great Britain and Germany have existed over a long period. In all probability, the differences were greater in 1800 than in 1900. The character of agricultural enterprise in Germany is therefore part of a larger whole. Certain kinds of agricultural work could be done because cheap labor was abundant. Conditions existing in 1914 were not primarily a result of the protective policy. In some cases the shelter of protective duties made it possible to postpone changes that would have otherwise been necessary. In other cases, such as the sugar-beet culture, the tariff was an important factor. But even in such instances it is easy to misjudge the actual effects of the tariff.

British agriculture cannot justly be criticized because of its relatively low rate of productivity per acre, but it is none the less true that there were grounds for grave concern. It is possible to justify the contraction of cereal production on the ground that English soils were better adapted to stock raising. But this invites criticism of the relative backwardness of British dairying. To be sure, large areas were devoted to sheep, but cattle were an important factor on British farms, stock breeding had been carried to a high level of attainment, and the British had long taken pardonable pride in their accomplishments with stock. But in the later decades of the last century Britain contributed little that was new in the field of dairying.

The British farmers complained of discriminating railway rates, and some bewailed the lack of any tariff to protect the London market from Danish butter and Dutch cheese. The patriotic farmers commonly ignored their own shortcomings. They were still making butter and cheese just as butter and cheese had been made for two, three, or even four generations. They were slow to recognize the importance of the changes taking place around them. No attempt was made to work out the applications of the new sciences to agriculture. The primary new work was done in France, Sweden, Denmark, and the United States. Systematic research and instruction in agriculture were developing rapidly in all these countries, partly because government funds were made available, but even more largely because interest in the subject was keen. In England, scientific work was confined to the privately endowed station at Rothamsted.

Towards the close of the century the government began to show a new sense of responsibility. Funds were made available for research and instruction. The Rothamsted station was given government aid, and the range of .its work was enlarged. Instruction in agriculture was established in the universities with government assistance. Important efforts were made by some landowners to assist in the reorganization of British agriculture. There can be little doubt but that these efforts were somewhat tardy. They were delayed, in part, by overconfidence in the adequacy of private initiative. At the critical moment, the landed gentry failed to maintain their place as leaders in agricultural advance. Empiricism, common sense, and even humanitarian ideals were no longer an adequate basis for adjustment to the changing world. New qualities of leadership were required, which were not formed by the habits of thought common among the landed gentry. The social system made it difficult for new leaders to rise to positions of importance. The concentration of ownership made it difficult to modify systems of farming that were closely identified with long-established units of tenancy and ownership.

# CHAPTER 29

# THE ECONOMIC DEVELOPMENT OF RUSSIA, 1861–1914

---◆---

## The Emancipation

Various factors were gradually undermining serfdom in Russia during the first half of the nineteenth century. In the course of time it was becoming more and more obvious that serfdom was an obstacle in the way of the country's economic progress. The development of industry was hampered by the scarcity of free labor, and by the low productivity of forced labor. The use of forced labor was discontinued whenever an opportunity presented itself. To a considerable degree, the same difficulty was experienced also by agriculture. Here, too, the low productivity of serf labor, as well as the rigidity of the whole system of serfdom, prevented many landlords from making a sufficiently quick and successful adaptation of their economy to the demands of the market. The influence of this rigidity was increasingly felt by the lords both as consumers and as producers. In the fertile south, where most of the largest estates were situated and where capitalistic agriculture working in a large measure for foreign markets was growing more rapidly than anywhere else in the country, the use of hired laborers from outside, to supplement the work of the serfs, was widely practiced as early as 1840. In the non-black-earth regions of central Russia and in the north the quitrent system was steadily growing at the expense of the *corvée*. In many cases this involved the reduction of the lord's home farm to a bare minimum, and in general this phenomenon can be regarded as a "degeneration" of serfdom, foreshadowing its ultimate disappearance.

However, it would be a mistake to assert that serfdom fell under its own weight, when and because it became economically unprofitable to the landlords. The black-earth regions of central Russia remained the citadel of serfdom to the very end, and here the tendency on the part of the landlords was to extend the direct exploitation of their land and to increase the pressure upon the serfs bound to perform the *corvée*. It is true that these efforts did not always give the desired result, and that on the whole the landlord's economy was far from being in a prosperous state. On the eve of the Emancipation, about 40 per cent of all the estates in European Russia and about 70 per cent of privately owned male serfs were mortgaged to state credit institutions.  But in spite of this the majority of the landlords were adamant in defense of their rights connected with serfdom.  To the usual reluctance of a privileged class to part with its vested interests was added the deficiency of the gentry in initiative and knowledge and the lack of capital funds necessary for the reconstruction of their economy on entirely new foundations. It is no wonder that during the last half century before the Emancipation only a relatively small number of serfs were able to buy their freedom, even with the assistance of governmental legislation designed to facilitate the procedure.

The pressure of noneconomic factors was necessary to put an end to serfdom.  One of these was the growing unrest among the serfs themselves, which led to a number of serious uprisings during the reign of Nicholas I.  This was the danger that Alexander II had in mind when he made his famous statement that it was "better to abolish serfdom from above than to wait till it begins to abolish itself from below."  Another factor of considerable importance was the growing influence of the abolitionist sentiment, not only among the liberals but also among the enlightened conservatives, which found its expression both in literature and in political movements. Finally, the immediate cause of the Emancipation can be seen in Russia's defeat during the Crimean War, as a result of which a thoroughgoing reform of the country's social structure became necessary.

These were the conditions that enabled the government of Alexander II to attempt what had been found impossible under his predecessors : instead of waiting for a gradual abolition of serfdom to come from the good will of the landlords themselves, the government now took the initiative by ordering an immediate reform. It was explicitly stated that a landless emancipation was excluded. With all its determination, however, the government could not ignore the gentry, of whom it demanded a cession of a considerable part of their property.  Under governmental pressure provincial committees of the gentry were formed to discuss the terms of the emancipation.  The next task consisted in trying to reconcile the various proposals emanating from the nobility with the governmental projects of reform.  For several years the discussion went on in the Main Committee in St. Petersburg, with the struggle centering around two questions : the size of the allotments of land to be given the emancipated serfs, and the amount of compensation to be paid the landlords.  As was to be expected, the landlords of the south and the agricultural center tried to retain in their hands as much land as possible, while the gentry of the non-black-earth regions directed their efforts towards obtaining the highest possible compensation for the loss of profits they used to derive from their serfs' earnings.  Under such conditions it was inevitable for the reform, in its final shape, to bear plentiful traces of compromise with the vested interests of the landed gentry.  On the other hand, a mere comparison of the final terms with the original proposals of the provincial committees would show that the advocates of peasant interests succeeded in obtaining from the landlords much larger concessions than the latter had at first been prepared to make.

One must emphasize the magnitude of the reform and the complexity of the problem it attempted to solve.  The Emancipation Edict of 1861 liberated about 20,000,000 serfs, while the land-settlement part of the reform, as well as the new administrative arrangement, affected in addition about 20,000,000 crown peasants of various categories.  A number of separate statutes had to be prepared to take care of local differences, and it was necessary to make temporary arrangements for the difficult transition period.  It is obviously impossible to give an account of all the details within the scope of the present chapter, and only the main features of the reform, as finally established, can be briefly summarized.

With the exception of the "household serfs" who merely were made personally free, all the former serfs received their homesteads and some arable land.  The homesteads became the property of each separate household; but wherever communal landholding prevailed, allotments of land were turned over to the village communes, which were required to distribute them among their members, according to the size of each household.  The size of allotments varied with the quality of soil, density of population, and general economic conditions existing in each region.  For the land received at the Emancipation, the peasants had to pay the landlords a specified compensation in money, the amount of which, for every region, was fixed by law.  In view of the fact that many peasants were not able to pay for land in full, the government undertook to finance the transaction.  The Treasury paid the landlords in bonds specially issued for this purpose, and the peasants had to repay the loan to the government, with interest, in annual installments spread over a period of forty-nine years (the so-called "redemption payments").

The defects of the Emancipation settlement will be discussed in one of the following sections. Here it should be noted only that with all its shortcomings it provided for terms more favorable to the peasants than those on which the abolition of serfdom was achieved in west-European countries. The right of every peasant to a land allotment was recognized, and credit facilities for the redemption of their holdings were offered all of them from the outset.

## Social Changes after Emancipation

In its legal aspect the Emancipation meant the abolition or human bondage, the doing away with the fundamental distinction between those who were and those who were not personally free. It was followed by a series of reforms, all tending in one direction : the breaking down of legal barriers which the old order had erected between the various classes. The establishment of the *zemstvos* (a system of local self-government institutions in charge of economic matters and public welfare in the country districts) provided for a co-operation, theoretically on a basis of equality, of various groups of population including the former serfs. The new courts introduced the conception of "laws equally just to all," while the army reform made military service a universal obligation of all the social classes without discrimination. Generally speaking, the old social structure, based on the division of the population into several "estates," began to undergo profound transformation in the direction of civil equality characteristic of a bourgeois society.

Perhaps the most outstanding single phenomenon in the social history of Russia in the period between the Emancipation and the Revolution was the gradual decline in the wealth and importance of the nobility. The abolition of serfdom deprived the gentry of about one third of their landed property and of the supply of serf labor. Moreover, it automatically abolished the landlords' "manorial" jurisdiction over the dependent population of their estates, and it dealt a blow to the general predominance of the nobility in the provincial administration. Economically, the majority of the noble landowners found themselves in a very difficult situation. The lack of capital from which they suffered was not remedied by the compensation they received for the land ceded to the peasants. About two fifths of the total amount due the landlords was withheld by the Treasury to cover their debt to state credit institutions. In need of ready cash and therefore pressed to dispose of the bonds, the landlords flooded the market with these securities and before long brought their price to a point reaching, at times, 30 per cent below par. To the lack of capital was added in most cases lack of initiative and special training. Only a few could adjust themselves promptly to new conditions. Even the new credit facilities opened to the nobility by the government were not used by the majority of the class to the best advantage, and by the end of the 1880's their indebtedness was considerably larger than on the eve of the Emancipation. There were many cases of downright bankruptcy, and still more numerous were the occasions when the owners of the estates preferred to sell their land rather than to struggle against adverse circumstances. In fact, the transfer of land from the nobles to non-noble owners continued without interruption to the end of the imperial regime. By 1877 the nobles had sold about 13 per cent of their land; by 1887, about 24 per cent; by 1897, about 35 per cent; by 1905, about 48 per cent; and by 1916, about 59 per cent.

Parallel with the decline of the nobility went on the steady advance of the middle classes. Only after Emancipation could one speak of the formation of a bourgeoisie in Russia, in the west-European sense of the word. The number of those engaged in trade and industry rose much more rapidly than before, simultaneously with the growth of their economic and social importance. Much of the land sold by the nobility passed into the hands of the merchants, and other forms of wealth also began to serve as a foundation for high social position. There was a noticeable progress of cultural standards among the merchants and the industrialists, and a corresponding development of "class-consciousness" among the members of the group. After 1870 the professional organization of the Russian bourgeoisie advanced steadily, while the new law on town administration, passed in 1870, placed in their hands the management of municipal affairs. The reforms, in general, opened new fields of activity which did not exist before. Work in the zemstvos required a constant supply of doctors, statisticians, and agricultural experts, and the reform of the law courts led to the growth of much work for lawyers. Economic development called for an increasing number of technical specialists, while the rising demand for education and a general intellectual awakening were responsible for a notable increase in the number of teachers, writers, and journalists. One may say that a new class, that of the professional men, made its appearance in Russia.

While the middle classes now enjoyed a status of practically complete legal equality with the former privileged order, the same could not be said of the peasantry. Even after the Emancipation the Russian peasants did not become full-fledged citizens. As members of the village commune they could not dispose of their property, and their freedom of movement was limited by the authority of the village assembly, which was held responsible by the government for the payment of taxes and redemption installments by its individual members. For minor offenses the peasants were tried by special township courts on the basis of the customary law. And the poll tax, which they still had to pay and from which other classes were exempt, was a mark of their social inferiority. The poll tax was abolished in 1883–1886, but the principle of joint liability remained in force until 1903, and it was only during the constitutional period that first measures were taken towards endowing the peasants with full civic rights.

From the economic point of view, the Russian peasantry had not been a homogeneous body even before the Emancipation, and after the abolition of serfdom the social differentiation inside of the peasant class went on increasing, in spite of the equalitarian tendencies of the village commune. Economic investigations of the late nineteenth century and the early twentieth revealed the existence in the Russian villages of a comparatively large group of well-to-do peasants on the one hand, and of a larger group of landless proletarians on the other.

Some of these proletarians had become agricultural laborers, while others joined the ranks of the growing class of factory workers. From about 500,000 on the eve of the Emancipation, the number of the factory workers rose to about 1,300,000 by 1890, and to more than 2,000,000 by 1900. It is true that in many cases the industrial workers in Russia still retained their connection with the villages, either living permanently in towns without their families or being employed only as seasonal laborers. But at the same time the number of those who became totally urbanized and who worked in the factories all the year round was steadily increasing, more particularly in the major branches of industry. In this sense, the formation of the modern industrial proletariat in Russia, like that of the bourgeoisie, dates from the Emancipation.

## The Agrarian Problem

There was an "agrarian crisis" in late nineteenth-century Russia, caused by the depression from which large-scale agriculture suffered in the 1880's and early 1890's. The plight of the peasants presented a still more serious problem. The crisis was a general European phenomenon caused by the growing competition with non-European regions overseas. The plight of the peasants was a peculiar Russian phenomenon, and for its explanation one must look to the conditions within the country.

In the discussion of this agrarian problem, which became painfully obvious to the government and public opinion during the severe famine of 1891-1892, two factors usually have been given prominence: the insufficiency of the allotments of land received by the peasants at Emancipation, and the weight of the financial burden that lay on the peasantry both in the form of redemption payments and in the form of taxes. While it is impossible to deny the highly unfavorable influence of these factors, one should be careful not to overemphasize their importance. So far as the *absolute* size of the allotments is concerned, in many cases it was not so very small. The average per male "soul" was $23\frac{1}{2}$ acres for the former state peasants and $9\frac{1}{2}$ acres for the former serfs, and the smallest of these two figures still compares favorably with the average size of a peasant landholding in France during the same period. Neither should one overlook the fact that as early as 1881 the redemption payments were reduced almost 27 per cent, and that a few years later the poll tax was abolished. If, in spite of this, the landholdings of the majority of the Russian peasants proved to be *relatively* too small, and the financial burden that lay on them *relatively* too heavy for the peasants to prosper, one obviously must seek the principal cause of the pressure in the general economic conditions within the country.

The whole situation can be summarized as a case of agrarian over-population. The chief trouble was that while the rural population was increasing very rapidly, there was little progress in agricultural technique, so that the yield of peasant farming, though somewhat increased towards the end of the period, still remained very low. At the same time the relatively tardy industrialization of the country made it impossible for the factories to absorb the excess labor of the rural districts at the required rate. Nor was large-scale capitalistic farming developing with sufficient rapidity to provide enough employment.

As a result, the majority of the peasants remained congested in the agricultural regions of central Russia without any immediate possibility of substantially improving their condition. In the eyes of the peasants, the only remedy for their ills was to obtain more land.  This they were trying to do both by buying and by leasing land from the landlords.  The extension of peasant landholdings, however, did not bring an immediate relief.  Of the land bought by the peasantry, a considerable part passed into the hands of the well-to-do peasants, while the land acquired by the poorer ones could not be used by them to the best advantage because of the lack of capital and backward methods of cultivation.  At the same time the financial sacrifices involved added considerably to the burden which the peasants had to carry.  This was particularly true in the case of the leased land, because the prevailing rents were high.

Under such conditions, some period of time had to pass before a necessary adjustment in national economy could be reached, to do away with the agrarian overpopulation.  Moreover, the prevailing communal type of peasant tenure in Russia proved to be a serious obstacle in the way to such an adjustment.  Curiously enough, the village commune was idealized not only by the early Russian radicals, who saw in it a nucleus for the future socialist society, but also by many of the conservatives, who expected it to play the part of a bulwark against class struggle and thus, indirectly, against socialism.  Partly because of these general considerations, and partly because of fiscal reasons, the commune was preserved in the Emancipation settlement both as an economic and an administrative unit.  But before long it became clear to many that it was not performing either of the two functions that had been expected of it.  In spite of the joint liability principle the peasants were not meeting their financial obligations towards the state, and the arrears in redemption payments and in taxes were growing with an alarming rapidity.  Likewise, the equalitarian features of the communal arrangement were not able to prevent social differentiation and the growth of economic inequality in Russian villages.  On the other hand, by its open-field system, its compulsory course of husbandry, and its periodical redistribution of land, the commune thwarted personal initiative and introduced an element of instability that was bound to react most unfavorably on all attempts at technical improvement.  At the same time, both the entailed character of the communal property and the authority of the village assembly over its members interfered with freedom of movement among the rural population of Russia and thus artificially kept in the overcrowded agricultural regions many peasants who might otherwise have moved elsewhere.

It must be said in addition that governmental policy of the period, while by no means neglecting the plight of the peasants, lacked the necessary vigor and consistency. Neither the activities of the Peasant Land Bank established in 1882, to grant the peasants credit for buying land, nor the organized assistance to peasant migration into Asiatic Russia, acquired real importance until after the revolution of 1905.

## Industrialization in the Late Nineteenth Century

While Emancipation opened the way for the eventual industrialization of Russia, its effect in this direction was not immediate. On the one hand, a certain period of time was needed to permit industry to readjust itself in accordance with changed social conditions, and as a matter of fact for the first decade after the abolition of serfdom the progress of industrial production was temporarily retarded. On the other hand, at the time of Emancipation Russia still lacked adequate means of transportation, a modern system of credit institutions, and a stable currency, all of which were necessary prerequisites of a large-scale industrial development. During the 1860's and 1870's Russian capital was attracted chiefly to railroad building and banking, which promised quicker and larger returns, and comparatively little was invested in industrial undertakings.

Extensive railroad building was one of the most characteristic features of Russian economic life in the second half of the nineteenth century. On the eve of Emancipation Russia had less than 700 miles of railroads, but by 1894 the mileage rose to more than 21,000, and by 1900 to more than 36,000. Until 1880 most of the lines were constructed by private companies, on the basis of concessions granted by the government. But thereafter the governmental policy was modified in the direction of state control. A number of privately owned railroads were purchased by the Treasury and new lines were built and operated by the government itself. State railroads finally became the predominant type in Russia,[1] while the private lines that were permitted to exist were subject to a rather strict supervision.

Prior to Emancipation Russia had had practically no privately owned credit institutions. The first joint-stock commercial bank was founded in 1864; by 1904 the number of such banks rose to about forty; and in 1914 there were about fifty banks with over seven hundred branches in the provinces. Joint-stock companies

[1] In 1913 the mileage of state railroads was more than twice that of the private lines.

in general were a comparatively recent phenomenon in Russian economic life.   Before the era of reforms their number was less than 80, while in 1861–1873 alone 357 new companies were formed, and there was an even more rapid development in the later part of the century.   Characteristically, the participation of the government in the field of banking was far more active than in any of the countries of western Europe, and besides a State Bank of the commercial type the Russian government established also a number of special credit institutions.   Another concern of the government during the decades in question was the improvement of the monetary situation. Throughout the period following the Crimean War Russia had lived under a most unsatisfactory regime of depreciated paper currency. After 1862 the Minister of Finance attempted to establish the gold standard by gradually increasing the Treasury's reserve.   But it was not until 1897 that this policy was successful.   The monetary reform created conditions of stability for commercial operations within the country, and by putting Russian currency on a basis of parity with those of other nations it also made possible a very considerable influx of foreign capital into Russia in the form of loans and investments.

By the late 1880's the ground was prepared for a rapid industrial progress, and in the last decade of the century Russia entered into her first phase of intense industrialization.   A few figures will give an idea of the rate of development.   The number of industrial establishments increased by 26.3 per cent, and about 700 new joint-stock companies were founded.   The increase in the production of oil was 132 per cent, of pig iron 190 per cent, of manufactured iron 116 per cent, of coal 131 per cent, and of cotton manufactures 76 per cent.   Of particular importance was the rise of new industries and new industrial regions.   The Russian coal industry dates from the discovery of vast deposits of coal in the Donets district of south Russia, about the middle of the nineteenth century.   The discovery of iron in the same district led to the creation of a new metallurgical center in the south, which in 1900 was already far ahead of the old mining and metallurgical center of the Urals.   After 1870 the Russian oil industry began to develop in the Caucasus, principally around Baku, and at the beginning of the twentieth century Russia occupied the second place in the world production of petroleum, supplying about one fourth of the total.

Among the older branches of industry, a particularly notable development took place in the field of cotton manufacture.   The

Moscow district remained the most important in the country, but production grew rapidly until on the eve of the World War Russia had attained the fourth place among the cotton-manufacturing countries of the world, ranking after Great Britain, the United States, and Germany. The acquisition of Turkestan in Central Asia furnished an important supply of raw cotton from domestic sources. In 1890 Russia still relied on foreign sources for 75.1 per cent of her cotton supply, but in 1910 this proportion had fallen to 49.1 per cent, and wide irrigation works were in progress to increase still further the area of the cotton culture in Turkestan.

The Russian statesman of the period most closely connected with the country's economic progress was Witte, Minister of Finance from 1892 to 1903. He was a firm believer in industrialization, and kept the ideal of an economically self-sufficient Russia before his eyes. He spared no effort to support the development of Russian industry by a policy of tariff protection, governmental guarantees, and subsidies. It was Witte also who finally carried through the introduction of the gold standard. For some time he actually directed railroad building in Russia, being largely responsible for the construction of the great Trans-Siberian line in 1892-1904.

## The Labor Problem and the Socialist Movement

The growth of the working class meant the emergence in Russia of the labor problem in its modern aspects. In the early period of capitalistic advance, labor conditions were particularly unsatisfactory, as they had been to a greater or less degree in other countries during similar economic transformations. As a rule the factory hands were overworked, underpaid, and badly fed and lodged. To the ruthless exploitation of their labor by the pioneers of Russian capitalism the workers answered with sporadic outbursts of discontent and poorly organized strikes. The government felt that it must interfere and try to improve the situation. The years 1882-1886 saw the real beginning of labor legislation in Russia. These early factory laws were rather modest in scope, dealing partly with the protection of women and children, and partly trying to eliminate some of the most crying abuses, such as the irregular payment of wages or payment in kind. A decade later (1897) they were supplemented by a law which limited day work of adults to eleven and a half hours and night work to ten hours. In 1903 the first labor insurance law was passed, but it was rather unsatisfactory, for it applied to a limited number of workers only, gave a vague definition of industrial risks, and provided for very low rates of compensation.[1] To ensure the observance of this legislation the office of factory inspector was established. The authority of the factory inspectors, however, was not always sufficient to overcome the stubborn opposition on the part of many employers, especially in the earlier stages.

Furthermore, the situation was aggravated by the fact that until the constitutional period no trade-unions were permitted by the government. In the early years of the twentieth century a number of legally unrecognized trade-unions were formed by the workers in some branches of industry, but they led a precarious *de facto* existence. It was only in 1906, under the pressure of the revolutionary movement, that the unions were finally legalized. But even then conditions remained unfavorable to the real progress of trade-unionism in Russia. On the one hand, the law, while permitting local unions, still prohibited national organization, and in general the authorities continued to view the workers' organizations with suspicion, constantly interfering with their activities on political grounds. On the other hand, the comparatively low cultural level prevailing among the Russian workers was in itself a serious obstacle to the immediate success of the movement. In 1907, at the height of unionist development, there were some 650 unions in Russia, with a total membership of about 250,000. The majority of these were very small. About 350 unions had less than one hundred members each, and only 22 had a membership of more than two thousand.

No wonder that under such limitations the improvement in labor conditions was neither rapid nor substantial enough to prevent the growth of discontent among the working masses. Before long this discontent proved to be a fertile ground for revolutionary socialist propaganda. The early Russian socialism of the 1860's and 1870's, usually designated by the name of "Populism," was non-Marxian both in the source of its inspiration and in its general nature. It had a predominantly agrarian character, relying chiefly on the peasantry as the revolutionary class par excellence. It emphasized the individuality of Russia's historical development, and it denied the necessity for Russia of passing, on her way to socialist society, through the preliminary "bourgeois" stage. It had a profound distrust of parliamentary democracy, and it wanted to save Russia from capitalism by a timely "preventive" revolution. On the tactical side it was thoroughly revolutionary. Partly because of the

[1] It was greatly improved by a new labor insurance act passed in 1912.

political conditions in the country, and partly because of theoretical predilections, it chose the way of political conspiracy, contemplating a direct attack on the government by a revolutionary minority as the opening act of the social revolution.

Marxism, as an organized movement, appeared in Russia in the 1890's, and from the outset characterized itself as a scientific and realistic doctrine in opposition to the Utopian romanticism of the Populists. Pointing to the unmistakable evidence of the growth of capitalism in the country, the Marxists emphasized its "educational" and revolutionizing features, and expected the liberation of Russia by the urban proletariat. Theoretically, they distinguished between the bourgeois phase of the forthcoming revolution, which would establish a democratic political order, and the more remote "proletarian" phase, which would bring with it the full realization of the socialist ideal. In tactical matters they emphasized the importance of mass movement as opposed to the conspiratorial methods of their predecessors.

Officially the Russian Social Democratic Party was founded in 1897, but it was not effectively organized until 1903, and it was only during the revolution of 1905 that it definitely allied itself with the mass movement of the workers. Characteristically, at its second (actually first) convention it split into two factions which became known as Bolsheviks and Mensheviks.[1] While the latter, subsequently led by Plekhanov, on the whole remained within the boundaries of orthodox Marxism, as represented chiefly by the German Social Democrats, the Bolshevik doctrine, formulated by Lenin, introduced some significant modifications. Still professing his belief in the revolutionary hegemony of the proletariat, Lenin insisted on the necessity of its alliance with the peasantry in view of Russian conditions. Simultaneously, he rejected the possibility of co-operation with the Russian bourgeoisie, whose interests, according to him, were inseparably bound up with those of autocracy. In fact, because of this alignment of social forces in the country, it was for the proletariat to achieve the bourgeois — that is, the political — revolution, without the assistance and even in spite of the bourgeoisie. Such a course made possible an immediate transformation of the bourgeois revolution into a "proletarian-peasant" revolution. In this way Lenin was led to abandon the idea of intermediary stages in Russia's transition to socialism.

---

[1] The names mean "members of the majority" and "members of the minority," respectively.

Finally, while still insisting on the importance of the mass movement, Lenin in his tactical plans assigned a role of first magnitude to a centralized organization of "professional revolutionaries." In all these respects Lenin's thought differed considerably from the Marxian concepts of the types prevailing in western Europe; Lenin revived, in a modified form, some of the characteristic tendencies of earlier Russian socialism.

## Economic Progress during the Constitutional Regime

At the beginning of the twentieth century Russian industry experienced a severe commercial crisis from which recovery was slow. This depression was followed closely by the revolutionary disturbances of 1905–1906, which were bound to react most unfavorably upon the economic well-being of the country. One of the outstanding features of the revolutionary movement was the active participation of the factory workers. Beginning in the spring of 1905, a veritable epidemic of strikes, this time of a frankly political nature, spread over all the industrial regions of Russia. The movement culminated in the famous general strike of October, 1905, which forced the government to concede some of the demands of the opposition and to promise the establishment of a constitutional regime. In view of the partial character of this victory, falling short of the desires and expectations of the radical wing of the opposition, grave disturbances continued after the publication of the October Manifesto. Under the leadership of the *Soviet* (Council) of Workers' Deputies, organized in St. Petersburg, strikes went on, and an abortive armed insurrection, with the workers taking a prominent part in it, broke out in Moscow in December, 1905. Minor events of the same nature took place in other parts of the country. Under such conditions normal economic life was obviously impossible, and in 1905–1906 industrial production became thoroughly disorganized.

By 1907, however, the revolutionary movement was definitely suppressed, and order was restored throughout the Empire. Simultaneously, with the political pacification of the country, Russian capitalism resumed its advance along the lines established during the first phase of intense industrialization. While not so spectacular as in that earlier period, the progress was still impressive enough. There was a steady and fairly rapid growth of production in the manufacture of textiles, in the metallurgical industry, and in mining. One notable exception was the relative stagnation of the Russian oil industry in the decade preceding the World War. For this there were special reasons. At the beginning of the twentieth century the industry was concentrated in the Baku oil fields, and production in these fields was brought to a complete standstill during the revolutionary disturbances of 1905-1906. Almost three fifths of the wells were ruined, and the problem of starting the work anew presented great difficulties. Moreover, the Baku oil wells had already begun to show some signs of exhaustion before the crisis, and development of other areas required time before it could give substantial results. On the whole, however, the constitutional period (1907-1914) was one of economic prosperity for Russia.

Perhaps the most interesting feature of Russian industrial life of the time was the striking tendency towards greater concentration of production. Establishments with more than five hundred workers formed over 50 per cent of all the industrial enterprises, while the proportion of concerns with more than one thousand workers was no less than in Germany. In the early twentieth century, combinations of western European and American types found their way into Russia. Syndicates were formed for the control of the market, such as *Prodamet* in metallurgical industry (1902) and *Produgol* in coal industry (1904). Somewhat later fusions of more important separate enterprises, in the form of trusts, took place in several of the principal industries. Partly because of this phenomenon, and partly because of the general progress in the professional, and to some degree even political, organization of the bourgeoisie consequent upon the establishment of the constitutional regime, there was a notable tendency on the part of the Russian industrialists to emancipate themselves from excessive governmental paternalism. Although the role played by the government in finance and industry continued to be a very important one, private initiative was asserting itself with more vigor than before.

The influx of foreign capital into Russia, naturally interrupted by the revolution of 1905, became again quite prominent after the restoration of order in the country, and on the eve of the World War a considerable proportion of capital invested in Russian industry was of foreign origin. Its real significance for Russian economic development is a debatable point. Some writers assert that after 1910 it was losing ground to native capital, which was gaining a clear ascendancy, while others insist that toward the end of the period Russia's dependence on foreign capital was growing rather than diminishing. Whatever position one is inclined to take in this controversy, there seems to be little foundation for the extreme assertion that Russia was gradually becoming an "economic colony" of foreign nations.   On the contrary, the general impression one gets from the study of Russian prewar economics is that native capitalism had taken firm roots in the life of the country and that it had proved its vitality.

## The Agrarian Reform of Stolypin

The grave peasant disturbances that broke out in 1902–1903, and again, with a greater force and on a larger scale, in 1905–1906, made the agrarian problem one of the chief concerns of both the government and the opposition.   It was only after the revolution of 1905 that governmental policy with regard to the problem acquired necessary vigor and determination.   The cancellation of the balance of redemption payments in 1905 substantially relieved the financial burden that lay on the peasantry.   In the same year the State Land Bank for the Peasants was given greatly increased powers, and in 1906 considerable tracts of state and crown land were sold through the Bank to the peasants.   Numerous estates of private landowners, many of whom were greatly frightened by the agrarian riots, likewise passed into the hands of the peasantry, with financial help from the Bank.   Organized assistance to peasant migration into the Asiatic provinces of the Empire now assumed really large proportions under the guidance of the newly established Colonization Department of the Ministry of Agriculture.   Every year the agents of the Department surveyed and assigned for settlement suitable areas mostly in Siberia, made immeasurably more accessible by the construction of the Trans-Siberian railroad.   The settlers were granted land in perpetual use, subject to the payment of a small rent, and they were entitled also to a number of other privileges such as reduced railroad fares, loans for traveling expenses, and temporary remission of taxes.   Both in European Russia and in the regions of new settlement, the government developed a system of expert agricultural assistance in co-operation with the zemstvos, which likewise paid great attention to this problem.

Important as all these measures were, they were still in the nature of palliatives, and there was a general feeling that something more fundamental had to be done for the solution of the agrarian problem. Among the opposition the most radical proposal emanated from the Socialist Revolutionaries, a party which became organized at the end of the nineteenth century and which revived the agrarian tradition of the earlier Populists by concentrating its attention on the peasantry. The chief plank in their program was the "socialization" of land — a term which they preferred to "nationalization" because in their scheme the land management had to rest with the self-governing communes and not with the central government. A more moderate program was formulated by the Constitutional Democrats, a political organization of the Russian liberals: it contemplated the distribution among the peasants of all the land belonging to the state, the crown, and the monasteries, and the compulsory alienation for the same purpose of some part of the privately owned land. The landlords, for the loss of their property, were to be compensated by the Treasury at an "equitable price."

None of these proposals was acceptable to the government. It refused to violate the principle of private property, and it expressed great concern for the fate of large-scale farming in Russia, which precisely at that time was making considerable progress and which was playing an increasingly important part in the general economic development of the country. Under the leadership of Stolypin, Prime Minister in 1906-1911, the government advanced an agrarian program of its own, designed to improve the conditions of the peasantry without attacking private property or compromising the success of capitalistic agriculture. The substance of that program lay in an attempt at a gradual elimination of the village commune and the encouragement of individual landownership among the Russian peasants. Under the terms of the Stolypin laws (1906-1911) every member of the commune had the right to claim his share in the common land of the village as his private property. The next step was the actual enclosure of the land thus appropriated. This would permit the owner to have his land in one compact holding and not in widely scattered strips as under the open-field system.[1] To supervise settlements between the commune and its seceding members and to assist the latter in their efforts to establish themselves as individual farmers, a special Land Settlement Department was organized, with a very large staff of local agents.

The promulgation of these laws met with vigorous objections on the part of the opposition, which attacked them as a mere political stratagem on the part of Stolypin and as an example of high-handed bureaucratic interference with established popular customs. Undoubtedly, political considerations played a considerable part in

---

[1] The whole procedure bore a rather close resemblance to the enclosure movement in England in its eighteenth-century phase.

Stolypin's motives; he wanted to create in Russia a numerous class of small landed proprietors as a conservative force and a bulwark against revolution.   But there is no reason to believe that his objection to the commune as an obstacle in the way of agricultural progress was a mere pretense.   As to the interference with popular customs, one might argue that Stolypin's legislation was in harmony with the general trend of the country's economic development.   For some time social differentiation had been going on in the villages, individualist tendencies had been coming to the fore, and the commune had been losing its vitality.[1]   More telling was the other criticism advanced by the opposition against the Stolypin policy — namely, that it favored the wealthy peasants to the detriment of the others.   Stolypin himself admitted that his was the "wager on the strong," and obviously it was somewhat difficult for the poorer peasants to start individual farming by themselves.

The agrarian legislation of Stolypin was in operation for too short a period of time to permit us to pass a final and categorical judgment upon its merits or shortcomings.   But it is significant that it had a rather striking initial success.   By the end of 1913, about 24 per cent of all the peasant households in European Russia had availed themselves of the opportunity to appropriate their communal holdings on the basis of individual ownership, and if we add all those whose applications still waited to be acted upon, the ratio will rise considerably higher.   No amount of governmental pressure could achieve such a result, and one feels forced to conclude that the reform found a favorable and sufficiently prepared ground.

---

[1] An investigation conducted by the zemstvos between 1897 and 1902, for thirty-five provinces of European Russia, revealed the fact that more than half of the communes among the former serf villages had dropped the practice of land redistribution.

# CHAPTER 30

# THE RETURN TO PROTECTION

———◆———

## The French and Other Treaty Systems, 1860–1879

By the middle of the nineteenth century Great Britain had opened the British market to the trade in grain by repealing the Corn Laws, had given up the policy, embodied in the Navigation Acts, of monopolizing colonial trade, and had virtually abandoned the system of tariffs on manufactures. In the Cobden-Chevalier treaty of 1860 the British were joined by France in a system of virtual free trade. This treaty in turn was the first of a network of reciprocal, most-favored-nation treaties embracing most of Europe. In this way there was established the most liberal system of trade ever experienced by the states of Europe. Adam Smith's views, in spite of his pessimism in regarding free trade as Utopian, appeared to have won the day.

The treaty of 1860 provided that articles hitherto barred were to be admitted. Mutual reductions in duties were made, and after 1864 French duties were 24 per cent ad valorem or lower. The most-favored-nation clause was incorporated for extending to each country the lowest rates accorded to other states. Similar treaties, containing the most-favored-nation clause, were concluded by France, within less than a decade, with Belgium, Holland, Prussia and the other states of the German Customs Union (the *Zollverein*), Sweden, Norway, Austria, Switzerland, Spain, Portugal, and the Papal States. The conventional tariffs (established by treaties) supplanted in large measure the autonomous French tariff (applying in the absence of a treaty). The autonomous tariff also was liberalized, as in the repeal of the surtaxes on goods imported in foreign ships not of the country of origin of the goods. The tariff was interpreted administratively in accord with liberal principles. There were also modifications of the monopolistic or preferential treatment accorded Frenchmen in shipping, shipbuilding, and trade with the French colonies.

The ascendancy of free-trade principles was more apparent than real. The treaty of 1860 was negotiated secretly and adopted arbitrarily by the autocratic government of Napoleon III. A similar treaty was accepted by Prussia largely as a weapon against

Austria, the great rival of Prussia in German affairs.   When the terms of the Anglo-French treaty were made known in France, there was much opposition, especially among the manufacturers, and this was accentuated by a commercial crisis in 1864.   Opposition was in part allayed by succeeding years of prosperity, but as the date (1870) of the expiration of the treaty approached (the term was ten years), demands for a reversal of policy became so strong that the government agreed to two legislative inquiries, one relating to industry and the other to the merchant marine.   These investigations were interrupted by the Franco-Prussian War.   The government of the Third Republic, established on the ruins of Napoleon III's empire, denounced the treaty with Great Britain. But in the meantime the treaty with Prussia (1862) had been recognized as giving most-favored-nation treatment to the new German Empire, and several other treaties of the previous decade were still binding.   Partly because of these earlier treaty commitments and partly because of the diplomatic weakness of the early government of the Third Republic, the treaty with Great Britain was renewed in 1873 without substantial change.   The efforts to return to protection were virtually abandoned, although minor changes were made in the autonomous tariff.

In most of the countries of Europe there was apparent, toward the end of the 1870's, a reversion toward protection.   In the United States, protection was firmly established as a result of the Civil War, which gave ascendancy to the industrialists of the east as against the farmers and southern planters.   In Europe, particularly significant was the action of Russia in 1876, when tariff rates were raised indirectly about 50 per cent by means of a law requiring payment of duties in terms of the value of gold.   Spain in 1877 established two sets of duties, one for countries according Spain most-favored-nation treatment, and the other, at higher levels, for other countries.   A public inquiry in Italy from 1870 to 1874 resulted in the conclusion that protection was desirable, and in 1878 there was a slight increase in duties.   The industrialists of Piedmont desired protection, but the government of Italy, like that of France, found its liberty of action restricted by treaties.   In Austria-Hungary, duties were raised at the termination, in 1877, of the treaty with France.   A new tariff, in 1878, was a compromise between the agrarians of Hungary, who desired free trade as an inducement to foreigners to buy their products, and the industrialists of Austria, who favored protection.   The German tariff of 1879, which has been described as the first decisive step in the return to protection, was in harmony with the tendency already apparent in various other countries.

## Assaults on the Theory of Free Trade

Leadership was assumed by Germans in the assault on the theory of free trade as well as in the actual reversion to protective policies. Even before the adoption of the treaty system beginning in 1860, a powerful voice had been raised against the doctrine of commercial liberalism.  Friedrich List, in his *National System of Political Economy* (1841), had insisted on the determination of policy in the light of national conditions and needs.  He pointed to Great Britain's unchallenged competitive supremacy and need for foreign markets as the basis of her free-trade policy.  Germany, on the other hand, was primarily agrarian, lacking in modern technological equipment, and, when List wrote, politically divided.  He held that a people fitted by training and natural resources, as were the Germans, for the development of manufactures should seek to achieve an industrial state as the most advanced stage of economic life; and that when hindered in doing this, as were the Germans, by the competition of a more advanced rival, protection became necessary.  List also criticized Adam Smith and his followers for applying to nations the rule of the individual merchant of buying in the cheapest market; for the aim of nations, List argued, must be not the utmost immediate profit but rather the development of a well-rounded national productive capacity and the assurance of future national wealth and safety under possible conditions of war and interrupted trade as well as peaceful intercourse.  List was profoundly influenced by his experiences in the United States, and there are many resemblances between his ideas and those of Mathew Carey and Henry C. Carey, American economists.

List's immediate influence was slight, for the example of Great Britain was followed even by Germany for a generation after the appearance of the *National System of Political Economy*.  But the book was extremely popular, the seventh edition appearing in 1883, and his ideas were incorporated in the writings of the historical school and especially in the views of a group of economists within the school known as the state socialists.  In 1863 appeared the first number of the *Yearbook of National Economy*, and in this influential organ of the historical school there was little trace of the abstract logic of the classical school or of reverence for individualism and *laissez faire.*  In 1872, at a conference at Eisenach, leading economists and some interested officials issued a formal declaration renouncing the doctrines of free trade and *laissez faire*, and formed a group known as the Union for Social Politics.  Liberal economic theory, stemming from Adam Smith, viewed governmental intervention with distrust and held that the free play of competing individual interests afforded the basis for automatic adjustments for the advantage of all.  The German economists exalted the state as the necessary instrumentality for reconciling conflicting interests and for achieving national aims, economic as well as political. Prominent among these aims were security for the workers and a well-rounded system of production.  These aims in turn required, in the view of the economists, the intervention of the state in the enactment of social legislation and the protection of national industries against the unequal competition of more advanced rivals, such as the English.

The newly achieved national unification of Germany and the accompanying intensification of national ambitions gave emphasis to these views in Germany.  But similar conceptions gained wide acceptance elsewhere, not only in Europe but in the United States, although in America social legislation as the correlative of protection was slow in winning support.

## The German Tariff of 1879

Napoleon III directed French commercial policy largely on the basis of political and diplomatic considerations in the face of strong opposition to free trade.  Similarly, Bismarck and his minister of commerce in Prussia, Rudolf von Delbrück, in forging the Zollverein and entering the French treaty system were moved by the desire to achieve political unity and to restrict the influence of Austria, which opposed free trade.  During the early years of the Empire they continued their free-trade policies as a method of strengthening their political and diplomatic position.  They were supported by two incongruous elements, the liberals and the agrarians — by the former on general grounds of theory and principle, and by the latter in order to promote the export of their products and the purchase of cheap imported farm tools and machinery.  These tendencies found expression, from 1873 to 1877, in reductions of rates on iron, ironware, shipbuilding materials, and various other goods.  Germany had become virtually a free-trade country.

But circumstances rapidly changed ; and Bismarck, who boasted that experience, not theory, was his guide, quickly adapted his policies to these new conditions.  The reductions in rates between 1873 and 1877 occurred at a most unfavorable moment, for the middle years of the decade were years of extreme depression, which was aggravated by the dumping of British goods.  The manufacturers had overextended their plants during the boom years following the victory over France, but they were inclined to blame free trade for the depression.  A Central Union of German Industrialists, formed in 1876, clamored for protection as the only way of escape from ruin.  The views of the agrarians were changing, for several reasons.  The landlords of Hungary and Russia were invading German markets; and the rapid extension of the area of cultivation in the United States, combined with the use of farm machinery, had raised the total of American agricultural exports to all countries, by 1874, to a value of $454,000,000.  The rapid growth of the industrial population of Germany greatly increased the German demand for farm products and caused the agrarians to place a greater value upon the home market.  The movement of population to the cities also tended to raise farm wages and to reduce the supply of farm labor.  The agrarians were therefore inclined to join the manufacturers in demanding a change in policy.

Bismarck was moved not only by these considerations but also by political realignments.  Before 1878 he had relied largely on the National Liberal party in the Reichstag.  Thereafter he sought support among the agrarians and the Catholic Center party.  He was also inclined to revert to a policy of protection for conciliating the industrialists of the newly acquired province of Alsace-Lorraine, whose free access to French markets had recently come to an end.  An additional reason for Bismarck's change of policy was his desire to obtain, by means of revenues from imports, a larger income for the imperial government from sources which would render it less dependent on the states and on tax levies requiring legislative sanction from year to year.  As was pointed out in the preceding section, prominent German economists were renouncing the doctrines of economic liberalism and exalting the functions of the state in fostering the national economy.  The result of these various circumstances was the tariff of 1879.

The German tariff of 1879 was designed by Bismarck to conciliate the agrarians and the manufacturers and to strengthen the financial position of the imperial government, and at the same time to avoid extremes such as would antagonize foreign powers or jeopardize his diplomatic position. The duties, which were largely specific rather than ad valorem, applied notably to grains, meat, and textiles. The duty on iron was restored, and a large variety of other manufactures received moderate protection. Raw materials, with few exceptions, were admitted free of duty as an encouragement to manufacturers, but timber, tallow, and oil, produced extensively in Germany, were subject to duties. Luxury goods of various kinds were taxed lightly, primarily for revenue. In general the law was moderate and conciliatory, but it committed the new imperial Germany unmistakably to a policy of protection. With the exception of Great Britain, other countries, already inclined in that direction, were not slow to follow suit.

### French Tariff Policies, 1881–1892

The German tariff of 1879 was adopted near the time of expiration of the more important French commercial treaties, and the trend toward protection in Germany and elsewhere naturally strengthened the protectionists in France. Steps had been taken as early as 1875 to learn the views of the French chambers of commerce and other organizations representing farmers as well as manufacturers and merchants. These groups indicated a preference for specific in place of ad valorem duties as a safeguard against frauds in the valuation of goods. Changes were proposed, also, in the commercial treaties. The most-favored-nation clause was opposed as limiting the government's freedom of action in dealing with varying conditions and degrees of protection in different countries. After 1875, the agitation for protection gained rapid headway and was stimulated not only by similar tendencies elsewhere but by conditions in France. The depression of the middle years of the decade affected France as well as other countries and was aggravated by a grape blight and by silkworm diseases which wrought havoc in the vitally important wine and silk industries.

The tariff of 1881 substituted specific for ad valorem duties, raised rates on many manufactured imports, especially woolens, and left agricultural products virtually without additional protection. A supplementary law of 1881 was designed to promote shipping and shipbuilding by means of bounties. The duties on manufactures from various countries were later lowered by new reciprocal treaties. The agricultural interests, disappointed with the treaty, organized an extensive movement for further changes.

The principal change, before 1885, was the protection of the beet-sugar industry. In that year the farmers succeeded in electing a majority of the Chamber of Deputies favorable to further protec-tion, and during the next two years there were new duties or upward revisions applying to animals imported for food, and to rye, barley, oats, wheat, and flour. France as an exporter of wine had bargained with other countries for low wine duties, and these treaty limita-tions prevented the granting of duties desired by the wine growers. This situation was one of the principal causes of the abandonment of the treaty system inaugurated in 1860.

## The French Tariffs of 1892-1910

The experience of France, after 1860, with the system of recipro-cal treaties was the subject of a special inquiry in 1890 among indus-trial and agricultural associations. These organizations indicated an overwhelming preference for a general or autonomous tariff as opposed to conventional tariffs embodied in commercial treaties containing the most-favored-nation clause. The latter plan, it was held, had unduly restricted the government's freedom of action. The Chamber of Deputies elected in 1889 was dominated by protec-tionists, and the approaching expiration of most of the surviving commercial treaties in 1892 occasioned a shift in policy to higher duties embodied in a general tariff law.

The demand for additional protection for agriculture became especially insistent, due to several circumstances. The plant louse which attacked the vineyards in the 1870's reduced the output so seriously that imports of ordinary wine were twenty times larger in 1887 than they had been in 1877. The silk industry also suffered severely from diseases which cut down the production of raw silk by more than 50 per cent. Wheat growers suffered from declining prices, the average price from 1886 to 1890 being about 25 per cent lower than from 1871 to 1875. The conservatism of the French peasants, combined with the small size of their farms, militated against reduction of costs by means of technological improvements. The competition of newer countries, especially of the United States, in the wheat-growing and cattle-raising industries became acute during the 1880's. Spanish and Italian wines competed in the French market; and German beet sugar, supported by subsidies, endangered French producers. Manufacturers also desired higher duties, and in addition called for abandonment of the treaty sys-tem and for the adoption of a more specialized and flexible tariff.

The tariff of 1892 increased agricultural duties approximately 25 per cent. Bounties were provided for silkworms, woven silk, hemp, and flax. By means of these protective measures France remained virtually self-sufficing in respect to agricultural products. Raw materials were not extensively taxed, but exceptions were coal, ferromanganese, and timber. Machinery and other metal wares and most of the textiles were highly protected. Subsidies for shipping and shipbuilding were continued and in 1893 were increased. Duties on manufactures embodied the system of maximum and minimum rates, the differential varying with different articles but approximating in general 15 per cent. The object of the differential was to give flexibility and bargaining power. It was intended that the maximum rates would ordinarily apply and that the minimum rates would be reserved for countries which accorded special privileges to Frenchmen. In practice the minimum rates applied to most countries, although grave controversies arose, especially with Switzerland, with which a destructive tariff war was waged from 1893 to 1895. The special agreements with regard to minimum rates were subject to termination on short notice; and this fact, combined with the highly specialized nature of the tariffs (comprising 721 articles), enabled the government to retain much greater autonomy and flexibility than had been possible under the earlier treaty system. The only countries with a higher degree of protection were the United States and Russia.

Although a new general tariff act was passed in 1910, no new principles or vital changes in policy were adopted. The schedules were revised to take account of new products such as automobiles and synthetic dyes; most manufacturers obtained additional protection; and both maximum and minimum rates were raised. The differential between the two sets of rates was increased for the purpose of strengthening the government's bargaining power with other countries.

## The German Treaty System, 1890–1902

The German tariff of 1879 gave moderate protection and at the same time kept Germany comparatively free from the entanglements of a complicated system of conventional tariffs such as France had developed after 1860. But it became apparent, as early as 1889, that France was determined to abandon her treaty system and to build a higher tariff wall by means of a general or autonomous tariff. The expiration of treaties brought to an end the advantages of Germany under the most-favored-nation clause, and in addition tariff rates were being raised not only in France but also in Germany's other principal markets, American as well as European.

The German tariff act of 1879 had been successful in raising revenue and in protecting the home market, but the rapid industrialization of Germany created a situation which called for expansion of markets beyond Germany. In addition, the rising prices of food due to increasing demand, bad harvests, and import duties were causing widespread discontent. Germans were therefore beginning to view with misgivings the building of tariff walls and to examine the possibility of surmounting barriers by means of reciprocal treaties in emulation of the system which the French were discarding. The dismissal of Bismarck in 1890 afforded an occasion for a reorientation of public policy.

As a result of these circumstances the German government undertook the negotiation of a series of treaties. In 1891, treaties were concluded with Austria-Hungary, Italy, and Belgium; and from 1892 to 1894, with Switzerland, Serbia, Rumania, and Russia. A treaty with Spain was rejected by the Spanish Cortes. Unlike the French treaties, all of the new German treaties with the exception of the one with Russia could be terminated after one year's notice on the same date — the end of 1903. The treaty with Russia was to expire the following year. The rates agreed to could not be altered during the treaty period. The treaties included the most-favored-nation clause, and there were reciprocal reductions of rates below the level of rates in the autonomous tariffs applying to nontreaty states, but the conventional rates were extended to various other states by means of most-favored-nation agreements. The reductions in rates were mainly on agricultural products — a policy adopted against the vigorous protests of the landlords. There were also reductions on many manufactured articles, and exports were stimulated by a system of private subsidies.

### The German Tariff of 1902 and the New Treaty System

The German tariff of 1902, adopted on the eve of the expiration of the treaties of 1891 to 1894, was designed frankly for bargaining purposes. The rates were raised above desired levels, the purpose being to grant reductions in return for concessions to Germany. The freedom of the government in making reductions by treaty was restricted by the inclusion in the law of minimum rates on important agricultural products. This was a hotly contested concession to the agrarians. The prices of wheat and rye had declined seriously under the reciprocal treaties, and were approximately one third lower in 1900 than in 1891. The agricultural interests contended also that stronger protection was necessary because of the loss of farm workers, who continued the earlier movement to the cities, and because of the increasingly competitive nature of agriculture. The expansion of the farming area, the adoption of improved methods, and the development of cheap transportation facilities contributed to the creation of a world market for farm products and progressively curtailed the advantages of German producers in the domestic market. The agrarians also asserted that the maintenance of self-sufficiency as a safeguard against the hazards of war required protection of agriculture, the basic industry. They contended that there had been an excessive growth of manufacturing and an artificial emphasis on the export trades. As in France in connection with the tariff of 1892, the agrarians exerted a decisive influence on the German tariff of 1902.

The industrialists desired cheap food and raw materials but demanded additional protection for many industrial products. The depression of 1901, with its curtailment of markets, was a factor in the demand for further protection. But the manufacturers were most insistent on a higher degree of specialization, with separate rates on a larger number of items, in order to give flexibility and to make possible minor concessions in bargaining with other powers.

The intended use of the tariff of 1902 for bargaining with other powers was indicated by the fact that it was to become operative only at the discretion of the government. The diplomatic aspect was apparent also in the concession to agrarians of minimum duties below which rates could not be granted by reciprocal arrangements with other countries. The minimum duties on wheat and oats were higher than the general rates in the preceding tariff. Virtually all agricultural products were protected, but efforts were made to protect consumers from shortages and extreme prices affecting basic foods, as in the provision for the free entry of potatoes during the winter season. Agrarian protection was undoubtedly a factor in the subsequent large increases in domestic production of grains. In the case of rye, an extremely important crop, within ten years there was even a small surplus for export.

As in other industrialized countries, the general tariff provided for an ascending scale of duties from normally free raw materials to highly protected finished products. There were various exceptions; and here again the influence of the agrarians was apparent. Timber, for example, was taxed, while such commodities as fertilizers and drain pipes were admitted free. The maritime ambitions of Germany found expression in the free entry of shipbuilding materials. The mass-production industries and large-scale agriculture were more highly protected than were the small-scale branches of production — a reflection of the political balance of power, and a factor in the subsequent weakening of the middle classes.

When it became apparent that the new German tariff was designed for bargaining purposes, other countries, notably Austria-Hungary, Russia, Rumania, and Switzerland, raised their duties for strengthening their position in the impending negotiations. Diplomatic jockeying increased the natural difficulty of the task of completing the new treaty system. The tariff act included nearly a thousand separate items, and the highly specialized nature of the rates made possible the extending of concessions to a given country on minor articles without the inclusion of similar items which would have been lumped together in a schedule of duties less differentiated in nature. But the progress of negotiations was impeded by the vast amount of detail involved in negotiations relating to so many separate items. In 1904 and 1905 treaties were concluded with Belgium, Austria-Hungary, Italy, Switzerland, Rumania, Serbia, and Russia, but it was not until 1906 that the new agreements, together with the general tariff, became effective.

Rates below those of the general tariff were granted not only to the states which negotiated special treaties during 1904 and 1905, but also to other countries which had most-favored-nation agreements with Germany. These countries included the United States, France, and the British Empire with the exception of Canada. As a result, most of Germany's trade was carried on under the conventional duties rather than the rates of the general tariff. The new duties, especially on manufactures, were comparatively moderate. With the exception of Great Britain, every major country had higher rates, and in the United States and Russia the general levels of duties were vastly higher. There was a continued upward tendency in some countries, notably in France in the tariff of 1910. More significant than the extent of protection were the tendencies toward the promotion of national self-sufficiency and toward the utilization of tariffs as an instrument of national policy in the field of diplomacy.

## The Protectionist Movement in Great Britain

Before the World War Great Britain continued to adhere to the free-trade policies which had been gradually adopted during the first half of the nineteenth century. The original economic basis of British free-trade policies was in the competitive advantages of superior technology, maritime ascendancy, pre-eminence in financial and industrial organization, an exceptionally strong and adaptable national government, and a world-wide empire. By the end of the century these advantages had been wholly or partly lost, and as a result there was a widely supported movement for "tariff reform." There were two main aspects of the movement: a demand for retaliatory duties against countries with high tariffs, and an effort to introduce preferential tariffs for the interchange of commodities within the empire.

Preferential trade arrangements between Great Britain and the dominions were discussed as early as 1897, during Queen Victoria's Diamond Jubilee. Somewhat later Joseph Chamberlain as Colonial Secretary became a determined advocate of imperialism and protection and at a conference of colonial prime ministers in 1902 he suggested a system of preferential imperial tariffs. The prime ministers were not as responsive as Chamberlain had hoped, nor were his ideas received with cordiality at home. In 1903, in a speech to his constituents at Birmingham, he boldly championed both retaliatory tariffs and a system of preferential duties within the empire. The speech created dissension not only in the country at large but in the cabinet as well. Salisbury, the Prime Minister, favored retaliatory tariffs for promoting "fair" trade but opposed duties on food and held that imperial preference must await colonial action. Some of the free-trade members of the cabinet resigned in protest, and Chamberlain also retired from the cabinet so that he could be free to devote his energies to a campaign for converting the country to protection. To this end he organized the Tariff Reform League and engaged in active propaganda.

Chamberlain contended that free trade was the cause of the rapid loss of ground by Great Britain to other countries. "Agriculture," he declared, "as the greatest of all trades and industries of this country, has been practically destroyed. Sugar has gone. Silk has gone. Iron is threatened. Wool is threatened. Cotton will go!" Other industries, he asserted, would suffer in their turn. The remedy he proposed, retaliatory tariffs, could readily be applied, he held, because of Great Britain's extensive purchases from countries with high tariffs: "We take from Germany about twice as much as she takes from us. We take from France about three times as much as she takes from us. From the United States of America we take about six times as much as they take from us. Who is it that stands to lose if there is to be a war of tariffs?" Furthermore, because of the vast populations and resources of her dominions, Great Britain's position could be made impregnable within the walls of the empire: "There is nothing we want that they cannot supply; there is nothing we sell that they cannot buy."

But his arguments failed to convince either his countrymen or the peoples of the dominions. Already the self-governing colonies had adopted protective tariffs against the home country as well as foreign states and were determined to build up their own industries. To be sure, minor preferences were offered to British citizens. Canada led the way in 1898 by granting a preference of 25 per cent to certain British goods (later increased to $33\frac{1}{3}$ per cent), and South Africa, New Zealand, and Australia, between 1903 and 1907, followed the example of Canada. But tariffs were retained on imports from Great Britain, and the colonists were mainly concerned on the one hand with protecting their "infant industries" and on the other hand with the buying of such goods as they imported in the cheapest markets, whether imperial or foreign. The British themselves, in the election of 1906, decisively defeated the protectionist candidates in most of the constituencies. Free trade had promoted the export of capital as well as of goods. The vast investments of Great Britain abroad, combined with her shipping, insurance, and financial services throughout the world, sufficed to sustain a progressive increase in imported goods as compared with exports. The fear of weakening Britain's position in respect to "invisible" imports and exports and of losing the advantages of cheap foods and raw materials accruing from free trade sufficed to maintain the traditional system until it was shattered by the shocks of World War and postwar maladjustments.

# CHAPTER 31

## THE GROWTH OF IMPERIALISM

---

### Nationalism and Industrialism, 1870–1914

For more than half a century after the downfall of Napoleon I in 1815, imperial interests beyond Europe occasioned comparatively little conflict between European powers. Toward the end of the nineteenth century there was renewed imperial rivalry not only beyond Europe but also in various European areas of strategic value, of coveted natural resources, or of racial tensions. The revival of imperialism resulted largely from the combined impact of nationalism and industrialism.

Newly achieved political unity gave to Italians and Germans a feeling of pride, an ambition for power, and an agency of centralized government for the achievement of their aims. Nationalism was stimulated in France by the defeat of the French in the Franco-Prussian War. In Austria-Hungary, the nationalistic ambitions of the two main peoples, the Germans of Austria and the Magyars of Hungary, were reconciled with imperial unity in the Compromise of 1867. Russian nationalism, combined with imperialism, found expression in the Pan-Slav movement. In the United States, national consolidation was made possible by the outcome of the Civil War and was achieved largely by the nation-wide extension of facilities for transportation and communication. In the Far East, nationalism found expression in the emergence of Japan as one of the great powers, in the gradual transformation of China, and in efforts to obtain autonomy for India.

Nationalism was stimulated by industrialism; and the further extension of industrialism as a source of national wealth and power was one of the main ambitions of those who controlled the various national governments. This is apparent, for example, from the growth of protective tariffs. The industrial revolution in Germany after the achievement of national unity in 1871 proceeded at an unprecedentedly rapid pace. French industry was at first retarded by the loss of Alsace-Lorraine and by the war indemnity imposed by Germany in 1871, but after 1890 advance was rapid. Steam power used in industry, excluding transportation, increased from 336,000 horsepower in 1870 to 863,000 in 1890, and to 2,913,000 in

1910. The generation of hydroelectric power also greatly increased. In Italy, merely a beginning, mainly in Piedmont under the influence of Cavour's nationalistic policies, had been made toward the establishment of industries of the modern type before the attainment of political unity. The rapid growth of industry in Austria before the World War was closely connected with the political ascendancy of Austria in the Austro-Hungarian Empire. In Russia, under the powerful stimulus of Witte's policies from 1892 to 1903, reinforced by French loans, large-scale business enterprise made rapid progress.

In Great Britain as well as in countries where the effects of the industrial revolution had been experienced more recently, the nature of industrialism was transformed. Profoundly important technological changes were connected with new processes for making steel, the new role of chemistry, electrical energy, the internal combustion engine, the transition from sail to steam and from wooden to iron vessels, and the perfecting of new modes of communication and transportation. There was a progressive increase in the size both of plants and of companies. The tendency toward concentration of ownership was counteracted to some extent by the joint-stock principle and the diffusion of stock ownership. At the same time there was a grave weakening of the responsibility of ownership, since the main tangible connection of many of the holders of stocks with the enterprises represented by the stocks was the drawing of dividends. The connection of governments with business became more intimate as a result of the decline of *laissez-faire* conceptions, even in Great Britain, and also as a result of the growth of rival nationalistic ambitions in the world of trade and empire. Powerful corporations and cartels made increasingly insistent demands upon the political and diplomatic agencies and the armed forces of their respective countries for the protection and promotion of their interests throughout the world. The growth of large incomes produced potential capital seeking investment far beyond the needs for capital equipment for supplying the effective demands of domestic markets, because these markets were rigorously limited by the small incomes and restricted purchasing power of most of the population. The result was an intensified competition for markets and opportunities for profitable investment of large incomes throughout the less highly industrialized regions of the world. Industrialism reinforced nationalism and tended to transform nationalism into an agency of imperialism.

## Unstable European Boundary Lines

The main economic causes of tension between the national governments of Europe were rivalry for markets, territories, and spheres
of influence outside of Europe, and the instability of European areas
where political, ethnic, and economic boundary lines failed to coincide.  An ideal national state has been defined as an area comprising
a natural geographical and economic unit, inhabited by a people
with similar racial and cultural traits, and governed by a single
political authority.  The impossibility of achieving ideal national
states as thus defined is apparent even from a casual comparison of
the main economic, ethnic, and political divisions of Europe.  The
increasingly complex and interdependent nature of the economic
life of the European peoples added to the problem of achieving
separate political sovereignties on the basis of ethnic and economic
units.  Nationalistic ambitions gave little heed to the ideal basis
of political sovereignty and accentuated rather than mitigated the
difficulties inherent in the natural and racial environment.

The formation of the United Kingdom had involved the sub-
jugation of Ireland.  Russian, Austrian, and Prussian ambitions
had led to the partitioning of Poland.  The Baltic provinces of
Russia were subjected to Russian rule contrary to the wishes of
important elements of the population.  Alsace-Lorraine, although
at one time more closely associated with the Germans than with
France, had been under French rule so long that the annexation
of this region to Germany in 1871 was a breach of ethnic unity.
But the existence of rich iron mines in Lorraine and of the principal
European source of coking coal in the Ruhr valley affords an illustration of the frequent divergence of economic, ethnic, and political
boundaries.  In Austria-Hungary a large number of racial groups
opposed the rule of the Germans of Austria and of the Magyars of
Hungary.  In the Balkans a confused medley of races maintained
for the most part a comparatively simple agricultural mode of life,
but because of the vital importance of the region in the expansionist
plans of Russia, Germany, Austria-Hungary, and Italy, they were
peculiarly subject to nationalistic and imperialistic stresses and
strains.  The progress of nationalism among the major peoples
intensified the discontent of racial minorities and made increasingly
difficult the maintenance of peaceful diplomatic relations.  The
incident which occasioned the World War — the assassination of
Francis Ferdinand, crown prince of Austria-Hungary — was an

outgrowth of the nationalistic ambitions of the Yugoslav minority racial group in the Austro-Hungarian Empire.

## The Revival of Overseas Expansion

Significantly, the revival of British interest in overseas territorial expansion was simultaneous with the triumph of nationalism in Italy, Germany, and the United States, with the Austro-Hungarian Compromise, and with the reorganization of Japan on Western lines. The expansion of British territory had in fact never ceased; but the wisdom of further expansion, and even of retention of many of the existing territories, had been widely questioned in official as well as private circles. Disraeli's dramatic campaign as a champion of imperialism culminated in the victory in 1874 of the Conservative party and the ascendancy of imperialistic policies. An important factor in the reversal of sentiment was the work of the Royal Colonial Institute, organized in 1868.

In Germany, Bismarck was at first opposed to colonial expansion. He rejected various opportunities to acquire colonies, as Mozambique, offered for sale by Portugal, and held that colonies were costly luxuries. He believed that Germany's destiny was purely European. But German traders were soon penetrating Africa and the islands of the Pacific; German manufacturers, equipped with new techniques, found available markets increasingly inadequate; German bankers associated themselves with merchants and shippers who were interested in the exploitation of unappropriated regions; and German missionaries, extending their activities to various remote regions, called upon the government for protection. A flood of propagandist literature deluged the country. In 1882 a group was formed for stimulating interest in colonial projects and policies, and two years later the Society for German Colonization undertook the task of raising money by the sale of shares for buying land in Africa and undertaking the actual work of colonization. Bismarck, sensitive to the currents of influential opinion, had already begun to turn with the tide. His protective tariff policy of 1879 was soon followed by various measures for the promotion of trade and the staking out of German claims in areas not already appropriated by other powers.

In France, Napoleon III attempted to win popularity by an expansionist policy, one phase of which was the ill-starred Mexican venture of Maximilian, his protégé. It was not until the early 1880's that the Third Republic, under the leadership of Jules Ferry, re-entered the race for colonies and spheres of influence. Italy's colonial ambitions were intensified by frustration when France seized Tunisia — a fact which Bismarck utilized in securing Italy as a member of the Triple Alliance. Russia's ambitions, thwarted earlier by the Crimean War, found expression, again unsuccessfully, in the Russo-Turkish War of 1878. Among the lesser powers, Belgium entered the race for empire as early as 1876. In that year Leopold II, under the guise of promoter of scientific exploration and the Christianizing of the natives, sponsored a conference in Brussels and organized the International Association for the Exploration and Civilization of Africa.

Humanitarianism and science were brought into the service of imperialism. The enlightenment of backward peoples, the shouldering of "the white man's burden," and the advancement of geographical and scientific knowledge were conceptions which played a large part in imperialistic propaganda. The penetration and profitable exploitation of remote areas were facilitated by tropical medicine, modern communication and transportation, and new modes of utilizing natural resources, such as the vulcanizing of rubber and the refining of petroleum.

Essential factors in the revival of imperialism were the needs of a rapidly expanding industrialism. The growth of industrial states in Europe called for raw materials and foods and for markets where the products of machine technology could be sold. Restricted demand in home markets made necessary the expansion of external markets if the productive plants were to be operated profitably; and the building of tariff walls intensified the desire of merchants and manufacturers to obtain external markets under the national flag. But the utmost efforts to expand markets failed to provide sufficient opportunities for disposing of the output of industry and therefore for the profitable investment at home of all the rapidly accumulating surpluses of large incomes. The result was a keen rivalry for opportunities for investment abroad, preferably under the national flag.

Nationalism contributed to the revival of imperialism because the national state was the most effective instrumentality at the disposal of imperialistic industrialists and investors. Furthermore, the gratification of national pride and ambition could readily be associated in the popular mind with expansion of territory, the conquest of markets, and the prestige of world power. Such sentiments made possible the obscuring of the costs of imperialism by their absorption in part in the national budgets. Much of the capital invested abroad was dissipated in fruitless ventures, but losses were not serious. Large incomes were accumulating beyond the limits of opportunities for profitable investment, so these private losses, combined with tax burdens chargeable to imperialism, tended to reduce the sums available for investment to such proportions as to make possible the profitable use of surviving surplus income. There was an alternative use of surplus income for increased consumption and expanded production at home, but under the prevailing systems of income distribution this alternative was merely theoretical.

### The Decline of European Influence in America

The one region where European imperialism declined from 1870 to 1914 was the New World. In the Americas the extension of European imperialism was restricted by the policy of the United States centering around the Monroe Doctrine, formulated in a message to Congress by President Monroe on December 2, 1823. This declaration, although not recognized as a part either of American or of international law, became a symbol of the attitude of the United States. Numerous minor actions occurred contrary to the doctrine, but its existence and the growing strength and assertiveness of the United States after the Civil War in upholding and extending it undoubtedly account largely for the decline of European imperialism in the New World during a period of intensified search for new territories and spheres of influence. A particularly significant extension of the Monroe Doctrine was the claim by the United States of the right of intervention on account of revolutionary disturbances in nations of the Western Hemisphere, or on account of failure by these nations to make payments on debts due to foreigners. This was described by President Theodore Roosevelt in 1904 as "the exercise of an international police power."

When, in the 1820's, Spain's continental American colonies revolted, Great Britain championed their independence as a method of gaining access to their markets. As a result, British influence, already powerful, was greatly strengthened. Especially important from the point of view of the interests of the United States was the ascendancy of Great Britain in the Caribbean region and Central America. In the Clayton-Bulwer Treaty of 1850 the government of the United States succeeded in obtaining an agreement that neither country should control or fortify any isthmian canal that might be constructed, or colonize or control any part of Central America.

Briefly, the treaty provided for equality of status. Although the British regarded the agreement as a recession from their dominant position, it was opposed in the United States because it gave mere equality and also on the ground that it was contrary to the Monroe Doctrine. Nevertheless, the treaty was not abrogated until 1901. The Civil War, the westward movement, and the building of transcontinental railways and of a railway across the Isthmus of Panama caused a decline of American interest in the canal question and in the southward extension of American influence. But during the final decade of the century a series of events caused a revival of American interest and brought about not only a further decline of British influence but also the expulsion of Spain from the island remnants of her once dominant empire in the New World. In the meantime an abortive effort had been made under French auspices to construct a Panama canal.

Great Britain's boundary controversy with Venezuela led in 1895 to an unprecedentedly forceful reminder of American adherence to the Monroe Doctrine and caused Great Britain to yield to the demand for arbitration. The Spanish-American War, growing out of the Cuban revolt, brought under the American flag or under direct American influence the Spanish West Indian possessions and the Philippine Islands. These new territories and spheres of influence, combined with American interests in Hawaii, Samoa, and the Far East, made inevitable a revival of interest in the canal question. In the meantime Great Britain's grave problems in South Africa and her diplomatic isolation preceding the formation of the Triple Entente with France and Russia, created a situation favorable for reconsideration of the Clayton-Bulwer Treaty. The result was the Hay-Pauncefote Treaty of 1901. The new treaty withdrew the prohibitions of the Clayton-Bulwer Treaty on the acquisition of territory in Central America by the United States. It conceded to the United States, so far as Great Britain was concerned, the right to construct and fortify a canal. Although Great Britain gave up her position of equality under the Clayton-Bulwer Treaty, she nevertheless obtained a significant provision in the new treaty to the effect that there should be no discrimination, even in time of war, against other nations in the use of the canal.

### Territorial Expansion of European Empires, 1870–1914

Although Great Britain possessed a vast empire in 1870, the additional areas acquired by the British before the World War exceeded in importance the acquisitions of any other nation. In addition to obtaining new territories, the British made rapid progress in the settlement and development of the older empire. The area of colonization was rapidly extended. About two thirds of the 470,000 emigrants from the United Kingdom in 1913 remained within the British empire. Immigration and natural growth of population rapidly extended the settled areas of Canada, Australia, New Zealand, and South Africa and supplied the man power for carrying on the exploration, conquest, and control of other regions not adapted to colonization, either because of climatic conditions, as in tropical Africa, or because of the existing density of population, as in the Far East.

The positions already occupied by the British, and their world-wide connections and experience, gave to the British an outstanding advantage in obtaining any additional territory they desired. Thus in South Africa, expansion from areas long occupied eliminated the Dutch republics and brought about the occupation of Bechuanaland, Zululand, Rhodesia, and various other important territories. Walfisch (Walvis) Bay, commanding the coast of the area later claimed by Germany as German Southwest Africa, was acquired in 1878. In 1890 a protectorate was declared over the island of Zanzibar on the eastern coast, strategically important in relation to German East Africa. From early slave-trade centers on the west coast, especially Lagos, British rule was extended to Nigeria. After the opening of the Suez Canal in 1869 and the buying of shares in 1875 by Disraeli, the British obtained control of the more strategic points along the new route to the Far East. Cyprus in the eastern Mediterranean was acquired in 1878. British influence in Egypt was gradually extended to include the Sudan and the area south of Ethiopia. In 1884-1886 the principal harbors of Somaliland south of the southern Red Sea gateway were occupied. The control of the route to India and the checkmating of Russian expansion led to the establishment of a British sphere of influence in southern Persia. In the Far East, the area of British control was extended widely in India and Burma. British power in the Malay Peninsula was greatly expanded and strengthened. The northern part of Borneo and the southeastern part of New Guinea were acquired. Weihaiwei was leased from China. The Fiji group and a large number of other small islands in the Pacific and the Indian Ocean were added to the empire.

Next to the British, the French added most extensively to their imperial possessions from 1870 to 1914. A few additions had been made between 1815 and 1870. Louis Philippe extended French rule to Algeria and established posts in Guinea and the Ivory Coast of western Africa. Napoleon III acquired the island of New Caledonia, obtained footholds in Cochinchina and Cambodia (Cambodge), southeast of Siam, and occupied some of the harbors of Somaliland on the southwestern shores of the Red Sea. Under the Third Republic, expansion was resumed. A large and populous area extending northward from Cochinchina and including Annam, Laos, and Tonkin was joined to Cochinchina and Cambodia to form French Indochina, a region larger than France. In addition, China was later forced to lease to France for ninety-nine years the strategic Kwangchowan Bay region, with exclusive mining rights in certain adjacent areas. Expansion in Africa was also resumed. Tunisia was made a protectorate in 1881. French West Africa and the French Congo were connected with Algeria and Tunisia, and the French claimed Morocco, outside of the Spanish area in the northwest, as their sphere of influence. Madagascar and adjacent islands were occupied. In 1914 more than a third of Africa, excluding Morocco, was under French control, but a comparatively large part of the French empire was desert area.

The Germans not only had no non-European territories when the empire was founded in 1871 but had no ambitions, so far as their government was concerned, to acquire an empire. This attitude, however, was soon reversed by the impact of numerous and powerful forces interested in overseas expansion, and strenuous efforts were made by the government and by various private agencies to obtain territories and "a place in the sun." In 1914 Germany held four large areas in Africa — Kamerun (Cameroons), Togo, German Southwest Africa, and German East Africa — with an aggregate area of almost 1,000,000 square miles. In the Pacific, a portion of New Guinea was obtained and renamed Kaiser Wilhelm's Land. This area, together with various other Pacific islands acquired by Germany, aggregated almost 100,000 square miles with a population of more than 500,000. Kiaochow, a strategic coastal area of 200 square miles in the Shantung province of China, was leased by Germany and declared a German protectorate.

Italy in 1870 lacked great industries, powerful armaments, and diplomatic prestige. Nevertheless the Italians dreamed of ancient imperial glories and looked upon Tunis, the site of ancient Carthage, as the cornerstone of a new empire. When France seized Tunis in

1881, Italian imperialists were so affronted as to bring about an alliance between Italy and her late oppressor, Austria-Hungary. Italy then turned toward Ethiopia by way of Eritrea to the northeast and Somaliland to the southeast of Ethiopia. These two areas were almost valueless except as approaches to Ethiopia. The attempt to conquer the latter country failed, but Eritrea and Italian Somaliland were retained and made the bases of the victorious attack on Ethiopia in 1935. In the Far East, Italy in 1902 obtained from China a small concession at Tientsin. In 1911–1912 Italy, at the cost of a war with Turkey, obtained control of Libya, consisting of the comparatively sterile provinces of Tripoli and Cyrenaica between Tunisia and Egypt. During the Balkan wars Italy extended her influence over Albania, thus assuring control of the Adriatic.

Russian imperialism from 1870 to 1914 was marked by continued efforts to gain control of outlets to the Mediterranean, the Indian Ocean, and the Pacific. The more important territorial additions and new spheres of influence included Bessarabia, the Batum region, northern Persia, central Asia, outer Mongolia, and northern Manchuria. Toward the Mediterranean, Russian advance was barred by European rivals, using Turkey as a buffer state. ˙ Toward India and the Indian Ocean, the advance was opposed by every device at the disposal of Great Britain, including the establishment of rival spheres of influence in Persia and Afghanistan. In the Far East, Japan, aided diplomatically by the British, not only checked the Russian advance but turned the Russians back and won for herself the control of Chosen (Korea) and predominant influence in southern Manchuria, particularly by the transfer to herself of the vitally important Chinese concessions in the region of Port Arthur.

Among the lesser powers of Europe, the principal territorial gains were made by Belgium in the acquisition of the Congo region, about eighty times the size of Belgium. The Spanish empire suffered further decline as a result of the revolt of Cuba and the Spanish-American War. The Portuguese and Dutch empires, survivals from the seventeenth century, underwent little change after 1870. Since Portugal was a satellite of Great Britain and was unable to make extensive use of her territories, the British derived peculiar advantages, especially from Angola and Mozambique, without suffering the costs and responsibilities of imperial administration. In the principal ports of Mozambique even the monetary system was predominantly British.

## Imperialism and Colonization

An argument frequently advanced in favor of imperialism was the need of land for colonization by the rapidly growing populations of Europe. Most of the available areas suitable for colonization by Europeans were controlled by the British, Russians, and French or were in the New World where European domination was barred by the sovereignty of the several countries and by the Monroe Doctrine.

British colonization continued at an increasing rate before 1914. The average number of emigrants from the United Kingdom from 1870 to 1914 was 238,000 a year. Toward the end of the period the numbers were much larger than earlier, and the proportion of emigrants going to countries within the British Empire increased. In 1913, 78,000 went to Australia and New Zealand, 26,000 to South Africa, and 196,000 to Canada. The settlement of the sparsely occupied areas of Russia in Asia resembled the westward expansion in the United States. Large numbers of Russian Jews and other minority races emigrated to other countries, the main cause being racial discriminations. The French, among the major European peoples, were least inclined toward emigration, but they possessed, next to the British and the Russians, the principal areas adapted to colonization by whites. Before the World War the total number of Frenchmen in Algeria and Tunisia was hardly more than half a million, and in other parts of the French empire the number of Frenchmen other than officials and soldiers was negligible.

German migration was extensive during the last quarter of the nineteenth century, the largest number of emigrants in a single year being 221,000 in 1881. Toward the end of the century there was a decline. In spite of efforts to encourage colonization, emigration to the German colonies was negligible. The total white population of all the German dependencies in 1913 was less than 25,000. The Italian government estimated that in 1910 there were 5,558,000 Italians abroad. Emigrants in 1911 numbered 711,000. In Eritrea and Italian Somaliland there were only a few thousand Italian settlers, and ten years after the acquisition of Libya the number of Italian colonists there was probably not more than 20,000.

The conspicuous lack of success of Italy and Germany in utilizing their overseas territories for colonization was partly due to the fact that these territories were not so well adapted for colonization as the regions which other countries had already acquired. This fact tended to embitter them in their struggle for territories and to emphasize the expatriation of Italians and Germans, many of whom were becoming British and French citizens in the overseas dominions which they felt they had a right to share. The rapidly expanding industries of Germany absorbed the population except in periods of depression, and the immediate problem of surplus population was not acute. In Italy, on the other hand, population continued to grow more rapidly than opportunities for productive employment at home. The desire for territories suitable for colonization arose in part from prospects of future surpluses of population, from ambitions for future expansion, and from national pride and envy of states with abundant land.

Territories not suited to colonization were held to be valuable in supporting larger populations at home by virtue of the opportunities they afforded for investment, trade, and the expansion of industry and national wealth. Nevertheless, the experiences of the various countries in their efforts to secure overseas territories, whether suited to colonization or not, were costly in the extreme and were a principal cause of controversy and war. There is evidence in support of the view that intercourse with other regions without the risks and expenses of political and military control would have been more profitable and advantageous than ventures in imperialism, alike to the subject and to the dominant peoples.

### Imperialism and Trade

Territorial expansion was frequently advocated on the ground that dependencies under the national flag were necessary for national security in obtaining essential raw materials and maintaining export markets. The experiences of the older imperialistic powers, notably Great Britain, were cited as proving the value of imperial connections in promoting trade. Trade statistics gave a degree of plausibility to the argument.

In 1912 exports from the United Kingdom to the principal British possessions were as follows: to Australia and New Zealand, about two thirds of their total imports; to the Straits Settlements, one tenth; to India (1912–1913), almost two thirds; to the Union of South Africa, almost three fifths; to Canada, 45 per cent; and to the British West Indies, more than one third. Exports from the same dependencies to the United Kingdom were as follows: from Australia, about two fifths of all exports; from New Zealand, more than three fourths; from India, about one fourth; from the Straits Settlements, somewhat less than one fourth; from the Union of South Africa, nine tenths; from Canada, one fifth; and from the West Indies, one fourth. In addition, much of the trade not carried on directly with the United Kingdom was within the empire, and because of the predominance of the United Kingdom financial and shipping interests, intercolonial trade was presumably more beneficial to the home country than trade between imperial areas and foreign countries.

In 1912 more than two fifths of the trade of the French dependencies was with France. With the exception of rice, the products of the Dutch East Indies went mainly to Holland. The trade of the dependencies of Belgium, Germany, and Italy was largely with these countries, but the amount of colonial trade in comparison with total trade was almost negligible.

Trade statistics were often cited to support the policies of territorial expansion for increasing the volume of trade and for obtaining control of raw materials. But various considerations must be taken into account in evaluating the prevailing view. Even on the assumption that existing imperial connections were commercially profitable, after deducting the costs of empire, to the peoples already possessing empires, this alone is not sufficient evidence that the acquisition of territories by other peoples would have been profitable to them. Great Britain, Holland, and to a lesser extent France had early acquired maritime experience and facilities, financial resources, and industrial skills. Their world-wide contacts and the flexibility of their institutions favored them. If the territories of these countries had been divided among the other powers of Europe with newly acquired imperialistic ambitions, even without the devastating cost of war and conquest, the advantage to these countries would have been doubtful; for success in the imperial relation depended on geographical, historical, and political qualifications in part bestowed by nature and in part evolved in the costly school of experience.

The attempts of Italy and Germany to establish empires cost the peoples of these countries, even before the World War, many times the returns obtained from their territories. Even the British, favored as they were by nature, history, and experience, found their empire to be increasingly burdensome. In South Africa, for example, individuals and groups found profit in trade, gold, or diamonds, but the Boer War alone cost the British people approximately £250,000,000.   Colonial markets, although valuable under imperial controls, could hardly have been less valuable to the peoples of commercial countries if the subject countries had been independent or, in the case of uncivilized areas, under appropriate international arrangements.

Trade between the sovereign nations before the World War was vastly more important in volume and value than colonial trade. Even in the case of Great Britain, imports from the British possessions in 1910 were only one fourth of the total imports; exports of British produce to the possessions were only one third of the total; and re-exports of foreign and colonial produce to the possessions were only about one tenth of total re-exports.   With few exceptions, access to colonial markets by countries other than the possessors of colonies was on a basis of virtual equality.   Producers of raw materials and foods in the various colonies were eager to sell their products to the nationals of any country which could use them and pay for them; and consumers in the colonies were equally eager to buy what they needed abroad from the nationals of any country which offered them the best prices and terms.   The remarkable expansion of German trade before the World War was in part attributable to the penetration of the colonial markets of other countries without the costs and responsibilities of administering the colonies.

### Imperialism and Investments

The propagandists of imperialism emphasized the view that territorial expansion was necessary for commercial growth and security, in respect both of export markets and of supplies of food and raw materials.   This view could be expressed persuasively and with popular appeals for the support of imperialism as being in the national interest.   The promotion and protection of private investments abroad played a much less prominent part in public discussions but perhaps an even more vital role in the actual shaping of imperialistic policies.

British national wealth has been estimated as exceeding fourteen billion pounds in 1914, with more than four billion pounds invested abroad.   Almost half of the four billions was invested in the empire. More than half a billion was invested in Canada and Newfoundland, and approximately half a billion in Australia and New Zealand. India and Ceylon accounted for about four hundred millions, and South Africa for almost the same amount.   Investments in the less extensively developed areas outside of the empire included more than three hundred million pounds in Latin America and large sums throughout the rest of the world.  The Board of Trade, the Bank of England, Lloyd's, and other agencies had gradually developed information services and staffs for expert advice which contributed effectively to maintaining the position of Great Britain as the world's chief banker.

French foreign investments in 1914 totaled about forty-five billion francs, approximately 15 per cent of the country's national wealth.  Investments in the French colonies amounted to only about four billion francs.  The largest amount invested in any one country was in Russia — eleven billion three hundred million francs. Loans to Russia were particularly significant because of their connection with the political and military alliance between France and Russia.  Loans to Latin America amounted to about six billion francs.  Germany's foreign investments were probably not more than twenty-five billion marks, perhaps 7 per cent of the national wealth.  The investments were widely scattered, with three billions in Latin America and two billions in Africa.  Foreign and imperial investments of other European countries were comparatively unimportant with the exception of the investments of the Dutch and the Belgians in their dependencies, and of the Russians in their Asiatic empire.

British loans to foreign governments before the World War amounted to about three hundred million pounds.  French and German loans to governments formed a much larger proportion of total investments.  Next to the securities of governments, the stocks and bonds of railroads were the most popular forms of foreign and imperial investments.  Loans were often intimately connected with political alliances, with economic concessions to the nationals of the creditor countries, and with the establishment of spheres of influence.  Notable instances were the British military occupation and financial control of Egypt, and the French "peaceful penetration" of Morocco.  Enforcement of the conditions embodied in loan contracts was a frequent cause of intervention in various forms. These contracts often involved not merely repayment of principal with interest but also intricate details regarding security, fiscal control, and economic concessions.  It was largely in connection with loans by Europe and the United States to Latin-American countries and the threats of European intervention on behalf of creditors that President Theodore Roosevelt in 1904 reinterpreted the Monroe Doctrine as involving "the exercise of an international police power" by the United States. The new financial imperialism, with long-term investments abroad, put increasing pressure on the governments of the investors to extend political control over areas to which capital was being exported. Financial imperialism thus became even more aggressive than commercial imperialism.

### Concessions, Strategic Areas, and Spheres of Influence

The "battle of concessions" was a term applied by a British diplomat to the situation in China near the end of the last century. But the battle was not confined to that period nor to China. It is possible merely to mention some outstanding instances of the struggles throughout the world among imperialistic powers for concessions involving loans, extraterritoriality, railroads, mining rights, construction contracts, strategic areas, spheres of influence, and other aspects of the intricate game of imperialism. Available information is restricted by limited access to diplomatic archives and company records and by the destruction of records, as those of the late Sir Basil Zaharoff, international munitions magnate.

British control of Egypt grew out of concessions, originally to Frenchmen for the most part, relating to loans and the construction of the Suez Canal. The virtual bankruptcy of Ismail, Khedive of Egypt, enabled Disraeli to buy the Khedive's canal shares. Continued financial difficulties led to international fiscal control in the interest of the French and British creditors. When Ismail tried to throw off this control, the British and French governments sent armed forces. Later the French withdrew, leaving the field to the British, who had become keenly aware of the strategic value of Egypt in relation to their Red Sea route to India. Ultimately the British claimed the entire Nile valley as their sphere of influence, won joint control of the Anglo-Egyptian Sudan, checked the French in their efforts to win exclusive concessions for a railroad from Djibouti through Ethiopia to the Nile, and turned back the tide of French expansion eastward in the region of the sources of the Nile.

The French occupied Tunisia largely because the government of Tunis favored Italians in making concessions. In Morocco the advantages of the French in respect to concessions for loans, public works, railroads, and mines precipitated crises which more than once threatened war.

Annexation of primitive African areas was often preceded by

concessions embodied in "treaties." Thus in 1884 four chieftains in East Africa were induced to "sign" papers presented to them by an enterprising German adventurer, and they found later that they had virtually surrendered their kingdoms to a German company. This was the beginning of German East Africa. In 1888 a powerful chieftain in South Africa "signed" a document which in his view merely permitted certain visitors to dig for gold in return for arms, a steamboat, and specified sums of money. He later discovered that the "treaty" gave to the British exclusive rights to minerals in his kingdom, which soon became Southern Rhodesia. Another form of concession in primitive areas was devised in the Congo. The International Association for the Exploration and Civilization of Central Africa, sponsored by Leopold II of Belgium, was transformed in 1885 into the government of the "Congo Free State," with Leopold II as sovereign. All "vacant" lands were declared the property of the state, that is, in effect, of Leopold II as sovereign. Concessions were then granted to private companies, Leopold reserving shares for himself, the companies being granted virtually sovereign powers over both natives and natural resources in specified areas. In 1899 the French government adopted a similar system in the French Congo.

A concession which attained outstanding international importance was granted in 1888 to a group of Germans by the Turkish government. The original concession was for the building of a railroad to connect Constantinople (Istanbul) with Angora (Ankara). After long delays due largely to the opposition of Russia and Great Britain, the concession was extended in 1903 to include the building of a railroad to connect Constantinople with the Persian Gulf — the Bagdad Railway — and the construction of branch lines to tap contiguous areas, including Persia. The Turkish government agreed to sell bonds to finance the project, the money to be loaned to the company and secured by a mortgage on the railroad, which was ultimately to revert to the government. The company was guaranteed against operating losses, was exempted from taxation, and was granted mineral rights in an area forty kilometers wide along the right of way.

The financing and control of the road involved increasingly the rival imperial interests of Germans, Britons, Russians, and Frenchmen. The British feared the project would menace their line of communications through the Indian Ocean and extend the influence of Germany at their expense. The Russians opposed the project because they feared it would strengthen Turkey as a buffer state under German control and would cut off their southward expansion toward the Mediterranean and the Red Sea. Diplomatic and financial difficulties, the Balkan Wars, and the Young Turk Revolution combined to prevent the completion of the project, which became one of the outstanding issues culminating in the World War.

Another area important alike because of imperial strategy and natural resources, particularly petroleum, was Persia. William K. D'Arcy, a British adventurer and promoter, obtained an oil concession from Persia in 1901. Out of this concession emerged in 1909 the Anglo-Persian Oil Company, which, in 1914, was bought by the British government. The struggle for oil and for control of southern Persia as a highly strategic area on the Indian Ocean involved Great Britain in bitter controversies with Russia, which desired access through Persia to the ocean. The controversies were compromised in 1907 by the Anglo-Russian Entente.

The battle for concessions in China began with the mid-century breach in China's wall of isolation. But intensified rivalry began in the last decade of the century. Important episodes were the leasing of ports in 1898 — Kiaochow to Germany, Port Arthur to Russia, Kwangchowan to France, and Weihaiwei and also land near Hong Kong to Great Britain. Accompanying the leasing of the ports was the staking of claims to spheres of influence — by France in the three southern provinces; by Great Britain in the rich Yangtze valley of central China with an area connecting with Peking (now Peiping); by Germany in Shantung; by Russia in Manchuria and Mongolia; and by Japan in Chosen (Korea) and, after the Russo-Japanese War, in southern Manchuria. In each of these areas concessions were obtained for the building of railroads and for exploiting mineral resources. By the end of the century, the British had obtained concessions to build 2,800 miles of railroad; the Russians, 1,530; the Germans, 720; and the French, 420.

The main battles for concessions were not between other countries and China, which was virtually helpless, but between the rival empires. Between Great Britain and Germany an agreement at length was reached in 1898 for excluding Germans from Shansi and the Yangtze valley in the interest of the British, and for excluding the British from Shantung in the interest of the Germans. In 1899 Russia agreed to keep hands off the British sphere of influence and the British agreed to stay south of the Great Chinese Wall.

In 1899 the American Secretary of State, John Hay, announced the Open Door policy in opposition to the exclusive rights claimed by European powers and Japan. In 1900 the Chinese were aroused sufficiently against the "foreign devils" to stage the Boxer uprising. The chief result was international action to suppress the uprising. Extreme and humiliating penalties were imposed upon the Chinese government. Although Americans had little part in the concessions, American bankers desired to share the financing of railroads and other enterprises, and after personal intervention by President Taft in 1909, they obtained this right. In the so-called Consortium of 1912 there was agreement for a loan of $125,000,000 to the new government of China after the revolution of 1911. Bankers of Great Britain, France, Russia, Germany, Japan, and the United States were to participate, with the backing of their governments. Final arrangements were not made until after the inauguration of President Wilson. He objected to American participation on the ground that the loan was granted on conditions which forced excessive concessions from the Chinese government and infringed its independence and sovereignty.

## Imperialism and the System of Alliances

The imperialistic ambitions of the principal national states involved these states in almost continuous controversies over boundaries, tariffs, territories, investments, concessions, and spheres of influence. During the half century preceding the World War, grave diplomatic differences or actual conflict characterized the relations even of the countries which later were leagued together in the World War. Austria and Prussia waged war in 1866, and although Austria-Hungary and Germany were later in alliance, they had serious conflicts of interest, especially in the Balkans. Italy, which joined the Allied Powers during the World War, was earlier in league with Germany and Austria-Hungary. Great Britain and Russia had clashes over various strategic areas, and in 1898 Great Britain and France seemed on the point of war over rival claims in Africa.

Gradually the principal differences between Germany, Austria-Hungary, and Italy were adjusted to such an extent as to enable these countries to join forces in the Triple Alliance, and as a counterpoise democratic France and absolutist Russia entered into a Dual Alliance. Bismarck's policy was designed to isolate France diplomatically as a method of thwarting revenge for the defeat of 1871.

To this end he attempted to keep Russia, Austria-Hungary, and Italy within the orbit of German diplomacy. In 1873 he succeeded in forming the Three Emperors' League of Germany, Austria-Hungary, and Russia, but this was disrupted by the rival ambitions of Austria-Hungary and Russia in the Balkans and by the thwarting of Russia's aims in the Russo-Turkish War of 1877–1878. In 1882 Bismarck succeeded in bringing Italy into the alliance with Austria-Hungary, in spite of the traditional hostility between Austria and Italy. A principal cause of Italy's action was Bismarck's support of Italian claims in Africa after the occupation of Tunisia by France. Russia was again induced to enter into mutual agreements with Germany and Austria-Hungary, but conflicting ambitions in the Balkans soon made it apparent that Germany must choose for an ally either Russia or Austria-Hungary, and she naturally favored the latter. The French government, on the other hand, supported the imperialistic ambitions of Russia by approving the loan of vast sums of money for Russian armaments and the modernizing of Russian industries in return for diplomatic collaboration and for aid in the event of war with Germany. A diplomatic understanding was arranged in 1891, and this was followed in 1893 by a military alliance, ratified January 4, 1894.

Great Britain at first played her traditional role of utilizing Continental differences while avoiding definite commitments either to the Triple Alliance or to the Dual Alliance. Both groups sought British support, but at first British imperialism seemed to be more seriously challenged by the Russians and the French. For a time British policy veered toward the Triple Alliance, although in any case German hegemony in Europe depended not on active British support but merely on British neutrality. But German policy after the dismissal of Bismarck made British neutrality increasingly difficult. By the turn of the century Germany was rapidly emerging as a world power, with commercial, financial, colonial, and naval ambitions in conflict with British imperialism. These soon overshadowed British controversies with the French and the Russians. Furthermore Great Britain had grave diplomatic and imperial problems, such as the Venezuelan boundary controversy and the Boer War, which made diplomatic isolation seem less tolerable. Gradually the British accepted the view that they could no longer safely remain detached from Continental alliances or effectively utilize Continental differences by alternately playing one nation or one alliance against another.

The British government first undertook to settle its outstanding differences with the French. These involved rival imperial claims in various parts of the world — fishing rights near Newfoundland, the sovereignty of the New Hebrides islands, territories in West Africa, old claims in Madagascar and Zanzibar, and, chiefly important, spheres of influence in Egypt, Morocco, and Siam. An agreement was reached in 1904. France recognized Britain's special position in Egypt, and the British agreed to give the French virtually a free hand in Morocco. Other aspects of the entente were similar — essentially they were demarcations of the areas over which each of the two countries was to rule or exert predominant influence. In 1912 a military agreement between the diplomatic agents of the two countries further strengthened the entente.

The British also attacked the problem of Russian relations, and agreements were signed in 1907. Russia recognized Great Britain's "special interests" in the Persian Gulf and yielded to the British in the matter of political and commercial concessions to be obtained from the Persian government in southern Persia, "such as concessions for railways, banks, telegraphs, roads, transport, insurance, etc." Great Britain similarly conceded the predominance of Russian claims in northern Persia. Agreements were also entered into in regard to Afghanistan and Tibet. The essence of the latter agreements was the assurance that these regions would remain as buffer states between British India and Russia. The Anglo-Russian understanding of 1907 was the final step in the formation of the Triple Entente, which, with the Triple Alliance, set the stage for a major historical tragedy — the World War.

# PART VI. THE NEW EUROPE

# CHAPTER 32

## THE PRODUCTION AND CONSUMPTION OF POWER, 1910–1930

———◆———

### The Development of Central Electric Stations

The telegraph used so little electricity that its requirements were long served by batteries.  No effective dynamo was available until the work of Pacinotti laid the foundations for the modern types, and even then it was some time before the development of the electromagnet afforded the means of building powerful machines. The perfection of the dynamo and the motor in the late 1870's made possible applications to lighting and transport which soon developed a demand for power.  The pioneer work in this field was done by Edison in the United States, and the Siemens brothers in Germany. Despite important work in pure science, England was a little slow to make the primary practical applications.  The United States led in the development of the incandescent light.  Germany was first, by a small margin, in the development of the electric railway. Both of these applications required large amounts of power.  The first practical electric railway was opened in Germany in 1881. The first lighting systems with a central station were put into operation in the United States in 1882 : in Appleton, Wisconsin ; Sunbury, Pennsylvania ;  Pearl Street, New York City.

The requirements for power developed rapidly as the systems of lighting became more comprehensive, and as the networks of the street railways embraced larger areas.  Within a very short space of time, the central stations began to produce power on a scale never before realized.  After 1890 electric stations were installing great triple-expansion engines of a type previously used only in marine transport, and these units were quickly pushed to the practical limits of safe construction.  In less than a decade these stations surpassed any units previously constructed for the production of power. But these developments were no more than a beginning : there were new problems of investment and utilization which were destined to carry centralization of power production to much greater lengths.

Throughout this period the lighting companies and the street railways ordinarily maintained independent power stations. Both types of service, too, were divided among different companies serving a single area or adjoining areas. This arrangement proved to be uneconomical, because the demand for electric energy was unequally distributed through the twenty-four hours. Even in winter, the demand for electric light was largely confined to the interval between dusk and ten P.M. There was some demand for the early morning hours, but it was a shorter period and the total amount of energy required was much less. Furthermore, even within these periods, there were variations in demand. The heaviest daily demand for lighting is concentrated in an interval of scarcely more than half or three quarters of an hour. Much of the capacity of the plant lies unutilized for the greater part of the day. A plant designed to supply a single type of service might well be using less than one tenth of its full capacity to produce power. This ratio between total capacity and actual utilization is commonly defined as the "load factor"; the proportion of useful load carried by the plant.

The large amount of capital invested in electric power stations and in their transmission systems makes it a matter of great importance to secure the fullest possible degree of utilization. There were two means by which plant utilization could be increased. The production of power could be more completely centralized so that all the different demands for power would be served by single power systems. New uses for electricity could be developed at the hours during which the plant was least fully utilized. In practice, both lines of action have been followed. Both procedures are directed towards building up a greater diversity in the demand for power, so that the intervals of idleness shall be reduced to a minimum.

The attempt to secure economy of operation set in motion a tendency towards centralization of power production which seems likely to continue until complete consolidation is reached, not only in particular localities but even over large areas. The importance of the economies that can be achieved is indicated by the differences in the cost of power in two districts of England. In 1917 Lancashire was supplied with electricity by twenty independent municipal plants. The region is densely populated, and electricity was extensively utilized. Costs per unit, however, ranged from a minimum of .66 pence to 2.42 pence; the average cost was about 1.50 pence. In the North East Coast industrial district, where power production was more completely centralized, the cost per unit averaged less than .50 pence.  This stage of centralization began simultaneously in the first decade of the present century, in the United States, Great Britain, and Germany, and concentration proceeded rapidly in the years immediately preceding the World War, and during the war.

## The Production of Electricity

The development of the electrical services created many new opportunities and problems in power engineering.  The possibilities of the use of water power were greatly increased.  Hitherto, water power could be used only for the production of motion, and the limited possibilities of transmission of motion restricted the effective use of water power to waterworks and to industrial plants that could be conveniently located at the power site.  It now became possible to convert water power into a generalized form of energy that could be converted into light, or heat, and, even in the earliest period, transmitted over considerable distances.

In less than ten years after the invention of the incandescent lamp, hydroelectric lighting systems were being installed in the mountainous sections of central Europe and Scandinavia.  Tramways were built in sparsely settled districts that had been dependent on the simplest facilities for transport.  Large industrial plants, already using water power at great power sites, found it more convenient to produce electricity and to apply motors to the various machines in the plant.  It soon became evident that even the largest power sites could be utilized.

The development of water powers did not require any new inventions outside the electrical field.  The hydraulic turbine, invented in 1832, had already been fully developed.  In 1880 it was possible to design a turbine to meet the requirements of any power site.  Wheels could be designed to utilize a small mountain stream falling through a great height, or a large flow of water with a drop of only a few feet.  The great volume of Niagara combined with the height of the fall made it necessary to build equipment of unusual strength, but the elements of novelty were confined to these matters of scale.  The first electric plant at Niagara Falls, opened in 1881, was equipped with two turbines; but only a part of the energy produced was converted into electricity.  Plans for a larger development were drawn up in 1890, and construction of a new powerhouse began in 1891.  This unit was provided with 10 turbines connected with generators rated at 5,000 horsepower each. This successful and ambitious project did much to emphasize the importance of water power, but for many years it remained one of the largest hydroelectric installations in the world.

The characteristic feature of the early development in Europe was the large number of relatively small installations. In 1900 only one hydroelectric plant in Austria was rated at a capacity of more than 1,000 horsepower, and many of the plants were of less than 500 horsepower. In Switzerland in 1914, the scale of the plants was largely determined by the possibilities of marketing the power, and prior to 1900 the electrical systems were predominantly

WATER POWER PLANTS OF MORE THAN 20 H. P. IN OPERATION IN
SWITZERLAND, JANUARY 1, 1914 [1]

| Minimum Constant Capacity, H. P. | Number of Plants | Total Mean Capacity, H. P. |
|---|---|---|
| 20–99 | 561 | 36,042 |
| 100–999 | 217 | 92,909 |
| 1,000–4,999 | 41 | 139,927 |
| 5,000–9,999 | 10 | 100,940 |
| 10,000 or more | 6 | 117,400 |
| | 835 | 487,218 |

local. The smaller power sites were being rapidly developed, and the general features of the technique were established, but the major sites could not at this time be successfully used.

The development of the electrical industry was even more profoundly influenced by the application of the steam turbines. Small units, ranging from five horsepower to several hundred, were commonly based on the de Laval patents of 1882. The larger units, ranging from several hundred to several thousand horsepower, were based on the Parsons type, invented in 1884. The first notable installation of the Parsons turbine was in 1894, at the Manchester Square Station of the Metropolitan Electric Supply Company of London. The turbine was especially suitable to the requirements of electric generating stations because of the high speeds of revolution. Dynamos were run, even in the early days, at speeds of 1,000 to 1,500 revolutions per minute. The reciprocating engine was not capable of such high speeds, so that gears were necessary to increase the speed of the driving shaft. The early turbines attained speeds that were inconveniently high: 10,000–30,000 revolutions per minute in the de Laval type; 1,000–18,000 in the Parsons type.

[1] U. S. Atlas of Commercial Geology, vol. II, p. 25.

Later developments in steam turbine design, notably by C. G. Curtis in the United States, achieved economies of operation of very great importance to the electrical industry.

The steam turbines have been a noteworthy achievement in power engineering. The turbine is a more efficient mechanism than the reciprocating engine, and large units can be built with substantial economies in construction and operation. In 1900 the reciprocating engines of 6,000–8,000 horsepower were presumed to have reached their limit. Larger engines of these types have since been constructed, but the turbines have been carried far beyond these limits. By 1912 turbines of 20,000 horsepower had been built, and in 1919 the Berlin station at Klingenberg installed a turbine rated at 108,000 horsepower. These very large units are still rare; most of the current is generated in plants whose basic units range between 10,000 and 20,000 horsepower. It is quite clear, however, that the dominant tendency today is towards the larger units. The turbines have largely displaced the reciprocating engines. In England and in Germany more than 80 per cent of steam-generated electricity is produced by turbine units.

The large turbines achieve fuel economies of great importance. Conditions are difficult because of the substantial variations in the demand for power during the day. The marine engine, operating continuously at its most favorable speeds, achieved good results. The best marine records of the late nineteenth century reduced coal consumption to 1.9 pounds per horsepower hour. In 1900 the highly efficient plant of the Commonwealth Edison at Chicago used 5.17 pounds of coal per horsepower hour (6.90 pounds per kilowatt hour). The great central stations show rapid improvement in fuel economy. At Chicago, coal consumption was reduced from 6.90 pounds per kilowatt hour in 1900 to 2.87 pounds in 1913. In 1924 the Colfax station at Pittsburgh consumed 1.29 pounds of coal per kilowatt hour. In 1928 the best practice in the United States reduced coal consumption to .89 pound. In Germany the results of improved methods were closely comparable. The best works report the following records for production of electricity in terms of high-grade bituminous coal: in 1913, 2.53–2.31 pounds per kilowatt hour; in 1924–1925, 1.93 pounds; in 1929–1930, .99–.88 pound.

## The Technique of Long-Distance Transmission

The development of the technique of transmission was also of primary importance. Experiments with long-distance transmission began at an early date.   In connection with the Electrical Exhibition at Munich in 1882, Marcel Desprez of Paris operated a fountain with a pump driven by electricity generated at Miesbach, 37 miles away.   The installation was small; less than one half a horsepower of energy was available at Munich, only 38.9 per cent of the electricity generated.   The tension was rated at 1,343 volts.   In the following year further experiments were made near Paris and Grenoble.   More significant was the demonstration at Paris in October, 1885.   A current of 5,469 volts was used.   The generator at Creil operated at an average rate of 53.5 horsepower, and 41.4 horsepower was available at the motor in Paris, 36 miles distant. The loss in transmission was only 23 per cent.   These experiments attracted much attention, but costs were high and no considerable practical results followed.   Development was impeded by Edison's fear of the high voltages necessary for economical transmission, and though the direct influence of Edison was greatest in the United States, it was by no means unimportant in England and Continental Europe.

Effective achievement of long-distance transmission was accomplished by the group working with alternating currents. The first experiments with the transmission of such currents were made by Circhi in Italy in 1886.   The three-phase system ultimately used for transmission was developed shortly after by the independent but simultaneous work of Tesla, Ferrario, and Bradley.   In 1891 experiments were made between Frankfort on the Main and Lauffen with an alternating current of 25,000 volts.   In the course of the decade the commercial details of such transmission systems were fully developed, though the distances involved were short.   In the early years of the present century, transmitting systems worked at tensions up to 30,000 or 40,000 volts.   The first work in Europe with tensions in excess of 100,000 volts was done in 1912, between Lauchhammer and Riesa;   the system developed a tension of 110,000 volts.   In 1922 work was done with tension of 220,000 volts.   At 110,000 volts, energy could be transmitted 125 miles with a loss of 10 per cent.   At 220,000 volts, the radius of transmission was doubled.

## Projects for the Integration of Power Production

The developments in the technique of long-distance transmission opened up a wide range of new opportunities for the development of power installations.   Power systems were still essentially local in the years immediately preceding the World War, and even in particular localities the production of power was very incompletely centralized. In England and in Continental Europe, lighting systems were commonly controlled by the municipality. Street traction was commonly in the hands of private companies, and in the larger cities the streetcar lines were rarely in the control of a single company. The larger industrial companies using electricity were still producing their own power. But new tendencies appeared in all the leading countries; small territorial power systems developed in Germany, England, and the United States. In the Newcastle area, in the Ruhr, and in the industrialized area between Chemnitz and Berlin, power systems were being developed which embraced considerable areas, though no single company or authority possessed complete control of the production and distribution of electricity. The great companies, however, were able to demonstrate concretely the advantages that might be secured by greater integration in power production.

The significance of these developments was clearly perceived. In 1910 Mr. Z. D. de Ferranti proposed the comprehensive coordination of the generation and distribution of electricity in Great Britain. In 1912 Mr. Insull declared that it would be possible to develop a comprehensive interconnected power system for the entire industrial area between Boston and Philadelphia. Although no comprehensive plan was suggested in Germany, consolidation proceeded rapidly by voluntary combination of private companies and the active participation of the state and imperial governments in the acquisition of electrical systems.

Curiously enough, no country of Continental Europe proceeded as rapidly as Great Britain with a program of deliberate central planning. The proposals rather lightly made by de Ferranti were studied (1917) with care by a Sub-Committee on Coal Conservation appointed by the Ministry of Reconstruction. The report of this committee led directly to the passage of the Electricity Supply Act of 1919 (December 23). This action was inspired by the recognition of the gravity of the situation in Great Britain. The early development of municipal ownership had resulted in the establishment of a large number of relatively small undertakings. The general level of efficiency was low; fuel consumption was excessive, and poor load factors made the cost of electricity high even in the municipal plants. It was freely admitted that power production was, on the whole, much less efficient than in Germany or the

United States.   In a few sections there were large efficient systems, but the general condition was bad.   There was determined opposition to change, both from private companies and especially from the municipal corporations.   The act of 1919 was designed to meet these objections.

## The British Electricity Supply Acts of 1919 and 1926

The act of 1919 provided for the appointment by the Minister of Transport of five Electricity Commissioners.   The commissioners were given authority to conduct experiments for the improvement of methods for the supply of electricity, or for the more efficient utilization of fuel or water.   The general purpose of the act was to bring about a complete co-ordination of the production of power, so that all primary users and producers should be connected with a comprehensive electric network.   Companies producing power for their own use were to deliver all excess over their needs to the general system.   On account of the sharp opposition no positive pressure of authority was placed upon existing companies to join the system.

The commissioners were authorized to designate specified areas to be organized as electricity supply districts, but no orders were to be put into effect until local authorities and producers of electricity had been heard.   Existing interests were then called upon to submit a scheme or schemes for the improvement of electricity supply.   If no scheme was submitted, the commissioners were authorized to prepare a scheme.   A joint electricity authority might then be set up in the district.   This authority would be in effect a cartel or a complete consolidation of all the producers of electricity willing to join the association.   Through these authorities it was intended to bring about the standardization of equipment necessary to form a well co-ordinated power system.   New construction was obliged to conform to the requirements of the commissioners and even stations outside the system were required to follow the orders of the commissioners as to the voltages and frequencies of the current produced.

Joint electricity authorities were set up under this act in London and in a number of other areas, but progress was slow.   The problem was studied by a small committee consisting of Lord Weir, Lord Forres, and Sir Hardman Lever.   The report of the committee became the basis of the Electricity Supply Act of 1926.

This act of 1926 created a Central Electricity Board with substantial powers of initiative and control.  The board consists of seven members appointed by the Minister of Transport.  It has corporate powers, and though it was not intended that it should acquire or build generating stations, it is allowed to do so in special cases.  The primary function of the board is to make provisions for the planned production of electricity throughout Great Britain, and to act as a wholesale distributing agency within the system. Stations in the system are required to make contracts with the board even for the electricity required for their own use.  The board has, however, no direct contact with consumers.  The individual stations are responsible for all contracts with consumers.

The mechanisms of the Electricity Act of 1919 were preserved for the preparation of schemes for systematic development within particular districts.  There were important changes in detail. Stations were guaranteed against any increase in their costs for a period of seven years — so that the burden of rearrangements of machinery to conform to standard requirements of current would fall upon the board, unless absorbed by economies of integrated production.   If the owners of existing stations prove to be unwilling to co-operate, the board is authorized to purchase the station. The board may build new stations if private interests are unwilling to provide facilities.  The authorities were thus in a position to proceed with the general plan even if private interests in particular localities were hostile or lukewarm.  The board is to acquire, lease, and construct all transmission lines essential to the scheme, and to bear the capital cost of standardizing frequencies of current.  The act authorized a capital expenditure of £33,500,000.  Control is exercised over all important aspects of the enterprise.  Investment is controlled directly because all new investment is planned by the board.  Production policies are determined by the board.  Rates are controlled indirectly through the rates charged the select stations, which generate the electricity available for general distribution.

The grid work of high-tension transmission lines was finally completed in 1936.  There are 3,000 miles of primary high-tension lines of 132,000 volts.  Actual transmitting distances are short, so that the voltage was not set as high as the international committee suggested.  There is also a considerable mileage of secondary lines. In 1926, when the act was passed, the annual consumption of electricity was 113 kilowatt hours per capita.  It was hoped that the per capita consumption would be increased to 500 kilowatt hours by 1940.  In 1932–1933 consumption stood at 227 kilowatt

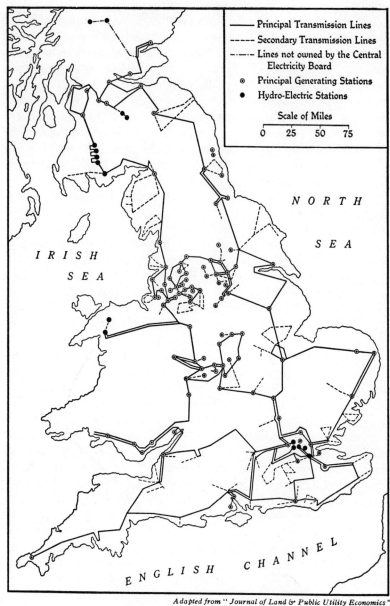

Principal Transmission Lines
----- Secondary Transmission Lines
---·- Lines not owned by the Central
        Electricity Board
⊙    Principal Generating Stations
●    Hydro-Electric Stations

Scale of Miles
0    25    50    75

*Adapted from " Journal of Land & Public Utility Economics"*

**The British Electricity Network, 1936**

hours. It was expected that the number of generating stations would be quickly reduced. Estimates called for a reduction to 124 plants by 1940, but down to 1937 this process was not working out so nearly to schedule. The number of plants increased slightly until 1929, and then fell off a little. In 1926, fully half the power was produced by 32 plants. The full realization of the extensive economies possible was dependent upon actual abandonment of the small inefficient plants, but despite all criticisms these plants survived. British experience is not widely different from that of other countries in this respect.

### The Socialization of Power Production in Germany

The development of a high-tension network has progressed as rapidly in Germany as in any country of Europe. As the area involved is large, interconnections do not cover the entire territory as comprehensively as is now the case in Great Britain. Within important zones, the high-tension network is already extensively developed, and new connections are still developing rapidly. International contacts are especially important. There are lines connecting France and Germany all along the eastern boundary of France. Connections with Switzerland and with Austria are of even more importance in terms of the exchange of current.

The history of the network presents many special features. In the earlier period (1900–1918), the development of high-tension lines proceeded much more rapidly than in England or in other parts of Europe. The movement was fostered by the great concentration of coal resources in the Ruhr and Saar, and by the relations between fuel resources and the industrial districts of Bavaria, Saxony, and Berlin. Development proceeded around these focal points, so that the elements of three territorial groups emerged in the Rhine valley, in Bavaria, and in the region between Dresden, Chemnitz, Leipzig, and Berlin. The Rhine valley was dominated from the outset by a combination, which became in 1906 the Rhenish-Westphalian Electric Works. Further consolidations have resulted in variations in the corporate name, but the identity of the corporation has been substantially continuous. In its earlier years the company was dominated by the great coal owners and the steel producers — the Stinnes-Thyssen group. Latterly, large stock holdings have been acquired by the state. The earlier history of concentration in this region was dominated by private capital.

The central zone and Bavaria were more largely dominated by

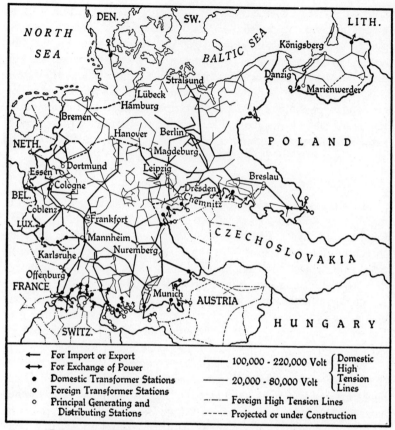

*Primary High-Tension Transmission Lines in Germany, 1931* [1]

state-controlled enterprises. Production of electricity was at first
controlled by the municipal undertakings for lighting and street
traction. After the World War the German government took the
initiative in developing an interconnected network. Connections
have developed very rapidly since 1926. By 1930 the Bavarian
network was tied into the network of the central zone, and the
central zone had connections with Breslau in Silesia and with
Stralsund on the Baltic. The Bavarian network was also tied in
with the Rhenish network, and an important connection was projected to join the north-central network with the Ruhr via Magde-
burg and Hanover.

[1] Adapted, by permission, from Werner Kittler, *Der Internationale Elektrische
Energieverkehr in Europa*, München, 1932.

The German network differs in one important respect from the British network. The British grid connects all selected stations and all primary industrial works producing electricity. In Germany a sharp distinction persists between central stations and industrial companies producing electricity for their own use. Many of these stations are very small, and one must presume them to be hopelessly uneconomical, but the movement towards integration still leaves them untouched. The official returns for 1932 are given in the following table.

ESTABLISHMENTS PRODUCING ELECTRICITY IN GERMANY, 1932, CLASSIFIED BY SIZE

| Capacity in Kilowatts | Central Stations | | Private Industry and Transport | |
|---|---|---|---|---|
| | Number | Installed Capacity in Kilowatts | Number | Installed Capacity in Kilowatts |
| 1–100 | 576 | 27,000 | 2,260 | 97,000 |
| 101–1,000 | 659 | 220,000 | 1,816 | 584,000 |
| 1,001–5,000 | 189 | 436,000 | 457 | 1,075,000 |
| 5,001–10,000 | 39 | 275,000 | 112 | 793,000 |
| 10,001–100,000 | 122 | 4,222,000 | 89 | 2,082,000 |
| Over 100,000 | 13 | 2,815,000 | 2 | 247,000 |
| Total | 1,598 | 7,995,000 | 4,736 | 4,878,000 |

About 40 per cent of the total production of electricity is thus produced outside the general network of central stations. A small amount of privately generated current is actually sold to other firms; but only 3 or 4 per cent of the total product comes from these firms which stand outside the general distributive system. The general reasoning, upon which consolidation is based, would lead us to presume that this large amount of highly individualized production involves a serious loss in efficiency. Industrial load factors are seldom good, and the general system would gain something through complete co-ordination of production. More than half the total industrial demand is withdrawn from the general network. The territorial extension of the network has thus progressed more rapidly than actual co-ordination of production.

The central stations represent three types of ownership: public, private, and mixed ownership. Before the war the municipalities and other local public bodies were the only authorities significantly interested in the production of electricity. The law of December 31, 1919, laid the foundations for the extension of public ownership to all primary producing plants and to the primary transmission lines. The effective accomplishment of the policy laid down has been beset with difficulties, and actual progress has been slow. These extensions of public ownership involved participation both by the central government and by the individual states. In order to secure greater flexibility of organization, the publicly owned central stations have become more and more independent of the general administration. The finances of the electrical works were made completely independent at an early date, and latterly the state-owned systems have been organized as corporations, or holding companies.

The holdings of the central government were combined in 1923 as a "concern," or syndicate — the Concern of United Industrial Enterprises, commonly known as the VIAG (Vereinigten Industrie-unternehmungen Aktien Gesellschaft). The combination included a large "Electric Works Company," and companies for the production of nitrogen and aluminum. Subsequent acquisitions added largely to the capacity for production, so that this combination controlled about 14 per cent of central station capacity.

PROPORTIONS OF CURRENT GENERATED BY DIFFERENT CLASSES OF CENTRAL STATIONS, IN GERMANY

|      | Public Ownership | Private Enterprise | Mixed Ownership |
|------|------------------|--------------------|-----------------|
| 1913 | 40.3             | 42.7               | 17.0            |
| 1924 | 44.0             | 28.7               | 27.3            |
| 1925 | 43.9             | 25.6               | 30.5            |
| 1928 | 56.6             | 14.6               | 28.8            |
| 1929 | 56.3             | 11.8               | 31.9            |

OWNERSHIP OF CENTRAL STATIONS IN GERMANY, 1933

| Ownership | Number | Current Generated, in Kilowatt Hours |
|-----------|--------|--------------------------------------|
| Public: |  |  |
| Central Government | 13 | 1,828,900,000 |
| Imperial Railways | 62 | 219,800,000 |
| The States | 28 | 1,400,900,000 |
| Provinces | 10 | 36,400,000 |
| Circles | 46 | 192,900,000 |
| Communes | 566 | 2,070,100,000 |
| Other public corporations | 85 | 2,189,800,000 |
| Mixed | 208 | 4,922,000,000 |
| Private | 609 | 1,650,600,000 |
| Total | 1,627 | 14,511,400,000 |

The systems under control of particular states are also largely organized as corporations. These corporations are able to enter the open market to meet certain capital requirements. The mixed companies are most characteristically represented by the Rhenish-Westphalian Electric Concern. The common stock is held jointly by public bodies and by private individuals. The development of public ownership and the relative importance of the different forms of ownership are shown by the tables on page 664.

Transfers of power over international boundaries began in Europe in 1914 with exchanges between Sweden and Denmark by submarine cables under the Sound. Other connections have developed over many of the national boundaries, most especially across the German border. Considerable pains have been taken to develop standard modes of dealing with the technical and legal problems involved. A conference at Geneva in November and December, 1923, drew up a general form for treaties between states proposing to exchange electric energy. The immediate result was not very important. There were further discussions at Basel in 1926, and at the second world power conference at Berlin. In the meantime actual connections were developing on a considerable scale. The exchanges between France and Germany are so nearly balanced that they must be treated as a purely local phenomenon. Contacts with Austria and Switzerland are of substantial importance; both countries export considerable amounts of electricity. Connections between Austria and Bavaria were established in 1923; and in 1931 an important high-tension line was run from Austria to Württemberg. The Swiss connections were made in 1926. Contacts have also been made with Poland and with Czechoslovakia, but the amounts of electricity moving across these borders in 1937 was as yet insignificant. The total international movement was still small, but the development was of such recent date that there was no indication of its importance for the future.

## Coal and Competing Sources of Energy

The importance of the changes in the modes of producing power has tended to distract attention from the profound changes in the total demand for power since 1913. During the World War, the production of coal ceased to expand, and there was no recovery after the war. It is not easy to appreciate the magnitude of this change. The production of coal, the primary source of power, had increased at substantial rates over a long period. We have some

WORLD PRODUCTION OF ENERGY, 1928, CONVERTED INTO EQUIVALENT WEIGHTS OF COAL, IN MILLIONS OF TONS [1]

| | Coal | | Petroleum | | Water Power | | Total | |
|---|---|---|---|---|---|---|---|---|
| | Mill. Tons | Per Cent | Mill. Tons | Per Cent | Mill. Tons | Per Cent | Mill. Tons | Per Cent |
| Germany | 187.8 | 14.5 | 0.1 | | 6.4 | 4.8 | 194.3 | 11.2 |
| England | 241.6 | 18.6 | | | 1.0 | 0.7 | 242.6 | 14.0 |
| France | 51.4 | 4.0 | | | 8.4 | 6.3 | 59.8 | 3.5 |
| Russia | 31.5 | 2.4 | 19.6 | 6.6 | 1.0 | 0.7 | 52.1 | 3.0 |
| Other Europe | 134.7 | 10.4 | 9.6 | 3.2 | 38.0 | 28.5 | 182.3 | 10.6 |
| Total Europe | 647.0 | 49.9 | 29.3 | 9.8 | 54.8 | 41.0 | 731.1 | 42.3 |
| United States | 514.7 | 39.7 | 202.5 | 68.0 | 46.8 | 35.0 | 764.0 | 44.2 |
| Canada | 13.2 | 1.0 | | | 18.4 | 13.7 | 31.6 | 1.8 |
| Mexico | | | 12.4 | 3.8 | 1.2 | 0.9 | 13.6 | 0.7 |
| Other America | 2.9 | 0.2 | 34.7 | 11.7 | 3.2 | 2.5 | 40.8 | 2.4 |
| Total America | 530.8 | 40.9 | 249.6 | 83.5 | 69.6 | 52.1 | 850.0 | 49.1 |
| China | 16.0 | 1.2 | | | | | 16.0 | 0.9 |
| Japan | 31.7 | 2.4 | | | 7.2 | 5.4 | 38.9 | 2.3 |
| British India | 21.6 | 1.7 | 3.0 | 1.0 | 0.7 | 0.6 | 25.3 | 1.5 |
| Dutch East Indies | 1.0 | | 6.4 | 2.2 | | | 7.4 | 0.4 |
| Siberia | 3.7 | 0.3 | | | 0.4 | 0.3 | 4.1 | 0.2 |
| Other Asia | 14.0 | 1.1 | 9.9 | 3.3 | 0.1 | | 24.0 | 1.4 |
| Total Asia | 88.0 | 6.7 | 19.3 | 6.5 | 8.4 | 6.3 | 115.7 | 6.7 |
| Africa | 13.4 | 1.1 | 0.5 | 0.2 | 0.1 | | 14.0 | 0.8 |
| Australia | 17.6 | 1.4 | | | 0.8 | | 18.4 | 1.1 |
| World | 1,296.8 | 100.0 | 298.7 | 100.0 | 133.7 | 100.0 | 1,729.2 | 100.0 |
| Per Cent of Total Energy | 75.1 | | 17.3 | | 7.6 | | 100.0 | |

[1] Meisner, M., Weltmontanstatistik, Stuttgart, 1932, vol. II, p. 40.

statistical record of production for the world as a whole after 1864. The use of lignite in Central Europe makes it necessary to adjust the figures for the production of lignite to the heating value of this fuel; so that the production of lignite is figured as equivalent to about one fourth as much as good bituminous or anthracite coal. With this adjustment the record of coal production in the world shows an average rate of growth of 4.4 per cent per year for the whole period 1864 to 1913. There were minor fluctuations in the rate of growth, but the average rate for the period as a whole has genuine significance. In 1913 this rapid expansion of the coal trade came to an abrupt end. Between 1913 and 1933 the world production of coal exceeded the figure for 1913 only in 1929, when the total product was 1,380 millions of tons as compared with 1,320 millions of tons in 1913. In 1933 production fell to the level of 1905, and despite some recovery in 1934 and 1935, production did not exceed the level attained in 1913.[1]

The significance of this arrested growth will be most readily appreciated if we compare current levels of production with the level that would have been attained if growth had continued at a constant rate of 4.4 per cent per year. If it had done so, the production in 1936 would stand at about 4,000 millions of tons of coal.

Many have assumed that the decline in the production of coal is due to the development of the use of petroleum as a source of power, and to the use of water power on a large scale in the generation of electricity. These sources of power have been important, and the extension of their use has been a contributing factor, but careful computation of the energy equivalents of the various sources of power shows that these supplementary sources are not sufficiently important to account for any large part of the decline in demand for coal. The notable computations by Meisner are given in the table on page 666.

Petroleum accounts for 17.3 per cent of the total energy produced in 1928. The consumption of gasoline in motorcars is hardly a direct substitution for coal, though the reactions upon railroads and urban transit must not be ignored. The use of fuel oil for merchant shipping and for naval use causes, of course, an important reduction in the demand for coal. The use of oil as a source of domestic heat has affected the demand for coal. But the displacements are not large. If there had been no increase in the use of oil and all equiv-

[1] Figures not adjusted for lignite follow a somewhat different course.

alent energy had been drawn from coal, coal production in 1928 would have stood at 1,597 million tons. This would imply growth in coal production at a rate of 1.12 per cent per year. Allowing for some independent development in the use of oil, we can assume a decline of only a fraction of one per cent per year as the net result of displacement of coal by oil.

Water power is even less important as a factor in a reduced demand for coal. Water power contributed only 7.6 per cent of the total energy produced in 1928. Furthermore, it is essential to remember that the aggregate importance of the small water powers had long been a considerable source of energy. European records are so incomplete that we cannot deal with the problem on any comprehensive basis. The German returns are indicative of the general character of the development. In 1875 water powers supplied 10.2 per cent of all the power used in industry and transport in Germany. In 1895 water power accounted for 17.8 per cent of the total supply of power; in 1907, only 10.9 per cent. In the United States there was a sharp decline in the importance of water power as a source of power. The census of manufactures, excluding mines and railroads, in 1870 reported water power as 48.5 per cent of the total power used. In 1900 water power supplied only 15.5 per cent of the power used in manufactures. The application of water power to the generation of electricity on a large scale is not a new addition to our resources.

The actual percentage of the contribution of water power to total energy supplied is frequently misjudged because popular discussion fails to attribute sufficient importance to the amount of energy currently used solely for the production of heat. About forty per cent of the total consumption of coal occurs in uses requiring heat rather than motion. The following table shows the distribution of world consumption among the various uses of coal. The statistics of world consumption present many difficulties; but, even with some elements of error, the generalized table is more significant than the records for particular countries. The nature of the demand for coal explains completely the differences between the relative contribution of water power in the narrower and larger fields. The demand for power as motion is only a fraction of the total demand for energy. Recent changes in the use of petroleum and water power do not, in any substantial measure, account for the extraordinary cessation in the growth of the demand for coal. Substitutions have been only a minor factor.

RELATIVE WORLD DEMAND FOR THE VARIOUS USES OF COAL, ABOUT 1929 [1]

| | Per Cent | | Per Cent |
|---|---|---|---|
| Domestic fuel | 17 | Industry: | |
| Transport: | | Metallurgy | 17 |
| Railroads | 23 | Gas works | 5 |
| Ships' bunkers | 3 | General industry | 29 |
| | | Central electric stations | 6 |

## The Reduced Demand for Energy

This long-continued absence of sustained growth in the demand for coal must be ascribed in large measure to a decrease in the total demand for energy. Demand has been sharply arrested by the stabilization of population, by disturbances of trade caused by the World War, and by improvements in the technique of utilization. The significance of these factors cannot be established with any great degree of precision, but rough approximations are possible.

The growth of population has been sharply arrested. The inadequacy of materials for Asia and Africa makes it desirable to confine attention to Europe and North America. For these continents, statistics are sufficiently trustworthy since 1850 to afford significant results, as follows:

POPULATION OF EUROPE AND NORTH AMERICA, 1850-1929 [2]

| | 1850 | 1900 | 1910 | 1929 |
|---|---|---|---|---|
| Europe | 266,000,000 | 401,000,000 | 447,000,000 | 478,000,000 |
| North America | 39,000,000 | 106,000,000 | 134,000,000 | 162,000,000 |
| Total | 305,000,000 | 507,000,000 | 581,000,000 | 640,000,000 |

These figures indicate an average rate of growth of 1 per cent per year for the period 1850-1900; and a rate of 1.125 per cent per year for the period 1900-1910. From 1910 to 1929 the rate of increase was only .58 per cent per year. This rate is actually lower than the average rate for this area in any half century since 1750, though the rate for the second half of the eighteenth century was not significantly higher. The important fact is the magnitude of the decline in the rate as compared with the decade prior to the World War. The abrupt fall to about one half of the rate of the prewar decade cannot be explained by ordinary economic changes. We must assume that this reduction in the rate of growth was

[1] Moutté, Frédéric, La question de l'organisation internationale de l'industrie charbonnière, Paris, 1929, p. 31.
[2] National Bureau of Economic Research, International Migrations, vol. II, p. 46.

due to direct losses of life in the war, to the unfavorable age distribution of the postwar period, and to unfavorable economic circumstances.

There can be no doubt of the development of important improvements in the technique of utilization of coal. Completely generalized figures are not available. The reduction in coal consumption in central electric stations amounted to more than 2 per cent per year. There have been savings in the use of domestic fuel, and important savings in the use of fuel in steam locomotives and in other forms of traction. As the central electric stations were operating on a very low standard in 1913, it is fair to presume that the net economies in the use of coal were less than the economies realized in electricity production. We may say then that the improvements might account for a decline of consumption of 1 per cent per year. By elimination, this reasoning leads to the conclusion that the disturbances directly due to the World War are responsible for more than half of the reduction in the demand for coal.

The age of the motorcar, the airplane, and the radio thus seems to be a period of hardship, pressure, and stabilization. Some writers, who seem to have little interest in totals, have characterized this period as the "new industrial revolution." But it is difficult to look towards the future with such optimism and confidence. It is not easy to see today any net additions to our primary resources equal in importance to the changes brought about in the eighteenth century. The perfection of the techniques for the working of aluminum and for the fixation of nitrogen affords the greatest possibilities. If we are indeed entering upon a new age in resource utilization, we are still too near the earliest stages of the new development to recognize any new influences in the secular trends of production. The records of economic activity today show most vividly the evidences of slackened growth and the ending of a great period of economic advance.

### The Computation of the Power Resources of Europe

Determination of the extent of the resources available for power production presents serious difficulties. The extent and richness of coal measures can be determined with some degree of accuracy, though it is difficult to anticipate specific possibilities of working at great depths or in thin seams of coal. Oil resources are extraordinarily difficult to estimate, and only the roughest appraisal of resources is possible. Water-power resources can be computed within reasonable limits of error, but it is not easy to make any quantitative comparison with coal resources.

Meisner has suggested a method which, with modifications, is fully adequate to the needs of economic discussion. It is possible to compute with considerable accuracy the relative equivalence between the amounts of energy generated by water and by coal. We know the amounts of coal consumed per kilowatt hour. Water power saves coal in just such a ratio. In 1925–1926 the average rate of coal consumption in Germany and the United States was 1.95 pounds of coal per kilowatt hour. Each unit of water power utilized for a full year would take the place of 7.8 tons of coal for each kilowatt per year, or 5.75 tons for each horsepower per year. Meisner assumed that it would not be possible to secure more than 60 per cent utilization, so that the effective saving would be 4.67 tons of coal per kilowatt year, or 3.5 tons of coal per horsepower year.

This is a very generous allowance on two separate counts. The consumption of coal in the best plants is already scarcely more than half the average rate of consumption, so that there is clear certainty that coal will not long be saved at this rate. Furthermore, few electric stations secure more than 30 per cent of full utilization. The relative value of water power as compared with coal might be estimated at only one fourth the figure used by Meisner; on a very conservative basis it might be reduced to .83 ton per horsepower year. Plant utilization will doubtless improve in course of time, so that it is best not to be too conservative.

The next step in the computation is to state the approximate stock of coal in the ground that corresponds to the amount of coal saved each year by the use of water power. Meisner assumed that the stock in the ground could be rated as low as one hundred times the annual product. For this there is no evident justification. The annual product of England, Germany, France, and Belgium in 1913 was about one four-hundreth of the certain reserves of coal, and about one thousandth of the total reserves, probable as well as certain. The stock of unused coal needed to yield the amount of energy produced by water power must be estimated at not less than 400 times the annual saving, if comparison be made with actual reserves, or 1,000 times the annual saving if the figure for total reserves is used. The tables for Europe and for the world, on pages 672 and 875, have been computed on these principles.

The figures used by Meisner have also been corrected in the light of the latest Russian and Italian material. Energetic exploration

POWER RESOURCES OF EUROPE, EXPRESSED AS MILLIONS OF TONS OF COAL [1]

| Country | Per Cent of Total Area | Coal Certain Reserve | Coal Per Cent | Oil | Water Power | Total Energy Amount | Total Energy Per Cent |
|---|---|---|---|---|---|---|---|
| Great Britain | 2.23 | 141,499 | 41.000 | 12.0 | 1,700 | 143,211.0 | 30.000 |
| Germany | 4.67 | 88,763 | 25.500 | 15.0 | 4,000 | 92,778.0 | 19.400 |
| Russia (European) | 46.60 | 76,600 | 22.048 | 1,571.4 | 29,400 | 107,571.4 | 22.510 |
| Poland | 3.82 | 10,497 | 3.060 | 36.5 | 295 | 10,828.5 | 2.263 |
| Czechoslovakia | 1.37 | 7,030 | 2.040 | | 705 | 7,735.0 | 1.617 |
| Austria | .82 | 98 | .028 | | 3,590 | 3,688.0 | .770 |
| Yugoslavia | 2.42 | 843 | .240 | | 4,030 | 4,873.0 | 1.020 |
| Hungary | .91 | 74 | .021 | | 262 | 336.0 | .070 |
| France | 5.49 | 5,124 | 1.480 | 3.4 | 16,450 | 21,577.4 | 4.510 |
| Belgium | .03 | 6,600 | 1.890 | | | 6,600.0 | 1.380 |
| Netherlands | .03 | 3,165 | .910 | | | 3,165.0 | .660 |
| Spain | 5.00 | 5,984 | 1.730 | | 3,500 | 9,484.0 | 1.953 |
| Italy | 3.04 | 22 | .006 | | 27,250 | 27,272.0 | 5.678 |
| Switzerland | .04 | | | | 3,680 | 3,680.0 | .769 |
| Norway | 3.16 | | | | 20,600 | 20,600.0 | 4.320 |
| Sweden | 4.38 | 106 | .030 | | 7,575 | 7,681.0 | 1.605 |
| Rumania | 3.11 | 13 | .005 | 195.5 | 1,921 | 2,129.5 | .445 |
| All others | 12.98 | 24 | .012 | | 4,900 | 4,924.0 | 1.030 |
| Total Europe | 100.00 | 346,442 | 100.000 | 1,833.8 | 129,858 | 478,133.8 | 100.000 |

[1] Adapted from material in Meisner as cited on page 875.

has revealed large mineral resources in Russia previously unknown, and the known resources have been more accurately estimated. The coal reserves are much greater than was formerly supposed. In Siberia about nine times as much coal has been discovered as was known in 1913, when the primary data on coal resources were compiled by the Geological Congress of the World. The resources of European Russia have been found to be somewhat greater than was supposed.

In respect of Italy, the recent development of water power makes it necessary to use only the latest returns. The figure used in the table on page 672 is based on the official estimate that there are now available about 11.6 million horsepower. In 1921 the U. S. Geological Survey gave the potential water power of Italy as 5.5 million horsepower. Apparently, too little allowance was made for regulated flow of rivers.

The tables thus represent the most favorable statement of the relative value of water power that can reasonably be made, and the corrections for Russia and Italy should make the tables truly representative of the best information now available. Discussion of the situation in the world as a whole will be postponed until a later chapter. The problems of Europe itself can best be considered at this point.

## The Regional Distribution of Power Resources

Study of known resources is important, because disparities between current production and available resources indicate very clearly the likelihood of rapid economic development with attendant displacements among various regions. Thus, in the nineteenth century, the great difference between Germany's current production and her resources in coal pointed very clearly to the great change in the position of Germany. One cannot predict the timing of the development, but it is obvious that great resources will not long lie unutilized unless there are very serious technical or social obstacles to be overcome. Sooner or later these resources will come into use.

We must now ask if there are any disparities between primary power resources and current utilization in Europe at the present time. The table on page 672 gives the results of the comparisons that can be made of the resources of coal, oil, and water power. It is clear that Great Britain and Germany are in an essentially stable position: production and resources are balanced. Great

Britain in 1928 produced 32 per cent of the power produced in Europe, with 30 per cent of the effective resources. Germany produced 26.6 per cent of the power with 19.4 per cent of the resources. Russia, on the other hand, produced in 1928 only 7 per cent of the power with 22.51 per cent of the resources. The potentialities of Russia are obvious. It is important to note, however, that these resources are not fully proportionate to the area of the country. European Russia embraces 46.6 per cent of the total area. Her area is so large that significant study of her problems would properly call for much geographical detail. Industrialization is possible on a large scale; but, except in particular regions, agriculture will necessarily continue to be a dominant factor in Russian life. The precise influence of Russian development upon the economic life of Europe cannot be foreseen. In some respects, Russia will become less dependent upon European markets; in other respects she may well become more dependent upon western Europe. In some degree, power resources afford a measure of the productivity of labor that can be achieved. Productivity is roughly proportional to available power. In so far as this relationship holds, it will not be easy for Russia to achieve the measure of productivity that has been achieved in Great Britain, Germany, and the United States.

The utilization of large-scale water power adds significantly to the power resources of Italy, Norway, and France. The figure for Italy may be unduly high, as it is based on recent estimates of Italian engineers which involve an unusually comprehensive survey of possible development. It would perhaps be wise to make the other elements in the computation a little more conservative. It is fairly clear, however, that Italy has resources which are at least directly proportionate to her area, and perhaps slightly better. Her other resources are much more important than those of Norway, whose supply of power is closely comparable; but the other resources of Italy are certainly very much less significant than those of France. Hydroelectric developments have affected Italy more profoundly than any of the other large powers, but without primary minerals and more fuel it is unlikely that Italy will become an important center of the heavy industries.

Recent developments of power engineering make some changes in the relative position of the countries ill supplied with coal. But coal clearly remains the primary source of power, and a controlling factor in the location of the heavy industries. There are new opportunities for some development of specialties and light industries, but these changes will not radically alter the general structure of economic life in western Europe.    In the light of this fundamental division of labor among the regions of Europe, it is difficult to find any permanent justification for the extreme forms of economic isolation that have characterized the postwar period.    Serious interference with interregional trade of western Europe can only bring poverty and distress to all alike.    The great industrial districts can prosper only by selling their products to their neighbors. Their neighbors will have a good market only if the industrial regions are prosperous.

# CHAPTER 33

## ECONOMIC ASPECTS OF THE WORLD WAR

———————◆———————

### Summary View of the Economic Antecedents

The antagonisms which culminated in the World War were prominently associated with nationalism. But nationalism was more than a political ideal or a system of government. It involved conflicting economic ambitions for the control of natural resources, trade, strategic areas, and regions for settlement and for the export of capital, combined with a desire for self-sufficiency in the face of an increasingly interdependent economic system. The stronger these nationalistic ambitions and desires became, the more intense were the antagonisms which they generated. As the nations of the Continent successively acquired modern techniques and forms of economic organization, the area of the competitive struggle was extended, while at the same time its intensity was increased. The spread of industrialism involved an increasing dependence of the industrialized nations on external supplies of food and raw materials, external markets for manufactures, and external opportunities for the investment of large surplus incomes.

There was a serious disequilibrium between regions. The industrialized countries had scientific techniques and strong governments; the backward regions retained their primitive or traditional economic and political patterns. The countries of Europe also experienced disparities of opportunity for controlling and utilizing the trade and resources of the backward regions. It was this disparity which gave significance to the historic urge of the hinterland populations of Russia toward the seaways and to the ambitions of Germans for "a place in the sun." The World War was preceded by an intensification of commercial, colonial, financial, and diplomatic rivalries.

Classical economic theory held that economic liberty, involving local, regional, and international freedom of exchange, would remove conditions of disequilibrium, bring about and maintain flexibility in economic relations, and furnish the best assurance of peace. The equitable operation of a regime of economic liberty called for a start from scratch and for the maintenance of fair competition; and certain regions, notably Great Britain, had initial advantages when the classical theory became popular. Neverthe-

676

less, even with grave limitations, the earlier period of extensive acceptance of the theory was exceptionally peaceful.

Another conception advanced as a necessary basis for the maintenance of peace was in some respects the antithesis of the classical doctrine of free competition and automatic adjustment by the forces of the market place. This conception emphasized the idea of international control. Long before the League of Nations was organized, it was held by many that national sovereignty as popularly conceived involved dependence on brute force in the relations between peoples, just as the absence of a central authority within a country would mean the rule of might in the relations between individuals or groups within a nation. Treaties and alliances imposed certain limitations on national sovereignty, especially in the realm of international law, but the judicial and administrative functions, on which the validity of law depends, remained almost entirely in the realm of national sovereignty.

Before the World War there was an increasingly influential group which accepted the idea of an international authority for supplementing the work of national governments, but which held that the economic basis alike of national and of international authority must be altered if war was to be avoided. This conception, although not confined to the socialists, was emphasized by them. The general point of view was summarized in the concluding passage of the famous resolution against war adopted in 1907 by the Stuttgart International Socialist Congress: "Wars, therefore, are part and parcel of the nature of [private] capitalism; they will cease only when the capitalist system declines, or when the sacrifices in men and money have become so great as a result of the increased magnitude of armaments that the people will rise in revolt against them and sweep capitalism out of existence. The working classes, who contribute most of the soldiers and make the greatest material sacrifices, are, therefore, the natural opponents of war. Besides which, war is opposed to their highest aims — the creation of an economic order on a socialist basis, which shall express the solidarity of all nations."

Among the antecedents of the World War were many forces and circumstances not primarily economic, such as the antagonisms resulting from racial and cultural differences and the conflicts of personalities and of political systems. So obvious a fact calls for mention merely as a reminder that in an economic history only the economic factors can be emphasized.

## War Finance

The basic problem which confronted governments in carrying on the war was financial. It was of course necessary to fight the war not with money but with men and with essential commodities. But in the various belligerent countries, production had been carried on by private enterprise, and the use of the products of private enterprise for war purposes required vast financial resources. Although conscription already was either in vogue or was generally adopted, men were viewed in a measure as free agents, and even the conscripted forces were paid at least small stipends in addition to being provided with sustenance and the means of warfare. Since production was not a governmental function, governments were confronted with the alternatives of conscripting capital as well as men and transforming private production for profit into a self-liquidating system of public production, or else of obtaining money for paying private producers for the goods and services required for war. With minor exceptions, the second alternative was chosen. But the question remained as to methods of obtaining funds — by taxation or by borrowing.

In most of the belligerent countries there were extensive discussions of the relative merits of taxation and of borrowing. It was held by many that taxation was unjust to the war generation and that a large part of the burden should be passed on to the future by means of borrowings. The real costs could not of course be postponed, for the real costs were not marks or pounds or other monetary units but munitions of war, essential commodities, and the lives of participants. A belligerent nation might obtain goods on credit from other nations and thus shift some of the immediate costs to others. But credits for production within a nation involved curtailment of normal consumption for supplying war needs, combined with future obligations of consumers, as taxpayers, to the government's creditors; while payment by means of taxation meant curtailment of current normal consumption without future obligations. Various related questions were discussed, as the comparative effects on prices, on volume of production, and on economic reconstruction after the war. But in the actual decisions regarding fiscal policies, the underlying principles received slight consideration. In most countries the line of least resistance was followed — a progressive expansion of credit, with comparatively slight increases in taxation.

German ordinary imperial revenues for the year 1913–1914 totaled less than 3,600,000,000 marks. During the early war period taxation actually declined, but later increased materially. The imperial funded debt in October, 1913, totaled 4,800,000,000 marks; in 1915, 12,800,000,000; and on March 1, 1919, 92,400,000,000. In addition there was a vast unfunded or floating debt. Loans from the beginning of the war to March 31, 1920, totaled 222,000,000,000 marks.

In France, as in Germany, revenues from taxation declined during the early war period, but some of the wealthier areas of France were in the occupied zones. In 1913 French revenues, including a small amount from loans, totaled 4,739,000,000 francs. On July 31, 1914, the French national debt was 34,000,000,000 francs, and on January 1, 1920, it was 240,000,000,000. Of this sum, 137,000,000,000 francs made up the fixed debt, the remainder being floating debt, made up largely of directly inflationary bank loans and treasury bills with early maturity dates. The annual debt service alone on January 1, 1920, totaled 9,442,000,000 francs.

The government of Great Britain obtained less than £200,000,000 in revenues other than loans during the fiscal year ended March 31, 1914. Throughout the war period there was a continuous increase. Receipts during the year 1918–1919 were £889,000,000. But in comparison with borrowings, the increases in taxes were small. The national debt at the beginning of the war amounted to £678,000,000, and by March 31, 1920, had grown to £7,859,000,000, including large sums borrowed to aid the dominions and the allies.

In the United States the national debt in 1916 was only $1,188,000,000; in 1919, it was $25,482,000,000. But almost half of this debt was for the purpose of extending loans to the Allied Powers. In 1916 ordinary Federal revenues were $782,500,000, and there was a progressive increase to $6,694,600,000 in 1920. Most of the other belligerents pursued policies of dependence on loans and monetary inflation resembling the policies of France and Germany.

The vast expansion of funded and floating obligations in the various belligerent countries was accompanied by the issue of increasing amounts of paper money, such as currency notes in Great Britain, German Reichsbank notes, and French notes based on credits established at the Bank of France. The notes of the Bank of France in circulation increased from 5,713,000,000 francs at the end of 1913, to 37,274,000,000 at the end of 1919.

The German loans were almost entirely domestic.  France and most of the other belligerents borrowed extensively from other countries.  Germany extended credits to Austria-Hungary, Turkey, and Bulgaria; while the Allied Powers opposed to Germany established a complicated system of inter-Allied loans, with Great Britain bearing the chief burden before the United States entered the war, after which time American credits predominated.  Inter-Allied loans continued after the armistice, and in the case of the United States, the credits extended increased from \$7,077,000,000 at the time of the armistice to \$11,861,000,000 in 1923.

## Prices and International Exchange Rates

The inflation of currency and credit, combined with abnormal demands for goods and services and curtailment of the facilities for production, resulted in rapidly rising prices.  For certain countries the percentages of increase in the average of wholesale prices in 1919, over the average of 1913, are estimated as follows:

### RISE IN WHOLESALE PRICES, 1913 TO 1919

| | | | |
|---|---|---|---|
| Great Britain | 155 per cent | Netherlands | 204 per cent |
| France | 256 per cent | Sweden | 230 per cent |
| Italy | 266 per cent | Japan | 136 per cent |
| Germany [1] | 315 per cent | United States | 106 per cent |

Thus even in the United States wholesale prices in 1919 were more than twice as high as in 1913.  The vital needs of warring countries called for restriction of nonessential consumption and for stimulation of the production of essentials required for war.  The net effects of fiscal policies on prices and on these needed reorientations of consumption and production cannot be estimated with assurance, but it is known that the policies were extremely demoralizing.  The immediate effects on prices were held in check in a measure, however, by emergency controls, as for example in the case of the international exchanges.

The maintenance of prewar exchange parities and the automatic regulation of the markets on the basis of the gold standard soon proved to be impossible because of the extreme variations in fiscal policy, prices, and demands for goods from nonbelligerents. Early efforts of the British and the French to maintain exchange rates by gold shipments and sale of foreign securities were inadequate, and arrangements were made with American bankers to

[1] Rapid inflation began in Germany toward the end of 1919.

pay for purchases in the United States at stabilized rates of exchange. The credits established for this purpose were secured in part by the deposit of collateral. Thus Americans were enabled to continue the sale of their products to the Allied Powers but not to the enemies of these countries. The later government loans to the Allied Powers were without collateral security but were similarly used to stabilize exchange rates.

By the piling up of debts, monetary inflation, artificial pegging of exchange rates, and an elaborate system of inter-Allied loans, the Allied Powers were able to finance the purchase of the goods and services necessary for carrying on the war with comparatively slight increases in taxation. Some of the effects of these policies will be described later.

### Economic Mobilization of the Central Powers

To an unprecedented extent the World War involved the entire populations of the belligerent countries and called for the centralized control of all economic activities. At the same time, most of the warring countries had become accustomed to private initiative and comparative freedom from governmental control of business enterprise, although *laissez-faire* traditions were less influential in the Central Powers than among their enemies.

Austria-Hungary possessed great natural resources, but industry and transportation were not as advanced as in Germany, France, and Great Britain, and efficient utilization of resources was retarded by the cumbersome system of dual government in Austria and Hungary and by the many discontented racial minorities within the empire. Turkey and Bulgaria, which joined the Central Powers, were able to furnish important food supplies and raw materials but were backward both politically and economically and were largely dependent on Germany for financing war operations.

From the point of view of economic resources and the readiness with which they could be directed effectively to military ends, Germany was in a favorable position, not only among her allies but also in comparison with her enemies. To her own vast and geographically concentrated resources were added, early in the war, the extremely important coal, iron, textile, chemical, and agricultural resources of Belgium, Luxemburg, and northern France. German industry, although based on private initiative and ownership, was characterized by centralized control under great corporations and cartels, and was accustomed to intimate relations with government alike as to regulation and as to tariffs and other protective policies. The comparative amenability of the people to the discipline of a central authority simplified the problems of restricting the production and consumption of nonessentials, of stimulating the production of essentials, and of making most effective use of both human and natural resources. Even the blockade of German ports contributed indirectly to industrial mobilization by creating among the people a spirit of unity and sacrifice.

Early in the war the German government made an inventory of available and needed materials and took steps to commandeer all essential supplies. Possible means of acquiring resources from abroad were thoroughly studied and steps were taken to counteract as far as possible the Allied blockade. Nonessential industries were curtailed, and the facilities of production were directed, by means of a rationing of credit, materials, and labor, to the production of essentials. Scientists and technicians were set to work on the problems of substitute materials and products to take the place of supplies lacking in Germany and no longer available from other countries.

Late in 1916 there was adopted a comprehensive system of compulsory civilian service. As described by the chief of the Emergency War Office, this was designed to effect a complete mobilization of labor and the facilities for production and to make the maximum use of the nation's resources, human and material, for war purposes. The system was described as being centered about a pyramid based on coal and iron, rising through transportation, the auxiliary materials for making munitions, and the semifinished products, and finding its apex in cannon, shells, and other instruments of warfare. All available labor was mobilized and fitted as far as possible into the most appropriate field of work.

The food problem was handled by rigorous control of the supply, which was allocated in accordance with relative urgency of need. In virtually all of the cities and larger towns community kitchens were established. Food tickets for the urban population became almost universal. For the purchase of many basic foods, such as meat, fats, milk, and potatoes, it was necessary for individuals to register with a designated dealer, whose shop was supplied only with the amount of food allocated to the registered purchasers. For the more effective mobilization of the entire nation, rigorous measures were taken to control the press and all agencies of opinion. Control of the modes of utilizing capital was attempted by the regulation of credit and prices and the allocation of labor and resources. But industry remained largely within the limits of private ownership; and profits in many cases rose to abnormal levels.

## Economic Mobilization of the Allied Powers

In Great Britain, France, the United States, and Italy, the comparative strength of *laissez-faire* traditions and of the idea of government by consent accentuated the difficulty of governmental control of economic life. The Russian government had extreme political power but exhibited less competence in controlling the national economy than the more democratic governments of Western Europe. More than 15,000,000 men were called to the colors, but no adequate program was attempted for maintaining essential auxiliary and civilian services. The importation of munitions and other supplies was greatly restricted by the closing of all ports except Archangel and Vladivostok, both remotely located. Industrial mobilization was made more difficult by Germans and German sympathizers as owners or managers of some of the important enterprises. Munitions when made or imported could be sent to the front only after disastrous delay, due partly to failure to maintain such strategic services as those connected with railway shops. When the peasants found that their supply of manufactured goods, normally meager at best, was being seriously curtailed, they resisted the demands of the government for increased supplies of food and raw materials. These various difficulties and shortcomings of the Russian government in its handling of the economic aspects of the war were cumulative in their effects. The result was increasing demoralization and ultimate breakdown.

In France there was a comparatively strong central government, but its economic functions before the war had been slight. Individualistic and *laissez-faire* traditions prevailed among the predominantly small-scale businessmen. There were a few powerful groups connected mainly with the Bank of France and the basic heavy industries, but most of the areas of the heavy industries and some of the leading textile centers were occupied by the Germans early in the war. Early mobilization included an indiscriminate drafting into the armed forces of all individuals in specified age groups. Later this policy was reversed and efforts were made to maintain noncombatant services and essential industries by a selective process based on specialized training, skill, and experience. In the United States there were many peculiar difficulties connected with

American individualism and constitutional limitations. But on the basis of European and particularly French and British experience, America was able to achieve a comparatively rapid and efficient mobilization of economic resources.

The slow and painful experience of Great Britain was substantially characteristic of the initial difficulties and the ultimate efficiency and success of the more democratic countries in putting national economies on a war basis. The general British organization that finally emerged was headed by a small, compact War Cabinet capable of obtaining Parliamentary consent because it was a coalition of the political parties. Most of the ordinary departments of government were not represented in the cabinet. The five main divisions of the emergency government were the three ministries of Munitions, Food, and Shipping; the War Office; and the Board of Trade. Subject to the War Cabinet were numerous specialized agencies, such as the War Trade Department, concerned with the regulation of exports and imports, the office of the Director General of National Service, authorized to prevent the employment of labor in nonessential activities, and the extremely important War Priorities Committee, which exercised vital control by means of its power to allocate labor and materials.

During the first month of the war several important steps were taken. The government suspended the Bank Act and inaugurated a controlled system of currency and credit in place of the gold standard. Public operation of the railways was undertaken. Complete control of the sugar supply was vested in a royal commission (a forerunner of later comprehensive control of food). Parliament enacted the Defense of the Realm Act, which, with various amendments, gave legal sanction for the public control of agencies of opinion and for the public operation or supervision of virtually all business enterprises. But during the first year of the war the prevailing conception was "business as usual" and there was no serious attempt to interfere with supply and demand under competitive bidding, public and private, for materials, labor, and output.

The first important change was forced by the munitions crisis on the western front. The urgency of need for guns, ammunition, and other essential military supplies, not only by the British forces but by all the Allied armies, led to the creation in May, 1915, of the Ministry of Munitions. This agency efficiently reorganized the basic industries and successfully met the crisis in this most vital aspect of industrial production. The control of shipping was attempted by the requisitioning, early in the war, of about 20 per cent of available tonnage. In November, 1916, all ships not requisitioned were subjected to a licensing system for allocating tonnage to appropriate uses. The Ministry of Shipping, organized late in 1916, subjected shipping to additional controls which placed all tonnage at the disposal of the government as needed. In January, 1917, an Interallied Shipping Committee was formed. Later a Tonnage Priority Committee and an Allied Maritime Transport Council pooled and co-ordinated all shipping facilities and promoted shipbuilding. From time to time various agencies were formed to deal with particular food problems. Late in 1916 a Ministry of Food was organized to co-operate with the Board of Trade and other agencies in buying and importing food. The Ministry of Food also worked with the Food Production Department. The public buying and control of food supplies made possible some degree of control of prices. Later a food-rationing system was introduced.

Outstanding among the problems of economic mobilization was the utilization of labor. In Great Britain there were strong trade-unions, an influential Labor party, and traditions which called for action by mutual agreement. Coercion by government was therefore long delayed. But it was discovered that voluntary enlistment for military service was removing sorely needed individuals with special training from essential war industries. On the other hand, the experience of other countries, notably Russia and France, demonstrated the futility of general conscription for the armed forces without selective measures for retaining men of special training or skill for war industries and for maintaining civilian as well as military services. The British government, in characteristic fashion, did little at first and later effected a series of compromises between voluntary service and selective control of man power. The measures adopted applied both to the armed forces and to civilian service. There were numerous exemptions from military service and frequent "combing" of the exemptions to counteract charges of favoritism.

In respect to trade-unionism, the government proceeded in accordance with its general principle that consent and co-operation were better than compulsion. An important agreement was made in March, 1915, with the unions in the munitions industries. The various Munitions of War Acts included provisions based on this agreement, and much of the administrative work of the Ministry of Munitions was entrusted to trade-unions and to special agencies with union representation.  There were similar agencies in various other industries, notably the Cotton Control Board and the Wool Control Board.  Unions were also utilized in the administration of the recruiting acts.  A joint committee of unionists and employers served in an advisory capacity on problems of general policy.  The unions agreed to compulsory arbitration and to temporary modification of union rules and standards to speed up the production of essentials.  For the same reason they agreed to the "dilution" of labor in the unionized crafts by the employment of women and of workers from other occupations.  The government, in addition to admitting unions to representation in various agencies, agreed to special measures for the limitation of profits and for safeguarding working conditions and living standards.

### Problems of Economic Mobilization Confronting Governments

In most of the belligerent countries there had been a sharp distinction between the functions of business enterprise and the work of governments.  Public officials, although credited with certain distinctive qualifications, were popularly viewed as lacking the traits of business insight and efficiency essential to the directing of large economic activities.  But economic demoralization and lack of co-ordination of economic and military activities soon demonstrated the fallacy of the popular dictum of "business as usual" and thrust upon governments the functions of directing and co-ordinating business activities.  The conditions under which these unaccustomed functions were assumed put the efficiency of public officials and governmental agencies to an extremely severe test.

The authority of governments was vastly extended during the emergency, but not without grave opposition or obstruction. There were many who continued to adhere to traditional views of individualism and *laissez faire*.  Large numbers were willing to place personal advantage and profit above national aims.  Problems were created also by those who conscientiously dissented from national aims or from the war as a method of achieving them. In most countries there was a prevailing view that the war would be short, and long-range plans were therefore opposed.  Even when this view was shown to be erroneous, there were innumerable problems of judgment and foresight involved in meeting the rapidly changing military situation.

Governments assumed responsibility for the control and use of the facilities of production without acquiring authority of ownership or freedom from obligations to the private owners of these facilities. The labor supply, the materials, and the facilities available for use were subnormal. The normal labor supply was drafted largely into the armed forces, and it was necessary to utilize the aged, those who were incapacitated for military service, and untrained women and young people. Materials were extremely scarce and often inferior in quality, and substitutions and ingenious adaptations were frequently necessary. The maintenance of the facilities of production at normal levels of efficiency was impossible because of the necessity for diverting all possible resources from capital investment and upkeep into channels of immediate consumption. Adequate judgment regarding the efficiency of public agencies in the exercise of economic functions during the war must take account of these various considerations.

### The Status of Neutrals; Contraband of War and the Blockade

The moves and countermoves of Great Britain and Germany in respect to neutral trade and in particular the trade of the United States resembled in many ways the Anglo-French maritime struggle of the Napoleonic era. As in the earlier period, the United States finally abandoned neutrality, but this time on the side of Great Britain. Several of the smaller European powers maintained a technical neutrality but found it necessary to yield, economically, to the pressure of the belligerent nations.

A long series of international agreements had created a code of international law defining the rights and duties of neutrals, but when the war developed into a desperate struggle between the major powers, little remained of the law of neutrality. Before the war there had been general agreement that neutrals had the right to carry on ordinary trade not only with other neutrals but with belligerents as well. The main exceptions or qualifications were the right of belligerents to establish an effective blockade of enemy ports, and the right to seize contraband of war on the high seas even when carried in neutral vessels. An effective blockade required such a naval patrol of enemy harbors as to make hazardous an attempt to reach a blockaded port; and notification was required as to the nature and date of establishment of the blockade. Blockade running was punishable by confiscation of ship and cargo.

The law of the blockade was vague as to what constituted effectiveness, but the law of contraband was even more indefinite. There was agreement on an extensive list of articles absolutely contraband, essentially munitions of war or other goods used directly for war, but agreement regarding articles conditionally contraband was impossible. Any agreement could hardly have stood the test of war because of the rapid changes in technology, the varied military and civilian uses of the same commodity, as cotton, and the possibilities of substitution and release for war purposes of domestic products as a result of importations for civilian use. It was in connection with the ill-defined limits of the blockade and of contraband that the Allied Powers adopted early measures for throttling neutral trade with the Central Powers.

Before March, 1915, Great Britain depended largely on an extension of the list of contraband of war to check the flow of goods to enemy countries. In March, new "measures to intercept the seaborne commerce of Germany" involved in effect, although not at first in name, an attempt to blockade German ports and also to prevent goods with a German destination from entering the ports of the northern neutrals — the Scandinavian countries and the Netherlands (Holland). In order to avoid unnecessary hostility as a result of such obvious departures from international law, vessels and their cargoes ordinarily were not confiscated. Such an extensive blockade could not be effectively enforced, partly because of the extent of coast line and partly because of German use of submarines, mines, and airplanes. The United States refused to recognize the legality either of the blockade or of the expanded list of contraband. The American government also challenged the associated policies of requiring neutral vessels to submit to search and to stop at a British port for clearance to neutral as well as belligerent ports.

### Blacklists, Embargoes, and Other Policies Affecting Neutrals

As a result of these various difficulties the British adopted additional measures for bringing pressure to bear on neutrals to prevent them from "assisting or rendering services to the enemy." One of these methods was the blacklist. British citizens were forbidden to trade not only with the enemy but with neutral persons or groups suspected of having "enemy associations." These persons or groups formed the blacklist. Their identity was disclosed to the British by virtue of British control of communications and by the censorship not only of cable messages but also of the mails. All foreign trade of the British was controlled with increasing rigor by licenses and by the allocation of tonnage, cable facilities, credits, etc. Much of the neutral trade and shipping depended on British connections, Allied coal supplies and coaling stations, Allied cable and port facilities, etc. The cutting off of British connections with persons or firms on the blacklist was therefore an effective method of bringing pressure to bear to prevent neutral trade with the enemy. In addition, favorable inducements were offered to neutrals for the sale of their goods to the Allied Powers and for the placing of their shipping profitably in the service of the Allies. Pressure was also exerted by means of embargoes, as a general embargo on all exports to a given country pending an agreement, or an embargo applying to a specified commodity.

As a result of the blockade, the expansion of contraband, the blacklist, and the embargo, the British succeeded in forcing most of the neutral states of Europe into the making of agreements highly favorable to the Allied cause. Early in the war the Dutch formed the Netherlands Overseas Trust for the centralized management of commercial relations. In July, 1915, this organization made an agreement with the British government by which the trust acted as consignee of goods imported by the principal Dutch companies and undertook to guarantee that such goods would not be forwarded to Germany and would not be used as substitutes for Dutch goods sold to Germany. Agreements resembling in principle this arrangement with the Dutch were made also with Switzerland and the Scandinavian countries and with various associations, such as the Textile Alliance, in the United States.

The cutting off of American trade with the Central Powers and the offering of inducements to American traders to sell their goods to the Allied Powers and to place their tonnage at the service of these powers led to a vast expansion of trade and shipping. The value of American exports to Great Britain in 1910 was $506,000,000; in 1913, $597,000,000; and in 1916, $1,527,000,000.[1] The value of exports to France in 1910 was $118,000,000; in 1913, $146,-000,000; and in 1916, $629,000,000.[1] The value of exports to Russia in 1910 was $18,000,000; in 1913, $26,000,000; and in 1916, $310,000,000.[1] There was also a vast expansion of credits to the Allied Powers, and the validity of these credits depended on Allied victory. These economic interests thus reinforced the resentment aroused by the unrestricted German submarine campaign.

[1] The increase in value was of course in part a result of higher prices.

When the submarine campaign and the general havoc of war gravely menaced Allied supplies of food, materials, and munitions, an elaborate system of rationing was applied, with American co-operation, to the European neutrals. On the basis of statistics of trade, production, consumption, and the vital needs of the neutral populations, goods permitted entry into neutral countries were restricted in nature and amount as far as possible to the domestic requirements of neutrals. Germany also entered into various rationing agreements, but the economic pressure and commercial inducements of the Allied Powers were in most cases far more effective in controlling neutral trade and economic life.

### The Economic Significance of Territorial Changes

The mobilization and gradual co-ordination of the economic as well as military resources of the Allied Powers, combined with effective pressure brought to bear on neutrals, led to the virtual isolation of Germany and a progressive exhaustion of German resources. Economic attrition undermined the material bases of German morale; and when the Germans were faced with the failure of their submarine campaign, their surrender was merely a question of time and of diplomatic strategy.

The treaties which ended the war were unprecedentedly detailed and complicated. The territorial changes, although concerned in the first instance with political boundaries and the regrouping of racial elements, were profoundly important in their effects on European and world economy. Changes affecting Germany were embodied in the Treaty of Versailles of 1919. The loss of Alsace-Lorraine by Germany included approximately three fourths of the iron-producing resources of Germany on the basis of prewar production. The natural coal supply for reduction of the Lorraine ores was in Westphalia east of the Rhine. The Saar basin also possessed vast coal beds, and this area was transferred for fifteen years to the jurisdiction of an international commission, with title to the mines themselves transferred outright to France. This transfer minimized the dependence of the French on coal under German control for exploiting the iron of Lorraine, — a significant illustration of the dislocation, for political purposes, of natural economic relations. Upper Silesia, which produced about one fourth of Germany's prewar output of hard coal, was tentatively transferred to Poland, but a plebiscite in 1921 was made the basis for the return of part of the region to Germany. All of the non-European territories of

Germany were ceded to her enemies and by them allocated to themselves under League of Nations mandates. The economic significance of the territorial curtailment of Germany was vastly accentuated by other provisions of the treaty, to be discussed later.

The empire of Austria-Hungary was dismembered by the Treaty of St. Germain of 1919 with Austria and the Treaty of the Trianon of 1920 with Hungary. The territories of the empire were divided among Austria, Hungary, Poland, Czechoslovakia, Yugoslavia, Rumania, and Italy. The economic basis of Austria and of the great city of Vienna had been partly political but it rested more largely upon its varied economic resources, its strategic location, and free intercourse with other areas in the empire. The territorial changes destroyed Austria's political importance; deprived the country of iron, a large part of its coal, and many of its most important agricultural provinces; and severed the contacts between its large industrial populations and those areas with which complementary economic relations had long been maintained. Hungary was also reduced to comparative insignificance, without maritime outlets, with few nonagricultural resources, and with its frontiers cutting across long-established routes of trade and severing integrated economic areas.

The mere establishment of new political boundary lines was not economically significant. But the states which fell heir to the territories of the empire at once established tariff walls, elaborate administrative controls, and policies based on the conception of national economic self-sufficiency. The racial minorities had long been repressed by the Austrians and the Hungarians (the Magyars), and these minorities, now in the ascendancy, and inflamed by the passions of war and extreme nationalism, utilized their political sovereignty in a manner which forced profound alterations of the economy of eastern Europe.

As in the case of Austria and Hungary, Bulgaria, in the Treaty of Neuilly, was forced to yield extensive territories, including all of her Aegean coast line. The final territorial arrangements with Turkey were influenced by disputes between Allied Powers and by the unexpected transformation of Turkey under the revolutionary leadership of Mustapha Kemal. But Turkey yielded to the French in Syria and to British influence on the Arabian shores of the Red Sea, in Palestine and Trans-Jordan, and in the extremely important region of Iraq, embracing the historic Tigris-Euphrates river basin.

## The Throttling of German Economy

Aside from the provisions for territorial changes, the terms of the treaties of peace were particularly significant and severe in application to Germany. Germany indeed was forced to acknowledge and "accept" the responsibility of her allies as well as her own responsibility "for causing all the loss and damage" of the war. It was on this compulsory admission of "war guilt" that the more extreme provisions of the Treaty of Versailles were based.

Some of the numerous temporary provisions of the treaty may be mentioned by way of illustration. In spite of the loss of extremely important coal-producing areas in the west and in Upper Silesia, Germany was required to make extensive coal deliveries to France, Belgium, Italy, and Luxemburg. On the basis of the prewar output in the areas remaining in her possession after the war, the deliveries required under the treaty left to the Germans less than three fifths of the amount of coal consumed by them before the war; and prewar production standards could not at first be maintained. The loss of three fourths of Germany's prewar production of iron ore by the transfer of Alsace-Lorraine to France was not accompanied by any agreement, such as the Germans requested, for the exchange of coal and coke for ore. Thus the treaty gave to the French the power to disrupt the complementary economic relations, decreed by nature, between the Lorraine iron area and the Westphalian coal basin — a situation on which German economy vitally depended.

The internal economy of Germany was affected by various other provisions of the treaty. Germany was required to transfer to the victors 5,000 locomotives and 150,000 railroad cars in good repair. Nonreciprocal provisions required favorable treatment of goods and passengers of the Allied Powers on German railroads. Control of river transportation on the Elbe, the Oder, and the Danube as well as the Rhine was transferred to international commissions. Utilization of the Rhine for power and irrigation along the Franco-German frontier was given exclusively to France, and ownership of all bridges was made entirely French. Not less than 20 per cent of German tonnage used for inland navigation was to be transferred to the Allied Powers. In respect to trade relations, the treaty included a series of nonreciprocal advantages. Thus Alsace-Lorraine could send exports to Germany without duty for five years but might impose tariffs on goods from Germany. Germany was prohibited for three years from restricting the importation of various goods, including such luxuries as wines, during a period when her economy called for rigorous limitation of the consumption of luxuries and the utilization of all available foreign exchange for the purchase of materials essential for reconstruction and the payment of reparations.

With the exception of the provisions relating to coal, these and many similar clauses of the treaty were perhaps more provocative and humiliating than really vital in throttling German economy. More important were the provisions relating to the merchant marine, the status of German property and interests outside of Germany, and the imposition of reparations and indemnities. All merchant vessels larger than 1,600 gross tons were given up, and, in addition, half the vessels from 1,000 to 1,600 tons and one fourth of the fishing fleets. Vessels owned by Germans under neutral flags and vessels under construction were included.

Private as well as public interests in the former German overseas territories, including all concessions and contracts, and the rights of Germans even to reside in these territories, were surrendered. All private as well as public property in Alsace-Lorraine held by German nationals was to be expropriated. The treaty also gave to the victors the right "to retain and liquidate all property, rights, and interests belonging . . . to German nationals or companies controlled by them within their territories, colonies, possessions, and protectorates." These properties, which included extremely important patents and copyrights, were to be utilized primarily as the basis for compensation of nationals of the victor countries on account of injury or damage to them or their property in German territory. Furthermore, the Reparation Commission, created by the treaty, was authorized to require Germany to dispossess her nationals of "rights and interests" in "any public utility or in any concession operating in Russia, China, Turkey, Austria, Hungary, and Bulgaria," and to transfer such rights and interests, together with any similar rights and interests of the German government itself, to the Reparation Commission. A notable exception to the general policy of confiscating German private investments was the ultimate return to their owners of a large part of the properties originally confiscated in the United States. Control of the economic interests and properties of Germans was further assured by the sections of the treaty dealing specifically with reparations, to be discussed in Chapter 36.

## CHAPTER 34

# THE RUSSIAN REVOLUTION

### Russia and the War

The World War caught Russia in the process of a profound internal transformation, and at a time when this process was still in its early stages. The constitutional experiment was less than a decade old, while the educational reform, which had for its purpose the establishment of compulsory universal instruction, was on the point of achieving its first concrete results. In a similar fashion the industrialization of Russia, despite its rapid tempo, had not as yet proceeded beyond the initial stages of development. More than 80 per cent of the population still lived in the country districts, and agriculture continued to play the predominant part in national economy. New tendencies in agriculture had not had enough time to dominate any extensive area. Large-scale capitalistic agriculture was a comparatively recent phenomenon, and the agrarian legislation of Stolypin, aiming at the substitution of individual farming for the communal system, had been in operation for only a few years.

The war interrupted all the political, cultural, and economic progress that had been going on during the preceding decades, and it was bound to produce serious disturbances in the economic life of the country. In fact, it can be argued that Russia's unpreparedness was more of an economic than of a military nature. None of the countries that took part in the war were adequately prepared for an armed struggle of such magnitude and duration, but in comparison with the more industrialized countries of the West, it took Russia longer and she had to make greater efforts to adjust her economic system to the wartime requirements.

On the eve of the war Russia was still far from having attained any high degree of economic self-sufficiency. Russian industry imported large amounts of machinery and in some cases imported fuel. Many of the manufactured articles intended for wide consumption also had to be imported from abroad. The outbreak of the war brought with it a drastic curtailment of Russia's foreign trade, and the country was really subjected to a partial economic blockade. Neither the overland route to Central Europe nor the two principal sea outlets were any longer available.[1]  The ways of communication with the outside world that remained open were obviously insufficient.  The ports of the extreme north, such as Archangel and the recently constructed Murmansk, together with the transit route via Finland and Sweden, offered but limited opportunities, while Vladivostok on the Pacific shore was separated from European Russia by an enormous distance.  After the early summer of 1915 the situation became aggravated by the loss of Poland and part of the Baltic provinces which were among the most important industrial regions of the empire.

Almost from the outset the condition of railroad transport presented a grave and extremely difficult problem.  Russia's railway system, in spite of all the extensive construction of the prewar period, was still insufficient to satisfy the needs of the country, even in time of peace.  The loss of the western provinces was a particularly heavy blow, as it was precisely in that part of the empire that the railway system was developed more than anywhere else.  What remained was taxed to a very large degree of its capacity by the heavy demands of the military traffic.  Industry had to suffer from the consequences.  It must be added that in Russia the geographical distribution of some of the basic industries was particularly unfortunate.  For instance, the whole metallurgical industry of the St. Petersburg region was dependent upon raw material and fuel that, after the closing of the Baltic, could be obtained only from the south, while the Moscow textile industry relied regularly on the supplies of cotton from Turkestan.

To the difficulties with raw material and fuel was added that of labor shortage.  The repeated mobilizations made throughout the war brought the total number of men mobilized, by 1917, to over 15,000,000, which constituted a very high percentage of the whole male population of working age.  The results were felt much more acutely in industry than in agriculture.  In peasant farming the situation was met by the increased work on the part of the older members of peasant households as well as of their women and children, while on the large estates the drastic decrease in the available supply of hired labor was somewhat remedied by the extensive employment of war prisoners.  In industry the problem did not lend itself to such an easy solution.  Particularly

---

[1] Before the war about 87 per cent of goods imported into Russia came either through the western land frontier or via the Baltic Sea, while about 69 per cent of Russian exports went either through the Black Sea ports or the Baltic ports.

grave was the situation with regard to skilled labor. In the beginning of the war the practice of exempting skilled workers from mobilization was not systematically adhered to, with the result that many of them were lost to industry forever, while others were not recalled to their factories until much harm had been done by their prolonged absence.

In general, no attempts at economic control were made until the autumn of 1915. It was only at that time that under the pressure of aroused public opinion, and upon the initiative of the Duma, there were established several central boards, with the participation of the representatives of the legislative chambers and of various public bodies, to take care of war industries as well as of fuel and food supplies. The system of control thus established was essentially similar to that adopted by the other nations participating in the war, but in Russia its efficiency was impaired by the mutual distrust of the government and the opposition. In spite of this difficulty, however, war industries showed an impressive progress, and it was due to their increased production, together with assistance received from abroad, that the Russian army was at last adequately supplied early in 1917, paradoxically enough, almost on the eve of the revolution.

## The Revolution of 1917

Although the accumulated social discontent of the popular masses was the most potent single factor in the ultimate destruction of imperial Russia, and although the March revolution of 1917 started with bread riots on the streets of St. Petersburg, it would be a mistake to place all the emphasis on the economic interpretation. Grave as were the immediate economic difficulties which the government had to face, they did not affect the whole of the country, and they certainly had not reached catastrophic proportions. As yet there was no sharp decline in the amount of industrial production, and in fact there was even an increase of production in some of the branches of industry. There was no scarcity of food in the country, and the problem of transporting food supplies to the consuming regions of the north, and to its urban centers in particular, while difficult, was by no means insoluble.

The fall of the imperial regime was made immediately possible not by these economic troubles but by the acute political crisis caused by the war: the complete isolation of an unpopular and discredited government, the universal loss of respect for the dynasty, the breakdown of the national morale, and the war-weariness of the people. It was only after the revolution that the economic disintegration of the country began to proceed at an alarmingly rapid pace. The Provisional Government which replaced the imperial regime in March, 1917, was faced with a problem of tremendous difficulty. Committed to a policy of continuing the war in common with Allied Powers to a "victorious democratic peace," it had at the same time to undertake a complete reorganization of Russia along the new democratic lines. In the economic field it had to face not only the specific problems created by the war but also the persistent demands of the popular masses for immediate and drastic social reforms. It lacked, however, even that imperfect administrative apparatus which the old government had possessed, and it actually was deprived of any means of compulsion.

In industry the necessity for increased production clashed with the demands of labor for shorter hours and higher wages, while the factory discipline was greatly undermined by the hostility of the workers towards the employers and the management. In agriculture the successful solution of the problem of food supplies was compromised by the threat of an immediate distribution of all the land among the peasants. While the government was preparing to meet the demands of the masses in an orderly way by elaborating a corresponding legislation, the peasants and the workers often refused to wait, and took matters into their own hands. There were cases of attacks upon the landlords' property by the peasants, and of the ejection of owners and managers from the factories by the workers.

Under such conditions the Provisional Government was perhaps foredoomed to fail in its struggle against the opposition of the Bolsheviks. Originally a small minority not only in the country but even in the recently organized Soviets (Councils of Workers', Peasants', and Soldiers' Deputies), the Bolshevik party succeeded towards the end of the period in winning over a considerable part of the working class and the soldiery in and around St. Petersburg. They obtained also strong hold on the imagination of large masses of population throughout the country. This, however, did not mean the conversion of the people to communism. At that time, communism was not an issue in Russia, and the Bolsheviks themselves as yet did not emphasize such a program. In their propaganda they concentrated on immediate demands, and used slogans that could be easily understood by the masses. They advocated the transfer of political power from the "bourgeois" Provisional Government to the Soviets, the cessation of war, and the establishment of "workers' control" over industry. They encouraged the peasants to undertake an immediate seizure and distribution of land. It was the growing popularity of this program, and above everything else the longing of the Russian people for peace, that enabled the Bolsheviks in November, 1917, to overthrow the Provisional Government and to establish in Russia a Soviet Socialist Republic.

## The Period of Military Communism

The period of the first three and a half years of the Soviet regime in Russia is usually designated by the name of "Military Communism" or "War Communism." The name was used by the Bolsheviks themselves, and the implication is obvious. It was designed to convey the idea that the system of rigid control over the economic life of the country which prevailed during those years was an inevitable consequence of civil war and intervention.

It must be admitted that there is an element of truth in this contention. Many of the measures passed by the Soviet Government during that period were forced upon it by the stern necessity of an armed struggle with its enemies, both domestic and foreign, but as a complete explanation of the policies of the time the theory is inadequate. There are reasons for asserting that it was not only a *military* but also a *militant* communism. Long before Lenin's advent to power, he envisaged the possibility of transforming a successful "bourgeois" revolution in Russia into a "socialist" one. He was now determined to use the "dictatorship of the proletariat" in order to bring about such a transformation. In this determination he was strengthened by a confident expectation that the victory of the Communists in Russia would be followed in the near future by a similar revolution in Germany and eventually in the whole world. Accordingly, in his first public address after the victory, he declared that "we should now occupy ourselves in Russia in building up a proletarian socialist state." On the other hand, we have his own admission in March, 1921, at the time of the introduction of the New Economic Policy, that, "lifted up by the wave of enthusiasm . . . we assumed without sufficient calculation to be able, by the direct fiat of the proletarian state, to put in shape state production and state distribution of products in communist style." Thus the policies of military communism should be viewed as a combination of theory and expediency, and it is only from this double angle that they can be properly understood.

At first the chief concern of the new government was to remain in power. It was not secure in its control of the country, and in addition it still had on its hands the war with the Central Powers. With the complete disorganization of the army and the administrative machinery, it needed time to rebuild both. No wonder, therefore, that in the course of the first winter (1917–1918) the policies of the Soviet Government were of a tentative nature, and that in many cases it simply drifted along with the tide of events. In legalizing the "workers' control" over the factories or in sanctioning the seizure and division of land estates by the peasantry, the Bolsheviks were following the line of least resistance.

Nationalization of industry likewise proceeded piecemeal and without any evidence of a well co-ordinated plan. It was only in June, 1918, that a general decree of nationalization was passed affecting all larger industrial establishments, while the smaller enterprises were not nationalized until November, 1920.[1] Gradually a system of bureaucratic control was built up to take care of the whole nationalized industry. The task was assigned to the Supreme Council of National Economy, with about fifteen "sections," one for each of the major branches of industry, and about fifty "chief committees," each dealing with a particular industry. The efficiency of this control, however, was greatly impaired by conditions prevailing in the factories where the committees of workers had to be consulted over programs of production and questions of labor discipline. There was a considerable slackening of the latter, and a correspondingly sharp decline in the productivity of labor. An acute labor shortage began to be felt in the winter of 1918–1919, partly because of the enlistment of many workers in the Red Army, but chiefly because of a mass migration from the cities to the country districts, in quest of food. In an attempt to meet the situation the Soviet Government gradually tightened its grip over the working class. The trade-unions were turned into government-controlled organizations, with obligatory membership, and the right to strike was denied the workers. The principle

[1] In September of the same year the cottage industries were placed under government control, and the peasant craftsmen were obliged to turn their produce over to the state.

that work was a social duty, at first applied to the bourgeoisie rather than the proletariat, and for emergency work only, was later extended to the whole field of labor. The system of labor conscription was adopted in January, 1920. In its extreme manifestation it took the form of the militarization of labor, with the workers treated as soldiers and made subject to military discipline. Side by side with these measures of compulsion went attempts to create new work incentives. "Socialist competition" was encouraged as between individual workers, factories, and whole regions, and "shock establishments" were made out of some factories from which a greater output was expected in return for extra allowances of food, fuel, and raw material.

With the prohibition of private trade, which managed to survive only in the form of illegal and irregular peddling, the state tended to become the sole dispenser of food, clothing, and other necessities of life. While the country districts in this respect were left very much to their own fate, in the cities a system of food rations was introduced. The inhabitants were grouped into several categories in accordance with their respective social usefulness, and living quarters, transportation facilities, gas, and electricity were afforded free of charge. Co-operative societies, like the trade-unions, lost their former independent and voluntary character, and after March, 1919, they became governmental agencies of distribution, with compulsory membership. Under such conditions, with wages paid in commodities to the extent of 80 per cent, and with the catastrophic devaluation of currency, money practically lost all importance, and Soviet economists were discussing its complete elimination as an ideal to be striven for.

### The Peasants and the Revolution

The political strategy of Lenin, in its first stages, included an attempt to enlist on the side of the revolution the whole peasant class of Russia. Therefore an unqualified support was given by the Bolshevik party to the spontaneous agrarian movement which aimed at a general redistribution of land in the country. Immediately after the establishment of the Soviet regime a governmental decree transferred all the larger estates, whether belonging to the private landowners or to the state and the church, to the hands of township land committees and district Soviets of Peasants' Deputies. A further step was taken in February, 1918, when all ownership in land was abolished forever, and the right of cultivation was granted to all citizens who were willing to till the land personally or with the assistance of their families. The use of hired labor was forbidden. It was provided that land should be distributed according to a "labor-consumption" norm, but the form of cultivation (whether communal or individual) was left to the choice of the local peasant communities. The nationalization of land, an idea which Lenin had borrowed from his opponents, the Socialist Revolutionaries, remained, however, to a large degree a pure theory. The new government had no means to regulate its operation, and in practice land in each case was simply appropriated by the local peasantry. Inside a village equal distribution was more or less a rule, but equalization of allotments between the villages of the same township was less common. Cases of equalization throughout a district were extremely rare.

From the point of view of the direct increase in peasant land-ownership the results of the agrarian revolution were less impressive than many people would suppose. On the eve of the revolution, the Russian peasants already had in their hands about 75 per cent of the arable land, and it has been figured out that the average increase per capita was less than one and a half acres.[1] More important was the redistribution of land between the various groups of peasantry. Investigations made by Soviet economists have shown that as a result of redistribution, the middle groups of peasants, possessing less than ten acres of cultivated land, have acquired land at the expense of the landless rural proletariat, on the one hand, and of peasant households with a larger acreage, on the other. A heavy blow was dealt in particular to enclosed individual farming which had begun to develop on the eve of the revolution, on the basis of Stolypin's legislation. Epidemics of land partitioning continued throughout the period 1918–1920, and in some localities reapportionment reached such proportions that the Soviet Government was forced to issue laws aimed at limiting the practice and introducing more stability into the agrarian relations.

The most serious problem, however, from the governmental point of view, was to insure a regular flow of food supplies from the country districts to the cities. For a government which undertook to feed the population of the urban centers, and which had to take care of the provisioning of a large army, this was, without exaggeration, a question of life or death. Almost from the outset it became obvious that the peasants would not be inclined to part

[1] *O Zemle*, vol. I, Moscow, 1921, p. 9.

with their grain voluntarily, as they could not expect to get in return what they needed. The solution found by the Soviet Government was drastic. In May, 1918, a "grain dictatorship" was established. The government made it obligatory for the peasants to deliver to the organs of state all their produce above the specified subsistence minimum which they were permitted to retain for their own consumption. In the form of this "food levy" the agricultural produce was nationalized while production itself as yet remained outside of government control. As the peasants displayed a considerable reluctance in performing this obligation, the next step was for the government to undertake collection of grain by means of state coercion. The Commissariat of Supply organized a "Food Army" of its own, which by 1919 numbered some 45,000 armed men, and special "Workers' Detachments" were created in addition, to assist the government in this task. A similar duty was imposed upon the "Paupers' Committees" organized in the villages in June, 1918, from the poorer peasants, and with their appearance the class war in Russia entered a new phase. In this case, to reasons of expediency were added those of revolutionary strategy. If in the first stage of the revolution the Bolshevik appeal was to the peasantry as a whole, now, with the destruction of the czarist regime and the landowning nobility, one had to organize the poorer and the middle group peasants against the village bourgeoisie, the *kulaks*. In this way there would be created in the country districts a firm foundation for the final victory of the "dictatorship of the proletariat."

No vigorous attempts were made during this period at establishing socialistic forms of agriculture. The government sponsored the creation of agricultural communes, of various degrees of collectivization, trying to attract the peasants to these collectives (Russian name, *kolkhozy*), by granting loans and distributing agricultural implements. Also governmental "grain factories" were begun in the form of "soviet farms" (Russian name, *sovkhozy*). More radical measures were discussed, such as state regulation of peasant farming, compulsory sowing, and standardization of the technique of cultivation, but all these projects had to be dropped because they were obviously impractical under existing conditions. In fact, even the more modest attempts at collectivization were not very successful. Even at the end of the period both the *kolkhozy* and the *sovkhozy* played a very small part in the agricultural life of the country.

## The Crisis of 1921

By 1921 Russia's national economy was in a state of decline which had reached threatening proportions. The total product of industry was only about 15 per cent of what it had been on the eve of the war.[1] In agriculture the percentage was considerably higher (it has been variously estimated between 40 and 60 per cent), but even so, production was drastically reduced and the problem of distribution still presented unsurmountable difficulties. The urban centers, more particularly in the north, experienced an acute shortage of food, and for some time their population was subject to a regime of semistarvation. Equally catastrophic was the situation with regard to the supply of fuel, the lack of which, together with other factors, contributed to the well-nigh complete disorganization of transport.

One should bear in mind that to a large extent the economic breakdown was caused by circumstances over which the Soviet Government had no direct control. The loss of Poland and the Baltic provinces, made permanent by the provisions of the Brest-Litovsk and Riga treaties, was made more serious by the temporary loss of many other provinces as a result of the civil war. As long as this war continued, the Soviet Government was deprived of food supplies in the Ukraine, the Volga provinces, and Siberia; it was also cut off from important supplies of coal in the Donets basin, of iron both in south Russia and in the Ural region, of oil in Transcaucasia, and of cotton in Turkestan. To this must be added the effect of foreign intervention which made the economic blockade of Russia much more complete than it had been during the World War. But even when allowances are made for these difficulties, the governmental policies of the period of "War Communism" must be held responsible in part for the country's economic collapse. Even under such adverse circumstances industrial production could have been maintained on a higher level had it not been for the inefficiency of the management and the extremely low productivity of labor.

The detrimental effect of governmental policy was particularly obvious in agriculture. The peasants met the nationalization of their produce and the ruthless attempts at coercion with passive resistance. Unable to dispose of their surplus products on the

---

[1] For particulars concerning the various branches of industry, see *Za piat let, 1917–1922*, Moscow, 1922, pp. 404–408.

market, and unwilling to turn them over to the state in return for nothing, the peasants reduced their sowing area and slaughtered many of their cattle.  This was undoubtedly the chief reason why the famine of 1921–1922, caused partly by drought, assumed such appallingly large proportions.

The opposition on the part of the peasants was not always limited to passive resistance.  In 1920–1921 there were serious peasant uprisings in western Siberia, in southern Russia, and in the central province of Tambov.  From the peasantry the dissatisfaction penetrated into the ranks of the workers and the armed forces of the country, and there were strikes and factory riots in Petrograd, and in March, 1921, a mutiny of sailors and soldiers at Kronstadt.

## The New Economic Policy

The political aspect of the movement forced Lenin to hasten the promulgation of the New Economic Policy (or NEP) which had been under consideration for some time.  In his plea for the adoption of the NEP, made at the tenth convention of the Communist party in March, 1921, Lenin emphasized the danger of the peasant revolt which in his opinion presented a far greater menace to the safety of the Soviet regime than the now defeated White armies ever had been.  Consequently, the first aim of the NEP was to placate the peasants.

Instead of the food levy, which forcibly deprived each peasant of all of his surplus produce, there was introduced a definite tax in kind, later on replaced by one in money.  The rest of his surplus was left the property of the peasant, who could now sell it on the market.  The inevitable corollary was the re-establishment of freedom of trade within the country.  Further concessions to the peasantry were embodied in the new Land Code published in 1922.  While the principle of nationalization was left intact, the peasants' longing for a secure possession of land was satisfied by a system of practically permanent tenancy.  Somewhat later, leasing of land was allowed, subject to certain limitations, and the use of hired labor was permitted in exceptional cases.

The scope of the NEP, however, was not limited to agrarian relations.  It was a general and a fairly far-reaching change in the economic policies of the Soviet Government.  The end of the civil war created possibilities of a peaceful economic reconstruction.  It became clear to the Bolshevik — or Communist — leaders that chances for an immediate world revolution were very slight, and that capitalism in foreign countries had entered the phase of "temporary stabilization." The end of intervention and the lifting of the blockade offered opportunities for co-operation with foreign capital which could be used for the purpose of strengthening socialist economy at home. The promulgation of the NEP significantly coincided with the signing of the first Anglo-Soviet trade agreement. The new policy was clearly intended to make such co-operation possible. The government adopted the practice of granting industrial concessions to foreign capitalists, on the basis of partnership with the Soviet Government.

As far as small industry was concerned, a limited participation of private initiative was admitted : some of the plants were returned to their former owners, and licenses were granted to start new enterprises. The government, however, kept in its hands the control of large industry and the railroads; and foreign trade remained a government monopoly. These were considered to be the "commanding heights" which the Communist dictatorship could not abandon under any circumstances. A significant change, however, was introduced into the management of the nationalized industry. The general principle was that it should be run on a sound commercial basis. An attempt was made to do away with the excessive bureaucratic centralization of the preceding period. Although the Supreme Economic Council still retained general supervision over industry, the actual management of its various branches was delegated to some five hundred trusts, into which plants of the same type were combined. Obliged to account for their expenditures and revenues, and to submit to the Council their annual plans of production, the trusts were allowed a relative independence in their activities, and they were placed on a "self-supporting" basis. To increase the efficiency of the nationalized factories, individual management was given preference over the committee system, and capitalistic wage incentives, such as piece-rates and payment of bonuses, were introduced to supplement the devices of "socialist competition," and to replace those of compulsory labor.[1]

With the re-establishment of freedom of trade within the country, the reorganization of the nationalized industry on a commercial basis, and the partial abolition of the rationing system, money

[1] Compulsory labor was formally abolished in the revised Labor Code of 1922. It was retained, however, in emergency cases and as punishment for offenses against the law.

economy regained considerable importance. Consequently a semi-capitalistic organization was given Soviet finance. In 1922 the State Bank, which was made the center of the national banking system, was empowered to issue bills backed by either gold or foreign bonds. In 1924 the old devalued paper currency was withdrawn from circulation and replaced by the new *chervonets* bills; a chervonets was made equal to ten gold rubles.

The New Economic Policy was an ingenious compromise between communism and individualism, government control and private initiative, monopoly and freedom of trade. Under this system, which Lenin on occasions called "state capitalism," socialist and private "sectors" co-existed in the national economy. In agriculture private interests were largely predominant, but socialization retained its primary importance in industry and to a great extent in commerce. The socialist ideal was by no means abandoned, and its ultimate victory still was confidently expected. It was to be achieved, however, not by means of coercion, but by successful competition of the socialist sector with the private one. The Communists were to learn how to run the factories and how to trade, while the peasants were to be won over to socialism by a practical demonstration of its economic advantages. Apparently, a fairly long process of economic reconstruction and popular education was involved in the program. The NEP was declared to be a temporary retreat only, but Lenin insisted that the retreat was undertaken "in all earnestness and for a long period of time."

# CHAPTER 35

# PROBLEMS OF POSTWAR RECONSTRUCTION

───◆───

## Conflicting Proposals

Events so catastrophic as those of the World War inevitably affected vitally the subsequent economy of the world.  But human nature has remarkable recuperative powers; and the way in which these powers were directed and utilized (or, in the view of many, misdirected and thwarted) during the period of transition from a war to a peace economy is a phase of economic history rivaling in importance the war itself.

The immediate sources of many of the problems of reconstruction were the treaties of peace.  When it became apparent that the Allied Powers and the United States would win the war, a sharp conflict of opinion developed regarding the policies to be pursued in dealing with the defeated nations.  A policy of conciliation and of moderate demands was embodied in the pre-Armistice agreement, but in the making of the treaties other counsels prevailed.  The economic activities of the Germans, the Austrians, the Hungarians, and the Bulgarians were subjected almost completely to the will of the victors; and under the guise of reparations, obligations were exacted which in reality were indemnities.  At the same time, the conditions imposed made impossible the payment of the reparations demanded.  The Turks, because of their location, the revolutionary energy of their leaders, and disagreements among the victors, were able soon after the war to throw off the more extreme restraints imposed by the original treaty of peace (the Treaty of Sèvres) and to obtain comparatively favorable terms in the Treaty of Lausanne of 1923.

President Wilson, the chief official spokesman for those who favored a moderate and conciliatory peace, yielded repeatedly to the advocates of extreme measures.  He obtained in return the Covenant of the League of Nations and provisions for the International Labor Organization as integral parts of the Treaty of Versailles.  The proposals for international organization brought into sharp contrast the two conflicting points of view regarding the nature of the peace.  Even in this aspect of the final settlement, after yielding in the specific details of the terms imposed upon the defeated countries, the advocates of moderation and conciliation won an uncertain victory. The defeated nations and Russia were denied membership in the League until such time as the original members, acting by a two-thirds vote of the League Assembly, agreed to grant the privilege of membership. The League was widely viewed as essentially an instrument, in its early stages, for enforcing the terms of the treaties and maintaining the ascendancy of the victors.

Problems of reconstruction within the several warring nations evoked proposals no less contradictory than the conflicting views in the realm of international relations. The axis of controversy was the connection of governments with economic life. There were three main points of view. Socialists held that governments should utilize their wartime experiences in the directing and utilizing of enterprise and should go farther by socializing the ownership as well as the control of business. In Russia this view prevailed. In other countries many who opposed the socializing of capital held, nevertheless, that the extremely disorganized and difficult conditions of the transitional era could best be met by temporary continuance of governmental controls, with a gradual return to a modified and socially responsible individualism. But in most countries a third point of view gained wide acceptance and rapidly grew into a demand for an immediate return to prewar individualism. In the United States this mood was characteristically expressed by the demand for a "return to normalcy." This natural desire to discard wartime disciplines and restraints made extremely difficult the exercise of the centralized controls required for the adequate handling of the abnormal conditions of the period immediately following the war. It was out of this extreme reaction toward prewar individualism and its accompanying undisciplined encounters between conflicting groups that the Fascist conception emerged. Fascism attempted to use organized violence and dictatorial political methods for the purpose of rescuing private capitalism from the menace of undisciplined individualism and for preventing the transformation of private capitalism, under socialistic auspices, into a system of socialized enterprise.

### Loss of Life and Morale

A conservative estimate of the direct loss of life among the armed forces of the various belligerents exceeds 8,000,000. The number wounded was more than 20,000,000, and those reported as captured or missing totaled nearly 8,000,000. The casualties affected most vitally the male population of working age. This fact tended to give continuing status to the industrial employment of women, begun on a large scale during the war. There was also a significant change in the age distributions of the population, with disproportionately large numbers, during the early postwar period, of children and aged persons outside the productive periods of life.

Reconstruction policies had little direct bearing on the problems resulting from the irrevocable loss of life and the altered proportions of the ages and the sexes, but the care of the wounded and the rehabilitation of those who were not permanently disabled presented grave problems demanding immediate action and imposing heavy economic burdens. Care of the wounded and rehabilitation of the temporarily or partly disabled combatants involved concrete problems of hospitalization, medical treatment, and vocational training and placement. Far more difficult and in many countries more urgent was the problem of coping with the widespread demoralization of the population, both civilian and military. In Germany and the countries allied with her, the demoralizing effects of defeat and of the collapse of political authority were accentuated by the exhaustion of supplies of essential foods and materials. The blockade was continued until the signing of the treaty of peace in June, 1919. Later in that year Germany was described by a British official as "broken in body and spirit." The immediate and most pressing problems of physical relief were met with measurable success by such agencies as those created by the Supreme Economic Council at the Paris Peace Conference. The basic problems of rehabilitation and restoration were far more difficult, alike among the vanquished and among the victors. The mentality of war, created in part deliberately by propaganda and by the disciplines and habits of nations transformed into war machines, could not suddenly be cast aside, as a uniform, in favor of a mentality adapted to civilian needs and peaceful pursuits. The fundamental problem of reconstruction was the demobilization, figuratively speaking, of entire populations and the return to attitudes of mind and patterns of action suited to the pursuits of peace.

### Return of the Armed Forces to Civilian Life

The immediate and inescapable aspect of the general problem of demobilization was the reduction of the armed forces and the return of the discharged men to civilian life. The magnitude of the problem in terms of mere numbers is indicated by the fact that the mobilized forces of the European belligerents totaled almost 60,000,000. The mobilized strength of the German army alone at the time of the Armistice was about 6,000,000. A serious related problem was the demobilization of the vast numbers of civilian war workers whose functions ceased with the end of the war.

Before the end of the war, detailed studies were undertaken in most of the belligerent countries and also in some of the neutral nations, for the purpose of preparing for the transitional period after the war. Reconstruction agencies were established as early as 1916. In Great Britain a Ministry of Reconstruction was created in August, 1917, and before the end of the war fifteen groups of committees and commissions were organized and directed to make preliminary plans for dealing, during the transition, with the chief problems growing out of the war. Even earlier (in August, 1916) the German government created an Imperial Commission for Economic Transition. Its duties included preparations for returning soldiers to suitable civilian occupations; the care, rehabilitation, and re-employment of disabled soldiers; revival of labor legislation suspended for the purpose of speeding up the production of war materials; and removal of women and children from jobs normally held by men. This commission was later absorbed by a new Imperial Ministry of Economics. The British Ministry of Reconstruction and the German Ministry of Economics were typical pre-Armistice organizations for dealing with questions involving reconstruction.

The German and Austrian plans for demobilization included a novel method of releasing men not by military divisions or branches of the service but in accord with the need for workers as determined by careful analysis of industrial conditions. Elaborate plans were prepared for an interval of rest with pay for discharged soldiers, a public employment service, housing facilities, unemployment insurance, and retirement pensions. The carrying out of these plans was thwarted or delayed by the terms of the Armistice and by the breakdown of the political and economic systems of Germany and Austria. In France and Belgium the problems of fitting the demobilized forces into civilian life were comparatively simple. Captured and surplus war supplies, the resources of Alsace-Lorraine and the Saar, payments of reparations in kind, and credits for purchases abroad enabled these countries to obtain ample materials. Ironically enough, the problems of unemployment and of utilization of wartime plant facilities were solved by the need for labor and materials for the rebuilding of the war-torn areas.

The British plan for demobilization, although less elaborate than the German plan, was similar in principle. It was declared in 1916 that "demobilization is primarily an industrial and social question and only in a minor degree a military question." The Ministry of Reconstruction organized eight committees for formulating plans for demobilization not only of soldiers but also of civilian war workers. An official announcement early in 1918 stated that both the Admiralty and the War Office had agreed that "men must be released from the forces in accordance with civil rather than naval or military requirements." A Labor Resettlement Committee was formed with representatives of employers and trade-unions under the chairmanship of the Minister of Labor. Local advisory committees, also representing both employers and unions, were formed to handle local details and individual cases. The local employment offices or labor exchanges of the Ministry of Labor were expanded and adapted to the special requirements of demobilization. Representative groups were formed for putting into effect, with necessary modifications, the government's pledge to restore prewar trade-union rules and standards. Special schools and rehabilitation services were provided for disabled soldiers.

In view of the magnitude of the problem, the demobilization of the armed forces in Great Britain was accomplished in an efficient as well as democratic manner. It soon became apparent, however, that the permanent reabsorption of a considerable part of the working population was impossible under existing economic arrangements, in spite of the enormous casualties of the war. Among the factors which created a labor surplus were the decline of the basic industries, especially the textiles and shipbuilding; the continuance of women in gainful employments; and the increasing productivity of labor without a corresponding expansion of market demands for the output of labor.

### Restoration of the Peace Basis of Industry

The primary aim during the war was to obtain munitions, foods, and other supplies required by the combatants. This called for emphasis on basic industries such as agriculture, coal, iron and steel, and chemicals; the suppression of nonessential industries; and the adaptation of the facilities of production to war purposes. Controls were no longer sought in the competitive or semicompeti-

tive operation of normal market demands but in the public allocation
of materials, transport facilities, labor, and credit under an elaborate
priority system.

At the end of the war the production of war supplies was in full
swing, and many of these supplies were useless for postwar purposes.
In addition they absorbed vitally needed materials, glutted the
systems of transportation, and obstructed the conversion of plants
to nonmilitary uses. And yet the sudden cessation of war industries
would have caused large-scale unemployment, a breach of innumerable contractual relations, and the disruption of a complex and
highly integrated system of production. The demobilization of
war industries, like the demobilization of the armed forces, was
not merely a negative process of bringing industrial war activities
to an end but a positive problem of fitting the productive facilities,
the materials, and the labor supply into the radically different
pattern of production for peace.

The problem could not be solved by merely returning to prewar
industrial patterns, for adaptations were required to meet important alterations in European economy and economic relations.
Public and private credit was so expanded as to be described
only in astronomical figures. The elaborate and highly sensitive
organization of national and international markets was gravely
disrupted. Monetary and exchange systems were no longer regulated by the gold standard, and were without a sound or uniform
alternative basis. Prices were inflated and price relations were
out of balance because of abnormal demands for goods required
for war. The capital structure was seriously impaired.

It was primarily the abnormal demand for labor and materials
for the restoration of the capital structure that enabled private
enterprise to absorb the demobilized combatant forces and to
re-establish itself on a peace basis. The cessation of employment
and of income from employment in connection with war activities
involved a grave curtailment of demand for consumption goods,
but the production of capital goods could be financed by means of
credits, and the restoration of the capital structure created an
abnormal demand for capital goods, such as new machinery and
raw materials. Thus the transition from the wartime economy to
a peace basis was facilitated, ironically enough, by the wartime
impairment of the capital structure. The pressing problems of
utilizing the vast war industries organization and of allocating the
supplies that had been intended for war purposes were handled by

the Supreme Economic Council, created at the Paris Peace Conference. The Council took over many of the emergency economic agencies, directed the work of relief, and allocated supplies for the rebuilding of the devastated areas.

## Restoration of the Capital Structure

Impairment of the capital structure was not confined to actual destruction or damage in the areas of armed conflict. There was serious deterioration due to deferred maintenance and replacement. Investments in enterprises designed purely or mainly for supplying war needs had no value or comparatively small value after the war. In many industries there was overinvestment in capital facilities due to the stimulus of war demands, and as a result after the war there was an abnormal amount of marginal and submarginal investment requiring liquidation or retarding the profitable use of other facilities. In the United States an outstanding illustration was the extension of agriculture to grazing lands and other areas not suited to farming. Financially, the capital structure was subjected to severe strain by the sudden shifts in prices, the vast expansion of credit, and the disturbed relations between debtors and creditors. In the defeated countries additional disruptive factors included loss of territories and trading connections, the burden of reparations, and the confiscation of property beyond the treaty frontiers.

The estimates of actual destruction of capital during the war can be little more than intelligent guesses. A noted British statistician, Professor Bowley, hazards "a rough guess" that all property destroyed, excluding armaments, munitions, and other military supplies, approximated £2,000,000,000 in terms of prewar prices, or about one thirtieth of all property values. British wholesale prices in 1919 were more than twice as high as in 1913. The same authority states that in 1920 the world's productive capacity had so rapidly revived as to be at least as great as might have been anticipated before the war even if there had been no war. He cites with approval a significant statement by M. Theunis, president of the World Economic Conference at Geneva in 1927. "The eight years of postwar experience have demonstrated the outstanding fact," said the president of the Conference, "that, except in the actual fields of conflict, the dislocation caused by the war was immensely more serious than the actual destruction. The main trouble now is neither any material shortage in the resources of nature nor any inadequacy in man's power to exploit them. It is all in one form or another a maladjustment — not an insufficient productive capacity but a series of impediments to the full utilization of that capacity."

## Economic Readjustments to New Political Boundaries

Prominent among the causes of dislocation and maladjustment impeding economic reconstruction was the political reorientation after the war. Almost everywhere except in Russia there was a demand for individualism and *laissez faire* at a time when the intricate problems of reconstruction required an exceptional degree of discipline and co-ordinated action. Both the older states and the newly created national sovereignties encountered difficult problems of adjustment to new political institutions. The new political boundaries tended to become economic frontiers which severed long-established economic relations.

New international boundary lines resulting from the World War totaled almost 8,000 miles. Whatever may have been the justification and the ultimate advantages of many of these changes, such extensive political readjustments necessarily created grave problems which were aggravated by intense nationalism, racial and religious animosity, and the passions of war. New states in Europe included Czechoslovakia, Poland, Lithuania, Latvia, Estonia, and Finland. Austria and Hungary became separate political units greatly reduced in size. Russia, Germany, Bulgaria, and Turkey suffered diminutions, while France, Belgium, Denmark, Italy, Greece, Yugoslavia (the former Serbia), and Rumania made extensive gains. Numerous territorial changes outside of Europe affected Great Britain as well as Continental countries.

The problems of economic readjustment to new political boundaries as affecting the defeated countries were mentioned in the discussion of the treaties of peace. But even the countries which expanded their boundaries experienced grave difficulties in consolidating their gains, in organizing their rule over populations partly hostile to the change, and in developing economic systems within their own frontiers after the severing of long-established economic relations. The "Succession States" (the countries which inherited various portions of the Austro-Hungarian empire) exhibited in aggravated form the general problem of readjustment. Most of the Succession States imposed prohibitions on imports from their neighbors for the purpose of developing and protecting "national" industries. Prohibitions were also imposed on the export of products which were deemed essential for national self-sufficiency and for the promotion of manufactures. A limited amount of trade was carried on by licenses and special agreements.

Railway transportation was disrupted by the new boundaries. There were conflicting claims to ownership of the rolling stock of the Austro-Hungarian state railways, and a country in possession of cars and locomotives refused to allow them to cross its frontiers in fear of seizure and detention by rival claimants. Traffic was impeded also by the elaborate customs arrangements of the new states, by lack of facilities for expediting traffic at the new international boundaries, and by obstacles in the way of adequate use of international telegraph and telephone systems.

These obstructions incident to the new political frontiers, and especially the commercial restrictions in the Succession States, were similar to the obstacles created by territorial changes elsewhere. But in the Succession States they were particularly significant because they broke into economic as well as political fragments the formerly integrated system of the Austro-Hungarian empire. Instances of necessary economic readjustments are to be found in the new political barriers between the coal fields of central Czechoslovakia and the iron mines of Austria; between the Austrian spinning industry and the weavers of western Czechoslovakia; between the Croatian and Transylvanian wheat fields, annexed to Yugoslavia and Rumania, and the milling industry of Hungary; between the hinterland northeast of Italy and its natural outlets on the Adriatic Sea; between the industrial centers of the new Baltic states and the agricultural hinterland of Russia; between the iron industry of Polish Upper Silesia and the coal industry of the German portions of the same area; and between the iron of Lorraine and the coal of the Ruhr.

## New Political Institutions

Political institutions and policies are conspicuous, and the readily observable actions of governments tend to give an exaggerated view of their influence on economic life. It is nevertheless true that economic behavior is conditioned significantly by the political environment. Opinions differ as to whether or not the political changes of the war period promoted ultimate economic improvement either within nations or in the economic relations between peoples. But in any case the changes required vital economic readjustments and created immediate economic problems.

The Baltic provinces of the Russian empire — Lithuania, Latvia, Estonia, and Finland — broke away from the empire and attempted to transform their parts of the autocratic Russian system into republics and to isolate themselves from the Russian economy as well as from Russian politics. Poland was formed by the union of territories previously under German, Austrian, and Russian rule and was confronted by the problem of fusing these diverse areas and local institutions into a national system  The newly formed republic of Czechoslovakia and the other states which fell heir to the territories of the Austro-Hungarian empire faced the necessity of organizing new agencies of government or of extending existing governments to new areas with conflicting nationalistic ambitions and racial minorities.

The governments of the older states with few exceptions were reorganized both in structure and in economic policy. Russia, Germany, Austria, Hungary, Turkey, several of the smaller states, and (after a brief postwar interlude) Italy underwent revolutions requiring radical readjustments to new political institutions. Extremes of political change are represented by Russia and Italy, with subsequent struggles in other countries to maintain parliamentary institutions in opposition alike to Russian Communism and to Italian Fascism.

The revolutionary and inexperienced government of Russia undertook to reorganize the entire national economy on the basis of national ownership of capital. In this huge task the difficulties it encountered included the German invasion; the disintegration of the old regime; armed intervention after the war by nonsocialistic powers in support of internal enemies of the government; diplomatic and commercial isolation; and lack of technical facilities and skills. In Italy the postwar demoralization was aggravated by a struggle between socialism and private capitalism. The outcome was the triumph in modified form of the latter under Fascism, with an unprecedented degree of governmental control of enterprise as a method of preventing socialization on the one hand and demoralization or disintegration on the other hand.

Particularly significant internationally were postwar attempts at political readjustment in Germany and Austria. Both countries introduced parliamentary democracy, and in both countries the principal parties had socialistic aspirations. But the revolutionary governments were confronted by conflicting views of socialistic strategy and by the extreme hostility of opponents of the socialization of capital. Furthermore, the treaties of peace subjected both countries to indirect control by foreign governments, which, however, assumed no responsibility for the maintenance of German and Austrian economic life. To the burdens of reparations were added the financing and administering of vast programs of housing and social insurance demanded by the workers. Various other economic groups in both countries brought pressure to bear on their governments. Group interests and conflicts, finding expression through proportional representation, gave rise to the multi-party system. In place of unified party responsibility for the conduct of government, there was a succession of blocs and temporary compromises, frequently ending in resort to decisions by executive decrees. The ultimate results were the discrediting of the democratic principle and the rise of Fascism, which had already gained ascendancy in Italy.

## Minority Groups

The problem of minority groups had long disturbed most of the countries of Europe, but in spite of underlying discontents the powerful prewar governments had maintained racial relations on the basis of minimum interference with economic life. Many of the territorial changes after the World War were designed to recognize the legitimate claims of national groups, such as the Poles, the Finns, the Czechs, and the Slovaks. Other changes aggravated old minority problems or subjected new groups to persecutions, as the Magyars in Rumania, the Germans in Poland, and the Austrians of the Tirol under Italian rule. At the peace conferences emphasis was placed on the lack of adequate safeguards for the rights of minorities within the several political units. An effort was made by the victorious powers to provide such safeguards in the treaties which defined the boundaries of Poland, Czechoslovakia, Austria, Hungary, Yugoslavia, Bulgaria, Greece, and Turkey. Special declarations, conventions, and bilateral treaties concerned the minorities of the new Baltic states, Upper Silesia, Danzig, and other areas.

These treaty provisions and special agreements for safeguarding the rights of minorities were opposed to the principle of assimilation and were designed to perpetuate the linguistic, educational, religious, and racial separateness and integrity of minorities. The enforcement of the safeguards was acknowledged by most of the states concerned as an international obligation embodied in their member-

ship in the League of Nations. The League itself thus assumed
a measure of responsibility. But minorities in France, Italy, and
Great Britain were beyond the jurisdiction of the League; and its
work in dealing with the groups nominally under its protection was
restricted largely to conciliation proposals for mutual agreement
between the minorities and the national authorities to which they
were subject.

Racial ambitions and animosities were intensified by the World
War and were reflected in a spirit of revenge which characterized
many of the liberated groups. So intense was the spirit of nationalism and so embittered were racial relations in Greece, Bulgaria,
and Turkey that arrangements were made for a large-scale exchange
of populations. Greece, a country of limited natural resources and
a population of about 5,000,000, added about 1,500,000 Greeks from
Turkey and Bulgaria. About 400,000 Turks were transferred from
Greece to Turkey. An agreement between Bulgaria and Greece, in
1919, provided for the voluntary emigration of minorities under
the supervision of a commission composed of two League of Nations
appointees and one representative of each of the two countries.
Problems of Jewish minorities led to the establishment of a Jewish
"national home" by Great Britain in Palestine. a British mandate
under the League of Nations.

## Obstructions in the Way of Enterprise

An outstanding contrast between the economy of the war period
and that of peace under private enterprise was the basis of the
demand for goods. In a system of specialized production and
exchange and competitive prices, effective demand depends on
the possession of means of payment by consumers and on the
adequate allocation of income to the purchase of the output of
enterprise. In an industrial society where the population belongs
largely to the nonpropertied classes and to small proprietors, the
possession of means of payment depends predominantly on jobs.
But jobs, especially in an era of rapid technological advance, depend
on volume of production. The central problem of private enterprise is therefore to maintain without obstruction or interruption
the cycle of production, income, consumption, and production.
During the war the cycle was maintained by governmental control
of all stages of the cycle, and particularly the income stage, through
the utilization of credit.

The end of the war was also the end of the artificially stimulated demand for the output of private enterprise. For a short time after the war the restoration of the impaired capital structure created an abnormal demand, as was previously stated, for labor, capital, and materials and aided in the transition to a peacetime basis. A significant feature of the employment of both capital and labor is the interrelationship between the production of capital goods (for use in further production) and the production of ordinary consumption goods. A small increase, actual or anticipated, in the demands of consumers for goods and services brings producers into the market in quest of profits and stimulates the production of capital goods. The making of capital goods in turn increases employment, purchasing power, and demand for consumption goods. On the other hand, a small decrease in the demand for consumption goods puts an end to the profits to be derived from new capital goods and curtails or even suspends the demand for capital-goods replacement. This in turn throws out of employment a large part of the labor and the capital used in producing capital goods. When consumers who have depended on income from the production of capital goods are no longer able to obtain income from this source, the curtailment of their consumption means in turn the impairment of the income of those who are engaged in the consumption-goods industries. These relations are affected by price changes and by the fact that production must be based in part on fallible estimates of future demand and future prices and on particularly fallible estimates of the shares of the aggregate demand which the several producers will be able to supply.

After the World War, when abnormal reconstruction and capital-goods replacement reached their peak and began to decline, private enterprise was faced with an acute form of its normally recurring problem of a lack of balance between the capital-goods industries and the consumption-goods industries and by disequilibrium in the allocation of means of payment to consumption and investment. Under prevailing economic controls, there was available no method for directing the necessary flow of income into consumption within each country, either directly or through price changes, for the purchase and needed utilization of the potential output of the new and comparatively efficient facilities for production. The traditional mode of relieving the disequilibrium, namely, an expansion of external trade, was thwarted by intensified competition and by postwar international maladjustments.

The high degree of specialization among the principal countries of Europe created an economic interdependence which increased their business activity and their prosperity when the flow of trade was unobstructed and which, conversely, interfered gravely with their well-being when economic relations were severed or seriously impaired. During the postwar period the normal obstacles, such as tariffs and an unbalanced allocation of income to consumption and investment, were magnified and reinforced by other obstructions in respect not only to international trade but as well to the economic processes within nations. Among the postwar impediments to the full employment of labor and capital were the maladjustments, already described, connected with territorial and political changes and with the disruption of long-established economic relations. Other obstacles included the reparation sections of the treaties of peace, which proved to be economically unsound and unworkable, and the vindictive spirit of the treaties and of enforcement policies, which impeded the return of good will and mutual confidence essential to normal interchange. The burdens of debt called for interest payments alone in excess of current means of payment. The fluctuations in prices vitally altered creditor-debtor relations and made impossible any sound long-range policy of allocating income on the one hand to consumption and on the other hand to investment. Trade and the payment of international balances were difficult and frequently inequitable because of the highly variable monetary systems and exchange rates. These obstacles call for brief explanatory comment.

## Unstable Monetary and Exchange Systems

The restoration of the impaired capital structure was accompanied, in 1919 and 1920, by further monetary and credit inflation and by a brief industrial boom. Governmental as well as private debts were increased even beyond the vast proportions of the war period. The British government, to be sure, began a slight reduction of its debt in 1920, but this was made possible by taxation so severe that taxpayers, in spite of the temporary business boom, were forced in many cases to borrow money for the payment of taxes. The French government's receipts in 1920, other than from loans, were less than half of its expenditures. The International Financial Conference of the League of Nations at Brussels in 1920 estimated that German expenditures for 1920, exclusive of reparation payments and other obligations under the treaty of peace, were almost twice as large as the receipts provided for in the

budget. Among other important countries of Europe, the estimated ratios of receipts to expenditures as provided for in the
budgets ranged from 21 per cent for Poland to 95 per cent for
Sweden.

Prices fluctuated widely. In Germany the general level of
wholesale prices, on an index basis with the average for 1913 as
100, had risen to 262 by January, 1919. The figure for October,
1919, was 562, and for January, 1920, 1,256. Thereafter there was
comparative.stability until the summer of 1921, when riotous
inflation began which soon destroyed the value of money and the
meaning of the price figures. Even in Great Britain price fluctuations seriously disturbed economic relations. The index number
for January, 1919, was 224, or 124 per cent above the average for
1913. For July, 1920, the index number was 299, and for January,
1922, 156. Fluctuations in the general price level were less disturbing in some countries than were the divergent trends of the
prices of important types of commodities. Disproportionate
changes in the prices of raw materials, partly finished goods, and
finished products, and in the prices of industrial and agricultural
products, were brought about by changes in tariffs, monetary
policies, exchange rates, and other factors which had slight connection with the basic conditions of supply and demand. Such changes,
combined with abnormal fluctuations in supply and demand, vastly
increased the hazards of business enterprise and disturbed the
equilibrium of the various economic groups.

When the artificial measures of the war period for stabilizing
exchange rates were abandoned, it was impossible to return to the
prewar gold standard, and exchange rates fluctuated wildly. The
pound sterling, least subject, among the currencies of the belligerents, to fluctuations in terms of the dollar, fell from par of $4.87
to an average of $3.66 in 1920, and gradually rose thereafter. The
French franc fell from 19.3 cents to an average of 7 cents in 1920,
rose to an average of 8.2 cents in 1922, and then rapidly declined.
The reichsmark fell from 24 cents to an average of less than 2 cents
in 1920, and soon thereafter the orgy of inflation rendered the quo-
tations meaningless. The exchange rates of these currencies and of
most of the others varied widely from month to month and even
from day to day; and they fluctuated, of course, in relation to each
other as well as in terms of the dollar.

Before the World War, exchange rates were based on the gold
standard. The principal currencies were assigned a standard gold

content and were backed by gold reserves.  Ordinarily, international transactions (including not merely the exchange of goods but expenditures by tourists, debt payments, investments, etc.) were handled by the buying and selling of bills of exchange, and only when the balances became so large as to cause the premium on bills of exchange to exceed the cost of gold shipments was there an actual transfer of gold.  After the war the balances connected with international transactions of ordinary types were so variable and of such magnitude, and the reserves of gold were so impaired, that the gold standard was no longer practicable.  Neither could the emergency wartime "pegging" of exchange rates be continued.  Wild fluctuations in the comparative values of the various currencies naturally resulted from the highly variable quantities and values of irredeemable currencies; from the speculative buying and selling of foreign currencies; and from the flight of capital from country to country as a result of the disturbed and uncertain conditions, both political and economic.

Unstable exchanges adversely affected international transactions and business activity in several ways.  Speculation was encouraged, and this in turn aggravated the instability of the exchanges.  Countries urgently in need of capital were frequently deprived of funds for investment as well as of the resources required for stabilizing their monetary systems.  Business transactions, especially those involving long-term commercial and financial operations with obligations payable in the future, were discouraged by the uncertain nature of the obligations in terms of future exchange rates.  A country with depreciated exchange rates could sell to other countries advantageously, because persons in other countries could buy its currency at reduced rates.  On the other hand, such a country could buy abroad and meet its debts or other obligations abroad only by paying a premium for foreign currencies.  Since the industrialized countries of Europe required extensive imports of food and raw materials, the export advantages of depreciated currencies were at least in part neutralized.  Nevertheless, the desire to stimulate exports tended to encourage the depreciation of exchange rates; while other countries, placed temporarily at a disadvantage, were inclined to resort to the same artificial stimulus and also to raise higher their protective walls in the form of tariffs, quotas, and prohibitions, in order to keep out the goods of countries with depreciated currencies.

# CHAPTER 36

# INTER–ALLIED DEBTS AND REPARATIONS

## The War Loans of the Allies

The financial problems of the war soon created a serious crisis. The Continental Allies required direct assistance from Great Britain, and the purchases of supplies from neutral countries made it essential to use effectively the facilities of London as a market for foreign exchange.   Credits were opened in Paris and in London for the Balkan powers and for Russia.   The specie resources of the Allies were pooled, and much of the gold moved to London.   As early as February, 1915, France, Russia, and Great Britain reached a formal agreement for the establishment of financial solidarity for the period of the war.   It was further agreed that although complete accounts should be kept of all transactions, the precise amount of the ultimate obligation would be determined at the close of the war. All grants of assistance among the Allies were thus expressed as loans, although it was recognized that many of the grants were in fact subsidies.   The purpose underlying this policy was to encourage economy in expenditure.   If the beneficiary states were convinced that they would be asked to repay some stated proportion of the total credit, it is evident that they might wisely attempt to achieve what little economy is possible in wartime.   This general purpose is clearly suggested by the actual practice of Great Britain.   The needs of her borrowers were carefully scrutinized, but little attention was given to the acknowledgment of indebtedness.   Large sums were lent to Serbia for which no evidence of obligation at all was received for many months.

In the early months of the war, France was able to make some loans, but her resources were soon exhausted.   Great Britain thus became the primary source of credit.   Loans were also placed in neutral countries.   We are not, however, concerned with the administrative problems of war finance.   It will suffice, therefore, to present the summary of war borrowing, up to April 1, 1917, given in the table on page 724.   In addition to these intergovernmental loans, the Allies had borrowed $2,891,000,000 in the United States and in other neutral countries.   The burden of war debt was thus already large before the United States entered the war.

AMOUNTS OF INTERGOVERNMENTAL LOANS OF THE ALLIES TO APRIL 1, 1917 [1]

| Borrowing Country | Lending Country | | Total Borrowing |
| --- | --- | --- | --- |
| | Great Britain | France | |
| Russia | $1,657,500,000 | $426,500,000 | $2,084,000,000 |
| Italy | 673,500,000 | | 673,500,000 |
| France | 555,000,000 | | 555,000,000 |
| Belgium | 242,800,000 | 48,300,000 | 291,100,000 |
| Serbia (Yugoslavia) | 59,000,000 | 35,800,000 | 94,800,000 |
| Rumania | 60,800,000 | | 60,800,000 |
| Portugal | 9,700,000 | | 9,700,000 |
| Greece | 7,100,000 | 3,900,000 | 11,000,000 |
| Belgian Congo | 4,500,000 | | 4,500,000 |
| British Dominions | 544,500,000 | | 544,400,000 |
| Total | $3,814,400,000 | $514,500,000 | $4,328,800,000 |

## The War Loans of the United States

In April, 1917, the financial situation was as critical as the military situation — in some respects more critical, because more immediate. The financial expedients devised to facilitate purchases of war material in the United States were very nearly exhausted. The declaration of war by the United States relieved the immediate financial pressure. The financial resources of the United States were placed at the disposition of the Allied Powers without limitation; within a few days, a credit to the amount of $250,000,000 was placed at the disposition of the British Treasury.

The United States, however, attached a meaning to war loans that differed in every vital respect from the attitude of the French and British. There was not the slightest evidence of any intent to treat the loans as subsidies. The credit extended was a pure business transaction, in fact as in form. All loans to the Allies were covered by short-term notes bearing the same rate of interest as the Liberty Bonds issued to provide the funds. It was intended that these notes should be soon replaced by foreign bonds maturing at the same date as the Liberty Bonds issued. The United States government merely acted as an intermediary. It was further provided that none of the funds should be spent outside the United States. This limitation was not of great significance, because the chief need of the Allies was for funds available in the United States.

French writers have contended that the United States as an ally had in effect pooled her resources for a common cause. Unofficial

[1] Moulton, H. G., and Pasvolsky, Leo, *War Debts and World Prosperity*, New York, 1932, p. 425.

statements of French writers go to great lengths to establish this point. They attribute a technical legal meaning to the official term "associated power," because the French translation may be given the meaning of the term "partner." Emphasis is also placed upon the use of the funds in the United States, and more strangely still upon the details of centralized purchase of food and materials of war. It is seriously suggested that these war contracts were "tainted" by compulsion in such a fashion as to make them invalid. There can be no manner of doubt in respect to the nature of the war loans of the United States. Whatever might be said by particular members of Congress or by private persons, and whatever might be said of an "unstinted use of the resources of America," the actual affair was intended to be a strictly commercial transaction. The American point of view was expressed with precision by the Committee of Ways and Means in its report on the first Liberty Loan bill: "It will be observed that the credit proposed to be extended to foreign governments will take care of itself and will not constitute an indebtedness that will have to be met by taxation in the future."

During the debate on the first Liberty Loan, it was proposed that a gift, limited in amount, be made to France in recognition of French assistance during the Revolution. At the request of the Premier of France, this resolution was not pressed, and no action was taken.

THE INTER-ALLIED DEBTS, OCTOBER, 1919, IN MILLIONS OF DOLLARS [1]

| Loans to: | By U. S. | By United Kingdom | By France | Total |
|---|---|---|---|---|
| United Kingdom | 4,210 | | | 4,210 |
| France | 2,750 | 2,540 | | 5,290 |
| Italy | 1,625 | 2,335 | 175 | 4,135 |
| Russia | 190 | 2,840 | 800 | 3,830 |
| Belgium | 400 | 490 | 450 | 1,340 |
| Serbia and Yugoslavia | 100 | 100 | 100 | 300 |
| Other Allies | 175 | 395 | 250 | 820 |
| Total | 9,450 | 8,700 | 1,775 | 19,925 |

The amount of the Allied debts as known in October, 1919, is given in the above table. The United States and Great Britain were the only countries having a net credit balance. Assuming all debts paid, Great Britain would have had a balance of $4,490,000,000; but the Russian debt would certainly not be paid, and it would

[1] Keynes, J. M., *Economic Consequences of the Peace*, Macmillan & Co., Ltd., London, 1919, p. 271.

be clearly unwise to attempt to collect the full amount of the sums due from France and Italy. The official attitude of the United States, with its emphasis upon prompt settlement in full, inevitably became a serious factor in the financial policies of all the Allies as soon as the Armistice brought hostilities to an end. The policy of the United States was not technically related to the problem of reparations, but a group of debtors could hardly fail to consider all their assets with care when their creditor was pressing them for payment. The attitude of the United States on the repayment of the war debts of the Allies gradually became associated in their minds with the problem of reparations.

### The Problem of Reparations

The fourteen points proposed by President Wilson as a basis for peace (January 8, 1918) recognized the justice of the restoration of devastated territory in Belgium and in France. The restriction of reparation to these countries is perhaps as significant as the language used: "Belgium must be evacuated and restored"; "All French territory should be freed and the invaded portions restored. . . ." Apparently, only primary work of reconstruction was contemplated. In the text of the Armistice, a more general phrase was used: "With the reservation of any future concessions and claims by the Allies and the United States, reparation for damage done. While the Armistice lasts, no public securities shall be removed by the enemy which can serve as a pledge to the Allies for the recovery of reparation for war losses."

The insertion of the reparations clause in the Armistice was urged by Clemenceau after some deliberation. Correspondence shows that President Wilson became concerned over the change of phrase, and not without just grounds. The Allied governments, in a note of November 2, 1918, admitted their intention of making the nature of the obligation more precise. "The Allies feel that it is important to leave no possible doubt as to the meaning of the condition. They take the phrase to mean that Germany must give compensation for all the losses suffered by the civil populations of the Allied nations, and for all damage to their property caused by the aggression of Germany, on land or on water, or by reason of aerial bombardment."[1] The extended meaning to be given the clause in the Armistice was not generally known until a few weeks later.

[1] Calmette, G., *Recueil des documents sur l'histoire de la question des réparations*, Paris, 1924, p. 71.

The new concept of reparations was brought dramatically before the public by the general election announced in Great Britain for December. The earlier platforms and speeches paid no attention to reparations, but as the campaign failed to yield the desired prospect of success, the boldest spirits appealed to popular sentiment on the issue of the cost of the war. On December 6, Lloyd George declared that "All the European Allies have accepted the principle that the Central Powers must pay the cost of the war up to the limit of their capacity." In the course of the following week even this qualification was abandoned, and the electorate went to the polls on the explicit promise of the government to demand the whole cost of the war. It was even declared that a Committee of the Cabinet believed that Germany could in fact be forced to pay. We know now that the principle had been accepted, before the election was planned, but the publicity of the campaign did much to complicate the discussions at the Peace Conference.

## Negotiations during the Peace Conference

Within a month of the signing of the Armistice, Great Britain, France, and the United States had become, in some measure, committed to economic policies that were inconsistent with the achievement of a workable peace. France was convinced that she could secure large compensation from Germany, and large concessions from Great Britain and the United States. Great Britain felt little real hope of securing the full cost of the war from Germany, but she was deeply committed to exacting all Germany could pay. She was thus closer to France than to the United States on the basic economic issue. The United States was committed to a policy of restricting reparations to the minimum requisite for the reconstruction of devastated areas. The United States, however, insisted upon prompt funding of the debts of the Allies. From the point of view of the United States, these issues were distinct. From the point of view of the Allies, the problems were necessarily parts of a larger whole. If Germany was to pay the cost of the war, the debts due the United States were obviously a most conspicuous and specific item in the cost. If the United States insisted upon payment in full, the Allies would have to get at least that much from Germany.

Consideration of reparations at the peace conference was largely based on the presumption that Germany was responsible for the whole cost of the war. Until a late stage in work on the treaty, the capacity of Germany to pay was scarcely considered. Claims of various countries were submitted and discussed, but no change in policy was suggested.

In the meantime, Klotz, the French Minister of Finance, had suggested a joint conference on the problem of the debts of the Allies to the United States. It was implied that something less than a full settlement would be necessary, but the primary objective was to avoid the creation of privileged positions by the grant of large concessions to the weaker powers. The British, also, discussed the matter with the agent of the United States Treasury. Nothing was done. Finally, January 15, after further informal discussion, the point was formally raised by a letter from the French Deputy High Commissioner to the American Secretary of the Treasury. Two points were made: that privileged situations could be avoided only by a general negotiation; that the capacity of the various countries to pay would be affected by their expectations of payments from Germany.

Secretary Glass replied that he saw no need of any general negotiation, though he was ready to recognize that the capacity of a country to pay might be affected by the amount received from Germany. He insisted upon independent settlements with each country, but recognized the expediency of postponing settlement until after the signature of the treaties. It became evident later that Secretary Glass had no authority to suggest even by implication any reduction in the amount of the debt.

Until the early months of 1919 there is no evidence of any adequate appreciation of the economic adjustments that would be required to restore Europe to effective economic activity. The problems did not escape the attention of economists, but there was little public discussion, and political leaders showed no true consciousness of the gravity of the disturbed condition of currency and trade. It had been assumed that the problems of establishing peace were predominantly political. By March, 1919, it was becoming painfully evident to many that it would not be an easy task to restore the economic adjustments of the prewar period.

The most explicit expression of these views is afforded by the letter of Lloyd George to President Wilson (April 23, 1919) enclosing the full detail of the Keynes plan for a loan by the Allied powers and the United States to the states of Central Europe and the Baltic states. It was recognized that the scheme would need to be tied into the reparations settlement, but the whole problem of reparations was still open.   President Wilson refused to accept this scheme.   He pointed out that the position of Germany could be improved by a more moderate policy in respect of reparations. He expressed complete disagreement with the reparations policy of the Allies, but said that the United States would not withhold its assent because it was an issue which concerned only the Allies. The President, however, promised to have the American experts study the problem.

The report of these experts, Davis and Lamont, was a notable document in every respect.   They emphasized the need of American co-operation in Europe.   They recognized that it was urgently necessary that loans be given the Central European states, that France and Belgium should have credit for reconstruction, that demands for reparations be reduced to proportions which would assure Germany sufficient working capital, that the United States should fund all payments on the Allied debt for a period of three years.   They recognized that the situation was unknown or misunderstood in the United States, so that a vigorous effort would be required to educate public opinion and bring the United States to a realization of its interest in the welfare and prosperity of Europe.

These suggestions were not entirely without effect.   An organized attempt was made to provide for the immediate needs of Europe in food.   Credits were provided for the more urgent work of reconstruction in France and Belgium.   The British delegation finally threw its whole weight into a revision of the reparations clauses of the treaty.   The attempt to fix the amount of reparations was abandoned.   The responsibility of Germany for the whole cost of the war was defined in general terms, but it was recognized that she could not possibly pay the full cost.   A Committee on Reparations was charged with the duty of establishing the precise amount of reparations to be paid the various countries, on or before May 1, 1921.   Provision was made for the immediate delivery of certain commodities and a considerable amount of property.   Even with this compromise on the earlier concept of reparations, the Treaty of Versailles still ignored many of the distressing economic problems which threatened the economic stability of the world.

## The Keynes Scheme

The views of economists were developed further by a conference of bankers and economists at Amsterdam in October, 1919.   But the most comprehensive formulation of the misgivings of the experts was furnished by the publication of J. M. Keynes's *Economic Consequences of the Peace.* Although the book is in many ways an intensely personal document, it is in a larger way an expression of a point of view that was shared by large numbers of economists and bankers. Subsequent events have given the book a new significance. It affords positive evidence of precisely how much clarity of judgment was then possible to a well-informed observer. In the light of this criticism of the treaties and the debt settlements, it is not possible to say that wiser decisions were beyond the capacity of the responsible ministers of state.

The proposals of an essentially economic character involved two basic reversals of the policies that were then developing. Reparations payments were to be limited to $10,000,000,000 with a credit of $2,500,000,000 for the shipping and other property surrendered. It was held that the sum of $7,500,000,000 could be paid, and that it would suffice to meet the primary costs of reconstruction within the devastated areas of France and Belgium. Great Britain and the other countries would have to sacrifice all claim to further compensation from Germany. It was suggested that the sum of $7,500,000,000 be paid in thirty installments without interest.

"With the reparations problem cleared up it would be possible to bring forward with better grace and more hope of success two other financial proposals each of which involves an appeal to the generosity of the United States. The first is for the entire cancellation of Inter-Ally indebtedness. . . . It would be an act of far-seeing statesmanship for the United Kingdom and the United States, the two powers chiefly concerned, to adopt it." [1]

The second financial proposal called for an international loan. Keynes felt that the United States would necessarily be involved, because adequate funds would not be accessible elsewhere.

In addition to these proposals, it was suggested that a European customs union be formed under the auspices of the League of Nations. Membership should be made compulsory for the Central European states, optional for other states. Such a project may seem visionary to many, but it is scarcely more remote from current accomplishment than a German Customs Union seemed in 1815. In 1919 the primary obstacle to a Central European Union was not the ill will of the states most directly involved, but the unwillingness of the other powers to create so broad an element of unity among

---

[1] Keynes, J. M., *op. cit.* (page 725), p. 270.

the "nationalities" which the Versailles congress had been at pains to create. The essential issues in November, 1919, however, were the reparations claims and the inter-Allied debts. Events have since shown that Keynes was fully justified in his estimate of the critical importance of sound decisions of policy on both of these points. The economic recovery of Europe and the re-establishment of world trade could be achieved only by a reduction of reparation claims to a bare minimum, and by general cancellation of the inter-Allied debts. The processes of reasoning by which this judgment was then reached need not now be examined in detail. Nothing more is involved than a thorough understanding of international trade and foreign exchange. Most economists and international bankers could doubtless have agreed with Keynes at that time, though many might have held that a sound economic policy was politically impossible. Many remained silent because they felt that the cause was hopeless.

We cannot know what measure of actual success was even then possible, for no significant changes in policy actually occurred, but it is important to recognize that these were the critical months in the development of the economic policies for the reconstruction of Europe. The treaty did not commit the Allies to heavy reparations claims, for the final determination of the amount of reparations payments rested with the Reparation Commission, and action might be postponed until May 1, 1921. No real decision had been reached in respect of the inter-Allied debts. Statements of policy had been made on both issues by all the leading statesmen, but no decisions had been made.

It was most unfortunate that the critical decision rested with the United States. As the principal creditor nation, the United States commanded the European situation. The peoples of Great Britain and France were in a mood that precluded generosity to their debtors and to Germany except on condition of American generosity to them. Their own debt structures were gravely out of hand; and their tying up of their debts to us with reparations from Germany was natural and inevitable. The United States thus had it in her power to determine the amount of the German reparations. There was more and more appreciation of the dangers involved in a crushing indemnity, and if self-interest were not sufficient, the generosity of the United States could have been made directly conditional upon a defined degree of moderation in the prosecution of the claims upon Germany.   The American view that the issues were essentially distinct was legally correct; but as a matter of actual statecraft the two issues were inextricably interwoven.

## The United States Insists upon Payment in Full

The immediate American contribution to the crisis at this moment was a formal invitation to proceed at once towards the funding of the war loans.   To the various European debtors there was sent a memorandum (November 1, 1919) suggesting a plan for the funding of the outstanding debts.   The plan provided for the issue of two series of bonds corresponding to the series of United States bonds under the Liberty Loan acts.   The first series would mature June 15, 1947; the second series, October 15, 1938.   All bonds were to provide for interest at 5 per cent, but no interest should be chargeable for three years.   These interest payments were not canceled, but merely deferred; they were payable without compounding over a period of twelve years.   In the tenth year, payments on capital account would begin, and the total annual payments would amount to 7.5 per cent of the principal after the twelfth year.   By these operations, 17.8 per cent of the issues of 1938 would have been retired prior to maturity, and 55.7 per cent of the bonds of 1947.   The balance was evidently to be paid off at maturity.   This plan was merely a demand for prompt payment in full.

This proposal produced a most painful impression in France. The British agreed to accept the plan as a basis for negotiation, and suggested the need of settlement of the general question of inter-Allied indebtedness along broad lines.   Mr. Rathbone replied for the Treasury: "I note that the Chancellor attaches great importance to the ultimate settlement along broad lines of the general question of inter-Allied indebtedness.   Just what is meant by that expression I do not know, but I feel confident there is no such question now under discussion or consideration." [1]   From this, and other American materials, it seems likely that ·official policy in the United States was already determined and that no serious reconsideration was likely.   Public opinion was hostile.   The Treasury really had no authority to make any concession whatsoever, and no one wished to raise the issue of concessions and cancellation in Congress.   It is easy to appreciate the attitude of the

[1] Cited, Moulton, H. G., and Pasvolsky, Leo, *War Debts and World Prosperity*, p. 59.

President and the cabinet, but their indifference to the gravity of the decision is none the less tragic.

Despite the discouraging effect of the Treasury plan, the British officials continued to work for a general consideration of the entire economic problem. Informal discussion continued, and February 4, 1920, the representative of the British Treasury submitted a formal request for a broad consideration of war debts looking towards cancellation. The official reply by the Secretary of the Treasury, Houston, took the position that cancellation was not necessary. The debtor governments should levy more taxes, balance their budgets, deflate their currencies, reduce military expenditure, remove trade barriers, and make "a prompt and reasonable definite settlement of the reparation claims against Germany."

France and Great Britain presently decided to link the problems of debts and reparations, and further attempts were to be made to secure the adhesion of the United States to such a plan. The negotiations between the Treasury departments were suspended, and, after an interval, Lloyd George addressed himself directly to President Wilson. A long letter was sent August 5, which went over all the issues with great care. The linkage of the various problems was carefully stated, and considerable assurance was given of a willingness to fix the liabilities of Germany within her "reasonable capacity to pay."

The reply of President Wilson was withheld until after the election of 1920. The note as it stands contains nothing new, nor anything that might not have aided the Democratic party in a campaign which involved not a little criticism for their failure to collect the war debt. It is possible that the tone of the note was affected by the results of the election. The note was largely devoted to an exposition of the legal position of the Treasury of the United States, emphasizing the absence of any authority to make any concessions. But it was made perfectly clear that the President did not desire any such authority. He failed "to perceive the logic in a suggestion in effect either that the United States shall pay part of Germany's reparation obligation or that it shall make a gratuity to the Allied governments to induce them to fix such obligation at an amount within Germany's capacity to pay." This was the final decision in the long series of negotiations over the economic issues arising out of the war. The isolationist policy of the United States made any adequate solution of the problem impossible. The United

States had still to learn that not even its great continental area can live in prosperity, if the other major industrial continent is distracted by a continuing sequence of political and economic disorders.

## The London Schedule of Reparations Payments

Negotiations on reparations were not at this time very far advanced. Arrangements had been completed for deliveries of coal (July 5), and shipments of coal had been begun August 1. The broader issues were still unsettled and it was not clear that any attempt would be made to arrive at a final statement of Germany's obligation even at the date set in the treaty (May 1, 1921). The precise connection between these negotiations and the discussions with the United States cannot be satisfactorily established. Several conferences were held. The work of the Reparation Commission was subordinated to the discussions of these conferences and to meetings of the Supreme Council of the Allies in Paris and in London. The schedule of payment was largely the work of the Supreme Council, though it was adopted by the Reparation Commission. The resulting plan was presented to Germany (May 5, 1921) as an ultimatum coupled with a threat to occupy the Ruhr.

The total amount of the claims upon Germany was fixed at $33,000,000,000, but distinctions were made between sums involving immediate payments of interest and sums involving only remoter and uncertain liabilities. Provision was made for the issue of two series of interest-bearing bonds amounting in all to $12,500,000,000. A third series of bonds amounting to $20,500,000,000 was to be issued only if it should be clear that there were means of meeting interest payments. Bonds in this class, too, were to be retired upon the surrender of various kinds of property. This total figure of 33 billions was only one third of the amount suggested at Boulogne ten months earlier, and a still smaller fraction of the vast sums considered at Versailles. But it was more than four times as much as Keynes's suggestion in 1919.

The annuities are perhaps more significant than the capital sums. With some appreciation of difficulties of payment and transfer, the plan did not call for a rigidly defined annuity. The payments were divided into three classes: a sum of 2,000,000,000 gold marks; a sum equivalent to 25 per cent of the annual value of German exports in each twelve-month period beginning May 1, 1921, or an equivalent amount computed by some alternative formula; a further sum equivalent to 1 per cent of the exports or such other index as might be proposed. The magnitude of the annuity is best appreciated when we compare it with the volume of German trade. In six months, from May to October, 1921, German imports amounted to 2,443,000,000 gold marks; and exports amounted to 1,864,000,000 gold marks. The reparations payments would absorb 80 per cent of her total annual exports. It is difficult now to understand why anyone should have presumed that it was possible for Germany to make such payments by the necessary decrease in imports or increase in exports. Fluctuations of more than 15 per cent in the volume of export or import trade usually involve serious economic disturbance.

The schedules of the London scheme were not strictly observed even during the first year. As early as September, 1921, it was necessary to grant delays in making the cash payments. In March, 1922, cash payments were officially reduced to 720,000,000 marks for the year 1922; and on August 31, cash payments were suspended for six months. Payments in kind continued, though not according to schedule, but cash payments were not resumed. Under these circumstances, Great Britain and France rapidly drifted apart. The British were now convinced that Germany was unable to pay; the French assumed that she was merely unwilling to pay. At a meeting of the premiers of the four principal Allies, Great Britain proposed to reduce the amount of reparations and to suspend all cash payments for four years. France, however, raised the question of willful default in the Reparation Commission (January 9, 1923), and secured authority from it for the occupation of the Ruhr.

Passive resistance to the occupation of the Ruhr led to the heavy issues of paper money, which through negligence or deliberate purpose resulted in the complete devaluation of the mark. This was the first major calamity directly created by the reparations problem, but it was by no means the last.

It was during this unhappy period that the negotiations for the funding of the debts to the United States were actively begun. The entire transaction had been removed from the jurisdiction of the Treasury, and by act of Congress vested in the World War Foreign Debt Commission. The act as originally passed forbade the extension of any debts beyond 1947, or the acceptance of any rate of interest lower than 4.25 per cent. It proved necessary to modify these provisions, and to afford the Commission some reasonable latitude in negotiation. In the period between May 1, 1923, and May 3, 1926, arrangements were concluded with thirteen countries,

The settlement with Great Britain was the second to be concluded, preceded only by the agreement with Finland. The British agreement established the general type. The loan was funded for a period of sixty-two years; for the first ten years at a rate of 3 per cent, for the remainder of the period at 3.5 per cent. The annuities were computed to combine interest payments and payments on account of principal. Other agreements provided for variations in detail, especially in respect of the rate of interest charged. The entire amount borrowed was taken as the capital of the funded debt, but some concessions were made in respect of the rate of interest. The normal rate was 3.3 per cent for the period as a whole, but Belgium, France, Greece, Italy, and Yugoslavia were charged rates ranging from 0.3 per cent to 1.8 per cent.

The French negotiators were anxious to secure the inclusion of a safeguarding clause, designed to make payment to the United States contingent upon the receipt of reparations. The Commissioners of the United States, however, refused to accept this qualification, and the agreement was signed without it (April 29, 1926).

## The Breakdown of the Reparations Settlement

In the meantime some attempt had been made to readjust the amount of the reparations payments. In December, 1922, Secretary of State Hughes suggested the appointment of a neutral committee of experts to determine Germany's capacity to pay. Great Britain and Germany were ready even at that juncture to accept such a procedure for the settlement of the reparations problem, but France was without faith in the sincerity of Germany and was preparing to occupy the Ruhr. This experiment proved to be so disastrous that by the fall of 1923 even France was ready to approach the problem with some measure of realism. It was agreed that the Reparation Commission should appoint two committees of experts to consider the whole problem of reparations. The members of the committees were drawn from five countries, France, Great Britain, Italy, Belgium, and the United States. Charles G. Dawes and Reginald McKenna acted as chairmen. The reforms proposed were put into effect September 1, 1924, as the Dawes Plan.

The Dawes Plan reduced the amount of the annuities due from Germany; it provided a new means of control; and specified in more detail the precise method of securing the credits necessary to make the payments. The amount of the indemnity was reduced for the first year to 1,000,000,000 gold marks; this amount was to be increased progressively in the course of the succeeding years until in the fifth year it reached the permanent level of 2,500,000,000 gold marks. The funds were to be derived from the profits of the state-owned railways; from the returns of a selected list of industrial companies; from a tax on transport; and from specified items in the general budget.

For the first time, serious attention was given to the problem of transferring credits from Germany to the recipients of reparations payments. An Agent General for reparations payments was appointed, to be assisted by a Transfer Committee. Provision was made to separate the operation of transfer from the payment in Germany. Provision was also made for some readjustments of the shares of reparations payments allotted to the various countries.

The general public was disposed to treat the plan as a permanent settlement, but the experts regarded it as a purely temporary measure, designed to promote confidence and permit a more leisurely canvass of the entire question. The temporary character of the settlement was further emphasized by the question of bringing to an end the military occupation of the Rhineland. It was finally decided (September 16, 1928) to appoint a new commission to reach a final decision on reparations, and to include as members of the commission representatives of Germany. The United States was invited to participate, and the chairmanship of the new committee of experts was given to Owen D. Young. This committee sat in Paris from February 9 to June 7, 1929, and its work was then discussed by an official conference of representatives from the various nations. At a session held at the Hague (August, 1929) a number of preliminary agreements were signed, and seven committees were appointed to deal with the primary features of the scheme. These committees reported to a second conference, also at the Hague (January, 1930), at which a series of agreements and conventions were concluded.

The agreement between Germany and the Allies embodied the outstanding features of the Young Plan, with minor amendments of detail. It provided for the termination of the Reparation Commission, and the establishment of a Bank for International Settlements. Comprehensive arrangements were made for all quotas, both deliveries in kind and payments in currency or exchange. The percentages for the division of payments among the Allies were further revised. The annuities were reduced to a slightly lower level than under the Dawes Plan, and the discretion with reference

# THE NEW EUROPE

to postponement of transfer was increased. Germany remained under obligation, however, to meet in some manner the full amount of the scheduled annuity. After a short period of transition, this reached the amount of 2,350,000,000 gold marks. The reduction from the permanent level of the Dawes Plan was not considerable.

The burden of all these payments increased rapidly soon after the new machinery was established. The period of expansion came to an end in 1929, and the year 1930 was marked by increasing strain. Much apprehension was felt in many quarters, but few had anticipated the severity of the collapse which followed the failure of the Credit Anstalt in Vienna in May, 1931. Germany and Great Britain were immediately affected, and during June it became evident that the difficulties could not be localized. Reparations payments were met, and the payments due the United States were made, but the future was uncertain and it seemed dangerous to attempt further payments of any kind until the nature of the emergency was fully known.

The development of the crisis had been watched with the gravest apprehension in the United States, where Owen D. Young and Parker Gilbert were in close touch with the administration. For want of authority, no attempt was made to postpone the payments on the debt due June 15, although the emergency was clearly recognized somewhat earlier. Shortly afterward (June 20, 1931) it was resolved that the President should suggest postponement of all intergovernmental reparations and debt payments for the period of one year. Subject to ratification by Congress, the President offered to postpone payments to the United States, provided that the creditors of Germany should relieve Germany of obligations to them. The United States for the first time recognized officially the relationship between inter-Ally debts and the reparations payments.

The moratorium was well received in many circles, and high hopes were entertained that a solution would be found for the economic problems of reconstruction. These expectations were promptly disappointed by the attitude of France. The French government refused to accept the terms of the moratorium, because such action would involve the abandonment of all claims to the unconditional indemnity. Negotiations were necessary. A preliminary agreement was reached July 6, but the arrangement was then discussed by a Committee of Experts so that it received final approval only on August 11. This arrangement provided for the postponement of conditional annuities only, and set forth a system for the funding of the payments suspended. Conditions were further complicated by delay in the United States. The moratorium was not ratified by Congress until December 22, several days after the semiannual debt payments were due. By mutual agreement, no attempts were made to cover these payments.

The suspensions covered only the current year, then already far advanced, so that negotiations for a permanent settlement began before the moratorium was ratified.   M. Laval, then Prime Minister of France, conferred informally with President Hoover in Washington. It was agreed that the next steps should be taken at the initiative for the European powers.   Germany made a formal application to the Bank of International Settlements for the appointment of an Advisory Committee under the Young Plan.   This committee met at Basel, December 7, 1931.   After hearing a large amount of evidence, the committee reported that Germany was in no position to continue the payments scheduled.   A comprehensive survey of the entire problem was recommended at an early date.

It was proposed to hold the conference at Lausanne January 18, 1932, but the wide divergence of opinion between France and Germany made it essential to set a later date.   The Germans declared that further payment of reparations was impossible. France was willing to postpone, and even to reduce, the amount of the obligation, but she was not then ready to abandon reparations. The conference, opened June 16, reached a compromise.   Reparations were to be abandoned, but Germany was to deposit bonds with the Bank for International Settlements amounting in all to three milliards (billions) of marks.   These bonds were to be sold under stated conditions and the proceeds devoted to expenditures for reconstruction in Europe.   This final act of the conference was signed by representatives of the powers on July 9.   It made a most favorable impression, until it appeared (July 13) that its effect was significantly modified by the "Gentlemen's Agreement" of July 2.   Belgium, France, Great Britain, and Italy had agreed that the final act should not be given effect until each of the Allies had arrived at a satisfactory settlement with its creditors.

Not a little resentment was felt in the United States when the "Gentlemen's Agreement" was made known.   It was held that undue pressure was being brought to bear upon the United States. The impending election made negotiation unwise, and it was agreed that nothing should be done until November.   The decisive defeat of President Hoover was a serious blow.   Greece defaulted two days after the election, and Hungary gave notice of default. The major powers approached the question with new misgivings. As only a few weeks remained before the date of the next payment, Great Britain urged postponement of all payments pending a complete review of the entire question. President Hoover consulted with President-elect Roosevelt, as it was evident that no settlement could be reached before March 4, but there were differences of opinion both as to procedure and as to policy. No substantial progress was made. The President, and perhaps even Congress, were ready to make some concession to Great Britain, but there was no disposition to reduce the obligations of France. The United States was, therefore, especially anxious to continue the procedure of negotiation with individual powers.

Several exchanges of notes merely served to reveal the magnitude of the differences between the parties; and, as the President assumed that he possessed no discretion, it became evident that no formal action could be taken to postpone the payments due December 15. As the transfer problem was itself a serious factor, Great Britain announced that she would pay the amount due in gold, but only as a partial payment of the capital sum due. The United States did not accept this interpretation of the payment, but Great Britain declared with equal insistence that her previous note defined precisely the meaning she attached to the act. The French government proposed to make a similar payment, but was unable to carry the necessary vote in the Chamber of Deputies. This decisive defeat, on December 14, led to the resignation of Herriot as Premier. France was left in default. A number of other countries also made no payments. Negotiations were not at once discontinued, but nothing was accomplished. The banking crisis in the United States, however, created an emergency which made discussion of a permanent settlement impractical.

In the following June, Great Britain offered a token payment of $10,000,000 in silver bullion. The majority of the debtors of the United States made no effort to meet their payments. Technically, the Lausanne agreement is not in effect, and the various powers are still liable for the full amount of their funded debt with interest. But in fact, "we have reached the end of reparations, the wreck is completed. . . . It has taken the statesmen of the world a fatal thirteen years and thirty-five conferences to discover the truth which Professor Keynes preached in 1919. . . ."[1]

[1] Wheeler-Bennett, John W., *The Wreck of Reparations*, New York, 1933, p. 255.

CHAPTER 37

## ECONOMIC ASPECTS OF INTERNATIONALISM

———◆———

### International Economic Relations before the World War

The economic relations between peoples became increasingly intimate and vital as a result of the industrial revolution. At the same time, the element of conflict in these relations was intensified by the economic concepts of individualism and competition and by the political concept of national sovereignty. The sovereignty of a nation has required that individuals and groups within a nation yield their power of independent action, in the spheres covered by law, to the authority of government exercised through public agencies. Within a nation, the use of force for settling disputes is reserved exclusively to the public authority. Nations, on the other hand, under the theory of absolute sovereignty, have played a dual role. They have claimed the right to exercise the functions both of plaintiff (or defendant) and judge and have reserved to themselves the right to use force in carrying out their decisions. Independence of action in carefully restricted fields has been limited, to be sure, by treaties or other agreements, but these agreements, previous to the League of Nations Covenant, failed to surrender the right of national appeal to force or to abandon the dual role of plaintiff or defendant and judge — a role wholly repugnant to the principles of national or municipal law. Even the collective sanctions provided for by the League of Nations Covenant proved to be largely inoperative.

Internationalism in the political or legal sense may be described as the movement to substitute the basic principle of law for the absolute sovereignty of national force in regulating the relations between nations. Just as nationalism and national law do not exclude the ultimate alternative of revolution, so internationalism and international law would not exclude the ultimate alternative of war. But internationalism would surrender the principle of national resort to force just as nationalism surrenders the principle of resort to force by individuals or groups within a nation. War would thus become an ultimate resort of nations for the establishment of a new system of international law, just as revolution is an ultimate resort of individuals within a nation for the establishment of a new system of national law.

741

Such a far-reaching change can occur only as the culmination of increasingly intimate relations between peoples, and especially of relations involving economic interests vitally dependent on the orderly processes of law. In the growth of these relations and in the development of international agreements and agencies connected therewith are to be found the significant economic aspects of internationalism.

An outstanding factor in the growing importance of economic relations was the extension of the industrial revolution. Prominent features of the industrial revolution were the growth of urban population and the development of specialized industries. These populations and industries were increasingly dependent on imported foods and materials and the export of manufactures. Accompanying these developments were the export of capital, the internationalizing of corporate activities, and the emergence of problems relating to the international status of patents and other forms of industrial property. Before the World War such conditions gave increasing importance to the economic aspects of treaties and other international agreements and found significant expression in the rise of consular systems. Some of the cities of medieval Italy maintained consular offices for adjusting commercial disputes, but the modern system as maintained by national governments was an accompaniment of the increasing intimacy of economic relations in the nineteenth century. Earlier, certain private citizens residing abroad had occasionally been given a semiofficial status without pay, but not even the British government organized a paid consular service until 1825. The present French system dates from 1833, and that of the United States from 1852. The Germans maintained virtually no consular service before the founding of the Empire in 1871.

Before the World War there was an extensive development of international public agencies, most of which had economic functions. The nineteenth century marked the rise of international conferences other than those concerned with the making of treaties of peace. Several such gatherings occurred after the Congress of Vienna in 1815. A notable later instance was the Congo Conference of 1884, which dealt with international policies in the Congo region. Usually these special conferences created no international agencies of a continuing character, although notable exceptions are the commissions for supervising navigation on international waterways such as the Danube. With the formation of the International Telegraph Union in 1865 (resulting from a typical technological change transcending national boundaries), and the International Postal Union in 1874, later known as the Universal Postal Union, a new era of international administration may be said to have begun. These Unions hold periodical conferences, maintain international bureaus, and derive their authority from a surrender of national sovereignty in restricted but important fields. Among numerous other agencies formed before the World War for dealing primarily with international economic relations were the Latin Monetary Union, the Metric Union, the International Institute of Agriculture, and the Radio-Telegraphic Union. Permanent offices or commissions had been created for dealing with the international aspects of railroad transportation; the Suez Canal; patents, copyrights, etc.; sanitation; the slave trade; various phases of the sugar industry; and the navigation of international waterways.

Unofficial congresses, conferences, and agencies for dealing with international economic relations had become numerous before the World War. An early instance of a large international conference was the World Anti-Slavery Convention of 1840 at London. Agencies of this type included, in the economic field, purely technical associations and conferences, such as the International Association for Testing Materials (which was partly financed by governments); numerous trade-union and socialistic groups; associations of businessmen, such as the International Congress of Chambers of Commerce; and cartels in many industries. In addition, mention should be made of corporations with stockholders, offices, and activities transcending national boundaries.

## Immediate Effects of the World War

Although the World War disrupted normal economic relations and created conditions unfavorable to internationalism in a cosmopolitan or comprehensive sense, it nevertheless intensified internationalism among the allied nations on both sides. Furthermore, it focused attention sharply on the problem of regulating international relations in such manner as to avoid war. It thus gave rise to the League of Nations and associated agencies.

During the first month of the war an Anglo-French commission was formed for co-ordinating the buying of war supplies. This agency, the *Commission internationale de ravitaillement*, later had representatives from the other Allied countries and from the United States. It supervised purchases totaling about $3,350,000,000 in value. The Allied Export Provisions Commission bought food other than cereals and sugar to the value of about $1,300,000,000. Special inter-Ally arrangements were made for wheat and sugar. Later in the war an Allied Food Council and an Allied Munitions Council were created. In 1917, after the declaration of war by the United States, an Inter-Ally Council of War Purchases and Finance was formed. One of the most comprehensive and vitally important agencies was the Allied Maritime Transport Council. This organization with its numerous committees combined the advisory functions of an international body with the executive authority of the several governments. The council operated by means of direct relations with the numerous specialized agencies for dealing on the one hand with transport facilities and on the other hand with the various types of commodities — agencies such as the Inter-Allied Meats and Fats Executive, and the Nitrates Executive. The activities of the Council extended virtually throughout the Allied and neutral countries.

The international economic organization for war was transformed, at the Paris Peace Conference, into the Supreme Economic Council, which was described as "the most powerful economic organization the world has yet known." Its purpose was to take over and co-ordinate the numerous economic agencies of the war period. It supervised the ending of the blockade, the allocation of shipping to transitional and postwar uses, the distribution of food and other supplies, and the restoration of facilities for communication and transportation.

The League of Nations was not an application of merely theoretical principles of internationalism ; it was substantially a continuation of the practices developed by the inter-Allied war agencies and by the postwar Supreme Economic Council. The Allied Maritime Transport Council was particularly significant in providing not only experience in international government but also a personnel embodying that experience. The British, French, and Italian members of the executive committee of the Allied Maritime Transport Council became members of the Secretariat of the League. The technical committees of the League were similar in principle and often in detail and personnel to the corresponding groups associated with the Allied Maritime Transport Council and the Supreme Economic Council. The League embodied also the same general conception of a central agency, not for administering world affairs (except in restricted technical fields), but rather for maintaining direct and continuous contacts between governments and thus facilitating harmonious decisions and co-ordinated action by the national governments.  Outstanding differences between the League and the Allied war organization are the more extensive membership of the League, the greater diversity of interests, and the lack of the impelling war motive.

### The Economic Work of the League of Nations

The League of Nations as a political agency and policy-forming body encountered obstacles which prevented it from functioning as effectively as many of its founders had hoped.  It was designed, however, to serve other purposes which, though inconspicuous, were important in facilitating the economic and social relations of peoples. The boundaries of European countries intersect many areas with relations hardly less intimate than those of the states of the United States.  Many of their relations and activities require not far-reaching changes in policy and often not even a common administrative agency but rather a mechanism for maintaining constant contacts between governments and for providing technical information and guidance.   Some of these functions were performed, long before the formation of the League, by such agencies as the Universal Postal Union and the International Telegraph Union.   Article 24 of the Covenant provided for the incorporation of various agencies in the League system and for the inclusion of all future agencies. Most of the earlier international agencies, however, retained their autonomy and merely collaborated with the League.

The League established several permanent agencies for administering or for facilitating the handling of the more intimate and less controversial phases of international relations.   The Secretariat was established at Geneva as a permanent office with a continuing staff for routine work, registering of treaties and conventions, furnishing information, and aiding the various specialized agencies.   There were three main groups of technical committees and commissions.

The technical agencies included the Economic and Financial Organization, with a financial committee and an economic committee.   The financial committee deals with the problems of national and international finance, exchange rates, bills of exchange, etc.   It arranged for aid by the League to Austria, Hungary, and other countries.   It also deals with such special problems as the prevention of counterfeiting and the development and interchange of financial statistics on a uniform basis.   The economic committee deals largely with trade.   Its work includes the development and

interchange of commercial and industrial statistics, the simplification of customs procedure and nomenclature, the promotion of the
arbitration of disputes between nationals of different countries, the
elimination of unfair practices, and the removal of trade restrictions.

Another technical group is the Communications and Transit
Organization, with a general Advisory and Technical Committee on
Communications and Transit. This general committee has organized numerous subcommittees and commissions, permanent and
temporary, has employed experts in various fields, and has held
various general and special conferences. It has encouraged the
collaboration of private and public agencies. It has carried on
either administrative or advisory work in such varied fields as ports
and maritime navigation; navigable waterways and inland navigation; transportation by rail, particularly the intricate problems
of the new frontiers and the competition between railways and
waterways; road transport; air transport; uniform practices in
regard to passports; rules for the measurement and registration
of vessels; telephonic, telegraphic, and radio communication; and
electric and hydraulic power, especially transmission problems and
the utilization of the water of international streams.

Still another technical group is the International Health Organization. Numerous committees, commissions, and conferences have
dealt with a wide range of problems. These have impinged vitally
on the economic field and have involved international interests
mainly noncontroversial but requiring informational, advisory, and
administrative agencies for concerted action.

Several commissions and committees not a part of these three
technical organizations have exercised important temporary or
continuing functions essentially economic in nature. Prominent
among these have been the agencies for administering the Saar valley previous to its return to Germany, for dealing with refugees,
emigrants, and minority groups, and for supervising the government of the mandated territories.

In the work of most of the technical organizations, participation
is not restricted to member states. Many nonmember states
have shared the work of both the economic and the noneconomic
agencies, such as the committees on intellectual co-operation,
health, disarmament, and the trade in opium and dangerous drugs.
Participation by the United States has included official representation on some of the League's agencies and at many of the conferences held under the auspices of the League.

Other important international agencies active during the early postwar period include the Reparation Commission, committees of experts concerned with reparations, and the Bank for International Settlements. These agencies, which are discussed in connection with reparations and war debts, have sometimes been erroneously associated with the League system.

## Mandates and the Colonial Question

Turkish territories in Asia which had been conquered by the Allied Powers, and the various German colonies, were described by the League Covenant as "not yet able to stand by themselves under the strenuous conditions of the modern world." The Paris Peace Conference refused to return them to Turkey and Germany, and devised a somewhat disingenuous plan for disposing of them. It was declared in the Covenant that "there should be applied the principle that such peoples form a sacred trust of civilization and that securities for the performance of this trust should be embodied in this Covenant." For the avowed purpose of giving effect to this principle, these territories were assigned as mandates of the League to victor nations.

Three types of mandates were created. The "A" class consisted of territories which could be "provisionally" recognized as "independent nations" subject to the "administrative advice and assistance" of the mandatory powers. This type included Palestine, Trans-Jordan, and Mesopotamia (Iraq), assigned to Great Britain, and Syria and Lebanon, assigned to France. The "B" class consisted of areas less advanced in culture, to be subjected to more direct control by the mandatory powers. Control was to be subject to certain restrictions, particularly the prohibition of the slave trade and of traffic in arms and liquor; prohibition of the use of the natives for military purposes other than native police and defense; protection of the natives as to religious and other rights; and a guarantee of the open door — that is, of "equal opportunities for the trade and commerce of other members of the League." The "B" mandates included Tanganyika and parts of Togoland and the Cameroons, assigned to Great Britain; parts of Togoland and the Cameroons, assigned to France; and Ruanda and Urundi, assigned to Belgium. The "C" class consisted of the other German territories, which were described as remote, sparsely settled, or small, and for these or other reasons best suited to direct administration under the laws of the mandatory powers as integral parts of their territories but subject to safeguards for the natives similar to the provisions for "B" mandates. The "C" class included German Southwest Africa, assigned to the Union of South Africa; Western Samoa, assigned to New Zealand; the German Pacific islands south of the equator, assigned to Australia; Nauru (a phosphate-bearing island), assigned to Great Britain and Australia; and the German Pacific islands north of the equator, assigned to Japan.

For the purpose of supervising the exercise of mandatory powers, the Permanent Mandates Commission was established. The members were appointed by the League Council. To this commission the mandatory powers were required to make annual reports and to furnish supplementary information when requested. The commission was given authority to obtain expert assistance, hear petitions, render advisory decisions, and make reports to the League Council.

The work of the Mandates Commission proved in general to be in accord with the spirit of the provisions of the Covenant for maintaining the open door in the "A" and "B" mandates and for protecting the natives from the grosser forms of exploitation. But if the principles set forth in the Covenant were valid for the former Turkish and German territories, they appear to have been equally valid for the territories of other nations. It was urged by many that the general application of these principles, and possibly their extension by vesting the actual administration of the less advanced areas in agencies subject to the League, would have done much to remove the causes of conflict between the industrialized nations over access to the natural resources and markets of the unindustrialized regions. Such an arrangement would presumably have mitigated some of the incitements to war, because inequalities of imperialistic opportunities have tended to promote alliances of the "have-nots" for improving their status, and among the "haves" for checkmating the "have-nots." But inequality of opportunity among imperialistic nations has not been the primary source of imperialistic conflicts; these have been the natural results of the dependence of capitalistic enterprise on continuous expansion for avoiding the unprofitableness of accumulated surpluses when invested exclusively at home. Equalization of opportunity under mandates, unless accompanied by changes in national economy for absorbing surplus profits by domestic consumption, would merely postpone the dependence of investors among the "have-nots" on further expansion beyond the status of mere equality, and, in so far as it reduced the opportunities of investors among the "haves," would aggravate their problems of profitable use of surpluses.

## The International Labor Organization

The International Labor Organization (the I. L. O.), like the League of Nations, established a twofold system of international activity. It was designed both as a policy-making agency, notably in the formulation of draft conventions, and as an instrument for international collaboration by serving as a clearinghouse of information and a center for international contacts. Like the League, its work in formulating international policy proved to be more difficult than its activities as an agency of contacts, discussion, and co-operation. But even in the field of international policy, numerous labor conventions were drafted by the International Labor Organization and extensively ratified by national governments.

Both the League and the I. L. O. have been described as agencies for democratic discussion and compromise. The distinctive work of the I. L. O. is in the field of labor legislation, industrial relations, and the maintenance of minimum standards among competing national groups. The constitution of the I. L. O. was embodied in the Treaty of Versailles, which contained a separate section, not a part of the League Covenant, with provisions for the structure and activities of the Organization. Members of the League were to be members of the I. L. O., but states not members of the League were also eligible for membership. The location is the same as that of the League — Geneva — and various arrangements are made for collaboration.

Part XIII of the Treaty of Versailles, containing the constitution of the I. L. O., based that organization on two premises. It was declared, in the first place, that prevailing conditions of labor brought "such injustice, hardship, and privation to large numbers of people as to produce unrest so great that the peace and harmony of the world are imperiled." Measures required for improving these conditions were declared to include the regulation of hours of work; prevention of unemployment; provisions insuring a "living wage"; social insurance in connection with sickness, accidents and industrial diseases, old age, etc.; special protection for children, young persons, and women; protection of emigrant workers; assurance of the right to organize freely; and provisions for vocational and technical education. The second premise was the assumption that "the failure of any nation to adopt humane conditions of labor is an obstacle in the way of other nations which desire to improve the conditions in their own countries."

The same section of the treaty provided for a General Conference, to meet at least once a year, as the central authority for formulating policies designed to give effect to the purposes of the I. L. O. The General Conference embodies the group-representation principle. Each member government has the right to send four delegates, two representing the government, one representing workers, and one representing employers. The worker and employer delegates are chosen in agreement with the "most representative" organizations of workers and employers. The principle of representation is functional and the plan as applied in the I. L. O. has been described by an official as "valid under any system of economic and social organization. The employers in essence represent the principle of management and direction, the workers the principle of execution, and the government represents the interests of consumers and the public as a whole."

To the General Conference belongs the function of passing on draft conventions and recommendations. The conventions that have been adopted deal with such subjects as social insurance, child labor, hours and periods of work, industrial accidents and diseases, maritime employment, emigration, compulsory labor, and the right to organize. Many of the conventions deal with technical and essentially noncontroversial subjects and merely provide information and machinery for the more efficient handling of activities universally regarded as desirable. Such, for example, was the convention adopted in 1935 for the maintenance of the rights of migrant workers in respect to payments made by them to national insurance funds. Most of the conventions embody standards not above the level of national standards already adopted by many of the member states. It was expected, however, that these countries would at least have the advantage of the protection of the standards already attained from the competitive pressure of other nations which, without the conventions, would presumably have lower standards. But when standards already achieved are protected by international conventions, it was expected that they could more readily be made the basis for a further raising of national standards in the more advanced countries. Recommendations by the General Conference, in contrast with draft conventions, embody principles or policies favored by the Conference but not reduced to the form of conventions proposed for ratification by the member states.

Many economists held that the efforts of the I. L. O. to raise labor standards by international agreement were largely futile due to a necessary increase in production costs.   It was held that the country with the greatest advantage or least disadvantage in cost of producing a given article tends to specialize in its production on the principle of the international or interregional division of labor, and that a rise in cost of production in certain countries as a result of an international convention would merely reduce their comparative advantage or increase their comparative disadvantage and lead to unemployment.   Other economists urged, however, that the international division of labor on the basis of comparative costs under free competition was an assumption of theoretical economics.   Labor standards under imperfect competition depend in part, it was held, on bargaining power in the distribution of the product; and one of the most effective weapons of employers against higher labor standards is the prevalence of lower costs in other countries.   In any case, a large part of the work of the I. L. O. was beyond the field of the theoretical controversy of the economists in regard to the possibility of raising or maintaining labor standards by means of a change in comparative labor costs in the member states.   A rise in labor standards may, in fact, within certain limits result in lower labor costs.

A convention adopted by the General Conference is not applicable to a given country until that country's government ratifies it; and the only obligation of a member state is to accept it for consideration.   The total number of ratifications as reported to the General Conference of 1936 was more than 700.   A government which ratifies a convention assumes the obligations of enforcing it as in the case of other treaties or conventions and agrees to make annual reports to the I. L. O. regarding the enforcement of the convention.

Provision was also made in the treaty for a representative Governing Body.   This group was to meet at least four times a year, for the purpose of drawing up general plans, outlining the work of the I. L. O., and appointing committees for the preliminary study of subjects for consideration by the General Conference.

The continuing work of the I. L. O. was put in the charge of the International Labor Office, with a Director General and a permanent staff.   This Office provides the factual basis of the activities of the conference, serves as a general clearinghouse of labor information, and makes possible the maintenance of constant relations between the labor offices and industrial and labor associations of the member states.  The dependence of the General Conference on the democratic processes of debate and compromise gives peculiar importance to the work of the International Labor Office in collecting international labor information on a comparable basis and in maintaining intimacy and continuity of international contacts.

### International Economic Conferences

International conferences became increasingly prominent during the nineteenth century and the early twentieth, but before the World War they remained incidental.  After the war the League of Nations and the I. L. O. provided for periodical gatherings partly in the nature of conferences.  The League Assembly, in respect to matters requiring the concurrence of the member states in the form of conventions or treaties, was given merely the advisory powers of a conference.  The Council of the League was entrusted with extensive duties, as the supervision of the government of mandated territories; but in so far as it lacks the power of final approval of changes in policy, it is essentially a conference.  Similarly, the General Conference of the I. L. O. can adopt conventions but their final ratification and enforcement require the separate action of the member states.  There are also numerous meetings of permanent committees, frequently held in connection with sessions of the Council or the Assembly or the General Conference.  In addition, there are many temporary committees or other agencies which hold special conferences, such as the meeting of representatives of central banks in 1928 to promote uniformity of bank statistics.

There have been several special conferences primarily economic in nature, besides the conferences which dealt with reparations, discussed in another connection.  In 1920 the League of Nations convoked the International Financial Conference at Brussels.  This was the first postwar conference at which Germany was represented.  The report of the conference, describing it as "a gathering unique in the history of the world," was warranted in the sense that it was a gathering under official auspices not of statesmen but "of experts from all nations working for the solution of the common problem of the whole world."  But in view of the unprecedented problems of war debts, reparations, and urgent demands for relief and reconstruction then facing the governments of Europe, the orthodox recommendations of the experts for stopping inflation, returning to the gold standard, and balancing budgets had an element of unreality as the basis for an immediate program.  The way was prepared, however, for minor remedial measures, later carried out by the League, in extending financial aid to Austria, Hungary, and other small states.

More realistic and more immediately successful was a conference at Portorose, near Trieste, in 1921, representing the countries which had fallen heir to the territories of the Austro-Hungarian Empire. The economic impasse resulting from the establishment of new frontiers was described in Chapter 35. The recommendations of this conference included specific measures for removal of the more serious barriers in the way of international transport, communications, and trade. The protocol proposed by the conference was not ratified, but its detailed recommendations were made the basis of a number of special agreements between several of the states of eastern Europe.

The International Economic Conference of 1922 at Genoa was initiated by the Allied Supreme Council and was dominated by the Allied Powers; but Germany, Russia, and many other nations were represented, and the United States sent "observers." Its proposals included stabilization of currencies and exchange rates on the basis of the gold standard; lowering of trade barriers; freeing of transport and communication facilities from disabilities imposed by nationalistic policies; and a return to "normal" conditions assuring the free international movement of capital. This Genoa Conference exhibited a nostalgic desire for economic liberalism. At the same time, as at the Brussels Conference, comparatively little attention was paid to the main obstacles: reparations, war debts, the financing of reconstruction, and adjustment of relations with Germany and Russia. These two countries, encountering an uncompromising attitude toward their respective points of view, arranged, in the Treaty of Rapallo, for mutual concessions regarding war claims and reciprocal trade. The Genoa Conference achieved little of immediate value, but its three technical commissions (dealing with economics, finance, and transport) made extensive reports and prepared the way for action on minor matters.

The Genoa Conference was followed by an impasse in the reparations situation, discussed elsewhere, and by the collapse of German finances. After the temporary adjustment of reparations under the Dawes Plan, the restoration of German finances, and the admission of Germany to the League, another ambitious attempt was made to solve the outstanding problems of economic instability by a general conference. The International Economic Conference of

1927 assembled at Geneva under the auspices of the League of Nations. This conference was composed of representatives not only from League states but also from the United States, Russia, and Turkey.

The Geneva Conference declared that "the time has come to put an end to the increase in tariffs and to move in the opposite direction." Subsidies, prohibitions, quotas, dumping, and retaliatory policies, as well as high tariffs, were condemned. In the field of industrial production, qualified approval was given to international cartels and other industrial agreements as offering a possible method of planning production, eliminating the more destructive forms of competition, and promoting the rationalization movement. Rationalization included not only mergers and combinations (in so far as these tended to reduce costs) but also mechanization, standardization of materials and output, scientific management, and a more effective co-ordination of production, transportation, and marketing. The conference held that rationalization should be encouraged. It recognized the difficulty, during rapid rationalization, of increasing the effective demand and the volume of production to such an extent as to maintain existing levels of employment of labor and capital, but anticipated expansion through a lowering of prices due to reduction of the costs of production. The effects of lower prices on the relations between debtors and creditors were not adequately analyzed. The freeing of commerce, the stabilization of currency and exchange rates on the basis of the gold standard, and the checking of monopolistic price fixing by combinations were viewed as the best assurances of price reductions and industrial expansion accompanying rationalization. The conference also made recommendations relating to agriculture, notably a reform of credit policies for the cheaper and more adequate financing of farmers. An important achievement of the conference was the impetus it gave to the effort throughout the world to place agricultural economy on an equality with other phases of economic life.

In its consideration of rationalization, prices, volume of production, and agriculture, the Geneva Conference made distinct advances over earlier conferences in economic thinking and constructive proposals. Agreement was achieved, however, at the price of ignoring many basic problems of inequality and disequilibrium between nations and economic groups. The report of the conference was more than "a glimpse into the obvious" but less than "the Magna Charta of future world economics."

Following the Geneva Conference there was an ambitious attempt to achieve international stability and security by means of the Pact of Paris of 1928 and a network of treaties agreeing to "renounce war as an instrument of national policy." The League of Nations Committee on Arbitration and Security promoted similar treaties; and the League also attempted with renewed energy but without success to obtain agreement on disarmament. For a time industrial production and general business activity expanded. But the main obstacles in the way of stability, security, and freedom of interchange remained, and the expansion of business proved to be largely unsound and speculative. There followed the reparations crisis, the Young Plan, rejection by the World Court of the proposed Austro-German Customs Union, the collapse of Austrian finances, the Hoover Moratorium on intergovernmental debts, the cancellation of reparations, and the cessation of debt payments to the United States, as international episodes in world-wide depression.

The Lausanne Conference of 1932 on reparations conditionally canceled reparations and proposed another general economic conference to consider remaining problems, notably intergovernmental debts. The result was the World Economic and Monetary Conference held at London in the summer of 1933. The Preparatory Commission's proposal for including a settlement of intergovernmental debts (in effect their cancellation) was rejected by the American government. Other proposals included measures for achieving monetary and exchange stabilization, checking deflation of prices and of the debt structure, and removing some of the obstacles to trade by agreements regarding tariffs, prohibitions, and quotas.

In regard to monetary and exchange policies, the American government was confronted by the fact that most of the countries of the world had earlier resorted to currency inflation and monetary devaluation, and exchange rates in terms of the dollar had been greatly lowered, giving foreign producers a corresponding advantage in American markets. The United States had not resorted to devaluation for reduction of internal debt, lowering of exchange rates, and maintaining equilibrium in debtor-creditor relations. These relations had been disturbed by price deflation, especially in the case of agricultural prices. The fall in prices had increased the real debt burden of the government as well as of private debtors; and at the same time the loans extended to foreign governments and in many cases to private borrowers abroad were virtually in default. Under these circumstances, the American government decided to adopt the policy of devaluation previously pursued by other governments, and to postpone stabilization agreements until the dollar had been allowed to find its competitive level unsupported by the gold standard. American emphasis was therefore placed on other items on the program of the London Conference, especially the relaxation of tariffs and trade restrictions. Other governments, however, were unwilling to give up their advantages in exchange rates based on their depreciated currencies. They insisted on monetary and exchange stabilization as a prerequisite for changes in tariff policies. The resulting stalemate led to the adjournment of the conference after agreement had been reached only on minor matters. After the conference the American government undertook an independent program of reciprocal trade agreements for lowering tariff barriers; and in 1936 the breakup of the gold-standard bloc led by France prepared the way for a tentative program of stabilizing the principal exchanges and for an acceleration of the movement toward lower trade barriers.

### Unofficial Agencies: the International Labor Movement

The relations between peoples have found expression in an extremely large number of unofficial agencies of a cultural and technical as well as economic nature. Prominent among the economic agencies are those connected with the international labor movement.

The international labor organizations that are described in Chapter 26 opposed the World War before its outbreak but fell apart into their respective national units during the war. Labor and socialistic groups in most cases supported their governments, but toward the end of the war they became increasingly assertive in their efforts to bring the war to a close on the basis of a negotiated peace, with an economic and political reorganization designed to eliminate the causes of war. Unsuccessful efforts were made during the war to convene representatives of the belligerent countries on both sides as well as of neutral countries. In February, 1918, prominent representatives of labor and socialistic groups among the European Allied Powers met in London in the Inter-Allied Labor and Socialist Conference. The outstanding war aims set forth by the conference were the following: a peace without punitive indemnities or an economic boycott of the defeated countries; territorial adjustments in Europe based as far as practicable on internationally supervised plebiscites for ascertaining the will of the populations; international administration of such areas as tropical Africa (including territories of the Allied Powers), with safeguards for the native populations; the maintenance by international authority of the free use of "the main lines of maritime connection"; the elevation of industrial and labor standards by international agreements for limiting competitive pressure on hours, social insurance costs, etc.; and a league of nations with independent authority. These proposals are typical of the comparatively moderate and conciliatory attitude and of the tendency toward internationalism among working-class groups.

After the war both the Second International and the International Federation of Trade Unions experienced much difficulty in reorganizing and achieving unity. One obstacle was the refusal of governments to issue passports to delegates. But two conferences, one by socialists and another by trade-unionists, were finally held at Berne in February, 1919. The socialist conference included delegates from twenty-six countries. War passions flared, and the Germans, who had previously assumed leadership in the Second International, were relegated to a secondary position. A more fundamental problem was the old question of revolutionary versus evolutionary tactics, now concretely associated with the Russian Revolution. At a later conference held in Geneva in 1920, disagreement had become so serious that representation was restricted to a few groups — those which favored parliamentary tactics, no fight with private enterprise during reconstruction, and a gradual advance toward socialism. The principal groups represented were the British Labor party and the German Social Democratic party.

In the meantime the Russian socialists had formed the Third (the Communist) International, with an uncompromising advocacy of revolutionary methods similar to those used in Russia, and with an appeal for the support of left-wing groups throughout the world. Large groups of socialists were unwilling to support either the right-wing views of the Second International or the left-wing policies of the Third International. These groups therefore sent delegates to a conference at Vienna, which met in February, 1921, and formed the International Working Union of Socialist Parties. This group disavowed the purpose of forming a new international, but it was popularly called the Two-and-a-Half International or the Vienna International. It proposed merely to work out a program more in keeping with varied national conditions, not confined rigorously to using "democratic methods only," as demanded by the Second International, or to "the mechanical imitation of the methods of the Russian peasants' and workingmen's revolution," as proposed by the Third International. The main delegations at Vienna were from the British Independent Labor party, the German Independent Socialist party, and the Austrian Social Democratic party. Groups in ten other countries also were represented.

The Third International remained inflexible in its support of revolutionary methods and in its conditions for membership. Its affiliates in most countries were therefore comparatively small left-wing groups. For a time, the cleavage of the Second International and the Vienna group also continued. At length the differences were adjusted, and at a conference at Hamburg in 1923 the two groups were united and renamed the Labor and Socialist International. The Second International as thus reorganized distinctly opposed the Third International and collaborated, as before the war, with the Amsterdam International Federation of Trade Unions. The conference at Hamburg represented groups from thirty countries with about 7,000,000 members. Plans were formulated for a congress to be held once in three years and for machinery of a simple nature for carrying on the activities of the organization between congresses. Parliamentary and evolutionary methods and participation in nonsocialistic governments were approved, but the policies advocated were far in advance of those actually pursued by governments and by the League of Nations. An illustration was the persistent demand for cancellation of reparations as a necessary basis for international reconciliation and reconstruction.

When the Berne Conference of the Second International met in February, 1919, trade-union representatives from sixteen countries also held a meeting at the same place. The conference formulated an International Labor Charter embodying demands for an advanced program of labor legislation. It included a 36-hour week, social insurance, free compulsory education, and an International Labor Parliament somewhat resembling but much more powerful than the International Labor Organization later formed under the Treaty of Versailles. Steps were also taken to reorganize the International Federation of Trade Unions.

The reorganization was brought about at the Amsterdam Congress of July, 1919, soon after the signing of the Treaty of Versailles. The Congress was extremely critical of the treaty. This fact and its socialistic tendencies alienated the American delegation led by Samuel Gompers. At the same time, the failure to support the Russian revolution led to a countermove for the establishment of a more radical federation. The result was the organization of the Red Trade Union International at Moscow in 1921, but its non-Russian membership was restricted to comparatively small left-wing groups. The International Federation of Trade Unions (the Amsterdam International) survived as the principal international organization of the working classes.

Both the Amsterdam International and the Labor and Socialist International (the Second International) opposed the Third (or Communist) International. But both groups exerted strong influence on governments for recognizing the Russian government and for maintaining friendly relations with Russia. After the rise of Fascism, especially in Germany, and the decline of Russian expectations of an imminent world revolutionary movement, the Third International moderated its demands for revolutionary tactics. It blamed the compromising attitude of the other internationals for the advance of Fascism, but recognized the urgency of a united front. Labor and socialist leaders in other countries read the warning of the destruction of their organizations in Fascist countries. In France and Spain, "popular front" movements united the principal groups in opposition to Fascist tendencies.

In the handling of detailed problems of international working-class relations as distinguished from the larger questions of policy, the international trade secretariats occupied a prominent place. These numerous agencies are illustrated by the offices maintained by the Miners' International Federation, the International Federation of General Factory Workers, and the International Transport Workers' Federation. They were associated in most cases with the International Federation of Trade Unions. After the World War, when the International Labor Organization was attempting to raise the international level of labor standards, the trade secretariats contributed effectively to this work. They regarded as desirable the free movement of workers from country to country, but held that safeguards were necessary to prevent a competitive lowering of standards. To this end the secretariats worked out arrangements for a mutual interchange of trade-union benefits and controls for enabling migrating workers to conform to the standards of the country to which they went in quest of work. Other activities of the secretariats included international co-operation in connection with strikes and lockouts, concerted action for the adoption of higher standards in countries with low standards, and the interchange of information on industrial and labor conditions.

## Unofficial Agencies: Industrial Associations and Corporations

The first International Congress of Chambers of Commerce was held in 1906. At the International Trade Conference held at Atlantic City in 1919, steps were taken to form a permanent international organization. Plans were adopted at Paris in 1920, a general office was established there, and in the following year the first annual meeting of the International Chamber of Commerce was held in London. The organization was modeled largely after the Chamber of Commerce of the United States. It was composed of representatives of national associations, but firms and individuals were allowed associate membership. Committees were formed to deal with such subjects as statistics, trade terms, monetary exchanges, trade policies, the simplification of tariff formalities, double taxation, and arbitration of disputes between nationals of different countries. An international court of arbitration was set up. The International Chamber of Commerce early established co-operative relations with public international bodies such as the technical committees of the League of Nations.

A form of agency associated directly with the actual carrying on of business enterprise was the international cartel or combine — an association of independent firms or undertakings in a given field operating in different countries. These associations were maintained for one or more of several purposes, such as the division of markets or sales territories; joint sales arrangements; the allocation of sources of materials; joint purchasing arrangements; agreement as to fields of specialization; interchange of patents; standardization of products; control and allocation of output; and regulation of prices. In most cases the general purpose was to enable the national producers to command their domestic market and if possible to allocate the general market on a relatively noncompetitive basis.

Before the World War there were more than a hundred international combines, mainly in the basic fields of mining, metals, chemicals, and transportation. Many of them were disrupted by the war, but after the war conditions favored a return to industrial agreements. The new political frontiers severed established economic units and areas of trade. In these regions international arrangements were promoted both by inertia in the formation of new economic units and by the economic interdependence of politically severed areas, as Lorraine and the Ruhr. The rapid advance of rationalization, alike in the fields of technique and of organization and management, vastly increased the productive capacity of the capital structure. At the same time, the obstacles in the way of a free flow of trade, both domestic and international, restricted effective demand and suggested agreements for controlling output, allocating markets, reducing costs, etc. Many governments were inclined to view such agreements as possible beginnings of a rational and planned system of production. The movement was one of the main subjects of inquiry at the International Economic Conference of 1927 at Geneva, and the League of Nations made studies and published reports on the subject.

A cartel which attracted much attention was the International Steel Agreement of 1926, designed not for direct price regulation but for production control. It included the steel producers of France, Germany, Luxemburg, and Belgium and later also those of Czechoslovakia, Austria, and Hungary. A prominent factor in bringing about the agreement was the industrial dislocation resulting from the separation of Lorraine from Germany and the severance of the resources and markets of Austria-Hungary. Production quotas were assigned by the original agreement, and the total estimated demand composing the sum of the quotas was calculated on a quarterly basis. Penalties were imposed for exceeding the quotas, and compensations were allowed for falling below them. The agreement was subject to revocation under various conditions, but it survived the depression, partly by virtue of a system of arbitration for adjusting conflicting interests, and was renewed in 1933 with a revised quota system.

International cartels exemplified the interrelations of national groups of producers and they embodied a significant aspect of unofficial international relations. Their monopolistic tendencies entailed, at the same time, a vital argument in favor of the development of public international machinery for coping with the problems of monopoly transcending national boundaries.

Another significant phase of the internationalization of enterprise was the extension of corporate activities beyond national boundaries by means of branch factories, sales offices, or subsidiary organizations. The United States Department of Commerce estimated that in 1930 American direct investments in Europe (as distinguished from indirect investments by purchase of securities through investment bankers) exceeded $1,350,000,000. Most of the large American corporations established direct connections and in many cases built factories in the principal European countries. European corporations adopted similar methods for penetrating the American market and especially for surmounting the tariff barriers and other nationalistic obstacles in the way of access to the markets of their neighbors.

Professor F. A. Southard in his *American Industry in Europe* contrasts this process of internationalizing industry with the internationalization which was envisaged by Mill and the classical economists. According to the doctrine of comparative costs, "competition will tend to allot to each area in the world those forms of activity in which it has the greatest comparative advantage or the least comparative disadvantage." The result, under a free, competitive flow of capital and enterprise, would be geographical specialization and division of labor and international interdependence. But nationalistic ambitions and policies favor the development of a varied economy with a minimum of dependence on neighbors and potential enemies. As a result, the specialized producer in a given area best adapted to his specialty, as automobiles, encounters obstacles designed to protect the producers in other areas. At the same time, his advantages in respect to comparative costs, although greatest in his own area, are likely to be superior in the protected country to those of other producers. He therefore exports his superior productive facilities to the protected market instead of exporting his product. Corporations thus became increasingly international in their investments, organization, management, and interests; while peoples became increasingly conscious of their nationality.

Regional specialization on the basis of comparative costs fixed by free competition (the system envisaged by Mill) suggested many advantages, notably maximum production and interchange at minimum cost. But regional or national interdependence was so one-sided as to mean in reality an excessive dependence on the part of some areas, particularly nonindustrial areas, and a dangerous power on the part of other areas — a power which could be used arbitrarily and not by free competition to maintain the *status quo*. Industrial retardation and dependence resulted not only from natural deficiencies but also from externally imposed obstacles in the way' of the development of resources and techniques. The advantages of a well-rounded economy in enriching the life of a people and in preventing excessive dependence on overpowerful neighbors undoubtedly provided a basis for economic nationalism without justifying the monopolistic and belligerent extremes to which it was often carried.  Internationalism may ultimately be promoted not only by interdependence but as well by the development of nationalities able to command mutual respect and impelled toward mutual agreement by such forces as corporate interpenetration.

CHAPTER 38

## RUSSIA AND THE FIVE-YEAR PLANS

### The Contradictions of the New Economic Policy

The immediate effects of the New Economic Policy proved the wisdom of the course advocated by Lenin in March, 1921. The NEP successfully performed the task of providing the Soviet regime with a much needed respite, and probably saved the country from a complete breakdown. Of course, other factors have to be taken into consideration. The cessation of civil war made available to the government the resources of the whole country, while the end of the blockade and of diplomatic isolation permitted it to use foreign assistance for economic reconstruction. No such reconstruction, however, would have been possible without the temporary abandonment of militant communism, the reorganization of the nationalized industry along more rational lines, partial concessions to private initiative, and restoration of freedom of trade within the country. The process of recovery developed with an unusual rapidity. By 1926 production both in industry and in agriculture equaled the prewar amount. Progress was particularly striking in industry, where it had started from a much lower level than in agriculture. Simultaneously, there was notable improvement in the living conditions of the urban population, which had achieved a degree of well-being far above the near-starvation standard of the early revolutionary years.

Almost from the outset, however, it became obvious that the NEP contained inner contradictions. Designed as a temporary retreat only, it attempted to use the forces of private initiative and economic freedom without permitting them to gain the upper hand in national economy. In practice, it became increasingly difficult to decide how far these forces should be allowed to go. Economically they should have been encouraged if it was desired to increase production of articles of wide consumption, and to improve the distribution of goods throughout the country. Politically they should have been kept in check and occasionally even suppressed lest their undue development should threaten the "dictatorship of the proletariat." The original thought of Lenin, who formulated the famous question "Who shall prevail?" seems to have been that

764

the victory of the "socialist sector" over the "private" economy would be achieved by a process of economic competition. But while the communists were learning how to trade and to manage business enterprises rather slowly, their economic rivals were displaying alarming vitality and resourcefulness. To combat this danger, to the devices of economic competition were added those of governmental discrimination and direct pressure. The "nepmen" of the cities, whether they were engaged in industry or in trade, were obliged to work under severe handicaps. They were subjected to heavy, at times almost punitive, taxation, and unlike the governmental establishments they did not enjoy the benefits of credit, rebates, and preferential rights to supply of materials and goods. At best they were merely tolerated as an inevitable evil, and they were always in danger of being persecuted as "profiteers." It is surprising that under such conditions the private traders were able to hold their own, and in some cases even to force the co-operatives to beat a retreat.

## The Peasantry under the NEP

In the field of industry and urban trade the government on the whole remained in a position to retain its control, but it had to face a much more serious difficulty in its relations with the peasantry. It was here that the contradictions of the NEP were felt in the most acute form. Under the stimulus of the regained economic freedom individualist tendencies in the Russian countryside began to develop with great vigor. The government-sponsored collective farms failed to attract any considerable number of peasants and continued to play an insignificant part in Russian agriculture, but there was a strongly pronounced tendency towards individual enclosed farming on the basis of a permanently secured land tenantship. In some parts of European Russia the movement reached such proportions that to some observers it looked like a resumption, after the interruption caused by war and revolution, of the process originated by Stolypin's agrarian legislation. There were also visible signs of increasing social differentiation among the peasants. With the class war in the villages temporarily called off, and with the general relaxation of government control over the country districts, the well-to-do peasants again had a chance not only to hold their own but even to strengthen their position. In spite of the rather strict limitations provided by the law, they availed themselves of the permission to lease land and to use hired labor to a much greater extent than the government was prepared to allow. Here, then, these "kulaks" were a counterpart to the city nepmen, the resurrected village bourgeoisie. The kulaks were a much larger group than the city nepmen (official estimates made their number about 5 per cent of the peasants), and they also were more strongly entrenched, more difficult to control, and economically more important.

Consequently, the agrarian policy of the Soviet Government during the NEP period vacillated. The peasants were encouraged to increase their production and to improve their agriculture, but discriminating regulations were issued against those who were doing too well. There was a considerable practical difficulty in determining at what stage an enterprising and relatively prosperous peasant would become a political menace, and a good deal of arbitrary caprice was displayed in the attempts to draw a line between the average peasant and the kulak.

As a matter of fact, not only the kulaks but the average peasants as well presented a problem which had not been definitely solved by the inauguration of the NEP. With the Soviet farms and the collectives together still covering less than 3 per cent of the planted area, the government had to rely on the mass of the peasantry both for food supplies and for an agricultural surplus that could be exported. As the requisition policy of the "war communism" period had been done away with, it was necessary to provide incentives for the peasants to increase their production and make them willing to part with their surplus. This could be done in one way only, by offering them in return the manufactured articles of which they were badly in need. And it was precisely in this respect that the NEP was not a success. As the efforts of the government were concentrated on heavy industries, the increase in the production of articles of wide consumption remained insufficient, and this insufficiency was bound to be felt more acutely when the population of the country again began to grow at a very high rate. At the same time the government, which retained the monopoly of foreign trade, refused to import any large amount of manufactured goods from abroad.

In spite of some improvement in the management and the technique of the nationalized industry, it continued to suffer from an unreasonably high cost of production which was inevitably reflected in a high level of prices for all manufactured articles. From this situation the peasants suffered the most, not only because they were the largest group of consumers in the country, but also because the prices of agricultural products remained on a very low level, in sharp contrast with the prices of manufactures. In many cases freedom of trade assumed for the peasants a purely theoretical character, as they were confronted on the market with the actual predominance of state purchasing organizations able to dictate the prices. The discrepancy reached its highest proportions in 1923, when the purchasing power of agricultural products, in relation to industrial products, became from one third to one fifth what it had been before the war. Although subsequently the ratio was noticeably improved, through the strenuous efforts on the part of the government to lower the prices of manufactured goods, the situation remained unsatisfactory to the very end of the period during which the NEP was in force. There was a widespread discontent among the peasants which on some occasions tended to acquire a definitely political character. While not so acute and not so outspoken as in 1920–1921, it was serious enough to produce considerable alarm in government circles, and to force the communist dictatorship to "face the village" (that is, the peasant village).

## The Controversy in the Communist Party

The peasant problem was the main question in the acute controversy which took place within the Communist party in the period 1923–1928. The growing discontent on the part of the peasants, and the rising threat of another grave food crisis, led some of the communists to advocate further concessions to the peasantry and a general extension of the NEP. The most radical elements of the party, on the contrary, expressed great concern over the large extent of concessions that had been made to the bourgeois tendencies in the country. They pointed out the alarming growth of "capitalist" elements, more particularly in the villages, and they insisted on ending the retreat and resuming the socialist offensive. Their program included a vigorous speeding up of Russia's industrialization, a resolute struggle against the nepmen in the cities and the kulaks in the country districts, and a general attempt at the "socialization" of agriculture. Essentially, what they advocated was a return to the policies of the "war communism" period. The central groups of the party condemned both the "right deviation" and the "left deviation," and they professed to be in favor of a "general line" of policy that would be equally removed from the two extremes. They accused the right wing of abandoning communism and of preparing the way for the eventual restoration of capitalism in the country, and they branded the "leftists" as irresponsible political adventurers who were ready to disrupt the "revolutionary alliance" between the workers and the peasants in order to promote their own unrealizable projects.

The dissension within the party became especially acute after the death of Lenin in January, 1924. While Lenin was alive, his authority and prestige remained unquestioned, and it was his will that usually prevailed at the end of each controversy. With his disappearance the field became open to a contest for leadership in the party and in the government. Almost from the outset this contest assumed the nature of a personal strife between the two strongest men in the party, Stalin and Trotsky, representing the central position and the "left deviation" respectively. The opposition from the right did not produce any vigorous leadership, and consequently it never presented any real danger to the unity of the party as did the movement headed by Trotsky. The strength of the latter lay in his dynamic personality, combined with outstanding literary and oratorical gifts, as well as in the wide popularity created by the prominent part he had played both in the conquest of power and during the civil war. On the other hand he had joined the party only in 1917, and to the party members it was known that on several occasions he had had serious disagreement with Lenin. By many old Bolsheviks, therefore, he was regarded with distrust and suspicion. Stalin, on the contrary, was known for his lifelong party regularity and his unswerving loyalty to the "chief." Moreover, while lacking Trotsky's intellectual ability and dramatic personality, he proved to be a more astute and resourceful politician. The position of the executive secretary of the party's Central Committee, to which he had been elected several years before Lenin's death, had given Stalin an opportunity to build up a strong party machine of his own. It was with the help of that machine, and by means of clever political maneuvering, that he ultimately succeeded in defeating both groups of opponents.

The personal strife for power was somewhat disguised by a theoretical dispute over the problems of revolutionary strategy. While Trotsky insisted that the victory of communism in Russia was inseparably bound up with the progress of a world proletarian revolution, Stalin came forward with the theory of "socialism in one country." Strictly speaking, the difference between the two points of view was not so wide as heated polemics would make it appear. After all, Trotsky did not advocate a postponement of gradual realization of socialism in Russia until its final victory on an international scale. On the contrary, it was he who insisted on the immediate resumption of the socialist offensive in Russia. Neither did Stalin subscribe in theory to an abandonment of the idea of world revolution. In his conception, socialist Russia still had to provide a base for such a world-wide transformation. The difference lay in the concept of the immediate aims of the Russian Communist party. While Trotsky wanted it to conduct the socialist offensive inside and outside of Russia simultaneously, Stalin found it necessary to concentrate for the time being on the task of socialist construction at home. Thus in practice Trotsky's position was imbued with the earlier internationalist spirit of Bolshevism, while that of Stalin reflected its gradual evolution towards a more nationalist attitude.

## The Origin and the Purposes of the Five-Year Plan

The Fifteenth Convention of the Communist party, held in December, 1927, registered the decisive victory of Stalin over the opposition. It confirmed the previous expulsion of Trotsky from the party, and it voted in favor of excluding all the other "leftist" leaders. At the same time it condemned in no less definite fashion the "right deviation" by proclaiming the end of the retreat and the beginning of a new socialist offensive. This meant the official termination of the NEP. After having crushed the left opposition, the majority led by Stalin actually took over from its defeated opponents several of their principal proposals.

One of the most important decisions of the Fifteenth Convention was the approval in principle of a Five-Year Plan of intensified economic activity. The idea of planning, of course, was not a radically new departure. In fact, it was inherent in that program of building up a socialist state in Russia which Lenin had proclaimed at the very outset of the Soviet regime. But during the first decade of its existence the communist government had very little opportunity to attempt economic planning on a large scale and in a systematic fashion. During the earlier years, when it was absorbed in the struggle for power, it was forced to concentrate on problems of immediate importance and to follow, on the whole, a hand-to-mouth policy. The years of the NEP were a period of recovery. All efforts had to be directed towards repairing the damage done by civil war and militant communism. Before it could advance any further the country had to regain that level of economic development which it had reached before the war and the revolution. As far as the amount of production was concerned, this was achieved by 1926–1927. It was done in a large measure by using the accumulated stocks and the equipment which the new regime had inherited from prerevolutionary Russia. Now the point was reached when it became necessary to make a new vigorous effort in order to continue along the road of economic progress.

Viewed from this angle, the Five-Year Plan was but another chapter in that historical process of Russia's gradual economic transformation. The earlier high points were the periods of industrialization under Witte and Stolypin. Both Witte and Stolypin, however, had merely tried to assist and to speed up the growth of capitalist tendencies in the country; Stalin's industrialization, on the contrary, was designed to supplant capitalism as a system, and to direct the whole economic activity of the Russian people into entirely new channels. In other words, it was a political as well as an economic scheme, and one even might say that politics predominated over economics in the motives for its adoption. The problem it was called upon to solve can be expressed in the words of Trotsky, who, on one occasion, spoke of the "contradictions inherent in the position of a workers' government functioning in a country where the large majority of the population is composed of peasants." In this he did not disagree with Stalin, who in one of his addresses, made in support of the Five-Year Plan in October of 1928, quoted Lenin to the effect that "so long as we are living in a country of small peasants, capitalism has a firmer economic base in Russia than communism." [1] The supreme task, therefore, was to *create* in Russia an economic and social base for the political "dictatorship of the proletariat" that had been established in 1917. Hence the forced tempo of industrialization which would increase the economic resources at the disposal of the communist government, and hence also the other fundamental feature of the Five-Year Plan, the collectivization of agriculture. In both cases the Soviet government had definite social objectives in view : the strengthening of the "proletarian" elements in the country, and the ultimate elimination of all the "parasitic classes," such as the city nepmen and the village kulaks. This meant the resumption of the class war on a grand scale and in an acute form, and under such conditions it was inevitable that economic planning would be combined with increased political pressure and a drastic suppression of all opposition.

[1] See the third Russian edition of Lenin's works, vol. XXVI, p. 46.

With regard to the outside world, the Five-Year Plan was a declaration of the Soviet Union's intention to attain the highest possible degree of economic self-sufficiency. While the idea itself had been present in the minds of the earlier sponsors of Russia's industrialization, such as Witte for instance, it now assumed a widely different character because of its connection with the theory of "socialism in one country." An economically self-sufficient Russia was to become the bulwark of socialism in the world, and by "overtaking and outrunning" all the other countries Russia was to demonstrate the inherent superiority of the socialist system over capitalism. Finally, with the advent of Hitler in Germany and the intensification of the Russo-Japanese conflict in the Far East, there arose also much concern for the strengthening of national defense, and military considerations began to play a prominent part in the framing of Soviet economic plans.

## The Progress of Industrialization

The First Five-Year Plan, after having undergone several upward revisions, was put in operation on October 1, 1928. Its termination was announced on December 31, 1932, so that it was declared to have been completed in a period of four years and three months. A Second Five-Year Plan, prepared by the State Planning Commission (Gosplan), immediately went into effect, and in 1937 was in the last year of its fulfillment. More Five-Year Plans were then to follow until the entire program of socialist construction in Russia should be realized.

In accordance with the chief aims of the scheme, the emphasis was laid on the development of heavy industries, the building of new large industrial establishments, and the modernization of their equipment. During the first Five-Year-Plan period more than 1,500 huge enterprises were built, and under the second Five-Year Plan industrial construction was developed on an even larger scale. In 1933-1935, of 64 billion rubles spent on construction over half was invested in industry, and of this sum over 27 billion rubles went to heavy industries as against 6 billion rubles left for industry producing articles of consumption. With such distribution of capital, and with a corresponding concentration of effort and attention, one should not wonder that the outstanding successes of the Five-Year Plans are registered in the field of heavy industry. From the quantitative point of view the achievements of the Plans with regard to industrialization should be recognized as remarkable.

The following table will give an idea of the rate of increase in the output of some of the basic industries : [1]

|  | 1928 | 1935 |
|---|---|---|
| Coal | 35,500,000 tons | 108,900,000 tons |
| Pig iron | 3,300,000 tons | 12,500,000 tons |
| Steel | 4,300,000 tons | 12,500,000 tons |
| Rolled steel | 3,400,000 tons | 9,400,000 tons |

The figures for 1935 indicate not only a great progress since the inauguration of the Five-Year Plans but also a considerable increase over the prewar level. Of particular importance is the vigorous growth of some industries which before the war had still been in the original stages of development. In generation of electricity the country, which in 1913 occupied fifteenth place in the world, had moved to third place by 1935. There has been a striking progress in chemical industry, and in the production of machinery. The automobile industry, which still is rather modest as compared with that of the United States, is a new departure for Russia, and so is the manufacture of tractors, the output of which in 1936 was larger than anywhere else in the world. Simultaneously, significant changes have been taking place in the geographical distribution of centers of industrial production. In many cases industrial establishments have been brought nearer the sources of supply, and special efforts have been made to speed up the industrialization of eastern regions. New industrial centers of importance have been developed in Siberia, where the Magnitogorsk and the Kuznetsk plants already play a prominent part in Russian mining and metallurgical industry.

With all their indubitable achievements, however, the Five-Year Plans have not been free from some serious defects. Even in the field of heavy industry, where they have been most successful, there have been frequent instances of considerable disparity between rates of progress in the various branches of industry. In contradiction to the very idea of planning, the development does not seem to be sufficiently even and steady, and fairly often spectacular achievements are subsequently compromised by unforeseen "breaks in the industrial front," the effects of which have to be remedied by use of extraordinary measures. In spite of the quantitative growth of both coal and oil industry, as registered in official statistics, there have been recurrent fuel crises, and railroad transportation seems to be lagging far behind the industrial progress. In fact, if industrial

[1] *The Second Five-Year Plan*, New York, 1937, p. xxiv.

construction on the whole has been wider and more rapid than that of the prerevolutionary period, the opposite is true of railroad construction.[1]

The shortcomings of the system become more evident when one passes from the heavy industries to the production of food and other articles of wide consumption. At the introduction of the second Five-Year Plan it was officially announced that more attention would be paid to the production of consumers' goods, and that an effort would be made to give the population three times as much food and manufactured articles as they received in 1932. But it is extremely doubtful whether this goal of the second Plan can possibly be attained. As we have seen, under the second Plan as under the first, the emphasis has continued to be placed on heavy industries. Light industry has been assigned but a small part of the total capital invested in industrial construction. There seems to have been some improvement during the last years, and in January of 1935, presumably in view of the increase of manufactured goods and foodstuffs in the country, the government found it possible to abolish the rationing system which had been partly re-established in 1928. But the general impression one gets from a careful perusal of the Soviet press is one of scarcity, not of abundance, and the average standard of living apparently continues to be rather low. With regard to food and other articles of wide consumption, official statistics are likely to be misleading: they indicate only the relative increase of production in the nationalized industry, and they do not take into account the complete elimination of small private establishments and a great reduction of output of city artisans and peasant craftsmen, which had taken place since the beginning of the new socialist offensive. On the other hand, there is enough evidence available in the official Soviet publications to show that as yet neither the problem of improving the quality of manufactured goods nor that of reducing their cost has been satisfactorily solved.

Another problem which awaits solution is that of raising the productivity of labor to a sufficiently high level. With regard to this question, claims of substantial success alternate in the Soviet press with frank admission that even in the most advanced establishments of heavy industry productivity of labor is considerably lower than that prevailing in capitalist countries.[2] In its efforts to improve the

[1] For a fully documented discussion of this point see P. Vostokov, "Les chemins de fer russes, autrefois et aujourd'hui," Le Monde Slave, vols. III–IV (1935).
[2] See, for instance, a statement to this effect in Pravda, March 2, 1937.

situation the Soviet Government has used a policy combining
elements of idealistic propaganda with an appeal to self-interest.
On the one hand, the crusading nature of the undertaking has been
stressed, and the workers have been asked to participate to full
extent in the work of socialist construction. On the other hand,
the system of a differentiated wage scale, with larger material
rewards going to those who work more and better, has been used
under the Five-Year Plan more widely and more consistently
than under the NEP. In the last few years a good deal of attention
has been attracted by the so-called Stakhanov movement. It
originated in the coal mines of the Donets basin, where, in the spring
of 1935, a hewer, Aleksei Stakhanov, tried a new method of extracting coal which permitted him greatly to exceed the established rates
of output. Within a few weeks his example, which had been given
a tremendous publicity by the government, began to be emulated
by individual workers in various trades all over Russia. The
Stakhanov movement has been officially described as "a new and
higher stage in socialist competition." But it can be regarded also
as an attempt on the part of the more enterprising workers to raise
their wages as high as possible on the basis of the piece-work system.

## The Collectivization of Agriculture

The drive for collectivization of agriculture began with great vigor
in 1929. The forcible methods employed during the earlier stages of
the campaign apparently produced serious discontent among the
peasants, and in the spring of 1930 Stalin found it necessary to
rebuke the overzealous local officials, and to prescribe a more cautious handling of the problem. Since that time the official policy of
the government has been to attract the peasants into the collectives
by demonstrating their advantages over the individualist peasant
economy, and by granting them all kinds of preferential treatment.
There can hardly be any doubt, however, that in conjunction with
this policy of persuasion, coercion continued to play a prominent
part in the process of collectivization. The recalcitrant peasants
were always in danger of being treated as kulaks, and with regard
to the latter a policy of complete "liquidation" was officially
announced. The whole upper group of the peasantry was actually
dispossessed, and hundreds of thousands of well-to-do peasants were
sent into exile or to concentration camps. What it amounted to
was a second agrarian revolution, this time effected not from below,
by the peasants themselves, but from above, by the government.

All together, about 900,000 peasant households were ruined, and if one remembers that in 1928 the kulaks had been responsible for over 14 per cent of the whole sowing area, the economic significance of this fact is obvious. Simultaneously, a wholesale slaughter of cattle seems to have been widely practiced both by the kulaks threatened with "liquidation" and by the average peasants forced to join the collectives against their will. The inevitable result was an acute crisis in Russian agriculture, which, combined with a drought, produced a grave famine in 1932–1933. Among the regions especially affected were some of the most fertile and prosperous farming districts of prewar Russia, such as the Ukraine and the Northern Caucasus. While no official statistics are available, careful foreign observers have estimated loss of human life as high as 5,000,000.

The ultimate success of the drive for collectivization can be illustrated by these facts: [1] from 1928 to 1936 (April 1), the number of noncollectivized peasant households was reduced from over 24,000,000 to over 2,000,000; the number of collectivized farms was increased from over 33,000 to over 245,000; the percentage of collectivization was increased from 1.7 to 89; and the sowing area under the collective system was increased from 1.2 per cent to 98.2 per cent. The total number of peasant households fell from about 24,500,000 in 1928 to about 20,500,000 in 1936. The disappearance of some four million households should be ascribed to the "liquidation" of the kulaks, the famine of 1931–1932, and a partial movement of rural population to the urban centers.

The organization of the collective farms — the kolkhozes — did not assume definite form until 1935. At present the overwhelming majority of collectives belong not to the more advanced "commune" type, in which all the resources of members are pooled together, but to the *artel* type, which combines communal features with individual ownership of homesteads, minor implements, and some livestock. To perform their communal work the members of the artel are organized into "brigades," each under the command of a "brigadier," and they have to follow the instructions received from the managing board of the kolkhoz, which in turn is responsible to the governmental agencies of control. Since 1933 every kolkhoz is obliged to supply the state with a specified amount of agricultural products at fixed prices. In addition, the

[1] *Sotsialisticheskoe Zemledelie*, June 6, 1936, and *Plan*, 1936, No. 24.

members of the collectives have to pay an agricultural tax, and a special tax to cover building and cultural expenses in the country-side. It should be noted that in the case of the noncollectivized peasants the grain quota is from 5 to 10 per cent higher, and the amount of agricultural tax 25 per cent higher than that paid by the members of the collectives.

The government, on its part, comes to the assistance of the collectives by supplying them with mechanical power. Mechanization plays a very great part in the whole scheme of reorganizing agriculture along new lines, and strenuous efforts have been made to increase the production of agricultural machinery in the country. In 1936 about 450,000 tractors and 85,000 combines were available for service. The collective farms are not permitted to buy large machinery, but during the planting and harvesting seasons they are supplied with tractors and combines from some 5,000 machine-tractor stations organized by the government. For this the collectives have to pay a fee in kind that may run as high as 20 per cent of the crop.

State property as well as the communal property of the collectives is heavily protected by law, and its intentional destruction or theft is punishable by death (decree of August 7, 1932). The same punishment is prescribed for sabotage and fraudulent misinformation with regard to amount of labor and production (decree of January 1, 1933). The latter decree also establishes fines for refusal to perform the assigned work without good cause, while in case of a repeated refusal the guilty are subject to expulsion from the collective.

Side by side with these drastic disciplinary measures, one finds also attempts on the part of the government to appeal to the self-interest of the collectivized peasants. The preference for the artel rather than the commune type of collectives is characteristic of that tendency. As explained by Stalin, the advantage of the artel consists precisely in that it combines the personal interests of the individual members with their communal duties, while in a commune the former are totally suppressed. The new Soviet constitution, adopted in December, 1936, guarantees the personal property of the collectivized peasants and its inheritance by their descendants. It is equally significant that for their work the members of the collectives are remunerated in accordance with its quantity and quality, and not on the basis of the equalitarian principle ("to each according to his needs"), typical of the commune. Finally, the peasants are permitted to dispose of their surplus on the "market" provided they sell it directly to the consumers.[1]

A law published in February, 1935, guaranteed the collective farms a permanent tenure of land which they held. To this effect every artel was to receive from the government a deed in which the boundaries of the given kolkhoz were definitely stated. The issuance of these documents was accompanied by a large-scale land settlement as between the neighboring collective farms. During the earlier period of forced collectivization the kolkhozes had been formed in such a haphazard fashion that the rectification of their boundaries became an urgent necessity. It is interesting to note that in a number of cases the collective farms were given more land at the expense of the government "Soviet farms." The latter seem to be in a state of partial decline, and by March, 1937, they had been liquidated to the extent of one fourth of the total area which they had occupied.

With the amount and character of information now available (July, 1937) it would be premature to attempt a definite judgment as to the general economic results of collectivization. It is obvious that one of its principal aims, to increase the food supplies at the disposal of the government, has been achieved with a large measure of success. As compared with the NEP period, state grain collections have more than doubled. But whether there has been a corresponding improvement in the well-being of the rural population is open to doubt. While the population has continued to grow very rapidly, the increase in sowing area has been a rather slow one (from 282,000,000 acres in 1928 to 335,000,000 acres in 1936).[2] Neither has there been noticeable any considerable increase in crops. Apparently, the impressive progress of mechanization in itself is not sufficient to bring about a commensurate rise of productivity. Bad management, inefficient work, and lack of mechanical training have often been complained of in Soviet periodicals. Among other unfavorable factors, the situation with regard to livestock should

|  | 1928 | 1934 | 1936 |
|---|---|---|---|
| Horses | 33,500,000 | 15,600,000 | 16,600,000 |
| Big-horned cattle | 70,500,000 | 42,400,000 | 56,500,000 |
| Sheep and goats | 146,700,000 | 61,100,000 | 73,300,000 |
| Pigs | 26,000,000 | 17,400,000 | 30,400,000 |

[1] Every attempt at resale is punishable as "speculation." It is obvious that under such conditions permitting the peasants to sell part of their products does not mean a restoration of the freedom of trade.
[2] *Plan*, 1936, No. 24.

be singled out as having great importance. While showing some improvement since 1934, it was unsatisfactory two years later, as shown by the preceding table.[1]

It is obvious that as yet the country had not recovered from the destructive effects of the second agrarian revolution.

### Changes in Population and in Social Organization of Russia since the Revolution

During the period of civil war and militant communism the population of Russia had sharply decreased, and in 1922 it was only 131,000,000 as against 141,000,000 in 1917, within the same area. After the NEP period, however, it again began to grow rapidly, and it continued to increase at a very high rate. The estimated population of the Soviet Union at the end of 1937, within its boundaries of 1922–1937, is over 180,000,000, — some 5,000,000 greater than the population of the Russian Empire on the eve of the World War. Perhaps the most important single fact, with regard to the distribution of population, is the definite trend eastward which has become particularly noticeable since the revolution. In 1913, out of 175,000,000 inhabitants of the Russian Empire, about 20,000,000 lived in what was known as Asiatic Russia (Siberia and Central Asia). In 1933, out of the 166,000,000 total population of the Soviet Union, about 30,000,000 lived to the east of the Ural Mountains and the Caspian Sea. In other words, the population ratio of the Asiatic regions had risen from about 11.5 to about 18 per cent.

Of course, the rise of this ratio is explained in part by changes in the political boundaries of Russia. It is significant that while Russia retained her Asiatic possessions intact, all the territories she lost as a result of the war and the revolution were along her western frontier (Finland, the Baltic provinces, Poland, parts of White Russia and Ukraine, and Bessarabia). But in a large measure the eastward trend of the population must be ascribed to the growing settlement and development of both Siberia and Central Asia, a process which had started before the revolution but which was intensified by the policy of the Soviet Government.

A similar historical continuity can be observed in another phenomenon — that of the gradual urbanization of Russia. Here again, after a temporary setback during the earlier years of the revolution when there was a movement out of the cities into the

[1] *Plan*, 1936, No. 19.

country districts, the growth of the urban population assumed even larger proportions than before, due to the progress of industrialization. By 1937 its percentage rose to 25.5 as against 18 on the eve of the war.

The revolution has completely destroyed some of the old social classes, and it has radically changed the nature of others. The old landowning nobility has disappeared forever, beyond the possibility of any restoration. If in this case the revolution dealt a mortal blow to a social group which had been on the decline even before the upheaval, it was different with the Russian bourgeoisie. The bourgeois class was just coming into its own, and it had every reason to expect further growth of its importance in the social life of the country. This possibility was forcibly eliminated by the revolution, and the upper stratum of the bourgeoisie was destroyed from the outset, during the earlier years of the Soviet regime. The lower middle class lingered for a while, and it was not finally eliminated until the beginning of the new socialist offensive.

A somewhat similar fate befell the upper group of the peasantry. Badly shattered during the first agrarian revolution, the well-to-do peasants were able to attempt a comeback under the NEP, but they were finally abolished in the course of the second agrarian revolution. Simultaneously, the whole peasant class radically changed its nature. As a result of collectivization, both the member of the prerevolutionary village commune and the individual farmer have been replaced by the members of the collectives who represent a new social formation widely different from the prerevolutionary peasantry. From the point of view of their relation to land, they are hereditary tenants, with the state playing the part of the landlord. As far as conditions of work are concerned, they also depend entirely on the state.

The industrial workers likewise have to deal with the state as their only employer. Theoretically they are the ruling group in the country which is governed in the name of the "dictatorship of the proletariat," and in practice they have greatly gained in social prestige, in striking contrast with their inferior position before the revolution. As a result of the industrialization, their number increased from about 2,500,000 on the eve of the war to about 6,500,000 in 1936.

The professional class has lost its identity and has become completely absorbed in governmental bureaucracy, the growth of which, in accordance with the totalitarian nature of the Soviet

780       THE NEW EUROPE

state, has reached truly prodigious proportions.  The total number
of persons employed by the government in one capacity or another
(including the workers) had risen to about 29,000,000 in 1937.[1]

The avowed purpose of the Soviet social policy is the formation
in Russia of a classless society, and some of the recent official pro-
nouncements can be interpreted as an assertion that this purpose
already has been achieved.  At the same time, however, there has
been no lack of repeated appeals to the Communists to continue
the struggle against the class enemies within the country.  Whatever position one is inclined to take on this question, it is certain
that no state of complete equality exists in the Soviet society.  To
be sure, there is no inequality based on the ownership of means of
production or on private property in general, but there is a social
gradation involving rather strongly pronounced differences in
social prestige, political influence, and material well-being.  The
members of the ruling party, the higher governmental officials, the
indispensable technical specialists, and other "notables" form
what might be called the new aristocracy of the country.  Likewise,
the "stakhanovists" among the workingmen and the more successful "kolkhozniks" in the collective farms form the nucleus of a
labor aristocracy separated from the mass of average workers by a
distance which certainly is not shorter than that existing between
the various groups of labor in capitalist countries.

In the official theory the inequality is explained as being characteristic of the transitional stage of development.  As yet Russia
cannot go beyond a *socialist* society in which "each works according
to his ability, and receives articles of consumption according to the
work he performs."  Only when sufficient abundance of goods will
be secured by further economic progress, would it be possible to
have a *communist* society where everybody will be supplied with
articles of consumption "according to his needs."

Whether the Soviet society will develop in the direction of communism or whether, on the contrary, the inequalities of the transitional period will tend to become permanent, must remain an open
question.  Any attempt to answer it would be based not so much
on factual information as on some general theory concerning the
evolution of human society.  But a theoretical discussion of such
nature does not lie within the scope of this study.

[1] *The Second Five-Year Plan*, pp. 624-625.

CHAPTER 39

## ITALY AND FASCISM

———◆———

### The Limitations of Italian Liberalism

Italy was the home of the individualism of the Renaissance, which first broke down the authoritarian ideas and disciplines of the Middle Ages. Before national unification, political separatism and foreign domination prevailed. Unification was achieved under the influence of the liberal traditions of the French Revolution, British parliamentary institutions, and the classical system of economic thought. Before the rise of Fascism, the government and the system of private enterprise therefore resembled the liberal regimes of western Europe. Ministers were responsible to a popularly elected parliament; economic individualism was tempered by a mild system of governmental regulation and social legislation; and socialistic groups advocated national socialism and the international solidarity of the working classes.

After the World War, Fascism intervened as a system avowedly hostile alike to liberalism, democracy, and socialism, which were declared to be "logical derivations one of the other." Fascism emerged as primarily a political and not an economic system, but it differed from liberal and democratic regimes alike in its political absolutism and in its degree of control of economic life. In its avowed aims if not in its achievements, Fascism is a term applicable to Italian economy as well as government.

The earlier liberal regime had encountered many difficulties. Regional differences and traditions of separatism had never been fused into a harmonious national system. The country was predominantly agricultural. Land tenures exhibited the extremes of very large estates, especially in the south, and farms too small or infertile to afford an adequate living. Absentee ownership of the large estates was prevalent. Most of the laborers and tenants and many of the farmers who owned small tracts were illiterate, dependent, and extremely poor. In 1921, 8,294,000 persons, or 21 per cent of the total population (38,756,000), belonged to the families of hired farm laborers, shepherds, etc. The families of cash tenants and share-croppers combined included 4,689,000 persons, or 12 per cent of the population. The families of farmers who owned and

781

tilled their farms included 7,115,000 persons, or 18 per cent of the population. The agricultural resources were varied but were not adequately conserved. The pressure of the rapidly growing population, formerly relieved by emigration, was intensified by restrictions on immigration in the United States and other countries.

The needs of the agricultural population for land, combined with the increasing demand for food and materials by the expanding industrial centers, called for large-scale, expensive projects of land reclamation and conservation. These in turn required a strong national government and continuity of policy. The rapid growth of industry called not only for an expansion of the food supply but also for large importations of coal, petroleum, cotton, wool, iron, and other materials. Industrial growth also gave rise to demands for hydroelectric development, control of the credit and capital structure and of the forms of industrial organization, regulation of the relations between employers and employees, and the extension of social legislation. All of these problems called for co-ordination and continuity of national policy.

The responsibilities of the national government after the World War were magnified by acute problems of demobilization and were made more difficult by opposition arising from the failure to achieve Italian territorial ambitions at the Peace Conference. Its tasks proved to be beyond its capacity. Although the Italian system before the rise of Fascism resembled the older liberal and democratic regimes of western Europe, it exhibited characteristics which foreshadowed Fascism. The governmental system had been superimposed on an inadequate social and economic structure. The percentage of illiteracy was large. Experience in democratic self-discipline was slight. Before 1912 the masses of farm laborers, tenants, and subsistence farmers and many urban workers had virtually no share in national politics. The conditions of the succeeding decade were far from conducive to training for an intelligent part in the momentous decisions of that decade. The new industrial workers were politically self-conscious but were divided by the conflicting claims of traditional liberalism, evolutionary socialism, and revolutionary syndicalism. The church long opposed the national government and participation by Catholics in national affairs. This virtually removed conservative opposition and assured the ascendancy of leftist (liberal, not radical) groups. Political blocs centered around personalities with no well-defined party principles and organizations. Government was

dependent on fluctuating and opportunist coalitions of blocs able
to command votes in the Chamber of Deputies but with few positive
and long-range commitments in the field of national policy. Maintenance of a solid and dependable majority as the basis for continuity of policy was made more difficult by two measures which, at
a critical time, put a new strain on liberal institutions. Untested,
inexperienced, and diversified groups were allowed to vote after
1912 without corresponding measures for raising their cultural and
economic standards; and proportional representation, adopted in
1919, gave impetus to the formation of obstructive minority groups
in the Chamber of Deputies.

The influence of businessmen had been dominant. The typical
business enterprise was small, even in manufacturing, but in the
basic industries (mining, metals, textiles, power, etc.) joint-stock
undertakings grew rapidly during the decade before Fascism.
From 1912 to 1922 the capital invested in joint-stock companies
in the principal industries had doubled and in some cases almost
trebled. In metals and engineering, for example, these investments
increased from 710,000,000 gold lire in 1912 to 1,794,000,000 in
1922. In the electrical industries the increase was from 463,000,000
to 1,211,000,000 gold lire. The land, as already stated, was largely
in the hands of absentee owners, who rented it to cash tenants or
to share-croppers or engaged bailiffs to employ hired labor. Many
members of the middle classes (owners of small factories, shopkeepers, contractors, independent farmers, and the professional
groups) had a direct financial interest in large-scale enterprise
and in government through investments in corporate and public
securities.

These groups — the great industrialists, bankers, landlords,
and the middle classes — had given direction to public policy.
But after the extension of the franchise and the emergence of new
social forces from the war, political realignments occurred. Large-
scale industry rapidly increased the numbers and stimulated the
group consciousness of industrial workers. In 1919 the Socialists
won 156 seats in the Chamber (the total membership of which was
508). A Catholic party, formed in 1919, obtained 101 seats in
that year. It opposed socialism but advocated social reforms and
the compulsory sale of lands for distribution to peasants. The
division into blocs in the traditional left and right groups, both
opposed to socialism, was accentuated after 1919 by proportional
representation. The ministry found it necessary to rely increas-

ingly on the Socialists and on the uncertain voice of the newly enfranchised peasants.

### Group Conflicts and the Rise of Fascism

Italian society after the World War was divided into sharply defined groups. The liberal government was faced with the responsibility of reconciling the conflicting interests and ambitions or of dominating and directing them either by constitutional methods backed by the Chamber of Deputies or by the use of the armed forces. Its failure in this urgent national responsibility was in part a result and in part a cause of the rise of Fascism to a commanding position.

After the war there was a rapid rise in prices, a curtailment of war industries, and a sudden increase in the labor supply due to demobilization. Real wages fell, unemployment became serious, and discontent, demoralization, and disillusion were prevalent. Hunger riots as well as strikes ensued. The strikes of 1919 and 1920 began as protests or as demands of a traditional trade-union character. When employers retaliated with lockouts, the strikes were given a revolutionary direction, not so much in a political as in an economic sense. The metalworkers of Milan, when a lockout order was issued, refused to evacuate the plants. Lockout orders were then extended to other parts of Italy, and the occupation of factories was also extended, but in a peaceful manner. Councils were formed, a police force was organized, and efforts were made to operate the factories.

There were demands by the owners that force be used by the government against the workers, but Giolitti, the prime minister, preferred negotiation. The workers were not averse to negotiation, for they were unable to obtain the aid of technicians and bankers, necessary for operating the factories. The more moderate leaders recognized, also, that even if they could command the necessary Italian resources, Italy was vitally dependent on other countries for materials and markets, and they knew that the governments of these countries were in no mood to permit another experiment such as was being made in Russia if it could be prevented. Under these circumstances, labor leaders and owners met with the prime minister and worked out an agreement, to be embodied in law, for joint employer-employee control of industry.

This agreement was denounced by employers as having been forced upon them by the premier's desertion of their cause, and their hostility to the government was so extreme that they prevented the agreement from being enacted into law. Some of the labor leaders, on the other hand, held that the agreement was a virtual betrayal of the workers at a moment when the resources of the state could have been utilized peacefully for the socialization of industry. There was a split in the Socialist party, although only a small minority actually seceded. The fears of the employers were further aroused by an organized movement among the peasants to force concessions from the landlords — a movement which had been promoted both by Socialists and by the Catholic party. The landlords and the industrialists made common cause and found little difficulty in stirring up many of the middle classes in opposition alike to the workers and peasants and to the government.

During the same period of acute industrial and agricultural unrest, the government was subjected to violent attacks from the extreme nationalists over the terms of the treaty of peace. The Italian representatives at the Peace Conference had demanded the port of Fiume on the northeastern Adriatic, but representatives of the other powers held that the interests of Yugoslavia should take precedence. A conciliatory tone on the part of Premier Nitti in the summer of 1919 promised a compromise, but the nationalists, inflamed by the poet D'Annunzio, seized the city. Premier Nitti appealed to the Italian masses for support of his plan of compromise, but the opposition of the industrialists and the extreme nationalists was intensified against the government as well as against the Socialists and the working classes.

In the meantime the Fascist movement was taking shape. Its creator, Benito Mussolini, had been a left-wing Socialist, but he broke with his party in 1914 over Italy's war policy and was expelled from the party. He became an extreme nationalist and attempted with slight success to win the workers to the view that Italy should join the Allied Powers and extend her territories by means of war. Early in 1919 he formed at Milan a small group called the *Fascio di Combattimento* and adopted the fasces of the ancient Roman lictors as the group's emblem.

Mussolini still sought to win the support of the working classes, and to this end he adopted for his new organization such slogans as the confiscation of church property, nationalization of munitions plants, abolition of the monarchy and of the senate, minimum wages, high inheritance taxes, and seizure of war profits by the state. During the hunger riots of 1919, Mussolini's newspaper printed such inflammatory statements as the injunction to "Hang the starvers of the people to lampposts." Fascist groups were formed in various places, and candidates for the Chamber of Deputies were entered in the election of 1920, but without success. The Socialist party, on the other hand, made extensive gains and revealed to the Fascists the difficulty of winning the workers.

The popularity of D'Annunzio's defiance of the government strengthened the nationalistic tendencies of the Fascists and suggested a more or less covert alliance with nationalistic employers and landlords against the socialistic trade-unions and the peasants. Many antisocialistic and antigovernmental groups not connected with Mussolini's clubs were being formed throughout Italy. Veterans without jobs, adventurers, professional strikebreakers, and vagrants swelled the numbers of such groups, many of which were merely loose and temporary bands incited to violence and depredations by the prevailing demoralization and unemployment. These groups, together with local vigilance committees of various kinds, were widely utilized to break strikes, suppress socialistic demonstrations, and preserve law and order as interpreted by the antisocialistic groups.

The leaders of Fascism were not slow to recognize the possibilities of welding these various groups into a national movement supported by employers, landlords, and army officers. They co-operated, in 1920, with the Agrarian Association of Bologna in suppressing the peasants of that region, and received increasingly the support of the landlords. Municipal governments controlled by the Socialist party, as well as party offices, clubs, and newspapers, were attacked by Fascist bands, often led by army officers and transported without cost in public conveyances. Thus the violent tactics were not restricted to attacks on revolutionary extremists among the socialists or even to the suppression of strikes of workers' and peasants' organizations, but were extended to the overthrow of municipal governments based on constitutional elections and conducted by constitutional methods.

In the elections of 1921, the Fascists won only 35 seats in the Chamber of Deputies. Mussolini, convinced of the difficulty of victory in a popular election, moved rapidly toward the overthrow of the constitutional regime. The numerous loosely organized local groups were thoroughly reorganized, given a definite military form, vigorously disciplined, and required to swear allegiance not to the government but to the Fascist party and its head.

Violent tactics were renewed on a more definitely organized and efficient basis. The reorganized "voluntary militia" continued to seize municipalities, break strikes, and destroy the offices and newspapers of the socialists and the trade-unions. Co-operative stores, opposed by the merchants, were also molested. The plants of *Avanti* and *Il Lavoro*, two prominent socialistic journals, were burned. All of this was in the name of "service to the state." In protest against such tactics and the failure of the government to control the situation, a strike broke out in August, 1922. The Fascists declared that if the strike was not ended in 48 hours they would seize the national government. The strike soon ended, but violent seizure of municipal governments continued, and in October the final step was taken. The Fascist militia marched toward Rome, the king refused to sign an order declaring a state of siege, the city was occupied, and Mussolini was confirmed by the king as prime minister.

### Beginnings of the Fascist System

Before the march on Rome the program of the Fascists was designed not for the exercise of responsibility but for the attainment of power. Their proposals were inconsistent and vague as to specific policies but more and more unmistakable in the avowal of extreme nationalism, in the demand for dictatorial power and antiparliamentary methods, and in hostility to anti-Fascist unions and to socialism. Resistance to Fascism was denounced as violence and at the same time Fascist violence was glorified as service to the state. Businessmen and landlords, however, had ample assurance as to the economic policies of the new regime alike in the more recent statements of the leaders, in the direction given to Fascist violence, and in the dependence of the movement on their support.

Although extremely bold, Mussolini recognized the fact that he had no definite and detailed program for national policy, and also the fact that his party held only 35 out of 508 seats in the Chamber of Deputies. He had proclaimed his opposition to parliamentarism, but instead of dispensing with the Chamber he overawed it with threats and also obtained a measure of support by offering cabinet posts to leaders of several of the blocs. He then demanded and received a grant of emergency power for one year. The party, which had been held together by vague promises and the ardor of the quest for power, was reorganized on the basis of strict allegiance and of rewards in the form of governmental appointments. The party militia was demobilized for the purpose of purging it of undesirable elements, but was immediately reorganized under rigorous discipline and sworn allegiance to the party. Fascists were appointed to public posts throughout the country. Many of the local governments were abolished and new governments controlled directly by the party were put in their place. In other local governments and in the national service, replacements were made in various ways. Party appointments to the judiciary were facilitated by a reorganization of the courts of appeal, by changes in many of the lesser courts, and by the establishment of special tribunals. A hundred thousand carefully selected men were added to the army. The staffs of the state-owned railways were reorganized. The natural desire to avoid displacement put a premium on evidence of loyalty to the new regime.

With these preliminary safeguards, combined with a new electoral law and thorough arrangements for supervising the elections, the party in 1924 obtained a majority in the Chamber of Deputies. But the methods used led to a widespread reaction against Fascism. There followed a new wave of violence, a series of attacks on the opposition, and the establishment of a one-party dictatorship in control of virtually every aspect of Italian life.

In 1926 a Special Tribunal for the Defense of the State was established with broad powers and martial-law procedure. Even elective officials of local governments were supplanted by officials appointed by the central government. In 1925 the prime minister had been given authority by law to fix the number and duties of the ministers, to appoint them, and to make all final decisions. Legislation by decree was authorized. Parliament became, by its own action, an agency for registering the will of the prime minister. In 1928 the Chamber of Deputies was transformed into a body selected by the Fascist Grand Council from lists submitted by organizations controlled by the party, and qualified voters were then required to vote "yes" or "no" in approval or disapproval of the entire list. A vote of "no" was an anti-Fascist vote; and Mussolini himself in 1927 had declared that "there is no place for anti-Fascists in Italy."

### Fascist Trade-Unions and Employers' Associations

The Labor Charter of 1927 states that the nation is a moral, political, and economic unity, which finds its complete expression

in the Fascist state. "What is the state?" Mussolini had asked
this rhetorical question in the Chamber of Deputies in 1923. "The
policeman!" was his own reply. In the same year he had declared:
"If consent should fail, there is still force." Again, on the eve
of the "yes" or "no" plebiscite of 1929, he wrote: "Let no one
delude himself by thinking that a pile of ballots will jeopardize
the regime, which will be more totalitarian tomorrow than it was
yesterday."

The methods, already briefly outlined, of achieving political
unity under Fascism were extended to the economic field. A notable
instance was the formation of Fascist trade-unions and employers'
associations for the making of so-called labor contracts. The early
stages of this development are to be found in the Fascist trade-
unions (syndicates) formed before the march on Rome. In 1922
these groups were directed to form a national confederation with a
comprehensive plan. All kinds of workers, intellectual and manual,
were to be included. It was asserted that the impulse to organization, although originating with labor, should extend to all classes
and become the institutional expression of the whole population.
By this means the social functions of the different groups would be
defined and their economic and juridical relations would be established and maintained. But it was declared that these institutions
cannot be independent but must be incorporated in the state and
become subject to the will of the state. It was further declared,
in the general plan (the "statutes") of the confederation, that
there must be no class struggle; each class has its necessary function,
and employees must co-operate with employers; and the only
permissible struggle is the effort of those in the lower classes who
have special ability to rise above their group and take the places
of those in the upper classes who fail to perform their functions
adequately.

When the Fascists gained control of the government, they gave
every possible encouragement to the Fascist unions. But it was
not until 1925 that they succeeded in obtaining enough members
for these unions to give them the boldness necessary for their next
step. This was an agreement between the Fascist unions, called
the Confederation of Fascist Corporations, and the Industrial
Employers' Federation. Each organization recognized the other
as having the exclusive right to represent all workers, or all employers. Actual labor contracts were to be made by local affiliates
of the two organizations. Later the idea of a comprehensive single

organization for each group was abandoned — a decision which was influenced by the ancient maxim *divide et impera*.

In 1926 an antistrike law was passed. The law provided for the legal recognition of associations of Fascist employees and employers. An association of workers which included as many as 10 per cent of the workers of a specified industry or area might qualify as the exclusive legal representative of all of the workers. In the same way, an association of employers whose workers numbered as many as 10 per cent of all of the workers in the specified industry or region might qualify as the exclusive legal representative of all of the employers. Legal recognition of any association might be revoked at any time. Officers had to be approved by the government, and the associations were subject to constant governmental supervision. Public employees were not allowed to organize.

The formation of these associations was primarily for preventing strikes, but lockouts were also forbidden. The legally recognized associations were to make collective agreements, which had to be deposited with public authorities and officially published. Since the associations were in no sense "free" and were dominated by the government even in respect to the choice of officials, the nature of the collective agreements as well as their acceptance by both associations was ordinarily assured. Any controversies either as to the making or as to the enforcement of agreements were to be handled by labor courts controlled exclusively by the government, and access to these courts was granted only to the legally recognized associations. Associations not legally recognized were subject to supervision by government officials with discretionary power to administer their property and to dissolve them.

The underlying principles of this legislation were set forth in 1927, in a law called the Labor Charter. This law reaffirmed the faith of the government in private initiative, proclaimed the responsibility of the employer, and demanded the collaboration of employees with the employer. It adopted in principle the weekly rest on Sunday, the annual holiday with pay, and the "improvement" of social insurance. There were some general statements regarding security of tenure as affected by illness, by a call to military service, etc. Employers' and workers' associations were required to co-operate with public agencies for recreation, relief, and propaganda. Employers were required to patronize the official employment bureaus and to give preference to "members of the Fascist party and of Fascist unions."

The associations recognized by law were classified under six heads : industry (manufacturing and mining) ; agriculture ; trade ; transportation by sea and air ; inland transportation and communication ; and finance. In addition there were associations of artisans, artists, and professional workers. In 1933, 166 national and interprovincial labor agreements and 1,517 provincial agreements were registered.

## The Corporate State

The associations of workers and of employers were mainly local and regional, and their work was largely concerned with collective labor contracts. They were corporations neither in the sense of being independent juridical bodies nor in the sense intended by Italian authorities in their references to the institutions supposedly composing the "corporate state." It was intended that a "corporation" (in essence an agency for comprehensive economic control by the state) should be formed of representatives, loyal to the party, from each main branch or "category" of production. The functions were to include the handling of all the larger problems of production, and "above all, that of co-ordinating and rationalizing production."

The Labor Charter and other laws referred vaguely to such a plan, and a Ministry of Corporations was established. A National Council of Corporations, to be under the Ministry of Corporations, was authorized in 1926. The Ministry and the Council were designed for the purpose of extending the functions and co-ordinating the work of the legally recognized associations already described. Grave problems were encountered, such as organization by craft and occupation or by industry ; organization by industry or by region ; integration in a single organization of overlapping industries, as in the making of textiles and of clothing ; and the assimilation of workers and employers not included in the legally recognized associations. As a result, the corporate state, outside of the control of labor, remained largely a paper organization.

In 1934 a new law was enacted and renewed effort was made to utilize the imposing machinery of organization. The prime minister authorized the formation of 22 corporations in three groups. Eight corporations were to be connected with agriculture and the production and preliminary fabrication of nonmineral materials. These were to be concerned with cereals ; fresh fruit, vegetables, and flowers ; vineyards and wine making ; edible oils ; beets and sugar ; animal husbandry, fisheries, and allied industries ; forestry, lumber and wood industries; and textile fibers and their products. A second group of eight corporations was to include mining, construction, and most of the manufacturing and engineering industries. They were concerned with metals and engineering; chemicals; clothing; paper and printing; building trades; water, gas, and electricity; mining and quarrying; and glass and pottery. The third group, of six corporations, was to include transportation, finance, and the service industries. They covered insurance and banking; the arts and professions; sea and air transportation; inland transportation and communication; public entertainment; and hotels, restaurants, and other agencies of public hospitality. Each corporation was to be representative of an integrated branch of business activity. In manufacturing, for example, the essential phases of the cycle of production were to be included, from the principal materials used to the finished products.

The administrative machinery for this ambitious project included a council for each corporation, a National Council of Corporations, a Central Corporative Committee, and industrial trade associations (consortia) organized nationally on an industry basis. There was also a regional organization which included for each province a Provincial Council of Corporate Economy. Over the whole presided the Ministry of Corporations. The membership of the various agencies was rigorously controlled by the party and their functions were largely confined to discussion, technical criticism, and formal approval of policies desired by the party heads. The dominant elements in the party remained sympathetic with private enterprise and opposed the direct assumption by the government of responsibility for the productive process. The imposing structure of industrial associations and corporations was primarily an instrument for use by the party leaders in harmonizing private enterprise with the party's aims, such as the curbing of elements opposed to the party, the promotion of national self-sufficiency, and the mobilization of the national economy for war. Within these general limits, decisions regarding ordinary business policies continued to be made by businessmen themselves. Taxation, trade policy, public purchases, and the allocation of credit and materials, backed by absolutism, were the most vital means of economic control.

### Private Enterprise under Fascism

The course of business activity under Fascism followed substantially the same patterns as in other nonsocialistic countries, although in Italy economic depression and a declining standard of living preceded the world economic crisis of 1929. Mussolini, it is true, asserted in 1933 that "the method of capitalistic production is vanquished," and that "Italy is not a capitalistic country." He defined capitalism as "a mode of mass production for mass consumption, financed in mass through the national and international issue of joint-stock capital." Italy, he asserted, was predominantly a country of small-scale enterprise and should remain so.

On the other hand, in the year following Mussolini's speech proclaiming the vanquishing of joint-stock capitalism, the General Fascist Confederation of Italian Industries declared that "the joint-stock company as a financial power in the land has been a comparatively recent and for a long while a slow growth in Italy," but that "it has acquired the stature of a giant, overshadowing all other forms of industrial and commercial organization." The Confederation stated that the capitalization of joint-stock companies had increased from about 15,400,000,000 lire in 1922 (the year of the march on Rome), to 52,300,000,000 in 1930, and that thereafter, during the financial crisis, the government went to the rescue of these enterprises and even encouraged further combinations, especially in finance, electric power, and transportation. The prevailingly dependent nature of the agricultural population was indicated by the prime minister himself when he stated that in 1931 the number of tenants, crop-sharing farmers, wage workers on farms, and casual agricultural laborers was about 5,000,000.

The Fascists rose to power with the support of industrialists and landlords and many of the middle classes. When Mussolini became prime minister, the official journal of the federation of industrialists expressed firm confidence in him and offered him the support of the organization. "Guild or corporate economy," the prime minister stated in 1934, "respects the principle of private property. . . . It respects private enterprise." Consistent support, including the granting of extensive subsidies, was extended to private enterprise. The government undertook numerous public works, but these resembled the enterprises of other governments. They included such typical activities as road building, land reclamation, port and harbor development, forest conservation, the construction of hydroelectric plants, and housing. As in other countries, the postwar financing of industry was supervised and aided by official or semiofficial credit institutions of various kinds.

The first four years of Fascist rule, from 1923 to 1926, were marked by industrial expansion in Italy as well as in other countries. Italy profited notably by two good harvest years, by the demand for Italian labor in other countries, especially in France, and by a revival of the tourist trade. Italy obtained exceptionally favorable terms for the funding of the inter-Allied war debts. Expansion was stimulated also by the inflation of the lira, with a rapid rise in prices, while money wages remained almost constant. In 1927 the stabilization of the lira at a comparatively high value stopped inflation. There followed a deflationary tendency, a checking of expansion, and a further decline in real wages.

In some industries, expansion was resumed. Italy's lack of coal, gas, and petroleum and her exceptional water-power resources suggested an ambitious program, public and private, for the development of facilities for generating hydroelectric energy. The steel and chemical industries and shipbuilding were promoted by an increasingly ambitious national program for the expansion of armaments and by the desire to promote self-sufficiency in the industries most important for war. Various types of construction were stimulated by subsidies and by grants for public works. But so serious had been the depression before the world economic crisis that the prime minister in December, 1928, described Italian economy as convalescent.

Although Italy had already suffered a severe depression during the years of general expansion elsewhere, culminating in 1929, her economy during the world depression declined more than in most of the other countries of Europe. Comprehensive figures for Italy before 1928 are not available. Between 1929 and 1932, the available official indexes of industrial production (manufacturing and mining) for various European countries show declines (or increases as indicated) as follows:

CHANGES IN THE VOLUME OF INDUSTRIAL PRODUCTION, 1929 TO 1932

| | Per Cent Decrease | | Per Cent Decrease | | Per Cent Decrease |
|---|---|---|---|---|---|
| Germany | 46.7 | Belgium | 30.9 | Sweden | 9.9 |
| Poland | 46.1 | Hungary | 23.1 | Denmark | 9.0 |
| Netherlands | 37.7 | Estonia | 21.7 | Norway | 7.3 |
| Czechoslovakia | 36.5 | Finland | 16.7 | | Per Cent Increase |
| Austria | 35.7 | Great Britain | 16.5 | | |
| Italy | 33.1 | Spain | 11.6 | Greece | 0.9 |
| France | 31.2 | Rumania | 11.5 | Russia | 82.9 |

Only five European countries for which statistics of industrial production are available showed greater declines than Italy. In all of these countries production had greatly expanded from 1926 to 1929, during the Italian depression. After 1932 production and employment were accelerated by armaments and war.

The Italian government fought a sensationally dramatized "battle of wheat." By means of costly land reclamation and conservation projects, propaganda, and protective policies, the average production of wheat from 1930 to 1934 was increased 10 per cent above the average from 1925 to 1929, while the increase for Europe as a whole, excluding Russia, was 13 per cent. The importation of wheat was restricted and there was an increased dependence on inferior breads.

## Labor Conditions under Fascism

A large part of the burden of deflation and depression was borne by wage earners through part time, unemployment, and repeated reductions in wages. Even during the upturn in business from 1923 to 1926, real wages declined. The cost of living increased about 30 per cent, while industrial wages remained almost constant. A report made in 1925 by the International Labor Organization on real wages in seventeen countries stated that real wages were lower in Italy than in any other country except Portugal. After the stabilization of the lira in 1927, prices fell, but wages fell more rapidly. The labor contracts were revised for the purpose of reducing wage rates. A series of wage reductions also accompanied the deepening of the depression after 1929. The Secretary of the National Confederation of Fascist Syndicates stated in 1932 that wage rates fell about 20 per cent from June, 1927, to December, 1928, about 10 per cent in 1929, and from 18 to 25 per cent in 1930, and that further downward adjustments were made in 1931. Additional reductions were ordered in 1934. During the same period the cost of living declined but much more slowly than wage rates. The standard of living was also reduced by part time and unemployment.

Contrary to the expectations of many economists, the elasticity of the wage structure failed to relieve unemployment or even to check its increase. In the face of greatly increased part time, a large expansion of the civil and military services, and an ambitious public works program, unemployment was more than three and a half times as great in 1932 as in 1927. Although many economists advocated wage reductions as a method of increasing employment, in the belief that lower wage costs would make employment profitable to employers, others held that wage reductions would reduce employment by curtailing the buying power of workers and thereby undermining the demand for goods, on which production and employment depend.

The wage reductions were accompanied by an increase in the number of industrial disturbances, but these were readily curbed. The antistrike law of 1926 provided heavy fines for workers who, in groups of three or more, went on strike or worked in an undisciplined manner; and the law imposed imprisonment as well as fines on leaders or promoters of such actions. In addition, employers were authorized by law to fine employees or suspend them or discharge them without compensation for "infractions of discipline" and "acts disturbing to the normal functioning of a concern" — a provision which went far toward nullifying the prohibition of lockouts. A factor which enabled workers to survive the reductions in wages already extremely low was the work of public agencies for relief, recreation, and propaganda. In this way a part of the income deducted from wages was returned to the workers but in forms wholly beyond their control. Even the social insurance benefits accruing to workers were in part diverted to publicly controlled expenditures.

Italian economy, like that of every other country after the World War, was confronted by grave problems. In most countries there was a recognition of the inadequacy of individualism and *laissez faire* even when tempered by the extensive public regulation and social legislation of the period immediately preceding the war. In Russia and to a lesser extent in some other countries, governments attacked these problems by acquiring ownership of enterprise and assuming direct responsibility for carrying on the productive processes. In Great Britain, France, and most of the other countries, especially in western Europe, private enterprise was retained, as in Italy, and economic as well as other problems were handled within the framework of democratic institutions by the processes of discussion, compromise, and consent. From various causes, one of which was undoubtedly the disruptive and violent tendency of the Fascist movement, Italy failed in her efforts to retain democratic methods. Fascism intervened and gained ascendancy at the moment when the first postwar depression was receding.

It is in the light of these circumstances that the historian must interpret Mussolini's declaration in 1933 that "the corporations supersede socialism and supersede liberalism; they create a new synthesis." The Italian system was a new synthesis in time and circumstance, but it was essentially a revival of predemocratic systems. It bears a notable resemblance especially to the mercantilistic national state such as Colbert developed in France on the basis of royal absolutism, which perished in the French Revolution.

A significant aspect of the experience of Fascist Italy was the appearance of economic depression, with a downward trend of the standard of living, before the world economic crisis. The acceptance of repeated reductions in wages by the workers was praised by the Fascist leaders as patriotic sacrifice and as "a preparation for tomorrow by the renunciations of today." And yet in 1934 the prime minister asserted: "We are probably moving toward a period of humanity resting on a lower standard of living. Humanity is capable of asceticism such as we perhaps have no conception of." Accompanying the declining standard of living was a persistent governmental encouragement of large families and a rising birth rate.

## Fascist Imperialism

The statements of the prime minister, and the official statistics already cited, indicate a discouraging response of Italian industry and agriculture to the stimulus of Fascist policies, an increase of unemployment, and a decline in the standard of living already exceptionally low. These circumstances intensified the imperialistic ambitions inherent in Fascist theory and policy and hastened the Ethiopian adventure. Mussolini's expulsion from the Socialist party had been a result of his advocacy of Italian participation in the World War. After the war he supported D'Annunzio's Fiume adventure. When he failed to win the support of the working classes, he became increasingly imperialistic, and in 1921, in the Chamber of Deputies, his party formed a coalition with the Nationalists, the most extreme of the imperialistic groups.

In the first important statement of Fascist doctrines, a speech in 1925 by A. Rocco, Minister of Justice, the theoretical basis of Fascist imperialism was made clear. In this address, which the prime minister personally endorsed, the social group was described as an organism and was identified with the national state, and the following views were expressed: The aims of the national state

798 THE NEW EUROPE

cannot be determined, nor its authority controlled, by the people, but only by "the chosen few." (The method of choice was not defined.) The aims of the state are distinct from the aims of individuals — "so distinct, in fact, that they may be in opposition. Hence the necessity, for which the older doctrines make little allowance, of sacrifice, even up to the total immolation of individuals in behalf of the society." In another section of the address, the Minister of Justice discussed an apparent exception to the rule. Fascism recognizes, he stated, that "the most powerful spring of human activities lies in individual self-interest"; and in the formation, ownership, and inheritance of capital, self-interest must not only be permitted to function but must be protected by the national state.

Among the essential aims of the national state, the Minister of Justice further asserted, is expansion; and he said that it is in the pursuit of this and other essential aims of the social organism that the state must be supreme over individuals even to the extent of the total immolation of individuals. In this fact, he continues, lies "the true explanation of war, eternal law of mankind, interpreted by the liberal-democratic doctrines as a degenerate absurdity or as a maddened monstrosity."

Thus within the national state, according to Fascism, there must be "social unity" and peace maintained not by "popular sovereignty" but by "state sovereignty" on the basis of "the duty of the individual" and "the right of the state." On the other hand, in the external relations of the national state, "social unity" and peace are impossible. Because of the sovereignty of the state and the right of the social organism to expand, external relations are necessarily, in principle, on the basis of "war, the eternal law of mankind."

An early incident indicating the imperialistic trend of Fascist policy was the seizure, in 1923, of the Greek island of Corfu; but in this instance Italy yielded to the League of Nations and withdrew from that island. The resentment then aroused found expression later in the point of view stated in 1929 by a responsible Italian League of Nations representative and editor of a prominent Italian journal. Italy, it was asserted, should not resign from the League but should remain a member for the explicit purpose of hastening its end, and in the meantime influencing its policies while Italy was preparing for independent military action. In keeping with this attitude was the retention of League membership in 1935 and 1936, throughout the conquest of Ethiopia, another member of the League, while Italy defied the League in its attempt to prevent the conquest by means of economic sanctions against Italian trade.

Expansion by means of diplomacy, as in the extension of Italian influence in Austria and the Balkans, and by means of war, as in the conquest of a member of the League, was frequently avowed as in keeping with the doctrines of Fascism. But there is a basis for the view that this particular manifestation of Fascist doctrine and policy was little more than an exceptionally frank and unrestrained expression of the general spirit of modern imperialism. A major unsolved problem of capitalistic enterprise in Italy as elsewhere was the maintenance of its operation on a profitable basis by means of the domestic market and friendly, mutually profitable trade relations. At the heart of the problem was the difficulty, under prevailing social controls, of maintaining income and production in equilibrium and of allocating income in a suitable manner on the one hand to production and on the other hand to consumption. The invariable experience of modern industrial societies was a failure to control the income nexus between production and consumption in such manner as to maintain a free flow of output into consumption. The facilities for production therefore sooner or later exceeded the buying capacity of consumers. Capital thus failed to find full employment. On the employment of capital depends, in an industrial society, the employment of labor. Unemployed workers further diminished effective demand and enlarged the obstructions between production and consumption.

One of the traditional modes of maintaining the employment of capital and the profitable operation of the productive plant was the control of markets in other countries. Surplus profits and other forms of income, representing claims on production, accumulated to such an extent that they could neither be used for consumption by the owners nor, because of the limited buying power of other consumers, be profitably invested at home. These accumulations were therefore invested in other countries, particularly in unindustrialized regions. This process of investment, combined with the desire to control essential raw materials or other resources, provided the main economic basis of modern imperial expansion. The diversion of income from domestic investment and consumption often resulted in its destruction, but even in that case the diversion checked investment at home and tended to make possible the profitable investment of the surviving capital. When this process failed to maintain the basis for the profitable operation of enterprise, depressions or wars intervened to wipe out accumulated savings, to destroy or render obsolete much of the existing capital structure, and thus to make possible a renewal of enterprise on a profitable basis.

The opportunities of Italian business enterprise for profitable expansion were exceptionally limited. Before the latter part of the nineteenth century, Italy lacked a strong national government, and in the meantime the choicer areas were taken by other countries and Italian emigrants were expatriated. Many of the essential materials had to be imported. Landlords and manufacturers alike found the Italian market extremely restricted by the exceptionally low standards of living — a situation which was aggravated by the Fascist policy of reducing wages. Wage reductions were based on the theory that they would reduce labor costs and thus increase competitive power in foreign markets; but the effects in stimulating foreign trade were far from satisfactory. Other countries were not without recourse to protective measures, even on the assumption that wage reductions lowered unit costs. At the same time, Italian production costs were increased by heavy taxation for party uses and for armaments and by the policy of promoting self-sufficiency through industries for which Italy was not best adapted. It was held that Italy lacked capital, and yet the existing productive plant found profitable operation increasingly difficult because of the limited market.

During the first four years of Fascist rule, the problem of the profitable use of capital was deferred by internal expansion connected with such factors as inflation and the expenditures for reconstruction and public works. The Italian depression beginning in 1927 and later merging with the world depression focused attention on the problem. The government, which claimed complete control of all phases of Italian life, was faced with grave alternatives. One was the internal adjustment of the national economy for expanding the domestic market, combined with peaceful efforts to obtain favorable alterations in colonial and commercial opportunities. The other alternative was resort to conquest and attempted expansion by force. In keeping with the Fascist doctrine of force and of expansion by means of war as the eternal law of mankind, the second alternative was chosen.

# CHAPTER 40

# THE SURVIVAL OF LIBERALISM IN FRANCE AND GREAT BRITAIN

————◆————

## Nature of Economic Liberalism

Economic liberalism is intimately connected with political and cultural liberalism, and its meaning has varied from generation to generation. In its theoretical aspects early liberalism was influenced by the individualism of the Renaissance; by the doctrines of the social contract, popular sovereignty, and "the natural rights of man"; and by "the system of natural liberty" of the early classical economists. In the sphere of action and policy, it was a reaction against guilds, corporate monopolies, mercantilism, and political autocracy. In place of these, liberalism stood for a wide range of occupational choice, an extension of competitive enterprise, the elimination of numerous restraints on freedom of trade both domestic and international, a restriction of the economic functions of government, and a relative dependence on the competitive price system as a mechanism for automatic adjustment.

Although there was wide acceptance of the view that the mercantilistic system of public regulation should be abandoned, important governmental functions in the economic field were always conceded; and when the imperfections of competition and of automatic adjustments became apparent, liberalism assumed a new aspect. Toward the end of the nineteenth century, the typical liberal still accepted private capital and private enterprise as basically sound, but attempted to defend them, as did John Stuart Mill, on rational and utilitarian grounds and not as "natural rights of man." At the same time, there was a predominant sentiment among liberals in favor of expanding the functions of government for the regulation of economic life and for the assumption of direct governmental responsibilities in such matters as the protection of labor, social insurance, and the control and even operation of monopolistic public utilities.

After the World War, the distinctive significance of liberalism was its contrast with communism and Fascism. From the economic point of view, the countries in which liberalism survived were characterized, in the first place, by comparative freedom of economic thought and criticism. In communist and Fascist countries alike, the economic regime, whether socialistic or capitalistic, was identified with the state, and opposition to the one was viewed virtually as treason to the other. The Russian constitution of 1936 gave promise of a trend toward liberal and democratic methods to be applied within the limits of socialistic economy, but a serious obstacle was the threat of war in the expansionist ambitions of Germany and Japan.

A second distinctive feature of the countries where liberalism survived was the maintenance of freedom of association on the part of economic groups. The prevailing ideal called only for a general framework of public policy and of legal sanctions for the maintenance of voluntary contractual relations. Freedom of association survived in a more distinctively liberal form in connection with the adjustment of group relations as exemplified by trade-unions, employers' associations, trade associations, and consumers' leagues.

A third feature of liberal economies was the continued reservation of a comparatively large area for private initiative and private enterprise for profit. In Russia, under public ownership, the government assumed direct responsibility for carrying on the productive processes, and private profits were barred. In Germany and Italy, governments claimed full authority without assuming direct responsibility. Private profits were protected but were diverted to those who supported the political regime, and enterprise was directed into channels which the autocratic state authorities considered essential to their purposes. In France and Great Britain, on the other hand, businessmen as well as others were much less restricted in their economic choices and were free, within the legal and constitutional framework, to support or oppose the government of the day and to support or oppose changes in the constitutional framework itself.

A fourth characteristic of liberal countries was their price policy. These countries made comparatively slight departures from the price system as a competitive mechanism of adjustment. Everywhere there was increasing recognition, to be sure, that in some fields, as agriculture, prices were too yielding or "soft" and that production might continue even at a loss. As a result, subsidies, or protection, or other policies were adopted, even in liberal countries, to maintain or raise price levels or to sustain production on a noncompetitive basis. It was also widely recognized that in certain other fields prices were inelastic or "sticky," and policies were adopted, even in liberal countries, to lower prices or keep the price level down, notably in monopolistic public utilities. But liberal countries retained the general conception of an elastic price structure as in itself a regulatory mechanism; whereas, in other countries, prices came to be viewed more largely as mere instruments to be used by the controlling authority for directing the country's productive resources into desired channels and for influencing the allocation of income viewed as purchasing power. Intrinsically, however, there seems to be no reason for debarring a politically liberal regime from using price policies for similar purposes, provided the policies are economically feasible and are adopted in accordance with liberal political principles. The economic "laws" of an earlier generation are no longer divorced from human controls.

The historical sources of liberalism were predominantly in Great Britain and France. In these countries liberalism took deep root in favorable soil. Liberal traditions were maintained in opposition alike to revolutionary socialism and to Fascism by the comparatively large numbers of small entrepreneurs — businessmen, farmers, and professional men — and by holders of public securities. Liberalism was more readily maintained in France and Great Britain by virtue of their comparative security, political, economic, and military, which obviated the necessity for rigorous and long-continued subordination of the individual to the group for the purpose of group preservation.

It was only in France and Great Britain, among the major powers of Europe, that liberalism survived the storms of the World War and world depression. Even in these countries grave doubts arose as to the efficacy of the traditional system of private enterprise in maintaining both freedom and security, especially for the masses of nonpropertied citizens. The limitations on liberty imposed by economic inequality and insecurity became increasingly apparent. But the urgent nature of economic problems gave renewed vigor to the advocates of the liberal principles of social adjustment by the process of democratic discussion, free association, and general acceptance of lawfully made decisions. It is particularly significant that the liberalism of Great Britain and France even abandoned the doctrine of private ownership of capital as an inviolable and "natural" right, permitted a large measure of freedom of discussion of the relative merits of private enterprise and socialism, and even utilized legal and constitutional methods for introducing a wide range of socialized investment. Economic liberalism in its more recent manifestations may perhaps best be described not as a peculiar system of business enterprise but as a method of social adjustment.

## " Normalcy " after the World War

In the United States after the World War a popular political slogan was "the return to normalcy." In France and Great Britain similar sentiments prevailed and found expression in the early abandonment of wartime controls. The rationing of materials, labor, transportation facilities, credits, and consumption goods was given up. Exports and imports were freed from the more extreme controls, although Great Britain adopted protection and France extended her prewar protective system. There was a relaxation of wartime controls of agencies of information and of unofficial controls finding expression in the coercive influence of group opinion. There was a temporary reaction against social legislation and restrictive reforms designed to limit war profits and to assure the co-operation of labor in carrying on the war. Governmental purchasing activities, efforts to control prices, and the pegging of international exchange rates were largely abandoned.

The most difficult phase of the attempted "return to normalcy" was the struggle for financial solvency and equilibrium. War finance and the burdens of debt, discussed elsewhere, bore much more heavily on France than on Great Britain, but both countries were altered profoundly by wartime financial problems and policies. In Great Britain the process of inflation by note issues was checked in 1919, and of inflation by credit in 1920. Deflation and heavy taxation followed, and in 1925 the Gold Standard Act required the sale by the government, on demand, of gold bullion in quantities of not less than 400 ounces at prewar prices, but the interchangeability of notes and gold coins was not restored. The severe deflation accompanying the introduction of the gold bullion standard on the basis of the prewar value of gold temporarily benefited British holders of obligations, domestic and foreign, payable in British money, but increased the difficulties of debtors and of exporters. Foreigners, especially in countries with depreciated currencies, could ill afford to buy pounds sterling at prewar rates for purchasing British goods and for servicing British loans.

In France inflation continued after the war. Public expenditures were financed extensively by advances to the government by the Bank of France and by the sale of bonds. The advances made by the Bank of France took the form of bank notes turned over to the government for use in meeting its obligations. In 1920, 69 per cent of the total bank-note circulation consisted of advances which were in reality loans without collateral or reserves. In succeeding years the proportion declined somewhat, but in 1926 rose again to 67 per cent. By means of bond issues the advances were repaid in part from year to year, but the repayment of advances and the use of the bank notes by the government for meeting its obligations provided funds for the purchase of additional bonds, which could be used as the basis for additional note issues. Bonds were also frequently bought by means of bank loans secured by property, and the bonds thus purchased could be deposited at the banks and made the basis of still further note issues.

The vast expansion of currency and credit, combined with the lively demand for goods and services for the rehabilitation of the devastated areas and the reconstruction of business, led to a rapid rise in prices. The accompanying table of index numbers shows approximate changes in wholesale prices in France and in the cost of living in Paris, with similar changes in Great Britain:

WHOLESALE PRICES AND COST OF LIVING IN FRANCE AND GREAT BRITAIN, 1913–1926

|  | Wholesale Prices (1913 = 100) | | Cost of Living (July, 1914 = 100) | |
|  | France | Great Britain | Paris (July) | Great Britain |
| --- | --- | --- | --- | --- |
| 1913 (or July, 1914) | 100 | 100 | 100 | 100 |
| 1919 | 356 | — | 261 | 215 |
| 1920 | 509 | 307 | 373 | 249 |
| 1921 | 345 | 197 | 306 | 226 |
| 1922 | 327 | 159 | 397 | 183 |
| 1923 | 419 | 159 | 321 | 174 |
| 1924 | 489 | 166 | 360 | 175 |
| 1925 | 555 | 159 | 421 | 176 |
| 1926 | 703 | 148 | 574 | 172 |

The critical state of French public finances, the rapid rise in prices in 1925 and 1926, and a realization of the exaggerated nature of anticipations from German reparation payments combined to bring about a drastic reform of the French fiscal system. Tentative stabilization of the franc in 1926 was followed in 1928 by legal stabilization on a gold bullion basis at approximately one fifth of the franc's prewar value.

### Expansion of French Industry

As a result of the World War, France was temporarily impoverished by the devastation of the war-torn areas and by the exhaustion of reserves and man power. At the same time, the annexation of Alsace-Lorraine, the addition of colonial territories as mandates of the League of Nations, the temporary control of the Saar, and the receipt of reparation payments in various forms vastly enlarged the base and expanded the resources of French economy.

Alsace-Lorraine added to France highly developed industries associated with iron and coal, although the coal has too high a percentage of volatile oils for most advantageous conversion to metallurgical coke, and postwar animosities created grave problems in the interdependent development of the Lorraine-Westphalian iron and coal industries. The potash deposits of Alsace enabled France to deprive Germany of her prewar monopoly of potash, particularly important in the fertilizer industry and the maintenance of soil fertility. The textile industries in the recovered provinces, mainly in Alsace, increased the capacity of France in woolen manufactures by about one fourth and in the cotton industry by more than a fourth, and virtually doubled the existing facilities for the production of rayon. The facilities for transportation as well as mining and manufacturing were in many respects more advanced technologically than were those of France beyond the recovered provinces.

The expansion of French industry was facilitated by the payment of reparations in various forms. Germany's loss of her mercantile marine, foreign investments, and other sources of revenue forced the Germans to depend largely on the export of goods or, for immediate payments, on foreign credits for financing reparations. As a result France, as well as other countries which received reparations, was confronted by the problem of German competition. Nevertheless, it was assumed that Germany would be able ultimately to finance her international obligations, and extensive reparation payments in cash were made by her from foreign credits, especially American loans, and these payments, as well as reparations in kind, aided materially in the postwar industrial expansion of France.

Expansion was also stimulated by monetary and credit inflation. Extensive inflation is inevitably accompanied and followed by serious disadvantages. But inflationary methods of financing such abnormal public burdens as those of the World War and reconstruction could hardly have been avoided, even in the case of domestic obligations, save by confiscatory taxation or perhaps even by a virtually complete socialization of the national economy and a rigorous and comprehensive system of rationing.  There would have remained the question of the advisability of financing the purchase of supplies and services from other countries by surrendering claims to future production.  The warring countries had little experience and inclination either for confiscatory taxation or for socialization and a complete system of rationing.  As a result of the choice of credit finance, the mountainous burden of debt, if unrepudiated or unrelieved by further inflation, could hardly have been borne by the country's productive facilities, although the disadvantages of inflation could undoubtedly have been kept within more restricted bounds by more careful expenditures and by a more rigorous system of taxation.  The huge war debt, the reconstruction debt, and even private debts were to some extent liquidated by means of inflation.  Obligations incurred at comparatively high levels of franc values were paid off with depreciated francs.  Much of the foreign debt was allowed to lapse, although not formally repudiated.

Payment of obligations in depreciated money has been described as merely a transfer of income from creditors to debtors, from holders of public obligations to taxpayers, and from those with comparatively fixed incomes to those with incomes more responsive to changes in the value of money.  But under the prevailing conditions of resistance to taxation and to direct intervention by the government in the carrying on of enterprise, combined with urgent need for reconstruction of the country's productive facilities, inflation seems in fact to have been more than a mere transfer of income.  It seems to have been a method, costly and in many ways disadvantageous, but nevertheless effective, for increasing the nation's real wealth and income.  It made possible the carrying on of the processes of reconstruction.  It stimulated businessmen to employ labor and to expand their capital facilities, and it enabled foreigners, by virtue of the cheapness of the franc, to increase their purchases of French goods.  The postwar expansion of currency through note issues and of credit through the sale of bonds was mainly for two purposes: the payment of war debts as they matured, and the financing of the vast productive enterprises connected with postwar reconstruction and rehabilitation. The additional borrowings for reconstruction flowed rapidly into

THE DECLINE OF BASIC BRITISH INDUSTRIES

| | Unit: Thousands of | 1913 | 1929 | 1932 | Index of Production or Trade: 1913 = 100 | |
|---|---|---|---|---|---|---|
| | | | | | 1929 | 1932 |
| **Coal:** | | | | | | |
| World output | Metric tons | 1,215,720 | 1,286,628 | 917,220 | 106 | 75 |
| British output | Tons | 287,430 | 259,907 | 208,733 | 90 | 73 |
| British exports | Tons | 73,400 | 60,267 | 38,899 | 82 | 53 |
| **Pig iron:** | | | | | | |
| World output | Metric tons | 78,819 | 95,688 | 38,088 | 121 | 48 |
| British output | Tons | 10,260 | 7,589 | 3,574 | 74 | 35 |
| **Steel: ingots and castings:** | | | | | | |
| World output | Metric tons | 76,620 | 116,568 | 49,356 | 152 | 64 |
| British output | Tons | 7,664 | 9,636 | 5,261 | 126 | 69 |
| **Shipbuilding (merchant vessels launched):** [1] | | | | | | |
| World | Gross tonnage | 2,962 | 2,794 | 733 | 94 | 25 |
| United Kingdom | Gross tonnage | 1,825 | 1,481 | 330 | 81 | 18 |
| **British woolen goods exported:** | | | | | | |
| Woolen and worsted yarns | Pounds | 80,415 | 63,612 | 47,498 | 79 | 59 |
| Manufactures | Square yards [2] | 176,977 | 161,947 | 85,330 | 92 | 48 |
| **British cotton goods exported:** | | | | | | |
| Yarns | Pounds | 210,099 | 166,637 | 141,463 | 79 | 67 |
| Piece goods | Linear yards | 7,152,459 | 3,825,517 | 2,330,158 | 53 | 33 |

[1] Three-year averages: 1911-1913, 1928-1930, 1931-1933.
[2] Partly linear yards in 1913.

the channels of wages, profits, and productive enterprise and apparently aided in expanding the real as well as the monetary wealth and income of the country as sources of taxation for the ultimate liquidation of the obligations incurred.

The industries which gained most by the postwar influences promoting expansion included coal, iron, steel, building materials and the building trades, electricity, machinery and machine tools, chemicals, and rayon. The growth of these industries, although in part a temporary response to the needs for reconstruction, indicated nevertheless an important shift of French enterprise toward the heavy industries and mass-production methods. The reconstruction of the war-torn areas afforded an opportunity for the thorough modernization of factory buildings and equipment and facilities for mining. Modernization was accompanied by extensive mergers and administrative reorganization. The stimulus of these changes in the devastated areas extended to other parts of France. During the first decade of the postwar period, the output of manufactured goods and minerals more than doubled.

### The Decline of Basic Industries in Great Britain

The prewar industrial and commercial power of Great Britain had been based largely on coal, iron and steel, shipbuilding, woolen goods, and cotton goods. Although her relative position had declined before the World War, Great Britain still maintained an outstanding importance in these various industries. Some aspects of her decline after the World War are indicated by the table on page 808.

Total exports of the produce and manufactures of the United Kingdom were much greater in 1929, in monetary value, than in 1913; but when the price changes in the various groups of exports are taken into account, total exports appear to have been between 15 and 20 per cent less in 1929 than in 1913, and almost 50 per cent less in 1932 than in 1913. Imports, on the other hand, remained large. Net imports (excluding goods re-exported), even in 1932, were somewhat in excess of net imports in 1913, although in value slightly lower. It was possible for Great Britain to maintain her imports while exports were declining, because of the so-called invisible exports. British capital invested outside of Great Britain amounted in 1914 to about four billion pounds. This vast sum was diminished by the abnormal requirements of the war period to approximately three billions, much of the capital being used to finance the importation of munitions and foods. Before the world depression of 1929 set in, overseas investments had again expanded to substantially the prewar figure, and the annual income amounted to almost a quarter of a billion pounds. The low point of income from overseas investments was reached in 1933, when it amounted to only about £150,000,000.

The monetary policy of the government in restoring the prewar gold value of the pound had much to do with the revival of overseas investments, but in view of the depreciation of currencies and restriction of trade in other countries, the dearness of the pound proved to be a serious handicap to British exporters and ultimately contributed to world economic disequilibrium. But the futile effort to maintain the pound at its prewar value was not a permanent or fundamental factor in the decline of British basic industries. Some economists have assigned much importance to the comparatively high labor costs as a factor in the decline of British industry. But as in the case of the dearness of the pound in international exchange, there were compensating advantages. The maintenance of living standards and purchasing power of workers and of the morale of the labor force may more than counterbalance the apparent competitive disadvantage in wage rates, especially in the long run. Even with depreciated currencies and comparatively low wages, the Continent of Europe suffered a relative decline in the export trade almost as great as that of Great Britain. The Royal Commission on Unemployment Insurance estimated that in terms of value the Continent's share of world exports declined 17 per cent from 1913 to 1928, while Great Britain's share declined 20 per cent. The consequences of the decline to Great Britain were mitigated by her vast overseas investments and her comparatively large income from international services.

Nevertheless the decline of British exports was exceptionally serious because it marked a fundamental change in the country's status in world economy and because it afflicted the country with the problems of the depressed areas, which had formerly been outstanding centers of industrial activity. The growth of the heavy industries such as coal, iron, steel, machinery, shipbuilding, and chemicals in other countries, especially in the United States, Germany, Belgium, France, and Russia, and of the textile industries in these areas and in Italy and Japan, made impossible Great Britain's continued utilization of an expanding world market on the basis of her nineteenth-century superiority in competitive power.

The extremely rapid reorientation of British economy after the World War is indicated in part by the following table showing changes in the geographical distribution of employment from 1923 to 1928, and from 1928 to 1935, among workers insured against unemployment.

THE GEOGRAPHICAL DISTRIBUTION OF EMPLOYMENT AMONG INSURED WORKERS IN GREAT BRITAIN AND NORTHERN IRELAND, 1923–1935

| Division | Estimated Number of Insured Workers in Employment Aged 16–64 | | | Per Cent Change | |
|---|---|---|---|---|---|
| | June, 1923 | June, 1928 | June, 1935 | 1923 to 1928 | 1928 to 1935 |
| London | 1,760,000 | 2,038,000 | 2,267,000 | + 15.8 | + 11.2 |
| Southeastern | 672,000 | 830,000 | 1,001,000 | + 23.5 | + 20.6 |
| Southwestern | 669,000 | 757,000 | 834,000 | + 13.2 | + 10.2 |
| Midlands | 1,467,000 | 1,558,000 | 1,727,000 | + 6.2 | + 10.8 |
| Northeastern | 1,686,000 | 1,669,000 | 1,612,000 | − 1.0 | − 3.4 |
| Northwestern | 1,712,000 | 1,839,000 | 1,741,000 | + 7.4 | − 5.3 |
| Scotland | 1,079,000 | 1,124,000 | 1,084,000 | + 4.2 | − 3.6 |
| Wales | 564,000 | 463,000 | 428,000 | − 17.9 | − 7.6 |
| Northern Ireland | 207,000 | 203,000 | 208,000 | − 2.0 | + 2.5 |
| Total | 9,816,000 | 10,481,000 | 10,902,000 | + 6.8 | + 4.0 |

Comparable figures before 1923 are not available, but the shifts indicated were already under way, due to the postwar decline of the coal, iron, shipbuilding, and textile industries in Wales and the various northern divisions and the rise of new industries in the south. Nor do the figures of employment among insured workers tell the whole story. Thus in the coal industry the total number of insured workers fell from 1,244,000 in 1923 to 1,075,000 in 1929, and a further decline occurred thereafter. The population of certain depressed or "special" areas in England and Wales in 1931 was 2,894,000, which was 74,000 less than in 1921. In England and Wales as a whole, the population in 1931 was 39,952,000, an increase of 2,066,000 over 1921. Unemployment remained most serious in the areas of declining industry and population. An exceptional but significant instance is the case of Jarrow, once a prosperous shipbuilding and engineering center. The insured population in 1927 was 9,940; in 1932, after the conditions of unemployment insurance had been liberalized, 9,330; and in 1935, 7,950. During the months of January and July from 1927 to 1935, the number of insured workers who were unemployed was never less than 26.3 per cent of the total number of insured workers (July, 1927), and in January, 1935, the number was 81.5 per cent of the total number of insured workers.

Furthermore, much of the employment, especially in the areas of declining industries, was maintained by such means as public works and housing subsidies; and much of the regular employment was on a part-time basis. A special inquiry in October, 1931, showed that more than a third of the workers in the bleaching, printing, dyeing, and finishing of textiles were on part time with an average loss of 14.9 hours per week. In the smelting and rolling of iron and steel and related processes a fourth of the workers were on part time, with an average loss of 15.3 hours per week.

### British and French Phases of the World Depression

As was indicated in the preceding section, serious difficulties during most of the postwar period characterized British heavy industries, textiles, and trade. British economy suffered severely during the early stages of the depression, but with certain exceptions exhibited an early tendency toward revival. France, on the other hand, was able to withstand the forces of depression for a time but experienced a tardy recovery. Some of the principal aspects of British economy in comparison with world economy in 1929 and 1932 were indicated in the table showing the decline of basic British industries (page 808). British and French comparisons for 1929 to 1932 and 1935, as indicated by figures published in the *Monthly Bulletin of Statistics* of the League of Nations, are given in the table on page 813.

Comparisons of British and French economic developments during the depression beginning in 1929 must take account of conditions before 1929, and of essential differences in the economic life of the two countries. Industrial production, for example, during the depression was maintained at much higher levels in Great Britain than in France when the 1929 level is the basis of comparison, but British production had been at abnormally low levels during most of the postwar period. The extreme decline in France after 1929, in trade and industrial production, was therefore less serious than would have been a similar decline in Great Britain. Agriculture remained predominant in France, and agricultural production, with the exception of certain internationally commercialized products such as wine, was not in excess of domestic needs. There was in fact opportunity for expansion of important types of farm output without glutting the markets or interfering as seriously as

ECONOMIC CHANGES IN FRANCE AND THE UNITED KINGDOM, 1929–1932, AND 1935

| | 1929 | 1930 | 1931 | 1932 | 1935 |
|---|---|---|---|---|---|
| Indexes of industrial production | | | | | |
| United Kingdom | 100.0 | 92.3 | 83.8 | 83.5 | 105.7 |
| France | 100.0 | 100.4 | 88.9 | 68.8 | 67.4 |
| Exports (monthly averages) | | | | | |
| United Kingdom (millions of pounds) | 60.78 | 47.56 | 32.55 | 30.42 | 35.49 |
| France (millions of francs) | 4,178 | 3,570 | 2,536 | 1,642 | 1,289 [1] |
| Imports (monthly averages) | | | | | |
| United Kingdom (millions of pounds) | 92.59 | 79.76 | 66.45 | 54.22 | 58.47 |
| France (millions of francs) | 4,852 | 4,376 | 3,517 | 2,484 | 1,745 [1] |
| Unemployment | | | | | |
| United Kingdom (registered unemployed insured workers) | 1,263,000 | 1,994,000 | 2,717,000 | 2,846,000 | 2,028,000 |
| France (unemployed in receipt of relief) | 928 | 2,514 | 56,112 | 273,412 [2] | 426,879 [2] |
| Indexes of wholesale prices | | | | | |
| United Kingdom | 100.0 | 87.5 | 76.8 | 74.9 | 77.9 |
| France | 100.0 | 88.4 | 80.0 | 68.2 | 54.0 |
| Indexes of cost of living | | | | | |
| United Kingdom | 100.0 | 96.3 | 89.6 | 87.8 | 87.2 |
| France (Paris) | 100.0 | 104.5 | 102.3 | 94.6 | 86.9 |

in Great Britain with vital trade relations. The government and the banks had comparatively ample gold and financial resources for coping with a temporarily unfavorable balance of imports over exports. Great Britain's population was much more highly industrialized and much more dependent on imported food and raw materials and on the prosperity of other countries.

[1] The Saar excluded after February, 1935.
[2] Including recipients of aid from Social Welfare offices as well as unemployment insurance beneficiaries.

Particularly significant as an indication of the nature of French economy was the fact that the extreme decline of industrial production was accompanied by a relatively small amount of unemployment. In Great Britain the number of unemployed workers insured against unemployment had never fallen, between 1921 and 1929, below a million. In France, on the other hand, reconstruction work combined with ordinary agricultural and industrial enterprises had called for large numbers of immigrant workers in addition to native labor. During the depression unemployment was mitigated by the exodus of large numbers of immigrant workers. Before the depression there had been a serious shortage of farm labor, and when the demand fell off for labor for reconstruction work and industrial enterprises, farming absorbed many of the unemployed. The continued predominance of agriculture, the existence of much agricultural land not fully utilized, and the prevalence of small-scale peasant ownership made possible a reversion to subsistence farming as a cushion against unemployment.

The unemployment statistics of European countries are in most cases incomplete. The figures for France are for recipients of unemployment benefits and, after 1931, of aid from public agencies. Unemployed persons living by other means, as personal savings or the aid of relatives, are not included. The British figures include all insured workers registered with the employment exchanges as unemployed, such registration being a necessary qualification for unemployment insurance benefits. In both countries and in most of the other countries where official figures of unemployment are published, the unemployed in important groups of workers are not included. Unofficial figures of unemployment in the United States have included estimates of the number unemployed in all groups classified by the census as normally having gainful occupations, whether as wage earners, salaried employees, or self-employed workers. Estimates of unemployment in European countries, if placed on a comparable basis, would therefore show much larger numbers as unemployed than are shown by the official figures.

### The Reorientation of British Policy

British history has been distinguished by a gradual adaptation of policy to changing conditions. The world depression beginning in 1929 resulted merely in the extension of policies long in the making. Even the abandonment of free trade had long been widely discussed and was initiated before 1929.

Before the present century, modern British economy was sustained by an almost continuous expansion in the world market under conditions peculiarly favorable to the British. A gradual slowing up of the rate of expansion was followed, after the World War, in the words of the Royal Commission on Unemployment Insurance (1932), by a "loss of the power to expand." Inelasticity or contraction of demand was accompanied by an increase in the working population and by a curtailment of opportunity for emigration — even by immigration.

At the same time, the historic process of technological improvement continued, with a progressive increase in average output per worker or reciprocally a reduction in the amount of labor required per unit of output. The figures of employment and production in the Censuses of Production of 1924 and 1930 include manufacturing, mining, public utilities, and many of the governmental agencies. They indicate a general increase of about 12 per cent in the average output per wage earner. A comparison of the index numbers of industrial production constructed by the Board of Trade for the years 1928 to 1934, with the employment statistics for the same industries, shows an increase of approximately 16 per cent in average output per wage earner. Even in agriculture, available statistics indicate an increase from 1921 to 1931 of not less than 14 per cent in average output per person engaged in agricultural pursuits. In coal mining, average output from 1924 to 1934 increased 27 per cent per miner and 30 per cent per man shift. Stated in another way, in 1934 less than 80 miners produced the same amount of coal that 100 miners produced in 1924.

Assuming that a miner's output of coal was formerly four tons per week (a hypothetical figure) and that a thousand miners were at work, their total production was 4,000 tons. If the individual output is now five tons and all of the thousand miners remain at work, the total production is now 5,000 tons. This requires an increase in the demand for coal at the same rate as the increase in the output per miner. If in the meantime the number of persons seeking work as miners has increased to 1,100, the total demand must be for 5,500 tons if all of the applicants for jobs at the mines are to be employed as miners. Some of the miners may find work in other industries or trades. But if a general increase in the average output of all workers is not to be accompanied by unemployment, the total volume of production must increase at the same rate, even when the supply of workers is not increasing.

The essence of the British problem has thus been an expansion of production such as would afford employment to an increasing number of workers with a rising rate of average output. A reduction of average output would not solve the problem, for in competitive markets technical efficiency and a high rate of labor productivity are essential even for preventing a reduction of demand and therefore a reduction of the volume of production and of employment. Furthermore, there has probably never been any surplus labor or efficiency even in Great Britain for maintaining the level of production high enough to provide merely a moderate standard of living for the entire population.

The main ingredients of the traditional British prescription for maintaining elasticity of demand were competitive private enterprise at home and free trade in the world's markets. The nearest approach to a competitive regime under international free trade was in the nineteenth century, when British political and economic advantages were at their maximum and when vast areas of the world were being rapidly settled and were calling insistently for British emigrants, capital, and manufactures, especially machinery and capital equipment. Even then there was frequently a large amount of unemployment alike of labor, of funds for investment, and of the physical facilities for production. Each period of economic recession was accompanied, however, by obsolescence, by extensive loss of investments, and by the using up of surpluses; and this depletion of resources and deflation of capital made possible a renewal of expansion on a profitable basis. Even before the World War attention was directed repeatedly to the slowing up of expansion and to the unemployment of labor and capital accompanying the growth of labor productivity under conditions of inelastic demand for the products of labor. It was this situation in Great Britain and to a less extent in other industrialized countries that gave such grave intensity to the prewar struggle for world markets and for opportunities for external investments. After the World War, the British controlled an even greater empire, but world conditions were such that its utilization in the former manner was no longer possible. There were significant departures from the traditional dependence on competition, free trade, and *laissez faire;* and there was a tendency to examine the possibilities of an expansion of domestic demand.

For the purpose of ameliorating the conditions prevailing in the coal, iron, steel, shipbuilding, and textile centers, and for utilizing some of the surplus labor of these areas, several new policies were adopted. Efforts were made to refinance and reorganize the declining industries; aid was extended for introducing new industries in the depressed areas; and facilities were created for the retraining and transfer of workers to industries and areas of expanding activity. Assistance was also offered to workers desiring to emigrate to the dominions, but with little success. In 1920 contributory unemployment insurance was extended to most of the wage earners in manufacturing, mining, and the service industries, but because of the rapid growth of unemployment, extensive benefits were granted on a noncontributory basis. In 1931 the disadvantage of the overvaluing of the pound in international exchange was overcome by the abandonment of the gold standard and a reduction of exchange rates for facilitating the payment by foreigners of their international balances to the British. Ironically enough, an unprecedented expansion of armaments afforded opportunities for the temporary employment of much idle capital and labor.

These various measures were viewed as merely ameliorative and as embodying no vital changes in prewar policies. The new monetary policy, to be sure, was more than a mere revaluation of the pound in relation to other currencies. It was an effort to control the monetary system on a more flexible basis in adjustment to the changing volume of production and to the changing needs for credit as well as currency not only for meeting the fluctuating international balance of payments but also for financing domestic production and consumption. This policy was a significant departure from the comparatively inflexible gold basis formerly viewed as a normally unalterable part of a "free" or self-regulating economy. But a more serious breach in the traditional conception of liberal policy was the resort to protection. This first assumed the form, after the wartime controls had lapsed, of a tentative and presumably temporary "safeguarding" of certain industries against dumping, but soon grew into a combination of tariffs, quotas, subsidies, imperial preferences, and propaganda for buying domestic and empire goods.

The British people had long given up the idea of agricultural self-sufficiency and had come to view their economic relations as complementary — the buying of overseas food and raw materials and the export of manufactures, capital, and services. But the threatened severing, during the war, of Britain from her sources of supply and the later sharp curtailment of exports led to a reorientation of agricultural policy.  Self-sufficiency was not anticipated, but an expansion of agriculture was desired, both for increasing the proportion of home-grown foods and raw materials and for absorbing a portion of unemployed industrial workers.  On the basis of subsidies and revenue abatements (reduced domestic excise duties as compared with customs duties on imports) the sugar-beet industry was created and enabled, by 1934, to supply a fifth of the country's sugar requirements.  The wheat, milk, and livestock industries were also subsidized.  Direct payments to agricultural producers totaled, by early 1935, about £57,250,000.  Quotas as well as tariffs limited the amount of imports from other countries.  Agricultural marketing boards regulated almost the whole range of agricultural production.

Subsidies were granted to the coal industry for maintaining wage rates and competitive prices.  Tariffs on manufactured goods were greatly extended.  The tariff act of 1932 definitely adopted the principle of protection.  An outstanding feature of the act was its arrangement for flexible rates as a weapon against discrimination, as an instrument for negotiating reciprocal agreements, and as a basis for granting preferential exemptions to the dominions.  It was in connection with these provisions that preferential agreements were made in 1932 at the Ottawa Imperial Conference.  An indirect protective device was the abandonment of the gold standard in 1931, followed by the reduction of the value of the pound in international exchange.  British importers were thus required to pay more for foreign currencies to meet their import bills.  At the same time, exports were stimulated by the cheapening of the pound.

An immediate advantage accruing from protection was the stimulus to the capital-goods industries.  New opportunities for sales in the protected home market led to the building of new factories, the renovation of old establishments, the extension of agricultural facilities, the investment of idle funds, and the employment of additional workers.  These circumstances largely account for the rapid expansion of British enterprise in the south of England. But the ultimate and general effects of protection depended on a complicated set of interdependent factors, national and international, largely unforeseeable.  Many economists, while recognizing the difficulties of British free trade during an era of extreme economic nationalism, nevertheless persisted in viewing protection with misgivings.  They feared that the abandonment of free trade and the depreciation of the pound would lead to still further protective measures and monetary depreciation in other countries. Many were also apprehensive of adverse effects on the capacity of British customers to meet their obligations for British manufactures, credits, and services, and on the ability of the British themselves to buy necessary foods and raw materials. Many who favored protection viewed it merely as a necessary expedient dictated by prevailing restrictions on trade and depreciation of currencies in óther countries. But in any case the new policy was a significant departure from the historic policy of dependence on economic "laws" underlying the free-trade school of thought.

### The " Social Wage " in Great Britain

There were similar differences of opinion regarding another vital change in British policy in connection with the effort to adjust the national economy to its "loss of power to expand " in the world market. This other policy involved in effect if not in original intent a public control of the national income by means of taxation, social legislation, and an increase of socialized investment. Beginnings were made by the Liberal party in its prewar program of health insurance, unemployment insurance, old-age pensions, and social services; by the growth of publicly owned utilities; and by the co-operative societies in their distributing of the net real income of their enterprises among their millions of members.

The expansion of the policy of taxation for increasing the indirect income or "social wage" of various classes, particularly of wage earners, the professional classes, and small proprietors, is indicated by figures of national revenues and expenditures. The total receipts of the United Kingdom Exchequer in 1934–1935 were more than four times as large as in 1913–1914, wholesale prices being approximately the same in the two years. Expenditures classified under the general heads of health, labor, and insurance, comprising the principal social services, were eleven times as large in 1934–1935 as in 1913–1914. Taxation in the meantime had shifted significantly to surtaxes and supertaxes.

Revenues of local authorities in England and Wales were more than three times as large in 1932–1933 as in 1913–1914. Approximately a third of the local revenues other than from loans for capital works came from the "trading services" or publicly owned utilities embodying socialized investment, low-cost services, and in many cases reduced rates of taxation. Expenditures by local authorities were mainly for the maintenance of services falling in general under either public utilities or social services, both of which embodied the principle of indirect compensations or the social wage as distinguished from direct wages, profits, interest, and rent. The principal local expenditures, aside from capital investments in public utilities and their maintenance and operation, were for such services as education, libraries, public health, parks, recreation, and housing. Housing facilities owned by local authorities were rented substantially at cost and often below cost in connection with grants for the aid of unemployed or part-time workers. Housing was aided extensively by national grants. The number of houses (family units) thus built by local authorities in England and Wales from 1921 to 1935 (March 31) was 790,145, while public aid was extended during the same period for the private construction of 422,565 units. After 1930, public aid in England and Wales declined, but in Scotland it increased.

The policy of utilizing taxation and public credit for expanding socialized investment and especially for increasing the indirect income or social wage of the small-income classes met with much criticism, largely on the basis of traditional economic conceptions of the free, competitive flow of labor, capital, and income as the best available method of maintaining economic efficiency and well-being. Others criticized the policy as failing to go far enough and as embodying excessive governmental powers over industry unless these powers were accompanied by governmental responsibility for the actual operation of the economic system, as in the case of publicly owned utilities.

Those who favored the policy of the social wage attempted to justify it on both social and economic grounds. It was held that neither employers nor workers were responsible for the basic conditions creating unemployment, low wages, and unwholesome standards of living, and that society must assume a larger measure of responsibility. This was viewed as a necessary measure of self-defense against the dangers of demoralization, degeneracy, crime, disease, and even revolution inherent in an attitude of irresponsibility. On economic grounds the policy was favored on the basis of the view that it was the most readily available and most practicable method of correcting the ill effects of rigidities in the economic system such as those created by debt and other inflexible costs and by interest, rent, and other income not based essentially on the ability and productivity of the recipients. These factors, affecting costs of production, and embodying claims on production, tend to prevent a properly allocated flow of income and enterprise into consumption and into the most productive channels.

A characteristic feature of an economy with limited external outlets is likely to be a concentration of income in the hands of those who are unable to use it productively. They fail to consume the goods and services to which their income gives them title; and if they attempt to invest their surplus income in production or capital goods, they are likely to find that existing facilities can more than supply the effective demand. Therefore the new investment is likely to be either unprofitable or to force out of use existing facilities. When national income under conditions of idle labor and capital fails to flow adequately into consumption, the flow of production is correspondingly restricted unless external outlets are enlarged. A limitation of workers to marginal wages profitable to employers and of entrepreneurs to marginal or competitive profits would not suffice, without altering other costs of production, to expand the external outlets for British products enough to maintain either labor or capital in full employment.

Such circumstances, it was held, afford a sound economic basis as well as social justification for governmental intervention. Government may intervene directly and, independently of profits, set the unemployed workers and idle resources to work in producing needed goods and services on a self-liquidating basis. This, however, would mean the abandonment of private enterprise, a step entailing grave problems as well as popular approval not extended in Great Britain except in limited fields, such as local public utilities. Within the limitations of private enterprise, government may take indirect action to prevent the formation of "stagnant pools" of income. By means of taxation and public credit, income which, if uncontrolled, would become stagnant may be directed into the active flow of purchasing power, demand, and production and not merely maintain but expand the volume of production and employment. The actual policy was gradually developed in Great Britain not so much on theoretical grounds as on the basis of expediency. Its effects are to be judged in the light of the fact that the costs were derived not merely from surplus income but in part from wages and other comparatively small incomes which, if untaxed, would have been effectively used by their recipients. Nor was the policy based on a scientific or consistent effort to solve the central problem of achieving a continuously balanced and controlled allocation of income and resources to consumption and to capital investment.

## Reorientation of French Economic Policy

French economic policy during the world depression was affected vitally by the earlier period of inflation and the difficult struggle for monetary stability, which was achieved in 1928 at the cost of a reduction of the franc to about one fifth of its prewar value. There was general opposition to further monetary changes, especially by the numerous holders of public securities. But the maintenance of the financial structure on the new basis became increasingly difficult.

Soon after stabilization the reduction and later cancellation of reparations deprived the French budget of anticipated revenues at a time when other revenues were dwindling — a significant fact regardless of the unsound basis of French anticipations from reparations. In 1931 Great Britain abandoned the gold standard and headed the sterling bloc of states based on the conception of currency control by public agencies. Their exchange rates were generally unfavorable to the French export and tourist trades. Germany and Italy adopted a direct rationing of credit and exchange facilities and direct control of the import and export of commodities as well as money. Japanese monetary devaluation interfered with the French silk and novelty industries. In 1933 the United States abandoned the gold standard and reduced the exchange value of the dollar, thus greatly curtailing French income from American tourists and from American purchases of luxury goods, although the repeal of prohibition increased the import of French wines.

French trade, industry, and tourist income, which had been at comparatively high levels, declined after 1930 with such rapidity as to restrict dangerously the government's sources of revenue, while at the same time a large volume of unemployment was increasing the government's financial burden. The servicing of the foreign debt was largely allowed to lapse, but the internal debt alone increased from 280 billion francs on March 31, 1930, to 335 billion francs on September 30, 1935.

Before the Popular Front ministry took office in June, 1936, French policies centered around the "defense of the franc." A rapid succession of ministries formulated budgets based on economies in expenditures, higher taxes, restriction of imports, and control of prices. The most extensive efforts to achieve recovery on the predepression monetary basis were made by the ministry of Premier Pierre Laval (June 7, 1935, to January 22, 1936). By means of extraordinary powers granted temporarily by parliament, numerous emergency decrees were issued. These included measures for reducing expenditures by reductions in government salaries, pensions, and family allowances and in the interest payments on government securities. There were also decrees for increasing taxes, for reducing prices, rents, and interest on mortgages, and for expanding public works.

Other decrees during the Laval ministry affected social insurance. In February, 1930, a revised and greatly extended system of social insurance had gone into effect. The law originally applied to about 8,500,000 workers and provided insurance against sickness, invalidity, maternity, old age, and death. Rights were maintained during unemployment, but unemployment insurance was not included. The system was supported by public grants and by compulsory contributions from workers and employers. In October, 1935, the Laval ministry issued decree laws reducing temporarily the contributions of workers and employers and liberalizing the conditions for receipt of benefits, especially in connection with the maintenance of rights during unemployment.

The various governments of the depression period also extended the protective system, especially by means of quotas for limiting imports from particular countries to specified amounts. While efforts were made to reduce the general level of prices, aid to farmers included attempts to support the prices of wheat and other farm products above competitive levels. At the same time steps were taken to reduce the costs of agricultural production by means of lower prices for fertilizers and lower interest rates on farm loans.

The persistence of the depression in France, after extensive progress toward recovery had been made in many other countries, aggravated the difficulties of the French government and created conditions favorable to Fascist and communist propaganda. Fascist groups, especially the *Croix de Feu*, and royalist or ultra-conservative groups such as the *Camelots du Roi* organized uniformed, armed units and fomented violent opposition against the socialists and trade-unionists and even against the government, in a manner resembling the methods of the Italian Fascists and the German Nazis during their rise to power. In France these tactics were met by the formation of the Popular Front, an alliance of the Socialist party, the Radical Socialists, and the Communists, together with some minor groups. The Radical Socialists were in reality a group somewhat resembling American "progressives" but had been committed philosophically to associative or co-operative socialism as a compromise between individualistic liberalism and coercive state socialism. The Popular Front profited by a strong national reaction against antiliberal armed organizations, and in the elections of May, 1936, obtained a majority of seats in the Chamber of Deputies. Under the leadership of Leon Blum, a Socialist, the new ministry undertook to carry out a program for the more thorough regulation rather than the supplanting of private enterprise — a program essentially in defense of republican liberalism and social reform in opposition to Fascism.

The new ministry was confronted not only by the numerous problems inherited from earlier governments but by nation-wide "stay-in" or "folded-arms" strikes and in some industries by lockouts. The premier lost no time in calling a national conference of representatives of employers and employees and insisting on a general agreement for attempting an improvement in living standards and industrial relations — a prominent phase of the political program of the Popular Front. Following the conference, a law was enacted to provide for a general maximum working week of forty hours, with increases in wage rates designed to prevent a lowering of weekly earnings as a result of the reduction of hours. Legal provision was also made for vacations with pay. Another law repealed earlier decrees which had reduced the pay of public employees, forbidden promotions, and curtailed family allowances and pensions. Legislation was also enacted for promoting collective bargaining and trade agreements between representatives of employers and of employees. This legislation authorized the ultimate intervention of the Ministry of Labor for bringing about collective agreements and for compulsory application of such agreements to all employers and workers concerned.

A bold measure promised by the Popular Front was the democratization of the Bank of France. This historic institution, with a monopoly of issuing notes and of serving as a deposit bank for state funds, and with a network of branches and auxiliary offices throughout the country, was controlled by the two hundred largest stockholders, although the total number of stockholders was about 47,000. The reorganization, voted by the Chamber of Deputies in July, 1936, provided for a governor and two vice-governors appointed by the state, serving as heads of an administrative council of twenty-six. The other members of the council, largely advisory, were to be chosen in part by the whole body of stockholders but mainly by the ministers of finance, commerce, and agriculture to serve as technical experts and as guardians of the various interests served by the bank. Another measure advocated by the Popular Front was the nationalization of the principal munitions industries, and the initial steps were taken in October, 1936. The distinctive aims of the socialists and the communists were frankly held in abeyance pending a possible future successful appeal to the electorate.

Increasing governmental costs due to restoration of salaries, to relief and public works, and to the expansion of armaments were not paralleled by increases in revenues, nor was the rate of industrial recovery satisfactory. The export trade and income from tourists remained abnormally low, due at least in part to the dearness of the franc in international exchange. The outward flow of gold increased. Under these circumstances the gold standard was finally abandoned. Agreements of September 28, 1936, with Great Britain and the United States were made the basis of a law of October 1 for a tentative devaluation of the franc between the limits of two thirds and three fourths of its former value. Devaluation was followed by the abandonment of more than a hundred import quotas, by reductions ranging from 15 to 20 per cent in numerous tariff rates and trade license fees, by the formation of a committee for tariff revision, and in general by the initiation of a policy favorable to the promotion of reciprocal trade.

From the point of view of the country's economy as a whole and its relations to the world, the most important aspects of the regime of the Popular Front were its conciliatory international attitude and its demonstration of the continued adherence of the French people to the liberal tradition and the democratic method of meeting national problems.

### Growth of Voluntary Associations

In both Great Britain and France, regulatory policies in application to private enterprise were continued and even extended, as in the reorganization of the Bank of France, a qualified support of industrial combinations and rationalization, and intervention for influencing production, prices, and labor relations. But free associations of businessmen and agricultural proprietors were encouraged. A significant development was the growth of such associations. They were viewed as possible agencies for the voluntary improvement of trade practices, restriction of wasteful or unfair competition, planning and co-ordination of production and marketing, and the negotiation of collective agreements with employees. They remained within the general orbit of the liberal method of social adjustment. In Italy and Germany, on the other hand, the "corporations" and "chambers" were essentially organs of administration, subject to the avowedly antidemocratic governments, thus losing their liberal and voluntary character.

There was a continued growth of co-operative societies. A British authority on co-operation, H. J. Twigg, estimated that the total capital employed by the British industrial co-operative societies, excluding the agricultural associations, was £54,920,888 in 1913; £143,331,216 in 1926; and £221,725,055 in 1933. Wholesale prices in 1913 and 1933 were approximately the same. The same authority estimated that from 1924 to 1933 co-operative retail trade increased in volume about 40 per cent. Members of co-operative societies and their families make up almost half of the total population. A significant feature of the co-operative movement in its various forms was its resistance to the forces of depression. The total sales of retail stores fell from a high point of £216,327,000 in 1930 to £196,357,000 in 1933, but the physical volume of sales as indicated by price changes was somewhat larger in 1933 than in 1930. In 1935 sales were greater both in value and in volume than in any previous year.

A form of voluntary association mainly among the working classes and antedating both the co-operative society and the trade-union was the friendly society. The membership of friendly societies without branches reporting to the national government was 3,818,048 in 1913, and 4,695,776 in 1933. Benefits paid to members increased from £3,335,776 in 1913 to £7,438,644 in 1933.

The French co-operative movement also made progress, although it encountered serious difficulties, and information is less adequate because of the comparative decentralization of the societies. Consumers' societies were adversely affected by legislation in 1933, withdrawing certain tax exemptions and imposing a turnover tax on annual business. Later a more favorable attitude was apparent. In August, 1936, legislation encouraged both consumer and agricultural co-operation by promoting the establishment of mixed associations under joint managing committees and extending facilities for long-term advances from a national agricultural credit fund. In Italy and Germany, co-operation as an autonomous and voluntary movement virtually disappeared.

Trade-unions improved their status, especially in respect to collective bargaining with employers and in their political influence, in both France and Great Britain, although some of the newer industries, especially in the south of England, successfully resisted unionization. The British Labor party twice (in 1924, and again from 1929 to 1931) held office, but without a majority in the House of Commons and therefore without a mandate for the carrying out of the party's program for socializing the major industries. The short-lived British general strike of 1926 led to a limitation by Parliament of legal strikes and lockouts to industries in which there were specific disputes between employers and employees. In France, the trade-unions were able to extend their membership in the rapidly growing large-scale industries, but from 1921 to 1934 they were divided into two main groups, one group being affiliated with the Second International and the other with the Third or Communist International. In 1934 the two groups formed a "united front" against Fascist organizations. Later a formal union was brought about under the General Confederation of Labor, with a moderate program for the socialization of the major industries. The consolidation of labor organizations provided a working-class basis for the Popular Front of political parties, already described. It was largely the support of the working classes in alliance with many farmers and independent voters that enabled the Popular Front to obtain a majority in the election of May, 1936, and to enact legislation favorable to labor organizations and co-operative societies. Like the British Labor party, the French socialists were without a majority except by foregoing their distinctive policies in their immediate program. In Italy and Germany, free trade-unionism was destroyed, and labor organizations were made adjuncts of the antidemocratic one-party systems of these states.

The prevailing conception of the modern national state embodied the doctrine of national sovereignty; but the sovereignty of the liberal and democratic state was identified with popular sovereignty and with limitations on governmental power. An essential function of the liberal state was the maintenance of the right of voluntary association for purposes not inconsistent with the national authority, including criticism of the nature of that authority as well as the manner of exercising it. So vital was the role of voluntary associations that many students of political science have preferred to describe the modern state as pluralistic rather than unitary. But if the general authority allows voluntary associations to transcend their limited fields of activity, to interfere with the free functioning of other associations, or to challenge even the authority of the government itself, it surrenders its essential reason for existence and is supplanted sooner or later by an antiliberal regime, as in the case of the former liberal governments of Italy and Germany. The fate of these governments was not a defeat at the hands of revolutionists who assumed the risks and responsibilities of revolt, but a gradual surrender to subversive antiliberal groups which took advantage of the false tolerance of the liberal regimes.

Such a danger confronted the government of France when uniformed and armed groups such as the *Camelots du Roi* and the *Croix de Feu* attempted to overthrow opposing organizations and to nullify the authority of the government itself. In defense of its liberal traditions the government of France in December, 1935, enacted legislation for disbanding all associations "having the character of groups of combat or private militias." On the authority of this legislation the government of the Popular Front took steps to dissolve such organizations, without preventing their reorganization on a basis of equality with other associations. With the support of leading Conservatives, Liberals, and Laborites, the British government took similar steps to debar political uniforms and to check the disruptive tendencies of British Fascists. This policy was justified by the Home Secretary in his speech on November 16, 1936, moving the second reading of the Public Order Bill, as a necessary defense of political and civic toleration and of "all the things which we prize — freedom of opinion, freedom of speech, and freedom of meeting."

# CHAPTER 41

# GERMANY: LIBERALISM AND REACTION

## The Transition to the Republic

The outstanding importance of Germany in European economy is apparent from the country's central location, great natural resources, advanced technology, vigorous and disciplined population, and ambitions for world power. Exceptionally significant, therefore, is an understanding of her semiautocratic prewar system, her troubled and unsuccessful efforts to articulate her government and economy with other countries on the basis of Western liberalism, and her abandonment, under Nazi control, of Western ideals.

The contrast between the German system and the governments of western Europe and America was accentuated during the World War for propagandist purposes, but it is true that the German government retained important features of eighteenth-century bureaucratic autocracies. The efforts of nineteenth-century German liberals to achieve national unity had failed, and the imperial government was established as a result of brilliant military victories over Austria in 1866 and over France in the Franco-Prussian War. The Prussian system, which became dominant in the Empire, remained largely autocratic, under control of powerful landlords and the military caste. It is true that Germany was strongly influenced by Western liberalism stemming from the British parliamentary system, the French Revolution, and the classical doctrines of economics. Freedom of organization and discussion was allowed, business enterprises and labor organizations were not radically different from those in other industrialized countries, and the Reichstag became at least an influential debating society and an instrument for influencing as well as registering government decisions. Cities enjoyed virtual autonomy in handling their economic and social problems. Rapid industrialization, widespread prosperity, policies favorable to business, and an advanced system of social legislation enabled the imperial government to win extensive support without acceding to the demands for full parliamentary authority and for ministerial responsibility to parliament.

In such essentials as private enterprise, joint-stock finance, corporate organization, trade-unionism, and dependence on imported materials and markets for manufactures, the prewar German economic system resembled the economies of western Europe and the United States. But there were important distinctive characteristics. The encouragement of cartels facilitated an exceptional integration of industry. Mechanization on a comparatively efficient basis was achieved by means of emphasis on technical education and as a result of recent industrialization. The country contained exceptional resources of iron and coal; and the deposits of potash, combined with facilities for producing nitrates, provided an unequaled basis for soil conservation and agricultural production. Transportation facilities by railways and waterways were well planned and co-ordinated, largely under government ownership. Germany had the advantages of direct and economical access, except for political obstructions applying also to other countries, to the markets of practically the whole of Europe. In most of the neighboring states and in America influential elements of the population were of German origin, and they tended to strengthen economic and cultural ties with Germany.

Near the end of the war there was an increase of opposition to the imperial government. There were widespread strikes and even mutinies in the armed forces. On November 8, 1918, the heads of the Social Democratic party and the Social Democratic Parliamentary party sent an ultimatum to the "bourgeois" government, demanding the abdication of the Kaiser and the Crown Prince, the inclusion of additional Social Democrats in the ministry, and the formation of a Prussian cabinet responsible to the majority in the Reichstag. Delay in meeting the terms of the ultimatum precipitated a peaceful strike and forced not only the flight of the Kaiser but also the establishment of a republican government headed by Friedrich Ebert, chairman of the Social Democratic party. This party had vigorously opposed the war, but after war had been declared, a caucus of the party's Reichstag members, while reasserting the criticisms of policies which had brought on the war, had voted to support the government against "the menace of foreign invasion." During the course of the war the party had become increasingly critical of the government and insistent on democratic reforms.

### Group Conflicts and Compromises

The groups which assumed responsibility on the collapse of the imperial regime were socialistic in theory but were divided as to the extent of socialization and the methods of achieving it.  During the war there were three socialistic groups: the Social Democrats, the Independent Socialists, and the Spartacists.  The third group, organized during the war, formed the nucleus of the later Communist party.  The first two groups joined forces to proclaim the republic and to form a revolutionary government, the Independent Socialists foregoing their demand for immediate socialization.  In spite of the extremely disturbed conditions, a decree was issued on November 12, the day after the Armistice, proclaiming the end of the censorship, the introduction of complete freedom of the press, of speech, of assembly, and of association, the liberation of political prisoners, the annulling of various wartime decrees, and the restoration of social legislation for the protection of labor.  Even earlier, on November 9, when the republic was proclaimed, a completely democratic National Assembly was promised for the purpose of adopting a constitution.

Thus the majority socialists accepted without reservation the doctrines prevalent in western democratic countries, including recognition of private enterprise.  They put their faith in their ability to obtain popular support in the subsequent elections for ultimately carrying out such socialistic measures as seemed practicable.  A contributing factor was probably their desire to give evidence of literal conformity to President Wilson's demands for a democratic representative government to make treaties for Germany.  The exhaustion of Germany's food supplies and the dependence on imports and exports may well have inspired fears of external pressure against a socialistic policy.  Such pressure was being exerted at the time by the Allied Powers against communist Russia, a former member of the entente.

The radical socialists were bolder.  They recognized the opposition of the Allied governments to German socialism as well as to German autocracy, but made an appeal to the working classes of other countries.  They contended that under existing economic conditions freedom of the press, universal suffrage, and similar measures would play into the hands of the militaristic and reactionary groups by virtue of their control of newspapers and other agencies for influencing the electorate and of enterprises on which food and jobs depended.  They believed that the establishment of the republic on the basis of the existing system of private capital would merely return political control to the reactionary groups with intensified hostility to socialism, and they therefore favored the use of force if necessary for the immediate socialization of enterprise and the founding of political institutions on the basis of socialism. The moderate socialists, now in control of the government, were forced either to accede to these demands for immediate socialization or to suppress their fellow socialists by force. They chose the second alternative, made a secret alliance with the monarchical general staff for the overthrow of those who favored economic as well as political revolution, and abandoned their own liberal doctrines of freedom of association, assembly, and the press. Their plea was for the maintenance of law and order pending elections to a general assembly.

These conflicts among the socialists greatly strengthened the antisocialistic groups, and they were further aided in checkmating socialism by the adoption of proportional representation in the elections, held in January, 1919, to the National Constituent Assembly. The dangerously divided condition of the nation was apparent from the numerous factions represented in the Assembly, which met at Weimar. Although the Social Democrats obtained the largest number of seats, they were helpless except in such measures as commanded the support also of antisocialistic groups. They succeeded only in securing the adoption of certain mild clauses authorizing but not directing the new government to advance toward socialism. The constitution gave to the state the right to obtain lands for settlement or other purposes, to superintend the distribution and use of land for promoting homesteads and small holdings, and to supervise the use of subsoil and power resources. Subject to laws and legal procedures, and without prejudice to claims for compensation, private enterprises suitable for socialization might be converted into public property. Industrial relations were to be regulated by district works councils and a federal council representing the main occupational groups. The duties of these councils were to be defined by federal statutes and subordinated to federal authority. Extensive social legislation was authorized by the constitution, and among the notable developments in this field under the republic was unemployment insurance.

The general dissatisfaction in Germany with the arbitrary powers of the Kaiser and his ministers led to the adoption of democratic ideas more extreme than those in vogue even in the older democracies. The ministers individually, and as a whole, were to be subject to the will of the Reichstag. Provisions were included for popular initiative and referendum in respect to legislation and for the recall even of the president of the republic.  Proportional representation was adopted, and by its encouragement of minority groups it contributed materially to the "pluralistic stagnation" and impotence of the national government preceding the formation of the "totalitarian" or one-party state by the Nazis.  In contrast with these extreme innovations, the new constitution retained the economic arrangements which were the essential supports of the political power of landlords and industrialists.  In addition, the constitutional provisions for safeguarding the continuity of the civil service virtually imposed upon the new government a powerful organization which had been built up largely on the basis of aristocratic and conservative traditions.

### German Economy from Versailles to Locarno

The territories retained by Germany after the World War were virtually unscathed by war.  Her war debt was internal.  The prohibitions in the Treaty of Versailles on arms, although humiliating, promoted industrial rehabilitation while her former enemies diverted vast resources into armaments that rapidly became obsolete.  These circumstances were comparatively favorable.  On the other hand, the shackling of German economy by the economic and territorial clauses of the Treaty of Versailles was one of the main causes of the impotence and final overthrow of the republican system under the Weimar constitution.

The extensive financial and material aid extended by Germany to her allies was lost, and there were no compensating war borrowings abroad which could be repudiated or canceled.  By the Treaty of Versailles and the confiscatory policies of her enemies she lost her colonies, her mercantile connections and foreign concessions, extremely important patent rights, and a large part of her foreign investment.  The European territories which she lost had been the source, in 1913, of four fifths of her total production of iron ore in tonnage although not in value, almost half of her pig iron, a fourth of her coal, three fifths of her zinc (metallic content), and more than a third of her lead (metallic content).  The loss of arable land was greater than the loss of population.  The burden of reparations not only taxed with extreme severity her curtailed productive resources but subjected both her economic and her political life to external controls.  These losses and burdens, combined with trade barriers resulting from the general rearrangement of political boundaries, made necessary a thoroughgoing reorganization of the national

economy.   An instance was the effect of the severing of the Lorraine iron area from the coal basins of the Ruhr and the Saar.   Germany's dependence on foreign markets was increased while her
access to them was impeded.

Private capital was diminished and public credit was exhausted
by the war.   The war had been financed largely by credits, partly
in anticipation of the fruits of victory and partly as a result of
constitutional limitations on the taxing power.   The Weimar constitution increased the federal power over taxation but left the
government in a weak fiscal position because of the vast war debts
and the political turmoil and delay accompanying the revolution,
the transition to federal control of taxation, and the adoption of
tax policies.   As early as December, 1919, however, a national
emergency contribution was voted, calling for a capital levy up to
65 per cent payable over a period of years.   When the antisocialistic
parties became stronger, this was modified and in 1921 abandoned
in favor of forced loans and a comprehensive system of taxation.

In the meantime the burden of internal and external obligations
pressing on a diminished and demoralized productive system caused
a loss of faith in Germany's economic position and brought about a
rapid flight of capital.   Throughout the world there had been a
tendency toward inflation of credit and currency.   In Germany,
ordinary currency circulation in June, 1922, was more than twice as
great as in January, 1921.   A committee of international bankers
then attempted to arrange a foreign loan for stabilizing the German currency.   This move was blocked by French objections to
the conditions proposed for the loan.   The impasse was followed
by further inflation, the failure of Germany to make reparation
payments when due, and the occupation of the Ruhr valley by
French and Belgian troops.

During the ensuing complete demoralization of German economy
the mark rapidly depreciated until it became worthless.   France
and the other creditor nations were faced with the alternatives of
occupying the whole of Germany and assuming direct control of the
political and economic life of the country or of agreeing to a compromise for reducing the German burden and extending foreign
aid for the revival of the country.   The second alternative was
chosen.   The Dawes Plan was adopted in 1924 for dealing with
reparations and German finances.   In the following year the
Locarno agreements embodied a settlement of outstanding territorial
and political questions, largely on the basis of the Treaty of Versailles,

and by means of mutual guarantees and arbitration treaties involving Germany, France, Great Britain, Belgium, Poland, and Czechoslovakia. New arrangements effected a tentative solution of the Ruhr-Lorraine problem. In 1926 Germany was admitted to the League of Nations; and in the same year an international steel cartel formed the basis for adjusting some of the more important economic relations.

## Combination and Rationalization

The orgy of inflation liquidated a large part of Germany's internal debts. Individuals and institutions dependent on fixed or relatively inelastic incomes, including large numbers among the middle classes, were virtually beggared. Wage earners also were adversely affected by the failure of wages to rise as rapidly as prices. Rapid depreciation led to the immediate spending of incomes and reserves, either for consumption goods or for investments which would respond to the rise in prices. Foreign exchange rates made importation difficult and thus protected the home market, while exportation was artificially stimulated. At the same time, the bringing in of needed raw materials and foods was obstructed. The reconstruction of industrial plants was encouraged not only by the "flight from the mark" to avoid depreciation of liquid assets but also by the fact that wage payments and other contractual costs rose less rapidly than the price level.

The building of new plants and the reconstruction of old plants during inflation initiated the postwar rationalization movement. Rationalization was defined by the German Federation of Trade Unions, in 1926, as the use of technological and organizational methods for increasing the productivity of labor and of the industrial plant. Closely connected with rationalization was the combination movement. Some forms of combination, such as the older cartels, which were essentially associations, tended to stabilize the existing situation and by enabling less efficient companies and plants to survive, checked some forms of rationalization. Other types of combination, especially mergers, frequently promoted the elimination of inefficient companies and plants, although by encouraging price controls or other monopolistic practices they tended to make profitable operation possible without dependence on competitive efficiency. In so far as they deflated excessive capital investments, eliminated less efficient units, reduced the needless duplication of plants and of purchasing and marketing facilities, and in other ways reduced production costs, combinations were a part of the rationalization movement.

Although the trade-unions accepted and even favored rationalization, they held that economies in production should find expression in higher wages, lower prices, and increased output. The aim of those actually in charge of combination and rationalization was primarily the profitable operation of their establishments. The government as arbiter enacted a law in 1923 (slightly amended in 1933) for regulating combinations. This law set up a special court; it required that agreements affecting prices and the control of materials be in written and contractual form (not merely "gentlemen's agreements"); and it gave to a cabinet minister authority to intervene for the purpose of nullifying any agreement which improperly restricted supply and demand, raised prices unduly, or promoted the use of unfair methods. This law merely supplemented the general legal and administrative arrangements for public supervision of industry.

Both rationalization and combination had previously been prominent features of German economy, but the postwar period was peculiarly favorable. The World War demonstrated the advantages of industrial co-ordination and of a progressive technology. The period of inflation forced a flow of income and of reserves into capital investments and encouraged such speculative combinations as the Stinnes enterprises. The unequal effects of inflation and deflation on debts weakened some concerns and strengthened others. Stabilization in 1923–1924 and the accompanying deflation required a series of major operations for stabilizing industry as well as finance. The acceptance by Germany of the heavy burdens of reparations imposed by the Dawes Plan brought a realization of the necessity for the most efficient available system of production for competing in world markets and thereby acquiring the foreign credits necessary for meeting reparation payments. Extensive foreign credits facilitated the movement. The efforts of the government to check abuses and to protect labor were accompanied by trade-union support. The example of the United States was widely heralded as the "economic miracle" of technological progress and high standards of living. The treaty ban on German armaments also contributed to the use of resources for rationalization.

The most significant phase of the combination movement after the war was the advance beyond the older cartel or mere association of companies, and the formation of more closely integrated groups.

This tendency facilitated rationalization and at the same time intensified the problems of monopoly and of public control. Combination found notable expression in mergers and consolidations, in holding companies, and in "concerns." The last-named type consisted of companies which retained their legal identity but which went beyond mere association and entered into definite affiliation or federation by exchange of shares, continuing contractual relations, interlocking directorates, or other methods. Definitions of the different types of combinations vary widely because the methods and purposes were experimental and variable, with a broad area of common characteristics. The outstanding combinations were in mining, iron and steel, machinery, chemicals, and power. Combination and rationalization included a rationing of output and markets, especially during monetary stabilization and deflation; reorganization of enterprises for combining related units, for introducing greater plant and regional specialization, for standardization of materials and products, and for eliminating surplus units; the introduction of technological and managerial improvements; and efforts to co-ordinate the various branches of mining, manufacturing, transportation, and trade on a national basis.

An instance of rationalization accompanying combination was the reduction of the number of blast furnaces and the concentration of production in larger, more efficient, and more satisfactorily located plants. The number of units in operation was reduced from 141 in 1925 to 115 in 1929, while total output increased from 7,914,000 to 13,240,000 tons. The effects of rationalization on the productivity of labor cannot be measured exactly in most industries, but for coal and lignite there are significant figures. In bituminous coal mining, the average output per worker increased 33 per cent from 1925 to 1929; and in lignite mining, 39 per cent.

## Indications of Economic Revival

The feverish activity of the inflation period with its artificial stimulus to consumption and to speculative investment was abruptly halted late in 1923. It was followed by a sudden contraction of currency, credit, business activity, and employment. The announcement of plans in October, 1923, for a new monetary system was followed immediately by a rapid rise in unemployment. The estimated percentage of unemployment had already risen from 3.5 in July to 9.9 in September, and there was a further rise to 28.2 in December. Recovery began in 1924, and although there was a recession in 1925 and 1926, revival again gained headway and was sustained until 1929.

Factors affecting recovery included the restoration of stable monetary and credit conditions in Germany. The deflation of internal debts by currency depreciation, although disastrous to many individuals and groups in Germany, and the cause of grave losses to many foreign investors, established nevertheless the basis for the new monetary and credit structure. The adjustment of reparations by the Dawes Plan proved to be temporary but was accepted in good faith and was made the basis of foreign credits totaling about 1,200,000,000 marks in 1924 and much larger sums early in 1925. In addition, there was a renewal of foreign purchases of private securities. Long-term investments by foreigners increased from about a billion marks in 1924 to more than four billion marks in 1926. Short-term investments in 1926 also amounted to about four billion marks. Both types, and especially short-term investments (endangering solvency at any moment of crisis), continued to expand rapidly after 1926. Foreign capital facilitated rationalization, payment of reparations, the purchase of food and raw materials, and the extension of credits by German exporters to their customers. Secondary factors which tended to give Germany temporary trade advantages were the British coal strike, the stabilization of the French franc in 1926, and the Locarno agreements.

Among the evidences of revival was the rise of the index of production in manufacturing and mining. Industrial production in 1925 was 20 per cent higher than in 1924; and in 1927, 46 per cent higher than in 1924. Thereafter, until 1930, it remained substantially unchanged.

German trade expanded rapidly. The value of exported commodities was 22 per cent greater in 1925 than in 1924; the value of imports, 25 per cent greater. In 1929, the value of exports was 75 per cent greater than in 1924, and the value of imports, 42 per cent greater. In 1924 the value of imports exceeded the value of exports by almost two billion marks; in 1929, the values were virtually equal. The trade balance was usually against Germany, and her surplus income after the war from investments and services abroad was insignificant. It was by means of foreign credits that Germany was able to pay the import balance as well as reparations.

Another criterion of economic revival was the status of labor. When the monetary system was stabilized, wage-earner income in terms of purchasing power was probably not more than three fourths of prewar income. By 1928 the prewar level seems to have been restored; but in the meantime the productivity of labor had been greatly increased, and the relative position of wages as an element in national income and consumption had declined. Rationalization without an expansion of demand for the output of the improved productive plant corresponding to increased productivity and growth of the working population made full employment impossible. In 1928, the year when the index of industrial production reached its highest point, a monthly average of 1,353,000 persons registered as unemployed at the public employment offices.

## German Aspects of the World Depression

When the world depression began in 1929, Germany was in a peculiarly vulnerable position. Among the unfavorable factors were her international obligations, including a large volume of short-term debts; her dependence on foreign trade, which, in turn, depended largely on foreign credits; and the reliance of her government on unstable compromises and coalitions among essentially antagonistic groups. Economic revival from 1924 to 1929 had been based on such precarious foundations as the repudiation of internal debts by inflation, the incurring of additional external debts, and an excessive stimulation of capital-goods production. Caught between the demands of the victor nations and the severely restricted possibilities of her postwar economy, Germany in effect was forced either to thrust responsibility back upon the victors or to adopt a temporizing hand-to-mouth policy.

During the period of revival, employment was one of the phases of the national economy that responded slowly to the forces of recovery. It was also one of the first to be affected adversely by the world depression. The average number of registered unemployed persons increased from 1,353,000 in 1928 to 1,892,000 in 1929, and to 5,575,000 in 1932, with approximately 1,500,000 additional unemployed persons not registered at the employment offices. After the extreme decline of real wages during inflation, there had been a return to prewar levels. From 1929 to 1932 wage rates, weekly hours, and retail prices all declined, but the net result for workers whose wages are a matter of record was a decline of about 6 per cent in real weekly earnings. Because of the great increase in unemployment and the fall in wages, total pay rolls were drastically reduced.

Employers and many economists held that in spite of the increase in labor productivity, wages during the period of recovery had been higher than the country's competitive position and international obligations warranted, and that the decline after 1929 was too small. The alleged rigidity of the wage structure was credited with retarding employment during recovery and accelerating unemployment during the depression. According to the widely accepted doctrines of marginal utility as applied to wages and employment, an increase or decrease in the number of workers depends on whether more or fewer workers will add to the profits or reduce the losses of the employer, whose decision will be determined primarily by the wage scale. Low wages therefore tend to increase employment and high wages tend to create unemployment. It was therefore held that when the German workers forced wages up during the recovery and resisted reductions during the depression, they made unemployment inevitable.

Trade-union leaders held that this analysis of the way in which the economic system operates necessarily placed the main burden of production costs and of Germany's international obligations on the wage-earning classes. Indeed it was the acceptance of this view that led many to advocate the socialization of enterprise as the only method of achieving a more equitable sharing of the costs of production and of maintaining employment on the basis of the need for output within the limits of available resources.

But others held that the currently accepted analysis of the causes of unemployment was faulty. They agreed that employers will not employ additional workers or retain all of their existing force at a loss but held that the profitable employment of workers depends on the demand for output. Demand in turn depends on various factors. Among these are prices, which employers attempt to maintain on a rigid basis while demanding elasticity of wages; the adaptation of the product to consumer needs and tastes; and ultimately the possession of means of payment by consumers, including wage earners as a major consumer group. It was held that wages, instead of being above their proper economic level, had lagged behind the productivity of labor and behind other forms of income. This in turn had overstimulated investment in production goods, had withheld income from consumption, and had undermined market demands required for profitable investment and employment.

The fact remained, however, that the primary problem of the

individual employer, who depended on the general market for disposing of his output, was the reduction of his wage bill as a part of his production costs, and not the increase of the purchasing power of his employees. The depression in Germany and elsewhere was evidence of the failure to solve the problem. In 1930 industrial production in Germany was 14 per cent lower than in 1929; in 1931, 32 per cent lower; and in 1932, 47 per cent lower. The extreme curtailment of activity in the capital-goods field, following a period of overstimulation, is shown by the fact that the output of investment goods in 1932 was only a third as large as in 1929, while the output of goods for current consumption was three fourths as large as in 1929. Agriculture in Germany as in many other countries had shared only in slight degree the benefits of the period of recovery; and it suffered during the depression from the deflation of prices accompanied by a rigid debt structure. The usual interest rate on farm mortgages was 9 or 10 per cent, and rates on short-term loans were higher.

The recession of foreign trade was even more extreme, in terms of value, than the decline of industrial production. The value of imports in 1932 was approximately a third of the value of the 1929 imports; and the value of exports was slightly more than two fifths of the 1929 value. Special trade measured by weight was reduced 50 per cent from 1929 to 1932 in the case of imports, and 25 per cent in the case of exports.

Germany had been unable to pay reparations without an extensive trade for building up foreign credits. But she was unable to extend her trade without incurring further obligations for reconstructing her industries, buying materials and foods, and arranging for credits to her customers. Her creditors built up tariff walls against her exports but granted further credits for the extension of her trade. These credits were predominantly of the short-term types. Long-term foreign investments in Germany in 1929 totaled about 7,300,000,000 marks, and short-term investments about 11,700,-000,000 marks. The extensive withdrawal of these credits and the curtailment of further credits before Germany could acquire a favorable trade balance marked the beginning of the end of the remarkable postwar structure of reparations, inter-Allied debts, and German loans. There followed at length in 1932 the canceling of reparations and inter-Allied debts; but the economic and political advantages of these adjustments were dissipated by the long delay.

## The Nazi Movement

The position of the government had been extremely difficult even during the upturn in business from 1926 to 1929. The Social Democratic party, unable to obtain a majority in the Reichstag, continued its policy of subordinating its socialistic principles to collaboration with antisocialistic parties in unstable coalitions. The continued concentration of industry gave the great industrialists and financiers increasing influence. The middle classes, chief sufferers from inflation, were unable to regain their former status. The failure of the movement for general disarmament and the refusal of France and other nations to consent to German rearmament, to the abrogation of the war-guilt clause of the treaty, and to other modifications of the treaty, caused increasing discontent in Germany. Imports continued in excess of exports, with minor exceptions, and the international balance of payments for imports as well as reparations was met by borrowings. The government was attacked with increasing vigor by the Communist party, by the groups on the extreme right, and by the German National Socialist Workers' party — the Nazis. During the depression political as well as economic disintegration culminated in the overthrow of the republic and the establishment by the Nazis of a system resembling Italian Fascism.

The National Socialist Workers' party was neither a socialistic nor a labor party. The group which served as its nucleus was the German Workers' party, formed in 1919. Adolf Hitler, an Austrian corporal in the German Reichswehr, joined the party in July. In 1920 a formal program was adopted. This program, known as "the twenty-five points," made lavish promises to virtually all except the Jews, who were to be denied citizenship. To the militaristic and nationalistic groups were promised the overthrow of the peace treaties, the restoration of a national army, the union of all Germans, the acquisition of new territories, and the control of the press. The working classes were told that it was the duty of everyone to work, that unearned incomes would be abolished, that war profits would be confiscated, and that great industries or trusts would be nationalized. The middle classes would be favored by the taking over of large stores, the granting of low rental rates to small tradesmen, giving preference to small business in the buying of supplies by national and local governments, and the opening up of the universities and the higher offices of state, army, and navy on an equality with the aristocracy. Farmers and agricultural workers were encouraged by promises of agrarian reforms such as the confiscation of estates, abolition of interest on mortgages, and prohibition of speculation in land.

In 1926 the constitution of the party affirmed that "the twenty-five points" were unalterable. But interpretation was necessary, and the way in which they were made to mean different things to different groups is illustrated by the clauses relating to land reform. In reply to attacks by landlords in 1928, on the proposal relating to confiscation of land, Hitler declared that the party recognized and protected private property; that the phrase "confiscation without compensation" meant only the creation of legal means for confiscation; and that the program was directed primarily against the Jews. The "breaking of interest slavery" was similarly interpreted as referring to "Jewish money lenders."

The appeals to national pride against the war-guilt clause of the treaty of peace, the burden of reparations, the inequality of Germany in respect to armaments, and other clauses of the treaty were popular with all classes. The workers were disillusioned by the compromises of the Social Democratic leaders and by their conflicts with the heads of the Communist party, while the violent tactics of the Nazis were condoned by the government in the name of constitutional liberty. Some were misled by the socialistic promises of the Nazis. Even as early as 1922, Hitler had declared that socialism merely meant devotion to the national cause. To the propertied classes other than Jews and "traitorous" elements he clearly disavowed public ownership or any form of confiscation. His bitterest attacks were against Marxism and its "horrible" denial of the right of private property. There were many, nevertheless, who interpreted the socialistic phrases of the "unalterable" official program at their face value as late as the "blood purge" of June, 1934.

The party obtained the support of some of the workers, especially among the unemployed, who joined the Storm Troopers in large numbers, but most of its adherents were debt-burdened farmers and members of the urban middle classes. Crushed by inflation, by large-scale business and cartels, by heavy taxes, and, especially in the case of farmers, by extremely high interest rates, falling prices, and foreign competition, they were convinced that they had little to lose by supporting the Nazis. Desiring to retain their traditional superiority to the wage-earning classes and to resist the forces of economic and social decay, they were attracted by the promises of aid against big enterprises and of positions in public offices and the armed forces on an equality with the aristocracy. Marx had prophesied the growth of big business and the crushing of the middle classes. He held that they would be forced into the ranks of the proletariat and would recognize their community of interests with the wage-earners. The Nazis unceasingly denounced Marx, played upon the class pride and ambitions of the middle classes, and promised to raise them to a superior economic and social status among the "elite" — the leaders who would rule the country and elevate the superior German race to new heights of power.

The capitalistic classes had successfully utilized the coalition governments of the republic for the maintenance of a balance of power in the state against the Communists and the extreme nationalists. Some of the great industrialists and many of the extreme nationalists and militarists supported the Nazis, but a large proportion of businessmen were not disposed to abandon the coalition governments as long as they functioned without serious discord or disturbance to business. But when the structure of reparations, borrowed capital, and trade based on foreign credits collapsed under the impact of depression, government by coalition of parties and factions became increasingly difficult. Businessmen then began to view the Nazi movement with favor, but their support was given discreetly lest it drive away the middle classes and unemployed workers who gave to the party the appearance of a mass movement.

### Transition to the Nazi Regime

The Nazis, like the Italian Fascists, were contemptuous of representative government, liberalism, and democracy. They continually reviled the "Weimar System" based on the republican constitution adopted at Weimar. Hitler early denounced parliamentary methods and majority votes and proclaimed reliance on the strength of "a few resolute men." In 1920 the party organized a military section and in 1921 transformed it into the Storm Troopers. In 1923 an armed rebellion was crushed and Hitler was for a short time imprisoned. Thereafter the armed force was vigorously developed, composed largely of unemployed workers, but was used for propaganda, parades, and the suppression of the meetings and activities of opposing groups, mainly the Communists, who were opposed also by the government. The party changed its tactics and posed as a mass political movement as well as a military force. The purpose was to win a majority vote and control the republican government in order to destroy it.

Inflation and the Ruhr invasion, together with a Nazi alliance with an anti-Semitic group, drew extensive support from the hard-pressed middle classes as well as extreme nationalists, and in 1924 the party won 32 seats in the Reichstag and a popular vote of 1,918,000. In a later election in the same year, only 14 seats were won; and four years later, on the eve of the depression, the party obtained only 12 seats.

The depression brought rapidly mounting unemployment, increasing public burdens and declining revenues, impairment of social insurance, widespread discontent among the workers and middle classes, and fears among businessmen of a socialistic revolution. The Social Democrats and the Communists still fought over tactics. The Center party organized a coalition government and proposed as a remedy for depression a deflationary policy of higher taxation, curtailment of public expenditures, and reduction of wages and prices together with higher protective tariffs as an aid to hard-pressed farmers. Unable to obtain a majority in the Reichstag, the Chancellor resorted to emergency presidential decrees. The victor nations evacuated the Rhineland and canceled reparations, but the crisis continued.

The Nazis, supported by many of the extreme nationalists, had made spectacular gains in 1930, polling 6,406,000 out of 35,224,000 votes, and winning 107 out of 577 seats in the Reichstag. In the presidential election of April, 1932, Hindenburg, with the support of the Social Democrats and the Center party, received 53 per cent of the total popular vote; Hitler received 36.8 per cent; and the Communist candidate, 10.2 per cent. In spite of this popular verdict, and the fact that Chancellor Bruening commanded a majority in the Reichstag, the aged president was persuaded to dismiss the chancellor and appoint a representative of the extreme right — a prelude to the appointment of Hitler as chancellor and the filling of strategic posts by his followers. In the last election in which the forms of the Weimar constitutional procedure were followed, in March, 1933, the Nazis controlled the propagandist facilities and electoral machinery, but were able to obtain only 17,277,000 votes out of a total of 39,655,000, and to elect only 288 deputies out of 647. Thereafter the national elections were merely "yes" or "no" plebiscites, held under conditions dictated by the party and controlled by its coercive machinery. The failure of the liberal experiment resulted from a series of circumstances which began with the assumption in the treaty of peace of obligations which could not be met and which ended with the conferring of powers by President Hindenburg on a minority group, the Nazis, who were avowed enemies of the "Weimar System."

### Labor and Capital under the Nazi Regime

Out of the flood of propaganda and promises of the era of the quest for power certain basic party doctrines emerged. Among these were the supreme power of the national government over all political units; the right of the state to intervene in all aspects of life, social, cultural, and economic; the subordination of individuals to their "leaders" in economic as well as political life; and the culmination of the leadership principle in the absolute authority of the head of the state, *der Fuehrer* (the Leader). The general policy of the new government was described by Dr. Goebels, Minister of Propaganda and Enlightenment: "Germany is to have only one goal, one party, and one conviction, and the state organization is to be identical with the nation. . . . The state must stand for the principle of totality."

The first and most rigorous application of these conceptions in the economic field was in connection with labor. After the war the trade-unions had grown rapidly. In 1931 the German unions associated with the International Federation of Trade Unions had approximately five million members, and many of the unions were not connected with the International Federation. In the same year the number of manual workers covered by collective agreements with employers was more than twelve million. The party name (National Socialist) and its official program, when viewed literally, called for emphasis on the subordination of business rather than labor to the state. But the party's interpretations of its program and its close association, during the later stages of its rise to power, with ultraconservative groups provided ample evidence that its efforts would be directed primarily toward the suppression of working-class organizations and the subjection of the workers to employers as delegated "leaders." Steps were taken in this direction before the party acquired political power. A National Socialist Cell Organization was formed and every wage earner who joined the party was required to join a "cell" in his establishment or aid in forming one. The purpose of the "cells" was to gain control of the trade-unions. This process of "boring from within" accomplished little, and the unions for the most part successfully resisted Nazi penetration.

After Hitler's appointment as Chancellor one of the party's first moves was the dissolution of the unions. There were external signs at first of a policy of toleration. On May 1, 1933, the unions were permitted to stage extensive May Day demonstrations. The next day, however, carefully prepared secret plans for the forcible dissolution of the unions were carried into effect. During the next few days not only the trade-unions but the Communist party, the Social Democratic party, and even some of the co-operative societies found their records, banks, newspapers, and other properties confiscated and many of their leaders imprisoned. The Nazi journal, *Arbeitertum*, was made the "official" organ of the wage-earning classes. The unions, nominally surviving, were transformed into party agencies with party appointees in charge.

On May 10, 1933, the formation of the Labor Front was announced. This organization was designed to absorb all non-Jewish workers. Dues-paying membership in the organization or in its constituent "unions" was compulsory and was made virtually a condition of employment. A new conception was proclaimed — the identity of interests of employers and employees. Strikes were forbidden. Robert Ley, head of the Labor Front, announced that decisions must be left with the employer as the responsible "leader" and "master in the house."

The Law for the Organization of National Labor, January 20, 1934, embodied the so-called "leadership" principle, which in fact resembled the long-abandoned master-and-servant doctrine of the English common law. It provided, to be sure, for consultations between workers and employers, but the workers' representatives were not only required to be loyal and active Nazis but must have the approval both of the employer and of the "leader" of the party "cell" in the establishment. If such persons, when their names were submitted to the workers, were not accepted, the representatives of labor were to be chosen by the Labor Trustee. The elaborate organization of Labor Trustees and "honor" courts was designed to place ultimate decision in labor relations beyond dispute by vesting authority in officials appointed directly by the government. Workers were further restricted by a law for forcing former agricultural workers in the cities to return to the farms. Much more important was the adoption of a detailed worker's record book or "labor passport" for keeping a complete record of each worker and for controlling his movements and employment.

Under the new labor policy employers were given pre-eminence but were expected to exercise their authority as "leaders" subject to the superior authority of their own organizations in the several fields of enterprise and to the supreme authority of the state. Cartels and trade associations, already prominent, were further encouraged and utilized by the new government. The first and most rigorous measures of control by the state were applied to enterprises connected with the press, communications, advertising, the theater, and the arts. These were organized in September, 1933, into a Chamber of Culture and were subjected, largely for political reasons, to the Ministry of Propaganda and Enlightenment.

Early in 1934 a Law for the Organic Reconstruction of German Business provided for the supervision of enterprise by the Ministry of Economics. Thirteen groups of industries were formed, with trade associations somewhat resembling the Italian corporations or guilds. Later a new classification was undertaken, with a central organization known as the Chamber of Economics. Under this Chamber were national associations classified by industries and local or territorial chambers of commerce and industry comprising in most cases various types of enterprises. These organizations, national and local, were not innovations. The new policy was merely an attempt to effect a more logical and comprehensive classification and to bring about a more thoroughgoing integration and centralized control. To this end, the appointment of the principal officials was subject to governmental approval. The associations were utilized for such purposes as the allocation of materials, credits, and labor, and the control of prices.

Similar efforts were made, under the Ministry of Agriculture, to organize and co-ordinate farm production. To the older agricultural associations, long prominent, many new agencies were added, connected not only with the production but with the processing and distributing of farm commodities, particularly foods. Like the industrial associations, those connected with agriculture (called collectively the Agricultural Estate) comprised two types: local and regional associations, and associations interested in particular branches of agricultural production. As in the case of the industrial groups, the principal changes were the expansion of such agencies and increased governmental control. The Agricultural Estate was utilized for such purposes as the control and expansion of production, the regulation of prices, and even the rationing of products for reducing the amount of imported food.

The Chamber of Economics and the Agricultural Estate merely reclassified, expanded the membership, and co-ordinated the activities of industrial and agricultural associations. The Labor Front, on the other hand, destroyed the associations of workers, confiscated their properties, and compelled workers to become dues-paying members of the new organization. The Labor Front, although theoretically composed of all producers, was primarily designed for handling labor problems. In 1935 the Chamber of Economics and the Agricultural Estate formally joined the Labor Front. It was expected that by means of a centralized organization a better co-ordination would be effected and that the Minister of Economics, whose affiliations were with businessmen, would be able to exert a restraining influence on the Labor Front. The elaborate administrative machinery called for frequent experimental adaptation, but the complete control of labor by employers under governmental supervision was consistently maintained.

## Employment, Wages, and Production

The primary aim of the government in the reorganization of economic agencies was the achievement of political power in the economic field. The exercise of power was for purposes which were gradually evolved. The country's most obvious needs were re-employment and increased production. The Nazis attained power at a time when economic recovery was being experienced in a large part of the world, but they proved to be unequal to the task of formulating policies for sharing in the expansion of world trade. Unemployment was slowly declining before the Nazi regime began, and under the new government the decline was accelerated. At the party congress at Nuremberg in September, 1936, Hitler stated that unemployment had fallen from six millions to one million. The methods used included compulsory work by young men in the State Labor Service at nominal pay; *Landhilfe*, composed of young persons sent to the farms to work for their board and lodging; a virtually compulsory system of part time for sharing available jobs; a large reduction in the number of women workers; provisions forbidding the holding of jobs by the wives and children of public employees; an extensive program of public works and subsidized housing; a great expansion of employment in government service and the armed forces; and rearmament on a gigantic scale. From 1933 to 1935 about 80,000 Jews and an indeterminate number of non-Jewish critics of the government sought refuge in other countries, and their displacement made available many public and private positions.

Hourly wage rates in the principal industries were about 4 per cent lower in 1935 than in 1932, according to official figures, and prices, especially of the staples of working-class diet, were materially higher. Weekly earnings were affected by extensive work sharing and by deductions and "voluntary" contributions of various kinds. Only the wage rates in the principal industries are included in these figures. A large part of the re-employment was in the Labor Service and in other activities affording merely a subsistence.

While real wages even in the basic industries were falling, production was increasing. The general index of industrial production, which had fallen from 100.0 in 1929 to 53.3 in 1932, rose from this low level to 94.0 (an increase of 76.4 per cent) in 1935, although after March, 1935, the increase was partly due to the inclusion of figures for the Saar basin. Building activity was approximately doubled from 1932 to 1935, and railway freight traffic increased 44 per cent. Imports, on the other hand, declined 11 per cent in value and exports fell off 25 per cent in value, in the face of rising prices.

The increase of 76.4 per cent in industrial production from 1932 to 1935 was predominantly in iron and steel, machinery, and engineering. The output of iron and steel more than trebled (an increase of 219 per cent), and production in the machinery and engineering industries more than doubled (an increase of 114 per cent). These increases, together with the doubling of building construction, reveal the predominant importance of rearmament, public works, and subsidized housing in the expansion of employment and business activity.

### Germany's International Economic Position

The rearmament program was a natural reaction against the restraints of the treaty of peace and a logical expression of the Nazi conception of Germany's proper place in the world. The constantly reiterated aims of the Nazi leaders from the beginning of the movement included the overthrow of the economic and political system established by the treaties of peace; the rearmament of Germany; the absorption in the Reich of all Germans in the territories adjacent to Germany; and even the acquisition of territories occupied by non-Germans.

The official German editions of Hitler's autobiography, *Mein Kampf*, give in detail the aims and even the tactics of the party in relation to Germany's world position. War, *der Fuehrer* asserts, makes mankind great, peace is its ruin. Germany's lost territories must be regained, and lands needed by the German people must be acquired by means of armed force. Territories needed by Germany in Europe are primarily the lands of Russia and some of the states bordering on Russia. For assuring the triumph of German arms, Germany must cultivate the good will and if possible obtain the positive aid of Great Britain and Italy and thereby isolate France, Germany's deadly enemy. These policies, combined with an internal racial "purification" and national unity on the basis of Nazi principles, will ultimately make Germans the masters of the world.

These views were written in *Mein Kampf* before the withdrawal of Allied troops from the Rhineland and the cancellation of reparations. But it was after these events that the autobiography was given the leading place in German literature and in the schools as the authentic voice of the head of the party and of the government. In September, 1936, at the party Congress at Nuremberg, Hitler asserted that "if Germany possessed the Ural Mountains with their immense wealth of raw materials, Siberia with its vast forests, and the Ukraine with its extensive wheat fields, the country and the National Socialists would be bountifully supplied." The chief significance of such statements was not so much in the indicated direction of proposed expansion, eastward, westward, or overseas, as in their evidence regarding the fundamental aims and methods of Nazi policy.

The lack of external territories under German control was assigned as the principal reason for the adoption, in 1936, of an elaborate four-year program of economic development. It was officially stated that the purpose was to make Germany "wholly independent of foreign countries" in respect to all those materials which German resources and ingenuity could produce. Plans were adopted for a rigorous limitation of consumption of articles not produced at home. Wages were further restricted to check consumption and to keep production costs at a low level. Efforts were made to utilize more effectively the industrial and agricultural associations and the direct agencies of government for the regulation of prices, the control of exports and imports, and the allocation of materials, credits, and labor to the enterprises most needed, in the first place, to achieve a maximum of self-sufficiency, and in the second place, to provide exports, in part subsidized, for the purchase of necessary foods and materials abroad.

In the meantime Germany, it was declared, would not relinquish her right to acquire additional territories consistent with the needs of the nation and its growing population. The demand for additional territory was based on lack of land and resources to support the existing population, and at the same time every effort was made to encourage early marriages and large families. "Germany," declared Dr. Schacht, Minister of Economic Affairs, "is a country without land enough for its population." Attempts by other countries "to repress a great people dependent on expansion must lead first to misery and discontent and at length to some kind of explosion."

CHAPTER 42

# THE ROLE OF THE LESSER STATES

———◆———

## Limited Role of the Lesser States before the World War

Among the forces which directed the activities and shaped the institutions of economic life before the World War, nationalism acquired increasing strength. The economy of Europe as a whole was overshadowed by the major powers, and the lesser states tended to conform to the larger patterns. But the extension of nationalism, especially after the World War, had important repercussions on the small countries and was accompanied by distinctive developments. Among these was the growth of peasant proprietorships, the erecting of artificial economic boundaries, the struggle on the one hand for natural resources and self-sufficiency and on the other hand for collective security, and the conflict between advocates of liberalism and advocates of autocratic authority. An account of the extremely diverse and rapidly shifting developments in the numerous lesser states is beyond the scope of a general economic history. It is sufficient to indicate the limited role of these states before the World War, to mention some of the complications introduced into European economy by postwar nationalism, and to describe briefly some of the more distinctive and significant general trends.

Before the World War, European economy was dominated by Great Britain, France, Germany, Russia, Austria-Hungary, and Italy. In most cases the independence and economic interests of the smaller states commanded respect. Among the causes of their comparative security were their isolation or insignificance; geographical features and ethnic traits which made them separate entities and afforded them a measure of natural defense; and jealousy among the great powers.

In the extreme southwest, Portugal, with the remaining fragments of her empire, survived as a satellite of Great Britain. Spain, with the defenses of her natural frontiers and without the hazards of her former imperial ambitions, maintained her semifeudal traditions in seemingly successful resistance alike to internal change and to the expansive forces of the peoples who succeeded her on the imperial stage. Possessed of important nonagricultural resources, especially

854 THE NEW EUROPE

iron, lead, copper, and mercury, the Spaniards allowed ready access to foreigners.  Most of the output was exported, although in the decade before the World War efforts were made by the government to promote the metal-working as well as the mining industries and to limit foreign financial control of mineral resources.

The Netherlands, Belgium, Switzerland, and the Scandinavian states were closely integrated economically with neighboring countries, but with the exception of Belgium they were able to maintain their independence and even their neutrality during the World War.  This was due to such factors as their geographical position, their well-developed economies, their ethnic unity (although in the case of Switzerland the unity was cultural, not racial), and their vigorous and adaptable political institutions.  Belgium, partly because of its great wealth and the highly developed state of its industries peculiarly important in war, but mainly because of its strategic location, became involuntarily, as in earlier wars, a vital battleground between the major powers.

The other comparatively unimportant states were in southeastern Europe.  This region, center of ancient traditions and of nationalistic ambitions, had long been subject to Turkish rule.  With the gradual nineteenth-century recession of Turkish power, the Greeks, Bulgarians, Serbs, and Rumanians organized the principal states.  All of these countries were largely agricultural and were backward economically and politically but were extremely nationalistic and aggressive.  Their nationalistic aspirations encountered the difficulties associated with an exceptionally confused geographic and ethnic pattern and with conflicting and bitterly contested territorial claims.  Even more significant from the European point of view was the fact that with the recession of the Turks the great powers of Europe attempted either to thwart the nationalistic ambitions of the region or to utilize them for the promotion of imperialistic aims.  Italian and Austro-Hungarian interests clashed in the eastern Adriatic.  Germany sought, in alliance with Austria-Hungary and Turkey, to obtain control of a route from Berlin to Bagdad.  Russia sought control of the South Slavs and of the straits between the Black Sea and the Aegean for access to the Mediterranean Sea.  France had extensive interests in the Near East and looked with suspicion on the efforts of Germany and Austria-Hungary to gain ascendancy in the Balkans.  Great Britain desired to thwart both the southward advance of Russia and the eastward extension of German influence.

## Postwar Status of Minor Countries

The countries which maintained their neutrality during the World War (Spain, Switzerland, the Netherlands, Norway, Sweden, and Denmark) greatly increased their income and their productive facilities. But all of these countries found difficulty, after the war, in readjusting their capital structure, overextended to meet wartime needs, to the modified and more restricted demands of peace. The economy of Belgium for a decade after the war, even more than that of France, was dominated by reconstruction activities and German reparations. In general, the relations of these lesser countries of western Europe underwent few vital changes as a result of the World War.

Four of the six new states — Finland, Estonia, Latvia, and Lithuania — had been Russian Baltic provinces, although a small strip of German territory was added to Lithuania. Poland was carved from the Russian, German, and Austro-Hungarian empires; and Czechoslovakia had been the heart of the industrial area of Austria-Hungary. These new states were almost entirely without distinctive natural frontiers, although the lakes of Finland gave it a unique aspect, and the Pripet marshes formed a part of the Polish-Russian border. The avowed principle of boundary determination at the Peace Conference was ethnic rather than geographic or economic, but the victorious powers interpreted numerous doubtful cases in their own favor and in many instances ignored ethnic considerations for the purpose of acquiring important resources or strategic areas.

The Russian Baltic provinces had come under the influence of German capital, trade, and landlordism, and the anti-Russian elements obtained German aid in resisting the authority of the Soviet government. After the defeat of Germany, the victorious Allied powers, especially Great Britain, took the place of Germany in supporting the anticommunistic elements and sanctioned the establishment of independent governments. But the natural bonds with the Russian hinterland were so strong that in spite of anticommunistic sentiment the new governments responded to the overtures of the Russian government and entered into nonaggression pacts. Special arrangements were also made for the use of certain free ports by Russia and for the promotion of reciprocal trade. Under the former Russian regime the Baltic provinces had profited by their maritime location and by governmental encouragement of manufactures for sale to the predominantly agricultural hinterland. As independent states they lost some of these advantages. Their location and control of ports sufficed to maintain important trade relations with Russia, but the Soviet government naturally preferred to develop its own manufactures and to divert much of its trade to Black Sea ports under its own control. The new states therefore tended to revert to a condition more largely agricultural.

The new Poland, although sixth in size and sixth in population among European states, and although in possession of varied natural resources, nevertheless encountered serious obstacles in the way of independent economic development. The boundaries diverged sharply from the Polish ethnic frontiers. In language, almost a third of the population was non-Polish. With the exception of the Pripet marshes, which were beyond the Polish ethnic frontier, there was a natural continuity of Polish territory with that of neighboring countries. Access to the sea was obtained by the cumbersome and troublesome Danzig Corridor, but since the Poles were not given control of the "free city" of Danzig, they developed at great expense the rival port of Gdynia under their direct control. The severing of the principal industrial centers from their former German, Austrian, and Russian markets, as the German market for Silesian coal and iron, tended to retard the already slightly developed industries of Poland, although strenuous efforts were made to develop a self-sufficing system and to expand manufactures in a protected home market. Manufacturing, mining, trade, and transport in 1921 occupied only about 15 per cent of the working population, while approximately three fourths were engaged in agriculture, which suffered even more than industry from the curtailment of neighboring markets. Unfriendly relations with other countries, the lack of natural frontiers, and unrest, both racial and economic, caused the diversion of immense resources and credits into armaments. The methods adopted for rectifying the eighteenth-century destruction of Polish independence introduced new and gravely disturbing factors, both economic and political. The predominance of agriculture and the variety of natural resources made possible for Poland a comparatively self-sufficing economy, although the dependence of the large estates on agricultural exports and the dependence of industry and government on foreign finance militated against self-sufficiency even on the basis of the extremely low prevailing standard of living.

The new state of Czechoslovakia, south of Poland, was even more dependent than Poland on the maintenance of favorable relations with other countries. The effects of the World War and the treaties on the fragments of the Austro-Hungarian Empire and the Balkan states have been mentioned in another connection, but the peculiar importance of Czechoslovakia demands a brief additional statement. The treaties of peace sanctioned the inclusion in Czechoslovakia of exceptionally rich and varied resources, both industrial and agricultural. The new state fell heir to a large part of the more highly developed areas of the Austro-Hungarian Empire. The country depended on the export of manufactures for the maintenance of its varied industries, including textiles, shoes, ironware, sugar, glass, and porcelain. At the same time most of the foods and raw materials required could be produced at home, and this rendered difficult the making of reciprocal trade agreements with adjacent agricultural countries for the exchange of manufactures for food and raw materials. Furthermore, access to distant markets was complicated by the inland position of the country. The Elbe River provided access to the Baltic, and the Danube to the Black Sea, and railway lines connected the country directly with the port of Trieste and with several of the main European centers. But the adequate use of these facilities for exports and imports depended on agreements with other powers. In respect to the use of waterways, there had long been international agreements. The Congress of Vienna of 1815 adopted the principle of freedom of navigation. In 1856 an international commission was formed for regulating the use of the Danube. The treaties of peace after the World War greatly extended the idea of international control of inland waterways, and particularly in the case of Czechoslovakia attempted to safeguard its interests by giving it representation on some of the commissions and by requiring Germany to extend free-port privileges at Hamburg and Stettin. But in November, 1936, the German government, in keeping with its general attack on the treaty system, denounced the clauses providing for the international control of navigation on rivers flowing through Germany. Czechoslovakia's position was further complicated by its racial diversity and by the land hunger and keen economic rivalry as well as political animosity of some of its neighbors.

## Economic Nationalism

The theory of nationalism which found expression in the wartime aspirations of the Czechs and Slovaks, the Poles, and other peoples, in President Wilson's Fourteen Points, and in some measure in the redrawing of frontiers after the World War, was self-determination on the basis of racial groups. The conception of a self-governing national group bound together by common ties of race, language, culture, and congenial political institutions, while admirable as an ideal, encountered grave obstacles. The ideal was reinforced, to be sure, in the Fourteen Points by a proposal for an international organization for the just and peaceful settlement of disputes and by the principle of freedom of trade for supplementing the economic life of the various autonomous national units.

The actual outcome was a hardly recognizable translation of these principles. There was a scramble for natural resources and strategic areas, with slight regard for ethnic frontiers, as seen in the struggles between Poland and Germany for the mineral resources of Upper Silesia and between Yugoslavia and Italy for Adriatic ports. The tracing of political frontiers even approximately in accord with ethnic boundaries, which were rarely clear-cut, necessarily restricted the economic basis of nationalism and made imperative a liberal system of international exchange and intimate economic co-operation in such matters as currency, transportation, and movement of population, if even the former low standards of living were to be maintained. But the more restricted were the natural resources and the economic foundations of nationalism, the more ambitious seemed to be the new nations for economic self-sufficiency. The causes were partly the racial antagonisms engendered by long periods of domination of minority groups, especially by the prewar governments of Austria-Hungary, Russia, and Germany. Nor can the earlier status of the Irish under British rule be overlooked as a factor in the economic nationalism of the Irish Free State. But there were many causes of restrictive policies and of diminished interchange, such as the disordered monetary systems, the difficulties incident to organizing administrative systems for supervising international relations, the desire to foster industries essential for war, the lack of means of payment of international balances, and the clamor of local producers for protection in the home markets.

Some of the obstacles in the way of international exchange between the Succession States of eastern Europe were mentioned in the discussion of postwar reconstruction. Many of these were incidental to the dismemberment of the Austro-Hungarian Empire. But without exception the lesser states of Europe, whether newly formed or in existence before the World War, adopted restrictive and regulatory measures, either by means of traditional tariffs or by quotas or by the depreciation of currencies or by rationing or by subsidies or by a combination of a number of methods.    Before the world depression began there were signs of a relaxation of restrictions, but after 1929 they became increasingly rigorous and were frequently necessary measures against production or export subsidies, depreciated currencies, and dumping.

These policies of the lesser states were essentially similar to the policies of the great powers and were in some cases designed as measures of defense against economic penetration and domination by the great powers.    The adoption of protective measures by the small states gave added significance to the protective system for a number of reasons.    The increased number of states with economic barriers added to the difficulties of production and trade, by virtue of the mere diversity of regulations and increased number of frontiers. The fact that the boundaries of many of the states severed natural economic units and cut across long-established channels of trade aggravated the maladjustments.    The multiplication of barriers in small areas was a reversion toward medieval localism in the control of economic life in an age when local self-sufficiency had given place to an unprecedented degree of interregional and international interdependence and division of labor.    Intensified and localized economic nationalism necessarily increased the friction and disorder, diminished the economies of regional specialization, and added to the menace of war.    Localized national sovereignties in areas of such intimate economic relations were inherently inconsistent alike with free trade and *laissez faire* and with a rational and co-ordinated system of economic control.

## International Agreements and Collective Security

Extreme nationalism was somewhat mitigated by a counter-tendency toward international agreements and by efforts to utilize the various international agencies.    These tendencies were discussed in relation to Europe as a whole in Chapter 37 on the economic aspects of internationalism.    In that connection reference was made, for example, to the Portorose Conference in 1921 of representatives of the Succession States.    Attempts were made later by the states of eastern Europe to work out a customs arrangement by which the agricultural states would admit the products of the industrial states, Czechoslovakia and Austria, on favorable terms in return for reciprocal concessions on agricultural products.    But

Czechoslovakia was unwilling to make such an arrangement if other industrialized countries, notably Germany, were included, while these other countries opposed any arrangement which excluded them. Germany made counterproposals to Austria for a customs union, but this was blocked by other signatories to the Treaty of Versailles, especially by France, as a violation of the treaty. Thus negotiations among the lesser states became enmeshed in the net of European policy as manipulated by the larger states.

But in spite of difficulties, certain significant arrangements among the lesser powers proved to be feasible. Limited agreements were made among the states of eastern Europe, such as reciprocal trade arrangements between Austria and Hungary. An arbitration agreement was signed in 1925, by Estonia, Finland, Latvia, and Poland, and an economic agreement affecting tariffs and other mutual interests was adopted in 1934 by Latvia, Lithuania, and Estonia. Belgium and Luxemburg in 1922 formed a customs union. The Netherlands and Belgium in 1932 agreed to a gradual reduction of tariffs. In 1930, representatives of the Netherlands, the Belgium-Luxemburg Union, Denmark, Sweden, and Norway signed a Convention of Economic Rapprochement for limiting the field of tariff restrictions and for mutual consideration of proposed changes. These regional agreements suffice to indicate a significant effort among the lesser states to mitigate the effects of the extreme economic nationalism of the postwar period.

The international agencies established after the World War were utilized extensively by the lesser states. The membership of the League of Nations and of the International Labor Organization included twenty-three smaller nations of Europe. The detailed fact-finding and administrative work of these agencies proved to be particularly helpful to the lesser states. The expense and duplication of effort of independent national agencies and the difficulties they would have encountered prevented unbiased fact finding and effective common action without central agencies. Through the international agencies much progress was made in dealing with tariff procedure, international transportation and communication, sanitation and public health, labor standards, the maintenance of rights of migratory workers in social insurance schemes, and numerous other important but relatively noncontroversial questions.

In regard to larger international problems and policies, notably the question of collective security, the lesser states at times exhibited

an independence of the great powers and took the lead in attempting
to maintain the League as an instrument for checking aggression
and maintaining the rights of members.   This was apparent in the
attitude of the League Assembly, in which all members of the
League are represented, toward Italy's attack on Ethiopia, a League
member.   But in most of the larger questions of policy the lesser
states tended to fall within the orbits of the great powers and to
vote in accord with these powers, especially on problems affecting
the maintenance or the alteration of the treaty system established
after the World War.

### Relations with the Great Powers

The new states were a joint creation of local nationalistic groups
and of support by the victorious nations in the World War.   Great
Britain and France attempted to draw these states into their orbits
by recognizing their independence, supporting them in most of their
territorial claims, and in many cases granting them financial aid.
A new French "system" was created by means of treaties with
Poland and the Little Entente (Czechoslovakia, Rumania, and
Yugoslavia), the countries which profited most by the territorial
readjustments.   In 1934 a treaty between Poland and Germany
recognized the existing territorial status for ten years, but the alliance with France was not abandoned.

Austria, Hungary, and Bulgaria lost heavily under the treaties
of peace and became spheres of influence for German and Italian
diplomats and merchants.   The League of Nations, supported by
France and Great Britain, undertook the financial rehabilitation of
Austria and Hungary, but the desire of these countries and of
Bulgaria to obtain revisions of the treaties of peace naturally tended
to align them with Germany or Italy.   But Italy supported France
and Great Britain in opposition to every move for union of Germany
and Austria, which was forbidden by the Treaty of Versailles.
German-Austrian rapprochement was based largely on the close
economic ties of the two countries — ties which were strengthened
by Austria's loss of vital industrial resources and trade connections
in the former Austro-Hungarian Empire and by the postwar growth
of Austrian agriculture.   But after the rise of the Nazis in Germany,
there was strong Austrian opposition to Germany, and Italian
influence gained ascendancy.   Austria became a victim of clashing
international ambitions and of the resulting internal discord.   The
clash of interests of the great powers in eastern Europe resembled

the prewar conflicts but assumed new forms associated on the one hand with the maintenance and on the other hand with the alteration of the postwar treaties.

The relations of Russia to the lesser states were strengthened by Russia's adoption of a system of autonomy within the Union of Soviet Socialist Republics and by a series of nonaggression pacts recognizing the independence of the new states and pledging with them and other states the use of peaceful methods for settling controversies. Special economic arrangements were also made, especially with some of the Baltic states, and in 1935 a mutual assistance pact was signed with Czechoslovakia. After Russia joined the League of Nations she ardently supported the League doctrine of collective security, notably in connection with efforts to prevent Italy's conquest of Ethiopia — a doctrine which naturally appealed to many of the weaker states. In the Spanish civil war of 1936 Russia agreed to a nonintervention pact but frankly expressed sympathy with the loyalist forces. Covert intervention by various countries in this internal Spanish conflict demonstrated the inclination of the great powers to direct the course of events in lesser countries to their own advantage.

## Liberalism and Fascism in the Lesser Countries

The terms "liberalism" and "Fascism" are here used to designate in broad terms differing methods of social adjustment. The origin of the Spanish civil war of 1936 and the attitudes of the great powers toward the struggle are significant illustrations of the essential differences between the two methods.

Before the World War, Spain had maintained her semifeudal institutions with relatively little change. The country was predominantly agricultural, although the valuable mineral resources had been extensively utilized, largely for export and by means of foreign financial aid. The agricultural system was dominated by aristocratic landlords, the peasants remaining for the most part uneducated and with an exceptionally low standard of living. During the war, agriculture flourished, industry expanded, and the standard of living somewhat improved. With the cessation of wartime demands and with the postwar depression came resistance on the part of the workers to unemployment and falling income. There was an insistent demand for the breaking up of large estates, for alteration of peasants' and farm workers' obligations to the landlords, and for industrial reforms and social legislation. The monarchy was overthrown, and dictatorial regimes alternated with administrations which made little more than gestures of reform. In February, 1936, however, a combination of groups known as the Popular Front won a decisive electoral victory on a definite program of reform.

Among the Popular Front groups were a comparatively small number of socialists, most of whom agreed to a policy of collaboration with the dominant nonsocialistic groups of the Popular Front. But the defeated parties of the Right attempted to discredit the entire Popular Front program as alien and communistic; and violent opposition of a Fascist nature culminated in a revolt by a large part of the professional army. The country was invaded by the garrisons from Morocco, aided by Moors.

Here was clearly a situation in which a minority attempted by force to prevent a lawfully elected government from carrying into effect the mandates of the electorate. Premier Blum, head of a similar Popular Front government in France (though agrarian and tax reforms and various other changes proposed in Spain had been accomplished more than a century earlier in France), recognized that to prevent Frenchmen from sending arms or other aid to the Spanish government was in effect an advantage to the rebels, who were in command of the professional army. But in view of the dangerous international situation, Premier Blum, aided by Great Britain, took the lead in the formulation and adoption of a general nonintervention agreement. Italy and Germany, on the other hand, while at length formally signing the agreement, gave legal recognition as well as extensive material aid to General Franco, the Fascist leader.

Outstanding among the lesser countries which maintained the liberal tradition were Switzerland, the Netherlands, Belgium, the Scandinavian countries, and Czechoslovakia. Most of the other countries maintained at least the forms of the liberal method but surrendered from time to time to dictatorial regimes. With few exceptions, however, these regimes avowed no intention to supplant, at least permanently, the liberal, democratic, or constitutional principle. In this respect they perhaps resembled the dictatorships of certain Latin-American countries more closely than the Fascist regimes of Italy and Germany, which boldly challenged the principle of liberalism and claimed for Fascism inherent superiority, permanence, and even ultimate universality.

There were two main factors which accounted for the rise of

regimes either frankly Fascist in principle or merely dictatorial in an opportunist sense.   One of these was the long-continued subjection of the people to stresses and strains and to the pressure of problems which seemed to be beyond solution, at least by the methods of tolerant discussion and popular decision.   Another condition was lack of self-governing experience and of cultural and economic standards required by the liberal method.   Without exception one or both of these conditions prevailed in Germany and Italy as well as in the various lesser countries where Fascist or dictatorial regimes found footing.   For the first of these conditions the liberal countries were in part responsible by virtue of their failure to put into effect the principles of liberalism in their postwar dealings with the defeated countries.   The second condition was particularly characteristic of Poland and of most of the countries of eastern Europe. These countries were largely agricultural, with illiterate and oppressed peasant classes dominated by landlords who were themselves the victims of inefficient methods of production, extreme economic nationalism, and the forces of world depression.

## Land Reform

In almost every country of Europe after the World War efforts were made to simplify land tenures and to promote the ownership of land by those who tilled the soil.   Aside from the changes in Russia, described in Chapters 34 and 38, land reform was notably important in the new Baltic states, Poland, and eastern Europe.   Opposition to plans for dismemberment of the large estates, private and ecclesiastical, in Spain was a principal cause of the Fascist revolt there in 1936.   In western Europe it was only in the Iberian Peninsula that medieval landlordism survived both the storms of the French Revolution and the rising tide of industrialism.   But in Russia, in eastern Europe, and even in the Polish portions of Germany and parts of Italy, agriculture retained many of its earlier characteristics of land tenure, class relations, and even methods of production.

In the new states formerly controlled by Russia, Germany, and Austria-Hungary, noblemen of Russian, German, Austrian, and Hungarian origin had obtained ownership of much of the land, while large additional tracts had been granted to the church. There were also extensive crown lands.   Public acquisition and redistribution of these lands were therefore possible by the new national governments with a minimum of resistance.   The seizure of estates by the Russian peasants without compensation to the landlords inspired hopes in the peasantry of adjacent countries and at the same time forced from the landlords and governments promises of reform.

Land was promised to the peasants of Rumania in 1917, largely for the purpose of placating them and maintaining their morale during the war. The dramatic initiation of reform is described by a Rumanian scholar, Dr. David Mitrany. In 1917, when the Allied eastern front was virtually in collapse, the new Russian slogan of "'peace and land' was running like wildfire along the lines." King Ferdinand visited the front and addressed the troops: "Sons of peasants, who, with your own hands, have defended the soil on which you were born, on which your lives have been passed, I, your king, tell you that besides the great recompense of victory which will assure for every one of you the nation's gratitude, you have earned the right of being masters, in a large measure, of that soil upon which you fought. Land will be given you. I, your king, am the first to set the example; and you will also take a large part in public affairs."

The concentration of ownership in prewar Rumania is indicated roughly by the fact that approximately 50 per cent of the land was owned by less than 1 per cent of the total number of proprietors. The status of tenants and of many small owners was semiservile. The land reform measures reduced the aggregate number of hectares (a hectare is 2.471 acres) in holdings of more than 100 hectares from 3,398,000 to 621,000, and increased the aggregate number of hectares in holdings up to 100 hectares from 4,593,000 to 7,370,000. In the newly acquired territories a similar transformation occurred. The land was not confiscated, nor was it given to the peasants. The landlords were compensated, and the peasants were burdened with heavy taxes and long-term debts.

In Czechoslovakia many of the large estates were traceable to the confiscations of the seventeenth century, when the Austrian Hapsburgs rewarded their adherents, during the wars of religion, with gifts of land seized from Czech subjects. In 1919 the new government passed a law transferring to the state the titles of all estates of more than 150 hectares (370 acres) of arable land or of more than 250 hectares whether arable or not. Compensation was arranged for, and owners were permitted to retain estates variable in size. Most of the arable land not retained by the landlords was allotted to the former tenants and workers under conditions making possible its purchase from the state but providing for public supervision to protect the new owners' titles and at the same time to require efficient use of the land. Forests were retained as public property, either national or local.

Land reform in Poland was complicated by the diverse conditions in the several areas formerly ruled by Russia, Germany, and Austria-Hungary. The area of largest estates was in the east, and it was there also that the land was most extensively divided into fragments or strips in "checkerboard" fashion — a medieval survival which seriously interfered with efficient farming. The many types of agriculture and stages of economic development also complicated the plans for reform. In 1920 a law was passed for limiting the size of estates, the stated maximum ranging from 60 hectares (148 acres) to 300 hectares in the various regions. This law remained largely inoperative, and a new act was passed in 1925, providing for a gradual process of expropriation with compensation and for gradual allocation to the peasants. The plan also called for the elimination of such earlier customary rights as pasturage on fallow land, use of timber, etc. — rights which had frequently been in the interest of the peasants. Efforts were made to consolidate small parcels or strips into unified holdings and in other ways to promote efficient farming.

Changes in the new Baltic states are illustrated by the experience of Estonia. Before the World War more than half of the land was owned by about 250 families of German origin. Most of the large estates were tilled by hired laborers or by semiservile tenants under conditions not far removed from those of medieval serfs. There were also many share-croppers, especially on the smaller estates. In 1919 the new government passed a law which established state ownership not only of the estates of the nobles but also of lands which had belonged to the Russian government and rented lands belonging to the church. The former landlords were permitted to retain farms of limited size and were compensated for equipment and livestock. In 1926 a law was passed granting limited compensation also for the land. The allocation of lands gave preference to the workers who were already occupiers, each peasant being allotted no more than he could normally cultivate without hired help. Provision was made for purchase from the state, subject to regulations for promoting good husbandry.

Land reform measures were also carried out in Yugoslavia, Greece, and Hungary, and to a slight extent in Austria, although in postwar Austria large estates formed a comparatively small proportion of agricultural land. In western Europe, the Irish Free State carried out and extended earlier land reforms, notably by the land act of 1923, which vested ownership of tenanted lands not already purchased by the tenants in the Land Commission for retransfer to tenants under revised purchase plans. The Scandinavian countries, where there had long been a comparatively independent, vigorous, and prosperous class of small farmers, made extensive further progress in land reform with a greater emphasis than in eastern Europe on co-operative methods.

In most of the countries where land reforms were carried out, compensation to the former owners imposed a heavy burden of taxes on the peasants; and the purchase of the land and of improvements, equipment, and livestock created debts largely in the form of long-term fixed costs. Taxes and debts in turn required production for markets in place of subsistence farming. The reduction of perquisites in kind, as the elimination in parts of Poland of rights of pasturage and use of forests, intensified the demand for cash income from crops. At the same time, the restrictions on international trade, the curtailment of markets during the depression, and the extreme decline of prices added to the burdens of fixed costs. The resulting discontent was aggravated in many regions by dissatisfaction with the extent of the reforms and the methods of administering the laws and by the difficulties of developing efficient methods of production and marketing on the basis of small-scale farming. These circumstances, combined with the desire of the landlords to retain their political power and to regain their economic privileges or to sabotage the reform movement, were among the principal causes of dictatorial tendencies in eastern Europe and even in Germany and Italy.

The beneficial effects of land reform policies were thus gravely restricted during the difficult transitional period, and the ultimate results were unforeseeable. There was nevertheless a basis for the view expressed in 1928, at a meeting of the International Institute of Agriculture: "The agrarian change, which offers the necessary basis for a better social order, will no doubt give to the twentieth century one of its characteristic marks."

## The Evolution of Liberal Economic Controls

The efforts of France and Great Britain to adapt the historic principle of liberalism to the difficult conditions of the postwar period are described in Chapter 40. Many of the smaller countries also made significant contributions in this field. The most distinctive and successful efforts were made by the Scandinavian countries, and especially by Sweden. Swedish policies during the world depression included the abandonment of the gold standard and the adoption of monetary controls for preventing extreme fluctuations in prices; but these measures merely supplemented a general program which, in main outlines, the government and the co-operative societies had been carrying on during most of the post-war period. These policies included the curbing of monopoly prices by co-operative production and distribution, and an expansion of production and employment by public works involving a large measure of socialized investment.

The numerous co-operative agencies utilized by farmers, especially in Denmark, in connection with their purchases, their credit needs, the processing and marketing of their products, the maintenance of standards, and even the regulation of production, were primarily for reducing their costs and maintaining a moderate margin of profit. These agencies were designed not to supplant private enterprise but to maintain it on a profitable basis. But enterprise thus conducted was radically different from the traditional conception of individualism and free competition, and its success marked a significant evolution, indeed a transformation, of economic liberalism.

In other fields of co-operation from which profits were eliminated, namely, wholesale and retail trade and industrial production, there were also significant developments in the Scandinavian countries. One of these was a closer integration of urban and rural groups in the membership and activities of the societies. The consumers' groups, formerly made up largely of urban workers, attracted increasing numbers of farmers. The Swedish Co-operative Union joined forces with the Farmers' Union to resist the organized opposition of livestock dealers to the Farmers' Union, and provided the farmers with a dependable market for their products. In 1928 the two organizations collaborated in the operation of a fertilizer factory for the purpose of breaking down monopolistic control of fertilizer prices.

This latter episode illustrates a second important feature of Scandinavian co-operation — the distinctive role played by co-operative production. There were two reasons for ventures into this field: either to attack monopolistic controls of important articles required by their members or to perform essential functions, such as the supplying of housing facilities, in which private enterprise for profit had failed. The Swedish Co-operative Union entered several branches of production in addition to the manufacture of fertilizers. It materially reduced prices and raised the standards of quality, not only for its members but for the country as a whole, by successfully engaging in the baking industry, the milling of flour, and the manufacturing of shoes, tires, rubber overshoes, and other articles. It even broke down, in Sweden, the powerful international control and monopolistic prices of electric lamps by successfully operating an electric lamp factory. Co-operative methods, supplemented by public aid, succeeded in meeting the serious housing shortage in Sweden and in raising housing standards while reducing housing costs. The grave inadequacy of the milk supply system of Stockholm was remedied by co-operative action.

A third distinctive feature of co-operation in Scandinavia was the formation there of the first international co-operative organization which functioned not as a mere association but as a business enterprise. This was the Scandinavian Co-operative Wholesale Society, composed of the Swedish, Danish, Norwegian, and Finnish wholesale groups.

In the field of enterprise operated by governmental agencies, the Scandinavian countries made perhaps few distinctive contributions. As in some other countries, the governments engaged in the production of power but not on a monopolistic basis. The main purposes were the control of power production and of rates by the force of example and of competitive cost, and the promotion of the wider use of electricity, especially in the rural districts, by the aid of co-operative groups. In a similar manner the Swedish government engaged in the extremely important industries connected with the utilization of the forests, and by example as well as formal regulation promoted the conservation and efficient use of the forests by private enterprise. The iron mines, although largely owned by the government, were leased to an operating company in which the government retained half ownership.

Private enterprise for profit remained, in the Scandinavian countries, the main form of economic activity. Its fields of activity and its methods were restricted in comparatively slight degree by legal prohibitions and regulations. Control was more largely an accompaniment of positive action, by co-operative societies and public agencies, at strategic points of monopolistic price or natural resource utilization. The positive action assumed the form of demonstrations of their capacity to meet economic needs more efficiently than was being done by private enterprise.

In the relations of government to business a significant development was a form of corporate organization first extensively utilized in connection with the liquor and tobacco industries of Sweden. Public monopolistic corporations were formed for these industries. Some of the stock, paying limited dividends, was owned privately, and the direct management of the corporations was private, but subject to public intervention. Most of the profits went to the government. A similar plan was applied to the radio broadcasting industry. It was desired, especially in the case of the liquor and tobacco industries, to obtain revenues for meeting the costs of social legislation without taxation which, if added to profits, would result in higher prices. But it was held that direct governmental administration of such enterprises for profit, or even on a cost basis, would lack the initiative and flexibility of a nonpolitical corporation charged with the actual administration but subject to ultimate public supervision and responsibility.

Later organizations in Great Britain somewhat resembling these Swedish corporations included the Central Electricity Board, the British Broadcasting Company, and the London Passenger Transport Board. The general principle underlying such corporations was approved by virtually all political parties both in Sweden and in Great Britain. Conservative groups opposed the application of the principle except in narrowly restricted fields. Other groups favored its more extensive use as a means of obtaining the benefits of socialized investment and ultimate public responsibility without the disadvantages of the direct administration of business enterprises by political agencies.

# CHAPTER 43

# THE CHANGING WORLD

—◆—

## The Individual and the World of " Law "

The nineteenth century was dominated by concepts of law which restricted within narrow limits the importance of the individual. The individual was held to be free, but his action could only accomplish a prescribed and foreordained destiny. The nineteenth century had its Utopians, but the Utopians were not representative of their age. Even the Marxian philosophy was more largely concerned with the evils of capitalism than with the analysis of the constructive problems of organization in a socialist state. Furthermore, the doctrine of necessity underlying the materialistic interpretation of history tended to minimize the importance of individual choices and decisions. In a world dominated by great forces, the individual seemed to count for little. Scientific socialism, like the economic science of the time, formulated laws which reduced the decisions of individuals to some kind of mechanistic reaction. Thought and judgment might seem to be a free expression of the individual mind, but action was presumed to be dominated by external forces which lay outside the control of any human agency.

Classical economic thought had no positive theory of statecraft. Little attempt was made to explain the origins of institutions, and it was held that the fullest utilization of resources would be achieved through the efforts of each individual to seek his own immediate welfare. This concept of policy rested upon assumptions about competition which were without foundation. In actual practice, statesmen even of the most liberal turn of mind pursued policies which involved considerable elements of social control. But these acts of policy were not characteristic of the age. The most typical expression of the attitude of economists toward public policy is to be found in the controversy on banking policy in Great Britain in the first half of the century. Neither the Currency school nor the Banking school felt that the Bank of England should attempt to control the money market. The Banking school maintained that the Bank could wisely supply all the "legitimate" needs of traders. A cautious scrutiny of each individual loan was all that was necessary, they said. They recognized that there should be no discounting of accommodation bills or of any paper that did not originate in a bona fide transaction. Faithful performance of such a routine would in their minds achieve the highest welfare of the community.

The Currency school held no higher opinion of the banker's task, but the routine they advised was of a different kind. This group feared an overexpansion of credit. They held that this could certainly be avoided if the Bank were not allowed to issue notes freely. By setting a rigid limit to the note issue, all changes in the volume of currency would be produced by changes in the amount of gold in circulation. The monetary system would therefore behave precisely as if there were no bank notes. The banker would be unable to overexpand, and the money market would be undisturbed by individual acts of judgment. This theory involved a number of errors which need not concern us here. The characteristic point lies in the notion that banking would not in any case involve difficult judgments of policy of recognized importance to the community. The automatic gold standard seemed desirable not only because it was honest, but because it would "necessarily" produce the best results.

The Bank Act of 1844 was a faithful attempt to give explicit effect to the concepts of the Currency school. Three years later, in the midst of a serious crisis, the act was suspended. The Bank of England extended its issues of notes and assumed responsibility for the money market. Ever since that crisis, it has been more and more clearly recognized that central banking is not a mere routine business, but an agency for the deliberate and continuous control of the credit structure.

This development of conscious credit control marks the first great break between practice and the classical concept of the automatic character of market adjustments. The importance of the change in point of view was not recognized at the time; perhaps it is not very clearly recognized now. But the policy of the Bank of England after 1847 involves a complete abandonment of the fundamental notion of seeking social welfare through essentially routine adjustments of individual interests. The Bank began to work directly and consciously for the welfare of the industrial and commercial community which it served. The "guiding hand" which Adam Smith recognized as a vital factor in human affairs was at last associated with concrete individuals seeking social rather than individual ends.

Marxian socialism was itself a characteristic expression of nineteenth-century thought. Like the classical economic theory, it laid little emphasis upon the conscious acts of policy of individuals. The materialistic interpretation of history set forth a rigid concept of determinism which left individuals literally powerless in the grasp of relentless forces operating over long periods of time. Even the adepts find it difficult to reconcile the evolutionary elements of Marxian thought with the revolutionary aspects of the teaching. If the impending doom of the capitalist order were indeed foreordained, it is not easy to see why a revolution need be so elaborately prepared. But it is not necessary to attempt any reconciliation of these elements. These divergent trends of thought were never fully reconciled in the writings of Marx, and his followers ultimately divided into two groups. Attention was concentrated upon the criticism of capitalistic society rather than upon the structure or policies of an actual socialist commonwealth.

The newer thought has been dramatized most effectively by the Soviet leaders, and the general outlines of the first and second Five-Year Plans have captured public imagination to an extraordinary degree. There has been some tendency to take it for granted that social planning must necessarily assume the bureaucratic form characteristic of the authoritarian states, and all these versions of planned economies inevitably seem to be far removed from a free society. This is an excessively narrow position. The broad change in the concepts of public policy involves only the acceptance of the notion that social welfare and the best utilization of resources demand deliberate and conscious acts of judgment and policy. There is no longer any issue between planning and not planning. The vital problems are the method of planning, the choice of objectives, and the establishment of acceptable standards of social welfare and resource utilization. Planning is already far advanced in some of the great free societies, but it is not the same kind of planning that we find in Russia.

The appointment of the Dominions Royal Commission in Great Britain in 1912 was an important indication of tendencies of thought there. The Commission was instructed to investigate the resources of the self-governing dominions and the best means of promoting their development. The work of the Commission marked a great advance toward co-ordination of economic policy within the Empire, though little was done to establish any formal or continuous agencies for action. A more notable innovation in policy came with the appointment of the Committee on Reconstruction in 1916. Al-

though the direct incentive was furnished by the anticipated difficulty of demobilization, the range of work was broad.  The committee undertook to formulate policies for the adjustment of labor
relations, for the more effective conservation of primary resources,
and for the reorganization of basic industries.

### The Meaning of Economic Planning

The studies of the British Committee on Reconstruction have
led to the passage of several broad statutes providing for the gradual
introduction of new modes of organization in the field of labor and
industry.  The Whitley Councils, the Electricity Supply Acts,
and the Coal Mines Acts are the most notable results.  The attempts
to deal with the mining crisis failed.  The Electricity Supply Acts
finally resulted in the establishment of the comprehensive system
of supply already described.  The Whitley Councils were established in several industries, with results that were not very impressive.  These and other schemes have certain common features
which are significant.  There is no emphasis upon any large extension of government ownership.  When controls are established,
the controls are exercised by administrative boards whose ownership
of basic resources is narrowly restricted.  There is a great increase
in the centralization of authority, but a delicate balance is preserved
between the central authorities and the local bodies or enterprises.
Some of the new authorities are organized as corporations, rather
than government departments.

Only an extended survey of the activity of the central government
over a large field could adequately reveal the changes in the direction
of economic and social policy in Great Britain.  There is nothing
to suggest the "planned economic system" that is commonly
discussed in contemporary literature, but there can be no doubt of
the great increase in planned action.  It is hardly too much to say
that we can already see the primary outlines of the new social
structure that is rapidly emerging.  There is nothing anywhere
in evidence that is inconsistent with the continuance of a free
society.  It promises to become a system of planning by compart-
ments carried out by various public and private agencies.  Central
authorities of various kinds will possess more power than any such
officers have held in the past, but the general structure presents
few elements of novelty.  The novelty lies not so much in the
details of the framework as in the point of view which pervades the
whole system.

## The Prestige of Europe in the World of the Future

The nineteenth century was marked by great changes in the relations among the countries of Europe and in the relations between Europe and the world at large. These changes have already been discussed. The comparison of the current production of energy with the reserves of primary energy suggests important changes in the future. The reserves of primary energy for the world as a whole are shown in the following table:

THE WORLD RESERVES OF PRIMARY ENERGY, CALCULATED IN MILLIONS OF TONS OF COAL [1]

|  | Coal | Oil | Water Power | Total | Per Cent of Total |
|---|---|---|---|---|---|
| Germany | 240,715 | 15.0 | 8,000 | 248,730.0 | 2.86 |
| England | 189,533 | 12.0 | 3,400 | 192,945.0 | 2.22 |
| France | 32,406 | — | 32,000 | 64,406.0 | .74 |
| Russia [2] | 142,245 | 1,571.4 | 8,000 | 151,816.4 | 1.75 |
| Other Europe | 255,408 | 235.4 | 181,200 | 436,843.4 | 5.06 |
| Total Europe | 860,307 | 1,833.8 | 232,600 | 1,094,740.8 | 12.63 |
| United States | 2,735,527 | 1,618.6 | 140,000 | 2,877,145.6 | 33.07 |
| Canada | 667,095 | 223.1 | 104,000 | 771,318.0 | 8.91 |
| Mexico | — | 1,045.0 | 24,000 | 25,045.0 | .28 |
| Other America | 32,580 | 2,175.0 | 212,400 | 247,155.1 | 2.85 |
| Total America | 3,435,202 | 5,061.7 | 480,400 | 3,920,663.7 | 45.11 |
| China | 995,228 | 308.6 | 80,000 | 1,075,536.6 | 12.37 |
| Japan | 7,570 | 277.2 | 56,000 | 63,847.2 | .73 |
| British India } Dutch East Indies } | 77,445 | 927.1 | 29,600 60,000 | 167,972.1 | 1.93 |
| Siberia [2] | 1,077,990 | — | 204,000 | 1,281,990.0 | 14.77 |
| Other Asia | 23,068 | 1,312.4 | 62,800 | 87,180.4 | 1.00 |
| Total Asia | 2,181,301 | 2,825.3 | 492,400 | 2,676,526.3 | 30.80 |
| Australia | 148,709 | — | 26,000 | 174,709.0 | 2.02 |
| Africa | 57,229 | 213.7 | 760,000 | 817,442.7 | 9.44 |
| Total World | 6,682,748 | 9,934.5 | 1,991,400 | 8,684,082.5 | 100.00 |

Before the regional distribution of power resources is discussed, it should be observed that the present positions of oil and water power are profoundly changed. Water power now provides only

[1] Adapted from Meisner, M., *Weltmontanstatistik*, Stuttgart, 1932, II, p. 41. For description of the modifications and corrections of Meisner's table, see pp. 670–673.

[2] As known Jan. 1, 1934. See Mikhaylov, N., *Soviet Geography*, Leningrad, 1935, p. 33.

7.6 per cent of the current supply of energy, but the reserves of water power constitute 23.3 per cent of the total reserve of energy. The computed value of the water-power reserve is perhaps high, but the potential water power of Asia is less adequately reported than the coal. Preliminary estimates of Russian engineers in Siberia would add largely to the reserves of water power, but the reports are still so vague that it did not seem wise to add them to the table. If accepted, recent reports would add the energy of 916,000 million tons of coal to the water powers of Siberia. In all probability the water power of Africa is understated. On the whole, therefore, it seems clear that water power will be a more important source of energy than it has been in the past. The reserves of oil will seem very small. This accords with currently accepted views of experts, but all agree that estimates of oil reserves are very uncertain. The general implication of the table is fairly representative of expert opinion. The reserves of oil are small and are likely soon to be exhausted. New stocks will undoubtedly be uncovered but none presume it likely that oil will figure largely as a producer of primary energy.

The regional distribution of reserves differs notably from the present production of energy by regions. Europe, with 12.63 per cent of the total reserve, produced in 1928 42.3 per cent of the energy. Asia with 30.8 per cent of the reserves produced 6.7 per cent of the energy. There is, therefore, a strong presumption in favor of a profound displacement of economic activity between Europe and Asia. Asia will become relatively more important. Europe need not become less prosperous, but her place in the economic world will be different. Africa will become more important than she is now, but the differences will not be so striking. South America seems to have little prospect of an important future. The history of South America is an eloquent commentary on the economic importance of resources and ease of access. Though generally settled earlier than North America, South America has made little progress in industry.

If we examine the position of particular countries, it appears that for European Russia the relative amount of energy now produced is greater than her relative stock of power resources. Siberia is clearly a region that is as yet very inadequately developed. Siberia, with 14.77 per cent of the total resources, now produces only 0.2 per cent of the present annual output of power. If we credit Siberia with water powers recently reported, she would have

22.9 per cent of the total power reserve. This is, indeed, a vast opportunity. It means, however, that the Russia of the future will be more specifically an Asiatic than a European power.

China is likewise a country of vast opportunity. Credited in 1913 with reserves of 12.37 per cent of the world total, she produced in 1928 only 0.9 per cent. Recent surveys reveal serious exaggerations in earlier estimates. Reports in 1929 give much smaller figures for reserves of coal. These returns seem to be over-cautious and not comparable with figures for other countries.[1] Japan, like European Russia, already produces power out of proportion to her reserves. There are, therefore, strong grounds for presuming that the present rate of development in insular Japan is not likely long to continue. The lure of Manchuria can easily be understood.

How remote is the ultimate equilibrium between power production and power resources? No question is more hopelessly insoluble. We must remember, however, that two generations were sufficient to bring the United States to the position of a maturely developed industrial power, and that in the case of Germany the period of transition was somewhat shorter. It is idle to speculate, but it must be evident that the industrialization of China and Siberia need not be exceedingly remote. Once this development is far advanced, the position of Europe in the world will be profoundly changed. Economic changes will carry in their train political stresses and strains. The narrowest concept of self-interest would seem to show that the nations of Europe have urgent need of peace and security at home.

[1] "The Coal Reserves of China," *World Power Conference, Tokyo, 1929*, Vol. I, pp. 319–351.

# APPENDIX

## THE SCALES AND THE PROPERTIES OF THE SEMILOGARITHMIC GRAPH

Several systems of graphic presentation have been developed. Each system has distinctive properties because in each case the scales are really designed to facilitate specific kinds of comparisons. Arithmetic scales make it easy to compare magnitudes; logarithmic scales make it possible to compare rates of change. When graphic methods are used, it is essential to use the scales that are appropriate to the kinds of comparisons it is desirable to make. The choice of scales can never be a matter of indifference. For some purposes, the arithmetic scales are unsuitable; for other purposes, the logarithmic scales will be unsuitable. Analysis of the problems of growth shows that the rate of change is the most important feature of series of statistics that are to be used as a measure of growth. For this reason, the analysis of historical statistics requires the use of a logarithmic scale for the vertical axis of the graph. As intervals of time must be treated as constant increments, the horizontal axis remains an arithmetic scale. This form of graph is commonly described as the "semilogarithmic graph," and at times as a "ratio chart."

The general features of the scale are shown in the accompanying diagram. In this scale the distance from 1 to any given number is equal to the logarithm of the number. Expressed in terms of the values of equal spaces, any given unit of length on the scale measures equal ratios for all portions of the scale. The linear distances from 1 to 2, from 2 to 4, and from 4 to 8 are all equal. Similarly, the distances from 1 to 3 and from 3 to 9 are equal. If greater length is necessary in the vertical dimension, the sequence of rulings from 1 to 10 is repeated, but the values are increased by ten because the base line of this series is ten. The coefficients of the second series would be 10, 20, 30, 40, 50, 60, 70, 80, 90, 100. The scale may be extended to any desired length, but the coefficients always increase at the stated ratios. Different actual values may be given the scale by using a different unit as base; the higher values remain multiples of the base in the ratio indicated. With values other than 1 or a simple fraction, the intermediate values sometimes become confusing. Five and its multiples can be used without inconvenience, but odd numbers are likely to result in serious error or inconvenience in plotting items. It is not essential that the various series plotted on a given graph should be plotted in terms of a single scale. The curves can be compared only in respect of their slopes, and as these are identical for all positions on the graph, the precise location of any given curve is a matter of indifference. The curves in the graphs on page 15 were plotted in terms of values which avoided confusing intersections. The general principles hold for any length of the vertical scale; equal distances on the scale represent equal ratios of change. Consequently, straight lines on a semilogarithmic graph represent growth at a constant rate of change. The steeper the slope of the line, the greater the rate of change.

This property of the graph makes it possible to study the rates of change in a given series of items or among different series. When the rates of change vary, the movement must be conceived as a continuous curve. If the points are connected with straight lines, the graph represents the chords of the various arcs of which the curve is composed. This common practice has advantages, but the meaning of the graph should be clearly present to the mind.

The semilogarithmic graph does not admit of any comparison between specific magnitudes, whether we attempt to compare different items in a given series or items in different series. As it is frequently necessary to compare magnitudes in different series, separate graphs must be made for that purpose. Bar graphs on arithmetic scales are suitable to such a purpose and they cannot be misleading, as they emphasize the fact that the comparison involves only the condition at a given moment of time.

The errors involved in the use of the arithmetic scale in place of the semilogarithmic scale are not always of the same magnitude. Both axes of the scale are involved. The errors are small if the period of time involved is relatively short, five or ten years, and the horizontal axis relatively large in proportion to the vertical axis. Similarly, if the values of the items in the series are all of the same general order of magnitude, the errors are small. Confusion in respect to the use of the two types of graph is undoubtedly due to the large number of graphs that fall within this general class. The widespread practice of using only a portion of the arithmetic scale is an additional factor in fostering the use of arithmetic scales for purposes that strictly call for the semilogarithmic scale. The elements of error rapidly become serious as the length of the time period increases, and as the range of difference between the items becomes greater. For periods of fifty and one hundred years, the curves of the arithmetic graph are hopelessly misleading.

The extensive use of index numbers creates a special problem, which emphasizes in a different way the special properties of the semilogarithmic scale. If an arithmetic scale is used in plotting index numbers, the slope and shape of the curve will be different for every possible base. If the semilogarithmic scale is used, the slope and shape of the curve will be the same irrespective of the base used. This will be readily apparent from the simplest possible numerical illustration. Suppose that we have a series of prices for a given commodity for moments at equal intervals of time: if the prices are 25, 50, 100, 200, four different series of index numbers can be constructed, using each year as a base.

| I | II | III | IV |
|-----|-----|-----|------|
| 100 | 50 | 25 | 12.5 |
| 200 | 100 | 50 | 25 |
| 400 | 200 | 100 | 50 |
| 800 | 400 | 200 | 100 |

As index numbers, all these series have equal claims upon our attention, though experience with the practical difficulty involved has created a preference for using as base some value intermediate between the extremes. The choice of a base year is of palpable importance if arithmetic comparisons are made. The curves are profoundly different in character and the arithmetic differences correspondingly wide in their range. But when plotted on a semilogarithmic chart, these four series yield straight lines of equal slope located at different positions on the figure. As we know that the position of the curve is a matter of indifference, the semilogarithmic graph tells us the same story for all the series. The index number series are equivalent. This graph, therefore, possesses at least the merit of yielding a certain result, and it implies correctly that this result is the only meaning that can safely be read from the index numbers. They can tell us only the relative differences between the various items in a series. Expressed in graphic form on a semilogarithmic scale, the index number series reveals the only true meaning that it can possess. The relatives of the series express relations only and not amounts.

As in growth series, there are circumstances in which the errors of the arithmetic graph are not very serious. When the time period is short and the differences in the range of items is small, the errors are not serious. But in the case of index numbers this last condition is never really fulfilled. The difference between the largest and smallest items is commonly altogether too large to make it safe to present the series of relatives in arithmetic form. It is difficult to avoid the conclusion that the use of graphic methods of analysis has been seriously retarded by indifference to the properties of the various types of graphs.

## Numerical Values of the Primary Functions of the Semilogarithmic Graph

The emphasis upon rates of change in the semilogarithmic graph makes it possible to compare many different series in respect to the rate of change. Different magnitudes cannot be compared directly unless they can be reduced to similar units, and consequently the range of comparison upon arithmetic graphs is really very limited. It is seldom possible to make comparisons between the curves on different graphs. When the logarithmic scale is used, comparisons of the relative rates of change may be made for an entire series of graphs if care has been taken to use comparable scales, and the properties of the scale make it a simple matter to preserve comparability over an extensive series of graphs. It is only necessary to maintain a fixed proportion between the arithmetic scale of years and the distance between 1 and 10 on the logarithmic scale. The nature of the units used in plotting items on the vertical scale merely affects the position of the curve on the graph and does not alter the slopes of the chords drawn between selected points on the curve. Every different ratio between years and the distance 1–10 on the logarithmic scale produces a different scale for the graph as a whole, but the values of the scale are constant for all numerical expressions of a given ratio. Thus, if we take the distance 1–10 on the logarithmic scale as equal to the distance for 100 years the values of the graph are the same for all values of the distance 1–10.

The values of the slopes in rates per cent per year can be obtained from the larger compound interest tables by plotting the amount of 1 for the various rates per cent.   The values of the angles may be obtained by use of tables of trigonometric functions, so that slopes may be measured with a protractor if that method is more convenient than direct comparison of the graph with a scale of numbered slopes.   A small scale of slopes is shown in the figure below.

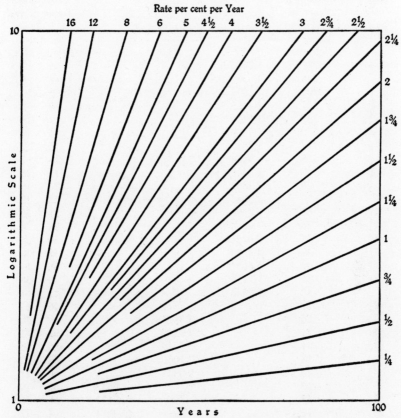

Rates of Change in Per Cent per Year, Shown by Slopes Anywhere on a Semi-logarithmic Graph in Which the Distance 1–10 on the Logarithmic Scale Is the Same as the Distance for 100 Years on the Horizontal Arithmetic Scale.

The following table of values gives also the number of years required to double the value of 1 at the designated rate of increase. The rates of increase are relatively small quantities, and as the compound interest functions are relatively unfamiliar to many, the length of this time interval is likely to bring better realization of the full significance of these rates of change.

### VALUES OF THE PRIMARY FUNCTIONS OF THE SEMILOGARITHMIC GRAPH

When $y = \log .10$
$x = 100$ years
$x = y$

| Rate of Increase Per Cent per Year | Number of Years in Which the Value of 1 Doubles | Value of 1 at the End of | | | Slope of the Linear Trend as Value of the Angle: | |
|---|---|---|---|---|---|---|
| | | 100 Yrs. | 50 Yrs. | 20 Yrs. | Degrees | Min. |
| $\frac{1}{4}$ | 277 | 1.2836 | | | 6 | 10 |
| $\frac{7}{24}$ | 238 | 1.3380 | | | 7 | 8 |
| $\frac{1}{3}$ | 208 | 1.3948 | | | 8 | 13 |
| $\frac{5}{12}$ | 167 | 1.5155 | | | 10 | 9 |
| $\frac{1}{2}$ | 139 | 1.6466 | | | 12 | 18 |
| $\frac{7}{12}$ | 120 | 1.7889 | | | 14 | 2 |
| $\frac{5}{8}$ | 112 | 1.8646 | | | 15 | 7 |
| $\frac{2}{3}$ | 105 | 1.9434 | | | 16 | 7 |
| $\frac{3}{4}$ | 93 | 2.1110 | | | 17 | 23 |
| $\frac{7}{8}$ | 80 | 2.3862 | | | 20 | 46 |
| 1 | 70 | 2.7048 | | | 23 | 25 |
| $1\frac{1}{8}$ | 62 | 3.0609 | | | 25 | 56 |
| $1\frac{1}{4}$ | 56 | 3.4634 | | | 28 | 20 |
| $1\frac{3}{8}$ | 51 | 3.9182 | | | 30 | 35 |
| $1\frac{1}{2}$ | 47 | 4.4320 | | | 32 | 50 |
| $1\frac{3}{4}$ | 40 | 5.6681 | | | 36 | 59 |
| 2 | 36 | 7.2446 | | | 40 | 38 |
| $2\frac{1}{4}$ | 32 | 9.2540 | | | 41 | 1 |
| $2\frac{1}{2}$ | 29 | | 3.4371 | | 46 | 53 |
| $2\frac{3}{4}$ | 26 | | 3.8823 | | 49 | 38 |
| 3 | 24 | | 4.3839 | | 52 | 1 |
| $3\frac{1}{2}$ | 21 | | 5.5849 | | 56 | 10 |
| 4 | 18 | | 7.1066 | | 59 | 40 |
| $4\frac{1}{2}$ | 16 | | 9.0326 | | 62 | 21 |
| 5 | 15 | | | 2.6532 | 64 | 40 |
| $5\frac{1}{2}$ | 13 | | | 2.9177 | 66 | 36 |
| 6 | 12 | | | 3.2071 | 68 | 22 |
| $6\frac{1}{2}$ | 11 + | | | 3.5236 | 69 | 57 |
| 7 | 10 + | | | 3.8696 | 71 | 10 |
| $7\frac{1}{2}$ | 9 + | | | 4.2478 | 72 | 17 |
| 8 | 9 | | | 4.6609 | 73 | 20 |
| $8\frac{1}{2}$ | 8 + | | | 5.1120 | 74 | 14 |

# SELECT BIBLIOGRAPHY

The following titles have been selected with a view to affording the reader an adequate and significant guide to the basic literature in this field. Emphasis has been placed upon the more recent works, and upon secondary treatises rather than sources. The older literature and the sources are described in detail in the general and special bibliographies contained in the titles listed. Treatises containing important bibliographical material are marked with an asterisk.

Some titles have been included which deal in part with the period prior to 1750, when knowledge of the earlier period is essential to an understanding of conditions in the late eighteenth century. The arrangement of titles under the general headings has been governed by the content of the book in preference to the precise wording of the title. Many books are in fact more general than the title would lead one to expect. Such books have been classified under more general headings than might seem appropriate if the wording of the title were taken literally. Government documents and the publications of international bodies have not been listed. Adequate treatment would exceed the limits of space available. References in the general and special bibliographies should meet the requirements of the student.

## CLASSIFICATION

# BIBLIOGRAPHY

## I. General

### A. Bibliographies

Studies in Bibliography: *The Economic History Review*, London, IV, pp. 219–249: "Medieval Capitalism," M. M. Postan. IV, pp. 336–378: "Modern Capitalism," R. H. Tawney. V, no. 1, pp. 104–109: "The Industrial Revolution," T. S. Ashton. V, no. 2, pp. 99–112: "The Basic Industries of England," H. L. Beales.

Power, Eileen, *The Industrial Revolution, 1750–1850: A Select Bibliography*, London, 1927.

Williams, J. B., *A Guide to the Printed Materials for English Social and Economic History, 1750–1780*, 2 vols., New York, 1926.

Allison, W. H.; Fay, S. B.; Shearer, A. H.; and Shipman, H. R., eds., *A Guide to Historical Literature*, New York, 1931.

Haering, H., *Dahlmann-Waitz, Quellenkunde der deutschen Geschichte*, 9th ed., Leipzig, 1931.

International Committee of Historical Sciences, *International Bibliography of Historical Sciences*, 1926, and annually thereafter, New York.

### B. Historical Method

Bober, M. M., *Karl Marx's Interpretation of History*, Cambridge, Mass., 1927.

Hook, Sidney, *From Hegel to Marx*, New York, 1936.

Lifschitz, F., *Die historische Schule der Wirtschaftswissenschaft*, Bern, 1914.

Ogburn, William Fielding, *Social Change with Respect to Culture and Original Nature*, New York, 1922.

Rickert, H., *Die Grenzen der naturwissenschaftlichen Begriffsbildung*, Tübingen dun Leipzig, 1921.

Schmoller, G., *Über einige Grundfragen der Socialpolitik und die Volkswirtschaftslehre*, Leipzig, 1898, 1904.

Seligman, E. R. A., *The Economic Interpretation of History*, 2d ed. rev., New York, 1924.

Usher, A. P., "The Application of the Quantitative Method to Economic History," *Journal of Political Economy*, Chicago, Ill., vol. XL, pp. 186–209, April, 1932.

### C. General Treatises on Europe

Birnie, Arthur, *An Economic History of Europe, 1760–1930*, New York, 1930.

Clapham, J. H., *The Economic Development of France and Germany, 1815–1914*, New York, 1921; 4th ed., 1936.

Cole, G. D. H., and Cole, M., *The Intelligent Man's Review of Europe Today*, New York, 1933.

Day, Clive, *Economic Development in Modern Europe*, New York, 1933.
—— *A History of Commerce*, rev. and enl. ed., New York, 1922.

Eyre, Edward (ed.), *European Civilization, Its Origin and Development*, vol. 5, *Economic History of Europe Since the Reformation*, Oxford, 1937.

Hammond, J. L., and Hammond, B., *The Rise of Modern Industry*, New York, 1926.

Hauser, H., *Les débuts du capitalisme*, Paris, 1927.

* Heaton, Herbert, *Economic History of Europe*, New York, 1936.

Hobson, J. A., *The Evolution of Modern Capitalism*, 1st ed., 1897; new and rev. ed., New York, 1926.

Jennings, W. W., *A History of the Economic and Social Progress of European Peoples*, Lexington, Kentucky, 1936.

Johnson, E. A. J., *Some Origins of the Modern Economic World*, New York, 1936.

Knight, M. M.; Barnes, H. E.; and Flügel, F., *Economic History of Europe in Modern Times*, New York, 1928.

Kulischer, Josef, *Allgemeine Wirtschaftsgeschichte des Mittelalters und der neue Zeit*, vol. II, *Die neue Zeit*, München und Berlin, 1928–1929.

Nussbaum, F. L., *A History of the Economic Institutions of Modern Europe*, (a careful summary of Sombart's *Der moderne Kapitalismus*), New York, 1933.

* Ogg, F. A., and Sharp, W. R., *The Economic Development of Modern Europe*, rev. ed., New York, 1926.

Renard, G. F., and Weulersse, *Life and Work in Modern Europe*, New York, 1926.

Sée, Henri E., *Modern Capitalism, Its Origin and Evolution*, trans. by H. B. Vanderblue and G. Doriot, New York, 1928.

Sombart, Werner, *Der moderne Kapitalismus: Das Wirtschaftsleben im Zeitalter des Hochkapitalismus*, München und Leipzig, 1927.

Wagenführ, R., *Die Industriewirtschaft: Entwicklungstendenzen der deutschen und internationalen Industrieproduktion, 1860 bis 1932*, Berlin, 1933.

* Waltershausen, A. Sartorius von, *Die Entstehung der Weltwirtschaft*, Jena, 1931.

D. General Treatises on Particular Countries or Regions

1. England and the British Empire

Bland, A. E.; Brown, P. A.; and Tawney, R. H. (comps. and eds.), *English Economic History; Select Documents*, Part III, 2d ed., New York, 1915.

* Treatises marked thus with an asterisk contain important bibliographical material.

Brentano, L., *Eine Geschichte der wirtschaftlichen Entwicklung Englands*, vol. 3, Jena, 1929.

British Association for the Advancement of Science, Economic Science and Statistics Section, *Britain in Depression*, London, 1935.

Cheyney, Edward P., *Introduction to the Industrial and Social History of England*, rev. ed., New York, 1920.

Clapham, J. H., *An Economic History of Modern Britain;* vol. 1, *The Early Railway Age, 1820–1850;* vol. 2, *Free Trade and Steel, 1850–1886*, New York, 1931–1932.

* Cunningham, William, *The Growth of English Industry and Commerce in Modern Times*, 4th ed., Cambridge, Mass., 1904. (The later portion is also published separately under the title *The Industrial Revolution*.)

Davies, D. J., *The Economic History of South Wales prior to 1850* (largely since 1750), Cardiff, 1933.

Dodd, A. H., *The Industrial Revolution in North Wales*, New York, 1933.

Fay, C. R., *Great Britain from Adam Smith to the Present Day*, London, 1928.

Hamilton, Henry, *The Industrial Revolution in Scotland*, Oxford, 1932.

Jones, Evan J., *Some Contributions to the Economic History of Wales*, London, 1928.

Knowles, L. C. A., *The Economic Development of the British Overseas Empire*, 3 vols., London, 1924–1936.

—— *The Industrial and Commercial Revolutions in Great Britain during the Nineteenth Century*, London, 1921.

Lipson, E., *The Economic History of England*, 3 vols., London, 1920–1931.

* MacInnes, C. M., *An Introduction to the Economic History of the British Empire*, London, 1935.

Mantoux, P. J., *The Industrial Revolution in the Eighteenth Century* (trans. from the French ed. of 1906), London, 1928.

Moffit, Louis W., *England on the Eve of the Industrial Revolution*, London, 1925.

Redford, Arthur, *The Economic History of England (1760–1860)*, London, 1931.

Rees, J. F., *A Short Fiscal and Financial History of England, 1815–1918*, London, 1921.

—— *A Social and Industrial History of England, 1815–1918*, New York, 1920.

Slater, G., *The Growth of Modern England*, London, 1933.

Toynbee, Arnold, *Lectures on the Industrial Revolution of the Eighteenth Century in England*, New York, 1884.

Usher, A. P., *An Introduction to the Industrial History of England*, Boston, 1920.

## 2. FRANCE

Jaurès, Jean (ed.), *Histoire socialiste, 1789-1900*, 12 vols., Paris, 1900-1908.

Lavisse, Ernest, *Histoire de la France contemporaine depuis la Révolution jusqu'à la paix de 1919*, 10 vols., Paris, 1920-1922.

Lefebvre, Georges; Guyot, R.; et Sagnac, P., *La Révolution française*, Paris, 1930.

Levasseur, E., *Histoire des classes ouvrières en France avant 1789*, 2 vols., Paris, 1900-1901.

—— *Histoire des classes ouvrières en France depuis 1789 à nos jours*, 2 vols., Paris, 1903-1904.

Martin, Germain, *Histoire économique et financière de la nation française*, Paris, 1927.

Renard, G., et Dulac, A., *L'évolution industrielle et agricole depuis cent cinquante ans*, Paris, 1914.

Sée, Henri E., *Economic and Social Conditions in France during the Eighteenth Century*, New York, 1927.

—— *Esquisse d'une histoire économique et sociale de la France depuis les origines jusqu'à la guerre mondiale*, Paris, 1929.

*—— *L'évolution commerciale et industrielle de la France sous l'ancien régime*, Paris, 1925.

—— *La vie économique de la France sous la monarchie censitaire, 1815-1848*, Paris, 1927.

Thorez, M., *France Today and the People's Front*, New York, 1936.

Weill, Georges, *Histoire du mouvement social en France*, 3d ed., Paris, 1924.

## 3. GERMANY

Barker, J. E., *Modern Germany*, London and New York, 1909, 6th rev. and enl. ed., 1919.

Brady, Robert A., *The Spirit and Structure of German Fascism*, New York, 1937.

Cambon, Victor, *L'Allemagne au travail*, Paris, 1910.

—— *Les derniers progrès de l'Allemagne*, Paris, 1914.

Dawson, William Harbutt, *The Evolution of Modern Germany*, London, 1908.

Ehrenberg, Richard, *Grosse Vermögen, ihre Enstehung und ihre Bedeutung*, rev. ed., Jena, 1905.

Ermarth, Fritz, *The New Germany*, Washington, 1936.

Heiden, Konrad, *History of National Socialism* (trans. from the German), New York, 1934.

Hoover, Calvin B., *Germany Enters the Third Reich*, New York, 1933.

Howard, Earl Dean, *The Cause and Extent of the Recent Industrial Progress of Germany*, Boston, 1907.

Lichtenberger, Henri, *Germany and Its Evolution in Modern Times* (trans. from the French by A. M. Ludovici), New York, 1913.

Neuhaus, G. G., *Deutsche Wirtschaftsgeschichte im neunzehnten Jahr-hundert*, Kempten und München, 1919.

Prösler, Hans, *Die Epochen der deutschen Wirtschaftsgeschichte*, Nürnberg, 1927.

Schuman, F. L., *The Nazi Dictatorship: A Study in Social Pathology and the Politics of Fascism*, New York, 1935.

Sombart, W., *Die deutsche Volkswirtschaft im neunzehnten Jahrhundert*, Berlin, 1919.

* Waltershausen, A. Sartorious von, *Deutsche Wirtschaftsgeschichte, 1815-1914*, Jena, 1923.

4. OTHER COUNTRIES

Childs, Marquis W., *Sweden, the Middle Way*, New Haven, 1936.

Douglass, Paul F., *The Economic Independence of Poland*, Cincinnati, 1934.

Goldmark, Josephine C., and Hollman, A. H., *Democracy in Denmark*, Washington, 1936.

Howe, Frederick C., *Denmark, the Coöperative Way*, New York, 1936.

Lémonon, Ernest, *L'Italie économique et sociale, 1861-1912*, Paris, 1913.

McGuire, C. E., *Italy's International Economic Position*, New York, 1926.

Pitigliani, F., *The Italian Corporative State*, London, 1933.

Royal Institute of International Affairs, *The Balkan States*, vol. 1, *Economic: A Review of the Economic and Financial Development of Albania, Bulgaria, Greece, Roumania, and Yugoslavia since 1919*, New York, 1936.

—— *The Economic and Financial Position of Italy*, 2d ed. rev., New York, 1935.

Salvemini, Gaetano, *Under the Axe of Fascism*, New York, 1936.

Schneider, H. W., *Making the Fascist State*, Oxford, 1928.

Tibal, A., *La Tchécoslovaquie: étude économique*, Paris, 1935.

Van Houtte, H., *Histoire économique de la Belgique à la fin de l'ancien régime*, Gand, 1920.

II. POPULATION AND ECONOMIC GEOGRAPHY
A. POPULATION AND ITS PROBLEMS

Bowen, Ezra, *An Hypothesis of Population Growth*, New York, 1931.

Buer, M. C., *Health, Wealth, and Population in the Early Days of the Industrial Revolution*, London, 1927.

Carr-Saunders, A. M., *The Population Problem*, New York, 1922.

—— *World Population; Past Growth and Present Trends*, New York, 1936.

Dublin, L. I., and Lotka, A. J., *Length of Life*, New York, 1936.

East, Edward M., *Mankind at the Crossroads*, New York, 1923.

Gini, Corrado (ed.), *Proceedings of the International Congress for Studies on Population* (Rome, 7-10 Sept. 1931), 10 vols., Rome, 1934-1935.

Gregory, J. W., *Human Migration and the Future*, Philadelphia, 1928.

\* Griffith, G. Talbot, *Population Problems of the Age of Malthus*, Cambridge, England, 1926.

Knibbs, G. H., "The Laws of Growth of Population," *Journal of the American Statistical Association*, vols. 21, 22, Dec., 1926, March, 1927.

—— *The Shadow of the World's Future*, London, 1928.

Levasseur, Pierre Émile, *La population française*, Paris, 1889–1892.

National Bureau of Economic Research, *International Migrations* (ed. by Walter F. Willcox), 2 vols., New York, 1929.

Pearl, Raymond, *Studies in Human Biology*, Baltimore, 1924.

Pitt-Rivers, G. H. L. F., *Problems of Population* (report of the Proceedings of the Second General Assembly of the International Union for the Scientific Investigation of Population Problems), London, 1932.

Taft, Donald R., *Human Migration; A Study of International Movements*, New York, 1936.

\* Thompson, W. S., *Population, a Study in Malthusianism* (Columbia University Studies, 1915), New York, 1915.

Usher, A. P., "Population and Settlement in Eurasia," *Geographical Review*, New York, vol. XX, pp. 110–132, 1930.

Weber, A. F., *The Growth of Cities in the Nineteenth Century*, New York, 1899.

Wright, Harold, *Population*, New York, 1923.

## B. ECONOMIC GEOGRAPHY AND NATURAL RESOURCES

Andrée, K., Heiderich, F., und Lieter, H., *Geographie das Welthandels*, 3 vols., Wien, 1926–1930.

Bengston, N. A., and Van Royen, W. *Fundamentals of Economic Geography*, New York, 1937.

Blanchard, R., *La Flandre*, Paris, 1906.

\* Bowman, Isaiah, *The New World; Problems in Political Geography*, Yonkers-on-Hudson, 1928.

Brunhes, Jean, *La géographie humaine*, 3 vols., Paris, 1925.

\* Darby, H. C. (ed.), *Historical Geography of England*, New York, 1936.

Emeny, Brooks, *The Strategy of Raw Materials*, New York, 1935.

Huntington, C. C., and Carlson, F. L., *The Geographic Basis of Society*, New York, 1937.

Huntington, Ellsworth, and Cushing, S. W. *Principles of Human Geography*, 3d ed. rev., New York, 1923; 4th ed., 1934.

Huntington, Ellsworth; Williams, F. E.; and Van Valkenburg, S., *Economic and Social Geography*, New York, 1933.

Jefferson, Mark, *Man in Europe*, New York, 1926.

Jones, L. Rodwell, *North England; An Economic Geography*, London, 1921.

Lefèvre, M. A., *L'habitat rural en Belgique*, Liège, 1925.

Mackinder, H. J., *Britain and the British Seas*, London, 1902; 2d ed., New York, 1922.

Simonds, F. H., and Emeny, B., *The Great Powers in World Politics*, New York, 1935.
Taylor, Griffith, *Environment and Race*, London, 1927.
Vidal de La Blache, P., *Principles of Human Geography*, New York, 1926.
—— "Tableau de la géographie de la France," in Lavisse, E., *Histoire de France*, vol. I, part 1, Paris, 1911.
Zimmerman, E. W., *World Resources and Industries*, New York, 1933.

III. General Studies of Industry: Its Evolution, Its Location, Its Organization, and Its Control

Brady, Robert A., *The Rationalization Movement in German Industry*, Berkeley, 1933.
Brown, W. J., *The Prevention and Control of Monopolies*, New York, 1915.
Bücher, Carl, *Industrial Evolution* (trans. from the 3d German ed. by S. M. Wickett), New York, 1901.
Carter, G. R., *The Tendency Toward Industrial Combination*, London, 1913.
Dimock, Marshall E., *British Public Utilities and National Development*, London, 1933.
Evans, G. H., *British Corporation Finance, 1775–1850; A Study of Preference Shares*, Baltimore, 1936.
Gras, N. S. B., *Industrial Evolution*, Cambridge, Mass., 1930.
Hirst, F. W., *Monopolies, Trusts, and Kartells*, New York, 1906.
Hoover, E. M., *Location Theory and the Shoe and Leather Industries*, Cambridge, Mass., 1937.
Hunt, B. C., *The Development of the Business Corporation in England, 1800–1867*, Cambridge, Mass., 1936.
Levy, Hermann, *Industrial Germany; A Study of Its Monopoly Organizations and Their Control by the State*, London, 1935.
—— *Monopoly and Competition: a Study in English Industrial Organization*, London, 1911.
—— *The New Industrial System; a Study of the Origin, Forms, Finance, and Prospects of Concentration in Industry*, London, 1936.
Liefmann, Robert, *Beteiligungs- und Finanzierungsgesellschaften; Eine Studie über den modernen Effektenkapitalismus*, Jena, 1923.
—— *International Cartels, Combines, and Trusts*, London, 1927.
Lucas, A. F., *Industrial Reconstruction and the Control of Competition; The British Experiments*, New York, 1937.
Macrosty, H. W., *The Trust Movement in British Industry*, London, 1907.
Meakin, Walter, *The New Industrial Revolution; A Study for the General Reader of Rationalization and Post-War Tendencies of Capitalism and Labor*, New York, 1929.
Michels, Rudolf K., *Cartels, Combines, and Trusts in Post-War Germany*, New York, 1928.
Palander, Tord, *Beiträge zur Standortstheorie*, Upsala, 1935.

Passow, R., *Die Aktiengesellschaft*, Jena, 2d ed., 1922.

Piotrowski, Roman, *Cartels and Trusts; Their Origin and Historical Development from the Economic and Legal Aspects*, London, 1933.

Predöhl, A., "Das Standortsproblem in der Wirtschaftstheorie," *Weltwirtschaftliches Archiv*, 1925, vol. 21, pp. 294–321.

Pribram, Karl, *Cartel Problems; An Analysis of Collective Monopolies in Europe with American Applications*, Washington, 1935.

Robson, William A. (ed.), *Public Enterprise: Developments in Social Ownership and Control in Great Britain*, London, 1937.

Rousiers, P. de, *Les grandes industries modernes*, 3 vols., Paris, 1924–26.

—— *Les syndicats industriels de producteurs, en France et à l'étranger*, Paris, 1912.

Scott, W. R., *The Constitution and Finance of English, Scottish, and Irish Joint-Stock Companies to 1720*, 3 vols., New York, 1910–1911.

Shadwell, Arthur, *Industrial Efficiency: A Comparative Study of Industrial Life in England, Germany, and America*, new ed., London, 1913.

Stockder, Archibald Herbert, *German Trade Associations*, New York, 1924.

Strieder, J., *Studien zur Geschichte der kapitalistischen Organisationsformen*, 1914; 2d ed., 1925.

—— *Zur Genesis des modernen Kapitalismus*, Leipzig, 1904.

Weber, Alfred, *The Theory of the Location of Industries* (trans. from the German by C. J. Friedrich), Chicago, 1929.

## IV. INVENTION AND TECHNOLOGY

* Beck, Theodor, *Beiträge zur Geschichte des Maschinenbaues*, 2d ed., Berlin, 1900.

Byrn, Edward W., *The Progress of Invention in the 19th Century*, New York, 1900.

Clark, George N., "Early Capitalism and Invention," *Economic History Review*, vol. VI, pp. 143–156.

Crozet-Fourneyron, Marcel, *L'invention de la turbine*, Paris, 1925.

Dessauer, Friedrich, *Philosophie der Technik*, Bonn, 1928.

Dickinson, H. W., *James Watt, Craftsman and Engineer*, London, 1936.

* Dickinson, H. W., and Jenkins, Rhys, *James Watt and the Steam Engine*, New York, 1927.

Dickinson, H. W., and Titley, A., *Richard Trevithick, the Engineer and the Man*, New York, 1934.

* Gilfillan, S. Colum, *The Sociology of Invention*, Chicago, 1935.

* Gould, Rupert T., *The Marine Chronometer: Its History and Development*, London, 1923.

Hart, Ivor B., *The Great Engineers*, London, 1929.

Jenkins, Rhys, *Links in the History of Engineering and Technology from Tudor Times*, London, 1936.

* Kirby, R. S., and Laurson, P. G., *The Early Years of Modern Civil Engineering*, New Haven, 1932.

Marshall, Thomas H., *James Watt, 1736–1819*, Boston, 1925.

Matschoss, Conrad (ed.), *Beiträge zur Geschichte der Technik und Industrie*, Berlin, 1909.

—— *Geschichte der Dampfmaschine: Ihre kulturelle Bedeutung, technische Entwicklung, und ihre grossen Männer*, Berlin, 1901.

—— *Ein Jahrhundert deutsches Maschinenbau, 1819–1919*, Berlin, 1919.

Müller, W., *Die Francis-Turbinen und die Entwicklung des modernen Turbinenbaues in Deutschland*, Hannover, 1905.

Mumford, Lewis, *Technics and Civilization*, New York, 1934.

Neilson, Robert M., *The Steam Turbine*, 4th ed., New York, 1908.

The Newcomen Society for the Study of the History of Engineering and Technology, *Transactions*, London, 1920 and thereafter.

Quennel, Marjorie, and Quennel, C. H. B., *A History of Everyday Things in England (The Rise of Industrialism, 1733–1851)*, New York, 1934.

Richardson, Alexander, *The Evolution of the Parsons' Turbine*, London, 1911.

* Robertson, J. Drummond, *The Evolution of Clockwork*, London, 1931.

Roe, Joseph W., *English and American Tool Builders*, New York, 1926.

* Rossman, Joseph, *Psychology of the Inventor*, Washington, 1931.

Spengler, Oswald, *Man and Technics*, New York, 1932.

* Usher, A. P., *A History of Mechanical Inventions*, New York, 1929.

## V. History of Industry in Particular Countries
### 1. England

Allen, G. C., *British Industries and Their Organization*, London, 1933.

—— *The Industrial Development of Birmingham and the Black Country*, London, 1929.

Anonymous, *Britain's Industrial Future, Being the Report of the Liberal Industrial Inquiry*, London, 1928.

Bowden, Witt, *Industrial Society in England towards the End of the Eighteenth Century*, New York, 1925.

Cole, G. D. H., *British Trade and Industry: Past and Future*, London, 1932.

Cook-Taylor, R. Whately, *The Modern Factory System*, London, 1891.

Day, Clive, "Distribution of Industrial Occupations in England, 1841–1861," *Transactions of the Connecticut Academy of Arts and Sciences*, vol. 28, pp. 79–235, New Haven, 1927.

Fong, H. D., *The Triumph of the Factory System in England*, Tientsin, 1930.

Great Britain, Board of Trade, *An Industrial Survey of the North East Coast Area*, London, 1932.

Great Britain, Committee on Industry and Trade, *Factors in Industrial and Commercial Efficiency*, London, 1927.

Hamilton, Henry, *The English Brass and Copper Industries to 1800*, London, 1926.

Hammond, J. L., and Hammond, Barbara, *The Skilled Labourer*, 2d ed., London, 1926.

—— *The Town Labourer*, 2d ed., London, 1925.

—— *The Village Labourer*, 4th ed., London, 1927.

Hower, Ralph M., "The Wedgwoods: Ten Generations of Potters," *Journal of Economic and Business History*, Vol. 4, pp. 281–313, 665–690.

Lord, John, *Capital and Steam Power, 1750–1800*, London, 1923.

Melchett, Sir Alfred M. M., *Industry and Politics*, London, 1927.

Page, William (ed.), *Commerce and Industry*, 2 vols., New York, 1920.

Redford, Arthur, *Labour Migration in England, 1800–1850*, Manchester, 1926.

Siegfried, André, *England's Crisis*, London, 1931.

Westerfield, R. B., *Middlemen in English Business*, New Haven, 1915.


2. FRANCE AND BELGIUM

Ballot, Charles, *L'introduction du machinisme dans l'industrie française*, Paris, 1923.

Bourgin, Georges, et Bourgin, Hubert, *Le régime de l'industrie en France de 1814 à 1848*, 2 vols., Paris, 1912–1921.

Capot-Rey, Robert, *La région industrielle sarroise*, Paris, 1934.

Charriaut, Henri, *La Belgique moderne; Une terre d'expériences*, Paris, 1910.

Comité des Forges, *La sidérurgie française, 1864–1914*, Paris, 1920.

Constantin, Albert, *L'économie sarroise entre la France et l'Allemagne*, Nancy, 1934.

* Cornelissen, F. C., *Les industries des Pays-Bas; Leur localization géographique et leur évolution*, Paris, 1932.

* Dechesne, Laurent, *Histoire économique et sociale de la Belgique depuis les origines jusqu'en 1914*, Paris, 1932.

Deiss, Edouard, *Études sociales et industrielles sur la Belgique*, Paris, 1900.

Des Cilleuls, A., *Histoire et régime de la grande industrie en France aux XVIIe et XVIIIe siècles*, Paris, 1898.

Guillet, L., et Durand, J., *L'industrie française*, Paris, 1920.

Julin, A., *Les grandes fabriques en Belgique vers le milieu du XVIIIe siècle*, Bruxelles, Paris, 1903.

Lewinsky, Jan de St., *L'évolution industrielle de la Belgique*, Bruxelles, Paris, 1911.

Martin, Germain, *La grande industrie sous le règne de Louis XV*, Paris, 1900.

Martin-Saint-Léon, Étienne, *Histoire des corporations et métiers*, 3d ed., Paris, 1922.

—— *Le petit commerce française: Sa lutte pour la vie*, 2d ed., Paris, 1911.

Moreau de Jonnès, Alexandre, *Statistique de l'industrie de la France*, Paris, 1856.
Ogburn, W. F., and Jaffé, W., *The Economic Development of Post-War France*, New York, 1929.

### 3. GERMANY

Bein, L., *Die Industrie des sächischen Voigtlandes*, Leipzig, 1884.
* Benaerts, P., *Les origines de la grande industrie allemande: Essai sur l'histoire économique de la période du Zollverein (1834–1866)*, Paris, 1934.
Berdrow, Wilhelm, *Krupp, a Great Business Man Seen through His Letters* (trans. by E. W. Dickes), New York, 1930.
Blondel, Georges, *L'essor industriel et commercial du peuple allemand*, Paris, 1900.
Dawson, William Harbutt, *Industrial Germany*, London, 1912.
Grothe, H., *Bilde und Studien zur Geschichte der Industrie und des Maschinenwesen*, Berlin, 1870.
Hauser, Henri, *Germany's Commercial Grip on the World*, New York, 1917.
Howe, Frederick C., *Socialized Germany*, New York, 1915.
Huber, F. C., *Deutschland als Industriestaat*, Stuttgart, 1901.
Lichtenberger, Henri, *L'impérialisme économique allemand*, Paris, 1918.
National Industrial Conference Board, *Rationalization of German Industry*, New York, 1931.
Schmidt, C. T., *German Business Cycles, 1924–1933*, New York, 1934.
Schmoller, G., *Zur Geschichte der deutschen Kleingewerbe in neunzehnten Jahrhundert*, Halle, 1870.
Troeltsch, W., *Ueber die neuesten Veränderungen im deutschen Wirtschaftsleben*, Stuttgart, 1899.

### 4. OTHER COUNTRIES

Anselmi, A., "Trade Associations and Corporations in Italy after Recent Reforms," *International Labor Review*, vol. 31, pp. 6–27.
Confederazione Generale Fascista dell' Industria Italiana, *L'industria italiana*, Roma, 1929.
Einzig, Paul, *Economic Foundations of Fascism*, 2d ed., London, 1934.
General Fascist Confederation of Italian Industries, *Fascist Era Year XII*, Rome, 1934.
Gomez de la Serna, Javier, *España y sus Problemas*, Madrid, 1915.
Greenfield, K. R., *Economics and Liberalism in the Risorgimento; A Study of Nationalism in Lombardy*, Baltimore, 1934.
Hubbard, G. E., *Eastern Industrialization and Its Effect on the West*, London, 1935.
Mitzakis, Michel, *Les grands problèmes italiens: L'économie, les finances, les dettes*, Paris, 1931.

VI. History of Particular Industries
1. Textiles

Anonymous, *The History of Silk, Cotton, Linen, Wool and Other Fibrous Substances*, New York, 1845.

Baines, Ed., Jr., *History of the Cotton Manufacture*, London, 1835.

Barlow, Alfred, *The History and Principles of Weaving by Hand and Power*, London, 1879.

Beaumont, Gaston, *L'industrie cotonnière en Normandie*, Paris, 1901.

Chapman, Sydney John, *The Cotton Industry and Trade*, London, 1905.

—— *The Lancashire Cotton Industry*, Manchester, 1904.

Clapham, J. H., *The Woolen and Worsted Industries*, London, 1907.

Daniels, G. W., *The Early English Cotton Industry, with Some Unpublished Letters of Samuel Crompton*, Manchester, 1920.

Dehn, R. M. R., *The German Cotton Industry*, Manchester, 1913.

Despature, Paul, *L'industrie lainière*, Paris, 1935.

Ellison, Thomas, *The Cotton Trade of Great Britain*, London, 1886.

Felkin, William, *A History of Machine-Wrought Hosiery and Lace Manufactures*, London, 1867.

* Forrester, R. B., *The Cotton Industry in France*, Manchester, 1921.

Fox, Joseph Hoyland, *Woolen Manufacture at Wellington*, London, 1914.

French, G. J., *Life and Times of Samuel Crompton*, Manchester, 1860.

Gill, Conrad, *The Rise of the Irish Linen Industry*, Oxford, 1925.

Guénau, Louis, *Lyon et le commerce de la soie*, Lyon, 1923.

Heaton, Herbert, *The Yorkshire Woolen and Worsted Industries, from the Earliest Times up to the Industrial Revolution*, Oxford, 1920.

Henderson, W. O., *The Lancashire Cotton Famine, 1861–1865*, Manchester, 1934.

Hirst, W., *History of the Woolen Trade during the Last Sixty Years*, Leeds, 1844.

Hooper, Luther, *Hand-Loom Weaving, Plain and Ornamental*, London, 1910.

—— "The Loom and Spindle; Past, Present, and Future," Smithsonian Institution, *Annual Report*, 1914, pp. 629–678, Washington, 1914.

Horner, John, *The Linen Trade of Europe in the Spinning Wheel Period*, Belfast, 1920.

Houdoy, Jules, *La filature du coton dans le nord de la France*, Paris, 1903.

James, John F. S. G., *History of the Worsted Manufacture in England*, London, 1857.

Lévy, Robert, *Histoire économique de l'industrie cotonnière en Alsace*, Paris, 1912.

* Lipson, Ephraim, *The History of the Woolen and Worsted Industries*, London, 1921.

Murray, Malcolm W., *L'industrie cotonnière anglaise, 1913–1923*, Lille, 1925.

Pariset, E., *Histoire de la fabrique lyonnaise, étude sur le régime social et économique de l'industrie de la soie à Lyon depuis le XVI<sup>e</sup> siècle*, Lyon, 1901.

Reybaud, Louis, *La laine*, Paris, 1867.

Schultze-Gaevernitz, G. von, *The Cotton Trade in England and on the Continent*, London, 1895.

Tupling, G. H., *The Economic Development of Rossendale*, Manchester, 1927.

Unwin, George, *Samuel Oldknow and the Arkwrights; The Industrial Revolution at Stockport and Marple*, New York, 1924.

Wadsworth, A. P., and Mann, J. de L., *The Cotton Trade and Industrial Lancashire, 1600–1780*, Manchester, 1931.

Warner, Frank, *The Silk Industry of the United Kingdom, Its Origin and Development*, London, 1921.

2. COAL

Ashton, T. S., and Sykes, J., *The Coal Industry of the Eighteenth Century*, Manchester, 1929.

Beaumont, Maurice, *La grosse industrie allemande et le charbon*, Paris, 1928.

Jevons, W. S., *The Coal Question*, London, 1865; 3d ed., 1906.

Leseure, E., *Historique des mines de houille du departement de la Loire*, St. Étienne, 1901.

Lozé, Ed., *Les charbons britanniques et leur épuisement*, 2 vols., Paris, 1900.

Lubin, Isador, and Everett, Helen, *The British Coal Dilemma*, New York, 1927.

Meyer, Hermann, *Die rheinische Braunkohlen-Industrie und ihre wirtschaftliche Organization*, Bonn, 1910.

Mezzatesta, Vittorio, *Carbone ed elettricità in Italia*, Città di Castello, 1920.

Moutté, Frédéric, *La question de l'organization internationale de l'industrie charbonnière*, Paris, 1929.

Nef, J. U., *The Rise of the British Coal Industry*, 2 vols., London, 1932.

Neuman, Andrew Martin, *Economic Organization of the British Coal Industry*, London, 1934.

Raynes, J. R., *Coal and Its Conflicts*, London, 1928.

Rouff, M., *Les mines de charbon en France au XVIII<sup>e</sup> siècle, 1744–91*, Paris, 1922.

Smart, R. C., *The Economics of the Coal Industry*, London, 1930.

Stockder, Archibald H., *Regulating an Industry; The Rhenish-Westphalian Coal Syndicate*, New York, 1932.

Twelfth International Geological Congress, Toronto, 1913, *Coal Resources of the World*, 3 vols., Toronto, 1913.

Vieillard, E. F., *Le terrain houiller de Basse-Normandie*, Caen, 1874.

## 3. Iron and Steel

Ashton, T. S., *Iron and Steel in the Industrial Revolution*, Manchester, 1924.

Baedeker, Diedrich, *Alfred Krupp und die Entwicklung der Gusstahlfabrik zu Essen*, Essen, 1912.

Beck, L., *Die Geschichte des Eisens in technischer und kulturgeschichtlicher Beziehung*, 5 vols., Braunschweig, 1884–1903.

Bell, Sir Lowthian, *The Iron Trade of the United Kingdom — Compared with That of the Other Chief Iron-Making Nations*, vol. 8, British Iron Trade Association, 1886.

Bessemer, Sir Henry, *An Autobiography*, London, 1905.

Brooks, A. H., and LaCroix, A., *The Iron and Associated Industries of Lorraine, the Saare District, Luxemburg, and Belgium* (United States Geological Survey, Bull. 703), Washington, 1921.

Burat, Amédée, *Situation de l'industrie houillières in 1861*, Comité des houillières françaises, Lacroix, 1862.

—— *Les houillières en 1868* (avec atlas contenant la suite des documents produits à l'exposition universelle), Paris, 1869.

Eleventh International Geological Congress (Stockholm, 1910), *Iron Ore Resources of the World*, Stockholm, 1910.

Fairbairn, William, *Iron: Its History, Properties, and Process of Manufacture*, Edinburgh, 1869.

Jeans, J. S., *The Iron Trade of Great Britain*, London, 1906.

Jeans, W. T., *The Creators of the Age of Steel: Bessemer, Siemens, Whitworth, Brown, Thomas, Snelus*, New York, 1884.

Krupp, A., *A Century History of the Krupp Works, 1812–1912*, Essen, 1912.

Levainville, J., *L'industrie du fer en France*, 1922.

Lloyd, G. I. H., *The Cutlery Trades, An Historical Essay in the Economics of Small-Scale Production*, London, 1913.

McKay, Donald C., *Essays in the History of Modern Europe*, New York, 1936.

Martin, R., *Die Eisenindustrie in ihrem Kampf um den Absatzmarkt*, Leipzig, 1904.

Meisner, M., *Weltmontanstatistik, Die Versorgung der Weltwirtschaft mit Bergwerkserzeugenissen*, I, 1860–1926; II, 1926–1930; III, 1930–1935, Stuttgart, 1925–1936.

*The Mineral Industry*, annually, New York, 1892–1937.

Percy, John, *Metallurgy: The Art of Extracting Metals from Their Ores, and Adapting Them to Various Purposes of Manufacture; Iron and Steel*, London, 1864.

Pole, William, *Life of William Fairbairn*, London, 1877.

—— *The Life of Sir (Charles) William Siemens*, London, 1888.

Roesler, Max, *The Iron-Ore Resources of Europe* (United States Geological Survey, Bull. 706), Washington, 1921.

Roll, Erich, *An Early Experiment in Industrial Organization; Being a History of the Firm of Boulton & Watt, 1775-1805*, London, 1930.

Scrivenor, H., *A Comprehensive History of the Iron Trade throughout the World from the Earliest Records to the Present*, London, 1841, 1854.

Stillich, O., *Eisen und Stahl-Industrie*, Berlin, 1904.

United States Geological Survey, *World Atlas of Commercial Geology*, Part I, "Distribution of Mineral Production"; Part II, "Water Power of the World," Washington, 1921.

Wilkins, C., *History of the Iron and Steel Trades of South Wales*, Merthyr Tydfil, 1903.

4. ELECTRICAL INDUSTRIES

American Academy of Political and Social Science, *Giant Power, Large Scale Electrical Development as a Social Factor (Annals,* vol. 118), Philadelphia, 1925.

Barham, G. B., *The Development of the Incandescent Electric Lamp*, New York, 1913.

Barut, Victor, *L'industrie de l'électro-chimie et de l'électro-metallurgie en France*, Paris, 1924.

Chazeau, Melvin G. de, "Rationalization of Electricity Supply in Great Britain," *Journal of Land and Public Utility Economics*, vol. 10, 1934.

Fleming, J. A., *Fifty Years of Electricity*, New York, 1921.

Great Britain, Ministry of Transport, *Committee on the Supply of Electrical Energy* (Report of the Weir Committee appointed to review the national problem of the supply of electrical energy), London, 1926.

Howell, J. W., and Schroeder, H., *History of the Incandescent Lamp*, Schenectady, 1927.

Kittler, Werner, *Der internationale elektrische Energie Verkehr in Europa*, Würzburg, 1932.

Köpke, Max, *Probleme der Elektrizitätspolitik in Deutschland*, Eberswald, 1931.

Neubauer, Johannes, *Die Strukturveränderungen der deutschen Kraftwirtschaft seit dem Ende des vorigen Jahrhunderts*, Halle, 1934.

Pring, J. N., *Some Electro-Chemical Centres*, Manchester, 1908.

Quigley, Hugh, *Electrical Power and National Progress*, London, 1925.

Siemens, Ernst Werner von, *Lebenserinnerungen von Werner von Siemens*, 4th ed., Berlin, 1895.

Wendlandt, Kurt, *Die Entwicklung der Kommunalen Elektrizitätswerke und ihre Stellung zu den Expansionsbestreitungen der Grosskraftwerke*, Berlin, 1931.

Whyte, A. G., *The Electrical Industry*, London, 1904.

—— *Forty Years of Electrical Progress*, London, 1930.

Winterfeld, Ludwig von, *Entwicklung und Tätigkeit der Firme Siemens & Halske in den Jahren 1847-97*, Kiel, 1913.

Zipfel, Richard, *Die preussischen staatliche Elektrizitätswerke im Weser-Main Gebiet*, Kassel, 1930.

## 5. Petroleum

Anninos, E. G., *Der wirtschaftliche Einfluss Deutschlands auf die Petro-leum-Industrie Rumäniens und ihre Bedeutung für die internationale Wirtschaft*, Giessen, 1926.

Apostol, P., et Michelson, A., *La lutte pour le pétrole et la Russie*, Paris, 1922.

Arnot, R. Page, *The Politics of Oil; Studies in Labour and Capital*, London, 1924.

Brackel, O., *Der dreizigjährige Petroleumkrieg*, Berlin, 1903.

Davenport, E. H., and Cooke, S. R., *The Oil Trusts and Anglo-American Relations*, New York, 1924.

Delaisi, Francis, *Oil, Its Influence on Politics*, London, 1922.

Denny, Ludwell, *We Fight for Oil*, New York, 1928.

Fischer, Louis, *Oil Imperialism*, New York, 1926.

Garfias, V. R., *Petroleum Resources of the World*, New York, 1923.

Hoffman, K., *Oilpolitik und angelsächsischer Imperialismus*, Berlin, 1927.

L'Espagnol de le Tramerye, P., *La lutte mondiale pour le pétrole*, Paris, 1922.

Lopez, Pedro N., *Politica petrolifera*, LePas, 1929.

Mohr, Anton, *The Oil War*, New York, 1926.

White, David, *The Petroleum Resources of the World* (American Academy of Political and Social Science), Philadelphia, 1920.

Zanguench, Azami, *Le pétrol en Perse*, Paris, 1933.

## VII. Social Conditions, Labor, and Social Legislation
### A. Social Conditions and Classes

Bagge, G.; Lundberg, E.; and Svennilson, I., *Wages in Sweden, 1860–1930*, vol. 2 of *Wages, Cost of Living and National Income in Sweden*, London, 1933, 1935.

Beveridge, William H., *Unemployment; A Problem of Industry*, London, 1909; new edition, 1930.

Bonenfant, Paul, *Le problème du paupérisme en Belgique à la fin de l'ancien régime*, Bruxelles, 1934.

* Botsford, Jay B., *English Society in the Eighteenth Century, as Influenced from Oversea*, New York, 1924.

Bowden, Witt, "The Productivity of Labor in Great Britain," *Journal of Political Economy*, vol. 45, pp. 347–369, June, 1937.

Bowley, Arthur L., *Wages in the United Kingdom in the Nineteenth Century*, Cambridge, England, 1900.

Carré, Henri, *La noblesse et l'opinion publique en France au XVIIIᵉ siècle*, Paris, 1920.

Clark, Alice, *The Working Life of Women in the Seventeenth Century*, New York, 1920.

Clay, Henry, *The Post-War Unemployment Problem*, London, 1929.

Dawson, William Harbutt, *The German Workman*, London, 1906.

Dubreuil, H., *Employeurs et salairés en France*, Paris, 1934.

Ducros, Louis, *French Society in the Eighteenth Century* (trans. from the French by W. de Geijer), New York, 1927.

Dunlop, Jocelyn, and Denman, R. D., *English Apprenticeship and Child Labor*, New York, 1912.

Ford, Percy, *Work and Wealth in a Modern Port, An Economic Survey of Southampton*, London, 1934.

George, M. Dorothy, *England in Transition; Life and Work in the Eighteenth Century*, London, 1931.

—— *London Life in the Eighteenth Century*, New York, 1925.

Gilboy, Elizabeth W., *Wages in Eighteenth Century England*, Cambridge, Mass., 1934.

Gillespie, F. E., *Labor and Politics in England, 1850–1867*, Durham, N. C., 1927.

Hagen, H., *Der Einfluss der Maschine auf die Arbeitslosigkeit: ein Beitrag zur Wirtschafts- und Sozialreform*, Stuttgart, 1935.

Hammond, J. L., and Hammond, B., *The Age of the Chartists, 1832–1854; A Study of Discontent*, London, 1930.

Howard, L. E., *Labour in Agriculture; An International Survey*, London, 1935.

Jewkes, John, and Gray, E. M., *Wages and Labour in the Lancashire Cotton Spinning Industry*, Manchester, 1935.

Kuczynski, Jürgen, *Die Entwicklung der Lage der Arbeiterschaft in Europa und Amerika, 1870–1933*, Basel, 1934.

*—— *Labour Conditions in Western Europe, 1820 to 1935*, London, 1937.

Kuczynski, Robert R., *Arbeitslohn und Arbeitszeit in Europa und Amerika, 1870–1909*, Berlin, 1913.

—— *Postwar Labor Conditions in Germany* (U. S. Bureau of Labor Statistics, Bull. No. 380, Misc. Series), Washington, 1930.

Lascelles, E. C. P., and Bullock, S. S., *Dock Labour and Decasualization*, London, 1924.

Lefebvre, Georges, *La grande peur de 1789*, Paris, 1932.

Lockwood, H. D., *Tools and the Man*, New York, 1927.

Moon, Parker T., *The Labor Problem and the Social Catholic Movement in France*, New York, 1921.

Myrdal, Gunnar, *The Cost of Living in Sweden, 1830–1930*, vol. 1 of *Wages, Cost of Living and National Income in Sweden*, London, 1933.

Palm, F. C., *The Middle Classes, Then and Now*, New York, 1936.

Pigou, A. C., "Prices and Wages from 1896 to 1914," *Economic Journal*, vol. 33, pp. 163–171; also in *Essays in Applied Economics*, pp. 70–79.

Pinchbeck, Ivy, *Women Workers and the Industrial Revolution, 1750–1850*, London, 1930.

Postgate, R. W. (ed.), *Revolution from 1789 to 1906*, Boston, 1921.

Royal Institute of International Affairs, *Unemployment; an International Problem*, London, 1935.

Simiand, François, *Le salaire, l'évolution sociale, et la monnaie*, 3 vols., Paris, 1932.

Wiggs, K. I., *Unemployment in Germany Since the War*, London, 1933.

Wood, G. H., "Real Wages and the Standard of Comfort Since 1850," *Journal of the Royal Statistical Society*, London, 1909, pp. 91–103.

Woytinsky, W., *The Social Consequences of the Economic Depression*, Geneva, 1936.

—— *Three Sources of Unemployment: The Combined Action of Population Changes, Technical Progress, and Economic Development*, Geneva, 1935.

### B. Co-operative and Labor Organizations

Beales, H. L., *Chartism*, Oxford, 1937.

Beer, Max, *Fifty Years of International Socialism*, London, 1935.

Braun, Adolf, *Die Gewerkschaften: ihre Entwicklung und Kämpfe*, Nürnberg, 1914.

Cole, G. D. H., *A Short History of the British Working Class Movement*, 3 vols., London, 1927.

Delsinne, L., *Le mouvement syndical en Belgique*, Paris, 1936.

Elliott, Sydney R., *The English Coöperatives*, New Haven, 1937.

Fay, C. R., *Co-operation at Home and Abroad; Description and Analysis*, 4th ed., vol. 1, *Pre-War*, London, 1936.

Gammage, R. G., *History of the Chartist Movement, 1837–1854*, Newcastle, 1854; rev. ed., 1894.

Gide, Charles, *Consumers' Co-operative Societies* (trans. from the French), New York, 1922.

Gjöres, Axel, *Co-operation in Sweden* (trans. by J. Downie), New York, 1935.

Goetz, R., *Les syndicats ouvriers allemands après la guerre*, Paris, 1934.

Hall, Fred, and Watkins, W. P., *Co-operation: A Survey of the History, Principles, and Organization of the Co-operative Movement in Great Britain and Ireland*, Manchester, 1934.

Horace Plunkett Foundation, *Co-operation and the New Agricultural Policy*, London, 1935.

Hovell, Mark, *The Chartist Movement*, London, 1918.

International Labour Office, *Collective Agreements*, Geneva, 1936.

* Levine, Louis (Lorwin, L. L.), *Syndicalism in France*, 2d ed., New York, 1914.

* Lorwin, Lewis L., *Labor and Internationalism*, Washington, 1929.

Louis, Paul, *Histoire du mouvement syndical en France, 1789–1910*, 3d ed., Paris, 1921.

Mehring, Franz, *Geschichte der deutschen Sozialdemokratie*, 12th ed., 4 vols., Stuttgart, 1922.

Milne-Bailey, Walter, *Trade Unions and the State*, London, 1934.

Pierre de Grece, Prince, *Les co-opératives agricoles danoises et le marché extérieur*, Paris, 1935.

Redfern, P., *The Story of the C. W. S.*, Manchester, 1913.

Saposs, David J., *The Labor Movement in Post-War France*, New York, 1931.

Sassenbach, J., *Twenty-five Years of International Trade Unionism*, International Trade Union Library, Amsterdam, 1926.

Shields, B. F., *The Labor Contract*, London, 1936.

Tawney, R. H., *The British Labour Movement*, New Haven, 1925.

Twigg, H. J., *The Economic Advance of British Coöperation, 1913 to 1934*, Manchester, 1934.

Vandervelde, E., *Le parti ouvrier belge, 1885–1925*, Bruxelles, 1925.

Warbasse, James P., *Co-operative Democracy*, 3d ed., New York, 1936.

* Webb, Sidney, and Webb, Beatrice, *History of Trade Unionism*, rev. ed., London, 1920. Extensive bibliography in earlier editions.

Weinstein, H. R., *Jean Jaurès*, New York, 1936.

### C. SOCIAL LEGISLATION

Adams, L. P., *Agricultural Depression and Farm Relief in England, 1813–1852*, London, 1932.

Ashby, Arthur W., *One Hundred Years of Poor Law Administration in a Warwickshire Village*, Oxford, 1912.

Bloch, C., *L'assistance et l'état en France à la veille de la Révolution*, Paris, 1908.

Bowden, Witt, "Surplus Labor and the Social Wage in Great Britain," *American Economic Review*, vol. 27, pp. 31–44, March, 1937.

Carroll, M. R., *Unemployment Insurance in Germany*, rev. ed., Washington, 1930.

Chegwidden, T. S., and Myrrdin-Evans, G., *The Employment Exchange System of Great Britain*, New York, 1934.

Cheyney, Edward P., *Modern English Reform*, Philadelphia, 1931.

Clark, Colin, *National Income and Outlay*, London, 1937.

Cohen, Percy, *The British System of Social Insurance*, New York, 1932.

Dawson, William Harbutt, *Social Insurance in Germany, 1883–1911*, London, 1912.

Egger, Alois, *Die Belastung der deutschen Wirtschaft durch die Sozialversicherung*, Jena, 1929.

Frankel, L. K., and Dawson, M. M., *Workingmen's Insurance in Europe*, New York, 1910.

Hallsworth, J., *Protective Legislation for Shop and Office Employees*, rev. ed., London, 1935.

* Hampson, E. M., *The Treatment of Poverty in Cambridgeshire, 1597–1834*, Cambridge, 1934.

Hayes, Carlton, *British Social Politics*, New York, 1913.

Hill, A. C. C., and Lubin, Isador, *The British Attack on Unemployment*, Washington, 1934.

Hohman, H. F., *Development of Social Insurance and Minimum Wage Legislation in Great Britain*, Boston, 1933.

Hutchins, B. Leigh, and Harrison, Amy, *History of Factory Legislation*, 3d ed., London, 1926.

McKay, D. C., *The National Workshops; A Study in the French Revolution of 1848*, Cambridge, Mass., 1933.

McKay, Thomas, *Public Relief of the Poor*, London, 1901.

Marshall, Dorothy M., *The English Poor in the Eighteenth Century: A Study of Social and Administrative History*, London, 1926.

Mess, H. A., *Factory Legislation and Its Administration*, London, 1926.

Nordskog, J. E., *Social Reform in Norway*, Los Angeles, 1935.

* Pipkin, Charles W., *Social Politics and Modern Democracies*, 2 vols., New York, 1931.

Ratzlaff, C. J., *The Scandinavian Unemployment Relief Program*, Philadelphia, 1934.

Rubinow, Isaac M., *Social Insurance*, New York, 1913.

Sykes, Joseph, *British Public Expenditure, 1921–1931*, London, 1933.

United States Bureau of Labor, *Workmen's Insurance and Compensation Systems in Europe*, 2 vols., Washington, 1911 (Twenty-fourth Annual Report, 1909).

Webb, Sidney, and Webb, Beatrice, *English Poor Law History*, 2 pts., London, 1927–1929.

Weigert, Oscar, *Administration of Placement and Unemployment Insurance in Germany*, New York, 1934.

Williams, Gertrude, *The State and the Standard of Living*, London, 1936.

## VIII. Money and Banking

Andréadès, A., *History of the Bank of England*, London, 1909.

Bigo, Robert, *La caisse d'escompte (1776–1793) et les origines de la Banque de France*, Paris, 1927.

Bisschop, W. R., *Rise of the London Money Market: 1640–1826*, London, 1910.

Conant, Charles A., *A History of Modern Banks of Issue*, 4th ed., New York, 1909.

Courtois, Alphonse, *Histoire des banques en France*, Paris, 1881.

Crick, W. F., and Wadsworth, J. E., *A Hundred Years of Joint Stock Banking*, London, 1936.

Dierschke, K., und Müller, F., *Die Notenbanken der Welt*, 2 vols., Berlin, 1926.

Feavearyear, A. E., *The Pound Sterling*, Oxford, 1931.

Galvarriato, Juan Antonio, *El banco de España*, Madrid, 1932.

Harris, S. E., *The Assignats*, Cambridge, Mass., 1930.

—— *Exchange Depreciation*, Cambridge, Mass., 1936.

Kaufman, M. E., *La Banque en France*, Paris, 1914.
King, W. T. C., *History of the London Discount Market*, London, 1936.
Labrousse, Camille Ernest, *Esquisse du mouvement des prix et des revenus en France au XVIII<sup>e</sup> siècle*, Paris, 1932.
Laughlin, J. Laurence, *A New Exposition of Money, Credit and Prices*, 2 vols., Chicago, 1931.
Patron, Maurice, *La Banque de France and le crédit national*, Paris, 1908.
Ramon, Gabriel, *Histoire de la Banque de France*, Paris, 1929.
Richards, R. D., *The Early History of Banking in England*, London, 1929.
Riesser, Jacob, *German Great Banks and Their Concentration*, Washington, 1911.
Robey, Ralph (ed.), *The Monetary Problem, Gold and Silver*, New York, 1936.
Sayous, André E., *Les banques de dépots, les banques de crédit, et les sociétés financières*, Paris, 1900, 1904.
Shaw, William Arthur, *The History of Currency, 1252–1894*, London, 1895.
Silberling, Norman J., "British Prices and Business Cycles, 1779–1850," *The Review of Economic Statistics*, Oct. 1923.
—— "Financial and Monetary Policy in Great Britain during the Napoleonic Wars," *Quarterly Journal of Economics*, vol. 38, pp. 214–233, 397–439, Feb.–May, 1924.
Simiand, François, *Recherches anciennes et nouvelles sur le mouvement des prix depuis le XVI<sup>e</sup> siècle*, Paris, 1932.
United States National Monetary Commission, *The Reichsbank, 1876–1900*, Washington, 1910.
Viner, Jacob, *Studies in the Theory of International Trade*, New York, 1937.
Weber, Adolf, *Depositenbanken und Spekulationsbanken, ein Vergleich deutschen und englischen Bankwesens*, München, 1915.
Whale, P. Barrett, *Joint Stock Banking in Germany; A Study of the German Credit Banks before and after the War*, London, 1930.
Willis, H. Parker, *A History of the Latin Monetary Union*, Chicago, 1901.

IX. Commercial Policy and Imperialism
A. Commercial and Fiscal Policy
1. General

Ashley, Percy, *Modern Tariff History*, 3rd ed., New York, 1920.
Bastable, C. F., *The Commerce of Nations*, 9th ed., London, 1922.
Birschel, H., *Die Bedeutung der Brüsseler Zucker-Konvention für Deutschland*, Berlin, 1909.
Borchard, F., *Entwicklungsgeschichte der Meistbegünstigung im Handelsvertrag-System*, Königsberg, 1906.
Bose, L., *Zollalliancen und Zollunionen*, Berlin, 1907.
Crister, J., *L'union douanière européenne, ses conditions et ses difficultés*, Paris, 1928.

Dretzel, H., *Retaliatory Duties*, London, 1906.
Farrer, T. H., *The Sugar Convention*, London, 1889.
Gregory, T. E. G., *Tariffs: A Study in Method*, London, 1921.
Grunzel, Josef, *Economic Protectionism*, Oxford, 1916.
Heckscher, E. F., *The Continental System*, Oxford, 1923.
Láng, L., *Hundert Jahre Zoll-Politik*, Wien und Leipzig, 1906.
Manoïlesco, Mihaïl, *The Theory of Protection and International Trade*, London, 1931.
Pentmann, Juda, *Die Zollunionsidee und ihre Wandlungen*, Jena, 1917.
Penty, A. J., *Protection and the Social Problem*, London, 1926.
Spencer, J. P. S., *The Brussels Convention and Free Trade Speeches by Earl Spencer and H. Campbell-Bannermann*, London, New York, 1903.
Wittschewsky, V., *Russlands Handels, Zoll- und Industrie-Politik*, Berlin, 1905.

2. GREAT BRITAIN

Armitage-Smith, George, *The Free Trade Movement and Its Results*, New York, 1904.
Ashworth, Henry, *Recollections of Richard Cobden and the Anti-Corn Law League*, London, 1877.
Atton, Henry, and Holland, Henry H., *The King's Customs*, 2 vols., New York, 1911.
Aubeigné, R. de, *Historique de la législation douanière sur les blés en Angleterre, 1750-1846*, Paris, 1909.
* Barnes, D. G., *A History of the English Corn Laws from 1660-1846*, London, 1930.
Brady, Alexander, *William Huskisson and Liberal Reform*, London, 1928.
Carr, A. S. C., and Evans, D. R., *The Lure of Safeguarding*, London, 1929.
Chatterton, E. K., *King's Cutters and Smugglers, 1700-1855*, Philadelphia, 1912.
Clark, George Kitson, *Peel and the Conservative Party*, London, 1929.
Cunningham, W., *The Rise and Decline of the Free Trade Movement*, 2d ed., London, 1907.
Dowell, S., *A History of Taxation and of Taxes in England from the Earliest Times to the Present Day*, 2 vols., London, 1884.
Empire Economic Union, Research Committee, *A Plan of Action*, London, 1932.
Fay, C. R., *The Corn Laws and Social England*, London, 1932.
Findlay, Ronald M., *The British under Protection*, London, 1934.
* Fisk, Harvey E., *English Public Finance from the Revolution of 1688*, New York, 1920.
* Galpin, W. Freeman, *The Grain Supply of England during the Napoleonic Period*, New York, 1925.

Great Britain, *Accounts Relating to the Public Income and Expenditure of Great Britain and Ireland* (pub. in each financial year from 1688 to 1869, with historical notices, appendices, etc.), 2 parts. (Report by H. W. Chisholm), *Commons Papers*, 1868–1869, vol. 35, p. 366.

Hargreaves, E. L., *The National Debt*, London, 1930.

—— *Restoring Currency Standards*, London, 1926.

Harper, C. G., *The Smugglers*, London, 1910.

Hirst, F. W., *From Adam Smith to Philip Snowden*, New York, 1926.

—— *Gladstone as Financier and Economist*, London, 1931.

Holland, Bernard, *The Fall of Protection, 1840–1850*, London, 1913.

Huskisson, William, *Papers* (ed. by Lewis Melville), New York, 1931.

Hyde, Francis Edwin, *Mr. Gladstone at the Board of Trade*, London, 1934.

Morley, John, *The Life of Richard Cobden*, 2 vols., London, 1881.

—— *The Life of Gladstone*, 3 vols., London, 1903.

Parker, Charles Stuart, *Sir Robert Peel, from His Private Papers*, 3 vols., London, 1899.

Parnell, Sir Henry B. (First Baron Congleton), *Financial Reform*, London, 1830.

Peel, George, *The Private Letters of Sir Robert Peel*, London, 1920.

—— *The Tariff Reformers*, London, 1912.

Prentice, Archibald, *The History of the Anti-Corn Law League*, 2 vols., London, 1853.

Ramsay, Alexander, *The Economics of Safeguarding*, London, 1930.

Robertson, J. M., *The Political Economy of Free Trade*, London, 1928.

Shore, H. N., *Smuggling Days and Smuggling Ways*, London, 1892.

Smart, William, *The Return to Protection*, London, 1904.

3. FRANCE

Amé, L., *Étude sur les tarifs de douane et sur les traités de commerce*, 2 vols., Paris, 1876.

Arnauné, A., *Le commerce extérieur et les tarifs de douane*, Paris, 1911.

Aubert, Louis, *L'assimilation douanière dans les rapports de la France et de ses colonies*, Paris, 1911.

Augier, C., et Marvaud, A., *La politique douanière de la France*, Paris, 1911.

Chevalier, Michel, *Examen du système commerciale connu sous le nom de système protecteur*, Paris, 1852.

Clément, P., *Histoire du système protecteur en France*, Paris, 1854.

Dunham, Arthur Louis, *The Anglo-French Treaty of Commerce of 1860 and the Progress of the Industrial Revolution in France*, Ann Arbor, 1930.

Funck-Brentano, et Charles Dupuis, *Les tarifs douaniers et les traités de commerce*, Paris, 1895.

Girault, Arthur, *The Colonial Tariff Policy of France*, New York, 1916.

Gomel, C., *Histoire financière de l'assemblée constituante*, 2 vols., Paris, 1896–1897.

—— *Histoire financière de la legislative et de la convention*, 2 vols., Paris, 1905.

Guyot, Yves, *La question des sucres en 1901*, Paris, 1901

Haight, F. A., *French Import Quotas*, London, 1935.

Marion, Marcel, *Histoire financière de la France, depuis 1715*, 6 vols., Paris, 1914–1931.

Melvin, F. E., *Napoleon's Navigation System*, Philadelphia, 1919.

Meredith, K. O., *Protection in France*, London, 1904.

Nogaro, B., et Moye, Marcel, *Le régime douanier de la France*, Paris, 1931.

Nussbaum, F. L., *Commercial Policy in the French Revolution: A Study of the Career of G. J. A. Ducher*, Philadelphia, 1924.

Stourm, R., *Les finances de l'ancien régime et de la Révolution*, 2 vols., Paris, 1885.

### 4. GERMANY

Brodnitz, G., *Bismarck's nationaloekonomische Anschauungen*, Jena, 1902.

Dawson, William Harbutt, *Protection in Germany; A History of German Fiscal Policy during the Nineteenth Century*, London, 1904.

Eisenhart Rothe, W. v., und Ritthaler, A., *Vorgeschichte und Begründung des deutschen Zollvereins: 1815–1834*, 3 vols., Berlin, 1934.

Franz, Eugen, *Der Entscheidungskampf um die wirtschaftlichspolitische Führung Deutschlands, 1856–67*, München, 1933.

Gaertner, A., *Der Kampf um den Zollverein zwischen Österreich und Preussen von 1849 bis 1853*, Strassburg, 1911.

Gerloff, Wilhelm, *Die Finanz und Zollpolitik des Deutschen Reiches nebst ihren Beziehungen zu Landes- und Gemeindefinanzen, von der Gründung des Norddeutschen Bundes bis zur Gegenwart*, Jena, 1913.

Hirst, Margaret E., *Life of Friedrich List, and Selections from His Writings*, New York, 1909.

Kumpmann, Karl, *Friedrich List als Prophet des neuen Deutschland*, Tübingen, 1915.

Lenz, Friedrich, *Friedrich List, der Mann und das Werk*, München und Berlin, 1936.

List, Friedrich, *Schriften, Reden, Briefe*, 10 vols., Berlin, 1932–1935.

Lotz, W., *Die Ideen der deutschen Handelspolitik 1860–91*, Leipzig, 1892.

Mender, Fritz, *Das moderne Zollschutz-System*, Zurich, 1916.

Menn, Walter, *Zur Vorgeschichte des deutschen Zollvereins, Nassaus Handels und Schiffahrts-Politik vom Wiener Kongress 1815–1827*, Greifswald, 1930.

Rachel, Hugo, *Handels-, Zoll- und Akzisepolitik Brandenburg-Preussens*, 3 vols., Berlin, 1911–1928.

\* Robinet de Clary, Adrien, *La politique douanière de l'Allemagne depuis l'avènement de Caprivi jusqu'en 1925*, Paris, 1935.

Sieveking, H., *Auswärtige Handelspolitik*, Leipzig, 1905.
Treitschke, Heinrich von, "Die Anfänge des deutschen Zollvereins," *Preussische Jahrbücher*, vol. XXX, pp. 397, 409, 479, 648, 1872.
—— *Die Gründung des deutschen Zollvereins*, Leipzig, 1913.
Wagner, A., *Agrar- und Industriestaat*, Jena, 1902.
Weber, W., *Der deutsche Zollverein*, Leipzig, 1871.
Worms, E., *L'Allemagne économique ou histoire du Zollverein allemand*, Paris, 1874.
Zimmermann, A., *Die Handelspolitik des deutschen Reiches, 1871–1900*, Berlin, 1901.

B. IMPERIALISM AND ITS PROBLEMS

Angell, Norman, *Raw Materials, Population Pressure, and War*, Boston, 1936.
Bakeless, John, *Economic Causes of Modern War; A Study of the Period 1878–1918*, New York, 1921.
Beer, George L., *The Old Colonial System, 1660–1754*, 2 vols., New York, 1913.
—— *British Colonial Policy, 1754–1765*, New York, 1907.
Bining, A. C., *British Regulation of the Colonial Iron Industry*, Philadelphia, 1933.
Buck, N. S., *Development of the Organization of Anglo-American Trade, 1800–1850*, New Haven, 1925.
Carrothers, W. A., *Emigration from the British Isles*, London, 1929.
Clark, Grover, *The Balance Sheets of Imperialism*, New York, 1936.
—— *A Place in the Sun*, New York, 1936.
Day, Clive, *The Policy and Administration of the Dutch in Java*, New York, 1904.
Dutt, R. Palme, *World Politics, 1918–1936*, New York, 1936.
* Earle, Edward M., *Turkey, the Great Powers, and the Bagdad Railway*, New York, 1923.
Feis, Herbert, *Europe, the World's Banker, 1870–1914*, New Haven, 1930.
Foerster, R. F., *The Italian Emigration of Our Times*, Cambridge, Mass., 1919.
Foster, Sir William, *England's Quest of Eastern Trade*, London, 1933.
Giffen, Sir Robert, *The Growth of Capital*, London, 1889.
Glass, D. V., *The Struggle for Population*, Oxford, 1936.
Hall, Walter P., *Empire to Commonwealth; Thirty Years of British Imperial History*, New York, 1928.
Hobson, Charles K., *The Export of Capital*, London, 1914.
Hoffman, Ross J. S., *Great Britain and the German Trade Rivalry, 1875–1914*, Philadelphia, 1933.
*Italy and Ethiopia*, No. 314, *International Conciliation*, New York, 1935.

Jenks, Leland H., *The Migration of British Capital to 1875*, New York, 1927.

Jessup, Philip C., and Others, *Neutrality, Its History, Economics, and Law*, 4 vols., New York, 1935–1936.

Johnston, Sir Harry H., *History of the Colonization of Africa by Alien Races*, rev. ed., Cambridge, England, 1913.

* Keller, Albert G., *Colonization: A Study of the Founding of New Societies*, Boston, 1908.

Kindersley, Robert, "British Overseas Investment: 1934–35," *Economic Journal*, vol. 46, pp. 645–661.

Langer, W. L., *The Diplomacy of Imperialism, 1890–1902*, 2 vols., New York, 1935.

Leroy-Beaulieu, Paul, *De la colonisation chez les peuples modernes*, 2 vols., 6th ed., Paris, 1908.

Lippincott, Isaac, *Development of Modern World Trade*, New York, 1936.

* Merriman, Roger B., *The Rise of the Spanish Empire in the Old World and in the New*, 4 vols., New York, 1918–1934.

* Moon, Parker T., *Imperialism and World Politics*, New York, 1926.

Morrell, W. P., *British Colonial Policy in the Age of Peel and Russell*, Oxford, 1930.

Newton, Arthur P., *The European Nations in the West Indies, 1493–1688*, London, 1933.

Prestage, Edgar, *The Portuguese Pioneers*, London, 1933.

Puryear, Vernon J., *International Economics and Diplomacy in the Near East; A Study of British Commercial Policy in the Levant, 1834–1853*, Stanford University, 1935.

Ragatz, Lowell J., *The Fall of the Planter Class in the British Caribbean, 1763–1833*, New York, 1928.

Richardson, J. Henry, *British Economic Foreign Policy*, New York, 1936.

Robinson, Howard, *Development of the British Empire*, Boston, 1922.

Southard, F. A., Jr., *American Industry in Europe*, Boston, 1931.

Townsend, Mary E., *The Rise and Fall of Germany's Colonial Empire, 1884–1918*, New York, 1930.

* Williamson, James A., *Short History of British Expansion*, new ed., 2 vols., London, 1930.

Woolf, Leonard S., *Economic Imperialism*, New York, 1920.

—— *Empire and Commerce in Africa*, New York, 1920.

## X. Oceanic and Inland Water Transport

Beyerhaus, E., *Der Rhein von Strassburg bis zur holländischen Grenze in technischer und wirtschaftlicher Beziehung*, Coblenz, 1902.

Bowen, Frank C., *A Century of Atlantic Travel, 1830–1930*, Boston, 1930.

Broodbank, Sir J. G., *History of the Port of London*, 2 vols., London, 1921.

Cadbury, George, and Dobbs, S. P., *Canals and Inland Waterways*, New York, 1929.

Candace, Gratien, *La marine marchande française*, Paris, 1930.

Charles-Roux, J., *L'Isthme et le Canal de Suez*, Paris, 1901.

Dussol, Aimé, *Les grandes compagnies de navigation et les chantiers de constructions maritimes en Allemagne*, 2 vols., Paris, 1908–1912.

Gilfillan, S. C., *Inventing the Ship*, Chicago, 1935.

Kirkaldy, A. W., *British Shipping, Its History, Organization, and Importance*, London and New York, 1914.

Lafitte, L., *Étude sur la navigation intérieure en Allemagne*, Nantes, 1900.

Lindsay, W. S., *History of Merchant Shipping and Ancient Commerce*, 4 vols., London, 1883.

Meeker, Royal, *History of Shipping Subsidies*, Cambridge, Mass., 1905.

Michon, Georges, *Les grandes compagnies de navigation anglaises*, Paris, 1913.

Palmer, J. E., *British Canals, Problems, and Possibilities*, London, 1910.

Rossignol, L. M., *Le Canal de Suez (étude historique, juridique, et politique)*, Paris, 1898.

Roux, Louis, *La marine marchande*, Paris, 1923.

Sargent, A. J., *Seaways of Empire*, London, 1912.

Wilson, Arnold T., *The Suez Canal; Its Past, Present, and Future*, Oxford, 1933.

Wright, Charles, and Fayle, C. E., *A History of Lloyd's*, London, 1928.

## XI. Highway and Railroad Transport

Alberty, M., *Der Übergang zum Staatsbahn-System in Preussen*, Jena, 1911.

Anderson, R. M. C., *The Roads of England*, London, 1932.

Brunner, Christopher T., *Road Versus Rail, the Case for Motor Transport*, London, 1929.

Cleveland-Stevens, E. C., *English Railways, Their Development and Their Relation to the State*, New York, 1915.

Dugelay, P., *De l'intervention de l'état français sur les lignes de chemin de fer d'intérêt général*, Lyons, 1930.

Girard, P., *L'exploitation rationelle des chemins de fer en France*, Montpellier, 1923.

Haufe, Helmut, *Die geographische Struktur des deutschen Eisenbahnverkehrs*, Langensalza, 1931.

Kaufmann, R., *La politique française en matière de chemins de fer* (trans. by F. Hamon), Paris, 1900.

Kidd, Howard C., *A New Era for British Railways*, London, 1929.

Koulomzine, A. N., *Le Transsibirien*, Paris, 1904.

Lambert, R. S., *The Railway King, 1800–1871, A Study of George Hudson and the Business Morals of His Time*, London, 1934.

Lavie, Paul, *La concurrence du rail et de la route*, Lyon, 1933.

Lewin, H. G., *Early British Railways, 1801–1844*, London, 1925.

Owen, D. J., *The Port of London, Yesterday and Today*, London, 1927.

* Pratt, Edwin A., *A History of Inland Transport and Communication in England*, New York, 1912.

Raper, Charles Lee, *Railway Transportation; A History of Its Economics and of Its Relations to the State*, New York, 1912.

Reverand, Max, *Les chemins de fer français d'intérêt général depuis la fin de la guerre*, Paris, 1931.

Rochefoucauld, Eugène de la, *La co-ordination des transports ferroviaires et routiers*, Paris, 1934.

Sherrington, C. E. R., *The Economics of Rail Transport in Great Britain*, 2 vols., London, 1928.

* —— *A Hundred Years of Inland Transport, 1830–1933*, London, 1934.

Shoemaker, Michael Myers, *The Great Siberian Railway from St. Petersburg to Pekin*, New York, 1903.

Young, Robert, *Timothy Hackworth and the Locomotive*, New York, 1923.

## XII. Agriculture and the Structure of Rural Life
### A. General Treatises on Europe

Ciriacy-Wantrup, Siegfried von, *Agrarkrisen und Stockungs-Spannen*, Berlin, 1936.

Garsonnet, Eugène, *Histoire des locations perpétuelles et des baux à longue durée*, Paris, 1879.

Gras, N. S. B., *A History of Agriculture in Europe and America*, New York, 1925.

Hanssen, G., *Agrarhistorische Abhandlungen*, Leipzig, 1880.

Kowalewski, Maxime, *Die oekonomische Entwicklung Europas*, Berlin, 1901–1914.

Lacombe, Paul, *L'appropriation du sol, essai sur le passage de la propriété collective à la propriété privée*, Paris, 1912.

Lewinski, Jan St., *The Origin of Property and the Formation of the Village Community*, London, 1913.

Maine, H. J. Sumner, *Village-Communities in the East and West*, London, 1871.

Morgan, O. S. (ed.), *Agricultural Systems of Middle Europe; A Symposium*, New York, 1933.

Probyn, J. W., *Systems of Land Tenure in Various Countries*, 2d ed., London, 1881.

Schlitte, B., *Zusammenlegung der Grundstücke*, 3 vols., Leipzig, 1886.

Scholz, Karl (ed.), " Foreign Land Problems," *Annals of the American Academy of Political and Social Science*, vol. 150, pp. 220–293, July, 1930.

Sée, H., *Esquisse de l'histoire du régime agraire en Europe aux XVIIIᵉ et XIXᵉ siècles*, Paris, 1921.

Shaw-Lefevre, George, *Agrarian Tenures*, London, 1893.

Sugenheim, Samuel, *Geschichte der Aufhebung der Leibeigenshaft und Hörigkeit in Europa, bis um die Mitte des XIXen Jahrhunderts*, St. Petersburg, 1861.

Timoshenko, V. P., *World Agriculture and the Depression*, Ann Arbor, 1933.

## B. Agriculture and Land Reform in Particular Countries
### 1. England

Astor, Viscount W. A., and Murray, K. A. H., *The Planning of Agriculture*, Oxford, 1933.

Brodrick, G. C., *English Land and English Landlords*, London, 1881.

Curtler, W. H. R., *The Enclosure and Redistribution of Our Land*, Oxford, 1920.

Davies, E., "The Small Landowner, 1780–1832, in the Light of the Land Tax Assessments," *The Economic History Review*, vol. 1, pp. 87–113.

Dunlop, O. J., *The Farm Laborer*, London, 1913.

Ernle, Lord R. E. Prothero, *English Farming, Past and Present*, 3d ed., London, 1922.

Gonner, E. C. K., *Common Land and Inclosure*, London, 1912.

Gray, H. L., *English Field Systems*, Cambridge, Mass., 1915.

Hasbach, W., *A History of the English Agricultural Laborer*, London, 1908.

Johnson, A. H., *The Disappearance of the Small Landowner*, London, 1909.

Levy, Hermann, *Large and Small Holdings: A Study of English Agricultural Economics*, New York, 1911.

Marriott, John Arthur Ransome, *The English Land System*, London, 1914.

Middleton, Thomas Hudson, *Food Production in War*, Oxford, 1923.

Pash, Harold, *The English Village, the Origin and Decay of Its Community*, London, 1922.

Pomfret, John E., *The Struggle for Land in Ireland, 1800–1923*, Princeton, 1930.

Slater, Gilbert, *The English Peasantry and the Enclosure of Common Fields*, London, 1907.

Tawney, R. H., *The Agrarian Problem in the Sixteenth Century*, London, 1912.

Venn, J. A., *The Foundations of Agricultural Economics*, 2d ed., Cambridge, England, 1933.

### 2. France

Artz, F. B., *France under the Bourbon Restoration, 1814–1830*, Cambridge, Mass., 1931.

Augé-Laribé, M., *L'agriculture pendant la guerre*, Paris, 1925.

—— *L'évolution de la France agricole*, Paris, 1912.

Aulard, Alphonse, *La Révolution française et le régime féodal*, Paris, 1919.

Bloch, Marc, *Les caractères originaux de l'histoire rural française*, Paris, 1931.

Bloch, Marc, *La lutte pour l'individualisme agraire dans la France du XVIII^e siècle*, I, *L'œuvre des pouvoirs de l'ancien régime* (*Annales d'histoire économique et sociale*, vol. 2), 1930.

Calonne, A. de, *La vie agricole sous l'ancien régime dans le Nord de la France*, Paris, 1885.

Gain, André, *La restauration et les biens des émigrés*, Nancy, 1928; Paris, 1929.

Göhring, Martin, *Die Frage der Feudalität in Frankreich am Ende des Ancien Régime und in der französischen Revolution* (*bis zum 17 Juli 1793*), Berlin, 1934.

Graffin, Roger, *Les biens communaux en France*, Paris, 1899.

Herbert, Sydney, *The Fall of Feudalism in France*, New York, 1921.

Kareiew, E., *Les paysans et la question paysanne en France dans le dernier quart du XVIII^e siècle*, Paris, 1899.

Kovalewski, M., *La France économique et sociale à la veille de la Révolution*, Paris, 1909.

Lecarpentier, G., *La vente des biens ecclésiastiques pendant la Révolution française*, Paris, 1908.

Lefebvre, Georges, *Les paysans du Nord pendant la Révolution française*, Lille, 1924.

—— *Questions agraires au temps de la terreur*, documents, Strasbourg, 1932.

—— "Les recherches relatives à la répartition de la propriété à la fin de l'ancien régime," *Revue d'Histoire Moderne*, vol. 3, Paris, 1928.

Loutchisky, Jean, *L'état des classes agricoles en France à la veille de la Révolution*, Paris, 1911.

—— *La petite propriété en France avant la Révolution et la vente des biens nationaux*, Paris, 1897.

Marion, Marcel, *La vente des biens nationaux*, Paris, 1908.

Sagnac, P., and Caron P., *Les comités des droits féodaux et de législation et l'abolition du régime seigneuriale*, Paris, 1907.

Sée, H., "Les progrès de l'agriculture en France de 1815 à 1848," *Revue d'histoire économique et sociale*, vol. 9, 1921.

—— *La vie économique et les classes sociales en France, au XVIII^e siècle*, Paris, 1924.

Sion, J., *Les paysans de la Normandie orientale, étude géographique sur les populations rurales du Caux et du Bray*, Paris, 1908.

Société des Agriculteurs de France, *Rapport de la commission d'enquête sur la situation du métayage en France*, Paris, 1913.

### 3. GERMANY

Buchenberger, A., *Agrarwesen und Agrarpolitik*, 2 vols., Leipzig, 1892–1893.

Dönniges, *Die neueste preussische Gesetzgebung über die Befreiung des Grundbesitzes*, Frankfurt und Berlin, 1849–1852.

Ford, Guy Stanton, *Stein and the Era of Reform in Prussia, 1807–1815*, Princeton, 1922.

Gerdes, H., *Geschichte des deutschen Bauernstandes*, 3d ed., Leipzig, 1928.

Grünberg, Karl, *Die Bauernbefreiung und die Auflösung der gutsherrlich-bäuerlichen Verhältnisse in Böhmen, Mähren, Schlesien*, Leipzig, 1894.

Hausmann, Sebastien, *Die Grundentlastung in Bayern* (Séminaire des sciences sociales), Strasbourg, 1892.

Knapp, G. F., *Die Bauernbefreiung und der Ursprung der Landarbeiter in den älteren Theilen Preussens*, Leipzig, 1887.

—— *Grundherrschaft und Rittergut*, Leipzig, 1897.

Knapp, Theodor, *Neue Beiträge zur Rechts und Wirtschaftsgeschichte des württembergische Bauernstandes*, Tübingen, 1919.

Lette, W. A., *Die Vertheilung des Grundeigenthums*, Berlin, 1858.

Lette, W. A., und Rönne, L. von, *Die Landeskulturgesetzgebung des preussisches Staats*, Berlin, 1853.

Meier, E. von, *Französische Einflüsse auf die Staats- und Rechtsentwicklung Preussens im neunzehnten Jahrhundert*, 3 vols., 1907–1909.

—— *Der Minister von Stein: die französische Revolution und der preussische Adel*, 1908.

Meitzen, August, *Der Boden und die landwirtschaftlichen Verhältnisse des preussischen Staates*, 8 vols., Berlin, 1868–1908.

Middleton, T. H., *The Recent Development of German Agriculture* (Great Britain, Parliament, *Commons Papers*, 1916, vol. 4, Cd. 8305), London, 1916.

Ritter, Gerhard, *Stein, ein politische Biographie*, Stuttgart-Berlin, 1931.

Schneider, E., *Die Landeskultur-Gesetzgebung des preussischen Staates für Auseinandersetzungen*, Berlin, 1879–1882.

Seeley, J. R., *Life and Times of Stein*, 3 vols., Cambridge, 1878.

Stadelmann, R., *Preussens Könige in ihrer Thätigkeit für die Landeskultur*, 4 vols., Leipzig, 1878–1887.

Wittich, Werner, *Die Grundherrschaft in Nordwest Deutschland*, Leipzig, 1896.

## C. AGRICULTURAL SCIENCE

Amery, G. D., "The Writings of Arthur Young," *Journal of the Royal Agricultural Society of England*, November, 1924; reprinted 1925.

Boussingault, Jean Baptiste, *L'économie rurale considérée dans ses rapports avec la chimie, la physique, et la météorologie*, 2d ed., Paris, 1851.

—— *Mémoires*, 5 vols., Paris, 1892–1903.

Drohojowska, La Comtesse de, *Les grandes agriculteurs modernes: Olivier de Serres, Duhamel Dumonceau, Parmentier, Matthieu de Dombasle*, Tours, 1909.

Fraas, Karl Nikolas, *Geschichte der Landbau und Förstwirtschaft*, München, 1865.

Goltz, Freiherr Theodor von der, *Geschichte der deutschen Landwirtschaft*, 2 vols., Berlin, 1902–1903.

Hall, Sir Alfred Daniel, *The Book of the Rothamsted Experiments*, 2d ed., New York, London, 1918.

—— *Fertilizers and Manures*, New York, 1920.

Haslam, C. S., *The Biography of Arthur Young, F. R. S., from His Birth to 1787*, Rugby, 1930.

Hjelt, Ed., *Geschichte der organischen Chemie*, Braunschweig, 1916.

Körte, Wilhelm, *Albrecht Thaer; sein Leben und Wirken als Arzt und Landwirth*, Leipzig, 1839.

Liebig, Justus von, *Die Grundsätze der Agricultur*, Braunschweig, 1855.

—— *Organic Chemistry in Its Applications to Agriculture and Physiology*, London, 1840.

Macdonald, William, *Makers of Modern Agriculture*, London, 1913.

Roscoe, Sir Henry E., *Justus von Liebig, His Life and Work*, New York, 1895.

Russell, E. J., *Soil Conditions and Plant Growth*, London, 1921; 7th ed., 1937.

Schorlemmer, Carl, *The Rise and Development of Organic Chemistry*, London, 1894.

Thaer, Konrad Wilhelm Albrecht Daniel, *Geschichte meiner Wirtschaft zu Möglin*, Berlin, 1815.

—— *Grundsätze der rationellen Landwirtschaft*, Berlin, 1880.

Volhard, Jakob, *Justus von Liebig*, Leipzig, 1909.

Young, Arthur, *The Autobiography of Arthur Young* (ed. by M. B. Betham-Edwards), London, 1898.

—— *A Course of Experimental Agriculture* (*transacted during 5 years on near 300 acres at Bradfield Combust, near Bury, in Suffolk*), 4 vols., Dublin, 1781.

### XIII. THE WORLD WAR AND RECONSTRUCTION
### A. THE WAR AND ITS PROBLEMS

Angell, J. W., *The Recovery of Germany*, rev. ed., New Haven, 1932.

Antonucci, A., *La liquidation financière de la guerre et la reconstruction de l'Europe centrale*, Paris, 1933.

Bergmann, Karl, *The History of Reparations*, Boston, 1927.

*Bogart, Ernest L., *Direct and Indirect Costs of the Great World War*, 2d ed., New York, 1920.

Bowley, Arthur L., *Some Economic Consequences of the Great War*, London, 1930.

Braunthal, A., "The New Economic Policy in Belgium," *International Labour Review*, vol. 33, pp. 760–789.

Calmette, Germain, *Recueil de documents sur l'histoire de la question des réparations* (1919 – 5 mai, 1921), Paris, 1924.

Clark, John M., Hamilton, Walton H., and Moulton, Harold G. (eds.), *Readings in the Economics of War*, Chicago, 1918.

Clarkson, Grosvenor B., *Industrial America in the World War*, Boston, 1923.

Dawes, Rufus C., *The Dawes Plan in the Making*, Indianapolis, 1925.

Dexter, Philip, and Sedgwick, J. H., *The War Debts; An American View*, New York, 1928.

Einzig, Paul, *Germany's Default*, London, 1934.

—— *World Finance, 1914–1935*, New York, 1935.

Eisenmann, Louis, and Others, *The Problem of Minorities* (International Conciliation, no. 222), New York, 1926.

Fisk, H. E., *The Inter-Ally Debts; An Analysis of War and Post-War Public Finance, 1914–1923*, New York, 1924.

Fontaine, Arthur, *French Industry during the War* (trans. from the French), New Haven, 1926.

Friedensburg, Ferdinand, *Kohle und Eisen im Weltkriege und in den Friedensschlüssen*, Munich, 1934.

Friedman, Elisha M., *Labor and Reconstruction in Europe*, New York, 1919.

Guichard, L., *Histoire du blocus naval, 1914–1918*, Paris, 1929.

Harris, C. R. S., *Germany's Foreign Indebtedness*, Oxford, 1935.

Heaton, Herbert, *The British Way to Recovery; Plans and Policies in Great Britain, Australia, and Canada*, Minneapolis, 1934.

Jessup, Philip C., *American Neutrality and International Police*, Boston, 1928.

Kellogg, Paul U., and Gleason, Arthur, *British Labor and the War*, New York, 1919.

Keynes, John M., *The Economic Consequences of the Peace*, New York, 1920.

—— *A Revision of the Treaty*, New York, 1922.

Ladas, S. P., *The Exchange of Minorities: Bulgaria, Greece, and Turkey*, New York, 1932.

Lloyd, E. M. H., *Experiments in State Control at the War Office and the Ministry of Food*, Oxford, 1925.

Macdonald, William, *Reconstruction in France*, New York, 1922.

Mahaim, E. (ed.), *La Belgique restaurée*, Bruxelles, 1926.

Manchester Guardian Commercial, *Reconstruction in Europe* (a series edited by John M. Keynes, beginning April 20, 1922).

Marcé, Victor de, *Le problème des dettes de guerre*, Paris, 1934.

Mitrany, David, *The Effect of the War in Southeastern Europe*, New Haven, 1936.

—— *The Land and the Peasant in Rumania; The War and Agrarian Reform* (1917–1921), New Haven, 1930.

Moulton, Harold G., and Pasvolsky, L., *War Debts and World Prosperity*, New York, 1932.

Ponsonby, Arthur, *Falsehood in Wartime*, London, 1928.
Rogers, J. H., Maffry, A., and Landman, R. E., *The Process of Inflation in France, 1914-1927*, New York, 1929.
Rogers, Lindsay (ed.), *The Problems of Reconstruction, International and National* (International Conciliation, no. 135), New York, 1919.
Salin, Edgar, *Das Reparations-Problem*, 2 vols., Berlin, 1929.
Salter, J. A., *Allied Shipping Control; An Experiment in International Administration*, New Haven, 1921.
Shotwell, James T. (ed.), *Economic and Social History of the World War*, (sponsored by the Carnegie Endowment for International Peace), 152 vols., New Haven and Oxford, 1921-1937.
Squires, James D., *British Propaganda at Home and in the United States from 1914 to 1917*, Cambridge, Mass., 1935.
Thomas, Brinley, *Monetary Policy and Crises; A Study of Swedish Experience*, London, 1936.
Walling, William E. (ed.), *The Socialists and the War*, New York, 1915.
Wertheimer, Mildred S., *The Lausanne Reparations Settlement* (Foreign Policy Association Reports, vol. 8), New York, 1932.
Wheeler-Bennett, John W., *The Wreck of Reparations*, New York, 1933.
Withers, W., *The Retirement of National Debts*, New York, 1932.

### B. INTERNATIONAL ORGANIZATIONS

Berenstein, A., *Les organisations ouvrières: leur compétences et leur rôle dans la Société des Nations et notamment dans l'organisation internationale du travail*, Paris, 1936.
Cheyney, Alice S. (ed.), *The International Labor Organization* (*Annals of the American Academy of Political and Social Science*, vol. 166), Philadelphia, 1933.
Donaldson, J., *International Economic Relations*, New York, 1928.
Hubbard, Ursula P., *The Coöperation of the United States with the League of Nations and with the International Labor Organization* (International Conciliation, no. 274), New York, 1931.
—— *The Coöperation of the United States with the League of Nations, 1931-1936* (International Conciliation, no. 329), New York, 1937.
International Labour Office, *The International Labour Organization; The First Decade*, Boston, 1931.
Keppel, F. P., *The International Chamber of Commerce* (International Conciliation, no. 174), New York, 1922.
Lorwin, Lewis L., "The I. L. O. and World Economic Policy," *International Labour Review*, vol. 33, pp. 457-467.
Lowe, B. E., *The International Protection of Labor*, rev. ed., New York, 1935.
* McClure, Wallace, *World Prosperity as Sought through the Economic Work of the League of Nations*, New York, 1933.

Myers, Denys P., *Nine Years of the League of Nations, 1920–1928* (9th yearbook), Boston, 1929.
Plummer, Alfred, *International Combines in Modern Industry*, London, 1934.
Sayre, Francis B., *Experiments in International Administration*, New York, 1918.
Schacher, Gerhard, *Central Europe and the Western World* (trans. from the German edition published at Prague), New York, 1936.
* Shotwell, James T. (ed.), *The Origins of the International Labor Organization*, 2 vols., New York, 1934.
Sly, J. F., *The Genesis of the Universal Postal Union* (International Conciliation, no. 233), New York, 1927.
Wilson, Francis G., *Labor in the League System*, Stanford University, 1934.
Woolf, Leonard S., *International Government*, New York, 1916.
Zimmern, A., *The League of Nations and the Rule of Law, 1918–1935*, London, 1936.

### XIV. Economic Doctrines and Views of Social Policy

Beer, Max, *A History of British Socialism*, 2 vols., London, 1919–1920.
Bernstein, Eduard, *Evolutionary Socialism* (trans. from the German by E. C. Harvey), 2d ed., London, 1912.
Blease, W. L., *A Short History of English Liberalism*, New York, 1913.
Böhler, E., *Korporative Wirtschaft, eine kritische Würdignung*, Zürich und Leipzig, 1934.
*Britain Without Capitalists: A Study of What Industry in a Soviet Britain Could Achieve* (by a group of economists, scientists, and technicians), London, 1936.
Chamberlin, W. H., *Collectivism; A False Utopia*, New York, 1937.
Clark, John M., "Adam Smith and the Currents of History," *Preface to Social Economics*, pp. 170–195, New York, 1936.
Cobban, Alfred, *Rousseau and the Modern State*, London, 1934.
Cole, G. D. H., and Others, *What Is Ahead of Us?* (Fabian Society Lectures), London, 1937.
Dewey, John, *Liberalism and Social Action*, New York, 1935.
Dicey, A. V., *Lectures on the Relation between Law and Public Opinion in England*, 2d ed., New York, 1905.
Dutt, R. Palme, *Fascism and Social Revolution*, New York, 1934.
Feder, Gottfried, *Hitler's Official Programme, and Its Fundamental Ideas* (trans. from the 5th German ed.), London, 1934.
Florinsky, Michael T., *Fascism and National Socialism: A Study of the Economic and Social Policies of the Totalitarian State*, New York, 1936.
Ford, Guy Stanton (ed.), *Dictatorship in the Modern World*, Minneapolis, 1935.

Furniss, Edgar S., *The Position of the Laborer in a System of Nationalism; A Study in the Labor Theories of the Later English Mercantilists*, Boston, 1920.

Gide, Charles, and Rist, Charles, *A History of Economic Doctrines* (trans. from the 2d French edition by R. Richards), New York, 1915.

Hamlin, Scoville, *Balance or Chaos*, New York, 1935.

Haney, Lewis H., *History of Economic Thought*, 3d ed., New York, 1936.

*Heckscher, Eli F., *Mercantilism* (trans. by M. Shapiro), 2 vols., London, 1935.

Higgs, Henry, *The Physiocrats*, London, 1897.

Hitler, Adolf, *Mein Kampf*, 40th ed., München, 1933. (The authorized English translation diverges seriously from the German editions.)

Hobhouse, L. T., *Liberalism*, New York, 1911.

Hobson, John A., *The Economics of Unemployment*, rev. ed., New York, 1931.

Homan, Paul, *Contemporary Economic Thought*, New York, 1928.

Kautsky, Karl, *The Economic Doctrines of Karl Marx* (trans. from the German by H. J. Stenning), London, 1925.

Keynes, John M., *The General Theory of Employment, Interest, and Money*, London, 1936.

*Laidler, Harry W., *History of Socialist Thought*, New York, 1927.

Laski, Harold J., *The Rise of European Liberalism; An Essay in Interpretation*, London, 1936.

Lippincott, Benjamin E. (ed.), *Government Control of the Economic Order; A Symposium*, Minneapolis, 1935.

Lippmann, Walter, *The Method of Freedom*, New York, 1934.

Maccoby, Simon, *English Radicalism, 1832–1852*, London, 1935.

* MacKenzie, Findlay (ed.), *Planned Society; Yesterday, Today, Tomorrow*, New York, 1937.

Matteotti, G., *The Fascisti Exposed; A Year of Fascist Domination* (trans., by E. W. Dickes), London, 1924.

Michelis, Giuseppe de, *World Reorganization on Corporative Lines*, London, 1935.

Mussolini, Benito, *Fascism; Doctrine and Institutions*, Rome, 1935.

Norlin, George, *Fascism and Citizenship*, Chapel Hill, N. C., 1934.

Orth, Samuel P., *Socialism and Democracy in Europe*, New York, 1913.

Peck, H. W., *Economic Thought and Its Institutional Background*, New York, 1935.

Pirou, G., *La crise du capitalisme*, Paris, 1936.

—— *Le corporatisme*, Paris, 1935.

Robbins, Lionel, *Economic Planning and International Order*, London, 1937.

Rocco, Alfredo, *The Political Doctrine of Fascism* (International Conciliation, no. 223), New York, 1926. By the Minister of Justice.

Rowse, A. L., *Mr. Keynes and the Labour Movement*, London, 1936.

Strachey, John, *The Nature of the Capitalist Crisis*, New York, 1935.

Thomas, P. J., *Mercantilism and the East India Trade*, London, 1926.

Treitschke, H. G. von, *Politik*, 3d ed., Leipzig, 1911–1913.

Usher, A. P., "Laissez Faire and the Rise of Liberalism," *Explorations in Economics: Notes and Essays Contributed in Honor of F. W. Taussig*, pp. 403–411, New York, 1936.

Viljoen, Stephan, *The Economic Tendencies of Today*, London, 1933.

Wagner, Donald O. (ed.), *Social Reformers; Adam Smith to John Dewey*, New York, 1934.

Webb, Sidney, and Webb, Beatrice, *A Constitution for the Socialist Commonwealth of Great Britain*, London, 1920.

Weulersse, Georges, *Le mouvement physiocratique en France de 1756 à 1770*, 2 vols., Paris, 1910; abbr. ed., *Les physiocrates*, 1931.

Whitehead, T. N., *Leadership in a Free Society; A Study in Human Relations*, Cambridge, Mass., 1936.

Wootton, Barbara A., *Plan or No Plan*, London, 1934.

World Social Economic Congress, *World Social Economic Planning*, The Hague, 1932.

## XV. RUSSIA

Brutskus, B. D., *Economic Planning in Soviet Russia*, London, 1935.

*Chamberlin, W. H., *The Russian Revolution, 1917–1921*, 2 vols., New York, 1935.

—— *Russia's Iron Age*, Boston, 1934.

Dobb, M. H., and Stevens, H. C., *Russian Economic Development since the Revolution*, New York, 1928.

Florinsky, M. T., *World Revolution and the U.S.S.R.*, New York, 1933.

Grinko, G. T., *The Five-Year Plan of the Soviet Union*, New York, 1930.

Gurian, Waldemar, *Bolshevism: Theory and Practice*, New York, 1932.

Hindus, Maurice, *The Great Offensive*, New York, 1933.

Hoover, C. B., *The Economic Life of Soviet Russia*, New York, 1931.

Kovalevsky, W. de (ed.), *La Russie à la fin du 19ᵉ siècle*, Paris, 1900.

Lawton, Lancelot, *An Economic History of Soviet Russia*, 2 vols., London, 1932.

Leroy-Beaulieu, H. J. B. A., *Empire of the Tsars and Russians*, 3 vols., New York, 1904.

Mavor, James, *An Economic History of Russia*, 2 vols., 2d ed., New York, 1925.

Mïkhaïlov, N., *Soviet Geography: the New Industrial and Economic Distributions of the U.S.S.R.*, London, 1935.

Miliukov, P., *Essais sur l'histoire de la civilisation russe*, Paris, 1901.

*Miller, M. S., *The Economic Development of Russia, 1905–1914*, London, 1926.

Pavlovskïï, G. A., *Agricultural Russia on the Eve of the Revolution*, London, 1930.

Pazhitnov, K. A., *Die Lage der arbeitenden Klasse in Russland*, Stuttgart, 1907.

Preyer, W., *Die russische Agrarreform*, Jena, 1914.

Raffalovitch, A. (ed.), *Russia: Its Trade and Commerce*, London, 1918.

\*Robinson, G. T., *Rural Russia under the old Régime*, New York, 1932

Rosenberg, Arthur, *A History of Bolshevism*, London, 1934.

Shotwell, James T. (ed.), *Economic and Social History of the World War, Russian Series*, 12 vols., New Haven, 1928–1932.

*Socialism Victorious*, New York, 1935.

Stalin, Joseph, *Leninism*, 2 vols., London, 1932–1933.

—— and Others, *From the First to the Second Five-Year Plan*, New York, 1934.

Trotsky, Leon, *The Revolution Betrayed*, New York, 1937.

Tugan-Baranovsky, M., *Geschichte der russischen Fabrik*, Berlin, 1900.

Turin, S. P., *From Peter the Great to Lenin: The History of the Russian Labor Movement*, London, 1935.

Union of Soviet Socialist Republics, State Planning Commission, *The Soviet Union Looks Ahead; The Five-Year Plan for Economic Construction*, New York, 1929.

—— *The Second Five-Year Plan*, New York, 1937.

Wallace, D. M., *Russia*, New York, 1912.

Webb, Sidney, and Webb, Beatrice, *Soviet Communism: a New Civilization?*, 2 vols., New York, 1936.

\*Williams, A. R., *The Soviets*, New York, 1937.

Witte, S. J., *Memoirs*, New York, 1921.

Yugoff, Aron, *Economic Trends in Soviet Russia*, London, 1930.

## Books in Russian

Balabanov, M., *Ocherki po istorii rabochego klassa v Rossii*, 3 vols., Moscow, 1926.

Finn-Enotaevski, A., *Kapitalizm v Rossii, 1890–1917*, Moscow, 1925.

Kulisher, I., *Istoriia russkoi torgovli*, Petrograd, 1923.

—— *Ocherk istorii russkoi promyshlennosti*, Petrograd, 1923.

Lenin, N., *Razvitie kapitalizma v Rossii (Sochineniia*, vol. 3), Moscow, 1934.

\*Liashchenko, P., *Istoriia russkogo narodnogo khoziaistva*, Moscow, 1927.

Maslov, P., *Agrarnyi vopros v Rossii*, 2 vols., St. Petersburg, 1908.

Sarabianov, V., *Ekonomika i ekonomicheskaia politika U.S.S.R.*, Moscow, 1926.

Tugan-Baranovski, M., *Russkaia fabrika v proshlom i nastoiashchem*, 1926.

# INDEX

(Continued on next page.)